1 MONTH OF
FREE
READING

at
www.ForgottenBooks.com

By purchasing this book you are eligible for one month membership to ForgottenBooks.com, giving you unlimited access to our entire collection of over 1,000,000 titles via our web site and mobile apps.

To claim your free month visit:

www.forgottenbooks.com/free916125

ISBN 978-0-266-96200-7
PIBN 10916125

HISTORICAL MANUSCRIPTS COMMISSION.

[ ]

REPORT

ON THE

MANUSCRIPTS

OF

THE FAMILY OF GAWDY,

FORMERLY

OF NORFOLK.

Presented to both Houses of Parliament by Command of Her Majesty.

LONDON:
PRINTED BY EYRE AND SPOTTISWOODE.

To be purchased, either directly or through any Bookseller, from any of the following
Agents, viz.,
Messrs. HANSARD and SON, 13, Great Queen Street, W.C., and 32, Abingdon Street,
Westminster ;
Messrs. EYRE and SPOTTISWOODE, East Harding Street, Fleet Street, and
Sale Office, House of Lords ;
Messrs. ADAM and CHARLES BLACK, of Edinburgh ;
Messrs. ALEXANDER THOM and Co., Limited, or Messrs. HODGES, FIGGIS, and Co.,
of Dublin.

1885.

C.—4576.—III.] *Price* 1s. 4d.

THE GAWDY PAPERS.

THE collection of letters chiefly relating to the Norfolk families of Gawdy, Knyvet, Hobart, Hare, and Le Neve, the first part of which is calendared in the following pages, has hitherto been generally known under the general title of the Gawdy Papers.

Many of them (*i.e.*, those comprised in this Calendar,) certainly relate to the Gawdy Family and passed, by the marriage of its heiress with Oliver Le Neve, into the hands of Peter Le Neve, Norroy, to whose industry, it will be remembered, Blomefield was indebted for the greater part of the material for the County History, which bears his name.

Many family papers of the Le Neves and much of the Herald's own correspondence, were, however, added to the collection, the whole, containing 3,276 MSS., being bound up in 17 folio volumes by, I believe, the late owner Mr. Daniel Gurney, of Runcton, who printed 29 of them at pp. 840 and 1029 of his "Record of the House of Gournay."

No arrangement, either chronological or otherwise, was attempted by the binder, so, since the MSS. have been added to my library, I have cancelled the old numbers (the more especially as no references to such old numbers have ever been made), and have re-arranged the papers into as many divisions as families, keeping each division in chronological order.

I should have liked to have included in this Calendar the Gawdy letters which, like many others of Le Neve's MSS., are in the possession of Mr. George Edward Frere, of Roydon, 110 of which were calendared by the late Mr. A. J. Horwood in the Appendix to the Seventh Report of the Historical MSS. Commission, but was unable to do so.

Another volume of Gawdy letters is at Oxford, being Tanner MS. 241, and containing 61 folios of letters to Bassingbourne Gawdy, High Sheriff of Norfolk, from the Lords of the Council and others, with some of his answers, 1576–1589.

The 1,222 documents calendared and indexed in the following
pages comprise the Gawdy Letters proper, and range in date from
1509 to 1675, thus forming a welcome continuation of the other
and better known county correspondence, the Paston letters, the
last dated of which was written in 1506 (ed., Gairdner, iii.,
p. 403).

It is intended to calendar the letters of the other four families
in a future report.

WALTER RYE.

GAWDY MSS

COLLECTION OF LETTERS AND DOCUMENTS FORMED BY PETER LE NEVE, NORROY KING-AT-ARMS (BORN 1661, DIED 1729), CHIEFLY RELATING TO THE NORFOLK FAMILIES OF GAWDY, KNYVET, HOBART, HARE, AND LE NEVE.—EDITED BY WALTER RYE.

PART I.

CORRESPONDENCE and DOCUMENTS relating to the GAWDY FAMILY and their CONNECTIONS, from A.D. 1509 to the death in 1606 of SIR BASSINGBOURN GAWDY, *twice Sheriff of Norfolk.*

[Note.—Suggestions and explanations, for which the Editor is responsible, are placed between square brackets [']. Where no name of a county follows the name of a place, the place may be assumed to be in Norfolk; the exceptions being well-known localities such as London, Hampton Court, &c.]

1509.

1.—1 April 1509. *John Gawdy* to *William Fuller, Thos. Gawdy,* senr., and *Thomas Gawdy,* jun., his brother [sic], and *John Fuller,* jun.

Copy deed of feoffment of 5 acres (*a*) in Woodhalefield abutting on manor of Haukers, land of John Fuller and lane from Woodhalefield to Harleston-market (*b*) next land of John Fuller (*c*) between land of George Hemingham and Thomas Ward's close (*d*) abutting on land of manor of Redenhale-hall in tenure of Ward, and lane called Strowbreglane. Thomas Fyske of Harleston attorney to give seisin. Witnesses, Thomas Ward, Robert Cotton, William Oby. Witnesses to seisin, Thos. Ward, barber, Robert Warde, Thomas Burgis, jun., John Fuller, jun., Will. Oby.

Memorandum ; that Thomas Fuller, living in the house of Mr. Copping, sometime Jo. Maslie's, afterwards Locke's, at Wortwell, has the original deed.

1511.

2.—28 May 1511. *Thomas Orwell,* late of Aylsham, Raffman, [*i.e.,* Tallow Chandler] to *Henry Reppes* late of Heveningham, Suffolk.

Receipt by Orwell for 24*l.* 13*s.* 4*d.* on account of purchase money of lands in South Repps, Thorpe Market, and adjoining towns.

3.—6 June 1512
4.—5 July 1513
5.—27 December 1513
6.—25 December 1514

Similar receipts, for 19*l.* in all, dated at Aylsham. Reppes is described as "the young gentleman" and "late of Thorpe Market." The land is identified as "late William-att-Lownds."

7.—26 October 1541. *Bettys* or *Beterys Reppes* [? Beatrice] of Walpole, Widow, to *Henry Reppes.*

Receipt by Bettys Reppes for 6*l.* 13*s.* 4*d.* due at the feast of St. Edmund the King next.

GAWDY MSS.

8.—14 August 1542. *Thomas Gawdy* of Shottesham Hall J.P.

Memorandum: *John Haylet* of Ditchingham bound over.

9.—4 December 1544. *Beterys Reppes* to *Henry Reppes*.

Receipt by B. Reppes for 106*l.* 13*s.* 4*d.* due at feast of St. Edmund the King last.

10.—April [1547 or earlier ?]. *Edmond* . . . of Sybeton, Suffolk, to *Elizabeth Holland* [daughter of Thos. Holland of Swinested, Linc.].

Receipt (mutilated) for 100*l.* from Mrs. ᵈHolland by hands of Mr. Henry . . . . [to be paid] unto my Lord of Norfolk his grace.

1547.

11.—[1547 or 1548?] *Symon Lowe* [of London, see No. 15] to *William Andros*, Bechall.

Andros' son Edmond, who is with Lowe, is in good health. Harry Reppes married Elizabeth Holland of Mendham, who died in childbed, the Cæsarean operation being performed. Reppes says the child was born alive and claims tenancy by the curtesy in her lands. Lowe thinks it impossible and, fearing foul play, asks Andros or his friends about Mendham or Harleston to make cautious enquiry. Thomas, Elizabeth's eldest brother and heir, sold the land to Lowe, but unthriftily spent the money and more (to the amount of 1,000*l.*) within a year, so cannot defend the title except at Lowe's charges. Phillipa Oon, of Mendham, was the midwife; Richard Spayne of Harleston was the surgeon who operated; Edmond Halle, another surgeon of Mendham or Harleston, was present but refused to operate. One William Rochester of Mendham or Harleston has been tampering with the witnesses; he is "truly the falsest and craftiest man in the country," for "a forty shilling" he will confess all, if well handled. Get the witnesses to a tavern, make them talk, and have men by to hear them.

[Between these dates Henry Reppes married his second wife Ann Wotton, relict of Thomas Wodehouse of Waxham.]

1548.

12.—10 July 1548. *Sir William Woodhouse* to his brother-in-law *Henry Reppes*.

Requests payment to his brother Croppe (?) of 56*l.* of the debt Reppes owes him due next Lammas.

13.—30 September 1548. Extract from settlement on marriage of *Thomas* (second son of *Thos. Gawdy* of Harleston) and *Awdry Knightley* (niece of William Pawe of Bylow, clerk). Pawe settles land in Rokelond, Bramerton, and Surlingham which came to him as son and heir of Andrew Pawe of Norwich, deceased. Feoffees in trust, Thomas Gawdy of Harleston, Thomas Gawdy of Shottesham, John Stubbe of Buxton, Simon Hylle of Estbergholt, Suffolk, Robert Coke of Heydon, Henry Attemere of Norwich, and John Plombe of Topᵇcroft. Witnesses to seisin, Thomas Gedge, William Ecok, Robt. Gedge, and John Tory.

[Thomas Gawdy of Harleston had three families by three wives, the eldest son in *each* case being named Thomas. From the *eldest* Thomas (of Shottesham and Redenhall, serjeant-at-law 1552, ob. 1556) sprang the family of Bassingbourn Gawdy. The *second* Thomas (his settlement given above) was serjeant 1567, and Judge of K.B. 1574; he died 1588, from him came the Gawdy's of Claxton Hall. The *third* Thomas changed his name at confirmation to Francis (Co. Litt. 3*a.*), was serjeant 1577, Judge of K.B. 1588, L.C.J.C.P. 1605 and died 1606.]

14.—8 April 1550.　*Thomas Gawdy* [of Shottesham] to *Henry Reppes.*

Receipt for 35*l.* due Gawdy on bond.

15.—3· July 1551.　*Thomas Holland* of Swynested, Linc. (son and heir apparent of Thos. Holland, Esq., sen.) to *Simon Lowe,* Citizen and Merchant Scissordealer of London.

Statute staple for 40*l.* payable to Lowe next Bartholomew-tide (Radm̄. Warey, Robert Broke, record).

16.—12 January 1551-2.　*Henry Reppes* of Mendham, Esq., to *Sir William Woodhouse* of Hickling, and *Sir Thomas Woodhouse* of Waxham.

Acknowledgment by Reppes of his indebtedness in 100*l.* payable Lady-day next. Receipt for 10*l.* paid by Mr. Banyerde. Receipt for 100*l.* paid by Mr. Gawdy, signed John Gostling.

17.—6 March 1551-2.　*Thomas Gawdy* of Shottesham to *Henry Reppes* of Mendham.

Receipt by Gawdy for 25*l.* due him on bond.

1554.

18.—10 September [1554].　*Thomas Gawdy* of Shottesham to his son *Bassingbourn Gawdy,* " at my Lord Chancellor's, Black Friars, Norwich."

My Lord of Norfolk has written to the Lord Chancellor for the latter's pleasure concerning the late Duke his grandfather's burial; let Bassingbourn get himself sent back to my Lord from the Chancellor. Urge the Chancellor that it is "most meetest" for Lady Surrey to have the ordering of her daughters Ladies Jane and Margaret Howard. Brooke has untruly informed the Lord Chancellor and my Lord of Norwich that Thomas Gawdy was present when the late Duke was asked if he would have "my Lord that now is" to be one of his executors and "at the holding up of his hand." Gawdy in fact neither saw nor spoke with him within ten days before his death. Will wait on the Chancellor on Saturday. Commendations to my Lord of Ely.

19.—August 1556. Extract from p. 180 of Plowden's Commentary on the death of *Thomas Gawdy* of Shottesham and *Richard Catlyn,* both of Norfolk, both of the Inner Temple, both made serjeants-at-law 19 May 1552, both burgesses for Norwich in the Parliament of 1553, and both died this month. Cites epitaph, commencing

"Munere Gaudœo junctus, virtute, labore,
Temporibus, patria, fortuna, moribus, annis,
Funere conjunctus, terras Catilina reliquit,
Felices ambo," &c.

1558.

20.—[March 1557-8.] Fragment of account of funeral expenses of *Henry Reppes* of Mendham who died 10 February 1557-8, by *Ann Reppes* his widow and executrix.

	£	s.	d.
Further for 3 yards of black cloth for my gown and my hood.	3	0	0
Item for 2½ yards for my maid - - -	1	13	4
Item for 14 yards for my men - - -	3	19	2
Item for 17¾ yards for the hearse - - -	0	13	6
Item for 6 " cutchings " - - -	0	4	0
Item for 4 " stafe-torches " - - -	0	4	0
Item to the doole at the burying - - -	15	0	0
Item to the Priest and Clerk that day - -	0	5	0
Item to the Vicar for his mortuary - -	0	10	0
Item to the doole at the 30th day - - -	5	0	0
Item to the Priest and Clerk that day - -	0	3	0

His Bequests.

	£	s.	d.
Item to the Church of Mendham - - -	1	0	0
Item to the poor people of Stowe - - -	1	0	0
Item to John Balles - - - -	2	0	0
Item to John Barmie - - - -	1	0	0
Item to William Bonet - - - -	1	6	8
Item to Mother Purdye - - - -	0	6	8

[26 September 1558 Anne Reppes married Bassingbourn Gawdy, and on 19 May 1560 their eldest son Bassingbourn Gawdy, junr., was born.]

21.—3 July 1561. Memorandum by P. Le Neve that *Anthony Gawdy* of Mendham, Suff., was a party to deed of this date; refers to deed of 31 January 1564-5 in his possession.

1561.

· 22.—9 October 1561. *Charles Framlingham* of Debenham, Suff. Esq. and *Philip Tylney* of Shelley, Suff. Esq.

Post-nuptial settlement on Anne only sister and heir presumptive of Framlingham. Recites birth of son. On Framlingham's decease without issue the manors which came to him from his father Francis are to go (after his widow's death) to issue of Anne Tylney. Similarly, Tylney's manor of Shelley-hall and other lands (to amount of 120*l*. a year) are to go to his son. The parties to enter into cross recognizances in sum of 2,000*l*. &c.

[Bassingbourn Gawdy's second son Philip born about this time.]

1562.

23.—7 May 1562.—*Thomas Gawdy* [of Claxton Hall] to *Sir Thomas Gresham.* .

Receipt by Gawdy for 14*l*. fees due last Michaelmas ; viz. 2 years fees for receivership and stewardship of Mileham granted him by Lord Maltravers at 5*l*. a year and 2 years like fee granted him for life by Sir T. Gresham (including services as Counsel) at 2*l*. a year.

24.—5 October 1562. *Charles Framlingham* to his father-in-law *Sir Clement Heigham* [formerly L.C.B. Exch.].

Receipt by Framlingham for 30*l*. by the hands of Lady Heigham in part of a larger sum.

25.—20 March 1562-3. *Thomas Hampton*, of Inner Temple to *Edward Flowerdew*, of Inner Temple, gent.

Recites a report that Hampton had given or lent Flowerdew 20*l*., 30*l*. or 40*l*. Confesses all such reports are false, untrue and unjust.

Acknowledges he never lent him over 10s. and, for further declaration of the truth, gives Flowerdew a general release; and further promises not to challenge any such debt, and yet further, if he or any one by his procurement starts such a report, he will forfeit 40l.

1563.

26.—27 November 1563.   *John Reppes* [brother of Henry Reppes deceased] Walpole in Marshland, to [*Bass. Gawdy*].

Asks a loan of 5l. 6s. 8d., and encloses his bill for 20 marks. Sends a crane with two mallards, which is all the fowl they can get, it is so scarce. Has spoken for knot, which will cost 5s. the dozen. These fowl are commonly taken at Terrington, where has been such great loss of sheep, owing to the last storm breaking their banks, that fowlers have no leisure to lay for fowl. Thanks for the cheesevat [" cheasfatt "] and cheese.

27.—15 November 1566.   *John Houghton*, Gunthorpe, to *Bassingbourn Gawdy.*

Sends a new warrant for some oaks at Bunwell, addressed to the present bailiff there; instead of one Gawdy had from Houghton's master directed to William Browne, now deceased.

28.—17 June 1567.   *William Dodds*, Hertfordshire, Esq., to *Edward Flowerdew*, of Inner Temple, Esq.

Receipt by Dodds for 7l. 10s. on bond due 12 May last.

1570.

29.—[April 1570 ?]   *Thomas Gawdy*, Norwich, Esq. [afterwards Justice of K.B.] to *Queen and Privy Council.*

Petition to be excused lending the Queen 100 marks on privy seal. Alleges he lent the late Queen 10l. which has not been repaid. Has since then been at great charge in building, and has borrowed of friends, merchants in London and elsewhere, 1,000 marks to complete a purchase and the said building and to support his wife and many children. Moreover he had no advancement from his ancestors, neither is he " any great meddler in the trade of the law."

30.—14 December 1570.   *John Holland* of Hethersett, husbandman, to *Edward Flowerdew* of Hethersett, Esq.

Acknowledgment that Holland owes 58s. 3d. upon account for arrearages of wood sales of Hethersett manor; Thomas Amyas, gent., being auditor of manor.

31.—25 April 1574.   *John Reppes* of Clifford's Inn, gent. [nephew of Henry Reppes, dec.] to *Bassingbourn Gawdy* of West Harling, Esq.

Receipt for 10l., ten marks of which is for annuity under Henry Reppes' will, and balance allowed by goodwill of Gawdy. Witness, James Berdewell, Perceval Thornton, Robt. Bowlton.

32.—20 January 1574–5.   *John Reppes* to *Bassingbourn Gawdy* and *Ann* his wife, executrix &c.

Similar receipt for 5l., half year's annuity: witness R. Bowlton.

33.—29 September 1575.   *Same* to *same.* Similar receipt for ten marks. Witness, Nicholas Saier, Robert Bowlton.

34.—31 October 1576. *Lady Dorothy Stafford,* the Court at Hampton, to [*Bass.*] *Gawdy.*

If Gawdy is appointed sheriff asks post of under-sheriff for Nicholas Fermor, one of my Lord of Leicester's gentlemen.

35.—6 November 1576. *Nicholas Fermor,* Blo Norton, to [*Bassingbourn Gawdy*].

Had he not been ill would have waited on Gawdy for his answer to the letters of the Council on Fermor's behalf.

[Between these dates John Reppes of Clifford's Inn died.]

1577.

36.—26 November 1577. *John Reppes* of Emneth, gent. [formerly of Walpole] to *Bassingbourn Gawdy.*

License [as remainderman under will of Henry Reppes], for Gawdy to fell four good oaks growing in the grounds of Gawdy's present mansion called Middleton Hall in Suffolk [which he held in right of his wife].

37.—4 February 1577–8. *Thomas Heyward,* Thetford, to *Bassingbourn Gawdy.*

Asks loan of a strong ambling gelding to ride to London, Heyward having lent one of his to his brother Clere. Gawdy can use the horses he leaves behind. Sends a mason and lime burner, whose advice should be taken about the stone work. Has ready landed in his yard for Gawdy 5 chaldrons of coals ["chawlder colles"].

1578.

38—26 June [1578]. *John Marsham* [Court of Exchequer], London, to cousin [*Edward*] *Downes.*

Has searched the records and finds none to charge Downes with any such service. The opinion of the most ancient and experienced in the office agrees with that of Marsham, viz., that Downes should not offer to do the service. If there were any record to charge him, and now at her Majesty's coming he did not perform it, he would not forfeit his estate ; at the worst a petty fine of 10s. or 13s. 4d. would be assessed.

It would be a bad precedent to do it, as after he died the escheator's office would find it accordingly so that the estate would thereafter be charged with it by record.

[August 1578.   Queen Elizabeth came into Norfolk on progress and Mr. Downes presented her with a pair of gilt spurs as service for Earlham. She was said to have stopped at Gawdy's at Harleston, and Thomas Churchyard's pamphlet (Nichols progresses, vol. 2, p. 224), incorrectly states that she knighted Gawdy.]

39.—27 October 1578. *Robert Dudley, Earl of Leicester,* the Court, to [*Bassingbourn Gawdy*].

Understanding Gawdy is to be sheriff, the Earl prays he will appoint the bearer Thomas Wingfield (the Earl's servant) to be under-sheriff.

40.—5 November [1578]. *Thomas Gawdy,* [eldest son of Thomas Gawdy of Shottesham], London, to his brother, *Bassingbourn Gawdy.*

Hears Bassingbourn is in the bill for Sheriff of Norfolk ; begs he will not promise the under-sheriffship for Suffolk until further advice.

[Most authorities incorrectly make Bassingbourn Gawdy, jun., then only 18, sheriff this year, instead of his father.]

.41.—18 November 1578. *Richard Day*, Lincoln's Inn, to [*Bassingbourn Gawdy*].

·Earnestly recommends the· bearer, Butfyld, for the: post of ¡clerk¡ to the under-sheriff.

42.—18 November 1578. *George Gawdy*, London, to his cousin, *Bassingbourn Gawdy*, High Sheriff, Mendham.

Asks his help to the bearer, Tolwyn, "my old·acquaintance," to the arrantship of Loddon and Clavering hundreds; Tolwyn having bought the letters patent to the bailiwick from one Lancaster. ·

43.—19 November 1578. *Sir·Arthur Heveningham*, Heveningham, to·*Bassingbourn Gawdy*.

Heard at Court on Sunday night from·my'Lord Chamberlain that· Gawdy was to be sheriff. Begs the bailiwick of Humbleyard hundred.

44.—21·November 1578. *Sir·Christopher Heydon*, Baconsthorpe, to *Bassingbourn Gawdy*.

Asks the nomination of the bailiff of Holt hundred, which he has been accustomed to have.

45.—21 November 1578. .*Francis Gawdy*, Serjeant's Inn, Fleet Street, to his nephew, *Bassingbourn Gawdy*, Mendham.

Asks the bailiwick of Clackclose hundred for·his servant Stephen Carrowe, who has had it of other sheriffs before at the writer's request. Let the under-sheriff direct warrants to Carrowe by name, or it will·be no benefit.

46.—22 November 1578. *John Nonne* to [his kinsman] *Bassingbourn Gawdy*.

Nonne has waited on the Bishop [of Norwich] for·the enlarging of Mr. Everard. He is contented that Everard be kept in good safety in' any house Gawdy likes in Bury. "Howbeit lest his enemies should gather occasion·of quarrel or complaint, he requireth to. be·advertised in writing from any of credit that the sickness is so set either in or near the jail that there appeareth fear of ·infection." Application must be made to the ·Privy Council for a warrant if it is required for him to leave the town, as was done in Mr. Bedingfield's case, who'was·sent to Leyston Abbey [Suffolk]. Please retain·the bailiwick of·Henstead for one of Nonne's friends. [Henry Everard,·of· Lynsted, married ·Catherine, Gawdy's sister of the whole blood, and was, a popish recusant. ,. See post Nos. 66 to 71.]

47.—23 November [1578].·· *Henry Gawdy*, Claxton, to his cousin, *Bassingbourn Gawdy*, Harling.

· Begs arrantship and stewardship of·Loddon and Clavering for Tolwyn, and bailiwick of Hensted for the bearer, whose wife nursed seven of Henry's children. [This letter·may·· possibly have.. been written,·in 1593.]

48.—[December 1578.] *John Nonne* to [*Bassing. Gawdy*]:-

Nonne has sent Law home, who will answer for himself touching " your·netherstock and my sister's doublet." Nonne· has perused·the wines for his sister, the best coloured old wine is·but reasonably strong; there *is* stronger, but high coloured, like red wine. Bailiwick of Tunsted is vacant, Mr. Crofts sues. for it. for one Moone, recommended by Mr. Roger Drury; 5*l*. is offered. The Clerk of the Peace (whose friendship is material) applies through one Palmer for the bailiwick of

Tayersham, the least in the county, and offers forty shillings. Neither Rolf, the late sheriff's clerk, nor Bradshaw, the gaoler. have returned, which detains Nonne. The bailiwick is only worth 18*l.* to Mr. Drury. Que Bretton challenges Gawdy's promise to him of Tunsted bailiwick; if he gets it, a very honest bailiff and five pounds are lost !

1579.

49.—8 January [1578–9].   *John Nonne* to [*Bassingbourn Gawdy*].

The extremity of the Exchequer appears notably by the enclosed bundle. Let Sir Henry Woodhouse know that the extent for 240*l.* against him and Mr. Ro. Townshende is come and must be executed; let him say if he will have the latter extended or not. Nonne is con- strained to return the execution against Twynne. Were it not for Mr. Bedingfield's letter, Nonne would favour the poor man, for he sees no hope of " any good consideration for the doing of it."
Sends also the attachment out of the Court of Wards, as being nearer Gawdy, and very perilous to be omitted.
Complains of the trouble and responsibility caused by such important process, and wishes himself free from it.

50.—17 January 1578–9.   *John Nonne,* Norwich, to [*Bassingbourn Gawdy*], Harling.

Sends two persons who are to be carried to Bury Sessions by order of Sir Nicholas Bacon.

51.—21 January 1578–9.   *John Skot,* Hingham, to *Bassingbourn Gawdy,* Esq., East Harling.

After he left Gawdy, Skot heard at Market Harling that "the said Jacob " dwelt at Gissing. This he finds is not true. Jacob has left word that he can be seen at Great Ellingham. Skot asks the favour of a special bailiff to catch him.

52.—24 January 1578–9.   *Anthony Flowerdew* of Hethersett, gent., and *Henry Hammon,* yeoman, to *William Moore,* of Intwood, yeoman.

Joint bond to secure payment of 5*l.* and delivery by Flowerdew to Moore of 500 " good wood and hable fagots, well filled." Witness, Thomas Gay, Thomas Margeay, William Sheaking.

53.—26 January 1578–9.   *John Nonne* to [*Bassingbourn Gawdy*].

Sir Roger Woodhouse objects to the panel for the attaint " because the best sort are not returned, the parties being of worship and the cause of weight." He does not object to Sir Henry Weston, though half-brother to Mr. Knyvet ; the other side are less careful as to the panel, which makes Nonne think the attaint is " for policy." Nonne has joined Mr. Bolton in striking an indifferent panel ; if he cannot content both sides shall content himself. He did the like between Mr. Drury (for my Lord Dacre's cause) and Mr. Southwell, and had to fall back upon his own uprightness " that is able to bear me." Mr. Morryson, of Costessy, has set 25*l.* against Gawdy without cause ; Nonne will justify what services he rendered. Tomson and Younger might easily agree.

54.—27 March 1579.   *John Nonne,* Walsingham, to [?].

Has received surety from Mr. Godfrey for Nonne's brother's [*i.e.* Gawdy's] indemnity, either by discharge from Mr. Guybon or payment.

Mr. Robert Sturges need not therefore complain; if. Godfrey could have got a proper discharge from Guybon it would have been paid long since. Godfrey paid Guybon's son 10*l.* [see No. 57].

55.—27 March 1579. *John Owles,* Diss, to *Bassingbourn Gawdy,*
High Sheriff, Harling.

Owles is to receive money of Gawdy for wine not yet all delivered ; he also owes money to Gawdy's farmer, Henry Topas [?], who has shortly to pay his rent ; asks Gawdy to allow on the rent what is coming to Owles, who will deliver the wine in 15 days.

56.—22 April 1579. *John Nonne,* Norwich, to [*Bassingbourn Gawdy].*

Disclaims having anything to do with the arrest of Mr. Dade, who was taken " by the long care and great charges of divers his creditors upon common warrants. . . . I presume to foresend my wife's maid with her linen, as the state of the city occasioneth me thereunto by increase of deaths, which many fear and flee. I would have sent my wife also, but she misliked to leave me behind. . . . I can hardly tell how to bring my wife and her rest without your help of a man and horse." Nonne leaves the procuring a cook for Mrs. Gawdy, as the woman is in the hottest part of the infection. Hopes Sir Henry Wood-house will give a good bond with surety ; he must be spoken with before he comes to Norwich.

57.—25 April 1579. *John Nonne* to [a son of Mr. *Anthony Guybon*].

Nonne has received 18*l.* 13*s.* 4*d.* from Godfrey for Anthony Guybon's use and has seen Guybon's son's receipt for 10*l.* more, leaving 6*l.* due. Send a receipt by A. Guybon to Gawdy for the whole sum and Nonne will see the balance, 24*l.* odd, paid to Guybon, less " what is reason " for his own trouble. [See No. 54.]

58.—2 June 1579. *Nicholas Hare,* London, [eldest son of John Hare] to *Bassing. Gawdy.*

Hare refers to their conversation when last at Sneterton as to a venire facias in an action of replevin between Edward Smyth, Hare's farmer, and John Steward and William Cambridge defendants. "I have no great opinion of some that be dealers for you in the returns." Let honest, indifferent men be chosen and a list given him, lest any be changed on the return ; the man Steward is " well acquainted with shifts." Let none of the Pratts, Butts, Morrises, or Drapers be re-turned. The panel will be indifferent if it comes from Marshland and Wells, but Hare fears Mr. Yelverton and other " bearers in the cause " if it be laid on the other side of Norfolk.

There are likely to be trials at the Assizes between Hare and Gawdy's uncle, Serjeant [Francis Gawdy]. " If he were as reasonable as he is learned, or as a great many be of his kindred " the causes would have been settled. In one case Serjeant Gawdy is plaintiff, and Humphrey Marshall, Richard Giles and John Winter (Hare's servants) are defen-dants. In the other Thomas Smith (Hare's servant) is plaintiff, and Edmund Philip defendant. Hare will not challenge the array for cosenage if indifferent men, not neighbours of the Serjeant, are returned. The other actions are replevins, William Mychell v. Henry Burrow (Hare's man), and Humphrey Marshall v. John Smith.

59.—6 June 1579. *Robert Pennyng,* Frandeston, Suffolk, Cooper, to *Bassingbourn Gawdy.*

Receipt for 12*l.* debt and 39*s.* damages on *ca. sa.* against Thomas Bostocke of Cranworth, Clerk. Witness, Lawrence Sutton, Robert Bowlton.

60.—26 June 1579. *E[dward] Lord Morley,* "my lodge at Hockering" to [*Bassingbourn Gawdy*].

Asks Gawdy's personal attention to two enclosed executions, as the under-sheriff and deputies are absent.

61.—26 June 1579. *William Howse,* Walsham, Suffolk, Husbandman, to *Bassingbourn Gawdy.*

Receipt and release for 5*l.* debt and twenty shillings damages on *ca. sa.* against Edward Bunnet at Oyse. Witness, Robert Puntinge, Robert Catchepole, Thomas Browne, William Davies.

62.—30 June 1579. *Sir Christopher Heydon,* Saxlingham, to [the *Keeper of Norwich Jail*].

Considering the sickness in Norwich, asks that his cousin John Smythe now in custody may be allowed out into the country by leave of the sheriff. Smyth will pay his keeper's charges.

63.—2 July [1579]. *John Nonne,* London, to *Bassingbourn Gawdy.*

"Mr. Attorney desireth that good choice be made of the fittest open place for the seat of the Judge . . . . he was informed that the place proposed, near behind their lodging, would not be had; he also was informed of a convenient place near the Cross ; they look that substantial care be had both of the place and frame.

"Mr. Dowening very lately received from the B[ishop] of London that the Monsieur desisteth from his purpose of coming into England, the tidings whereof are nothing tedious to the best. From the number of venire faciases Nonne expects a small assize. But for Lord Surrey's cause and four other remanets, the Common Pleas "standeth very empty," whereby many "conceive that the law is in declination." Write to Sir Henry Woodhouse that his cause against Peapes will ease him little, except he pay a "convenient sum" this term : he will be "deeply extended or roundly amerced," so Mr. Morrant his attorney tells Nonne, who would write to Sir Henry himself, but the Exchequer, the attaint, Mr. Drury's panel and Younger's cause have kept him "as waking as ever he was." Nonne has to attend Mr. Buxton and Mr. Dyxe for his discharge of an amerciament. "Mr. Thomas Gawdy, I fear, attendeth a dangerous conclusion by purchase. The Chancery suspendeth the trial between Mr. Serjeant [Gawdy] and Mr. Hare."

[A letter of Sir Francis Walsingham in the Domestic State papers of about this date refers to the great losses by law-suits suffered by Thomas Gawdy, who was then speculating in alum.].

64.—12 July 1579. *Sir Christopher Heydon,* Saxlingham, to *Bassingbourn Gawdy.*

"Has received a letter calling on him, Sir William Butt, and others, to appear before the Justice of Assize, which letter is not in the accustomed form. Owing to his distance from the assizes he will not attend unless it be for the Prince's service, which he would in no wise slack. Asks particulars.

65.—27 July [1579]. ' *William Methwold,* South Pickenham, to *Bassingbourn Gawdy.*

Sends by the bearer Henry Rame [?] a dozen and a half of teal.

66.—[July 1579.] *Catherine Everard* [Lynstead, Suffolk], to her brother *Bassingbourn Gawdy.*

Begs his letters to the Earl of Leicester or other Lords of his acquaintance for the enlarging of her husband. Hears Mr. Hare has got his liberty. Hopes her brother will "stick to them." Mr. Back's friend, who formerly hindered the suit, is now in the country. [See ante No. 46.]

67.—[August 1579. *Bassingbourn Gawdy* to the *Privy Council*].

Draft petition for the enlarging of Gawdy's brother-in-law Henry Everard, "as others have been enlarged, committed for the like cause in Norfolk and Suffolk." The sickness continues at Bury, and Gawdy's sister is like to die and would fain see her husband both for her own comfort and for the better providing for their 14 children.

68.—14 August 1579. Sir *Thomas Bromley,* Chancellor, *A[mbrose]* Earl *of Warwick, Sir Francis Walsingham, Earl. of Lincoln, Sir James Crofts,* and *Sir Thomas Wilson,* Greenwich, to [*The Bishop of Norwich*].

Permission for the enlargement of Henry Everard, "theretofore committed prisoner at Bury for matters of religion," on account of the infection there and his wife's sickness. A bond to be taken of him and his brother-in-law for his good behaviour and due forthcoming [a copy only].

69.—15 August [1579]. *Anne Everard,* Lynstead, Suffolk, to her uncle *Bassingbourn Gawdy.*

Her mother has had no fit since Gawdy's departure, but the physician says there is no way but one with her. He says further the fit comes from the corruption that is in her, ascending to her heart. Lowe has brought her father's discharge from London; they do not know what terms will be enforced till Lowe has been to the Bishop.

[Mrs. Everard, her husband, and Barberye, Lowe's wife, were still returned as Popish recusants in 1596, see post 124.]

70.—17 August 1579. *Henry Everard,* Lynstead, Suffolk, Esq., and *Bassingbourn Gawdy,* Harling, Esq., to *the Queen.*

Joint bond in penalty of 200*l.*: recites Everard's committal to Gawdy's custody till further order taken by the Privy Council or the Bishop: the bond is conditioned to secure the forthcoming of Everard when required, and his good demeanour and behaviour, &c. [a copy only].

71.—17 August 1579. *Edward, Bishop of Norwich,* Ludham, to the *Keeper of Bury Jail.*

Warrant for Henry Everard's release.

[The following undated letters from two of Everard's daughters, probably belong to this period.]

GAWDY MSS.   72.—[December 1579 ?] *Katherine Everard to Mrs. Gawdy.*

Thanks her uncle and aunt for placing her where she now is. Her master and mistress have given her leave to tarry with them till Mr. and Mrs. Gawdy come home. She has been sent for to Weston, where she will be glad to go when she has learnt more. [She married Henry Brampton at West Harling in 1587.]

73.—[1579?] *Mary Everard to Bassingbourn Gawdy.*

Begs Gawdy to pity her distress and to mitigate his displeasure against her. If his displeasure be not hindered " alas! silly wretch, I know not what shall become of me! " She believes all this trouble has come upon her through " conceiting the counsel of so bad and vile a woman."

74.—15 December 1579. *John Nonne*, Wymondham, to *Bassing-bourn Gawdy* at Sir E. Clere's house in Holborn.

Gawdy's affairs at Mendham and Harling are all well. Sedgeford sends word that the " woolpullers " are caught ; he paid Nonne 9*l.*, being the balance of 10*l.* 2*s.* due by Mr. Kempe's man for ewes, and a further sum of 5*l.* 16*s.* for 29 ewes sold by him. The cash is at Weston's to be sent to Gawdy by Heyward. Complains that he cannot get free from charge of the jail [see No. 75]. Has called for Sandly's inventory ; his wife says she has paid Gawdy more than the debt. The plague increaseth here afresh. If any suit be made for Roger Watson, delay promising it.

75.—19 December 1579. *John Nonne* to [*Bassingbourn Gawdy*].

Has left money with Mr. Heyward (as above), also 9*l.* and twenty-two pence received of the late Bailiff of Holt.

Nonne considers himself hardly used by Sir Thomas Knyvet [the incoming Sheriff], having waited three weeks, including four special days of Knyvet's own appointment, and yet cannot tell when he shall be quit of [Wymondham] jail. Has been there with his indentures ready for sealing, but is always put off with fair words and devices. Sir T. Knyvet's proposed under-sheriff hopes for the Clerk-of-the-Peace-ship. Nonne will be with Gawdy before the prefixed time.

P.S.—Oats are scarce, on account of the plague and the " extremity of the travel " into Marshland. A messenger Nonne sent to his b[rother ?] Cressiner, fell by the way into a ditch, and broke his arm.

1580.

76.—[February 1579–80, or later]. *In the Consistory Court of Nor-wich. Fleete v. Manne.*

Before the Venerable William Maisters and the Bishop's Consistory Court, Robert Fleete of Pessenall charges against Joan Manne, wife of Thomas Manne ; that the said Joan in the months of March 1579 (and so on to) January of this present year, scandalously and lyingly spoke these words against the good fame of the said Fleete, viz. ; " That he was a cuckoldy knave, and so she would prove him to be a cuckold." [The same charge, with the enormous consequences flowing therefrom, is set out in four more counts, ending with a demand that Joan be punished and made to pay costs.]

GAWDY MSS.

77.—29 February 1579–80. *Francis Gawdy*, Wallington, "to" his nephew *Bassingbourn Gawdy*, Esq., at Sir E. Clere's house, Holborn.

Has Bassingbourn spoken to my Lord of Huntingdon? or has he heard more of the matter his uncle made him privy to when he last waited on my Lord Chancellor?

78.—20 March 1579–80. *John Nonne*, Weston, to [*Mrs. Gawdy*].

Sends his wife's regrets to his good sister for the death of Lady Clere. She is too ill to write herself.

79.—20 March 1579–80. *John Nonne* to [*Bassingbourn Gawdy*, London].

[This letter is torn; words in brackets are conjectural.] Nonne has travelled almost continually since [last sun-]down [?], collecting from the bailiffs [who are] extremely slow and afraid of collecting sums due by men of worship. No penny from Sir Henry Woodhouse or Sir R. Shelton. As to Mr. Sturge's dishonest outcries, he pretends an inhibition from Gawdy to stay Nonne demanding any money from Sir. H. Weston, whose debt is 48*l.* 10*s.* 14*l.* is due by Thomas Townesend. Godfrey cannot pay. [Send] Bolton to Mr. Bedingfield to hasten him. [Nonne hears] he has promised discharges to several; Mr. Heyward, Slater, and he [met] at the assizes, and Heyward promised them payment or security for the amount of the execution. The tailor of Norwich is one Quynch, for 10*l.* or so due by Dade, whereof Sir E. Clere can advertise Gawdy. Tyler's prisoner made no escape, he will be found in fetters in Norwich Castle. Brierton's complaints are due to the spleen. Nonne has sent his men and horses for Mrs. K. Everarde,—she cannot come before Easter.

Nonne has sent 55*l.* 18*s.* 10*d.* to Heyward to convey to Gawdy, and is going again to Norwich collecting. His wife has an ague which "taketh away her stomach and loadeth her head with extreme pain."

[June 1580. Bassingbourn Gawdy jun. and his brother Philip went up to London about this time, Serjeant Flowerdew getting them lodgings till chambers were vacant in Clifford's Inn, where they were to study.]

80.—15 June 1580. *Bassingbourn Gawdy*, of West Harling, to *Richard Fysher*, of Diss, Yeoman.

Bond in penal sum of 200*l.* to indemnify Fysher against his liability as surety for Gawdy on bond of even date to Sir Nicholas Bacon to secure 100*l.* Witness, Robert Bowlton.

81.—28 June 1580. *Thomas Heyward*, Thetford, to [*Bassingbourn Gawdy*].

Cannot tell how the dispute between the Earl of Arundel and Sir E. Clere will end; it would have been better if the latter had contented himself with that which he might quietly have enjoyed, as Richard Fulmerston did. Sends 2 gilt spoons (3oz. 9gr.) which at six and eightpence the ounce comes to 26*s.*, the money for these he received of Bardwell; also 2 quarts of "sallet oil," which cost half a crown, in a pewter that cost as much. Cannot get any sturgeon under twenty shillings a . . . (word torn off). Has a gilt bottle, which will come in his trunk by the next London carrier; he received it from Mr. Wolmer.

82.—13 July [1580.   *Sir John Fortescue,* Salden, [? Bucks], to his brother-in-law [*Bassing. Gawdy*].

Asks Gawdy to release a poor man from prison who owed him 20*l.* whereof 6*l.* 13*s.* 4*d.* was paid. Sends the balance, which was raised among the friends of his old master, Sir Ed. Ashefilde, and asks Gawdy to forego the charges. Hopes they will see "my good sister your wife" this winter at London.

83.—18 August 1580.   *Elizabeth Framlingham,* "my house at Croweshall " [Suff.], to *Bass. Gawdy,* Harling.

Has Gawdy spoken with Sir Robt. Jermyne and Mr. Ashefeld as to a matter wherein they are to deal between her husband and another ?

84.—6 October [1580 ?].   *John Nonne,* Norwich, to [*Bassingbourn Gawdy* ?]

Nonne has paid the bearer fifty-five shillings and eighteen pence towards his charges in collecting money. Asks to have the further remuneration fixed, and Nonne will pay it. Bearer will also want his bond ; he has collected about 32*l.* or 33*l.*, a good part of it near Dereham.

85.—11 October 1580.   *Charles Framlingham,* Crowshall [Suff.], to cousin *Bassing. Gawdy,* Harling.

His wife is ill and has kept her bed two days, so they must excuse themselves from the pleasure of a visit from Mrs. Flowerdew, who is now at Harling. Asks Gawdy to name a day to meet Mr. Ford at Crowshall to act on my Lords of Bedford's letters concerning one Simon Jefferye [alias Sponer].

86.—12 October [1580].   *John Nonne* to [*Bassingbourn Gawdy*].

Asks loan of his sister's coach to help his wife and himself home; his leg is so bad he cannot sit a horse "go he never so easily." Can accommodate Gawdy with two horses.

87.—6 November 1580.   *Francis Gawdy,* Serjeant's Inn, to *Bassingbourn Gawdy,* Harling.

Sir E. Clere is in the bill for Sheriff, ask him for the bailiffship of Clackclose hundred before Mr. Hare can move for it.

88.—17 November [1580].   *Charles Framlingham,* Crowshall, to *Bassingbourn Gawdy,* Harling.

Asks a day to be appointed [as above, No. 85].

89.—26 November 1580.   *Humfrey Moseley* to [*Bass Gawdy* ?].

Moseley is willing to purchase land in Suffolk near the little he owns there ; would like to know about quantity and quality of land in " your moiety of Towling " (?) before making an offer.

90.—7 December 1580.   *Charles Framlingham* to *Bassing. Gawdy,* Midleton Hall, Mendham.

The 9th December will not suit Forde for the Sp^{o}ner enquiry. [*See* next letter.]

91.—18 December 1580.   *Charles Framlingham,* Croweshall [Suff.], to *Bassingbourn Gawdy.*

Gives a history of the Sponer affair. Sponer brought an "action of perjury" against one of Framlingham's servants, apparently on a matter of Framlingham's·title· to·certain lands which Sponer claimed. Sir,.Gilbert,Gerrard, the Attorney-General, at last Bury Assizes, referred the matter to Sir Robert Jermyne and Mr. Ashfelde, their order to be set down by Christmas. · Gawdy was present and helped at the enquiry, and knows their conclusion, viz., that Sponer had no title, and that Framlingham and his servant had suffered wrong at his hands. Asks Gawdy (as the limit of time draws near) to urge them to make their order forthwith, and punish Sponer as it is in their power to do. [*See* No. 96.]

92.—19 December 1580. *Sir Arthur Heveningham*, Ketteringham, ., to *Bassingbourn Gawdy.*

Sends the confession of *Elizabeth Jeakes, sometime servant 'to Nicholas Fox. Bind her over to the sessions, examine Nicholas and his wife, and take recognizances of Hacon and Blobolde of Mendham, and other witnesses. This will be a kindness to the poor men, as otherwise, Sir Arthur will send his warrants for them to Ketteringham, as " the matter belongs unto the prince," although done four or five years ago.

93.—27 December 1580. *Robert Damont*, Stow-market [Suff.]· to [*Bassingbourn Gawdy ?*].

One Christopher Otway, of Stowe Market, a farmer under Sir Drue Drury, has agreed to set over his term of years to Damont. Asks help in obtaining the necessary consent from Sir Drue.

1580-1.

94.—[January 1580-1.] *John Nonne* to· *Bassingbourn Gawdy*, Midleton ·Hall, Mendham.

Nonne thanks his sister and Gawdy for that they are received " here " by Gawdy's appointment from Harling. Nonne is lame, and fears the result of his suit, he being at issue with " yonder lewd fellow Henry Heyward and his mate." He hopes for Gawdy's influence at the Sessions, as he himself will not be present. Get a panel returned including men of knowledge in Sheriff's matters, if possible, some who have been undersheriffs or clerks, " of which sort there be store about Shipdham," where the venue is laid. Mr. Hoogan favours Heyward, having spleen against Nonne for his conduct in a suit between Hoogan's man and Sir D. Drurie's. Have the panel filed in Court, lest the other side, mislik. ing it, defer and dally for better opportunities. Kyrby is clerk to the under-sheriff, he will help by conference with Mr. Brett and others, whom Gawdy may appoint to confer with Mr. Gilbert. Tell Bridgs to fetch the two loads of wainscot hence ; this idle time will serve well for such work.

95.—9 January 1580-1. *John Nonne to Bassingbourn Gawdy*, the Sessions, Norwich.

See that Bradshaw looks better to Gawdy's discharging ; Bradshaw's sureties " became housekeepers " when Nonne tried to have them arrested. Mr. Seman has written of some causes touching Gawdy through Bradshaw's default. As to Gawdy's execution against Mr. Blakes, Mr. Steads wrote to Nonne, and he wrote to Seman, asks Gawdy to take order in it. [The rest of the letter is almost identical with No. 94 as to Nonne's suit with Bullocke or Heyward, ending with " the extremity of my peril terrifieth me."]

96.—13 January 1580–1. • *Sir John Fortescue*, Ipswich, " very sick
in my chamber," to *Bassingbourn
Gawdy.*

· Asks an appointment to meet and prosecute the enquiry touching the
good behaviour of the bearer Simon Jefferyes, alias Sponer, as directed
by the Earl of Bedford's letters.

Has never heard but well of the man, except from cousin Framlingham, who urges dispatch. Jefferyes is anxious to ride to London,
thinking to find his Lord there, it being Parliament time.

97.—22 January 1580–1.   *Charles Framlingham*, Crowshall, to
Bassingbourn Gawdy, Mendham.

· Is Gawdy riding to London this term ? If so, asks him to take
Crowshall on his way, upon a matter of business.

1581.

98.—3 April 1581.   *Nicholas Hare*, Denyngton, to *Bassingbourn
Gawdy.*

Has talked with Thurston as to the matter between Seman and the
inhabitants of Denyngton, and asked proof of the articles on oath. Such
is the practice of justices before binding over to good behaviour,
" unless they conceive very well of them that exhibit the articles."
Recommends the granting of application, and to take Seman's bond " in
some deep sum," to appear at the assizes. His peddling practices do
the country much harm.

· 99.—10 April 1581.   *Margaret Darby's* confession.

That Robert Arthure, the neatherd of Roudham, is the " only father "
of her child.

100.—18 April [1581]. *Anthony Gawdy*, Arundel House, London,
to brother *Bassingbourn Gawdy.*

Applies to his brother to forgive his son " Bas," who confesses his
offence and broken promise by "playing." He promises amendment and
asks pardon and payment of his debts (26*l*.) and that his mother may
not hear of it. " He does not desire to live unless he has your favour .
. . . The news is here of the ' [French] ' Commissioner's arrival and
the great triumph that is towards."

[Between the dates of these letters Bassingbourn Gawdy, jun., was
evidently recalled from town. |

101.—1 June [1581].   *Bassingbourn Gawdy* [junior], Crowshall,
[Suff.], to his uncle *Anthony Gawdy*,
London.

After thanking Anthony for pecuniary help towards his debts, Bassingbourn tells of some notable thieves lately brought before him, who
robbed shops and mills near East Harling, and one church, having pick-
lock keys that will unlock nearly every door in Bassingbourn's father's
house. The worst is that one of them is Anthony's own man, William
Dowset. Another of the gang is one Jasper Sturten, who was helped
out of Newgate lately by Dowset. He confesses that the night
Anthony and Bassingbourn lay together at Redgrave, Dowset returned
to Sturten's house and borrowed 8 picklocks, the two then riding
double to Larlingford on Anthony's horse, thinking to have robbed his
trunk there containing 30*l*. The other blaming Dowset for robbing his
master, he said Anthony could spare it, being " as rank a churl and

arrant an usurer as any in England."' The trunk having been taken by the carriers to Thetford they rode to Kenninghall windmill, Sturten commending the beast for its paces. They each stole a combe of meal and took it home on the horse. The other fellow [Busbey ?] says Dowset showed him a key he and Sturten had made. Bassingbourn urges his uncle to prefer his credit and Bassingbourn's good name and oath, to his man's life.

102.—20 September 1581. *Bassingbourn Gawdy*, West Harling, to *Richard Fysher* of Diss, Yeoman.

Bond to secure payment of 50*l.* to Fysher at Suddon Hall, Renton, Suffolk, on St. Luke the Evangelist next. Witness, Robert Bolton, Reynold Chamberlen, Thomas Tyte, John Bowser. [See post No. 106.]

103.—11 October 1581. [*Sir*] *J*[*ohn*] *Heigham*, Barrow, Suffolk, to *Constables*, &c.

Judith Rust and one Halsted, with whom she has departed, are lewd and incontinent livers. Requests assistance to the bearer in apprehending and returning them to Suffolk for punishment.

104.—20 October [1581]. *Anthony Gawdy*, Arundel House, to brother *Bassingbourn Gawdy*, Harling.

Monsieur is speedily coming ; his chamber at Court is hanged and a cloth of estate hanged up and direction given for all things necessary. The plague is ceased in London. Mr. Norris hath had a great overthrow in Flanders, many of our knights, gentlemen and soldiers slain.

1582.

105.— 31 March 1582. [A brother-in-law of *John Houghton*] to *Bassingbourn and Mrs. Gawdy*.

Gives a doleful account of the writer having sued his brother-in-law John Houghton for detaining two bonds and for false imprisonment. It was tried at the Guildhall, Norwich, last assizes, when one John Marshall of that City, Tailor, seeing it was going against Houghton did "wickedly and ungodly" swear that Houghton had delivered the bond sued on to Mr. Pecke, Alderman of Norwich, when he was mayor. Pecke can prove this false, but the jury believed Marshall and found against the writer to his "great and intolerable loss." Being a man he cannot wage law for his remedy. Sues for a "piece of money for a time" and hopes to bring Houghton to reason yet (signature cut off).

106.—12 May 1582. *Richard Fysher*, of Diss, to *Bassingbourn Gawdy*.

Receipt by Fysher for 20*l.* on account of 150*l.* due him for his interest in Bridgham lease [see No. 102 and 116].

107.—31 May 1582. *Nicholas Hare*, London, to *Bassingbourn Gawdy*.

Stewarde has exhibited a bill in the Star Chamber against Hare and nine others. The Chancellor has granted a *dedimus potestatem* to receive the answers, Gawdy being a Commissioner ; they are to sit at Lynn on Trinity Monday. Hare does not wish to trouble Gawdy to go so far and has written to Fermor who lives nearer Lynn. If Stewarde calls, do not let out that Hare wrote to Fermor.

108.—[5 June] Whit Tuesday 1582. *Nicholas Hare,* Stow-Bardolph, to *Bassingbourn
Gawdy.*

Understands by Ralph Gawdy [a son of Thomas] that Bassingbourn
has been ill. Sketches out a letter for him to write and send by Ralph
to satisfy the Chancellor why he does not attend.

109.—8 June [1582]. *Nicholas Hare,* Stow Bardolph, to *Bassingbourn Gawdy.*

Had he not heard Gawdy was too ill to travel, Hare would gladly
have had the Commission executed by now. The Chancellor appointed
Mr. Justice Windham, Gawdy, Mr. Peyton, and Mr. Fermor to be Commissioners, without nomination either by Hare or Stywarde. Would
like to have Gawdy's letter of excuse to show the Chancellor.

110.—June 1582. *Sir Thomas Bromley,* Chancellor "my house
near Charing Cross," to *Sir Thomas Wing-
field, Sir Nicholas Bacon, Sir Robert Jermyn,
Sir John Higham, Sir Roger Woodhouse,
Sir William Springe, James Ryvett, Esq., and
Bassingbourn Gawdy, Esq.*

Her Majesty having appointed Commissioners by Letters Patent to
speedily repair a lane called Christmas Lane near the town of Metfield,
Suffolk, the above Justices are to see that the head and under constables aid in the work. [This appears to be a circular copy and has this
note at the end : " Received this letter 25 June in my chamber at London,
of Edmonde Curteys, one of the Commissioners."].

111.—7 July 1582. *Sir Arthur Heveningham,* Ketteringham, to
Bassingbourn Gawdy.

Has received letters from the Privy Council for certain weighty
services. Calls a meeting of the Justices for the 10 July at the White
Horse in St. Stephen's [Norwich] ; the Sessions are on the following
Thursday.

112.—11 August 1582. *Thomas Heyward,* Thetford, to [*Bassingbourn Gawdy*].

Heyward is sorry to hear that Gawdy's servant Bobbet has indirectly
sought to leave his service. [The man has apparently charged Heyward with enticing him away.] " My Lord " sends the enclosed
warrant for a buck. Heyward has tried without success to get Gawdy
a long Turkey carpet.

113.—11 August 1582. *Robert Sucklyng,* Mayor, Norwich, to *Mr.
Serjeant Flowerdew,* Stanfield.

To apprise him of meeting of the Subsidy Commissioners. The
bearer is a suitor for the poor minister Mr. Metcalfe, and can offer
sureties such as Mr. Serjeant may accept on behalf of that "distressed
man."

114.—15 August 1582. *Sir Arthur Heveningham,* Ketteringham, to
Bassingbourn Gawdy, West Harling.

Asks a benevolence on the marriage of his cook, who has served him
10 or 12 years. The wedding is at Wymondham on 19th.

115.—20 August [1582?].   *Anthony Gawdy*, Hawsted [Suff.], to his brother *Bassingbourn Gawdy*, Harling.

Riding with Sir William [Drury] has hindered Anthony from coming to his brother. Sir William and his wife marvel that they do not see [Bassingbourn?] and Philip.

116.—8 September 1582.   *Richard Fysher*, of Diss, Deputy Attorney of *Thomas Brampton*, of Renton, Suff., gent., to *Bassing. Gawdy, Esq.*

Irrevocable Power of Attorney to Gawdy to recover, &c. in Brampton's name all monies, &c. due from Thomas Foster, George Kempe, and John Vincent under any Indenture, bargain, sale, or writing obligatory, &c., assigned or set over by Brampton and Alice his wife to Fysher. Witness, Robert Bolton, Nicholas Sayer. [See Nos. 102 and 106.]

117.—17 September 1582.   [*Arthur*] *Throckmorton*, Beaumanoir, [?] to *Lady* [*Drury*].

Thanks Sir William and Lady [Drury] for their kindness to his daughter "Bes." Mr. Stocks and he are so grateful, that next to my Lady Stafford, Throckmorton will hold himself indebted to them. As to the proposed match with their friend, he begs it may stand over ; she is his only daughter and very young.

[The proposed match was with Bassingbourn Gawdy, junr., who with his brother Philip visited Throckmorton next month.]

118.—25 September 1582.   *Richard Fysher*, Diss, to *Bassingbourn Gawdy*.

Receipt for 10*l.* on account of bond for 30*l.* due at Hallowmas ; money sent by hands of Robert Bolton.

119.—28 September 1582.   *Robert Coon* to [*Bassingbourn Gawdy*]

Coon cannot come to keep Gawdy's Court at Harling in October as he promised. He has received precepts from the Court of Wards for three cases at Ipswich on the 4th and 5th October ; being interrogatories exhibited by Mr. Felton's executors against Widow Nonne of North Pickenham, one Johnson (an Ipswich merchant) and one Bull, of Bossehall, near Ipswich. Sends his son-in-law to take his place, and hopes that he with Bolton's help will see to the charge of Mr. Brett's lands to Gawdy's profit.

120.—12 October 1582.   *Henry Appleyard* and *Christopher Flowerdew*, both of Wymondham, Gents., to *Robert Kyrby*.

Joint bond to secure payment of 10*l.* at Christmas 1583 at the house of Marion Sterling, Wymondham, widow.

121.—22 October [1582].   A[*rthur*] *Throckmorton*, Beaumanoir, [? where] — to *Bassingbourn Gawdy*.

Begs that the motion of marriage made by Sir William Drury between Throckmorton's daughter and Gawdy's son may stand over, on account of the former's "unmeetness" in age and growth, and the distance Throckmorton is from his friends, with whom he and Mr

B 2

GAWDY MSS. Stocks would fain consult. • Thanks Gawdy for his willingness to entrust Throckmorton with his "jewels, . . . which truly be jewels indeed."

1582-3.

122.—22 February 1582-3.   A[rthur] Throckmorton, Beauma-noir, to Bassingbourn Gawdy.

Throckmorton goes to London before the term, but not by my Lady Hynes, as she is gone up to her daughters. He will go by Northamptonshire. If Gawdy has nothing else to come up for but the proposed match between his son and Throckmorton's daughter, better put off coming till the young people have met, as she is unwilling to take anybody. Has had bad health since Gawdy's sons were there. If the weather and ways wax fairer, he will go up, tho' it were in his litter; as being nearer his native air he may recover his health.

123.—1 March 1582-3 [?].   Sir Thomas Gawdy to his nephew, Bassingbourn Gawdy [?].

Asks his nephew to treat with Mr. Flegg and get him to leave Gawdy Hall at M[icbelmas] next. Bear him in hand that it is not Sir Thomas' desire, but that B. Gawdy wants his uncle to come there. If Flegg wants a house, Sir Thomas is going to sell his.

124.—12 March 1582-3.   Henry Everard, Linsted [Suffolk], to brother-in-law, Bassingbourn Gawdy.

Hears that process has come to the Sheriff to levy the money the recusants were condemned to pay at last assizes. Gawdy knows Everard's estate, that he is greatly indebted and has great charge of children which he could not support if Gawdy and other friends did not help keep some.

Asks Gawdy's good word to the Sheriff to favour Everard and his friends as much as possible.

125.—17 March 1582-3.   John Holden, Ellingham-Magna, Clerk, to Bassingbourn Gawdy.

Master Francis Woodhouse will meet Gawdy and the witnesses on the 22nd March at Stowe Church according to Gawdy's warrant. Asks him to notify William Tymperley.

1583.

126.—12 May 1583.   Thomas Leventhorp, Aldebury, to Bassing-bourn Gawdy.

Lawrence Attcocke, "a little fellow with a red face," now in gaol at Thetford as a rogue, and who was burnt in the ear by Leventhorp for the same offence, is wanted in Hertfordshire for burglary. Please pass him from constable to constable to Royston or Barley, where a warrant will be for taking him to Hertford gaol.

127.—22 May 1583.   John Laurence, Fressingfield, Suffolk, to Bassingbourn Gawdy.

Apologises for not having waited on Gawdy for so long a time.

128.—23 May [1583 ?].   Thomas Leverington, Wyndham, to Bassingbourn Gawdy.

Leverington's honest poor neighbour, Richard Cattawaye, is in prison in London by order of the High Commission on the accusation of the

Vicar of Wymondham, " a very lewd and ungodly man." The Vicar had railed in Cattawaye's presence at a man who found fault with the Lord's prayer.

" Cattawaye answered that the man did but ask a question, not that he do hold any such thing. As for example (said Cattawaye), I should ask you this question, ' Why do we say Our Father, which. art in heaven, rather than Our Father, which art in earth '? " Cattawaye did this to make him understand it was a question, not that he held any such opinion. The Vicar, being full of malice, accused him of desiring men to alter the Lord's prayer, which is false. Such is. his malice and envy against all who would have the Word truly preached."

129.—28 May 1583. *Francis Gawdy* to his cousin, *Bassingbourn Gawdy.*

Asks benevolence for their poor kinsman Daniel Plumbe, on his marriage. The bride's father requires him to be made worth 300 marks, whereof Mr. Gawdy and "my brother Serjeant" have given 200.

130.—28 September 1583. *Augustine Dyxe*, Longstratton, to *Bassingbourn Gawdy.*

On 27 January 1582–3, Daniel Reve and Cicely his wife consented to surrender at the next Court for Seckford Manor, 10 acres in Quiddenham to John Baxter and Mary his wife, which Nicholas Baxter had bought from Reve. Dyxe entered this in his book, Reve to be bound in 20*l.* to fulfil his promise.

131.—17 October 1583. *Bassinglourn Gawdy*, W. Harling, to *Thomas Heyward*, Thetford, Esq.

Bond to secure payment to Heyward of 20*l.* at Michaelmas next. (Witness, Robert Bolton.)

1583–4.

132.—17 March 1583–4. *Bassingbourn Gawdy*, West Harling, to *Thomas Heyward*, Thetford.

Bond to secure 200*l.* payable to Heyward next Michaelmas. (Witness, Robert Bolton.)

1584.

133.—2 May 1584. *William Hewyck*, Norwich, draper, to *Anthony Flowerdew*, gent., *Humphrey Flowerdew*, gent., *Edmund Flowerdew*, gent., and *Thomas Inne.*

Receipt and acquittance by Hewyck (or Hewke) of all debts, &c.

134.—23 June 1584. *Thomas Heigham,* Bury, to *Bassingbourn Gawdy.*

Heigham lost a mare and her foal some ten weeks past, and having searched the "book of entries for such occasions" at Thetford, found that Mr. Futter had had them cried there. ' Hears they were found within Gawdy's manor, who has them. The bearer will pay for their keep.

135.—25 June 1584. *Sir John Heigham*, Bury, to *Bassingbourn Gawdy.*

To excuse Mr. Gosnold from being trained as a soldier, he being sufficiently charged with provision of arms, &c.

136.—22 July 1584. *Sir Charles Framlingham,* **High Sheriff** Suffolk, to his bailiffs, *John Jubye* and *John Baxter.*

Warrant to arrest Stephen Burrell, formerly of Lowestoft, yeoman, outlawed in Norfolk 13 April 1584, at suit of Robert Ringword, for debt. Robert Crispe [Under-sheriff? *See* No. 193].

137.—29 July 1584. *John Nonne* to sister-in-law [*Mrs. Gawdy?*].

(Letter mutilated.) Is encouraged by his wife to expect "in you a favourable mind." Begs correspondent to . . . [send to?] Weston some time tomorrow, also to get [Gawdy?] (if back from the Assizes) to signify where Nonne may wait upon him.

138.—26 August 1584. *Francis Gawdy,* Wallington, to his nephew, *Bassingbourn Gawdy,* Harling.

Understands dispute between Smyth of Tarleton and William Ingram. of Bunwell is referred to B. Gawdy and Mr. [Buxton?], begs the former to be "good master" to Ingram.

139.—14 September 1584. *Sir Nicholas Bacon,* Redgrave, to *Constables of Lopham.*

Warrant to take Henry Sporle before B. Gawdy to be examined.

140.—19 October [1584?]. *Anthony Gawdy,* Hawsted [Suffolk], to brother *Bassingbourn Gawdy* [senr.], Harling.

Asks Bassingbourn to come with all his friends and freeholders to Ipswich on 2 Novr., where Sir William Drury desires their voices ["woyesis"] to elect him knight of the shire.

141.—[? October 1584.] *Thomas Heyward* to *Bassingbourn Gawdy.*

It were well for Gawdy to write at once to the Mayor and Burgesses of Thetford, Heyward will forward and further it.

142.—22 October 1584. *Thomas Heyward* to *Bassingbourn Gawdy.*

Has sent again to the Mayor of Thetford to do what he can for the answering of my lord of Arundel's letters if they come. Heyward sends below the copy of the letters he first sent in Gawdy's behalf. Prays Gawdy to help his wife to-morrow to Mr. Cotton's of Barneham. Sends by her the £20 he borrowed last week. Tell Mrs. Gawdy that he has sent the other £20 to London to be paid to Mr. Asheley.

(Copy Letter.)

Understanding there shall be a Parliament called for the 23 November, and knowing you are to appoint two burgesses, Heyward has moved Gawdy "to continue his care and travail to the increase of your commodity therein." Gawdy if elected "meaneth freely to discharge you of the whole charge incident to the same."

143.—13 November [1584?]. *Anthony Gawdy,* Hawsted [Suffolk], to brother *Bassingbourn Gawdy* (senr.).

Please deliver to Borde, Anthony's man, the £90 which he has occasion to employ.

[Bassingbourn Gawdy, sen., goes up to London.]

144.—8 December 1584. *Edward* [*Flint* ?], "my lodgings" [London], to *Bassingbourn Gawdy*.

Asks him to sign a petition for a poor man their countryman, the former certificate having been lost after Mr. [Heggon ?] saw it. Did not like to trouble him with this the last day at Arundel House.

1584–5.

145.—12 February 1584–5. *James Quarles*, Clerk of Her Majesty's Kitchen, to *Mr. Serjeant Flowerdew*.

Grant of a yearly buck in summer and doe in winter from any of the Royal Parks in Norfolk or elsewhere.

1585.

146.—9 April 1585. *Revd. John Thaxter*, Bridgham, to [*Bassingbourn Gawdy*].

[A long letter with texts cited in the margin.] Wishes to do his duty to the small flock over whom he has been placed by Gawdy, especially by means of the ancient exercise of public catechizing, which he has used for six or seven years both at Cambridge and in the country, and which has proved more profitable than " other preachings." At Bridgham it does *not* succeed ; the people have no copy in print and few or none can read or write out the written copy Thaxter has given them ; also he conjectures they cannot understand it " being wholly bent to the toil of manual affairs and the tilth of the ground." Begs Gawdy to have the enclosed two small catechisms printed, and send him 20 or 30 copies ; he would not have them published at present altho' he has been advised to do so. Thaxter has nothing to say against other catechisms, but " every man's spittle savours best in his own mouth." One is for young people, the other more advanced.

147.—16 April 1585. *William Rushbroke*, Hoxene [Suffolk], to *Bassingbourn Gawdy*, London.

Asks Gawdy to hire of Mr. Southwell for him the piece of ground " lying by my glebe " called Pasture Close, with the meadows adjoining, at the price Mr. William Cornwalleys paid four years past for it. It is in great request by wealthy neighbours, &c., and would not benefit Rushbroke if he paid for it " at their pitch." There comes from London on Thursday to Hoxne, one Mr. Boadley, merchant, living not far from the 3 Cranes in Whittington College parish in Maiden Lane, whose son is to marry neighbour Barker's daughter ; Rushbroke would like word sent by him. Remembrances to Mrs. Gawdy, "your sons, Mrs. Katherin [Everard ?], &c.

148.—21 April 1585. *Simon Foppesfeld*, Mettingham Hall [Suffolk,] to *Bassingbourn Gawdy* [London.]

Gawdy's letters were delivered to Thurston on Friday and sent by him to Sir Nicholas Bacon, who is fixed in his determination for Brame. The man has not yet been sworn. News came to Harleston that Sir Nicholas had been sent for by a pursuivant and had ridden to London or to the Court. Sir Nicholas wrote to Thurston that the stay of swearing Brame was by Foppesfeld's means. In truth he believes it was, and if he had not spoken Thurston would not have remembered Gawdy. " Beccles' (?) outrageous babble for the common " is pacified by Justice Clenche, Sir Philip Parker and·" my uncle" Ashefeld. Sir Arthur·Heveningham, "my uncle Ashefeld and my father . . [?]" were at the Sessions on Monday. William Wrott who comes to London this week can let Gawdy know the proceedings. Does not know how his man the bearer will succeed in collecting the money Foppesfeld has appointed him to receive. Asks Gawdy if necessary to help him with 20*l.* or 30*l.* which will be repaid at his coming up. Remembrances to his brother Anthony.

(The postscript to the letter is dated Harleston.)

149.—3 May 1585. *Sir Arthur Heveningham*, Ketteringham, to *Bassingbourn Gawdy.*

Has received letters from the Privy Council. Calls a meeting for Thursday next at Norwich at the Crown in St. Stevens which he understands " to be the clearest place."

150.—June 1585. *Francis Gawdy to Mr. Coote*, Lopham.

Asks the present of a buck to the bearer.

151.—26 August 1585. *Francis Gawdy*, Wallington, to his nephew *Bassingbourn Gawdy* [Sen.], Harling.

Sends bearer to fetch away his daughter, and acknowledges B. Gawdy's kindness to her. Would have visited him but had been in pain and troubled with " thundering in my head."

152.—27 September 1585. *Thomas Heyward*, Brettenham, to *Bassingbourn Gawdy.*

Heyward's meeting at Thetford with Lord St. John's assignees as to settlements between that nobleman's sister and " my cousin Edwd. " Clere " was broken off for two reasons. They wanted 100*l.* a year in possession and 600*l.* in reversion. Also that the son's debts be paid, they say 4,000*l.* at least. They waited on Sir E. Clere and report that he agreed to the increase, provided that 40*l.* or 50*l.* a year of the reversionary land might be sold to pay the debts, and Sir E. Clere not be otherwise charged with them. This is a dear bargain, as he gets no money nor certainty of living with the gentlewoman ; they have gone to get my lord's decision. Sends Gawdy's basin and ewer. Asks a warrant for the service of one Roger Saulter, a husbandman, who is Heyward's covenanted servant *till to-morrow* (sic) and has been inveigled away. Constables names are Richard Conestall and Marten Toller.

153.—21 October 1585. [Sir] *Francis Hynde*, Maddingley [Cambridge], to *Mr. Baron Flowerdewe.*

At last Wisbeach Assizes Hynde was a suitor to the Judge on behalf of himself and his neighbours of Marche within the Isle having causes between them and the Bishop's farmer of Stone, within the lordship of Marche, as to the former having procured an injunction removing the cause into the Exchequer. Begs him to get the cause returned into the Isle.

154.—13 December 1585. *Thomas Heyward*, Brettenham, to *Bassingbourn Gawdy.*

Mr. Lovell's officers continue intruding on Mr. Warren's liberties Before the proposed survey of the latter, and whilst Gawdy is with

Mr. Warren, it would be well to look into his evidences, and go over the title with Mr. Donne. Heyward has resumed possession for Warren of 40 acres from sundry tenants, viz., John A-bretnehm̄, the College of Rushford, Ric. Purrye, Edmund Smythe, Thos. Huggan, Ric. Welles, John Watts his oatfield, Tebald, Swanes, Osteleyne, Pike, &c., and expects to find more. Unless Warren can divide his manor [Calton Hall] from Lovell's, and prove the waste to be his fee, a survey will only damage him, and he had better rely on his use and possession, and only seek to restrain Lovell's attempts to bring the 5 new tenements on the green within his manor of Rothyng-hall in Brettenham, which is the "lewd devise" of Blak his Steward, so as to get enough tenants to hold a Court and in time make by-laws for all Brettenham as he pleases.

[Thomas Lovell bought Rothyng-hall manor of the Earl of Arundel in 1583.]

1585–6.

155.—18 January 1585–6. *John Thurston*, Hoxne, Suffolk, to *Bassingbourn Gawdy*.

James Richardson, of Denham, and Clemence his wife, have brought up the wife's niece, one Elizabeth Filby, from childhood, and kept her 24 years or more. Clemence also gave her 10*l.* lately, which was left with a nephew Richard Wright for the niece's use. A month ago the girl ungratefully left them, taking more than was her own with her, and Thurston hears that Wright brought her to Gawdy's. He wishes the maid sent that he may examine her ; her relations being willing she should return to Gawdy's service afterwards.

1586.

156.—15 September 1586. *Sir Arthur Heveningham*, Ketteringham, to *Bassingbourn Gawdy*.

Entreats Gawdy on behalf of the bearer Mr. Robert Chamberlayne of Attleburgh and his mother to get their rate on the subsidy roll reduced again. The mother is 100*l.* poorer than she was and the son has spent part of the little he had from his father in a suit with Mr. Flynte.

157.—24 September 1586. *Christopher Heydon* [*Esq.*] to *Bassingbourn Gawdy*.

Heydon is induced by the "immoderate brag" of Farmor to stand in election for one of the places in Parliament. Asks for Gawdy's and his friends' assistance ; he would "ride a hundred mile to do them any pleasure" in return.

[This was the celebrated double election so much debated in the House of Commons. Fermor and Gresham were returned on the first writ, which was not in the Sheriff's hands soon enough to be properly proclaimed. The Court of Chancery issued another writ and Heydon and Gresham were returned. The House finally supported the first return.]

158.—24 October 1586. *William Stone to Bassingbourn Gawdy*.

Receipt by Stone for 8*l.* 13*s.* by hands of Luke Wolmer.

159.—13 December [1586 ? or earlier]. [*Sir*] *Charles Framlingham*, Croweshall, to his cousin [*Bassingbourn Gawdy*, *Sen.*]

The bearer, Thomas Gescolfe, was maliciously indicted at the last quarter sessions at Beccles for refusing to work with John Bonne, "because he was otherwise in work at the time." Framlingham asks Gawdy if he thinks the indictment was brought by ill will to cause the "bock" to be withdrawn without fine, or such reasonable one as he conveniently may. Remembrances to "my cousin your bedfellow and "the rest of our young cousins."

1586–7.

160.—6 January 1586–7.   *Alexander Duke*, Rising, to *Bass. Gawdy.*

Writes for a pair of breeding swans Gawdy once promised his master.

161.—3 February [1586–7].   *Elizabeth Nonne*, Tostock, Suffolk, to her sister [*Mrs. Gawdy*], Harling.

Hears Mr. Nashe the minister is dead, which makes "a way for my "brother and you to provide the ministry of His Word . . . for "His glory and your comfort . . . Not every learned man, no, not "every good man, is fit to be a minister, as you have already had "experience." Mrs. Nonne can recommend one whose gifts, and godliness they know, Mr. Harvey, whose present living is so small and his charge so great that there is talk of moving him. While loth to part with him, she would rather her correspondents enjoyed that "which the "Lord hath denied me."
[Harvey was presented to West Harling 30 March 1587.]

162.—5 March 1586–7.   [*Sir*] *William Heydon*, Baconsthorpe, to [*Bassingbourn Gawdy.*]

Having received last night very late copies of a letter from the Privy Council to the lord lieutenant, and the latter's letter to his deputies, Heydon advertises [Gawdy] that all captains of footmen and horsemen are to have their men warned from "man to man" to be ready by a day to be named before the 20 March. Vacancies are to be filled up by then. Will meet at Norwich if necessary to confer.

163.—7 March 1586–7.   *William Maister*, Norwich [See No. 76 ?], to *Bassingbourn Gawdy*, Harling.

Apologises for intermeddling on behalf of the poor man Jeffrye Griffin of Brockdish, whose wife was formerly in Maister's service. Asks the calling back of Gawdy's warrant for his punishment, as undeserved. Griffin never offended Mr. Gibson "by lewd speech or behaviour," if he did it was four years ago, and the charge is brought by "hypocritical bodies who seem to cloak their uncharitable affections with a dissembled zeal to preserve the reputation of a preacher who meaneth no such bitterness."

1587.

164.—[? April 1587.]   *William Cardynall* to *Bassingbourn Gawdy* [senior ?].

Is well satisfied with the loving disposition of Gawdy and his wife towards their son [? Philip]. Cardynall will leave his daughter of inheritance immediately after his death 50*l.* a year, whether he has a son or no. And if no son he will leave her 50*l.* a year more after his and his wife's deaths. Cardynall has 100*l.* a year besides to leave at his pleasure. Will agree with Gawdy as to the present maintenance of the young couple. He cannot come to Gawdy's house as he is not well, and dare not take so far a journey. Asks Gawdy to come to his house to meet his cousin Gurden in Easter week.

[June 1587. *Anne, Bassingbourn Gawdy's* wife, died. He, held Middleton Hall in her right under will of her former husband, Henry Reppes.]

165.—11 June 1587. *John Nonne to Bassingbourn Gawdy.*

Nonne has talked with the "greatest dyers" near him, who advise Gawdy to have his greens changed to black in London, there is peril of it taking a good colour otherwise. In the country he would have to wait his turn, and would not be charged less than 14*d.* or 15*d.* a yard. Nonne sends 20*l.*, all he can scrape together on short notice, and will wait on Gawdy on Thursday. Sends consolations for Gawdy's loss.

166.—20 June 1587. *Bassingbourn Gawdy* and *John Reppes* [of Emneth, remainderman under his brother Henry Reppes' will].

Agreement leasing to Gawdy Middleton Hall and grounds till next Hallowmas; with special arrangements as to hay, &c. on the Pricke, the Common Ground, and the Somer-ley. Gawdy to use barns, lower houses, and corn-chamber till Candlemas; the higher houses, garden, and orchard till Hallowmas. Gawdy to have use of implements and household stuff. As to ground occupied by John Balles, John Nedham, and John Goebold, they are to pay Reppes 10*l.* rent at Michaelmas. Nothing said about Gawdy paying rent, but Reppes is to have all fire-wood lying felled in the grounds, and to have ingress at pleasure, and right to keep his horse in the pasture.

(Witness, James Berdew, Robert Bolton, John Nedham, William Pells, John Balles.)

167.—1 August 1587. *Thomas Fermor*, East Barsham, to cousin *Bassingbourn Gawdy.*

Asks benevolence on marriage of his old servant, William Reymes.

168.—15 August 1587. *Sir William Heydon*, Baconsthorpe, to *Bassingbourn Gawdy*, with speed, speed, speed.

Has received commission from the Exchequer, and a letter from the Attorney-General to himself, Serjeant Gawdy, B. Gawdy, and Mr. Buxton, to inquire and seize for her Highness's use all the goods and two parts of the lands of certain recusants. Fears they will be delayed waiting Mr. Serjeant's return from circuit. Asks Gawdy to meet him at Attleborough on Monday next.

169.—24 August 1587. *John Reppes*, Mendham, to *Bassingbourn Gawdy.*

Sir Henry Woodhouse has asked Reppes to lay up all the hay and wood he can, being minded to pass the winter at Mendham. Reppes asks for hay off the meadows and pastures for the provision of the house. Also Sir Henry asks the price of Gawdy's two coach-horses. He is likely to be at Mendham next week on his way to Sir Nicholas Bacon.

170.—3 September 1587. *Francis Gawdy*, Wallington, to his nephew *Bassingbourn Gawdy*, senior.

Appoints his nephew to meet him and Sir Will. Heydon next Wednesday at Lytcham, some four miles from Soffham [Swaffham], to

GAWDY MSS. sit on a Commission [as to Recusants]. Francis is ·keeping Bassingbourn's son Philip with him, having·deferred journeying till next week.

171.—22 September 1587.   *Sir William Heydon*,. Baconsthorpe,
                              to *Bassingbourn Gawdy*, Harling.

Heydon and Gawdy's uncle consider there will not be convenient provision at Litcham to entertain the assembly, they think Fakenham more
convenient, and the juries are to be summoned there.   The appointment
is for Tuerday next at 9 a.m.

172.— [Autumn of 1587 or sooner.]   *W. Lukin* [or Lakin] to *Bassing-
                                     bourn Gawdy* [senior], Middle-
                                     ton Hall.

Thanks Gawdy for inquiring him out a house.   Mr. Reymes' house
does not suit, Lukin knows no one in that neighbourhood.   Did Gawdy
succeed yesterday in inducing Mr. Herynge to delay promising his
house?

173.—2 December ·1587.   *John Oseley*, Courtenhall, Northampton·
                          shire, gent., and *William Moore*,
                          Winge, Bucks, gent., to *Philip Gawdy*,
                          West Harling, Esq.

Recognizance for 50*l.* to be paid Gawdy at Christmas.

174.—20 December 1587.   *Joan Moyse*, Sancroft, Suffolk, widow, to
                          Bassingbourn Gawdy [senr.], W. Har-
                          ling.

Release of all claims.   Witnesses, John Nyddam and John Carlton.

1587-8.

175.—1 January, 1587-8.   *John Nonne* to *Bassingbourn Gawdy*,
                           West Harling.

In answer to Bretton's "importunity and clamorous speeches," the
truth is that Gawdy while Sheriff took bond for his appearance *ats* one
Guye : Bretton failed and process went out against Gawdy's lands and
goods next year.   Sir Thomas Knyvet returned the writ against Gawdy
and his clerk John Rolf at London notified Nonne of it, who thereupon
had Bretton's bond sued on.   Bretton settled the original. action and
made divers journeys to Harling, his surety finally confessing judgment
on the bond.   Afterwards at Blome's house, Sir Henry Woodhous and
Gawdy "being on the leades there," Bretton agreed to pay 5*l.* in full.
If Nonne has taken aught from Bretton since, he will pay treble ; the
5*l.* was paid Gawdy's attorney ; the matter cost Gawdy 100 marks
costs, and my Lord of Arundel's officer's amerciaments, Mr. Plumbe, &c.
Shrievalty will be "a mean office" if such things go on ; Nonne has
paid some 20*l.* in such matters out of his own pocket rather than trouble
Gawdy with the "outcries of such shameless and unthrifty fellows."

176.—2 January 1587-8.   *William Dyer*, Jailor of Melton Common.
                          Jail, Suff., to. *Bassingbourn Gawdy*,
                          West Harling.

Certificate that Gawdy (by the hands of Lawrence Okeley, of South
Elmham, Suff., husbandman, his assignee and deputy) has bestowed on
the poor prisoners in said Jail in 'bread, meat, and drink two several
times in the year, 3*s.* 4*d.* yearly, out of a certain close called Roose's

close under the will of Sir Richard Fulmerston. Witness, Thomas Cosen. [Gatfride ?] Rose [Nicholas ?], Byrche.

177.—15 February [1587–8]. *Anthony Gawdy,* lodgings at Wilson's in the Strand, to cousin *Bassingbourn Gawdy,* jr., at Mendham, to be left at [Thetford ?].

Sends house furniture and bill for same ; has made as good a bargain as if dealing for himself. Would have written before, but "the world is dangerous and I never so discontented since I came from you " ; they are happiest who have good wives and can live in the country, " the court is such a new world . . . I know not how to bestow myself in it." Plenty of news but dangerous to send ; letters being searched everywhere. Remembrances to his servant Calterope, Ralph and Mr. Arnold ; when will Bassingbourn's father be at Harling ?

[Between these dates, Bassingbourn Gawdy, jr., married Anne, daughter and heiress of Sir Charles Framlingham, of Debenham, Suffolk.]

178.—19 March 1587–8. *Sir Charles Framlingham,* Crowshall, to his brother *Bassingbourn Gawdy* [senr.], Harling.

To enquire after health of Gawdy and " my son and my daughter " and cousin Philip. Sir Charles is going to London. Thanks Gawdy for forbearing the money from Christmas to this Lady day, would like it left over till Michaelmas.

1588.

179.—16 April 1588. *Sir John Heigham,* Bury [Suff.] to [*Bassingbourn Gawdy*].

To recommend the bearer, Henry Byrd, of Bury, whose servant has run away to one Smyth of Wilby. Send for the man and Smyth the father and Jeoffrye Smythe his son, &c. Remembrances to nephew and niece.

180.—8 May 1588. *William Forster,* " Camerwell (?) at my son Bowyer's," to *John Thurston,* Hoxne, Suffolk.

Recommended the gentleman Thurston moved him for to the lady, who liked well of him and will receive him courteously for Forster's sake, of which he thought the gentleman had been apprised. " She is very pleasantly seated and wealthily, with very great commodity," worth about 400*l.* a year at least.

[Probably relates to a proposal of marriage for Philip Gawdy.]

181.—10 May 1588. *Agnes Haiward,* London, to *Bassingbourn Gawdy,* the elder, Harling.

About a year ago she lent Gawdy's son Philip 17*l.* ; he has repaid 10*l.,* but only gives fair promises for the rest, saying that his father has undertaken payment and deducted the amount from his exhibition. Is this so ? Begs Gawdy to see her paid.

182.—20 May [1588]. *Anthony Gawdy,* London, to brother *Bassingbourn Gawdy,* the elder, West Harling.

Since Anthony's coming to London, there have been many changes ; it is doubtful if Sir Wm. [Drury] remains governor of Bergen, or if

Sir Thos. Morgan shall have it : the Queen, Lord Leicester, and Mr. Secretary have " all together bestowed it of Sir Thos. Morgan." It is unknown if he shall have it. Sir Thos. [Leighton ?] being at dinner at Mr. Treasurer's drank to B. Gawdy and his son and to " us," and commended Bassingbourn and all his company, saying he had acquainted the Queen with his enviable entertainment and she would write her thanks to "them." No certain news of peace or war. Sir Wm. Russell has lost 200 men by an ambuscade. All the Queen's "shippine" lies still at the Land's End; Anthony's instructions are to take ship this day. Remembrances to "you," Bass[ingbourn,] his wife and my servant Calterope [? Calthorpe]. Sir Thos. [Leighton] spoke openly how proudly and foolishly Mr. Lovell [abused?] him since his coming to court, and Mr. Treasurer promises he shall not be grieved again. Anthony and Philip spoke what *they* knew of Lovell which "was ill enough."

183.—30 May [1588]. *Anthony Gawdy,* Bergen-op-Zoom, to nephew
               Philip Gawdy àt his lodging, Fleet St.
               by the " Hanging Sword " [?].

Announces safe passage to Flushing in two days, came next day to Bergen, which is full of captains and good soldiers in want of money and apparel. Sir William [Drury] hath a great commandment and well beloved. Ostend is beseiged, none are to relieve it from hence. There is good hawking, but not without 50 foot and as many horse, for the enemy comes to the very walls. Has not yet seen a Spaniard. Commends himself to Philip's father. The Governor and his lady send commendations.

184.—10 June 1588. *John Thurston,* Hoxne, Suffolk, to [*Bassing-
               bourn Gawdy*].

Asks to know what answer Gawdy will make the "party in Essex"? The "party here" does not care to travel into Essex unless assured of success. Recommends a meeting at the house of Gawdy's kinsman, Southwell, in Suffolk.

185.—13 June 1588. *Sir William Heydon,* Baconsthorpe, to [*Bas-
               singbourn Gawdy*].

Both Heydon and Sir Edward Clere are desirous of complying with Gawdy's request in favour of Roger Lowdale, but their assistant Mr. Lane had left before Gawdy's messenger arrived. Will "undelayedly" forward the letter to Lane "for the delivery of the said ' Roger Lowdaye," (*sic*). Remembrances to cousin Calthorpe.

186.—10 July 1588. *Anthony Thwayt,* Norwich, to [*Bassingbourn
               Gawdy*].

The bearer John Johnson of Attleboro' was called to serve at the last muster. A friend of Thwayts had previously hired him against Michaelmas next and will be unfurnished if he is not discharged.

187.—3 August 1588. *Sir William Heydon,* Deputy Lieutenant, to
               Mayors, Bailiffs, Constables, &c.

Mr. B. Gawdy the younger being appointed Captain of two hundred men levied in the country of Norfolk to be sent to Tilbury in Essex by the direction of the right honourable Lords of Her Majesty's Privy Council, he is authorised to demand post-horses for himself and his men at ordinary prices.

188.—4 August 1588. *Thomas Methwold*, Langford, to *Bassingbourn Gawdy.*

Begs to have the bearer excused service, as at the last muster, he being not altogether well of his late hurt.

189.—4 August 1588. *Henry Hoogan*, Quidenham, to *Bassingbourn Gawdy.*

To interest Gawdy in the bearer, George Godfrey, who is summoned before him. Let him be "spared from pains," he is greatly charged with children and serves Hoogan's kinsman John Wingfield.

190.—17 September 1588. *Sir John Peyton*, Blickling, to *Bassingbourn Gawdy*, Harling.

Sends word by Mr. Drury that he cannot attend the subsidy meeting at Watton, being one of 3 knights and 3 squires specially directed by the Council to compose the old differences between divers gentlemen in Lincolnshire. Cannot meeting be postponed till 12 October?

191.—21 September 1588. *Edward Suliarde*, Tolshunt, [Essex], to *Bassingbourn Gawdy*, Harling

The "unreasonable foul weather" has prevented Suliarde from reporting verbally his conference with his sister touching Gawdy's suit. Takes the opportunity of this bearer (who is going to Mr. Jermyn) to say, that, like a wise woman, she keeps her own counsel; but she has spoken well of Gawdy in his absence. Has no doubt Gawdy will be forward in offering a convenient jointure.

[4 November 1588. Sir Thomas Gawdy died.]

192.—9 November 1588. *John Thurston*, Hoxne [Suffolk], to *Bassingbourn Gawdy.*

Thurston understands by Robt. Aldows that Gawdy wishes to know Thurston's position towards Robert's brother John concerning a close Thurston has from year to year by Gawdy's grant, now occupied by Henry Woodwarde. Thurston is to give Gawdy 60*l.* for it, whereof he paid John Aldows 40*l.* before last Feast of the Purification, to be repaid by 6 Oct. last, and paid him the balance, 20*l.*, before last Lady-day, to be repaid last Michaelmas. Thurston was to receive the rent; and to give Aldows back his bond on receipt of the deed from Gawdy. Thurston gave him a draft deed for Gawdy's perusal, which he returned approved before Whitsuntide. Aldows has taken the rent and done nothing, forfeiting two bonds of 120*l.* and one of 8*l.*, yet Thurston dealt favourably with him (as being Gawdy's servant) in the presence of his neighbour Grudgfeld. Aldows now dares Thurston to do anything.

[15 November 1588. *Francis Gawdy* made Judge of K. B.]

193.—19 December 1588. *Sir Charles Framlingham*, Crowshall, to brother *Bassingbourn Gawdy.*

Asks that the money he has to pay at Christmas may stand till Lady-day, when he will pay the whole. His lately deceased Under-sheriff Crispe [or Cruspe?] did not pay the money in his hands into the Exchequer, but he and Lord Manners [?] his master put Sir Charles off with fair speeches. Now Crispe is gone "out of this world," and the Serjeant, my Lord Treasurer's mace-carrier, was coming down to bring

GAWDY MSS. Sir Charles to London to answer Crispe's account. 'Sir Charles' London friends write him that his lands are all extended; so he must hurry to London with 300*l.* or 400*l.*, pay the account, and sue out his quietus.

1588–9.

194.—2 January [1588–9?].   *Christopher Heydon*, Mannington, to [*Bassingbourn Gawdy*].

Understands there is a Parliament expected, does not mean to stand himself, but wishes to oppose the election of a stranger.   Asks [Gawdy] to hold his votes in suspense until the election, when he does not doubt out that a good Norfolk candidate may be produced.

[*C. Heydon* was elected Knight of the shire for the Parliament commencing 4 February 1588–9.]

195.—17 March 1588–9.   *Lady Elizabeth Framlingham*, "my house at Hogesden" [? where], to her daughter [*Mrs. Bassingbourn Gawdy, jun.*], Harling.

To ask her daughter to speak to her uncle, Mr. Nonne, about a lease he bought from one Mr. Richman, which lease belongs to Lady Elizabeth's friend Mr. Covell.   To avoid trouble Covell will buy the lease; if Nonne will not sell, tell him "to tackle with Mr. Covell concerning the covenants" between Richman and Covell's predecessors.   Certainly the ground cannot be ploughed up (as is proposed) without Covell's consent.   Encloses letter to forward to Nonne.

1589.

196.—2 May [1589?].   *John Thurston*, Hoxne [Suffolk], to [*Bassingbourn Gawdy*].

Thanks [Gawdy] for his offer as to an exchange of land.   There is a ground rent of 13*s.* 4*d.*   Thurston pays him for leased lands which he bought of Mr. Everard.   He will accept a release of this land.   Thurston has prepared the deed to himself, and given it to [Gawdy's] servant Aldhowse.   If it is approved he will send his servant to witness [Gawdy's] execution, and will himself execute the deed to [Gawdy] in the presence of Aldhowse.   The latter has forfeited his bonds to Thurston, and is so stubborn that he will hardly give Thurston 20*s.* to discharge them over and above the arrearages of the rent.

197.—14 June 1589.   *John Springe* to *Bassingbourn Gawdy.*

At Gawdy's late muster one William [Sasser?] made his appearance as belonging to Gawdy's division although not discharged out of Springe's father's band.   Asks to have him sent back.

198.—16 June 1589.   *Thomas Fermor*, East Barsham, to *Bassingbourn Gawdy.*

For a benevolence to his servant Robert Armstrong on his marriage at Walsingham the Sunday after Midsummer.

199.—14 July 1589.   *Sir William Heydon* to *Bassingbourn Gawdy* [sen.].

Isabell Hampton, widow, is charged with finding armour, &c. to the same extent as her late husband was.   Yet she is much poorer, part of his estate being divided among children, &c.   Commends her to Gawdy's consideration. Remembrances to "cousin Bassingbourn and his wife and cousin Philip Gawdy."

[August 1589. Framlingham Gawdy, Bassingbourn Gawdy, jun.'s eldest son, born.]

200.—2 September 1589. *Bassingbourn Gawdy*, West Harling, to *George Dawdrie*, Bunwell.

To request Dawdrie's attendance at West Harling on Friday at 8 a.m., that an end may be made of the controversy between him and this poor man, the bearer.

201.—5 September 1589. *William Rugge*, Bylaugh, to *Bassingbourn Gawdy*.

Sends by Mr. Rookwood a book drawn concerning an order to be set down betwixt Rookwood and Francis Shilling. Mr. Corbut and Rugge commend the book to Gawdy to alter or confirm it, "that it may at the last be ended."

[20 January 1589–90. Bassingbourn Gawdy, senior, died. The date is incorrectly given by all authorities except Mr. Carthew.]

1590 or earlier.

The following undated letters are addressed to Bassingbourn Gawdy, senior.

202.—1 March. *Thomas Gawdy*, Snitterley, to his uncle *Bassingbourn Gawdy*, Harling Hall.

To excuse his servant Cobye from serving as a trained soldier.

203.—Whit Sunday. *Rev. Thomas Symonds*, Thorndon, to *Mr. Gawdy*, Mendham.

Mr. Kene in his testament bequeathed to the daughters of Willm Seman, of Eye, 40s. This bringer, Thomas Fenne, hath married one of Seman's daughters, who ought to have the legacy as she has no sisters living. Asks Gawdy to pay 20s., and Mr. Bacon has promised to pay the other.

204. —— *Thomas Holland* to [*Bassingbourn Gawdy*].

"There is lately come into the town of Kenninghall to inhabit divers foreigners who be young people, and likely hereafter to be chargeable to the town. . . . To prevent this mischief the Lord Chief Justice hath directed a course to the Justices of the Peace, which is to impose a weekly contribution from the owner and letter and bringer-in of such out-town body."

The owner of the house to pay if his farmer not able. The townsmen are factious, part of the better sort loving ale-houses as well as the meaner and slow to reprehend vice. Those who are for the town's good are spurned at and discountenanced. The inn and ale-houses do decay daily those who are well left. Holland lately made James Foister constable against the will of some chief inhabitants, because he is severe against ale-houses.

[*Also see* post No. 354 *et seq.*, for other letters possibly addressed to B. Gawdy, Senr.]

Letters to *Bassingbourn Gawdy*, son of *Bass. Gawdy*, deceased, afterwards knighted.

205.—18 April 1590. *Richard Futter* to *Bassingbourn Gawdy*.

Asks if he is to hold his present farm at Bretnam after next Michaelmas ; if not, he is minded to plough up the close before his gate.

206.—25 April 1590. J. [? Henry] Holdyche to Bassingbourn
Gawdy.

To save him 40s. or so on Gawdy's account, which he will see paid.

207.—10 May 1590.   Thomas [Gawdy ?] to his cousin Gawdy.

To bespeak his friendship for a man who has been arrested [letter
much damaged.]

208.—15 May 1590.   William Methwold, South Pickenham, to
Bassingbourn Gawdy.

Commends the bearer, a poor woman, Mother Jone, who asks for
protection under Gawdy's license, whereby she may the more boldly
travel as a mendicant.

P.S.—Would gladly have the pigeons now.

209.—2 July 1590.   William Neashe, Lopham, to Bassingbourn
Gawdy, West Harling.

This Assizes a trial comes off between Neashe and Pannell for
Pecoke's seven neat [cattle], one of which Barton (Gawdy's servant)
had. Neashe's neighbour, Segeford, delivered one milch cow, which,
if Pannel recovers from him, he must look to Barton for. Thinks
Gawdy might help him. Wenn, of Middle Harling, is Pannell's lewd
witness.

Alludes to James Love's robbery, and fears that, as in that case, the
fraud will be carried by lewd witnesses.

210.—3 October 1590.   John Sporle, Framlingham Erle, Brickmaker, to Robert Sporle, his son.

Bargain and sale to Robert of all John's personal estate. Schedule:
—3 heifers, one red shild, one red dowed, one red grymble; one black
and one red bull; 4 weaning calves, 2 bay mares, one black mare,
15 swine. Witness, Loye Kett and Thomas John. [See post No. 273.]

211.—30 November 1590.   Michael Hare, Norwich, to cousin Bassingbourn Gawdy.

Gawdy has execution against the bearer, Mr. Blak, and his surety
("my host Bredshawe") for 100 marks on an obligation for the non-
appearance of one Mr. Fenn in the time of Gawdy's [father's] late
shrievalty. Asks it may be stayed till the end of next term, and they
will either have Fenn arrested or compound with the parties who are
suing Gawdy and pay all the latter's expenses, &c. Remembrances to
"my cousin your wife."

212.—[circ 1590 or 1591.]   Anthony Gawdy, Redgrave, to
cousin Bassingbourn Gawdy.

Sends thanks to Sir Charles and his lady for their courteous favours.
Sir Nicholas will meet your [Justices ?] at Norwich on Monday; that
night Anthony lies at Harling, and so to Bury. The end of his journey
concerns Sir Robert Dury. Remembrances to Bassingbourn Gawdy,
his wife, "and little Fram."

1591.

213.—22 January 1590-1.   Anthony Gawdy, West Harling, to
nephew Bassingbourn Gawdy.

Power of Attorney to prosecute and sue trespassers on sheep courses
of Bridgham and Brettenham. Witnesses, Robert Bolton and Tho⁸
[Pyte ?].

GAWDY MSS.

: [April 1591.ᵗ Philip Gawdy sails under Sir Rich. Grenvile in Lᵈ Thoˢ Howard's fleet, and is captured on board the " Revenge " at the celebrated fight in the Azores when Sir Richard died.]

214.—16 May 1591. *Ralph Playsted*, Baconsthorpe, to *Bassingbourn Gawdy.*

Excuses himself for not personally attending with his Master's letters on the ground of the " multiplicity of young men's cares drawing so near to a new alteration of life."

215.—20 May 1591. *Rev. George Gurney*, Tacolneston, to [*Bassingbourn*] *Gawdy*, Harling.

To excuse breach of his half-promise to Mr. Harvey to come to Harling, being hindered by a christening. Will come whenever wanted, even if it be next Sābt. [Sabbath].

216.—30 May 1591. *Geffray Gate*, Carbroke, to *Bassingbourn Gawdy.*

In answer to Gawdy's question, by his servant William Wyston, as to Gawdy's safety in purchasing a copyhold which Wyston's wife holds as guardian for her son, Gate gives very guarded advice; pointing out the necessity of protecting not only Gawdy against the boy when he comes of age, but also the boy against his step-father, in assuring the boy the benefit of whatever consideration Gawdy gives for the land.

217.—8 July 1591. *Anthony Thwaytes*, Quidenham, to [*Bassingbourn Gawdy.*]

The bearer Richard Briante, one of the trained soldiers, is warned for these present services into France. He is to be married at Banham on Sunday to Thwaytes' wife's maid. His poor friends have laid out for the occasion all they can make shift for, and are likely to be undone if he is not excused serving.

218.—12 July 1591. *Robert Mulhe*, Kenninghall Lodge, to [*Bassingbourn Gawdy*].

On Sunday next his son's daughter is to be married at Botholp's dale [Suffolk], where he would be much obliged if [Gawdy] would send his benevolence.

219.—[16 ?] October 1591. *John Springe to Bassingbourn Gawdy*

Intreats Gawdy to go to Bury and act on Springe's commisaion, which will otherwise be of no use. Sir John Higham and Springe will be there, but not the latter's father, there must be three to form a quorum.

220.—5 October 1591 [? 1592]. [Account, probably imperfect, of *Bassingbourn Gawdy's* sheep flocks.]

Flock I. at *Levele's* [*Manor*, Walton]. The flock numbered 500 at last count, 223 are accounted for, and 498 remain ; showing an increase of 221.

Flock II. at *Bridgham* (Silvester's ewes) numbered 409 at last count, and that number still remain, the increase of about 70 is accounted for in different ways.

Flock III. at *Bridgham* (wethers) numbered 355 at last count, was raised by drafts from other flocks to 462, 96 are accounted for and 366 remain.

Flock IV. at. Bridgham (Cooke's ewes) numbered 347 at last count, was increased to 417,,73, of which are accounted for (sent to Gasthorpe holms, Crowshall, &c.) and 344 remain.

Flock V. at *Brettenham* (Jo. Heyden) started with 434, received 138 hogs and sent away in all 139.

Flock VI. [? at *Brettenham*] (Largent) started with 470, was increased to 548, 69 are disposed of and 479 remain.

Flock VII. at *Brettenham* (Clarke). Started with 712, received 3 rams and accounted for 62 skins, leaving 653 in his charge, but at the clipping he turned over 663 to Thos. James, the new shepherd. (James) started with 663, was increased to 885, accounted for 162 and had 708 remaining, being short on his account.

Flock VIII. at *West Harling* (ewes). Clarke started with 601 and ended with the same number, all the increase (122) being drafted off to other flocks.

[The accounts further show that at least two other flocks existed, the first of which was evidently a new one, viz. :—

Flock IX. at *Crowshall* (Suffolk). 569 sheep were drafted thither from the other flocks.

Flock X. at *Gasthorpe Holms*, whither 91 were sent.

39 sheep were sent "to the kitchen," 3 were killed by dogs, "Maubyn's dog" being named. There is much shifting about from flock to flock, making it impossible to state the natural increase in any one flock.]

1592.

221.—13 January 1591-2. *Thomas Marche*, Trymley [Suffolk], *Bassingbourn Gawdy*.

Whereas Gawdy has written to Marche's master, who is not at home, for some account, concerning land in Scarning, my lady says that 8 or 9 years ago she sent Mr. Gawdy's late father two or three such accounts. She thinks it was Mr. Bolton fetched them.

222.—14 January 1591-2. *Robert [Doon ?]* to *Bassingbourn Gawdy*.

Could not come to Croweshall at Christmas, the way was so dangerous to ride, would rather go twice to Harling. Mr. Cornwallis is not at home, encloses my lady's answer in writing.

223.—15 February 1591-2. *Edmond Moundeford*, Feltwell, to *Bassingbourn Gawdy*, West Harling.

Returns one of Gawdy's warrants signed, the other he will have delivered. Bring to the meeting the High Commissioners' letter to Moundeford concerning Edward Turner.

224.—17 [June ?] 1592. *Michael Stanhope*, the Court at Theobalds to *Bassingbourn Gawdy*.

Has a matter to be tried at the Queen's Bench by a Norfolk Jury, asks the favour of Gawdy's *personal* care in preparing the panel. Jurors to be men not afraid of Sir Arthur Heveningham nor living under any of the [Cornwallises ?].

· 225.—4 September 1592. *Henry Calton* and *Robert Watts*, West
Harling, yeomen, to *William Smith*,
Banham, singleman.

Joint bond to secure payment of 5*l.* on feast of St. Matthew the
Apostle, 1593, at South porch of Banham Church. Witness, Robert
Lulpeck, Thomas Clark, William Clark.

[29 September 1592. Philip Gawdy returns to London, having been
a prisoner of war at Lisbon.]

1592–3.

· 226.—23 January 1592–3. · *Rev. John Trendle,* Ovington, to *Bassingbourn Gawdy,* Harling.

Complains of a fellow in his congregation who "interprises" to keep
an unlicensed ale-house; where "poor men spend their thrift, poor
women spend their husbands' earnings . . . . children are made drunk
there," &c. Never had a tavern before in the village.

1593.

227.—2 April 1593. · *Edmond Moundeford,* Lynford, to *Bassingbourn
Gawdy.*

The Lord Chief Justice has appointed Gawdy and Moundeford to
enquire into the petition of William Inglish of Illington against Christopher Gasken for detaining a tenement called Dollers and certain lands.
Moundeford appoints Wednesday in Easter week.

228.—8 June 1593. *Robert Bedingfield* and *John Parker* to *John
Hotte* or ? *Holte,* Wymondham, yeoman.

Receipt for 8*l.* 10*s.* on writ directed to Henry Gawdy, High Sheriff
[son of Sir Thomas Gawdy, Claxton Hall]. Witness, John Foster,
Roger Woodhouse, John Brewster.

229.—28 June 1593. *Sir Edward Stanhope* and *Dr. B. Swale,*
Doctor's Commons, to *Bassingbourn Gawdy.*

Mr. Anthony Gawdy has brought a counterfeit warrant from Her
Majesty's Commissioners for causes ecclesiastical, purporting to be
signed by Drs. Cosin, Swale, and Drury. The Archbishop of Canterbury and Dr. Cosin being at Croydon they will keep the warrant and
beg Gawdy not to discharge the man he arrested for attempting to serve
it.

230.—3 July 1593. *Sir Edward Stanhope,* Doctor's Commons, to
Bassingbourn Gawdy, Norwich.

The Archbishop of Canterbury thanks Gawdy for arresting "so bad
a fellow as 'Tompson." The warrant was forged, Gawdy's cousin
saying it is none of his hand. The Archbishop wrote by Stanhope to
the Lord Chief Justice to request a severe punishment. The latter and
Mr. Justice Fenner saw the papers and will have special care of the
matter when at Norwich, meantime Mr. Pemberton (the Lord Chief
Justice's man) keeps the papers. Stanhope had promised his old
acquaintance Mr. Anthony Gawdy the warrant should be forthcoming.
Hopes Gawdy will yet further discover the "knot of these cozeners, ,. .
and disburden the poor people of such filthy cormorants."

231.—4 August [1592 or 3.] *Elizabeth Nonne* to her. nephew *Bassingbourn Gawdy.*

Asks him to pay her nephew Cressinor the exhibition Gawdy promised him at her entreaty, which (with her husband's help) is all he has to depend on. A "heavy occasion" prevents her coming to Harling.

232.—11 October 1593.   *Edmund Newman*, Hingham, Tanner, to *Peter Moore*, Hingham, Grocer.   ·

Bond to secure payment to Moore of 3*l.* 13*s.* 4*d.* at his house in Hingham in two instalments. Witness, William Bathecome senr. and William Mallowse "the scribe."

233.—15 October 1593.   *Edward Sulyard*, Langley Park, to *Bassingbourn Gawdy.*

When he sends to London after Hallowmas will forward acquittance for the last money Gawdy had of Sulyard's brother Sheldon for Sulyard's use ; needs the balance to enable him to pay what he is bound for next Christmas. Is furthering the passing of the conveyance, and for that purpose is selling timber to pay debts, &c.

234.—2 November, 1593.   *John Nonne* to [*Bassingbourn Gawdy*].

Nonne's letter is to the same effect as Mr. Jeff's. [Gawdy] should get some friends to see that the assurance sufficiently conveys the manor and discharges arrearages of rent. He had better send Bolton or some one well furnished as to particulars of Lymborne [Suffolk] to some good counsel, Mr. Sannfield or Mr. Godfrey, and get Mr. Wolmer's help if he be at St. Albans. As to payment, better borrow the money ; Nonne knows a widow who will advance it "at reasonable reckoning."

235.—24 November 1593.   *Sir Charles Framlingham*, Croweshall, to his son *Bassingbourn Gawdy*, Harling.

Sir Charles willed Sutton to ask Gawdy to speak to Sir Nicholas Bacon to apply to Sir Robert Wingfield to remove old Taylor from the head-constableship. His "badness and his stomach" are known to those who have been in Commission, as Sir Philip Parker, Mr. [Grise ?], Mr. Garneys, and Sir Charles himself : he is a bad example to the other constables. It is time to "put off his bells, or else he will not stoop to any quarry." The "crafty fox" pretends to be willing to go, desiring to get the place for his kinsman, one Tiller, who dwells in the same town, under cover of whose authority he would still rule and "play the merchant." Sir Charles is very sorry little Charles is not yet over his ague ; remembrances to his daughter and little Fram.

236. [End of November] 1593.   *Henry Gawdy*, Claxton, to cousin *Bassingbourn Gawdy.*

Had sent seven hogsheads of beer before Gawdy's man came, the rest shall follow. His butt being in some decay, had to send it to be mended, so cannot sooner finish the brewing. Bassingbourn's man will therefore return home and leave the brewing to Henry's man. Remembrance to cousin Anthony.

237.—29 November 1593.   *Edward Moundeford*, Feltwell, to *Bassingbourn Gawdy*, West Harling.

Will meet him at time appointed. Wishes Gawdy joy of his troublesome office.

238.—29 November 1593. *Bassingbourn Gawdy*, West Harling, and GAWDY MSS.
John Nonne, Tostock, Suffolk, gent., to
William Tipper, London, gent.

Joint Bond to secure payment by Gawdy to Tipper of 40*l.* on
10th February then next at the dwelling-house of William Cooke,
Esq., Bury St. Edmonds. Witness, Matthew Cryspe and Henry
Gibson ; William Cooke.

Two receipts endorsed "to use of William Tipter (sic) " signed
Thomas Hervey for 10*l.* each, dated 22nd and 28th January.

[This was for purchase money of Lymborne Manor, Suffolk, *see* 286.]

239.—1 December 1593. *Henry Gawdy* to cousin *Bassingbourn
Gawdy*.

Asks him to oblige the bearer, a poor man, by keeping office at the
latter's house.

240.—3 December 1593. *Thomas Holms*, Burrow Green, J. P. for
Cambridgeshire, to *Constables* for
Dullingham, and so from town to town
the nearest way to Thetford,

Is informed by Martyn Brice and the confession of Edward Grigson,
that the latter married his wife Ann 14 or 15 years ago, and has 3
children by her. He left her 3 months ago and married Alice Pedder
(by the temptation of the devil and the enticement of the said Alice)
who lives at Dullingham. Warrant for his apprehension and passing
from hand to hand to the town of Bretnam (sic.).

241.—4 December 1593. *Sir William Heydon*, Saxlingham, to
Bassingbourn Gawdy, High Sheriff.

Thanks Gawdy for his friendly message sent by Heydon's man, who
was with Gawdy for the bailiwick of Holt. Asks Gawdy to take the
bearer, Robert Orwell, into his service or the undersheriff's.

242.—9 December 1593. *Lady Elizabeth Framlingham*, Crowshall,
to her son *Bassingbourn Gawdy*, High
Sheriff, Harling.

At request of Bullarde the sadler, of Ipswich, she asks Gawdy to give
the man what work he has this year.

243.—21 December 1593. *William Randall*, Stilton, Lincolnshire,
yeoman, to *Bassingbourn Gawdy*.

Receipt for 7*l.* 10*s.* on writ of *ca. sa.* against William Warner, gent.
Witness Christopher Ballard, junr.

244.—23 December 1593. *Sir John Fortescue*, Hampton Court, to
Bassingbourn Gawdy, High Sheriff.

No return has been made to process from the Exchequer between
Her Majesty's servant Ralph Rabberds and John Shering and John
Thaxter. Requires special attention to such process, and statement of
the reason why, if it cannot be executed.

245.—27 December [1593 or earlier]. *Thomas Gawdy*, [junr.],
Waybread [Suffolk], to uncle
Bassingbourn Gawdy.

Asks Gawdy to use his wife's influence with her father Sir Charles
[Framlingham] to procure the presentation of the bearer, who has been
tutor to Thomas' son Thomas for 2 years, to the living of Kenton

GAWDY MSS. [Suff.]. . . If it has been already promised to Mr. Morre perhaps the latter will give it up. [*See* No. 344.]

246.—28 December 1593.   *Thomas Harrys*, Catfield, Yeoman, to
                          Bassingbourn Gawdy, High Sheriff.

Receipt for 3*l.* 13*s.* 4*d.* levied by fi. fa. on goods of Edmund Warde. Witness, Christopher Ballard, jr., George Wobell.

247.—29 December 1593.   [*Rev.*] *William Downyng*, Beccles, to
                         Bassingbourn Gawdy, High Sheriff. .

Downing delivered Gawdy's letter to under-sheriff Crispe at Norwich and also sent his deputy and his wife to Martham on the day Gawdy appointed. Understands that Mr. Bolton was there on Thursday but the writ was not executed. The expense is great, Downing and his family lying as guests for money in other men's houses, scattered in sundry places. Urges Gawdy "by the sincerity of justice and a Sheriff's oath" to act indifferently and expeditiously. Let him give no credit to the vaunts which his clerk Bolton heard Downing's adversary utter. If Gawdy cannot give him possession, asks his letter to the nobleman that wrote to him on Downing's behalf. Divers loads of corn have been carried from the parsonage and more will probably follow. Downing had appointed a man to see to the "indifferent severing" of the corn.

248.—   1593.   *Nicholas Raynberd* to *Bassingbourn
                         Gawdy.*

A hasty confused letter written from the Tower [? Town] as to Mr. Ward's [?] business. Has also written to Mr. Finshe [?].

249.—   1593.   *Sir Arthur Heveningham*, Kettering-
                         ham,   to   *Bassingbourn   Gawdy*
                         High Sheriff.

Begs a benevolence on marriage of Sir Arthur's Falconer.

250.—   1593.   *John Smithe* to *Bassingbourn Gawdy*,
                         High Sheriff.

As by former letter from Sir Edward Clere, Smithe entreats a favourable letter to the under-sheriff for the delivery of his bullocks, so unjustly detained, not seeing any reason that he should be charged with what another is to make payment of. If the under-sheriff refuse, Smithe will be enforced to fly to the law. He was evil dealt with by the late under-sheriff the last year. If Gawdy so pleases ease may be wrought to Smithe and kindness to Sir Edward, whom the matter doth only concern. Sir Edward desireth return of answer touching Mr. Cross. Remembrances to Gawdy and his wife.

251.—[1593 ?] *John   Smithe* to [*Bassingbourn
                         Gawdy*].

Forepointed occasions restrained him from attending on [Gawdy] and enforce him to send the bearer "with an Angell to your servant." Asks [Gawdy's] favourable acceptance of this small trifle as a matter better agreeing with the means of his fortunes than with the inwardness of his mind.

1593-4.

252.—7 January 1593-4. *Robert Cobbe,* Yarmouth, yeoman, to *Bassingbourn Gawdy,* High Sheriff.

General release of all claims &c. Witness, John Jenkinson and William Hurrey

253.—14 January 1593-4. *Robert Hooke,* Trouse, yeoman, to *Bassingbourn Gawdy.*

Receipt for 10*l.* debt and 50*s.* damages levied by *ca. sa.* against Henry Sotherton, gent. Witness, Robert Bedingfield.

254.—18 January 1593-4. *John North,* Ellmun Hall [? Elmham, Suffolk], to *Bassingbourn Gawdy,* Harling.

Has heard that Gawdy has been ill of a hectick fever within a year or two. North would be glad to know by what means he was cured, he himself having been sick for 4 months at Ellmun Hall and within the last fortnight has fallen into the same fever: "After meat very hot, "especially my hands; my forehead sweateth often, my breast is almost "continually pained," and he also suffers from faintness of the heart, unusual and unnatural heat and from general faintness.

255.—18 January [1593-4 ?]. *Edmund Moundeford,* Feltwell, to *Bassingbourn Gawdy,* West Harling.

Moundeford and his cousin Spilman were assigned by the late Chief Justice, Sir Christopher Wrey, to view the land in controversy between the bearer and his adversary. This they did and took evidence and Moundeford drew a "platte" of the ground. Had Justice Wrey lived Moundeford thinks he would have given judgment according to their certificate for the bearer, who is wronged by his adversary, or old Mr. Downes long since deceased. [Wrey died May 1592].

256.—20 January 1593-4. *Mathew Crispe,* Blythburgh, Suffolk, [Under-sheriff,] to *John Nonne,* gent.

Bond for 50*l.* to be paid on 17th February next. Witness, Robert Bolton.

257.—4 February 1593-4. *Thomas Smyth,* gent., to *Bassingbourn Gawdy,* High Sheriff.

Receipt for 12*l.* debt, 40*s.* damages on *ca. sa.* against John Warde of Walcote, yeoman. Witness, Thomas Cooke, Willm Mullins, John Flowerdew.

258.—4 February 1593-4. *Thomas Smith,* gent., to *Bassingbourn Gawdy,* High Sheriff.

Receipt by Smith for 16*l.* debt, and 2*l.* damages on *ca. sa.* against Thomas Ward. Witnesses, John Flowerdew, William Mulley (?), John Perkas (?).

259.—6 February 1593-4. *John Nonne* to *Bassingbourn Gawdy.*

Reminds Gawdy that Tipper's bond [ante No. 238] falls due on 10 inst. They have been to Harvie, who has no money to lay out at this time of year. If Gawdy sends his man on Saturday, Nonne will

GAWDY MSS. accompany him "though it be a·day that wise foresight might have
prevented." Desires to hear of the success of Gawdy's weightier affairs.
Assizes at Thetford are this day fortnight.

260.—19 February 1593–4. *Henry Gawdy* to his cousin *Bassingbourn Gawdy.*

The javelins shall be ready whenever sent for and Henry will attend
at the assizes in spite of his lameness. Remembrances to cousin Anthony
and Philip. Mr. W. Branthwayt has sent his brother word as to Dr.
Barrow's answer, which is enclosed.

261.—22 February 1593–4. [*Rev.*] *William Downyng*, London, to
Bassingbourn Gawdy, High-
Sheriff, or his under-sheriff.

Downyng spoke this forenoon with the Lord Chief Baron and the two
other Barons of the Exchequer as to a judgment unlawfully entered and
execution "stolen out" against him by Eden and Franklin. As soon
as the Queen's business in hand against certain traitors is finished, they
have promised to examine the matter, which they greatly find fault with,
and punish this malicious practice. Meantime asks to have the execution stayed.

262.—   1594.   *Anthony Gawdy* to cousin *Bassingbourn Gawdy*, High Sheriff.

Sir William Springe has heard by Mr. Richards, Chaplain to my
Lord Chief Justice, that he is determined to be " here " next Saturday.
Takes the opportunity by Sir Nicholas Bacon to advise the sheriff to
send a man to Newmarket to know their pleasure.

263.—22 February 1593–4. *John Scamler*, lodging in Gray's Inn
Lane, to *Bassingbourn Gawdy.*

Has sent Gawdy his horse by Titley, Scamler's father's servant; he
is for sale, a good pennyworth, and will make a good roadster. He cost
40*l.* when a colt, bought from one Mr. Jobson, of Essex, and 10*l.* to
Alexander, of the Queen's stable, for breaking him. This last is probably lost by his not being used to his "manadg." Titley is empowered
to agree on a price. With remembrances "to my brother Phillipe,
your brother."

264.—23 February 1593–4. *Edmond Moundeford*, Feltwell, to his
cousin *Bassingbourn Gawdy*, High
Sheriff.

Moundeford's brother, Fowler, has been summoned to appear as one
of the great inquest next assizes. Fowler is away from home on important business, pray let him be put out of the bill. Suggests fixing
day to renew innkeepers' licenses immediately after the assizes. Would
go to receive the Judges if he knew time and place.

265.—24 February 1593–4. [*Rev.*] *William Downyng*, London, to
Bassingbourn Gawdy, High Sheriff,
or his under-sheriff.

Downyng writes further as to stay of execution, and also that proceedings are to be taken at 'the Sessions or Assizes as to some alleged
irregularity by the Under-Sheriff in making restitution to Downyng.
The 'return' to the writ is full enough. The·Earl of Essex means to
write soon again to Gawdy in reply to the latter's letter. o ⌐ʊ ɪ ɪ∎

266.—25 February 1593–4. *Francis Gawdy*, Wallington, to nephew *Bassingbourn Gawdy.*

Requests the Sheriff to excuse his neighbour, Mr. Wilughby, "an outer barrister in Court," from serving on the great inquest at Thetford Assizes.

267.—3 March 1593–4. *Thomas Methwold*, Langford, to *Bassingbourn Gawdy.*

Has only got some of the coneys Gawdy wrote for to "store a new ground withall ; " he will send them soon to Harling. Will Mr. Undersheriff " wipe Methwold's name out of " the grand jury list ? He has a great pain in his back, and cannot stand the press of people.

268.—10 March 1593–4. *Thomas Styward*, Gressenhall, to *Bassingbourn Gawdy*, High Sheriff, Harling.

Asks the benevolence of Gawdy, "with the rest of his town," for Styward's kinswoman, who has served him 13 years, and is to be married. To save labor has sent a note of the " names within Gawdy's manor," and begs him to send someone round with the bearer to collect the money.

269.—15 March 1593–4. [*Rev.*] *William Downyng*, Martham parsonage, to *Mathew Crispe*, Undersheriff.

According to Gawdy's directions given at Thetford, Downyng and witnesses attended yesterday expecting an officer to see to the severing of the mingled corn, but no one came. It was clear Eden had acted colorably, and pretended to bring some grain of his own sowing to the parsonage grounds. Witnesses can show he took away corn, and thus prevented the severing ordered by the Court of Exchequer. Since Downyng was restored to his possession he got Mr. Blennerhasset to come, but though Eden's arbitrator, Mr. Clipwell, only lives two miles off, Eden would do nothing. Yesterday Eden refused to send anyone, though Clipwell and Anthony Eden were within 100 yards of the house.

270.—15 March 1593–4. *Thomas Lane*, London, to *Mathew Crispe.*

Asks to have two writs executed, one against Robert Godfrey, Bailiff, of ——, who owes 4*l.*, the other against Thomas Geps, of Cromer, who is to be arrested on the attachment of privilege, and not the capias utlagatum *unless* Cromer be a liberty, in which case take him on the capias.

271.—22 March 1593–4. *J. Ferrour* to [*Mathew Crispe*], Undersheriff.

Sends a warrant to be sealed ; has underwritten it to save the clerks trouble. Begs an immediate levy. Hopes [Crispe] will let Ferrour have such warrants as he may desire at the suit of Sir Robert Southwell. When Ferrour was under-sheriff he never took fees from any sheriff or under-sheriff his predecessors. Asks what order he has taken with [Twaffe ?] and Johnson, the prisoners, and [Wursche ?] the jailor.

272.—24 March 1593-4. *John Ferrour* to [*Mathew Crispe*], Under-sheriff.

Ferrour has sent again for the warrants which he hopes Crispe has now examined according to his "curious desires." His predecessors never showed such mistrustful minds. Crispe treats him over-hardly in refusing a special warrant upon the capias utlegat against William Jener, which was sent yesterday, especially as no execution was had of the former capias. Jener dwells in Downeham Market. Asks for special warrants against the parties named in the enclosed warrants. The man who made out the warrant against Jener did but cobble it. Let the warrant against Page and Watson name Robert Page in the same way as he is named in the writ. Ferrour suspects that some of Crispe's underlings (whose favours he desires not), have moved the under-sheriff to be dainty of his friendly disposition towards Ferrour.

273.—24 March 1593-4. *Robert Sporle*, Framlingham, Brickmaker, to *Mathew Crispe*, gent.

Replevin bond, Sporle claiming three mares, valued at 50s. taken on *fi. fa.* against John Sporle *als* Topcliffe, gen. Witnesses, Henry Gibbon, and Robert [Bryndlemarshe?]. [*See* No. 210.]

1594.

274.—25 March 1594. *Christopher Soame*, Citizen and Alderman, Norwich, to *Bassingbourn Gawdy*, High Sheriff.

Release of all claims, &c., on *ca. sa.* executed against George Waffe for 20*l.* debt, and 5*l.* damages. Witness, Christopher Ballard, John Gybson.

275.—[29 March] Good Friday 1594. *J[ohn] Ferrour* to *Mathew Crispe*, Under-sheriff, Norwich.

Sends certain warrants which are as effectually made out as Crispe or any of his factors could make them; so need not be examined, let them be sealed and given to the bearer with word what exigent or proclamation there is in the office against Ferrour, Sir Robert Southwell, or Clemente Rolle of Gressenhall.

276.—31 March 1594. *Henry Farrar*, Beccles, to *Mathew Crispe*, Westwood, Under-sheriff.

Peter Gleane of Norwich has sued Farrar, who gave Gleane a bond with 4 sureties for 33*l.* payable 10*l.* a year. One payment was due last Candlemas; but Farrar has paid 25*l.* to one of his sureties, so is not to blame. Asks Crispe's favour. Does Mr. [Hanges?] claim more of Farrar? he has been paid 65*l.* and if he asks more must have it, but Farrar would wish to pay it in person and try to get an abatement.

277.—5 April [1594?]. *John Dover*, Ellingham, to [*Bassingbourn Gawdy*].

Thomas Chamberleyne sued William Davye about 3 years ago for 40s. debt. At Davye's request Dover paid Chamberleyne the money at the Griffin in Attleborough, in spite of which he has now taken Davye in execution.

278.—5 April 1594. *John Nonne to: nephew [Bassingbourn Gawdy].*

Asks that Mr. Onslow may have some scions for grafting from [Gawdy's] winter and summer "pearmeynes."

279.—7 April 1594. *John Heyes, senior, King's Lynn, Merchant, to Bassingbourn Gawdy, Esq., High Sheriff.*

Receipt for 9*l.* 10*s.* on fi. fa. against Christopher Haws of Tilney. Witness, Ch. Fisher, Notary Public, and Bartholomew Adryan.

280.—9 April 1594. *Robert Skathe, Little Brandon, yeoman, to Bassingbourn Gawdy, High Sheriff.*

Receipt for 11*l.* 10*s* levied by *ca. sa.* against William Leake. Witness, Richard Duffylde, William Dixon.

281.—13 April 1594. *Michael Hawkes, of Debham, Norfolk, Miller, to Bassingbourn Gawdy, High Sheriff.*

Release of all claims arising from *ca. sa.* against John Kirkeman for 6*l.* and 33*s.* 4*d.* damages. Witness, Christopher Ballard, Robert Orwell.

282.—13 April 1594. *John Nonne to his nephew Bassingbourn Gawdy, High Sheriff, West Harling.*

Urges the return of the *venire fac.* concerning Mr. Crowe which he left with Gawdy. Nonne is going to London. If the freeholders have been sent by the Under Sheriff let this messenger bring them to Nonne. Hears his niece is at Cambridge. P.S.—Forwards a letter from his nephew Nicholas Cressener at Cambridge; expect it contains "such requests as he is driven to make to others his poor friends."

283.—23 April 1594. *Thomas Heigham, Wonringford [? Wormingford, Essex, second son of Sir John Heigham] to his nephew Bassingbourn Gawdy, High Sheriff.*

Asks Gawdy's furtherance of his suit on bond against Richard Haynwright of Foxley, living near Mr. Rugge; and encloses his attorney's letter and the writ. When the arrest is made let the [bail] bond be sent to Furnval's Inn and Heigham (who is going to London with his wife) will deliver the bond sued on there. In case of settlement, states he has sent twice to Denver where defendant then dwelt and to Gregory Prats (where his unlucky bargain was made), then there is the attorney's fee, writ, and expense of arrest, besides the debt 14*l.* 10*s.*, on payment of all which he will stay proceedings.

284.—26 April 1594. *Sir Charles Framlingham, Croweshall, to his daughter [Ann] Gawdy, Cambridge.*

Is 'sorry' to hear of her ill health; will gladly do anything for her a father can do. Has sent Brame; if she likes to keep him to pass the time with music, or for any service, pray do so: he can also bring back word if she wants anything. Will write his wife to hasten to Cambridge and see what "her poor skill" can do; she is now at London and in better health. [A very affectionate letter.]

GAWDY MSS.   - 285.—4 May 1594.· *Thomas Fayrclough*, London, Goldsmith, to
                                    Bassingbourn Gawdy.

Receipt for 30*l.* received from Mr. Crispe, under sheriff, on account
of statute of 60*l.* against the body of John Brotone of Walton Abbey
Suffolk.

                ⎧ Two releases (same parties, Fayrclough
(*a.*) 7 February 1594–5. ⎫ described in the first as "Silkman") of
(*b.*) 22 July 1596.   ⎬ all demands. Witnesses, Robert Bolton,
                ⎩ Rich. Sutton.

286.—13 May 1594.   *Robert Dayle*, at his master, Mr. Tipper's
                   house, Aldergate, London, to [*Bassingbourn
                   Gawdy*].

Asks payment for preparing the conveyance from Tipper, his master,
to [Gawdy] of Lymborne Manor, Suffolk, which was made last term at
St. Albans, also what he paid for the acknowledging of it before a
Master in Chancery. Mr. Bristowe, who took the conveyance, promised
to mention it. It comes to 20*s.*, besides "some other consideration in
regard that I am patentee with my master."

287.—22 May 1594.   *Robert Newham*, Norwich, grocer, to *Bassing-
                   bourn Gawdy*, High Sheriff.

Receipt for 7*l.* 10*s.* levied on *ca. sa.* against Walter Sabarne of
Fundenhall, yeoman. Witness, Christopher Ballard, John Gybson.

288.—29 May 1594.   *John Pigeon*, Redenhall, Yeoman, to *Bassing-
                   bourn Gawdy*, High Sheriff.

Release of all claims, &c. arising from an outlawry after judgment
(C.P.) against Alice Kylby, now the wife of John Ballyston, for 19*l.* 10*s.*
at suit of John Pigeon and Honor his wife. Witness, Gregory . . .

289.—30 May 1594.   *Robert Purdye*, Harleston, to *Matthew Crispe*,
                   Under-sheriff, or Mr. Henry Gibson, his
                   deputy.

To say that the suit of Pigeon and Alice Kylby is settled, and she
is to be released; encloses the acquittance (supra).

290.—1 June 1594.   *Robert Hornesey*, Norwich, Woollen-draper, to
                   Bassingbourn Gawdy, High Sheriff.

Release of all demands arising from outlawry of Thomas Reve of
Aslacton. Witnesses, Christopher Ballard, Robert Bedingfield.

291.—6 June 1594.   *Nicholas Hooker*, Goldsmith, to *Bassingbourn
                   Gawdy.*

Receipt for 1*l.* 1*s.* 6*d.* in full of debt of Mrs. Ann Gawdy, by hands
of William [Pagram?], servant to Mr. Gawdy.

292.—12 June 1594.   *Mathew Crispe to Bassingbourn Gawdy.*

Crispe has received the enclosed writ to return a jury for Sir Arthur
Heveningham. As he is forbidden to return it, he sends a book of
freeholders for Gawdy to select from, he must join 4 hundredors where
the venue is laid, or jury will be quashed. P.S. by Sir Arthur
Heveningham to speed the return and he will pay the messenger.

293.—13 June 1594. *John Pettus* to *Bassingbourn Gawdy*, High Sheriff, Harling.

Gawdy's two bonds to David Le-maire, merchant-stranger, for 100*l.* each (due respectively 1 August 1594 and that day twelvemonth) are offered for sale in London. Before buying, Pettus would like to hear if Gawdy has any objection to being bound to him for that sum.

Postscript by *Thomas Pettus* (father of John) dated 16 June, asking for an answer by "this carter," who will pass through Thetford. John Pettus' address is at Mr. Hawes' house in St. Martin's Lane by Canwicke St., London.

[These bonds were given for ransom of Philip Gawdy, formerly imprisoned at Lisbon and released by David Le-maire's son, Lucas Phelix, becoming surety for him.]

294.—14 June 1594. *Gyles Fleming,* London, Grocer, to *Bassingbourn Gawdy,* High Sheriff.

Release of all claims arising from a *ca. sa.* against Gyles Symonds, late of Hilderston ———, Esq., for 23*l.* debt, and 1*l.* 3*s.* 8*d.* damages. Witness, John Fawcett, Robert Bunell.

295.—15 June 1594. *Henry Gawdy* to cousin *Bassingbourn Gawdy.*

Has heard bad news of Bassingbourn Gawdy's wife's health; asks for certain intelligence.

296.—17 June 1594. *Thomas Oxburgh* to *Bassingbourn Gawdy,* High Sheriff.

Receipt for 70*l.* levied on goods of Nicholas Browne, late of Hampton, out of which Oxburgh has paid Mathew Crispe, under-sheriff, his fee on the *fi. fa.,* 3*l.* 8*s.*

297.—23 June 1594. *Stephen Hart, Jr.,* Hempstead, yeoman, to *Bassingbourn Gawdy,* High Sheriff.

Release of all claims concerning a *fi. fa.* against Hart's goods. Witness, Christopher Ballard, Gabriel Cooke.

[23 June 1594. Bassingbourn's wife Ann died.]

298.—27 June 1594. *Edmond Moundeford,* Feltwell, to *Bassingbourn Gawdy,* High Sheriff.

Again asks to have his brother Fowler excused serving on the great inquest. Prays Gawdy may be comforted in his sorrow.

299.—27 June 1594. *Peter Morphewe,* Pulham St. Mary, yeoman, and *Peter Wales,* Thorpe, yeoman, to *Bassingbourn Gawdy,* High Sheriff.

General release. Witness, John Gibson, Thomas Crispe, Anthony Colphax.

300.—29 June 1594. [*Sir*] *Francis Hynde,* Maddingley [Camb.], to *Bassingbourn Gawdy,* High Sheriff.

Condoles with Gawdy on his loss. A "troublesome lewd fellow," Robert Banks, boasts of his influence with the jury in an action against Hynde, who begs Gawdy to counteract this by saying a word to the jurors, &c.

GAWDY MSS. 301.—1 July 1594.   *Thomas Fastolfe, Senr.*, Pettaugh (?), Suffolk,
               to *Bassingbourn Gawdy*, High Sheriff.

Release of all claims on *ca. sa.* against William Wrenche and ———
Snyler for 20*l.* and 53*s.* 4*d.* damages.   Witnesses, Henry Gibson,
Christopher Ballard.

302.—2 July 1594.   *Edward Lewkenor*, Denham, to *Bassingbourn
                     Gawdy*, High Sheriff.

To interest Gawdy in the bearer, a servant of Lewkenor's, who wishes
party taken in execution ; Crispe delays matters very much.

303.—3 July 1594.   *Henry Smythe* to *Bassingbourn Gawdy*, High
                     Sheriff.

Receipt for 21*s.* 8*d.* levied by *ca. sa.* on Willm. Ashwell.   Witness,
William Hunt.

[Between the dates of these letters Mathew Crispe, under-sheriff,
died.]

304.—13 July 1594.   *Thomas Funston*, Wymondham, to *Bassing-
                      bourn Gawdy*, High Sheriff.

Offers to serve him as under-sheriff in place of Crispe, deceased ; as
it may help Funston to the post next year.

305.—13 July 1594.   *Henry Gawdy to Bassingbourn Gawdy.*

Since the under-sheriff's death the office has been taken from poor
man Baker's house and kept at the Crown.   Begs it may be retrans-
ferred.   Remembrances to cousin Anthony.

306.—20 July 1594.   *John Owen*, Collector of Customs, Lynn Regis,
                      to *Bassingbourn Gawdy.*

Requests Gawdy to charge the Executors of his late deputy
[Mathew] Crispe with 33*l.* 14*s.* 10*d.* he collected on writ of extent
sent down by the Treasurer and Sir John Fortescue against the goods
of Edward Stone, Merchant, of Lynn, who was drowned one night in
the haven, being at the time indebted to the Queen for customs and
subsidies.

307.—20 July 1594.   *Thomas Gawdy*, Weybread [Suffolk], to
               · " brother   and   friend "   *Bassingbourn
                      Gawdy.*

To persuade Bassingbourn [who was his nephew, not brother] to be
" a mean " and peacemaker between Sir Nicholas Bacon and Thomas'
neighbour, Thomas Flatman, the matter (he understands from "my
uncle Justice ") is of no great importance.

[This Thomas died between the date of this letter and January
1596-7.]

308.—28 July 1594.   *Thomas Gawdy* [Junr.], Weybread [Suffolk],
               to *Bassingbourn Gawdy*, Harling.

Begs the Sheriff's favor in expediting a warrant to, oblige " his poor
kinsman Thomas Gawdy's " mother-in-law.

309.—1 August 1594. *John Pettus' to Bassingbourn Gawdy,* W.
Harling.

When dealing for the two bonds mentioned in (293) a contention
arose through a third person claiming the promise of their being sold to
him, whereupon Le-maire would not sell them to either. Le-maire has
now sent the first bond to Pettus with a letter of attorney to receive the
money for him.

310.—[End of July or beginning of August] 1594. *Thomas Funs-
ton,* London, to *Bassingbourn Gawdy,*
High Sheriff. Directed to Mr. Eden, of
Thetford.

Has got good favor in Gawdy's business [*Re* Crispe]. Got together
my Lord Treasurer, the Lord Chief Baron, and Mr. Fanshawe, and promised the latter the best gelding the late under-sheriff had. By Fanshawe's advice has obtained a commission to seize everything until
Her Majesty be paid. The Commission is directed to Sir Nicholas
Bacon, Sir Philip Parker, Mr. Ward, Mr. Nonne, and Funston. Funston hopes to return on Monday; in the meantime better summon
Nonne and Gibson. Crispe's sureties should be much bound to
Gawdy.

311.—[4 August] 1594. *Thomas Funston,* Ware [Herts], to *Bassingbourn Gawdy,* High Sheriff.

Fanshawe does not like the gelding, thinking it will prove a lame
jade, but Funston has arranged for it to stop a week to be shod and
trimmed, when Fanshawe will try it again. Funston wishes Fanshawe had had the blind gelding, which might have appeared without
fault. Fanshawe advises either that the administrator sell the corn,
good security being taken to see the Queen paid, or better, to buy the
corn of the administrator or take an assignment of him of enough to pay
the Queen, and then have a supersedias to avoid the Commission. Mr.
Nonne saith if we keep the goods they must pay for their own keeping.
Better let the sheriff buy of the administrator, so as to pay himself and
the Queen, or let the goods be kept underhand. Gawdy has keeping
enough for the sheep, and if the administrator will not be ruled, overrule him. This is Nonne's advice, "but I know you have the bent of
his bow." . . . . . "You know how bold Mr. Wentworth and
the widow have been with the administrator, let us be so likewise.
Blush not, but through with it." [Sunday night.]

312.—4 August 1594. *John Nonne* to his nephew [*Bassingbourn
Gawdy*].

[Gawdy's] case is full of peril, 3 or 4 of his sureties are insufficient
and almost undone by Crispe. Has seized much corn and cattle,
which must be watched day and night. Send two men "with money in
their purses" to reap the rye, &c. All the sureties but Codd attend to
their own business. Nonne will wait for the men, but must be at
Norwich on this business on Tuesday [he writes on Sunday]. Barnes,
the administrator of Crispe's goods, is arrested, which is another
difficulty. [Gawdy] should not make any grant for any felon's or
outlaw's goods in Crispe's possession; they have been taken to Mr.
Bedingfield's and will be begged of Gawdy for her [? Crispe's widow],
she is well provided for otherwise by indirect means. Let the men
come on foot to avoid charge.

GAWDY MSS.   P.S. The men must be at Westwood before noon Tuesday, and 10*l.*
with them.   Write Mr. Rous to assist.

313.—18 August 1594.   *John Nonne* to his nephew [*Bassingbourn Gawdy*, while on a visit at
Sir Charles Framlingham's, Crowes-
hall].

All the cattle must be sent away.   Send help to drive them; there
are 900 sheep and 60 great beasts.   Nonne dare not deliver them to
the sureties, for they care little for the cause.   The corn and hay-
stacks must abide all adventures, for the creditors combine to overthrow the Commission.   Mr. Rous and his wife are from home at
Broome.   Mentions Mr. Codd's possible arrival.   These toils both
distemper Nonne's body and mind.   Sends his duty to Sir Charles
Framlingham and my lady.   If [Gawdy] comes himself let him come
early so as to return to Croweshall after the cattle are sent away.   The
creditors will not stick at a little.   Do not send Aplewhin [?] nor Morris,
but some one who will be careful.

314 to 325.—19 August 1594.   Receipt by *Thomas Bridges*,
lieutenant, to *Henry Morgan*,
captain of 158 foot, from
Sir Thomas Shirley, Trea-
surer-at-War for France and
the Low Countries, pay from
8 June to 31 July, viz., 5*l.*

				£	s.	d.
7 September 1594. Similar receipt by H. Morgan for relief of his company		-	28	18	6
14 ,, ,,	,,	,,		28	18	6
20 October ,,		..	..	8	17	0
28 ,, ,,	,,	,,	,,	20	11	0
4 November ,,	,,	,,	,,	20	11	0
19 ,, ,,	Similar receipt by Lieut. Bridges	-	10	0	0
25 ,, ,,	,,	,,	,,	7	13	6
16 December ,,	,,	;, Thos. Bridges, lieutenant, to Captain Morgan, late deceased -	-	-	-	8	0	0
28 ,, ,,	,,	.,	8	0	0
10 January 1594-5.	,,	..	,,	8	0	0
3 February ,,	,,	,,	,,	12	0	0

326.—17 September 1594.   *Timothy Brewster*, Norwich, to *Bassingbourn Gawdy*, High Sheriff.

At the last assizes Brewster was left in the calendar to be bailed
before Mr. Houghton and Mr. Hubberd, and so to be discharged from
imprisonment on payment of fees.

In order to pay these he sent to his mother at Crowshall for money.
Gawdy's man Sanderson being there, Brewster's mother entrusted him
with eight shillings, which he has detained for over a fortnight, so that
the fees will amount up to more than that money comes to. ... .

327.—19 September 1594.   *Thomas Stywarde*, Gressenhall, to
Bassingbourn Gawdy, High Sheriff.

Last term a venire facias was delivered to the under-sheriff in a case
between my Lord Cromwell and Mr. Taverner.   Henry Gibson made a
return that the writ was delivered to Stywarde, who made no answer.

Taverner now brings the writ, with an order of Court to return '48 jurors, as each party may take exception to 12.

Stywarde will explain at the sessions why he dare not return the writ, which he encloses with the order.

328.—28 September [1594 ?]. *Thomas Osborne*, Garboldisham, to *Bassingbourn Gawdy*.

Some time ago, at the direction of the Lord Chief Justice and Privy Council, enquiry was made into the misdemeanours of former mayors of Thetford. . Mr. Eden, late mayor, and Edmund Downyng, his jailer, were indicted at last assizes for the wilful escape of a felon. Eden has three other escapes and Downyng six more charged against him. Gawdy has used influence to prevent these charges coming on in hopes of amendment. Now Richard Cocke, one of Gawdy's servants and Downyng's brother-in-law, lies in wait for Osborne, who preferred the indictment, "with great oaths to kill or have a leg or arm " of him. If they meet, " the event of fighting will be hanging or killing," which is an alternative Osborne "utterly dislikes " in so mean a quarrel. Osborne came hither last night, and already Downing and Cocke are lying in wait. Begs Gawdy will summon them and take their promise to keep the peace.

[Eden was mayor for the last time in 1591.]

329.—16 October 1594. *Thomas Styward*, Gressenhall, to *Bassingbourn Gawdy*, High Sheriff.

Has told Bolton of the arrest of Anthony Thwaytes on Styward's warrant, which Curtyes (the present under-sheriff), who came to his place through Crispe's creditors, doth disallow, notwithstanding composition between Styward and Crispe. The warrant was made last assizes, but not executed to oblige Mr. Attorney. The time is short, let Gawdy say if he will support the warrant or not. Styward makes no penny by it; he offered half the fee to Bolton and half to Curtyes at Norwich (5l. a piece), but the latter declined to take charge of Thwaytes, showing Gawdy's letter directing great regard to be had of him on account of his friends and subtilty. As Curtyes refuses to obey this letter, order has been taken for Thwaytes' "sure imprisonment and fast carrying up," if the warrant be allowed.

330.—20 October 1594. *Thomas Funston*, Wymondham, to *Bassingbourn Gawdy*, High Sheriff.

Funston directed Buxton to give Gawdy Funston's bond. Mine host at Ware says Mr. Fanshawe returned the gelding seven weeks ago, " much misliking him for stumbling." Wishes him sold to some horse-courser at London and that Fanshawe had the price. Hopes when he comes to Gawdy he can have the 40l. for his account.

331.—5 November 1594. *Thomas Funston*, London, to *Bassingbourn Gawdy*, care of Mr. Eden, of Thetford.

Has conferred about their exchequer cause ; the commission must be altogether altered. Pray send Mr. Nonne, it cannot be done without him. Funston has " substantially dealt with our attorney," but has not seen Fanshawe yet. Let Gawdy ride up on the gray gelding; Fanshawe's forwardness will be very necessary. The Court comes to Somerset House this week. Woodhouse is in the bill for sheriff. Let Barnes write a special letter to Mr. Walker to confess judgment in Funston's suit against him for 80l.

332.—15 November 1594. *Thomas Funston*, London, to *Bassing-bourn Gawdy*, High Sheriff.

London is full of strangers, and the Court this night at Somerset House, so Funston cannot provide Gawdy the lodgings he would, but may manage it by Thursday. Let him alight at the Black Swan in Holborn, where he will be met. Fanshawe longs greatly for his gelding, which he does not consider a gift, but claims as a heriot for some land Crispe held of him in Essex. Funston told him that Gawdy was trying it on the way up. Must get a special order from the Court to return the commission, if it is done without they will be answerable for the whole 700*l.* Has received a "cutting letter" from Nonne, who will not come up. Barnes and his friends delay his coming. Nonne is "so peremptory grown and so lazy" that Funston knows not how to use him.

333.—19 November 1594. *William Rugge*, Bylaugh, to *Bassing-bourn Gawdy*, Hingham.

Rugge is hindered by his ancient enemy the rheum from attending the meeting of Justices called at Hingham for the 20th. Let his men take copies of the new orders, or one of the newly printed copies, if they are to spare.

334.—4 December [1594 ?]. *Lady Elizabeth Framlingham* to her son-in-law *Bassingbourn Gawdy*, High Sheriff, Harling.

Cannot come to Gawdy as she cannot endure to ride one way or the other. She has besides causes for tarrying at home which cannot be put on paper, but which Gawdy shall know when they meet. Offers to give anything in her house that will pleasure him.

335.—11 December [1594 ?]. *Henry Daveney*, Thetford, to *Bassingbourn Gawdy*, West Harling.

Begs Gawdy's presence at the Sessions for that borough on the 18th inst. Thanks him for notifying them as to the Assizes and for other kindnesses to the town. [The Lord Chief Justice was reported by Philip Gawdy as promising to hold the assizes at Thetford this once more at Bassingbourn Gawdy's request.]

336.—30 December 1594. *Bassingbourn Gawdy*, West Harling, to *Lady Frances Gawdy*, widow [of Sir Thomas Gawdy], Gawdy Hall.

Bond to secure payment of 40*l.* on 22 January next; delivered into hands of Richard Sutton.

337.— 1594. *Nicholas Raynberd* to *Bassingbourn Gawdy*.

If Gawdy will "accept any of mine to attend" on him, Raynberd will furnish him accordingly with horse. Is going Londonwards; can he do anything there for Gawdy?

338.— [1594 ?]. *Rev. William Herringe*, Tittles-hall, to *Bassingbourn Gawdy*, High Sheriff.

Receipt for money due on outlawry against Cuthbert Sponner, of Babingley, brick burner. Witness, Richard Sponner, William Mulley.

1595.

339.—8 April 1595. *William Smyth*, St. Michaells, South Elmham, Suffolk, Yeoman, to *Bassingbourn Gawdy*, Harling.

Release (as Executor of Roger Corbet, of Hickling) to Gawdy, late Sheriff, of all demands, &c. Witness, Robert Bolton, Reynold Chamberlen.

340.—18 May 1595. *Bassingbourn Gawdy*, West Harling, to *Henry Daveney*.

Bond to secure 31*l.* 10*s.* payable to Daveney at Harling Church porch on 15 November 1595. Witness, Robert Bolton, Richard Sutton. (Note that 48*l.* paid at that time and place.)

341.—17 June 1595. *Bassingbourn Gawdy*, West Harling, to *Richard Smyth*, Carleton Road, gent.

Bond to secure payment of 50*l.* to Smyth on 6 November next. Witness, Robert Bolton, Thomas Lyle [?].

[29 June 1595. *Sir Charles Framlingham* died.]

342.—Memoranda as to the *Framlinghams* in writing of *Peter Le Neve*, Norroy.

3 Edward I. [?]	William de Framlingham. Inquisitions, hundred of Diss.
1446.	John Framlingham, Esq., and Margery his wife, Quer. in fine levied 24 Henry VI. of manor of Hoowys, Alderton, Suffolk.
1453.	John Framlingham, Esq., mentioned in fine levied 31 Henry VI., lands in Bawdesey, Suffolk.
1480.	Henry' Framlingham, Esq., witness to will of Nicholas Rumpe, of Felmingham. (Ex libro Caston Regr. Norw. fo. 81.)
1497.—3 October.	John Framlingham died, and buried with Alice his wife in church of St. Peter le Poore, London (Glover's Collectanea).
1538.	Recovery acknowledged by Charles Duke of Suffolk, to —— Framlingham (29 Henry VIII.) of manors of M[andevill?] and Abbottshall.
1545.	Elizabeth Latham [?], widow, Quer. and Francis Framlingham, Esq., deft., lands in [Ikyn?], Suff. (Fines 36 Henry VIII. No. 328.)
1595. 14 May.	Refers to lease of Pettaugh of this date [*see* same recited post, No. 350] and to another lease of Abbotshall Manor in Le Neve's Pettaugh Papers.
1595. 29 June.	Sir Charles Framlingham died, he married (1) [Dorothy] a daughter of Sir Clement Heigham, by whom he had Clement [born circ. 1564] (died in father's lifetime), and Ann, married Sir Bassingbourn Gawdy ; and (2) Elizabeth, daughter of Sir Thomas Barnardis—

ton, of Ketton, Suffolk, who survived him, and married Sir Henry Gawdy, of Claxton, by whom she had no issue.

1595. 19 August: Inquisition held at Eye. Jury find Sir Charles' will dated 20 June 1595; that his daughter Ann pre-deceased him, leaving Framlinghan Gawdy (aged 6) son and heir, and Charles Gawdy second son: Sir Charles died seised of Crows-hall in Debenham, Butlers, Abbottshall, Mun-develd's Manor, Ashfield Manor and Rectory; also Thorpe Rectory, and the site of the Manor of Harborow. (Old's Abstract of Inquisitions, v. 2, p. 193.)

(Undated.)   Sir Charles Framlingham, of Crowshall, married Anne, d. and h. of Robert Horne, by Margaret his wife, d. and coh. of John, Marquis Mon-tague, and relict of Sir —— Mortimer.

(Undated.)   Robert Framlingham, of Twyford, Inn-keeper and Shoe-maker; his eldest son was William F. of Lynn, Baker, High Sheriff of Norfolk [this is a mistake]; he pretended to arms and left Joan his d. and h., who married Sir Peter Sea-man, of Norwich [Sheriff 1710], and had a son, Thomas, and two daughters.
Richard Atteley, Esq., buried at St. Cuthbert, 18 Dec. 1600. Richard, son of Sir Edwin Richards [?] baptised at . . . . . . 1593. [? Any connection with Framlingham.]

343.—[July 1595.] Deposition of *John Pecke.*

The Friday before Sir Charles died (he died on Sunday), he called his wife to him and said to this effect, " Bess, I have given thee all my moveable goods upon this condition, that you shall be good to my ser-vants and the poor of Debenham, and that you shall not leave this house with bare walls, for I leave you as a mother among children." She answered, " Sir, I will leave this house in such manner as the heir shall have no cause to complain." Mistress Anne Barnardiston, her niece, was there at the time, as Pecke is persuaded in his conscience. Further-more, Pecke was a witness to Sir Charles' will, as far as the land is mentioned, and saith that the same was read to Sir Charles so far, and when the reader came to the gift of the goods he then stayed, and read not the same to him nor to any of the witnesses.

344.—[July 1595.] Deposition of *Rev. George Hals*, Minister of the Word of God at Kenton [Suff.].

Being with his patron Sir Charles after his will was made, and a little before his death, Hals heard him say to his wife, " Besse, I have given thee all, but I would not have the house defaced when thou diest, but I would have the children well dealt with, that they should not come to the bare walls." She answered, " Sir, by the power of God it shall be far from me to deface the house, but when I die I will so deal that they shall have no just cause to complain." Mrs. Brampton [? Barnardiston] heard the same. Hals further states that after Lady Framlingham's death, that is 21 Dec. 1604, having reported these words to Sir Bassing-bourn Gawdy in Crowshall parlour, he presently reported them to John Wrythoke, "standing by the fire," who said, " O yea, yea! but these words are not to be spoken now." [Although made after 1604, the above statement comes in most appropriately now.]

345.—27 July 1595. *Thomas Heigham*, gent.; second son of Sir John Gawdy Mss. Heigham, and *Sir Nicholas Bacon.* ·

Agreement : recites that Lord Burleigh, Lord High Treasurer and Master of the Wards, had bestowed on the said Thomas Heigham, his servant, the lease of the lands belonging to the Crown ·on the· death of Sir Charles Framlingham. Heigham covenants (after office found) to sue out the lease in the case name and at the expense of Bassingbourn Gawdy. Sir Nicholas is to pay Heigham 200*l.* at his father's house at Barrow on 31 July, and give his bond for 46*l.* 13*s.* 4*d.*

Witness, Sir John ·Heigham, Bassingbourn Gawdy, and ·Thomas Griggs.

346.—27 July 1595. *Sir Nicholas Bacon*, Culford, Suff., to *Thomas Heigham*, of Barrow, Suff.

Bond to secure 46*l.* 13*s.* 4*d.* payable 31 October next.

347.—31 July 1595. *Thomas Heigham* to his cousin, *Bassingbourn Gawdy.*

Receipt for 200*l.* paid at Mr. Fayrcliffe's house, Bury.

348.—[December ?] 1595. Attorney's bill for proceedings after the death of *Sir C. Framlingham.*

Mr. Gawdy.

	£	s.	d.
Trinity Term, 37 Elizabeth.			
For a warrant- for the· Commission to inquire after			
Sir C. Framlingham's death - - -	0	3	6
For the Commission - - - - -	0	18	0
Michaelmas Term, 37 & 38 Elizabeth.			
To Mr. Dewe, for a copy of the office - -	2	2	8
To Mr. Barker's man, writing the survey · - -	0	3	4
For the particular to Mr. Lovelace, Mr. Tock's clerk	1	5	0
To Mr. Pickeryll, for his fee - - -	0	4	4
For drawing the lease - - - -	0	3	4
For Mr. Attorney's fee, and his man's - -	0	11	0
For ingrossing the lease - - - -	0	13	4
For Mr. Hare's fee for the same - - -	0	18	0
For the obligations - - - - -	0	4	0
For the Commission - - - -	0	5	6
To the clerk for his pains - - -	0	5	0
For the fine of the lease ' - - -	33	6	8
For the acquittance for the same fine - -	0	1	0
	£41	4	8

Receipts for 8*l.* 6*s.* 8*d.* and 30*l.* on account.

1595–6.

349.—4 January 1595–6. *Thomas Wythe* [steward to Nathaniel Bacon] to [*Bassingbourn Gawdy*].

A much damaged letter as to compounding with Mr. Hare at 6*l.* 13*s.* 4*d.* for the fines on admission of Sir Charles Framlingham and his heir. This, together with the arrearages since he sold the manor to Mr. Bacon, comes to·12*l.* 13*s.* 4*d.* As to·the sheepwalks, my Lady [Framlingham] wrote to Wythe and Wrethock [see No.·344] to talk with Mr. Bacon, who suggested an arbitration by Sir Nicholas Bacon and Mr. Knyvet.

GAWDY MSS.
This cannot be done till after next term ; meantime Wythe must lie out
of the rents.   One White begs for a lease.

1596.

350.—9 April 1596.   *Bassingbourn Gawdy*, West Harling, to
                           John Peache, of Debenham, Suffolk,
                           Yeoman.

Indenture of confirmation of lease. Recites that Sir C. and Elizabeth
Framlingham by lease dated 14 May 1595, demised to Peache their
tenement called Woodward's in Pettaughe [Suff.] (wherein John
Smyth lately dwelt) for 21 years from Michealmas 1595 (if Peache so
long lived and for one year after his decease), at the rent of 21*l*.   Recites that on conference between Dame Elizabeth Framlingham and
Bassingbourn Gawdy it was agreed that the latter should take this land
(inter alia) in satisfaction of the one third of Sir Charles' lands during
the minority of Framlingham Gawdy, the heir at common law. Bassingbourn Gawdy confirms the recited lease.   Peache covenants to
spend 20 marks on the houses and buildings within six years, according
to the order of Edmond Stricklond and Richard Folkar.   Witness,
Robert Bolton, Richard Sutton.

351.—27 May 1596.   *Bassingbourn Gawdy*, West Harling, to
                           Henry Daveney.

Bond to secure payment to Daveney of 30*l*. on 29 June next.   Witness, Robert Bolton.

352.—2 December 1596. · *John Nonne* to [*Bassingbourn Gawdy*].

Mr. Follegate asks Nonne's help to prevent his niece (who is in
Gawdy's service) from "casting herself away in marriage" with her
fellow-servant Isaac. "All masters . . should rule and overrule their
servants, chiefly of that sex, &c."   Follegate would like her sent home,
their remaining in the same service would not be safe, &c.

1596–7.

353.—19 January 1596–7.   *Sir Arthur Heveningham*, Kettering-
                                 ham, to *Bassingbourn Gawdy.*

The Council has directed that the whole company of the trained
bands, both horse and foot, should be mustered and made fit, according
to martial discipline. Notify Captain Cottrell, who alone is appointed
to view and muster them. The justices have fixed his pay at 40*s*. a
week ; let this be collected from the several hundreds.

· [As Bassingbourn Gawdy was knighted before 17 January 1597–8,
the following undated letters addressed or referring to him as
" Esquire" must have been written before that date. Some of the first
division may relate to his father.]

I.—*Undated Letters relating to B. Gawdy (father or son).*

354.—*Henry Gawdy* [son of Sir Thomas] to *Bassingbourn Gawdy.*

Sends an indenture, a matter of great weight.   Remembrances to
cousins Anthony and Philip.·

355.—*Henry Gawdy* to cousin *Bassingbourn Gawdy*, Harling.   ⏐{

Lady Browne, my nephew North and his wife, and my sister Warner
will be with Bassingbourn next day. Does not know if Sir Thomas
will come, he came so weary from Warwick. ·

356.—*Owen Gawdy* [son of Thomas] to kinsman *Bassingbourn*   GAWDY MSS.
      Gawdy.

Asks a supersedias for the bearer, who has been bound to keep the peace without cause.

357.—[*Bassingbourn Gawdy ?*] Harling, to cousin *Gawdy.*

Draft letter renewing request made when cousin Gawdy was last at · Harling for the latter's favour to the writer's neighbour, Mr. Smyth, for whose reputation he vouches. Complaints have been made against Smyth, who desires to be helped to knowledge of the circumstances.

358.—   *Downying* (?) to *Bassingbourn Gawdy.* 9 November.

Is charged more than others of his living; this is especially unfair since he has "departed one half" among his sons.

359.—*Anthony Fryre*, Thetford, o *Bassing. Gawdy*, Harling. 17 February.

Mrs. Heyward cannot lodge Gawdy as Sir Edward Hinsell, Sir William Heydon, and the Sheriff are to be there. Heyward will be back from London to-morrow. P.S. Has been with Fisher at Mr. Lovell's, who will keep two rooms for Gawdy and his servants, but a bed and furniture must be sent, unless only one judge comes on circuit.

360.—*Roger Harvy*, Thetford, servant to the *Earl of Leicester*, to *Bassingbourn Gawdy*, West Harling. 25 April.

"If it may please your good worship, you have here within your liberty an obstinate parson, Edward Howlton, which sheweth himself very undutiful, not only himself but the rest of his company, which I trust in God your good worship will see it amended; for he maketh a jest at the Queen's authority, and he cometh with his boats in his neck" (*sic*). Trusts it may be amended before he comes again "or else he shall hear further of it. There be more which I will not name at this time. Trusting in God they live to amend both towards God and to our prince," &c.

361.—*Thomas Hayward*, Norwich Castle, to *Bassingbourn Gawdy*, West Harling. [This is *not* Thomas Heyward, of Thetford.]

Beseeches Gawdy, whose cook he once was, to stand good master to him with his late master Mr. Reppes, who is displeased with him, and by whom he has been confined in Norwich Castle, where he is " in great misery, without both money and meat."

362.—*Michael Henshaw*, Deputy Manciple of Clement's Inn, to [*Bassingbourn Gawdy ?*]. The bearer "George Fyton" is certified to be "Fellow and Companion of this House or Inn of St. Clement, of honest behaviour and conversation without any debt or arrearages."

363.—*Anne Heyward* [London] to *Mrs. Gawdy.* Sends by bearer the things Mrs. Gawdy wrote for. "Your sipers cost 4s. 4d., your border and your crippin 11s., your gett pendants 12d., 6d., and 3d., your bugle 9d., your satin silk half an ounce 16d." Remembrances to Mrs Gawdy's husband and father-in-law. Is sorry for the loss of her and their good friend.

364.—*Thomas Hinlon* to *Bassingbourn Gawdy.* Gawdy's brother had no authority to cancel Hinlon's wife's bond. Begs the money may be paid, he has bought land and counted on it.

365.—*Christopher Highnone*, Lopham, to *Bassingbourn· Gawdy.* Sends his mare ; had ridden her poor this summer, but now she is "fat and unbreathed . . ˙. . . taken from grass this morning." Is starting for West of England, leaves price to Gawdy, who can give his bill to bearer. Mare is valued at 12*l.*

366.—*William Hopkinson*, Martin Hall, to *Bassingbourn . Gawdy.* West Harling. 14 July. Hears by Mr. Gray's servant that a stray nag has come to Gawdy's hands. Hopkinson claims it on behalf of Mr. Fincheam. It was on its way back from wintering with Mr. Parris at Norton, and has been proclaimed at Thetford, Walton and Cambridge.

367.—*William Methewold* to [*Bassingbourn Gawdy* ?] Methwold has talked to Mr. Rookwood's man who will not receive Methwold's lambs before Lammas. Begs they may be taken back to [Gawdy's (?)] flock to save him from loss.

368.—*H. Manny* to his brother *Flowerdew*, Bury. At the instance of the bearer Kyllyon, Manny is willing that Flowerdew should send for Mr. Lychfell (lodging in Helton), and having taken a bond of the bearer in 500*l.* to abide the end of the matter that one of the jury may be withdrawn. to-morrow, and in the meantime they may eat and drink. Dated, Sunday.

369.—*Robert Mully*, Kenninghall Lodge, to *Bassingbourn Gawdy.* West Harling. 13 April. Informs Gawdy of the misbehaviour of Thomas Burdeis, now of Kenninghall, Sawyer. Last year he was very troublesome, "barryting and fighting" with any one who wrought in the ground within Mully's charge. Burdeis hath greatly misused the bearer, throwing him out of work, where he had taken great store of work of Robert Clowth, also struck him and his fellows and threw them and the pieces of timber in the pit ; he has done the like in Bullymer's carke and the common of Kenninghall. The controversy was referred to Mully and Goodman Davye, when Burdeis was. "so stout and so full of law that no reason would rule him."

370.—*Thomas Osburne*, Brissingham, to *Bassingbourn Gawdy.* 3 November. Requests Gawdy to send his cart or man and horse for his governes [? harness, reins] which have been done for a sen'net.

371.—*Richard Pead* to [*Bassingbourn Gawdy*]. "It is true I sold Brett ten loads of hay to be taken out of my hay house for 20 marks, but with this limitation, if there were so much there, otherwise to be abated rateably . . . . he urgeth two things against this, the note under my hand which mentioneth no such exception . . . . and my taking of hay after I had sold it." The note was an imperfect memorandum given "for mortality's sake ;" admits he took 6 cwt. of hay with Brett's consent for which he will allow at 2 shillings a hundred. Brett was told "to look in the hay house and peruse the hay," and before he approached it "he would have lumped for it" at 20 marks : will leave it to [Gawdy's] arbitration.

372. —— *Pecke* to *Bassingbourn Gawdy.* Reminds Gawdy that it was he who referred Pecke's complaint against his son Richard of Larling to the parson of that place. Complains that the parson does nothing, being friendly to the son. Moreover since then his son's wife has beaten him. Pecke bought the house and land for 27*l.* (thinking to dwell in it for his life), but he has no dwelling in it ; the son has also received 30*s.* of Pecke's money, sold his cow for 5 nobles, also a piece of land he sold and took the money and 12*s.* for his books, 10*s.* for a clock, and 28*s.* for land, besides keeping from his father a cupboard and other things.

373.—[*Re N. Raynberd*] *Lord Hunsdon*, Court at Theobalds, to *Sir William Spring, Bassingbourn Gawdy*, and *Robert Gelding.*

Lord Hunsdon formerly wrote them on behalf of Robert Browne of Thetford to call before them Browne and Nicholas Raynberd of the same town of whose hard dealing Browne complained. Is now informed that Browne's complaint is false and that the man is practising cunningly with his brother, a minister, to defraud Raynberd of certain goods and a lease; he has also fraudulently transferred his goods to his brother. Lord Hunsdon associates Mr. Golding of St. Edmundsbury with them as being acquainted with the causes. Browne is to give surety to put in bail to Raynberd's action, if he refuses, bind him and his brother to appear before Hunsdon wherever the Court may be.

374.—*Nicholas Raynberd* to *Bassingbourn Gawdy*, Esq.

Goes to London to-morrow, can he do anything there or at Court? Asks Gawdy to join with Mr. Townshende and Mr. Gresham in granting a warrant that the town of Brisingham may be charged with this bearer's daughter and the town of Fersfield discharged.

375.—*Nicholas Raynberd*, Thetford, to *Bassingbourn Gawdy*, West Harling, 26 December. Is riding to Court on Friday before new year: will execute any commission there. (Memo. below. Robert and Agnes Godderham (?), of Winfarthing; Adam Clarke, of Gissing; Christian Warner, wife of William Warner. Supersedias for the peace, John Knowles of Rowdham 10*l.*, Barttemewe Knowles 5*l.*, Leonard Levalde (?) 5*l.* sureties against Thomas Chamberlyne of Rowdham.)

376.—*John Snellinge* to *Anthony Rawlings*. To get his master Gawdy to send the promised protection for John Cressenhalle, who will deliver it again in a month or so. Remembrance to Mrs. Rawlings.

377.—*William Spryng*, Pakenham, to *Bassingbourn Gawdy*, 25 June. Asks a licence for bearer John Baker, there being no ale-houses at Stanford.

378.—*Thomas Styward*, Norwich, to *Mr. Bassingbourn Gawdy*. 13 January. Has had a conference with Gawdy's attorney as to Styward being repaid the money he has disbursed, which is 50*s.* Asks Gawdy to send it by his man, Bullocke. Styward has promised the attorney to join with him for Gawdy's discharge.

379.—*Petition of the town of* . (Heading of petition damaged and illegible.) One George [Nonne?], Gent., denies their right of common. They demand first the use of the furze, in shacke food for their horses; mares, and colts from Lammas till . . . . . item their neat beasts to feed "with the lord. as the lord hath done with us," item the use of their closed commons from that time till Lammas. Item the bailiff or haywarde has always been allowed eight shillings and for the dinner of the steward and the lord's deputy other eight shillings, item that they may have a pynfold so as not to be driven to pen "any stray cattle in our yards noisome unto us," item that they may pay the old fines, 4*d.* an acre and not as the lord thinks good. Item that they may have a certain sheep going in the lord's flock without disturbance. Whereas they have two or three new reared up tenements which are denied common, although rated, and the lord wisheth the homage to set a "pain" of 10*s.* on their heads, which they refused to do and then willed them to return that the occupiers did common . . . . (mutilated).

II.—*Undated Letters prior to* 17 *January* 1597–8, *probably relating to Bassingbourn Gawdy (the son).*

380.—*Rev. Thomas Barsham*, Eccles, to *Bassingbourn Gawdy*, West Harling. Barsham understands that some of his neighbours are to be before Gawdy that day at Harling, namely, such as keep ale-houses and tippling houses, for the appointing of orders to be observed in their houses, " the execution of which is oftentimes by them but slenderly performed, nay almost not at all regarded, as I (their poor minister) find by experience." Barsham hears abroad to his great grief that the town of Eccles, in the sins of gaming, blasphemy, riot, gluttony, licentiousness, drunkenness, &c., passeth all the towns about. He has laboured by all possible means to cut them down, and craves Gawdy's aid to put down all the unlicensed houses, and as to licensed houses to give such charge unto him that shall be still continued ("for one is sufficient, yea too many for our town ") that God's name be not abused as heretofore. The constables cannot do much as they live two miles from the town, " such was the wise choice of our townsmen of their officers."

381.—*Robert Dawbeny* to *Bassingbourn Gawdy*, Esq., Harling, 12 May. After diligent search can find no writings concerning Gawdy or his lands. If any such were committed to Sir Nicholas Bacon he trusts Mr. Colby has them.

382.—*Robert Dawbeny* to *Bassingbourn Gawdy*, Esq., 17 September. Will recommend to his master anyone Gawdy commends to serve in Elizabeth Fowle's place. Knows that Mistress Anne Brampton is desirous of serving his master.

383.—*Richard Fysher* to *Robert Boulton*. Asks Boulton to speak to Fysher's master and get him eased 3 or 4 pounds. He is rated at 16*l.* in goods and 5*l.* in land, but only owns 41 acres, and is charged higher than his neighbours who own twice or thrice as much land.

384.—*John Fysher* to [*B. Gawdy ?*]. Begs that he and his partner may be discharged to-morrow at Wymondham, and sends a note of the store of powder, &c. which " our hundred of Grymshoe " is charged withal.

> Inprimis, lbs. 260 of powder ⎫ We have them both to the
> 　　　　　lbs. 360 of match ⎭ 　full.
> 　　160 bullets. 　The lead was bought by Mr. Wryght, and it remains in the hands of Mr. Tom Wryght, his son, who has been several times asked for it but denies he ever had it.

9 Pioneers.	All appointed and in readiness.
12 Shod shovels.	Ten of them in readiness.
12 Pickaxes.	Ten of them in readiness.
12 Bare shovels.	Ten of them in readiness.
5 Axes.	Not any provided.
3 Beetles.	Not any provided.
12 Baskets.	Ten of them in readiness.
2 Carts.	Ready.

385.—*Barbarie Hart* to *Mr.* [*Framlingham*] *Gawdy*. Gawdy having been so kind to her son on his marriage, Mrs. Hart asks him to do as much for her daughter, who is to be married on Twelfth-day next. Asks him to come to the wedding and to desire Mrs. Dorothy to come also.

386.—*William Heringe* to *Bassingbourn Gawdy* (" my very good captain "), Harling　The Commission is to sit on the Saturday after

Michaelmas at Harleston, at Cookes. Begs Gawdy's and Mr. Sayer's GAWDY MSS. attendance, as Mr. Thurston and others will be there.

387 —*Robert Lillie* to [*Bassingbourn Gawdy*]. Has been dismissed from [Gawdy's] service, and writes to explain away his offence. He accompanied Mary Freeman's brother, to whom he was much beholden, to East Harling (a place then suspected of God's visitation). He did not stay there above two hours, went into no house, consorted with no one in the parish. Some of his fellow servants were there the same day, and can be a warrant of his good behaviour while there. Asks [Gawdy] to receive him again into favour.

388.—*Francis Moundeford*, Feltwell, to his friend *Bassingbourn Gawdy*, West Harling. 28 January. Sends enclosed the lieutenant's letters received this evening. Shropham and Guiltcross are parcel of this limit and next to Gawdy, who should direct his warrant to them for the collecting of the money. Moundeford has done the like to Wayland, Grimshoe, and South Greenhoe.

389.—*Francis Moundeford*, Feltwell, to [*Bassingbourn Gawdy*]. 4 May. Sends the lieutenant's letters which Mr. Guybon and Mr. Reppes have seen. Will attend according to appointment.

390.—*Peter Myne, Junr.*, to [*Bassingbourn Gawdy?*]. 11 August. Wishes to let [Gawdy] understand his poor substance. He has but 39 acres of land, out of that has to pay his mother 20 nobles a year, and, besides discharging Lord and King, when the heir comes of age he has to pay him 55*l.* He serves in a corslet, but the man, though of great substance, gives him no wages. He has already served six days. Asks Gawdy to think of him.

391.—*Roger North*, Kirtling [Cambridgeshire], to *Bassingbourn Gawdy, Mr. Colbie* and other *J.P.'s.* 9 January. Understands his farmer at Elmham (?) [Suffolk] and servant John Selling were assaulted in the grounds about North's house there by young Bateman and a " cutter or slight person " who belongs to one Mr. Gleman. North's man was in danger to have been slain by the "roister," if he had given him any cross language. They came under pretence to hawk "hard at the house side," but had planned beforehand the "match of destroying his man." All will to wrack if such doings are allowed.

392.—*Roger North*, Kirtling [Cambridgeshire], to *Bassingbourn Gawdy*, Harling. 25 January. To favour this poor bearer so as to do him justice in Gawdy's [manorial] Court, or license him to draw the suit to the common law.

393.—*Roger North*, Mildenhall, to *Bassingbourn Gawdy.* 23 March. Asks Gawdy's warran to attach the bearer's servant, who has run away from him.

394.—*Roger North*, Kirtling [Cambridgeshire], to *Bassingbourn Gawdy*, Mendham. 17 September. Is going to set forward his work at Elmham and purports to visit Gawdy at Mendham the Friday after Michaelmas, staying with him Saturday and Sunday. Trusts they may be bold to trouble Mr. Lawrence for that Sabbath. Goes to the sessions at Beccles on Monday and is like to bring Robert Ashfield with him. Sir Robert Wingfield [?] will be there also. Please send the enclosed to Downing, the attorney, at Beccles.

395.—*Roger North*, Bury, to *Bassingbourn Gawdy.* 11 October. The bearer, William Martin, informs North that one Richard Smith a shepherd died in Gawdy's manor of Bridgham owning a copyhold tenement. Smith left two daughters, one named Awlyn and the other Ann; the latter married one Lawrence and lives in the place. Martin pretends some claim to the house. North begs that he may be given a copy of the Court Rolls.

396.—*John Spurforde*, of East Wrotham, to *Bassingbourn Gawdy*, Esq. Is a schoolmaster and has been "inbylled" doubtless from the envy of John Harwarde, who was a grievous enemy of Spurforde's father, as the latter could not favour Harwarde's evil and crooked dealings.

Reminds Gawdy of his favourable promises to Spurforde and his father.

397.—*Bassingbourn Gawdy* to kinsman *Michael Stanhope*, Esq., one of the Privy Chamber, &c. Asks his furtherance in a matter touching Gawdy in credit, particulars of which are in letter to Sir John Townsend. The captains Gawdy has appointed are his uncle Anthony Gawdy and the bearer, one Mr. Barwicke.

Remembrances to "my cousin your wife and (your) mother."

1597–8.

398.—17 January 1597–8. *Sir Bassingbourn Gawdy,* Harling, to *Anthony Gawdy.*

Bond to secure 100*l.* to be paid to Anthony at West Harling Church porch on 18 January 1598–9. Witness, Robert Bolton, Richard Sutton.

1598.

399.—25 April 1598. *Edmund Moundeford,* Feltwell, to his cousin, *Sir Bass. Gawdy,* West Harling.

John Browne, licensed by Gawdy to keep an alehouse at Tottington, suffers unlawful games. George Fytt, of the same place, "whom I have suppressed," still sells ale and suffers bowls, cards, tables, dice, and such like unlawful games to be played, besides encouraging very lewd company. Will Gawdy deal with them, or shall Moundeford proceed at Swaffham Sessions ?

400.—4 June 1598. *William Sprynge,* Buckenham, to *Sir Bassingbourn Gawdy,* Harling.

Sprynge has "used means to the escheator" who will stay proceedings till Friday. Will be much obliged if Gawdy will be at Swaffham at 9 a.m. on that day.

401.—13 August 1598. *Rev. John Trendle,* Ovington, to *Sir Bassingbourn Gawdy*, East Harling.

Since Ambrose Longwood has been encouraged by Sir Robert Southwell, he proceeds to disturb and vex Trendle in his sermon time. " Yesterday by frowning, putting out his mouth, setting his teeth, " knitting his brows, whispering to himself, clapping his hand upon his " knee with malcontented gestures the same as heretofore, stamping " with his feet to the offence of others." Trendle could not proceed, and has charged the constable with him, but the justices are afraid of him. Asks Gawdy to bring up the case ; the witnesses are, John Pickas, Nicholas Weightman, Ambrose Clement, and Israel Trendle. Trendle spoke to Mr. Hassett [?] about it who was at the Sessions, but heard no motion made, and marvels that the recognizance should be in Sir Robert's pocket. As to going to Sir Robert that is out of the question, as he has threatened to whip Trendle naked. **fi**

402.—22 August 1598. *Same to Same.*

GAWDY MSS.

Encloses a letter which he begs to have forwarded with Gawdy's good word to Sir Nicholas Bacon. Trendle is "as a man perplexed . . . " I have preached the gospel this twenty four years in Norfolk," . . . and was never so hardly dealt with before.

403.—4 September 1598. *Sir John Heigham,* Bury [Suffolk], to his loving nephew, *Sir Bassingbourn Gawdy.*

Heigham's honest neighbour, Thomas Saddleton, is indebted to Francis Warner, Gawdy's servant, and wishes to repay principal and interest. Asks Gawdy to get Warner's consent.

404.—10 October 159[8]. *Thomas Wythe,* Sternfield [Suffolk], to *Sir Bassingbourn Gawdy,* Harling.

Acknowledges receipt of award to which he will conform himself. Cannot see how Mr. Bacon can think himself wronged therein, but has had no time to see him. Is sorry he was away when Gray came for the rent. Will wait on Gawdy before going to London, at present the waters are so great, he can hardly travel that way.

405.—22 October 1598. *Peter Pett,* Limehouse [Middlesex], to *Sir Bassingbourn Gawdy,* Harling.

Apologises for delaying his coming. Has to be next Sunday with the Earl of Nottingham at the court at Richmond, and next week will be with Gawdy. Remembrances to my lady, Mr. Framlingham, and Mr. Charles.

P.S.—A letter was sent to him at Harling since he came to London, brought by Nicholas Pyne. Pett thinks Gayford has it.

406.—4 November 1598. *Edmond Moundeford,* Feltwell, to his cousin *Sir Bass. Gawdy,* West Harling.

Moundeford and his cousin Spilman wrote to his cousin Guybon touching the desire of Gawdy and themselves to have the proposed house of correction erected, and asked him to send his warrants to the chief constables to collect the money that was yet unpaid and to certify any obstinate persons refusing to pay, to the nearest justice. Has not heard in reply from Guybon and suggests Gawdy should write and fix a day for a meeting.

[This relates to the Bridewell at Swaffham, formerly the prison of the Earls of Richmond.]

407.—[1598.] *Jasper Meller* to *Sir Bassingbourn Gawdy.*

"Though Humanity do blush to see my rash presumption yet your " exceeding courtesy so emboldeneth my illiterate pen that, after " craving pardon for my arrogancy, you may add more honour to " your own glory in shewing kindness to an so-undeserved peasant."

Two days ago he caught with some labour this Tasslegentle and afterwards found on him the Queen's Varvaile [a small silver ring round the hawk's leg] and one Mr. Throgmorton's name on the "mayle." Dares not disobey the Statute which directs the hawk to be sent to the Sheriff, but as he "knows not the knight . . . would rather hazard a " touch of impudency from your honorable conjecture than . . . " from a stranger." Asks Gawdy to acquaint the Sheriff and asks " if the letter of the law be satisfied" that *he* may not be unregarded.

408.—[1598.] *Jasper Meller* to *Sir Bassingbourn*
Gawdy.

" Sir, If acknowledgement may pass for a Badge of Gratuity, or en-
" deavour countervail so honorable favours, the world shall witness
" my desire to blazon your virtue . . . for as in Pristine ages it
" hath been held death to a man of means, so in these days. I hold it
" more than Inhuman not to confess such gracious kindness . . .
" Pardon me, Good Sir, if I seem too importunate to beg your service
" because I have ever held Forgetfulness a greater vice than Mortality
" can comprehend, therefore I pray you . . . that wherein my
" Imbecilious power may stead you, or my Banqueroute means
" pleasure you, you will increase my bond," &c. . . Remembrances
" to brother Philip . . : " I will as howsoever die your debtor,
" and cry with the Spaniard, ' Oxala ' !" [Would to God].

1598–9.

409.—10 February 1598-9. *Edmond Moundeford*, Lynford, to his
cousin, *Sir Bassingbourn Gawdy.*

Moundeford has just heard a cause in controversy between Mr. Conye
and Clement Egmore of West Wrotham. Asks Gawdy to join him in
granting " a warrant of the good behaviour " against her. The Constable
of East Wrotham will report her doings and speeches with her neighbours.
She is too poor to find sureties and imprisonment would be too great
punishment. Suggests setting her in the stocks and so dismissing her.

410.—13 March 1598-9. *John Morrys*, Hockham, to *Sir Bassing-*
bourn Gawdy, Harling.

Last Sabbath afternoon Morrys and his neighbours met to make a
rate for charges directed to be collected by the Constable's warrant
and to be paid at Harling Market. They wanted to rate Morry's
sheep course under the last statute, which he would not consent to.
Has since been told by counsel that it can only be rated for relief of
the poor and for providing stocks for the town.

1599.

411.—25 March 1599. *Earl of Essex*, the Court, to the *Commissioners*
for the Muster and *Justices of the Peace.*

Holograph letter commending his servant, Thomas Elyott, who has
been appointed by the Council one of the Muster Masters for Norfolk.
" He hath served me many years and followed me in sundry of my
" employments for Her Majesty's service, whereby he hath well
" enabled himself for his charge."

412.—29 March 1599. *Rev. John Trendle*, Ovington, to *Sir B.*
Gawdy, Harling.

Asks Gawdy to get one Mr. Button, a neighbouring minister, to come
to terms with the bearer, Christopher Hutchinson, without law.

413.—30 March 1599. *Henry Gawdy* [of Claxton], Norwich, to
cousin, *Sir Bassingbourn Gawdy*, Harling.

Recommends George Fytte, of Tottington, for a license to victual
within that town.

414.—31 March 1599.   *Edmond Moundeford*, Feltwell, to *Sir Bassingbourn Gawdy*, West Harling.

It is nearly time to take accounts and appoint new churchwardens and overseers of the poor. Will Gawdy and Bartlett take Shropham, Guiltcross, and Wayland in Easter week? Moundeford and Pratt will join for South Greenhoe, Grimshoe, and Clackclose, or Moundeford will join Gawdy if preferred.

Sir Philip Woodhouse summons Moundeford to meet Gawdy at Attelboro' on Monday on the Recusants' Commission; it is too near our sessions at Lynn, and Moundeford has to be on the same Commision at Walsingham on Thursday, so must be excused.

415.—[? circ. April 1599.]   *John Hill* [the writing varies from that of John Hill, a foster brother of Sir Thomas Knyvet, and auditor of the Crown,] to *Sir Bassingbourn Gawdy.*

His master bids Hill write that there is intelligence of much to do in the Exchequer about the Recusants' Commission, the return of which Gawdy is supposed to be witholding so that nothing may be done therein. Urges its return.

416.—2 April 1599.   *Henry Gawdy,* Claxton, & *Lady Eliz. Framlingham,* to *Sir Bassingbourn Gawdy.*

Asks Gawdy's influence with Sir Nicholas Bacon to procure discharge of their neighbour, a widow, Mrs. Heryng, living at Eye [Suffolk], from furnishing a light house. She is well disposed, has lent on Privy Seals (25*l*. out of pocket now), and is in litigation about lands she purchased.

417.—7 June 1599.   *Robert Dade,* Lincoln's Inn, to [*Sir Bassingbourn Gawdy*].

Has acquainted my Lord Chief [Justice] of [Gawdy's] care in " committing the man to Norwich Gaol for affirming and publishing to " such as he took to be his servant Frame, that he and 20 others had " determined to kill his Lordship, and that if he should not ride " strongly he should be made sure never to ride circuit again." His Lordship took it very kindly of [Gawdy] but said he cared not for them at all, whereupon Dade mentioned it to my Lord Keeper and my Lord Treasurer, who send this bearer to fetch the man and the examinations [Gawdy] has taken, names of accusers, &c.

418.—10 June 1599.   *Richard Sutton,* Feltwell, to *Sir Bassingbourn Gawdy,* West Harling.

Sutton is sent by my Lord Treasurer, and Mr. Chancellor of the Exchequer with a commission under the Great Seal directed to himself Gawdy, Mr. Edmond Bell, and Mr. Edmond Moundeford to survey and value the manors of Feltwell and Northwold which the Queen means to resume from the Bishop of Ely's possession. The commission must be executed on the land itself, and that forthwith, as it extends to five other shires and is returnable the 26th inst. Does not wish to draw Gawdy to come so far, and at the same time would like to have his seal to the certificate which he can do without being present. Will wait on him for that purpose to-morrow night after Sutton and Moundeford have performed the service.

GAWDY MSS.   419.—11 June 1599.   *Edmond Moundeford*, Feltwell, to *Sir Bassingbourn Gawdy*.

They have valued Feltwell and its demesnes at 27*l*. 4*s*. 8*d*. per ann. and Northwold at 18*l*. 12*s*., and have entered on part of Feltwell Manor in the name of the whole to resume it for Her Highness.

420.—26 July 1599.   *John Reynolds*, Attelboro', to *Sir Bass. Gawdy*.

The men who have heretofore trained in the harness supplied by Reynolds have habitually either lost or exchanged it for worse, to his great loss. May not his servant, John Francke, train with Reynolds' caliver ? Would wait on Gawdy in person but for " want of sight and other impediments."

421.—2 August 1599.   *Rev. John Trendle* [of Ovington] to *Sir B. Gawdy*.

Has come to wait on Gawdy, and finding him from home leaves his request in writing, viz., " if you wish a tailor for your house to attend upon you at Michael [sic] next," to take Trendle's son, a youth of 20, now at Mr. Claxton's.

422.—9 August 1599.   *Sir John Heigham*, Barrow [Suffolk], to *Sir B. Gawdy*, Harling.

Asks Gawdy to spare William Myles, servant to widow Martyn of Asheby, a trained soldier, from going forth this muster.

423.—10 August 1599.   *Lord Nottingham*, Somerset House in London, to *Constables* and principal officers of *Brentwood and Ingerston* in Essex.

The foot and horse companies out of Norfolk were given their rendezvous at Brentwood and Ingerston, but " the necessity of the present service will not permit them to stay there." Advise their chief leaders, Sir Christopher Heydon, Sir John Townshend, Sir Clement Heigham, and Sir William Woodhouse, to march " hither to me at London without any stay there."

424.—[? September 1599].   *Henry Gawdy* to his cousin, *Sir B. Gawdy*.

Has received the commission for the subsidies. Expects Mr. Attorney, when he will write again.

425.—1 September 1599.   *Edmond Moundeford*, Feltwell, to *Sir Bassingbourn Gawdy*, West Harling.

Asks Gawdy to appoint a collector for their division of the subsidy, and appoint him to be at the next meeting at Watton with his sureties.

426.—15 September 1599.   *Robert Dade*, Bury St. Edmond's [Suffolk], to *Sir Bassingbourn Gawdy*, Harling.

Asks payment of the " remanet " of his bill on Monday after Michaelmas. Had hoped to meet Gawdy at Redgrave [Suffolk], and to have taken instructions for the conveyance for my Lady your wife and " the purchasers who have joined with you in the fine."

427.—29 September 1599. *Edmond Moundeford*, Feltwell, to Sir *Bassingbourñ Gawdy*, West Harling.

Sends four blank warrants for a collector of the subsidy, and a note of substantial men in Wayland, Grimshoe, and South Greenhoe, for Gawdy to select names from.

428.—25 October 1599. *John Dixon*, Norwich, to *Sir Bass. Gawdy*.

Gawdy's "poor beadsman" begs intercession with Sir Nicholas Bacon that he may be bailed. Considering he is "in danger of debt," . . . his "lying here will be to his utter overthrow." Explains why he withstood Sir Nicholas' warrant ; the man who served it would not say what it was for, and Dixon "doubted nothing but it had been for debt."

429.—4 November 1599.   *Sir Nicholas Bacon* and *Sir Bass. Gawdy*, Redgrave [Suffolk], to [*Sir John Pop-ham*] *Lord Chief Justice of England*.

Recommends Henry Holdiche, Esq., to be in the Commission of the Peace, there being none other within eight miles of his residence. [Mem. by P. Le Neve. "Dudlington."]

430.—14 December 1599.   *Thomas Wythe*, Sternfield [Suff.], to *Sir Bassingbourn Gawdy*, Harling.

Gawdy's servant Grey will bring him 8*l*. rent of hop ground. Wythe has written to Mr. Grigges to pay his fine. Reminds Gawdy of his old suit to Mr. Nathaniel Bacon, whom he meant to have seen at Twelfe [sic] Sessions, but as he is now High Sheriff, fears to miss him. Begs Gawdy to be earnest with Bacon, not to put Wythe out of his steward-ship ; for which (with Bacon's privity) Wythe gave 13*l*. 6*s*. 8*d*. to Mr. Horneby and a score of trees of the best fruit, which cost 30*s*., and did lay out to Mr. Auditor Hill 20*s*. to renew his patent. Wythe has only enjoyed the office seven years ; half a dozen tenants have com-plained and another has been appointed in his place without Wythe having an opportunity to answer their complaints.

431.—24 December 1599. *Da. Hughes*, Woodrising, to *Sir Bass. Gawdy*, Harling.

My lady [Southwell] has ordered Gawdy a doe "of the best," which Hughes fear will be but poor owing to the wet season. Let him have warning before Gawdy sends his man for it.

432.—13 January 1599–1600.   *Edmond Moundeford*, Lynford, to cousin *Sir Bassingbourn Gawdy*, West Harling.

Robert Newporte, a miller of Ashill, purchased a windmill which cost him all his substance, and for which he is indebted 40*l*. It is now "blown down and overthrown by tempest of wind" to his ruin. Can he be helped by the charitable contribution of the county without waiting for the sessions ? [Endorsed by Sir B. Gawdy " *Sir Ed*. Moundeford ; " he was not knighted till 1603.]

433.—1 February 1599–1600. *Martin Manne*, Norwich, to *Sir B. Gawdy*.

Encloses proceedings touching the horses ; certificate of default is deferred. " There is come a letter to set Transportation at liberty again . . . sent by my Lord Treasurer upon your letters written when the restraint was received." Mr. Attorney thanks Gawdy for remembering Mr. Phillips. Manne's master, and Sir Christopher have written to the officers of the Peace to "deal with the merchants for some reward." Let Gawdy move any who benefit by transportation to contribute voluntarily.

1599–1600.

434.—17 February 1599–1600. *William Howes*, late soldier under Gawdy's band, to his good captain *Sir Bassingbourn Gawdy, Knt.*

"Umblie desires" excuse as he has been sore sick since coming from Stratford.

435.—21 March 1599–1600. *Sir Arthur Heveningham*, Ketteringham, to *Sir Bassingbourn Gawdy*, West Harling.

Gawdy's hundreds have not paid in their composition money for Her Majesty's privy diet. The Purveyors . . . would have had Sir Arthur certify the chief Constables' names that a Marshall's man might have come down for them. . . . The money should be paid to-morrow or they will be returned in contempt.

436.—22 March 1599–1600. *Edmund Moundeford*, Lynford, to *Sir Bassingbourn Gawdy*, West Harling.

Moundeford and his cousin Holdiche take the account of the Church-wardens and Overseers of the poor for Grimshoe next Wednesday; when does Gawdy for Wayland? Sir John Townshend, Mr. Guybon, and Mr. Bell appoint 31 March to take account of the Stock of the house of Correction at Swaffham. Some of the company much mislike the order taken by Gawdy and Moundeford for "the farme of the house and the use of the Stock." Who has Mr. Chabnor's bond for the delivery of the stock?

437.—4 April 1600. *Francis Gawdy*, Wallington, to *Sir Chris. Heydon, Sir Philip Woodhouse*, and *Sir Bass. Gawdy*.

To beg that the hundred of Clackclose may be relieved from contributing 4l. to repair bridges in Trowse; they have been at unusual charge this winter in repairing banks and bridges, there being many breaches and decays, the hundred being most subject to waters.

1600.

438.—13 April 1600. *Da. Hughes*, Woodrising, to [*Sir Bass. Gawdy*].

Complains of Widow Fitt, who keeps an unlicensed victualling house and brews strong drink at Carbrook. As she has no other means of firing, she and such as she spoil "my lady's woods and hedges."

439.—7 June 1600. *John Sprynge*, Pakenham, to *Sir Bassingbourn Gawdy*, West Harling.

Informs Gawdy that a little man he has taken into his service is "a very disordered fellow and very often drunk," and has often run away

from Sprynge and his father before. Let him be punished, or send him GAWDY MSS.
back for correction ; but not alone, or he "will give the slip."

440.—22 July 1600. *Henry North*, Mildenhall [Suffolk], to *Sir
Bass. Gawdy.*

At request of his good neighbours of Brandon, North asks a licence
for Robert Toller of Weeting, who has kept a victualling-house there,
but has been dismissed. He is of "very modest and civil behaviour."

441.—. July [1600?]. *Ruth Gawdy*, Waybread [Suffolk, wife of
Thomas Gawdy], to cousin *Sir Bass.
Gawdy*, Harling Hall.

Presumes on Sir B.'s "precedent courtesies" on behalf of her child
to ask that he may be educated with Sir Bass.' sons: does not wish to
charge Gawdy with his apparel or the "Content to the Schoolmaster."
[See next letter.]

442.—27 September 1600. *Thomas Gawdy*, Waybread [Suffolk],
to cousin *Sir Bassingbourn Gawdy*,
West Harling.

My Lord Keeper's decree against Thomas *ats* Mr. Russell will "come
down very strong and hard" against him this term and he must absent
himself, and has but little means to leave for his wife and children.
Begs Sir Bassingbourn to take Thomas' son Francis to educate with *his*
sons ; does not desire either his diet, apparel, or learning to be burden-
some to Sir Bassingbourn.

443.—3 October [1600]. *Robert Dawbeney*, Redgrave [Suffolk], to
Sir B. Gawdy, Harling.

After Gawdy came from Norwich yesterday the challenge between
Sir Robert Mansfield and Sir John Heyden took effect: Sir John is
thought to be dead. Some passengers came at the end of the fray.
'Tis reported they went out about twelve o'clock from Norwich to fight
about half a mile distant from Barford [?] Bridge, without friend on
either side. The passengers before their near approach saw Sir John
Heyden fall, hurt in many places, but the deadly wound is by a thrust
at his throat and out at the top of his head. Sir Robert went to Norwich with the arms of the other, who lay on the ground till the passengers
conveyed him to a house.

444.—4 October 1600. *Thomas Methwold* to *Sir Bass. Gawdy*
Harling.

Is sorry he cannot lend 100*l.*, wishes he had known when they had
last met at Watton. Can get 50*l.* from a friend, who is so precise as to
want a surety for 50*l.* and two sureties for 100*l.*

445.—8 October 1600. *Dr. Daniel Reve*, Banham, to *Sir B. Gawdy*
West Harling.

"I am sorry your worship is troubled with the complaints of this perverse woman, who cannot be any way intreated or urged to have her
daughter (a forlorn wretch) brought to any goodness, but thus from time
to time molesteth them who endeavour to fit her for some service."
Advises the mother be sharply rebuked and he will see to the girl being
brought up to earn her livelihood, lest (if she associate with her mother)

" our town be forthwith pestered with her beggaries. I leave your worship to the saving zeal of Israel."

446.—10 October 1600.   *Edmond Moundeford*, Lynford, to *Sir Bassingbourn Gawdy*, Harling.

Asks appointment to meet at Swaffham about the house of correction. Lawes is to make account and either " lay in new bond or deliver up the stock."

447.—[? Before 17 November 1600].   *Sir Robert Mansfield to Sir Bass. Gawdy.*

Would have been with Gawdy on Tuesday night, but this weather is such an enemy to his right arm that he dares not stir from the fire side. Hears from London that Sir Christopher Heydon is so earnest for his coming up that he will have to go in spite of his discharge from my Lord Admiral. Would have liked to have examined these poor men first, for the falsehood of what Heydon fathers on them is so apparent that they will not by any means permit speech of them. Sir Robert is going to send one of his servants to enquire for them and get them to come before Gawdy without frightening them. Sir Robert will bring his nephew Hungatt with him and if the meeting be at Norwich Sir Robert will offer for Sir Arthur and his son to be present.

448.—17 November [1600].   *Sir Robert Mansfield*, Pentney, to *Sir Bassingbourn Gawdy.*

Has placed such confidence in the honesty of his cause that he did not even enquire where the men dwelt that first came in after their fighting. Nor did he know their names till he read them in Sir John Heydon's apology, being Thomas Gaxham and Henry Harding. Begs Gawdy to send (not his servant but some discreet countryman) for them and Chief Constable Shardloe.

Sir Robert will meet them either at Gawdy's or his own house. His speedy procuring their testimony will mar his unworthy antagonist's report.

449.—[About 22 November 1600].   *Sir Robert Mansfield*, Pentney, to *Sir Bassingbourn Gawdy*, Harling.

Has just received a letter from Sir John Townshend advising the speedy procurement of the examination. "As you love me meet me to-morrow at my house by dinner-time though we are like to have no one bit to eat for I purpose not to have my being in town known . . . . . I pray you come in as secret a manner as you can and light not till you come to my house through Chappellyfield which gates shall be open for you."

Bring Shardloe, but do not let him know beforehand that they are going to Norwich. The bearer, Sir Robert's footman, may come with them.

[On 23 November 1600 *Sir Bassingbourn Gawdy* took the depositions of the two witnesses, which are preserved with his subsequent correspondence with C. J. Popham. Add MSS. Brit. Mus. 27,961.]

450.—27 November 1600.   *Henry Gawdy*, Claxton, to Cousin *Sir Bassingbourn Gawdy*, Harling.

Asks for indenture " that was for my undersheriff," cannot tell if Sir Bass. or Cousin Woodhouse have it.

451.—13 December [1600]. *Sir Robert Mansfield*, London, to *Sir Bassingbourn Gawdy*.

Thanks Gawdy for his journey to Norwich. The examination of the poor men pleases him much. Everyone Sir Robert talks with blames Sir John " not more for his base humour of lying than for his cowardly disposition." Sir John's friends begin to entreat Sir Robert to forbear publishing his disgrace that he may be able to show his head thereafter. Sir Robert has resolved since he spake with Mr. Attorney to stand with Gawdy for the election as knights of the shire. Gawdy need not regard any unkindness from the Heydons, people seek as much to shun the elder brother since the mortgage of Baconsthorpe as to talk of the younger.

452.—13 December 1600. *Henry Gawdy*, Norwich, to cousin *Sir Bass. Gawdy*.

Has spoken to Sheriff as to bailiwick of Diss, but there had been a prior promise. As to the election, has spoken to his brother Barnes, the Sheriff, Mr. Clere, Mr. Hobart, Mr. Berney's Chief Constables, free-holders and tenants at Henry's Courts.

The other proposed candidate (whom he will not name) is not liked and if they stand together both will fail.

453.—20 December 1600. *Augustine Styward*, Thetford, to *Sir Bass. Gawdy*.

One Margaret Fraunces, by " the hasty censure of some and by neglecting the ordinary means to know the truth " has been accused of bewitching a maid at Hockham named Joane Harvey. Fraunces was brought before Gawdy and has been " a long time committed," of which Stywarde was notified by divers of the same town who have now re-formed their opinion. He visited the maid on Friday and makes bold to state " according to the experience I have had both of ordinary and extra-ordinary diseases, the effect and operations of divers humors, of sick persons' qualities and several dispositions that this (that some carrying the show of learning there do so much wonder at, and as it were make uproar about it together with others like-ignorant) is nothing else but a disease called the Mother commonly, or as Phisicke calleth it *uteri suffocatio* or *strangulatio* which hath her natural cause, and all the strange fits they affirm to proceed of witchcraft to be only passions and symptoms of the same and other mixed disorders in her nature ; yea greater have I seen than this and more admirable . . . neither are there any such strange matters as they report which are now ashamed of what they have done and therefore strive to uphold their credit herein with falsehood ; as that she is not able to be held in the time of her fit with 3 or 4, which I myself in presence of divers both learned Divines and others did alone ; and that " [*she*, the word is struck out] " the spirit spits at the name of Jesus and divers other fopperies." Stywarde will give this evidence publicly and begs that the " present misery " of Margaret Fraunces so wrongfully inflicted may induce Gawdy to ponder means for her " deliverance out of prison, or other provision in this hard extremity."

1600–1601.

454.—1600.—Norwich Sessions.

	£.	s.	d.
Received of Mr. Rayner, Chief Constable of South Erping-ham for King's Bench and Marshalsea.	1	9	3

	£	s.	d.
Then of Mr. Neve, his partner, by said Reyner - -	4	6	2
Laid out to the 5 parishes at Norwich at 13s. 4d. each - -	3	6	8
For horse-meat there - - - - -	6	10	9
For fire there - - - - -			7
For our wages there, self, Isack, Lulpeck and Henry -		4	8
Balance in hand - - - - -	1	12	7

455.—January 1600-1. *Thomas Might to Sir Bassingbourn Gawdy.*

Will not be able to attend the election himself, but will send his friends. He takes it the last county [day] was on the 29 of last month, and the next county [day] shall be on the 27 of this month; before which day he must be in London, and the election must be on the county day next after the sheriff gets the writ.

Advises Gawdy to write to Godbould (his uncle, Mr. Justice's servant,) at Fyncham to procure the Chief Constables of Clackclose, Freebridge-Lynn, and Freebridge Marshland.

Also to Valentine Pell (Gawdy's uncle's steward of the hundred of Freebridge). Moreover, procure my lord Bishop of Norwich's favour for his tenants, and Sir John Townsend's for his friends and tenants, and his letters to Mr. Richard Bunting, bailiff of the Duchy, who with Gawdy's uncle Henry (who may procure many of Mr. Attorney General's friends), will furnish him well.

If he gets these Might knows none who can stand against him for the first voice. Warns him lest the Sheriff dispatch the election before the freeholders come in, many having to journey 30 miles and not starting before 4 a.m.

1601.

456.—9 January 1600-1. *John Hill,* Burgatt [Suffolk], same man as in No. 415, *to Sir Bassingbourn Gawdy.*

This poor man John Simpson being very lately removed from Palgrave, a town within two miles of Redgrave [both in Suffolk], into Diss. . . . Hill asks a licence for his keeping an alehouse at Diss: he did the like at Palgrave for some 14 years, licensed by Mr. Thurston and Mr. Edmiston. Discontinuing his licence, he was presented (with others) before the Lord Chief Justice.

He is commended by the best sort and is "fit for nothing else, . . . being so gross a man," . . . that he cannot work.

457.—14 January 1600-1. *Sir Bassingbourn Gawdy,* Harling, to *Henry Gawdy, Esq.,* Norwich.

Bond to secure 102l. 10s. to be paid at H. Gawdy's dwelling-house in Norwich on 16 April next. Witnesses, Roger Browne, Robt. Bowlton.

458.—21 January [1600-1]. *Sir Robert Mansfield,* London, to *Sir B. Gawdy.*

Sir Robert and Sir John have been at the Council table where they were commanded to find sureties. Sir John can get none till his brother comes up. The Council appointed my Lord Chief Justice, Mr. Secretary Herbert, the Attorney and Solicitor General to examine the cause which they did yesterday. Sir Christopher Heydon's letter to the constables against Sir Robert is also to be examined into. Means are being taken to prevent Sir Robert standing for the county.

459.—20 May 1601.   *Captain George Ruthall*, Chester, to *Thomas Morris, Gent.*   GAWDY MSS.

Receipt for 3 horses levied in Norfolk for service in the realm of Ireland, described (with rider's names) as follows :—

1. Robert Shuickfield of Garson ; [? Garveston], a black trotting horse 17 handfulls high, &c.
2. Ellis Androes of Wootton ; bay trotting gelding, 16 handfulls, and 14 years old.
3. Edmund Gooch of Berry, Suff. [sic] ; bay trotting gelding, 15 handfulls, 6 years old ; all riders well furnished.

460.—28 May 1601.   *Edmond Moundeford*, Lynford, to his cousin *Sir Bassingbourn Gawdy*, West Harling.

The "poor bearer," Henry Harward, was enforced to forsake Rushford where he dwelt, some four years past leaving his wife big with child, and household stuff worth 3*l.* Three years ago the wife died, leaving the stuff in charge with one Edmond where she dwelt, who holds it for a debt of 6*s.*, and refuses to give it up.

461.—13 July 1601.   [*Commissioners of the Muster*] Norwich, to *Thomas Hewar, Esq.*

Copy Certificate of Hewar's discharge at his own request on ground of ill health from charge of the band of light horse and petronels in the hundred of Freebridge Marshland, Freebridge Lynn, and Clackclose. William Cobb, Esq., to take over the charge.

462.—14 July 1601.   *Thomas Lestrange*, Gressenhall, to *Sir Bass. Gawdy*, the Crown, St. Stephen's, Norwich.

Recommends the bearer, formerly servant to Sir Nicholas L'Estrange, and who has since remained with Thomas, at Hunstanton, and is to marry a maid of "my cousin, Henry Spillman's," at Fakenham. If Gawdy gives his "good will" to the man himself, he will deliver it to L'Estrange, who will present it at the wedding in Gawdy's name.

463.—30 July 1601.   *Royal Commissioners of the Musters,* Court of Greenwich, to the *Commissioners for Norfolk.*

Copy circular letter (original signed by Thos. Egerton, C.J., J. Buchurst, E. Worcester, E. Stanhope, J. Fortescue, Nottingham, Robt. Cecil, J. Harbert, and Thos. Smith) to the Commissioners for Norfolk (viz., the Sheriff of Norfolk, Sir A. Heveringham, Sir Edw. Clere, Sir John Townshend, Sir Ph. Woodehouse, Sir Robt. Maunsel (sic), Sir B. Gawdy, Nathaniel Bacon, Esq., and Henry Gawdy, Esq.), and to Sir Thos. Lovell. Recites the Commission under Great Seal, dated 7 Dec. 1597 (renewing a former Commission), and empowering them to appoint gentlemen to take the general musters, see soldiers trained and armed, and provisions of warlike service, supplied, &c., in counties where no Lieutenant has been appointed. Appoint accordingly Sir Thos. Lovell to join with the rest of the Commissioners of Norfolk in such duties.

464.—2 August 1601.   *Edmond Moundeford*, Moundford, to *Sir Bassingbourn Gawdy*, West Harling.

Encloses a letter of Sir William Paston's recommending the bearer Christopher Pepper for a license. Moundeford and Holditch lately committed Pepper to gaol for victualling without license. Refers the decision to Gawdy.

.465.—10 August 1601. *Henry Gawdy* to cousin *Sir B. Gawdy.*

Begs to borrow the books. Hears Sir B. is bidden to Mr. Attorney's daughter's marriage—is he going?

466.—26 August 1601. *Edmond Moundeford,* Moundford, to *Sir Bassingbourn Gawdy,* West Harling.

Mr. Oxborough is not in the Country. "My brother Gawdy lodged with me last night," his answer to the letters will agree with Moundeford's in substance, but he thinks we "should not all use one form of answer." "The credit we reposed in the petitioners, the good of her Majesty in maintaining Merchant and Marquers (?) and. the general good of the country to have salt at reasonable price are causes sufficient for our request." The country complains generally of the patent.

467.—28 September 1601. *Sir Bass. Gawdy,* W. Harling, and *Richard Sutton,* Norfk., Yeoman, to *Richard Smyth, Gent.,* Snetterton.

Joint bond to secure 120*l.* to be paid at Smyth's house at Snetterton on 29 Sept. 1602. Witnesses, Thomas Townshende and Geo. Rogers.

468.—[September 1601.] *Henry Gawdy* to cousin *Sir Bass. Gawdy.*

Henry and his brother Bacon are determined to stand for Parliament. Last time it was against his will; asks his cousin's influence with Sir Nicholas and others. Hears that the electors will have no young and inexperienced men, "but mean to have their free election."
[Henry and Sir Bassingbourn Gawdy were elected].

469.—6 October 1601. *Francis Gawdy,* Wallington, to nephew *Sir Bassingbourn Gawdy.*

Has moved many to give Sir Bass. their first voice for Knt. of the Shire, and Sir Robert Mansfield the second; some have asked to be at liberty as to their second voice. Cannot send his servants as he rides perforce to London that day, but Mr. Scott and his neighbours will be there.

470.—7 October 1601. *Sir Bassingbourn Gawdy,* W. Harling, to *Anthony Gawdy.*

Bond in penal sum of 400*l.* to idemnify Anthony for having joined Bassingbourn Gawdy as surety in bond of even date to Francis Sherman of Blow Norton, gent., to secure 200*l.* Witnesses, Robt. Bowlton, Richd. Sutton, George Rogers.

471.—[? October 1601.] *John Holland* to *Sir Bassingbourn Gawdy,* Harling.

Has received Gawdy's and Lord William Howard's letters. Will gladly speak to the tenants and others to give their votes to Gawdy and Sir Robert Mansfield. Will send to Mr. Hovell and other gentlemen on Monday. Mr. Thwayte was from home, his wife promises he shall be at Norwich for the election. (Note.—The letter has been addressed by mistake in the first instance to Mr. Richard Hovell, Flitcham).

; 472.—20 October 1601. *Edward Gosse* and *Christopher Heye,* Watton, to *Sir Bass. Gawdy,* Harling hall.

Recommend their well-beloved kinsman, John Olley, to be licensed to keep an Inn, the house into which he moved at Michaelmas having always been " used an ancient Inn in Watton."

473.—[End of October 1601 ?]. *John Holland* to [*Sir Bassing-bourn Gawdy*].

Sends apologies for not having visited Gawdy ; the reason he has forborne seeing him is secret to himself, and no way toucheth Gawdy. Hears that Gawdy is shortly for London.

474.—11 November [1601 ?] *Henry Gawdy* to his cousin *Sir Bass. Gawdy,* Mendham.

Hears he is to be Sheriff. Asks the appointment of undersheriff for a friend (unnamed), who will give 30*l.* and good bonds, &c. Henry's wife is *enceinte.*

475.—23 November 1601. *Sir John Peyton,* Lieutenant of the Tower, to *Sir Bass. Gawdy.*

The bearer, John Bennett, of Wymondham, gentleman, has "by course of law been arrested; prosecuted, and condemned within Her Majesty's Tower of London," at suit of Peter Warberton. Believing him willing to pay his creditors, Sir John has " granted him the prosection and privilege of Her Majesty's said Tower for the space of one whole year to travel abroad with his keeper " to make interest among his friends and collect monies due to him, so as to " satisfy the debt for which he hath been here arrested " and his other creditors. Let this be notified to the Undersheriff, &c., lest he molested through ignorance of the ancient privileges and prerogative of " this Her Majesty's Castle."

476.—26 November 1601. *Sir Arthur Heveningham* to *Sir Bass. Gawdy.*

Asks the office of Steward of the Hundred-Court of Happing for " my solicitor, Henry Skarburghe of North Walsham . . . being the next hundred to him." He will gratify Gawdy as usual.

477.—[November] 1601. *Rev. Thomas Daynes* to *Sir Bass. Gawdy,* High Sheriff, Harling.

Understands Gawdy has a place of government in this commonwealth. Writes on behalf of a christian friend and kinsman who desires to employ a son (a toward, good natured youth) with Mr. Boulton the under-sheriff. " You see I come not to beg a benefice of your worship, this benefit shall content me for this time." Remembrances to " my good lady with petition to her ladyship for some benefice with tithes juice of liquorice " [sic, apparently a standing joke between them, see post No. 638]. Remembrances to Mr. Anthony Gawdy, " if he be with you."

478.—4 December 1601. *Francis Gawdy,* Serjeants Inn, to nephew *Sir Bass. Gawdy.*

Asks that his servant John Neave 'of Thorpe may be reappointed as deputy to the under-sheriff " to break up writs " and make warrants for this part of the country " for the ease of the people thereabouts." .

479.—6 December 1601. *Henry* ʟ*Basham,* Lynn Regis, to his kinsman *Sir Bass. Gawdy,* High Sheriff.

The bearer Edward Gryffin is the man Basham named by Gawdy's leave for the bailiffship of Freebridge Lynn, in place of the late bailiff Edward Goodshawe, who had been selected by Mr. Bowlton the under-sheriff.

480.—9 December 1601. *Edward Symonds,* Hindolveston to *Sir Bass. Gawdy,* West Harling.

Begs stewardship of Holt Hundred : would wait on Gawdy but is employed on weighty business by Sir John Townshend.

481.—10 December 1601. *Francis Gawdy,* Sergeants Inn, to nephew *Sir Bassingbourn Gawdy,* High Sheriff.

Recommends his cousin Appleyarde who has "occasions" in Norfolk.

482.—12 December 1601. *Henry Gawdy,* Norwich, to cousin *Sir Bassingbourn Gawdy.*

Commends the bearer Mr. Yonger, for the living of Bridgham vacant on the death of Mr. Thacster.

483.—16 December 1601. *Henry Gawdy,* to cousin *Sir Bass. Gawdy.*

Asks Sir Bassingbourn to take William Andrewes into his service "and that he may have your cloth this year," he will be at the charge thereof.

484.—22 December 1601. *Henry Gawdy* to cousin *Sir Bass. Gawdy.*

On behalf of the bearer [Josse ?] an old "bailiff-arrant," that he may serve this year.

485.—22 December 1601. *Sir Richard Lee,* London to *Sir B. Gawdy.*

Mr. Freston, one of Gawdy's neighbours has a vicarage in his gift which Sir R. Lee is earnest to have bestowed on "a very sufficient minister, whose name is Mr. Richardes, who was with me this late journey into Muscovia ; . . . himself and I marrying two sisters," . . . Sir R. Lee hopes Gawdy will assist his suit.

486.—30 December 1601. *Edmond Moundeford,* Lynford, to his cousin *Sir B. Gawdy,* High Sheriff, W. Harling.

Moundeford has received letters from my Lord Bishop for a meeting to dispatch the subsidy next Saturday at Norwich. He cannot attend on account of a sickness that "hath hanged on" him for 6 weeks and a sore cut in his hand which makes him unable to bear the rein of his bridle.

'1601-2.

487.—3 January [1601-2]. *George Fowler*, Bromhill, to *Sir Bassingbourn Gawdy*, High Sheriff.

Fowler admits he has a gelding belonging to the prisoner who broke from jail, where " my brother " Moundeford had committed him. He claims it both as waif [" wefe."] and felon's goods, being taken within his manor of Weeting. It is unshod, having been fired as it could " scant stand " when taken. (P.S.) The party Fowler has an execution against "keepeth in Thetford at cards and dice every night."

488.—6 January [1601-2]. *George Fowler*, Bromhill, to *Sir Bass. Gawdy*, High Sheriff.

Sends further particulars of the " lame old jade " which is spavined, foundered, &c. The prisoner tied him in Willton-field and cast him off, thinking to hide in a gravel pit. The gelding strayed over Methold warren down to Weeting town, two miles from the prisoner. Fowler can show evidence for 300 years as to his right, waifs, &c., being taken by Lords Plays [" Place "] and Howard, the earls of Oxford, Lord Latimer, and the copartners, &c.

489.—14 January [1601-2]. *Edmond Moundeford*, Lynford, to cousin *Sir Bass. Gawdy*, High Sheriff.

On his return to his sick wife Moundeford saw Fowler, who was quite willing to give up the gelding, the cause of his stay was " by mistaking of a book-case " as will be showed to Gawdy. Moundeford would like the sword as a present, it is very light and he has no weapon for his own use "in a sudden in privy watch or otherwise." Sends Mr. Pratt's letter to have one excused as a soldier. Pratt is uncle Gawdy's good neighbour, " sed utere tuo judicio."

490.—14 January 1601-2. *Roger Dalyson*, Langhton [?], to cousin *Sir Bassingbourn Gawdy*, High Sheriff.

Presumes on their old acquaintance to request Gawdy to supply the defects in the execution of a writ of elegit for a friend of Dalyson's which was sent last term to " your late sheriff."

491.—22 February [1601-2?]. *John Smythe*, to *Sir Bassingbourn Gawdy*, Thetford.

A mischance has happened to Smythe's kinsman Thomas Johnson, a barrister of Lincolns Inn. " Upon a sudden chance in a chamber, his man, assaulting him with his dagger, my cousin taking up his rapier and beating by his dagger struck the same an inch into his eye, so as shortly after he died. Yet the surgeon hath deposed that the wound was not mortal, neither did he in conscience conceive the same to be [the cause of] his death, and upon the coroner's quest he standeth clear." Knowing that " my Lord " is strict in such causes and wishing to save his cousin from disgrace and his practice from ruin, Smythe begs Gawdy's intervention, through Sir Nicholas Bacon and others, to prevent public disgrace.

492.—26 February 1601-2. *Anthony Thwaytes* to *Sir Bassingbourn Gawdy*.

Robert Banes of Shelfhanger continually hunts and kills my Lord's deer in Kenninghall Park and grounds with greyhounds and guns.

He killed one on the evening of the 16th. Asks warrant for his arrest.

493.—2 March 1601-2. *William Brewster*, London, to kinsman *Sir Bassingbourn Gawdy*, Harling.

Asks Sir Bassingbourn and Henry Gawdy to move my Lord Chief Justice at Thetford assizes to "clear the city of Norwich of those dangerous infecting Papists which be there imprisoned and doeth much hurt in the City." "Let him do it even as he doth clear the City of London now at this time, and send them all to the Castle of Framlingham, so as to keep them but in one only place." If Brewster himself moved this, it might be supposed he aimed at his own particular benefit. Indeed, "seeing it is my fortune thus to spend my days, I had as lief keep many as few. These of Norwich be well able to find themselves ; most of those I have be poor and yield me no benefit. . . . I have room for 30 prisoners more."

494.—8 March 1601-2. *Sir John Peyton*, Great Bradley [Suffolk], to *Sir Bassingbourn Gawdy*, High Sheriff.

Applys on behalf of a minister his neighbour to have discreet men returned to try his Nisi Prius case.

495.—27 March 1602. *Thomas Howse*, of Rushford, from County Jail, Norwich, to *Sir B. Gawdy*, High Sheriff.

Howse is imprisoned at the suit of Mr. George Fowler of Bromhill near Brandon "upon a great execution for debt," which Fowler will discharge on Howse giving his bond for payment "by small portions yearly," provided the Sheriff and his officers are satisfied all fees, &c. Begs on score of poverty that Gawdy will accept 20s. or "some rabbits to that value" between now and midsummer, and ease him of the fees.

496.—4 April 1602. *Thomas Peade*, Bury [Suffolk], to *Sir Bass. Gawdy*, Harling.

Please pay bearer, John Turner, "that little sum due me" and he will give up bond.

1602.

497.—19 April 1602. *Roger Dalyson*, Langhton [?], to kinsman *Sir Bass. Gawdy*, High Sheriff.

Repeats request in previous letters [see No. 490].

498.—26 April 1602. *Edmond Moundeford*, Lynford, to *Sir Bassingbourn Gawdy*.

Moundeford's cousin Osbert Pratt never paid more than 13s. 4d. tax on Hockwold cum Wilton. Mr. Pygeon and other neighbours have raised him to 18s. besides taxing his brother for part of the land. Asks a letter to bid collector not to distrain for the tax.

499.—30 April 1602. *Sir Francis Vere* [?], London, to [*Sir Bassingbourn Gawdy* ?].

Warrant appointing Thomas Bartly to receive the 150 men raised in Norfolk and conduct them to the port of Yarmouth.

500.—8 May 1602. *Charles Rawlyns,* Nórwich, to his father [*Rev.* *Jo. Rawlyns*], Parson of Attleborough.

Dog-latin letter written in answer to his father's "exhortations and clamors;" no news to tell; hopes his barbarous language will move his father to laughter. P.S.—Uncle shall hear from Yarmouth by goodman Hill.

501.—14 May 1602. *Edmond Moundeford,* Lynford, to *Sir Bassingbourn Gawdy,* High Sheriff.

Intercedes for the poor bearer, who has offended by error and not obstinately in omitting to conduct the soldiers "lately to be shewed before you and the other Commissioners at Norwich."
P.S.—"The great T. L. [? Thomas Lovell] hath made complaint at Court," that the Justices combine against him. "I was there in the presence 3 or 4 hours yet no man ever said anything to me."

502.—28 May 1602. *William Dey,* or *Dye,* Deputy Keeper of the Bridewell at Acle, to *Sir Bass. Gawdy.*

Receipt for 33s. 4d. from Gawdy (by hands of Robt. Bowlton) as Treasurer for King's Bench and Marshalsea as per order made by Sir B. Gawdy, Sir A. Heveningham, Sir Philip Woodhouse, Sir Miles Corbet, Henry Gawdy, Charles Cornwallis, and Henry Holdiche, Esqs. Dated Norwich.

503.—[? May 1602.] *Sir Robert Mansfield,* [London], to *Sir Bassingbourn Gawdy.*

Sir Robert has taken such course with my lord Admiral, my lord Thomas Howard, and his cousin Trevor that Gawdy will not be forgotton when deputy lieutenants are appointed which will be very shortly. Sir Robert will also leave behind him a letter to Sir John Townshend as to the authorization of superintendents of regiments for he does not think the name of Colonel will be allowed. Sends remembrances to his honoured brother Sir Nicholas Bacon.

504.—[? May 1602.] *Sir Bassingbourn Gawdy* to [*Lord Thomas Howard*].

Draft of a letter thanking Lord Thomas for his favour. Sir John Townshend has told Gawdy that Lord Thomas hopes for some good end for Gawdy of Mr. Knyvet. Has requested Sir John Townshend to signify Lord Thomas's pleasure as to Gawdy waiting on him at London.

505.—[? May 1602.] *Sir Robert Mansfield* to *Sir Bassingbourn Gawdy.*

Returns Gawdy's sketch of letter to Lord Thomas Howard which he apologises for forgetting in the stress of business. It will come time enough by the next carts.

506.—2 June 1602. *Lady Elizabeth Mansell* [or *Mansfield*], Pentney, to her nephew *Sir Bassingbourn Gawdy,* High Sheriff.

Asks an upright Jury in Clackclose Hundred on behalf of her servant in suit between him and Mr. Holl.

507.—9 June [1602?] *Sir Robert Mansfield,* from my lodging near Friarbridge [London], to *Sir Bass. Gawdy* and *Sir Philip Woodhouse.*

Sir Robert received their letters in the absence of Sir John Townshend now at Bath, in the afternoon of the 8 June, just as he left Court having received the dispatch for his voyage to sea. No countermand could have been obtained however forcible the reasons, the lords being all gone to their houses in London. Sir Robert thinks they are both mistaken as to the meaning of their lordships' letters, which is not to deprive the 7 commanders of their superintendency but to reduce every private company to or under the number of 200. Can see no reason for an alteration unless they suppose Sir Arthur's greatness or insolency can appoint what Captains he pleases in their limits. This will go by votes, and they will have the majority when Sir John or Sir Robert should be in the country, and in their absence thinks Mr. Nathaniel Bacon, who stands equal in commission to Sir Arthur, will join with Gawdy and Woodhouse. When a lord lieutenant is appointed their superintendency will be ratified.

[In September 1602 Sir R. Mansfield fought Spinola's galleys off Cezimbra.]

508.—9 June 1602. *Thomas Hunston*, Walpole [in Marshland], to *Sir Bass. Gawdy, Sir A. Heveningham, Sir Ph. Woodhouse*, and other Commissioners.

Owing to deaths and removals and the County being "generally impoverished," Hunston's hundred cannot furnish its full tale of 130 men; which by the Commissioner's letters of 15 June 1601 were to comprise 50 pikes 50 muskets and 30 "collevers" [calivers]. Asks a reduction in the charge, and as he is going to London this term and is not sure of his return in time to take a fresh view of the levies and give his certificate, that the Commissioners will authorise John Reppes and Thos. Hewar and Hunton's Lieutenant the Muster-Master to take the view and certify same.

509.—13 July 1602. *William Brewster*, Framlingham Castle, [Suffolk], to his kinsman *Sir B. Gawdy*.

Please send him the recusant prisoners who are at Norwich. The bearer Mr. Berrye is a messenger of her Majesty's lately from London and will take charge of them. Do not let the Lord Chief Justice know of this request; do it as of Gawdy's own motion.

510.—16 July 1602. *Strange Mordant*, Massingham, to *Sir Bassingbourn Gawdy*.

Begs to be excused attending on the Grand Jury.

511.—17 July 1602. *Henry Davy*, Norwich, to *Sir B. Gawdy*.

Cannot attend the wedding of Gawdy's servants at New Buckenham but incloses a riall. [The word sovereign first written and then struck out.]

512.—19 July 1602. *Ralph Hare* to *Sir Bassingbourn Gawdy*.

Sends benevolence of 6s. 8d. for Gawdy's servant.

513.—24 July 1602. *William Hall* to *Sir B. Gawdy*, Harling.

Sends a "small token" for Gawdy's servants who are now to be married.

514.—24 July 1602. *Sir Thomas Mounsen*, Lincoln, to *Sir Bassingbourn Gawdy*.

Asks [Gawdy's] favour in executing two writs brought him by Mr. Yonger "against two sea foules." The matter concerns Sir Thomas's friends.

GAWDY MSS.

515.—28 July 1602.　*Dr. Edmund Sucklyng*, [Heloden ?], to *Sir Bassingbourn Gawdy.*

Sends a benevolence for Gawdy's servant.

516.—28 July 1602.　*Nicholas Garneys*, Reedham, to [*Sir Bassingbourn Gawdy*].

Sends a French crown for Gawdy's servant Morris. Garney's servant is also to be married at Bungay [Suffolk] when [Gawdy's] benevolence will be acceptable.

517.—2 August 1602.　*Jo. Hill*, Queen's Auditor, London, to [*Sir Bassingbourn Gawdy*], Farmer of Royal Manor of Bridgeham.

Precept to appear before Hill at Thetford on 16 Oct., pass accounts and have lease enrolled. [Jo. Hill was a foster brother of Sir Thomas Knyvet.]

518.—9 August 1602.　*Jo. Pettus* to *Sir Bassingbourn Gawdy*, High Sheriff.

Receipt for 175*l.* to be repaid in London to Sir Thos. Tasborough one of Her Majesty's tellers.

519.—18 August 1602.　*Edmond Moundeford*, Lynford, to *Sir Bassingbourn Gawdy.*

Asks benevolence for his servant's marriage at Watton.

520.—26 August 1602.　*Edmond Moundeford*, Lynford, to *Sir Bassingbourn Gawdy.*

One Raby in the under-sheriff's office has an execution in his hands against John Starre of Geyton *ats* Mr. Stephen Bull. Moundeford wishes it served, he is the real plaintiff himself and Bull is dangerously ill, which will make further costs, if he die before Starre is attached.

521.—2 September 1602.　*Thomas Lane* to [*Sir Bassingbourn Gawdy*].

Asks payment for 6½ yards of 3 pile black velvet delivered to Mr. Under Sheriff Boulton on 27 Feb. 1601 for Gawdy's use which at 26*s.* the yard comes to 8*l. 9s.*

522.—3 September 1602.　*Sir Arthur Heveningham*, Ketteringham, to *Sir Bass. Gawdy*, High Sheriff.

Sir Arthur is sorry the Pursuivant delivered his message wrongly. Letters have come from the Lords [of the Council] to "four of us," touching the "hurt the Dunkirkers had done upon our coast," and Sir Arthur had warned them to meet him next day at Norwich. If Gawdy will change his proposed place of meeting to the Griffin at Wymondham, Sir Arthur will notify Sir Miles Corbet and Mr. Henry Gawdy so that a general meeting may be had there of the Commissioners. Send word by the Constable of Attleborough.

523.—[3 September] 1602.　*Henry Gawdy* to cousin *Sir Bass. Gawdy*, High Sheriff.

Had received Sir Arthur's appointment for Norwich before he got Gawdy's for Wymondham. Suggests that Norwich should be adhered to "lest that between 2 stools &c."

524.—21 September [1602 ?] *Lady Elizabeth Mansell* [or *Mans-field*] *to her nephew Sir Bassingbourn Gawdy.*

Will deliver Gawdy's letters. Mr. Mansell is at sea and likely to continue there.

525.—24 September 1602. *John Topclyff*, Honingham, to *Sir B. Gawdy.*

Although unknown to Gawdy, Topclyff sent a crown in gold by Capt. Elyot on the marriage of his two servants. For 3 years Topclyffe has had an execution for 200*l.* against Edward Downes ran outlawry against the latter's sureties (Edward Walgrave of Stanninghall and Thos. Lovell of Beechamwell), and cannot get them served. He is out of pocket 20*l.* as his attorney Mr. Grene knows. Has promised the undersheriff a "further recompense" if he will serve the execution or the outlawry on Walgrave, whose friends would then settle.

526.—25 September 1602. *Thomas Myne*, Walsingham, to his cousin *Sir Bassingbourn Gawdy*, High Sheriff.

Two extents have come down against Myne's land in Walsingham, one from the Exchequer, the other from the Court of Wards. Gibson, the under sheriff, has had sent him the order Myne got from the Exchequer that no writ should issue until the Court of Wards debt was satisfied. In the latter Court Myne pleaded, and the matter was referred to the Queen's auditors-general, with stay of proceedings; which order Gibson is also privy to, "but I can find no grace in his eyes." "Money in your officer's hands is hardly gotten out again," even if Myne succeeds in clearing his land. Begs delay till this term be past.

527.—28 September 1602. *Francis Gawdy*, Wallington, to nephew *Sir Bassingbourn Gawdy.*

Asks Gawdy to receive Henry Bekyswell, "youngest son of my Cousin Francis Bekyswell," into his service; his father will bestow 10*l.* a year to maintain him.

528.—29 September 1602. *Thomas Myne*, Walsingham, to *Sir Bassingbourn Gawdy*, High Sheriff.

Myne is not so unreasonable as to expect Gawdy to lose by obliging him, and if he fails to clear his land will pay the Queen's extents whenever Gawdy sends for the money.

529.—19 October 1602. *Rev. Jo. Rawlyns*, Attleborough, to *Sir Bassingbourn Gawdy.*

Rawlyns is bold "like a bad debtor, ready when he should pay to be further indebted," to remind Gawdy of his suit touching his son, and of Gawdy's kind promise to consider it.

530.—22 October 1602. *Sir Christopher Heydon*, Baconsthorpe, to *Sir Bassingbourn Gawdy.*

Begs Gawdy to withhold executions against Heydon's surety, Mr. Thetford. He will satisfy the parties by next term and pay the undersheriff's fees, so that the latter will be no loser. If he could have sold land would not have let matters go so far.

This favour will prevent "much infamy, grief, and other inconveniences."

531.—29 October 1602. , *Sir Arthur Heveningham,* Ketteringham, to *Sir Bassingbourn Gawdy.*

˙, Asks Gawdy to take the bearer into his service, he is of "good behaviour and sufficient to be a clerk."

532.—4 November 1602. *John Reppes,* West Walton, to *Sir Bassingbourn Gawdy,* High Sheriff.

Reppes' poor kinsman, William Harte, imprisoned in Norwich Castle for debt beyond his power to pay, has got a *habeas corpus* to transfer him to the King's Bench, hoping to get some relief from the High Commissioners. The Undersheriff returns this writ "*languidus in prisona,*" only to make delay and put the poor man to costs. ˙ Begs Gawdy's assistance.

533.—16 December 1602. *Thomas Gawdy,* Waybread [Suffolk], to Cousin *Sir Bassingbourn Gawdy,* Harling.

Sends a pedigree, which please return if no good.

534.—16 December 1602. *Rev. Thomas Scot,* to *Sir Bassingbourn Gawdy.*

Applies for the gift of the benefice of Stanton Downeham [Suffolk], for himself or his friend, a very good preacher and a Master of Arts. If Gawdy has already promised it and will recall his consent, " the party shall in some measure be gratified "

535.—18 December 1602. *George Fowler,* Bromhill, to *Sir Bass. Gawdy,* Harling.

Sends an execution against Howes, the warrener of Thetford warren. Gawdy knows the man ; he put in false bail in the King's Bench, and troubled Mason, of Nayghton [? Neaton]. Fowler would take his money (30*l.*) in instalments on good security. ˙

536.—19 December 1602. *Rev. Thomas Scot* to *Sir Bassingbourn Gawdy.*

Finds he has been mistaken ; it is the benefice of Bri[d]gham, not Stanton, that is void. Repeats his request, which is for his son-in-law.

537.—   . 1602. *Sir Clement Heigham* to *Sir Bass. Gawdy.*

Begs the discharge of one John Brown, a neighbour of Heighams's, in Bungay [Suffolk], who was " injuriously pressed " while travelling through Norfolk.

538.—   1602. *John Holland,* Kenninghall, to *Sir Bassingbourn Gawdy,* at Eccles.

Thanks Gawdy for his favour about Holland's armour. In faith his pikes were stolen from the place where he left them in Norwich, also two Spanish headpieces. Is uncertain if he shall stay here; if he does, will be in better sort the "next show." His cold prevents him being at the muster to-day.

539.—   1602. *John Holland* to *Sir B. Gawdy,* Harling.

Has received letters from my lord [Howard], which oblige him to use money. Please deliver to the bearer the money Holland troubled him with. If Holland could have endured putting on a doublet he would have come himself.   Hopes Gawdy will recover his wonted health.

1602–3.

540.—11 January 1602–3.   *Thomas Nonne*[?], Culford [Suffolk], to *Sir Bass. Gawdy*, Harling.

Encloses a letter by order of his master.

541.—16 January 1602–3.   *Thomas Wythe*, Sternfield [Suffolk], to *Sir Bass. Gawdy*, Harling.

Sends a scutcheon with Sir Charles Framlingham's quarterings. If Gawdy compares these with the coats of arms in his window [at Bardewell Hall, Harling,] he will be able to identify them, and perceive that from Horne to Jefferie all were noblemen. Is not sure of Nevill, but thinks he was Marquis Mountecute. Once saw a pedigree of the Framlinghams made by procurement of Mr. Clement Framlingham. Hopes to see Gawdy after the end of term; is so ill-horsed he cannot travel both to Gawdy and to London.

542.—16 January 1602–3.   *Edmond Moundeford*, Lynford, to *Sir Bass. Gawdy*.

Informed "our uncle Gawdy" of Sir Bassingbourn's answer for the money which is yearly collected for the Marshalsea. Moundeford reckoned in 50*l.* for 3 years paid to . . . . . [?]. The judge examined one of that hundred who denied that such sum was paid to the town. Let Gawdy send him the statement in writing to show the judge before going to London, as he is much discontented.

543.—26 January 1602–3.   *Sir Arthur Heveningham*, Ketteringham, to *Sir B. Gawdy* and *Sir Thomas Lovell*, "from one to another."

Encloses copy letter just received. Appoints them to meet him at Norwich next day.

544.—23 February 1602–3.   *Henry Gawdy*, Norwich, to cousin *Sir Bass. Gawdy*.

On behalf of one Palmer asks Sir B. Gawdy to write to the Lord Chief Justice as to the conversation and bad behaviour of Edward, Thomas, and Margaret Coppinge. Mr. Thomas Sponer and other Justices can speak of their troublesome contentious humours. .

545.—27 February 1602–3.   *Henry Gawdy*, Norwich, to *Sir Bass. Gawdy*.

The bearer will draw the oak for Henry for 20*s.* If Sir Bass. will pay him when he has finished, Henry will repay it.

546.—16 March 1602–3.   *Sir Bass. Gawdy* to *Thomas Hillersdon*, of Amptell, Bedford, gent.

Bond (unexecuted) to secure payment of 52*l.* 10*s.* at Gray's Inn Hall, Holborn, on 10 November next. (Memorandum "Thomas Hinton of Wake, Bedfordshire, gent., bound with.")

547.—19 March 1602–3. *Edmond Moundeford,* Lynford, to cousin GAWDY MSS.
                           Sir Bassingbourn Gawdy, West
                           Harling.

Begs to be excused attendance on subsidy-meeting, as he is engaged
in business about ale-houses.

548.—19 March 1602–3. *Francis Gawdy,* Wallington, to nephew
                           Sir Bassingbourn Gawdy.

Thanks his nephew for notifying him of meeting of Subsidy Commissioners, but cannot attend on account of ill-health.

549.—22 March 1602–3. *Anthony Thwayts* to *Sir Bassingbourn
                           Gawdy.*

" These bearers have made pitiful suit to Mr. Holland and myself "
to intercede with Gawdy to pardon his offence. Most of the town join
in the entreaty, by reason of their poverty. If he be punished con-
dignly. half a dozen poor children will be thrown on the charge of the
town.

550.—[Before 24 March 1602–3].

Á BREVIAT OF SWIFT'S CASE.

Ingratitude. He was brought up by his master's charity from 10 till
he was 26. After he was 18 his master gave him 12*l.* a year, meat
drink, and livery.

The Cosenage conspired. Notwithstanding, he thought his master
miserable towards him, and complotted with his brother-in-law Watson
to get some greater gain from his master. They resolved on account of
his master's love for his daughter to bring her name in question ; this
he confessed before Henry Gonchingham, gent., and Richard Edy, his
keeper in the Marshalsea.

Devised. By advice of the said Watson, a learned and a lewd man,
he tendered a bargain to the gentlewoman being under 14 years of age,
offering her 10 angels in regard of a greater sum to be paid him on
her marriage. This she agreed to suspecting no villany and being
indebted in some small sums for idle expenses. (*See* her depositions.)

Acted. He causeth a bill to be made with words to bind her to be
at his disposition during her life; then at fitting time and place he brought
it to her with pen and ink, gave her the 10 angels in the presence
of two witnesses, and desired them all to set their hands to it speedily
for that Mistress Hinton, her governess, was coming. (*See* her deposition and the evidence of the witness, and he confesses the bill was
not read.)

Published. He concealed the bill for over 2 years, till speech was
had for her marriage, and then published it as a contract, labouring by
letters by Sir John Peter, Mr. Grevell, Mr. Monson, Robert Sprignall
and others to persuade his master to redeem the bill to save his daughter's
credit, sometimes asking 30*l.* a year and 300*l.* down, sometimes 20*l.* and
200*l.* He confessed to John Bitteringe, gent., he had no intention to
marry her.

Improbability of Pretence. He could produce neither witness,
letter, token, proof, or probability besides this cosening bill. She constantly deposed both in this Court and before Her Majesty's high Commission that she never was so disposed towards him.

Judgment. · This Court declared her free from all his imputations, and found him guilty of the whole practice, but as the cosenage was committed before the last general pardon and thereby his corporal punishment remitted, the Court only sentenced him for his publication, ordered him to be pilloried in Cheapside and Westminster, fined 1,000 marks, imprisoned during her Majesty's pleasure, and to make a public confession on his knees in the place and manner to be appointed by my Lord Grace of Canterbury.

In Pillory, behaviour Slanderous. He was set upon the pillory in Cheapside, where he behaved slanderously and contemptuously; slanderously in making the people believe he was so punished for such a gentlewoman's love, and that he willingly sustained it for her sake imputing perjury to the witnesses against him.

Contemptuous. Contemptuously against this honourable Court and and her Majesty's high Commission Ecclesiastical declaring himself innocent after they had found him guilty, procuring pity and commiseration instead of shame and detestation. In his libel he calls his just punishment infamous penance and scorning the order for his confession. Lastly, refusing to be examined by Mr. Mill who went thrice with my Lord Keeper's order therefore. Woollfall and Goulborne his two counsellors in framing the libel being examined wherein any of the witnesses had perjured themselves could answer nothing.

551.—24 March [1602–3 ?]. *Simon Herne to Sir Bassingbourn Gawdy*, W. Harling.

Understands Gawdy wants a teacher in his house for the young gentlemen his children. Is a suitor unto him on behalf of the bearer, his eldest son, Bachelor of Arts of a year's standing. Herne confesses himself (in regard to his many children) not able to maintain him at Cambridge any longer. "Young, very young, yea too, too young he is to step into the ministry, and wanteth that portion of the Spirit to discharge so weighty a calling until such time as he be Master of Arts." Hopes Gawdy will make trial of him. If he receives him into his family Herne will be "twice happy, trusting that your worship will prefer him as his desert shall deserve."

1603.

552.—25 March [1603]. *Robert Hawys to Sir Bassingbourn Gawdy*, West Harling.

Apologises for these "few hasty, scrawling, blotted lines." The suit he made for his friend for the tutorship of Gawdy's sons he now makes for himself. Should have done so before but for the following doubts, first will the service last after the two young gentlemen go to Cambridge, "yea or no"? The second whether he might also serve the cure at Harling under neighbour Rouse, being so nigh, "yea or no," or whether Gawdy would give him greater wages and keep him altogether as preacher and chaplain.

Intimates that it may not be worth his while to forego his present certainty. Can give references to Mr. Nathaniel Bacon, Mr. Rouse, Mr. Conney, Mr. Michael, and others. Suggests that a trial would be preferable. Hopes to speak with Gawdy as he returns from Harling in the afternoon.

553.—26 March 1603. *Anthony Thwaytes to Sir Bassingbourn Gawdy.*

Requests Gawdy to spare John Walker who is pressed out of Kenninghall. He is a coal-burner and works for Thwaytes.

554.—29 March 1603. *Edmond Moundeford,* Lynford, *to [Sir Bassingbourn Gawdy].*

Apologises for not attending the meeting of the Justices. Had " an evil fit " on Sunday morning, but had to attend Uncle Gawdy early on Monday about the subsidy, as Mr. Pratt is very sick and there was none else to join with him. Is very weary but must ride 30 miles on the same business on Wednesday. Will proclaim the King if desired at Watton on Wednesday market day. Uncle Gawdy would know if the other Commissioners here and in Suffolk proceed with the subsidy or no.

555.—2 April 1603. *Edmond Moundeford,* Lynford, *to Sir Bassingbourn Gawdy.*

On Wednesday last after the proclamation made at Watton " I made a desperate journey against the wind to Setchey," to join with Uncle Gawdy in proceeding for the subsidy, but the latter dismissed the Assessors without giving them any charge. " News I have none but that all is quiet at London, and the King daily expected, as my brother Do . . . advertiseth me, and that all the reports of the Lord Beauchamp are untrue."

Is about to ride to Swaffham to proclaim the King. The following peers, Oxford, Scrope, and Norris have signed the new proclamation besides those who signed the first one.

556.—2 April 1603. *Sir Arthur Heveningham,* Ketteringham, *to Sir Bassingbourn Gawdy.*

Asks Gawdy's vote and interest at the next election for knight of the shire.

557.—22 April 1603. *Sir Bassingbourn Gawdy to Thomas Marryot,* of Wethersett-cum-Brockforde, [? Wetheringsett, Suffolk,] *Clothier.*

Acknowledgement of indebtedness in 35*l.* to be paid to Marryot 1 August next.

558.—22 April 1603. *Thomas Wythe,* Sternfield [Suffolk], *to Sir Bassingbourn Gawdy,* Harling.

Has forwarded Gawdy's letter to Mr. Smith, of Stutton [Suffolk], by his son ; he dwells beyond Ipswich. Will give Mr. Nelson his letter next day. Returns the letter for Mr. Ockelie who now lives at Lynn.

559.—1 May 1603. *John Nonne,* Bury [Suffolk], *to Sir Bassingbourn Gawdy,* West Harling.

Cannot help Gawdy with money. Has agreed to buy Sir James Scudemore's manor of Dunkeston [Suffolk], for 3,600*l.*, and has bound himself to pay 1,200*l.* of it this term, and the balance in 6 months. Moreover Mr. Bokenham has disappointed him of 300*l.* due on statute, which Nonne counted on as surely as if it had been in his chest. This has driven him to try Mr. Webbe and other friends to raise 300*l.*

560.—5 May 1603. *Henry Gawdy to cousin Sir Bass. Gawdy.*

A writ has come to the Sheriff to appoint Collectors for the subsidy, but Henry has stayed it till they can apprise the Lord Keeper that they had not been neglectful and had made an appointment. Does not know who has the certificate. Despatch the enclosed letter to my Lord Keeper by this messenger, and add in the postcript the names, Henry's cousin F . . . (?) Denny on his part, and —— Rendall on Sir Bassingbourn's part. Does Sir B. know if one Edwards (bailed by Henry), committed the felony ? if so he will surrender him.

561.—[? May 1603.]   *Rev. George Hals* [of Kenton, Suffolk,] to *Sir Bassingbourn Gawdy*, Harling.

Has sent Mr. Pierson to be schoolmaster, he is known to Mr. Cresnar and will profit the children more in a quarter than they have profited heretofore in 2 years. Has talked with Debenham men concerning money. Simon Sponer, Simon Tovel, George Tovel and others are in debt and cannot lend. Old Collame will lend 20*l.* and his son Collame of Wethersell [? Wetheringsett, Suffolk,] 20*l.* Send for the latter and more may be got. Brampton and Grymble of Hals' parish are to let him know on Sunday if they can raise 10*l.* each.

562.—7 May 1603.   *Edmond Moundeford*, Lynford, to *Sir Bassingbourn Gawdy.*

Sends the subsidy book for the hundred of Wayland. Hopes he may be excused attending on the score of his wife's sickness and want of company. Expects Sir Philip Woodhouse will attend.

563.—19 May 1603.   *John Holland* [Kenninghall], to *Sir Bassingbourn Gawdy*, Harling.

Holland has had 3 fits of very extreme ague, "the two first held me very painfully 12 hours." If Holland receives any good news touching the "advance of this poor house" [*i.e.*, the Lords Howard, *see* next letter] he will let Gawdy know. "My Lord and Lord William [Howard] threaten a restraint for these grounds this year, for the King meaneth next summer to see Norfolk." Remembrances to Mr. Anthony.

564.—[May or June 1603.]   *John Holland to Sir Bass. Gawdy.*

Received last night letters from my Lord William Howard who had been with my lord to see the king. "My lord Henry Howard at their first coming to Burleigh brought them presently unto the king and my lord and he kneeling down the king gave my young lord his hand and then came unto my lord William in like sort and willed them to stand up and turning unto my lord Henry said ' Here be two of your nephews, both Howards, I love the whole house of them,' and then turning again unto my young lord said, ' I love your whole house,' and then my lord kissed again his hand, and the king said they should never repent his coming into this kingdom, and so drew my lord Henry along the gallery with him."

The king appointed them to visit him at Theobalds [Essex] whither he went yesterday to remain 10 days. He is to be crowned on the 25th July.

565.—12 July 1603.   *Thomas Wythe*, Furnival's Inn, to *Sir Bassingbourn Gawdy*, Harling.

In answer to Gawdy's charge that Wythe has felled timber to build a house of his own, the latter explains the facts. One Nicholas Smith, farmer to my Lady [Eliz. Framlingham, now married to Henry Gawdy], had built a barn's end of 3 loads of his own timber, which Henry Gawdy and my lady both by letter and by John Cullie desired Wythe to allow Smith for. Wythe afterwards needed timber to "groundsale" a barn and bought the right to this 3 loads from Smith, but fearing it would be questioned made the carpenter measure it and be sure not to exceed the allowance. Mr. Henry Gawdy is in the bill for Knight of the Bath.

566.—6 September 1603. *William Rugge*, Felmingham, to *Sir Bass. Gawdy*, Wymondham.

Recommends the bearer Francis Flewde, a poor joiner of Northelmham, whose house and tools were lately burnt. He is honest, wellgiven, and a very good workman, no loiterer gamester, or alehouse haunter.

Hopes Gawdy as one of the Treasurer for the county will bestow the "more liberal portion" upon him.

P.S.—One Mrs. Hoo complains at these Wymondham Sessions of one Goodeman for "a very great disorder and misdemeanor done against her to the hurt of her body"; see her righted.

567.—19 September [1603 ?]. *Elizabeth Nonne*, Tostock [Suffolk], to her nephew *Sir Bassingbourn Gawdy*, Harling.

Complains on behalf of a maid Jane who has been dismissed with great displeasure by Lady Gawdy and without cause "but only that she discovered some things to you which you greatly urged her unto. . . At her last being at Harling she neither could get lodging in the house and so hardly in the town that one night she sat up without a bed." Jane's best friends have turned against her owing to Lady Gawdy's displeasure, and Mrs. Nonne is keeping the girl with her till she hears further from Gawdy. "It were better she departed with good will than thus be provoked to make her own defence with the discredit of others."

568.—1 October 1603. *Sir Edmond Moundeford*, Lynford, to [*Sir Bassingbourn Gawdy*].

Thanks [Gawdy] for advertising him of the Lord Marshal's letters by which he understands [Gawdy] is required to certify the places of abode and the antiquity of such gentlemen as have been lately knighted by the king.

Has lived for 4 years at Lynford and before that at Feltwell; where his ancestors have "remained gentlemen bearing arms since the reign of Edward III." as appears by certain deeds bearing their seal, which he encloses for Gawdy's inspection. Sends the money due to the Lord Marshall.

Owing to the increase of the infection at Norwich he will not attend the Sessions. P.S.—His Cousin Osbert Pratt, of Hockwold, having a complaint unto the Lord Chief Justice against John Pygeon, of Wilton, the same was referred to [Gawdy] and Sir Philip Woodhouse. Moundeford can assure them that Pygeon is a very troublesome man.

569.—2 October 1603. *Sir Henry Gawdy*, Claxton, to his cousin *Sir Bass. Gawdy*.

Has kept the messenger until he got the things ready for "my godson's deafness." Sends a letter from cousin Birche with directions

GAWDY MSS. how to use them. Would like a copy of the letter Bassingbourne sent to brother Berney and others for fees for their knighthood to my Lord of Norfolk.

570.—20 October 1603. *Sir Bassing. Gawdy*, West Harling, to *Sir Henry Gawdy*, Claxton.

Bond to secure 110*l.* to be paid at Claxton Hall on 20 October 1604. Witnesses, Anthony Gawdy, Robert Bolton, Anthony Rawlyns.

571.—2 November 1603. *Francis Gawdy*, Wallington, to *Mr. Havers*, keeper of Winfarthing Park.

Warrant for a buck for Francis' nephew, Sir Clippesby Gawdy.

572.—19 December 1603. *Francis Gawdy*, Wallington, to his nephew, *Sir Bass. Gawdy.*

Francis' servant Blome says Sir Bassingbourn has a goshawk that will kill a pheasant. Would like to borrow it for a week. Tell Blome when the doe is required.

573.—20 December 1603. *Thomas Wythe*, Sternfield [Suffolk] to [*Sir Bass. Gawdy*].

Wythe was sorry to send Gray away without the money which has been "so dainty here" owing to lack of ready sale for commodities. Now sends 15*l.*; all that is due, considering the out-rents paid at St. Michael. Expected to have sent 4*l.* in fines, but the tenant could not raise it. Mr. Okeley will do nothing, Wythe will seize his land for non-payment of rent. Has got a good fellow to take two coveys ["coves"] of partridges "and yet they are but eight" (which he sends) being the first taken by a long-winged hawk since Wythe came there. Although Gawdy has two good sling hawks, yet "the one will range, the other often miss." After Wythe sold the billets to Mr. Lawrence, Vicar of Freston [Suffolk], Smith took them away in Wythe's absence. Lawrence did "so take on" with Mrs. Wythe that she had a load of bush-faggots made for him, for which Wythe will pay at next accounting. He suspects Smith was "willed to take the faggots."

1603–4.

574.—18 January 1603–4. *John Straffe*, or *Starf*, to *Sir Bass. Gawdy*, West Harling.

Cannot get a second surety, and if he is sent to jail he will be ruined as he is in debt.

575.—28 February 1603–4. *Martyn May*, Stiffkey, to *Mr. Bolton*, Thetford.

Please send the 15*s.* to be allowed by Sir Bassingbourn to one Thurlce. Roger Browne paid the other 15*s.*

576.—28 February [1603–4 or later]. *George Fowler*, Bromhill, to [*Sir Bass. Gawdy*].

Fowler has no cause to show favour to his "hard neighbor Fisher." Few lords would put up with such wrongs from their tenants, most of Fisher's living being copyhold under Fowler. His misdemeanour was "in haying up my warren and beating my warrener ['warner'] and his man who was stroken down and sore hurt of his head. My warrener, left alone against four . . . ran in at my outward gate to raise my men to rescue his man." Fisher has threatened to ruin the warrener if he seeks any remedy and has slandered Fowler, saying he gave one of the men (who has run away) 40s. to confess the matter. Fowler will not "put up" this slander, but will leave the assault to [Gawdy] and Sir Edmond [Moundeford?] to end, if they will see the warreners paid for their hurts and the stolen conies. If the Lord Chief Justice tried it, there would be a fine of 40l., and Fisher and his sons imprisoned. The poor neighbours dare not witness against Fisher by reason of his office, and would have "put up a supplication" against him this assize, had not Fowler prevented them.

577.—29 February 1602-4. *Sir Henry Gawdy*, Claxton, to *Sir Bass. Gawdy*, [Thetford]..

Sends apologies to my Lord for this, Sir Henry's first absence from Thetford assizes, he has "such a cold." His man Birche will explain anything that is asked. Commendations to cousins Anthony and Philip and the latter's wife and Bassingbourn's two sons. Please join with Sir Philip Woodhouse to aid Mr. Webbe in a matter brought against him by Mr. Myrrell.

578.—8 March 1603-4. *John Holland*, to *Sir Bass. Gawdy*, Harling.

Holland on his return from Gawdy found Mr. Thomas Havers and his wife who asked if Gawdy had recovered perfect health, which Holland said he had. They then said they were sorry "of the late ill chance fallen in your house" [see ante No. 567] and asked if the woman were gone "and if my lady were promised of another." Holland said she was gone and they offered their daughter (now with Mrs. Holland) "a very honest, sober, modest, and very well disposed maid" as Holland can say, having "summered and wintered her." Holland wishes "all unkindnesses between you and my lady trodden underfoot and perfect love between you."

579.—1 March 1603-4. *Anthony Thwaytes* to *Sir Bassingbourn Gawdy*.

James Duffilde against whom Thwaytes complained has submitted to Thwaytes' father and mother. Begs Gawdy's favour for Duffilde especially in a "very undue" complaint of Parson James against him. Please take order for Kenninghall and Banham "men's dogs."

1604.

580.—12 April 1604. *John Holland*, to *Sir Bassingbourn Gawdy*, Harling.

Holland understands by Shuckforde that he cannot prevail with Gawdy. He had thought neither Mr. Davye nor Mr. Colby nor Mr. Lytton could have carried Gawdy to break his promise. It was Holland's first suit and such that no justice in Norfolk would have refused, "but since a clown can so far prevail with you before a gentleman, I shall from henceforth leave to trouble you, and it may be cry quittance with them."

581.—15 April 1604. *Sir Edmond Moundeford*, Lynford, to *Sir Bassingbourn Gawdy*.

"My neighbour Fisher" having desired at Larlingford to be discharged from being constable, Moundeford moved the matter to the

Justices at Lynn [?] Sessions and proposed as fit substitutes John Martine and Richard Seaman of West Tofts. Martine was chosen and Fisher discharged.

Martin now says he has broken up house-keeping and lives in Suffolk and wishes to be discharged. Suggests their joining to appoint Seaman, but cannot travel on account of his lame leg. Asks the truth as to a proclamation against recusants who "grow more than bold in speech and action." Moundeford was much misliked at Lynn Sessions for giving in charge the inquiry of the statute against them.

> 582.—23 April 1604. *Sir Edward Moundeford*, Lynford, to *Sir Bassingbourn Gawdy*.

Hears that Gawdy has received "a note of such statutes as are to be debated upon this present parliament." Asks for a copy.

> 583.—30 May 1604. *John Holland* to *Sir Bassingbourn Gawdy*, Harling.

"I know you shall be earnestly borded (sic) for the killing of an out deer at Lopham, but remember your warrant and let this be secreted."

> 584.—1 June 1604. *John Nonne* to *Sir Bassingbourn Gawdy*, West Harling.

Nonne is bestowing all his money into land again and hopes he may reckon on 100*l.* from Gawdy before September.

> 585.—14 June 1604. *Ar.   Everard*, Gillingham, to *Sir [Bassingbourn Gawdy ?]*.

For the clearing of Robert Raynbearde, Everard can testify that on the 1st of June Sir Arthur Heveningham and Sir Edward Pyttes rode in his company from his house to Yarmouth, and on their return that night Everard's wife told him that Robert Raynbearde came to the house with Mr. Turrell about 11 a.m. and they dined there in company with one Mr. Hamonde.

> 586.—3 July 1604. *William Rugge*, Felmingham, to [*Sir Bassingbourn Gawdy*].

Repeats his request for help to Francis Floud, whose loss was over 30*l.*, out of the surplusage of the stock in the county formerly bestowed on such cases. Commends Gawdy to the protection of "the celestial God."

[See ante No. 566.]

> 587.—7 June 1604. *Francis Morice* [spelt by Gawdy "Morrys"] "my poor house in the old Palace in Westminster," to *Sir B. Gawdy*, West Harling.

Since Gawdy's servant Mr. Boulton was with Morice, the King's letter (which Boulton could not wait for) has been printed. Gawdy will find the enclosed copy better than any of the ordinary written ones that went abroad. Morice also sends a lately published poem "concerning the whole life and death of the late Earl of Essex, . . . well and feelingly written and I think will not hereafter be had as they are already called in and the printer called in question." Expects Gawdy will have heard how the lords and others who were called in question on Sunday night are all discharged and the Earl of Southampton in favour again. "But yesterday at Court one Jo. Sharpe, sometime a chaplain to my late Lord Essex but now a chaplain to the King and by appointment waiting ordinarily upon the Princes was sent for before the Council," and sent to the Tower. "It seemeth that upon the former restraint of the lords and the rest the Sunday before, he either solicited thereunto. by others or out of his own brain, without any grounds or warrant, went about to persuade divers gentlemen of special worth and ability about London, that (the King's Majesty being in danger to be surprised by some conspiracy or fancy) they should give their names to be in a readiness upon a warning to come to the Court to defend the King's person and should also procure as many more of their friends of like quality to be likewise ready." The names to be given to Sir Thos. Erskine, Captain of the Guard, and not to include papists "puritants" (sic) or followers of any nobleman. Concerning the Deputy Lieutenantship, Morice's master is most willing to serve Gawdy, who had better however write Morice a letter which he could show his Master so as to keep the matter in remembrance.

588.—23 July [1604 ?] *Anthony Thwayts* to *Sir Bassingbourn Gawdy.*

Asks a hue and cry after Thomas Dunte "a roguish young fellow, about 18 years old," who committed divers burglaries and robberies last week, "apparelled in an old white doublet and a pair of great round black hose." He broke into the house of John Pretiman, gent., at Cranworth, and besides stealing divers things found the key of his closet and came again next night and got things of good value. Next night he broke into Thwayts' house at Hardingham and stole a couple of young hounds he was training for "my good Lord of Arundel." The thief has confederates, and "under the color of stealing dogs" (sic) they break and rob continually. Asks that particular description may be given of the dogs; one white with black ears and the hair " scalt " off the top of his shoulders, the other white with blue ears and blue spots. Let warrant be directed to Diss and so on to Suffolk and Essex. A reward will be given if dogs brought to Hardingham, Quiddenbam, or Kenninghall. [This letter, written " in haste," is plainly dated 1640, which is an impossible date.]

589.—22 July 1604. *Sir Arthur Heveningham,* Ketteringham, to *Mr. Sayer,* Pulham.

Did not think neighbour Sayer would have dealt so dishonestly with him " as to feed him with so many fair words with nothing but deceit in them." If the promised cast of hawks are not sent Sir Arthur may have to take them. [Ends with some jocose threats.]

590.—31 July 1604. *Richard Mountague,* New Buckenham, to *Sir Bassingbourn Gawdy.*

About a month ago Sir Bassingbourn Gawdy, at the request of Sir Julius Cesar, consented to be one of Mountague's Commissioners at New Buckenham on 1 August.
Sends word that he will not proceed on that day.

591.—2 August 1604. *Sir Edmond Moundeford,* Lynford, to [*Sir Bassingbourn Gawdy*].

At last assizes there was much talk of altering the order of keeping Quarter Sessions ; begs to be advertised of what the Lord Chief Justice said on that head.

592.—7 August 1604. *Francis Morice*, Old Palace, Westminster, to
  Sir Bassingbourn Gawdy, West Harling.

Morice expects soon to be in the country, meanwhile reports that the
Constable of Castile landed on Sunday night at Dover and the King
will probably return from his pleasures in the country to finish the
treaty of peace, which only lacks " the mutual oath of the Princes
themselves." Thinks that haste may be expected in dispatching the
business the rather because the ambassador is to be defrayed here at the
King's charges at the " incredible rate " as he hears) of 400*l.* a day.
Morice got a friend to mention Gawdy to my Lord of Northampton
in case he had occasion to employ any one in the matter " of the loan
in Norfolk which was committed to his charge." Does not know the
result, as he has been out of town a fortnight.

593.—8 August 1604. *Edmund Doyly*, Shottesham [High Sheriff],
  to cousin [*Sir Bassingbourn Gawdy*].

The Lord Chief Justice directs the immediate execution of the
prisoner who escaped, and that Pye should be bailed till next assizes.
Understands the Jailor is to wait on [Gawdy] with the other prisoner,
so he sends Pye.

594.—14 August 1604. *Francis Morice* [Westminster], to *Sir
  Bassingbourn Gawdy*, West Harling.

" The great Constable of Castile arrived at London on Friday last at
night. He is lodged in Somerset House, which is most richly
apparelled with the King's furniture, and he attended by the King's
officers and servants, and all his charges defrayed by his Majesty, and
so is also Count Arrenbergh and the Archduke's Commissioners, who
were also brought the same night to Duresme House, which was in like
sort made ready for them : the daily charge is said to be 300*l.* at the
least . . . for their train of gentles of worth and other followers is
exceeding great, the provision for every meal in both houses being for
64 several messes of meat. The same day the Constable arrived here,
Sluys [' Sluce '] was rendered upon composition ; the soldiers departing
with colors flying and bullets in their mouths, and with bag and
baggage, leaving all munitions, seven great galleys, the galley-slaves,
and some hostages for the delivery of some men of worth which were
prisoners with the Archduke. The King is expected here this night ;
it is said he will give the Constable and the rest audience upon Thursday next, swear the peace and feast them upon Sunday (for which great
provision is made), and they shall take their leaves on Monday,' so as
to shorten the time of expense and let the King get back to his progress
and pleasures in the country, " whence he cometh in post and bringeth
but part of his company and carriages." The Peace Commissioners,
viz., the Lords Treasurer, Admiral, Devonshire, Northampton, and
Cecil will also feast the Ambassadors. The book for Privy Seals for
Norfolk is not yet signed by the Lords, but is set down by my Lord of
Northampton ; Mr. Kerry, the Clerk of the Privy Seal, has seen " how
you are rated," but the book is not yet in his hands. Sir Charles Cornwallis is appointed ; Morice had hoped Gawdy would be, but did net
perfectly know his mind therein.

595.—18 August 1604. *John Holland*, " Grastocke " [? Gray's
  Thurrock, Essex], to *Sir B. Gawdy*.

" My good Lady," [Howard] came hither in good health, and " with
as little weariness as if she had ridden but 10 miles." She was so well

pleased to come to her own that she shows small disposition to return. Holland often wishes Gawdy and "my cousin Anthony" were there. "My Lady" is much visited by the best of the country, yet her "southern friends" would have hearty welcome. She keeps an honourable house, her alms in meat, drink, and money are great, and she has won the love of many who were her enemies. Holland wishes himself at Harling, but dare not hasten my lady's return, lest she think him "weary of the country which she so well loveth."

596.—21 August 1604.　*Francis Morice*, the Court [London], to *Sir Bass. Gawdy*, West Harling, to be left with Mr. Bolton or Mr. Chapman, Thetford.

The King posted in from "his sports in his progress" this day se'nn'et, swore to the Peace in his Chapel at Whitehall, and feasted the Ambassadors "with great sports and pleasures" on Sunday, the peace being proclaimed at the Court gates and in the City. Yesterday the Constable of Castile "being not well able to come to Court to take his leave . . . the King (to hasten back again to his country pleasures) went himself to Somerset House about six o'clock to bid him farewell, and from thence immediately took horse and rode post the same night to Ware, and so to his further delights, dispensing rather with his own greatness than willing to expect the Ambassadors coming unto him." Lord Cecil was yesterday made Viscount Cramborne in Dorsetshire. Morice has seen the book of Privy Seals. Mr. Justice Gawdy is rated at 100*l.*, Sir Henry Gawdy at 100*l.*, Sir Clippesby Gawdy 30*l.*, Sir Bassingbourn 40*l.*, and Lady Gawdy 40*l.*

597.—25 August 1604.　*Sir Edward Moundeford*, Linford, to [*Sir Bass. Gawdy*].

Went to Wellington on Thursday to inform [Gawdy] of the orders agreed on by the justices at Norwich. Mentions arrangements as to the hundreds they are to deal with.

598.—31 August 1604.　*Same* (Feltwell) to *Same*.

Encloses two warrants; Gawdy can execute either. If the party goes to jail, the king may never get the fine. Better bind him to appear at next sessions.

599.—3 September 1604.　*Same* to *Same*.

Has no answer to his last.

600.—16 September 1604.　*Sir John Heigham*, Barrow [Suffolk], to *Sir B. Gawdy* and *Sir Philip Woodhouse*, Thetford.

The untimely death of his niece's husband makes him unable to keep his engagement to meet them at Thetford "about the view of the river between that and Brandon" fixed for 17th September. Excuses to Mr. Mayor. They had better enter into the cause with effect to save time.

601.—17 September 1604.　*John Nonne*, to *Sir Bassingbourn Gawdy*, West Harling.

Mr. Holdych presses Nonne to "prevent" his payment. As Dudlington is no further from Harling than Bury is, Nonne begs the 100*l.* may be sent there at latest the Wednesday after Michaelmas.

602.—24 September 1604. *George Mynors*, the Court, Hampton
Court, to *Sir Bassingbourn Gawdy*,
Harling.

Delayed writing, as he could not get a copy of the Commission as he
promised. As to the business of Gawdy's horse, Mynors has made
means to my Lord and Mr. Somerset that "they being satisfied you
may enjoy your horse and my lady hawk with patience notwithstanding all unkind proceedings by some which you and she know well."

603.—25 September 1604. *Francis Morice*, Westminster, to *Sir
Bassingbourn Gawdy.*

Morice has given good reasons to his friend Mr. Kerry [Clerk of the
Privy Seal] to be imparted to my Lord Northampton why Gawdy
should be spared this loan. Kerry has already made out 209 privy
seals by way of supply more than at the first and expected directions
from my Lord for at least as many more. The King came to Hampton
Court on Saturday [22nd] the Commissioners of Scotland for the
Union are come hither already : the assembly is the 20th of next month.
The King purports to be at Roiston again next week. Ostend is
certainly said to be lost, and some 1,400 of the garrison slain.

604.—27 September 1604. *Da. Hughes*, Woodrising, to *Sir
Bassingbourn Gawdy*, Harling.

Recommends the bearer, William George, who was lately forbidden
to victual in Carbrook. He has "lived in more awe of offending than
most of that trade," and has proved himself honest as my lady's bailiff
in that town. Begs he may be licensed, "having fitted himself for
such a course of life"; Gawdy has always favored "this decayed
house" which emboldens Hughes to ask this. [The reference is to the
Southwell family.]

605.—2 October 1604. *Sir Christopher Heydon*, to *Sir Bass. Gawdy*,
Harling.

Heydon has hopes of farming the customs of Norfolk, and has been
bold with divers of his friends, most of them not under Gawdy's rank,
to be his sureties, not pressing them beyond a 100*l.* a year. Assures
Gawdy there will be no risk.

606.—7 October 1604. *Sir Edmond Maundeford*, Lynford, to *Sir
Bass. Gawdy.*

Returns the certificate and letter to the Lord Chief Justice, which he
has signed but cannot forward.

607.—9 October 1604. *Francis Morice* [London ?] to *Sir Bass.
Gawdy*, Thetford.

Morice has been in danger of losing a good wife in child-bed. Mr.
Kerry, too, has been "in danger to be lost" and kept his chamber 12
days. Morice scribbles these lines at the "weak elbow" of Mr. Kerry,
who puts him out of doubt that he will do Gawdy some good in *re* the
Privy Seals.

608.—16 October 1604. *Francis Morice*, Westminster, to *Sir Bass.
Gawdy.*

Mr. Kerry's illness hinders matters, his influence with Lord Northampton is the only thing to be depended on. An opportunity will offer
soon, as the King, Queen, Prince, Duke Charles and Lady Elizabeth

came in great state to Whitehall to-day and are to be met by the Lord Mayor and Aldermen, as was often done in the late Queen's time. Anthony Drury's name cannot be substituted for Gawdy's. After searching the certificates of the 3 several supplies for Norfolk made since the first, it seems Drury is down for 20l. already, and he lent 50l. in the last Privy Seal. Cannot propose Bradbury's name either. It is usual in asking exemption to have the signatures of several to the reasons; perhaps as Gawdy "is so public a person" it may not be needed.

[24 October 1604 Francis Gawdy is nominated for the post of Lord Chief Baron, but does not get it.]

609.—6 November 1604. *Francis Morice*, Westminster, to *Sir Bass. Gawdy*, West Harling.

All business is at a stand, probably on account of "this weighty business of the Union, which is intended so much on all hands as all time almost is spent in it, either in private committees and conferences or in public assemblies of the Commissioners on both sides." Lord Northampton will do nothing till Sir Charles Cornwallis comes up; if he supports Kerry it will be all right.

610.—12 November 1604. *Sir William Fletewood*, Receiver General of the Courts of Wards, to *Sir Bass. Gawdy*.

Receipt for 13l. 6s. 8d. half year's rent due Michaelmas, of the lands late of Sir Charles Framlingham.

611.—22 November 1604. *Francis Morice*, Westminster, to *Sir Bassingbourn Gawdy*, West Harling.

Regrets that his endeavours and Gawdy's own presence have been unavailing. As requested by Mr. Boulton has given Gawdy's privy seal to his brother Mr. Philip Gawdy and encloses the other two letters. There is yet a chance that the amount may be reduced, and Mr. Kerry will move for this, unless "the increase of your ability and state" may peradventure make Gawdy wish to have nothing more done.

612.—4 December 1604. *Mrs. Frances Gawdy* [wife of Owen Gawdy] to *Sir Bassingbourn Gawdy*, Harling Hall.

Asks to have one of his farms let out to her, she has already selected some stock which she does not want to squander. If he is willing she will send her husband to confer.

613.—10 December 1604. *Francis Morice*, Westminster, to *Sir Bassingbourn Gawdy*, Harling.

The lords have committed the right to discharge or abate privy seals to the lieutenants and collectors of counties. "This day the late Lord Bishop of London was confirmed and installed Archbishop of Canterbury the young prince and all the lords were present and dined with him at Lambeth." The Bishops are enjoined to enforce conformity themselves, not committing the matter to their officials or chaplains. A petition sent in on Friday from Lancashire gentlemen and Justices on behalf of their ministers who are not conformable is said to have been taken very ill by the King.

[About this date Lady [Elizabeth] Gawdy (formerly Lady Framling-ham) died.]

614.—15 December 1601.   *Thomas Wythe*, Crowshall, [Suffolk,] to *Sir Bassingbourn Gawdy*, Harling.

John Wrethock and John Cullie met Wythe at Abbotshall [Suffolk] and the former fell debating as to the tenants attorning. Wythe bade him hold his peace and not "buzz anything into the tenants' ears." Wythe then told the tenants he had met Gawdy at Bury and been advised there that they were to attorn to him, which they readily did, both there and at Debenham [Suffolk]. Mr. Moyse was the first tenant to come forward at Crowshall. Ralph Talmach surrendered 19 acres to Richard Wythe of Pettaugh [Suffolk] fine was cessed at 7*l.*, Wrethock getting 6*l.*, and the balance awaits Gawdy's pleasure. Nicholas Bell was admitted to the Camping Close (1½ ac.) Wrethock is to get the fine 26*s.* 8*d.* If the frost holds Wythe hardly expects Gawdy. John Cully says there is yet 100*l.* worth of goods left, which Sir Henry [Gawdy] would let Sir Bassingbourn have for the asking. The other goods that are gone might have been had "at a very small rate" had Gawdy and his kinsman met. Wythe urges a reconciliation with Sir Henry, pointing out that Gawdy has throughout "lighted on the gain" while Sir Henry hath lost. Urges them to arrange a meeting. "As for things past and attempted against you, I mean for Garden in Socage, &c., you have got the gold.

[The deposition of Rev. George Hals, ante No. 344, taken now.]

615.—29 December 1604. *John Holland* to *Sir B. Gawdy*, Harling.

The Constable of Fersfield was with Holland this morning at Harling having arrested the maid who "carried our pales, and confesses she did it by her dame's command. She says at Christmas her master and his brother brought home 6 turkeys, which they said Lone's wifes mother gave them. a very unlikely tale. They have companions at Brisingham, a miller and one Knights and others of the like sort come to them out of Suffolk.

Knapswood, the farmer at Boyland, says he has lost over 30 turkeys and geese this winter and has noticed Lone's brother viewing them, the day before they were stolen and so vehemently suspects them.

Linen has also been stolen. They keep at their house a wench who is with child by one Richard Doner [?] of Thetford. Holland would like the girl freed after examination, unless Gawdy thinks she should "justify her confession." Send warrant for apprehension of John and Robert Lane.

616.—   1604. *Lewes Pickering*, Thetford, to *Sir Bass. Gawdy*, Harling.

Having occasion to employ his servant, Pickering is enforced to set down one of his hawks. Hearing Gawdy has a skilful falconer, Pickering begs the man may mew the hawk (a heroner) or get some honest man to it. If she is mewed with Sir William Woodhouse's heroner they will be fit to fly together next year.

1604 to 1604-5.

617.—   1604. *Sir Christopher Heydon* to *Sir Bass. Gawdy*.

Asks Gawdy to be his surety in taking up 100*l.* Hopes it is the last time he will be driven to the like plunge.

618.—   1604. *William Morris*, Redgrave [Suf-   GAWDY MSS.
folk], to *Sir Bass. Gawdy.*

Morris offered his master 10*l.* for the gelding, and finally bought him for Gawdy for 11*l.*

619.—   1604. *John Flight*, Norwich [Jail], to *Sir Bass. Gawdy,* Harling.

Can tell Gawdy no more of "certain truth" than he has. Pray "send word to the jailer to release me of some irons, for I think they will lame me else."

1604-5.

620.—12 January 1604-5.   *John Nonne*, Bury [Suffolk], to *Sir Bass. Gawdy,* West Harling.

Nonne would be loth to be used in testimony between two whom he esteems, but cannot refuse his evidence as a witness to the bond made before my Lady Framlingham last married. It was made to Mr. Everarde, "now, I hear, Sir Anthony Everarde," in the penal sum of 1,000*l.* as he thinks. Hopes all unkindness will be avoided.

621.—25 January 1604-5.   *Barnabe Moyse*, Debenham [Suff.], to *Sir Bass. Gawdy,* West Harling.

On Friday Sponer is to be paid the money which Moyse was Gawdy's surety for. Moyse has spoken to Mr. Fuller, who will let it stand over.

622.—28 January 1604-5.   *Sir Edmond Moundeford*, Feltwell, to [*Sir Bassingbourn Gawdy*].

The Constables of Breccles wish to have Mary Whitbye, of that town (lately delivered of a base child which is dead) punished by two Justices for her offence. Asks [Gawdy] to meet him for that purpose, but it requires no great haste. Expects [Gawdy] has received letters concerning vintners and taverners, and has warned those within his limit, and also the corporation of Thetford. Moundeford has sent to Wayland, Grimshoe, and Clackclose hundreds.

623.—25 February 1604-5.   *Henry Felton*, Fakenham, to [?].

Will wait on his correspondent in in the evening "to pay the last respects to the corpse of my honoured uncle" [?]. His brother Bacon will also be there.

1605.

624.—April 1605.   *Elizabeth Everard*, Holme, to sister *Mrs. Sayer,* at Pulham.

Mrs. Everard's husband died without a will. Sir Francis Gawdy has taken an inventory of all the goods and demands 150*l.* besides this half year's rent, for which and for the next half year's rent he asks surety. If Sir Francis gets his full demand, she will be ruined. Can find no writing to show what her husband paid in his life-time. Thomas Tayler has offered to be her surety.

625.—12 April 1605.   *Sir Francis Gawdy*, Wallington, to nephew *Sir Bassingbourn Gawdy.*

Begs the continuance of his nephew's good offices on behalf of Sir Francis' servant John Bloome with Sir Francis Lovell, and to get the latter to perform his promises, or at least to come to some conclusion in writing.

626.—14 April 1605. *John Holland* to *Sir Bassingbourn Gawdy,* Harling.

Had Holland known of the woman's lewd behaviour to Gawdy he would not for 40*l.* have moved on her behalf. He did it out of compassion hearing that she had disbursed 40*s.* or 50*s.* in jail, and at Shuckford's entreaty that the house might be licensed so that she could recover her loss. "Dany" may storm at it; his "malice is much to Shuckford," let him be careful, he knows not how long he may be in office. But for Gawdy countenancing Dany, Shuckford would care but little for him.

627.—15 April 1605. *Sir Henry Gawdy,* Claxton, to cousin *Sir Bassingbourn Gawdy.*

Understands that Sir B. Gawdy sent on Easter Thursday his servants to Croweshall to join Sir Henry's servants in the pricing of the latter's stuff. Sir Henry did not send as he heard Sir Bassingbourn had fallen sick, and was gone to Cambridge. Makes another appointment as he is going to London the following week.

628.—2 June 1605. *Sir Henry Gawdy* to cousin *Sir Bassingbourn Gawdy.*

Smythe of Sternfield [Suffolk] owes Sir Henry a great deal of money. Please look up his lease and bond in the closet, and send it by nephew Whetcroft that Smythe may be sued.

629.—3 June 1605. *William Derehaugh,* Soham Lodge [Cambridgeshire], to [*Sir Bass. Gawdy*].

Sends the mare that Mr. Writhoke told [Gawdy] of. She is about 10 years old, has never been ridden, been kept for breeding. Derehaugh is putting away his ground and selling his cattle. [Gawdy] shall fix the price.

630.—12 June 1605. *Robert Dey,* Skoulton, to *Sir Bass. Gawdy,* Crowshall [Suffolk].

Thomas Dawes of Skoulton travelled to London to the late Lady Southwell last assize time merely to get leave to keep an alehouse. He has kept an unlicensed house two years and was committed by Gawdy for contempt. Dey has taken out new warrants, but he betaketh him to his house and will not obey. Let his petition stand over till my Lady come to Rising when the unfitness of the place (according to my Lord Chief Justice's order) may better appear.

631.—26 June 1605. *William Derehaugh,* Debenham [Suffolk], to *Sir Bassingbourn Gawdy.*

Relates a mischance at last Debenham Fair ; a young man, son of a gentleman, old Ellice Brame, had a quarrel fastened upon him by a drunken companion. Although he acted beyond the discretion of young men the other party drew on him suddenly and the young man after giving back as far as he could, unhappily killed his adversary. Earlier in the day the dead man had tried to put an impudent quarrel on the bearer of this letter. An envious neighbour has laid the matter very bitterly before Gawdy's father [in law] Sir Nicholas Bacon. Derehaugh hopes that Gawdy will write to Sir Nicholas and induce

a better opinion of the case before the Assizes. Remembrances to Philip GAWDY MSS.
Gawdy.

632.—26 June 1605. *Francis Morice*, Westminster, to *Mr. Boulton*,
Thetford.

Begs Boulton to procure from Sir Bassingbourn Gawdy a warrant
for a buck out of one of the Earl of Arundel's parks nearest to Yarmouth, for one Dr. Felton, a "principal friend" of Morice's. Dr.
Felton was born at Yarmouth, but his charge is in London ; he is noted
for his learning, virtues, "painful preachings and studies," and has
"almost consumed himself." "We expect daily a great ambassador
from the Emperor and my lord Admiral's return, with a new ambassador-
Leiger for Spain. My lord of Worcester went this morning towards
Wales about ordering the disorders lately committed by the Recusants
in those parts. Yesterday was condemned and this day executed one
Douglas, a Scot, for counterfeiting the King's hand and seal to letters of
his own devising which he delivered to the B.B. Electors, viz., '[the
Bishops of] ' Treves, Mentz, and Cologne, and to other Princes of the
Empire, wherein he made the King to write as if he had been of their
pretended Catholic religion, &c."
[Enclosed by Boulton who forwards letter from Thetford to Gawdy.]

633.—12 August 1605. *John Holland* to *Sir Bassingbourn Gawdy*,
Harling.

Renews his suit for Shuckford's license, lest others try to "erect
more alehouses to cross him." That town is very riotous, "some have
geese to roast, seeth and bake pies, and have resort to spend them and
for that they will not have it said they keep an alehouse, they send for
beer by the pot and by that means great riot and company meets."

634.—28 August 1605. *John Holland* to *Sir Bassing. Gawdy*,
Harling.

Holland understands Gawdy and Sir Francis Lovell are to hear a
cause between John Clarke and the bearer, William Lownds, who is
only interested as " our bailiff." If Lownd's evidence does not satisfy
Gawdy, Holland begs an adjournment till the 4th September that the
Steward may attend.

635.—23 September 1605. *Thomas Gawdy*, Waybread [Suffolk]
to cousin *Sir B. Gawdy*, W. Har-
ling.

John Shothowe of Shimpling has investigated the removal of a windmill belonging to Thomas in right of his wife. One Tebbould, who is
the farmer till Michaelmas, is to remove it. Asks Gawdy's letter or
warrant.

636.—4 November 1605. *John Holland* to *Sir Bassing. Gawdy*,
Harling.

Having to make up over 300*l.*, Holland is driven to acquaint Gawdy
with a debt of 10*l.* money he lent "my lady" [Gawdy] who cannot
pay it.

637.—8 November 1605. *Nicholas Fowle*, Bodesdale [Suffolk], to
Sir B. Gawdy.

Being importuned by the bearer, Fowle reports the very rude and
unbeseeming behaviour of one Barker ; who twice came to his house

GAWDY MSS. while he and his wife were away and laboured to entice their servant, Jane Culham.

On Monday 4 November he came to the Crown at Bodesdale, and complotted with the wench to carry her away. On Wednesday following he returned before daybreak " well appointed with horse and man armed with their swords and daggers." The host of the Crown notifying Fowle, they went to the White Horse, "and there were swaggering the most part of the day," sending secret messages to the wench that they were ready. Sends thanks for the token received by " your little sweet son " [Framlingham, who appears to have been on a visit to his Uncle Philip at London, and may have taken Bodesdale on his way].

638.—21 November 1605.   *Rev. Thomas Daynes*, Norwich, to *Sir Bass. Gawdy.*

" Grace and peace," &c. Has no matter of moment to write about but to signify his Christian love [at some length] and hearty thanks for entertainment at Harling. "I never begged anything but wine of liquorice " [*see* No. 477], now asks for any farm fitting for him which Gawdy may be disposed to grant. " Grace be with us, Amen."

639.—21 November 1605.   *Christopher Cooke* and *William Hornebye* to *Sir Bass. Gawdy*, West Harling.

Request that " our poor neighbor " Simon Master may sell beer and bread out of doors, not within the house. He will amend former faults.

1605-6.

640.—15 February 1605-6.   *Sir Bass. Gawdy*, West Harling, and *Thomas Wythe*, of Sternfield, Suff., Gent., to *Elizabeth Wrottle*, St. John St., Middlesex.

Joint Bond to secure 32*l*. 5*s*. payable 15 Nov. next at house of William Bowes, Esq., St. John Street. Witness. Bennet Clark, Francis Maldanbye, Anthony Rawliyns.

[Sir Bassingbourn Gawdy died 23 May 1606, aged 46.]

UNDATED LETTERS

Addressed to *Sir Bassingbourn Gawdy* (*i.e.* between January $\frac{1596-7}{1597-8}$ and May 1606).

641.—   *William Brewster*, Wisbeach Castle, Cambridgeshire, to *Sir Bass. Gawdy.*

(21 September.) Brewster's friend, John Coles of Wisbeach (who is my Lord Chamberlain's man), has a controversy with one Sturman of Wisbeach, and desires to retain Mr. Attorney General. Asks a letter from Gawdy.

642.—   *Robert Dawbeney*, Redgrave [Suffolk], to *Sir Bassingbourn Gawdy*, Harling.

(21 March.) Was advertised that Goodman Clark of Berdelay [Suffolk] would willingly give Gawdy a load of hay. Dawbeney went.

out and enquired of him, who said he would willingly perform his promise if Gawdy would send his horse and cart.

643.—   *Robert Dawbeney to Sir Bassingbourn Gawdy*, Harling.

Sends his gelding for Gawdy to try, the price is 7*l.* 10*s.* Hopes his proof will be his praise.

644.—   *Fyrmyn Denny to Sir Bass: Gawdy.*

(9 April) [after 1603.] Denny has received a warrant from Gawdy and Mr. Bartlett concerning Agnes Wyxe, and referred the cause to Mr. Archdeacon Stokes, who settled the matter to her satisfaction. She is a clamorous woman and now wants more. If Gawdy thinks there has been any unfair dealing Denny will deal with it in his own Court as lord of the manor and chancellor. He is making up the King's money, will Gawdy pay him the 25*l.* at London or at Norwich? Gawdy's man sold Denny a company of rotten sheep, of which 40 at least died.

645.—   *Fyrmyn Denny to Sir B. Gawdy*, Harling.

(6 August.) Wishes to buy 100 wethers or ewes; asks the price. Hears that Gawdy's man Morrys was at Mr. Henry Jenny's after a falcon. Denny bought one of his cousin Jenny for Henry Cornwallis last year, giving 5*l.* 6*s.* for her. She turned out a very strong, lusty falcon, too full of mettle for a woodland country, "ever raking out at crows." Gawdy can have her at the same price.

346.—   *Fyrmyn Denny to Sir Bassingbourn Gawdy,* Harling.

(30 November.) Expected to have received 50*l.* on the 15th of the month to send to London. Please send it to Mr. George Byrch's by Saturday.

647.—   *Thomas Fermor,* Barsham, *to his cousin Sir Bassingbourn Gawdy.*

(12 May.) Asks for a benevolence for his servant, who is to be married at Fakenham on Trinity Sunday next.

648.—   *Henry Gawdy* [of Claxton] *to cousin Sir Bassingbourn Gawdy.*

[Before 1603.] Thanks him for remembering the business at Wyndham.

649.—   *Henry Gawdy to cousin* [*Sir Bass. Gawdy?*]

To borrow 20*s.* to help him to London ; expects to get money this term to repay all his kind friends, &c. [This is not Henry Gawdy of Claxton who was knighted 1603.]

650.—   *Sir Clement Heighham to Sir A. Hevening-ham, Sir Ph. Woodhouse, Sir Bass. Gawdy,* and *Sir Nathaniel Bacon.*

[After 1603.] Has received their peremptory command "for the viewing certain Lances appointed to be shewed for this county." Considering in what place he serves his Majesty, Heigham thinks they might have known that neither he nor his horses are to be commanded by them. If he ever does that kind of work he expects a higher place than they can appoint, or for the matter of that can execute themselves.

651.— *Sir Christopher Heydon* to *Sir Bassingbourn Gawdy.*

(1 October.) For upwards of 40 years there has been an Inn at the sign of the White Horse in Kenninghall, where William Mulley lately dwelt. He has left and Heydon asks Gawdy to join him in licensing the bearer William Cheffley, alias Blackwill.

652.— *Henry Holdych,* Dudlington, to *Sir Bassingbourn Gawdy,* at Watton.

(23 May.) Asks Gawdy to discharge the bearer, a poor old crazed man from training. Excuses himself for not seeing Gawdy when he passed by a-hunting but did not know Gawdy had returned from the Bath and had heard that my lady was gone to Sir Nicholas Bacon's.

653.— *Henry Holdych,* Dudlington, to his cousin, *Sir Bassingbourn Gawdy,* Harling.

(22 June.) Asks Gawdy to help the bearer, a poor cripple, who has lost all that she hath by fire. The Justices at the Sessions allotted her 3*l.*, but she has lost above 20*l.* in stuff besides her tenement.

654.— *John Holland* to *Sir Bassingbourn Gawdy,* Harling.

(20 March.) To release the bearer from the fine upon him for keeping an unlicensed ale-house.

655.— *John Holland,* Norwich, *Esq.,* to *Bassingbourn Gawdy, Esq.,* Harling.

(4 September.) If Gawdy wishes to sell the house that John Nedham lives in Holland will buy it or exchange for it other land nearer Gawdy as at Brakland [?] or Larling.

656.— *John Holland* to [*Bassingbourn Gawdy*].

Asks Gawdy to bring his cook with him to help as the cook which should have dressed their dinner is sent for by his master Mr. Kempt.

657.— *John Holland* to *Sir Bassingbourn Gawdy,* Harling.

(5 December.) To be easy in rating the fines on some poor women who are committed to gaol for having drawn beer. One has a very poor, lame husband : some others have left their houses and are afraid to come home for fear of being committed. There has been great disorder these holidays at Spinkes' both at play and drunkenness, and when Spinkes was reproved he said he would answer it.

658.— *Thomas Moundeford* [London] to *Sir Bassingbourn Gawdy.*

(17 February.) Sends certain drugs. Of the electuary in the pot take the quantity of a great nutmeg every morning fasting and within half an-hour drink a draught of warm posset ale made of equal parts of ale and white wine,—" Take your emplaister, warm it a little and lay the silk side next your skin on the left side, so let it lie day and night, if it wrinkle roll it smooth, if it dries, renew it with some of the roll spread with a warm knife." Trusts to see Gawdy in London. Remembrances to my lady.

659.— *Barnaby Moyse* to *Sir Bassingbourn Gawdy*.

Could not borrow the money of Michael Fuller as he was out, so was driven to borrow it upon his bond of Simon Sponer till Candlemas day next. He has sent the sum of 30*l.* to Gawdy by John Bonde.

660.— *Nicholas Raynberd*, Kenninghall Lodge, to *Sir Bassingbourn Gawdy*.

(20 March.) Would like to see Sir Bassingbourn before Nicholas goes to London. Begs his promise to favour William Mulley.

661.— *Daniel Reece* to *Sir Bassingbourn Gawdy*.

The poor of the town are likely to starve whilst the inhabitants quarrel about their assessment. Cannot Gawdy come or send some one to settle it? For instance, Mr. Thomas Colbye has 7 times as much land as Reece and will only be rated at 4 times in value more; at least 60 of the inhabitants wished to wait on Gawdy in a body, but Reece persuaded them to let him try the effect of a petition.

662.— *John Spurgin*, Kenninghall, grocer, to the *Lord Keeper*.

Petition, showing that one Lionel Griggs of Bridgham, yeoman, upon divers matters of accounts got into his hands a good amount of Spurgin's goods and will not come to any composition for them. Griggs is a troublesome contentious person, and Spurgin being a " poor young man " cannot contend with him. Begs letters to Sir Bassingbourn Gawdy, Knight, and Mr. Edward Bartlett to call the parties before them and determine the matter.

663.— *Michael Stanhope*, from his house at S . . . . [?], to cousin *Sir Bassingbourn Gawdy*.

(30 September.) Sends thanks for a hawk; would gladly see her on the wing if he could stay in the country but has not time, nor any falconer to entrust her to. Begs that he may return her and next year if Gawdy will meet him in Suffolk with the hawk he will "show you patridge to weary both you and your hawk." Thanks Gawdy also for unsolicited attempts to forward Stanhope's interest. His friends started the idea without his notion, he thinks they are likely to be " overshot in their own bows " [" oen boes "].

664.— *Christopher Taylor* to *Bassingbourn Gawdy*.

Chapman told Taylor that [Gawdy] wanted a boy, so he presently enquired about one and has sent him by chance to Thetford, not knowing where [Gawdy] is. He is a very good gentleman born, but his father was undone by reason of the wars in Ireland. Chapman and his wife have been arrested for felony and are in close prison. Taylor went to the Sheriff, whose name is Mr. Ratclef, and asked him in [Gawdy's] name to take Chapman's cloak from him and not suffer him to say that he was [Gawdy's] man, and if any jewels came to his hands that were in Chapman's and his wife's custody to take care of them till he heard from [Gawdy]. If the cloak is delivered to Taylor he will make a pair of hose and a cassock of it for the boy. Asks [Gawdy] to send him word about the clothes that he caused his friend to (redeem?). [No Sheriff named Ratclef for either Norfolk or Suffolk during this period.]

PART II.

CORRESPONDENCE and DOCUMENTS relating to the FAMILY of GAWDY, of West Harling (Norfolk), and their CONNECTIONS, from the death of SIR BASSINGBOURN GAWDY, in 1606, to the death of his son, FRAMLINGHAM GAWDY, in 1654. (NOTE.—Most of the letters in this part bear date prior to the year 1640.)

[The following undated letter comes in most appropriately here, as it introduces Sir Robbert Knollis, who became Framlingham Gawdy's guardian upon Sir Bassingbourn Gawdy's death. Probably written after 1589, when Sir John Fortescue was made Chancellor of the Exchequer.]

665.—   *Sir Edward Stanhope* to his friend
                              Mr. Robert Knollis, Esq., one of
                              the Esquires of Her Majesty's
                              body in Ordinary.

Sir,—When I gave her Majesty humble thanks from you and that I entered into the particularities of your suit, she answered in this manner, "Let me alone for Robyn, it is more than time something were done for him, I will speak with John Foskew or with my Lord Treasurer," and with heat concluded. Wherefore my opinion is you drive not the time as you did last year, till the matter be forgotten or otherwise greater occasions make yours have the worse passages, and believe me it must be your own attendance and following that will bring this suit to a good issue and wherein you shall be ever assured of my poor credit and travail, &c.

1606.

666.—   Case for Counsel's opinion Re *Sir Charles
                         Framlingham* dec[d] [Exparte *Sir Robert
                         Knollis*].

[circ. 1606.] Sir Charles Framlingham died seised of the manors of Crowshall, Debenham, Butters, Scottnetts [cum le Hang ?] Abbotshull and Mendevilles, Suffolk, held *in capite.* He left them to his wife for life (she is now dead) and assigned Mendevilles for the King's full third (which it is not).

The manors of Crowshall, Debenham, Scottnetts and Abbotshull were to go to Charles Gawdy, his youngest grandchild, and Mandevilles manor to Framlingham Gawdy, both in tail special, with cross remainders over. His cousin Wolmer and Sir Bass. Gawdy to enter and account for rents during the children's minority. Wolmer and Sir Bassingbourn are both dead: Framlingham Gawdy (yet a minor) being his father's sole executor. The King, by the advice of the Court of Wards, demised 1/3rd of all the manors to Sir Bassingbourn.

Query. Who is to enter on Charles Gawdy's
          two parts and who shall hold the Courts?

Sir Charles made feoffments of some of the manors to the use of his will, &c., and covenanted to suffer a recovery of another to use of him and his heirs: but tenants did not attorn.

Query. Shall not the King
[Sir R. Knollis] have
the manors
spite of the

. . Shall not Framlingham Gawdy have a third, he having less than that devised to him ?

[A short and damaged note of the *Opinion* is endorsed ; apparently to this effect. The Crown lease transferred all the King's rights to Sir Bassingbourn, the Committee cannot therefore set them up again in his own person. A bill must be filed by Sir Robert on behalf of himself and the heir; *he* can only claim the 1/3rd leased by the Crown, the heir must join as having to account for the profits of the other 2/3rds during his brother Charles' minority.]

1607.

667.—8 October 1607. *Richard Lewis*, alias *Davis*, of Westminster, Yeoman, to *Sir Robert Knollys*, of same place, Knight.

Receipt by Lewis, under letter of attorney from Henricke Williamson of St. Martin in the fields, Tailor, for 50s., in full payment and satisfaction of £7 10s. due and owing by Knollis to Williamson : Release of said debt of 7l. 10s. Witness, William Swetenham, notary, and John [P ?]lukenett, his apprentice.

1608 or 9.

668.—28 April [circ. 1608 or 9]. *Laurence Stephens*, Harling, to his master, *Sir Robert Knollis*, St. Martin's Lane [London].

The hawks in Stephens' keeping are well, but Guy could keep his no longer. Has found a man at Deepham who kept Sir Robert Gardiner's hawks, and engaged him to mew a pair for 3l., 30s. to be paid down. Stephens could only pay him 6s. earnest, and begs the rest may be sent; also money to buy green geese and ducks for the hawks. These are very necessary ; especially as Stephens' nag is so poor that he cannot kill hawksmeat enough.

The dutch falcon is well.

669.—[May 1608 or 9.] *Lawrence Stephens*, Harling, to his master *Sir Robert Knollis*, St. Martin's Lane, [London].

Has received Sir Robert's letter and 20s. by "my fellow William." "Your hawks are well and mewed to the long feather," expects them to mew them every day. Cannot draw the Tassel ; as Thos. Morrys is very sick. "Your old hawk was taken with the cramp and the quack[?]" and continued in the mew three weeks "and then we threw her out and she is dead."

Sir Guy has been very sick and unable to go to Mr. Jermyn's about Sir Robert's bond. His black haggard is well mewed to the long feather.

1610.

670.—4 April 1610. *William Southwell* to *Framlingham Gawdy*, *Esq.*, and *Thomas Wyth*, gent.

Receipt for 105l. due Southwell. Witness, Thomas Godbould.

[About this time Framlingham Gawdy married Lettice, daughter of guardian, Sir Robert Knollis.]

1611–12.

671.—15 January 1611–2. *Henry Felton* to brother [in-law] *Framlingham Gawdy*, Harling Hall.

Asks for the copy of the annuity of 20 marks to be paid to his wife and sisters during their minority. Also can Gawdy remember the very words which cousin Colbie spoke to Sir Nicholas Bacon concerning the 1,000*l.* which he promised at Fornham [Suffolk], which brother Charles says were related to himself and Gawdy.

672.—2 March 1611–2.   *George Gawdy* to cousin *Framlingham Gawdy*, Harling.

Is sorry he cannot return homeward by Harling, as he had promised ; but is enforced to ride to Eye in Suffolk. Service to Sir Robert Knollis and my lady. George will impart to his father the business Sir Robert spoke to him about ; and when cousin Charles comes to Claxton he shall also speak of it.

Remembrances to Mrs. Gawdy, cousin Charles, and his wife. " My man hath served your privy seal on Mr. Heigham."

[Framlingham's eldest son, William Gawdy, born about 1612.]

1612–3.

673.—6 February 1612–3.   *Thomas Gascoigne*, Maydewell [Northamptonshire ?], to *Sir Robert Knollis*, at his house in St. Martin's Lane.

Writes for payment of his debt. What Knollis writes to him now is to the same effect as what he said at his house in Tothill fields in the late queen's days when Gascoigne first sued on the bond. Knollis spoke then of his extraordinary charges and expectation of recompense from the Court, just as he now writes " of great expences and charges in Triumph, &c., since his Majesty's coming into England as yet without any penny recompense." Understands Knollis' proposition to be that Gascoigne should wait and take his debt in order as it shall be set down. Perceives he is to be " in the last rank." He supposes there is none more ancient than his debt. When he sent his friend Knollis denied owing him anything. Calls to Knollis' remembrance how many suits he has begun and then forborne at his request. He has paid interest on the money himself for 15 years, and " suffered even until my back is broken."

674.—[circ. April 1613 ?]   *Sir Henry Gawdy* certifies that Mr. Colby promised at Thetford, before Henry and Sir John Heigham, to cousin Framlingham Gawdy to procure a release from cousin Charles Gawdy of the monies received by Sir Bassingbourn Gawdy in his time for the lands of Sir Charles Framlingham ; which was the consideration for the settlement then made.

1613.

675.—12 April 1613.   *George Gawdy*, Claxton, to cousin *Framlingham Gawdy*, Harling.

Has spoken to his father [Sir Henry], who never had Sir Charles Framlingham's will, and says it is at Crowshall with the other writings. George is glad that Framlingham and his brother agree to refer the suit to arbitrators, but as there are so many he fears it will be in vain. Mr. Colby spoke of 100*l.* a year to be given besides the land bequeathed to Framlingham. George thinks it would be well to end the suit if Charles gave say 30*l.* or 40*l.* more. George and his brother Anthony will be at Harling " towards London " next Monday.

676.—26 May 1613. *Framlingham Gawdy, of West Harling, to Thomas Morrys, of Bridgham, Yeoman.*

Acknowledgment of Gawdy's owing 10*l.*, to be paid next Michaelmas. Witness, Anthony Rawlyns.

677.—12 December 1613. *Anthony Gawdy* [of Claxton, son of Sir Henry] to cousin *Fram. Gawdy,* Harling.

Anthony's haste to London made him neglect seeing Framlingham. Sends the bond, not to trouble him, but for his satisfaction.

1613–14.

678.—18 January 1613–4. *Anthony Gawdy* [of Claxton, son of Sir Henry Gawdy] to cousin *Framlingham Gawdy,* Harling.

Acknowledges receipt of news that Framlingham's wife has been brought to bed, and will not fail to be with Gawdy as appointed. Is sorry it fell out now as it may prevent Anthony having Framlingham's company to London.

[Birth of Framlingham Gawdy's second son, Framlingham.]

679.—30 January 1613–4. *Thomas Wythe,* Sternfield [Suffolk], to *Framlingham Gawdy,* Harling.

Sir Henry Gawdy has arrested Smith and declared last term for his occupying the lands he did by [leave ?] of Sir James Bacon. Wythe has not seen Mr. George Gawdy this term, and fears unless Framlingham gets a stay that they will go to trial at Suffolk Assizes.

[Between the dates of these letters Framlingham's third son, Bassingbourn, was born.]

1615.

680.—27 March 1615. *Richard Brewster,* of West Harling, yeoman, to *Anthony Rawlyns,* of same place, yeoman.

Bond in penal sum of 60*l.* to secure payment to Rawlyns of 8*l.* 16*s.* on 27 March 1616, at Rawlyns' house in West Harling, in a certain street called Thursmere Street, to the use of Margaret Warren, one of the daughters of William Warren, late of West Harling, dec^d. Witness, Robert Lulpeck, Mary Thaxter, and others.

681.—27 March 1615. *Richard Brewster,* of West Harling, yeoman, to *Anthony Rawlyns,* of same place, yeoman.

Similar bond (mutilated) in penal sum of 10*l.* to secure payment of 5*l.* 6*s.*

682.—3 October 1615. *William Dye,* Governor of House of Correction, Acle, to *Framlingham Gawdy,* one of the County Treasurers for King's Bench and Marshalsea.

Receipt for 3*l.* 6*s.* 8*d.*, one quarter [salary] to Michaelmas.

683.—30 October 1615. *Richard Sutton,* of Starston, yeoman to *Framlingham Gawdy,* of West Harling.

General release. Witness, Charles Gawdy, Anthony Rawlyns.

684.—20 November 1615. *Nicholas Oldom* to *Framlingham Gawdy,* one of the county treasurers.

Receipt for 2*l.* for the "poor prisoners of the King's Bench and Marshalsea," for one year to Michaelmas.

1615-6.

685.—11 March 1615-6. *William Dye* [as in No. 682] to *Framlingham Gawdy.*

Receipt for 3*l.* 6*s.* 8*d.* "my pension for keeping of the house of correction at Acle " to Lady-day.

1616.

686.—10 April 1616. *William Garway* to *Sir Robert Knollis,* at St. Martin's, London.

Reminds Sir Robert that he is indebted to Garway, yet neither answers his letters nor will speak with his man. Can wait no longer.

1617.

687.—20 October 1617. *Martyn Folkes* to *Framlingham Gawdy.*

Receipt for 50*l.* to the use of the Hon. Sir Thomas Jermyn for moneys lent by him to Mr. Philip Gawdy. Enclosed as an exhibit shown to Folkes "on his examination to the 6 interrogatory " before Thos. Reve and Fr. Sandroffe. 11 March 1634.

[Philip Gawdy probably died before this date (he was alive early in 1614) leaving his children slenderly provided for.]

688.—27 October 1617. [Unsigned letter dated near Hereford] to [?] *Sir Robert Knollis.*

Inferred the success of his correspondent's letters in his behalf to Mr. Humfreyes before his departure from London. About 22 October one Richard Caple, of Howecaple, Herefordshire, died, a gentleman of good worth, whose son will be one of his Majesty's wards, being about 12 years of age, and his estate about 200*l.* a year. Leaves it to his correspondent what shall be done.

689.—2 December 1617. *Henry Fortesque, Esq.,* to *Framlingham Gawdy,* of Harling.

Receipt for 40*l.* due by Gawdy, paid by John Sherdekow, gent.

[About this time Framlingham's fourth son, Thomas, was born.]

1618.

690.—15 May 1618. *Jo. Harrsson* [? Harrison], London, to *Sir Robert Knollis,* knight.

"I am sorry you are sick, and sorrier your friend Conway is dead," will help Sir Robert "in suit or means " against Conway's wife and son. If Sir Robert will clear interest and charges on the bond, the 20*l.* may stay on 6 months.

691.—23 June 1618. *Peirce Morgan to Framlingham Gawdy.*

Morgan has given the bearer, Mr. John Sherdeloe, for Gawdy, 7½ yards of the best rich crimson velvet in grain to line his cloak, which comes to 9*l.* 3*s.* 9*d.*, cheaper than he would sell it to any one not being a customer.

1618-9.

692.—13 January 1618-9. *Henry* and *Dorothy Felton to Framlingham Gawdy.*

Release. Henry Felton, of Ipswich, Esq., and Dorothy his wife, one of the daughters of Bassingbourn Gawdy, deceased, to Framlingham Gawdy, of all claims under Sir Bass. Gawdy's will and all other claims except upon a bond given by Framlingham to Dorothy in the penal sum of 400*l.*, conditioned for payment of 200*l.*, and dated 7 October 1612. Witness, John Bulwer, Elizabeth Gawdy.

693.—[Before 20 January 1618-9.] *Francis Delavale to Sir Robert Knollis,* at his house in St. Martin's Lane.

Asks Sir Robert to let his man Arthur keep Delavale'a falcon a few days and to have his opinion of the bird, which he distrusts. Has the ague.

[Sir Robert Knollis buried 20 January 1618-9.]

694.—1 February 1618-9. *Thomas Moore,* St. Martin's Lane [servant to Sir Robert Knollis], to *Framlingham Gawdy,* Harling.

Has been with Lord Wallingford [Sir William Knollis] at his house in Oxfordshire twice since Moore came up to London. On the first occasion acquainted him with my master's death, whereat he was sorrowful yet said little, but in the evening "as he was making unready to prepare to bed," he saw Moore in his withdrawing chamber. Moore said he thought Sir Robert died of an imposthume which broke, caused by the fall he had at Causam [Caversham, Oxfordshire] last summer Also told him that there were about 500*l.* worth of debts, besides the bond to Moore, which he hoped would be paid by Lord Wallingford's means, who answered that he would not meddle with his brother's debts, but Moore might keep the goods. Moore said there were 3 judgments against him, " with that, my lady called him to bed." Next day Moore saw his counsel in London, who advised him to administer, whereupon he returned to Lord Wallingford, and asked his letter to Sir John Bennett, judge of the prerogative Court, which he would not do without Mrs. Gawdy's consent. Asks for such a letter accordingly. All the benefit he will get is in the " underpraising " of the goods as he will have to account for all that they are appraised at. My lord has resigned the mastership of the wards to Sir Lionel Cranfeild without consideration except he continues his ward.

1619.

695.—3 April 1619. *Thomas Moore,* London, to *Framlingham Gawdy,* West Harling; " Larlingford— letter paid."

Has had a world of trouble since he last wrote. Begs a favourable letter to my lord [Wallingford] in regard to Moore's great loss by the death of his brother. Besides what Sir Robert Knollis owed Moore and his six and a half year's service he has paid almost 80*l.* for a grant under the Privy Seal of the goods. These goods the bailiffs of West-minster have seized claiming under a former grant of all outlaw's goods in the liberty. When Mr. Therle was last in town he said Mrs. Gawdy wished for some of her late father's things; she shall have such of those she mentioned as are in the house. Would have waited on Gawdy, but the land-lady and creditors have so tormented him both "in purse and prison" that he has had no time. Will try and come the latter end of next term.

696.—13 April 1619.   *Mary Gawdy*, Wenham [Suffolk], to cousin *Framlingham Gawdy*, Harling.

[The actual writer of this letter, probably Sir Clippesby Gawdy,] writes at request of "your kinswoman Mary Gawdy" who wants 5*l.* interest and 10*l.* "of her stock" [or capital], which latter she hopes to replace some day. She has owed the money since last Midsummer in London for a gown; the mercer and tailor having trusted her for the writer's sake, but will now probably sue her. "She has made very hard shift ever since she come to me, by reason she had neither clothes nor linen to wear but an old loose gown which was not fit for her wearing." Had not the writer been fain to keep her she would have owed 10*l.* more. She takes it very unkindly that her friends, who give her nothing, will not let her "make bold with her own without so many messages."

Love to Gawdy's wife. [See post as to this Mary Gawdy who married Anthony Mingay.]

697.—7 May 1619.   *Thomas Hall*, of Kingston Lacey, Wimborne minster, Dorsetshire, gent., to *Fram. Gawdy* and *Anthony Rawlings*, of West Harling, yeomen.

General release. Witnesses, Bartholomew Hall, George Lane, Jo. Shardelowe.

1620.

[20 July 1620. Henry Felton created a Baronet.]

698.—[? before 1621]. *William Springe* (?) to *Framlingham Gawdy*, Harling.

Asks appointment to meet Gawdy and "my brother Drury" to-morrow to journey together; proposes to meet at Quidenham town. His wife sends service to Mrs. Gawdy.

[Framlingham Gawdy and Sir Thomas Holland, M.P.'s for Thetford.]

1621.

699.—13 April 1621. *Anthony Gawdy* [son of Sir Henry], Hen ham [Suffolk], to cousin *Fram. Gawdy*, Harling.

Is sorry his cousin should have cause of distaste against him and suspect his good dealing. He never heard of Grige's exigent but from Framlingham, and never looked after it, as (altho' he is principal in the bond) it is his brother's debt who will no doubt pay it next term. As to Sir John Taseborough Anthony promised him his money at Beccles' sessions.

Sir John [Rous] and his lady send commendations.

700·—29 June 1621.   *George Davye*, London, to his brother *William Davye* "at Gonville in Caius College, Cambridge," [sic].

If George were sure to meet his sister Duffield he would strain his leisure with his brother to be "there" as he promised. He is not now an apprentice, but in some respect his own man. Sends an 8 gallon runlet of sack for them to remember his health in. Uncle Webb will not pay his creditors a penny unless they all " underwrite for to accept of a noble in the pound, which is as much as his money would extend for to do."

Will try to persuade brother Robert to come down, thinks brother Harry cannot afford the charges. Has heard from brother Ricas [? mutilated] at Rotterdam; troops are making ready for the field. England is the only place in Christendom free from wars. [The Davys were connections of the Duffields.]

701.—24 September 1621.   *Thomas Pecke*, Bury, to [*Anthony*] *Rawlings*, Harling.

Sends "3 yards w^t koste hollou" [?]. Had no time to make out Rawlings' bill, which is some 14*l.* 7*s.* 6*d.* Commendations to Mrs. Rawlings.

1621-2.

702.—5 February 1621-2.   *John Snelling* [Bury, Suffolk], to *Mr.* [*Fram.*] *Gawdy.*

Mr. Longe of Bury reports that the warrant has come for the chosing of Burgesses for the Parliament. Expects Sir Charles [Gawdy ?] will have notified Framlingham and that the latter will certify Sir [Gros ?] of his intention to try his friends in the town. He had then better come and see the Mayor, &c. Snelling will meantime use his influence.

1622.

703.—1 May 1622.   *Edmund Michell* [Tutor, Gonville, and Caius Coll.], Cambridge, to [*Fram. Gawdy*, Harling].

Michell has given Gawdy's kinsman [Anthony Gawdy, son of Philip], the note of all his charges from the time of his admission, and would have sent it sooner, but expected Mr. Davy at Easter. It is 8*l.* 0*s.* 7*d.*, far above the allowance Gawdy's kinsman must look to have; but it includes charges which " ran from the very day of his admission [21 March 1620-1]; add also to these his gown, surplice, chest, " together with the income into his chamber and study," amounting to about 5*l.*

Michell has received 3*l.* and would like the balance speedily. ·

704.—6 May 1622 [? 1621].   *Sir John Tasburgh*, Flixton, [Suffolk], to *Framlingham Gawdy*, Harling.

Thanks Gawdy for his "so just payment of this money " and wishes Sir Robert [Gawdy] had played his part as well.

Has spoken to his cook Lucas "about the child he is accused to have begot," who will attend Gawdy shortly and asks his favor in the cause.

705.—17 October 1622. *Edmund Michell,* Cambridge, to *Framlingham Gawdy,* West Harling.

Has given [Anthony Gawdy] the note of his expenses for the quarter from Midsummer : it is ₁5*l.* 4*s.* and Michell would like the money, having to pay for commons for him and many more. Dr. Gostlin (the Master) and the fellows have "pre-elected" him to the scholarship he wrote about, one of Dr. Branthwayt's late foundation and worth 5*l.* a year, "it is one of the best that belong to our college, our ordinary places be but 40*s.* a year."

There are only four of these scholarships : the man now actually in the place will not vacate it till Michaelmas next, unless Gawdy pleases to buy him out at once, which would only be paying 5*l.* beforehand and will give [Anthony] seniority and other rights.

706.—27 November 1622. *Edmund Michell,* Cambridge, to *Framlingham Gawdy,* West Harling.

Has received the 5*l.* sent up by Mr. Cresswell, and the arrangement with Dr. Munden (Dr. Branthwayt's Scholar) has been carried out. Michell expected his own 5*l.* 4*s.* before now.

707.—5 December 1622 [or ? 1611]. *Nicholas Meade,* the George Inn, Ware [Herts], to *Framlingham Gawdy,* West Harling.

Sends Gawdy's bay mare, her keep at 6*d.* a day comes to 13*s.* The farrier charges 5*s.* and advises her to be let run till March.

708.—26 December 1622. *Edmund Michell,* Cambridge, to *Framlingham Gawdy,* West Harling.

Wonders he has not been paid [Anthony's] charges to Michaelmas and sends new bill to Christmas for 51*s.* 10*d.*, not including his commons, which, as he is now a scholar of the house, he will not have to pay till the half-year is ended, viz., at Lady Day, when his stipend will be allowed him.

1622–3.

709.—[circ. 1622–3]. *Henry Rochford,* to cousin *Framlingham Gawdy,* West Harling.

Sir Francis Lovell is dead, having made a bargain and sale of his chattels to Henry's mother, Lady Hundsdon, for 600*l.*

The bearer is Thomas Fisher, my Lady's servant, who is a stranger in the country. Asks Gawdy to assist him in taking an inventory and disposing of the goods [about which he appears to expect there will be some contest. Sir Francis married Anne, daughter of John Carey, Lord Hunsdon].

710.—5 March 1622–3. *William Stanhope,* Harrogate, to his brother *Framlingham Gawdy,* Harling.

Sends an acquittance from his wife and himself : and if Gawdy does not want to employ the money he would like it paid at Lady Day, when he has an opportunity to send it away into Derbyshire.

1623.

711.—23 April 1623. *Edmund Michell,* Caius Coll., Cambridge, to *Framlingham Gawdy,* West Harling.

Sends note of Anthony's quarter's expenses 5*l.* 12*s.* 9*d.*, his scholarship being set off at the audit against half a year's commons.

He will be wary and careful in his expenses, which he expects next half year to be 33s. or 40s. lower at least.

, " You must provide him suddenly of convenient bedding ; what he has been using is to be " otherwise disposed of."

712.—21 May 1623. *Edmund Michell*, Caius Coll., Cambridge, to *Framlingham Gawdy*, West Harling.

In answer to Gawdy's enquiry as to Mr. Anthony Bartlett, " late student in our house," Michell would refer him to the college letters as to his " sufficiency and good carriage," which Bartlett lately obtained. Personally Michell can say he was esteemed " a very good scholar and sufficient, and therefore when the proctor-ship was last at our college he was appointed public Moderator for the University for the philosophy-disputations held in the public schools by the sophisters," which he performed creditably.

713.—28 May 1623. *Edmund Michell,* Cambridge, to *Framlingham Gawdy*, West Harling.

Michell has received 5l. 12s. Gawdy has not paid the carrier, whose due is 4d. in the £. [Anthony] has lately been sick and was forced to take physic. He was let blood for a pleurisy by the advice of Dr. Wells ; his physic comes to 13s. 5d.
Fears his allowance will not be sufficient.

714.—24 August 1623. *Edmund Michell,* Norwich, to *Fram. Gawdy*, West Harling.

Asks for 47s. 7d. due on last bill to Midsummer : please send it by Peter Aspinall.

715.—1 December 1623. *Edmund Michell*, Cambridge, to *Framlingham Gawdy*, West Harding.

As Gawdy has changed his intention of getting [Anthony] a suit of apparel of Cambridge and means to have it made for him in the country, Michell thinks it " high time to send him down that he might the better be fitted." He has done this the rather because of an opportunity of riding a friend's horse without charge. [Anthony] must be provided with bedding and sheets.

1623–4.

716.—23 January 1623–4. *Anthony Gawdy* [son of Sir Henry] Henham [Suffolk], to cousin *Framlingham Gawdy.*

The weather is so ill it will probably hinder many freeholders attending the election, much more Anthony who would be but a spectator. Sir John Rous desires to be remembered and suggests that Framlingham and some other neighbours and friends associate together during Parliament, and Framlingham may have a lodging in the house where Sir John lies.' They expected to have met Framlingham at honest Anthony Hobart's last week. Sir John is Burgess for Dunwich [Suffolk], so " being both for neighbour towns and neighbours and familiar acquaintance it is fitting you should keep your Randevous together."

H 2

1624.

717.—27 March 1624. *Edmund Michell's* account for *Anthony Gawdy's* expenses for half-year from Christmas 1623.

	£	s.	d.
Paid the carrier for bringing up his suit and other things from Harling.	0	2	0
Paid the tailor for work done - - - -	0	2	8
„ „ barber - - - - -	0	1	0
A pair of new shoes, as also shoes and stockings, soled and mended.	0	7	4
Given him at sundry times for dinners and other necessaries.	0	9	7
Laundress - - - - -	0	2	6
Chamber-rent - - - - - -	0	2	6
Commons and sizings from Michaelmas 1623 to 27 March 1624 (his scholarship deducted and allowed).	1	17	1
Tuition - - - - - -	0	10	0
	£3	14	8

718.—3 May 1624. *John Rendall* to *Mrs. Rawlyns*, West Harling.

Rendall bought 10 combes of barley from Mr. Gawdy and sent for it, but Mr. Rawlyns being from home, he could only get seven. If he may not have the rest, will get it elsewhere.

719.—2 June 1624. *Edmund Michell*, Cambridge, to *Framlingham Gawdy*, West Harling.

Has given [Anthony] his last quarter's bill, 3*l.* 14*s.* 6*d.* If Gawdy sends 5*l.* Michell will not trouble him again till Michaelmas. Anthony's gown is quite worn.

720.—[? 15] July 1624. *Edmund Michell*, Cambridge, to *Framlingham Gawdy*, West Harling.

Acknowledges receipt of 5*l.* by Peter Aspinall, the Norwich carrier. Divers of the College have been sick of small-pox, "it is somewhat dangerous . . . . and very chargeable, physic running in a high rate and good attendance hard to be had." The master will probably send the young scholars into the country.

721.—14 September 1624. *Martin Stuteville*, Dalham [Suffolk], to [? *Framlingham Gawdy*].

The church of Dalham has been some time defaced by the ruins of the steeple. Stuteville and his neighbours took the work in hand, but after dealing with sundry workmen found the charge would be too heavy without outside help. "It hath been a manner amongst us (still used) to make marriage dinners and to invite our friends in the favour of our well deserving servants." Stuteville has never done this, but begs leave "to exchange my suit for a servant into a suit for this service and to request your presence at the Guildhall in Bury on 11 October at dinner for the said purpose."

722.—[Before 18 September 1624]. [*Sir*] *Henry Felton* to brother GAWDY MSS.
Fram. Gawdy.

Sends another acquitance, and apologises for sending the other before the money was due, which was only done to save his horses a journey, having other business near. Remembrances to "my sister and cousin Doll." [Dorothy Gawdy, probably daughter of Philip Gawdy who lived with Framlingham, and is often mentioned in these letters.]

723.—18 September 1624. *Bassingbourn Gawdy* to his brother [*Framlingham Gawdy*].

Announces the death of [Sir] Henry Felton this morning at 4 o'clock. His brother's attendance on Monday at Foxall [near Ipswich, Suffolk], will much comfort the widow. He died without a will.

724.—*Peter Le Neve's* Memoranda concerning the pedigree and family history of the *Feltons.*

20 Edward II.	*Sir John Felton* captured about 120 sail of Normandy. (*See* Hollinghead, Harrison's Edition, p. 337.)
29 Edward III.	*Sir Thos de Felton* held manor of Fynbergh, Suffolk, for life. (*See* fine levied of the inheritance of John de Insula of Rougemont, of Fen-ditton, Camb. Fines. Lib. 5, n. 6.)
30 ,,	He also had letter of protection (dated at Bamboro' [?] 3 Feb.) to go into Gascoigny with the Prince of Wales. This year he was Seneschal of Aquitain.
32	He had an interest in Langford Manor (Norff.).
34	Sir Thos. and Joan his wife mentioned in a fine levied of Old Newton manor; also in 36 [or ? 37] E. 3, of manor of Ikene, both in Suffolk.
37	He was Seneschal of Aquitain under the Black Prince, and was one of the Commissioners to treat of Peace between Edw. III. and Don Pedro of Castile. (*See* Pat. Roll, 37 Edw. III., xi. m. 43 [?]. Rymer's leaques, vol. 6, p. 402, 525.)
40	He was a witness (23 Sept. 1366) to the deed by which Don Pedro granted that Edward III. and his heirs should have the leading of his vanguard against the King of Granada. This year he was elected one of the Knights of the Garter.
41	He and his brother, *Sir William de Felton*, were both in Spain with the Black Prince on the expedition against Henry the Bastard. A few days before the battle of Najara Sir William was killed, and Sir Thomas and Sir Hugh Hastings, of Elsing, were cap-

tured. (*See* Hollingshead, pt. 2, p. 398.)

II. Commissioner to treat with King of Arragon about peace. Rot. franc. 47 E. 3 m. 23. Rymer v. 7, p. 4.

Berard de la Brett (Sir Thomas' prisoner) had licence to go into France for his ransom. (Rot. Franc. 48 E, 3 m. 9 Rymer, vol. 7, p. 48.)

He was still Seneschal of Aquitain (Rot. Franc. 49 E, 3 m. 20, Rymer, v. 7, p. 63), and empowered to treat with the King of Navarre and Earl of Fois.

Thomas de Felton and John de La Sale, Justiciarius Regis Cestriae at plac. Reg. (Pat. Roll, 1 R. 2, pt. 2.)

Sir Hamo de Felton, knight of shire for Norfolk. Second son of John de Felton, son of Robert, who was called son of Paganus de Felton. (Parl. Reg. v. 4, p. 312, 325.) Hamo's will (dat apud Glosthorp) is dated 13 April 1379, and proved 1 Aug. 1379. (Ex. lib. Haydon Reg. Norwich, fo. 132.) He left his body to be buried at the church of the Carmelites at Lynn (in another place Le Neve says " London ").

Sir Thomas de Felton had a grant of 15,000 marks. (Rot. Franc., 3 Ric. 2, m. 23.)

Lieutenant to King Richard in Acquitain. When a prisoner in France had leave to come home for his ransom. King Richard (ut sup) granted him 30,000 francs out of the Earl of St. Paul's ransom towards the moneys due him for his services. Also gave him, Sir William de Bordes, a French prisoner. (*See* Pat. Roll, 4 Ric. 2, p. 1, m. 22, Rot. Franc., 4 Ric. 2, m. 22.) He then went to France, having the King's letters of protection. (Rymer, v. 7, p. 267, 276.)

Sir Thomas and Joan his wife held manor of Fordham (Camb.) in capite. Mary, Sybil, and Alianor were his daughters and co-heirs. (Lib. Rel. penes Rememb., Thesaur., 4 Ric. 2, m. 22.)

Joan, his widow, held manor of Ryburgh, by grant of Sir Oliver Calthorp (I suppose as feoffee).

Richard II. Joan, his widow, mentioned in fine of Barwe (Suff.).

„ She was Lady of Manor of Aslacby (Linc.). Cl. Roll, m. 23.

20 Richard II.	*John Felton*, Esch. Ac.	GAWDY MSS.

20 Richard II.　　*John Felton*, Esch. Ac.　　GAWDY MSS.
Sybilla de Felton ' (daughter of . Sir Thomas) was abbess of Barking, Essex, in 1404. She and her father and mother were all buried near St. Hildithe's shrine in Barking Church.

8 Henry IV.　　Joan (widow of Sir Thomas) held Aslacby for life, remainder to Edmund Stafford, Bishop of Exeter [?], and others for the life of Sybilla de Felton, Abbess of Barking. (Fines, Lincoln-shire.)

10　　Mary (daughter of Sir Hamo de Felton) married John Breton, of Wychingham, who had issue Cecilia, who settled or sold Lycham Nether Hall alias Feltons, to Sir Thos. Erpingham. (4 Claus., 10 Hy. 4, m. 34.)

5 Henry V.　　Sybilla (Abbess, &c.) held manors of Banham, Mareschalls, Greys, and moiety of Beckhall for life. (Fines Norf., H. 5, n. 31.)

9 Henry V.　　*Sir Thomas de Felton*, governor of Gamaches, in France. (Goodwin's H. 5, p. 332.)

30 April 1498.　　Will of *John Felton*, alias Chapman of Kirketon, gen., gave lecacies to marry Felicia and Parnella Felton ; had sons William Felton, clerk, and Robert Felton, (? daughter) Eliz. Sharington. William Felton and Robt. Pisbaron, executors. Proved 15 May 1498. (Ex. lib..Multon Reg. Norwic.)

24 Henry VII.　　*Edmund Felton*, of Sudbury, gen., deed of land in Cavendish, Suff., 23 Feb. (Preston's Collect. 58.)

1 James I.　　*Anthony Felton*, Playford, Suff., made Knight of the Bath.

30 September 1678.　　*Anne* (d. of Sir. Anthony) married first Robert Rich, of Mulbarton, and (2) Thos. Aldrich, of Swardeston, where she was buried 30 Sept. 1678 æt. 80.

[Undated.]　　*Sir Roger de Felton*, witness to deed by . · · Philip de Columbariis, of Batesford . ,. manor, Suff., to John de Grey, Bishop . of Norwich.

The arms of ·the Feltons of Lycham (or Lutcham) are supposed by Sir Henry Spelman (Apology p. 49) to be derived from the Lestranges as holding half a knight's.fee of.them in this place. Le Neve refers to his MSS. of old Rolls, p. 94, for arms of. Sir Robert, Sir John, and Sir William de Felton, of Gloucestershire (which he gives). ·

.·, Le Neve cannot agree with the genealogists.who havei pieced the Norfolk Feltons on to the more ancient .Northumberland family.. · In 39 Ed.¡III. (contemporary with l¹he Norfolk Feltons), there ,was one William, son and heir of Wm..de Felton, knight, who held 60 acres, &c. in Malfen and Natterton [?] in. Northumberland in capite. As to the lately extinct family of Felton of Playford (Suffolk), their original was

John Felton alias Chapman of Codenham [?], Suffolk, and not the Norfolk family, "but they having been allowed, I have no more to say."

725.— 10 October 1624. *Anthony Gawdy* [son of Sir Henry], Henham [Suffolk], to *Framlingham Gawdy*, Harling.

Writes of a pair of mares belonging to Mr. Duke for Mrs. Lettice Gawdy's use. As they are in years their price is but 10*l.* Hears Framlingham has been ill. Anthony has "my Lady Gawdy's horse here at 100 marks price." Remembrances to cousin Doll and ".all my cousins."

726.—11 October 1624. *Frances Gawdy* [wife of Owen Gawdy], Waybread to cousin *Mrs. Dorothy Gawdy*, at Harling Hall.

Sends 3*l.* to pay towards the beasts Mr. Rawlyns bought for her, which she begs to have sent when this messenger returns from Cambridge.

727.—27 October 1624. *Edmund Michell*, Cambridge, to *Framlingham Gawdy*, West Harling.

Sends Anthony's bill from Easter to Michaelmas 5*l.* 10*s.* 8*d.*, deducting balance in hand, there is 4*l.* 5*s.* 4*d.* due Michell.

728.—2 December 1624. [Rev.] *Jo. Rawlyns*, Pagrave [Palgrave], to brother *Anthony Rawlyns*, Harling.

Asks Anthony to pay their mother 40*s.* for him, either through Thomas Cockle or brother West. On Wednesday before St. Thomas, Crane shall come for Kate and bring home Anthony [Rawlyns, jr. ?] for Christmas.

"My brother Wilton Reymond will come too, he desires to see Harling Hall and is without a master. Try and get him into service there or at Ridleswerth.

"I think I shall not have 10 combes oats and I am very loth to send them to Purgatory after my old chapman, unless you will give 5*s.* the combe. Though Sir Fr. would not pay Peter's debt, yet I hope Peter did not lock the gate against him."

729.—8 December 1624. *George Gawdy* to cousin *Framlingham Gawdy*, West Harling.

Writes to complain of Framlingham's conduct about the bond to Mr. Griggs in which they both stand surety for Sir Anthony [Gawdy, George's brother]. George at the last assizes gave Framlingham 37 twenty-two shilling pieces (40*l.* 14*s.*), to be forwarded to town, but owing to his delay in so doing, George was arrested for it in Westminster Hall, to his "great discredit and extraordinary charge." He could not get the money from Mr. Wales even then and had to borrow it of Sir Thomas Jenkinson for a day or two. Wales again failed him and Sir Thomas is much prejudiced. George has now promised him his money at Norwich next Saturday, and hopes Framlingham will send it by bearer. It is a great loss, a little over 20*l.* would have paid the debt which has now cost George 73*l.* or 74*l.* If the arrest is not generally known keep it private. George's wife does not know of it yet.

730.—10 December 1624. *Jo. Dyx,* Arundel House [London], to *Framlingham Gawdy.*

"My Lord" has sold Rushford and hopes Gawdy will not hinder it. Encloses another conveyance of as good or better security as to value, and refers Gawdy to Sir Thomas Holland as to particulars.

731.—15 December 1624.   *Edmund Michell,* Caius Coll., Cambridge, to *Framlingham Gawdy,* West Harling.

Michell has refrained from troubling Gawdy · for the Michaelmas bill, having heard of his sickness. [Anthony Gawdy's] late illness has caused much expense, and, though recovered, Dr. Gostlin recommends change of air and better diet. He is as one raised from the grave, so violent was his sickness.

Encloses bill for physic, diet, firing and keep, 6*l.* 6*s.* 6*d.*, also the apothecaries note of particulars. Anthony may stay down 5 or 6 weeks and on his return will want the fees for commencement, his degree will cost some 12 nobles, besides apparel.

732.—[circ. 15 December 1624].   *George Gawdy* to *Framlingham Gawdy,* Harling.

Expected to have received the money for Sir Thomas Jenkinson at Dickleborough or Norwich and failing same had to borrow it. Hopes Gawdy will have it for him at Christmas when he is coming to stay at Mr. Lovell's house.

733.—15 December [pridie Sapientiœ] 1624.   *Rev. Jo. Rawlyns,* Pagrave, to brother *Anthony Rawlyns.*

Please speak to goodman Stallan who promised to speak to their mother and brother Dan to pay "that little money." Let him do it before Candlemas, or else take up the bond which Rawlyns will otherwise sue Stallan's son on. Proposes their leasing a sheepcourse together. Will sell a score of wheat at 16*s.* to be received at Stanford. Has sent Anthony home for Christmas, return him home about Plough Monday, meantime "help him to write and peruse him sometimes in his book and let him bring with him some new copies. Pray your Kate to send me some more net patterns by her cousin or brother at furthest. Let Kate bring home her samplers. Nan hath sent my sister by Crane 2 geese, one fit to kill extempore, the other to be better fed than taught against New Year." Nan [Jo.'s wife] expects her confinement.

1625.

734.—20 January 1624–5.   *Edmund Michell,* Cambridge, to *Framlingham Gawdy,* West Harling.

Michell has received 5*l.* by Aspinall, leaving 5*l.* 11*s.* 10*d.* due, which he has urgent use for. Anthony Gawdy will also need 5*l.* for his commencement charges, "for his grace now is past in the college."

735.—3 March 1624–5.   *Edmund Michell,* Cambridge, to *Framlingham Gawdy,* West Harling.

Approves of Gawdy's resolution as to Anthony taking his degree, and hopes it will " spur him to his duties."

736.—10 [?] April 1625. *George Gawdy*, Shipdham, to cousin *Framlingham Gawdy*.

George has heard from [his brother] Sir Robert Gawdy that the County day for election of Knights of the shire will be on Easter Monday, for which Sir Robert means to stand. George requests Framlingham's attendance (if his health permit) with his friends and tenants. Does not know of any other candidate; would like to be advised of any that "publishes himself to stand." [Sir Robert was not elected.]

737.—2 May 1625. *Edmund Michell* to *Fram. Gawdy*.

Begs speedy payment of the last bill; understands Gawdy is going presently to London.

738.—20 June 1625. *Thomas Hyrne* to [? *Framlingham Gawdy*, Burgess for Thetford].

Asks a meeting on serious business in Westminster Hall to-morrow morning "about 8 o'clock before we go to Parliament."

739.—6 September 1625. *William Norwich*, Thetford, to his neighbour *Fram. Gawdy*, Harling.

Apologises for not being with him this day, having appointed business that must be dispatched.

740.—30 October 1625. *Edmund Michell*, Caius College, Cambridge, to *Framlingham Gawdy*, West Harling.

Sends by Anthony his half-year's bill, viz., 8*l.* 10*s.* 4*d.* If his commons are not paid within 15 days after the audit, he forfeits his scholarship by the Statutes.

Michell thinks Anthony himself the best messenger, so as to avoid this danger.

741.—31 December 1625. *Sir Thomas Holland*, Quidenham, to *Framlingham Gawdy*.

"Though it be unreasonable to desire your Company out of your own house at Christmas," yet Sir Thomas asks Framlingham and "my cousins" to meet my lord of Sussex and his Countess at dinner on Monday. Lord Hobart died last Thursday night.

742.—31 December 1625. [*Sir*] *Anthony Gawdy*, Henham [Suffolk], to *Framlingham Gawdy*, Harling.

Sir Anthony, Sir Charles [Gawdy], "your brother," and Sir John Rous have appointed a meeting with "honest Anthony Hobart and some few more of honest lads" at Lowestoft to hunt on the 6 February. If Framlingham comes all will come, and if he fails, none will come. Bring Sir John Breane [?] and cousin Moundeford.

1626.

743.—16 January 1625-6. *Edmund Michell*, Cambridge, to *Framlingham Gawdy*, West Harling.

"The time of our Bachelor's commencement is at hand," the examination is at "our Regent house" on 23rd inst. Sends Anthony as the fittest messenger for his fees, 20 nobles, part payable to the college, part to the proctors, &c.

744.—19 June [1626]. *Edmond Moundeford* [son of Sir Edmond], "at Mr. Lee's house in the Strand, the Horse and Sun " to [*Fram. Gawdy*].

" How I found London we beforehand truly judged. What I heard or daily hear I may not write. The project for money is yet unknown . . . . . they say we shall be very gently used and a Parliament at Michaelmas. Digby " [the Earl of Bristol] " is Towered, and they say he shall suddenly be arraigned ; Arundel and his company again confined. There is a proclamation more coming for Papists' coming to Court; no toleration will be permitted. You must provide to go to Wayborn Hoop" [a place on the Norfolk Coast where troops can disembark] "the Council intend to billet 1,200 soldiers more than your own, if your deputy lieutenants may avoid it not. This town is melancholy and empty in computation now you left it. The Great Seal is in some fears." From the weariness of his journey Moundeford will stay in London till he goes to Cambridge.

745—3 August 1626. *Ma*[?] *Holland*, Quidenham, to *Framlingham Gawdy*, Harling.

Asks Gawdy to sound his noble guest Sir John Hare "whether he will be willing to sojourn me, my two daughters, a man and a maid."

746.—8 November 1626. *Nathaniel Dod*, Caius Coll., Cambridge, to [*Framlingham Gawdy*].

Is willing to see to the discharging of Anthony Gawdy's college expenses. 1*l.* 5*s.* of old reckonings is due to Mr. Michell.

1627.

747.—6 April 1627. *Jo. Rawlyns*, Pagrave, to his brother *Anthony Rawlyns*, Harling.

Now their brother is dead, let old Stallan know that Thomas Stallan must pay or be sued. My Lady [Paston] is gone 14 days since. Service to good Mrs. Gawdy, cousin Kate, &c. " My Lady saith you have an unmerciful knife."

748.—16 April 1627. *Edmond Moundeford*, London, to [*Framlingham Gawdy*].

Moundeford intended to send the rumours of the town, but no sooner is anything affirmed, but it is immediately disputed. " Our Lord Admiral swears he will immediately go in person with his fleet, and to this end he wears a great feather ; it is perilous to confess infidelity in it, but I sent my men aboard one of the ships which had command of speedy readiness, but knows not where or when to get victuals. The lord of Warwick is gone." Lord Holland's patent for the sole exchange of plate and bullion much angers the goldsmiths. " The loan goes on coldly in London. Our committed gentry are very well and merry and have the liberty of the adjacent fields. There have been none lately committed, but Gloucestershire and Lincolnshire give a tedious attendance. . . . Mr. Coventry is married to Mrs. Craven at 30,000*l.* The buzzing multitude talks of a Parliament and of a sudden release of the imprisoned. My lord of Dorset hopes a recovery. . . . We long to hear what you resolve upon the letters sent you for aid in shipping. The king wants money and I [want] further news and a better pen." Service to his good cousin and Valentine and doubling their prosperity to the two virgins.

749.—17 April, 1627.   *Nathaniel Dod,* Caius College, Cambridge, to
             Framlingham Gawdy.

Has to acquaint Gawdy with a business concerning his pupil Anthony
which he wishes some other man had' to tell.   " Not long since your
kinsman being in the college buttery at beaver at the permitted hour
between 8 and 9 of the clock at night, the dean came in [and] charged
him to begone; he told him he would, and was presently departing.   The
dean tells him, ' unless Sir Gawdy you had forthwith gone, I should
have set you out ' ; upon that your kinsman, not brooking these speeches,
turns back and pulls on his hat and tells him, seeing he used him so he
would not get out ; upon that the dean strikes him with his fist on the
face.   He being a man and of a spirit could not forbear, but ·repays the
dean with interest.   For this he was convented before the Master and
Fellows and a severe censure passed on him ; he was deprived of his
scholarship and warned within a month's space to provide for himself
elsewhere."   Hopes Gawdy being "his best father " will be more
lenient.   Encloses bill of expenses.   " I make no benefit by your kinsman,
I pray you let me sustain no damage."

750.—22 April 1627.   *Sir John Hare,* Stow[-Bardolph] to *Fram-
             lingham Gawdy.*

Excuses himself for delay in giving an account of the books he
received from Gawdy ; it is the fault of the writer of them.   Did not
forget Gawdy when my Lord Keeper was here and will labour it again.
Is to be at Moundeford this winter [Hare married the daughter of Lord
Keeper Coventry].

751.—2 May 1627.   *Nathaniel Dod,* Cambridge, to *Framlingham
             Gawdy,* West Harling.

Dod has placed Anthony Gawdy in " an honest private house, where
he hath his diet, his chamber and washing for 5 shillings a week."
Dod lived there himself before he was made a fellow.   Payment is
expected weekly, so send his " quarteridge " beforehand by Peter
Aspinal the carrier.

752.—3 May 1627.   *Jo. Rawlyns,* Foulden, to his brother, *Anthony
             Rawlyns* [Harling].

Old Stallan's son is sued and will be outlawed.   He got all the
money from their deceased brother ; it comes to 18*l.*   " My Lady
Paston was again at my house last week," unexpectedly, with most of
her company.

753.—16 May 1627.   *Nathaniel Dod,* Cambridge, to *Framlingham
             Gawdy,* Harling.

P. Aspinal, the Norwich carrier, brought 7*l.* 5*s.,* which was 11 grains
(22 pence) light.   Report goes well of Anthony ; Dod will wait for the
board money.

754.—4 June 1627.   *Edmond Moundeford,* the Horse and Sun,
             Strand, to *Fram. Gawdy,* Harling (to be
             left at Thetford).

Had meant to write ever since his return from Bath.   " The Duke
has been often going and gone, but as yet is at York House ; on Wednesday it is said the King goes with him to Portsmouth."   It is not
known where he is to sail, " he is victualled but for a short time.   Sir
Thomas Glemham goes with him ; sale of honors furnish his Captain's

pay. The rumour of the Spanish Fleet was soon blown over and became a score of Easterlings. The prizes . . . amount by report to 300,000*l.*" Two Frenchmen are sent to the Tower as spies; the refusers of the loan remain in durance and have added to them Sir John Elliott and Mr. Corrington, " they expect daily to be removed into remote shires. Sir Harbottle Grimston and Sir Edmond Hamden, being both sick," are out on bail " for more open air. This project takes a general denial in Ireland."

Postscript.—The letter having " come short of the carriers " Moundeford can add that the King went to Portsmouth without the Duke. Six Londoners are committed for refusing the loan ; the Lords who refused are to be questioned. The King of Sweden is reported to be shot through the body.

755.—8 June 1627.   *Sir John Hare,* Stow, to *Framlingham Gawdy,* Harling.

Returns one of the borrowed books, which he has copied. Will speak with Gawdy at Norwich Assizes touching Banham living.

756.—8 August 1627.   *Nathaniel Dod,* Cambridge, to *Framlingham Gawdy,* Harling.

3*l.* are due for Anthony's first quarter's board. Also for new shoes and mending 4*s.* 8*d.,* the tailor mending his old apparel 2*s.* 4*d.,* barber 1*s.* Often sees Anthony at " our religious exercises " and meets him walking alone in the fields, " which I can no otherwise interpret but with an intent to his studies and meditations." Anthony is out of apparel, although careful. Dod hopes he may re-enter the college after Michaelmas.

757.—14 September 1627.   *Edmond Moundeford,* Feltwell, to *Framlingham Gawdy,* Harling.

Moundeford's cousin [Rowland] Fowler thanks Gawdy for the offered loan of cousin Mall's money, but he is furnished elsewhere.

758.—17 September 1627.   *Edmond Moundeford,* Gawdy Hall, to *Framlingham Gawdy,* Harling.

Has acquainted my Lady Gawdy with the money which Sir Charles pays for cousin Mall, " but before I came her pay-day grew so near as she durst not be unprovided." She will send 10*l.* cash towards the 50*l.* she promised Mall Gawdy.

759.—3 October 1627.   *Rowland Fowler,* Bromhill, to *Framlingham Gawdy,* Harling.

Will be glad to borrow the 100*l.* on his own and his son's bond.

760.—30 October [1627].   *Edmond Moundeford,* Feltwell, to *Framlingham Gawdy,* Harling.

Sir John Hare cannot accompany Gawdy to London before the 20th November.

761.—6 November 1627.   *Same to same.*

Moundeford has employed Gawdy's sergeant, Mr. Whight, whose " civil conversation (being somewhat rare in a soldier) will much advance the service." Will comply with Sir William de Grey's and Gawdy's directions as to Whight's pay and the manner of exercising the companies. Will follow Gawdy to London as fast as possible.

762.—18 November 1627.   *Henry Gawdy* [probably son of Thomas and Ruth Gawdy], Wood Street Counter [London], to his friend *Fram. Gawdy* " at his lodging " [London].

Sends Mr. Perrin " the steward of the house " to acquaint Framlingham with the " miserable durance " he suffers. Perrin has been the means of saving Henry's life and can procure his release for 5*l.*, if Framlingham will give it to " his poor suppliant ". and earn the prayers of a " poor miserable man."

763.—30 November 1627.   *Sir Anthony Gawdy*, Claxton, to *Framlingham Gawdy*, High Sheriff.

Is suitor for his cousin Birche, whose mean suit is so poor it will surely be granted. Framlingham once promised him the under-shrievalty, but withdrew his liking upon a supposed injury.

764.—20 December 1627.   *Thomas Ducket*, Little Glemham [Suffolk], to [*Fram. Gawdy*].

Encloses note of sums " streated by the Schedules out of the Exchequer " on lands in Stanfield [Sternfield, Suff.] formerly of Sir O. Framlingham's. Sir Thomas Glemham orders their collection under a grant from the King to the Dean and Chapter of Ely " within this liberty of St. Ethredling."
Ducket collected money from Sir Charles Gawdy 9 or 10 years since for Debenham lands, who " stopped it presently," a course Gawdy had better follow.

765.—26 December 1627.   *Henry Mingay*, Ameringhall, to *Framlingham Gawdy*, High Sheriff.

Excuses himself for detaining their kinswoman, Mary Gawdy. Proposes a match for her with Anthony Mingay, second brother to Henry's cousin John Mingay of Norwich, and whose estate exceeds that of his elder brother. Anthony would take her with 300*l.*, she has but 200*l.* Lady Gawdy would make up the balance if she were not in debt, and will at any rate give 20*l.* Sir Charles and Framlingham should do the rest. Will keep Mary till they all come to Harling the Monday after Twelfth Sessions, when Henry goes to Bury " with young youths which keep their Christmas with me."

1627-8.

766.—3 January 1627-8.   *Nathaniel Dod* to *Fram. Gawdy*. Receipt for 5*l.* 3*s.* (by hands of P. Aspinal) for Anthony Gawdy's half year's expenses to Michaelmas.

767.—10 January 1627-8.   *Lady Dorothy Felton*, Ipswich, to her brother *Framlingham Gawdy*, Harling.

A commission has come down to Mr. Cornwalles for the sealing of the lease for the wardship of her boy and the bonds to be taken for 200*l.* in instalments of 25*l.* Begs Gawdy to come and seal, bond (as promised) before expiry of Commission. Come to her house at Ipswich and she will notify Cornwalles and cousin Sakford. Postponement would prejudice her.

768.—13 January 1627–8.   *Henry Mingay*, Ameringhall, to *Framlingham Gawdy*, High Sheriff.

This furious weather prevents the proposed visit to Harling, &c. The messenger can go on to Mingay's brother at Cavendish [Suff.]. A postscript (signed by Mary Gawdy) asked that the promised assurances by Sir Charles and Framlingham Gawdy for augmenting her portion may be sent soon, "as the gentleman will be asked in the Church three Sundays before the consummation . . . . . in haste and desperate haste." [A further slip (dated the 14th) explains that a foot-messenger could not be got, so this is sent to be left at Larlingford.]

769.— 14 January 1627–8.   *John Reeve*, Hepworth [Suff.], to *Mr. Rawlyns*, Harling Hall.

Reeve will sue Rawlyn's brother Thomas Muryell, unless the 23*l.* due at Candlemas be then paid.

770.—16 January 1627–8.   *Henry Mingay*, Ameringhall, to *Framlingham Gawdy*, High Sheriff.

Acknowledges receipt of the "loving lines" enclosing the bounty of the family for cousin Mary. Anthony asks that the bonds may be renewed a few days before the ceremony in his name and left with some friend.

771.—12 February 1627–8.   *Jo. Rawlyns*, Pagrave, to brother *Anthony Rawlyns* [Harling].

The oats shall be at Tottington alehouse to meet Anthony's cart on 15th inst. Pray send an apricock tree by bearer, no doubt Anthony can get one from "your gardener" for the asking. If brother Ch[arles] come to Harling to the christening, ask him to take Pagrave on his return.

772.—25 February 1627–8.   *William Stanhope*, Bury [Suffolk], to his brother [in law] *Framlingham Gawdy*, High Sheriff.

Sir Harry Spiller, who was commended by my Lord of Arundel to the town of Thetford, has been already elected Knight of the Shire for Middlesex with Sir Francis Darcy. Gawdy could therefore get Sir Charles Gawdy chosen in his stead without offence to his lordship. Sir Charles takes it unkindly that "you let Sir Dru Drewry prevent you, since you had notice of a parliament before him. Stanhope cannot leave his wife, who is very ill.

773.—25 February 1627–8.   *Sir John Hare*, Moundford, to *Framlingham Gawdy*, High Sheriff.

Hare's going to Castle Acre and his distempered disposition of body will prevent his being at Thetford. Sends 3 of his servants who are charged to serve Gawdy diligently.

774.—25 February 1627–8.   *Thomas Rugge*, Felmingham, to *Framlingham Gawdy*, High Sheriff.

Bayfield tells Rugge he must go to Thetford on 27th inst. to serve on the grand jury. Gawdy is the first Sheriff who ever summoned him. Rugge has to muster his troops of horse before the Lieutenants on the 26th; how can he possibly keep both appointments?

775.—28 February 1627–8. *Sir William de Grey* ———, and *Sir John Hare.*

Whereas Framlingham Gawdy is charged with a lance and a light horse, which is too heavy for one of his " estate, rank, and fashion," he is discharged of his light horse.

776.—3 March 1627–8. *Sir John Rous*, Henham [Suffolk], to [*Framlingham Gawdy*], High Sheriff.

Has received his horse safely and does not mean to sell him. Does not think he will go to London as the bailiffs of Dunwich [Suffolk] have chosen their burgesses, who are Sir Robert Brooke and Mr. Winterton, a servant to the Lady Denby. Complains of the vile way he has been used, and says that out of fourteen burgesses in his country ten are courtiers.

777.—15 March 1627–8. *Jo. Rawlyns*, Swaffham, to brother *Anthony Rawlyns* [Harling.]

The money for the oats and half year's annuity comes to 4*l.* 8*s.* 4*d.* Is very short of his farm and loth to go to the usurer, so begs payment. Wants a shepherd and to have Anthony send home Kate and Dor. or Fr. [sic.] " our maids are so ill with lame fingers that my wife doth miss Kate very much."

778.—15 March 1627–8. *Anthony Mingay*, Norwich, to *Framlingham Gawdy.*

Sir Charles Gawdy is to pay Mingay 104*l.* on 2 5th inst. at Framlingham's house, which Mingay asks may be received for him and sent to Norwich when a safe conveniency offers. Tenders his services at Norwich. " My wife was never in better liking."

779.—22 March 1627–8. *Anthony Mingay*, Norwich, to *Framlingham Gawdy*, High Sheriff, West Harling.

Mr. Charles Rawlings will take the bond, but cannot be at Harling till Wednesday se'nnet.

780.—22 March 1627–8. *Charles Rawlyns*, Norwich, to *Framlingham Gawdy*, High Sheriff.

Purposes to wait on Gawdy on 3rd April; Mr. Bayfield, who must give much light on the business, cannot be from home till then. Sir Robt. Gawdy and his brother George with his wife and (Rawlyns thinks) Lady Gawdy of Gawdy Hall will be with Framlingham on 2nd April. George Gawdy will doubtless give his best directions if consulted with Mr. Wright. This will be soon enough to give Sir Charles his answer.

781.—[March 1627–8.] *Jo. Rawlyns* to brother *Anthony Rawlyns*, Harling.

The shepherd is wanted at Midsummer. Sends two cheeses for sister Susan and sister Mary. " For tobacco, I was better satisfied before I had your book than now. I think it a needless thing to take too much, and his tedious discourse about it as needless." Bids Kate look to her cloak bag.

1628.

782.—26 March 1628. *Sir John Hare*, Ely House, London, to *Framlingham Gawdy*, High Sheriff (leave at Brandon, to be sent to the Bell at Thetford).

Sends list of names of members of both houses. The parliament as yet produces nothing, except the privilege of the subject by raising loans by commission, and imprisoning those who refuse to lend. This has "taken up the whole dispute. hitherto." Hopes a happy success for this parliament ; a day of fasting and prayer has been appointed ; viz., 21 April for the country, which was the day " appointed for the view of our Norfolk horses at Leicester," which is postponed two months.

783.—9 April 1628. *Nathaniel Dod*, Caius College, to *Framlingham Gawdy*.

Incloses particulars of Anthony Gawdy's expenses, 7l. 11s. for six months to Lady-day.

784.—12 April 1628.—*Jo. Rawlyns*, Swaffham, to brother *Anthony Rawlyns*, Harling.

Desires to be certain of Anthony's shepherd, or shall re-engage his old man.

785.—14 April 1628. *Ed. Moundeford*, London [M.P. for Thetford]. to *Framlingham Gawdy*, High Sheriff (to be. delivered to Mr. Ludkin living at the Green Dragon in Bishopsgate.

Writes to renew his " caractur " in Gawdy's memory.
" That we have voted 5 subsidies to the King is no news. He this morning sent a messenger to the Lords to require justice of them for words spoken by my Lord of Suffolk (that Selden was fit to be hanged ; swearing that he had rased a record thereby to advance the subject's liberty beyond the due limits). This Lord has absolutely denied them, but the proof is so strong as it will be the worse to his disgrace. He went this afternoon with our Speaker to the King to deliver him a petition for the billetted soldiers, what answer we shall have is not known. Our house proceeds not with that calm it did, God grant a good end." The Lord Keeper, Sir George Goring, Sir Edward Howard, and the Chancellor of the Exchequer are called this day to the Lords as Barons. " We expect hourly from the Lords their resolution to our declaration concerning our personal liberty and property of Goods."

786.—25 April [1628]. *Ed. Moundeford*, London, to *Framlingham Gawdy*, High Sheriff.

" Such is the stay of all our business in the upper house that I can write you no proceedings. We have daily feared our period, such is the division of the lords whose numerous new company have the power of voice. The lord-keeper hath not obtained the best opinion in this, for which I am sorry ; there be some ten lords made this parliament. We hear it goes ill with our neighbours Rochelle, Stade, and Denmark. Lord Carlisle is gone on Tuesday last ambassador for Savoy and Venice.

u   19269.

787.—5 May 1628. *Edmond Moundeford*, London, to *Framling ham Gawdy*, High Sheriff.

So sorry to be a messenger of sad tidings, " the fears of an ill ending of this parliament are now grown so great as they command belief ; our last day is appointed to-morrow seven-night, and we are as far from ending our work as when we began. We have been this day with the king from whom we have inhibition of proceeding in our intended way, and are laid up, to rely upon his promises; what the sequel will be I know not, I wish we could so be rid of our money as not to be worse than we were before. Our lords increase and multiply. . . . . 'tis reported that Sir Baptist Hicks shall be Viscount Campbell." Can write no more, being both sick and sad.

788.—7 May 1628. *Sir John Hare*, Ely House, London, to *Framlingham Gawdy*, High Sheriff.

My Lord Keeper is engaged for the living to Mr. Weston for one Mr. Taffey, but has promised to remember Gawdy's kinsman with a living near Harling at the first opportunity. Remembrances to "your noble neighbour Drue and his lady."

789.—8 May 1628. *Henry Gawdy*, Wood Street Counter [London], to his friend *John Howard, Esq.*, at his chambers in Barnard's Inn.

Begs Howard to be a means for his enlargement from " this loathsome endurance ;" seven pounds will do it, and Henry will in future " avoid the like imprisonment and enter a new course in this world." Asks his friends' help in his suit against Wm. Pully, clerk, " to right these infinite wrongs I have suffered by his means." Requests Howard to perfect and engross the draft of his bill [against Pully] and to move Mr. George Gawdy therewith.

790.—21 May 1628. *Nath. Dod*, Cambridge, to *Framlingham Gawdy*.

Receipt for 7*l.* 11*s.* (Anthony's expenses).

791.—4 July 1628. *Henry Gawdy*, Wood St. Compter, to his chief friend *Framlingham Gawdy*, West Harling, High Sheriff.

Confesses the extravagance of his former life, from which he has awaked as from a trance, and (after some amazement) collected his senses and brought himself within the limits of his own centre. He now so excruciates himself that he needs no other corrector. "I did not waste all my means vaguely but lent a good part of it in hope of gain to one that betrayed me to prison, where I have been about 2 years in distresses unspeakable." Mr. George Gawdy has helped him largely with counsel and money, so has Mr. John Howard. 8*l.* will set him free. Begs 40*s.* towards it so that he may the sooner finish his suit at law.

792.—14 July 1628. *Ed. Moundeford*, Gawdy Hall, to *Framling.ham Gawdy*, High Sheriff.

At Lady Gawdy's request he craves to be excused from attending at Harling, but on Saturday he and Dick Sutton will be ready to wait on Gawdy on his way to Norwich.

793.—9 August 1628. *Chr. Rous*, Gawdy Hall, to *Framlingham* GAWDY MSS. *Gawdy*, Harling.

Understood from Mr. Moundeford yesterday at Bungay [Suffolk] that Framlingham and Sir Charles were to be at Henham on Monday. Rous' father will be away on the Commission between himself and uncle Duke, so meeting had better be postponed till Friday.

794.— August 1628. *William Stanhope*, Bury, to brother-in-law *Framlingham Gawdy*, Harling.

Sister Felton has written to ask the Stanhopes to put off their journey to Harling till she and her husband can meet them, they being detained for the wedding of Felton's mother. Stanhope is · not sure if he and his wife will not go first to Redgrave.

795.—1 September 1628. *Edward Moore*, Thetford, to *Framlingham Gawdy*, High Sheriff.

Has forborne collecting the subsidy assessed in Thetford before Gawdy and himself, being ignorant how the collector's bonds are taken. Asks Gawdy's directions.

796.—5 October 1628. *Sir John Rous* to [*Fram. Gawdy*] High Sheriff.

Is sorry to hear of the visitation in [Gawdy's] house, the sickness is much dispersed round Henham. Sir John hears Kenninghall is to be disparked, and would like to get a brace of red deer or one hind, but has no acquaintance with Mr. Holland.

1628–1629.

797.—10 January 1628-9. *Edmond Moundeford*, Gawdy Hall, to *Framlingham Gawdy*, Harling.

Gawdy's servant Sutton was correct. Moundeford intends to sell his Yorkshire nag. Meant him for Hyde Park market, his paces are good; he is very sure of foot; Gawdy may have him for 16*l.*

798.—15 January 1628-9. *Edmond Moundeford*, Gawdy Hall, to *Framlingham Gawdy*, Harling.

Has received the 16*l.* and given Gawdy's servant the nag. Is about ' to start for London.

1629. ‧ ·

799.— 27 March 1629. *Edmund Eade* [Gonville and Caius College, - Cambridge] to ˙*Framlingham Gawdy*, Harling.

Eade has now " voided the study in that chamber " which he showed Gawdy when last at Cambridge, so the latter's son [William; who matriculated 30 April] can come whenever Gawdy pleases.

800.—30 March 1629. *Anthony Mingay*, Norwich, to *Framlingham Gawdy*, West Harling.

Anthony is in treaty, with the help of cousin Smith, for the purchase of Winfarthing park from the Commissioners. Smith advises him to take a lease for 60 years at 13 years' purchase, rather than buy the fee at 16 years. It is valued at 156*l.* per ann., out of which my Lord· to reserve to himself 6*l.* a year and Mingay to take the 150*l.* for 60 years. For this they ask 1,950*l.* Anthony would ˙give what Thomas Holl

I 2

(since deceased) would have had it for and is told by the latter's son-in-law, Mr. Gilliard, that Holl would have had the fee. The park contains about 300 acres. Will do nothing without Gawdy's advice, and proposes coming to consult him, when they can go over the park together. If Gawdy meets Mr. Holland or Mr. Havers and the captain, they can tell him about it ; two of these are Commissioners for my Lord.

801.—15 April 1629.   *Edmund Eade*, Caius College, Cambridge, to *Framlingham Gawdy*, Harling.

Gawdy need not fear that the moistness of the walls of his son's chamber will endanger his health ; the materials are such that "they are free from any dampish quality."

He will solely enjoy the bedstead with curtains, but bedding must be sent, unless it is bought at Cambridge, where it is sold "at none of the cheapest rates." Gawdy already knows about buying the stuff for his son's gown.

The chamber is fitted, and, being new trimmed, is "better than many of our upper chambers," yet if the young gentleman wishes to remove, Eade will endeavour to get him a chamber "a pair of stairs high."

802.—6 July 1629.   *Anthony Mingay*, Norwich, to *Framlingham Gawdy*, Harling.

Please inspect a gelding offered by Mr. Bedingfield for Mrs. Mingay's use. Gawdy will probably be troubled once more this summer "with a bold guest." Remembrances to sister Dorothy.

803.—14 July 1629.   *Edmund Eade*, Cambridge, to *Framlingham Gawdy*, Harling Hall.

Sends William Gawdy's first quarter's expense account. He is "very hopeful" and like to prove an ornament to his country. Dr. Batchcroft "our master" will bestow a middle chamber upon him at the first opportunity.

804.—4 November 1629.   *Anthony Mingay*, Norwich, to *Framlingham Gawdy*, Harling.

According to Gawdy's directions, Mingay spoke with cousin Smith of Ameringhall, Mr. Holl, and the Bishop, who all pretended much love unto him in this business. Robert Warner (one of Gawdy's retainers) could tell if the rent of 200*l.* a year will hold.

805.—10 November 1629.   *John Davy*, senr., of Kenninghall, Yeoman, and *John Davy*, junr., of same place, Clerk, to *John Godbold*, of Dennington, Suffolk, Yeoman.

Bond in penal sum of 200 marks. Recites that Frances, wife of John Davy the elder, has agreed to release to A. Mingay her estate in 3 enclosures called Heaseldicke in Kenninghall, containing 30 acres. Bond to be void if obligors convey the Wood-close in Kenninghall to secure her 16*l.* a year for life. Witness, Drue Drury, Fram. Gawdy.

1629–1630.

806.—10 January 1629–30.   *Chr. Rous*, Henham [Suffolk], to *Framlingham Gawdy*, Harling.

Rous' father did not send for the hind because Sir John Wentworth sent word that my Lord would not part with the red deer. Sir John also disappointed him of the toils. The "bringing of them" is also so dangerous that they got a tame hind near by; moreover Rous has moved all his deer into another park where he fears the stags will never keep, so that he shall have to kill them.

807.—15 January 1629–30. *Anthony Mingay*, Norwich, to *Framlingham Gawdy*, Harling.

Sends Gawdy's brother's writing [a bond apparently]; please return it. Has not heard of Mr. James. Believes Sir Owen Smyth will hardly part with the property. Has written to "my brother Osborne" and believes he will assist Gawdy, unless Sir Lionel affects it.

808.—15 January 1629–30. *Edmond Moundeford*, Ketteringham, to *Fram. Gawdy*, West Harling.

Moundeford spoke to Mr. Boswell as arranged, and he will take care of cousin Charles [Gawdy] till they return from London. Boswell does not wish Charles to keep a man at Cambridge yet. Neither Mr. Barrye nor the escheators know of any writ, yet it may be with the feodary. They must take gold ; Moundeford cannot provide it, but his coach can carry it. It were well to use means for young Smith's resignation ; cousin Anthony Gawdy shall then be settled in a religious calling and reap the benefit of Sir Charles' intentions ; "it were pity so great an honour should be lost to Sir Charles."

809.—24 January [1629–30 or later]. *Edmond Moundeford*, to *Framlingham Gawdy*, Harling.

Asks for a meeting at the Christopher, Thetford, to discuss Charles' affairs.

810.—13 March 1629–30. *Edmond Moundeford*, Gawdy Hall, to *Framlingham Gawdy*, at Mr. Ball's, on the Angel Hill.

Does not know of anything done at Court to cause such a confident rumour. Hopes Gawdy will speak with Sir Thomas Jermyn.

1630.

811.—8 April 1630. *John Wyth*, Sternfield [Suffolk], to *Framlingham Gawdy*, West Harling.

A confused letter, stating that Wyth has given up possession to Almone upon the terms that he (Wyth) was in to Newson.

Would have done this at first, but expected "some better comfort" for his house and grounds. Wyth was told that Almunde had a covenant from Gawdy (but Gissop would not let him see it). Sends his lease as promised : he has let the Harrow pitell to goodman Stannard, and asks this may be confirmed. Sends by Stannard 9l. rent received from Lawrence Newson.

812.—13 April [1630 ?]. *Edmond Moundeford*, Feltwell, to [*Framlingham Gawdy*].

The weather not agreeing with his feverish disposition, disables him from going to Harling. Will wait on Gawdy to London if next week will do.

813.—30 April 1630. *Henry Fortescue* to *Fram. Gawdy*.

Receipt by Fortescue (out of 50l. paid Gawdy to use of Lettice Gawdy) for 50s. due to his sister Hambling for Lettice's diet and lodging.

814.—2 June 1630. *William Hewes* to *Bacon Gawdy*, both of Bury St. Edmunds, gentlemen.

General release. Witness, Andrew Cocksedge, Thos. Knyvet, Anthony Rawlyns.

815.—11 November 1630. *Rev. Hurd* [?] *Smyth*, of Aspinall, Suffolk, to *Sir E. Moundeford and Framlingham Gawdy.*

Bond in penal sum of 40*l.* to secure performance by Smyth of deed of even date. Witness, Isabie [?] Bradly, Anthony Rawlyns, Robert Garlins, [?] Thomas Catton.

816.—[Before December 1630]. *Sir John Holland*, Blickling, to *Fram. Gawdy*, West Harling. ·

Sir John has not changed his opinion of Davy's deserts, but is obliged by the importunity of Gawdy and others to sign Davy's certificate, although it is going point blank against his "prœ-proceeding." Service to Mrs. Gawdy.

817.—[Before December 1630]. *Anne Hill* to her cousin *Mrs. Lettice Gawdy*, West Harling.

Anne cannot visit Lettice, being *enceinte*. She, her husband, and sister Kate send remembrances.

[Between the dates of these letters, Framlingham Gawdy's wife, Lettice, died.]

1630–1.

818.—1 March 1630–1. *Anthony Mingay*, Norwich, to *Framlingham Gawdy*, West Harling.

Sends consolations on Gawdy's great and unspeakable loss. Brother-in-law Sayer's 100*l.* can stand over till April. Mingay (of Ameringhall) is ill.

819.—March [1630–1.] *John Mingay* to *Fram Gawdy.*
Receipt for 11*l.* 10*s.* 8*d.* for physic delivered for Gawdy's wife after the direction of Dr. Rant.

820.—14 March 1630–1. *Anthony Mingay*, Norwich, to *Framlingham Gawdy*, West Harling.

Sir John Holland offers for sale a perpetual rent charge of 100*l.* per ann. out of my Lord of Arundel's lands. Being lately in Robert Edgar's company (who now boards with neighbour Alderman Anguish) it was offered to Mingay. Sir Thomas Holland is said to have given 1500*l.* for it, when money went at 10 per cent :— 1700*l.* is now asked. Asks Gawdy's advice. Doubts if he shall meddle with Eccles, for cousin John Smith of Ameringhall says Sir Owen Smith has sold land in Suffolk and will not be forward to sell this.

821.—17 April 1630–1. *Edward Pecke's* Bill of Parcels.
13 yards of ell-broad tufted stitched Taffety at 5*s.* 8*d.* = 3*l.* 3*s.* 8*d.* Receipt for same (dated 15 Dec. 1631) from Mr. Sothell attached.

1631.

822.—18 April 1631.   *Sir Anthony Gawdy*, Claxton, to *Framlingham Gawdy*, Harling.

Will pay what he borrowed within three weeks.

823.—21 April 1631.   *Sir Edmond Moundeford*, Feltwell, to *Framlingham Gawdy*, Harling.

They must sell timber at Crowshall ; Moundeford cannot go, but will confirm whatever Gawdy does.

824.—29 April 1631.   *Same* (Thetford) to *same*.

Moundeford has arranged to borrow 100*l*. of Thomas, his cousin Butler's man, and 150*l*. of Mr. Bacon, of Hockham. Appoints meeting at Butler's at Thetford to execute bond.

825.—3 May 1631.   *George Gawdy*, Inner Temple, to *Fram. Gawdy*, West Harling, (to be left at the Bell, Thetford).

Edward Games was surety for Sir Charles Vaughan in 50*l*. and is sued to outlawry, Vaughan having died. John Games does not know what became of Vaughan's estate, but there is a jointure of 700*l*. or so.

Cousin Charles and Framlingham's sons were well at Cambridge. The Earl of Castlehaven has been tried by his peers and found guilty of 3 indictments, but is reprieved.

826.—1 June 1631.   *George Gawdy*, Claxton, to *Fram. Gawdy*, West Harling.

Hears from Mr. Wales that Framlingham is going to Sternfield [Suff.]. George will come to Harling.

827.—3 June 1631.   *Sir Edmond Moundeford*, Feltwell, to *Framlingham Gawdy*.

His young pupil Charles Gawdy wants money for his Ipswich voyage. Moundeford has to pay 27*l*. for Charles' clothes in London. Bacon Gawdy has borrowed part of his quarter beforehand.   Charles' expense in diet and horsemeat since he came will take 100*l*. and other small sums coming in.

828.—23 June 1631.   *Samuel Moody*, Bury [Suffolk], to [*Framlingham Gawdy*].

Asks payment of 11*l*. due Wm. Sutton and assigned to Moody.

829.—[Circ.   June   1631.]   *Sir Anthony Gawdy* to *Fram. Gawdy*.

Sends old John, " a current paymaster," who can explain the honesty of Sir Anthony's intentions.

830.—25 June 1631.   *Anthony Mingay*, Norwich, to *Framlingham Gawdy*, West Harling.

Please bring the mare Mingay thought of buying. The chamber and bed shall be provided by assize-time. Mingay is forbidden fast riding or walking. Mary Mingay advises Gawdy to come and dwell "in Norreg."

831.—28 July 1631. *John Wyth,* Sternfield, Suffolk, to *Framling-ham Gawdy,* of Harling.

General acquittance. Witness Anthony Barthelett.

832.—29 August 1631. *Sir Edmond Moundeford,* Feltwell, to [*Framlingham Gawdy*].

Will meet Gawdy on the Commission at any time and wishes to see him as to those who viewed Crowshall timber for the King. Mr. Boswell has sent a bill which Charles should have paid ; " these expenses are very extravagant, but his tailor says he spends not anything in a disorderly manner."

833.—23 September 1631. *Peter Murforde,* Norwich, to *Capt. Fram. Gawdy,* Harling.'

Lord Maltravers and the other deputy Lieutenants desire Gawdy to fill up the enclosed warrant with the names of 2 or 3 of his most frequent and obstinate defaulters, and have it executed. Let the names be sent to Murforde's house near St. Andrew's Church to be entered in the list. Gawdy is to attend there and return his muster on 4th October.

834.—[Circ. Oct. 1631 ?] *Sir Edmond Moundeford,* Feltwell, to *Framlingham Gawdy.*

Is going to London and will take whatever Gawdy has received to furnish him with, together with Moundeford's 40*l.* Will bring Charles back from town ; has promised him Sir Robert Mordant's lanner if he will come. " My wife takes heavily the loss of her loving father."

835.—1 November 1631. *Same,* London, to *same.*

Moundeford is but new come to town. Mr. Godbold advises that Moundeford's uncle George Brook and John Chabenor should be examined, lest John Gardiner fall from his offer. Moundeford got 200*l.* of his sister Gawdy, Mr. Canham failing him. Money is not to be got in London, but she will lend 300*l.* more. Charles' expenses will exceed 50*l.* besides the tailor's bill for his winter riding suit, near 20*l.* ; he has begun to ride a great horse. News was brought by one John Castle from the King of Sweden of his overthrow of Tilly. Castle was knighted.

836.—8 November 1631. *Same,* the Flower de Luce, Princes St., London, to *F. Gawdy,* Harling.

Has been with the Council of the navy, who wish him to set a price for the [Crowshall] timber by the load, which Moundeford is loth to do. Tilly is reported dead, his army not able to reinforce. " The King of Sweden is stept to the side of the Upper Palatinate ; the King of Bohemia is going to him. 24,000 men by our King and the States are parlied of for him. Our brave city soldier the noble Lord Craven is coming for England to be employed in the service. He was going to the King of Sweden, but had a command to the contrary. Our Princess is christened and named Maria,—this haste to avoid mother's importunity. All our noise is of Sir William Noy, our Attorney-General, and his stoical comportment ; many fear he will prove too honest and too stout. There is a general reformation in hand for Court and country. Offices shall be given by desert. The King's Pensioners and Guard shall be moulded to the pattern of Queen Elizabeth's. Sheriff-wicks shall be given as rewards of honour to the best deserving of the counties.

Keeping of ordinaries prohibited point-blank. Our Judges are chidden for their rigid demeanour to the gentry in their circuits . . . . . . Mr. Pettus is Sheriff for Norfolk, &c."

837.—14 November 1631. *Same*, London, to *same*.

Has been thrice at Tower Street with Sir William Russell. Navy Commissioners will not decide about timber till their agent, Apsley, returns. Charles' charge is great.

838.—17 December 1631. *George Gawdy*, Claxton, to *Framlingham Gawdy*, W. Harling.

Mr. High Sheriff tells George that a "bold fellow, suited in red," going by the name of Warner from Loddon, had used Framlingham's name to commend himself to the Sheriff's service. Encloses the letter Warner delivered.

1631–32.

839.—9 February 1631-2. *Sir Edmond Moundeford*, Thetford, to *Framlingam Gawdy* [London].

Is glad Gawdy likes London no better. Sir Drew Drurie is the same. Charles is at Ketteringham, his tutor will not go with him to France; he squanders money fast. The match between "my sister Gawdy" and Mr. Stutevile is broken off. Mr. Bac. Bacon and Mr. Web of Breccles had their houses robbed last week. Service to Sir Thomas Barington. Will Prat will bring him a letter. Has received Gawdy's second letter, "I hope your news was made under a tailor's table, which some call Hell."

840.—16 February 1631-2. *Same to same* [London.]

John Gardiner has given the two bonds to Charles Gawdy "referring himself to his mercy," and has been promised 40*l.* Charles, Sir Thomas, and Nat are with Moundeford; "that knot of wags" send service to Gawdy. Has not heard of Sir Robert Bell, and will be well advised before venturing on the bargain for Deeping Fen.

841.—[? February 1631-2.] *Same to same* [London].

Moundeford is making up their great book of account with Rawlyn's help. No money from Crowsnall, and Charles has spent Moundeford almost as low as himself; he must be kept while at Newmarket with as little money as possible. As Mr. Boswell cannot accompany Charles to France, Moundeford suggested one Mr. Nash of the same house, of whom Boswell approved, but Nash is away from home. "We are much frighted with the strict keeping of Lent, I pray let me hear what is thought of it." Service to Sir Thoˢ Barrington. The King is expected at Cambridge on Tuesday week. "The letter-boy sends; I can write no more."

842.—23 February 1631-32. *Anthony Mingay*, Norwich, to *Fram. Gawdy*, at his chamber at Mr. Ward's, a barber, over against the King's Head Tavern, Fleet Street, London.

Mingay has sent to Orford [Suffolk] for his [brother Osborne's] answer to Gawdy's letter. Thanks for London news, Norwich is.

GAWDY MSS. barren of any by reason of the remoteness of the Court. Dr. Sherwood (sometime of Ipswich) gives Mingay hopes of a cure without going to London. Robert Edgar sends remembrances. [Postscript by Mary Mingay. " Your Coucke roben (sic. ? Cook Robin) is dead."]

843.—29 February 1631–32. *Thomas Osborne*, Oreford [Suffolk], to *Anthony Mingay*, Norwich.

Sends family news, " Sue is qualmish " in her stomach at meal times, &c, Will do his best for Gawdy [apparently in the matter of an election]; secrecy is impossible, let him make himself personally known in our town. " I heard of Lady Denny's death, and withal that George Gardiner, comforting the grieved knight, told him that he had rather bury two wives than flay one bullock." Remembrances to Mr. Skottow. " Dr. Sherwood is mine ancient acquaintance and . . an able physician, if not somewhat covetous." Would like the advowson of some small living without conditions.

844.—[? February 1631–32. *Sir Edmond Moundeford*, Thetford, to *Framlingham Gawdy*, London.

" Charles is at Newmarket, very busy in his observations of the garb of the place ; much amazed with the glory of the Court. I hope before his return out of France his judgement will be ripened and his appetite glutted with viewing others' braveries; then will the pleasure of his own possessions appear." Does not think Charles either plays or drinks. Moundeford will see as to the travelling tutor. Sir Robert Heath wins much love. Sends service to Sir Robert Bell. " Our King and Queen like Newmarket very well and will add to the building. The Earl of Holland hath had a fall from his horse hunting," which defers the King's return, as the Earl has to entertain the Court homewards.

845.—24 March 1631–2. *Anthony Mingay*, Norwich, to *Fram. Gawdy*, West Harling Hall.

Encloses brother Osborne's letter [No. 843]. John Sayer wants his interest, and Mary Mingay would like a pound of violet cakes.

· 1632.

846.—5 April [1632 ?]. *Sir Edmond Moundeford*, Gawdy Hall, to *Framlingham Gawdy*.

Sends an offering of " right ripon " [? spurs] ; will be satisfied if they please Gawdy but one day's riding.

847.—13 April 1632. *Anthony Mingay*, Norwich, to *Fram. Gawdy*, West Harling Hall.

Mingay intends going to London by carrier's coach to get cured. Who was the doctor who cured Sir Robert Knollis ?

848.—2 May [1632 ?]. *Sir Edmond Moundeford*, Thetford, to *Framlingham Gawdy*.

Has received 30*l.* They must raise money, so as not to have to spend their own. The money in Mr. Gorboll's and Mr. Barrie's hands will not be paid this term.

849.—11 June 1632. *Anthony Rawlyns* to his master *Fram. ·Gawdy*, sign of the Bear, Fleet Street.

Rawlyns sent Perry and Pett to Sternfield, but no money came. Gawdy's coach and horses are yet unsold. Sends 12*l.* borrowed of his son, Foyster.

. 850.—30 June, ·1632.· *Andrew Ruddock*, Debenham [Suffolk], to *Framlingham Gawdy*, Harling.

John Walton has asked Ruddock and John Flower to sign a release that his father may be discharged from prison. They refused, without Gawdy's written instructions. The enclosed document was produced. and Walton said his father had given bond in 100*l.* never to trouble those he had in the Star Chamber in time past. Walton also said Gawdy gave him a letter which he had lost ; "we think he lies."

851.—[June 1632 or later.] Fragment of *Account, Fram. Gawdy.*

Imprimis to Mr. Davys - - -	£2 0 0	
Lent Cousin George Gawdy - -	2 0 0	
To Mr. Wales for Sir Walter Vaughan -	1 16 0	
Paid Nelson the tailor in full, 20 May 1632.	1 10 0	
Item, more to Mr. Davys - -	2 0 0	
Lent my cousin Charles Gawdy [in all]	8 4 0 ·	
To Mr. Davys in full pay - -	4 1 2	

852.—3 July [1632 ?] *Sir Edmond Moundeford*, Feltwell, to *Framlingham Gawdy.*

Is sorry cousin Anthony Gawdy's modesty "hath so slacked his pace to this advancement." But for the promise of his lost friend, Sir Dru. Drury to Mr. Draper, Anthony should have Moundeford's interest. Charles' trunk has come, he left a suit of clothes at Cambridge to wear there at the commencement.

853.—10 July 1632. *Same to same.*

Cousin Charles is still in town. Does not know what to do with him, and if he returns, will send him to Gawdy.

854.—19 August 1632. *Samuel Moody*, Bury, to *Anthony Rawlyns.*

The claim on Gawdy which William Sutton assigned to Moody [*see ante,* 555]·may be paid to Sutton. Has very good frieze. Does not Gawdy want a winter suit of Spanish or Broad-cloth ?

855.—8 September 1632. *William Napper* [married a daughter of Philip Gawdy] to his cousin *Framlingham Gawdy.*

Acknowledges Gawdy's favours, but must assert his wife's rights. Harry Fortescue reproved him for his dulness in not doing this three years ago, seeing his father-in-law left such large sums of money and his wife has had nothing. Her sisters know that Mr. Philip borrowed 10*l.* of her shortly before his death. Napper has taken out administration and claims an account, having such confidence in Gawdy's "virtues, religion, and sweetness of disposition," that they are willing to take him for their judge. [See post Nos. 876, 877, 917, and 1038.]

856.—22 September 1632. *Sir Edmond Moundeford*, Feltwell, to *Framlingham Gawdy.*

Anthony Mingay has spoken to him of Gawdy's desire that they should contract their scattered debts (*re* Charles Gawdy) into one man's hand. He will provide money, 300*l.* of which may be paid sister Gawdy. The Crowshall tenants and the timber-masters are at variance.

857.—26 September 1632. *Anthony Mingay,* Norwich, to *Framling-*
ham Gawdy, West Harling.

Moundeford has sent word by Will. Heveningham for Mingay to pay
widow Gawdy 300*l.* How is the other 200*l.* to be disposed? Ward
of Bixley is dead.

858.—29 September [1632]. *Same* to *same.*

Mingay will arrange money as required. Wonders why brother
Napper should molest him.

859.—7 October 1632. *Sir Edmond Moundeford,* Feltwell, to
Framlingham Gawdy.

Mingay will advance 500*l.* If Sayer does not require 100*l.* of this,
Moundeford would like to keep 200*l.* himself to the shortening of cousin
Charles' debt.

860.—7 October 1632. *Samuel Snelling,* Thetford, to *Framlingham*
Gawdy, Harling.

Robert Leving's boy reported on his way to London that Mr. Charles
[Framlingham's son, *not* Charles of Crowshall] lay very sick and full of
the small-pox at Harling. Thinks it a great pity they [*i.e.,* Framlingham's sons] were taken away from him ; the change of air may alter
the constitution of the body, and so Mr. Rawlyn's was told when he
fetched them.

The pox has been in town five months : out of nineteen "housen"
visited but one has died. On Wednesday " our schoolmaster" Smith
gave up his place and the meeting at the town-hall elected Mr. Ward
of Bury. The town sent to him on Thursday, and on Friday he came
and promised to dedicate himself to the school, and if he does not do
his best for the children "he must and is to leave it." He begins to
teach on Monday, for most of the town and country children are back
again. Snelling and Mr. Butler told Mr. Ward what Gawdy had said
about sending his three children, and Ward hoped that at least he
should have his Bury scholar [Thomas Gawdy] who had been with him
nearly two years. Sir William de Grey's son comes with Mr. Ward.

861.—22 October 1632. *Anthony Mingay,* Norwich, to *Framling-*
ham Gawdy, West Harling Hall.

Widow Gawdy will receive 300*l.* and Sayer 100*l.* on the 24th. 100*l.*
shall be kept at Gawdy's disposal. Notice will be needed when the
balance of the 1,000*l.* is wanted.

862.—30 October 1632. *Sir Edmond Moundeford,* Feltwell, to
Framlingham Gawdy.

Sir Nathaniel Rich sends caution as to Charles Gawdy's proceeding
with mistress Cook, for reasons he would communicate in London,
whither Moundeford goes at once. Charles has privily fetched his
trunk, &c.

863.—6 November [1632]. *Sir E. Moundeford,* at Will Prat's,
Drury Lane, near the Horseshoe
Tavern, to *Fram. Gawdy.*

Has received a very strange ‘peremptory letter from Charles [Gawdy
of Crowshall]. If Moundeford and Gawdy had not withheld their consent the marriage would have been concluded ; the parties asked 1,000*l.*
per annum jointure and Charles had agreed to 800*l.* " God deliver

GAWDY MSS.

him well out of their hands !" Will Heveningham has sent up 100*l.* from Mingay, Moundeford wants another 100*l.* and 300*l.* at Twelfth Sessions. Sir John Hobart and Sir William Somers are sheriffs.

864.—10 November 1632. *Anthony Mingay*, Norwich, to *Framlingham Gawdy*, West Harling Hall.

On Thursday Sir E. Moundeford sent his brother Mr. William Heveningham for another 100*l.* "to be made him up to London." The balance shall be ready at Twelfth Sessions.

865.—13 November 1632. *Sir Edmond Moundeford*, Drury Lane, to *Framlingham Gawdy*, Harling.

Moundeford saw Lady Cooke, who seems to slight the match, because in fact she is too sure of it. They will give no portion, and believe the Crowshall timber will furnish a large sum. One Mr. Palmer was fined 1,000*l.* in the Star Chamber for living in London contrary to the Proclamation, yet he was a bachelor, and his mansion house in the country lately burnt. The constables search out in every ward the names of persons lodging in town last vacation.

866.—20 November 1632. *Same to same.*

Charles' mistress has left town, but he loves London as well for Lady Coke's sake. Moundeford has almost persuaded him not to marry till he is of age. The King of Sweden is said by the Pal[ace?] walkers to have fought Wallenstein and taken 125 colours. Monsieur has fled again from his brother, and is at Brussels.

867.—3 December 1632. *Anthony Mingay*, Norwich, to *Fram. Gawdy*, West Harling Hall.

Repeats substance of his last letters sent by Mr. James and goodman Cobbet. Anthony has paid 600*l.* by Sir Edmond's order "besides my own 100*l.* for Doll." Expects them at Norwich at Twelfth Sessions to give him security.

868.—7 December [1632]. *Sir Edmond Moundeford*, Feltwell, to *Framlingham Gawdy*.

Can give no good account of Charles Gawdy's doings at London. W. Prat wrote that Charles would come down with Sir D. Drury for a short time. "I never see an ungrateful man prosper. . . . I hope it is but this madding fit which thus makes him forget himself."

869.—12 December 1632. *Anthony Mingay*, Norwich, to *Fram. Gawdy*, West Harling Hall.

Advises Gawdy of a rich widow. Two months ago one Mr. Gooch (said to have been once a Chief Constable) died at Hove near Dereham. Some say she is worth 8000*l.*, some 10,000*l.*, and some 12,000*l.* She is a comely woman between 40 and 50. Philip Calthorp lives in her house and has much influence. Cousin [Henry] Mingay died on the 5th [buried at St. Stephen's, Norwich].

870.—[Circ. 13 December 1632.] *Mary Mingay* to *Fram. Gawdy*.

Sends a token of her love ; "eat them for my sake." Would like a collar of brawn as they can get none in Norwich. Please send the 30*s.* she laid out on cousin Sayer's clothing ; her husband would not pay it.

(Postscript by Anthony that he only heard of the Dereham widow on Friday.)

871.—13 December 1632.   *Sir Edmond Moundeford*, Feltwell, to *Fram. Gawdy*, Harling.

Begs Gawdy to visit Feltwell that they may speak to Charles, who came last night and goes toward London on Monday.

872.—26 December 1632.   *Anthony Mingay*, Norwich, to *Fram. Gawdy*, West Harling Hall.

Cousin Sayer will ride in search of reports about the widow. Do not defer it beyond Twelfth Sessions.

1632–3.

873.—4 January 1632–3.   *Edmund Hevisett*, Thetford, to [*Framlingham Gawdy*].

Samuel Snelling bids him write, not wishing to be "offensive" in writing himself. One of Samuel's brother's children has lately recovered of small-pox (not above seven or eight to be seen); he is lodged by himself with his keeper and no one else comes into his room. Robert and Samuel Snelling have spoken with Mr. Miles, who will receive Gawdy's children till their house is safe. The pox has not been in any house where any free-school scholar lodges, and Mr. Ward has special care of his scholars.

874.—9 January 1632–3.   *Sir Edmond Moundeford and Fram. Gawdy* to *Anthony Mingay*, of Norwich, Gentleman.

Bond to secure 1,080*l.* to be paid at John Mingay's mansion house, Norwich, on 10 January 1633–4. Witness, Edward Sayer, Francis Gawdy, Will Cady. Endorsed with receipt for 80*l.*, a year's interest.

875.—28 January 1632–3.   *Sir Edmond Moundeford*, Feltwell, to *Framlingham Gawdy*.

Moundeford can give no account of "your mad-cap lover . . . . . . he is bitten by a gad-fly, as I suppose. Did I suppose I was infectious to any in affecting London, I would purge and fast to starve the contagious humour."

876.—20 March 1632–3.   *William Napper*, Drury Lane, to kinsman *Framlingham Gawdy*, Little Harling. [*See* ante No. 855.]

Napper writes again to suggest how unpleasant a law-suit would be to a man of Gawdy's retirement and sweetness of disposition. Is [ironically] sorry that his wife had behaved herself so ill as to be an unfit object of Gawdy's charity like her brothers and sisters. "As she was here cast upon a shelf and must of necessity perish had it not been my fortune to have lighted upon her." Hints that he can prove that large sums came to Framlingham's hands.

877.—   *Same to Same* [undated].

Napper admits he does not love law-suits, but goes over the same ground as in two former letters, not understanding why his wife should not be treated like others of her family, who have tasted liberally of the favour of Gawdy and Sir Charles. Is sure Philip Gawdy made no will, in spite of Framlingham's bold swearing witness.

Framlingham told Napper at Harling that he durst not administer for fear of debts, yet there were none. Sister Dorothy wrote to Lettice that 50*l.* was reserved for her (Dorothy). Why should not father Gawdy do as much for Napper's wife ?

878.—23 March 1632–3.   *Sir Edmond Moundeford*, Feltwell, to *Framlingham Gawdy*, Harling.

Charles Gawdy insists on going to the expense of sending such "mean stuff" to London ; what is to be done ?

1633.

879.—1 April 1633.   *Anthony Mingay*, Norwich, to *Fram. Gawdy.* West Harling Hall.

Dr. Sherwood has taken Mingay in hand [for an affection of the bladder] and purged him already of 10*l.* ; another 20*l.* to be paid at Christmas if the cure is completed. The doctor cannot travel without a coach, but will send his apothecary, Mr. Dey, to see Gawdy. Thanks for pigeons.

880.—25 April 1633.   *Same to same.*

The treatment does Mingay little benefit, he will send word next time Mr. Dey visits Gawdy. Remembrances to brother Anthony [Gawdy] for whose wife Mingay has a "commodity" against her lying down. Hopes also to see him at Norwich as a Suffolk preacher. Cousin Sayer's wife "is of the Mendingham" [sic]. John Legat's mother is lately dead.

881.—14 May 1633.   *Same to same.*

After six weeks' trial Mingay has given up Dr. Sherwood, who made him worse than he was. Has now got Dr. Martin to ride to Cromer to try "a water thereabout," and if that proves no good Mingay will go to Tunbridge. Is persuaded he can only be cured by taking waters. Is glad Gawdy can travel to London. Has not met cousin Cresner.

882.—25 June 1633.   *Sir Edmond Moundeford*, Drury Lane, to *Framlingham Gawdy.*

Cousin Charles complains of unpunctual payments, but paid or not there is little chance of getting him out of London. "Our King is well, his entertainment great at his journey ; the Lord of Newcastle most famous for his meat, the Bishop of York most famous for his drink."

883.—[Circ. July 1633.]   *Same*, Feltwell, to *same.*

On his arrival at London Moundeford found Cousin Charles troubled for want of his money, so he borrowed 30*l.* for him which Mr. Wright was unable to repay. Charles spent this at once, "and lived without money till my coming down," when he bemoaning his folly and promising to return to the country in a fortnight, persuaded Moundeford to borrow 20*l.* more for him, and promise him as much more when he came to Feltwell.

Charles' humours are strangely changed ; he would prove a hopeful kinsman but for this unfortunate match. "There is a noise of letters coming for a benevolence for the Palatinate." The King is returning. Moundeford goes to Ketteringham on his way home.

[Memorandum endorsed.] Disbursed in London first 40*l.* To Charles in full of Midsummer quarter 30*l.*; in part of Michaelmas do. 20*l.* Promised him 20*l.*, in all 110*l.*

884.—13 July 1633. *Same to same.*

Moundeford acknowledges 20*l.* Cousin Charles feared lest Lady Cooke should take exception and break off the match. Cannot meet Gawdy at Stow, as his mother-in-law Lady Moundeford is stopping with them.

885.—[After 13 July 1633.] *Ruth Gawdy to kinsman Fram. Gawdy,* West Harling.

Ruth's husband [Thomas] died on 13 July after an irksome and miserable life, leaving her in extreme penury, unable to pay for his burial or his debts. Begs help to stop the mouths of these insatiable creditors [gives a list of small debts for meat, malt, groceries, &c., coming to 14*l.* 11*s.* 4*d.*].

886.—[Circ. July 1633.]   *Sir Edmond Moundeford,* Feltwell, to *Fram. Gawdy,* Harling.

Thanks Gawdy for the company of "my honest young kinsman" [Gawdy's son]. Crowshall tenants fail in paying, sheep will not sell, &c. Mr. Bacon has lent 100*l.*; Gawdy sent him 20*l.* so he will have 10*l.* in hand over the 110*l.* he sent a note of.

887.—20 July 1633. *William Spring to Framlingham Gawdy,* Harling.

Commends the bearer to Gawdy's help. She entertained in her house a woman going by the name of Mrs. Browne, and besides incurring great charge and expense the woman (who is now at Snitterton) stole a wrought waistcoat, stuff petticoat, and muff. Mrs. Browne "crept into our corner" and lived as one whom country-folk call a Good Woman, a pretended physician, Chirurgeon and Blesser. In truth she is "a very Cheater, and with a fair tongue and cunning deludes simple people" till she is discovered, when she flies (as she pretends) for religion's sake; although her seldom or never going to church is all the religion Spring can hear that she professes! A wilful froward knave wished to hang an honest woman as a witch, and accused her before Spring, saying Mrs. Browne and such folk as Cawdell, &c. had told him his wife was bewitched. Spring's attention being thus called to her, he sent to the officers to enquire her mode of living, whereupon she removed, carrying with her what she could get. If Gawdy interests himself, the bearer may get her things easier than by the regular course of law.

888.—9 August 1633. *Sir Edmond Moundeford and Fram. Gawdy,* to *Anthony Mingay.*

Bond to secure 104*l.* payable the 20th of next February. Witness, Osbert Pratt, Jo. Waie, Francis Gawdy.

889.—24 August 1633. *Anthony Mingay,* Norwich, to *Fram. Gawdy,* West Harling Hall.

Sues for the re-acceptance by Gawdy of his "old servant our cousin Francis Gawdy," who cannot subsist if thrown off. Although "the present fact" be "a very great and heinous one," yet Francis promises amendment. Sister Dorothy has arrived, but not Anthony. Mingay has paid Lady Moundeford her 100*l.*

. 890.—17 September 1633. *Sir Edmond Moundeford,* Feltwell, to *Framlingham Gawdy,* Harling.

Moundeford will visit Harling on his way to Crowshall. Gawdy should meet Charles at Feltwell to welcome him and make merry over a buck from Kenninghall. Stanton is appointed, please notify Bradley.

891.—3 October 1633. *William Dennye,* Rudd [? Rudham], to *Fram. Gawdy,* West Harling.

Dennye's master left the evidences which are to defend him against Mr. Godderde's claim at his chamber in London. They shall be brought, and Gawdy may inspect them for Godderde's satisfaction.

892.—19 November 1633. *Anthony Mingay,* Norwich, to *Fram. Gawdy,* West Harling Hall.

Sends "a small remembrance of our child's Banckett." Mingay's wife does reasonably well. Dorothy will give details.

893.—6 December 1633. *Alexander Fisher* [or ? *Foister*] to neighbor *Fram. Gawdy,* Harling Hall.

Begs Gawdy to help a poor widow, who harbored a man and his wife in her back room ; they have neglected to pay the small rent and have violently misused her.

894.—9 December 1633. *Sir Edmond Moundeford,* Feltwell, to *Framlingham Gawdy.*

The new Sheriff dines at the Cross Keys, Thetford, on Saturday, and would like Gawdy's experience as to the present to the Judge, &c.

1633–34.

895.—[26 January 1633–34.] *Anthony Mingay,* Norwich, to *Fram. Gawdy,* West Harling Hall.

(Sunday) Widow Barnes, Justice Sheaphard's daughter, whose first husband was one Sponer, died lately at Kirby near Norwich. Sponer's only daughter is just 21, and has 240*l.* per annum. Her uncle, young Richard Sheapard, is going to London to sell the land. How would this do for Gawdy's son William ? The day Gawdy left Norwich Mingay's cousin, Dr. Stubs, visited him and spoke of the proposed marriage of John Cook's daughter with young Doyly. Stubs seriously protested that had he known about Framlingham's son when my Lord Cooke was last in Norfolk he would have made a match. Sir Edward Cooke will not stand out for money to match with a good family. Will write to Gawdy at London ; please send news about the masque.

896.—31 January 1633–34. *Same* to *same,* London, care of Mr. William Prat, tailor, Drury Lane.

It is reported at Norwich that the Lord Mayor hath set forth a proclamation taxing the price of all manner of fowl. Asks news of the masque and of cousin Charles's business.

897.—7 February 1633–34. *Same* to *same* (London).

Mingay sends thanks for London news and for the book, which was "a most sumptuous thing," and has done him knight's service already, having been borrowed by Sir Charles and others. Anthony perceives "it will go hard with your new buildings . . . if it be suffered they will make the body too big for the head."

Send word what is done to Prynne, and whether Charles [Gawdy] is married or not. Will the decree for taverns and inns hold strictly or not? My Lord Mayor's rate for all kind of fowl is very reasonable. Mingay wishes the " reformation of the citizens might be amended ; the excess is infinite, only a limitation and difference to be had amongst them, whereas now they be worn vulgarly and too mechanically."

The City of Norwich was remiss in writing to the Judges to urge the holding of the Assizes here, and so lost it.

Has made enquiries about Mr. Taylor, and will advise Gawdy. Love to cousin William [Framlingham's son].

898.—28 February 1633-4.   *Same to same*, West Harling Hall.

Mingay has parleyed again with Sir Owen Smyth about purchasing Eccles, and believes Sir Charles will also consent ; Gawdy might mention it at the Sessions. Respects to Cousin Charles [Gawdy].

899.—6 March 1633-4.   *Ruth Gawdy*, Mendham, to *Framlingham Gawdy*, Harling.

Ruth and her maid having promised to pay her late husband's debts. are now threatened with arrest. She is so hardly dealt with by her son Henry that Sir Thomas Gawdy will not help her. Henry has sold her land over her head and got the assurances of her jointure, which he intends to sue when she is dead. No one has helped her except the 10s. Framlingham sent (of which the bearer would have 3s.). Mr. Wales told her that Framlingham would let her have 3l.

900.—11 March 1633-4.   *Sir Edmond Moundeford*, Feltwell, to *Framlingham Gawdy*.

Has heard from Mr. Rallings that Gawdy will pass within 8 miles of Crowshall. It were well for him to send to Bradly to bring him the monies now due, as it is reported that the Crowshall tenants begin to dispute " whether they shall pay us any more money or no."

Moundeford is perfecting the account.

1634.

901.—25 March 1634.   *Sir Edmond Moundeford* and *Framlingham Gawdy to Dorothea Moundeford*.

Bond to Dorothea Moundeford, of the City of London (daughter of the late Sir Edmond Moundeford of Norfolk), to secure 216l. payable on 26 March 1635 at the Inner Temple Hall.

Witness, Abigail Moundeford, Jo. Waie, Francis Gawdy.

902.—25 March 1634.   *Sir Edmond Moundeford* and *Framlingham Gawdy* to *Arthur Heveningham*, of Hock-wold, Esq.

Bond to secure 216l. payable on the 26th March 1635 at the Mansion house of William Heveningham in Hockwold. (Same witnesses as 901.)

903.—11 April 1634.   *Anthony Mingay*, Norwich, to *Framlingham Gawdy*, West Harling Hall.

Cannot send full satisfaction about Mr. Taylor ; he has sent to enquire of Cousin John Legate his neighbour. A book is come forth confirming the death of Wallenstein, there are like to be great wars in Germany. Three years' fine at a rack rent is required for all new buildings in and about London ever since the second year of King

James. Another strict proclamation out against selling tobacco except GAWDY MSS.
by license.

904.—23.April 1634. *Anthony Mingay*, Norwich, to *Framlingham Gawdy*, West Harling Hall.

The minister of Hardingham reports well of Mr. Taylor, his revenue is 400*l*. a year and he lives in good credit and fashion and his daughter is well brought up. Mingay will gladly deal with Cousin Charles [Gawdy] but will not touch a lease, or give more than 16 years purchase, he would "willingly leave something certain for the thing my wife." There is good store of land for sale, Mr. Anthony Hobart and Mr. Sheapard are both about selling. All goes not well with our Alderman Anguish.

905.—16 May 1634. *Same to same* at Mr. Ward's house, a barber over against the King's Head Tavern, Fleet St., London.

Mingay has a great desire to try "those waters" [apparently some recommended by Gawdy], and has written enquiring of a gentleman that has taken them. "Your sessions" will be on 1st July. Mingay's wife and sister Utting will not come to Gawdy till after our guild, which is at Midsummer, and not then if Mingay goes to the waters. Is grieved at Charles [Gawdy's] inconsiderate courses. Remembrances to Gawdy's two sons; good Mr. Ead also sends his service, "who nobly performed his task in this place with much credit."

906.—10 June 1634. *Same* to *same*, West Harling Hall.

Sessions are fixed for 8th, when they hope Gawdy will come in. No news, "we are as barren as your heath ground with you." Remains "in Canterbury haste," &c.

907.—21 June 1634. *Sir Edmond Moundeford*, Feltwell, to *Framlingham Gawdy*, Harling.

Charles Gawdy still desires to "come of" Thos. Gilder's money. Moundeford does not know what he will do with Lady Cooke, who "yet works upon his affection and is as unreasonable as ever . . . I hear that last [week ?] they were all to pieces, but are become whole again, which is worse." Every Thursday there is very good company meet at Moundeford, "but a very bad bowling green." Sir Ed. Cooke is dead : one died of the plague in London last week. The Attorney [General, Noy,] is very ill in his head. Mr. Sheriff will be at Hockwold next week.

908.—28 June 1634. *Anthony Mingay*, Norwich, to *Framlingham Gawdy*, West Harling Hall.

Thanks Gawdy for furthering Mingay's Cousin John in his match making. Cousin John was there himself and saw the old folks, the maiden herself being from home ; " he perceives by her parents that the maid is much in league with another young man . . . which they would willingly break off. Desires sister Dorothy to ride over and see them about it. Old Peck died at London and is brought to Norwich. Four witches are sent out of Lancashire to the King to be re-examined and " divers new ones more apprehended." A gentleman of Gray's Inn is in question for coining gold.

909.—15 July 1634. *Sir Edmond Moundeford*, Feltwell, to *Framlingham Gawdy*, Harling.

Last night Michael Dirgo [?] came from his master [Charles Gawdy] to attend the Sheriff and saith his master was married last Thursday ; " he is in a dangerous way to spoil his fortune for ever." Moundeford has received a letter from Gawdy Hall that Mr. Cotten, of Starston, captain of foot company, is dead, and that Sir Thomas Gawdy [brother of Sir Henry Gawdy] desires the office. Let Framlingham send to Sir Robert Kemp and Sir Anthony Drury and Moundeford will speak about it to Sir John Hare and Sir Hamon Strange, although he thinks the post scarce worth acceptance. It may, however, be a means to bring him to Gawdy Hall and " a more stayed brain."

Hopes soon to meet Framlingham at Norwich.

910.—27 July 1634. *John Smythe*, Ameringhall, to *Framlingham Gawdy*, Harling.

Has signed warrant for Commission between Constable and his kinsman to sit at New Buckenham on 20th instant ; but the poor man does not think he can draw his witnesses thither.

911.—1 August 1634. *Rev. Edmund Draper*, Riddlesworth, to *Framlingham Gawdy*, Harling Hall.

Certifies that the bearer his neighbour Francis Deane has lived " both civilly abroad and quietly at home," ever since he came to the town. The late Mr. Gabin trusted him and employed him as chief about his husbandry.

912.—5 September 1634. *Anthony Mingay*, Norwich, to *Framlingham Gawdy*, West Harling Hall.

Hearing from Ralph Sayer that Gawdy is to speak with Sir E. Moundford, Mingay begs to remind him of the 8l. interest : he is short of money, having laid out 40l. in repairs of other folks' houses.

913.—10 September [1634?]. *Sir Edmond Moundeford*, Feltwell, to *Framlingham Gawdy*, Harling.

Congratulates Gawdy on the happy recovery of himself and his company from this visitation. Recommends the bearer (son of a woman who has a farm of Sir Edmond's at Lynford, and who has been left " well to live ") for Gawdy's service.

Remembrances to Cousin Bell.

914.—29 October 1634. *Same to same.*

Sends a man for the vacant groom's place. William Peke will not take his money before his time, but Moundeford does not think Charles will suffer much through having the 1,000l. so ready. The commission at Creake does not hold.

915.—31 October 1634. *Anthony Mingay*, Norwich, to *Framlingham Gawdy*, West Harling Hall.

Acknowledges receipt by "Cousin Rawlyns your servant" of 109l. 10s. and 12d. for light gold, and gave up Gawdy's bond. Although he has no use for money, he will accommodate him by receiving the 200l. more which Gawdy wishes to pay.

The Friars is to be sold and Mingay will have his money. Some think it is for Lord Maltravers who has often viewed it since he came to Norwich. Our three Aldermen are at liberty again. " My brother

Rogers " brings word that 63 died of the pox in London last week. The
widow Lancaster has "lately fallen " at Bury ; leaves it to Gawdy to
enquire how she is left.

916.—[Before November 1634?]. *Mary Mingay* [Norwich] to
Framlingham Gawdy [Har-
ling].

Is glad to hear of Gawdy's recovery "and pretty good health."
Anthony Mingay would not presume to come to Gawdy on behalf of
" my brother and your poor beadsman " [Anthony Gawdy], but believed
that Gawdy out of his noble and sweet disposition would give Anthony
the living of Harling before any other.

"O, I am in a grievous caks [sic. : ? case], little Sue is weaned."
Thanks for late entertainment.

917.—1 November 1634. *Sir Gilbert Dethick* [Garter King at
Arms] to *Framlingham Gawdy.*

Sir Gilbert has received Gawdy's letter and the two enclosed notes.
It was only the double diligence of Napper [*see* No. 855] and his
proctor that gave occasion for the second, as if Gawdy could not have
been found by the first. Dettrick will appear for him. The prosecution
of Gawdy's appeal has been "dallied " too long.

Dettrick prepared a petition and a commission for the Lord Keeper
to sign appointing some extraordinary judges, but Mr. Wales (to whom
he delivered it) neglected it wholly.

Is now resolved by Mr. De Talbott's advice to proceed the ordinary
way, and will get out a commission himself, for which purpose he has
received 5*l.* from Gawdy's son.

918.—1 November 1634. *Anthony Mingay,* Norwich, to *Framlingham Gawdy,* West Harling Hall.

Mingay sent to the carriers, but there was no letter for Gawdy. To
make sure he then went himself and "perused them all over," and can
say positively there was none. Hopes to ease Gawdy of his 200*l.* in
December.

Lord Maltravers is going to London.

919.—14 November 1634. *Same to same.*

Asks word sent by cousin Edward Sayer if he may count on the
200*l.* by the 5th or 6th December.

" My brother [Anthony Gawdy] hath dispatched his business with
the Bishop and hath gotten institution " [of Garboldisham]. Hopes he
may keep quiet possession. Perceived the Bishop had some doubts
" because of the long pedigree." . Mingay let him have 5*l.* to defray all
charges. Has also advised him to " frame the contents of a letter to Sir
William Whittipoll," and Mingay will try and get Sir Charles Le Gros
to subscribe it on his behalf. Would rejoice if "the Belly-piece and the
Benefice should both be provided of together."

920.—27 November 1634. *Same to same.*

Squire Paston brought news from London (and told it to Sir Charles
Le Gros in passing) that on Tuesday se'nn'et Sir William Whittipole
fought Sir Arthur Gorge at Calais. The French post brought news to
my Lord Treasurer that one of them was slain and the other dangerously hurt. Sir Charles is persuaded that it is Sir William who sur-
vives. This would make it worse for Anthony [Gawdy] as all would
come to the King's hands; let him be careful to keep possession ; at

GAWDY MSS. present there is no word of Mr. Guest at any, of the offices. "We are terribly frighted here with news of setting forth a ship of 800 tons;" two of the aldermen are gone up to the Council about it.. Would rather *not* have that 200*l.* just now, so much money is coming in at Twelfth Session.

921.—29 November 1634. *Same to same.*

Since his last letter (sent by Goodman Goodson) Mr. Guest has been with the Bishop with a presentation (said to be from Sir Anthony Wingfield), and the party who told Mingay this says that Guest has "good cards to show for it." He went away without institution, the Bishop willing him to see Mr. Gawdy and try to compound. Let Anthony look about him. Our Chancellor's letters say the duel has not yet been fought, but both are in durance at Calais; this is not believed. Mr. Digby, who came along with Gawdy at the last assizes, is said to have killed one of Sir John Suckling's men. Sends a present of a small rundlet of sack by old Kempe.

922.—1 December 1634. *Sir Edmond Moundeford*, Feltwell, to *Framlingham Gawdy*, Harling.

Encloses letter from cousin Charles who *has* got the 1,000*l.* ready and will lose by it, and nobody will take their money before Ladyday. Makes suggestions as to appointing a meeting with Framlingham and Charles at Bury.

923.—[Circ. 1 December 1634.] *William Withers* to son-[in-law ?] [*Anthony Gawdy*].

[A short note endorsed on No. 921, to the effect that there need be no fear unless Mr. Geste procures institution, but advising enquiry if Garboldisham ever belonged to Lord Latimer, "for there lies a mystery in that."]

924.—5 December 1634. *Rev. Anthony Gawdy*, Aspinall, to his brother [? *Anthony Mingay*].

[A rather supercilious letter, also endorsed on No. 921, making light of Mr. Guest's claim.] "My father-[in-law ?] is fully persuaded Mr. Gest will come unto him, because they are of great acquaintance. Let him keep his good cards till Christmas and then play them. Gest is much laughed at. Let Joseph lay in some wood, and Anthony will pay him when he comes next week.

925.—8 December [1634?]. *Sir Edmond Moundeford*, Moundford, to [?].

Will meet at his brother Gawdy's house to-morrow at dinner.

926.—19 December 1634. *Anthony Mingay*, Norwich, to *Framlingham Gawdy*, West Harling Hall.

Has received the 200*l.* by the hands of Cousin Rawlyns. The High Sheriffs of Norfolk and Cambridgeshire, the Mayor of Lynn, the Bailiff of Yarmouth, the Burgess of Wisbeach, and 10 Chief Constables for the other maritime towns, are all in the City. They have agreed on a gross sum of 5,500*l.* to be levied as follows, Norwich 1,625*l.*, Lynn 1,250*l.*, Yarmouth 1,000*l.*, Wisbeach 400*l.*, "and the rest" [1,225*l.*] "of the maritime towns if they can get it. My counsel is to you in the Country not as yet to laugh right out at us . . . I doubt you in the Country in the end will not go free; and so much for the ship business, which will spoil all our Christmas pies." Edward Lewknor is dangerously ill of the pox. Sir William Whittipoll's great friend Carr Coventry wrote to Mr. Edgar last week ("our this week's letters are not yet come ") that they had been at Calais and St. Omer, and cannot tell if they have fought. It was thought [Sir Arthur] Gorge was coming over again for England. Is sorry to hear sister Doll should be so indiscreet in her old age as to neglect so great a fortune.

1634–5.

927.—6 January 1634–5. *Sir Edmond Moundeford*, Feltwell, to *Framlingham Gawdy*, Harling.

Supposes Gawdy will be at Norwich Sessions. Moundeford will meet him at Thetford Sessions on Saturday and bring 80*l.* for Cousin Mingay, lest Croweshall fail.

928.—9 January 1634–5. *Arthur Heveningham*, Hockwold, to *Charles Gawdy.*

Desires payment, as his sisters importune him for " their parts." If Gawdy cannot be furnished, Heveningham will help him to it, if Sir E. Moundeford gives security.

929.—6 February 1634–5. *Anthony Mingay*, Norwich, to *Framlingham Gawdy*, West Harling Hall.

Wishes to know if he is to rely on Charles Gawdy paying him 500*l.* on 1 April next. Does not want the money, but if he must take it, wants to know beforehand for certain, "you know he is mutable." Ask brother [Anthony] Gawdy to send Mingay his composuit which Mr. Walles takes out for him, perhaps Mingay may save him 30*s.* on it.
[Postcript by Mary Mingay asking Gawdy to bring with him a pair of " the fine old sheets" he was wont to have.]

930.—28 [February 1634–5]. *Same to same.*

Sessions are not till 7″ April. Has not heard of Anthony.

1635.

931.—27 March 1635. *Sir Edmond Moundeford*, Feltwell, to *Framlingham Gawdy*, Harling.

Moundeford's sister relied on their promise to repay 208*l.* due from Charles, and wrote for it so earnestly that Moundeford has disbursed the 38*l.* or so which was wanting to make it up and has taken up their bond. Would like to have a final account and discharge.

932.—2 April 1635. *Anthony Mingay*, Norwich, to *Framlingham Gawdy*, West Harling Hall.

Mingay has been with Anthony Gawdy to talk with Cousin Bacon, who puts him in good comfort and advises him to choose a very able attorney. Sir Thomas Gawdy, being now in Norwich, says Cousin Charles and his wife are at Croweshall and that he hath received the 500*l.*
If Framlingham and Sir E. Moundeford please they can pay 516*l.* at the sessions and seal a new bond for the remaining 300*l.* Mingay will probably let Sir John Hobart have the 500*l.*, the only difference is as to the surety.

933.—24 April 1635. *Same* to *same*, at Mr. Ward's, Fleet Street, London.

Hopes to hear of Gawdy's safe arrival. Mingay's wife is *enceinte*; he longs to be "jogging to the waters" at Midsummer. Hears there is a play made of "our country knight and your kinsman that came with you hither last summer assizes." Remembrances to Gawdy's sons. Hears that the Earl of Northumberland was made a Knight of the Garter and that Lady Purbeck is to do penance in St. Clement's church.

934.—[Circ. 26 or 28 April 1635.] *Sir Ed. Moundeford* to *Framlingham Gawdy* [London].

Should be glad if they had no more accounts with Charles. On sending to Croweshall for the money he disbursed to make up the 208*l.* he paid his sister, Moundeford received answer from Mr. Walgrave by Tho. Gilder that Charles had none to spare and they did not know how the money had been laid out. Sends remembrances to Charles and wishes him the happiness to be weary of London. Unless Charles sue a fine before he has a child he will never recover his thraldom; this is Sir John Finche's advice.

935.—[1 May 1635 (circ.).] *Anthony Mingay*, Norwich, to *Framlingham Gawdy*, London.

Thanks for letter and book. Hopes the plague (which is much dispersed in the town) will not disappoint the Judges of their progress to Yarmouth. Mingay has written by these carts to 3 several friends in London about getting lodgings in Tunbridge as he would be "loath to be destitute" at his coming. A play is made of Sir J. S. and his kinsman that came along with Gawdy and Mr. Dence. Altho' there be four queries [?] against Anthony, Mingay supposes, it is all to one effect. "Guest is put up in the new Suffolk Combination." John Anguish (or Captain Shugg) is elected for next year. Tom Grosse is a well-wisher to Nic. Bacon's daughter.

936.—[Circ. 1 May 1635.] *Mary Mingay*, Norwich, to *Framlingham Gawdy*, London.

Anthony Gawdy has gone to London: begs Gawdy's advice and help for him.

937.—8 May 1635. *Sir Edmond Moundeford*, Feltwell, to *Framlingham Gawdy*, London.

Sends thanks for news. Tell Cousin Charles that Moundeford will wait for his money. Is sorry old Bradley is put out of his farm. It is true his accounts were extravagant but the fault was in Sir Charles Gawdy's negligence. Old Lady Heveningham was suddenly taken last week with the "numb palsy." Letters have come from the Council to certify the number and quality of malsters. It is so cold they scarce know the time of year. Have taken some dotterels and wish Gawdy could have the sport, but the "view of the Lord of Northumberland's pomp will be a better sight."

938.—8 May 1635. *Anthony Mingay*, Norwich, to [*Framlingham Gawdy*] [London].

"The news we hear is altogether terrible and bad. It is credibly reported . . . from London that there shall be a list taken of every man's age from 16 to 60, and that the oaths of Supremacy and Allegiance are to be administered unto all men, and all Beacons to be repaired and watched and all.this to be done before Midsummer, which doth breed a great fear among us of some troubles this summer."

Cousin Charles has served Mingay " as formerly he did " ; consequently the latter will not take his money till it is all due, viz., on 10 January. Will expect sister Dorothy to be gossip to his child ; she can hold herself ready for the week after Whitsuntide. Fears brother Anthony will suffer detriment in his suit.

939.—20 [May?] 1635. *Sir Edmond Moundeford*, Feltwell, to *Framlingham Gawdy*, Harling.

Charles Gawdy's coming to Croweshall is uncertain, as his wife hourly expects her confinement. Moundeford hopes to be in better leisure after the assizes. Hears that Mr. Stanton's place is granted to one Ambler who also has a grant from Mr. Walgrave of the " next advowsons " [sic] of Pettaugh & Debenham [Suff.]. Ambler married a kinswoman of Moundeford, but the latter was not privy to the purchase, which fact he hopes Mr. Stanton knows as the affair will be ill taken at Ashfield.

940.—17 June 1635. *Anthony Mingay*, Norwich, to *Framlingham Gawdy*, West Harling Hall.

As there is no remedy for it, Mingay must receive the monies from Charles Gawdy 14 days after Michaelmas, but will hold Fram. responsible that he be not again disappointed. Would like to hear of a purchase near Gawdy. Sir Owen [Smyth] says Eccles is much improved. What rent does Legate *bonâ fide* pay for it ? Mingay will lend the money to be received from Charles Gawdy to Sir Ch[arles le] Gr[os] for his daughter's portion. Sends the reversion of " our bancket " after " eight score women " had tasted it; let Dorothy, Anthony, and his wife partake of it. Expects to make his journey in 3 weeks.

941.—1 July 1635. *Same to same.*

" We are this night for Barton Mill, next day Bishop Stafford [Bishops Stortford, Herts], and next London," where they will stay 3 days and so on to the waters. Gawdy's old lodging is ready for him at the assizes.

942.—1 August 1635. *Anthony Mingay*, Speldhurst [Tunbridge Wells, Kent], to *Framlingham Gawdy*, Harling.

Mingay has delayed writing, hoping to be able to announce his recovery, but now anticipates no benefit, except it be after his return. He drinks daily 120 ounces, above a gallon, and has done so for 3 weeks; the symptoms are only aggravated. Intends to stay a fortnight longer, then perhaps stop a week in London and so home, lodging with Gawdy one night by the way (this will be either Thursday 27 August or 3 September).

There are many nobles here, often " six earls and lords in a morning at the wells, besides very many ladies. knights, gentlemen, and gentlewomen, of the chief of all which " Mingay has taken a catalogue. "In the afternoons we have a young Hyde Park for the Lords and Ladies to frolic in, and their only game of pastime among all the great ones is our Country Scalebones, " which they play at here for great sums of money." His daughter Susan sends her duty. " I am at 5l. a week charges, 20s. a week each chamber, 20s. a piece our diets, and 10s. a piece our servants' diet and 5s. a week the [servan's'] chamber—lord-like ! "

GAWDY MSS.

[Postscript by Mary Mingay.]• Saw Cousin Bass in London twice. " I met a young widow in the street, Alderman Peare's widow. She hath a great voice; I heard her talk as she went. She is worth 10,000*l*. and she hath four daughters and they have 5,000*l*. a piece. She is child-bearing and tall and straight, she lives hard by the Old Exchange, near our lodging. Think of this."

943.—4 September 1635. *Sir Edmond Moundeford* to *Constables of Oxboro, Northwold, Dudlington, Moundford,* and *Weeting.*

Warrant to arrest Thomas Taylor, Thomas Gastin, and William Aldred, on suspicion of feloniously stealing goods of John Dickons of Northwold.

944.—[Before 11 September 1635.] *Anthony Mingay.* Flordon Hall, to *Framlingham Gawdy,* West Harling Hall.

Mingay and family arrived here safely and send thanks for their entertainment at Gawdy's, "little Sue's great love" being particularly remembered. The Alderman [Anguish] arrived to make peace with his wife "and puts his fault of not coming upon the Bishop" being at Norwich; Mingay suspects it was rather to be attributed to Lord Castleton and the bowling ground. "We are as yet weather-fast, for we hear not of my Cousin Mingay's coach, yet our honesties is such as we have returned yours; we hope of Doll's company to Orford." Expects Mr. Woods or Mr. Rich to furnish them with a coach. Mrs. Anguish sends best respects.

945.—11 September 1635. *Same,* Norwich, to *same.*

Mingay gives thanks for the "free and noble entertainment" of him and his [on his return from Tunbridge]. Let young Charles [Gawdy] know that Mingay has arranged to lend the money to Sir Charles [le Gros] in sessions week (beginning 5 October) and must not be disappointed in receiving it.

946.—[? 11 September 1635.] *Mary Mingay* to [*Framlingham Gawdy,* Harling].

Alludes to a business Gawdy "motioned" to her when at Harling. She has mentioned it to [her husband ?] in great secrecy, who is willing to content Gawdy. Anthony Mingay's illness renders him unfit to keep house, but she has got a place for Gawdy if he comes fit for a king, " that is Alderman Anguishes, a most excellent house and people."

947.—15 September 1635. *Sir Edmond Moundeford,* Feltwell, to *Framlingham Gawdy,* Harling.

Moundeford is glad their time of discharge is so near, since they " serve for no other use than pawns." Will meet at Bury as appointed. Moundeford has a lanner to spare if Gawdy knows any person who wants one, as "we have not partridges enough for a Jake-marlen" [sic].

948.—23 September 1635. *Anthony Mingay,* Norwich, to *Framlingham Gawdy,* West Harling Hall.

" Our five brave captains with the several troops of horse are marched into the field, being in all about 150 horse, together with the lances, which were 12; but what will be the issue of it, whether the masters or the men shall go on foot, time at night will manifest." Sir Miles.

[Hobart] and Warner are both bound in 10,000*l.* for peaceable appearance before my Lord Marshall, Sir Thomas Glemham and Sir Edward Walgrave being sureties. Capt. Browne of Elsing is restored to my Lord's favour by mediation of friends. Hopes Gawdy will bring Charles' money and the interest as well; Mingay has to make up 1000*l.* for Sir Miles and counts upon it.

949.—20 October 1635. *Sir Edmond Moundeford*, Feltwell, to *Framlingham Gawdy*, West Harling.

Moundeford goes to London next week. Apologises for not undergoing his part of the burden in paying the money to Cousin Anthony Mingay. Asks Gawdy to receive 38*l.* 2*s.* 6*d.* for Moundeford from Charles.

950.—28 November 1635. *John Mawling*, of Kettleboro', Suffolk, husbandman, to *Framlingham Gawdy*.

General release of all actions, &c. Witness, Richard Sutton, Anthony Rawlyns.

951.—[November 1635.] *Sir Ed. Moundeford*, London, to [*Framlingham Gawdy*].

" The Palsgrave is daily here expected, but the winds hinder [he arrived 21 November]. There is a proclamation to stop the importing goods out of France and Holland for fear of the plague which is very great there. The Archduke hath lately taken another town from the States. The French have been beaten in Italy; the Emperor's forces increase. We have no new Sheriffs pricked nor shall not it is said until the now Sheriffs have accounted for this ship money; in some countries they pay, in others not and make the Sheriff take distress. New impositions are set upon fruit, silks, pewter, pins, and divers other things, to the value of 80,000*l.* per annum. There is a patent to be granted for making salt which will make us all smart. The king hath caused his commission of grace to pass the Seal this term, that all imperfections in grants may be there mended, and compositions to be made for forests or any claim the king makes to any subject's lands . . . . The Turk has made peace with his late adversaries and has raised a great army for Christendom." Robert Wingfield's brother goes sergeant major to one of the two regiments the King is sending to France. It is time the King put some grains into the lighter scale.

952.—1 December 1635. *Anthony Mingay*, Norwich, to [*Framlingham Gawdy*, Harling].

This messenger is to go on to neighbour Onge, who keeps Mingay out of his rent, " I fear I shall pay dear for the pig sauce." Mr. Holl and his wife are bedded again by the Archbishop's command. Lords St. Albans and Savage are dead ; so is old Parr, 152 years old. The Palsgrave has much respect shown him by the King and Queen; two of his gentlemen were slain in the ship coming over by the carelessness of Capt. Peanington's gunner discharging a piece of ordnance by way of salute, which was loaded with a bullet. Last week Mr. Murray of the bedchamber married one of Viscount Baring's [?] daughters. "We are very much vexed here about our ship-rate which is now in agitation, and some say you countrymen were much too hard for us in the rating of us at a tenth part, whereas in very deed and truth we are not a fiftieth part . . . I am resolved, if you will take any boarders to come and live with you in the country to save charges, for here I am rated (and not worshipped) like a knight. They report that divers shires do wholly withstand it and how that the king hath declared that no High Sheriff shall be discharged of his place until he hath paid in the ship-money for that county." " This Christmas housekeeping will well nigh kill our High Sheriff's lady, if his under sheriff do not come off with a round and sound donative." Mingay sends a pound of macaroons, all Gawdy has left him after paying his ship-money. Sir John Hobart has buried his eldest son, and " for joy keeps Christmas here to spend all." Mingay has paid this messenger, but if Gawdy pleases to give him anything " he hath wit enough to take it."

953.—20 December [1635]. *Same to same.*

Thanks for brawn. " It is no marvel you be so plentiful in your brawn, seeing your Bacon die so fast about you, but the great old hog liveth still, whereby I cannot yet get my money." Cannot tell what is become of Ned Sayer "unless drowned in a dry ditch," believes he is at Mr. John Cooke's. The King has sent to fetch over the Palsgrave's second brother [Prince Rupert], and high and mighty preparation is made for masking. Augustine Holl is arrived, without his wife. The business between Sir Miles Hobart and Warner was heard before the Lord Marshall, resulting in a [seeming ?] friendship. " Some mad knave has abused all your fellow Justices in a song, yourself have not escaped his health and so it goes round, to the comfort of a friend of yours. Our great city dons refuse to pay their ship money, and are too big for our Mayor's rate when such poor snakes as myself is made their equal in payment." . . . Your High Sheriff hath kissed his hands and is rid of 7,000*l.* of his money, and yet I believe will not get off next term. Our city money is not yet minted that should pay him; he must be taught more conscience than to make us the tenth part, when indeed we are not the fiftieth, as by his own town rates and all other country rates appeareth. My good friend Munecason, the bookseller, is dead, and all my intelligence is buried with him. Our new bishop [Mathew Wren] was installed upon Wednesday last by a proxy. It is so dark this Christmas that our city gentlemen cannot see to keep good hospitality." Ends with " as many good wishes as there be plums in all the Christmas pies in England."—St. Thomas' night.

1635-6.

954.—[? February 1635–1636.]   *Anthony Mingay* [Norwich] to *Framlingham Gawdy,* West Harling Hall.

Mingay is glad to hear of the conclusion of the match for Gawdy's son [William, with Elizabeth Duffield, of East Wrotham]. As to the match for Gawdy himself, her jointure is 300*l.* a year and 1,000*l.* in her purse, besides jewels and plate, " it is thought her lady mother left her a good bag at her death." Gawdy is 16 miles nearer the news than Mingay is. Please send Onge with some money.

955.—8 February 1635-6.   *George Blennerhassett,* of London, Haberdasher, to *Wm. Davy,* of East Wrotham, Gent. [The Davy family were connected with the Duffields.]

Whereas Davy has secured certain tenants against disturbance in their possession of lands in Ixworth, Suff., taken in execution (Thomas

Goodwine of Stoneham, Suff., Esq., *v.* John Gibson), Blennerhassett
agrees to pay half of any liability Davy may incur thereby.

956.—16 February 1635-6. *Anthony Mingay,* Norwich, to *Framlingham Gawdy,* West Harling
Hall.

Mingay supposes Gawdy did not answer the letter sent by Mr.
Wotton on account of his being over-joyed at his son's match. Neighbour Onge owes near 20*l.* Gawdy may chide him and find Mingay
another tenant by Michaelmas.

957.—1 March [1635-6]. *Same to same.*

Onge did not come according to promise. Three of the townsmen
would have bought the land, which Mingay refused; one of them
(Hemson) would hire it. Mingay has made enquiries and finds "all
things well but the woman," who is 45 years old. Subscribes himself
in haste "to eat pancakes."—"St. David's Day in Welsh."

958.—[1 March 1635-6]. *Mary Mingay* [Norwich] to [*Framlingham Gawdg,* Harling].

The widow is very rich, aged 46, and is reported "a very ill-condi-
tioned woman, which kills my heart to stir any further in it." Wishes
both Gawdy and his son "as good sweet wives as you deserve."

959.—5 March 1635-6. *William Davy,* East Wrotham, to *Framlingham Gawdy,* Harling.

Understands Framlingham's son Bassingborn is riding to London
next Monday. Asks the use of his horse on the return journey for a
friend, if he "cometh down empty."

960.—[8 March 1635-6.] *Mary Mingay* to *Framlingham Gawdy*
[Harling].

Wants to see him to talk about the widow. She is homely and
very hard favoured, but wonderful rich and good. "I grieve for
the wet day you had home. If I live till Easter, I will see Harling."

961.—8 March 1635-6. *Anthony Mingay,* Norwich, to *Framlingham Gawdy,* West Harling Hall.

Mingay has received Gawdy's letters sent by the younger Mr. Catline
and Anthony Gawdy. He wrote to Gawdy last week by one of the
townsmen of Kenninghall, as to Onge's default. Asks advice as to
distraining, or arresting Onge. Has been told the widow's son should
marry Mr. R.'s daughter, and that her old uncle Anthony R. will
augment her portion with 500*l.*
25 ships are to be made ready against 10 April next.
Dr. Mainwaring was made Bishop of St. David's at Lambeth
House, where the Palsgrave and his brother dined on Shrove Tuesday;
at night the Lady Hatton entertained the King, Queen, Palsgrave, and
his brother, with a royal supper and brave masque. "I pray tell
your sons that the Red Bull company of players are now in town, and
have acted one play with good applause and are well clad and act by
candlelight." Brother Francis writes Mrs. Mingay for help, but
brother Anthony says his own present annuity and future reversion of
Mr. Roger's gift will nearly accomplish the sum desired. If not,
Mingay will readily come in for a share; old Rogers may supply the

GAWDY MSS. rest. Would not leave it to Anthony, who "doth not· much mind his own business, but would have things done alone to his hand." Cousin Bacon is very doubtful of Anthony's title, and says Guest in his declaration sets forth a very strong title. He advises Anthony to go to Mr. Bacon, of Suffolk, who married Sir Anthony Wingfield's sister, and see his evidences; hasten Anthony's doing this before the conference appointed at Bury assizes. Get Sir Drue Drury's letter to Wingfield, and speak to cousin Bacon at Thetford assizes.

962.—16 March 1635–6. *Same to same.*

Asks Gawdy to send a servant with this bearer, Mr. Thomas Miies, an attorney of Norwich, who is to distrain on Onge's sheep. Respects to honest Harry Berney, "who only doth appear unto the High Sheriff in his coullers [sic.]." Is the match for Gawdy's son concluded?

963.—18 March 1635–6. *Same to same.*

See that Miles is not put off by words; either proceed with the distress, or get security with interest, including 3*l.* 10*s.* for wood sold to Onge a year ago. Mingay thinks all men conspire to break him. Onge will owe him 30*l.* at Lady-day; Anthony Gawdy almost 10*l.*; Ned Sayer 12*l.*; "my wife hath lost 7*l.* or 8*l.* at gleeke lately, and it must be paid; Doll oweth me 30*l.*; these keep me bare of money, yet to do my brother [Francis Gawdy] a perpetual good," Mingay sends 5 new pieces to go towards procuring him "this place," otherwise let Gawdy keep it, "let us not part with our monies except he hath the place." The Countess of Bridgewater is dead. Lady Mount Norris is coming out of Ireland to petition the King about her Lord "that should have been shot to death." Three captains in the late fleet are discharged for refusing the oath of supremacy. One of the King's ships goeth to the Groyne to fetch the Spanish Ambassador. Asks news of the assizes. Remembrances to Harry Berney, brother Francis, and sister Dorothy.

1636.

964.—26 March 1636. *Same to same.*

If Mingay forbears distraining on Onge at Gawdy's request, he expects the latter to send Onge in with his security, and a note if the security offered be good or no. Hopes brother Francis is not putting a trick upon them. An Ambassador is come from the States, business not known. "This morning here was 8 of our Norwich Ministers suspended for not conforming to the diocesan's commands, but I believe most of them will be absolved this night again, upon promise of conformity. Mr. Bridg and Mr. Carter are two of them, and I fear will stand out to their own detriment."

965.—3 May 1636. *Same to same.*

Sends a gardener, recommended by his brother John Mingay, who promises to be industrious and free from drinking. Lord Carlisle is dead, and "Secretary Cooke (dead to all joys), and our Bishop in his place and a privy counsellor. Our new visitors are very strict here in taking of verdicts, viz., Dr. Paule and Mr. Nowell, the Bishop's Chaplain, and do menace much conformity by their presence, which I doubt will be as soon forgot in their absence."

966.—8 May 1636. *Same to same.*

Is sorry to hear that [Onge] has shown his heels and run away. Cousin Mingay desires to know about the estate, life, and conversation of the minister at Larlingford, who is a suitor unto one of her daughters. " Our visitors keep a fearful stir here against your nonconformist. Cooke of Fretton and Burroughs of Titshall are both suspended upon it."

967.—11 May 1636. *Same to same.*

Asks what Onge has left behind him: The bearer has promised to be a good servant to Gawdy, " if you cashier him again as you shall see just cause (sic.)." Mr. Spurling spoke about taking the farm.

968.—1 June 1636. *Sir Edmond Moundeford*, Feltwell, to *Framlingham Gawdy.*

Not having heard from Rawlings concerning the timber they should have had at Thetford at Sir Wm. Campian's, Moundeford doubts if the bargain can have been completed. The timber is for sale, and Mr. Evenall seeks a partner to buy it with him. Suggests a meeting at Bury at "the bowling," where "my brother Heveningham" will attend Gawdy. Sir Hy. Bedingfield desires Sir John Holland to be notified. Is cousin Will married ?

969.—7 June 1636. *Same to same.*

Moundeford, Sir Hy. Bedingfield, and Wm. Heveningham will meet Gawdy at Moundford on Monday, when they can parly about timber and other business. Charles Gawdy is notified.

970.—28 July 1636. *Anthony Mingay*, Norwich, to *Framlingham Gawdy*, West Harling Hall.

By Onge's not coming at Mr. Hamond about the Court, Mingay suspects his dishonesty. Unless Mr. Bedingfield will go security for the 40*l.* due at Michaelmas, Mingay will come over on Monday and enter on the growing crop of corn. If Mingay had not lent John Hobart the 40*s.* to lend him, he might have been in jail now.

971.—2 August 1636. *Same to same.*

Wants to know if any agreement is come to with Onge and Bedingfield. Gawdy should see that Mingay is at no loss, or he will send his wife and children to Harling to eat it out, which will take till Christmas, unless there is the expense of a confinement thrown in ! "I hope of a good end, and then you will thrive the better at Bowls next week ; if not I will send John Sayer, with all his fellow Rooks to prey upon you and blow you all up, if six to four will do it." Let sister Doll solicit Mr. Bedingfield, " or else no gloves."

972.—19 August 1636. *George Gawdy*, Norwich, to kinsman *Framlingham Gawdy*, West Harling.

The bearer, Robert Hoggs (lately George's servant), sold Framlingham's neighbour Mr. Bedingfield a house a long time ago covenanting that all rent was paid, &c., and giving a bond for performance of the covenants. Mr. Bedingfield has now had him arrested on the bond, supposing there was a small yearly rent of 2*d.* or 3*d.* unpaid a few years before the sale.

Even if this were so, as Bedingfield had a good pennyworth, he might come to terms with the poor man.

973.—7 September 1636. *William Davy*, West Barsham, to his friend and kinsman [*Framlingham Gawdy*].

Makes an appointment to meet at Wood Rising about the buck Davy promised his correspondent. Has received a note from Mr. Bayfield of the money he has laid out, nearly 4*l.* "for your business concerning Garboldisham."

[About this date *Framlingham's* eldest son, *William*, married *Elizabeth*, daughter of *John Duffield*, of East Wrotham.]

974.—14 September 1636. *Anthony Mingay*, Norwich, to *Framlingham Gawdy*, West Harling Hall.

Sends thanks for the entertainment he and his received at Harling. Understands by brother Sayer, of Framlingham's son's nuptials; and wishes him joy. Last week 1,069 died of all diseases in London, and 650 of the plague, which is very much increased in Lynn, and is feared to have begun anew in one house in Yarmouth. Norwich is "sound and free," only 13 died last week, being the smallest number for 3 months. Mr. Freeman, Vintner, and brother Utting, are the new Sheriffs. Widow Skottowe's office has gone well on her side, which makes her the richer.

975.—26 September 1636. *Same to same.*

Acknowledges receipt of letter sent by Cousin John Mingay. Has had much sickness in his house, "my sister Roger in very great danger to miscarry by reason of a violent fever ; my sister Sayer was lately taken with an apoplexy in her head, and one side of her was taken lame and numb . . . . my own daughter Mary hath been very dangerously ill", with an imposthume in her mouth." Has good hope "this very night" of all their recoveries. "It is a very sickly time now in Norwich ; there died last week with us 24 . . . . hitherto we have no infection, but our sins. I have sent you Ket's books to pass the evenings withal, wherein you may perceive what misery "the city was then in." In London the plague abated to 645 last week, and of all diseases 1,200 odd. It is reported that Lord Cottington and Secretary Windebank are commanded to their houses about the Spanish plate. "It is thought the Hollanders and we shall have bullets about the fishing." The King will be at Newmarket speedily. Expects Gawdy to come and do his homage to Lord Maltravers, who is said to be coming soon.

976.—8 October 1636. *Same to same.*

Mingay had expected Gawdy this week, his bed was provided. Doubts not but he hears a very strong report of the infection here. Mingay for his part believes it has come, but the magistrates oppose it. The figures are suspicious, next week will show. Mingay has a present of a rundlet of sack for Gawdy, it is of Mrs. Mingay's commending and choosing, so her taste must be blamed if it is not extraordinary good. "My Lord of Northumberland with 7 of the King's ships came into Yarmouth road on Thursday last, and stays the expectancy of his commission to come on shore and end his voyage for this year : the town doth entertain him with a dinner, and Sir John Wentworth comes in with his dish. My Lord of Arundel is coming over without any good success. As is reported, the Landgrave of Hesse is banished his country, and hath sent over his two eldest sons into England, who are now both at Court. The King comes to Newmarket on Tuesday next. . . . 23 died with us this week . . . . great hurly burly in France." Would like the 5*l.* got from Charles Gawdy ; wants money against his wife's confinement.

977.—12 October 1636. *Same to same.*

This small vessel [of sack] would have been larger, if Mingay had not met with so great a rub in Buckenham Bowling green." Let Doll keep it for Gawdy, "she will beguile you of none, but for her own palate and Mr. Rogers'." None have died since his last letter out of the houses that were suspected and shut up. Cousin Edward Sayer died last Sunday morning of the yellow jaundice, "a poor man." My Lord of Northumberland landed at Yarmouth about 9 a.m. on Sunday, went to Church with the bailiffs, and dined at Bailiff Lucas' house, lodged that night at Sir John Wentworth's, and went next day to Sir Edmund Bacon's, and so to Court. " My son John is not well, which makes my wife out of tune."

978.—19 October 1636. *Same to same.*

Mingay must defend his tenant against the townsmen of Kenninghall to maintain his right of feeding in the fields. He has for his assurance the covenant of Mr. Wright, old Caine, and parson Davy, and would just as soon have the matter tried while they are alive. One died on Monday, supposed of the plague ; seven have died since the first bruit of it, but the physicians say it is some other contagious disease, "which die with spots." Expects Gawdy will hear of the petition to the King about the Ministers. Fears it will make a great rout in the city, the Mayor having sent it off without the consent of most of the aldermen, who have disclaimed it under their hands to the Bishop. Mingay is confident the City will suffer therein for their folly. In London 1,302 died last week, 792 of the plague. Mrs. Mingay would know if Lady Felton's maid died at Ipswich or no. Kemp has not yet called for the sack.

979.—25 October 1636. *Sir Edmond Moundeford*, Feltwell, to *Framlingham Gawdy.*

'Cannot entertain this man," although ready to have done so for his father's sake ; will move Sir John Hare to take him. Charles is at Croweshall.

980.—2 November 1636. *Anthony Mingay*, Norwich, to *Framlingham Gawdy*, West Harling Hall.

Three have died this week out of suspected houses ; last week 14 died from all causes. None have yet been "given in" as dying of plague, but Mingay believes these 3 and the other 7 all died of it. Last week's bill in London was 900 of all diseases and 458 of the plague. The King left Newmarket Saturday. Mingay will write to Parson Davy to give instructions about the trial, which will concern him more than Mingay. Send word what Spirling and Cle . . . field did at Gawdy's Court. The proclamation for the fast is come down, but not yet proclaimed.

981.—20 December [1636]. *Same to same.*

Sends thanks for 7 collars of Brawn ; Gawdy's health shall be remembered at the eating of them in a cup of muscadine. Sends " some bancketting,"—for wet sweetmeals Gawdy has better than any Mingay has, "these are only for your own eating." Last week 405 died in London of all diseases and but 85 of the plague. A book is lately out at Ipswich, titled News from Ipswich ; it is "much against our Bishop and Visitors."

Mr. Carter has laid down his living. The parish have elected Mr. Chapple (lately of St. Andrews) to be their preacher, Mingay doubts if he will accept it "being now in Derbyshire. To morrow four of the parish ride to acquaint him with their election." Meantime the Bishop is said to have appointed Mr. Guest (Anthony's antagonist) to supply the place, which made the parishioners appoint another so speedily. "Our parson is put off till next Sessions, and yet there is matter enough come against him already to hang him." Sir Thomas [Gawdy?] is lately come to town, "we are pestered with your country knights thi‹ Christmas," who do no good except raise the price of provisions. Gawdy's son's box was left with Daniel Harman at Thetford, 12d. to pay. Mingay has paid this messenger 3s.

1636-7.

982.—24 January 1636-7. *Same to same.*

Parson Davy was here yesterday : much troubled about the suit. He protests the right is not worth ten groats a year, and wishes it referred and he will pay the damage. Ask Spirling what is the true yearly value and how much the sheep course would be the worse without it. The men of Kenninghall are willing enough to let the trial stand over. Mingay fears it will cost the poor man 40l. or 50l., and intends to come upon Mr. Wright.

983.—3 February 1636-7. *Same to same.*

Understands by Mr. Rawlings that his son Spirling values the feed in the field at 3l. a year instead of 3s. 4d.; let Mr. Davy know this and that he must help defend it. Assizes are to be at Thetford a month next Monday, the death of the High Sheriff's wife "hath helped you to them there."

No disease is heard of at Sir Augustine's house. It is true an unsealed letter to the King (supposed of Mr. Hedge's writing) was found in the Guildhall, a foolish thing, it was never forwarded. Is sorry to hear of the ill-health of Framlingham and of Anthony Gawdy's wife. There is great fear in London of the great increase of sickness this very week past. Mr. Edgar's letters report that Lord Craven is to lend the Palsgrave 30,000l. "to furnish ships to sea this summer, I conceive with letters of marque or else I know not for what end. There are divers of the King's ships speedily to go forth and mariners apressing at London. The King doth abate his court ; your monthly waiters are but to attend quarterly and debarred their diet but only when they wait ; it is to save charges." If any more news arrives, will send it by "your chaplain."

Get the money from Charles [Gawdy] lest he prove a worse paymaster than Frank.

984.—10 March 1636-7. *Same to same.*

Is sorry to hear that "my brother's trial went against him," fears it will prove an ill omen. The Emperor is said to be dead and his eldest son the King of the Romans very sick of a fever. "At Paris lately there hath been some contestation between my Lord of Leicester our .GAWDY MSS. Ambassador and the Swedish Ambassador for precedency." Mingay has been labouring to get a house to dwell in, and has offered as much as 20*l.* a year for one in vain ; this was to give Gawdy content, " for a far meaner would serve my turn ;" trusts Gawdy will pay half the rent "to be lodged so knight-like." Mrs. Mingay asks her cloth to be sent to Larlingford to be brought in " our carts as they pass that way."

1637.

985.—[April or May 1637.]   *Same to same.*

The widow has resignd her house into Mingay's hands ; he and his family go in on Friday night and will welcome Gawdy to four bare walls the following Monday. Would gladly come to an end in suit with Kenninghall men, let Mr. Howes see if he can settle it. Some of St. Peter [Mancroft] parish have been at Cambridge to choose a new minister and have "fastened upon" Mr. William Norridg, whose father was mayor of Thetford ; Norridg was of Trinity, but is now fellow of Peterhouse; he is coming to preach on Sunday week. " I see letters yesterday from London . . . that all ministers that will not bow at the blessed name of Jesus are to be suspended within 14 days after notice given unto them. The sickness is like to increase this week there."

986.—9 May 1637.   *William Davy*, the Golden Anchor, Fleet St., right over St. Dunstan's Church to [*Framlingham Gawdy*].

Davy has spoken to Mr. Fountaine about Eccles Manor, which Sir Chas. le Groos refused to buy. Serjeant Reeve asks the refusal of it, but Davy believes that "like the Boatsman, he roweth one way and looks another." It is rated at 19 years' purchase at near 80*l.* a year. Understanding [Gawdy's] desire for news, Davy went to " the most eminentest places," viz., Pauls and Westminster. The title of the books that were burned in Smithfield was " An Introduction to a devout life," made beyond seas in Latin, and translated by the late Archbishop Abbot's chaplain. It was now reprinted and approved by the chaplain of the present Archbishop [Laud] who corrected many things in it, which by some indirect dealings were reinserted. The Archbishop desired that it might be said in the Star-chamber that he had no hand in it " for what with the Papist and the Puritan he is much spoken of though it be undeservedly." The great cause in the Star-chamber is against one Dr. Bastwick, a physician, Mr. Burton a divine, Prynne, Peter Wetherick's son of Norwich, and others for divulging books against the Bishops. Bastwick humbly desired that he might answer for himself and put in a cross-bill against the Bishops " for which he had a precedent, even St. Paul (Acts 26), who was permitted to speak for himself."   .‸

The sickness decreased 26 last week and it is not nearly so much spoken of as *it* is in the country. Yet they are very strict in punishing delinquents. A fishmonger is now in prison with as much irons on him as he can bear both sitting up and lying down. This was for opening his shop and letting his servants go up and down, when one of his house was dead of the infection. " There is a strange opinion here " amongst the poorer sort of people who hold it a matter of conscience " to visit their neighbours in any sickness, yea tho' they know it to be " the infection." Has spoken with Mr. Brampton about [Gawdy's] land in Garboldisham, his best course will be to " settle the respect of homage," and as Gawdy has his assurance both from the Earl of Arundel and his feoffees, he will be enforced to a double pardon. Sir Thos. Hopton has just come in, who has much need of money to pay Sir Owen Smyth's debts and would like the purchase money [of Eccles] all paid down. He desires to know Serj. Reeve's answer. " The malting business for Norfolk staggereth " and will presently "fall to nothing." Many monopolies spoken of, among others, one that only 10 men may sell sea-coal throughout England. A proclamation is out for restraining going into New England. " A minister in Leicestershire upon Easter-day at the time of receiving the sacrament did persuade his parishioners to follow his example to drink healths in the church, who did begin 3, one to the Father, 2 to the Son, 3 to the H. G." (sic.).

987.—3 June 1637. *Peter Murforde*, Norwich to *Captain Framlingham Gawdy*, West Harling.

Asks Gawdy to summon those in Thetford who bear arms to meet there on 9 inst. when Murforde will inspect and (" if you shall give way "' instruct them.

988.—9 June 1637. *Anthony Mingay*, Norwich, to *Framlingham Gawdy*, West Harling Hall.

There died 12 last week of all diseases in Norwich, whereof 3 of the plague, this morning the bills came in, 23 of all diseases whereof 11 of the plague : 9 out of the 11 being in two parishes beyond the water and the rest of the city being very well. Knowing Gawdy's fear, Mingay was careful in getting a safe messenger. Is sorry to hear brother Anthony is out of his living, perhaps it will make him a better paymaster in future. He and Charles seem to conspire to break a young housekeeper, who is weary thereof already. Wishes " a happy hour to the good young gentlewoman, for we cannot hear of an old one for you."

989.—[? 9 June 1637.] *Mary Mingay* [Norwich] to [*Framlingham Gawdy*, Harling].

The sickness is much increased in Norwich but " not near us." Gawdy may safely come to the assizes, and if he has his coach come for him, Mrs. Mingay and her little one will go home with him.

990.—[13 June 1637.] *Anthony Mingay*, Norwich, to *Framlingham Gawdy*, West Harling Hall.

Mrs. Mingay will send some Brome (?) capers by Willm. Cannum. " News here is little stirring, only Hamsden case [sic, read Hampden's case] for the ship money; it is all the talk in London at present. Yesterday was the day of hearing and argument before all the Judges." The Portuguese [" Portingales"] are strongly reported to be up in arms against the King of Spain "in a high manner," and a " motion at the Hague about a general peace this Christmas time." Sir Jacob Ashley and his lady lay at an Inn in Norwich two nights this week and are gone to the High Sheriffs. " Our Norwich clergy " are said to have got an order from the King to have " 2s. in the pound for the rent of all houses towards their maintenance ; it will make us all run into cottages · and not affect great houses except we take inmates" [lodgers]. Ends " your sleepy friend."

991.—13 June 1637. *Barberie Hart* to [*Framlingham Gawdy*].

Troubles and crosses prevent Mrs. Hart from living any more " of her self." Begs [Gawdy's] word with cousin Cressner, the preacher, that

she may live with him the small remnant of her life, not charging him
for apparel or furniture for her chamber, and doing him besides the best
service she is able.

992.—[? June or July 1637.]   *Mary Mingay* to [*Framlingham
Gawdy*, Harling].

Sir Thomas [Gawdy] is gone with Hevenmgham [?] to Yarmouth to
fetch away his money, "poor silly man, the Lord help him ?" Begs
Gawdy and the "young father" to take order that Mrs. Mingay has
" a good part of all things to make me merry for the little heir's sake."
Pray send her sister, who shall be welcome.

993.—6 July 1637.   *Ruth Gawdy*, Mendham, to *Framlingham
Gawdy*, Harling Hall.

Ruth has "lessened" the debts her husband left, but cannot pay all
off. She is in great straights, being sued for her rent, 40s. When
Framlingham sent her a friendly token from Crowshall, the "uncon-
scionable messenger" only brought her 7s. Begs commiseration for a
" poor aged gentlewoman," and that whatever Gawdy sends may be
done up in paper and sent by the bearer, John Middleton, of Homersfield [Suff.].
[Endorsed by Gawdy with memo. of lambs sold, viz., 416 lambs for
74l. 14s. 6d. and 330 wether lambs and crowes for 85l. 10s. Charges
at the fairs 2l. 3s. 3d.]

994.—28 September 1637.   *Anthony Mingay* to *Framlingham
Gawdy*.

Receipt by Mingay for 6l. from Gawdy by the hands of William
Davy, gent.

995.—29 September 1637.   *William Davy*, West Barsham, to [*Framlingham Gawdy*].

Sir Thos. Hopton, Lady Smith and Mr. Smith of Winson [Winston ?]
had fixed a day for Counsel to inspect the evidences and proceed to find
an office. However all the writings were taken out of Sir Owen Smith's
closet (as the report is by Lady Smith) so nothing can be done, and Sir
Thomas is gone to London. Advises [Gawdy] not to keep his money
any longer for Eccles. Encloses Mr. Mingay's receipt for the 6l. Davy
promised to lay out for [Gawdy.] It is constantly reported at Norwich
that Breda is yielded up.

996.—2 November 1637.   *Anthony Mingay*, Norwich, to *Framlingham Gawdy*, West Harling Hall.

Would like to receive of Charles Gawdy (who is now at Harling)
the 5l. sent him by Francis two years ago: also wants a half year's rent
from Spirling and to know if Parson Davy paid Gawdy the 32s. Mingay
laid out for him. There is Anthony's money too ; " all your country I
think are bad paymasters."

997.—3 November 1637.   *William Davy*, the Golden Anchor, Fleet
St., to kinsman [*Framlingham Gawdy*].

Only sends half the quantity of olives and capers, as there will be
better in the market by the end of term. Davy lodged at Newmarket
on Monday night : the Greyhound was wholly taken up by Sir Edmund
Bacon, Sir Dru Drury, and Mr. Barrow, who with Sir Thos. Richardson
were all going to London. Crossed Newmarket Heath with his charge

GAWDY MSS. in safety; the company took away the fears [Gawdy.] put him into.
The greatest news is of the Morocco Ambassador, " whose present to
His Majesty of Barbary horses and saddles is of great value, and also
a great quantity of Barbary gold (*ut loquentur nonnulli*), because his
Majesty's ships this last summer did great service in driving certain
pirates out of an Island belonging to that Prince." It is thought it will
prove commodious to our traffic there. He will have audience on
Sunday and has not been well since his arrival. Much exception is
taken at the Poland Ambassador not having audience, though he has
been here longer than the other. His Majesty would have him take
notice of some wrong offered by the King of Poland fairly pretending
a match with the Palsgrave's sister and afterwards proceeding in the
Emperor's family. A Bill was preferred this term against the Bishop
of Lincoln, but was taken off the file; it is said another will be put
on very suddenly. Mr. Caesar, one of the 6 clerks, died last Sunday,
great means is used for his place: he left a rich young childless widow.
Davy's brother and Cousin Webb send respects.

998.—[16 (?) November 1637.]   *Same to same.*

Has arranged with Mr. Ashley Brampton to attend to Gawdy's
business, which, the longer it is delayed, the worse it will be; because
upon every license of alienation *aurum reginae* must be paid, being the
tenth part of what is paid to the King. Has not spoken to Sir Thos.
Hopton about the sale of Eccles. The Morocco Ambassador was
brought through London on the 5 November in the afternoon by the
City Captains, the present, being 4 Barbary horses, led before him by
4 Moroccos on horseback. The military band met him at Temple Bar
and conducted him to Whitehall. About 6 o'clock, after the audience, his
Majesty's coach brought him back. The Ship-money has been argued last
week and this in the Exchequer, and it is concluded that in case of necessity the King may call unto his subjects for money and that he is judge
of the necessity: the judges will deliver their opinion before the end
of the term. Davy hears it delivered for law that those marshes which
are overflown *per altos fluxus maris* are in *jure coronae*, " and I am certain that most of our Norfolk men do compound with the King." There
is a new building now at Whitehall for masques and shows right over
against the pulpit in the yard, very near finished. The Temple Church
is locked up, that none are suffered to walk there as they have used to
do, and at Divine Service morning and evening wax candles burning
upon the Communion Table, and the pulpit removed to the side of the
Church." A great mutiny in Scotland about our form of prayer, &c.

999.—20 November 1637.   *Anthony Mingay*, Norwich, to [*Framlingham Gawdy*, Harling.]

A dunning letter much to the same effect as No. 996.
In future will have wit enough to keep his money in his purse. No
news, " only a new book of Sully's (?) voyage and the King of Morocco's letter to our King, the best penned letter ever you read."
Hopes to see Gawdy at next Sessions, " and if a widow happen to fall
in the meantime she shall be kept in syrup for you."

1000.—14 December 1637.   *William Davy*, West Barsham, to
Framlingham Gawdy, West Harl-
ing.

Davy sends his servant for the bag of 50*l.* he left with Gawdy.

1001.—[? December 1637.] *Anthony Mingay*, Norwich, to *Framlingham Gawdy*, West Harling Hall.

There died this week of all diseases, 16 (3 of the plague). "I trust that it is not in our lane." It was suspected in one house in the lane but all in that house are still in good health and the last died on Wednesday week. Gawdy may safely set his horses at his old inn (where he will find a new host), "howsoever first light at our house and then you shall know more." Is glad Gawdy has his hawk again: neither that nor "any of her fellows" bring any partridges into town that Mingay can see. George Bayfield to-day marries Mun Anguishe's young daughter aged 16. James Barwicke the attorney died suddenly of an apoplexy on Friday night at Harry Barnie's house "and scared Harry out of that little wit he had, made him leave his house and lodged last night at Maid's Head [Inn] needlessly." Mr. Ferne of Trinity is like to be St. Peter's Vicar.

1637–8.

1002.—14 March 1637–8. *Robert Eade* [Cambridge] to *Framlingham Gawdy*, West Harling.

Concerning Gawdy's son's complaint, Eade does not profess any skill, "never having practised upon any cure of that nature," nor is there any in Cambridge eminent for such cures. He conceives it would be "effected chiefly by artificial bodies to be so fitted unto him that may reduce that part that is lunated into its proper place, by lacing them straight to his body."

Remembrance to Mr. William Gawdy and "the rest of your sons."

1003.—17 March 1637–8. *Anthony Mingay*, Norwich, to *Framlingham Gawdy*, Harling.

Sends thanks for his late kind entertainment. Has been with the Bodymaker who is desirous to see Gawdy's son to take measure of him which is "much more effectual;" when he comes he "shall be dispatched in 24 hours and have them home with him."

1638.

1004.—11 April 1638. *William Moore* [Gonville and Caius College], Cambridge, to *Framlingham Gawdy*, Harling.

Has received 5l. 13s. 9d. by hands of Jeffrey Weldon, which with moneys received of Mr. Pell, clears both Gawdy's sons' [Thomas and Charles] accounts to Christmas. Encloses Charles's account to Lady day, it is so low on account of his long intermission, which has thrown him much back in his studies. "Such is his incapacity of University learning" that more than ordinary diligence is necessary with him. As to Gawdy's younger son [Robert] do not delay his admission, provided he be ripe enough for these studies.

1005.—24 April 1638. *Anthony Mingay*, Norwich, to *Framlingham Gawdy*, West Harling Hall.

Believes his wife will visit Gawdy at Midsummer. His son John has had the measles. Four died this week "suspiciously," and Mingay believes that they will be given in as of the plague. A searcher was

GAWDY MSS. sworn to-day "for the same purpose." Gawdy's son Robert has been
very well, Mingay sees him twice or thrice a week and he sits with them
at Christ Church. "We heard that Judge Crooke was for the "Country
and did speak very boldly in that business" [*i.e.*, ship-money]. Mingay
will mention the other matter to his brother Osborne who will be in
Norwich after Whitsuntide. Speak to Parson Davy about the 40*s*. due:
"your cousin Sir Thomas" does not pay the 5*l*., he is now removed.
Hints that he should like some pigeons. Robin wants his new shirt
speedily.

1006.—14 May [1638]. *Same to same.*

Son Robin is well, but has run into debt; he will write by Charles
Rawlings. 18 in all died this week, whereof 7 of the plague. Expects
Gawdy has heard of Parson Harrison at Common Pleas Bar. The Lord
of Northumberland and "your high Sheriff" are sick of the small pox
at London. Lady Townsend has married the Earl of Westmoreland.
Only 3 died in London of the plague last week. Hears sister Dorothy
is returned; please hasten her to Norwich. Mingay may become
Gawdy's neighbour. Edmund Anguish will sell the land in Cressingham that his son had on marrying old Methwold's daughter. It is let for
150*l*. a year, and Sir Richard Barney is said to have offered 2,200*l*. for
it. Mingay would give 200*l*. more, but must have Gawdy's advice.
(Dated Whit-Monday.)

1007.—5 June 1638. *William Heveningham*, Hockwold, to *Framlingham Gawdy*, Harling.

Brother Moundeford and Heveningham have been from home so long,
that they want to see their friends. Begs Gawdy to meet them and the
High Sheriff at Mr. Adame's, Thetford, on Saturday.

1008.—7 June 1638. *William Davy*, Golden Anchor, Fleet St. to
[*Framlingham Gawdy*].

Sir Thos. Hopton says Lady Smith is very earnest with him to sell
both Eccles and Easton Manors, as Sir Owen Smith's creditors are
suing her. She has procured Mr. Jermie's son, the Counsellor, to buy
both, offering them for 2,300*l*., and is willing to give 2,200*l*. and see
no writing but the conveyance from Sir Owen to Sir Thomas and Sir
Arthur Hopton. Sir Thomas would rather sell to Davy. The Divine
who accused Judge Hutton of treason was fined 5,000*l*. in the King's
Bench "for offering affront to the place of Justice and also to wear a
paper in his hat written with certain letters, with which he is to go into
Westminster Hall and every Court of Justice," besides imprisonment
during the King's pleasure, and the Judge having his action at law
against him. Has spoken to the Clerk in the Exchequer touching the
Unhall business ; he cannot stay issues, the Sheriff must pay them,
which will come to 8*l*. Mr. Bayfield is the only man who can make a
stay and he is out of town. Will speak to him on his return. If Davy
is not at Harling next Thursday night it will be because the Eccles
business keeps him. Baronet Wiseman is fined 10,000*l*. to the King,
5,000*l*. to the Lord Keeper, 1,000*l*. to Judge Jones, and has to pay
1,000*l*. to Mr. Tomson, the Lord Keeper's Secretary. "One Pickering
a recusant is censured in the Star-Chamber to lose his ears and be bored
through the tongue for saying the King was a papist in his heart and
that all Protestants were heretics and making a Hogsty of the Churchyard."

1009.—19 June 1638. *Thomas Futter*, East Wrotham, to *Framling-ham Gawdy.*

Has not finished his "clipping business," so writes to beg Gawdy and Sir John Holland to hold him excused from serving again as constable for the next year.

1010.—25 June 1638. *Anthony Mingay*, Norwich, to *Framlingham Gawdy*, West Harling Hall.

Thanks Gawdy for recent entertainment at Harling. Gawdy's son Robert and all the family are well. 17 died this week, whereof 4 of the plague. John Southes did not receive so much harm in his house as he suffered last term from the High Commission. The Bishop will be here next Friday in a horse-litter, Gawdy would do well to entertain him, "he may deserve it.'

1011.—13 August 1638. *Same* to *same.*

Twenty-three died last week, whereof 5 of the plague. Most of the High Sheriffs were to meet at the Council-board yesterday about the ship-money. Sir Seaman Dewce [*sic* ? Sir Symond D'Ewes] is Sheriff of Suffolk. "Your servant George is fairly quitted having 12 good god-fathers." Let Gawdy's son Fram. remind Sir Thomas of the 5*l.* Lord Maltravers is expected. Sir Ralph Hopton is in town about the business of Sir Owen Smith's land. Both St. Peter's and St. Andrew's men strive for Mr. Carter. Mr. Cock leaves St. Andrews and Mr. Sumptor will lay down St. Peters again. Would have Gawdy enquire about Anguishe's land.

1012.—15 October 1638. *Same* to *same.*

Sends four ounces best tobacco, which cost 4*s.* Gawdy's son Robert wants another winter suit. Speak to Sir Thomas and "my brother Anthony Farmer" to send the money or Mrs. Mingay will have no new bed to lie in withal. Is sorry for Mr. Bedingfield's death.

1013.—20 October 1638. *Same* to *same.*

Gawdy's son Robert wants a new suit and "hopes his learning will bear it out." Mingay will want a new servant at Christmas, when his old man goes home to his father. Gawdy was much missed by his fellow Justices last sessions.

Sir Anthony Drury is dead. "For want of other delinquents the country was compelled to indict Justice [sic ? a name omitted] and found his man for extortion." Some 10 days ago a ship from Rotterdam was cast away, 52 passengers all lost, including Browne the Post and Will. Pettus' son, at least 20 were Norwich people. Only 2 died of the plague this week. The bearer can tell the news of the state between the Bishop and Chancellor.

1014.—4 November 1638. *William Davy*, the Golden Anchor, Fleet St., to *Framlingham Gawdy*, West Harling.

"Suffer me to use a little Court holy water, for the High Sheriff of Suffolk and myself have spent almost this whole day there ; where I did see the Queen-mother, who is a comely, matron-like woman ; who came through London upon Wednesday last, it being railed in on both sides the street from Allgate to Temple Bar (as I am informed) the Livery on the one side and the Artillery on the other She doth live as yet at St. James, but it is *vox populi* that his Majesty will purchase Hatton House and give it her. I am told his Majesty at the first meeting . . . . . did speak of her troubles, she answered that they were nothing in respect she was come to the place where now she is. I am glad to hear she shall have out of France 10,000*l.* sterling per ann. whereby his Majesty shall not be burdened." Sir Thos. Richardson, Mr. Peeke, and Mr. Wymondham were in the Bill for Sheriff of Norfolk "for whom means being made, a fourth man was chosen, viz., Mr. Holl." Sir William Harvey, Mr. Warner, and Sir Simon D'Ewes were named for Suffolk, who also succeeded in getting a fourth pricked, viz., Sir Richard Brooke. One Chaworth an Irish Baron is Sheriff for Nottingham, about which is much dispute. His Majesty will be at Newmarket on 20 inst. The Bishop of Lincoln is a close prisoner.

1015.—[Circ. November 1638.]   *Mary Mingay* [Norwich] to *Framlingham Gawdy.*

Her husband is very angry that his tenant [? Spirling] does not pay the 10*l.* due 3 years ago. She wonders why "her brother" [? Anthony] is so careless of his credit with so good a friend as her husband has been. Please see about getting Will Cannume's [? Canham] son for their servant "he shall have wages and cloak and a good master . . . . . his sister knows our use of a man. I knew he is raw for service but I like the fellow well." Ask cousin William "to send me a shirt to make clouts, and I hope he shall have good luck after it."

1016.—[About 10 November 1638.]   *Anthony Mingay*, Norwich, to *Framlingham Gawdy,* West Harling Hall.

Mrs. Hamond has a daughter and "your rich desired widow Skettow" died last Sunday. Sir Francis Ashley is Sheriff of Norfolk, Sir Anthony Wingfield of Suffolk, Sir Anthony Irby of Lincolnshire, and Sir William Lucking, Bart., of Essex. Has sent Gawdy John Godfrey's bill by Mr. Howse; has paid Cuddon his money and got Mr. Hamond's word for the delivery out of Gawdy's bill. Our sickness much abated, but 10 of all diseases last week whereof 3 of the plague.

1017.—26 November 1638.   *Same to same.*

Mingay has furnished Gawdy's son Robert with his suit of clothes. None have died of the plague this fortnight. "Mr. Sheriff Holl intends to trouble the city with your companies at both assizes if he can prevail."

Mrs. Mingay expects her confinement and will want Gawdy here "to make a Bridgett" and to see how well they have laid out Sir Thomas' money.

1018.—1 December 1638.   *Same to same.*

Charles Rawlyns proposes Gawdy's son Framlingham, for Mrs. Elizabeth Layer, reporting him to have 200*l.* per ann. She is conceived to be worth 3,500*l.*, besides the possibility of her sister's part for want of children. Send him over and he shall see her. Mr. Bayfield will give satisfaction at Twelfth-Sessions about the business spoken of to Mr. Rawlyns.

Henry Barney is dead at Tottenham, leaving a widow who will help Gawdy pay his ship-money "which writs are now come, we understand." (Charles Rawlyns also signs this letter.)

1019.—7 December 1638. *Same to same.*

Mingay wrote Gawdy last week by his cousin Butolph about a match for his son Framlingham which Mingay and Charles Rawlyns are desirous to bring about. If Gawdy were younger or the lady somewhat older she would do for Gawdy himself. If Gawdy were younger or the lady somewhat older she would do for Gawdy himself.

"A staid discreet maid and well spoken and qualified and an excellent gleeker." The High Sheriff's wife is dead of the pox, and Robert Jeegon's wife has died suddenly.

Gawdy's son Robert wants to come home. A parliament is talked of for next March, and 'tis said that 22 patents are called in. Cannot learn why the Lord Chamberlain should come into Norfolk. Harry Barney died in London.

1020.—15 December 1638. *William Moore* [Gonville and Caius College], Cambridge, to *Framlingham Gawdy.*

Moore has accomodated Gawdy's son [Charles] for his journey home. His efforts have not been successful with Charles; "he is averse for this condition he is in," so that the longer he is at Cambridge the more he will be prejudiced, as it is detaining him from some fitter course of life.

1021.—[December 1638.] *Anthony Mingay*, Norwich, to *Framlingham Gawdy*, West Harling Hall.

Mingay had written to Gawdy by Mr. Pell before he received Gawdy's letter by Mr. Bedingfield. Mr. Capps being at London, Mingay delivered Gawdy's letter to his father Bayfield, who says Sir John Hobart hath the promise of the hawk. Mingay cannot help Bedingfield, as they cannot find where he [*i.e.*, his father who died in Oct.] put out any monies in the City, nor hear of any scrivener he ever employed. Gawdy must be content with his "little crib-chamber" at Sessions time, as Mrs. Mingay will be lying in in the best chamber.

Many privy seals are talked of. "I wish you a good widow to help to pay yours . . . . Send Spirling away with my rent to pay for sugar plums."

1022.—21 December [1638]. *Same to same.*

Mingay wishes Gawdy to stand God-father to his expected child ; all Mingay's kindred have been "gone over" and as yet they have had none of his wife's relations. Mr. Loverine [School-master, Norwich] has gone to Cambridge; he advises that Gawdy's son [Robert] should stay till Easter and then go with the rest of his form. Charles Rawlyns agrees that Gawdy should in any event bring his son Fram. and seriously think of the business "and be not too backward for his preferment, we consider as he lives now he stands you in upon 100*l.* a year . . . . . she told me again that if he comes, for our sake she will bid him welcome." Mrs. Delny (?) has refused 4 great matches and "is yet clear, for ought I know."

Son Robert owes 4*l.* Charles Rawlyns thinks the business might have been effected for Tom Gawdy if it had been well followed; they were on with Sir John Mead but are off again.

[Postscript.] About 6 o'clock this morning Mrs. Mingay was brought to bed of a lusty boy. St. Thomas' Day.

1638-9.

1023.—14 January 1638-9. *Same to same.*

Charles Rawlyns spoke with Mrs. Layer who puts off the question of marriage, but young Framlingham thinks she is somewhat engaged to young Bacon of Hockam, "they seem so familiar together."

Mingay has advised Framlingham to desist for the present and see what happens. She has gone into Suffolk this morning with her brother Bence; Mingay could not speak with her himself, being so taken up receiving Skyp's money; he will see her on her return.

1024.—31 January 1638-9. *Same to same.*

Since Framlingham's son departed, "Bacon of Hockam is yet the only man in place." Bence has gone over to see the land and writings. Sir Ury le Neve has lately appeared, backed lovingly by his rich kinsman, and will be perhaps the most fitting match for her, "if she will consider him in his best coat." She thinks well of Bacon of Hockam, but is old enough to be his mother.

The Queen was brought to bed of a daughter, who was christened by the Archbishop and died in 2 hours. The King will be at York in April. Many churches in Kent hurt by the lightning last Monday fortnight. "My Lord Marshal had oysters sent him from Hales in Sussex from a tenant of his, that upon the opening of them were found to be all bloody." [See John Rous' diary, p. 102, and Lady Brilliana Harley's letters, p. 25 (Camden Soc. Publications)].

Baron Denham is dead. A gentleman carried his wife to London last week and died about 8 at night, leaving her 500*l.* a year in land. The next day before 12 she was married to a journeyman woollen-draper that came to sell mourning to her.

Sir Thomas Edmonds has his writ of ease, Sir Henry Vane succeeds him. Sir Thomas Jarmine hath his place, Lord Goring succeeds him. Sir Thomas Jarmine's son hath his place. The Earl of Ancrum is displaced from the Privy Purse and the Marquis of Hamilton's brother has it. Sir William Belfourd, Lieutenant of the Tower, is displaced, no one has it yet. Sir Henry Vane's son is made coadjutor with Sir William Russell, Treasurer of the Navy.

1025.—[? January 1638-9.] *Mary Mingay* to *Framlingham Gawdy*, Harling.

Sends George on purpose to ask how Gawdy is, not having heard since he was at Norwich.

1026.—22 February 1638-9. *Anthony Mingay*, Norwich, to *Framlingham Gawdy*, Harling.

Thanks for a brawn. "My cousin Gawdy Brampton hath bound out his son an apprentice to my brother Utting's son."

The King was at the Tower on Monday to view all the ammunition and went down the Thames to give order about the shipping. "This day fortnight was a most cruel fight at sea between the Hollander and the Dunkirker, and they report the Hollander had the best of it; there hath not been such a fight this 40 years; the pieces were heard plainly within 6 miles of Norwich." Sir Thomas Richardson and his wife have gone to London "to see if he can get off."

Sir Robert Kemp has a letter to the same effect from my Lord Chamberlain; "these be all I yet hear of in this country."

Mingay is sorry to hear the Scots fall out among themselves, "it will breed ill blood at last" . . . . . To conclude with the lass. If "Bacon [of Hockam] refuse her, I believe she will not be made use of this Lent." Agrees with Gawdy that her beauty only deserves a younger brother . . . . . there is room enough in the house to entertain now, " they be at good quiet."

1639.

1027.—27 March 1639. *Thomas Howlyn* "from the place of misery in Thetford" to *Captain Framlingham Gawdy.*

Begs Gawdy, who is appointed to mediate between Howlyn and his merciless creditors, to take some course for his enlargement, so that his industry and labour may be applied to pay his debts and recover his weak decayed fortunes.

1028.—5 April 1639. *Sir John Holland*, Quiddenham, to *Framlingham Gawdy.*

Andrew Reeders, who has been pricked by Gawdy for a "foot arms for his Majesty's present service to York," has already furnished a horse. Hears Gawdy has surplusage, so begs that the double and unexampled burden may be spared him.

1029.—16 April 1639. *Anthony Mingay*, Norwich, to [*Framlingham Gawdy*, Harling].

The trained men are at Yarmouth with 350 which came out of Cambridgeshire, ready to be shipped. The horsemen volunteers are said to have got away on the 24 to Swaffham.

1030.—19 June 1639. *Same to same.*

Thanks Gawdy for his letter sent from London. News is come by the London Post by the way of Suffolk of prospects of peace. The Scots petitioned by the Earl of Dunfermline to have nobles well affected to religion appointed to confer with some of their nobles. The King answered by the Knight Marshall Sir Edward Verney that they must first suffer his first proclamation of free pardon to be read in all the chief places in Scotland to which they have agreed. "We have now a new Mayor to bid you welcome. Will Heveningham graced him with his presence at dinner on the Guild-day."

1031.—29 June 1639. *William Moore*, Cambridge, to *Framlingham Gawdy.*

Receipt for Robert Gawdy's expenses [at Gonville and Caius Coll.] from Lady Day to Midsummer 1639.

Commons and sisings -	- -	£3	10	11
Tuition -	- - - -		10	
2 pair of stockings -	- - -		6	6
Shoemaker -	- - -		5	
Mending apparel -	- -		6	8
A round cap -	- - -		3	
Laundress -	- - -		3	
Books -	- - - -		5	.
Bands, cuffs, socks, gloves, &c. -	-		6	
Matriculation -	- - -		1	1
For fasting nights and diet one week in the town -	- -		11	.
Candles, Barber, and such necessaries -	- - - -		2	6

£6 11 3

1032.—12 July 1639. *Sir E. Moundeford,* Feltwell, to *Framlingham Gawdy.*

Forwards letters from Charles Gawdy, per Northern Post, 2s. to pay.

1033.—6 September 1639. *William Davy,* the King's Head, Norwich, to [*Framlingham Gawdy*].

Perceives by Gawdy's letter that he is in the same mind about buying the moiety of Eccles Manor. Sir Ralph Hopton's solicitor wrote that he would do Davy any courtesy, but by Mr. Bacon's advice Davy sent Judge Reeve the order out of the Court of Wards for the delivery of the writings to the Feodary of Norfolk. This, he said, did not satisfy him as he received them by consent of Sir Charles Gros, who is no party to the suit.

1034.—17 September 1639. *William Heveningham,* Feltwell, to cousin *Framlingham Gawdy,* Harling.

Has to pay 1,000l. on a match between his sister and Mr. Pottes' son. Asks loan of 150l.

1035.—18 September 1639. *William Davy,* King's Head, Norwich, to *Framlingham Gawdy,* West Harling.

The deeds have to be returned to Mr. Justice Reeve after office found, so Gawdy and his counsel had better come to inspect them, while in Davy's hands. Can promise Gawdy the refusal. The bearer is to have 4s., he would not come for less.

1036.—22 September 1639. *Will. Heveningham* to *Framlingham Gawdy.*

Thanks for promise of loan. Had been offered by Sir Robert Payne the refusal of his house and land at Snare's Hill near Thetford, for which Payne's father gave 2,500l. Would Gawdy like it? Will. is buying a manor at Hockwold.

1037.—2 October 1639. *Same to same.*

Heveningham sends his servant for the money.

1038.—17 October 1639. *Elizabeth Napper,* Drury Lane, near the Red Bull, to kinsman *Framlingham Gawdy,* Harling.

Her husband died on Monday, leaving her very poor and liable to be turned out on the streets with her children, as over 20l. is due for rent. Her husband's family will not help her a groat, "in regard that I am not of their religion." Begs his charity.

1640.

1039.—22 July 1640. *William Moore* [Gonville and Caius Coll.], Cambridge, to *Framlingham Gawdy* at Wreatham.
"Leave this at Cutberde's shop that sells Tobacco to be forwarded, &c."

Gawdy's son [Robert] is restored to his health; the sickness not very sharp, but somewhat chargeable. Has spent about 5l., and "some charge must still run for his diet and lodging in the town." He wishes Gawdy MSS. money for new apparel, having "but slender change for the present."

1040.—[After 1634, and before October 1640.] *John Davy* [of Kenninghall, Yeoman], Guildhall [prison], Norwich, to *Framlingham Gawdy*, West Harling.

A begging letter; asks Gawdy and Mrs. Dorothy for 5*l*. he lent her father 20 years since, which with the "use given to usurers," comes to 20*l*. From lending money and giving credit and going security, Davy has lost 1,000*l*.; which made him sell his lands, leaving him still surety for 200*l*., and owing 100*l*. of his own debts. He is now imprisoned, and has wife and children to support; his only comfort being that he was not ruined by play, drink, &c.; his fault was that he "would never be ruled by his wife." There was 40*s*. also due from Sir Charles [Gawdy] which Framlingham might have paid, but said Davy mentioned it too late, the account was made up. Mrs. Mingay has sent him 2*s*. Cannot his long service as Chief Constable be remembered? "Where any of my partners spent a penny it cost me 12*d*., besides the loss of my time . . . I would be loth to live of the basket as I daily see to my grief a gentleman of a great [Norfolk?] house do . . . 20*l*. a year will not defray all my charges in the jail, though I live very sparing." Has heard that one Dame Biby has showed Davy's bonds to her for 100*l*., and offered to sell them for 15*s*. It is true she has such bonds, but as much money is due him by promise of her sister, the widow Waters, "by whom she and hers were made, by my only means." The widow made one, Robert Fenne, her brother, a feoffee in trust, and put 400*l*. in his hands on certain conditions, which he did not perform and sought to carry away the estate. The widow sent to Davy for help, and offered him 100*l*. if he would get her money back, "whereupon I brought him and his confederates into Chancery," and recovered it for her. Widow Waters then at Davy's instigation put Dame Biby in trust with the money (who before that time was of the poorest and basest condition). Biby was bound to pay Davy and others 300*l*. out of the 400*l*., which she now refuses to do and rails and exclaims against him. Begs Gawdy to counsel his (Davy's) unfortunate son to leave vain expenses and idle company, and to pay his debts without suit, and live in his high calling to the Glory of God.

1041.—6 October 1640. *Same to same.*

Davy, by trusting cosening dissembling knaves, has wasted nigh 100*l*. of the little stock left him since his imprisonment.

But 20*l*. remained, owing him by Mr. Sam. Birch, who having died, Davy sued his widow as administrator. She did not act and Sir Anthony Gawdy took the estate into his hands for 40*l*. rent due him, the goods coming (as per inventory) to 200*l*. Sir Anthony Gawdy gave fair promises to pay Davy next after himself and induced him to forbear suing. On sending Mr. Okes the attorney for the money, it now appears all the assets have been paid to other creditors (to Gawdy's advantage, Davy thinks), so there is no remedy. Davy must be compelled to live in the "prison called the hole amongst the baser sort and take of the basket," having no wherewith to maintain himself and wife. Threatens to bring Sir Anthony to public disgrace, which will do him more harm than ever the money did him good.

Curses the time he ever trusted any man so far. Begs Framlingham's intercession.

1042.—[November 1640.]   *Sir John Holland*, Quidenham, to *Framlingham Gawdy*, West Harling.

Understands that John Howse's integrity towards Holland at the former election is become a fault, and that Gawdy has warned him to bring in the Court Rolls and depart his service. Sir John has for his part striven to pass by the discourtesies and injuries he received from many, doing this partly to satisfy the desire of Sir Edmond Moundeford, and also to avoid "sidings and faction" among the gentry of the country. He had hoped to find others " of the like constitution," and especially Gawdy, who has given testimony of a quiet and peaceable nature. [Sir John and Sir Edmond were elected knights of the shire for the short parliament that sat in April, Framlingham sitting for Thetford, having apparently wished to sit for the county. This was the "former election" alluded to. At the election in October for the Long Parliament, Sir John Potts took Sir John Holland's place, which explains the "injuries and discourtesies " the latter speaks of.]

1043.—[November 1640.]   *Sir John Holland*, Quidenham, to friend and ally, *Framlingham Gawdy*, West Harling.

Asks Gawdy to pass over Howse's offence. It would be a clear reflection on Sir John in the eye of the country if he deserted Howse. None would be more troubled to desert their true and ancient affection than Sir John.
[Written the day after No. 1042.]

1642.

1044.—22 November 1642. *John Dusgate to Framlingham Gawdy*.

Receipt for 50*l.* lent within the hundred of Shropham " according to the propositions of both houses of Parliament," at 8 p. cent.

1644–5.

1045.—9 January 1644–5. *Henry Davy* to kinsman *Framlingham Gawdy*, East Wrotham.

On receiving Gawdy's letter by Osborne, Davy saw Warde about renting his lower or middle chamber, he was willing to let the lower chamber at 3*l.* a quarter. Is confident the rooms will not be let by the time Gawdy comes up ;—if they are he can have choice enough elsewhere.

1646–7.

1046.—25 January 1646–7. *John Brett*, of Harling, yeoman, to *Framlingham Gawdy*, of West Harling, Esq.

General Release of all claims, &c. Witness, Edward Briggs, Thomas Catton.

1647.

1047.—16 August 1647. *Anthony Mingay* to *Framlingham Gaway* at the Golden Anchor, against St. Dunstan's Church, Fleet St., London.

Mingay sees little hopes of an accord. Judge Bacon and all his family will be here on Saturday night, "the younger brother that was hanged here on Thursday last took his death that he died innocently of that fact, his brother would then have died with him but was reprieved; there was much lamenting for the other." Parson Carter is leaving, having got institution of Barnham Broom where John Legate was the late incumbent " but we hope the Lady Frances will stay him ; he refuseth to administer the sacrament to his parishioners until an eldership be confirmed, which I believe will be a long time first except the Scots prevail who we understand have entered into England again." Sister Dorothy wishes to know when Gawdy returns; and for him to send her some prunella and candied citron pills. " I trust this day's full meeting in your House [of Commons] will produce some good effect. I perceive the Presbyterian party do again prevail in the House.

[Mr. Carter declined Barnham Broome, and the bells of St. Peter Mancroft were rung on the announcement.]

1649.

1048.—30 April [1649 ?] *F[ramlingham]* *G[awdy, jr.]* to [his brother] *William Gawdy*, Wrotham.

Takes the opportunity of Johnson's messenger, being " very inquisitive whether you have or fear soldiers where you are." " I would desire if Osbourne brought me anything from London you would send word by this bearer," but chiefly that " you would satisfy me by asking my father concerning the Colchester alarms, whether the Parliament injoins the landlord to pay those taxes by Ordinance. I did observe he refused it himself to his Suffolk tenants. I pray, satisfy me very punctually." My lady Gawdy sends service to William, his father and wife and all the rest. She goes away to-morrow week, "then I shall return."

1049.—4 September 1649. *Robert Snelling* to *Framlingham Gawdy.*

Asks payment to his servant John Fornete [?] of 2*l.* lent Mr. Robert Gawdy at Cambridge.

(On same paper, a discharge of all claims, dated 27 Oct., and witnessed by Arthur Nedham, Cleric.)

1649-50.

1050.—20 February 1649-50. *Samuel Moody* to [*Framlingham Gawdy*].

Receipt by Moody from Mr. Edmond Barker by the appointment of Mr. Davy for 7*s.* due from Mr. Robert Gawdy, viz., stockings 4*s.*, and gloves 3*s.* Witness, Thos. Wilson.

1651-2.

1051.—2 February 1651-2. *Mary Dowffylde*, East Wrotham, Widow, and *William Gawdy*, of same place, Esq., to *James Cobbes*, of Great Saxham, Suff., Esq.

Joint bond in penal sum of 200*l.* to secure payment of 106*l.* to Cobbes on 5 February 1652-3. Witness, William Davy, Thomas

Brewster, Ann Brewster. Endorsed memo. of 4 yearly payments of 6*l.* interest, sent by hands of Will. Cropley, Mr. Davy, &c.

1653.

1052.—12 April 1653. *Christopher Hey,* Watton, to [*Framlingham* or ? *William Gawdy*].

Sends 12 ells of holland, 2*l.* 2*s.*, and 10 yards [?] fine white thread, 8*d.*

1653–4.

1053.—[30 January 1653–4 ?]   *Susanna Felton,* Fakenham, to Cousin *Framlingham Gawdy,* Harling.

Her mother, the Lady Felton, died yesterday 29 January at Susanna's house in Fakenham, and desired to be buried with her father and mother in the cloister at Harling. Requests a place may be prepared there for the burial.

1054.—31 January 1653–4. *William Davy,* the Golden Anchor, Fleet St., to [*Framlingham Gawdy* ?].

Davy has asked about "our tickets and it is reported that the clerks demand 6*d.* in the pound." Asks instructions.

Davy desired Thomas Jermyn to get [Gawdy] to change him gold for silver, which Davy will replace when he comes down. (Memo. of account, received of Bennett in part of rent 20*l.*, &c.)

1654.

1055.—3 May 165[4 ?]. *John Pennynge,* Norwich, to his honored friend *Mr. Charles Gawdy,* at his father's house at Wrotham.

At Charles' request, Pennynge sends a fresh copy of the bill without any dates of delivery, which Charles can fill in to suit himself.

1056.—23 May 1654. *Roger Hawe,* Wymondham, to [*Framlingham Gawdy*].

Asks payment to his servant John Mallowes of 6*l.* 3*s.* 9*d.* for physic.

1057.—17 July 1654. *Henry Davy* to his nephew [*William Gawdy*].

Has received Gawdy's tankard [?] and wishes to know what he would have done with it.

Endorsed on this letter is an unsigned draft of a letter (possibly to W. Gawdy also), the writer defends himself against slanderous accusations. Considering how "we lived together for 14 years at Wrotham," the writer cannot believe a bad opinion will be entertained of him. If any cause of displeasure has occurred at [Gawdy's] house, "she would not have spared to tell me, as Nan Heigham can testify," who heard her say if "she should take any offence at me I should hear of it on both sides of my head . . . If anything had troubled her in her mind she could not have concealed it in her fits, when she uttered everything that disturbed her fancy and imagination."

1058.—17 August 1654.   *Thos. Rous,* Sternfield [Suff.], to *Framlingham Gawdy,* Harling.

Rous has now satisfied all his sister Alice's debts, as executrix to "my father Gawdy." He would have paid May too had he deferred his journey to Framlingham for two days; he knew Rous was going to Norfolk to get money for that purpose. For my sister Margaret I never hindered her choice of a guardian," but desired that some one at Framlingham's appointment might undertake for her. There is no money due to her from Rous, and as the goods are divided by Framlingham's appointment, Rous has nothing in hand on which to raise money to pay her debt to May.

1059.—4 October 1654.   *Henry Davy* to nephew [*William Gawdy*].

Sends the silk stockings but the shoes are not yet ready. Remembrances to friends at Harling and Ellingham.

1654–5.

1060.—23 January 1654–5.   *Barbara Hawtrey* to sister *Ann de Grey,* Barkshire (?)

Cousin Ann sends service and thanks for lesson. " Sister Jane salutes you." " Your letter moved me to laughter."

Has no news to send. They are invited to Mr. Pitt's funeral, Mr. Wilkerson's feast, and James Robins' house-warming. Service to uncle Lany and thanks for sack-posset and rambose.

1061.—[? 22 February 1654–5.]   Framlingham Gawdy, Dr., to Chris. Hey [of Watton].

	£	s.	d.
Amount of an old bill - - - -	10	8	6
Fish, herrings, and other wares (19 February) -	4	9	0
Sugar, fruit, and soap (22 February -	3	19	6
	£18	17	0

[*Framlingham Gawdy* died February 25 : 1654–5.]

1062.   27 February 1654–5.   *Robert Newson* to *Framlingham Gawdy,* West Harling.

Intercedes for Gawdy's tenant John Knight, that the writ may not be served on him. He will pay part of the rent and give up farm at Michaelmas and sell his stock. Asks Gawdy to accept a new tenant Knight will name, for whom Newson will go surety. Asks word by Mr. Charles if he is coming over suddenly.

UNDATED LETTERS, &c. belonging to *Framlingham Gawdy's* period. (1606 to 1654–5.)

1063.   *William Davy* to *Framlingham Gawdy.*

Receipted account.

	£	s.	d.
Two bills paid to Mrs. Cockaine - - -	9	8	6
Allowed cousin Thos. Gawdy for his sword which Mr. Tripp had - - -		10	0

	£	s.	d.
Due me on a former account - - -	2	8	0
„ „ six several bills - · - · -	2	18	7

I promised to pay to Mr Redman, which is due from
  my cousin Robert Gawdy   -   -   -   1   0   0
.   .   . all the particular sums above written are discharged.

1064.—*Dr. Jaspar Despotin* to [*Framlingham Gawdy*].

" The things which openeth in the beginning will cause some heat
and dryness, as I told you, although when the stoppings are taken away
this heat ceases by himself." Hopes [Gawdy] needs nothing but good
diet, exercise and good company.

1065.—*Same*, Bury, to *same*.

Mrs. Lambe reports Gawdy inclining to a tertian ague, which
is not a sickness worth troubling about. The "facility of sweat show
some abundance of humor," which as Gawdy will not purge, should not
at least be hindered from coming out by the skin. Might take an
ordinary clyster an hour before supper every other day. In the fits
drink broth in which the roots of fennell, parsley, and succory have been
boiled (twice as much succory as the others together). "Decline the
air till this distemper leaves you, eat nothing the ill night and give all
your sadness to my patient Mr. Frank Gawdy."

1066.—*Same to same.*

The humor Gawdy purged was not so sharp as it was wont to be
because the state of his body is altered and the melancholic humor not
so hot or so plentiful as it was. May use the spleen stone if he wishes,
it will do no harm being an indifferent thing.

1067.—*Jo. Dyx* to *Framlingham Gawdy.*

Has disposed of his buck at Earsham and intended to give his buck
from Kenninghall to his wife but to oblige Gawdy will direct Sir Thomas
Holland to let him have it. His wife and his friends must have patience
for another year.

1068.—*Lady Dorothy Felton* to nephew *Charles Gawdy* (or *Thomas Gawdy* in his absence) [sons of *Framlingham*].

Asks to have the whelp sent on Monday. Charles' not coming
"suits with all my other fortunes, cross."

1069.—*Lady Dorothy Felton* to brother *Framlingham Gawdy*, Harling.

Asks benevolence for her old servant, to be married at Ipswich.
Remembrances to sister and to cousin Doll. Send Charles Gawdy, as
she hopes to effect that business.

1070.—*Same to same.*

Cannot come to Harling to night as she cannot leave her sister Rich.
and has to meet her brother Bassingbourn at dinner at brother Stanhope's
to morrow, "which I must do in respect of my boy." Remembrances
to sister and cousin Doll.

1071.—(14 August.) *Henry Heveningham*, Ketteringham, to *Framlingham Gawdy*, Harling.

His cousin Heveningham coming from Henham, Sir John Rous sent
Mr. Gawdy word that himself, Sir Robert Gawdy, Mr. Hobert, and
Mr. Goulding(?) would be at Gawdy's house next Saturday.

1072.—22 March. *Sir John Holland*, Quiddenham, to *Framlingham Gawdy*, West Harling.

Owing to the miscarriage of Shuckford's son, Gawdy and Mr. Drury have taken away his licence. Asks that it may be regranted on promise of amendment.

Sends award between Kent and Page.

1073.—*Sir John Holland* to [*Framlingham Gawdy ?*].

Warns his correspondent that it is reported his trained men are un-meet for service " by reason of their greenness of years and lowness of stature," so that they will not pass muster at Yarmouth. From his affection he warns his correspondent of this, lest he receive a "public blame at the general muster."

1074.—*Sir John Holland*, Quidenham, to *Framlingham Gawdy*.

The bearer Okeley [?] complains of the burden Gawdy has put upon him, being no trained soldier and having no abundant estate. Better that Gawdy " should take him off here, than we at Yarmouth."

1075.—25 April. *Edward Moore* to *Framlingham Gawdy*.

Understanding by Mr. Abraham that Gawdy purposes to come to Thetford, notifies him that most of the company are just going to a marriage at Watton. To-morrow is Bury Fair so better not come till Wednesday or Thursday.

1076.—[25 December]. *Robert Moulton* to *Framlingham Gawdy's* steward.

Knowing " your respective mind, especially to scholars, serving men, and such as are distressed," Moulton is emboldened to ask relief among the " gentlemen and yeomen of this worshipful house." He is " by accident a stranger without money or means, out of place or employment   .   .   .   travelling to the City of London." He formerly served the late Sir Edward Clere as his clerk, with whom he led a happy life, but is now "like a ship unrigged, without pilot, mast, sail, or rudder; unguided, unstayed, unfriended, undone."

1077.—15 November. *Abigail Moundeford*, Feltwell, to Cousin [*Framlingham Gawdy ?*].

Returns an enclosed letter, with thanks for courtesy shewn her.

1078.—(6 February.) *Thomas Okeley*, Parham [Suff.], to [*Framlingham*] *Gawdy*.

Since Gawdy was last at Sternfield [Suff.] his "poor Copy-holder" Okeley has been advised by good counsel that open wrong was done him by terrifying him about the forfeiture of his land. He denies having committed waste and will not pay 10*l.*, but for the sake of peace will pay 5*l.* to buy Gawdy's good-will. Otherwise he knows what course to take and will have 5 or 6 poor men arrested about this matter. [? The homage who presented him for waste.]

1079.—*Thomas Okeley* to [*Framlingham*] *Gawdy*.

Stanmore has commenced a suit against Okeley touching the house and land where Okeley lives. Requests to know Gawdy's pleasure.

PART III.

CORRESPONDENCE and DOCUMENTS relating to the FAMILY of GAWDY of
West Harling (Norfolk), and their CONNECTIONS from the death of
FRAMLINGHAM GAWDY, in 1654 to 1675.

(NOTE.—*With this series of letters the Gawdy period ends.*)

1654–5.

1080.—[March 1654–5.]   *Robert Foister to [William Gawdy].*

Statement of evidence Foister can give as to John Blomefield having
promised to be his brother's surety if the late Framlingham Gawdy
would lease him a farm ; this was agreed on for 5 years, with the same
covenants (except one) which Framlingham had granted to Mr. Wales,
a former tenant.

1081.—[March 1654–5 ?]   *Robert Foister*, jun., to his father *Robert
            Foister*, Harford.

A boy's letter.   Love to grandmother and sister.   Wants a pair of
shoes.   Grandfather is well.

1082.—[March 1654–5 ?]   *George Hobart to William Gawdy.*

A lady and gentleman came a dozen miles to see the things Hobart
has of Gawdy's.   They offered 20s. for the glass which cost 50s. and
30s. for the two lemon trees, two orange trees and 4 of the best gilt pots.
This was not half what was asked.   If Gawdy wishes to "put off" his
pewter, Hobart can help him to that money he required for it to
Chr. Hey.

1655.

1083.—25 [March] 1655.   *Robert Foister*, Harling, to his master
            William Gawdy, Bury [Suffolk].

The wool chapmen failed in paying and none of the tenants have paid
since Gawdy was at Harling.   Mr. Charles has received 34*l.* of
Mr. Duffield, which (with what Foister has received for wool) will
satisfy Mr. Jermie.   Mr. Bride is to be paid at Christopher Heys to-
morrow week.   Has had much trouble in getting Gawdy's goods
together, the servants be all gone, but Galyord has not returned with
Gawdy's horse.   If he does not return suddenly to Harling will send to
his father's for him.   " Mistress Gawdy goes away to-morrow week and
" is very desirous to compose the business with you.   Mr. Cressner
" has not paid in the 20*l.*, but hath promised this week."

1084.—27 March 1655.   *Robert Foister* [Harling] to his master.
            William Gawdy, Bury [Suffolk].

Thos. Galyard has brought back the horse "in good tune."
Mr. Charles is gone to pay Mr. Jermie, and Foister expects the wool-
men soon and will then wait on Gawdy.
" Mistress Gawdy makes claim to the yellow rug upon the Parlor
" Chamber, but I am informed that your father lent it her, when she
" went to Kenninghall."   She also claims two new coverlets.

1085.—[Circ. 1655.]   *Mathew Snelling* to [*William Gawdy*].

Desires to receive his cousin's quarterage if convenient, as he has to pay his own half year's board to his father.

1086.—4 May [1655].   *Thomas Ogle* (his lodgings next door to the "Reyne-deere" in Russell Street, Covent Garden) to *William Gawdy*.

Would not trouble Gawdy sooner, but begs to tell him that his father (some 14 days before his sickness) borrowed 20*l.* in gold from Ogle. It will be a right to the dead and a civility to Ogle, if it is repaid, if not he had too much respect for the deceased to mention it again.

1087.—7 June 1655.   *Mathew Snelling*, London, to *William Gawdy*, at Mrs. Sharp's, Bury [Suffolk].

Snelling did not think when he left Bury that he would be kept so long. He is detained copying a fine picture of "Princes Royals" down to the knees which he will bring Gawdy next week. His care will then "recover the stop that has been made" in his cousin [John's] drawing. Bid him keep to the pattern Snelling set him and let him know there are some very fine things coming for him to draw by. Service to Lady Duncomb and the other fine ladies.

1655–6.

1088.—28 February 1655–6.   *Christopher Hey*, Watton, to [*Robert*] *Foister*.

Asks payment to bearer of his bill, as he has to make up 400*l.* to-morrow at Norwich. Service to Mr. Gawdy.

1089.—Annexed is receipt for 9*l.* on account, signed by Hey's servant Gardener Isham.

1090.—12 March 1655–6.   *T[homas] E[any]* [? Sonning, Oxford,] to [*Mistress Anne de Grey*, Bury, Suff.].

"And why, forsooth, would you not call me clown yourself, but must write to another to do it for you? . . . why, I am the only gallant of this quarter, and the divulging of this aspersion would be enough to rob you of the esteem you have here . . . Know thou art a trivial, despicable and contemptible wight and must wait your good hour when we are at leisure from more noble and considerable services. Besides two rich and lovely widows, we have here the Earl of Dover's daughters, my Lord of Exeter is expected and the Countess of Devonshire is to come very suddenly. A very good neigbor we have at Woodly" [Oxfordshire] "who has a handsome lady to her daughter, well bred, and (which pleaseth me best) sings very well. But, O the inconstancy of that which we call happiness here! The other lady soon after I had discovered her to you was snatched from me and now I, by a kind of violence, am taken from this. My brother John who is my purse-bearer forces me to quit these old barren quarters to satisfy his desires of having my Company at Laxfield" [Suffolk]. "If I come a horse-back I intend to take Bury in my way and as I pass through your town I may allow you half an eye or so. Jack comes with me, if the good woman will venture the child so far. I cannot tell if you have heard how my sister by the help of a good tough Tertian ague has at length shaken off Mall her Cook, who is since entertained by Mrs. Blagrave. My Lady Chapman is dead, so is honest Dr. Carter."

1091.—18 March 1655-6. *Christopher Hey to William Gawdy.*

Receipt for 9*l*. 17*s*. by the hands of Robert Foister, in full of the debt of the late Framlingham Gawdy, dec^d.

1092.—[Circ. 18 March 1655-6.]   *Robert Foister to [William Gawdy].*

Gibbs promises the 6*l*., but has not yet paid. Foister has paid Hey and sold the wool at a low rate, 6*s*. 6*d*. the stone.

1093.—20 March 1665-6. *Robert Foister [Harling] to William Gawdy, Bury [Suffolk].*

Gibbs promises the rent next week. Benet has been this last week "under the doctor's hands from his own house," but is now recovering and both he and Mr. Bridgs will pay their rents at Lady day. Foister has received 10*l*. rents and paid off Hey. All last week he was at Sternfield [Suff.], and could only get 6*l*.; has arranged for Mr. Charles to receive the remainder. The orchard and garden are done to Gawdy's order, the dove-house prospering and the sheep doing very well, in spite of the very sharp and cold weather. Foister does his endeavour to provide for them and force the tenants to keep the cattle out of the grounds. Mr. Will. Canham and John Bringloe will provide for Gawdy against his coming. "Be pleased to move Serjeant Fletcher concerning the Rivers, that you have no several, but have always been kept by the town, for they are now very earnest for the money and pretend they were advised by Counsel at the Assizes."

1094.—[Circ. 21 March 1655-6.]   *Robert Foister [Harling] to his master William Gawdy, Bury [Suff.].*

Goodman Bringlo and his son bid very low for the farm, 75*l*. a year. "I have satisfied him concerning the bettering of the several, and how beneficial it will be to him. I have alleged that town charges are taken off him."

Another will deal for 10*l*. a year abatement; some reduction must be made "in regard it lie all upon your corn." Bridgs and Benet will pay next week. Can send pigeons by Benet if desired.

1656.

1095.—22 April 1656. *Christopher Hey*, Watton, *to William Gawdy, of West Harling.*

General acquittance by Hey of all bills, debts, &c.

1096.—29 April 1656. *George Dey*, Norwich, *to William Gawdy.*

Receipt for 7*l*. for physic "appointed for Mr. Framlingham Gawdy, esq., late dec^d per Doctor Browne.

1097.—8 May 1656. *Mary Rous [Sternfield] to William Gawdy, Bury [Suffolk].*

Goodman Knight is arrested at suit of one Mr. Ald (?) and goes to jail on Monday unless he can pay." He wishes to sell 5 buds (?), 8 sheep and his colt to Goodman Stannard, but cannot without "your" consent. Sir John thinks there is enough stock, but "you" had better come and select stock to answer the rent so that Knight can sell the rest. Remembrances to "my cousins your brothers."

1098.—12 June 1656. *Henry Davy* to kinsman [*William*] *Gawdy* [Ellingham].

Has received Gawdy's two letters about his chariot and has delivered them to the Coachman [? Coach-builder].

Remembrances to friends at Ellingham.

1099.—[26 ?] June 1656. *Henry Davy* to nephew (or cousin) [*William*] *Gawdy.*

Davy has seen the chariot and the coachman promised it should be ready next day by 9 o'clock to go by the carrier. Davy pointed out that it wanted divers things doing to it, besides the painting, which could not dry in time so that it would gather dust by the road. This the man confessed, and Davy told him to leave it till next week. The boots and shoes from Gawdy's shoemaker can go in the chariot. Davy has received the box of plate, but has been too busy yet to sell it. Asks Gawdy to reconsider his directions about tying his box to the chariot, "I am afraid it will wrong it." Cannot get anything of the Coachman [? any reduction], he says he does not get 20d. by the chariot.

1100.—3 July 1656. *Same to same.*

Has received Gawdy's two letters. The chariot has gone by the carrier; in it are the boots, &c. and a belt for " my cousin Framlingham Gawdy."

1101.—25 August 1656. *James Reynolds,* Hengrave, to kinsman *William Gawdy,* at Harling or elsewhere.

Has no use at present " for such a sum," which he will gladly leave in Gawdy's hands. Did not get the letter, so could not leave an answer at Mrs. Sharp's.

1102.—22 October 1656. *Jo. Howse,* Carlton Rode, to *William Gawdy,* Bury, " he lives near the Angel Hill and is a sojourner [?] there."

Howse waited on the lady yesterday, but the proposition concerning Sir Thos. Hatton's son now pending, could get no full satisfaction. She said Gawdy might take exception " because there was propositions for her other daughter for him of Crowshall, but it was after the proposition for Mr. Needham."

This Howse believes is true. Service to Gawdy and " my young master."

1103.—24 October 1656. *Henry Davy* to [*William Gawdy,* Bury].

Has bespoken shoes, which will not be ready till next week. Please pay the 14l. to Henry's cousin Davy at Bury.

1104.—13 November 1656. *Thomas Roberts* to *William Gawdy.*

Receipt for 10l. 12s. 0d. on bond.

1105.—5 December 1656. *Thomas Lany,* Laxfield [Suffolk], to Cousin *Mrs. Anne de Grey,* Bury.

" Since I lately heard of the death of that imcomparable man . . Mr. Saxby, of Sonning [Oxfordshire], my mind has been like an untuned lute, it sends forth none but confused and jarring notes. Sorrow has got the upper hand . . . Methinks now I am under a kind of sequestration, for you know my friends are my greatest revenue, and he

GAWDY MSS. a very great part of my friends. But what is my loss to that of the
church, to that of his wife and 9 children, to that of the town of Sonning ?
which, of a fair village, by the fall of this reverend oak is become bleak
and unpleasant.

"But truly (setting one or two families aside) though they stand in
need of pity they do not deserve it, but rather the curse of a Sectarian,
dunstical [sic] covetous Presbyterian successor, for their want of respect
to him whom God had plentifully endowed with the contrary virtues."
Asks particulars of his death and burial, &c. if "my brother Barker"
has informed Mrs. de Grey of them. Service 'to my lady; "pray send
me the old, very old piece of a book I gave you to keep for me, it has
too long disgraced your study."

1657.

1106.—7 May 1657.   *Alice Pell*, the new Exchange, London, " at
the sign of the Holy Lamb, below stairs,"
to *William Gawdy*, at Mrs. Sharp's, Bury.

Sends 8 bands, &c. (as below). As for the laced linen, she could not
do it, there was a quarter of a yard short and the lace could not be
matched, so she returns it. Her shop is the Holy Lamb, the next shop
to Mr. Hanbury, the hosier.

8 holland bands and cuffs at 7s. - - -	£2 16	0
6 pair of boot-hose at 7s. - - -	2 2	0
Cambric and making laced bands and cuffs -	5	0
4 pair of band strings - - - -	1 3	0
	£6 6	0

[Endorsed " discharged by my uncle Henry Davy, 14 Dec. 1657."]

1107.—4 June 1657.   *Robert Daye*, Middle Temple, [London] to
" the honourable and truly virtuous the
Lady Elizabeth de Grey, at her house in
St. Edmond's, Bury."

Daye is bold to visit Bury before his time, and has to beg her
Ladyship's "entrustment with a new score before I have discharged
my former debt, thus I tally without cancelling, thus I receive without
returning, and what a strange kind of audit and account is this! Or
upon or (and so are your Ladyship's favours golden and weighty indeed)
I confess is very false heraldry, but no doubt 'tis true transcendent
courtesy. "Your brother Madam, is our Treasurer," [requests her
letters to him for permission for Daye to go to Bury?] "My words,
alas, would be but a cipher, mine but a mute, mine but a blank; yours
a real figure in the Arithmetic, yours a letter in the alphabet, your
Ladyship's a capital Name in the Grand Calendar of his account."
[Signs, "yours exceedingly much obliged kinsman."] Service to
daughter, Mrs. Anne de Grey.

1108. 16 August 1657.   *Barbara Hawtrey* to her sister *Mistress
Anne de Grey*.

Sends service to her uncle Lany, "from whom I received a charge of
many lines, but desire a treaty till next or t'other week, for my headpiece is so foul that it cannot perform any handsome execution. I
cannot be very sorry for your loss, for I have had a greater ; my tailor
(who I had a very good opinion of) hath taken in, in my name at our

shop 5*l.* or 6*l.* worth of silks for his own use, and about 3*l.* for my
sister Hawtrey's name, and is gone I know not whither. This will
I think prevent my having a new gown to wait on you with. Notwithstanding all this if myself and family be well, and my foot give me leave
(which hath now something breeding on it and makes me go lame)
I intend for London with my sister Cletherow," &c.

1109.—21 October 1657. *Henry Davy* [London] to *William
Gawdy.*

Hopes Gawdy has received the cloth Davy sent him. Please pay
the money to brother William Davy.

1110.—5 November 1657. *Same to same.*

Sends 3 yards of cloth : the baize to line the cloak cannot be got to
match in London. Please pay brother William before he comes to
London, as he has to pay money in the country for Henry. Davy gave
Gawdy's letter to cousin Bass, who is gone to France, only staying
3 or 4 days in London. He returned the money by the same merchant
Sir Henry recommended [?]. Gawdy's rent is paid at Eaton. College.

1658.

1111.—6 June [1658 ?]. *Anne Hawtrey Lee* to sister [*Mrs. Anne
de Grey,* Bury].

Is unwilling to leave the town without giving her sister notice that
"thy prayers may go with me to Rislip" [?]. Looks for the coach on
Saturday. All things are concluded with Mr. Row and Cousin Jones,
who will be married suddenly. Wishes there was as much certainty
of her well-doing, the match but small for her fortune, "and he a
sparkish man, loves to live well." Brother and sister Rogers accompany
them, houses are very scarce and he is willing to settle at the end of
the town. Service to my lady and brother Gawdy. Mr. Fram: was
very well, he came to take his leave last week.

1112.—20 July 1658. *Mary Rous,* Kettishall, to [*William Gawdy*].

Hears that Goody Pettit gives out that her son Robert Drane shall
continue the farm if "you" do not take her son Edmund Newson as
tenant ; or some one who will give Drane 20*l.* for it. Both sons are
coming this day about it to "you." Others are deterred from offering
by their "big words." If it were to let from Michaelmas twelvemonth
(instead of this Michaelmas) Copland would take it, and in the meantime
Mary Rous will rent it herself giving security for the rent on her stock
and crop.

1113.—25 October 1658. *Anne Hawtrey Lee* to sister *Anne de
Grey.*

"This last letter very well pacified my anger . . . I won't challenge
thy affection, but have a better opinion of thee than thou hadst of me,
and think as well of Prince Morrice [sic] as ever I did, and all that
belongs to it, and wish myself almost as near to it as the bed is every
night, and then thou shalt see how much I am his humble servant."
Is looking out a nurse in obedience to Mr. Lee's desires, and wishes
she could think so slightly of what she has to go through as Anne does.
Would much like her sister's "sweet company " at that time, but must
be content to remain "at this great distance." Thanks Mrs. Green
for her care of the butter. Service to my lady, Mr. Laney, Jack Gawdy

GAWDY MSS. and the rest of "my acquaintance." Mr. Lee and brother Ned send service.

1114.—19 November 1658. *James Simson to William Gawdy.*

Sends Mr. William's suit and coat. "I do not question their fit dimensions, for I had a more exact proportion of him according to order."

1115.—[? Circ. 1658.] *Mary Simson to William Gawdy*, Esq., at Mr. Robert Sharp's, Bury, [Suffolk].

Will try to give content according to instructions, "but they wear them broad, most extreme broad [?], but you may wear them as you please." Hopes Gawdy has not yet disposed of his old shirts. Will send the bands with the gloves and strings.

1658-9.

1116.—22 March 1658-9. *William Davy* [London] to Cousin [*William*] *Gawdy.*

Has paid Gawdy's Eton rent due at Lady-day, near 43*l.*, and will send the college acquittance for the Mich. rent, as the bursar talks of some small arrear then due. Failed to see Sir Robert Drury at his lodging, about the rent charge of Garboldisham. Will show Gawdy a discharge of all arrears thereof to Mich. 1656. Wishes to hear when Gawdy comes to Harling. Well wishes to self and children.

1659.

1117.—9 April 1659. *William Gawdy to Sir John Duncombe*, Knight (both of Bury).

Bond in penal sum of 200*l.* to secure payment of 103*l.* on 10 Oct. 1659. Witness William Cropley, Nich. Gyrling.

Endorsed, "please pay to Mr. Cropley Duncombe of Bury, 19 Sept. 1659."

1118.—19 May 1659. [*Framlingham?*] *Gawdy* to brother *William Gawdy*, at Mrs. Sharp's house in Bury, [Suffolk].

Has received William's letter [about Bassingbourn Gawdy's (?) not paying a debt] and is glad the crime is no worse. Will certainly write to him, if William's uncle Davy can direct the letter. Asks William to be cautious not to prejudice him, "pray consider what a young man is abroad without credit, where peradventure he may starve or meet with unknown calamities for want of trust," &c. "Remember he is a young man, and you have nothing else to find fault with him for." Hopes to be at Crowshall after Whitsuntide.

1119.—21 October 1659. *Edward Briggs*, Honingham, to *William Gawdy*, at his lodgings at Mr. Sharp's, Bury.

Asks for time till Candlemas to pay his [rent ?], the harvest has been tedious and it would be labour in vain to try and borrow it.

1120.—22 December 1659. *Henry Davy* to nephew *William Gawdy*, Mrs. Sharp's house, Bury.

Has sent the cloth, &c., by Bury carts. Has returned the 50*l.* into France for "my cousin Bass."

4 yards and half an ell of cloth at 25s.		£5	15	8
5 yards of baize at 3s. 4d.		0	16	8

		6 12 4
[Added in another hand] "bringing down"		0 1 0
Cropley's bill		2 17 10
Making		0 14 6
		£10 5 8

1660.

1121.—[Before May 1660.] *Do. Leeke* to *Bassingbourn Gawdy*, or in his absence to [his brother] *Charles Gawdy*, Harling.

Mrs. Leeke's affairs concerning her tenant Salter (who owes 5 half year's rent) have been ill handled by a careless or dishonest attorney. She therefore sends the bearer, Mr. Butt, whom she can trust, to follow her business. Begs help for him (as he is a stranger), especially if he should need an attorney, bailiff, or some honest countrymen to help him. If Butt collects the rent, will Gawdy keep it till she comes; and if he needs money; please advance it to him. Service to brother Charles, "whose help I beg," and your sister.

[Endorsed with Charles Gawdy's account of wages paid at washing and sheep clipping at Harling and Eccles, the laborers being divided into washers, clippers, the thrower into the wash-pot, the carriers, the wool-gatherers, the branders and the winders.]

1122.—24 May 1660. *Do. Leeke* [?] to *Charles Gawdy*, West Harling.

"Sweet Mr. Gawdy, your brother [William] and cousin are very well at the Hague, where the States of Holland entertain the King and all that are come out of England. The King and Duke of York knew your cousin, and are extremely kind to him. My Lord Monk went yesterday to meet the King, 'tis thought he will be landed as last night or this morning at Dover." Mr. Salter has given satisfaction, so get his bond back from the [? bailiff or bail] as it would prejudice him if it were returned to London. Service to Charles' wife, to Bass, and to Mr. Thomas.

1123.—18 June 1660. *Do. Leeke* to [*Charles Gawdy*, Harling].

Salter, her tenant, will not take a new lease. The heirs of the Sowwells will join with her and Lady Hart to grant a lease for 7, 11, or 21 years. Supposes it should be "set up in papers in the market towns," and asks Charles' help to get a tenant. "My hay is let for 121l. a year, and my lady Hart's for as much, the quit rents are 11l. 16s. a year besides." Will be vacant Michaelmas 1661. Service to Charles' wife and brothers.

1124.—15 October 1660. *Robert Hornebye*, of Botesdale [Suffolk], to *William Gawdy*, of Harling.

Acknowledgment of Hornebye's indebtedness in 18s. Witness, Thomas Pell, John Howse.

1125.—29 November 1660. *Bassingbourn Gawdy*, of West Harling, Esq., to *William Davy*, of Ellingham, Magna, gent.

Bond in penal sum of 120l., to secure payment of 101l. to Davy, on 1 February next. Witness William Gawdy, Ed. Ireland.

1126.—8 December 1660. *Cressy Tasburgh*, Bodney, to [? *Framlingham* or *Charles Gawdy.*

Tasburgh was told by Sir Ralph Skipworth 10 days ago to write " to my brother Jack about the election of your brother, Mr. William Gawdy, in one of Mr. Howard's boroughs." Jack will do all he can, but advises that William should write direct to Mr. Howard, "disclaiming any interest of his own to be considerable." Let my Lord Richardson and Sir Philip Woodhouse deliver this letter, giving Jack notice that he may be at Mr. Howard's elbow. "My service to your fraternity."

1127.—24 December 1660. *Robert Ayrs to Thomas Gawdy.*

Authority to pay 40s. (on account of score of malt delivered by Ayrs, at Crowshall) to Mr. Charles Gawdy, for Mr. Daniel Reve.

1128.—10 $\left\{\begin{array}{l}\text{Septem}\\\text{Octo}\\\text{Novo or}\\\text{Decem}\end{array}\right\}$ber 1660. *Sir John Holland* [London] to kinsman *William Gawdy*, Bury.

Sir John was glad to hear what was done at the meeting of the Deputy Lieutenants at Norwich, and also that Gawdy was one of their number. If Sir William Doyly laid down his pretences to Depwade Hundred, Sir John designed his cousin Knyvet to command that company, and be his Lieutenant-Colonel, as his father was. He also meant (if the old practice of letting Colonels chose their own officers continued) to make Gawdy Captain of Shropham and Guiltcross, and Major (as his father was). The rule of seniority was not observed in Gawdy's father's time, " nor shall it be now." Desires to know if this will be acceptable before he makes out his list. If parliament dissolves at the prefixed time, Sir John may spend part of Christmas in Suffolk. [Mentions his having been " beyond sea."]

1660–1.

1129.—15 January 1660–1. *Sir John Holland,* London, to *William Gawdy*, Bury.

Expected to have received the names of Gawdy's Lieutenant and Ensign, so that he could have taken out all the Commissions, "blanks are not to be expected. . . I doubt not but you will now look so far into the military Art that you will enable yourself to discharge the active place of a Major, whose office it is to draw up the Regiment upon all occasions, and to see all words of command to be observed through the Regiment, and I believe we shall muster by Regiments in the Spring." May have to get a new deputy lieutenant [?] so wishes to quicken his officers that no more may lie upon his own hand than is proper as Colonel.

1130.—12 March 1660–1. *Edward Drewett*, Oxburgh, to friend *Charles Gawdy*, Harling Hall.

Asks Gawdy to receive from Sir Robt. Drury for him 40l., four years arrears due last Michaelmas, and 5l. rent due Lady-day. Drewett will attend at Harling for the money about 8 April.

1131.—23 March 1660–1. *John Mingay* [Norwich ?] to [*Framlingham* or *Charles Gawdy ?*]

Is much honored by the proposed visit of " your brother " [? William] begs his correspondent to come also at the election. Would have taken it an even greater honour if they had commanded that " due debt without any notice."

1132.—23 March 1660–1. *William Gawdy*, of West Harling, to Sir *Thomas Harvey*, of Bury, [Suffolk].

Bond in penal sum of 100*l.*, to secure payment of 50*l.* 15*s.*, on 24 June next, at William Cropley's house in the "Cookerowe," in Bury. Witness Roger Kerington, Nich. Gyrling.

[About this time William's eldest son, *Bassingbourn*, died in London.]

1661.

1133.—1 April 1661. *Edward Peck* [Temple] to *William Gawdy*, at his house in Bury (leave this at Mr. Sharp's house).

The best expedient for the chamber that was Gawdy's sons would be to desire leave of the house that some relation (the nearer the better) may be admitted. If not too late (by reason of any promise made by the Treasurer, Mr. Goddard), this may be done for 60*l.* at most, probably less, and the nominee can then sell it. Send the name of the person who shall "really have it" or who is to act as a trustee, and Peck will do his best.

1134.—29 April 1661 *Same to same* [London].

Desires to see Gawdy that day or next on the business.

1135.—[30 April 1661 ?] *Henry North* [Mildenhall, Suffolk ?] to *William Gawdy, Esq.*, M.P., Westminster.

Thanks Gawdy for finding him a lodging near the Golden Lion in the Strand, there being no part of the town more to his liking, unless he could be nearer Gawdy and Sir Edmund Poley [M.P. for Bury]. Possibly Sir Edmund has got a lodging for North, if he has not, please secure this for the 14th of the next month, when "my brother Holland" is to call for North. Son Harry and the girls send their service.

Gawdy's neighbour at Bury, Sir William Russell, died last Monday night.

1136.—3 May 1661. *Henry Davy*, London, to *William Gawdy*. [Endorsed "Uncle Henry Davy's bills for the children."]

	£	s.	d.
Paid Mrs. Gawdy	15	2	0
„ Jack Gawdy's master	16	5	0
„ Mr. Symson (tailor)	5	0	0
„ for torches	0	16	0
„ for candles	0	4	6
Delivered your man to go post into Norfolk	1	10	0
Paid for two coffins	3	8	6
„ for putting my cousin Bass into a coffin	0	1	0
„ to our beadle to look to the pall and attending at the burial	0	1	0
„ to the clerk in the Temple for duties due to the church	9	13	0
„ to our maids	1	0	0
„ for William Gawdy's commons	1	15	0

GAWDY MSS.

					£	s.	d.
Paid Mrs. Gawdy's maids	-	-	-	-	1	10	0
„ Mrs. Gawdy	-	-	-	-	24	3	6
„ the haberdasher	-	-	-	-	39	10	0
„ for rosemary	-	-	-	-	0	1	0
„ for wine at the Horn Tavern	-	-	-	2	5	0
„ „ „ "Pope's Head"	-	-	-	2	5	0
„ to the herald[ic] painter	-	-	-	2	12	0
„ the porter for bringing the plate	-	-	0	1	0
„ for letters	-	-	-	-	0	3	6
„ Jack's master when he went out of town	-	17	0	0
„ Mr. Symson	-	-	-	-	5	0	0
„ Dr. Denton	-	-	-	-	10	0	0
„ the wax-chandler	-	-	-	-	4	0	0
„ the minister of the Temple for going to my cousin Bass	-	-	-	-	0	10	0

			£164	5	0

				£	s.	d.
Received of a merchant a bag sealed up	-	-	31	6	11
„ of my cousin Webb	-	-	-	50	0	0
„ for plate	-	-	-	-	35	0	0
„ by bill of exchange	-	-	-	50	0	0

			£166	6	11

[Account is receipted as of 3 May.]

1137.—11 June 1661. *John Earle*, Burnham Market, to [?].

Encloses Mr. Mandey's letters in relation to Lakenham. Hopes to be in London on Saturday to receive his correspondent's commands.

1138.—4 July 1661. *William Gawdy*, of Harling, to *John Hervey*, of Ickworth [Suffolk], Esq.

Acknowledgement of Gawdy's indebtedness in 70*l.*, witness, William Bell.

1139.—30 July 1661. *William Davy* to cousin *Charles Gawdy*.

Asks payment of 9*l.* 10*s.* due him by Will. Gawdy.

[Endorsed with memo. of 105 lambs, 20*l.*, 28 crones, 5*l.* 12*s.*, and other rough calculations.]

1140.—[Circ. July 1661.] *Henry Davy* to kinsman [*William Gawdy*].

The gentlemen in the Temple has never paid the 110*l.* [?] for Gawdy's chamber there, and Davy does not think "they" mean to have it. Has not heard from them since Gawdy went and does not know where they live.

1141. 31 July 1661. *Sir John Holland*, London, to *William Gawdy*, at the Abbey in Bury St. Edmund's, Suffolk.

Since "you left us on Monday last the Bill we sent up to the Lords to prevent the printing of seditious books was returned to us with a proviso to exempt the houses of the Peers from search." At a conference the Commons declined to add to the privileges of the Lords, which were attached to their persons, not their houses or estates.

They also argued that the houses of commoners were as free from such · GAWDY MSS.
search now as those of the peers. After a free conference and the
Lords vainly laboring to "convince us of the reasonableness of this
proviso" the Commons at another conference "answer the reasons by
the Solicitor and adhere: which warmed the Lords, they having vouched
some precedents (as they thought) ·.· . . . and at another conference
. . my Lord Privy Seal who managed all these conferences declared
to adhere . . . and offered us the Bill which was refused to be
received, they being possessed of it and offering to deliver it without
any alteration. Whereupon the Lord Privy Seal threw it down upon
the table, where we left it and where possibly you may find it on the
20 of Nov. to which day Parliament is adjourned.",

On Tuesday morning the Lords desired a conference on the Bill for
the Reparation of the highways about St. James and Piccadilly, "when
we found the [other] Bill upon the Table in the painted chamber, of
which neither the Lords nor we took any notice." The Lords had
originated and sent down a Bill of their own about the levying of rates
for these roads,· to which the Commons excepted as being matter of
taxation, and brought in a bill of their own. The Lords now desired a
proviso saving their rights [to bring in such bills] which was so altered
by the Commons on Tuesday as to mean next to nothing "and at a
conference whilst the King was come to the House and retired into the
lodgings we returned this proviso so amended, which the Lords after
some debate laid by and entered a saving in their Journal-Book and so
we were sent for by the King . . . Mr. Speaker made an elegant
speech and presented his Majesty with the Bill for the levying of the
arrears of the excise, which may be worth to him (if all dues can be got
up) near 200,000l. as Birch reports, who best understands it." . . .

"The oldest parliament man alive cannot give such another instance
that a bill should be left by both Houses upon the table at a conference.
. . . I hope before we meet again (the dog days being over, and that
we have all taken the fresh air, which I am going to fetch within very
few days beyond the seas) we shall cool, and so meet in better temper."
The king's revenue being yet unsettled, a good intelligence between the
Houses is desirable, otherwise the King may be persuaded and enforced
to call a new Parliament. Holland has taken leave of the King and
procured a pass for his journey and return with wife, family, and household stuff without search or molestation. He supplied Gawdy's place
at Mr. Harvye's [? Harryes] one evening "where we were engaged in
prattle until twelve."

1142.—9 September 1661. *Martha Brewster*, Lanshull [?] to
William Gawdy, Bury.

Asks for payment of "your son's quarter," a fortnight's board over,
and 7s. 8d. laid out for him for linen, &c., in all 4l. 8s. 8d.

Understands Gawdy questions the spoon and the linen, " Sir, when I
lived first in the North Gate Street you sent your man Elett [?] to me
to know whether I would board your sons at the same rate I had
formerly done, and I told him if I might have 2 pairs of sheets and for
each of them a spoon I should be contented."

Thinks she might challenge the return of the other spoon, rather than
give up this.

1143.—27 September 1661. *Same to same.*

Receipt for 4l. 8s. 8d. received of Edward Gregory.

u 19269.   N

1144.—5 December [1661]. *Barbara Hawtrey* to sister *Anne de Grey*.

Barbara never.heard any ill of the gentleman: Brother Ned has enquired of one Mr. Martin (the suitor's neighbour) from whom Barbara buys cloth, he gives a good account of him. Has received 2 letters which she sends to her mother. Does not like to advise, having been unfortunate in the like business of others, but thinks Anne's own inclinations had better be followed. " Mr. Allington is, in.all friends' accounts, a better match than Jack Gawdy."

1145.—5 December 1661. *Thomas Laney* to [*Anne de Grey*].

Advises her that her friends show their respect to her by being zealous for or against the suitor, when they do not intend their own advantage. Cousin Barker is an honest man and true friend, but was never Laney's privy Counsellor. Is confident " your friend " will go back to her old opinion and prefer the other man when she understands Sir John [Duncombe] is of his namesake's side.

" That which you say has filled your town is like Rodger's tobacco, it moveth in sundry places and tumbles up and down London and Westminster also. Heaven keep it from a public ·debate in the house of Commons! Many of the members I know are pleased to think themselves concerned in·it." Sir John Dun[combe] said.he was desired from Bury to enquire into the citizens' estate, but can tell no more than his intimate friend John Harvey reported. W. A[llington] is the only man who can correctly estimate it. He has enough to make Anne happy, if she could be satisfied in other particulars. Sir John has talked to Mr. Gawdy, and thinks my Lady broke off the former proposal for Jack Gawdy upon an unusual and unreasonable demand. Suggests that in such a less material and accidental point she should be governed by custom ; ask Mr. Maltard or any other they can trust. If they come to this opinion " let me know it and Jack shall soon be your humble servant." Has no leisure to buy her books.

1146.—[Circ. 5 December 1661.] *Barbara Hawtrey* to sister *Mrs. Ann de Grey*, at Lady de Grey's, Bury [Suffolk].

Ann's last letter moved Barbara to pity, and she has made every enquiry about the gentleman's repute in London ; has no certain news but is hard to believe his estate is so great. Did he not have a partner, one Baker, two years ago, or let part of his shop to him " which sounds not very well." She will write definitely on Thursday, which Anne will get Saturday. Wonders at nothing but Anne's " condescension to the City, where certainly they live well. . . .

" I admire he doth not offer to purchase land," supposes he wishes to avoid office in the City.

1147.—14 December 1661. *Edward Drewett*, Oxburgh, to [*Charles Gawdy*, Harling].

Request Gawdy to collect 20*l.* rent due Michaelmas from [Sir Robert. Drury's tenant, Mr. Howse].

1661-2.

1148.—4 January 1661-2. *Same*, Oxburgh, to [*Same*, Harling].

Understands by Mr. Bunce [?] that Gawdy gave Howse time, and that it is doubtful if Drewett would find Gawdy at home if he came for the money. Asks word whether the money is to hand.

Send letter by one Precious who comes from Harling to Swaffham market every Saturday to buy hemp ["hympe"]; he can leave it at William Bell's, the Spurrier, at Swaffham.

1149.—20 January 1661–2. *Robert Duxe* to his landlord *Charles Gawdy.*

Sends this bearer on purpose to speed Sir Thomas Smyth's letter.

Asks help in the difference between himself and fellow-parishioners and Mr. Rous. Rous declares for tithe of broom-wood burnt in town for bricks and for "herbige" of horses and colts which was never paid before. They are sworn to answer particulars in the Spiritual Court. " He refuseth references, saying to one of us ' Shall I refer it to another man to determine whether my coat on my back be mine own or another's ?'" . . . "I beseech you leave me not in a labarynth."

1150.—13 February 1661–2. *T[homas] L[any]* to cousin *Mrs. Anne de Grey,* Bury [Suffolk].

Lany heard of Anne's return from Norfolk by his brother Franklin, and (by another hand) of the new servant she has. It was Mr. Gawdy told him this, " and in truth, Coz, he did it with a great deal of concern as if it had been the breakneck of all his hopes and designs." He was most anxious to match his son " and to you before any other." Will send the books wanted, " a very proper entertainment for Lent." Anne will find nothing so good in Dr. Sanderson as she has already in Bishop Andrewes, "whose sermons sure will outlast all others." [In postscript.] Since getting her second letter, Lany, " to appease the storm raised in you by my cousin Cis," got up earlier than usual to procure the books. The impression of Dr. Hamond's life is all sold off, " but the Bishop this week comes down to you in the waggon, and I hope brings his blessing with him." Sir Robert Clinch's daughter " (that lived in London) was buried yesternight. [On separate slip] : The Queen of Bohemia died last night. Pray send the Holy Court and Clemens Alexandrinus, both folios—send them as the Bishop comes, wrapt up in brown paper.

1151.—4 March 1661–2. *James Simson* [tailor] to *William Gawdy,* of Harling.

Receipt for 41*l.* in full of all debts, &c.

1662.

1152.—1 May 1662. *Sir Jo. Tasburgh,* Arundel House, to *William Gawdy,* at Mr. Sharp's house, Bury [Suffolk].

On his return from Dover, Tasburgh found Gawdy's letter. He is sensible of Dr. Stephen's misfortune about the Parsonage of Wells. It was an accident unexpected by all. " If a man dies and revives again we must ascribe it to the providence of God." There are many suitors to Dr. Lewin for the living ; Tasburgh will be very willing to back Gawdy's recommendations to Dr. Lewin.

1153.—3 July 1662. *Sir John Holland,* London, to *William Gawdy,* Bury [Suffolk].

" Dear Major," Sir John Holland has received Gawdy's letter but not the news he expected, viz., "the assurance of your son's marriage and your resolution to retire from the pleasures of Bury to those of

GAWDY MSS. Harling," which would be "an invitation of great force" to Sir John,
who hopes to make himself of the neighbourhood next year. Sir John
is vexed that his name was left out of the Commission for the regulating
of the Corporations, on which Gawdy has been acting.

"Touching the scruple upon the Commission which occasioned your
adjournment, it is fit to be concealed what you can, even for your own
sakes." The Commission was sent up express to Sir John, who has
had it amended and new sealed, it was but a slip of the clerk. It is
now returned to Lord Townshend.

About 3 weeks since there was a current report of " our re-assembling
before the 28th February, but I thank God with you we hear no
more of that. Sir John Duncombe . . tells me they are full of
faction and division at Court, but I will not forestall him with his
own news . . . The Earl of Bristol is again ours, newly departed
from Rome to us, God keep him with us ! "

Sir John sets out for Norfolk about Monday week. If he comes
down with his Dutch mares he will take but short journeys, but if he
can buy geldings will come quicker in a chariot.

Asks Gawdy to call for him at Quidenham to go together to Norwich
Assizes. My Lord Townshend desired Sir John to come direct to
Rainham and would send his coach to Thetford to meet him, but Sir
John must take Quidenham on his way.

1154. — 11 November 1662.   *John Howse*, Buck[enham], to
                                          [*William Gawdy*].

Has been laid up with a fever or ague. "The attornies [are] all
going now for London and I must despatch all before they go."

Has often spoken to Bringloe to have his suit stayed. The Muster
Roll for Shropham hundred is not yet done ; there is no great haste,
Sir John Knyvet after appointing a day to muster has put it off and
Sir Robert Kemp has done nothing " but upon the old account."
[Postscript.] "Mr. Lovell tells me of trouble in London " [Ensign
Tongue's rising] "which I heard not of before, for I have been very
sick, but I will hasten the business."

1155.—5 December 1662.   *Aug[ustine] Briggs*, Norwich,   to
                              William Gawdy, Bury Abbey.

Sends 2 lbs. of Tobacco " special Spanish Snesh [?] " 1*l.*

1662-3.

1156.—2 February [1662-3 or earlier].   *Thomas Hervey*, to *William
                                  Gawdy*, Esq., the Abbey,
                                  Bury [Suffolk].

Would gladly leave the 40*l.* in Gawdy's hands, but cannot do so,
having engaged himself to others. Service to Mr. Holland.

[After July 1662 and before June 1663, *John Gawdy* married *Anne
de Grey*, daughter of *Sir Robert de Grey* of Merton.]

1663.

1157.—6 June 1663.   *Peregrine Tasburgh*, Bodney, to [*Charles
                         Gawdy*, Harling ?].

Tasburgh's brothers are absent, and will answer the letter next week.
[Endorsed with a rough account (? Charles Gawdy's of rents received
from 12th February 1662-3 to 12th June 1663, viz., 6 sums amounting

to 317*l*. received, and 8 sums amounting to 311*l*. 12*s*. disbursed GAWDY.MSS.
"Gurling owes me 1*l*."]

[13 July 1663. *William Gawdy* made a Baronet— first so styled in
letter of 2 October, post.]

1158.—27 August 1663. *Thomas Laney*, Westminster, to Cousin
Anne Gawdy [née de Grey].

Laney has to-day returned from Buckden [Hunts.] " the only place now
where the Bishop of Lincoln " [Benjamin Lany, formerly Bishop of
Peterborough, afterwards of Ely] " has a house standing fit to receive
him. We have been there 3 weeks and are now come to our old
dwelling in Westminster from whence before Michaelmas we remove
again to Buckden," till Parliament sits. Although Buckden is but
30 miles or so from Mrs. Gawdy " the conveyance for letters will be
nothing so speedy as now." Would like to hear of her condition
" not only from the contagion of the place you live in, but from the
hopeful burden you carry." Remember that others besides her
" very loving husband," will be glad to hear of her. " Whilst I am
writing Fram. [Gawdy] salutes me bonny and blithe : he tells me my
cousin Gawdy has not been well but now is brave. He has been
this afternoon at Mrs. Lees, it seems she is gone to Ruislip [Haw-
trey's seat, Middlesex]. Petty Bestbeer he found at home and she
told him Mrs. Betty Jermyn is married. Fram. would very gladly
hear from his brother or you or grandmother."

1159.—15 [?] September 1663. *John Harwyne*, Fakenham, to
Mr. Gawdy.

Desires payment of 21*l*. due him, or part at least to enable him to
pay his harvestmen, &c. Do not " disrespect the messenger, Robert
Taylor, my shepherd."

1160.—29 September 1663. *W. Doull*, London, to *William Gawdy*,
Bury.

Renews the application he made 3 weeks ago by my Lord Callan
(" who is in Suffolk ") that Gawdy would pay 40*l*. due by his son
[Bassingbourn] of worthy money. Had " your son lived to see me in
England . . . the payment of that money would have been the least
civility he would have shown me." Nothing but this stays Doull
from returning to France. " I am lodged at the great Pearl in James
Street, in Covent Garden." Begs not to be kept waiting for an
answer. [Post-mark $\left(\frac{SE}{29}\right)$.]

1161.—2 October 1663. *W. Doull*, London, to *Sir William
Gawdy*, Knight and Baronet, Bury,
[Suffolk.]

My Lord Callan informs Doull he has seen Gawdy, who will soon be
in town and satisfy Doull, whereupon he gave up Gawdy's son's bond.
Begs to be dispatched as soon as possible. [Post-mark $\left(\frac{OC}{3}\right)$.]

1162.—3 November 1663. *R. Dey* to friend *Charles Gawdy*.

Cannot meet Gawdy at Carleton on Wednesday, having appointed a
Court and Leet. Will Thursday suit ?

GAWDY MSS,   [Endorsed "with Memo. of· Charles Gawdy's accounts—wages ·calcu-
lated at 10*d.* a day. Receipts to 10th December 1663 for Crones, &c.
47*l.* 9*s.* 1*d.*, disbursements 37*l.* 15*s.* 10½*d.*]

1163.—18 November 1663.   *George Freeman*, London, to *Sir
William Gawdy*, Bury St. Ed-
monds [Suffolk].

Has received Gawdy's letter with enclosure for Mr. Bull, " I was at
Mr. Lilly's about four days ago with Mr. Framlingham and he said
he liked his drawing very well and that he was much mended but
did not do with ·freedom enough which cannot ·come but with time
and practice, for now he hath pretty well learned to handle his
crayon." Intends to set him to draw from plaster figures, " for there
must be a method observed that he may learn to be excellent without
intangling of his judgment." This must be done by degrees, the
opposite course " causeth many to take a bad manner or else to despair
through the difficulty of attaining to it. Mr. Lilly . . . told me he
would write to you . . . he is very desirous he [Framlingham] should
be perfect in his drawing, it being the chief ground of painting and
the want of it the cause that so few attain to perfection." The better
to teach him, Freeman does all the draughts that he has to do in his
presence. Framlingham sends love to his brother and sister and
Freeman sends respects to Gawdy and to Mr. John Tremaine.

1164.—1 December 1663. *John Stafford to Charles Gawdy.*

Hopes the wine will give content, the man has promised to send the
best he has. The painted calicoes [" caliquo "] are extremely dear and
scarce, sends 4 yards of painted dimity [" demothy "] which is twice as
strong and much more fashionable; the price is 10*d.* a yard. [Endorsed
with memo. by Charles Gawdy of wages, Wonock and his son at 1*s.* 4*d.*
a day, others at 10*d.*]

1663–4.

1165.—14 February 1663–4.   *Sir John Holland*, Quidenham, to
*Bassingbourn Gawdy, Charles
Gawdy, William Davy*, &c.
(Commissioners of Subsidy for
Shropham and Guiltcross.)
" These speed from one to
another."

The time for assessing the two last subsidies is so near at hand that
Sir John and Mr. Rendall have issued warrants to the chief constables
to warn the assessors to appear at Larlingford on Wednesday 17th inst.
Desires they will also attend and assist.

1166.—7 March 1663–4. *R. Dey to Charles Gawdy.*

Sends particulars of lands that Robt. Almon died seised of, for the
better assessing of distinct fines on admission. Also sends a precept
for the Court, let the persons named have 10 days' notice. Since Dey
came from .London he met Mr. Jolly, who said Robt. Almon had surrendered into Mr. Howse's hands to the use of his will. Concerning Sir
Will. Gawdy's business against John Bringloe, Dey went to advise
with Mr. Baldock who said Bringloe and Mr. Shardelow had been with
him and desired " a composure of it," which Baldock thought he could
effect.

Service to Sir William; let him know Dey spoke to Mr. Marryot GAWDY MSS.,
about the rent charge, and will either secure it or pay for a release.
If Sir William will set a price to discharge it, Dey is to see Maryott
next week at Thetford and can tell him.

1664.

1167.—22 April 1664.   *Thomas Newman to Bassingbourn Gawdy*,
at Mr. Dey's house, White Lion Lane,
Norwich.

Touching Gawdy's estate at Illington, no Court has been held of the
Manor there, nor is likely to be next week. The money will be paid
Gawdy on Thetford fair-day, and Newman hopes to render him an
account on the 30th inst. He left the letter which Mr. Bayspoole was
concerned in, with Mr. Clerke; hopes Gawdy got it.

1168.—28 September 1664.   *R. Day to Charles Gawdy*, Harling.

Encloses warrants for Courts of Manors of Bridgham, and West
Harling, for 19th and 20th Oct., if that will suit Sir William and
Charles. Could hold Gasthorp the day after. Hopes Wiffen has made
his peace with Sir William.

1169.—   October 1664.   *William Davy* [Ellingham], to [*Charles
Gawdy*].

Davy is going to Mr. Spelman of Narborough all next week, so cannot
come to Harling. Charles can receive 30*l.* Sir William Gawdy owes
Davy and pay himself for the sheep out of it.

1170.—19 October 1664.   *William Davy*, Ellingham Magna, to
[*Sir William Gawdy, Bart.*].

Davy has no money at London, and will not be there till next
month; had he been "so near" he would have seen to the paying of
Gawdy's rents [to Eton College?]. Gawdy had better remit by a Norwich merchant, and Davy will write to his cousin, Thomas Webb, to see
to the payment.

1664–5.

1171.—6 February 1664–5.   *George Freeman*, London, to *Sir
William Gawdy*, Bury [Suffolk].

Understands by a letter Framlingham [Gawdy] showed him that Sir
William is troubled that Freeman has moved so far from Westminster
[where Fram. is lodging]. Anyone who knows what belongs to
drawing will see how he has improved. The bargain was that he was
to draw in his own chamber, from Freeman's copies, coming sometimes
to the latter's rooms where "having sometimes great pieces to do, there
would not have been room for him. But I, taking a delight in his
company, and finding him good-natured and ingenious, was willing to
have him always by me . . . which was a great inconvenience to me,
for many that come to sit for their pictures are not willing there should
be strangers in the room." Freeman thinks he should deserve more
" if he have my drawings abroad at his lodgings, for they may be in
danger of being lost or spoiled by those who do not understand the
value of them; which I esteem since they cost me many a weary step
and night's watching and study to do them." Hopes Gawdy will not
abate him anything of what he has always received. " Mr. Framlingham has been sick this ten days, and we thought he would have had

the small-pox, but 'he is now pretty well . . . He was somewhat discontented that he had not black clothes for he made signs that the Court was in mourning, and that he was ashamed to go see his friends in his old ones. I spoke with Mr. Bull to be careful of him and get him a a good nurse, &c."

1172.—14 February 1664–5. *George Freeman*, London, to [*Sir William Gawdy*].

[Opening part of letter cut off.] Acknowledges receipt of letter by Mr. Bull. Sent a woman who understands the nature of small-pox to see Mr. Framlingham, and whether he were well tended, "who tells me that he is in no danger at all, and that the worst is past, for they are all come forth, and that her opinion is that he will not be marked at all if they follow the directions she hath given them . . . Since it is a disease that few do 'scape having he will hereafter be void of that fear.

Mr. Framlingham is unwilling to leave the place where he is, liking the diet very well, the walk to Freeman's (although rather far may be a divertisement to him. If Gawdy prefers, he may be very well boarded hard by but at a dearer rate.

In the house where Freeman is they ask 12*s.* a week, and the chamber hath no closet, which Framlingham dislikes.

1665.

1173.—20 May 1665. *John Doe* [Norwich ?] to *Sir William Gawdy*.

Receipt for 42*l.* 19*s.* 1*d* [Eton College rents due Lady-day] by the hands of Mr. Walter Clopton, for the use of Dr. [Nathaniel Ingelo, " received for my father, Sheriff Charles Doe."

1665–6.

1174.—30 January 1665–6. *Sir John Holland*, Quidenham, Colonel to *Sir Will. Gawdy*, Bart. and Major, West Harling, " on his Majesty's especial service."

Has received the King's letters apprehending an invasion, and calling out the Militia, which is to be " drawn together into a body and put into a good posture, and to be placed upon their guard at or near to such port or ports, or upon such places on the sea-coast as shall be most convenient to discover and oppose the landing of any forces." The soldiers are to be notified to be in readiness to march at an hour's notice. Each musketeer to bring half a pound powder and half a pound bullet, each matchlock, 3 yards of match, and every soldier a knapsack.

1175.—8 March 1665–6. *John Doe*, " for my father *Sir Charles Doe*, Sheriff," to *Sir Will. Gawdy*.

Receipt for 42*l.* 12*s.* 3*d.* for the use of the Provost and Fellows of Eton College, by the hands of Anthony Webb.

1666.

1176.—21 April 1666. *R. Dey* [Norwich] to *Sir William Gawdy*, Harling.

Dey has to hold Sir John Hobart's courts next Monday and Tuesday, but could take Harling on Wednesday. As to the writ, Dey had directions from Mr. Charles Gawdy to sue Thomas Brooke, not saying in whose name. Dey issued writ in Charles' name, hence the GAWDY MSS. mistake.

1177.—13 June 1666. *R. Dey to [Charles Gawdy,* Harling].

Dey has this day held a set court for Francis Fludd and *ux.*, who mortgage their house and lauds to Wormley Hethersett, to secure 40*l.* to be paid in 5 years. He took 16*s.* fine for Sir William. Execution against Mr. Chamberleyne for 4*l.* 10*s.* was neglected by the bailiff last term, and has been renewed. Brooke was arrested and gave bond to appear, but made default and the Sheriff is to sue on bond. Dey will bring Bringloe's suit to trial. Mr. Tuthill's lease is drawn: Service to Mrs. Gawdy.

1178.—28 June 1666. *William Denny,* London, to [*Charles Gawdy,* Harling].

Coming yesterday to London, Denny received Henry Lisseman's letter, who says he has found Flint, and will discover him for 5*l.* down, and 5*l.* more when Denny gets either the man or his money. He also demands a bond of 20*l.* that Denny will never discover that it was Lisseman told him where to find Flint. Denny finds it strange that such demands should be made, the agreement come to in Norfolk was to give Lisseman 5*l.* and his reasonable charges. These punctilios are unnecessary. Let Gawdy send for him, give him the enclosed letter, and then "as a courteous advocate discourse the business with him." Explain that Denny will not give 10*l.* for Flint's person, and perhaps not be able to recover his money. Try to bring him to the original bargain, but as a last resource, Gawdy may offer 5*l.* for Flint's person, and 5*l.* more if he recovers his debt. "I thought him a parishioner [sic.] would "have scorned so meanly to have capitulated with me." On receipt of word where Flint is (direct to Denny's brother Tilson, at Fetter Lane, opposite the Red Hart), Denny will take the writ himself into Huntingdonshire, and then come across to Norfolk and settle with Lisseman. Service to "good Mrs. Gawdy, Mr. Bass, Mistress Uty, Mr. Thomas, Mr. Cressner, and all." [Endorsed with Memo. of account, 130 lambs, 22*l.* 5*s.* 0*d.*, &c.]

1179.—2 October 1666. *William Davy,* to kinsman, *Charles Gawdy,* at his house at Harling.

Desires to have sent by bearer the note whereby Robt. Steward had 20*l.* of Gawdy, by Davy's order. Will Gawdy come with Davy to Lynn to buy coal ? "I do hear that the fleet is expected every day." The Swan, at Watton, would be convenient to meet at. [Endorsed, "Mr. Deny owes me for himself 12 weeks, 5*l.* 15*s.*; for his wife and maid, 6 weeks, 3*l.* 9*s.* Received for sheep, 155*l.* 18*s.* 3*d.*; paid my brother, 75*l.*; paid tithe, 12*l.* 18*s.* 0*d.*" Names of laborers (paid sundry small sums) "Wabie, Quanterill, Parkin, Knot, James Goding, Lovicke, for sowing."

1180.—9 November 1666. *R. Dey* [Norwich] to *Charles Gawdy,* West Harling.

Gives particulars of fine set on Mr. Chamberleyne's admission to a number of parcels of land (including tenement called Lovell's and Bryant's alias Dove's close), in all 31*l.* 15*s.* This was to be paid on 15 Oct., when a Court Leet was held and a seizure awarded in default of payment; Chamberleyne promising to pay at Harling Hall. Dey desires there were an end with Steggall; Lady Hobart cannot let her

GAWDY MSS.ᵖ farm till she be rid of him, and will sustain damage from her unfitness to use it herself. The interest is in Mr. Marryott, who is desirous to be rid of the trouble and clamor of Steggall.

1181.—26 December 1666. *Same to Same.*

Mr. Baldocke having promised to pay Sir William his demand against John Bringloe, Dey has only signed judgement against the latter, and will not enter it. Hears Baldock is at Rushford. If Mr. Brooke has concluded with Sir William, Dey will get the late Sheriff to stay his hand.

Memorandum of costs—Bill against Bringloe	-			£4	9	7
Costs this terme of signing judgment, &c.	-			2	0	10
Costs against Weffen	-	-	-	1	4	3
,, ,, Brooke	-	-	-	1	13	8
,, ,, ,, (this term)	-			0	4	4
,, ,, Chamberleyne	-	-		3	15	2
				£13	7	10

1667.

1182.—3 April 1667. *William Denny*, Beaconsfield, [Bucks] to *Charles Gawdy*, West Harling (" Leave this with the Stationer, nigh Temple Gate") and (" Leave this at Larlingford ").

Mr. Clark, of Banham, was directed by Denny to pay Gawdy 5*l.*, all he could then pay, being much troubled by the hardness of the times, and his loss of 45*l.*, "occasioned by Flint's being too honest." "As fast as I receive, so fast I'll pay." Hopes his trunk of books is at Gawdy's house. Expected to have been at Harling ere this, but his wife's condition forbids travel. "Speak to Goodwife Gore [? Gow] to take my cassock and girdle, which lie in one of the drawers of my wife's trunk, and likewise my Stuff Coat, which I did wear last summer . . and send them up to me by Hartley . . direct them to be left at Mr. Tilson's chamber in the Paper Buildings in the Inner Temple." Wishes Gawdy and his wife joy of their young daughter; is glad that "little Bass holds yet your only son." Service to Mr. Bass, Mr. Thomas, and all at Trorton, also to Mr. Cressner.

1183.—6 June 1667. *G. Downing*, Whitehall Treasury Chambers, to [*Sir William Gawdy ?*].

"Your 200*l.* is payable next after 716,707*l.* 15*s.* 11*d.*, so it will be due about August next." Tally and order must be brought into the exchequer. The Receiver General shall pay it in Suffolk if desired.

1184.—12 July [1667]. *Thomas Lany*, Bugden [Buckden, Hunts], to cousin [*Anne Gawdy*].

Rallies his cousin on her making her interesting condition an excuse for not writing to him. "Now in truth I have seen Anne, duchess of of York, in your condition look big and take a great deal of state upon her;—But for Anne Gawdy so to do there may not be altogether the same reason, for it must be confessed that there is some difference between her bearing an heir of Great Britain and yours of Great Harling. And yet I warrant you she writes sometimes." Respects to cousin Gawdy and Fram., "who I suppose is now with you."

1185.—18 July 1667. *Nicholas Lany*, the Wheat-Sheaf, York St., Covent Garden, to his cousin *Madam Anne Gawdy*, to be left at Mr. Girling's, the Mercers, Cooke-Row, Bury [Suffolk].

Sends some patterns, if they please her, will be happy to serve her. Has heard of her several times by cousin Hawtrey. "I wish you much joy of your son and heir." Sends his wife's and his own service to "my Lady, my cousin and yourself."

1186.—25 October 1667. *Framlingham Gawdy*, the Stone-cutters, Drury Lane, to his brother [*John Gawdy*].

Sends by Bull, the carrier, a box containing a cloak (1*l.* 12*s.*), gown (3*l.* 10*s.*), a handkerchief, which with the falls and the rest of the lace, comes to 2*l.* 15*s.* 0*d.*, two knives at 2*s.* 6*d.*, the box and porter 2*s.* 8*d.* Charles Cooper had to advance 1*l.* 2*s.* towards this. Cannot get gloves, either fingers were too large or there was some evil shape or other in them; has ordered some to be made, and will send the chocolate with them. Mr. Reme has lost one of his sons that was in Holland, very rare at painting. Framlingham is now in a place where he gets very good diet, and a good chamber, and hopes he shall improve. "I see Mr. Ogle the other day very fine, who they reported to be hanged."

1187.—30 December 1667. *Robert Lullman*, Norwich, to *Mr. James Ralphes*, East Harling.

Sends Sir William Gawdy's arms by the bearer, William Brightling. There are 11 corslets complete (by which is to be understood a back and breast [piece], a gorget, a headpiece, and two tases,) 20 sacks tied up, 58 loose head pieces, one hamper for Sir John Holland, and one partizan. Thinks he has sent one back [piece] too many by mistake.

1667-8.

1188.—24 February 1667–8. *Edward Nelson* to *Charles Gawdy*.

Nelson writes to explain the "unkind difference" between Mr. Rous of Sternfield [Suffolk] and his parishioners, wherein Nelson is attorney "on the clergy side." Rous commenced suit for rent of glebe leased to Cooke, and for tithes due by Cooke and others. There being no defence they "designed to pay the poor parson with actions of trespass, in number at least 7 or 8, but in value inconsiderable." One Hellwise brought 2 of these actions but dare not proceed because of an injunction out of the Exchequer. Cooke has brought down his two cases for trial at the assizes, both concerning a piece of land he holds by lease from Rous. Cooke covenanted to maintain the fences about the close, "so that Cooke, by breach of his covenant in not repairing those fences hath created to himself a cause of action" [*i.e.*, apparently means that Rous' cattle have entered by the decayed fences and done damage]. "Such tricks will make Cooke a poor man," he owes already 20*l.* rent, besides tithes, and "whatever he recovers in these two pitiful actions of trespass," Rous will assuredly get back by action on covenant to repair the fences. Nelson apologises for giving Gawdy this "impertinent trouble," but could not leave his friend's concerns subject to misconstruction ["mistruccon"]. Cooke's special bail will be answerable on the action of covenant as well as for the rent. [This letter was possibly written to deter Gawdy from becoming special bail for Cooke, see previous

GAWDY MSS. appeal from the other side. No. 1149.] Endorsed is a memo. of
Charles Gawdy's accounts of sale of lambs.

				£	s.	d.
187 lambs sold for	-	-	-	27	7	4
189 „ „	-	-	-	29	10	10
38 „ „	-	-	-	5	3	1
19 " Cullet Lambs " (*i.e.*, 15 of Dickerson's,						
3 of Well's, and 1 of Margerhum's)		-	-	2	7	10
207 lambs of mine sold for	-	-	-	34	13	11

1668.

1189.—3 April 1668.   *Rev. T. Rous*, Sternfield [Suffolk] to *Mr. Thomas Gawdy*, Crowshall, near Debenham.

Mr. Dade is under a course of physick and cannot attend at Saxmundham as appointed. Begs Gawdy not to " think me so rude as to spurn at or kick against Authority, which you seemed publicly to charge me with on Tuesday last. 'Tis well known what I have suffered in the late times of rebellion for owning lawful Magistrates and disowning Usurers and their impositions. . . . " And as I am ready to give subjection to the Gods on earth (Psalms 82. 6), so under the God of Heaven, from them I hope for protection. . . God, we read, (Gen. 20, 21.) would not condemn the very Sodomites upon hearsay." Rous is heartily sorry for the sufferings of his tenant Legate of Monks Soham [Suffolk] and hopes he may be indemnified by the person who occasioned them. His sheep were distrained, not for any defect in Rous' arms (which were not faulted at Aldeburgh, Feb. 1665), but for the soldier not appearing with them at Debenham in July 1666. Rous has ever denied that he was sufficiently warned of that muster, and it was " Sir Charles Gawdy's noble promise that till a general meeting of the Deputy Lieutenants or a particular meeting of 2 or 3 of them " to try the case, Rous should not be molested on this warrant. This meeting has never been held: if it is held and Rous is found in the wrong he will pay the fine. Service to Sir Charles Gawdy. Begs he may not be misrepresented by " clamorous or malicious tongues."

1190.—14 May 1668. *Nicholas Lany*, London, to his cousin [*John ?*] *Gawdy*.

Sends 4¾ yards of striped lustring " to make my cousin a short vest— it is near your pattern and will wear better." (2*l.* 5*s.* 0*d.*) Also 4 pieces of ribbon (2*l.* 4*s.* 0*d.*) Hopes to see " you and my cousin here with my lady at Midsummer."

1191.—August 1668. *R. Dey* to [*? Charles Gawdy*].

Sends Indenture of Lease between Sir William and Mr. Tuthill ; also trust deed of Gasthorpe, the lease for the lime-burner, a warrant for Sternfield Court and a bill of charges for Mr. Brooke.
Service to Sir William, " yourself, and your good lady."

1192. — 22 August 1668.   *Wormley Hethersett*, Thetford, to [*Charles ?*] *Gawdy*.

Hethersett has occasion for money at Sturbridge fair [Cambridge]. " Truly the forbearance of my money is twice as much as my profit on the goods." Begs the 9*l.* 14*s.* 7*d.* may be paid next week.

1193.—29 September 1668: *Anthony Mingay, jr.*, "the yard over against the great James, London," to *Charles Gawdy*, Harling Hall.

"My sweet cousin Madam Frances Gawdy is upon her preferment in marriage to the Duke of Albemarle's physician, Dr. Troutbeck, a widower of a plentiful estate and one who doubtless she may live a comfortable life withal." She desires to muster what sums she has abroad and asks Charles to pay her 20*l.* to Mr. Anthony Mingay, grocer in Norwich, to whom she will send Charles' bond.

1194.—21 December 1668. *William Tayler,* Old Buckenham, to [*Charles Gawdy*].

Tayler wrote before to say he had no money, but would deliver a score of oats at Brandon when the boats come up; not hearing from Gawdy he did not send them. Tayler lighted on Gawdy's shepherd and found out Gawdy had sent a message by Jack Barber that he was lacking oats; this was never delivered. Will ship some more in a month or so. His unlucky suit upon the forged bond cost him 5*l.* last term. Service to Mrs. Gawdy.

1195.—24 December 1668. *Clement Herne* (at Mr. Justice Barker's house, Clerkenwell) to neighbour *Edward Lombe*, Cawston. (Leave this with Mr. Thomas Lombe, weaver, St. George of Colgate, Norwich).

"After a refreshment of my wearied parts I marched towards the widow's lodgings, which in truth is such a distance as renewed my distempers." Could only leave Lombe's letter "being the lady was absent in the necessary employment of giving visits." A day or two after her attendant came to Herne's lodging with the reply, thinking he was returning into Norfolk. She would not send it by post, "being concerns of valuable worth." "The town affords little news, but variety of discourse, the temper of the people differing, each from other imitating grandeurs, or rather the fish that clothes itself with the colours of the next object. He that lives in this hemisphere must act Proteus, truth and plain-dealing being out of fashion and their contraries *à la mode d'Angleterre.* . . . If corn and cattle bore as good a price as vest and tunic 'tis probable better times might appear." Corn of all grains, especially barley is rising. Herne's wife joins in love to Lombe and his little ones.

1668-9.

1196.—28 January 1668–9. *Clement Herne* [London] to *Mr. Edward Lombe*, Cawston.

Herne has been at Mrs. Dickenson's lodgings a second time and again found her out. Understands from Mr. Ward that Mrs. Tolke is "pliable to a reference by the relation of Mr. Haleck to you. . . . I am always in my own concerns apt to embrace a certain peace before an uncertain conquest . . . but could have wished Mrs. Tolke would have accepted a treaty offered long since both by myself to Mr. Halacke and by others to the defendant." If their intentions are fair towards Richman, Herne would advise a settlement, although Richman, is at great charge and his Counsel ready for trial and adverse to a treaty. Would advise both sides to treat "as the most heroic and conquering English did with the despiseable and inconsiderate Dutch in the late war with a drawn sword in one hand and resolution in the other." If this be done, acquaint Mr. Rich. Wilson and principally Mr. Claxton. This nearly concerns Herne, as Richmond's landlord; he cannot expect the rent of the fold course unless the tenant makes some advantage by it. There is to be no sitting of Parliament, as the King is able to set out 40 sail to help the Dutch without another supply. Corn rises all over England, especially barley and malt, which are 12s. and 14s. a combe. Was sorry to hear of Lombe's " dangerous conflict with the footmen " [foot-pads] " but glad of your delivery and victory." Shall be glad to hear how the tenants pay and other country news, here is "nothing but vanity in the height, and an increase of vice, which is the present glory of the inhabitants and grief to strangers." True love to Lombe's sister and boys.

1197.—4 March 1668–9. *Same* to *same.*

Thanks Lombe for care taken in Herne's absence. Herne's debt to Lombe is due about 11 April : let him collect the interest or my lady's rent from tenant Brooke. Bouls ought to have paid 8l. 10s. and Herne has ordered Foster of Melton to pay Lombe 10l. " As you ride through Haverland incite my tenants to relieve their necessitous landlord." Has put off Richman's trial, hoping a cheaper settlement by reference. " I have been a fox-chase to retrieve our Cawston business and I have scented them and hope to obtain : nothing can prevent us but the late fire which devoured both office and records." Sir Ed. Sawer is officious to help us—he saw the survey taken 5 Jac.—he was formerly engaged in the same with the Lord Hobart and " said he had been Lord of Cawston if the attorney had not stept in." Mr. Auditor Phillips is friendly. Sends commendations to his brethren. Mother Fairfax and Mrs. Herne send love. " Accidentally I met Martin Earle, who kills me with his look, but vanished out of sight with all haste," hopes by next letter to say he does not care a rush for Earle. On the payment of the money, take out our security and acquaint Mr. Alewis [?].

1669.

1198.—28 April 1669. *Henry Felton* to cousin *Charles Gawdy,* Harling.

Sends the bag for the hop clover, as much as would sow 1½ acres. Should it be sown with barley, or alone ? How does Henry's credit stand ? Service to his " she cousin and the rest."

1199.—21 June 1669. *Robert Dey* to *Charles Gawdy,* Harling.

Dey's son went this morning through Attleburgh towards London. Gawdy's desire shall be signified to him, and all possible charges in the suit spared, in hopes of its being settled. [Endorsed with note of Charles Gawdy's accounts.

" Received for the ploughmen's board due Mich. 1669, 2l. 10s.

      „   Gray's wages due Mich. 1669, 3l. 5s."]

1200.—9 July 1669. *Thomas Morris,* Ipswich, to friend *Charles Gawdy,* West Harling Hall.

Sir Robert Brooke, of Nacton [Suffolk], wants to know if Gawdy can furnish him with 100 wether hoggs " which are very good, and at what rate ? " [Endorsed with accounts : Larner, 30 lambs sold 4l. 4s. Chapman 4 lambs 11s. 4d. Co Marke 2 lambs 5s. 8d., in all 36 lambs 5l. 1s. Hoodle (?) 8 lambs 1l. 2s. 8d. Salter, 8 lambs 19s. 8d. Note of wages—Bullock for work in Hackfordhall and " my hemp land."

Bullock for "my brothers work" and in the car. Knot for work for GAWDY MSS. Charles and "my brother."]

UNDATED LETTERS BEFORE SIR WILLIAM GAWDY'S DEATH.

1201.— *Basil Fielding to* [*Charles*] *Gawdy.*

Asks in his father's name for some partridges and wild fowl. Also some walnuts and a cabbage for his mother.

1202.— *B*[*arbara*] *H*[*awtrey*] *to sister Mrs. Anne Gawdy.*

Is glad to hear of her sister's health and intention to visit her. Almost thinks Anne can come to her house as cheap as to London. If the same cost would rather meet Anne at home and come up together. Thinks Betty is now resolved on Mr. Sitwell, it is left to her choice. "I have sent poor Mall to Bury. I do not think of that business for sister Sollomans, true friends are hardly to be found and therefore would be glad to keep those I have, &c."

1203.—22 July [1669]. *Frances Troutbeck* [née Gawdy, see ante No. 1193] *to Charles Gawdy,* Harling.

Does not expect to be at Harling this summer, so please pay the money to Mr. Anthony Mingay. The Doctor [her husband] presents his compliments to "my cousin and your wife." [Endorsed by Charles Gawdy—balance of 15*l.* 2*s.* 11*d.* due.]

[About this time *Sir William Gawdy* died.]

1204.—6 September 1669. *Ralph Hawtrey to* [*Lady Anne Gawdy,* Bury], [Suffolk].

Hawtrey will be delayed a day or two in waiting on [Lady Gawdy] at Bury. "If your uncles desire a meeting pray appoint it the beginning of next week," when Hawtrey will do her what service he can. "I hope when all things are stated we may come to a fair concord. If your father's debt be due to you, which I question not, I think then it were better for you to buy some part of the sheep." Sister Lee approaches her confinement.

[Endorsed with mutilated recipe for cooking a shoulder of mutton.] "Cut a shoulder of mutton like a shoulder of vension, take samphire, parsley, a little onion, a little green shalott, an anchovy, a few capers, then peel a very little nutmeg, salt, pepper, shred with beef suet, as small as can be : so stuff it outside and inside and place it on the spit. Pour into your [pail?] some samphire liquor with a spoon : when it begins to be dry [baste?] it with butter and lard : about a quarter of an hour before it is roasted [take?] an onion sliced in . . . . take up the meat and hold it over the . . . and slab it so that the gravy may run into it. Squeeze an orange into it . . . . The samphire and parsley must be twice as much as the other things. It will take good roasting."

1205.—13 October [1669 ?]. *Ann Lee to* [*Lady Anne Gawdy*].

Thanks for remembrance : niece Sitwell has been in the country. Rejoices at prospect of seeing Lady Gawdy this summer, "but you are a pattern to all wives, loving home so much and the two fine children." Expects her confinement early in December. Service to Sir John.

· GAWDY MSS.   1206.—8 November 1669. R[obert] Dey to Charles Gawdy, Harling Hall.

Mr. Tuthill has appeared to the scire fac. at Gawdy's suit: please send the defeasance of the judgment if it was sealed. If the Commission for Sir William Gawdy's will be executed, please send it by bearer. Dey sent it by Great Wickham [Suffolk] about a fortnight since. Dey's son is for London.

[Endorsed with memo. of Wretham rents and amounts due (?) to Thrower, Ellgood, Smith, Ro. Kevinginton, Sproutley, and Catton.]

1207.—15 November 1669. William Tayler, Old Buckenham, to Charles Gawdy, Harling.

Tayler fears that Jack Barber instead of paying Gawdy 5l. on Tayler's account, will want to apply it on a debt of Tayler's to cousin William Barber. "Do not divulge what I write," . . nor that. Tayler understands from John Pears that he was deceived some 10s. in the bargain over and above the 5l.

1208.—16 November 1669. Ralph Hawtrey, Ruislipp [Middlesex], to Lady Anne Gawdy, Harling (to be left at Lady de Grey's at Bury).

Hawtrey forwarded 14 days ago Dr. Angelo's letter as to the rent due Lady Day and Michaelmas, some 82l.; but the fine will bring it up to 120l., which must be paid before lease will be sealed. If uncle Charles comes up supposes he will enter for her. Is sorry Lady Gawdy's rents come in slowly, and wonders Mr. Tillett, of Wretham, has not paid: hopes they are responsible tenants. How does Lady Gawdy like Harling, now she has had some trial of it? Ask Aunt Grey to pay the rent for our land at Ellengam, "she proves as bad a tenant as the worst, my wife the last week fell into a violent fit of the wind colic mixed with vapours, she continued ill a night and a day," but was cured by some pills sent from brother Rodgers. She says it will prove a breeding fit . . . "I think we shall have a colony of our own begetting." Service to all your uncles and Aunt Gawdy—love to your pretty baby and a kiss to Bass. Sister Lee joins in remembrance.

1669–70.

1209.—4 February 1669–70. William Denny, London, to Charles Gawdy, West Harling ("deliver with a gross of corkes").

The corks were ordered before Christmas and ought to have gone down with Gawdy's hats, but were neglected. Is sorry he hears no news of Mrs. Gawdy's delivery, and hopes in a fortnight to see Harling. Denny has been kept longer than he meant at Beaconsfield, by his father-in-law's late distemper. Service to Mr. Bass and Mr. Thomas, &c.

[Endorsed with accounts. "I owe to Baley, mole-catcher, 2s. 6d., &c., also notes of the disposal of some barley, some going to the doves, some to the warren, some used as seed, feed for horses, and some rejected as "dross and again thrown out of doors, 10 combs."]

1210.—10 March 1669–70. Ralph Hawtrey, Ruislip [Middlesex], to Lady Gawdy, at West Harling, (to be left at Lady de Grey's, Bury).

Hawtrey made another "assay to Eton," but did not find enough Fellows to make a quorum. They gave good words and Dr. Ingello said the provost would be there next week, when they would consult, GAWDY MSS. and give their resolutions (which Hawtrey now encloses). Has promised them an answer before Easter. It will be useless appearing there without a terrier. Thinks the fine reasonable if the lease is so valuable, and hopes the survey will clear all doubts on the matter. As to Lady Gawdy's uncles and their demand of security from her for the appraised value of the sheep, to secure them against casual deaths, &c., this is unreasonable. As long as she is a wife she cannot be bound. The Estate also which the sheep feed on (both at Harling, Wretham, and Bridgham) was settled on her upon her marriage. If the sheep feed there, they must pay rent, and in case they die and Lady Gawdy replace them with her proper money, the trustees will have nothing to do with such new stock, which will be hers absolutely if she survive Sir John. As to their threats of impounding her sheep "these are but bugg's words." Send up a copy of Sir William's will and Hawtrey will consult Mr. Baldock.

Lady Gawdy's time for becoming a house-keeper draws near; she must set about it cheerfully,—Ralph will come at any time if she needs him, on having 14 days notice. Mrs. Hawtrey will be confined about Midsummer. Service to Sir John, "your uncles and aunt," &c.

1670.

1211.—25 April 1670 [or later]. *Charles Gawdy's* memo. of sheep.

Lome's (?) charge. Sheep at Harling, 3 Sept. 1669, 1278, 60 of which sent to Garboldisham. Garboldisham skins 22. Harling do. 32. Remainder of Garboldisham sheep, 38. Remainder of Harling sheep to Lerne's charge (?) 1206. Will's and Salter's charge, Wretham, 3 Sept. 1669, 1269, 50 of which sent to Garboldisham. G. skins, 30. W. skins, 100. Remainder of G. sheep, 20. Remainder of Wretham sheep that stayed to Well's account, 1119.

To 25 April, 1670.	Wretham skins together	-	130
	Harling ,, ,,	-	54
			184

Sent Harling sheep to fat at Saham 20, remaining there 1,186.
,, Wretham ,, ,, ,, 20, ,, 1,118.

1674.

1212.—7 May 1674. *James Reynolds* to *Lady Anne Gawdy*.
Receipt for 6*l*. 6*s*. in full of all debts.

1213.—25 May 1674. *Henry Gay* to *Constables* of *Witchingham* (magna and parva) and *Alderford*.

Warrant (by virtue of precept from Deputy Lieutenants) to summon a muster at Heydon Ollands on Tuesday 2 June at 9 a.m., persons to bring the Muster Master's fee and every Musketeer half a pound of powder; every matchlock, 3 yards of match; every pike furnished with a sword, back, breast, and head piece.

1214.—23 December 1674. *Ralph Hawtrey*, Ruislip [Middlesex], to *Lady Gawdy*, Harling (to be left at Lady de Grey's Bury).

Renders account of moneys received and paid for Lady Gawdy. He received from his son Sitwell on 12 March 1673-4 by a bill of John

GAWDY MSS. Staffords upon Jacob Breston 87*l.*, of which 25*l.* was (he presumes) sent by Lady de Grey to Sitwell, leaving of Lady Gawdy's £62 0 0

On 10 April 1674, by Caslipp, a bill on Mr. Hale   -   12 0 0

£74 0 0

Of this he paid the periwig maker, 31 January 1673–4 -	10	0	0
To John Mills, tailor, 4 April 1674 - - -	10	1	6
To " my daughter Sitwell " - - -	10	0	0
Balance toward Eton rent due Lady-day 1674 -	43	18	6

74 0 0

The Eton rent due Lady-day came to 53*l.* 15*s.* 9*d.* (wheat being 9*s.* and malt 4*s.* a bushel, the Michaelmas rent 55*l.* 5*s.* 5*d.* (wheat 8*s.* 2*d.* malt 4*s.* 4*d.*, "and for want of entertaining them this year, had to pay 2*l.* a cursed covenant. The balance due Hawtrey for rent and 1*l.* 10*s.* he paid Counsel when Lady G. sent up the writing about Garboldisham, comes to 63*l.* 12*s.* 8*d.* Sitwell has still 30*l.* in hand on her account. Would like to know what money she has received from his brother Richard's tenant. Expects to see all his children together this Christmas (with Lady Gawdy's leave) when she herself would have been welcome. Service to Sir John. Love to nephew and niece.

1674–5.

1215.—19 February 1674–5. *Edward Swift* to his cousin *Shillinge.*

Requests to have the enclosed papers dispersed in the towns, Bargewell and Foxley way ; send some to Cousin John Lombe and Mr. Hall. Swift has sent some to Aylsham.

1675.

1216.—25 March 1675. *Jo. Lany* to his niece [*Lady Gawdy*].

Lany sent his man to Harling this morning, who met Sir John and returned with him. Has since seen Lady Gawdy's letter which is fully satisfactory. Would like Lady Gawdy to let Ben have 5*l.*, and the remainder as mentioned in the letter.

UNDATED LETTERS AFTER SIR WILLIAM GAWDY'S DEATH.

1217.—   *D. May* to Lady [*Anne*] *Gawdy.*

May is overjoyed to hear of Lady Gawdy's recovery. She had mourned over her as one lost, so bad was the news received from cousin Sitwell. Considered that Lady Gawdy's family did not deserve such a blessing, and that all that was left to her was to persuade Sir John to let her be buried with Lady Gawdy [meaning not very plain]. Hopes nothing will hinder her or Mrs. Dorothy from coming to Lady Gawdy to rejoice over her.

1218.—22 December   . *Dr. John Troutbeck,* Hatton Gardens, London, to *Lady Anne Gawdy.*

Will send Sir John the pills and syrup as soon as the weather is open. The servant he recommended is engaged. His wife and Uty send respects. Thanks for kindness when he visited Sir John and Lady Gawdy.

1219.—   *Elizabeth Sitwell* to *Lady Anne*   GAWDY MSS.
                            Gawdy, Harling (care of Lady
                            de Grey, Bury).

Mr. Sitwell desires to let her ladyship know that the bill will be paid at the time. Uncle Lany brought Elizabeth up 30*s.*, leaving 10*s.* in arrear, "for there was 20 books [?] at 2*s.*" [Abominably spelt, "ladyship know "="lasph noue."]

1220.—17 October   .   *Barbara Hawtrey* to sister *Lady Gawdy*.

Excuses herself for not waiting before : she knew of her sister's health from their mother; and has only written one letter since she was at Harling. The small-pox is yet about. Sister Rodgers has left her jewels [children] with Barbara, who are heartily welcome. Barbara's brother has got a note for the half year's rent due Lady Gawdy, and will write her when it is paid. There is great joy at the hill and talk of a long feast before Christmas on the young son's coming of age. Mrs. Wellstead's tenant has not paid. Thanks for Robin ; hopes he is now safe at Cambridge. Love to Lady Gawdy's little ones.

1221.—[Before 1670.]   *Eliza[beth] Sitwell* to her aunt *Lady Ann*
                           Gawdy at Harling.

Embraces the opportunity to write by uncle Lany. Has been to Ruislip [Middlesex] for two days only to eat fruit, and has no news to tell. Has bought the frocks which cost 5*s.*, hopes her aunt will like them. [Endorsed with memo. of acreage in *barley*, under heads of "Upgat. shift, Braky Shift, white haies shift, White Haies, and Homeland," in all 108 acres in barley "for this year 1670." Also acreage in *rye*; viz., "Upgate Shift, Upgate, Infield piece, Tunstale [? Turnstile], Raphgate Thorpe, House land, over Place-land " in all 85 acres of rye " this year 1670."]

1222.—19 October   .   *D. May* to *Lady [Ann] Gawdy*, Bury
                             [Suffolk].

Would have waited on Lady Gawdy to thank her for civility shown to Ampton and to invite her "here once more before your remove," but was hindered by a visit from Lady Payton ; who also says that "all the women in Bury are in strict mourning " which is a further difficulty as D. May is "so unprepared for mourning that I have not a plain handkerchief in the world." Begs the favour of a visit as soon as she may hope to have the pleasure of it "out of my bed."

INDEX.

A.

Abbot, Archbishop, his chaplain ; 163.
Abbotshall manor ; 53, 54, 98, 106.
Abraham, Mr. ; 181.
Acle, Bridewell at ; 79, 109, 110.
Adams, Mr., of Thetford ; 168.
Adryan, Bartholomew ; 45.
Albemarle, Duke of, (1668), his physician ; 205.
Aldeburgh ; 20, 204.
Alderford, constables of ; 209.
Alderton, Hoowys manor ; 53.
Aldows:
    John ; 31.
    Robert ; 31.
Aldred, William ; 154.
Aldrich, Thomas ; 119.
Alehouses ; 60, 62, 68, 69, 72, 100, 101, 104.
Alewis (?), Mr. ; 206.
Allegiance, oath of ; 152.
Allington, Mr. ; 194.
Almon, Robert, his lands ; 198.
Almone or Almunde, — ; 133.
Ambler, one ; 153.
Ameringhall ; 126, 127, 132, 134, 148.
Ampthill ; 84.
Amyas, Thomas ; 5.
Ancrum, Earl of, (1639) ; 172.
Andrewes:
    Bishop, his sermons ; 195.
    William ; 76.
Androes, Ellis ; 73.
Andros, William, letter to ; 2.
Angelo, Dr. ; 208.
Anguish :
    Alderman ; 134, 147, 154.
    Edmund ; 168.
    John ; 152.
    Mun ; 167.
Appleyard :
    — ; 76.
    Henry, bond by ; 19.
Apsley, (Sir Allen ?) ; 137.
Aquitaine, seneschal of ; 117, 118.
Armstrong, Robert ; 32.

Arrenbergh, Count ; 94.
Arthur, Robert ; 16.
Arundel :
    Earl of, (1580) ; 13.
    —— (1604) ; 93.
    —— (1605) ; 101.
    —— (1626) ; 123.
    —— (1628) ; 127.
    —— (1636) ; 160.
    —— (1637) ; 163.
Asheby ; 66.
Ashefeld, — ; 24.
Ashefilde, Sir Ed. ; 14.
Asheley, Mr. ; 22.
Ashfelde, Mr. ; 15.
Ashfield ; 153.
    manor and rectory ; 54.
    Robert ; 61.
Ashill, windmill at ; 67.
Ashley, Sir Francis ; 170.
Ashwell, William ; 48.
Aslacby manor, Lincs. ; 118, 119.
Aslacton ; 46.
Aspinall :
    Suffolk ; 134, 150.
    Peter ; 116, 124.
Astley, Sir Jacob ; 164.
Attcocke, Lawrence ; 20.
Atteley, Richard ; 54.
Attemere, Henry ; 2.
Attleborough ; 25, 27, 30, 65, 66, 206.
    the Griffin in ; 44.
    parson of ; 79, 82.
Attorney's bill ; 55.
Aylsham ; 1, 210.
Ayrs, Robert ; 190.

B.

Babingley ; 52.
Back, Mr. ; 11.
Bacon :—
    the great old hog ; 156.
    young, of Hockham ; 172.
    Bac. ; 137.
    Sir Edmund ; 161, 165.
    Sir James ; 109.
    Judge ; 177.
    Mr. ; 144, 174.

Bacon—*cont.*
　Mr., of Hockham ; 135.
　—— of Suffolk ; 158.
　Nathaniel, manor sold to ; 55.
　—— high sheriff; 67.
　—— ; 73, 80, 86.
　Nic.; 152.
　Sir Nicholas; 8, 13, 18, 23, 27, 38,
　　42, 48, 49, 60, 63, 65, 67, 77, 79,
　　100, 104, 108.
　—— agreement, &c. by ; 55.
　—— letters of; 22, 67.
Baconsthorpe ; 7, 26, 27, 28, 30, 35, 71,
　82.
Baker, John ; 59.
Baldock, Mr.; 198, 202, 209.
Ballard, Christopher ; 39, 40, 44–48.
Balles, John ; 4, 27.
Ballyston, John ; 46.
Banes, Robert; 77.
Banham ; 35, 69, 91.
　church ; 37.
　living ; 125.
　manor ; 119.
Banks, Robert ; 47.
Banyerde, Mr. ; 3.
Barbary horses and gold ; 166.
Barber:
　Jack ; 205, 208.
　William ; 208.
Barford (?) Bridge; 69.
Bargewell ; 210.
Baring (?) Viscount ; 155.
Barington, Sir Thomas ; 137·
Barker:
　Edmond ; 177.
　Justice ; 205.
　Mr.; 55.
Barking :
　church, St. Hildithe's shrine ; 119.
　abbess of ; *ib.*
Barmie, John ; 4.
Barnardiston, Anne ; 54.
　Sir Thomas ; 53.
Barneham ; 22.
Barnes, widow ; 145.
Barney:
　Henry, death of ; 170, 171.
　Sir Richard ; 168.
Barnham Broome ; 177.
Barnie, Harry ; 167.
Barrow:
　Suffolk ; 17, 55, 66, 95.
　Dr.; 42.
　Mr. ; 165 ;
Barrye, Mr.; 133, 138.
Barsham ; 103.
　East ; 27, 32.
　West ; 160, 165, 166.
　Rev. Thomas, letter of; 60.
Barthelett, Anthony ; 136.
Bartlett,
　—; 65.
　Anthony ; 115.
　Edward ; 105.
　Mr. ; 103.
Bartley, Thomas ; 78.
Barton Mill ; 153.

Barwe, Suffolk ; 118.
Barwicke:
　James, death of ; 167.
　Mr.; 62.
Basham, Henry, letter of ; 76.
Bass, Mr. ; 201, 202, 208.
Bastwick, Dr. ; 163.
Batchcroft, Dr.; 132.
Bateman, young ; 61.
Batesford manor ; 119.
Bath ; 79, 104, 124.
Bathecome, William ; 38.
Bawdesey, lands in ; 53.
Baxter:
　John ; 22.
　John and Mary ; 21.
　Nicholas ; *ib.*
Bayfield:
　George ; 167.
　Mr. ; 128, 160, 168, 170, 171.
Bayspoole, Mr.; 199.
Beacons, repair of; 152.
Beaconsfield ; 202, 208.
Beauchamp, Lord, (1603) ; 87.
Beaumanoir ; 19, 20.
Beccles ; 23, 40, 44.
　sessions at ; 25, 61, 112.
Bechall ; 2.
Beckhall manor ; 119.
Bedingfield:
　Sir Henry ; 159.
　Mr., recusant ; 7, 8, 49, 132, 159.
　—— his death ; 169.
　Robert; 41, 46.
　Robert, receipt by ; 37.
Beechamwell ; 82.
Beckyswell, Henry, son of Francis; 82.
Belfourd, Sir William, Lieutenant of the
　Tower; 172.
Bell:
　Edmond, commission to ; 65.
　Mr. ; 68,
　Nicholas ; 98.
　Sir Robert ; 137, 138.
　William ; 192, 195.
Bence, —; 172.
Bennett:
　John ; 75.
　Sir John ; 111.
Berdew, James ; 27.
Berdewell, James ; 5.
Bergen, governor of; 29.
Bergen op Zoom ; 30.
Berney:
　Harry ; 158.
　Mr.; 71.
Berrye, Mr. ; 80.
Bestbeer, Petty ; 197.
Biby, Dame ; 175.
Birch, Sam.; 175.
Birche, —; 126.
Bird, Henry, of Bury ; 29.
Bishop Stortford; 153.
Bishops, the, books against ; 163.
Bitteringe, John ; 85.
Blagrave, Mrs.; 183.
Blakes, Mr.; 15.

Blennerhassett:
    George, letter of ; 156.
    Mr. ; 43.
Blickling ; 31, 134.
Blomefield, John ; 182.
Bloome, John ; 99.
Blow Norton ; 74.
Blythburgh ; 41.
Boadley, Mr. ; 23.
Bodesdale ; 101.
    the Crown at ; 102.
    the White Horse at ; ib.
Bodney ; 190, 196.
Bohemia:
    King of, (1631) ; 136.
    Queen of, death of ; 195.
Bokenham, Mr. ; 87.
Bolton:
    Mr. ; 8, 40.
    Robert ; 17, 19, 27, 34, 41, 46, 53, 56, 62, 72, 74, 90.
    —— letter to ; 60.
Bonde, John ; 105.
Bonet, William ; 4.
Bonne, John ; 25.
Books:
    burning of ; 163.
    seditions, debate on ; 192, 193.
Bordes, Sir William de ; 118.
Bostocke, Thomas ; 10.
Boswell ; 133.
    Mr. ; 136, 137.
Botesdale ; 189.
Botolph's dale ; 35.
Bowes, William ; 102.
Bowls ; 159.
Bowlton, Robert ; 5, 10.
Bowser, John ; 17.
Boyland ; 98.
Bradbury, — ; 97.
Bradley :
    Great ; 78.
    old ; 152.
    Isabie (?) ; 134.
Bradshaw:
    — ; 8.
    suit with ; 15.
Brame, Ellice, his son's quarrel ; 100.
Bramerton ; 2.
Brampton:
    — ; 88.
    Anne ; 60.
    Ashley ; 166.
    Gawdy ; 172.
    Mr. ; 163.
    Thomas, of Renton ; 19.
Brandon ; 69, 95, 205.
    Little ; 45.
Branthwayt:
    Dr. ; 114.
    W. ; 42.
Brawn and Bacon ; 156.
Breane, Sir John ; 122.
Breda, surrender of ; 165.
Brentwood, rendezvous at ; 66.
Breston, Jacob ; 210.
Bretnam ; 33.
Breton, John ; 119.

Brett:
    Berard de la ; 118.
    John, release by ; 176.
    Mr. ; 15, 19.
Brettenham ; 24, 39.
    sheep at ; 36.
    Rothyng hall in ; 25.
    John A ; 25.
Bretton :
    — ; 8.
    suit with ; 28.
Brewster :
    John ; 37.
    Martha, letter of ; 193.
    Richard, bonds by ; 109.
    Thomas and Ann ; 178.
    Timothy, letter of ; 50.
    William, letters of ; 78, 80, 102.
Briante, Richard ; 35.
Brice, Martin ; 39.
Bride, Mr. ; 182.
Bridge, Mr., minister ; 158.
Bridges, Lieut. Thomas, receipt by ; 50.
Bridgewater, Countess of ; 158.
Bridgham ; 34, 61, 105, 109.
    manor ; 81, 199.
    living of ; 76, 83.
    catechizing at ; 23.
    sheep at ; 35, 36.
Briggs :
    Aug., letter of ; 196.
    Edward ; 176.
    —— letter of ; 188.
Bringloe, John ; 184, 196, 198, 201, 202.
Brissingham ; 58, 59, 98.
Bristol :
    Earl of (1626) ; 123.
    —— (1662) ; 196.
Bristowe, Mr. ; 46.
Brockdish ; 26.
Bromhill ; 77, 78, 83, 90, 125.
Bromley :
    Sir Thomas, signature ; 11.
    —— letter of ; 18.
Brook, Brooke :
    George ; 136.
    Mr. ; 202, 204.
    Sir Richard, sheriff ; 170.
    Sir Robert ; 128, 206.
    Thomas ; 200, 201.
Brotone, John ; 46.
Browne :
    Capt., of Elsing ; 155.
    Doctor ; 184.
    John ; 62, 83.
    Nicholas ; 47.
    Robert ; 59.
    Roger ; 72, 90.
    Thomas ; 10.
    William ; 5.
    Lady ; 56.
    Mrs., her impositions ; 144.
Bryndlemarshe (?), Robert ;
Buckden, Hunts ; 197, 202.
Buckenham ; 62, 196.
    bowling green ; 161.
    New ; 80, 93, 148.
    Old ; 205, 208.

Bull :
    —, of Bossehall ; 19.
    Mr. ; 198.
    Stephen ; 81.
Bullarde, — ; 39.
Bulwer, John ; 111.
Bunell, Robert ; 47.
Bungay ; 83, 131.
Bunnet, Edward ; 10.
Bunting, Richard ; 72.
Bunwell ; 5, 22, 33.
Burdeis, Thomas, charges against ; 58.
Burgatt ; 72.
Burgis, Thomas ; 1.
Burglaries ; 93.
Burleigh :
    James I. at ; 88.
    Lord ; 55.
Burnham market ; 192.
Burrell, Stephen ; 22.
Burroughs, —, minister of Titshall ; 159.
Burrow :
    Green ; 39.
    Henry ; 9.
Burton, Mr., in the Star Chamber ; 163.
Bury St. Edmunds ; 29, 39, 66, 78, 113,
        126, 127, 131, 134, 135, 139, 140,
        180, 182, 186.
    Abbey ; 192, 196.
    sickness at ; 11.
    assizes ; 15, 158.
    Angel Hill ; 185.
    Cooke Row ; 191, 203.
    the Guildhall ; 116.
Butfyld, — ; 7.
Butt :
    Mr. ; 189.
    Sir William ; 10.
Butters manor ; 106.
Button, Mr., minister ; 64.
Buxton :
    Mr. ; 27.
    Norfolk ; 2.
Bylaugh ; 33, 52.
Bylow ; 2.
Byrch, George ; 103.
Byrche, N ; 29.

C.

Cady, Will ; 142.
Cæsar :
    Mr., death of ; 166.
    Sir Julius ; 93.
Caine, old ; 161.
Cakes, violet ; 138.

Calais, duel at ; 149, 150, 151.
Callan, Lord (1663) ; 197.
Calthorpe :
    — ; 30.
    Sir Oliver ; 118.
    Philip ; 141.
Calton :
    Hall ; 25.
    Henry, bond by ; 37.
Cambridge ; 137.
    commencement at ; 159.
    college expenses at ; 113–116, 120–
        122, 173.
    Caius College ; 113, 123, 124, 129,
        131, 132, 167, 171, 173, 174.
    —— scholarships at ; 114.
    —— assault on dean of ; 124.
    Peterhouse ; 163.
    Trinity College ; ib.
    William ; 9.
Campian, Sir William ; 159.
Canham or Cannum :
    Mr. ; 136.
    William ; 164, 170, 184.
Canterbury :
    Archbishop of (1593) ; 37.
    —— (1604), installation of ; 97.
    haste ; 147.
Caple, Richard ; 110.
Capps, Mr. ; 171.
Carbrook ; 35, 96.
    alehouse at ; 68.
Cardynall, William, letter of ; 26.
Carleton ; 197.
Carlisle :
    Lord (1628), ambassador ; 129.
    —— (1636), death of ; 158.
Carlton, John ; 28.
Carrowe, Stephen ; 7.
Carter :
    Dr. ; 183.
    Mr., minister ; 158, 162, 170.
    Parson ; 177.
Caslipp, — ; 210.
Castile, Constable of, in England ; 94, 95.
Castle :
    Acre ; 127.
    John ; 136.
Castlehaven, Earl of (1631), his trial
    135.
Castleton, Lord (1635) ; 154.
Catchpole, Robert ; 10.
Catechizing, public ; 23.
Catfield ; 40.
Catline, Mr. ; 157.
Catlyn, Richard, Serjeant-at-law ; 3.
Cattawaye, Richard, charge against ; 20,
    21.
Catton, Thomas ; 134, 176.
Cavendish, Suffolk ; 119, 127.
Caversham ; 111.
Cawdell ; 144.
Cawston ; 205, 206.
Cecil :
    Sir Robert ; 94.
    —— made Lord Cranborne ; 95.
Chabenor, John ; 136.
Chabnor, Mr. ; 68.

Chamberlayne, Robert; 25.
Chamberlen, Reynold; 17; 53.
Chamberleyne :
   Mr. ; 201.
   Thomas ; 44, 59.
Chapman :
   —, arrest of; 105.
   alias Felton, John ; 119, 120.
   Lady, death of; 183.
Chapple, Mr. ; 162.
Charles I. :
   and the Parliament of 1628 ; 129,
   130.
   reformation of his court; 136.
   his journey north; 143.
   new impositions by; 155.
   his court abated; 162.
   presents from Morocco to; 166.
   and the Queen mother ; 169, 170.
   at Cambridge ; 137.
   at Newmarket ; 138.
   at York ; 172.
Charles II. :
   at the Hague and Dover ; 189.
   and his parliament ; 193.
Chaworth, Baron ; 170.
Cheffley, William ; 104.
Chester ; 73.
Clackclose, hundred; 7, 14, 65, 68, 72, 73,
   79.
Clarke :
   Adam ; 59.
   Bennet ; 102.
   Goodman ; 102.
   John ; 101.
   Thomas and William ; 37.
   Mr., of Banham ; 202.
Clavering hundred ; 7.
Claxton ; 126, 135, 137.
   Mr. ; 66, 206.
Clement, Ambrose; 62.
Clenche, Justice ; 24.
Clere :
   Sir Edward ; 12, 13, 14, 24, 30, 40,
   181.
   Lady ; 13.
   Mr. ; 71.
Clerke, Mr. ; 199.
Clerkenwell ; 205.
Clinch, Sir Robert, his daughter; 195.
Clipwell, Mr. ; 43.
Clopton, Walter ; 200.
Cloth, price of ; 4.
Clowth, Robert ; 58.
Cobb, William ; 73.
Cobbe, Robert ; 41.
Cobbes, James, bond to ; 177.
Cobbet, goodman ; 141.
Cock, Mr., minister; 170.
Cockaine, Mrs.; 179.
Cocke, Richard ; 51.
Cockle, Thomas ; 120.
Cocksedge, Andrew; 134.
Codd, Mr. ; 50.
Coke, Robert ; 2.
   See Cooke.
Colbie, Colby
   — ; 108.

Colby, Mr.—*cont.*
   Mr. ; 60, 91, 108.
   —— letter to ; 61.
   Thomas ; 105.
Colchester ; 177.
Coles, John, of Wisbeach ; 102.
Collame, — ; 88.
College bills ; 113–116, 120–122, 173.
Cologne, Bishop of; 101.
Colphax, Anthony ; 47.
Columbariis, Philip de ; 119.
Common, disputed right of ; 59.
Conestall, Richard ; 24.
Conney, Mr. ; 86.
Conway, — ; 110.
Conye, Mr. ; 64.
Cooke or Coke :
   Lord (1634) ; 145.
   Lady ; 141, 144, 147.
   secretary ; 158.
   —, minister of Fretton ; 159.
   - , his lands at Sternfield ; 203.
   Christopher, letter of ; 102.
   Sir Edward ; 145.
   death of ; 147.
   Gabriel ; 47.
   John ; 145, 156.
   Thomas ; 41.
   William ; 39.
Coon, Robert, letter of ; 19.
Cooper, Charles ; 203.
Coote, Mr., letter to ; 24.
Copping, Mr. ; 1.
Coppinge, Edward, Thomas, and Margaret ;
   84.
Corbet :
   Sir Miles ; 79, 81.
   Roger ; 53.
Corbut, Mr. ; 33.
Cornwallis :
   Charles ; 79.
   Sir Charles ; 94, 97.
   Henry ; 103.
   Mr. ; 36, 126.
   William ; 23.
Corrington, Mr. ; 125.
Cosen, Thomas ; 29.
Cosin, Dr. ; 37.
Costessy ; 8.
Cotten, Mr., of Starston ; 148.
Cottington, Lord (1636) ; 160.
Cotton :
   Mr. ; 22.
   Robert ; 1.
Cottrell, Captain ; 56.
Courtenhall, Northants ; 28.
Covell, Mr. ; 32.
Coventry :
   Carr ; 151.
   Mr., marriage of ; 123.
Cranfeild, Sir Lionel ; 111.
Cranworth ; 10, 93.
Craven :
   Lord (1631) ; 136.
   Lord (1637) ; 162.
   Mrs., marriage of ; 12
Cresnar, Mr. ; 88.
Cresner, — ; 143.

Cressener or Cressner :
   Mr.; 182, 201, 202.
   the preacher ; 164.
   Nicholas ; 45.
Cressenhale, John; 59.
Cressingham; 168.
Cressinor, — ; 38.
Cresswell, Mr. ; 114.
Crispe :
   his goods, &c. ; 51, 52.
   Matthew ; 39.
   —— letter of; 46.
   —— bond by ; 41.
   —— letters to ; 43, 44.
   —— his death ; 48.
   —— his goods, &c.; 49.
   Thomas ; 47.
Crofts :
   Sir James, signature ; 11.
   Mr.; 7.
Cromer; 43, 143.
Cromwell, Lord (1594) ; 50.
Crooke, Judge, and ship money ; 168.
Cropley, William ; 178, 188, 191.
Croppe, — ; 2.
Crowe, Mr. ; 45.
Crowshall ; 14, 16, 25, 29, 31, 38, 39, 50,
   54, 98, 106, 135, 136, 137, 139,
   141, 144, 146, 151, 152, 153, 161,
   165, 185, 204.
   sheep at ; 36.
Croydon ; 37.
Culford ; 84.
Culham, Jane ; 102.
Cullie, John ; 89, 98.
Curteys, Edmond ; 18.

D.

Dade :
   Mr.; 204.
   —— his arrest ; 9.
   Robert, letters of; 65, 66.
Dalham church ; 116.
Dalyson, Roger, letters of ; 77, 78.
Damont, Robert, letter of; 15.
Darby, Margaret ; 16.
Darcy, Sir Francis ; 127.
Daveney, Henry :
   letter of ; 52.
   bonds to ; 53, 56.
Davies, William ; 10.
Davies, alias Lewis, Richard, receipt by ;
   107.
Davy :
   Mr.; 91.
   parson ; 161, 162, 165, 168.
   George, letter of; 113.
   Goodman ; 58.
   Henry, letters of; 80, 176, 178, 179,
   185, 187, 188, 192.
   —— his bills ; 191.
   —— John, bond by ; 132.
   —— letters of ; 175.
   —— his debts, &c., ib.

Davy, John —cont.
   William ; 44.
   —— letter to ; 113, 156.
   —— letters of; 157, 160, 163, 165,
   166, 168, 169, 174, 178, 188, 192,
   199, 201.
   —— account by; 179.
   —— witness ; 177.
Davys, Mr.; 139.
Dawbeney, Robert, letters of; 60, 69,
   102, 103.
Dawdrie, George, letter to ; 33.
Dawes, Thomas ; 100.
Day :
   Richard, letter of ; 7.
   Robert, letters of ; 186, 199.
   See Dey.
Dayle, Robert, letter of; 46.
Daynes, Rev. Thomas, letters of; 75, 102.
Deane, Francis ; 148.
Debenham :
   Suffolk ; 4, 45, 54, 56, 88, 98, 99, 106,
   126, 139, 153, 204.
   fair, mischance at ; 100.
Deepham ; 107.
Deeping Fen ; 137.
Delavale, Francis, letter of ; 111.
Delny (?), Mrs.; 171.
Denbigh, Lady ; 128.
Dence, Mr. ; 152.
Denham ; 25.
   Baron, death of ; 172.
Dennington ; 132.
Denny :
   Fyrmyn, letters of ; 103.
   Lady ; 138.
   William, letters of ; 145, 201, 202,
   208.
Denton, Dr. ; 192.
Denyngton, inhabitants of ; 16.
Depwade hundred ; 190.
Dereham ; 14.
   Hove near; 141.
Derehaugh, William, letters of ; 100.
Despotin, Dr. Jaspar, letters of; 180.
Dethick, Sir Gilbert, letter of ; 149.
Dettrick, — ; 149.
Devonshire :
   Earl of (1604) ; 94.
   Countess of; 183.
Dewe, Mr. ; 55.
D'Ewes, Sir Symond ; 169, 170.
Dey :
   Mr., apothecary ; 143.
   George, letter of; 184.
   R., letters of; 197-208, passim.
   Robert, letter of; 100.
   or Dye, William, receipt by ; 79.
   See Day.
Dickenson, Mrs.; 205.
Dickleborough ; 121.
Dickons, John ; 154.
Digby, Mr. ; 150.
Dirgo (?), Michael ; 148.
Diss ; 9, 13, 17, 19.
   alehouse at ; 72.
   hundred of ; 53.
   bailiwick of ; 71.

Ditchingham ; 2.
Dixon :
    John, letter of ; 67.
    William ; 45.
Dod, Nathaniel, letters of ; 123, 124, 126, 129, 130.
Dodds, William, receipt by ; 5.
Doe :
    Charles, sheriff ; 200.
    John, receipts by ; 200.
Dogs ; 93.
Doner, Richard ; 98.
Donne, Mr. ; 25.
Doon (?), Robert, letter of ; 36.
Dorset, Earl of (1627) ; 123.
Douglas, one, forgeries by ; 101.
Doull, W., letter of ; 197.
Dover ; 189.
    Earl of (1656), his daughters ; 183.
    John, letter of ; 44.
Downes :
    Edward ; 82.
    —— letter to ; 6.
    Mr. ; 41.
Downham market ; 44.
Downing :
    G., letter of ; 202.
    Edmund ; 51.
    Rev. William, letters of ; 40, 42, 43.
Dowset, William ; 16.
Doyly :
    Edmund, letter of ; 94.
    Sir William ; 190.
    young ; 145.
Drane, Robert ; 187.
Draper :
    Rev. Edmund, letter of ; 148.
    Mr. ; 139.
Drawing lessons ; 198, 199.
Drewett, Edward, letters of ; 190, 194.
Drugs, &c. ; 104.
Drury : -
    Sir Anthony ; 97, 148.
    —— letter of ; 169.
    Dr. ; 37.
    Sir Drue ; 15, 127, 132, 137, 139, 141, 158, 165.
    Mr. ; 31.
    Sir Robert ; 188, 190, 194.
    Roger ; 7, 8.
    Sir William ; 19, 22.
    —— governor of Bergen ; 29, 30.
Ducket, Thomas, letter of ; 126.
Dudlington ; 95, 104, 154.
Duels ; 69, 70, 149, 150.
Duffield :
    family ; 113.
    Mr. ; 182.
    Elizabeth ; 156.
    James ; 91.
    Mary, letter of ; 177.
    Richard ; 45.
Duke :
    Alexander, letter of ; 26.
    Mr. ; 120.
Dullingham, constables of ; 39.
Duncombe :
    Lady ; 183.

Duncombe—*cont.*
    Cropley ; 188.
    Sir John ; 194, 196.
    —— bond by ; 188.
Dunfermline, Earl of (1639) ; 173.
Dunkeston manor ; 87.
Dunkirkers, the ; 81.
Dunte, Thomas, a burglar ; 93.
Dunwich, members for ; 115, 128.
Dury, Sir Robert ; 34.
Dusgate, John, receipt of ; 176.
Duxe, Robert, letter of ; 195.
Dye, William, receipts by ; 109, 110.
Dyer, William, certificate of ; 28.
Dyx, Jo., letters of ; 121, 180.
Dyxe, Augustine, letter of ; 21.

E.

Eade :
    Mr. ; 147.
    Edmund, letters of ; 131, 132.
    Robert, letter of ; 167.
Eany, Thomas, letter of ; 183.
Earle :
    John, letter of ; 192.
    Martin ; 206.
Earsham ; 180.
Easton manor ; 168.
Eccles manor ; 163–168, 174.
    alehouses at ; 60.
Ecok, William ; 2.
Eden :
    Anthony ; 43.
    Mr., of Thetford ; 49.
    —— mayor of Thetford ; 51.
Edgar :
    Mr. ; 151, 162.
    Robert ; 134, 138.
Edmiston, Mr. ; 72.
Edmonds, Sir Thomas ; 172.
Edy, Richard ; 85.
Egmore, Clement ; 64.
Eliot, Sir John ; 125.
Elizabeth, Queen :
    loan to ; 5.
    in Norfolk ; 6.
Ellingham ; 44.
    Great ; 8, 20, 189, 199.
Ellmun Hall ; 41.
Elmham ; 61.
    North ; 89.
    South ; 28, 53.
Elsing ; 117, 155.
Ely :
    Bishop of, (1554) ; 3.
    —— (1599), his manors ; 65.
Elyot, Capt. ; 82.
Elyott, Thomas, muster master ; 64.
Emneth ; 6.
England, New, restraint of going into ; 164.

Erpingham :
    South ; 71.
    Sir Thomas ; 119.
Erskine, Sir Thomas ; 93.
Essex, Earl of, (1594) ; 42.
    —— (1599), letter of ; 64.
    poem on ; 92.
    his chaplain ; *ib.*
Estbergholt ; 2.
Eton College, rents ; 199, 200, 210.
Evenall, Mr. ; 159.
Everard :
    Ar., letter of ; 92.
    Anne, letter of ; 11.
    Sir Anthony ; 99.
    Catherine, letter of ; 11.
    Elizabeth, letter of ; 99.
    Henry, recusant ; 7, 11.
    —— bond by ; 11.
    —— letter of ; 20.
    Katherine and Mary, letters of ; 12.
Exeter, Earl of (1656) ; 183.
Eye ; 33, 65.

F.

Fairfax, mother ; 206.
Fakenham ; 28, 73, 99, 103, 178, 197.
Falcon, a, price of ; 103.
Faushawe, Mr., present to ; 49, 51, 52.
Farmer, Anthony ; 169.
Farrar, Henry, letter of ; 44.
Fastolfe, Thomas, release by ; 48.
Fawcett, John ; 47.
Fayrcliffe, Mr. ; 55.
Fayrclough, Thomas, receipt of ; 46.
Felmingham ; 53, 89, 92, 127.
Felton :
    family, Le Neve's account of ; 117–120.
    Dr. ; 101.
    Mr. ; 19.
    Lady ; 161.
    —— death of ; 178.
    Lady Dorothy, letters of ; 126, 180.
    Henry, letters of ; 99, 108, 206.
    —— and Dorothy ; 111.
    Sir Henry, letter of ; 117.
    —— death of ; 117.
    Susanna, letter of ; 178.
Feltwell ; 36, 38, 41, 42, 47, 61–67, 89, 95, 125, 133, 135, 136, 139, 141, 143, 174, 181.
Fen-ditton, Rougemont ; 117.
Fenn, Mr. ; 34.
Fenne :
    Robert ; 175.
    Thomas ; 33.
Fenner, Justice ; 37.
Fermor : —; 17.
    Mr. ; 18.
    Nicholas ; 6.

Fermor—*cont.*
    Nicholas, letter of ; *ib.*
    Thomas, letters of ; 27, 32, 103.
Ferne, Mr., minister ; 167.
Ferrour, John, letters of ; 43.
Fersfield ; 59, 98.
Fielding, Basil, letter of ; 207.
Filby, Elizabeth ; 25.
Finche, Sir John ; 152.
Fincheam ; 58.
Fisher :
    a constable, charges against ; 90, 91.
    or Foister, Alex., letter of ; 145.
    Ch. ; 45.
    Richard, of Diss ; 13.
    —— bond to ; 17.
    —— receipts by ; 17, 19.
    Thomas ; 114.
Fitt, widow ; 68.
Flatman, Thomas ; 48.
Fleete, Robert, his suit with Joan Manne ; 12.
Flegg, Mr. ; 20.
Fleming, Gyles ; 47.
Fletcher, Serjeant ; 184.
Fletewood, Sir William, receipt by ; 97.
Flewde, Francis ; 89.
Flight, John, letter of ; 99.
Flint, — ; 201, 202.
    Edward, letter of ; 23.
Flitcham ; 74.
Flixton ; 113.
Floud, Francis ; 92.
Flower, John ; 139.
Flowerdew :
    Anthony, bond by ; 8.
    —— ; 21.
    Edmund ; *ib.*
    Humphrey ; *ib.*
    Baron, letter to ; 24.
    Christopher, bond by ; 19.
    Edward ; 4, 5.
    John ; 41.
    Serjeant, letter to ; 18.
    —— grant to ; 23.
Fludd, Francis ; 201.
Flushing ; 30.
Foister :
    James ; 33.
    Robert, letters of ; 182, 184.
Folkar, Richard ; 56.
Folkes, Martyn, letter of ; 110.
Follegate, Mr. ; 55.
Foppesfield, Simon, letter of ; 23.
Fordham manor ; 118.
Fornete, John ; 177.
Fornham ; 108.
Forster, William, letter of ; 29.
Fortescue :
    Harry ; 139.
    Henry, letters of ; 110, 133.
    Sir John ; 106.
    —— letters of ; 14, 16, 39.
Foster :
    of Melton ; 206.
    John ; 37.
    Thomas ; 19.
Fountaine, Mr. ; 163.

Fowl, taxing of ; 145, 146.
Fowle:
    Elizabeth ; 60.
    Nicholas, letter of ; 101.
Fowler :
    — ; 42.
    George, letters of ; 77, 83, 90.
    —— suit by ; 78.
    Rowland ; 125.
    —— letter of ; *ib·*
Fox, Nicholas ; 15.
Foxley ; 45, 210.
Framlingham ; 44.
    castle ; 78, 80.
    family, pedigree, &c. of ; 84.
    Charles, settlement by ; 4.
    —— letters of; 14, 16.
    —— letters of ; 25, 29, 31, 38, 45.
    —— warrant by ; 22.
    —— death of ; 53.
    —— lands held by ; 54, 97.
    —— his will ; *ib.*
    —— his estates and will ; .106, 108.
    Eliz., letters of; 14.
    Lady Eliz., letters of ; 32, 39, 52, 65.
    Erle ; 34.
    Francis ; 53.
    Henry, witness; 53.
    John, his lands ; 53.
    Robert ; 54.
    William ; *ib.*
    William de ; 53.
Francke, John ; 66.
Frandeston; 10.
Fraunces, Margaret, accused of witch-craft ; 71.
Freebridge Lynn and Marshland ; 72, 73, 76.
Freeman:
    George, letters of ; 198, 199.
    Mr., sheriff ; 160.
    Mary ; 60.
Fressingfield ; 20.
Freston:
    Mr. ; 76.
    vicar of ; 90.
Fretton ; 159.
Fryre, Anthony, letter of ; 57.
Fuller:
    Mr. ; 99.
    John; 1.
    Michael ; 105.
    Thomas; 1.
    William ; 1.
Fulmerston:
    Richard ; 13.
    Sir Richard ; 29.
Fundenhall ; 46.¦
Funeral, a, cost of ; 3, 4, 191.
Funston, Thomas, letters of ; 48, 49, 51, 52.
Futter:
    Mr. ; 21.
    Richard, letter of ; 33. ·
    Thomas, letter of ; 169.
Fynbergh manor ; 117.
Fyncham ; 72.

Fysher:
    John, letter of ; 60.
    Richard, letter of ; 60.
Fyske, Thomas ; 1.
Fytt, George; 62, 64.

G.

Gabin, Mr.; 148.
Galyard, Thomas; 182.
Games:
    Edward ; 135.
    John ; *ib.*
Garboldisham ; 51, 149, 150, 160, 163, 188, 209, 210.
Gardiner:
    George ; 138.
    John ; 136, 137.
    Sir Robert ; 107.
Garlins (?), Robert ; 134.
Garneys:
    Mr. ; 38.
    Nicholas, letter of ; 81.
Garveston (?) ; 73.
Garway, William, letter of ; 110.
Gascoigne, Thomas, letter of ; 108.
Gasken, Christopher ; 37.
Gasthorpe ; 204.
    manor ; 199.
    Holms, sheep at ; 36.
Gastin, Thomas ; 154.
Gate, Geffray, letter of ; 35.
Gawdy:
    Ann, letters of ; 197, 207.
    Mrs. Ann ; 46.
    Lady Anne, letters to ; 207, 208, 210, 211.
    Anthony, of Mendham ; 4, 139, 149, 157, 158.
    —— letters of ; 16, 19, 22, 29, 30, 34, 42.
    —— letter to ; 16.
    —— letters of ; 109, 112.
    —— son of Sir Henry, letters of ; 115, 120.
    —— bond to ; 74.
    —— his expenses at Cambridge ; 113–116, 120–122.
    —— his dispute with the dean ; 123.
    Rev. Anthony, letter of ; 150.
    Sir Anthony ; 175.
    —— letters of ; 122, 126, 135.
    Bacon ; 134, 135.
    Bassingbourn, letters to ; 3, 5, *et seq.*
    —— letter of ; 33.
    —— petition of ; 11.
    —— bonds by ; 11, 13, 17, 21, 56.
    Charles ; 106, 110' 133–154 *passim*, 165.
    ——letters to: 178, 194, *et seq..*
    Sir Charles ; 122, 127, 128, 152.
    Sir Clippesby ; 90, 112.
    —— his assessment ; 95.

Gawdy—*cont.*
  Eliz.; 111.
  Framlingham, letters, &c., to; 107, *et seq.*
  Frances, wife of Owen, letter of; 120.
  —— her marriage; 205.
  —— Lady Frances, bond to; 52.
  Mrs. Frances, letter of; 97.
  Francis; 142, 144, 146.
  —— letters of; 7, 13, 14, 21, 22, 24, 27, 43, 68, 74, 75, 76, 82, 85, 90.
  Serjeant Francis; 9.
  Sir Francis, letter of; 99.
  Frank; 180.
  George; 130, 139.
  —— letters of; 7, 108, 120, 121, 122, 135, 137, 159.
  —— his arrest; 120.
  Henry; 146.
  —— sheriff; 37.
  —— letters of; 7, 38, 39, 42, 47, 48, 56, 64, 65, 66, 70–88 *passim*, 100, 103, 126, 130.
  —— knighted; 89.
  Sir Henry, letter of; 91.
  —— his assessment; 95.
  —— certificate by; 108.
  Jack; 194.
  John, deed by; 1.
  —— letter to; 204.
  Justice, his assessment; 95.
  Mrs. Lettice; 120.
  Lettice, letter to; 134.
  Mall; 125.
  Mary, letter of; 112.
  —— her marriage portion; 126, 127.
  Owen; 97.
  —— letter of; 57.
  Philip; 28, 29, 33, 35, 37, 47, 97, 142.
  —— his death; 110.
  Ralph; 18.
  Robert; 177, 180.
  Sir Robert; 113, 128, 180.
  —— candidate for Norfolk; 122.
  Ruth, letters of; 69, 144, 146, 165.
  Thomas; 1.
  —— his marriage settlement; 2.
  —— letters of; 3, 33, 39, 48, 69, 83, 101.
  Thomas; 179.
  —— of Shottesham; 2, 3.
  —— of Claxton, receipt by; 4.
  —— of Norwich, letter of; 5.
  Sir Thomas; 146, 148, 151, 165.
  —— letter of; 20.
  William, at Cambridge; 131, 132.
  —— letters to; 177, 182, *et seq.*
  Sir William, Bart., letters to; 197, *et seq.*
  Hall; 128, 130, 133, 138, 148.
Gaxham, Thomas; 70.
Gay:
  Henry, letter of; 209.
  Thomas; 8.
Gayford, —; 63.
Gedge:
  Robert; 2.
  Thomas; 2.

Gelding, Robert, letter to; 59.
George, William; 96.
Geps, Thomas; 43.
Gescolfe, Thomas; 25.
Geste or Guest, Mr.; 150.
Geyton; 81.
Gibbon, Henry; 44.
Gibson:
  Mr.; 26.
  Henry; 39, 46, 50.
  John; 44, 47, 48, 157.
Gilder, Thomas; 147, 152.
Giles, Richard; 9.
Gilliard, Mr.; 132.
Gillingham; 92.
Gissing; 8, 59.
Gleane, Peter; 44.
Gleeke; 158.
Gleeker, a; 171.
Gleman, Mr.; 61.
Glemham:
  Little; 126.
  Sir Thomas; 124, 126, 155.
Glosthorp; 118.
Gloves; 203.
Godbold:
  Mr.; 136.
  John, bond to; 132.
Godbould:
  —, of Fyncham; 72.
  Thomas; 107.
Goddard, Mr.; 191.
Godderde, Mr.; 145.
Godderham, Robert and Agnes; 59.
Godfrey:
  Mr.; 8, 9, 38.
  George; 31.
  John; 170.
  Robert; 43.
Goding, James; 201.
Goebold, John; 27.
Golding, Mr.; 59.
Goldsmiths, the, and Lord Holland; 123.
Gonehingham, Henry; 85.
Gooch:
  Mr.; 141.
  Edmund; 73.
Goodshawe, Edward; 76.
Goodson, goodman; 150.
Goodwine, Thomas; 157.
Gorboll, Mr.; 138.
George, Sir Arthur, his duel; 149, 150, 151.
Goring:
  Lord (1639); 172.
  Sir George; 129.
Gosnold, Mr.; 21.
Gosse, Edward, letter of; 75.
Gostlin, Dr., of Caius College; 114, 121.
Gostling, John; 3.
Goulborne, —; 86.
Goulding (?), Mr.; 180.
Grastocke; 94.
Gray, Mr.; 58.
Greenhoe, South; 65, 67.
Gregory, Edward; 193.
Grenville, Sir Richard, his death; 35.

Gresham :
  Mr. ; 59.
  Sir Thomas ; 4.
Gressenhall ; 43, 44, 50, 51, 73.
Grevell, Mr. ; 85.
Grey :
  Anne de, letters to ; 179, 183, 185, 186, 187, 194, 195.
  Lady Eliz. de, letter to ; 186.
  John de, Bishop of Norwich ; 119.
  Sir William de ; 125, 128.
  —— his son ; 140.
Griffin, Jeffrye ; 26.
Grigges, Mr. ; 67, 120.
Griggs, Lionel ; 105.
Grigson, Edward ; 39.
Grimshoe ; 65, 67, 68.
Grimston, Sir Harbottle ; 125.
Grise (?), Mr. ; 38.
Gros. See Le Gros.
Grosse, Tom ; 152.
Gryffin, Edward ; 76.
Grymble, — ; 88.
Guest, Mr. ; 150, 162.
Guiltcross hundred ; 65, 190, 198.
Gunthorpe ; 5.
Gurden, — ; 26.
Gurney, Rev. George, letter of ; 35.
Guybon, Anthony, or Mr. ; 8, 9, 61, 63, 68.
Gybson, John ; 46.
Gyrling, Nich. ; 188, 191.

H.

Hague, the, Charles II. at ; 189.
Haiward, Agnes, letter of ; 29.
Hale, Mr. ; 210.
Haleck, Mr. ; 205.
Hales in Sussex ; 172.
Hall :
  Mr. ; 210.
  Bartholomew ; 112.
  Thomas, of Kingston Lacy ; 112.
  William, letter of ; 80.
Halle, Edmond ; 2.
Hals :
  Rev. George, deposition of ; 54.
  —— letter of ; 88.
Hambling, — ; 133.
Hamden, Sir Edmond ; 125.
Hamilton, Marquis of (1639) ; 172.
Hammon, Henry, bond by ; 8.
Hamond :
  Dr., his life ; 195.
  Mr. ; 92, 159.
  Mrs. ; 170.
Hampden, John, and ship money ; 164.
Hampton Court ; 96.
  letter dated at ; 6.
Hampton :
  Isabel ; 32.
  Thomas, letter of ; 4.

Hanbury, Mr. ; 186.
Happing, hundred court of ; 75.
Harborow manor ; 54.
Harding, Henry ; 70.
Hardingham ; 93.
  minister of ; 147.
Hare :
  Sir John ; 123, 148, 161.
  —— letters of ; 124, 125, 127, 129, 130.
  Michael, letter of ; 34.
  Mr. ; 11, 55.
  Nicholas, letters of ; 9, 16, 17; 18.
  Ralph, letter of ; 80.
Harleston ; 24, 61.
  market ; 1, 2.
Harling :
  East, robberies near ; 16.
  West ; 13, 17, 18, et seq. passim.
Harman, Daniel ; 162.
Harrison :
  Jo., letter of ; 110.
  Parson ; 168.
Harrogate ; 114.
Harrys, Thomas, receipt by ; 40.
Hart :
  Barbarie, letters of ; 60, 164.
  Lady ; 189.
  Stephen ; 47.
  William ; 83.
Harvey :
  Mr., minister ; 26, 35.
  Augustine, letter of ; 71.
  John ; 194.
  Roger, letter of ; 57.
  Sir Thomas, bond to ; 191.
  Sir William ; 170.
Harward, Henry ; 73.
Harwarde, John ; 62.
Harwyne, John, letter of ; 197.
Hassett (?), Mr. ; 62.
Hastings, Sir Hugh ; 117.
Hatton :
  Lady, entertainment by ; 157.
  Sir Thomas ; 185.
Haukers, manor of ; 1.
Havers :
  Mr. ; 90, 132.
  Thomas ; 91.
Hawe, Roger, letter of ; 178.
Hawes, Mr. ; 47.
Hawkes, Michael ; 45.
Hawks and hawking ; 63, 90, 93, 98, 105, 107, 167.
Haws, Christopher ; 45.
Hawsted ; 19, 22.
Hawtrey :
  Barbara, letters of ; 179, 186, 194, 207, 211.
  Ralph, letters of ; 207, 208, 209.
Hawys, Robert, letter of ; 86.
Haylet, John ; 2.
Haynwright, Richard ; 45.
Hayward, Thomas, letter of ; 57.
Heath, Sir Robert ; 138.
Hedge, Mr. ; 162.
Heigham :
  Sir Clement ; 4, 53, 66, 103.

Heigham, Sir Clement—*cont.*
—— letter of ; 83.
Sir John ; 35, 63.
—— warrant by ; 17.
—— letters of ; 21, 29, 66, 95.
Nan ; 178.
Thomas, letters of; 21, 45.
—— agreement, &c. by ; 55.
Hellwise, one ; 203.
Helton ; 58.
Hengrave ; 185.
Henham; 115, 120, 122, 128, 131, 132, 180.
Henshaw, Michael, letter of ; 57.
Henstead, bailiwick of; 7.
Hepworth ; 127.
Hering, William, letter of ; 60.
Herne :
Clement, letters of; 205, 206.
Simon, his son ; 86.
Herringe, Rev. William, receipt by ; 52.
Hervey :
John ; 192.
Thomas ; 39.
—— letter of ; 196.
Heryng, Mrs. ; 65.
Herynge, Mr. ; 28.
Hesse, Landgrave of (1636) ; 161.
Hethersett manor ; 5, 8.
Wormley ; 201.
—— letter of ; 204.
Heveningham ; 1.
Sir Arthur ; 24, 36, 46, 56.
—— letters of ; 7, 15, 18, 25, 40, 68, 75, 81, 83, 84, 87, 93.
Arthur ; 146.
—— letter of; 151.
Henry, letter of; 180.
Lady ; 152.
William ; 140, 141, 146, 159, 173.
—— letters of; 168, 174.
Hevisett, Edmund, letter of; 142.
Hewar :
Thomas ; 80.
—— letter to ; 73.
Hewes, William ; 134.
Hewyck, William, receipt by ; 21.
Hey :
Chr. ; 182.
—— bill due to ; 179.
—— letters of ; 75, 178, 183.
—— receipt by ; 184.
Heydon ; 2.
Ollands, muster at ; 209.
Sir Christopher ; 66, 70, 72.
—— letters of; 7, 10, 25, 32, 68, 82, 96, 98, 104.
Sir John, duel fought by ; 69, 70, 71, 72.
Sir William ; 57.
—— letters of; 26, 27, 28, 30, 32, 39.
Heyes, John, receipt by ; 45.
Heyward:
Ann, letter of; 57.
Henry ; 15.
Mrs. ; 57.
Thomas ; 21.

Heyward, Thomas —*cont.*
—— letters of; 6, 13, 18, 22, 24.
Hickling ; 3, 53.
Hicks, Sir Baptist ; 130.
Higham, Sir John ; 18.
Highnone, Christopher, letter of; 58.
Highways in London, bill for repairing ; 193.
Hill:
Anne, letter of ; 134.
Auditor ; 67.
John, letters of ; 65, 72.
—— Queen's Auditor, precept by ; 81.
Simon ; 2.
Hillersdon, Thomas, of Ampthill ; 84.
Hinderclay ; 102.
Hindolveston ; 76.
Hingham ; 8, 38, 52.
Hinlon, Thomas, letter of ; 57.
Hinsell, Sir Edward ; 57.
Hinton, Thomas, of Wake ; 84.
Hobart:
Lord, (1625) death of ; 122.
Lord ; 206.
Lady ; 201.
Mr. ; 71, 180.
Anthony ; 115, 122, 147.
George, letter of; 182.
John ; 159.
Sir John ; 141, 151, 171, 200.
—— death of his son ; 156.
Sir Miles ; 155, 156.
Hockering ; 10.
Hockham ; 64, 71, 135, 172.
Hockwold ; 78, 89, 146, 147, 151, 168, 174.
Hoggs, Robert ; 159.
Holden, John, letter of ; 20.
Holdiche :
Henry ; 67, 79.
—— letters of; 34, 104.
Holdych, Mr. ; 95.
Holl:
Augustine ; 156.
Mr., and his wife ; 155.
—— sheriff ; 170.
Thomas ; 131.
Holland:
plague in ; 155.
Lord (1627), and the goldsmiths ; 123.
Earl of, (1632) ; 138.
Elizabeth ; 2.
—— of Mendham ; *ib.*
John, debt by ; 5.
—— letters of ; 74, 75, 83, 88, 91, 92, 94, 98, 100, 101, 104.
Sir John ; 159, 169.
—— letters of ; 134, 173, 176, 181, 190, 192, 195, 198, 200.
Ma (?), letter of ; 123.
Mr. ; 131, 132.
Thomas, of Swinestead ; 2, 3.
—— letter of ; 33.
Sir Thomas ; 112, 121, 134, 180.
—— letter of ; 122.
Holme ; 99.

Holms, Thomas, warrant by ; 39.
Holt hundred ; 7, 76.
Holte, John ; 37.
Homersfield ; 165.
Honingham ; 82, 188.
Hoo, Mrs. ; 89.
Hoogan, Henry, letter of ; 31.
Hooke, Robert, receipt by ; 41.
Hooker, Nicholas, receipt by ; 46.
Hopkinson, William, letter of ; 58.
Hopton :
    Sir Arthur ; 168.
    Sir Ralph ; 169, 174.
    Sir Thomas ; 164, 165, 166, 168.
Horne, Robert ; 54.
Horneby :
    Mr. ; 67.
    Robert ; 189.
    William ; 102.
Hornesey, Robert, release by ; 46.
Horses, description of ; 73.
Houghton :
    John ; 17·
    —— letter of ; 5.
    Mr. ; 50.
Hovell, Richard ; 74.
Howard :
    Lady ; 94.
    Mr., his boroughs ; 190.
    Sir Edward ; 129.
    John, letter to ; 130.
    Lord Henry, and James I. ; 88.
    Lady Jane ; 3.
    Lady Margaret ; ib.
    Lord Thomas, letter to ; 79.
    Lord William ; 74.
    —— and James I. ; 88.
Howecaple ; 110.
Howes :
    —, warrener ; 83.
    Mr. ; 163.
    William, letter of ; 68.
Howlton, Edward ; 57.
Howlyn, Thomas, letter of ; 173.
Howse :
    Mr. ; 170, 198.
    John ; 176, 189.
    —— letters of ; 185, 196.
    Thomas, letter of ; 78.
    William, receipt by ; 10.
Hoxne ; 23, 25, 29, 30, 31, 32.
Hubberd, Mr. ; 50.
Huggan, Thomas ; 25.
Hughes, Da., letters of ; 67, 68, 96.
Humbleyard hundred ; 7.
Humfreyes, Mr. ; 110.
Hungatt, — ; 70.
Hunsdon :
    Lord, letter of ; 59.
    Lady ; 114.
Hunstanton ; 73.
Hunston, Thomas, letter of ; 80.
Hunt, William ; 48.
Hurrey, William ; 41.
Hutchinson, Christopher ; 64.
Hutton, Judge, his accuser ; 168.

Hyde Park market ; 131.
Hynde, Sir Francis, letters of ; 24, 47.
Hynes, Lady ; 20.
Hyrne, Thomas, letter of ; 122.

I.

Ickworth ; 192.
Ikene manor, Suffolk ; 117.
Illington ; 37, 199.
Ingelo, Dr. Nathaniel ; 200.
Ingerston, rendezvous at ; 66.
Inglish, William ; 37.
Ingram, William ; 22.
Inne, Thomas ; 21.
Insula, John de ; 117.
Intwood ; 8.
Ipswich ; 16, 22, 111, 126.
    News from, book called ; 162.
    Bossehall near ; 19.
    Foxall near ; 117·
Irby, Sir Anthony ; 170.
Ireland, Ed. ; 189.
Ixworth, lands in ; 156.

J.

Jake-marlen ; 154.
James I. :
    and the Howards, at Burleigh ; 88.
    proclamation of, in Norfolk ; 87.
    his sports and pleasures ; 94, 95.
    and the Lancashire petition ; 97.
James :
    Mr. ; 133, 141.
    Parson ; 91.
Jeakes, Elizabeth ; 15.
Jeegon, Robert ; 171.
Jefferye, Simon ; 14, 16.
Jener, William ; 44.
Jenkinson :
    John ; 41.
    Sir Thomas ; 120, 121.
Jenny, Henry ; 103.
Jermie, Mr. ; 182.
Jermyn :
    Mr. ; 31, 107.
    Betty ; 197.
    Sir Robert ; 14, 15, 18.
    Sir Thomas ; 110, 133, 172, 178.
Jobson, Mr. ; 42.
John, Thomas ; 34.
Johnson :
    John ; 30.
    Thomas, of Lincoln's Inn ; 77.
Jolly, Mr. ; 198.
Jone, mother ; 34.
Jones, Judge ; 168.
Jubye, John ; 22.

K.

Kemp :
  Sir Robert ; 148, 172, 196.
  George ; 19.
  Mr. ; 12.
  old ; 150.
Kempt, Mr. ; 104.
Keue, Mr., legacy by ; 33.
Kenninghall ; 87, 91, 157, 161, 162, 163, 175, 180.
  common ; 58.
  disparking of ; 131.
  windmill ; 17.
  foreigners in ; 33.
  ale-houses in ; ib.
  Lodge ; 35, 58, 105.
  Park ; 77.
  the White Horse in ; 104.
  Heaseldicke in ; 132.
Kent, churches of ; 172.
Kenton ; 88.
  living ; 39.
  minister at ; 54.
Kerington, Roger ; 191.
Kerry, Mr. ; 94, 96, 97.
Kett, Loye ; 34.
Ketteringham ; 15, 18, 24, 25, 40, 56, 68, 81, 83, 84, 87, 93, 133, 137, 180.
Kettishall ; 187.
Kettleboro' ; 155.
Ketton ; 54.
Kingston Lacy ; 112.
Kirby, Robert ; 19.
Kirkeman, John ; 45.
Kirketon ; 119.
Kirtling ; 61.
Knapswood ; 98.
Knight :
  goodman ; 184.
  John ; 179.
Knightley, Awdry ; 2.
Knollis :
  Robert, letter to ; 106.
  Sir Robert ; 138.
  —— letters to ; 107, 108, 110, 111.
  —— his death and debts ; 111.
Knot, — ; 201.
Knowles :
  John ; 59.
  Barttemewe ; ib.
Knyvet :
  — ; 190.
  Mr. ; 8, 55, 79.
  Sir John ; 196.
  Thomas ; 134.
  Sir Thomas ; 28, 65.
  —— sheriff ; 12.
Kylby, Alice ; 46.
Kyllyon, — ; 58.

L.

Lambe, Mrs. ; 180.
Lambeth House ; 157.
Lambs, sale of ; 165.
Lancashire :
  ministers, petition about ; 97.
  witches ; 147.
Lancaster :
  — ; 7.
  widow ; 149.
Lancy, Thos., letter of ; 197.
Land's End ; 30.
Lane :
  Mr. ; 30.
  George ; 112.
  John and Robert ; 98.
  Thomas, letters of ; 43, 81.
Langford ; 31, 43.
  manor ; 117.
Langhton (?) ; 77, 78.
Langley Park ; 38.
Lany :
  Benj., Bishop of Lincoln ; 197.
  Jo., letter of ; 210.
  Nicholas, letters of ; 203, 204.
  Thomas, letters of ; 185, 194, 195, 202.
Larling ; 104.
Larlingford ; 16, 91, 163, 198.
  minister at ; 159.
La Sale, John de ; 118.
Latham, Elizabeth ; 53.
Latimer, Lord (1634) ; 150.
Laud, Archbishop, feeling against ; 163.
Lawes, — ; 70.
Lawrence :
  Mr. ; 61, 90.
  John, letter of ; 20.
Laxfield ; 183, 185.
Layer, Elizabeth, her lovers ; 170–172.
Leake, William ; 45.
Lee :
  Ann, letter of ; 207.
  Anne Hawtrey, letters of ; 187.
  Sir Richard, letter of ; 76.
Leeke, Do., letters of ; 189.
Legat, John ; 143, 146, 177.
Legate, — ; 153, 204.
Le Gros, Sir Charles ; 149, 153, 154, 163.
Leicester, Earl of :
  (1578), letter of ; 6.
  (1588) ; 30.
  (1637) ; 163.
Leighton, Sir Thomas ; 30.
Le maire, David ; 47, 49.
Le Neve :
  Peter, memoranda by ; 53, 117.
  Sir Ury ; 172.
L'Estrange :
  Sir Nicholas ; 73.
  Thomas, letter of ; 73.
Levalde, Leonard ; 59.
Leventhorp, Thomas, letter of ; 20.
Leverington, Thomas, letter of ; 20.
Leving, Robert ; 140.

Lewin, Dr.; 195.
Lewis *alias* Davis, Richard, receipt by; 107.
Lewkenor, Edward, letter of; 48.
Lewknor, Edward; 151.
Leyston abbey; 7.
Lillie, Robert, letter of; 60.
Lilly (Lely ?), Mr., artist; 198.
Limehouse; 63.
Lincoln; 80.
  Bishop of (1637), proceedings against; 166.
  —— (1638); 170.
  —— (1663); 197.
  Earl of (1579); 11.
Liquorice, wine of; 102.
Lisseman, Henry; 201.
Loddon; 137.
  hundred; 7.
Lombe:
  Edward, letters to; 205, 206.
  John; 210.
  Thomas; 205.
London:
  plague in (1581); 17.
  plague in (1636); 160–163.
  proclamation against living in; 141.
  fine for new buildings about; 146.
  the Queen mother in; 169.
  Aldersgate; 46.
  Aldgate; 169.
  Arundel House; 16, 17, 23, 121, 195.
  Barnard's Inn; 130.
  Bishopsgate, Green Dragon in; 129.
  Canwicke Street; 47.
  Charing Cross; 18.
  Clement's Inn; 57.
  Clifford's Inn; 5.
  Covent Garden, James Street; 197.
  —— Russell Street; 183.
  —— York Street; 203.
  Doctors Commons; 37.
  Drury Lane; 140–145 *passim*, 203.
  —— Red Bull; 174.
  Durham House; 94.
  Ely House; 129, 130.
  new Exchange; 186.
  Fetter Lane, Red Hart; 201.
  Fleet Street; 30, 152, 165, 168, 169, 178.
  —— the Bear; 138.
  —— King's Head; 137, 147.
  —— St. Dunstan's Church; 163, 177.
  Friarbridge; 79.
  Furnival's Inn; 45, 88.
  Gray's Inn; 147.
  —— Hall; 84.
  ——Lane; 42.
  Hatton Garden; 210.
  Hatton House; 170.
  Holborn; 12, 13.
  —— Black Swan; 52.
  "the great James;" 205.
  Lincoln's Inn; 65, 77.
  Maiden Lane; 23.
  Marshalsea; 109, 110.
  Piccadilly highway; 193.
  Princes Street; 136.
  Red Bull players; 157.

London—*cont.*
  St. Clement's church; 152.
  St. James's highway; 193.
  St. John Street; 102.
  St. Martin's Lane; 107, 108, 111.
  St. Peter le Poore; 53.
  Sergeant's Inn; 7, 75.
  Smithfield, books burned in; 163.
  Somerset House; 66, 94, 95.
  —— court at; 51, 52.
  Strand; 29.
  —— Horse and Sun in; 123, 124.
  —— Golden Lion; 191.
  Temple; 3, 4, 135, 191, 192.
  —— Bar; 166, 169.
  —— church, closing of; 166.
  Tothill Fields; 108.
  the Tower; 75, 172.
  Tower Street; 137.
  Treasury, Whitehall; 202.
  Westminster Old Palace; 92, 94.
  Whitehall, new building at; 166.
  —— chapel; 95.
  Whittington College parish; 23.
  Wood Street Counter; 126, 130.
  York House; 124.
Longe, Mr., of Bury; 113.
Longstratton; 21.
Longwood, Ambrose; 62.
Lopham; 24, 34, 58, 92.
  constables of; 22.
Love, James; 34.
Lovelace, Mr.; 55.
Lovell:
  Mr.; 24, 25, 30, 57, 121.
  Sir Francis; 99, 101.
  —— death of; 114.
  Thomas; 82.
  Sir Thomas; 73.
  —— letter to; 84.
Loverine, Mr.; 171.
Lovicke, —; 201.
Lowdale, Roger; 30.
Lowe, Symon, letter of; 2.
Lowestoft; 22, 122.
Lownds, William; 101.
Lucas, Bailiff, of Yarmouth; 161.
Lucking, Sir William; 170.
Ludkin, Mr.; 129.
Lukin, William, letter of; 28.
Lullman, Robert, letter of; 203.
Lulpeck, Robert; 37, 109.
Lycham Nether Hall; 119.
Lychfell, Mr.; 58.
Lyle (?), Thomas; 53.
Lymborne; 38.
  manor; 39, 46.
Lynford; 37, 64, 67, 76–96 *passim*, 148.
Lytcham, near Swaffham; 27, 28.
Lynn, or King's Lynn; 17, 45, 48, 76, 87, 92, 201.
  sessions; 65.
  Carmelites' church at; 118.
  mayor of; 150.
  assessment on; *ib.*
  plague in; 160.
Lynstead; 11.
Lytton, Mr.; 91.

M.

Maddingley ; 24, 47.
Mainwaring, Dr., Bishop of St. David's ; 157.
Maister, William, letter of ; 26.
Maldanbye, Francis ; 102.
Mallowes, John ; 178.
Mallowse, William ; 38.
Maltard, Mr. ; 194.
Maltravers, Lord :
—— (1562) ; 4.
—— (1631) ; 136.
—— (1634) ; 148, 149.
—— (1636) ; 160.
—— (1638) ; 169.
Maltsters ; 152.
Mandey, Mr. ; 192.
Manne :
    Joan, charges against ; 12.
    Martin, letter of ; 67.
Mansfield :
    Lady Elizabeth, letters of ; 79, 81.
    Sir Robert, duel fought by ; 69, 70, 71, 72.
    —— letters of ; 70, 71, 72, 79.
    —— candidate for Norfolk ; 72, 74.
Manny, H., letter of ; 58.
March, lordship of ; 24.
Marche, Thomas, letter of ; 36.
Margeay, Thomas : 8.
Marie de Medicis, in London ; 169.
Marshall :
    Humphrey ; 9.
    John, of Norwich ; 17.
Marsham, John, letter of ; 6.
Martham ; 40.
    parsonage ; 43.
Martin :
    Dr. ; 143.
    Mr. ; 194.
    widow ; 66.
    John ; 92.
    William ; 61.
    Hall ; 58.
Marryot :
    Mr. ; 199, 202.
    Thomas, letter to ; 87.
Maslie, Jo. ; 1.
Mason, —, of Neaton ; 83.
Massingham ; 80.
Master, Simon, letter of ; 102.
Mawling, John, letter of ; 155.
May :
    D., letters of ; 210, 211.
    Martin ; 90.
Maydewell ; 108.
Mead, Sir John ; 171.
Meade, Nicholas, letter of ; 114.
Meller, Jasper, letters of ; 63, 64.
Melton Common Jail ; 28.
Mendevilles manor ; 106.
Mendham ; 2, 3, 27, 146, 165.
    church ; 4.

Mendham, Midleton Hall ; 14, 15.
Mentz, Bishop of ; 101.
Metcalfe, Mr. ; 18.
Metfield, Christmas Lane near ; 18.
Methold warren ; 77.
Methwold :
    old ; 168.
    Thomas, letters of ; 31, 43, 69.
    William ; 58.
    —— letters of ; 11, 34.
Mettingham Hall ; 23.
Michael, Mr. ; 86.
Michell, Edmund, letters of ; 113–116, 120–122.
Middleton :
    John ; 165.
    Hall, Suffolk ; 6.
    Hall, lease of ; 27.
Might, Thomas, letter of ; 72.
Mileham, stewardship of ; 4.
Miles :
    Mr. ; 142.
    Thomas ; 158.
Mildenhall ; 61, 69, 191.
Mill, Mr. ; 86.
Mills, John ; 210.
Mingay :
    Anthony ; 112, 126.
    —— letters of ; 128–177 passim, 205.
    Henry ; 141.
    —— letters of ; 126, 127.
    John ; 126, 142, 158.
    —— letters of ; 134, 190.
    Mary ; 135, 138, 149, 151.
    —— letters of ; 141, 152, 154, 157, 164, 165, 170, 172.
Monck, General ; 189.
Monks Soham ; 204.
Monopolies ; 164.
Monson, Mr. ; 85.
Montague, Marquis ; 54.
Moody :
    Samuel, letters of ; 135, 139.
    —— receipt of ; 177.
Moone, — ; 7.
Moore :
    Mr. ; 40.
    Edward, letters of ; 131, 181.
    Peter ; 38.
    Thomas, letters of ; 111.
    William, of Intwood ; 8, 28.
    —— letters of ; 167, 171, 174.
    —— receipt by ; 173.
Mordant, Sir Robert ; 136.
Morgan :
    Captain Henry ; 50.
    Peirce, letter of ; 111.
    Sir Thomas ; 30.
Morice, Francis, letters of ; 92, 94, 95, 96, 97, 101.
Morley, Lord (1579), letter of ; 10.
Morocco ambassador in England ; 166.
Morphewe, Peter ; 47.
Morris :
    John, letter of ; 64.
    Thomas ; 107, 109.
    —— letter of ; 206.

Morris, William, letter of ; 99.
Morryson, Mr., of Costessy ; 8.
Moseley, Humphrey, letter of ; 14.
Mother, the, diseased called ; 71.
Moulton, Robert, letter of ; 181.
Moundeford :
    Abigail ; 146.
    —— letter of ; 181.
    Dorothea, bond to ; 146.
    Edmond, letters of; 36–88 *passim*.
    —— commission to ; 65.
    Sir Edmond, letters of; 89, 91, 92, 93, 95, 96, 99.
    Edmond, son of Sir Edmond, letters of ; 123–161 *passim*, 174.
    Francis, letters of; 61.
    Thomas, letter of ; 104.
Moundford ; 127.
Mounson, Sir Thomas, letter of ; 80.
Montague, Richard, letter of; 93.
Mount Norris, Lady, her petition ; 158.
Moyse :
    Mr. ; 98.
    Barnabe, letter of ; 99.
    Barnaby, letter of ; 105.
    Joan, of Sancroft ; 28.
Mulbarton ; 119.
Mulhe, Robert, letter of ; 35.
Mulley, William ; 41, 52, 104, 105.
Mullins, William ; 41.
Mully, Robert, letter of ; 58.
Munden, Dr. ; 114.
Mundeveld's manor ; 54.
Munecason, the bookseller ; 156.
Murforde, Peter, letters of ; 136, 164.
Murray, Mr. ; 155.
Muryell, Thomas ; 127.
Mutton, shoulder of, receipt for cooking ; 207.
Mychell, William ; 9.
Myles, William ; 66.
Myne :
    Peter, letter of ; 61.
    Thomas, letters of; 82.
Mynors, George, letter of ; 96.
Myrrell, Mr. ; 91.

          N.

Nacton ; 206.
Najara, battle of ; 117.
Napper :
    Eliz., letter of ; 174.
    William, letters of ; 139, 142.
Narborough ; 199.
Nash, Mr. ; 137.
Nashe, Mr., minister ; 26.
Neashe, William, letter of ; 34.
Neaton (?) ; 83.
Neave, John ; 75.
Nedham :
    Arthur ; 177.
    John ; 27, 104.
Needham, Mr. ; 185.

Nelson :
    the tailor ; 139.
    Mr. ; 87.
    Edward, letter of; 203.
Neve, Mr. ; 72.
Newcastle, Earl of (1633) ; 143.
Newham, Robert, receipt of; 46.
Newman :
    Edmund, bond of ; 38.
    Thomas, letter of ; 199.
Newmarket ; 42, 160, 161, 170.
    court at ; 137, 138.
    heath ; 165.
    the Greyhound ; 165.
Newporte, Robert ; 67.
Newson :
    Edmund ; 187.
    Lawrence ; 133.
    Robert, letter of ; 179.
Newton, Old, Suffolk ; 117.
Nonne :
    Mr. ; 51, 52.
    Elizabeth, letters of; 26, 38, 89.
    George ; 59.
    John, letters of ; 7 *et seq.*, 22, 27, 28, 38, 41, 45, 49, 50, 56, 87, 92, 95, 99.
    —— bond by ; 39.
    Thomas, letter of; 84.
Norfolk :
    wild fowl in ; 5.
    plague in ; 12.
    elections in ; 25, 32, 72, 74, 122.
    levy of men in ; 30.
    sheep in ; 35, 36.
    jury in ; 36.
    Recusants' commission in ; 65.
    musters in ; 73.
    commissioners for ; *ib.*
    horses levied in ; 73.
    men raised in ; 78, 80.
    deputy lieutenants for ; 79, 80.
    proclamation of James I. in ; 87.
    loan raised in ; 94, 96, 97.
    assessment of ship money in ; 150, 155, 156.
    malting business in ; 164.
    maltsters ; 152.
    marshes in ; 166.
    militia in ; 200.
    Duke of (1547) ; 2.
    —— burial of ; 3.
Norridg, William, minister ; 163.
Norris, Mr., in Flanders ; 17.
North :
    Henry, letters of ; 69, 191.
    John, letter of ; 41.
    Roger, letters of ; 61.
Northampton, Earl of (1604) ; 94, 96, 97.
Northumberland, Earl of (1635) ; 152.
    —— (1636), at Yarmouth ; 160, 161.
    —— (1638) ; 168.
Northwold ; 154.
    manor ; 65, 66.
Norwich ; 26, 44, 69, 128, 135, 136, 141.
    plagues at ; 9, 10, 89, 152, 160–170 *passim*.

Norwich—*cont.*
  musters at; 73, 154, 190.
  papists imprisoned in; 78, 80.
  assessment on; 150.
  ship money; 156.
  mayor of; 18.
  ministers, suspension of; 158.
  maintenance of clergy in; 164.
  assizes; 125, 146.
  sessions, expenses at; 71, 72.
  Black Friars; 3.
  castle; 57.
  the Crown; 24, 73.
  the Friars; 148.
  Guildhall; 175.
  King's Head; 174.
  the Maid's Head; 167.
  prison; 99.
  St. Andrew's Church; 136, 169.
  St. George of Colgate; 205.
  St. Peter Mancroft; 163, 167, 169, 177.
  White Horse; 18.
  White Lion Lane; 199.
  Bishop of (1579), warrant by; 11.
  —— (1601); 72.
  —— de Grey; 119.
  —— (1635); 156.
  —— (1638); 169.
  William, letter of; 122.
Nottingham, Earl of (1598); 63.
  (1599), letter of; 66.
Nowell, Mr.; 158.
Noy, Sir William; 147.
  honest and stout; 136.
Nyddam, John; 28.

O.

Oby, William; 1.
Ockelie, Mr., of Lynn; 87.
Ogle:
  Mr.; 203.
  Thomas, letter of; 183.
Okeley:
  Lawrence; 28.
  Thomas, letters of; 181.
Okes, Mr.; 175.
Oldom, Nicholas, letter of; 110.
Olley, John; 75.
Onge, — his debts, &c.; 155, 156, 157, 158, 159 *passim.*
Onslow, Mr.; 45.
Oon, Phillipa; 2.
Orford; 137, 138.
Orwell:
  Robert; 39, 45.
  Thomas, of Aylsham; 1.
Osborne, Thomas, letters of; 51, 58, 138.
Oseley, John, of Courtenhall; 28.
Ostend, siege of; 30, 96.
Otway, Christopher; 15.
Ovington; 62, 64.
  tavern at; 37.

Owen, John, letter of; 48.
Owles, John, letter of; 9.
Oxboro'; 154.
Oxborough, Mr.; 74.
Oxburgh; 190, 194.
  Thomas, letter of; 47.
Oysters, bloody; 172.

P.

Page, Robert; 44.
Pakenham; 59, 68.
Palgrave; 72, 120, 121, 123, 127.
Palmer:
  —; 7.
  Mr., fined; 141.
Palsgrave, the:
  in England; 155, 156, 157.
  loan to; 162.
Parham, Suffolk; 181.
Parker:
  John, receipt by; 37.
  Sir Philip; 24, 38, 49.
Parkin, —; 201.
Parliament of 1628; 129, 130.
Parr, old, death of; 155.
Parris, Mr.; 58.
Partridges; 90.
Paston:
  Lady; 124.
  Squire; 149.
  Sir William; 73.
Paule, Dr.; 158.
Pawe:
  Andrew; 2.
  William; 2.
Payne, Sir Robert; 174.
Payton, Lady; 211.
Peache, John, lease to; 56.
Pead, Richard, letter of; 58.
Peade, Thomas, letter of; 78.
Peare, Alderman, his widow; 154.
Pears, John; 208.
Pecke:
  —, letter of; 58.
  old, death of; 147.
  Alderman, of Norwich; 17.
  Edward; 134.
  —— letters of; 191.
  John, deposition of; 54.
  Thomas, letter of; 113.
Pecock, —, his cattle; 34.
Pedder, Alice; 39.
Peeke, Mr.; 170.
Peke, William; 148.
Pell:
  Mr.; 167, 171.
  Alice, account by; 186.
  Thomas; 189.
  Valentine; 72.
Pells, William; 27.
Pemberton, Mr.; 37.
Pennington, Captain; 155.
Pennyng, Robert, receipt by; 10.
Pennynge, John, letter of; 178.

Pentney ; 70.
Pepper, Christopher ; 73.
Perkas (?), John ; 41.
Perrin, Mr. ; 126.
Peter, Sir John ; 85.
Pett, Peter, letter of ; 63.
Pettaugh ; 53, 56, 98, 153.
Pettit, Goody ; 187.
Pettus:
    Mr., sheriff ; 137.
    John, letters of ; 47, 49, 81.
    Thomas ; 47.
    Will. ; 169.
Peyton:
    Mr. ; 18.
    Sir John, letters of ; 31, 75, 78.
    Phelix, Lucas ; 47.
Philip, Edmund ; 9.
Phillips, Auditor ; 206.
Pickas, John ; 62.
Pickenham, South ; 11, 34.
Pickering:
    a recusant ; 168.
    Lewes, letter of ; 98.
Pickeryll, Mr. ; 55.
Pierson, Mr. ; 88.
Pigeon, John, release by ; 46.
Pillory, the ; 86.
Pisbaron, Robert ; 119.
Pitt, Mr. (1655), funeral of ; 179.
Plagues ; 160. See Norwich.
Players, Red Bull company of ; 157.
Playford, Suffolk ; 119.
Playsted, Ralph, letter of ; 35.
Plombe, John ; 2.
Plumbe, Daniel ; 21.
Poland, ambassador from ; 166.
Poley, Sir Edmund ; 191.
Popham, Chief Justice ; 65, 67, 70.
Portsmouth ; 124, 125.
Portugal and Spain ; 164.
Pottes, Mr. ; 174.
Potts, Sir John ; 176.
Prat, Will ; 137, 140, 141, 145.
Prats, Gregory ; 45.
Pratt:
    Mr. ; 77, 87.
    Osbert ; 78, 89, 144.
Precious, one ; 195.
Prescriptions ; 180.
Pretiman, John ; 93.
Prices, illustrations of ; 57, 58, 81, 114,
    116, 120, 134, 153, 165, 173, 177, 178,
    179, 182, 186, 189, 191, 192, 198, 203,
    204, 206.
Prisoners, gifts to ; 28.
Prynne, (William ?) ; 146, 168.
Pulham ; 99.
    St. Mary ; 47.
Pully, William ; 130.
Puntinge, Robert ; 10.
Purbeck, Lady, her penance ; 152.
Purdye:
    mother ; 4.
    Robert, letter of ; 46.
Purrye, Ric. ; 25.
Pye, —, a prisoner ; 94.

Pygeon:
    Mr. ; 78.
    John ; 89.
Pyne, Nicholas ; 63.
Pyte (?), Thomas ; 34.
Pyttes, Sir Edward ; 92.

Q.

Quiddenham ; 21, 31, 35, 93, 112, 122,
    123, 173, 176, 181, 196, 198, 200.
Quanterill, — ; 201.
Quarles, James ; 23.

R.

Rabberds, Ralph ; 39.
Ralphes, James, letter to ; 203.
Rame, Henry ; 11.
Randall, William, receipt by ; 39.
Rant, Dr. ; 134.
Rawlings, Rawlyns:
    Anthony ; 90, 102, 109, 110, 112,
    134, 155.
    —— letters to ; 59, 113, 120, 121,
    123, 124, 127, 138.
    Charles, son of Rev. Jo. ; 79, 82,
    170, 171.
    —— letter of ; 128.
    Rev. Jo., letters of ; 120–129 passim.
    Mrs., letter to ; 116.
Raynbearde, Robert ; 92.
Raynberd, Nicholas, letters of ; 40, 52,
    59, 105.
Rayner, Mr. ; 71.
Raynham ; 196.
Recusants ; 92, 101, 168.
Redenhale Hall, manor of ; 1.
Redenhall ; 46.
Redgrave ; 16, 22, 34, 66, 67, 69, 72, 93,
    102, 131.
Redman, Mr. ; 180.
Reece, Daniel, letter of ; 105.
Reeders, Andrew ; 173.
Reedham ; 81.
Reme, Mr., his son ; 203.
Rendall:
    Mr. ; 198.
    John, letter of ; 116.
Renton ; 19.
    Suddon Hall ; 17.
Reppes:
    Mr. ; 61.
    Ann ; 3.
    Bettys or Beterys ; 1, 2.
    Henry ; 1–5 passim.
    John ; 80.
    —— letters of ; 5, 6, 27, 83.
    —— of Clifford's Inn ; 5.
    —— agreement by ; 27.

Reve, Reeve :
  Daniel ; 190.
  —— and Cicely ; 21. ..
  Dr. Daniel, letter of ; 69.
  John, letter of ; 127.
  Judge ; 174.
  Sergeant ; 163, 164.
  Thomas ; 46, 110.
Reymes :
  Mr. ; 28.
  William ; 27.
Reymond, Wilton ; 120.
Reynolds :
  James, letter of ; 185.
  —— receipt by ; 209.
  John, letter of ; 66.
Rich :
  Mr. ; 154.
  Sir Nathaniel ; 140.
  Robert ; 119.
Richards :
  Mr., chaplain ; 42.
  —— minister ; 76.
  Sir Edwin ; 54.
Richardson :
  James and Clemence ; 25.
  Lord (?) ; 190.
  Sir Thomas ; 165, 170, 172.
Richman :
  Mr. ; 32.
  — ; 205.
Richmond, Surrey ; 63.
Riddlesworth ; 148.
Ridlesworth ; 120.
Ringwood, Robert ; 22.
Rising ; 26.
Rivers, Lord (1635), death of ; 155.
Roberts, Thomas, receipt by ; 185.
Robins, James ; 179.
Rochester, William ; 2.
Rochford, Henry, letter of ; 114·
Rogers :
  Mr. ; 157, 161.
  George ; 74.
Rokeland ; 2.
Rolf:
  — ; 8.
  John ; 28.
Rolle, Clement ; 44.
Romans, the, King of ; 162.
Rookwood, Mr. ; 33, 58.
Rose, G. ; 29.
Rous :
  Mr. ; 50, 86.
  his tithes ; 195.
  Chr., letters of ; 131, 132.
  Sir John ; 112, 115, 122, 180.
  —— letters of ; 128, 131.
  Mary, letters of ; 184, 187.
  Mr., or Rev. T., his parishioners at
    Sternfield ; 203, 204.
  Thomas, letter of ; 178.
Rowdham ; 59.
Royston ; 96.
Ruddock, Andrew, letter of ; 139.
Rugge, Mr. ; 45.

Rugge—cont.
  Thomas, letter of ; 127.
  William, letters of ; 33, 52, 89, 92.
Ruislip ; 197, 208, 209, 211.
Rumpe, Nicholas ; 53.
Rupert, Prince ; 156, 157.
Rushbroke, William, letter of ; 23.
Rushford ; 73, 78, 121, 202.
  College of ; 25.
Russell :
  Sir William ; 30, 137, 172.
  —— death of ; 191.
Rust, Judith ; 17.
Ruthall, Capt. George, letter of ; 73.
Ryburgh manor ; 118.
Ryvett, James ; 18.

S.

Sabarne, Walter ; 46.
Sack, rundlet of ; 160.
Saddleton, Thomas ; 63.
Saier, Nicholas ; 5.
St. Albans ; 38, 46.
  Lord (1635), death of ; 155.
St. David's, Bishop of (1636) ; 157.
St. John, Lord (1585) ; 24.
Sakford, — ; 126.
Salt making, patent for ; 155.
Salter, — ; 189.
Sancroft ; 28.
Sanderson, Dr. ; 195.
Sandly, —, his debt ; 12.
Sandroffe, Fr. ; 110.
Sannfield, Mr. ; 38.
Sasser (?), William ; 32.
Saulter, Roger ; 24.
Sawer, Sir Ed. ; 206.
Saxby, Mr., of Sonning ; 185.
Saxham, Great ; 177.
Saxlingham ; 10, 39.
Saxmundham ; 204.
Sayer :
  — ; 134, 142.
  Mr., letter to ; 93.
  Mrs., letter to ; 99.
  Edward ; 142, 149.
  John ; 159.
  Ned ; 156, 158.
  Nicholas ; 19.
  Ralph ; 148.
Scalebones, game of ; 153.
Scamler, John, letter of ; 42.
Scarning ; 36.
Scot, Rev. Thomas, letters of ; 83.
Scotland :
  Union with ; 96, 97.
  affairs of ; 166, 172, 173.
Scott, Mr. ; 74.
Scottnetts manor ; 106.
Scudamore, Sir James ; 87.
Seaman :
  Sir Peter ; 54.
  Richard ; 92.
Seckford manor ; 21.
Selden, John, Lord Suffolk and ; 129.

Selling, John ; 61.
Seman :
    Mr. ; 15, 16.
    William, his daughters ; 33.
Servant, a, enticement of ; 102.
Servants, benevolences to ; 80, 81.
Setchey ; 87.
Shardelow, Mr. ; 198.
Shardelowe, Jo. ; 112.
Shardloe, Chief Constable ; 70.
Sharington, Eliz. ; 119.
Sharp, Mrs., of Bury ; 183, 185, 186, 188.
Sharpe, Jo., chaplain at court ; 92, 93.
Sheaking, William ; 8.
Sheaphard, Justice :
    his daughter ; 145.
    Richard ; 145, 147.
Sheep ; 103, 209.
    account of ; 35, 36.
    washing ; 189.
Shelfhanger ; 77.
Shelley, Suffolk ; 4.
Shelton, Sir R. ; 13.
Sherdekow, John ; 110.
Sherdeloe, John ; 111.
Shering, John ; 39.
Sherman, Francis ; 74.
Sherwood, Dr. ; 138, 143.
Shilling, Francis ; 33.
Shillinge, — ; 210.
Shimpling ; 101.
Shipdham ; 122.
Ship money in Norfolk, &c. ; 150, 155, 156, 164, 166, 169, 170.
Shirley, Sir Thomas, treasurer at war ; 50.
Shothowe, John ; 101.
Shottesham ; 94.
Shottesham Hall ; 2.
Shropham ; 65, 190.
    hundred ; 196, 198.
Shuckford, — ; 91, 100, 101, 181.
Shugg, Captain ; 152.
Shuickfield, Robert ; 73.
Simson :
    James, letter of ; 188.
    —— receipt by ; 195.
    Mary, letter of ; 188.
Sitwell, — ; 209, 210, 211.
    Mr. ; 207.
    Elizabeth, letters of ; 211.
Skarburghe, Henry ; 75.
Skathe, Robert, receipt by ; 45.
Skettow, widow ; 170.
Skipworth, Sir Ralph ; 190.
Skot, John, letter of ; 8.
Skottow, Mr. ; 138.
Skottowe, widow ; 160.
Skoulton ; 100.
Sluys, surrender of ; 94.
Smith, Smythe, &c. :
    Mr., of Stutton ; 87.
    Lady ; 165, 168.
    Edmund ; 25.
    Edward ; 9.
    Henry, letter of ; 48.
    Rev. Hurd, bond by ; 134.
    Jeoffrye ; 29.
    John ; 9, 10.

Smith, Smythe, &c.—cont.
    John, letters of ; 40, 77, 148.
    Nicholas ; 88.
    Sir Owen ; 133, 134, 146, 153, 164, 165, 168, 169.
    Richard ; 53.
    —— his daughters ; 61.
    —— bond to ; 74.
    Thomas ; 9.
    —— receipts by ; 41.
    Sir Thomas ; 195.
    William, of Banham ; 37.
    —— release by ; 53.
Snelling :
    John, letters of ; 59, 113.
    Mathew, letter of ; 183.
    —— painting by ; ib.
    Robert, letter of ; 177.
    Samuel ; 142.
    —— letter of ; 140.
Sneterton ; 9.
Snetterton ; 74.
Snitterley ; 33.
Snitterton ; 144.
Snyler ; 48.
Soame, Christopher ; 44.
Soham Lodge ; 100.
Somers, Sir William ; 141.
Somerset, Mr. ; 96.
Sonning ; 185, 186.
Sothell, Mr. ; 134.
Sotherton, Henry ; 41.
Southampton, Earl of (1604) ; 92.
Southes, John ; 169.
South Repps ; 1.
Southwell ; 100.
    Lady ; 67.
    Mr. ; 8, 23.
    Sir Robert ; 43.
    charge against ; 62.
    Wilham, receipt by ; 107.
Sowwell (Southwell ?) family ; 189.
Spain and Portugal ; 164.
Spayne, Richard ; 2.
Speldhurst ; 153.
Spelman, Mr., of Narborough ; 199.
Spiller, Sir Harry ; 127.
Spilman :
    — ; 41, 63.
    Henry ; 73.
Spinkes, —; his alehouse ; 104.
Spirling, —; 161, 162, 165.
Sponer :
    — ; 145.
    Simon ; 18, 105.
    —— action by ; 14.
    Thomas ; 84.
Sponner :
    Cuthbert ; 52.
    Richard ; ib.
Sporle :
    Henry ; 22.
    John ; 44.
    —— and Robert ; 34.
    Robert, letter of ; 44.
Sprignall, Robert ; 85.
Springe, John, letters of ; 32, 35, 68.

Springe—*cont.*
William, letters of ; 62, 112, 144.
Sir William ; 18, 42.
—— letter to ; 59.
Spurforde, John, letter of ; 62.
Spurgin, John, petition of ; 105.
Spurling, Mr. ; 159.
Stafford :
John ; 210.
—— letter of ; 198.
Lady Dorothy, letter of ;
Stallan :
— ; 124.
goodman ; 121.
Thomas ; 123.
Stanford ; 59, 121.
Stanhope :
Sir Edward, letters of ; 37, 106.
Michael, letters of ; 36, 105.
—— letter to ; 62.
William, letters of ; 114, 127, 131.
Stanmore, — ; 181.
Stannard, goodman ; 133, 184.
Stanninghall ; 82.
Stanton Downeham, benefice ; 83.
Stanton, Mr. ; 153.
Star Chamber ; 139, 141, 163, 168.
Starre, John ; 81.
Starston ; 109, 148.
Steads, Mr. ; 15.
Steggall, — ; 201, 202.
Stephen, Dr. ; 195.
Stephens, Lawrence, letter of ; 107.
Sterling, Marion ; 19.
Sternfield ; 63, 67, 84, 87, 90, 102, 109,
126, 133, 135, 136, 138, 179, 181, 184.
suit about tithes, &c. at ; 203, 204.
Steward :
John ; 9.
Robert ; 201.
Stiffkey ; 70.
Stilton, co. Lincoln ; 39.
Stocks, the ; 64.
Stokes, Archdeacon ; 103.
Stone :
Edward ; 48.
William, receipt by ; 25.
Stoneham ; 157.
Stow-Bardolph ; 18, 124, 125.
Stowe :
Norfolk ; 4.
church ; 20.
market ; 15.
Straffe or Starf, John ; 90.
Strange :
Sir Hamon ; 148.
Mordant, letter of ; 80.
Stratford ; 68.
Stricklond, Edmond ; 56.
Stubbe, John ; 2.
Stubs, Dr. ; 145.
Sturbridge fair ; 204.
Sturge, Mr. ; 13.
Sturges, Robert ; 9.
Sturman, — of Wisbeach ; 102.
Sturten, Jasper ; 16.
Stutevile, Mr. ; 137.
Stutevill, Martin, letter of ; 116.

Stutton ; 87.
Styward :
Augustine, letter of ; 71.
Thomas, letters of ; 43, 50, 51, 59.
Suckling :
Sir John ; 150.
Dr. Edmund, letter of ; 81.
Robert, letter of ; 18.
Sudbury ; 119.
Suffolk :
elections for ; 22, 115.
Duke of (1538) ; 53.
Earl of (1628) ; 129.
Suliarde, Edward, letters of ; 31, 38.
Sumptor, Mr., minister ; 170.
Surlingham ; 2.
Surrey, Lady ; 3.
Sussex, Earl and Countess of (1625) ;
122.
Sutton :
Dick ; 130.
Lawrence ; 10.
Richard ; 46, 52, 53, 56, 62, 155.
—— letters of ; 65, 109.
—— bond by ; 74.
William ; 135, 139.
Swaffham ; 27, 87, 128, 129, 173, 195.
Bridewell or prison ; 63, 68, 70.
sessions ; 62.
Swale, Dr. B., letter of ; 37.
Swans ; 26.
Swardeston ; 119.
Sweden, King of :
(1627) ; 125.
(1631) ; 136.
(1632) ; 141.
Swift :
breviat of his case ; 85.
Edward, letter of ; 210.
Sybeton ; 2.
Symonds :
Edward, letter of ; 76.
Gyles ; 47.
Rev. Thomas, letter of ; 33.

T.

Tacolneston ; 35.
Taffety ; 134.
Taffey, Mr. ; 130.
Talbott, Mr. De ; 149.
Talmach, Ralph ; 98.
Tarleton ; 22.
Tasborough :
Sir John ; 112.
Sir Thomas ; 81.
Tasburgh :
Cressy, letter of ; 190.
Peregrine, letter of ; 196.
Sir John, letters of ; 113, 195.
Taverner, Mr. ; 50.
Taversham, bailiwick ; 8.

Taylor :
  Mr. ; 146, 147.
  Christopher, letter of ; 105.
  Robert ; 197.
  Thomas ; 99, 154.
  William, letters of ; 205, 208.
Tebbould, one ; 101.
Terrington ; 5.
Thacster, Mr., minister ; 76.
Thaxter :
  John ; 39.
  Rev. John, letter of ; 23.
  Mary ; 109.
Theobalds, court at ; 36, 59, 88.
Therle, Mr. ; 112.
Thetford ; 6, 13, 17, 18, 24, 49, 57, 59, 71, 77, 95, 122, 127, 129, 131, 135, 138, 164, 199.
  mayors of ; 22, 51, 163.
  members for ; 112, 176.
  assizes ; 42, 43, 78, 91, 158, 162.
  prison ; 173.
  sessions ; 52, 151.
  warren ; 83.
  small pox at ; 140.
  schoolmasters at ; ib.
  Snare's Hill near ; 174.
  the Christopher ; 133.
  the Cross Keys ; 145.
  Mr. ; 82.
Thomas, Mr. ; 201, 202, 208.
Thorndon ; 33.
Thornton, Perceval ; 5.
Thorpe ; 75.
  market ; 1.
  rectory ; 54.
Throckmorton :
  — ; 19, 20.
  Arthur, letters of ; 19, 20.
Throgmorton, Mr. ; 63.
Thurston :
  John, letters of ; 25, 30, 31, 32.
  —— letter to ; 29.
  Mr. ; 72.
Thwayt, Anthony, letter of ; 30.
Thwayte, Mr. ; 74.
Thwaytes :
  Anthony, letters of ; 35, 77, 85, 87, 91, 93.
  —— arrest of ; 51.
Tilbury ; 30.
Tiller, one ; 38.
Tillett, Mr. ; 208.
Tilly :
  overthrow of ; 136.
  reported death of ; ib.
Tilney ; 45.
Tilson, — ; 201, 202.
Tipper, William ; 39, 41, 46.
Titshall ; 159.
Tittleshall ; 52,
Tobacco ; 128, 147, 169, 196.
Tock, Mr. ; 55.
Tofts, West ; 92.
Tolke, Mrs. ; 205.
Toller :
  Marten ; 24.
  Robert ; 69.

Tolshunt ; 31.
Tolwyn, — ; 7.
Tomson, Mr. ; 168.
Topas, Henry ; 9.
Topclyff, John, letter of ; 82.
Toppcroft ; 2.
Tory, John ; 2.
Tostock ; 26, 39, 89.
Tottenham ; 170.
Tottington ; 62, 64, 127.
Tovel :
  George ; 88.
  Simon ; 88.
Townshend :
  Lord (1662) ; 196.
  Lady ; 168.
  Mr. ; 59.
  Sir John ; 62, 66, 68, 70, 72, 76, 79.
  Ro. ; 8.
  Thomas ; 13, 74.
Tremaine, John ; 198.
Trendle :
  Israel ; 62.
  Rev. John, letters of ; 37, 62, 63, 64, 66.
Treves, Bishop of ; 101.
Tripp, Mr. ; 179.
Trouse ; 41.
Troutbeck :
  Dr. ; 205.
  Dr. John, letter of ; 210.
  Frances, letter of ; 207.
Trowse, bridges in ; 68.
Trymley ; 36.
Tunbridge ; 152, 153.
  waters ; 143.
  wells, visitors and amusements at 153.
Tunsted bailiwick ; 7, 8.
Turner :
  Edward ; 36.
  John ; 78.
Turrell, Mr. ; 92.
Tuthill, Mr. ; 201, 204, 208.
Twyford ; 54.
Twynne, — ; 8.
Tylney, Philip, settlement by ; 4
Tymperley, William ; 20.
Tyte, Thomas ; 17.

U.

Uphall ; 168.
Utting, — ; 147, 160, 172.
Uty, Mistress ; 201.

V.

Vane :
  Sir Henry ; 172.
  —— his son ; ib.

LONDON: Printed by EYRE and SPOTTISWOODE,
Printers to the Queen's most Excellent Majesty.
For Her Majesty's Stationery Office.

REPORT

ON THE

MANUSCRIPTS

OF THE

MARQUESS OF LOTHIAN

PRESERVED AT

BLICKLING HALL, NORFOLK.

Presented to Parliament by Command of His Majesty.

LONDON :

PRINTED FOR HIS MAJESTY'S STATIONERY OFFICE

BY MACKIE & CO. LD. 59, FLEET STREET, E.C.

And to be purchased, either directly or through any Bookseller, from
WYMAN AND SONS, LD., FETTER LANE, E.C., and
32, ABINGDON STREET, WESTMINSTER, S.W.; or
OLIVER & BOYD, EDINBURGH; or
E. PONSONBY, 116, GRAFTON STREET, DUBLIN.

1905.

[Cd. 2819.] *Price* 2*s.* 2*d.*

INTRODUCTION.

THE Manuscripts at Blickling Hall, Norfolk, passed with that property to the Lothian family through the marriage of Lord Ancram (afterwards sixth Marquess) with Lady Henrietta Hobart, daughter of John, 2nd Earl of Buckinghamshire.

The present publication is due to the initiative and active personal interest of the late Constance Marchioness of Lothian, who a few years before her death permitted Mr. D'Arcy Collyer to examine and arrange the numerous charters and papers in her possession at Blickling, which had not been accessible to the Inspector on behalf of the Commissioners on his visit in 1869. These on examination arranged themselves under the three heads which follow :—

1. Ancient deeds and documents.

2. Hobart papers, documents belonging to the period commencing with the first connexion of the Hobart family with the property.

3. Buckinghamshire papers, belonging to the time of John Hobart, second Earl of Buckinghamshire.

The last section comprises part of a large collection of diplomatic correspondence and memoranda collected and endorsed by Lord Buckinghamshire himself, which was discovered by Constance Marchioness of Lothian in a cabinet, enclosed in antique cardboard boxes of foreign make, in which they had probably rested undisturbed for just over a century. An instalment of these papers has already been published by the Royal Historical Society in 1900 and 1902 (3rd series, Vols. 2 and 3), together with the text of the official despatches from St. Petersburg, noticed, but not set out, in the Commissioners' first Report above mentioned.

The first two sections of the present Report contain gleanings from the Muniment Room, a remote turret room where the papers had been either stored in boxes which had made many a journey in the London "stage," or had been piled in miscellaneous heaps of rolls, charters and correspondence, relating to persons whose relative significance had long since been forgotten, and to estates long parted with. These are now arranged in nine large tin boxes and docketed. Not till the documents had been cleaned and sorted was it possible out of this mass to evolve order or coherence. There then revealed itself, however, a singular and unexpected element of continuity in the presence, among the earlier muniments, of charters and rolls belonging to the foundations of Langley and Horsham St. Faith, two religious houses founded by the family of Fitz Robert (Cheyney), the first lay tenants of Blickling after the Conquest. This family held their manor in Blickling by grant or exchange from the Bishop of Norwich, whose predecessors had received it from the Conqueror in succession to Harold. The St. Faith's documents comprise court rolls going back to 49 Hen. III., and a number of charters of endowment; and the coincidence by which the muniments reverted after the dissolution of the monasteries to the home of their origin, if fortuitous, is remarkable. By a like coincidence, a charter of Bishop Eborard (p. 39) is among the documents, the Bishop who is recorded as having attempted in the beginning of the 12th century to recover the Cheyneys' manor to the see, on the ground of some condition in the grant. It was the destiny, however, of the two divisions of the manor into which the grant to John Fitz Robert had divided it, to become at last reunited in the hands of the lay holders, and the site of the Dagworth Manor House (where Blickling Hall now stands) superseded that of the older structure (occupied by Harold) of which the traces are still discernible on the river's edge, north of the Park.

So large a collection of papers, of course, contains many matters of interest to the local antiquarian. The extract (at p. 61) of the Langley rental, which is only a minute specimen of the elaborate code of task work (filling many pages) detailed for a long list of tenants, calls to mind how old is the never ceasing dispute between master and men in a wet harvest; the 24 days' work must not be hurried over to the detriment of the crops, *mediante equitate et justitia ne nimis cito accipiantur.*

The records of Hevingham, once a favourite lodge of the Bishops of Norwich (whither, too, Edward I. came in his progress in 1277), supply a specimen of a manorial extent (p. 33) which exemplifies the great multiplicity of ownership which widely obtained from earliest times and the extremely artificial character of the subinfeudation.

It is noticeable that Bishop Askew, minister to De la Pole* (Earl of Suffolk) in the reign of Henry VI., emerged from the position of parish priest in this obscure village (p. 43).

Social life is illustrated by the covenant (of cosenage) of Humphrey Bourgchier (p. 65), and the letter of William Trussel on the education of a ward (p. 75). The letter appears to be a 15th century copy. The Trussels were connected with Weybourne, where the De Veres too left their name. A will of John Thetford of 1565 (p. 44), gives bequests of his "sylver salte," his " bow and quiver of arrows."

Of wider and more national significance may be noticed *e.g.* the original (duplicate) in good preservation of the subsidy roll for the county of Norfolk made on the occasion of the knighthood of the Black Prince ; the names of well-known members of the royal party of Henry III. in a few charters ; that of Joan Countess of Hertford (daughter of Edward I.), whose title is handed down into Richard the Second's time in connexion with Saxthorpe (p. 46) ; and (in the case of the Blickling records) a trace here and there of the distinguished statesmen and warriors who found here relaxation from the toils of peace and war. Blickling seems early to have been a favourite place for sport, and it is appropriate to find John Engaine† in 1307 promulgating for Blickling the very scientifically drawn custumary which appears here (on pp. 22-24). Poaching was rife in the 14th century (pp. 25-28), and later Sir John Fastolf's bailiff seems to have had before his eyes the possible complaints of overpreservation of game from the "Hommages of the Lordschepes"

---

* The De la Poles are chiefly remembered (locally) as the builders of the beautiful churches at Sall and Cawston.

† This warrior seems to have been official or hereditary master of the Pytcheley hunt. The lands which he held at Pightesley in the county of Northampton were held by the service of "finding at his own expense certain dogs for the destruction of wolves, foxes, martins and other vermin, within the counties of Northampton, Rutland, Oxford, Bucks, Essex and Huntingdon."

(p. 57). Devolving always among collaterals and following several ramifications of the Cheyney family,[o] the manor fell to several distinguished owners. Margaret Cheyney, Aileen le Mareschal, Dagworth (who commanded in Aquitaine and suffered imprisonment at the hands of the Barons), Holveston, Sir Thomas Erpingham, of Agincourt and Shaksperian fame, Sir John Fastolf, the Boleyns and Sir Edward Clere, are among the noble owners whose names appear in these charters, but in none of the documents prior to the sale by Clere to the Hobarts can the personal share of the house in public life be definitely traced.

Sir Henry Hobart, Knight and Baronet, Chief Justice of the Common Pleas, *temp.* James I., bought the Blickling estates from Sir Edward Clere, the representative of the Boleyns in the female line, and on the site of the Dagworth manor house built the mansion which remains so impressive and beautiful an example of the architecture of his time. Sir Henry Hobart's public character is best known from the sketch by Judge Jenkins comparing him with his great contemporary, Coke :—
" Two lights of the law, . . . the monument of whose genius
" and labour shall flourish so long as our most just and sacred
" laws, the splendour, majesty and fame of England shall
" endure. In Hobart were many noble things, an excellent
" eloquence, the éclat of ancestry, the most engaging sweetness
" animated with a singular gravity." Sir Henry's handwriting in several holograph leases attests the diligence and accuracy with which his private affairs were conducted. His son Sir John, who married, first, Philippa, daughter of Robert Sydney, dying without an heir male, left as his widow a second wife, Lady Frances. This lady, who was the daughter of the Earl of Bridgewater and sister of Lady Alice Egerton (the "Lady" of Milton's *Comus*), lived to old age in Chapel Field House in Norwich, for many years the local town house of the Hobarts.[†]

A note of Lady Frances to General Lambert and his reply to it (p. 89) show that the family was not without influence with the leaders of the Civil War ; for though one or two cadets of

---

* De Cressi, Fitz Roger, Engaine and Dagworth are all descendants of the Cheyneys in the female line.

† Recent excavations show that the chapel of this chantry foundation stood in the open ground north of the house and east of the bowling green. A parcel of title deeds relating to this property are preserved at Blickling.

the family were found in the ranks of the Royalists, its main influence was steadily on the Parliamentary side throughout the crisis, while the estates and title passed to Sir John, son of Miles Hobart⁰ and nephew of his predecessor.

This Sir John, who enjoyed power and repute during the Commonwealth, " a quondam lord of Oliver Cromwell," as he is styled by Tompson, the contemporary newswriter,† lived to present in 1659 a petition for the return of the secluded members, to see his friend Sir John Holland of Quidenham the next year taking part in the deputation to bring the King back, and himself to return to the Lower House of Parliament after the Restoration, as member for Norfolk.

Of these stirring and troublous times unfortunately no epistolary correspondence remains, and scarcely a trace of the visit paid by Charles II. to Blickling shortly after the Restoration, when he conferred knighthood on the ill-fated Sir Henry, Sir John's eldest son.

The Estreat of Subsidies for the year 1663 (pp. 89-116) gives a list of landowners in five hundreds ; the name of " Philip Skippon, Esq., ultra mare," whose house is still conspicuous at Foulsham, illustrates the vicissitudes of political influence ; a local tradition credits this noted republican general with profiting by his neighbourhood to Melton (p. 108) to become possessed by some illicit means of the plan of Naseby fight, from some follower of Sir Jacob Astley.

A volume of Lieutenancy Journals fortunately preserved (of which a few extracts only are here given) affords a valuable contribution to the county history of the later years of Charles II. and the Revolution, and supplements the scanty entries in the house books and other casual memoranda in affording glimpses of the party jealousies which the stress of civil strife had exacerbated and His Majesty's presence in the county soon after the Restoration had evidently not permanently allayed. The List of Deputy Lieutenants and Officers of Militia given on pp. 125-7 stands as it appeared after being reformed and

---

* The *Dict. Nat. Biog.* distinguishes this Miles Hobart from the Sir Miles who was conspicuous for locking the doors of the House of Commons during the vote on Tonnage and Poundage (1629). *Cf.* the passages there cited from the *Gentleman's Magazine* for the grounds of this conclusion.

† Unpublished Felbrigg papers. Sir John was in fact a member of Cromwell's Upper House.

expurgated in the interests of the Court by Robert Paston, Lord Yarmouth, who replaced Lord Townshend on his removal from that office in 1675. It is significant that none of the three first signatories of the manifesto for reducing the expenses of the High Sheriff (pp. 122-4) are included in the new commissions as Deputy Lieutenants or in the Militia, and this perhaps makes it probable that what appears to be a harmless sumptuary agreement for reducing extravagance was represented at Court as having a disloyal intention.[*] Barillon's confidential imputations in his reports to Louis XIV. about this time as to the accessibility of certain country politicians to foreign influence suggest that economy was a matter of sufficient concern in the county to make the movement a natural one.

The entry (at p. 129) below, referring to the trial at the Bar of the House of Commons and another mentioning Verdon by name, are almost the only memorials of two contested elections fought with much determination by Sir John Hobart for the county representation in 1678-9, which were both the subject of petition. The first of these figures more largely in Mr. Ketton's Felbrigg papers.[†] Mr. Windham on the first occasion had declined Sir John's overtures to engage him in Parliamentary life on the ground that his opponent, Sir Neville Catelyn, the Court candidate, was "encouraged from above and countenanced here," and his surmise seems to have had ample foundation.

The tide of Protestant and Parliamentary reaction on which Titus Oates was being floated to the surface was not yet flowing so turbulently as to discourage the Court party from making a bold bid for power at the general election in Jan. 1678-9, and Sir Christopher Calthorpe and Sir Neville Catelyn enjoyed a short-lived triumph in being returned as knights of the shire, though Sir John after the "trial at barr" on his petition was successful in replacing Sir Christopher Calthorpe, unseated.[‡] But the contest was persistent and severe. The Lord Lieutenant and High Sheriff had been strong for the Court. "To oppose

---

[*] *Cf.* Hist. MSS., Rep. VI., part I., 374, William Hughes to Lady Yarmouth.

[†] Hist. MSS., Rep. XII., App. IX., 183.

[‡] Dean Prideaux' impressions of this election given in the Camden Society's volume of his letters to Ellis (p. 176) may be compared. The Dean is in error in citing this election as for the last Parliament at Westminster of Charles II., and his general statements about it seem equally incorrect. He came to Norwich afterwards, and his report was probably at second hand.

"any interest sett up by the civil and military government of a
"country," Mr. Windham had written, "will be called faction by
"some, inconsiderate by others, and very improbable to be
"successful by most, and that he who is sole judge of the poll,
"and by whom the returne is to be made, is our open and
"declared enemie."* Mr. Windham, however, seems to have
been busy just at this time with the cielings of his house at
Felbrigg, that beautiful Italian work in high relief that
is still one of its chief ornaments, and was dragged a very
reluctant Cincinnatus into the strife of the second election.
The country gentry were perhaps· naturally unwilling to
renew the strife of a generation earlier and the acts
of fraud and intimidation charged in Sir John Hobart's
petition against Samuel Verdon, the under sheriff, support the
theory that the latter was backed "from above," and that
functionary's vigorous and defiant methods must have been
exceptional even in the days of unreformed elections. First
refusing poll books or writing materials to Sir John's voters and
throughout the day fraudulently hindering the record of votes,
tearing leaves from Hobart's poll books, several times "beating
and abusing" the freeholders, he ended by closing the poll
prematurely in the face of 1,000 unpolled electors, "violently·
"took the pollbooks away, and drew his sword in defence of it."†
Paston, the Lord Lieutenant, was believed to have taken a strong
part. The petition charges "that before the election several
"letters were dispersed as written by the said Lord as heynge
"Lord Lieutenant of the said county (Norfolk) to the gentry and
"clergy of the said county not only appointing persons by name
"to be the said knights of the shire, but assuming it would be
"an affront to him and his authority as Lord Lieutenant to elect

---

* Unpublished Felbrigg papers.

† Unpublished Felbrigg papers. An account of Verdon and his eccentric progress to London is given by North in his memorial of the Lord Keeper Guilford
(II., 21), where he also mentions how the insolence of this man secured him the
favour of Judge Jeffreys. "The sergeant's men went down and took him (Verdon)
. . . But in bringing him up he would not be prevailed with, either to mount or
dismount his horse, but forced the messengers at every town to lift him on and off.
and at the same time had his clerks taking notes in order to testify these assaults of
his person, for every one of which he intended to bring an action of battery. It so
fell out that as he was upon the road between Norwich and London the Parliament
was prorogued, by which the warrant ceased, and after that the custody was a false
imprisonment, and Verdon brought his action for it against the messengers, which
action was tried at the Exchequer bar."

"or to be elected without his consent or concurrence . . .,
"and the said Lord Lieutenant's Steward as by his Lordship's
"command required some of his Lordship's tenants to give their
"votes for Sir Christopher Calthorpe and Sir Neville Catelyn,
"who were threatened that if they did not vote for them, the
"farms which they had of his Lordship should be taken from
"them."

When Sir John's petition came on for hearing, the excitement
of the Popish Plot was rising high, and he records how he was
vexatiously shut into the house on one occasion, and detained
during the arrest and examination of a suspect parliamentary
lawyer, one Reading.

Sir John obtained the seat at the next election, and again with
his son Henry sat in the Oxford Parliament of 1681. The
Ryehouse Plot in 1683 marked the decadence of the Protestant
and popular party, and the turn of the wheel found Sir John
obnoxious to the ascendant faction. In execution of an order
in Council addressed to the Earl of Arundel, who had succeeded
Lord Yarmouth in the Lord Lieutenancy, his house was
searched in July of the latter year. The list of arms found
at Blickling (given at p..130 below), is the result of this search.
Mr. Scambler at Wolterton, Hamond Claxton at Aylsham, Henry
Marsham at Stratton Strayless, and Thomas Newman at
Baconsthorpe were at the same time subjected to a like ordeal.
Dr. John Collinges, the biographer of Lady Frances and the
Presbyterian chaplain of the Hobarts at Chapel Field, was
arrested as a nonjuring suspect in 1685.[*] A few years later
it was the turn of the Papists, and later, of the nonjurors proper,
to experience these reciprocal visitations. Christopher Layer, of
Booton, who is marked for search in 1696 (p. 142), is uncle and
namesake of the notorious conspirator who suffered at Tyburn
in 1723. But as is shewn in these Lieutenancy Journals, these
neighbourly inquisitions were rewarded on each succeeding
occasion with less satisfying results. The seizures even at the
period of the "horrid designe" of the Rye House in 1683 were
of less value than variety. "A back, breast and head piece of a
horse" are found at Colney, "three Olliverian swords" at

---

[*] He appears to have been arrested twice this year according to the entries in the
Lieutenancy journal.

Warham. In 1696 Sir Christopher Calthorpe yields only "9 old
" carbines, 4 old musketts, one brass blunderbuss, 3 old pistols,
"3 old swords." The four black coach horses seized by Sir
Frances Guybon from Sir Nicholas L'Estrange, " one mealy
faced and one with a white starr," are discharged by the Deputy
Lieutenants in conclave, who certify that none of them is 'worth
5l., " they being old and lame, and some of them blind." The
lowest point is reached in 1707 with the seizure of " one musquet
and a belt of bandoliers " from Mr. Lake at Sparham (p. 145).

Sir Henry Hobart on his succession in 1683 found the estates
largely encumbered, and had further to reduce them by sale to
meet the demands made by creditors. Taking an active part in
the politics of the time and on the constitutional side, he appears
to have presided over the counsels of the county in the absence
of the Lord Lieutenant and to have favoured a policy more
comprehensive than that of his superior (pp. 155-6).

It is no doubt to the appointment of his son, the first Earl of
Buckinghamshire, to the Lord Lieutenancy, that is due the
preservation of the Lieutenancy Journals of this period, which
give a vivid illustration of the Revolutionary crisis of 1688-9.
The militia force of the county is shewn to be in a high state
of organisation, and the action of the Protestant Duke of
Norfolk, cool-headed and constitutional. "Bel homme à cheval,"
as Evelyn calls the latter, it is evident (pp. 134-5) that his
personality counted for something in the period of transition.
He seems to have sat the fence with masterly firmness, and so
long as hopes were held out by James II. that a Parliament
would be summoned the forces of the county were engaged to
maintain the existing régime. Not till the cause was surrendered by the retirement of James II. was their weight thrown
on the side of the Revolution.

In 1690 Sir Henry Hobart served on King William's staff
at the battle of the Boyne, but on his return the embarrassed state of the country was not such as to afford any relief
to his encumbered finances, and in a quarrel which is asserted
to have had some connexion with his contested election for the
county, he met with the wound from a left-handed antagonist [o]

---

* Oliver Le Neve of Great Witchingham, whilom Captain of the Eynsford
(militia) Company. There was evidently political animosity involved in the quarrel.
(See Le Neve Papers, edited by Mr. Rye).

that proved fatal. A stone marks the spot at Cawston heath where this, one of the last duels fought with swords, took place. The long minority and succession of his son (three of whose sisters were borne in their infancy to the churchyard of Blickling) added little of public interest to the archives, and in the papers of his grandson begin what are practically modern politics.

The diplomatic papers collected by John second Earl of Buckinghamshire in the course of his long life (1723-1793) relate for the most part, 1st, to the period of his Embassy to St. Petersburg (Sept. 1762-Jan. 1765); 2ndly, to the American Colonies; 3rdly, to his momentous Vice-Royalty of Ireland. Among the private letters are eight bundles addressed to Sir Thomas Drury, of which Lord Buckinghamshire became possessed through his first wife Mary Anne, eldest daughter and co-heiress of Sir Thomas Drury. The chief public interest of these consists in the record which they contain of the feeling with which men in the more distant parts of the country viewed the invasion of '45' and of the fluctuations of the money market at the time.

The letters addressed by Lord Buckinghamshire to Henrietta Countess of Suffolk, the Lady Suffolk of Pope, Swift, and Walpole, are those of a son to an indulgent mother, for such she had been to him and his only sister since the death of their mother in 1726. They serve to complement and illustrate Lady Suffolk's letters to him in reply, which have been published in Croker's edition of her correspondence, while the curious narrative (pp. 166-170) of her interview with Queen Caroline on retiring from office at Court in 1734 goes far to support the belief of her friends, to which Horace Walpole refers while he dissents from it, that Lady Suffolk's "connection with the King was confined to pure friendship." The cryptic allusion to "Lord B." is probably to be explained by a passage in a contemporary letter from Lady Elizabeth Compton (*Hist. MSS. Comm. Report* XI, 4, p. 243) in which she mentions a rumour that Lady Suffolk had been too often seen in the company of Lord Bolingbroke at Bath, and that her retirement was the result of consequent suspicions cast upon her loyalty to the House of Hanover.

The Russian papers make a considerable contribution to the chronicles of British trade with Russia both before and after the first formal treaty of commerce concluded by Lord Forbes in 1734, and there is also a long series of documents relating to the disputed succession to the Duchy of Courland. This was an event which at the time passed with scarcely a comment in England, yet it was Frederick the Great's promise to support Catherine II. in her policy toward that Polish fief which was the first step to the conclusion of the alliance between Prussia and Russia in 1764, of which the direct result was the partition of Poland. The absorption of Courland by Russia had long been in contemplation. Since the dissolution of the Livonian State in 1561, the Duchy had had an independent existence as a fief of Poland, and it was to the interest of Russia that it should be looked upon not as an appanage to the Crown of Poland but as a vassal state of the Republic. In 1733, the Czarina Anna made it a condition of her consent to support the election of Augustus III. of Saxony to the Crown of Poland that the Duchy should be so considered, and that it should not be divided into Palatinates. In 1737, the death of the last Duke Ferdinand of the Kettler family enabled Anna to force upon the Courlanders her favourite, John Ernest de Biren, whose grandfather had been groom to the Dukes of the ancient house. For one month in 1740, during the reign of the infant Ivan, the new Duke of Courland was Regent of Russia. For twenty years from May 1741 he was an exile in Siberia. Meanwhile, on the 3rd of January 1759, Augustus III. invested his son Charles Christian of Saxony with the Dukedom, at the request, as he declared, of the states of the country. But with the accession of Peter III. in 1762, Biren returned from exile once more to claim his Duchy, to become in the hands of Catherine the Second a convenient instrument in her design of ridding both Courland and Poland of the rule of the House of Saxony. It is at this point that Lord Buckinghamshire's papers take up the tale and furnish an official statement of the case on both sides between Russia and Poland in the matter of Courland. Stanislas Poniatowski's letter of 31st May, 1764, congratulating Duke Biren on his re-establishment, is significant as giving a clue to one of the conditions upon which he received the support of the Czarina in his election to the Crown of Poland.

The events which led up to that election are related by Thomas Wroughton, British Envoy to the Elector of Saxony and King of Poland, from the point of view of a man who was strongly prepossessed in favour of Catherine II., with whom he had lived on terms of intimacy before her accession. Wroughton had at that time the office of Consul General at St. Petersburg, and it was said that his house became the place of rendezvous for the Archduchess Catherine and Stanislas Poniatowski. Whatever may have been the truth of this, Peter III., when there was a question of Wroughton's appointment as Envoy, refused to admit him to an audience, and he was in consequence recalled in March 1762, and sent as resident to Warsaw.

Lord Buckinghamshire's embassy to Russia, partly from the uncertainty surrounding the prospects of the new Empress, partly from the inadequate realisation at home of the importance of the Russian factor in politics (p. 371), was attended by no political success. He was, however, upon his return to England, offered the Embassy to Madrid, which he refused, and he held no other public office until he became Viceroy of Ireland in January 1777.

When Lord Buckinghamshire accepted the arduous task which Lord Harcourt had not reluctantly dropped, he encountered, without that cordial support from the Government at home enjoyed by his predecessor, a combination of difficulties which, having increased under Lord Harcourt's administration, offered at the close of that nobleman's tenure of office a prospect which he felt scarcely able to encounter. The advent of a new Viceroy, besides being the occasion for a renewal of unsuccessful claims for patronage, prompted fresh appeals for the redress of the commercial and financial disabilities under which Ireland was suffering, and a phase of more active agitation in and out of Parliament synchronised with the external disquiet caused by the unfavourable conduct of the American war.

During four years, however, of a period the most critical in English history, Lord Buckinghamshire contrived to maintain in some fashion the *status quo*. The like succeeding period of four years witnessed the advent and departure of as many Viceroys and the establishment of an independent Parliament. His partial success seems attributable to personal qualities of tact and temper, which, combined with a sincere zeal for the welfare of the Irish people, created, in the opinion of Grattan, " a passion in his favour approaching to love."

The impoverished and defenceless state of the country, indeed, seem amply to have justified the concessions granted during his Viceroyalty to the export trade and the Volunteers.

On the question of Free Trade a memorandum of Sackville Hamilton (p. 301) is worth notice. A number of such monographs was collected specially by Lord Buckinghamshire for the instruction of Government. These able and eloquent dissertations justified the economic reform which was precipitated by the growing danger of the trade with France, then inflated by the existing embargo on the export of provisions and other economical restrictions. "Two of her" (Ireland's) "provinces," says one writer, "may at this very day be called provinces of " France as much as provinces of Great Britain." The rupture of diplomatic relations with France following on her action in regard to the revolted colonies, forced on the concession of an outlet for a trade which, diverted in illicit channels to France, had up to this time supplied a large share of the taxable wealth of the island. Of the same financial depression the rise of the volunteer movement was another natural outcome. The proposed militia scheme being abandoned for want of money, fresh drains were made on the military establishment, and the constant drafts of troops for the American war could not be replaced, even though Scotland was laid under contribution, and we find the Athol Highlanders among the infantry of the garrrison (p. 330). In these papers, however, we find little trace of the "impotent dismay" which the writer of the article in the Dictionary of National Biography (following Mr. Lecky) discovers in the Viceroy at this crisis. His attitude of passive acquiescence in the growth of these voluntary associations is not obscurely invited in Lord Sandwich's significant reminder that "a coast cannot be protected by ships alone," a phrase suggesting the tacit assent of the Home Government to a condition of things which the Viceroy was expected to tolerate, without any overt sign of approval.

If the extent and importance of the volunteer movement were at first underrated by him, the famous epigram of Hussey Burgh° is proof that the nation itself stood startled and surprised at the sudden growth and formidable proportions of its own military

---

* "You have sown the dragon's teeth and they have sprung up armed men."

offspring. If official discouragement disparaged the movement
in the eyes of immediate aspirants to Court favour, as these letters
seem to show, that movement at least in its earlier stages was
strong in the high character and loyal disposition of its leaders.

With the termination of his Viceroyalty, Lord Buckinghamshire's public life came to an end, though it may be gathered
from these letters that the conduct of Irish business presented
no difficulties (except those factitious ones arising from his
unfortunate relation to his colleagues at home) that he felt
unable to grapple with, and that he would not have been
unwilling to utilise his experience in a second term of office.

Sir Henry Clinton's letters to Lord Buckinghamshire, written
at and about the date of Lord Cornwallis' surrender, may
interest students of the polemics of this episode, though they
cannot be said to throw much additional light on an unfruitful
controversy. The rude original prints of the manifesto of the
Pennsylvanian line are tacitly eloquent of a crisis that seems so
nearly to have wiped out the army of the revolted colonies.

Dying in 1793, the second Lord Buckinghamshire was buried
the following year in the mausoleum which he had designed,
but not lived to complete, in the centre of his park at Blickling.
Tradition till lately kept alive the impressive memory of the
torchlight procession which accompanied the translation from
the church to their final resting-place of the remains of one who
had filled an honourable place in the public life of his time, who
had moved, a stately and representative figure, in the social and
political scenes of his environment and generation.

This Report, with the Introduction and Index, has been
prepared, with some assistance in revision of the early documents
from the Rev. W. D. Macray, by Mr. D'Arcy Bedingfeld Collyer.

MANUSCRIPTS

OF

THE MARQUESS OF LOTHIAN,

AT BLICKLING HALL, NORFOLK.

SECTION I.—ANCIENT DEEDS, Etc.

In the First Report of this Commission issued in 1870, one
page is occupied by an account by Mr. A. J. Horwood of a few
historical papers which he examined in July, 1869.   But he
makes no mention of the voluminous contents of the Muniment
Room, which had not then been examined for probably a century
and a half, and were entirely unsorted and unarranged, and
evidently not then open to his inspection, as being no doubt
supposed to lie outside the objects of his visit.[o]   These have now
for the greatest part been sorted and are described below.

The manor of Blickling belonged to Harold at the Conquest,
and the alleged site of Harold's house can even now be traced in
dry weather in the cornfield adjoining the river which runs
beyond the extreme end of the park from the north of the present
Hall.   The manor, according to the return made in the Hundred
Roll of 3 Edw. I. (*Rot. Hundr.* vol. i. p. 513), was confirmed by
Henry I. to Herbert, first bishop of Norwich, who gave it in
exchange for Thorpe near Norwich to John le Cheny (*sic*), son
of Robert Fitz Walter.

---

* Mr. Horwood mentions the existence of certain classical MSS., with Missals and
Books of Hours, which he was unable to see.   These, which still have not been
open to inspection, are, it is understood. chiefly, if not entirely, of foreign origin,
possessing no English historical interest.

HORSHAM ST. FAITH.

Robert Fitz Walter, with Sibyl de Caineto his wife, founded the priory of St. Faith near Norwich, A.D. 1105-6, as a cell of the abbey of Conches in Normandy, in pursuance of a vow, under circumstances well-known and narrated by Dugdale. It became independent of the abbey in 14 Rich. II.

The Priory documents include a charter of confirmation by the founder's grand-daughter Margaret Cheyney, and a copy of one of her father, William de Kaneto, containing one of those ambiguities which sometimes gave rise (as it seems to have done in the present case) to disputed claims. A fine levied in 34 Hen. III., of which the record is among the papers, settled a dispute between Berengarius the Prior and Hugh de Cressy the patron as to the title to 5 acres of wood, "*utrum sit libera eleemosina pertinens ad ecclesiam dicti Prioris de Horsham an laicum feodum ipsius Hugonis.*"

Among other benefactions to the priory is one of Theobald Halteyn, who bestows 67 acres for the benefit of the soul of his lord King Henry [II.] and his lord Humphrey de Buun [Bohun], for which he receives 27 marks to assist him in his expedition to Jerusalem. The name of the first or second prior hitherto not recorded, Austorgius, is found in a charter which may be dated about 1120-30, and that of a successor, Bertrand, about 1140-60.

The manor rolls, commencing in 49 Hen. III., are very voluminous. The domestic discipline in regard to admitting strangers to sojourn in the village appears to have been strict, a number of presentments being made of persons who had entertained strangers without licence. A selection of presentments is given below.

There is also a small roll of the market court chiefly interesting in regard to the nature of the chattels 'attached' to answer the judgment of the court.

Among later documents, the probate of the will dated 1521 of Helen Carter (*see* Blomefield's *Norfolk*, vol. x. p. 438), providing for a Trental to be sung for twenty years by the monks, and providing for the repair of the cross in St. Faith's churchyard, is worth noting. Also the "testimonyall" or letter of commendation from Prior Stokes given to one Metcalfe, the bearer of a bede-roll.

BLICKLING.

The rolls of greatest interest and antiquity are those of Dagworth manor, in Blickling, which from the time of Bishop Eborard (Hen. I.) was separated from the episcopal manor until re-united in a grant from Henry VIII. to Sir John de Clere. It is recorded that Eborard sought a Bull from the Pope to restore it to the see on the ground that it was granted away in order to protect it during times of civil disturbance. The manor belonged to a series of historical families, Dagworth, Holveston, Engayne, Erpingham, Fastolf, Boleyn and Clere.

An interesting order in Chancery (in English), relating to the terms of purchase between Sir John Fastolf and Sir Geoffrey Boleyn, is copied at length.

A roll of 7 Edw. II. affords a good specimen of the varied and interesting matters which the early Blickling rolls contain. Presentments are made of a parochial chaplain prosecuting in a Court Christian, and for his usury; of the taking by a tenant the order of Exorcist without the lord's licence; of two parochial chaplains for being concerned in an affray; of hamsoken; breaking the assize; selling mead; raising the hue and cry unlawfully; regrating; purpresture; &c.

It is probably owing to the connexion of the Hobarts with Blickling that the muniments include so large and varied an accumulation of manor rolls. Lord Chief Justice Hobart, who amassed considerable estates in Norfolk in the time of James I., appears, with commendable carefulness, to have got into his hands the oldest muniments of the several properties which he acquired by purchase. It is probably owing to this that there is so large a collection of documents of the Priory of Horsham St. Faith's, which came to him after the Dissolution, when the connexion of the priory with the lords of Blickling as its founders had apparently long ceased to exist. Many of Hobart's leases to his tenants are apparently drawn in his own handwriting.

HEVINGHAM.

To Sir Henry Hobart is probably also due the early and interesting series of manorial documents of Hevingham (which was purchased from the Thetfords), a former "hunting-box" of the Bishops of Norwich on the road from Norwich to Blickling, where the bishops had a deer park, and a manor which appears to have flourished and increased under their ascendancy. A charter of Bishop William Turbus granting lands in the manor to Herbert Catte and Alda his wife, "nepoti ejusdem Willelmi," suggests the origin of the name of "Catt's manor," which is not elsewhere accounted for.

An extent of the manor of Hevingham in the time of Henry III., with sundry interlineations (apparently amendments sanctioned by the King's Commissioners in Eyre), seems to illustrate the method in which manorial jurisdictions sometimes grew. This is here printed in full, and the corrections are noted by being printed in italics.

The charters connected with this manor include also an interesting compact under seal granting a "peace of mayhem" to the son of one considerable tenant who had injured another. The document is witnessed by a number of the junior representatives of neighbouring families. Here, as a presentment in Bishop Middleton's time [1278-88] attests, it was the custom for the tenants to choose yearly "*tres homines ad officium prepositi, tres ad cornu gerendum, et unum ad officium porcarii.*"

The account-roll for the year of the Black Death is among these documents.

An entry on one roll relates that a number of the records were burnt by the mob at the time of Litester's rebellion (following Wat Tyler's), when Bishop Spencer was riding about after the rioters. North Walsham, where he defeated them, is only a few miles distant.

SAXTHORP.

There are two principal manors in Saxthorp, those of Mickelhall connected more especially with Valence, Earl of Pembroke, and Loundhall. The latter extends into a number of adjoining parishes. William de Valence had a castle in this place, and the records shew it to have been a place of much greater relative importance than at present. The Loundhall rental of the time of Rich. II. noted below shews 243 tenants. The deeds and documents connected with these manors comprise the names of Wendenual (the holders *temp.* Hen. I.), William Valence Earl of Pembroke (a good impression of his seal), Ralph Lord Cromwell, Sir John Fastolf, Sir Thomas Erpingham, W. Oldhalle, Grey de Ruthin, Gresham, Yelverton, and W. Waynflete and other feoffees of Sir J. Fastolf.

There is a specimen of the seal of Bromholm priory, almost perfect, attached to a release of a rent of 4s. payable to the foundation.

Among the deeds worthy of note (of which there are not many in a very large collection) is a grant by Heloisa de Wendenual to an old servant of her father.°

Another of interest is the grant (27 Edw. I.) of licence to Sir Simon de Crepping from Richard de Hertford, the rector of the parish church, to have divine service performed " per idoneum capellanum " in a chapel or oratory to be erected by Sir Simon near his court, provided that Sir Simon attends the parish church on the four principal feast days.

A record of assize of 41-50 Ed. III. gives a considerable contribution to the pedigree of the Dautre family.

The free chapel of St. Dunstan seems to have been connected with the Mickelhall manor ; it is not that for which the license above was granted.

The name of "Peddersty" for a path (deed of 6 Hen. VI.) may perhaps throw a light on the vexed question of the origin of the name Corpusty, the name of the adjoining parish. " Peddersty " is presumably " the pedlar's way." *Cf.* A. S. *Stig.*

The series of charters and rolls for Saxthorp gives evidence of the thicker population of these districts in the 14th century compared with that at present existing. A customary of the manor of Loundhall *temp.* Richard II. shews 104 tenants paying a money rental, with 56 who pay in kind altogether 210. The population of the parish of Saxthorp at the census of 1891 was 276.

---

* The Wendenvals or Wendevals are mentioned by Blomefield as the earliest tenants of the manor after the Conquest, but-he does not refer to the name as occurring in any charter which he had seen.

LANGLEY.

Of the manor and abbey of Langley there was an ancient link with Blickling in the fact of its foundation by Robert Fitz Roger. In this case also the abbey site came into the hands of Chief Justice Hobart after the Dissolution, by purchase from Sir Richard Berney, and with it a beautiful survey or rental of the monastic lands dated 1288 in excellent condition.

WYMONDHAM.

A mass of bulky manor rolls of Wymondham deserve more detailed examination than time has permitted ; the bailiffs' accounts (as in the case of all these collections) being fairly numerous. An interesting pedigree tracing the title of Buckenham from D'Albini to the Knyvetts deserves mention.

I. HORSHAM ST. FAITH'S.

MANOR COURT ROLLS, 1265-1640 ; viz. Courts and Courts General and Courts with Lete for the years :—
    Henry III. 49-55.
    Edward I. 2-6.
    Edward II. 5-20.
    Edward III. 6-20 and 42.
    Richard II. 3-10.
    Henry IV. 2-14.
    Henry VI. 1-37, 38, (36, 37 and 39 appear to be copies).
    Henry VII. 1-24.
    Henry VIII. 1, 3-17, 31, 34, 35, 36, 38, (3 is W. Castlety's first
        Court).
    Edward VI. 1, 2, 4-6.
    Mary 1, Philip and Mary 1-5.
    Elizabeth 1-18 (6 is the first Court of Richard Southwell,
        alias D'Arcy), 30-39, 44, 45.
    James I. 1-19, except 3. Sir Henry Hobart's first Court is
        James I. 10.
    1631-1640.
Account Rolls:—1390-1509. Collectors and Messors.
    Richard II. 13-23.
    Henry IV. 1-3, 14.
    Henry V. 1, 2, 4-9.
    Henry VI. 1-39. "The accounts of Receivers of Rent for
        Richard Lord Prior of the Priory."
    Edward IV. 2, 5, 6, 9-12, 16, 20, 21.
    Henry VII. 2-17 (except 6 and 14), 20, 21, 23, 24. Also the
        Bailiff of Ryburghs for 23, 24.

Rolls of the Market Court, Hen. VI. 18-21.
    Edw. IV. 1.
Bailiffs' Accounts, 1461-1545 :—
    Henry VI. 39-40.
    Henry VII. 23-24.
    Henry VIII. 1-2, 5-6, 8-9, 11-12, 17-21, 26-27. 36 is the
      first Court of Will. Rogers, Alderman of the city of Nor-
      wich, " ad usum Marie Leche, uxoris Robert Leche."
Cellarer's Account.
    Henry IV. 2 (1401).
Priors' Receipts, 1408-1452 :—
    Henry IV. 9.
    Henry VI. 16, 25, 30. For the year 16 : "Outgoings of
      Grange and tithes received from Haveringland."
Extent (draft) of the late Priory lands, completed 4 Elizabeth
(1562).

Extracts from Horsham St. Faith's Manor Rolls.

Betrothal without licence.

Presentant quod Sibilla Colbert et Radulfus le Savere affidaverunt se adinvicem sine licentia, etc. Morrow of SS. Peter and
Paul, 50 Hen. III.

Presentment of persons entertaining strangers without licence.

Seventeen tenants are presented " quia sunt consueti hospitari
extraneos contra statutum curie." Monday before St. Dunstan's
day, 51 Hen. III.

Entry into the Homage.

Herveus Bele devenit hominem (sic) prioris reddendo annuatim
pro capite suo unum caponem ad Natale Domini.
    Item Levota fil. Willelmi piscatoris de Thaverham, similiter
devenit hominem prioris reddendo annuatim pro capite suo
unum caponem ad Natale Domini. Wednesday after Nat.
B.M.V., 52 Hen. III.
    Ysabell Brunville devenit hominem prioris et fecit feoda-
gium priori et dabit annuatim pro chevagio unum caponem ad
Natale Domini.

Presentment against the Millers.

Item presentatio totius soce de Roberto mollendinario et de
Waltero mollendinario. Dicunt quod fraudulenter et inique
curam mollendinorum eis in plena curia traditam custodierunt,
et ad opus domini et totius soce incongruam adhibuere custodiam.
Dicunt item quod male mollant et tonn[ant ?]
    Et ideo in misericordia. Et invenere plegios de misericordia
et de pace reformanda eis qui conquesti sunt de ipsis. Plegii
Walteri, Willelmus Crobert, Will. le Forester. Plegii Roberti,
Will. Rust et Symon Lanke. Et dictus Robertus invenit plegios

Will. Rust et Symonem Lanke. Item dictus Walterus invenit plegios Johannem Pokoc, Robertum Eyward. Ita quod in hoc anno proximo venturo proficuum dictorum mollendinorum procurabunt tam de advenis quam de secta, et quod fideliter mollent et tonn[ent?] ad opus domini sine fraude facienda domino sive alicui alio.

Oath of Homage and licences of Marriage.

Memorandum quod Radulfus le Syrer devenit hominem Prioris et fecit sacramentum, et habet licentiam accipere in uxorem filiam quondam Alani Cole, scilicet Sibilam, et dedit vij$^{d.}$, pleggio W. Holcot.

Memorandum quod Robertus cementarius fecit pacem cum Priore ut habeat licentiam accipere in uxorem filiam Matilidis Cole, et devenit homo Prioris et dedit ij sol. Monday before St. Gregory's day, 52 Hen. III.

Presentment of Brewers.

The capital pledges (who are not enumerated) present that all the brewers broke the assize. St. Peter's day, 52 Hen. III.

Complaint against a wife.

Henricus le Porter conqueritur de uxore sua Alicia de transgressione. Pleggio Alano Coco ad prosequendum. Dicta Alicia atachat se ad respondendum et invenit plegium W. Holcot. Tuesday after St. Dunstan's day, 53 Hen. III.

Grant of land in perpetuity at a capon rent.

Memorandum quod Berengarius prior et conventus Sancte Fidis de Horsham dederunt et conceserunt Viello garcifero suo et heredibus suis unam peciam terre sue, videlicet que vocatur Prestcroft per metas positas, in qua pecia continet (sic) in longitudine sexaginta pedes et in latitudine duodecim pedes, pro servicio suo, habendum et tenendum sibi et heredibus suis in perpetuum; reddendo inde annuatim dicto priori et conventui et eorum successoribus ipse et heredes sui quolibet anno unum caponem ad Natale Domini pro omni servicio, consuetudine, exactione, et omnimoda seculari demanda. Data in curia apud Horsham die Martis proxima post festum St. Dunstani anno Regni Regis H. fil Regis Johannis quinquagesimo tercio, in tempore Berengarii Carbonel tunc temporis seneschalli.

Transgressions.

Memorandum quod capitales plegii presentant quod Willelmus le Frere cecavit (secavit) unum frenum contra defensionem et illud vendidit sine licentia domini Prioris.

Item presentant quod in curia Willelmi Hacun invenere magnum dampnum quod factum fuerit in alneto Prioris et de hayis fractis et hasportatis. Vigil of St. Andrew, 53 Hen. III.

Presentment as to freedom.

Capitales plegii presentant et dicunt cum aliis juratis quod W. Hacun non est liber, et quod non potest maritare filiam suam sine licentia, et quod ipsa debet solvere gersumam. St. Luke's day, 53 Hen. III.

Entering the homage on marriage.

Memorandum quod Petrus Swyft devenit hominem Prioris reddendo annuatim unum caponem pro omnibus consuetudinibus ad Natale Domini, et dat domino xij denarios ut maritaret Agnetem Cappe nativam Prioris. Plegg. Will. Holkot.

Building lease for life.

Memorandum quod Beatrix filia Alicie Henrici concessit Roberto Yve unam aream in tota vita ipsius R. super quam possit edificare in longitudine xl pedes et latitudine xxx pedes. Post decessum vero dicti Roberti, dicta area quiete revertetur una cum edificiis tunc in eadem inventis predicte Beatrici et heredibus suis. Et sciendum quod dicta area jacet inter messuagium Vielli in Upgate et messuagium Anse Croket; et dictus Robertus dat domino Priori vj. denarios. Friday after Epiphany, 53 Hen. III:

Marriage conditions on entering on land.

Johannes Colbert dat domini Priori vij₃. pro herieto terre ipsum contingentis, et etiam pro licentia habenda ducende uxoris ubicunque voluerit, et esse sine uxore quamdiu voluerit, excepto hoc quod si ducat aliquam de homagio Prioris quod ipsa faciat pacem pro se ipsa. Et seneschallus dicti Prioris posuit eum in plena seysina de predicta terra et fecit feutagium (*sic*) dicto Priori. Plegii de dictis vij₃. Henricus le Mey et Willelmus Rust. Tuesday before St. Hilary, 54 Hen. III.

Custody of an infant.

Margareta Lanke dat unum marcam domino Priori pro custodia Willelmi filii sui habenda usque ad etatem decem annorum, et pro licentia habenda maritandi filium suum predictum ubicunque et quandocunque voluerit. Salvo hoc, quod de consensu parentum ex parte patris et ex parte matris ducet uxorem, et dicti parentes videbunt catalla que debent dari in maritagium cum dicto Willelmo. Et dicta Margareta interim faciet consuetudines integre que pertinent ad tenementum dicti Willelmi et quod nullam faciet destruccionem arborum domorum nisi in emendacionem messuagii predicti Willelmi. Plegii de dicta marca solvenda et de predictis observandis Will. Lanke, Herb. Biscop, Will. Crobert, Henricus le Mey.

Becoming "Husbond" of a tenement.

Memorandum quod Walterus Hering factus est husbond de illo tenemento quod fuit patris et matris ejusdem Walteri, et positus est in seysinam dicti tenementi, et fecit domino Priori feudagium, et dat domino Priori unam marcam argenti pro seysina dicti tenementi habenda, et etiam pro eo quod possit ducere uxorem quando voluerit et ubicunque, et esse sine uxore quamdiu voluerit, et quietus de herieto (etc). St. Mark's day, 55 Hen. III.

Villein claiming to be a freeman.

Willelmus Molendinarius in misericordia pro pluribus transgressionibus domino Priori factis, ut dicitur, videlicet pro eo quod debuit asportasse sepem circa nidum cingni reparatam, et de asportatione straminis pertinentis ad dictum nidum, et similiter eo quod dictus W. et parcenarii sui detinuerunt dicto domino Priori unum percarium [precarium?] suarum carucarum prout fecisse debuerunt, et etiam super eo quod idem W. dicebat se liberum hominem memorati domini Prioris cum sit villanus ejusdem Prioris, et ita negavit dominum suum coram seneschallo ejusdem domini. Plegii de misericordia Henricus le Porter et Symon Jolle. Et sciendum est quod dictus W. spontanea sua voluntate posuit se in misericordia ut predictum est. Morrow of SS. Peter and Paul [49 Hen. III.]

Presentatio capitalium plegiorum.

(*Here follows a list of presentments, including several for wrongful encroachments in making footpaths.*)

Item Matilda Spole in misericordia quod sine licentia domini Prioris hospitavit quasdam, scilicet., Anwyt[am] et fil. ejus.

Item presentant quod magister Gwydo et dominus Prior levaverunt quandam injustam foveam in itinere regali juxta domum magistri Willelmi.

Item presentant quod Robertus de Brie hospitavit quosdam in domo sua sine licentia domini Prioris.

Item presentant quod Radulfus faber desponsavit quandam mulierem sine licentia, &c.

Item presentant quod Sibilla Colbert et Radulfus le Savere affidaverunt se adinvicem sine licentia, &c. Morrow of SS. Peter and Paul, 50 Hen. III.

Fine for false petition.

Willelmus Cut in misericordia pro sua falsa petitione super hereditate Alicie filie quondam Roberti Pitans, quia omnes de curia dicunt quod dictus Willelmus non habet jus in petitione sua, et quod nullus alius heres habet jus ad eandem hereditatem nisi illa Alicia cum viro suo et filiis suis et filiabus, nisi Galfridus Pitans, frater dicte Alicie, de transmarinis partibus arripuisset. Plegius Alexander Cocus.

Preceptum est in curia sub pena duorum solidorum ut nullus hospitetur aliquem vel aliquam ultra duos dies et duas noctes. Court held by R. the Cellarer, feast of St. Scholastica.

[But at the very next court on St. Dunstan's day seventeen persons are presented as "consueti hospitare extraneos contra statutum curie."]

Compounding an assault.

Matildis le May in misericordia pro verberatione façta filio suo
a filio Willelmi Mollendarii, quia reconciliati sunt per licentiam.
Pleg. Will. Mollend. Court held by Berengarius Carbonel,
rector of the church of Haveringlond, St. Bartholomew's day,
52 Hen. III. [1268].

CHARTERS.

[*c.* 1120-30 ?] SURRENDER and QUITCLAIM by ROLAND and
SIMON, sons of WILLIAM the PRIEST of HELETUNE, of land
and buildings in Heletune.

Sciant presentes et futuri quod ego Rolandus et ego Simon
filii Willelmi sacerdotis de Heletune resignavimus et concessimus
et quietam clamavimus pro nobis et omnibus heredibus nostris
Deo et ecclesie Sancte Fidis de Horsham et domino Austorgio
Priori, et conventui ejusdem loci, totam terram que fuit Willelmi
patris nostri in villa de Heletune et in campis de Heletune quam
nos aliquando de eis tenuimus, cum omnibus edificiis et omnibus
aliis pertinenciis suis, in liberam puram et perpetuam elemosinam,
pro animabus patris nostri et matris nostre et omnium antecessorum nostrorum et pro salute animarum nostrarum et
omnium successorum nostrorum, ita quod nos nec aliquis heredum
nostrorum nec aliquis nomine nostro aliquid juris vel clamii in
predicta terra de cetero habere aut ponere possit. Set tota
predicta terra cum omnibus pertinenciis suis in proprios usus
predictorum Prioris et monacorum integre et plenarie devolvatur.
Et ad perpetuam eorum securitatem sigilla nostra huic scripto
apposuimus. Hiis testibus : Willelmo de Sancto Martino,
Radulfo de Erlham, Willelmo de Pynkeny, Hugone filio ejus,
Godefrido filio Johannis, Radulfo de Seugham, Nicolao Bus,
Radulfo de Chaineto, Willelmo filio Alani, Godefrido fratre ejus.

COPY [*temp.* Edw. I.] of the CONFIRMATION of a CHARTER of
ROBERT FITZWALTER and SIBYL his wife (Founders *circa*
A.D. 1106 of St. Faith's Priory) by their son WILLIAM DE
KAYNETO (Cheyney), to the monks of Horsham, with grant
of the advowsons of St. Martin le Bailey and St. Michael
Berstrete, Norwich, &c.

Willelmus de Kaneto, filius Roberti filii Walteri, omnibus
hominibus suis Francis et Anglicis salutem. Sciatis me concessisse et hac presenti carta mea confirmasse Deo et Sancte
Marie et Sancte Fidi et monachis de Horsham terram de
Helgheton et advocacionem ecclesie ejusdem ville cum homagio
et aliis libertatibus in perpetuam elimosinam, sicut Robertus
pater meus et Sibilla mater mea predictis monachis dederunt.
Insuper ex propria mea donacione dono eisdem advocacionem
ecclesiarum Sancti Martini in Ballia et Sancti Michaelis de
Berstrete in Norwyco. Item dono eis totum alnetum quod jacet
inter eorundem curiam et boscum meum ex una parte et viam

regiam ex altera, et inter terram Gilberti Wade et Gunny (*sic*)
cum pastura interjacente, et molendinum cum stagno suo ex alia
parte vie regie cum omnibus suis pertinenciis. Et volo et
precipio ut bene et in pace omnia predicta teneant.

Testibus, Radulfo de Noers, Lamberto camerario, Alano
armigero, etc.

Copy, on the same parchment as the preceding, of a Grant and
Quit Claim by Robert son of Roger (*c.* 1280-90) of a right
of pasture in Gunnysmede, reciting a controversy apparently
arising from the terms of the preceding grant.

Universis sancte Matris ecclesie filiis ad quos presens scriptum
pervenerit Robertus filius Rogeri dominus de Horsford et de
Werkworth salutem in Domino sempiternam. Noverit universitas vestra, quod cum inter nos ex parte una et religiosos vivos
fratrem Reymundum, Priorem Sancte Fidis de Horsham, et
ejusdem loci conventum ex altera, controversia et materia
questionis oriretur, scilicet de communia cujusdem prati in
Horsham quæ vocatur Gunnyldesmedwe in quo quondam communiam ad animalia nostra et hominum nostrorum a festo
Sancti Michaelis usque ad Purificationem Beate Marie virginis
vendicavimus; Tandem ex nostra gratia speciali concessimus
pro nobis et heredibus nostris, etiam quiete clamavimus, nominatis
Religiosis et eorum successoribus communiam quam in dicto
prato petebamus in perpetuum. Ita videlicet quod habeamus
ingressum et egressum in dicto prato ad palicium nostrum cum
necesse fuerit emendandum. In cujus rei testimonium presenti
scripto sigillum nostrum fecimus apponi.

Original Charter of Confirmation by Margaret de Chesney.

Universis sancte Matris ecclesie filiis ad quos presens scriptum
pervenerit Margareta de Chesneto salutem. Noverit universitas
vestra quod ego Margareta de Chesneto et heredes mei debemus
manutenere et defendere et warantizare domum Sancte Fidis de
Horsham, videlicet personas monachorum et facultates et posses-
siones eorum, contra omnes, sicut patroni, et sicut puram et
perpetuam elemosinam a patre meo et antecessoribus meis
dedicatam Deo et Sancte Marie et beate Fidi Virgini ac martyri,
et ecclesie Conchensi. Et in hujus rei testimonium presentem
paginam sigilli mei appositione corroboravi.

Hiis testibus, Ada de Bedingfeld, Willelmo Peche, Toma de
Sancto Audomero, Andrea Malherb, Turgys de Chesneto, Henrico
de Hosa, Johanne de Poswic, Toma Bardolf, et multis aliis.

[*c.* 1140-50?]   Grant of Land by Theobald Halth[ein].

Theobaldus Halth' omnibus hominibus suis Francis et Anglis
salutem. Sciatis me dedisse et concessisse et hac presenti mea
carta confirmasse Deo et Beate Marie et Sancte Fidi, et monachis
de Horsham, xij acras terre in liberam et perpetuam helemosinam,

de dominio de Helesdh[on] quas pater meus eis in helemosinam dedit in brugario, videlicet quod est inter quinque hogas et terram quam dedicavit hospitali Ierusalem. Concedo quoque monachis prenominatis ex mea propria donacione viii acras terre in eodem brugario juxta predictas xij acras, in liberam et perpetuam helemosinam, pro salute anime mee, et anime Agnetis uxoris mee et pro salute animarum patris [mei] et matris mee et omnium parentum meorum. Hujus donacionis et concessionis sunt testes Walterus presbiter de Oxenede, Henricus frater domini Theobaldi, Theob. de Belhus, Robertus fil. Hug', Rogerus Dispensator, Petrus de Harch', Gislabertus, Willelmus Coqus, Alexander filius Eluuriz, Hugo, Raimondus nepotes Bertrandi Prioris et multi alii.

[c. 1160?] GRANT and CONFIRMATION by THEOBALD HALTEIN.

Notum sit omnibus Christi fidelibus quod ego Tedbaldus Haltein, filius Walteri Halt[ein], de consilio salutis mee et meorum, et concessu Angnetis uxoris mee, et voluntate filiorum meorum, dedi et concessi et presentis testimonio confirmavi carte, Deo et Sancte Marie et Sancte Fidi virgini de Horsham et monachis ibidem Deo servientibus et in perpetuum servituris, totam terram illam de dominio meo que est ultra stratam puplicam que est a Norvico ad Horsseford per domum ospitalis sub Sutwuda, scilicet lxvij ci[r]citer acras, in liberam et puram et perpetuam elimosinam, pro salute Domini Regis H[enrici] et filiorum suorum et domini mei Humf[ridi] de Buun, et pro salute anime patris mei et matris mee, et pro salute parentum meorum et parentum uxoris mee A., et Johannis et aliorum filiorum et successorum meorum et omnium amicorum meorum, liberam et quietam ab omni servicio et seculari exaccione et penitus absolutam, nichil de illa terra mihi vel heredibus vel successoribus meis retinens preter solam elimosinam. Pro hac autem donacione mea et concessione et confirmatione recepti sunt in communionem orationum et beneficiorum memorate ecclesie Dominus meus Rex H[enricus] et omnes filii sui, et dominus meus Humfr[idus] et omnes sui, et ego et A. uxor mea et liberi nostri, et omnes amici et benevoli mei. Et ego de beneficiis predicte ecclesie Sancte Fidis et fratrum ibidem Deo militantium accepi xxvij marcas argenti ad perficiendum peregrinationem meam in Ierusalem. Hanc quoque confirmacionem meam sub presentia domini nostri Willelmi Norwicensis episcopi et clericorum suorum, et aliorum plurium ecclesie Sancte Fidis, et predictorum fratrum, per manum Bertrandi Prioris Sancte Fidis feci. Hiis testibus : Maistro (sic) Nicolao, Magistro Ricardo de Dreit', Galfrido capellano episcopi, Maistro Rogero, Maistro Amicio, Rad. de Schechet', Roberto filio Ricardi, Tedbaldo Walter', et Hamone fratre ejusdem, Everardo et Henrico fratres (sic) domini Tedbaldi, Galfrido de Hicheligge, Will. filio Engelrami, Waltero fil. Reg[inaldi], Augustino de Taverham, Rob. de Chent, Alexandro, Rogero filio Herberd', Rob. filio Hugonis, Hugone nepote Prioris, Reinmudus (sic) nepos suus,

Willelmo filio Scule, Alexandro janitore, Rob. de Toppesfeld, et Johanne clerico de Posswic, et Roberto capellano de Rendlesham qui hanc cartam scripsit.

There is a duplicate of this charter written in a much clearer and better hand, and free from the grammatical and other mistakes in the attestations. In this "Maistro" becomes "Magistro," Robert "de Chent" is "de Kent," Ralph "de Schechet" is "de Sceget," and "Will. fil. Scule" is "Will. fil. Escole."

[c. 1180-1190?] CONFIRMATION by WALTER SON OF ROBERT DE BASINGHAM[*] of a grant of Salt.

Sciant presentes et futuri quod ego Walterus filius Roberti de Basingham dedi et concessi et hac presenti carta mea confirmavi Deo et beate Marie et ecclesie Sancte Fidis de Horsham et monachis ibidem Deo servientibus, in liberam et puram et perpetuam elimosinam, pro salute anime mee et omnium antecessorum et successorum meorum, v wais (sic) salis in marisco de Maltebi, scilicet ad accipiendum in salina Edrici Hare, secundum mensuram marisci de Maltebi; quam salinam avus et pater meus eis dederunt in liberam et perpetuam elemosinam. Et istum prefatum Edricum et heredes suos istum redditum in perpetuum reddendum predicte ecclesie assigno. Ita quod ego nec heredes mei aliquam molestiam nec calumpniam prefato Edrico vel heredibus suis de predicta salina, de prefata ecclesia bene et in pace tenenda, inferre possimus; reddendo semper annuatim integre prenominatum redditum ad Nativitatem Sancte Marie. Et si ita contigerit quod prefatus Edricus vel heredes sui antedictum redditum reddere non valuerint, ego et heredes mei prefatum redditum integre et sine omni diminucione de aliis redditibus nostris in dicta villa de Maltebi ad predictum terminum eis reddemus et inde satisfaciemus. Et ego et heredes mei sepedictam elimosinam prefate ecclesie contra omnes homines eis warantizabimus. Et ut ista mea donacio rata et inconcussa in perpetuum permaneat, presentis scripti testimonio et sigilli mei appositione eam corroboravi. Hiis testibus : Hugone capellano Sanctæ Fidis, Rodberto persona de Maltebi, Philippo de Verlt', Willelmo de Sundlond, Rodberto filio Scule, Symone preposito de Maltebi, Johanne milite, Ailmero filio Godwini, Willelmo de Winpou (?), Rodberto filio Sefredi, Bartolomeo de Nes, Osmundo de Nes, Bertrando de Wichingham, Huberto serviente Sancte Fidis, Ricardo coco, et multis aliis.

Fragment of seal; a horse courant.

[1240-50.] INDENTED DEED OF EXCHANGE between PRIOR BERENGARIUS and the CONVENT and RICHARD LE MOYNE.

Omnibus Christi fidelibus ad quos presens scriptum pervenerit, Berengarius humilis prior Sancte Fidis de Horsam et ejusdem

---

* The grantor died in 1198.

loci conventus salutem in Domino. • Noverit universitas vestra nos
unanimi assensu et communi voluntate Ricardo le Muyne de
Norwico, filio Ricardi le Muyne defuncti,—pro decem acris terræ
et dimidia quas idem Ricardus nobis et successoribus nostris et
ecclesie nostre sancte Fidis in villa de Hyntewde dedit, concessit,
et carta sua confirmavit, in perpetuum habendas et possidendas,
quarum quinque acre jacent inter boscum Radulfi de Tyvile ex
una parte et terram Rogeri de Stalam ex altera, et una acra jacet
in cultura que vocatur Rokeshage inter terram nostram et terram
Anabele Dunich (?), et tres rode jacent in cultura que vocatur
Chirchecroft inter terras Radulfi de Tyvile ex utraque parte, et
una dimidia acra jacet in eadem cultura inter terram
nostram et terram Radulfi de Tyvile, et una roda jacet inter
terram persone de Hyntewde et terram Johannis Bigge, et
una acra et dimidia jacet in cultura que vocatur Lampitlond,
inter terram dicte persone de Hyntewde et terram Rogeri Tubbing,
et habuttat unum capud super communem pasturam, et una acra
et dimidia jacent in cultura que vocatur Norgate inter terram
Radulfi de Tyvile et terram Simonis de Kesewic,—dedisse concessisse et hac presenti carta nostra confirmasse decem acras et
dimidiam terre nostre arrabilis in villis de Hyntewde, Manegrene,
et Kesewic, de terra quam Johannes Gochop ecclesie nostre ante-
dicte et nobis dedit in perpetuam elimosinam, quarum due acre
jacent in cultura que vocatur Surwong, inter terram ejusdem
Ricardi le Moyne et terram Agnetis Puttoch, et due acre jacent
inter terram Symonis de Kesewic et viam regiam, et habuttat
unum capud super terram Henrici le Waleys versus haustrum,
et tres acre et dimidia jacent in cultura que vocatur
Hunnolwesbrom inter terram Galfridi de Florindune et
terram Ade le Neve, et una acra jacet inter terram Rogeri
Hardekin et terram Sibille Lorewen, et habuttat unum capud
super Egelunde, et una acra jacet in cultura que vocatur
Larkebat inter terram Willelmi Carpentarii et terram Herberti de
Managrene, et una acra. jacet inter culturam que vocatur
Hunolwesbrom et terram Emme del Hyrne, eidem Ricardo et
heredibus suis in perpetuum escambium, sive plus contineant
dicte pecie terre sive minus ultra numerum antedictum, habendas
et tenendas de nobis et successoribus nostris et ecclesie nostre (*sic*)
sancte Fidis libere, quiete, integre et plenarie, prorsus
quietas et solutas ab omni servicio, consuetudine, secta curie,
exaccione et seculari demanda. Et nos et successores nostri
predicto Ricardo le Moyne et heredibus suis predictas terras
warantizabimus, defendemus, et acquietabimus, contra omnes
gentes in perpetuum. In cujus rei testimonium et securitatem
presenti scripto ad modum cyrographi indentato, quod residebit
penes dictum Ricardum le Moyne, sigillum commune capituli
nostri apponi fecimus. Alteri vero scripto quod residebit penes
nos idem Ricardus sigillum suum apposuit. His testibus :
Alexandro de Wallibus majore, et Alexandro filio suo, militibus;
Willelmo le dene (?), Waltero de Karletune, Willelmo de Hylingtune, Radulfo de Tyvile, Mylone de Muletune, Radulfo de

Taseburg, Henrico le Waleys, Thoma filio Nicolai, Willelmo de Mangrene, Nicolao le Waleys, et multis aliis.

[*c*. 1250-60 ?] GRANT by WILLIAM DE MULLERS of Caldwell Mill.

Universis sancte Matris Ecclesie filiis ad quos presens scriptum pervenerit Willelmus de Mullers, filius Hugonis de Mulers, eternam in Domino salutem. Noverit universitas vestra me divini amoris intuitu concessisse et dedisse et hac presenti carta mea confirmasse Deo et Beate Marie et ecclesie Sancte Fidis de Horsham et monachis ibidem Deo servientibus totum molendinum meum de Caldewelle propinquior [*sic*] de Tirninge versus le suth, cum aqua et stagno et secta et omni libertate integre et plenarie, sine omni retinemento, sicut illud unquam melius aut liberius in dominico tenui, in liberam et puram et perpetuam elemosinam, pro salute anime mee et Agnetis uxoris mee, et omnium antecessorum et successorum meorum. Quare volo et firmiter precipio ut predicti monachi prefatum molendinum habeant et teneant libere et quiete et honorifice ab omni calumpnia et reclamatione de me et omnium heredum meorum (*sic*) in tantum quod nichil in illud (*sic*) retineo mihi vel heredibus meis preter solam elemosinam. Et prohibeo ne aliquis heredum meorum predicte ecclesie de prefata elemosina aliquam calumpniam aut molestiam aut contumeliam inferre presumat. Ego autem et heredes mei warantizabimus et defendemus predictum molendinum prefatis monachis cum omnibus supradictis pertinentibus contra omnes homines. Hanc igitur donacionem et concessionem feci consensu et consilio et bona voluntate Agnetis uxoris mee. Et ut hec mea concessio et donacio perpetue firmitatis robur optineat presentis scripti testimonio et sigilli mei apposicione eam coroboravi. Hiis testibus: Rodberto filio Rogeri, Rogero de Cressi, Willelmo de Gisnei, Rogero de Kerdestun, Willelmo Pesche, Willelmo de Stallam, Rodberto Filiol, Rodberto filio Scule, Willelmo fratre suo, Hugone de Sancto Dionisio, Bertrando de Wichingham, Gervasio mercatore de Skothoth; Rogero Coco, Ricardo Peitevin, Benedicto de Lammesse, Radulfo de Lammesse, et aliis pluribus.

GRANT by SIR ROBERT HAUTEYN, knt., of right of pasture for 300 hoggets at Hellesdon.

Universis has litteras visuris aut audituris Robertus Auteyn, miles, salutem in Domino. Noverit universitas vestra me caritatis intuitu et pro salute anime mee, patris mei, et omnium antecessorum et successorum meorum, dedisse et concessisse et hac presenti carta mea confirmasse, in puram et perpetuam elimosinam, Deo et ecclesie Sancte Fidis de Horsham et monachis ibidem Deo servientibus, pasturam trescentorum bidentum in bruario meo de Heylisdune in perpetuum. Dicti vero monachi receperunt me in fraternitatem sui capituli et omnes antecessores et successores meos, et in omnia beneficia sua tam communia quam specialia. Et ego et heredes mei warantizabimus dictis

monachis et successoribus suis dictam pasturam contra omnes
in perpetuum. In cujus rei testimonium huic scripto sigillum
meum apposui. Hiis testibus: Magistro Reginaldo de London,
magistro Willelmo de Tukeby, Johanne capellano, Radulfo de
Rudham, capellano, Roberto Auteyn, Henrico le Porter, Johanne
de Camera, Simone Scule, et aliis.

*Seal of arms; three . . . . , in chief a label of five points;
" Sigill' Roberti Hautein."*

[1255-1265.] EXCHANGE between the ABBOT and CONVENT of
LANGLEY and the PRIOR and CONVENT of ST. FAITH of two
pieces of land in Ryveshale, each containing 6 perches in
width and 48 in length, the perch containing 16½ feet.

Hiis testibus: Magistro Johanne de Alvechirche, Archidiacono
Suffolchie, domini Norwicensis officiali, Ricardo de Witton,
Will. de Gysinghe, Henrico de Sancto Paulo, Rogero de
Hekingham, domino Henrico de Ryveshale milite, dominis
Willelmo de Wendlinge, Galfrido de Lodnes, Reynero de Werthe
capellano, Johanne filio dicti domini Henrici de Ryveshale,
Rogero de Dicleburch, Johanne de Holebeche, Henrico le Neve,
Waltero le Brun, Stephano Alvered de Ryveshale, et aliis.

GRANT of an acre in the field of HORSHAM, by SIMON SCULE, son
of the late ROBERT SCULE of ST. FAITH's, to the PRIORY, for
twenty-five shillings and sixpence.

Hiis testibus: Barthol. Cordel, magistro Thoma de Derham,
Henrico janitore, Johanne Fraunceys de Spykeswrthe, Willelmo ad
Ecclesiam de Spykeswrthe, Willelmo Palmer de Cattone, Rogero
de Feletorp, Rogero filio sacerdotis de Cattone, Alexandro fratre
ejus, Benedicto de Tungate, Waltero Aviz de Einford, Willelmo
Sceth de eadem, et aliis.

RELEASE by HENRY DE BRADEFEUD, formerly porter of the
Priory, of a messuage and 6 acres.

Sciant presentes et futuri quod ego Henricus de Bradefeud,
quondam janitor de Sancta Fide, remisi et quietum clamavi de
me et heredibus meis in perpetuum totum jus et clamium quod
habui aut habere potui in uno messuagio et sex acris terre cum
pertinenciis in villa de Horsham, que habui de dono Austorgii
quondam Prioris et Conventus Sancte Fidis de Horsham, que
fuerunt Johannis le Careter et Margarete Rygeday uxoris sue,
villanorum predictorum Prioris et Conventus. Ita videlicet quod
ego dictus Henricus nec aliquis nomine meo aliquid de cetero
inde poterimus exigere. In cujus rei testimonium huic scripto
sigillum meum apposui. Hiis testibus: Galfrido Rydel, Simone
Scule, Johanne fratre suo, Willelmo le Curtays, Willelmo
Huggemayden, Willelmo de Stanighale, Bartholomeo Cordel,
Rogero de Feletorp, Willelmo le Palmer de Catton, Willelmo
Gurnel, Willelmo de Spyheswrd, Willelmo Schet de Heinford, et
aliis.

GRANT of land and a villein by ROBERT DE MARHAM.

Sciant presentes et futuri quod ego Robertus de Marham concessi et dedi et hac presenti carta mea confirmavi Deo et beate
Marie et ecclesie Sancte Fidis de Horsham et monachis ibidem
Deo servientibus, totam medietatem terre cum omnibus
pertinenciis que fuit Roberti sacerdotis de Tirnigges, cum
messuagio Willelmi sacerdotis de Tirnigges et prato ejusdem
Willelmi clauso in Benetingesker. Concessi etiam et dedi
predicte ecclesie absque ullo retinemento humagium Emme filie
Ælurici cum omni sequaci progenie filiorum et filiarum, scilicet
ipsam et totam progeniem suam in liberam et puram et perpetuam
elemosinam ; [etc.]

Hiis testibus : Alexandro et Philippo capellanis de Sancta Fide,
Willelmo de Miliariis, Richero de Huuitewelle, Hugone Daubeni,
Willelmo filio Rocelin, Alexandro persona de Tirninges, Matheo de
Stred, Roberto et Willelmo filiis Scule, Roberto clerico de Scothoch,
Eudone clerico, Henrico Mercatore, Willelmo filio Radulfi,
Hunfrido de Tirninges, Waltero Coco, Roberto filio ejus, Willelmo
de Belache, et multis aliis.

CONFIRMATION by WILLIAM PYLLECROWE of a grant by his
    grandfather of land in Brockdish.

Sciant presentes et futuri quod ego Willelmus filius Nicholai
Pyllecrowe de Brokedis concessi et hac presenti carta mea confirmavi Deo et monasterio Sancte Fidis de Horsham et religiosis
viris Priori et Conventui ejusdem loci et eorum successoribus, in
liberam puram et perpetuam elimosinam, totam terram quam
Willelmus pater Nicolai patris mei dedit dictis Priori et Conventui
Sancte Fidis in campo de Brokedis, que quidem terra quondam
fuit Christine filie Willelmi Basseth, videlicet duas turneras in
campo qui vocatur Seveneacris, in quibus turneris sex acre terre
continentur, que jacent inter Wygate et terram que fuit Reginaldi
de Brokedis, quarum una turnera abutat super Ryvishalemerke
versus boream et alia super terram quondam Willelmi predicti
avi mei versus nothum (sic) ; [etc.]

Hiis testibus : Domino Johanne de Ryveshale, Mylone Pillecrowe, Reginaldo Pollard, Willelmo Alger, Rogero de Ketelleye,
Will. Gundolf de Brokedis ; [etc.]

GRANT of twenty-five acres of land by JOHN and WILLIAM, sons
    of GEOFFREY PALMER, of Marlesford.

Omnibus Christi fidelibus presens scriptum visuris et audituris
Johannes et Willelmus filii Galfridi Palmer de Marlesford
salutem. Noverit universitas vestra nos concessisse et hac
presenti carta nostra confirmasse et in puram et perpetuam
elemosinam dedisse Priori et Conventui Sancte Fidis de Horsham
viginti quinque acras terre, cum omnibus pertinenciis ad eandem
terram spectantibus, que fuit Alexandri capellani le Fraunceis,
et quam nos deracionavimus in curia domini Regis coram

justiciariis per breve directum contra Willelmum le Fraunceis ;
et omne jus ad eandem terram spectans ad predictum Priorem
et Conventum concedimus ; [etc.]

Hiis testibus : Johanne de Estrin, Willelmo Hamund de
Estrin, Hugone serviente de Horsford, Willelmo Russel,
Willelmo Curteis, T. Fowle, Adam le Schipper, Rogero Norreys,
Stephano le Chanu de Tibenham, Simone le FSrauncieys, Wydone
rectore ecclesie de Sorpesti [Corpesti ?], R. de Tynkebi.

RELEASE by CECILY, relict of Richard the baker of the house
of St. Faith, to the Priory of her right by reason of
dowry in 2½ acres and one rood in Westfeld, bounded by
land called Westaker and Chaungedelond; with a clause
barring herself by her corporal oath, "tactis sacrosanctis
evangeliis," against any future revocation "instigatione
inimici." For this release the Priory gives eight shillings.

Hiis testibus : Domino Thoma Bardolf, Will. Burel, Petro
fratre ejusdem, Steph. de Colne, Will. Pyam, Ric. Sket, Will.
Russel, Radulfo de Cattone, Radulfo de Staninghale, Johanne de
Wyniston, Johanne de Beston, Joh. de Salle, capellano, presentis
instrumenti scriptore, et aliis. .

[c. 1280 ?*] GRANT by ALAN SON OF JOHN DE REINHAM of villeins
to the Priory.

Universis ad quos presens scriptum pervenerit Alanus filius
Johannis de Reinham salutem in Domino. Noverit universitas
vestra me in liberam et puram et perpetuam elemosinam dedisse
et concessisse et hac presenti carta mea confirmasse Priori et
monachis Sancte Fidis de Horsham, Ywinum de Sudgate de Hegletune et Isabellam uxorem ejusdem cum omni sequela eorundem,
videlicet filiis et filiabus ab eisdem procreatis et procreandis et
omnibus ab eisdem descendentibus, et cum omnibus terris, tenementis et catallis que de me et antecessoribus meis tenuerunt vel
tenere debuerunt in villa de Hegletune et de Reinham, absolvendo
eosdem et quietos clamando pro me et heredibus meis ab omni
honere servitutis, auxilii, consuetudinis, et servitii in quibus mihi
et antecessoribus meis vel successoribus tenebantur vel teneri
potuerunt vel debuerunt. Ita scilicet quod ego vel heredes mei
nichil juris aut clamii in predictis hominibus vel eorundem
catallis terris vel tenementis possimus vendicare vel exigere in
perpetuum. Et ne in posterum aliqua oriri possit contentio
ratione alicujus pasture ab eisdem antiquitus use (sic) vel
percepte, concessi eisdem et successoribus suis leberas (sic) pas-
turas et immunes ab omni exactione prestatione et auxilio, in
omnibus locis in quibus averia eorum pascere consueverunt vel
debuerunt in villa de Reinham vel de Hegletune. Ego vero et
heredes mei warantabimus predictam donacionem et quietam

---

* The grantor died before 1291. Blomefield's *Norfolk* (8vo edit.), VII, 143.

clammationem dictis priori et monachis contra omnes. Et ut hec omnia firma et inconcussa permaneant huic scripto sigillum meum apposui.

Hiis testibus: Magistro Constantino de Ley, magistro Reginaldo de Londiniis, Galfrido de Rudham, Willelmo filio Petri, Waltero Schule, Bartholomeo de Aldreford, Galfrido de Secheford, Nicolao Buis, Johanne fabro, Radulfo fabro.

Seal in brown wax; an eagle displayed; "Sigillum Alani fil. Johannis."

[c. 1280-90 ?] Exchange of Land.

Sciant presentes et futuri quod ego Walterus clericus de Newetune filius Willelmi de Newetune concessi, relaxavi, quietam clamavi, et abjuravi in perpetuum de me et heredibus meis, Deo et beate Marie, et ecclesie Sancte Fidis de Horsham, et monachis ibidem Deo servientibus, in curia domini mei Roberti filii Rogeri, totum jus et clamium quod ego et heredes mei habuimus aut habere potuimus, aut habere poterimus, in quinque acris terre que quondam fuerunt toftum Walteri de Horsford, in villa de Horsham. Et pro hac relaxatione et quieta clamantia et abjuratione, dederunt michi predicti monachi, in excambium, quinque acras terræ in campis de Horsham ad valentiam predictarum quinque acrarum, et unum toftum quod jacet inter domum Walteri Brennecat et domum Godwini Lanke, videlicet tres acras in Longefurlond, citra cheminum acram et dimidiam, et ultra cheminum acram et dimidiam, et juxta toftum Willelmi le Mai unam acram et unam rodam, et tres rodas que abuttant super Derling. Et ut hec relaxatio et quieta clamantia et abjuratio rate permaneant et inconcusse, eam hujus scripti testimonio et sigilli mei appositione roboravi. Hiis testibus: Domino Roberto filio Rogeri, Alexandro de Dunham, Roberto de Kent, Galfrido le Gros, Willelmi Bataille, Rogero filio Willelmi, magistro Ada Daco, Waltero de Couele, magistro Hugone medico, Roberto capellano de Lings, Hugone et Johanne capellanis de Sancta Fide, Johanne de Stanford, Roberto filio Scule, et multis aliis.

Of this charter there is also a copy with the added confirmation of Robert Fitz Roger at the end. "Et ego Robertus filius Rogeri ad majorem hujus rei securitatem in hujus rei testimonium perpetuum, ad instanciam et peticionem predicti Walteri clerici de Newetune presenti scripto sigillum meum apposui." But the seal (in brown wax) is only "Sigillum Walteri Clerici."

[1280-90.] Release by Agnes, widow of Geoffrey le Svein of St. Faith's, to Prior Raymund and the Convent, for the sum of two marks, of all her right in eleven acres of land which her late husband held of the Priory.

Hiis testibus: Domino Johanne de Strus, Rogero Feltorp, Willelmo Russel, Ricardo Sket, Herveo Burel, Johanne Lomb, Ricardo Pluket, Simone Scule, et aliis.

1524, March 10. Grant from William Castleton, Prior of St. Faith's, and the Convent, to John Greye, gent., William Russel, citizen of Norwich, William Wolcy, William Birton, Robert Rynouse, John Burwode, and Robert Warden, and their heirs, of a Guild-house formerly built by and at the cost of Prior John Ryssley for the Guild of St. Andrew, "et pro potationibus ad [usum] ecclesie parochialis S. Andree de Horsham predicte in eadem domo tenend. et custodiend."

1525. CIRCULAR LETTER, sent with a bede-roll, requesting offerings and prayers for departed members of the Priory.

Omnibus Sancte Matris Ecclesie filiis ad quos presentes litere pervenerint Nos Johannes Stokes, permissione divina Prior monasterii Sancte Fidis de Horsham, et ejusdem loci conventus, ordinis Sancti Benedicti, Norwicensis diocesis (sic), salutem in Eo quem peperit uterus Virginalis. Si grata sit et laudabilis apud Deum compassio qua hic vivis pauperibus corporibus alimentum porrigitur, quanto commendabilior est apud Deum oblatio qua defunctis fidelibus panis vite qui de celo descendit proponitur, culpa quevis remittitur, et per precum suffragia defunctis in Christo venia, vivis in mundo gracia, et mortuis in celo gloria, feliciter comparatur. Divina siquidem clementia sic dignatur lapsibus humanus (sic) de congruo remedio providere, ut non solum peregrinantibus in via, verum etiam resolutis carne ad pene refrigerium per oblacionem Victime salutaris annuit benigne subvenire. Cum igitur salubre sit hic vivos reficere et defunctos in Domino per pias preces et hostias pacificas penis eruere, a culpis absolvere, et sanctorum consorciis post mortem aggregare, vestram rogamus et exortamus in Domino caritatem ut nostris in Christo mortuis quorum nonina vobis transmittimus oracionum suffragia et oblacionem (sic) solacia caritatis intuitu salubriter impendatis. Et Galfrido Metcalfe, latori presentium, ne deficiat in via, humanitatis officio favorabiles propicios et benignos prompta benignitate piaque munificencia liberales studeatis vos exibere. Vestris equidem pro nostris reciproca vicissitudine volumus obligari. In cujus rei testimonium has literas patentes sigillo nostro communi fecimus appenso. Datum apud Horsham Sancte Fidis in domo nostro capitulari, vicesimo sexto die mensis Agusti (sic) anno Domini millesimo ccccc vicesimo quinto.

A small parcel of documents relates to the family of Burel of Horsham ; viz. Hervey Burel, William son of Hervey Burel, Hervey son of William, and William Burel and Agnes his wife, in the time of Hen. III. and Edw. I.

There are about 77 other deeds relating to Horsham from the time of Henry III. to that of the Commonwealth.

BLICKLING.

MANORIAL AND OTHER DOCUMENTS.

In 2 Ric. II. is the first court of Joan Holveston. In the next year is the first court of Thomas Gyssing, knight. This Lord continues during 4 and 5 Ric. II. The Lady Joan

Holveston appears to resume the manor in the 6th year till the 12th, when there is a precept to distrain the tenants for homage and fealty and to shew their titles.

At the next court, viz. on Friday, St. Katherine, 12 Ric. II., in accordance with this precept, "ad istam curiam totum homagium veniunt et concedunt domine ex mera sua propria voluntate, pro recognitione predicta, xˢ." The vicar of Aylsham, who seems to have held the mill, is three times threatened with distraint, but not after this last entry, which seems to be a compromise. The very elaborate and particular customary of the manor made in the 35th year of Edw. I. expressly states that no recognition is to be paid on the accession of a new lord.

LIST OF THE BLICKLING MANOR ROLLS.

COURT ROLLS :—Edward I. 29.

> Edward II. For the years 2, 5, 14, 17. Besides two undated of this reign.
> Edward III. 1-17, 19-21, 25, 34-39, 40, 41, 43, 46, 47 (with others defaced).
> Richard II. 1-7, 12, 13, 15, 16, 18, 21.
> Henry IV. 1-13. (3 is the first court of Richard Pycot, Agneta Fransham and of Henry, Bishop of Norwich,* "ratione minoris ætatis Will. fil. Baudwini de Thaverham." 4 and 5 the court is held by Ric. Pykot, Agneta Fransham, William Taverham, Thomas Erpingham, knight, farmers of the dower of Eleanor relict of Nicholas Dagworth.)
> Henry V. 4 and 9.
> Henry VI. 8, 9, 14, 16-24, 25, 26, 28, 31-36, 39. Court General 49.
> Edward IV. 1, 13, 22.
> Edward V. 1.
> Richard III. 1, 2, 3.
> Henry VII. 1, 7, 8, 9.
> Henry VIII. 18, 19, 31-33, 34, 37, 38.
> Edward VI. 1-6.
> Mary 1-5.
> Elizabeth 1-14, (except 4) 17, 19.
> And for the years 1622-36, 1639, 1640.

LEET ROLLS :—

> Edward I. 34.
> Edward II. 10, 13, 19, 23 (and other rolls with dates defaced).
> Edward III. 16.
> Richard II. 2. 3, 5, 8, 9, 13, 14, 16.
> Henry IV. 1-8, 10-13. (8 is the first court of Thomas Langlee, Bishop of Durham, (Lord Chancellor) " et sociorum suorum." 13 is the first Court of John Pelham, John Ingoldesthorp, and Robert Barney, knights, co-feoffees.)
> Henry VI. 9, 11-14, 16-28, 31-36, 49.
> Richard III. 1-3.
> Henry VII. 1, with view of frankpledge.

---

* Henry Despenser *or* le Spenser, Bp. of Norwich 1370-1407.

Henry VIII. 35.
Edward VI. 1-6.
Mary 1-5.
Elizabeth 1-14 (except 4), 15, 20.
James I. 9, 19.
And for the years 1632-1636, 1638-1640.

ACCOUNT ROLLS.

Edward III. Collectors' accounts for the years 25 and 26.
Henry IV. Bailiffs' accounts for years 11-13.
Henry V. 8.
Henry VI. Bailiffs and Collectors for 10 and 11.
Edward IV. 3-4, 7-8, 11-13.
Henry VIII. 6-7.
Elizabeth 6.
A Rental. *temp.* Henry IV.

CUSTOMARY OF THE MANOR, 35 EDW. I. [1307.]

Omnibus Christi fidelibus presentibus et futuris et ballivis et fidelibus suis Johannes Engayne salutem. Quia per sacramentum proborum et legalium hominum de manerio nostro de Blyclinge et eorum visneto, scilicet Roberti Sket de Erpingham, Johannis Baldewyne, Henrici de Yernemuth, Bricii Sweyne de Ingeworthe, Roberti de Caldewode, Thome de Rystone, Edwardi Carpentere, Willelmi ad Ecclesiam, Walteri filii Johannis ad Ecclesiam, Nicholai Passe, Jacobi Attewode, Roberti Kenyng, Godwyni et Valentini le Doo, Invenimus quod dictum manerium est de antiquo dominio corone domini Regis, et homines nostri tenentes de eodem manerio sunt sokemanni et tenere debent tenementa sua in eadem villa per fidelitatem et certa servicia et consuetudines subscripta annuatim nobis facienda et reddenda, Reddendo nobis et heredibus nostris annuatim triginta duas libras cum redditibus provenientibus de liberis tenentibus manerii predicti ad quatuor terminos subscriptos, Et reddendo annuatim pro nobis et heredibus nostris domino Norwyci Episcopo ad finem triginta duarum septimanarum tres solidos sex denarios pro warda castri, et eidem Episcopo scutagium domini Regis cum evenerit quantum pertinet ad feodum unius militis, Et facienda secta ad curiam nostram in eodem manerio de tribus septimanis in tres septimanas. Et nos tenebimus visum franci plegii in eodem manerio quolibet anno die Sancti Petri ad Vincula. Et habebimus amendas de omnibus transgressionibus factis in boscis, aquis separalibus, warrennis, hutesiis injuste levatis, sanguinis effusione, wayf, stray, catallis felonum et fugitivorum, rapinis, hamsoken, rescussu, thesauri et armorum inventione, et purprestura in separali nostro. Et omnes tenentes dicti manerii sokemanni habebunt amendas de omnibus aliis purpresturis in villa factis, de assiza panis et cervisie fracta, de falsis ponderibus, ulnis, mensuris, et omnibus defectis capitalium plegiorum et eorum decennariorum ; et placita debent tenere omnium transgressionum et querelarum si prius querantur eis quam nobis et inde amendas habere. Et ipsi homines ad proximam curiam nostram tentam ante festum S. Michaelis quolibet anno colligere (*sic*) debent collectorem, messorem, et duos custodes bosci, pro quibus respondere voluerint. Ita quod messor respondeat de omnibus attachiis et districtionibus in dicto manerio faciendis. Et custodes bosci respondebunt nobis de omnibus transgressionibus in bosco et warennis factis et collectis de bosco et aliis proficuis bosci venditi. Et collector nobis respondebit de omnibus exitibus dicti manerii infra dictum manerium per rationabilem compotum ad quatuor terminos anni, videlicet ad festum Sancti Andree Apostoli, ad festum Annunciationis Beate Marie, et ad festum Nativitatis Sancti Johannis Baptiste, et ad festum Sancti Michaelis. Ita quod ad quemlibet terminum solutionis sue fidelem habeat acquietantiam. Et si in fine anni super compotum suum in arreragio fuerit, et inde ad solutionem non sufficiat, tota soca pro eo nobis respondebit.

Et ipsi reparabunt fossatam nostram circa boscum ne dampnum intus fiat defectu clausture. Et nos sustentabimus et reparabimus sumptibus propriis molendinum nostrum in omnibus vectariis, salvo tantum cariagio unius mole per annum et reparatione stagnorum et enclusarum, scilicet ad quod de terra operari debet. Et ipsi facient sectam ad molendinum nostrum. Et de jure molare debent ex antiqua consuetudine duo quarteria et dimidium frumenti vel ordei pro dimidio bussalo ejusdem bladi et tria quarteria brasii pro dimidio bussalo brasii.

Et piscare debent in omnibus communibus aquis dicte ville. Et heredes dictorum sokemannorum post mortem eorum antecessorum, cujuscunque etatis fuerint, habere debent hereditates suas sine relevio, herietto, aut aliqua fine inde nobis facienda. Et si quis heres eorum post mortem antecessoris sui infra etatem fuerit, proximi parentes ejus quibus hereditas descendere non debet habebunt custodiam ipsius heredis et tenementi sui usque plenam etatem quindecim annorum. Et placitari aut implacitari non debent de tenementis suis infra dictum manerium nisi per parvum breve domini Regis de recto clauso secundum consuetudinem manerii nobis aut ballivis nostris directo. Et si in amerciamentis nostris inciderint tam per breve quam sine brevi per pares suos inde debent afforari. Et maritare debent filios suos et filias suas tam extra manerium quam infra sine licentiam petere aut aliquam finem inde facere (*sic*). Non debent chevagium dare aut recognitionem facere in adventu alicujus novi domini dicti manerii, neque gersumam dare pro mulieribus parientibus extra matrimonium. Et si quis eorum aliquod tenementum de bassa tenura adquisierit, in curia nostra finem faciet rationabilem pro ingressu inde habendo secundum antiquam consuetudinem, pro meliori acra campestri quatuor solidos, et pro mesuagio clauso et prato et pejori terra secundum valorem tenementi. Et non debent talliari ad aliquam talliagiam nisi quando dominus Rex facit talliari dominica sua per Angliam, et hoc per breve domini Regis. Et cum aliquis forinsecus infra dictum manerium alicui mulieri heredi se maritaverit, ideo non faciet finem pro licentia ad ipsam mulierem ingrediendam.

Et quod de nullis consuetudinibus quam de predictis pro tenementis suis onerari debent.

Nos dictus Johannes Engayne dictas consuetudines approbantes, ratus habentes, volentes et concedentes, ex consensu Elene consortis nostre, pro salute animarum nostrarum pro nobis et heredibus et assignatis nostris, quod omnes dicti homines heredes de dicto manerio in perpetuum remaneant ut de antiquo dominio sicut compertum est, et quod habeant et teneant omnia tenementa sua predicta per predictas consuetudines et servicia predicta sine mutatione alicujus servicii aut consuetudinis. Et omnes alias consuetudines et servicia que vel quas ab eis exigebamus eisdem hominibus et eorum heredibus de nobis et heredibus et assignatis nostris remisimus et quietum clamavimus in perpetuum. Salvis nobis et heredibus nostris consuetudinibus et serviciis prenominatis. In hujus rei testimonium his duobus scriptis in modum cirograffi confectis die Annunciacionis Beate Marie anno regni Regis Edwardi filii Regis Henrici tricesimo quinto, quorum parti penes dictos homines remanenti Johannes Engayne sigillum suum apposuit, et parti penes dictum Johannem remanenti dicti homines sigillum eorum commune apposuerunt.

Testibus : Johanne de Erpingham, Rogero de Calethorp, Johanne de Colby, Henrico filio ejus, Rogero de Woltertone, Johanne de Irmynglonde, Radulpho de Irmynglonde, et aliis. Datum per copiam.

Court holden there on Monday in the feast of St. Peter ad Vincula in the 7th year of Ed. II. (*Translation.*) *Mutilated roll.*

Head Borghs. John Attwode, John Skyppyng, Adam de Bondeker, John Impe, Ralph . . , John Bemund, Adam Passe, Richard le Palmere, junior, Robert Prayd, John Haghene, John le Waler, . . . Ketchod, Thomas Belle, Stephen de Skothowe, Richard Keye, John le Munne, Henry Mort, Nicholas Sukke, Robert Rente, Will. Kythod, ... Sworn.

Say upon their oath that John le Chusser ought to repair a certain well at Lund ; therefore, etc.   6d.

And they present that Richard de Thorp drew blood of Thomas Wytlok against the peace, etc.   6d.

Also they present that Beatrice Prigge committed hamsoken on Maud Dolch by carrying away a belt of the said Maud from the house of the said Maud against the peace, etc.   3d.

And they present that Agnes de Thorpgate did not open a ditch through which water ought to have course ; by reason whereof, etc.   6d.

Also they present that Thomas Wrchipe drew blood of Henry Grys.   6d.

Also they present that Reginald, son of Robert Sucke, " fecit vetitum Matillidi uxori Roberti Dolch de bidentibus . . . voluit inparcasse pro damno facto.'"   3d.

Also they present that the said Maud drew blood of the said Reginald ; therefore, etc.   3d.

Also they present that Simon Fyn broke a certain division between himself and Richard le Palmer in length . . . and unlawfully removed a certain boundary placed by the consent of the parties ; therefore, etc.   6d.

Also they present that Margaret, the daughter of Simon Spye, is an habitual thief in autumn time of the neighbours' corn and . . . . and does great damage ; therefore, etc.
                                                                    3d. Pillory.

Also they present that Margaret, daughter of Agnes of Matelask, is an habitual thief in autumn time of corn and all the year through is used to steal hens and do damage to the neighbours ; therefore, etc. And the said Agnes is a receiver ; therefore, etc.
                                                                         Pillory.

Also they present that Beatrice, the wife of Semann the Smith, raised the hue and cry upon John Wodeman the hayward (*messorem*) unjustly ; therefore, etc.   3d.

Also they present that when John de Causton stood at his gate in the peace of the lady, thither came Richard and Robert, chaplains of the parson, with two forks and atrociously assaulted the said John ; whereupon John for fear of the assault raised the hue and cry upon them lawfully, but did not follow them to the hall because John the servant of the lady was present and Thomas.   1s.

And John de Causton, because he raised the said hue and cry and is not present, and therefore he is amerced.   6d.

Also they present that John Payn is a common fisher, fishing on the lady's banks.

Also they present that William Figge brewed and broke the assize ; therefore, etc.   6d.

Also they present that Will. Wildun did the like.   2s.
Also they present that Reginald le Palmer did the like.   1s.
Also they present that John Skipping did the like.   1s.
Also they present that Nicholas Caterine did the like.   1s.
Also they present that Adam Godsone did the like.   2s.
Also they present that Cecily Salve . . . but she is dead.
Also they present that Agnes Salve brewed four bushels.   6d.
Also that Agnes Grand did the like.   6d.
Also that Elviva Keninge did the like.   1s.
Also that Edmund Larke is a baker and broke the assize.   6d.
Also that Roger Rose did the like.   6d.
Also that Adam Bateman is a regrator ; therefore, etc.   3d.
Also that Nicholas Ffre is the like.   3d.
Also that Simnel Lewyn is the like.   3d.
Also that Margaret Edes brewed and broke the assize.   3d.

It is also presented that Robert son of John Demund, the parson's servant (*manupastus*), arrested Roger Hullerd with his cart on the King's highway and detained him by night against the peace, etc.

Also they present that Richard the Chaplain, attorney of the parson, prosecuted Roger Hullerd in a Court Christian about matters which do not concern our testimony. They are agreed.

Also that the said Richard prosecuted Hugh le Mune in the same way.

Also that Richard the parson has encroached upon the highway with a wall built 22 feet in length and a foot in breadth. 2s.

Also that Richard the parson's chaplain is an usurer 40d.

Also that the said Richard dug the King's highway and made it beyond measure deeper than before, to the great hurt of the whole vill. 6d.

Also that John de Thorp dug the King's highway and deteriorated it, to the detriment of passengers. 6d.

Also that Robert Luue ploughed under a certain division between the said Robert and John Impe to the length of sixteen feet. 6d.

And that Estrilda Prigge damaged the corn of her neighbours throughout the summer. 3d.

And that Margaret, daughter of Richard Grys, is an habitual doer of damage to her neighbours in summer. 6d.

And that John son of Beatrice entered the house of William Kytot and did damage to the amount of 6d. 3d.

And that Mariota wife of William Schirlok is a habitual doer of damage to hens and other things of the neighbours. 3d.

And that John Freysell and John his brother, John le Pillemere, and Nicholas son of Hugh, and John Payn came by night to the lady's closes for eels, against the peace, etc. 1s. 3d.

And that William de Holt fished on the lady's bank.

And that the Master of the Hospital did the like. 2s.

And that Thomas and Ralph sons of Richard son of Adam did the like. 1s.

And that Henry de Colby did the like. 2s.

And that the son of Payn Meye did the like. 10d.

And that Ralph the baker did the like. 6d.

And that the willows on the side of the sacrist of St. Edmund hang on the bank and hinder the course of the river so that the (fields) on that side of the village are inundated and submerged, to great damage, etc. 6d.

And that William Lytot and John Chusser, assayers of beer, did not fulfil their office as they ought; therefore, etc.

And that John Skyppyng brewed honey mead and sold it contrary to the assize.

And that Roger Palmer did the like.

And that Richard Waller came within the liberty of the lady and took one cow of John G . . . . and drove the said cow to Irmingland, to the great prejudice of the lady and her liberty; therefore, etc.

[There are a few more entries, of which the following are the more noticeable:

"All the capital pledges, for concealment, because they did not make their perambulation to the tenement between the lady and

Edmund the carpenter to see the boundaries broken between them, as had been ordered in the Court.

John son of Roger Adyolf is accustomed to take chicken (*pulcinas*) aud capons with nets which Robert Keye had at the lady's mill.

Juetta the wife of Richard le Palmere is an usuress, and sells at a dearer rate for accommodation.

And they ask to distrain the said Juetta to answer to the lady about the said usury."]

EXTRACTS FROM THE COURT ROLLS.

Taking the order of Exorcist without licence.

St. Peter ad Vincula, 13 Edw. II.

Preceptum est, sicut pluraliter, attachiare Andream Wardeyn per corpus suum eo quod cepit ordines exorciste sine licentia.

Levy for fabric of the church.

Tuesday after St. Barnabas, 13 Edw. II.

Preceptum est messori levare de communitate agistamentum ad fabricationem ecclesie ad opus Roberti Keye.

Prescriptum est levare de communitate agistamentum ad fabricationem ecclesie ad opus Roberti Keye eo quod pacavit pro eis et delib. . . . nomina eorum messori per billam.

Presentment of the Bishop.

3 Ric. II.

Present. est domine quod Episcopus fecit unum cursum aque apud Hallemedwe in aysiamentum plus vicinorum.

Of the Vicar of Aylsham.

Present. quod Ricardus vicarius de Ailsham exaltavit stagnum suum in ponendo blestas altius quam facere debet in . . . mergendo fossata de feodo domine injuste, etc.

Item present. quod predictus Richardus fecit purpresturam super pratum Johannis Impe ponendo . . . ad exaltandum vivarium aliter quam facere debet ad prejudicium domine, etc.

(This Richard was a benefactor to St. Peter's Coll. Camb.)

Swearing in of youths to the Tithings.

St. Peter ad Vincula, 5 Ric. II.

Nicholas filius Ricardi Kethod juratus est in decennium.

Johannes Kethod filius Johannis Kethod juratus est similiter.

Johannes filius Nicholai Kethod juratus est similiter.

Poaching.

12 Ric. II.

[Presentant] quod Johannes de London, capellanus, fugatus fuit infra warrennam captando lepores.

Leaving the manor.

St. Agnes, 12 Ric. II.

Robertus filius Symonis Fygge nativus domini est fugitivus et manet extra dominium, etc., et ubi ignorant, etc., et precipitur seisire [per] corpus.

Robertus filius Johannis Froysel nativus domini de sanguine, similiter et similiter, et manet in villa de St. Botulph ; ideo pres. etc.

Robertus fil. John Wederall nativus domini similiter et similiter, et manet in Hemesby.

Johannes filius Roberti Altholf, et Thomas et Radulfus fratres ejusdem Johannis sunt similiter, et manent in Cleye, et Radulfus manet in Salle, et precipitur similiter.

Pleading in a Court Christian.

15 Ric. II.

Item quod Johannes fil. Thome Wattys injuste vexavit Robertum Fanmakere in curia Christianitatis.

Tuesday aft. St. Agnes, 16 Ric. II.

Item quod Joh. Melior injuste vexavit Johannem servientem Johannis Love in curia Christianitatis pro re tangente curiam regalem; ideo precipitur est seisire omnes terras et tenementa que idem Johannes tenet in villenagio domini.

Poacher's assault on a keeper.

Distringere Radulfum filium Johannis de Irmyngland ad respondendum, eo quod fecit rescussam Roberto Berte, custodi bosci domini, de duobus leporariis, et ipsum verberavit et male tractavit contra pacem, etc.

Regrating.

15 Ric. II.

Quod Johanna Parys junior est regratrix panis et vendit contra assisam.

1368.   Henry de Berneye, William de Qualissal (?), and Thomas Hervy, grant to Sir James Holveston, and Joan his wife, the manor of Blicklyng to hold to them and the heirs male of the body of Sir James; remainder to Sir Nicholas Dagworth and the heirs male of his body; remainder to the rightful heirs of Sir James Holveston.   42 Edw. III.

1378.   Indenture between James de Holveston and Johanna his wife, of the one part, and John de Colby of the other part.

Compounding a dispute about the flooding of Holveston's land by the misuse of Colby's water mill at Ingworth. (*In French.*) Friday, St. Andrew's day, 47 Edw. III.

1415. Roger Brekes and William Annes, churchwardens of Blickling. Declaration of trust of three roods of land in one piece in Blickling at the Kirkegap, adjoining the common path through the churchyard on the east. To remain for ever a garden of the church of Blickling and all parishioners of the said church. Tuesday after Nat. B.M., 3 Hen. V.

1444. Edward Love of Bliclyng grants to Richard Chever and others all his messuages in Bliclyng called Bertrams, otherwise Dygardes, with right of keeping two running dogs to catch foxes, and liberty of foldage, bull and boar; and other tenements. Conditionally on payment of 160*l.* 1 Sept., 23 Hen. VI.

1448. Henry Inglose, knt. and John Lynford, release to John Fastolf, knight, all their right in the manor of Bliklynge, and a piece of land containing 7 acres which they had together with the said John Fastolf and others. 21 Sept., 27 Hen. VI.

1448. Sir William Oldhall, knt. releases to many co-feoffees his right in the preceding land, as conveyed in a feoffment of 7 July. 3 August, 27 Hen. VI.

1506. Wm. Multon, clerk, at the special request of Thomas Boleyn, son and heir and executor of the will of Will. Boleyn, knt. demises to Richard Davy, clerk, Robert Davy, his brother, Thomas Semann, clerk, and Thomas Lanyon, junr., all the messuages in Bliclyng which he held with Robert Heyles, and 2*d.* rent. 9 Nov., 22 Hen. VII.

[1551], March 3, 5 Edw. VI. Covenant for the conveyance by Sir James Boleyn, knt. to "the right noble ladie Elizabeth, daughter of the late King of most famous memorie, King Henry VIII., sister of our Soverayne Lord King Edward VI.," of all his manors, lands, &c., in Heveningham, Marsham, Buxton, and various other places in Norfolk.

1554. Sir James Boleyn, knt., and Dame Elizabeth his wife and Sir John Clere on the one part, and John Mason, of Erpyngham, on the other part; lease of Blicklyng Mill for 60 years, reciting that James Boleyn and Elizabeth his wife were seized of the manor of Blikling with remainder to Sir J. Clere. 7 Sept., 1 and 2, Ph. and Mary.

1554. Conveyance by Edward Lord North and John Williams of the advowson of Blykelyng to Sir John Clere and Edward Clere. 22 Oct., 1 and 2, Ph. and Mary.

1558. Probate of will of Thomas Wilkinson, of Blickling.

Chancery Order in a suit between Sir John Fastolf and Geoffrey Boleyn respecting the purchase of the manor of Blickling.

Beit remembred that the Tewesday the v. day of Septembre the yere of the reigne of our soveraigne lord King Henri the sixte . . . apperid afore my Lorde Cardynall the Chauncellor

of Englande at Fullham Sir John Fastolf, knight, and Geffrey
Boleyn, Alderman of London, with both theire counselles, where
it was desired at that tyme for the partie of the said Sir John
the delivery of two obligations eyther of them of the summe of
x. marc, thenne beyinge in the kepyng of Master Thomas
Eborall, and also a dede of an annuite of marc xx. and iiiis. &c.,
agenste the which desire it was answered for the partie of the
said Geoffrey that the saide obligations and dede of annuite oght
noght to be delyvered to the said Sir John afore that he hadde
fulfilled diverse conditions conteyned in certeyne Indentures
thenne rehersed, and the tenour of theyme redde by Byllyng,
Recorder of London, afore my saide Lorde, the whiche
conditions as it was thenne surmytte for the partie of the
said Geffrey in no wise wer perimplissht, and in especiall
a defaute was assigned in the nonne delyvery of certayn
stuffe of shepe and other that the saide Geffrey oughte to
have with his purches of the manour of Bliclyng, accordyng
to the saide indentures, etc., and the nonne attournement
of diverse tenantes holdyng of the saide manour. Wherto
it was replied and sayde by som of the counsell of the
said Sir John that he had no noumbre of shepe at his first pur-
chas of the said manour, and thenne my saide Lord answered
and reherced that thendenture specified that the said Sir John
hadde solde to the saide Geoffrey the saide manour with the stuffe
of shepe and other, etc. And also how the same Sir John as it
was thenne declared for the partie of the said Geffrey hadde sent
by his letter to Bliclyng aforesaide to his servant there to delyvere
to the said Geffrey dlix. shepe. Wherefore my saide Lorde thenne
saide that hym thoght it accordyd noght well to make any suche
allegeaunces, and so in conclusion forasmoche as it was thoght
that the saide Sir John oghte of reason to delyvere the stuff of
shepe and other accordyng to the saide indenture and also the
other condicions in the same indenture specified trewly performe,
etc., it was agreed at the laste for the partie of the saide Geffrey
at the reverens of my saide Lordes lordship that the dede of
annuitie and one of the saide obligations sholde be delyvered
to the saide Sir John, and that other obligation to remayne stylle
with the saide maister Thomas to [sic] the said stuff were
delyvered and the other conditions in the saide indenture
specified performyd, etc., and that Haydon and Genny the elder
sholde examyne and make reporte of the noumbre and value of
the said stuff, etc.

HEVENINGHAM.

MANOR ROLLS.

An undated Roll of Henry III. ?

Edward I. For the years 6-21, 25, 26. The 25th is the
9th of the Pontificate of R. (Walpole), 1297.
Also for Cattes manor 4-7.

Edward III. 2, 3, 5, 6, 13, 14, 16, 17. 2 and 3 are the 4th
of the Pontificate of W. (Ayermine *or* Armine), 1329.
13, 14 and 16 are the 2nd, 4th and 6th of the Pontificate
of Anthony (Bek).

There are " Letes " for the years 2, 5, 14, 16.

Richard II. 1, 2, 3, 5-23, except 12 and 15. That of the
year 5 has this note :—

"Prima curia ib. tent. die merc. prox. post festum
Sᵗᵃ· Petri ad Vincula anno Regis Ricardi II. post
conquestum quinto, postquam rotuli curiæ, custu-
maria, rentale et rotuli sectæ curiæ, et alia monumenta
dicti manerii cremati fuerunt per tenentes Domini
et alios communes quando communes comitatus Norf.
et aliorum com. surrexerunt contra pacem domini et
magna dampna fecerunt, etc."

18, Catts manor.

Henry IV. 1-14. 2 is the 31st of Episcopate of Henry
le Despencer, 1401 ; at his court in 3 John Spencer and
others are farmers of the temporalities. (2, 10, and 11
are also Lete courts.)

Henry V. 1 (Lete). 2-10. 3, First court of the King on
escheat following the death of Courtenay, Bishop of
Norwich, 1415. A° 4 is the first general court of
Bishop Wakering, 1417.

1-3 also Catts manor.

Henry VI. 1-38 (Courts, Courts General, and Letes). 7 is
the 2nd court of Bishop William Alnwick, 1429 ; 15 is
the first court of Bishop Thomas Brown, 1437 ; and 27 is
the 4th year of Bishop Walter Lyhert, 1449.

Also Cattes manor, 4, 5-8.

Edward IV. Courts and Courts General, with separate
jurors for Parkhalle, Ryptonhall and Keritoft, 1-3, 8-12.
(Letes, Hevingham cum Marsham, 1-6.)

Catts manor, 19-23.

Richard III. Catts manor, 1.

Henry VII. 1-24.

Henry VIII. Marsham cum Hevingham and Hevingham
Courts, and Marsham cum Hevingham Letes, 2, 3, 5-11,
13, 15-30 (Anno 30 is Marsham Regis and Hevingham
Regis), 31 (first court of James Boleyn), 32, 33, 34 (cum
visu franciplegii), 36, 37, 38.

Cattes manor, 1-37.

Edward VI. 4, 5 Hevingham ; Hevingham cum Marsham,
1-6.

Philip and Mary.

Cattes manor, 3-6.

Elizabeth. 1, 2, 4-8, 29-34, 37, (17, 18 is the court of
W. Yaxley). Also a roll for the year 1564.

Catts manor, 1-8, 17, 18, and between 32 and 42.

James I. 4, First court of Sir H. Hobart.

ACCOUNT ROLLS.

Edward III. Provost's and Messor's accounts for years 2,
3, 6-18, 36, 40, 41. (18 is the 1st year of the Episcopate
of W. (Bateman) Bishop of Norwich.)
Farmer's accounts, 20-21.
Bailiff's accounts, 27-28.

Richard II. Provost's account for year 13 and 14.
Bailiff's account, 20-21.
Account of works (task), 23 to 1 Hen. IV.

Henry IV. 1, Account of work (tasks).
Ripton and Critoft manors. Messor's account for years
5 and 7.
Cattes and Ripton manors. Messor's account, years 11
and 12. Account of work (tasks).

Henry V. Messor's account for years 2 and 3 (Parkhalle).
(Hevingham cum Marsham.) Bailiff's account for years
5 and 6.

Henry VI. Bailiff's account for years 23, 24, 27, 28.
(Rypton.) Bailiff's account, 8 and 9.
(Parkhalle.) Messor's account, 15 and 16.
(Critoft.) Messor's account, 24 and 25.

Edward IV. Provost's and Messor's accounts, 2 and 3, 8 and
9, 9 and 10.

Henry VII. Messor's account, 16 and 17. (The account of
John Helwyn, deputy. Same date, like account of Robert
Bushop.)
(Hevingham cum Marsham.) Provost's and Messor's
accounts, 8.

Henry VIII. Messor's account for year 24 (John Martyn).

MANOR ROLLS.

1381-2. *Ripton Hall.* Rental, Richard II. 5.
Customary, Rich. II. 8 ?
1384-5. *Parkhalle Manor.* Customary and Rental, Rich. II. 8, taken
before Henry Cat, Lord of the Manor, and his tenants.
1444. *Hevingham.* Rental, Hen. VI. 22. In part renewed,
Hen. VIII. 1.
1444. *Hevingham Cattes.* Rental and Customary, endorsed
Hen. VI. 22. (Also an extract of an ancient extent
undated.)
1500. *Hevingham Critofts.* Customary, Hen. VII. 15.
1534. *Hevingham with Marsham.* Abuttal and Rentals,
Henry VIII. 26.
1544. *Hevingham Cattes.* Book of Demesne Lands, Henry VIII.
36.
1569. An abuttal of Andrew Thetford, Esq. His free lands
in *Hevingham filde,* 1569. (Formerly Master's.)
1598. *Hevingham.* Rental endorsed E.T. 1598.
Tenant Rolls of the manors of Hevingham, Repton or
Rypton Halle, Crichetots, etc. (undated).

1347-48. Account of Geoffrey Horsford, servant of Sir Constantine [Mortimer], for the manor of Hevingham, from Mich. 20 to˙Mich. 21 Edw. III. The year before the Black Death.

✻ ✻ ✻ ✻ ✻

Idem re[cepit] de xxxvi quarteriis bladi multure r[eceptis] de firma duorum molendinorum quorum unum ventricum et aliud aquaticum per annum. Summa xxxvi. qu.

De quibus, liberat. Johannis Randolph, tenentis, carucantis ab in crastino S[ti.] Michaelis usque diem Veneris proximum post festum S[ti] Johannis ante Portam Latinam per xxxii septimanas, iii dies, iii qu. ii bus., capientis quarterium per x septimanas.

In lib. unius tenentis carucantis per totum annum preter iiii septimanas in autumpno iiii quarterios vi bus., capientis quarterium per x septimanas. In lib. ii fugantium carucantium ab in crastino S[ti.] Michaelis usque diem Veneris prox. post f. S[ti] Johannis ante Portam Latinam per xxxii septimanas et iii dies et a festo˙Nativitatis beate Marie Virginis usque festum S[ti.] Michaelis per iii septimanas vi quarteria, quorum quilibet capiat quarterium per xii septimanas. In lib. J. Daye per totum annum iiii quarteria ii bus. dim. capientis quarterium per xii septimanas. In lib. i [unius] bercarii per idem tempus v quarteria ii bus. et dim. capientis quarterium per x septimanas. In lib. i herciatoris per xiv sept. et tres dies i qu. ii bus. iii p. capientis quarterium per xii sept. In lib. i porcarii a festo S[ti.] Michaelis usque diem lune proximum post festum Augustini in Maye per xxxiii sept. et iii dies, ii quar. iv. bus. p. capientis qu. per xiii sept. Item lib. eidem versus Burnham pro porcis domini ibidem custodiendis iiii bus. precepto domine. In lib. i aucarum custodis, custodiendis bestiis in Heselholt ii bus. In lib. Willelmi Soukis, custodiendis bestiis in Heselholt in estate vi. bus. In pane frumenti pro stotis tempore sementis ordei vi. bus. Item datur Henrico precepto domine ii. . . . Item datur Johanni Randolph ii bus. precepto domine. Item datur Thome de Midilton i bus. precepto domine in expensis autumpnalibus ii qu. iiii bus. In venditione i quar. ut in fr. Item allocatur pro stacione molendini aquatici per unam xiv[m.] iiii bus. Item in stipendio i garciferi euntis ad carucandum ante festum Natalis Domini per iii sept. ii bus.

[c. 1250?] Extent of the Manor of Hevingham.

Episcopus Norwic. est capitalis dominus villæ. [Words added.]

Episcopus Norwic. habet in eadem villa unum messuagium et unum parcum [stagnum continentem. ii acras infra clausum —; words struck out] unam acram terre arabilis in dominio.

Villani ejusdem.

Habet quinque villanos qui tenent v messuagia et xxvii acras terre.

C

Tenentes.

Will. de Parco tenet unum messuagium xl acras terre arabilis, unam acram prati, unum molendinum aquaticum, cum stagno, de episcopo Norwic.

Villani.

Idem Will. habet ij villanos qui tenent ij messuagia et unam acram terre.

Cotarii.

Idem Will. habet v cotarios qui tenent v. cotagia.

Liberi tenentes ejusdum Willelmi.

Henry de London tenet 1 cotag. et reddit iij$^{d.}$
Galfridus Craske tenet 1 cotag. et reddit v. den.
Rich[erus] de Pagrave tenet medietatem unius messuagii et 1 · acram terre, et reddit per annum iij$^{d.}$ ob.
Ricardus Faber tenet unum messuagium et dim. acram terre et reddit per annum xx$^{d.}$
Willelmus fil. Christiane tenet unum cotag. et reddit iiij$^{d.}$
Agnes Bonpayn tenet unam cotag. et reddit iiij$^{d.}$
Et dictus Will. tenet predictum tenementum, villanos, cotarios, et liberos tenentes de episcopo Norwic. per socagium, et reddit xi sol. x$^{d.}$ ob.

Willelmus le Kat tenet xxiiij acras terre.
Richerus de Pagrave tenet de eodem Will. i acram terre et reddit iiij$^{d.}$ ob.
Johannes fil. Ade de Hipeton tenet acram terre, et dat per annum iiij$^{d.}$ Et dictus Will. tenet predictum tenementum et liberos tenentes de episcopo Norwic., et reddit per annum ij$^{s.}$ vj$^{d.}$ ob., et tenet per socagium.

Andreas de Bramton tenet v villanos qui tenent v messuagia et viij acras terre, et tenet de episcopo Norwic. et dat per annum iij$^{s.}$ iij$^{d.}$
Rich. de Pagrave tenet unum acram terre de episcopo Norwic., et reddit per ann. pro se et pro Joh. fil. clerici vj$^{d.}$ ob. ·
Johannes fil. clerici tenet dim. acram terre de Rich. de Pagrave et dat per ann. iij$^{d.}$
Et dictus episcopus est patronus ecclesie de Hevyngham, et ecclesia habet in proprios usus xx acras terre et unum messuagium et unum villanum qui tenet ij acras terre.
Will. Olok tenet j rodam terre et dat per annum j$^{d.}$
Will. fil. Simonis tenet dim. acram terre et reddit iij$^{d.}$
Et idem Episcopus habet visum franciplegii [aprum, taurum, wayf de aver. extranea, furcas, thumerell ; *struck out*]. Et tenet totum predictum tenementum cum libertatibus et predictos villanos cotarios et libere tenentes cum eorum tenentibus de Domino Rege per baroniam episcopatus Norwic.

Dominus Rex.

Andreas de Branton (*sic*) tenet decem villanos qui tenent decem messuagia, lx et xiij acras terre, et unúm cotarium qui tenet unum cotagium, et tenet predictos villanos, cotarium, de domino Rege de manerio de Aylesham de antiquo dominico pertinente ad suum manerium de Branton, quod quidem manerium tenet per servic. xv · et viij^d.

Willelmus de Ecclesia et ejus tenentes tenent xij acras terre de Andr. de Brantone et reddunt per annum xij^d. [De] rege sed quo waranto et per quod servicium jurati nesciunt. [*Last clause struck out.*]

· Rich. Cucuk et parcenarii sui tenent x acras terre et unum messuagium. Idem habent unum cotarium qui tenet unum cotagium. Et tenent de Domino Rege de manerio de Aylsham de antiquo feofamento, et reddunt per an. iiij^s. iiij^d.

Thomas Faber et parcenarii sui tenent iij acras et dim. terre de Domino Rege, et reddunt per an. viij^d.

Thomas fil. Galfridi tenet iij acras et dim. terre de Domino Rege, et reddit per an. viij^d.

Et tenent de manerio de Caustone de antiquo feofamento.

Comes Glovernie.

Willelmus le Chat tenet unum messuagium, lx acras terre et ij acras prati. Idem habet xiiij villanos qui tenent xiiij messuagia, quater viginti et xij acras terre arabilis. Item habet iij cotarios qui tenent iij cotagia.

Isti subscripti tenent de Willelmo le Kat. Liberi tenentes ejusdem Willelmi.	Rich. de Pagrave tenet dim. messuag. unam rodam et dim. terre, et reddit per ann. vj^d.
	Henry le Blunt tenet unam acram et dim. terre, et reddit per an. iiij^d.
	Willelmus fil. Walteri tenet unum messuagium et vj acras terre, et reddit per an. iiij^".
	Willelmus de Ecclesia tenet unum messuagium et iiij acras terre, et reddit per an. iij^d.

Et dictus Will. le Kat tenet predictum tenementum, villanos, cotarios, et libere tenentes de comyte Glovernie per scutagium scil. ad xl. sol. quinque sol, ad plus plus, ad minus minus, et ^{tenentes dicti Co[mitis]} *debet pro tenemento suo* [words interlined are substituted for those in italics] [debent] unam sectam hundredi de Erpingham quam Johannes Parys et heredes sui facere tenentur. Et Comes tenet de Domino Rege per baroniam comitatus Glovernie viij pars unius feodi militis. Et idem Will. habet liberum aprum et taurum et faldam. *Et debet unam sectam bis per annum comitatui Norvic.* [words struck out].

Henricus de London tenet v acras terre et j acram prati de comite Glovernie per serv. j$^{d.}$ et scutagium, scil. ad xl$^{s.}$ v$^{s.}$

Et habet duos villanos qui tenent duo messuagia et ix acras terre.

Rich. de Pagrave tenet unum acram et dim. terre et reddit per an. j$^{d.}$ ob.

Petrus ad Parcum tenet unam acram terre et dat per an. iiij$^{d.}$

Thomas Wayt tenet iij rodas terre et dat per an. ij$^{d.}$

Radulphus Bonde tenet j acram terre et reddit ij$^{d.}$

Thomas Faber tenet j acram et dim. terre et reddit per an. ij$^{d.}$

Henricus le Blunt tenet unam acram terre et dat per an. iiij$^{d.}$

Henricus Rake tenet unam acram terre et dat per an. j$^{d.}$

Johannes fil. clerici tenet dim. acram terre et dat per an. ij$^{d.}$

Et isti tenent de Will. fil. Walteri, et Willelmus tenet de Will. le Kat, et reddit per an. iiij$^{o.}$ pro toto tenement suo, et W. le Kat tenet de Henr. de London et reddit per an. j$^{d.}$

Et dictus Henr. de London tenet dictum tenementum, villanos, et liberos tenentes de Thoma Jurdon per scutagium, scil. ad xl sol. v sol., ad plüs plus, ad minus minus, et debet unam sectam hundredo de Erpyngham quam Willelmus fil. Walteri et heredes sui facere tenentur. Et Thomas Jurdon tenet de Comite Glovernie et Comes de Domino Rege per baroniam comitatus Glovernie.

Kerebrok.

Willelmus de Ecclesia tenet iij acras turbarie, et habet unum cotarium qui tenet unum cotagium.

Wulmere Bondes tenet unum cotagium de eodem Will. et reddit per an. iiij$^{d.}$ Et Will. de Ecclesia tenet de domo de Kerebrok et reddit per an. iij$^{d.}$, et domus tenet in libera eleemosina; de cujus feodo ignoratur.

Prior de Gyslingham.

Will. le Kat tenet lx acr. pasture de Will. de Ecclesia et reddit per an. dim. marc., et Will. de Ecclesia tenet de Priore de Kyslingham, et Prior tenet in libera eleemosina de honore de Ry ex dono antecessorum J. le Mareschal.

Prior de Bromholm.

Johannes fil. clerici tenet unum messuagium et xviij acras terre, ij acras et dim. prati, de Priore de Bromholm, et reddit per an. vij$^{s.}$ vj$^{d.}$, et Prior tenet *de domino Rege sed qualiter* [words inter-lined are substituted for those in italics] et per quod servicium tenet jurati nesciunt.

Honor Ry.

Dominus J. le Marchal tenet in Hevingham xl acras terre arabilis, unum messuagium, xi acras prati, xvi acras pasture, x acras turbarie, et cc acras bruerie. Idem habet ix villanos qui tenent ix messuagia et lx acras terre. Idem habet iii cotarios qui tenent iij cotagia.

Et dominus J. le Marchal percipit per annum de feodo Guyet xxij[d.] ob. ad wardam castri Norwic., et ad scutagium quando venerit ad xls. xx[s.] ad plus plus, ad minus minus, et habet visum franci plegii et faldam. Et tenet predictum tenementum cum libertatibus, villanos, cotarios, et liberos tenentes a principio tenure sue infrascriptos, de Domino Rege per baroniam de Ry.

Liberi tenentes ejusdem J.

Thomas Schade [tenet] ij acras per j[d.] de J. le Mareschal.

Henricus Prente tenet dim. acram terre.

Petrus Guyet tenet unum mess. et unam acram terre.

Ricardus Howard tenet unum mess. et vj acras terre.

Ric. de Pagrave tenet 4 acras et dim. per ij[d.] de J. le Marschal.

Willelmus ad Ecclesiam tenet vj acras terre.

Thomas Wayegrave (?) tenet ij acras.

Radulphus Belle tenet unam acram.

Willelmus Brese tenet dim. acram.

Radulphus fil. Roberti tenet iiij acras.

Willelmus Cucuk tenet dim. acram per j ob.

Johannes Cucuk tenet unam acram per j[d.]

Henricus Cucuk tenet iij rodas per ob.

Ricardus Faber tenet ij acras per j[d.]

Willelmus frater ejus tenet dim. acram terre de Ricardo fratre ejus per j ob.

Henricus le Kat tenet ij acras terre.

Ric. Mariot tenet vij acras terre per vj[d.] de J. le Mar[eschal].

Petrus Wiltam tenet unam acram.

Adam Knut tenet dim. acram.

Thomas de Alvingetun tenet dim. acram.

Elvida Schade tenet dim. acram terre per ij[d]

Philippus de Middelton tenet dim. acram terre.

Robertus serviens persone, tenet dim. acram.

Johannes atte Fen tenet dim. acram terre.

Robertus Faber tenet i. cottagium.

Radulphus le Pottere tenet i. cotagium.

Johannes le Minere tenet i. cotagium.

Adam le Minere tenet i. cotagium.

Robertus le Potere tenet i. cotagium.

Johannes Luve tenet i. cotagium.

Henricus capellanus tenet i. messuagium et viii acras terre de Willelmo le Kat et reddit Willelmo v$^{d.}$ et J. le Mareschal 2$^{d.}$, et Willelmus tenet eundem (*sic*) tenementum de J. Marchal per scutagium.

Radulphus Streyt tenet unum mess. et unam acram et reddit v$^{d.}$

Thomas Sade tenet unum mess. et iii acras de eodem Rad. et reddit v$^{d.}$; et Rad. tenet totum tenementum de W. de Lovesæ et reddit per an. v$^{d.}$ ob, et Willelmus tenet de J. de Marchal.

Johannes fil. clerici tenet 1 acram et unum cotagium de Joh. de Lem, et reddit vj$^{d.}$ et J. de Lem tenet de J. de Marchal per scutagium.

Wlvive (*sic*) Bondes tenet 1 acram terre de J. de Lem, et reddit vj$^{d.}$ et J. de Lem tenet de J. le Marchal per scutagium.

Ricardus serviens persone tenet 1 cotagium et reddit ecclesie de Hevingham per an. iij$^{d.}$ ob.

Radulphus Cappe tenet i cotagium de War. de Herford et reddit i$^{d.}$

Willelmus Veys tenet i cotagium de Will. de Ecclesia et reddit iij$^{d.}$ et Will. tenet de J. le Marchal.

Idem Willelmus de Ecclesia tenet unam acram prati de Johanne clerico et reddit viij$^{d.}$ et Johannes tenet de J. le Marchal et reddit vj$^{d.}$

Henricus de Branteston tenet unum messuagium, iiij acras et dim. terre de heredibus Henrici le Neuman, et reddit x$^{d.}$ ob. et ipsi tenent de Johanne le Marchal.

Item pater noster tenet j cotagium et j acram terre de eisdem heredibus, et dat per an. x$^{d.}$, et ipsi tenent de J. le Marchal.

Thomas Schade tenet dim. acram de eodem feodo et dat per an. j^a.

Rich. fil. Simonis tenet unum cotagium et reddit iij^d.

Alicia Guyet tenet unum cotagium et ij acras et reddit iij^d.

Willelmus Capellanus tenet unum messuagium et ij acras terre et reddit v^d. ob.

Mariota Leces tenet unum cotagium et dim. acram terre et reddit ij^d.

Wulvive (sic) Bondes tenet unum messuagium et ii acras terre et reddit vij^d.

Henricus Lante tenet unum cotagium et reddit iij^d.

Henricus Rut tenet unum cotagium et dim. acram terre de W. le Kat, et reddit v^{j}. ob.

Et Willelmus le Kat tenet eundem (sic) tenementum de Will. de Parco per eundem servicium.

Matilda Guyet tenet unum cotagium et j acram terre et reddit ij^d.

Filie Henrici le Neuman tenent vj acr. terre et reddunt vij^d.

Radulphus Goding tenet unum cotagium et dim. acr. terre et reddit viij^d.

Henricus le Blunt tenet v acras terre et redd. v^d ob.

Rich. de Pagrave tenet j acram terre et dim. et reddit 1^d. ob.

Simon le Blunt tenet dim. acr. terre et reddit 1^d. ob.

Wulvive (sic) Parker tenet unam acram et reddit 1^d.

Mirylda la Blunde tenet vj acras et reddit viij^d

Alexander de Feltorp tenet ij acras terre et reddit iij^d

Jocel[inus] Buleman tenet dim. acr. terre et reddit ij^d.

Omnes isti sub circulo scripti tenent de Willelmo de Parco per servicium subscriptum et per scutagium in cartis suis contentum, et Willelmus tenet de J. le Marchal per scutagium de feodo Guet.

[c. 1135-1145.] GRANT of EBERARD, Bp. of Norwich, to his officer PHILIP.[*]

✠ In Nomine Patris et Filii et Spiritus Sancti. Amen. Notum sit omnibus tam presentis quam futuri temporis fidelibus quod ego Ebrardus Dei gratia Norwic. Episcopus dedi et concessi prece et concessione proborum hominum meorum huic Philippo ministro meo pro servitio suo et pro dimidio marco (sic) de gersuma, in feudo et in perpetua hereditate iiii toftes (sic) terras inter Heuigham et Ripeteunam, et simul cum illis iiii. toftes lviii acras de terra lucrabili et boscum et prata atque pascua et omnia eidem terre juste appendentia. Concessi etiam ei molendinum quod fecit in prato suo de quo stagnum ligatum est in bosco meo licentia et concessione mea. Hæc omnia

---

[*] Qu. Philip, archdeacon of Norwich 1138-60?

supradicta eidem Philippo hereditarie dedi, faciendo mihi per annum v sol. de servitio. Preterea noscat dilectio vestra postea me concessise et dedisse prenominato Philippo et heredibus suis terram meam de Stratuna quam Herbertus bone recordationis Episcopus dedit Jordano cognato suo. Hoc autem feci prece et bona voluntate et concessione ejusdem Jordani per idem servitium quod Jordanus tenebat die qua Herbertus Episcopus fuit vivus et mortuus, videlicet per duos solidos per annum pro omnibus servitiis sicut carta Herberti Episcopi et carta mea, quas predictus Jordanus sua bona et spontanea voluntate liberavit Philippo, testant. Hec omnia supradicta volo et firmiter precipio ut bene, honorifice, et in pace teneat per prenominatum servitium. Et ut ista donatio rata permaneat impositione sigilli mei et nostre ecclesie sigilli confirmo. Sunt etiam testes ad hanc donationem corroborandam, Willelmus Prior et Conventus ecclesie Sancte Trinitatis, et Willelmus, et alter Willelmus, et Walkerel', Rogerus archdiaconus,ᵛ et Adam et Walterus, nep[otes] episcopi, et Toraldus et Gaifer capellani episcopi, et Johannes dapifer episcopi, et Petrus stab[ularius], et Symon de Nuers, et Rogerus de Fleg, et Gocelinus Grossus, et Willelmus de Ecclesia, et Herveus cam[erarius], et Adam dapifer, et Hugo de Blafer', et Osmundus Ruffus, et Rodbertus cocus, et Rand[ulfus] cocus, et Willelmus pistor.

[c. 1150.] GRANT by BISHOP WILLIAM TURB to HERBERT CAT.

Notum sit futuris et presentibus Christi fidelibus quod ego Willelmus Dei gratia Norwicensis Episcopus dedi Herberto Catto et Alde uxori sue, nepti mee, et heredibus suis totam terram que fuit Grimbaldi in Ripetunia, cum omnibus liberis consuetudinibus ad eandem terram pertinentibus, pro duobus solidis annuatim. Eapropter volo et precipio ut teneat ipse et heredes sui post eum predictam terram pro prefato servitio bene et in pace, libere et quiete, et in pratis et in pascuis et turbariis. Et ut hec donatio nostra firma et inconcussa permaneat sigilli nostri impositione eam confirmo. Teste (sic) Daniele Abbate de Hulmo,† Helya Priore, Johanne dapifero, Petro de Mall[ar]d, Petro constabulario, Ric. de Ferreris, Hernaldo Lupell, Turoldo capellano, Hemero presbytero, Philippo de Martham, Gwarino hostiario, Roberto Wandelardo.

[c. 1170-4.] GRANT by BISHOP WILLIAM TURB to WILLIAM CAT.

Willelmus Dei gratia Norwic. Episcopus, omnibus hominibus suis Francis et Anglis salutem. Sciatis quod ego reddidi et concessi Willelmo Catto terram que fuit Grimbaldi de feodo de Marsham, videlicet xxx acras quas pater ejusdem Willelmi Herebertus Cattus tenuit, ei et heredibus suis, tenendam de me

---

* No Roger is found in the printed lists of the archdeacons of the diocese in the time of bishop Everard.
† Died in 1153.

et de meis in perpetuum successoribus ita bene et libere et per idem servicium sicut pater suus melius et liberius eam tenuit. Volo igitur et precipio ut idem Willelmus et heredes sui habeant et teneant prefatam terram libere et quiete et hereditarie, honorifice et pacifice, per prenominatum servicium. Test : Willelmo et Staingro'ᵒ Archidiaconis, Gaufrido filio Petri dapiferi, magistro Nicholao, Roberto Crasso, Richerio de Marsham, Roberto Grisio, Johanne clerico filio Roberti, Osmundo, Ric. Daniel, Stephano Ruffo, Joscel[ino] fratre Willelmi Archidiaconi, Roberto Pincerna et Godefrido fratre suo.

GRANT of two pieces of Land by ROGER GUET of Hevingham to WILLIAM LE KAT and LAURETTA his wife, the one called Hevidlond and the other Brodlonde.

Hiis testibus : Willelmo de Parco de Hevingham, Willelmo filio suo, Willelmo de Monasterio, Willelmo et Andrea de Levishaye, Henrico de London, Nicholao et Herveo filiis suis, Willelmo de Marheshal, Johanne filio clerici, Thoma Schade, et multis aliis.

GRANT of Land by HENRY FITZ-SIMON to WILLIAM LE KAT in consideration of a "PEACE OF MAYHEM."

Sciant presentes et futuri quod ego Henricus filius Simonis de London concessi dedi et hac presenti carta confirmavi Willelmo le Kat unam peciam terre mee in campo de Dudewik jacentem super Langfurlong inter terram Willelmi Spendluue ex parte orientali et terram Hugonis del Hil ex parte occidentali, et abuttat super terram Gerard versus austrum et super terram Will. Aldman versus aquilonem. Et homagium et servicium Walteri de Mendham merkatoris quod mihi debuit per annum pro tribus peciis terre, scilicet unum clavum gariofili pro tribus peciis terre quas aliquando de me tenuit. Quarum una pecia est medietas de messuagio Alquen, et alia super Wotelond inter terram Roberti le Kniht ex parte orientali et terram Petri le Kat ex parte occidentali. Et tertia pecia in crofto quod fuit Radulfi Alyetti inter viam regiam ex parte orientali et terram que fuit Radulfi prenominati ex parte occidentali, cum releviis et eskaettis et omnibus aliis rebus que mihi accidere possent de prefato Waltero et suis heredibus. Habendum et tenendum eidem Willelmo et heredibus suis vel suis assingnatis bene et in pace in perpetuum sine aliquo seculari servicio, pro pace de mahenio formata per predictum Willelmum inter prefatum Walterum ex una parte et me et Richerum filium meum ex altera parte. Et ego Henricus et heredes mei vel assingnati mei warrantizabimus, acquitabimus, defendemus predicta tenementa et servicia cum eskaettis et releviis et aliis rebus

---

* Staingrin (*Taingrin* in Le Neve) was archdeacon of Norwich in 1174-5, in which latter year bishop William died in January ; but no William appears to be found in the lists of archdeacons of Norfolk, Suffolk, or Sudbury about that time.

inde accidentibus prefato Willelmo et heredibus suis vel suis assingnatis pro pace de mahenio facta, sicut predictum est, contra omnes homines et feminas in perpetuum. In cujus rei testimonium presens scriptum sigilli mei impressione corroboravi. Hiis testibus, Johanne de Leem, Johanne de Tudeham, Willelmo de Parco de Hevingham, Willelmo et Richero filiis suis, Henrico de Leveshaye, Willelmo et Andrea filiis suis, Reginaldo de Refham, Johanne filio suo, Willelmo de Monasterio de Hevingham, Henrico et Willelmo filiis suis, Eudone Toppais, Petro filio suo, Rogero Guet, Johanne filio Johannis clerici, Richero Streit, et multis aliis.

GRANT of VILLEINS by WILLIAM AT CHURCH to WILLIAM LE KAT.

Omnibus Christi fidelibus presens scriptum visuris aut audituris, ego Willelmus ad Ecclesiam de Hevigham salutem. Noverit universitas vestra me concessisse dedisse et hac presenti carta mea confirmasse Willelmo le Kat, de eadem, et heredibus suis de se et Laurota condam uxore sua procreatis et eorum heredibus vel asignatis (sic), corpus Johannis Popi et corpus Seyhive matris sue et corpus Cecilie filie dicte Seyhive servos meos, cum toto tenemento et tota sequela eorundem, pro vinginti (sic) solidis argenti quos michi dedit premanibus. Habendum et tenendum de me et heredibus meis illi et heredibus suis prenominatis et heredibus eorum vel asignatis in perpetuum. Reddendo inde annuatim michi et heredibus meis unum clave de gelofero pro omni servicio consuetudine et seculari demanda [etc.]. His testibus: Andrea de Branton, Petro filio suo, Roberto de Bolewik, Will. de Levishaye, Rogero de Refham, Johanne filio suo, Will. de Park, Joh. le Clerk, Will. de Thorp, Hen. de Lundune, Richero filio suo, et multis aliis.

WILLIAM LE KAT of HEVINGHAM

grants to Henry, his eldest son, his whole messuage in Marsham. Witnesses: Sir Tho. Bardolf, kt., Sir Will. de Whitwell, kt., Will. de Merceshalle, Will. de Leveshaye, John de Refham, Henry de London of Hevingham, Andrew de Braunthonne, John son of Philip de Stratehonne, John Huberd of the same, Richard Scyet, Henry de Belagh, John le Bond, Christopher de Botheby, Simon Wrantham, clerk.

Sarra, daughter of Ralph the Smith ("fabri"), of Hevingham, releases to Ralph Smith (sic) all right in the land formerly her father's in Hevingham. One of the witnesses is Walter Bukeskin, the King's seneschal at Causton, and another, Henry le Cat.

1277[-8]. Roger, bishop of Norwich, for himself and his "nativi" of Hevingham, restores to William de Parco, of Hevingham, seven acres of meadow and one of alder-wood "in stagno," of which he had been disseised by William le Kat and many others named in a writ returned before the judges at Norwich, "cujusmodi disseisine faciende quidem nativi nostri de Hevingham personaliter interfuere." Suthelmham xvij Kal. Feb. 1277.

1318. Fine for settlement of lands in Hevingham, &c., between William le Kat and Katherine his wife, and Robert Felbrigg and John his brother, comprising 83 messuages, two mills, 500 acres of land, &c.—Octave of Hilary 11 Edward II.

1359. Andrew le Smyth of Hevyngham grants to Will. Burel of Hevyngham and Andrew Huberd of Straton all his lands, tenements, and messuage, in Hevyngham and Marsham, except a small house at the east of the messuage "pertinente ad artificium fabri."—Hevingham, Monday after Purif. B.M.V., 33 Ed. III.

1371. John de Herlyngge, John de Berneye, Nicholas, parson of the church of Boton, and William Curszon release to Will. Cat and Margaret his wife their rights in Riptonhalle and Parkhalle. Witnesses : Sir Will. de Wychingham, Will. de Clere, and others. Hevingham, 45 Edward III.

1411. Robert Mauteby to Henry Katt. Covenant to settle Hevingham manor on marriage. *French.* Easter Monday, 12 Hen. IV.

1439. Deed of Henry Catt of Hevingham, reciting a feoffment of all his manors in Norfolk to William Bishop of Salisbury, by name of Master Will. Askewe, clerk, Will. Yelverton, and others, to the uses of his will ; directing the sale of certain manors for payment of debts, with gifts of residue; *inter alia*, his best Missal to his wife Dionysia for her life, afterwards to the chapel of St. Mary in the church of Hevingham for ever, or so long as the same should last.

Declaration under seal by WILLIAM [ASKEW] BISHOP OF SALISBURY about Catt's Manor of HEVINGHAM.

1442. To the Cristen people that this presente wryting see or here, I William by the grace of God Bishop of Salisbury sende gretyng in our Lord God. Inasmoche as it is said and I am enformed that Henry Catte late of Hevyngham in the county of Norff., squir, shuld have died seised in his demene as of fee in the manor of Hevyngham and other his manors lands and tenements rents and services with thappurtenances in the said county of Norff., and for as moche as it is merytory and byhofful (*behoreful*) to witnesse trouth and to put away perjurie and other perill, I by this my writyng witnesse and thus notifie that the saied Henrye the fiftene year of the reigne of our soverayne lord the King that now is, me at that tyme being person of the churche of Hevyngham aforesaid, made a lawful feoffment of the said manor and other of his said manors landes and tenementys in the said counte of Norff. to me and to William Yelverton, Robert Mortymer, and to other, and to our heires in fee for ever more, to thentent to do and performe thereof his will : and we, as commone cours is, suffered the said Henry to occupie by our suffrance all his lyve, and otherwise deyde he not seisd in his demene of fee ; and this wol I seyn and witnesse as ferre as mine estats axith or requireth, and for the more open evidence hereof to give my writyng I have sette my seall the xvii day of the moneth of Feverere, the xx yere of the reigne of King Henry the sixth after the conquest of Inglond.

1471. Will. Aynse of Hevyngham and Nicholas Lincolne of Skothowe demise to John Wotton, "jurisperito," John Abbes of Buxton, sen., and James Jurdon of the same, two messuages with closes and 14 acres of land in Hevyngham which they had by demise of John Hall of Stratton.—2 Nov. "anno ab inchoatione regni Reg. Hen. VI. 49, et readeptionis sue Regie potestatis anno primo." Witn., Rob. Brampton, Will. Vergeons, Rich. Arnold, esq., Rob. Bulley, Rob. Marsham, &c.

1479. Release by John Ryther to his son William; reciting that he held a moiety of the manors of Ripton Hall, Park Hall and Kerytoft in Hevingham, Marsham, Brampton, Stratton next Hevingham, and half the manor of Horsted, called Cattes in Horsted, for life, in right of Johanna his late wife, one of the daughters and co-heiresses of Margaret Calys sister and heiress of Henry Catte; with remainder to his said son William, heir of said John and his wife Johanna; which moiety he now releases to him.—20 May, 19 Edward IV.

1479. Edmund Auncell, of Hevingham, "husbondman," grants to Thomas Tyler and John Coduham, of the same place, five acres of land in Hevingham. Witnessed (inter alios) by "reverendo domino domino Thome (sic) Scroope, episcopo Dromorensi." 25 Aug., 19 Edward IV.

1553. James Boleyn, knight, grants by royal license to Edward Lomnour,° esq., and Thos. Payne, gent., the manors of Hevingham, Causton, Cardeston and Ryffehame, which he and his wife Elizabeth had by sale of Henry VIII., by letters patent, dated 22 March, 28th of his reign; to hold of the Queen in capite, by military service for the tenth part of one knight's fee, with the condition that they should make a recovery to the use of the said James and Elizabeth his wife and the longer liver, with remainder to the Princess Elizabeth, commonly called the Lady Elizabeth's Grace.—9 October, 1 Mary.

1550. Will of John Martyn of Hevingham. Probate, 15 March, 1555.

1557. Will of Robert Martyn, of Hevingham, and probate at Aylsham the same year.

1565. Will of John Thetford, of Heveningham, gent.

Forty-four other deeds relating to Hevingham between the reigns of Edward I. and Eliz. have been examined and summarized, and about thirty-three examined from the time of Hen. IV.

° This name is evolved from Le Mynor, through Lemynour, to Lomnour and Lumnor.

SAXTHORPE
With the MANORS of MICKELHALLE and LOUNDHALLE.

MANOR ROLLS. Between 1290 and 1623.

COURTS AND COURTS GENERAL.

Edward I. for the year 18.

Edward III. for the years 2, 6, 7, 8, 20, 22-36. For Loundhalle : 28, 30, 31, 32, 33, 34, 36-50, except 46. Copies (?) also of 41, 47, 50. (The roll for the year 2 much damaged.)

Richard II. 1-23 except 4. (The year 10 is the court of Edmund Gurney.) For Mickelhalle: 17.

Henry IV. For Loundhalle : 1-14, except 8 and 9.

Henry V. For Loundhalle : 1, 3-8.

Henry VI. For Mickelhalle : 8, 14-32, 35, 36, 37. For Loundhalle: 1-4, 7-12, 16-28, 31-32, 33, 35-38. (The year 4 is the first court of " Oldhalle and others." 6 is the first court of Sir John Fastolf and others.)

Edward IV. For Mickelhalle : 3, 5, 15, 18, 19, 21, 22.

Richard III. For Loundhalle: 1-3. For Mickelhalle: 1. For Saxthorpe : 1.

Henry VII. For Loundhalle: 1-24. For Mickelhalle: 1, 2, 6, 12, 15, 16, 18, 19, 20, 21, 23, (18, 19, 20, with Matlask). For Saxthorpe : 1, 2, 9, 10, 12, 13, 14, 17.

Henry VIII. For Loundhalle: 1-38. For Mickelhalle: 1-16 (except 3), 17, 18, 20-23, 25-28, 29. For Saxthorpe : 21.

Edward VI. For Loundhalle : 1-6.

Mary. For Loundhalle : 1 and 2 to 5-6, P. and M. For Saxthorpe : 4-6.

Elizabeth. For Loundhalle: 1-28. For Mickelhalle: 11-25. (18 is with Briston ; 19 is Sir Christopher Heydon's first Court.) For Saxthorpe: 1, 2, 3, 6, 7-17.

James 1. For Loundhalle : 15 and 18, Sir Henry Hobart's Court. For Mickelhalle : 14-20.

LEET ROLLS:—

Edward IV. for year 21. Mickelhalle with Byrsten.

Henry VII. For Mickelhalle : 6, 12, 15, 16, 17, 18, 21, 23 (18, with view of frank pledge). For Saxthorpe: 1, 2, 9 10, 12, 13, 14 (1, 2 and 14 with Briston).

Henry VIII. For Mickelhalle : 1-16 (except 3), 17, 18, 20-23, 25-29. For Saxthorpe : 21.

Elizabeth. 1, 2-18.

ACCOUNT ROLLS :—

Edward I. For Loundhalle : Provost's accounts for 25, and accounts for 31. Two fragments, *temp.* Ed. I.

Edward III. For Loundhalle: Account for 10 ; Provost's for 13 ; Bailiff's for 24 ; "Serviens" for 29 and 30.

Richard II. " Serviens " for 9 and 10.

Henry IV. For Loundhalle : Provost's (W. Skottowe) for 6.

Henry V. For Mickelhalle. Bailiff's for 20-21,

Henry VI. For Loundhalle: Bailiff's for 14, 15, 16, 17, 19,
20, 21, 23, 24, 25, 27-30, 36-37. For Mickelhalle:
Bailiff's for 18-21. For Saxthorpe: 12, 13, 25. Messor's
and Farmer's for 16. Account of John Bert, Bailiff to Sir
John Fastolf, 16, 17.
Mary. For Loundhalle: Bailiff's for 1-5, P. and M.
Elizabeth. For Loundhalle: 1-8. Sir Christopher Heydon's
Court.

Rental of Mickelhalle, of Edward Grey, Esq. Undated.

Rental of Loundhalle. Undated, *temp.* Henry III.

A very fine rental of Loundhall, *temp.* Ric. II.,° in good
preservation, entitled: "Manerii de Lound, de liberis custumariis
et nativis, termini solutionis, videlicet festis Pasche, Johannis
Baptiste, Michaelis Archangeli, et cetera. Nomina tenentium, et
cetera." Followed by particulars of 106 money rents, 54 fowl rents.
"Corpusty, Heidone, extenta eorundem; termini solutionis
redditus, videlicet fest. Purificationis, Pentecosten, S. Mich.
Archang. Nomina tenentium, &c." With particulars of 55
money rents, 16 fowl rents. Huneworth, with 6 money rents, 6
fowl rents. Memoranda as to rents payable to Dominus de
Brewse, Dominus de Valence, Dominus Ric. Nugun, and others.
Attached is an ancient list of tenements liable to the office of
messor in rotation.

Rental of Loundhalle, in the time of Joan, Countess of Hertford, daughter of Edw. I.

Summaries of Deeds.

Helvisa de Wendenval grants to Geoffrey le Cras the
land and tenement which Elgar Kide, merchant, held of her
ancestors in the vill of Saxthorp "et libere adquisivit," to
hold "ita quod non faciat venditionem terrarum nec more nec
turbarum, nec destructionem, sed accipiat ad mensuram quod ad
victum sufficiat ardendi in domo propria." After his death to
the heirs of him and his wife Elviva, daughter of the said Elgar.
Rent of 2s. 10d., quarterly, and one hen or one penny for
2 acres, of the fee of Wikemere; two shillings for scutage.
Record of homage by Geoffrey and delivery of deed sealed by
Helvisa, "pro salute anime Ruellenni fratris mei in cujus servicio
idem Galfridus multum laboravit."
Witnesses: Willam her chaplain, Ralph le Nugun, Nicholas
his son, Robert Tirel, Roger de Croft, Roger de Saule, Robert
de Kent, Simon de Crosdale, Godfrey chaplain, and many others.
Oblong seal, broken, in green wax, a fleur-de-lis; " . . . Avelise
de . . . . ."

* A faint note at the head, in a hand of late 15th cent., runs thus: "Patet esse
tempore Ric. 2 per rot. cur. in nominibus tenentium."

Ralph de Clere releases to Ranulph Fitz Robert, Lord of Lound in Saxthorp, all his right in a rent of 3s. which was paid for the submersion of his common by the mill pond of Lound Mill; also of his right of turbary in the pool beyond the old course of the river, with rights of fishery, &c. The said Ranulph grants to said Ralph de Clere half the profits of the mill of Lound, provided that he pays half the expenses and costs thereof, and that his whole suit of villeins of all the homage pertaining to his manor of Styntone grind their corn at the mill.

Witnesses: Richard de Langcroft, Ralph de Nuion, Richard his son, Ralph de Irmynglond, Godfrey de Irmynglond, Robert Parker, Adam de Aula, John Josep, Simon de Crosdale.

A copy, made probably about A.D. 1300.

Ralph de Brus, keeper of the manor of Lund in Saxthorp, grants to Sigar de Oultone, for sixteen marks, all his tenements in Iteringham (except the homages of Skut of Iteringham); also Legatemill in Saxthorp; to hold the tenement and mill of him and his heirs in fee and inheritance; rendering yearly 'de censu' 23s. and three halfpence and two capons; for the lord's aid, 14 pence to the mark, "et ad plus plus et ad minus minus," "et similiter ad omne servitium forinsecum."

Witnesses: Sir Roland de Averas, Sir Ralph de Clere, Ralph his son, Ralph de Irmigland, Richard de Nugun, William Bainard, Geoffrey de Beck "serviente domini," William Bainard, Ranulph de St. John, and all the lord's soke.

Ralph de Brus grants to Robert son of Sigar de Oweltune, for six marks of silver, all the tenement that Sigar his father held of him, as in the preceding charter.

[c. 1200-20.] Ralph de Nugun, grants to Roger son of Steingrim of Corpesti all the land which he holds of Warin de Salla in Corpesti, viz., in Mucclelund and Litelelund, for one mark and "pro uno bisantio quod dedit Sabine uxori mea," paying annually 26d. and two capons.

Witnesses: Ralph de Irmingheland, Symon son of Alan, Richard son of Nicholas, Warin de Tithebi, Benedict his brother, Robert the merchant, Richard Fitz Warin, Matthew de Storh', Adam de Aula, Everard son of Stengrim, Richard de Norwich, Everard son of Hugh.

[1252.] 36 Hen. fil. Joh. Gervase and John, sons of Roger son of Arnald, grant to Simon son of Roger de Birston all the land of Roger their father in the vill of Saxtorp, "de feodo Templi Gerosolomitani," to hold free of all secular exactions at a rent of 2s. yearly.

Witnesses: Godfrey de Irmigl[ond], Bartholomew his brother, Geoffrey son of Simon de Irmigl[ond], Ralph his son, Roger de Irming[lond], Arnald de Irming[lond], Simon de Crosedale, Nicholas Morel, Richard de la Croft, Richard the baker, Joh. Joseph, Geoffrey the smith, Robert son of Adam de Corpesti.

John son of Joseph de Saxtorp to William de Peletot. Grant of land called Marlepit, and buildings between the free land of Saxtorp church and land of Robert son of Eda de Lund.

Witnesses: Sir Nicholas de Bernigham, knight, Walter Tirel, Godfrey de Irmiglond, Bartholomew his brother, Geoffrey de Irmiglond, Ralph his son, Roger de Corpesti, Hugh his brother, Richard de Crufta, Nicholas Morel, Simon de Brisstune, Simon de Crosedale, Nicholas Cappe, Robert Coli, Geoffrey the smith. Seal.

Roger, son of the late Simon de Birston of Saxthorp, grants to Robert son of the late Robert Ode of Saxthorp, a piece of land at Saxthorp which Robert acquired from Robert Hunewyne, and two pieces which Adam son of John de Glosdale acquired from John Joseph.

Witnesses: Ralph de Hirminglond, John de Hirminglond, Roger le Cres of Saxthorp, Roger his son, John le Neuman, Simon de Crosdale, Nicholas the tanner, Robert the tanner, Luke Bate, Edmund Pilyng. Small seal.

Robert son of the late Lucy de Coventre, daughter of John de Coventre, grants to John his brother all his right in the land of his mother at Saxthorp, which she held of the lady Helewisa de Wendeval.

Witnesses: Walter Tyrel, Nicholas Morel, Simon de Birston, Simon de Crosdale, Geoffrey the smith, Ralph Mus, Richard de Croft, Nicholas Cappe, John le Quyit, Nicholas le Neuman, and William de Basingham.

John Covyn[tre], son of Lucy de Coventre of Ouletoune, grants to Robert Ode of Saxtorp, for the sum of 40s., one piece of his land lying in Saxtorp in the place called le Ride, one end abutting on the land of Sir William de Valence, "quae computatur pro quatuor acris et dim."; paying annually 2s. 3d., and 2d. for a scutage of 40s.; with power of assignment except to religious houses.

Witnesses: Walt. Tyrel, Walter his son, Nicholas Morel of Saxtorp, Simon de Birstune of the same, Roger his son, William the tanner of the same, Simon de Crosdale of the same, Geoffrey the smith, Ralph Mus of the same, Thomas de Croft of Birstonne, Nicholas Cappe of the same, Joh. Quyit of the same. Seal, a fleur-de-lis; "S' Johannis fil' Lucie de Coventre."

Odo de Peletot grants to Stephen son of Adam de Gloresdale all that messuage that was Nicholas Gibney's in Saxthorp and five acres of land which said Nicholas had in Saxthorp and Corpesty of Sir Robert Wendeval, and one piece of land which he held of Nicholas Morel, and a piece of land called Marlepit-lond which his brother William bought of John Josep, and 12d. annual rent from a cottage which Sibilla Gibny held of him in Saxthorp; "reddendo inde annuatim dominis feodi servicium sicut continetur in cartis quas habui de predictis dominis, et mihi et heredibus meis unum obolum ad festum St. Mich."

Witnesses : Walter Tyrel of Manyngton, Walter his son, Sir
William de Parc of Saxthorp, Nicholas Morel of the same, Simon
de Briston of the same, Roger his son, Robert Ode of the same,
William his son, Simon de Crosdale of the same, William the
tanner of the same, Thomas de Croft of Briston, and Nicholas
Cappe of the same.

[c. 1260-70.] William de Valence, "Dominus Panbroch',"
grants to Roger le Cras the land and tenement which his
ancestors held of the grantor's ancestors in the vill of Saxtorp,
at a rent of 2s. 10d., quarterly, and one hen or one penny for
half an acre held of his fee of Wykmere.

Witnesses : Geoffrey Scatelyn, Jordan de Sakevile, knights,
William de Saxtorp, chaplain, Walter de Bynetre, Simon de
Birston, Roger his son, Nicholas Morel, Nicholas Cappe, Robert
Ode, William his son, Ralph de Irmyngland, Geoffrey the smith,
Richard de Croft. Seal of arms ; barry of six, thereon eight
martlets : " Sigill' Will'i de Val . . . . . ."

John son of the late Lucy de Coventry grants to William son of
Rob. Ode of Saxthorp, for half a mark, 4½ acres " inter terram
Beatricis fil. Lucie versus austrum et terram Johannis fil. Joh.
Robyn versus aquilonem, et unum capud abuttat supra terram
Domini Will. de Valence et aliud super regiam viam."

Witnesses : Sir Richard de Creppingge, knight, Walter Tyrel,
Simon de Birston, Roger his son, Simon de Crosdale, Will. the
tanner, Nich. Neuman, Will. de Basingham. Seal.

John le Plomer and Agatha his wife grant to Sir Richard
de Creppyng and Margaret his wife, " pro quadam summa
pecunie," all their right and title in the Baililond in Saxthorp
"simul cum dote quando acciderit."

Witnesses : Sir John de Cokefeld, Sir Ralph de Nougoun, Sir
Roger de Wolterton, John le Pouere, Thom. de Burston, John de
Ermilaunde, Simon de Burston, Roger his son, William Ode of
Saxthorp, Thomas de Apedall, Ralph Godes, Godfrey de Brandeston.

Ralph son of the Lady Wlviva de Iteringham grants to
Gervase son of Richer Hare of Saxtorp one piece of land which
he holds of Robert Siger of Oweltune in Saxthorp, lying between
land which he holds of Sir William his brother, and the land
which the sons of Turkill hold of William son of Robert de
Iteringham, for ten shillings ; paying yearly 2d.

Witnesses : Walter Tyrel, Ralph de Irminglond, Roger his
brother, Godfrey de Irminglond, Bartholomew his brother, Richard
de Oweltune, Benedict his brother, John de Corpesti, Symon de
Crosedale, Nicholas Morel, John Joseph, Martin the clerk of
Saxtorp, Richard the baker of Corpesty. Seal, a cross ; " Sigill'
Radulfi de Hiteringham."

Simon son of Simon de Crosdale of Saxtorp grants to Godfrey
son of Ralph Totinger of Saxtorp three acres in Saxtorp for
three marks and a yearly rent of 8d. ; with power to give to
assigns, " exceptis domibus religiosis."

D

Witnesses: Ralph de Irminglond, John his son, Walter Tyrel de Manington, Walter his son, Nicholas Morel of Saxtorp, Simon de Birston, Roger his son, William son of Robert Ode of Saxtorp, William the tanner of the same, Nicholas le Neuman of the same, Robert Simenel of Irminglond. Dated Sunday after f. of SS. Peter and Paul. Seal.

[1275.] Hugh Tyrel and Matilda his wife release to Richard de Crepping, his heirs and assigns, all their right in a mill at Saxthorp called Gate mille, which they had by way of dowry on the death of Thomas Syger, former husband of the said Matilda, to hold for the lives of the said Hugh and Matilda, rendering yearly three quarters of barley as good as comes commonly to the mill; with power to seize the barley by their bailiff for the time being if in arrear for 8 days.—Saxthorp, Tuesday after f. of St. Katherine V., 3 Edw. I.

Witnesses: Ralph de Irmingland, John his son, Bawdwine de Cankewell, Hugo le Parlene, Simon de Birston, Roger his son, Roger de Crosdale, Robert Simenel, Walter de Appleby, clerk.

1277. Stephen son of Adam de Gloresdale grants to William son of Robert Ode of Saxthorp all the messuages that were formerly Nicholas Gibny's in Saxthorp, 5 acres which the said Nicholas held of Robert de Vendeual, and a piece of land called Marlepitlond, which William de Peletot bought of John Josep.

1277. Juliana daughter of Robert Tyrel of Saxthorp, widow, grants and quit-claims to Robert Ode of Saxthorp and Matilda his wife all her rights in all the tenement with the. houses, etc., that belonged to Robert Tyrel, her father, in Saxthorp, for 45s., with all liberties, etc., as contained in the charter of feoffment of Helewisa de Vendewal.—Dated Sunday before f. of St. Gregory the Pope, 5 Edw. fil. Hen. 1276[-7].

Witnesses: Sir William de Park of Saxthorp, chaplain, Walter Tyrel of Manington, Walter his son, Simon de Birston of Saxthorp, Roger his son, Nicholas Morel, William the tanner, Simon de Crosdale, Ralph Mus, all of the same, Thos. de Croft of Birston, Nicolas Cappe of the same, William de Bassingham of Manington. Seal: "S' Juliane fil' Rob' Tirel."

1299. Richard de Hertford, rector of the church of Saxthorp, grants to Simon de Creppingge, son and heir of Sir Richard de Creppingge, knight, permission to have, during his life, divine service performed in a proposed oratory or chapel near his court in Saxthorp, "per idoneum capellanum"; provided that he attend the parish church on the four greater feast days of the year, and that the offerings be paid over. Dated at Possewyk, Tuesday after the f. of St. Hilary, 27 Edw. [I].

PARDON to SIMON CREPPING by EDW. II.

1318. 1 Aug. Edwardus Dei gracia Rex Anglie Dominus Hibernie et dux Aquitanie, omnibus ballivis et fidelibus ad quos presentes litere pervenerint salutem. Sciatis quod cum Simon de

Creppingges nuper implacitasset, ut accepimus, Johannem le Neweman coram Justiciariis nostris de Banco per breve nostrum, de uno messuagio, sex acris terre, quatuor acris prati et tribus acris pasture cum pertinenciis in Saxthorp, idemque Simon coram prefatis Justiciariis nostris in curia nostra per consideracionem ejusdem curie messuagium, terram, pratum et pasturam predictam versus eundem Johannem per defaltam post defaltam recuperasset, ac postmodum idem Johannes suggerens in curia nostra coram eisdem Justiciariis quod ipse in loquela predicta summonitus, seu visus de eisdem tenementis factus non fuit, quodque tenementa illa in manum nostrum capta non fuerunt, ut est moris, breve nostrum de deceptione versus prefatum Simonem impetraverit, de qua quidem deceptione idem Simon coram prefatis Justiciariis nostris ad prosecutionem dicti Johannis convictus fuit et prisone nostre ea occasione adjudicatus, in qua sic adhuc ut dicitur detinetur : Nos eidem Simoni volentes super hoc gratiam facere specialem, perdonavimus ei id quod ad nos pertinet de imprisonamento et deceptione supradictis : Nolentes quod predictus Simon per nos vel heredes nostros, justiciarios, vicegerentes, seu alios ballivos vel ministros nostros quoscunque inde occasionetur in aliquo seu gravetur. In cujus rei testimonium has literas nostras fieri fecimus patentes. Teste me ipso apud Notingh. primo die Augusti anno regni nostri undecimo. Per ipsum Regem, nunciante magistro Thoma de Cherletone. Fragment of seal.

1312. Luke Bate of Saxthorp grants release to Sir Simon de Crepping, knight, of all actions, claims and demands which he might have against Richard de Creppinge and Margaret his wife.—Saturday after Easter, 4 Ed. II.

1319. John le Neuman of Saxthorp releases to Sir John de Merewrth, knight, and Margaret his wife, daughter and heiress of Simon de Creppingge, and to all their tenants, both free and serfs, and to Ralph Gerveys of Saxthorp, chaplain, and Reginald Fox of Corpesty, clerk, and all men whom it concerns, all actions, claims, debts and demands on account of any transgression or deception against him by the said Simon de Crepping or any in his name, for which he has recovered against the said Simon " sexcies viginti et decem libras in curia domini Regis."—Saxthorp, Sunday after Nat. of St. John Bapt., 12 Edw. fil. Edw.

1324. John le Neweman of Saxthorp releases to Sir John de Merewrthe, knight, and Marjory his wife and all their tenants in Saxthorp, Corpesti, Irminglond, etc., all actions, quarrels and demands occasioned by any transgression by them done to him in the time of Sir Simon de Crepping or after his decease.— Saxthorp, Sunday after Translation of St. Thomas the Martyr, 17 Ed. fil. Edw.

1336. Release by Reginald de Bilney of all actions and demands against Sir John Mereworth and Hugh de Derby.— Saxthorp, Tuesday before f. of St. Luke, 9 Edw. III. *French.*

1361. Indenture of grant by Sir Ralph de Cromewelle, knt., to Esmon Gurnay of the wardship and marriage of William son of William (Dautre), heir of Margaret widow of John de Mereworth, with the manor of Loundhall, for 36 marks of silver. —Westbarsham, Monday after St. John Bapt., 35 Edw. III. *French.*

1368-77. Record of Assize on a claim against Leonell Dautre and John de Bery for wrongful disseisin of Dautre's assigns at Saxthorp, showing the descent of the owner, William Dautre, from Simon Crepping through the marriage of Simon's daughter Margaret to Sir John de Mereworth.—Between 41-50 Edw. III.

"Mem. quod Edwardus Gurney anno xxxvi. E. tertii perquisivit de Radulfo Cromewell custodiam Willelmi Dawtery consanguinei Margerie Mereworth ac custodiam manerii de Saxthorp.

Mem. Johannes Gurney obiit anno ix. H. quarti et Johannes Drew super[vix]it."

1367. William Dautre grants to Ralph de Beston, parson of the church of Harpelee, Thomas de Beston, and Simon Gurwhant, the manor at Saxthorp. [This enfeoffment is defended and maintained in the preceding record of assize.]— Sauxthorp, Monday before f. of St. Katherine V., 41 Edw. III.

1372. William son of William Dautre grants and quit-claims to Thomas de Beston and Simon Gurquant, chaplain, all his right in the manor of Saxthorp called Loundhall.—West Lexham, Sunday after f. of St. Matthias, 46 Edw. III. [See the two preceding documents.]

1377. Thomas de Beeston and Simon Gurwhan, chaplain, grant to Hamon de Felton, William de Elmham, Ralph de Shelton, knts., William de Gunthorp, rector of the church of Fakenham, Edmund Gurnay, William Wynter, Clement de Bretthenham, Edmund de Clypesby, and John Gurnay, the manor of Loundhalle in Saxthorp.—Wednesday after f. of St. Agnes, 50 Edw. III.

1390. William Dautre grants to John Gurnay, John Wynter, Richard Creyke, and Simon Baret his manor of Saxthurp called Loundhalle, in exchange for the manors of West Lexham and Gurnays in Wotton, with the wards, &c. "et cum omnibus nativis et eorum sequelis," with all the appurtenances of the manor in the vills of Saxthorp, Corpesty, Irmynglond, Heydon, Bernyngham Parva, Plumstede, Briston, Eggefeld, Itringham and Honeworthe.—Saxthorp, Monday after Whitsunday, 13 Ric. II.

1391. Fine levied at Westminster before Roberd de Cherlton, Will. Thirnyng, Will. Rikhill, John Wadham and Richard Sydenham, justices, between Robert de Martham, John, vicar of the church of Saxthorp, Robert, parson of the church of Great Rakheythe, and Matthew, parson of the church of Little Rakheythe, and John de Yelverton and Margaret his wife, conveying to the four former a messuage, 50 acres of land and

2 acres of meadow in Saxthorp, for 100 marks paid to said John Yelverton and his wife. A previous fine in 14 Rich. II. had conveyed the property for 50 marks.—Octave of St. Joh. Bapt., 15 Ric. II.

1394. Simon Baret of Hecham releases to John Gurnay all his right in the manor of Saxthorp called Loundhalle which the said John Gurnay, John Wynter, Richard Creyk and the said Simon acquired from Will. Dautre.—Bakunsthorp, Monday before St. Bartholomew Ap., 18 Ric. II.

1406. Thomas Erpyngham, Robert Berneye, Ralph Shelton, knights, John Wynter and John Yelverton, demise to John Gurnay, esq., John Drewe, clerk, William Brygg and Thomas Taseburgh, the manor of Saxthorp called Loundhalle, which manor they lately had by feoffment of the said John Gurnay.— Saxthorp, Monday before Annunciation B. M. V., 7 Hen. IV.

Same date, Power of Attorney by grantors to deliver seisin.

1407. John Gurnay, John Drewe, parson of the church of Harpele, and Thomas Taseburgh grant to Robert Morle, knight, Thomas Astle, John Boson, Robert Brunham, burgess of Linn Episcopi, John Eyre of Skulthorp and John Person of Massingham 20*l.* of annual rent from their manor in Saxthorp called Loundhalle.—Saxthorp, 1 April?, ["xxxij *mensis Marcii*"!], 8 Hen. IV.

1409. Alice Gurnay, late wife of John Gurnay, releases to Simon de Felbrigge, Robert Berneye, Roger Drewry, knights, Robert Mauteby, Edmund Oldhall, Edmund Wynter, Clement Herward, Robert Wynter, clerk, and Will. Howlyn, clerk, all her right in the manor of Saxthorp called Loundhalle, which the said Simon, &c., had by feoffment of John Drury, clerk, and Thos. Tasburgh.—Saxthorp, Thursday before Nat. S. Joh. Bapt., 10 Hen. IV.

1410. Simon de Felbrigg, Robert Berneye, Roger Drewry, knights, Robert Martham, Edmund Oldhalle, Edmund Wynter, Clement Herward, Robert Wynter, clerk, and William Howlyn, clerk, demise to John Wynter, esq., and Alienora his wife the manor of Saxthorp called Loundhalle, which they lately had by feoffment of Roger Drewe, clerk, and Tho. Tasburgh, to hold to the said John and Alienora for their lives, with remainder to the grantors.—Saxthorp, Thursday in Whitsun week, 11 Hen. IV.

1412. Alice, widow of John Gurnay and of John Wynter, John Drewe, parson of the church of Harpelee, William de Snetesham, and William Morel, chaplain, execute deed of arrangement for sale of the manor of Saxthorp for payment of the debts of said John Gurnay.—Bakenesthorp, Tuesday after the week of St. Hilary, 13 Hen. IV.

1426. Clement Herward, John Grene, John Drew, clerk, and John Baxtere of Honyng appoint Nicholas Manne, chaplain,

and Walter Arnold, attorneys•to deliver seisin to William
Oldhalle, Thomas Kyngston, knights, William Alyngton of the
county of Cambridge, esq., William Fynderne, esq., W. Kynge,
chaplain, John Harleson, esq., and John Conteshale, of the manor
of Loundhalle.—31 July, 4 Hen. VI.

1428. The path called "Peddersty" and the way called
"Walsingham waye" are mentioned in a feoffment dated at
Saxthorp, St. George the Martyr, 6 Hen. VI.

1428. William Oldhalle, knt., and Thomas Kyngeston, knt.,
release to John Fastolf, knt., Henry Inglose. knt., John
Kirtling, clerk, Henry Sturmer and John Lynford, all their
right in the manor of Loundhall.—Saxthorp, 9 June, 6 Hen. VI.
Oldhall's seal, a lion rampant, remains.

1429. Edmund Wynter, esq., grants to John Fastolf, Henry
Inglose, knts., John Fastolf, esq., John Kyrtling, clerk, Henry
Sturman and John Lynford, their heirs and assigns, all his
tenement called Odes in Saxthorp and all his land in Saxthorp,
Briston, Manyngton, and Stafford Berningham, which he had
(in common with John Braunche, John Hagon and Thomas
Robyns, parson of the church of Berningham) from Thomas
Barker of Bernigham, son and heir of John Barker of Saxthorp
[by deed in 10 Hen. V.]—Saxthorp, 12 May, 7 Hen. VI.

1442. Will. Oldhall, kt., releases to John, Cardinal Archbp.
of York, John Archbp. of Canterbury, W. Bishop of Winchester,
Ralph Lord Cromwell, Ralph Lord Sudley, John Lord
Beauchamp, John Fortescue, Ch. Justice of the Common Pleas,
William Yelverton, Justice of the same, Richard Waller, esq.,
Will. Tolye, Clement Denston, Thomas Ludham, Thomas Howys,
clerks, Thomas West, esq., William Wangford, Nicholas
Gyrlyngton, William Genneye, and Thomas Grene, all his right in
the several manors and tenements formerly held by him jointly
with them under the grant of Sir John Fastolf, viz., in the
manors of Castre in Flegge by Great Yernemouth, Redham halle,
Vaux and Bosons, advowson of St. Jo. Baptist there, manor of
Hemsby, 25 marks rent of Hickling priory from Netherhall
manor, one third part of Runham manor, manor of Wynterton
called Begvyles, manor of Boyton called Pedhamhall, manor of
Mundham with the advowson of the church of St. Ethelbert,
manor of Heylesdon and advowson of the church and two
chantries there and the water mills, manor of Drayton and the
advowson, manor of Felthorp with the advowson, half the church
of Taverham, manor of Heynford with the advowson, manor of
Guton in Brandeston with the advowson, manor of Blyclyng with
the appurtenances, manor of Loundhall, in Saxthorp, with water
mill and appurtenances, manor of Tichewell with the appurtenances ; and all lands in Caistor, Great Ormesby, Scroutby, and
forty-five other places in Norfolk, tenements in Norwich, manor
of Caldecotys, and manors and lands in other places in Suffolk,
manor of Dedham, Netherhalle and Overhall in Essex with the
watermill, and the manor or messuage in St. Olaves, Southwark in

Horseydoun in Surrey, with the watermills and appurtenances, formerly Henry Yevele's, and seven houses and 25 acres of land in said parish of St. Olave, Southwark, called Dunleys. —12 Jan., 20 Hen. VI.

1442. Edmund Grey, Lord de Hastynges, Creysfford, and Ruthyn, grants to Robert Grey, esq., his manor of Saxthorp. Witnesses: John Fastolfe, Henry Ynglose, Thomas Todinam, knights.—11 June, 20 Hen. VI. Fine seal of arms.

1469. William Boleyn occurs as a witness, 9 Edw. IV.

1470. Edmund Grey, Earl of Kent, William Calthorp, knight, Henry Boteler, gent., demise to Humfrey Grey, esq., Thomas Tresham, knight, John Bellers, William Catesby, son and heir of William Catesby, knight, William Alyngton, William ffilddyngs and Everard ffilddyngs, the manor of Saxthorp with the appurtenances and advowson of the free chapel.—5 June, 10 Ed. IV.

1470. John Hunte of Burbage, co. Leicester, yeoman, releases to Humfrey Grey, esq., Thomas Tresham, knight, John Bellers, William Catesby, son and heir of William Catesby, knight, Wm. Alyngton, William ffylddyngs and Everard ffylddyngs, his right in the manor of Saxthorp and the advowson of the free chapel.—20 July, 10 Edward IV.

1472. John Paston, knight, releases to William Waynflete, Bishop of Winton, David Husbond, William Gyfford, clerk, Thomas Danvers, William Danvers, and Richard Burton, all his right to the manors of Heynford, Saxthorp, etc., formerly John Fastolf's, knight.—10 April, 12 Edward IV.

1472. Will. Wayneflete, Bishop of Winton, Thos. Ursewyk, knight, Chief Baron of the Exchequer, John Say, knight, David Husbond, William Gyfford, John Nele, William Tebard, Richard Bernes, Stephen Tyler, clerks, Thomas Pounde, Thomas Danvers, William Danvers and Richard Burton, demise to John Morton, John Selot, clerks, John Heydon, Hugh Fenne, Henry Heydon, John Fyncham, Richard Southwell and Thomas Brampton, the manor of Loundhall in Saxthorp and all the lands formerly John Fastolf's, and also all the lands, etc., formerly Alienora Wynter's, which they had by demise of Robt. Anketell and Nicholas Westcote.—10 May, 12 Edward IV.

1472. William Paston, esq., reciting the seisin of Wm. Waynflete, Bishop of Winton, and his co-feoffees of the manor of Loundhall and the land late Sir J. Fastolf's, and their demise of the same to John Morton, John Selot and others, releases all his right in the said premises to Sir John Morton, etc.— 1 July, 12 Edward IV.

1472: Similar release from Sir John Howard, Lord Howard, William Yelverton, knight, Thomas Littleton, one of the Justices of the King's Common Bench and Wm. Genney, Sergeant-at-law. —1 July, 12 Edward IV.

1473. William Gurnay, esq.,·releases to John ·Morton, John Selot, clerks, John Heydon, Hugh Fenne, Henry Heydon, Richard Southwell, esqs., all his claim in the manor of Lound Hall, with the lands, etc., formerly Sir John Fastolf's.--14 Jan., 12 Edw. IV.

1474. William Yelverton, knight, grants to Robert Wyngfeld, knight, Thomas Brewes, knight, William Yelverton, esq., son of the said William Yelverton and the lady Ela his late wife, Robert Brewes, jun., William Wayte and John Motte all his messuages, lands and tenements in Saxthorp and Irminglond.—27 Dec., 14 Edw. IV.

1547. Fine between Richard Heydon and Rowland Shakerley and Anna his wife, and Robert Bedyngfeld, deforciant, conveying to the said Robert the manor of Micklehall in Saxthorp, with 30 houses, 20 tofts, 300 acres of land, 40 acres of meadow, 100 acres of pasture, 20 acres of wood, 500 acres "camporum et bruarium," and the advowson of the free chapel of St. Dunstan in Saxthorp.—15 days after Easter, 1 Ed. VI.

[1549.] Sept 26, 3 Edw. VI. Sir Thomas Woodhous, of Waxham, knt., conveys to Christopher Heydon, esq. "totam illam nuper capellam S. Dunstani in Saxthorp, et totum scitum ejusdem nuper capelle, et omnes illas decimas garbarum, granorum, bladorum, lane, agnellorum, et feni, et alias decimas quascunque annuatim ut de tempore in tempus crescentes, provenientes, sive renovantes, in villa et campo de Saxthorp predicta, modo vel nuper in tenura sive occupatione Anthonii Temple, dicte nuper capelle S. Dunstani in Saxthorp predicta dudum spectantes et pertinentes." Recites a grant from the Crown of 29 Sept. in the previous year of the Chapel to Sir Thomas Woodhous. With seal and signature.

[1553.] March 31, 7 Edw. VI. Building lease from Sir Christopher Heydon, knt., to William Empson, of Saxthorpe, miller, of Lound Mill, for 21 years, at sixty shillings a year; the said lessee to " mak, frame, sett up, and fynyshe one watremylle with all things necessarye in all purposes for the goyinge of a corne mylle or fullers mylle, in the place where the olde fullynge mylle was sometyme edyfyed at Lounde Wood in Saxthorpe, and also that he the same Wyllym shall repare and make the dammes and cawnses, and repare and amende the olde mylle hous now ther edyfyed."

Bailiff's covenant with SIR JOHN FASTOLF for farming the manor. [Hen. VI.]

"This Indenture made at Castre the 15 day of August wytnesseth that John Bert baily of Saxthorp hath made covenant·wyth John Fastolf knyth that he at the said Sᵣ John Fastolf's costages shall done erye sowe and harwyn at Saxthorp lxx [acres] of divers cornes, that is to sayn xl acres of ote xx acres of barley x acre of pesen, which shall ben in due and sesonable tyme, the said John Bert takyng for erying and

sowyng and harwyng of yche acre of ote x^d, for yche acre of
barly at all erthes cutte thereof 2^s 2^d, and for yche acre of
pesyn at the sowyng and harwyng thereof ix^d, and the said
Sir John Fastolf wyl and graunteth that en cas the said John
Bert may lete sufficient ferme these said landis or part thereof
that he þanne for as many londes as he so leteth xal ben
discharged of the saith earth and sowyng; and if there be mo
londes in the said Fastolf is hands the said John Bert graunteth
to erye and sowe them under the same ferme.

(*Endorsed*.) Item, the said John Bert shal kepe and answer of
covynet partriches and fesaunts within the wareyn of Eynford
and Saxthorp, so that no defaute may be found in hym by the
hommages of the lordshepes."

Many other deeds relating to lands here have also been
examined and summarized, viz. :—

Nine *temp*. Edw. I.
Fifteen *temp*. Edw. III.
Sixteen *temp*. Rich. II.
Eight *temp*. Hen. IV.
Eight *temp*. Hen. V.
Three *temp*. Hen. VI.
Eight *temp*. Edw. IV.
Three *temp*. Hen. VIII.
Seven *temp*. Edw. VI.
One *temp*. Mary.
Three *temp*. Eliz.
Two *temp*. James I.

TINTERN ABBEY.

1513, March 10. Grant from Abbot Thomas and the Convent
of St. Mary of Tinterne to Henry Palmere, of Moughton, of
twenty-six acres of land, a piece of water called *The Pounds*, etc.,
at Acle, at an annual rent.

St. MARY'S ABBEY, YORK.

1513, Oct. 16. Letter of Proxy from Edward [Whalley]
Abbot of St. Mary's, and the Convent, to John Diatson, Prior
of their cell of Romburge in the diocese of Norwich, John
Longe, M.A., and Robert Burghe, Proctor General of the Consistory of Norwich, to appear on their behalf before the Bishop
of Norwich, his commissaries and delegates, in all matters connected with the cell.

1563-1567. A bundle of papers relating to an arbitration
by Thomas Gawdy and John Blennerhasset on a difference
between William Blennerhasset and Sir Richard Southwell as
to the partition of certain rights under a joint lease of Horsford
Park. The correspondence contains several letters of Sir
Richard Sackville, P.C., the father of Thomas Sackville, Earl of
Dorset.

1526. Will of Helen Carter, of Horsham.

"In Dei nomine Amen. I helyn Carter, widow, of Horsham
Saint Fethes, beyng in my good mynde this 30' day of August
in the yere of our Lord God MCCCCXXVI thus order my will.
Inprimis I commende my soul to Almyhte God, to Our Lady
Saint Mary, to the virgin and martyr Sente Feyth and all the
holy company of hevn, and my body to be buried in a covenient
place there as it shall please master prior of Sant Feythes or my
son Dawne John Carter to doo, to wit I leve and bequeath to
Master Prior of Sant Feythe and to Dawne John Carter my son
all my goodis movable and unmoveable upon this condition that
they dispose my said goodis in the manner following : First I
will that the said M. Prior and my son Dawne John Carter shall
kep me with my own goods unto the tym of my dethe, and
afterwards I dispose it to the most pleasure of God as follweth,
Item I will that all the profyghts of my tenement lying in the
parish of Saint Olave within Noruich remain to Dawne John
Carter my son for the term of his life soe that he offer every
fridaie in the year on penye, and after his decease I will it shall
remayne to the said prior and convent, as makith mention in a
deed of gift indented which remayneth with them. Also I will
that my tenement with the appurtenances thereto belonging
lying in the parish of Horsham foresaid remayn to the said
John my son for the term of his life so that he syng every yer
by the space of xx yeares or cause to be song Seynt Gregorys
trentall, and after his decease the said trentall to be song amongst
the brethren of the said place for the said term afore rehersed,
and so after the said term to remayn to Geoffrey Hagon and his
asseyns paying the some of ten pounds to my said son as is
before rehersed. Also I bequeth to the church of Horsham
Seyne Feythes one acre and half of free land lying in the field of
Seynte Feythe foresaid to thentent that the churchwardens of the
said churche shall find reparation of the crosse being in the
churchyard of Horsham newly edified by me. All the residew
of my goods nott bequethed I putt to the good disposition of
Daun John Carter be the licens of master prior and Robert
Warden, worstedman, of Noruyche foresaid, and I pray master
supprior of the said monastery to be my supervisor of this my
former and last will. These being witnesses, Raff —— (illegible)
and John Collett of the same town.

Also I will that Alice Parkes alias Saker have my said
tenement in the parish of Saint Olaves foresaid to ferme by the
space of lx yeares, according to an indenture and the obligation
made to the said helyn and to her assignes or her certain
attorney.

[Endorsement.] Be it remembered that I the said Daune John
Carter within Noruich have reseyved for my modyrs goodys Helen
Carter wyth in Norwich xlli., That ys to say for all the stuff of
howyssholde and all other utensyll be langyn to the same Helen.
Also here followeth the expenses. I the said Daun John Carter
disposyd for my said modyr at my own meynde without any com-
maundment of my said modyr, In primis, for hyr beryall govyn

in elmess xxx*s*. Item govyn to the prior and to the convent for her beryall x*s* . Item govyn for her vii[th] day kept at ye parish church xl[d] . Item for her xxx[th] day spent in elmess in ye said parish xxxiii*s* & 4[d] . Item hyr grave light the space of a yer or more vi*s* & viii[d]. Item the grave stone lyging upon her, at the monastery xlv*s*. viii[d]. Item her crosse in the said parish church yeerde iiii*li*. Item for her twelvemonths day pore folkys xii[d]. Item paye for the Probate of this Elens wille xiiii*s*. Item to Robert Wardon for holping of ministratyon, iiij*e*. Item for hyer beryall cloth called an herse cloth xiiii.[s.] Item ye latyn plate of her obite day in the monastery . . . viii*s* . . . . in any wyse said Robert Warden kepe the seyd will term of his life . . . . . Indenture of thre parts, on for the convent, anodyr for the parish church, the third for Alice Parker, and after the said Robertes deceas to be delivered on to the supprior of the monastery the supervysor of the said will to remain in a common coffyr of theyrs, that the said M. Prior and covent and the foresaid parish church may have ther bequests that the said Elen gave them by this present testament.

Summa totalis expensarum per me Joh. Carter xii*li*. xii*s*. iiii[d]."

LANGLEY ABBEY.

MANOR ROLLS. Between 1265 and 1648.

COURTS AND COURTS GENERAL (no Court Lete occurs) for the years :—

Henry III. 49.
Edward II. 16-20.
Edward III. 1-49.
Henry IV. 49.
Henry V. 1-9.
Henry VI. 31-39.
Edward IV. 1-3, 5, 8, 9, 12, 14, 15, 16, 18, 20, 22.
Richard III. 2. Also extracts.
Henry VII. 1, 2-18, 20, 23, 24 ; and for Carleton Bastewyk, 1. Also extracts.
Henry VIII. 1, 8-13, 30-35. For Carleton Bastwyk, 21, 23, 24. Also a bundle of extracts.
Edward VI. 3-7. Also extracts.
Mary. A bundle of extracts.
Elizabeth. 2-44 (some in draft). 9-10 is the first court of Richard Barney, with roll of tenants having rights of common on Lang Marshe. There are also a number of drafts relating to Richard Barney's rights in the manor. Also a bundle of various extracts.
James I. 1-5, 14-22. The latter are the courts of Sir Henry Hobart. Also a bundle of extracts.
Charles I. A bundle of extracts.

BAILIFFS' ACCOUNT ROLLS, between 1461 and 1608 :—

Edward IV. 1-8 (7-8 a copy ?)
Henry VIII. The Collector's account for 2 October, 28
(1537, the year of the Dissolution). Also an extract for 29.
Elizabeth. 26-45.
James I. 1-5.

1289. Extent and Rental of the Abbot's Manor of Langley,
17 Edw. I. Parchment; a fine folio volume, in excellent condition ; ff. 81.

"Extentum de manerio de Langele cum omnibus pertinentiis
suis ut in villis de Laungele, Hardele, Chategrave, Thurtone et
Bergh ac Carletune," made in 1288-9, in the time of abbot Adam
de Phileby, "per manum fratris Ricardi de Hanewrth, ejusdem
monasterii canonici."

On eight leaves at the beginning of the volume are these
miscellaneous entries :—1. Rents belonging to the office of
sacrist. 2. Full description of all the marshes belonging to
the abbey. 3. Tithes of Langley in Hardele. 4. "Noticia
diversarum aquarum jacentium apud mariscum de Lynes."
5. Writ dated 6 July, 2 Hen. IV., to abbot John to restore land
to Henry Inglose, esq. 6. Grant by abbot Nicholas of land to
Denis Wylles, 21 Hen. VI. 7. Particulars of lands in Hardele,
Langmershe, &c., with the free tenants in Hardele. 8.
"Extente herbagii in Chattgrave et Hardele pertinencia ad
manerium Grange." 9. "Rentale Johannis filii Thome Berneye,
militis, de manerio suo in Norton juxta Hekyngham." 10. Plea
at the assizes at Great Jernemuth, 49 Edw. III., in a case against
Sir Thomas de Verney, knt., and Nicholas Hardhend for unjust
disseisin of Katherine who was the wife of John de Berney.
11. Note of land held by Thomas de Berney, knt. 12. Note of
homage made to abbot Ralph at Hekyngham, 12 July, 28 Edw.
fil. Hen. 13. Rents acquired by the abbot from Sir John
Reveshale, knt., 5 Edw. II.

The personal services rendered by the tenants are very fully
set out in the Rental. Of these the following extract relating to
one holding affords a sufficient specimen.

" Galfridus Griel qui est quinque akering tenet de villenagio
Abbatis et conventus septem acras et unam rodam, quarum
duæ acræ et dimidia, in quibus continetur messuagium suum,
jacent in crufta sua inter cruftam quæ fuit de domo Pres et
Thome Bigot. Et debet operari annuatim pro tenemento suo
videlicet a festo S. Mich. usque ad festum S. Martini, per sex
septimanas, duodecim dimidios dies a mane usque ad nonam,
sine cibo ; prec. cujuslibet diei unius oboli. Et a festo S.
Martini usque ad Natale Domini, per sex septimanas, sex
dimidios dies a mane usque ad nonam, sine cibo ; prec. diei ut
supra. Non debet operari in prima septimana Natalis Domini.
Et a Circumcisione Domini usque ad festum Sancte Crucis in
Maio, per septendecim septimanas, septendecim dimidios dies, a
mane usque ad nonam, sine cibo ; prec. diei ut supra. Et a

festo Sancte Crucis predicto usque ad festum Johannis Baptiste, per octo septimanas, sexdecim dimidios dies a mane usque ad nonam, sine cibo; prec. diei ut supra. Et a festo Sancti Johannis Baptiste usque ad gulam Augusti, per quinque septimanas, decem dies integros, sine cibo; prec. cujuslibet diei unius denarii. Et a gula Augusti usque ad festum Sancti Michaelis, per octo septimanas, viginti quatuor dies integros, sine cibo; prec. diei cujuslibet trium obolorum. Qui quidem viginti quatuor dies accipiendi sunt circa blada secanda et colligenda, mediante equitate et justicia, ne nimis cito accipiantur. Et debet facere tres dies integros precarios in autumpno, cum uno repastu quolibet dierum; prec. diei unius denarii. Et debet arare cum una caruca integra a festo Sancti Martini usque ad Natale Domini qualibet quindena unam arruram; prec. cujuslibet arrure duorum denariorum et oboli. Et a Circumcisione Domini usque ad festum Sancte Crucis in Maio, per septendecim septimanas, qualibet quindena unam integram arruram; prec. unius arrure trium denariorum et oboli.

Si autem Prior et conventus in festo Sancte Crucis predicto non plene perseminaverint set necessario oportet ipsos uberius seminare, si seminaverint ultra dictum diem Sancte Crucis per unam septimanam, tunc faciet unam dimidiam arruram, et habebit in predicta dimidia arrura allocationem unius dimidii diei de minutis operibus suis. Sed ista ultima arruera non ponitur ad precium cum ceteris arruris quia raro accidit. Et debet facere unum averagium per annum usque Riveshal ut alibi ad tot leucas; prec. averagii duorum denariorum. Sed in faciendo dictum averagium habebit allocationem unius diei dimidii, qui valet obolum. Et sic averagium in se valet tres obolos. Et debet averagiare per aquam quotiens turnus ad eum venerit, sed habebit ea quæ sibi necessaria fuerint in cibo et potu. Et cum redierit et si super averagium per septimanam aut amplius moram traxerit, habebit allocationem unius diei aut dimidii tunc secundum diversitatem temporis anni. Et debet falcare in majori prato cum uno homine, et habebit cibum suum, videlicet unum repastum tunc. Et debet colligere et cassare in eodem prato cum uno homine sine cibo; prec. falcationis et cassationis unius denarii. Et debet unam gallinam ad Natale Domini, prec. unius denarii, et septem ova ad Pascham, prec. unius quadrantis. Et faciet tres cumbos brasii vel dabit duos denarios."

The last eight leaves are a cartulary for Langle, Hardele, Lodnes, and Nortun, and on the reverse of the last leaf is the descent of the family of Roger Fitz Roger the founder.

MISCELLANEOUS DEEDS.

1535. Extent of Langley Manor, and Copy of Roger Berney's Voucher to purchase the Manor from the King's Commissioners 27 Henry VIII.

1537. Patent of grant of Langley Abbey. 28 Henry VIII. (27 Jan.)

1576. A Draft Rental, 18 Eliz.

A number of 16th century Rentals.

Boundaries of Gilbert's land ? *Temp.* James I.

Extent and Rental of Roger Berney's manors of Chetgrave, Langley, etc. (undated). ·

A book containing copies of deeds, extents and rolls of the manor of Carleton Bastwyks, Banyards, etc.

There are between forty and fifty other Deeds relating to Langley from the time of Edw. II. to 1696.

A large and very minute map, on paper, of all the lands of the manor of Langley; *temp.* Charles I. (The watermark on the paper is a flower-pot with a crescent above ; this is found used from about 1630 to 1645.)

DISPUTED RIGHT of a PARISHIONER to ATTEND HIS PARISH CHURCH.

1603. "Dr. Redmayne's letter in the behalf of Burgh parish against Langley" (endorsement). Directed "To his lovinge freinds Mr. Cooe, parson of Burrough Castle, and to Mr. Butts, vicar of Langley." "Whereas the Inhabitants and dwellers in Ravenshall in Norff. have by the space of threescore yeares, or thereabouts, repayred upon Sabboth Dayes, ffestivall dayes and other tymes appointed for publique prayer by the lawes and statutes of this realme of England to the parishe churche of Burrough Castle, and not to the parishe churche of Langly, being distant from Ravenshall by the space of viii miles, and the inhabitants in that howse have by the tyme before mencioned receyved the sacraments in the parishe churche of Burrough Castle aforesaid, and ther' paid their offeringes and oblacions, and performed all other sacramental rites : And for that, the premisses notwithstanding, Edmond Gedge the now fermer or dweller in the said howse is lett and hindered by the needlesse contention of you and pretensed claim that you do make, to have him your parishioner to heare Devine service in the parishe church of Burrough Castle° as I am informed : theis are to require you without further disturbance to permitt and suffer the said Edmond and his famelye to repaire and resorte to the parishe churche of Burrough Castle aforesaid upon Sabboth dayes and holye dayes and at other tymes appointed for publique prayer by the lawes of this realme untill you shall by due course of lawe prove and evict him for your parishioner ; and further to require you the parson of the churche of Burrough Castle aforesaid to admitt him the said Edmond and his famely, without sufferinge the churche of Burrough Castle aforesaid beinge in possession of him to be dispoyled in that behalfe without lawfull and due proofe made by the parson or vicar of Langley in that behalfe required : And so I bid you farewell : Norwiche, this xiiij of March, 1602.

Your very lovinge freind,
R̂[OBERT] REDMAYNE."

° [*Read* Langley ?]

WYMONDHAM.

MANOR ROLLS. With the various MANORS of GRESHAUGH (or GREISHEIGHE), CROMWELLS, BARNAK, SUTTON, SILFELD, WATTELFELD, NORTON, RUSTEYNS, and KNYVETTS. Between 1272 and 1664.

COURTS, COURTS GENERAL AND COURTS LETE for the years :—

Edward I. 1-35.

Edward II. 1, 2, 4, 6-20, except 15. (2 is the first court of Joan de Tateshall; 4, the first court of Thomas de Cailly; 12, of Robert de Ufford ; 19 and 20, the courts of Joan de Driby, all in Wymondham Manor.)

Edward III. 1-9, 10, 12, 14, 17, 19, 21-28, 30, 33-51. (41 is the court of Ralph Crumbwell at Wymondham ; 48 is the first court of John Clyfton at Old Bukenham.)

Richard II. 1-10, 13-18, 20, 21.

Henry IV. 1-14.

Henry V. 1-10.

Hen. VI. 1-38. Year 12, for Wymondham, contains a copy of writ to the Escheator to give seisin to John, son and heir of Constantine Clyfton, of all the lands and tenements that Margaret, the widow of Constantine, had in dower and otherwise to the end of her life. 27 is the first court of the feoffees of Sir John Clyfton, R[oger] Lord Say, Andrew Oyard and others.

Edward IV. 1-22. 16 is the first court of William Knyvett and Joan his wife, daughter of Humphrey, Duke of Gloucester, for Wymondham and Wymondham Gryshaugh.

Richard III. 1, and various other rolls.

Henry VII. 3-13, 24.

Henry VIII. 1-28, except 11.

Mary. 1; and Philip and Mary. 1.

Elizabeth. 1-21, 30, 31, 34, 35, 37, 38, 39, 40. 12 is the first court for Gryshaugh of Roger Woodhouse, executor of the will of Thomas Knyvett, knight. 30-31 is the first court of Thomas Lovel, Francis Woodhouse, Philip Audeley, esquires, inquisitors of the manor of Wymondham under a settlement on Thomas Knyvett and Katherine his wife and their heirs. 39 is the first court of William Downs for Wymondham Gryshaugh.

James I. 1-22. 8 is the first court of Philip Knyvett for Grysaugh Knyvette. 9 is View of Frankpledge.

Charles I. 6-33, 1651-1664. 7 is for Wymondham Regis. For Wymondham Cromwells in 1651-1661 the courts are those of Lady Frances Hobart.

BAILIFFS' and PROVOSTS' ACCOUNT ROLLS, between 1281 and 1564:—

Edward I. For the years 9, 12, 13, 14, 18, 19, 22, 23, 24.

Edward II. 6, 7, 10, 15, 19.

Edward III. 1-9, 11, 12, 14-17, 24-27, 32, 34, 36-38, 41-50 (except 44). Ralph Lord Cromwell occurs as Lord of the Manor for the years 16-17, 45-48. There are "*Serviens*" Accounts for 4-5, 31-32; and an audit of Bailiff's Accounts for 26.

Richard II. 1-22. 1-2 are the accounts of the Receivers and Bailiff of John de Clyfton. In 8 and 9 Richard Kette is Provost for Wymondham. For 18 and 19 there are the accounts of the Receivers of Constantine de Clyfton for Wymondham manor. For 20 and 21 those of the Bailiff of Gilbert Talbot for Wymondham Grisaugh. For 21 and 22 those of the receipts in Lord Cromwell's manor following the date of the death of the lord. For 22 and 23 the Court is that of Lady Matilda Cromwell, of Tatishall. There are Messors' accounts for Sutton, Silfeld, Wattelfeld and Norton for the years 2-16, 21 and 22, and "*Serviens*" for 18 and 19.

Henry IV. 1-14, except 12. In 3 and 4 J. Parker acts for William Hervy, Provost of Wymondham Manor. In 8 a Deputy Provost acts for Elizabeth Sporell, also of Wymondham. In 5 Hugh Kette is Provost for Wymondham. There are Messors' accounts for Silfeld, Sutton, etc., 1-12.

Henry V. 1-8, except 6. 4 is for Bokenham Castle. There are Messors' accounts for Silfeld, etc. 2-10, except 6. John Hardenheth is Messor.

Henry VI. 1-38, with a few exceptions. There are Farmers' accounts for 27, 28, 36, 37. Messors' for 1-38, with a few exceptions. "Officium receptoris in com. Norff.": An account of manors, lands, tenements, and other possessions of Ralph Lord Cromwell for the years 9-10, 16-17.

Edward IV. 1, 2, 3, 10-20, except 19. There are Messors' accounts, 10-20, except 19.

Richard III. 1 and 2 for Bailiff's, Messor's and Market account.

Henry VII. 1-14, 17-18, 22-25. There are the accounts of Bokenham Castle for 3-4; of the Market Bailiff for 4-7, 9-10, 15, 16, 21, 22; of the Messor for 1-25, (3-24 is '*ex parte* Fitzwilliam'). The Woodman's accounts also occur for 12-25.

Henry VIII. 1-3, 7-10, 12-24. Also various accounts on paper.

Mary. Philip and Mary. 1-5. Also Provost's accounts for 4 and 5 for Rusteyns, Calthorp, Gunvile manor.

Eliz. 1 and 6.

James I. Various officers' accounts on paper from Henry VIII. to James I.

Miscellaneous Documents and Deeds.

A bundle of old Rentals, mostly undated. One of 19 Edward I. (1291) contains a return of the proceeds of a sale of oak timber.

An ancient extent, undated.

Rental (containing 16 leaves), *temp.* Edward III.

1399. An extent and customary of Wymondham Grisaugh. 1 Henry IV.

Another, undated, of Gresaugh and Norton.

1400-1. Rental and Customary of Wymondham Grysheigh; and Rental and Customary of Wymondham 'Crunqwelle.' 2 Henry IV.

1423. Sir Ralph Cromwell's Rental and Customary of manor of Rokels Lyttebar. (10 ?) Henry V.

1454. Extract of Ralph Cromwell's will.

1515. Rental for Wymondham Rusteyns. 6 Hen. VIII.

An abuttal of lands in Wymondham, with a Pedigree of the family of Barnard, *temp.* James I.

A rental of Wymondham Grisaugh and Norton, *temp.* James I.

1624, 4 Aug. A list of accounts and documents.

1638, 10 Oct. Finding of the jury as to Wymondham Common.

Five other deeds, Henry VI.—Eliz. One of 7 Eliz. is a release from John Flowerdew of Hethersett and his sons of their moiety of Wymondham Cromwelle to Edward Clere.

AGREEMENT between HUMFREY BOURGCHIER and JOHN KNYVET for assistance to the latter in recovering the MANOR of WYMONDHAM.

1457. " This Indenture the xviii. day of November the year of the reigne of King Henry the Sixt xxxvj, betwixt Humfrey Bourgchier, son of Lord Bourgchier, of the one part, and John Knyvet, cosyn and heir to John Clyfton, knight, on the other part, wytnesseth that the same Humfrey shall be good maister and frend to the said John Knyvet and support hym as far as the lawe will, and help him to recover all the manor, londes, and tenements in the Counti of Norfolk, the which were late the said John Clyfton knight, and of the which the said John Clyfton died seised; whos heyre the said John Knyvet is, that is to say sone to Elizabeth suster to the said John Clyfton knight, as it apperith of record in the chaunncerie be an office founde befor sertain commyssioners by vertue of a comyssion in nature of a *diem clausit extremum* to them direct, and forasmuch as the said John Knyvet is cousin to Johane the wyffe of the said Humfrey, the said Humfrey graunteth to the said John Knyvet that he shall bere and pay to the said John Knyvet as moch sylver as shall grow to the third part of the reasonable costys to the recovery of the said livelode, and that as well the counsel of the said Humfrey as the counsell of the said John Knyvet shall be helping, consorting and assisting to the recovery of the said livelode on assent whan they therto ben reasonable required, and that the said Humfrey or his servauntes or other persons for him shall ride and goo wit the said John Knyvet for the expedition of the said recovery when thei shall be required thertoo conveniently reasonable, as law will, consideryng the said cosenage between the said parties had. And the said John Knyvet bi theis presents willeth and graunteth that he within iii yere imediately folowing after the recovery of the said livelode bi his dede under his seal of armys, or ellys under the selys of his feffes if ony, be enfeffed in the two parts of the manor of Wymondham, and shall make or do to be made a sufficient seur and a lawful estate of and upon the said two partes of the said manor of Wymondham in the Counti of Norfolk to the said Humfrey, and to the said Johane his wyff: To have and to hold the said 2 parts of the said manor to the said Humfrey and Johane for term of both their lives, the remaynder therof to the said John Knyvet and to his heyres of his body lawfully begotten, and for defawte of the issue of them the remaynder ther of to the right heyres of the said Humfrey and Johane and ther bodies lawfully begotten and to ther heyres. Moreover the said John Knyvet willeth and graunteth and be the present writing assenteth that the said Humfrey imediately after that the said John Knyvet hath recovered the said livelode, shall resseyve and take all the issues profits and comodities of the said 2 partes as his owen proper godes with ought account gevyng to the said John Knyvet or to his executor. In the wytnesse wherof the parties aforesaid to these Indentures interchangeable have sette ther seales. Given the day and year above rehersed."

VARIOUS MANORIAL RECORDS.

KESWICK.*

MANOR ROLLS.

ACCOUNT ROLLS, between 1302 and 1500 :—

Edward I. Accounts for the years 30-31.

Edward II. Provost's accounts for the years 2 and 3. Messor's for 6 and 7. Servant's for 13 and 14.

Edward III. Accounts of corn and stores to the end of the year 4. Accounts for 19-20, 30-31, 41, 42, 44-50.

Henry VI. Farmer's accounts for the years 1-2, 35-36. Bailiff's for 23 and 34 for Freethorp Manor. Accounts for Keswick, Rusteyn, Raynesthorp and Tacolveston, years 33, 34.

Edward IV. Farmer's accounts for the years 7-8, 12, 17, 21-22. Bailiff's and farmer's for Rusteyns Manor for 16 and 17.

Richard III. Farmer's for the years 2 and 3.

Henry VII. Farmer's for the years 4-6, 8-11. Bailiff's for Freethorp Manor for 9 and 10. For Rusteyns Manor for 14 and 15.

---

* Keswick occurs as Kestwyk, *temp.* Edw. I,

MISCELLANEOUS.

Henry III. or Ed. I. A rental (in French), with endorsement by Ralph de Vaux, remitting talliage to his native tenants, they being bound in return to distribute a certain quantity of bread yearly to the poor.

6 Hen. IV. An audit of certain accounts with the lady of the manor.

A bundle of four deeds, the first, undated, being a grant from Alexander son of Alexander de Waus (Vaux), to his brother Ralph, Rector of the church of Keswyk, of one messuage, with two houses, &c., in Keswyk: witnesses, Ralph de Tyvill and others; two releases by John de Vaux, *temp.* Edw. I.; and a release by Peter, son of William le Monk of Gouthorp.

1-2 Henry VI. A list of rolls and accounts, with a copy of a writ summoning the Justices to Thetford "for the correction of such offences and riotes as of late have been doone in our citee of Norwyche."

There are also other deeds relating to land in Keswick: five *temp.* Ed. I., one of Ed. II., five of Edward III., one of Richard II., three of Henry IV., two of Henry V., three of Henry VI., and three of Edward IV.

AYLSHAM° AND AYLSHAM LANCASTER.

MANOR ROLLS. Between 1450 and 1610.

COURTS, COURTS GENERAL AND COURTS WITH LETE:—

Henry VI. 28-39.

Edward IV. 1-23. (The 5th year is the 1st Court of the Excellent Lady Elizabeth, Queen of England. The 8th year is the "Turn" of the Chief Steward, Lord Scales.)

Richard III. 1-2.

Henry VII. 1-24.

Henry VIII. 1-38. (Courts "Domin. Regis Ducat. sue Lancastrie,"—with and without view of Frankpledge and Lete. In the 28th year Henry is first styled Supreme Head of the English Church.)

Edward VI. 1-7.

Mary. 1-2. Philip and Mary. 1-6. (3-4 is for Aylsham Lancaster.)

Elizabeth. 1-43 for both manors. There is View of Frankpledge with Courts Baron.

James I. 1-7.

RENTAL.

1631. A rental of Aylsham Lancaster.

---

* Aylsham occurs as Aylysham *temp.* Hen. VIII. and Ed. VI. and as Ailesham *temp.* Elizabeth.

. INTWOOD.

Manor Rolls.

Courts and Courts Lete, between 1274 and 1509 :—

Edward I. 2 and 3.
Richard II. 17, extract.
Henry V. 9 and 10.
Henry VI. 1-18, 20, 28-35, 38, 39, 41.
Henry VII. 1, 3, 4, 7, 8, 9, 10, 12, 13, 18, 21, 24. (1 is the
1st Court of Catherine Jenny, widow. 12 is the 1st Court
of William Jenny, sen.)

Provosts' and Bailiffs' Account Rolls, between 1335 and 1603 :—

Edward III. 8 and 20.
Henry VII. 35-36 (with Mulbarton).
Elizabeth. 23, 24-29, 30, 32, 34, 35, 38, 40, 44. (40 is the
first Court of William Gresham. 42 is the first Court of
Sir Henry Hobart.)
James I. 1.

There are also a few Deeds relating to land in 'Intwode' :
one undated, one *temp.* Edward III. ; one *temp.* Rich. II.; and
one *temp.* Henry VI.

For the following Parishes in Norfolk there are detached
Manor Rolls :—

Ingworth.—Between 1571 and 1649.
Courts and Courts Lete :—
Elizabeth. 13-44. (The Queen holds the Court for Thomas
Hoo, esq., a minor.)
James I. 1-5.
Also for the years 1634-1637, 1638, 1642, 1644, 1649.

Erpingham.
Extracts of Lete Roll :—
Elizabeth. 39.
James I. 1, 2, 4.
View of Frankpledge for Ingworth, Colby, Tuttington,
Erpingham, *temp.* James I.
One Deed relating to land here, *temp.* Edward III.

Irmingland.
An undated Rental.
Three Deeds relating to land here, viz. two *temp.* Rich. II., one
of Henry IV. (John Eloynes occurs as a landowner *temp.*
Rich. II. Also Edmund Kempe, Nicholas Daunger, Roger
Barker, Robert Nally.)
1386. A house with appurtenances is mentioned 9. Rich. II.
as formerly " Symneles."

WABORNE.

MANOR ROLLS.

COURTS AND COURTS LETE :—

Edward II. 15(?) being then the manor of Oliver de Burdeaux.
Henry VIII. 2, 6-18, 38 (a copy).
Edward VI. 1-2.
Elizabeth. 36.

BAILIFF'S ACCOUNTS :—

Henry VIII. 14-37.

OTHER DOCUMENTS.

1519. Abuttal and survey of Lady de Veer's manor of Waborne for the year 11 Henry VIII.
A perambulation of bounds of the same year.

1572. A lease of Waborne by De Vere, Earl of Oxford, to — Clopton. 14 Eliz.

1656. A release of the manor, etc., by Sir William Paston to Sir John Hobart.

THE DUCHY OF LANCASTER.

ACCOUNT ROLLS OF THE RECEIVERS FOR NORFOLK, SUFFOLK AND CAMBRIDGE, between 1385 and 1408 :—

Richard II. 8, 9 (Adam Pope, Receiver), 23 (Edmund Oldhalle, " King's Receiver ").
Henry IV. 1, 2, 8-9 (Edmund Oldhalle, Receiver).
Indenture of arrears of officers' accounts, "anno xiii." (?)

MISCELLANEOUS MANOR ROLLS.

Gymingham.

Provosts' Account Rolls, between 1382 and 1410 :—.
Richard II. 5, 6, 8, 9, 16-20. In the Roll for 5-6 there is mention of forfeiture of John Trunch for treason and insurrection. For the 7th year, May 9, " quo die manerium ibidem cum pertinentibus liberatum comiti de Bukyngham ad firmam per dimissionem."
Henry IV. 10, 11.

Matlask.

Court Lete :—
Henry IV. 1, 2. (2 is the first Court of Robert de Braybroke, Bishop of London, John, Bishop of Hereford, and Roger Mallory de Braybroke, feoffees. Matlask with Saxthorp.)
Saxthorp Court held at the same place. Henry IV. 6.
A small bundle of Rolls, *temp.* Richard II., Henry VII., (drafts) and Elizabeth.

Causton.—1387-97.
 Court Lete:—
  Richard II. 10, 11, 16, 19, 20.

Wood Dalling and Dalling Hall Monceux :—
 General Court Roll :—
  Henry VIII. 10.
  Philip and Mary. 5-6.

Martham.—1351.
 Court Roll:—
  Edward III. 25, the 7th of the Priorate of Simon Bozoun
  [Prior of Holy Trinity, Norwich].

Tunstede.—1406-7.
 Provost's Account:—
  Henry IV. 7-8.

Methwolde.—1408-1492.
 Provosts' and Bailiffs Accounts for the years:—
  Henry IV. 9-10.
  Henry VI. ?
  Henry VII. 6, 7.

Congham.
 Court Roll :—
  Temp. Edward IV.

Burnham Thorp.—1384-5.
 Bailiff's Account :—
  Richard II. 7-8.

CaRROW ABBEY.

CELLARERS' ACCOUNTS, between 1457 and 1530 :—

   Henry VI. 34, 35.   (Margaret Pygotte, Prioress.)
   Richard III. 2, 3.   (Margaret Palmer, Prioress.)
   Henry VIII. 20, 21.

MANOR ROLLS.

Marlingforth.

COURTS AND COURTS GENERAL WITH LETE, 1489-1557 :—

   Henry VII.   4-15, 19, 20.
   Henry VIII.   12 is " Curia cum Leta prima Edwardi Ponyng,
    Willelmi Boleyn, militum et al., ad usum Johannis
    Paston militis et Agnetæ uxoris ejus et heredum."
   Philip and Mary.   1-4, the courts of Clement Paston.

Swerdeston.
   1506. Account Roll for the year Henry VII. 21.

Deeds Relating to Land there.

One undated.
One *temp.* Edward I.
Four *temp.* Edw. III.
Three *temp.* Henry V.
Three *temp.* Henry VI.
One *temp.* Henry VII.

1588. Sir Edward Clere, of Blicklinge, grants a lease of the Rectory of Swerdeston, late belonging to Carrow Abbey (granted to him by letters patent of Queen Eliz.), to Roger Styth.

MISCELLANEOUS DEEDS.

Deeds relating to the following parishes (for the most part in Norfolk) have been examined and summarized:—

Witham.
Deed relating to land *temp.* Henry III.?

Aslacton.
An undated Deed.

Itteringham.
One undated and one *temp.* Edward I.

Mannington.
Two undated.

Southwood (Suthwode.)
One undated.

Threkeston.
One *temp.* Edw. II.

Hemlyngton.
One *temp.* Edw. III.

Buxton.
One *temp.* Edw. III.

Heynesford.
One undated.
One *temp.* Edw. III.
One *temp.* Henry IV.
One *temp.* Edw. IV.

Plumstead.
One *temp.* Edw. III.
One *temp.* Rich. II.
One *temp.* Henry IV.
Two *temp.* Henry VI.
Two *temp.* Edward. IV.

There is also an extent for *Witton* and *Plumpstead* for the year 12 Henry VIII., 1520.

Witton.
One, *temp.* Henry IV.

Ketteringham.
One, *temp.* Henry VI.
One, ,, Henry VIII.
One, ,, James I. 7.
The last is the conveyance of the rectory of Ketteringham
to Mr. Henry Hobart.

Combes.
Two, *temp.* Edw. IV.
One, *temp.* Elizabeth.

Tacolneston.
One, *temp.* Edw. IV.
Two, *temp.* Henry VI.

South Walsham.
Record of Assize.

Horsford.
One, *temp.* Edw. VI.

Brampton.
One, *temp.* Edw. VI.

Marsham.
One, *temp.* Edw. VI.
Extent of manor of Marsham, *temp.* Charles I.?

Scottowe.
Six, *temp.* James I., mostly relating to a mill there.

Kelling.
One, *temp.* James I.

Hethersett.

Mulbarton and Brakne.—
1316. An extent, containing a transcript of the Escheat Roll
made on the suppression of the Templars in the Hundred
of Humbleyard.—9 Edw. II.

Acle.
One undated.
Two *temp.* Henry VII., one of which is a grant of land with
"leed querns and hayer and all that is rote fast and nayle
"fast;" 1485.
1544. An abuttal of the year 36 Hen. VIII.

Loddon.—1577.
Deed of assignment of a term of years in the Rectory of
Loddon. 19 Eliz.

Rivyshall (in Suffolk).—1587.
Conveyance of manors in Rivyshall and Rawlyns in Rivyshall,
with a schedule of tenants holding for a thousand years.

Chetgrave and Hardeley—
An extent; 1675.

SETCH.

Robert de Hastinges grants to Matilda, his daughter, and her
lawful heirs all his lands in the vills of Scethich, Midleton,
Rungetun, Westwinch, Ley and Herdewyc, with remainder to himself and his heirs if she should die without issue; reserving rent
of 6¾d., four " atilia " [implements] and one clove.—Not dated.

STRATTON.

1300. Alice, formerly wife of John de Lundres, of Stratton,
grants to Sarra daughter of Will. de Merkeshalle, of Stratton,
half an acre of her land lying on the field at Stratton.—Sunday
after St. Hilary, 28 Edward I.
Witnesses : Hen. le Cat, John de Refham, Will. de Leveshaye,
John Philip of Stratton, John the Clerk of Hevingham, Richard
de Lundres of Stratton, Alfred de Horning of Stratton, and
others.

1363. William Breton, " de comitatu Essex," grants to
William son of Robert Clere and Dyonesia his wife, all his right
in the third part of the manor of Stratton by Buxton, etc.

1378. Matilda, formerly wife of Henry de Berney, grants to
William Clere of Ormesby and Dionicia his wife, Hervey parson
of the church of Stratton by Hevingham, Robert atte Northous
of Ormesby, and the heirs of the said William, four pieces of land
in Stratton.—Vigil of St. Peter and St. Paul, 2 Rich. II.

1529. A Rental of John Wekythyll in Stratton.

There are also 14 other deeds relating to land here, *tempp.*
Edw. II.—Eliz.

BROMHOLM.

1312. A lease of the Priory lands at Wood Norton by William
Prior of Bromholm and the Convent.—5 Edward II.

1412. Clement, prior of the church of St. Andrew of Bromholm,
and the Convent, release to Simon Felbrigge and Robert Berneye,
kts., Edmund Oldhalle, Robert Wynter, clerk, John Drew, parson
of Harpelee, and William Howlyn, parson of Plumstede, a rent
of 4s. arising from lands and tenements in Corpesty leased to the
said feoffees for thirty years. Conventual Seal attached; red wax:
St. Andrew sitting in the porch of a church with a tower on each
side ; in his right hand a double cross, in his left a book ; and a
small nich above, the Virgin and Child ; " Sigillum . . . .
Andree de Bromholm." This is different from the seal engraved
in Dugdale's *Monasticon.*—1 March, 13 Henry IV.

West Barsham.

1361.   Indenture of grant by Rauf de Cromewelle to Osman
Gurnay of the wardship and marriage of William Fitzwilliam,
heir-at-law of Marjorie widow of John de Mereworth, for 36
marks.—Monday before St. John Baptist, 35 Edw. III.

Great Yarmouth.

1392.   Nicholas Wildgos, burgess of Great Yernemouth,
releases to John son of Robert de Rollesbi, all his claim in one
messuage with the "fisshus" and all other buildings and appurtenances, formerly Richard Fastolf's.   Witn., John de Rendle,
John de Elys, William Exneye, Robert atte Gappe . . ,
bailiffs of Yermuth.—Sat., f. of St. Petronella virg., 15 Rich. II.

Buttele.

1445.   William Poley, prior of St. Mary of Buttele, and the
Convent, demise to Edward Palmer, of Wytton in Bromholm, and
Robert his son, the manor of West Somerton for 7 years at a rent
of 24*l.*—St. Matthias, 23 Hen. VI.

West Somerton.

1552.   Sir E. Fynes, knight, Lord Clynton and Saye,
Admiral of England, conveys to Sir Thomas Woodhouse, of
Waxham, the reversion of the manor of West Somerton, formerly
belonging to the monastery of Butley, on the death of the Lady
Anne of Cleevys.—19 March, 6 Edw. VI.

1456-57.   Accounts of Robert Brampton, General Receiver of
Elizabeth, Lady Dacre.

1515-17.   An account of all the manors of John Veer, knight,
in right of his wife Elizabeth, sister and heir-at-law of William
Trussel.

1517.   A charter of the Lady Catherine (of Arragon) to her
tenants of the honour of Clare.

1527.   An account of the manors of John de Vere, Earl of
Oxford, in right of his wife Elizabeth, sister and heiress of
Edward Trussel.

1546.   Conveyance to trustees by Richard Southwell of all his
property for his own use, with remainder to Richard Southwell,
alias D'Arcy, gent.—37 Hen. VIII.

1550.   Audit of accounts of John Woodhouse, esq., supervisor of all the flocks of Richard Southwell, knight.

1557.   The account of the sheep of John Corbett the elder,
esquire, made by Robert Newman, "shepereve," and others, for
one year.

1572.   Indenture with schedule of manors included in the wardship of Richard Barney.   Signed by William Cecil and R. Keeling.

Papers referring to the property of Sir Richard Southwell and
a case in Chancery of Richardson *v.* Doyly.   *Temp.* James I.

1603. Benedict Camp to Sir H. Hobart. Conveyance of the wardship of Thos. Neve.

Letter of William Trussel.

Ma très chère dame,

J'ay entendu par vos lettres en partie la manière des alienacions et enfeffemens de terres Mons. Robert de Matteshale q'fuist votre mary, et auxuit que vous plest savoir coment jay doné conngé à Phelip votre filz, et auxuit que vous moi requeretz avoir respite de s'vīs que moi devetz à cause de les t'rēs que vous tenetz de moy en chief la quel je vous ottray. Madame tãq ma veux purra étre en vos parties et endroit de conngé Phelip votre filz ceo est d'aler et revenir come un autre gentilz home de meyne. Et de puis que joe ai hu sey'syng de luy, jeo luy ai effert mariage convenable come appartient soloin la loy en saluacion de mon droit. Et si vous plest en le même tems fere gré soloin réson pur son mariage et ceo que a moy partient a mesure la cause jeo dorrai pleyn poar a Mons. Robert de Salle et a Will. de Hastings et a Sir Thomas Hikelynge chanon de Wayburn de trêter et acorder en vous ma Dame soloin réson. Et si ceo ne vous plest ma Dame moy covendra pursuir mon recoverir par loy en saluacion de mon droit heritage.

A Dieu ma tr' chē Dame qui vous eyt en sa garde.

Escrit a Lonndres le xxx. jō de Martz.

WILLM. TRUSSEL DE CUBLESDEN.

[1551.] 28 May, 4 Ed. VI. Copy of letters patent granting to Thomas Audeley, Esq., in consideration "boni veri fidelis et magnanimi servitii in conflictu versus innaturales subditos nostros proditores ac nobis rebelles in Com. nostro Norf. per nos dudum habito et facto, et in correctione et subductione eorundem, multis variisque modis præstiti et impensi, quorum quidem rebellorum et proditorum quidam Robertus Knight alias dictus Robertus Kett, existit capitaneus et conductor," all our manors of Meliorshall and Lethers hall, alias Leters, now called Gunvyles, and all that manor called Gunvyles manor in Norfolk, parcel of the possessions of the said Robert Knyght otherwise the said Robert Kett.

There are also many deeds which have not been summarized but are arranged in parcels according to their dates, viz. :—

5	Miscellaneous deeds *temp.*		Rich. III.
85	,,	,,	,, Henry VII.
42		,,	,, Henry VIII.
4		,,	,, Philip and Mary.
102		,,	,, Elizabeth.
45		,,	,, James I.
23		,,	,, Charles I.
9		,,	,, Charles II.

SECTION II.

THE HOBART PAPERS. 1601—1751.

1601, March 5.—Copy of an Order of the Court of the Duchy of Lancaster.

Adjusting the rights of common in the " firre ground " or " bruery" at Aylsham.

N.D. [1592-1607 ?].—Resolucons and advise uppon a Statute touchinge the Releif of the Poore and vagabon by the L. Cheife Justice of England.[0]

None ought to be sente to the places of theire birthe or habitacons but such onlie as are vagrante or wanderinge and not any that hath any dwellinge in any parishe, or be settled with their parents or any other in any parishe.

Resolutions. The husband, wief and children that are vagrante and wandringe being borne in severall parishes must be delte with all in this manner, that is to saye, the wief must goe with the husband to the parishe where he was borne, and not to be divided the one from the other, the children that are above 7 yeres of age must after they are whipped be sent to the parishes where they were severally borne. But those children under the age of 7 yeres, bycause they are not within the degree of vagabondes, must goe with their parents, not where they were borne or last abidinge.

Advises. Where there are multitudes of poore through idlenesse in all places, which if they should be whollye relieved by charitie would be more burthensome than the better sorte are able to beare : therefore it is moste conveniente that for the children betwene seven and sixteen they be put to be apprentiss and especially to husbandrye and huswiefrye whereof there is greate lacke in most places; and herein to be reported of especiallye, to ease such thereby as are overburthened through charge of children : and for the rest of the children they must laye at the charge of their parentes to be relieved by the labour of the parents.

That all suche that are in any wise able to worke, may be provided for of meanes to sett them on worke wherby they maye be able to releive themselves and theire children.

That none be suffered to live merelie uppon almes, that are not merelie impotente.

---

* Sir John Popham (1531-1608), Lord Chief Justice 1592-1607

Orders concerninge the Statute for the Releif of the poore, agreed at Ilmyster, the 11th of April.

1. *Imprimis* it is ordered that all justices of peace of this sheire shall presentlie make precepts thereby commandinge the cunstables of the hundredes to bringe before them the names of the Churchwardens and 4 substantiall subsidye men of everye parishe: And in defaulte thereof fower of the most substantiall householders of every parishe within their hundred some daye in Easter weeke, the orders to be then assigned for the benefitt of the lawe to be lost (*sic*) this yere.

2. *Item* it is further agreed that upon the deliverye of the names of the Churchwardens and 4 substantiall men they shall that yere followinge be appointed overseers of the poore of ther several parishes under the handes and seales of two or more Justices of the peace of or nere the seide parishe. And at the same tyme direction given them how they shall setle and order poore accordinge to the statute.

3. *Item.* It is also agreed that the townes that are not able to releif theire poore and have noe landes or other helpes shalbe in some reasonable proportion releived by such elected persons of the parish of the same hundred as to the discretion of the Justice in or nere the parishes shall seme mete, either by takinge them apprentiss, or by yeilding some weeklie contribucon to the towne for that purpose.

4. *Item.* It is also agreed that every parish shalbe rated for the releif of hospitalls and spitlehowses and such as receive losse by water or fyer within this sheire, and for the releif of the poore persons of the King's Bench or Marshalsye, and the same sett downe what shalbe paide to eche hospitall, King's bench and Marshalsye; and a treasurer be appointed for this yere.

5. *Item* it is also ordered that no pore person be removed out of the parish where they now dwell so long as they doe or can take any howse for theire monye and doe live without charging the parish, and that no extraordinarye course be taken either to remove them, or to inhibite them to take a howse.

6. *Item*, that whosoever taketh an Inmate from henceforth excepte by assente of the Churchwardens or overseers or the most parte of them with the assente of two Justices of Peace of the lymitte, shall paye yerely or weeklie to the releife of the poore as much as he receiveth of that Inmate.

7. *Item* that such as receive any Inmate except as aforeseid, frelye shall paye weeklie to the releive of the poore of the same parishe 1$^{d.}$ and if the partie be or shalbe a burthen to the parish shall paye vij$^{d.}$ weeklie for every such Inmate, or enter into sufficiente bonde with good suertyes that the parishe shalbe discharged of any harme or burthen by any such Inmate.

8. *Item.* That none be suffered to goe from dore to dore in beginge but within theire owne parish and that to such houses in such order as they shalbe assigned by the overseers.

9. *Item*, that such as live idlelye and maye have worke or use any idle course of life as in breakinge hedges, robbing

orchyards or takeing any kynde of corne or grayne growinge in
the fielde, milkinge of kyne or such like without the consente of
the owners and not being able to give recompence for the same,
be sente to the House of Correction there whiped and dyeted as
shalbe appointed.

10. That gardening be —— ? amonge the pore sorte and that
the pore that doth worke in his owne gardinge to have 2ᵈ a daye
in weeke that he so worketh ; so that it maye appere to the
overseers that there groweth good to the partie and comonweale
therby.

11. *Item* that such as have any howse or cottage in any towne
or parish will without the consente of the Churchwardens and
overseers of the same parish, or the more parte of them lett out
the same howse or howses without laying in of 4 acres of ground
to the same at the least, so as the same howse have so much
grounde belonging to it shall paye as much to the poore of the
parish yerely as he is to receive for the howse so leaten.

12. *Item* and if any such lett such howse freelie or any
cottage without assente as aforesaid to any person, then to paye
weeklie for everye such tenemente to the releife of the pore
1ᵈ and if the partie be or shalbe a burthen to the parish then
to paye weeklie vijᵈ· for every such tenemente or enter into such
bondes as is aforeseid for the discharge of the parishe.

13. *Item* that the overseers assigne none to fetche releife at
any howse but as be merelie impotente or under the age of
7 yeres and such as the overseers shall well prove that theire
parents are not able to releife by theire worke or livelihoode.

14. *Item*, that such as shalbe assigned to fetche any releife
at any howse, be assigned to some howse nere and certeyne to
fetche it, not wander aboute or from howse to howse at theire
pleasures and the howers to be assigned when they shall fetche
theire releife.

15. *Item* that none be suffered to have any releife for themselves or theire children that doe robbe . . . (*paper
defective*) . . . or that take Inmates or succor Inmates
contrary to the true meaninge of these orders.

16. *Item*, that noe bastard be releived by the Parish but the
supposed fathers and mothers if they or any of them be founde
to be able, and if there be any that be not able to releive theire
owne bastards such supposed father and mother to be sente to
the Howse of Correction and by theire worke there to releive the
same.

Orders agreed and sett downe at Ilmyster the 11th of Aprill,
 concerninge the Statute of Rogues to be confirmed at the
 Sessions with such addicon as to the greater parte of the
 Justices there assembled should thinke meete.

1. *Imprimis* it is ordered that imediatelie uppon Easter after
precepte by all the Justices of the Countye to the Cunstables and
Tytheingmen to apprehend all manner of wandringe soldiours
and all other idle and wandringe rogues, the meaner rogues to

punishe by whipinge and conveyinge by pastporte accordinge to the Statute, and such as are men able of bodye and like to be wandringe soldiours or marryners or otherwise dangerous persons to be brought before the justices to be examined and dealte with as to theire discretions and accordinge to the direction of the Statute shall seme meete, and if upon examination there appeare to be wandring souldiours or marryners to be sente to the gaole to be tryed as fellons according to the statute in that behalf made or shalbe made.

2. *Item*, that a howse of correction shalbe erected at Ilchester and the howse of Taunton and Wells to be continued.

3. *Item*, it is allso ordered that a Howse of Correction shalbe erected at Willington [Wellington] to receive any rogues from the 4 wester tythings of Byngburye and the hundred of Mylverton, which our good Lord the Lord Cheife Justice of England intendeth to builde at his owne charge. And if any such orders as are sett downe for maynetenance and goverment of other such Howse of Correction in this countye shall allso extende unto that.

4. That the somes sett downe uppon the particulars, persons and hundreds under our Handes for the erecting of the Howse of Correction at Ilchester shall be levyed by distresse and sale of theire goodes if they refuse to paye. . . And that aswell occupiers of landes within any Hundred or parishe shalbe taxed as the Inhabitants are, and the like to be done for such somes as shalbe hereafter imposed uppon any person or place for the maynetenance or continuance of any of the saide howse of correction.

5. That such as shalbe committed as rogues shall at the ffirste entrance be whipped untill theire bodyes be blodye.

6. It is allso ordered that the cheife officers of everye parte shall by the next passenger conveye unto the partes of Ireland everye such Irish beggar as shalbe at any tyme sent them by virtue of the Statute made in this last Sessions of Parliamente for punishm^t of rogues upon payne the same officer shalbe bounde to his good behavior and to appe(ar) at the nexte Generall Quarter Sessions. And we doe order that the charge of such transportacon shalbe borne by the whole countye. And we doe order that the tresurer for the Hospitalles shall defraye such charge.

7. It is allso ordered that everye inhabitante within everye parishe or towne within this countye shall apprehende everye rogue and poore person that shall come unto howse to aske releife, or that he shall (find?) in any of his outhowses and groundes and them presentlye conveye to the Cunstable, to Titheingmen or other officers of the same place upon payne to be bounde to his good behavior, and if the officer doe not cause presentlie the same poore person or rogue to be whipped untill his bodye be blodye and then make him a pasporte out accordinge to the statute: that every suche officer shall forfitt likewise 10*s.* for every rogue he shall leave unpunished according to the Statute. And the same to be levyed by way of distresses and sale of his goodes and converted to the releife of the poore of the same place.

8. It is allso ordered that at or nere everye parishe churche within thes sheire there be a payer of stock and that there be presentlie provided a canvis shurte made with a bevar to come over the face of him that shalbe appointed to whippe them, and a whipp provided. And that everye rogue brought to any officer or appointed by him shalbe conveyed unto the Parishe Churche and thereupon sett into the stockes and whipped by the advise of the Minister and one other of the parishe. And then conveyed by passeporte accordinge to the Statute. And it is ordered that the minister shall register the substance of the testemoniall which he is to keepe for that purpose upon payne of 5s. forfeiture for everye rogue he shall leave unregistered to be levied by distresse and sale of his goodes and to be converted to the use of theire poore there.

9. It is likewise ordered that Notice and Charge be given to the Justices of Peace nere adjoyning to the Severne or other Sea Costes, they to give speciall orders to all officers of townes and places nere the same sea costes and Severne that they suffer noe Irishe to be sett on lande which are like to live here by beginge.

[1612.]—Memorandum of questions to be referred to LEET JURY [WYMONDHAM].

Now to this Court and leete some of the ancientest tennants that hold both of the Queene and Lord to be of the Jurie.

To fynde whether they common by their tenements and lands ancientlie belonginge to these tenements or whether Alsoe by usuall custome tyme out of mynde purchased geven or discended to Any person.

Item, whether yf they purchase more Lande to their ancient tenements they may common with more cattell there than they usuallie did before by reason of such purchase.

Item, whether a tenement decaied out of memorie of man can challenge commonage by such Tenement.

Item, if he may, then whether may he keepe any more or other cattell then he can prove he kept before such dounefall as yf he use other purchased Lands lease or hired lands of other men therewyth.

To fynd yf tenants to Sir Augustin Pagraves mannor may of right common and to searche the Rolls who have beene amerced thereabouts for wrongfull commoners.

Whether new erected tenements can common.

Item, whether Butchers have not been punished for wrongfull commoners. Yt is usuallie reported they have beene and noe Butcher to common.

Item, what Incrochments have beene made by taken in any part of the commons either by ditchinge or fencinge of such dikes as lie next to the Common of any mannor of person or persons or otherwise and what person or persons hath broken the Lord's soyle either by digginge of flaggs, planting of trees, loppinge or fellinge of trees on the Commons or any parte of them.

DUCHY OF LANCASTER.

1614 to 1680. A number of papers relating to the Bailiwick of the DUCHY OF LANCASTER held by SIR HENRY HOBART and his successors on lease from the Crown, with correspondence relating thereto.

The MAYOR OF NORWICH to CH. JUSTICE HOBART.

1616, Jan. 25. Norwich.—Wee have received your Letters in answer of ours touching the cleyme of wood for the Hospital of this Citty, beinge arere for 22 yeres past, we are sory that the remissenes of the officers in not urginge payment from those that were the former owners of the Manor of Horsham St. Faithes hath occasioned so greate an arrerage upon y^r Ldpp., whome we have always found our honorable Friend, Yet wee are well informed that there have been demand made thereof from tyme to tyme. We have sent herewithal unto y^r Ldpp. the copy of the deed whereby the same was graunted and as we thankefully acknowledge y^r Ldpp'^{s} good Inclinacon in not withholding the same from the poore, so we shall alwaies rest ready to performe any office of love whereby our thankefulness may be manifested to your Lordshipp.

Tho. Hyrne. M[ayor].
Thomas Pye.
Alexander Thurston.
Roger Runsye.
William Brown } Sherifs.
Tho. Cory
Henry Fawcett.
Bass. Throkmorton.

Endorsed:—The Mayor of Norwich touching the claim of wood out of St. Faith's to the Hospital.

THOMAS HYRNE to CHIEF JUSTICE HOBART.

1616[-7], Feb. 6. Norwich.—Relating to the city's claim to fuel at Horsham on behalf of the Hospital.

[1616] AYLSHAM LANCASTER. Extract from Liberty Rolls.
Mems.—The Balywicke of the Dutche my Lord Hobart had by lease for a term of yeares, unto which these severall offices be within the libertie doe belonge for which I paid 80*l*. per ann.
The office of coroner.
The office of ffeodarye and escheator.
The office of clarke of the markett.
The balywick of everye several hundred in all six : South Erpingham, North Erpingham, North Greenhoe, South Greenhoe, Smythdon and Brothercrosse.
The breaking up of writts, outlawres, felons, goods and deodands.

1616' Dec. 9. Receipt under seal of JOHN SYMTHE of Antingham, Esq, of £1,600 paid by Sir Henry Hobart, £1,100 for manor of Blickling bought of Sir E. Clere (and the purchase money assigned to Smythe), and £500 for purchase of his (Smythe's) own land.

MILES HOBART. CONTRACT ON MARRIAGE.

1624, April 4. To all to whome this writing shall come I, Miles Hobarte of Lincolns in in the County of Middlesex, Esq., send greeting. Know ye that whereas Sir Henry Hobarte of Blickling, in the County of Norfolke, knight and Baronett, Lord Cheefe Justice of His Majesties Court of Common Pleas, my father, by an Indenture bearing date the third day of Aprill in the year of our Sovereign Lord James, by the grace of God, King of England, France and Ireland, Defender of the faith, that is to say of England France and Ireland the one and twentieth, and of Scotland the six and fiftieth, in consideration of a marriage by God's permission to be solemnized betwen me the said Miles Hobarte and dame Francis Bedinfield of Dersingham in the County of Norfolk, widow, and for the better support and maintenance of me the said Miles Hobarte and Dame Frances, hath granted one anuety or yearly rent of three hundred pounds of lawful money of England issuing out of all the lands of the said Sir Henry Hobarte in the Countye of Norfolk to have to the said Miles Hobarte after the solemnization of the said marriage during the joint lives of the said Sir Henry Hobarte, the said Miles Hobarte and the said Dame Frances Bedingfeild, payable at the feast of S. Michaell the Archangell and the Annunciation of the Blessed Virgin yearly by equal portions, with claus of distress as by the said Indenture more fully may apear. Know ye now nevertheless in consideration that my said father reaps no manner of benefit from my said marriage nor by any thinge that she the said lady bringes, and yet on his part hath given to me and her and or children great and large portions and preferments in land I, the said Miles Hobarte, do by these presents freely releas to the said Sir Henry Hobart, my father, one hundred pound by the year part of the said rent of three hundred pound by the year, contenting myself with the other two hundred pound by the year payable by equal portions at the feastes and with the like claus of distress for that onely as aforesaid, and by these presents do covenant with the said Sir Henrye Hobarte to give him any father discharge of the said one hundred pounds by the year that he shall at any time require according to the true intent of these presents. In witness whereof I have hereunto put my hand and seal this fourth of Aprill in the year of our sovereign lord James, by the grace of God, King of England, France and Ireland, the one and twentieth, and of Scotland the six and fiftithe.

MILES HOBARTE.

HAMON LE STRANGE to SIR HENRY HOBART.

1625, June 28.—Ho[ble] The distraction of my last and short abode att London caused me to forgett a motion which I shall now recommend to your Lordship's acceptance. I understand that your Lordship hath the sole royalte from the King touching swans and swanneries in Norf., and am desirous to have a particular mark for my river and waters att Gressenhall, and else where in this countye. There is a marke proper to Hastings formerly lords of Gressenhall and Elsinge, which is now used by Sir Anthony Browne to whom I am willing to relinquish the same, and would have a distinct marke peculiar to my name and family, and to that end I crave that your Lordship will please to affoard me that favour and as speedy a grant or direction for disposing thereof as conveniently may be. I hear also that sundry times stray swans are taken up betwixt Linn and me and some aieries lately erected there by meane persons. If your Lordship have not granted your power there I would desire also that additament from you.

Lastly, to conclude against my selfe, I return your Lordship the due recognition of your honourable affections to have esteemed me worthy of the love and labours you have formerly bestowed to have added me to the number of your deputy lieutenants in Norff. I doe so well assure my selfe the steadiness of your dispose (and am so much told it by those that knowe as little of my deserts) as I now growe in some feare of my favour and therefore doe as seriously and humbly importune that you will be aquiescent from any further motion to my Lord of Arundel for me ; for if I might boast of or finde a grace in disgraces the last disfavour hath rather added then taken from me, howsoever the weakness of my body, obscurity of my situascon, and the great and contented fruition of my selfe att the plaine labours of the plough (to which I have putt my hand and will not pull backe) make me say with Jacob I have enough. I beseech you will be pleased to forgett what you have formerly levelled att that mark (though I must not) and suffer me to have rest in this banishment which, being restored, I cannot. Pardon my plaineness the best badge of a true hart and that the best heaven upon earth, and be pleased still to retayne in your honourable embraces,

Your ever faithfull nephew to serve you,
HAMON LE STRANGE.

Sir John Peyton to Sir John Hobart.

1629, 29 July.— Not doubting of your coming [to] towne by my Lord of Bullingbrooke I doe expecte to see you heare, and if my daughter Hobert and you come together I beseech you to persuade her to come with you.

Your grandfather in all faithfull love and affection,
JOHN PEYTON.

1632. DISPENSATION to Sir John Hobart to eat flesh during Lent

Sealed by George [Abbot], Archbishop of Canterbury.
Confirmation of the above by royal letters patent, dated 29 Feb., 1632.

1634, Jan. 31.—Letters of administration to the goods of Edward Hobarte who died beyond seas, a bachelor, granted to Sir John Hobart, Knt. and Bt., brother.

SIR ROBERT BELL to SIR JOHN HOBART [on the Fen Drainage].

1634, Nov. 16.—I received this morning a letter from you butt it bears no date, but of your affection which I shall study to continue. I shall in answer to itt and in satisffaction of your desires make a short relation of all business wh. concern us both jointly and severally, wherein itt shall appear to all the world that we are bothe the same wee ever intended. First my Lord of Bedford and I are perfectly (by the favour of my noble Lord St. John) made up and reconciled on Friday last, and I shall have my part in Whittlesy presently without scruple or difference. The business concerning your assurance will be made fitt and to your contentment, but cannot be finished without your companie as N. Earle gives to understand. How this sutes with your approbation or my Ladyes I dare scarce enquire, I hope itt the last trouble you shall undergoe by any argument of mine and you shall need to stay out above two days at ye most. Deeping ffenn is as fit for judgment as any land in England being all at this time three foot under soile, butt Sir Thomas Halton doeth play ye (   ) with us and if he be not more conformable will have cause to repent itt, for we will have it adjudged in despight of him. There is a sluice overthrown at Boston but no disparagement to the land nor disadvantage to the woork, but Sir Anthony Browne his private loss, you shall hear your part instantly sett out and be confident it will be exceeding beneficall.

[1636-1638.]—"Acquittances for 500l. towards the Repairing of the decayes and ruines of the Cathedrall Church of St. Paul in London, and the beautifying thereof according to the true intent and meaning of His Majesties Commission by Letters Patents granted for that purpose under the Greate Seale bearing date the 10th day of Aprill in the 7th yeare of H. M. reigne."

SIR ROBERT BELL to SIR JOHN HOBART.

1637, May 26.—Noble Sir. Questionless my sinns are greater then other menns and your exceptions against mee greater too or else I could not have failed an answer from you (having sent you divers letters) of your intention in my Lord of Bedford's business, 'tis true, I have had it suggested unto mee that you have long resolved to desert it, but I am free from jealosies myself and do beleve if you had ment so, you would have declared yourself and not have protracted me into so great a straite. The business is of greater consequence then ever, in respect that the King's 12,000 acres are sett out in Whittlesey and thereabouts, by which occasion there are such woorks begun and this summer to be finisht for the improving and securing that quarter as will render it of a farr greater value than former expectation made it. Unless you please to conclude it the next tearme (my Lord of

Bedford being fully prepared every way) I have no further hope unless you signifie your pleasure so that I may make triall time enough to satisfie my Lord if any other will befriend mee.

Sir Robert Bell to Sir John Hobart.

1638, August 14.—I presume ere this you are acquainted with ye law of sale made at Huntington where we had as much (by Counsell) alledged for us as could be said and that which neither ye Attorny or Sollicitor could answer at all or in parte, but by a new trick in law, or in their instructions (I know not which) called ' Sic Volo ' They condemn^d our taxe, our law, our proceedings, and in consideration of the improvement wee had made and ye expense we had been at (sufficient evidence to intityle ye King) they have given His Majestie both every foot of my Lord of Exiter's and our land that it may be made winter ground within 10 yeares, and whether we shall have relief in it or noe they must inform you that understand it more than I, but the best is most of us are better able to endure this then hanging though with some (of which I must be one) 'tis but an even lay. Now disadvantages come seldome singly, especially to those that cannot master them, of which (from your hand) some fall fresh on mee. . . . .

Part of Bardolf will lye upon my hands that am not furnisht how to stock itt, for there is 2 or 300 acres (being all lett from year to year) thus hangs upon hand till almost this season for two reasons, first because it is the last grounde that is mowne in the countrie, secondly because the tenants pay one half year's rent at entry, and I might say thirdly because the later they defer it the better penny worth (like crafty merchants) they expect.

1638, Aug. 16.—Probate of will of Henry Hobart of South Pickenham.

Mentions brothers of testator, John, Miles, Nathaniel and James.

Sir Robert Bell to Sir John Hobart.

1639, May 10.—If this Scotch rebellion (which tyes up all menns purses) be turned (as there is great hope) into conformetie there will be open and free mart again and every man will trade.

Sir Thomas Wilbraham, Thomas Legh, Peter Egerton to Sir Edward Moseley and Dame Mary his wife.

1639, April 16.—Agreement as to terms of marriage settlement.

Sir J. Hobabt and Sir John Hele of Wembury, Devon.

1640, Mar. 10.—Articles of agreement on marriage of Dorothy Hobart, daughter of Sir John.

Letter of JOHN COKE announcing his Shrievalty of Norfolk.

1643, March 15.—Whereas it hath pleased his Majestie and the Parliament to make mee Sheriffe of the Countye so that by vertue thereof I am to nominate Bayliffs of the severall hundreds of the said Countie and knowinge that it is the desire of all good men that the said Bayliffes office may be put into the hands of such as are able and honest, and not doubtinge of your readinesse to further so good a worke and of your assistance herein, my desire to you is that you would forthwith consult and advise with the freeholders of your hundred for the findinge out of such a one in your hundred who may bee everye [way] fitt and likewise willinge to undertake dureinge my time the executfon of the said office of Bayliffe in your hundred, and that wfth all speed, you would send unto mee the partie so nominated to the howse of John Blackett in Norwich at or before the four and twentieth of this instant March with sufficient sureties for the passing of his Accompt. And so I bid you heartilie farewell and rest

Your assured,
JOHN COKE.

Norwich.

Petition from the prisoners in AYLSHAM Duchy Gaol.

1644, April 15. Norfolk.—To the Right Wp[ll] the Standing Committee at Norwich and to the Justices of ye Peace for the County of Norfolk.

We at this present, Prissoners in the Duchie Gayle in Ailsham, whose hands are hereunto subscribed being much oppressed and disterbed with Thomas Turner, a Prissoner in execution at the sute of Richard Bell for six pounds, who to our knowledge wants no Meate or Drink but is better relieved then he deserves by Roger Moris keeper of the said Gayle albeit he hath no moneys nor other meanes to pay for the same by the consent and with the sute of the said Richard Doe most humbly beseech your wp[ll] powers for removing him from us to the Castle of Norwich, he being a very profane ill-mouthed and ungodly person and very dangerous, insomuch as he fileth his Irons put on him for his most vilde and notorious accons in breaking open doores and locks and most absurdly abuseing us and such other persons as come to any of us. And also in threatening to pull doune and lay waste or burne downe the prison house where we are, for that he affirmeth there is neither God nor divell, heaven nor hell.

(S[a])	Richard Howes, clerke.
	Willm. Barker.
Signum	John Spratt.
Rogeri Moris.	William Harmer.
	Robert Jeckes.
	John Cony.

1645, April 3 and 7, and May 10.—RECEIPTS FOR PARLIAMENT PAY.

LADY FRANCES HOBARTE to SIR JOHN HOBART.

1649, Ap. 7.—Conveyance of Langley Manor.

MEMORIAL on behalf of M. RANSOME.

1653, Jan. 10. Felbrigge.—" To the Right Worshippfull Sir John Hobert, Knight and Baront. at his Blicklinge these present: "

Sir,—The schoole of Windham being voyd and M. Ransome that was expelled his Benefices for a very small occasion and upon very slender proofe and being detained of his fift part for his wife and children, is now a sutour for the schoole of Windham, beinge void, for which employment he is and will be very fitt, being a man very able that way and one that carryes himselfe very inoffensively towards the present government and all men; his humble suit is, which I desire to recommend unto you, that you would be pleas'd to grant him your letter to Mr. Dey, to enterteyne a good opinion of him, as all the best of the Towne and others have, wherein you shall doe a worke of mercy and charitie at all times to be acknowledged by him in his prayers, and by me and my wife.

Your humble and faithful servant,
THO. WINDHAM.

1654, Jan. 25. Probate of the will of Phillippa Hobart, granted in the name of Oliver Cromwell, Lord Protector.

HOUSE ACCOUNTS.

1655, 21 Feb. to 3 Dec., 1656, 27 Dec. to 13 March. Book of Daily expenses at Blickling Hall. Kitchen, &c.

1656, July 3.—Marriage Certificate. Sir John Hobart and Mary Hamond.

BLICKLING HOUSE ACCOUNTS.

Servants' wages paid for the quarter ended the 29th of September, 1655.

	£	s.	d.
Edmund Wise, Steward	7	10	0
Mr. Edward Legard	2	0	0
John Haynes	3	0	0
John Hogan	2	10	0
John Capon	2	0	0
Chris fferrys, Cooke	2	10	0
Peter Browne	1	10	0
Robert Thompson, Gardiner	1	10	0
Symon Browne, Groome	1	5	0
Charles Cove, Groome	1	2	6
John Webster	1	5	0
Bichard ffooteman	1	15	0

Peter ffarthing	-	-	-	1	10	0
Henry Claybourne, Cater	-	-	1	0	0
Wm. Capon, Butler's boy	-	-	0	12	6
Michaell Steward, Cookes boy	-	-	0	12	6
Robert Hunt, Bayliff	-	-	1	10	0
W. Taylor, a Husbandman	-	-	1	5	0
John Flatman, a husbandman	-	1	5	0
Richard Curtys, a husbandman	-	1	0	0
Henry ploughman, a husbandman	-	1	0	0
John Hobart, ffarmers boy	-	-	0	15	0
Blith Sutton	-	-	-	-	0	12	6
Sicilya West	-	-	-	-	0	12	6
Suzan Heydon	-	-	-	0	15	0
Mary Heydon	-	-	-	0	10	0
Alice Bynks	-	-	-	0	12	6

| | 41 | 10 | 0 |

Petition of THOMAS PARMENTER.

[1656.]—To the Right Wpp^ll the Committee for the County of Norff.

The humble petition of Thomas Parmenter sheweth your petitioner, having an equitable right to a house and about two and thirty acres of land in Witton, did about three weekes before Christmas last enter the possession thereof having no stock to employ the said land, since which tyme your Petitioner by his freinds hath sowne some of the said land and is charged or speedily to be charged with monthly pay to the Parliament and advaunce money to the Scotts Three pounds five shillings. And your petitioner, being poore by reason of many former suits unjustly prosecuted apainst him, hath neither Neat cattell, horse cattell, swine, sheepe, corn, money, nor credit to borrow money. And thro a widow Gostling challenging her thirds out of that land and her sonn Thomas Gostling three or four acres of it for copyhold and one Richard Burr, who maryed the petitioner's daughter agains his will, challenging all the said land, your petitioner can get no task cattell to pasture by means whereof he is not able to pay the said charge taxed upon him for the said land.

In respect whereof and for that my Lord of Manchester by his warrant, dated about the 25th of November, as the Petitioner remembreth did appoynt two Shillings in the pound to any that could discover any delinquent's goods, since which tyme your petitioner did discover so much money and goods as there hath been £59 already paid to the Parliament's use thereupon, and a great deale more is to be paid upon the sale of goods already so taken. And your Petitioner having received nothing doth humbly pray all taxes charged upon him for the Parliament and Scots advaunce may be suspended untill such tyme as he shall have satisffaction according to his Lopp^s order and the warrant thereupon. And your petitioner shall ever pray for your worshipp's prosperous successe in all yor affayres.

LADY FRANCES HOBART to THE COMMITTEE OF SAFETY.

1659.—I pray pardon this trouble which is occasioned by my feare of my horses being taken now upon my sudden jorney to my oune house at Chaplefield in Norw^ch which I intend, God permitting, to begin the 8th August, this day their haveing bin one of my horses taken by Capt. Frier's command and a note taken of the rest, but my horse civilie returned upon my promise to get somwhat from the Councell of State for my keeping them, and now, Sir, I desire to give you a just account of mine, 2 bay sound horses, 2 bay geldings, all standing in my sister of Exeters stalls, a black gelding and a bay in Gibbes stalls in Salisbury lane and a gray nag and a sorrell now at grase, these, Sir, are the horses, I begg the favour to keepe without any further trouble either to myself or my friends amongst which I beseche you give me leav to rank you.

Sir, my request to you is that you would get me a protection for these horses.

Endorsememt on the letter :—

Wee desire you to forbeare meddling with the horses mentioned in this letter and belonging to the within mentioned Lady Fran : Hobart.

Signed Lambert.

Whytehall, fryday,
'59, July 30. Richard Salwey.

1660, Oct..—Receipt for £10 for a quarter's rent of Sir J. Hobart's house in Petty France, Westminster.

1661.—Fees for burial of a child of Sir John Hobart at Covent Garden.

1680, 2 Dec.—Appointment of Sir H. HOBART Steward of Duchy of Lancaster.

1680-[1], 25 Jan.—Received then by the hands of Jo. Brewster for a horse for Hen. Howard to ride on to London, as an assistant to con : Verdon up thither upon his being taken upon a warrant from the House of Commons.

John J H Holdinge,
his marke.

ESTREAT of the ASSESSMENT for SUBSIDIES, in the
HUNDRED OF EYNESFORD, 1663.

The writing and estreate; of all and every the sume and sumes of money by vertue of an Act of the Parliament now prorogued lately made for granting fower intyre Subsidys To his M^atie by the Temporality assessed charged and taxed in the said hundred of Eynisford, in the sayd County of Norff, for and towards the pay^t of the first two of the said fower subsidys, also of the names and surnames of all and evry the person and persons upon whome the said sume and sumes of money are respectively so assessed, charged and taxed and also the yeerly or other best value or values or other qualifications for which or by reason whereof every of them were so assessed, charged and taxed this 28th day of Sept., anno Domini, 1663, by us whose seales and signes manuall are hereunto sett being amongst others named Com⁵· for the sayd County in and by the said Act or by virtue thereof assigned unto the Lymitt in the sayd County whereof the sayd hundred is part by and with the assent of Edward Bulwer, Esquire, the High Collector of the sayd Lymitt delivered unto

Lands.

Alderford.

Thomas Hall, gen.	xlˢ	xviˢ
Nicholas Chapman, gen	xlˢ	xviˢ
Richard Kett and others as Guardians of Sarah hankes	}xxˢ	viiiˢ
Sum̄a hujus ville		iiˡⁱ

Baudswell.
Lands.

Richard Chambers, gen.	xxˢ	viiiˢ
Henry Eglinton, gen.	xlˢ	xviˢ
Thomas Leman	lˢ	xxˢ
Robert Bucke	xlˢ	xviˢ
Willᵐ Wells	xxxˢ	xiiˢ
John Abbott	xxˢ	viiiˢ
Thomas Cotts	xxˢ	viiiˢ
Robert Philipes	xxˢ	viiiˢ
Ralph ffunnell, gntn. for the heyres of John Hare, sen. dec.	xxˢ	viiiˢ
Elizabeth Castleton, widow	xxˢ	viiiˢ
John Grange	xxˢ	viiiˢ
James Muddyshift	xxˢ	viiiˢ
Summa hujus ville viˡⁱ viiiˢ		

Brandeston.
Lands.

Robert Kinge, gen.	xlˢ	xviˢ
Henry Fuller	xlˢ	xviˢ
Timothy Stotton, gen. (*sic*)	iiiˢ	xxiiiiˢ

Goods.

John Jempson	iiiˡⁱ	xviˢ
Summa hujus ville iiiˡⁱ xiiˢ		

Bylaugh.
Lands.

Henry Beddingfield, esq.	xiiˡⁱ	iiiiˡⁱ xviˢ
Mrs. Frances Paston, widdow	xlˢ	xviˢ
John Bendish, gen.	iiiiˡⁱ	xxxii
Henry Hay, gen.	iiiˡⁱ	xxiiiiˢ

Thomas Raymer	xx^s	viii^s
John Westmor	xx^s	viii^s

GOODS.

John Porter	iii^{li}	xvi^s

Summa hujus ville x^{li}

Billingford.

LANDS.

Willm Boddy	xl^s	xvi^s
Richard Springall	xl^s	xvi^s
John Hase	xx^s	viii^s
Anthony Cooke	xx^s	viii^s

Summa hujus ville ii^{li} viii^s

Bintrye.

LANDS

John Hinks	iii^{li}	xxiiii^s
Christopher Andrews	xl^s	xvi^s
Andrew Poynter	xx^s	viii^s
John Browne	xx^s	viii^s
John Cubitt	xx^s	viii^s

GOODS.

Willm Lynn, gen.	iiii^{li}	xxi^s iiii^d

Summa hujus ville iiii^{li} v^s iiii^d

Elsing.

LANDS.

Thomas Browne, esq.	v^{li}	xl^s
John Robinson, cler.	xx^s	viii^s
Thomas Hewitt	xx^s	viii^s
John Drapitt	xx^s	viii^s
Bridget Copland, widow	xx^s	viii^s
Anne Southgate, widdow	xx^s	viii^s
Elizabeth Beacon, as guardian to her daughter	xx^s	viii^s

Summa hujus ville viii^l viii^s

Foulsham.

LANDS.

William Money, gen.	iiii^{li}	xxxii^s
Will. Keeling, gen.	iii^{li}	xxiv^s
Rob. Dey, gen.	xl^s	xvi^s
Phillup Skippon, esq., ultra mare		
Wm Parlett his farmer and bayliff	vi^{li}	ii^{li} viii^s
Will. Atthill	iiii^{li}	xxxii^s
Will. Parlett	xx^s	viii^s
John Wild	xx^s	viii^s
John Ives	xx^s	viii^s
Katherin Altcocke, widdow	xx^s	viii^s
Seth Chapman	iii^{li}	xxiiii^s
James Burton	xx^s	viii^s

Will. Nicholls	xl^s	xvi^s
Richard Nicholls	xx^s	viii^s
Robert Sparrow, gen.	xl^s	xvi^s
John Chapman	xx^s	viii^s
Henry Chapman, jun.	xl^s	xvi^s
Henry Chapman, sen.	xx^s	viii^s
Robt Chapman, Butcher	xx^s	viii^s
Edward Wild	xx^s	viii^s

GOODS.

Martha Alcocke, widdow	v^{li}	xxvi^s viii^d
Robt Chapman, draper	ix^{li}	ii^{li} viii^s
Symon Butler	iii^{li}	xvi^s

Summa hujus ville xx^{li} ii^s viii^d

ffoxley

LANDS

Anthony Howlett	iii^{li}	xxiiii^s
Richard Walker	xl^s	xvi^s
William Porter	xx^s	viii^s
Anne Burton, widdow	xx^s	viii^s
Robert Copeman of Barton	xl^s	xvi^s

GOODS.

ffrancis Porter	v^{li}	xxvi^s viii^d
Thomas Porter	iii^{li}	xvi^s

Summa hujus ville v^{li} xiiii^s viii^d

Geyst.

LANDS.

Henry Mynn, gen.	xl^s	xvi^s
Rice Wickes	xl^s	xvi^s
John Reymer	xx^s	viii^s
Wm Reymer	xx^s	viii^s
Edward Astly	xx^s	viii^s

GOODS.

Christopher Mynn, gen.	iii^l	xvi^s
John Duningham *alias* De Pree	iii^{li}	xvi^s

Summa hujus ville iiii^{li} viii^s

Geistwicke.

LANDS.

Edward Bulwer, esq.	xxiiii^{li}	v^{li} xii^s
Will. Bulwer, jure uxor.	v^{li}	ii^{li}
John Jermie	xl^s	xvi^s
Joseph Symonds, gen.	iii^{li}	xxiiii^s
Jsaacke Asshly	xx^s	viii^s

GOODS.

Roger Bulwer, gen.	iii^{li}	**xvi^s**

Summa hujus ville x^{li} xvi^s

Hackford.

LANDS.

Augustin Messenger	vi^{li}	ii^{li} viii^{s}
Elizabeth Coxfer, widdow	xx^{s}	viii^{s}
Thomas Munsey	xl^{s}	xvi^{s}
Henry Dewing	xl^{s}	xvi^{s}
Willm Bayfeild	iii^{li}	xxiiii^{s}
Richard Chamberlayne, esq.	xl^{s}	xvi^{s}
Thomas Breese	xl^{s}	xvi^{s}
Willm Parke	xx^{s}	viii^{s}

GOODS.

Thomas Norton	iiii^{li}	xvi^{s}

Summa hujus ville viii^{li} viii^{s}

Heverland.

LANDS.

Clement Hyrne, esq.	vi^{li}	ii^{li} viii^{s}
Mrs Anne Hyrne, widdow	iiii^{li}	xxxii^{s}
John Jeckes	xx^{s}	viii^{s}

Summa hujus ville iiii^{li} iiii^{s}

Hyndolveston.

LANDS.

Samuel Lynn	xl^{s}	xvi^{s}
And as guardian for John Lynn	xl^{s}	xvi^{s}
Daniell Brown	xx^{li}	viii^{s}
James Claybourne	xx^{s}	viii^{s}
Margaret Shinkwyn, widdow	xx^{s}	viii^{s}
Thomas Beddingfeild, gen.	iii^{li}	xxiiii^{s}
Willm Lynn	iii^{li}	xxiiii^{s}
Ryce Ollye	xx^{s}	viii^{s}
Robert Daniell, gen.	xl^{s}	xvi^{s}

GOODS.

Thomas Johnson	iiii^{li}	xxi^{s} iiii^{d}
Thomas Hallman	iii^{li}	xvi^{s}
Edmond Sconce	iii^{li}	xvi^{s}
Joseph Arlston	iii^{li}	xvi^{s}

Summa hujus ville ix^{li} xvii^{s} iiii^{d}

Lynge.

LANDS

Elizabeth Locke, widdow	xl^{s}	xvi^{s}
Thomas King, sen.	xl^{s}	xvi^{s}
John Abell	xx^{s}	viii^{s}
Thomas Stoughton	xx^{s}	viii^{s}
Thomas Kinge, jun.	xx^{s}	viii^{s}
Mrs Becke, widdow	xx^{s}	viii^{s}
Will. Couldwell, cler.	xx^{s}	viii^{s}

Summa hujus ville iii^{li} xii^{s}

Morton.

Goods.

Hugh Murrell   iii^{li} xvi^s

Summa hujus ville xvi^s

Reepham cum Cardeston.

Lands

John Dennis	xl^s	xvi^s
Edmond Skilling	xx^s	viii^s
Will. Dacke	xx^s	viii^s
Mary Dacke, widdow	xx^s	viii^s
John Hartston	xx^s	viii^s
Ralph Outlaw, clk. of Necton	xl^s	xvi^s

Summa hujus ville iii^{li} iiii^s

Ringland.

Lands.

Francis Heyward, gen.	vii^{li}	ii^{li} xvi^s
Thomas Kett, gen.	v^{li}	ii^{li}
Barnard Laverocke, gen.	xl^s	xvi^s
John Parfitt	xx^s	viii^s

Summa hujus ville vi^{li}

Sall.

Lands.

James Fountayne, esq.	vi^{li}	ii^{li} viii^s
Nathaniel Brett	xx^s	viii^s
John Barbour	xx^s	viii^s
Rob. Dey	xx^s	viii^s
Thomas Marker, gen.	xl^s	xvi^s
Willm Stewart	xl^s	xvi^s
Thomas Margatson	xx^s	viii^s

Summa hujus ville v^l xii^s

Sparham.

Lands.

Geoffrey Fuller	xx^s	viii^s
Elizabeth Batch, widdow	xx^s	viii^s
Thomas Sedly, gen. of Backton	xx^s	viii^s

Goods.

ffrancis hamond	iii^{li}	xvi^s
Godfrey Ridgwell	iii^{li}	xvi^s
Robert Ivory	iii^{li}	xvi^s

Summa hujus ville iii^{li} xii^s

Swannington

Lands.

Will. Jealons	xl^s	xvi^s
The same William as guardian to the children of John Allen, deceased	xl^s	xvi^s
William Moy	xl^s	xvi^s
Hamond Thurston of Drayton	xx^s	viii^s

Willm Bladwell, esq.   iiii^{li}   xxiiii^s
John Pikarell, gen.   vi^{li}   ii^{li} viii^s
     Summa hujus ville vi^{li} viii^s

Thimblethorp.

LANDS.

Edward Cooper   iiii^{li}   xxiiii^s
Anthony Brett   xx^s   viii^s
Nicholas Riches   xx^s   viii^s
Thomas Mowting of Norw^{ch.} gen.   xl^s   xvi^s
Thomas Copeman of G^t Yarmouth   xx^s   viii^s
     Summa hujus ville iii^{li} iiii^s

Thurning.

LANDS.

Peter Elwyn, sen., gen.   iiii^{li}   xxiiii^s
Peter Elwyn, jun., gen.   iiii^{li}   xxiiii^s
Thomas Elwin, gen.   xl^s   xvi^s

GOODS.

Christopher Pay   iiii^{li}   xvi^s
     Summa hujus ville iiii^{li}

Twyford.

LANDS.

Willm Raylye, gen.   iiii^{li}   xxxii
James Ward, gen.   iiii^{li}   xxxii^s
John Harnye   xx^s   viii^s

GOODS.

Henry Lynne   iii^{li}   xvi^s
     Summa hujus ville iiii^{li} viii^s

Weston.

LANDS.

Mrs Margaret Rookwood, widd.   vi^{li}   ii^{li} viii^s
Spencer Chapman   iii^{li}   xxiiii^s
Willm Bunn   xx^s   viii^s
Willm Hewitt, sen.   xl^s   xvi^s
Will. Hewitt, jun.   xx^s   viii^s
Thomas Andrews   xx^s   viii^s
John Mann   xx^s   viii^s
Th^{os} Fryer   xx^s   viii^s
Elizabeth Bunn, widdow   xx^s   viii^s

GOODS.

Thomas Rookwood, gen.   iii^{li}   xvi^s
Willm Lambe, g^{t.}   v^{li}   xxvi^s viii^d
Charles Bun   iiii^{li}   xxi^s iiii^d
     Summa hujus ville x^{li}

Wood Dawling.

Lands.

John Gallant, gen.	iii^{li}	xxiiii^{s}
Charles Kempe, gen.	iii^{li}	xxiiii^{s}
Edward Gay	xl^{s}	xvi^{s}
Roger Joyce	iii^{li}	xxiiii^{s}
Robert Sealth	xx^{s}	viii^{s}
Edward Messenger	xl^{s}	xvi^{s}
Richard Bell	xx^{s}	viii^{s}
William Sealth	xx^{s}	viii^{s}
Mrs Dorothy Astely	iii^{li}	xxiiii^{s}

Goods.

Rob. Johnson	iiii^{li}	xxi^{s} iiii^{d}
Will. Bell	v^{li}	xxvi^{s} viii^{d}
Zachariah ffuller	iii^{li}	xvi^{s}
John Bell	iii^{li}	xvi^{s}
Robert Starling	iii^{li}	xvi^{s}
Thomas Swallow	iii^{li}	xvi^{s}

Summa hujus ville xiii^{li} iiii^{s}

Whitwell.

Lands.

Augustin Breese	xx^{s}	viii^{s}
John Cawsey	xx^{s}	viii^{s}
William Greene	xx^{s}	viii^{s}

Goods.

William Barron	iii^{li}	xvi^{s}

Summa hujus ville ii^{li}

Wood Norton.

Lands.

Richard Springall	xl^{s}	xvi^{s}
Goodwyne, widd.	xx^{s}	viii^{s}

Summa hujus villa xxiiii^{s}

Witchingham Magna.

Lands.

Oliver Neve, esq^{re}	xx^{li}	viii^{li}
George Boid	iiii^{li}	xxxii^{s}
Stephen Dewing	iiii^{li}	xxxii^{s}
Thomas Allen, gen.	iii^{li}	xxiiii^{s}
Thomas Shackle, gen.	xl^{s}	xvi^{s}
Willm Pratt	xx^{s}	viii^{s}
Ralph Andrews	xx^{s}	viii^{s}
Thomas eu Styth	xx^{s}	viii^{s}

Summa hujus ville xxii^{li} viii^{s} (*sic*)

Witchingham Parva.
LANDS.

Ralph Outlaw, gen.	xl^s	xvi^s
Thomas Outlaw, gen.	xl^s	xvi^s

Summa hujus ville xxxii^s
Summa totalis hujus hundredi clxxviii^{li}

ESTREAT OF THE SUBSIDIES granted by the temporalty in the HUNDRED OF NORTH ERPINGHAM, 1663.

Antingham liiii^s

Edmond De Gray, esq.	iii^{li}	xxiiii^s
Robert Harmer	xx^s	viii^s
Andrew Rose	xx^s	viii^s
Robert Harmer, clerk	xxxv^s	xiiii^s

Cromer iiii^{li} viii^s

Sir George Windham, knight	vi^{li}	xlviii^s
Thomas Baxter, gent.	iiii^{li}	xxxii^s
Dennis Rounce	xx^s	viii^s

Gimingham vii^{li} xii^s

George Gryme, gent.	iii^{li}	xxiiii^s
John Matchett, gent.	iii^{li} x^s	xxviii^s
Thomas Gogle, gent.	xxx^s	xii^s
Myles Skerrett	xx^s	viii^s
Richard Johnsons	xxx^s	xii^s
William Cubitt	xx^s	viii^s
Nicholas Tompson	xx^s	viii^s
John Mingay, gent.	iii^{li} x^s	xxviii^s
Richard Gryme, gent.	xx^s	viii^s
Robert Gryme, gent.	xl^s	xvi^s

Gunton xxiv^s

Anne Jermy, gentlew.	iii^{li}	xxiv^s

Hanworth vi^{li} xiiii^s

Robert Doughty, esq.	vi^{li}	xlviii^s
Frances Doughty, gentlew.	xl^s	xvi^s
Robert Hogan	xlv^s	xviii^s
Robert Jell	xl^s	xvi^s
Elizabeth Miller, widd.	xxx^s	xii^s
Robert Miller	xx^s	viii^s
Thomas Love	xl^s	xvi^s

Knapton iiii^{li} xii^s

John Wortes	xxxv^s	xiiii^s
Thomas Everard, merchant	xl^s	xvi^s
John Harmer, gent., and his mother	xx^s	viii^s
Edward Wiggett	iii^{li}	xxiiii^s
Thomas Gryme	xx^s	viii^s
Philup Alcocke, gent.	xxv^s	x^s
John Flight	xxx^s	xii^s

Mundesley xxiiii^s

Edward Bradfield, gent.	iii^{li}	xxiiii^s

G

Northrepps xv^{li} x^s

Thomas Rugge, gent.	vi^{li}	xlviii^s
Riches Browne, gent.	iiii^{li} xv^s	xxxviii^s
Henry Playford, gent.	iii^{li}	xxiiii^s
Yallop, relict of Robert Yallop, gt. dec^d	iii^{li}	xxiiii^s
John Ellis, gent.	v^{li}	xl^s
Ward, relict of Alderman Ward, dec.	xxx^s	xii^s
John Spilman, gent.	v^{li}	xl^s
Thomas Outlacke, gent.	xx^s	viii^s
William Payne	xx^s	viii^s
Elizabeth Powell, widd.	xxxv^s	xii^s
Nicholas Carr, esq.	vi^{li}	xlviii^s
John Emerson	xx^s	viii^s

Overstrand lvi^s

Reymer, relict of John Reymer, esq., dec.	xl^s	xvi^s
John Manninge, clerk, guardian to or for William Reymer, gent., an infant	iiii^{li}	xxxii^s
Symson Rice	xx^s	viii^s

Roughton v^{li} viii^s

James Tennant, gent.	vii^{li} x^s	iiii^{li}
John Reynolds, clerke	xl^s	xvi^s
Robert Priest	xx^s	viii^s
Robert Hamond, gent.	xl^s	xvi^s
William Sudbury, clerk	xx^s	viii^s

Sidestrand iii^{li} vii^s

Thomas Deedes, gent.	xl^s	xvi^s
William Clerke, gent.	iii^{li}	xxiiii^s
Edmund Elden	xl^s	xvi^s
Giles Grey and his father	xx^s	viii^s
Roger Browne, gent.	xx^s	viii^s

Southreps ix^{li} viii^s

John Cubitt	iiii^{li}	xxxii^s
Robert Bateman	iii^{li}	xxiiii^s
Robert fflight	iii^{li}	xxiiii^s
Robert Primrose	xx^s	viii^s
Sara Rice, widdow	xx^s	viii^s
William Bateman	xl^s	xvi^s
Richard Doughty	xx^s	viii^s
Thomas Harmer	xx^s	viii^s
The heires of Joseph Snow, gent., deceased	v^{li}	xl^s
Robert Withers	xx^s	viii^s
John Crome	xxx^s	xii^s

Suffield vii^{li} viii^s

John Symonds, esq.	vi^{li}	xlviii^s
Thomas Symonds, clerke	iii^{li}	xxiiii^s
Henry Symonds, gent.	iii^{li} x^s	xxviii^s
John Porter, gent.	xxx^s	xii^s

John Starre   xx^s viii^s
John Wentworth, esq., here and at
   Roughton   iii^{li} x^s xxviii^s

Thorpe Market viii^{li} vi^s
Sir Thomas Rant, knight   xv^s vi^{li}
William Langwade and Elizabeth
   Langwade   xl^s xvi^s
Dame Cleyton   xxxv^s xiiii^s
Samuel Langwade   xl^s xvi^s
William Rant, gent.   v^{li} xl^s

Trimingham xxxviii^s
John Gryme, sen.   xxx^s xii^s
John Gryme, jun.   xx^s viii^s
Edmond Jewell   xxv^s x^s
Robert Parr   xx^s viii^s

Trunch vii^{li} xii^s
William Wortes, gent.   iii^{li} xxiiii^s
Richard Wortes, gent.   l^s xx^s
Robert Harmer   xl^s xvi^s
Robert fflight, g^t xl^s xvi^s
William Bates   xl^s xvi^s
William Mason   xxx^s xii^s
Samuel House   xx^s viii^s
Thomas Daynes   xl^s xvi^s
John Gogle   iii^{li} xxiiii^s

Alborough iii^{li} ii^s
Richard Hutchinson, esq.   xl^s xvi^s
John Miller, gent.   xl^s xvi^s
William Gay, gent.   xxx^s xii^s
Richard Whittacre   xx^s viii^s
Henry Gunton   xxv^s x^s

Aylmerton xlviii^s
Nicholas Monyman   xxx^s xii^s
William Johnsons   xxx^s xii^s
Edmond Pawle   xx^s viii^s
Richard Abbes   xx^s viii^s
• Richard Pawle   xx^s viii^s

Norwood Barningham vi^{li} viii^s
Sir John Palgrave, knight and
   baronet   x^{li} iiii^{li}
Augustine Palgrave, esq.   vi^{li} xlviii^s

Towne Barningham iii^s iiii^s
Sir Henry Beddingfield, k^t· and b^t·,
   Henry Beddingfield, esq., John
   Bendish of Elsing, gent., feoffees or   viii^{li} iii^{li} iiii^s
   trustees of Clem^t· Paston, esq.,
   deceased.
Dorothy Paston, relict of Clem^t Paston   vi^{li} xlviii^s
Rob. Miller   xx^s viii^s

Robert Billington, a non-comunicating
Popish recusant of 21 years   xvi^{d}
Richard Shaw, a non-com. Popish
recusant of 21 years of age   xvi^{d}
James Candler, a non-com. Popish
recusant of xvi yeares of age   xvi^{d}

Bassingham xx^{s}
  Robert Swaine   xxx^{s} xii^{s}
  Jerome Blofield, gent.   xx^{s} viii^{s}

East Beckham iii^{li} iiii^{s}
  Richard Chamberlayne, esq.   viii^{s} iii^{li} iiii^{s}

Beeston Regis l^{s}
  Anne Sherwood, gentlew.   xxx^{s} xii^{s}
  Richard Greene, gent.   l^{s} xx^{s}
  Edmond Hooke   xxv^{s} x^{s}
  Elizabeth Lombe, widow   xx^{s} viii^{s}

felbridge x^{l} xii^{s}
  John Windham, esq.   xxv^{s} x^{s}
  Richard Pawle   xxx^{s} xii^{s}

Gresham xxviii^{s}
  Elizabeth Ulfe, widdow   xxx^{s} xii^{s}
  Henry Johnsons   xx^{s} viii^{s}
  Richard Marys   xx^{s} viii^{s}

Matlaske iiii^{li} ii^{s}
  Phillip Pawle, gent.   iiii^{li} xxiiii^{s}
  Robert Gay   xl^{s} xvi^{s}
  Thomas Miller   xxx^{s} xii^{s}
  John Miller   xx^{s} viii^{s}
  Thomas Liggons   xxv^{s} x^{s}
  John Gay   xxx^{s} xii^{s}

Metton xvi^{s}
  Edward Crosby, gt.   xx^{s} viii^{s}
  John Carryer   xx^{s} viii^{s}

Plumpstead iiii^{li} viii^{s}
  Edmond Bretiff, gent.   iiii^{li} xxiiii^{s}
  Bartholomew Plumstead, gent.   xxx^{s} xii^{s}
  Nicholas Wilson, gent.   iiii^{s} xxxii^{s}
  Anne Britiff, widd.   l^{s} xx^{s}

Runton iiii^{li} i^{s} iiii^{d}
  William Blofield, gent.   l^{s} xx^{s}
  Mary ffirmary, widd.   xx^{s} viii^{s}
  John Smith, clerke   xx^{s} viii^{s}
  John Woodrow   l^{s} xx^{s}
  Thomas Smith   xl^{s} xvi^{s}
  Elizabeth Suggate, widd.   xx^{s} viii^{s}
  Jacob, an infant alien dwelling with
  Roger flint, clerk   xvi^{s}

Sheringham iii^{li} vii^{s}
  Robert ffeltham, gent.   l^{s} xx^{s}

Richard Jennys	xxv^s	x^s
Samuel Jennys	xx^s	viii^s
George Grey	xxv^s	x^s
Robert Yaxley	xx^s	viii^s
William Cooke	xx^s	viii^s
Thomas Cooke, sen.	xx^s	viii^s

Sustead xl^s

Leonard Blofield, gent.	iii^{li}	xxiiii^s
Thomas Cooke, gent.	xl^s	xvi^s

Thurgarton v^{li} vi^s

John Pettus, gent.	iii^{li} x^s	xxviii^s
Edmond Cooke	xx^s	viii^s
Christopher Blacke	iiii^{li}	xxxii^s
William Spurrell	xxxv^s	xiiii^s
Thomas Risbrough	xx^s	viii^s
William Druery	xx^s	viii^s
Samuell Soame	xx^s	viii^s

The grosse and totall summe of this hundred is cli^{li} xv^s iiii^d before any alteration, change or discharge had or made.

HUNDRED OF SOUTH ERPINGHAM, 1663.

Aylesham.

LANDS.

James Allen	xx^s	viii^s
Robt. Burre	xl^s	xvi^s
Thomas Browne	xx^s	viii^s
Elizabeth Bradie	xx^s	viii^s
Thomas Barker	xl^s	xvi^s
Francis Curtis, clerke	xl^s	xvi^s
Robert Doughty, gent.	lxxx^s	xxxii^s
John Durrant	xl^s	xvi^s
Thomas Lawes	xx^s	viii^s
Robert Russells	xl^s	xvi^s
Henry Some	xx^s	viii^s
ffrancis Curtis, as guardian to Thomas Leaman }	xx^s	viii^s
Richard Curtis	xl^s	xvi^s
Robert Hall	xl^s	xvi^s
John Ellis	xx^s	viii^s
Martha Smyth, wid.	xx^s	viii^s
Anne Brytiffe, wid.	xx^s	viii^s
William Doughty	xl^s	xvi^s
John Brady	xx^s	viii^s
Elizabeth Lubbocke, wid.	xx^s	viii^s
William Willson	xx^s	viii^s

Alby.

LANDS.

William Langwood	xl^s	xvi^s
Robt. ffisher	xx^s	viii^s
Jeremy Blofeyld	lx^s	xxiiii^s
William Parke	xx^s	viii^s

Baningham.

Humphery Carter	xx^s	viii^s
Thomas Knivett	xx^s	viii^s
Phillip Graye	xl^s	xvi^s
Richard Clark	xx^s	viii^s
Jeremy Barnes	xx^s	viii^s
ffrancis Wiggett	xx^s	viii^s

Barneingham pva.

Christopher Page	xx^s	viii^s
Thomas Page	xx^s	viii^s
William Bacon	xx^s	viii^s
Christopher Graye	xx^s	viii^s

Baconsthorpe.

Robert Beare	xx^s	viii^s
Edmund Warnes	xx^s	viii^s
Edmund Britiffe	v^{li}	xl^s
Longfer, wid.	xx^s	viii^s
Anne Vathecke	xx^s	viii^s

GOODS.

Mrs Susan Longe	vi^{li}	xxxii^s

Brampton.

Thomas Smyth	lx^s	xxiiii^s
Richard Curson	xx^s	viii^s

Buxton.

Thomas Bulwer	lxxx^s	xxxii^s
John Hurton	xx^s	viii^s
Thomas Edridg	xx^s	viii^s
John Watker	xx^s	viii^s

GOODS.

Mrs Anne Gosnald	lx^s	xii^s

Booton.

Catherine Malham	lxxx^s	xxxii^s
William Shillinge.	xl^s	xvi^s

Burrough.

Edmund Burre	xx^s	viii^s
Catherine Suffeild	xx^s	viii^s
William Parker	xx^s	viii^s
Robt Howse	xx^s	viii^s
James Fecsor	xx^s	viii^s

West Beckham.

Richard Cooke	xx^s	viii^s
Edmund Clucke	xx^s	viii^s
James Tower	xx^s	viii^s
William Clarke	xx^s	viii^s

Belough.

Edward Puttocke	xx^s	viii^s

Blicklinge.

Sir John Hobart, knight and baronet com.	xxx^{li}	xii^{li}

Thomas Sayers	xx^s	viii^s
Richard Smyth	xx^s	viii^s
Rob. Smyth	xx^s	viii^s
William Smyth	xx^s	viii^s
John Payne	xx^s	viii^s
James White	xx^s	viii^s

Coulteshall.

William Parkings	xl^s	xvi^s
Nathaniell Blaxter	lx^s	xxiiii^s
Henry Whitwell	lx^s	xxiiii^s
Richard Lubbock	xx^s	viii^s
Edmund Goslinge	xl^s	xvi^s

Calthorpe.

Bartholomew Plumsteade	xx^s	viii^s
John Tubbinge	xx^s	viii^s
William Webster	xl^s	xvi^s
Alice Muntford, wid.	xx^s	viii^s

Colby.

William Smyth	xx^s	viii^s

Corpustie cum Irmingland

Dame Alice Smyth	x^{li}	lxxx^s

Causton.

John Earle, esq., comr	v^{li}	xl^s
John Lombe	xl^s	xvi^s
John Hamond	xx^s	viii^s
Mary Vawle, wid.	xx^s	viii^s
Edward Lombe	lxxx^s	xxxii^s

Erpingham.

ffrancis hyrne	xl^s	xvi^s
Frederick Tylney	xx^s	viii^s
Henry Empson	xx^s	viii^s
John Warner	xx^s	viii^s
Thomas Lubbocke	xx^s	viii^s
Thomas Wolsey	xx^s	viii^s
William Spirall	xx^s	viii^s
Willm Lubbocke	xl^s	xvi^s
Thomas Hawes	lx^s	xxiiii^s
William Héwett	xx^s	viii^s

Heydon.

Erasmus Earle, serjeant-at-law, com.	xx^s	viii^s
William Sympson	lx^s	xxiiii^s
John Vrary	xx^s	viii^s
William Scottowe	xl^s	xvi^s
Richard Robins	xx^s	viii^s
Thomas Robins	xx^s	viii^s
Richard ffulcher	xx^s	viii^s
Thomas Newman	xl^s	xvi^s

Hevingham.

Thomas Scamler, gent.	lx^s	xxiiii^s

Itteringham.

Hevingham.
- Thomas Scamler, gent.   lx^s   xxiiii^s
- John Tolke   xl^s   xvi^s
- William Haylett   xl^s   xvi^s

Itteringham.
- Richard Robins   xx^s   viii^s
- Edmond Chapman   xx^s   viii^s

Ingworth.
- Briget Wolsey   xx^s   viii^s

Houtebys m^a
- Edward Warnes, cl.   xl^s   xvi^s
- Edward Denny   xl^s   xvi^s
- Henry Palmer   xl^s   xvi^s

Lammas cum Houteboys parva.
- Thomas Sadler   lx^s   xxiiii^s
- Robert Symth   xx^s   viii^s
- Rob Chapman   xx^s   viii^s
- Humphery Prattant   xl^s   xvi^s
- John Allen, sen.   xx^s   viii^s

Marsham.
- Edmund Gall   xx^s   viii^s

Manington.
- Sir John Potts, k^t and barr., com.   xv^{li}   vi^{li}
- John Potts, esq., com.   viii^{li}   lxiiii^s

Oxnett.
- Sir Robt. Paston, k^t and barr com.   xxx^{li}   xii^{li}
- Joane Kilbie, wid.   xx^s   viii^s

Oulton.
- William Bell   xl^s   xvi^s
- Edmund Bell   xx^s   viii^s
- John Bell   xl^s   xvi^s
- Wm Lombe   xx^s   viii^s

Saxthorpe.

LANDS.
- John Dey   lx^s   xxiiii^s
- Mary Dey   xl^s   xvi^s
- John Page, esq.   lxxx^s   xxxii^s
- John Vahan, cl.   xl^s   xvi^s
- Isadora Edmunds, wid.   xx^s   viii^s
- Mary Cooke, wid.   xx^s   viii^s

GOODS.
- Thomas Allen   lx^s   xvi^s

Swanton.
- William Coulsen, sen.   xx^s   viii^s
- Richard Beare   xx^s   viii^s
- Mrs Elizabeth Garrard   xx^s   viii^s
- Willm Cooper   xx^s   viii^s

Skeyton.

Edmund Spendlowe	xx^{s}	viii^{s}
Henry Empson	xx^{s}	viii^{s}

Scottowe.

Thomas Picroft	xl^{s}	xvi^{s}
John Spendlowe	xl^{s}	xvi^{s}
Thomas Lockton	xx^{s}	viii^{s}
John Warnes	xx^{s}	viii^{s}
William Durrant	xl^{s}	xvi^{s}
Martha Lubbocke	xx^{s}	viii^{s}
Brigett Edwards	xl^{s}	xvi^{s}

Stratton Straylesse.

Mrs Anne Marsham	xx^{s}	viii^{s}
Mr Henry Marsham	xl^{s}	xvi^{s}
William Marsham	v^{li}	xl^{s}

Tuttington.

Mrs Mary Rolfe	lxxx^{s}	xxxii^{s}
M$^{r\cdot}$ Barnard Utbard	xl^{s}	xvi^{s}

Twayet.

John Wolsey	xl^{s}	xvi^{s}
John Bande	xx^{s}	viii^{s}

Wickmer.

John Ramsey, esq.	v^{li}	xl^{s}
Henry Miller, sen.	xl^{s}	xvi^{s}
Henry Miller, jun.	xx^{s}	viii^{s}
Henry Gunton	xl^{s}	xvi^{s}
Robt Lubbocke	xx^{s}	viii^{s}
Amy Larwood	xx^{s}	viii^{s}
Martha Breese	xx^{s}	viii^{s}
Xpofer Parkine	xx^{s}	viii^{s}

Wolterton.

James Scamler, esq.	viii^{li}	lxiiii^{s}

Summe is 141^{li} 06^{s} 00^{d}

In the Hundred of HOLT, 1663.

Holt Hundred.

" The Assessment for the said Hundred of the first two subsidies of the fower granted to his Matie in the fifteenth yeare of his highness' raigne rated by William Symonds, Robt Hunt, Thomas Wright, Edmond Hobart, George Bulleyn, John Dey, and Henry Pane, gent., Assessors, and John Sorrell and Owen Palmer, gent., Cheife Constables there, the 19th day of Sept. in the year of our Lord God 1663."

Holt.

LANDS.

Edmond Hobart, gent., Assessor	iii^{li}	xxiiii^{s}
Sam Butler	xx^{s}	viii^{s}
Michaell Butler	xx^{s}	viii^{s}

John Millner	xx^s	viii^s
Will. Carre, sen.	xx^s	viii^s
Will. Carre, jun.	xx^s	viii^s
Rob. Shepheard	xx^s	viii^s
Will. Leake	xx^s	viii^s
James Bulleyn, gent.	xxx^s	xii^s
Phillip Feake	xx^s	viii^s
William Evered	xx^s	viii^s
Willm Spurrell	xx^s	viii^s

Goods.

Henry Ampleford, gent.	vi^{li}	xxxii^s
Stephen Allen	vi^{li}	xxxii^s
Thomas Donne	vi^{li}	xxxii^s
George Spurrell	iii^{li}	xvi^s

Bafeild cum Glandford.

Lands.

Rob. Jermy, Esq.	x^{li}	iiii^{li}
Rob. Jermy, jun.	iii^{li}	
Peter Critoft	xxx^s	xii^s
John Castor	xx^s	viii^s

Bathely.

Lands.

George Bulleyn, gent., Assessor	ii^{li}	xvi^s
James Brame	xx^s	viii^s
Lucy Shaxton, wid.	xx^s	viii^s
Thomas Poroditch	xx^s	viii^s
Bridget Bulleyn, wid.	xx^s	viii^s
Richard Thasher	xxx^s	xii^s

Gunthorpe.

Lands.

Thomas Might, gent., Assessor	v^{li}	xl^s
John Sorrell, gent.	i^{li}	viii^s
John Houghton, gent.	iii^{li}	xxiiii^s
Judah Houghton, wid.	ii^{li}	xvi^s
Alice and Elizabeth Houghton	xxx^s	xii^s
Jeffery Might, gent.	iiii^{li}	xxxii^s
Thomas Davies	iiii^{li}	xxxii^s
Samuel Beckham	xx	viii^s

Morston.

Lands.

Th^{o.} Shorting	xl^s	xvi^s
James Apoditch	xxx^s	xii^s

Blakeney.

Lands.

Sam Bacon, gent.	viii^{li}	iii^{li} iiii^s
Th^{o.} Youngman	xl^s	xvi^s

Th^{o.} Russell	xl^s	xvi^s

Th^o. Russell — xl^s — xvi^s
Th^os. Abraham — xx^s — viii^s
John Cressey — xx^s — viii^'
Henry Bassett — xx^s — viii^s

Wiveton.

LANDS.

Edmond Day, clerke — v^li — xl^s
John Loades — xx^s — viii^s
Richard Yaxley — xx^s — viii^s

Stodey.

LANDS.

Will. Symonds, gent., Assessor — iiii^li — xxxii^s
Rob. Critoft, gent. — xl^s — xvi^s
Rob. Feazer — xx^s — viii^s

GOODS.

Elizabeth Hastings, wid. — iii^li — xvi^s
Martin hastings, gent. — iii^li — xvi^s

Hempstead.

Robert Hunt, gent., Assessor — xl^s — xvi^s
Owen Palmer, gent., chief constable — xx^s — viii^s
Nicholas Gotts — xx^s — viii^s
Martha Preist, wid. — xx^s — viii^s
Willm. Worts — xx^s — viii^s

Salthausen.

LANDS.

Hen^y Parre, gent., Assessor — xl^s — xvi^s
Edward Dawney, Clerke — xx^s — viii^s
Henry Standforth — xxx^s — xii^s
John Goulding — xx^s — viii^s
Robert Leverington — xx^s — viii^s

Kelling.

LANDS.

Anne Gilbert, wid. — xx^s — viii^s
John Hamond — xx^s — viii^s
Richard Balls — xx^s — viii^s
Elizabeth grene, wid. — xx^s — viii^s

Wayborne.

LANDS.

Th^o. Wotton, gent. Discharged xx^s
  uppon his oath
John Munford — iiii^li — xxxii^s
Giles Preist — xx^s — viii^s
Sam Yaxley — xx^s — viii^s
John Cooke — xxx^s — xii^s

Langham.

LANDS.

John Dey, gent., Assessor	iii^{li}	xxiiii^{s}
Willm Mann, sen.	v^{li}	xl^{s}
Willm Mann, jun.	xl^{s}	xvi^{s}
Tho. Earle	xl^{s}	xvi^{s}
John Locksmith	xxx^{s}	xii^{s}
George Boise	xl^{s}	xvi^{s}
John Boise	xx^{s}	viii^{s}
Shorting, wid.	xxx^{s}	xii^{s}

GOODS.

John Brighmer	iii^{li}	xvi^{s}

Hunworth.

LANDS.

Phillip Britiffe	v^{li}	xl^{s}
Edmund Britiffe, sen., guardian to } Clement Britiffe	iiii^{li}	xxxii^{s}
Elizabeth Russell, wid.	viii^{li}	iii^{li} iiii^{s}
Rob$^{t.}$ Rogers	xx^{s}	viii^{s}
Will$^{m.}$ Newman	xx^{s}	viii^{s}

Briningham.

LANDS.

Thomas Burllingham, gent.	iiii^{li}	xxxii^{s}
Rob. Spurrell	xx^{s}	viii^{s}

Bodham.

LANDS.

Robt Watson, Clerke	iiii^{li}	xxxii^{s}
Thos Smith	v^{li}	xl^{s}
Th^{os} Franck	xl^{s}	xvi^{s}
Edward Franckling	xx^{s}	viii^{s}

GOODS.

Francis Roberts	iii^{li}	xvi^{s}

Swanton Novers.

LANDS.

John Fincham	xx^{s}	viii^{s}

Melton Constable.

LANDS.

Sir Jacob Astley, knight and baronett	xxx^{li}	xii^{li}

Burrow parva.

LANDS.

Thomas Reynor, clerke	xx^{s}	viii^{s}
John Lee, gent.	xx^{s}	viii^{s}

Letheringsett.

LANDS.

Edward Worsley, clerke	xxx^s	xii^s
Richard ffitts, gent.	l^s	xx^s
John Dix	xx^s	viii^s
Robt Pearetree	xx^s	viii^s

Edgfeild.

LANDS.

James Marting, clerke	xx^s	viii^s
Martin, wid.	xx^s	viii^s
John Buxton, gent.	iiii^{li}	xxxii^s
Bartholomew grene	iii^{li}	xxiiii^s
Robert Martin	xxx^s	xii^s
Henry Wodrow	xx^s	viii^s
Rob. Castor	xxx^s	xii^s
Rob. Butler	xx^s	viii^s
Tilney, wid.	xx^s	viii^s
Ann Hobart, wid.	xx^s	viii^s

GOODS.

Edward Denney, gent.	x^{li}	ii^{li} viii^s iiii^d

Briston.

LANDS.

Robt Jeoffery	xx^s	viii^s
Katherine Taylor, wid.	xx^s	viii^s
Cates, wid.	xx^s	viii^s
John Cates	xx^s	viii^s
Will. Jervis	xl^s	xvi^s
Will. Roper, discharged by oath		
Richard Roper	xl^s	xvi^s
John More	xx^s	viii^s
Richard Athow	xx^s	viii^s
Thomas Garrett	xx^s	viii^s
John Browne	xx^s	viii^s

Thornage.

LANDS.

John Parkin	xx^s	viii^s
John Pyke	xx^s	viii^s
Tho. Girdleston	xx^s	viii^s
James Dix	xx^s	viii^s

Sharrington.

LANDS.

Thomas Hunt, esq^{re}	viii^{li}	iii^{li} iiii^s
Will. Hunt, gent.	xl^s	xvi^s
Nicholas Wild	xx^s	viii^s
Tho. Chapman	xxx^s	xii^s
Will. Alborough	xx^s	viii^s

Brinton.

	LANDS.		
Edmond Cooke	iiii^{li}	xxxii^s	
John Cooke	xl^s	xvi^s	
John Rogers	xx^s	viii^s	

Saxlingham.

	LANDS.		
John Harmer, cler.	xxx^s	xii^s	
Rob. Chevely	xl^s	xvi^s	
Th^{o.} Keltham	xx^s	viii^s	
Andrew Athill	xx^s	viii^s	
William Browne	xx^s	viii^s	
Elizabeth Cheavely, wid.	xx^s	viii^s	

Cley.

Simon Britiffe, esq.	xii^{li}	iiii^{li} xvi^s
Robt. Burton	iii^{li}	xxiiii^s
Roger Uther, gent.	xxx^{li}	xii^s
Will. Crockley	iii^{li}	xxiiii^s
Richard Flaxman	xxx^s	xii^s
Tho. Rayner	xx^s	viii^s

The names of persons having estates in the hundred of Holt
living elsewhere.

Holt.

The heires of Malling in ferme of Michael Butler	xxx^s	xii^s
Widow Ringall in ferme of Stephen Allen	xxx^s	xii^s
The Company of fishmongers in London in ferme of James Ward, esq.	xxx^s	xii^s
grene of Norwich in the ferme of Thomas Armestrong	xx^s	viii^s

Bately.

Mr. Timothy ffelton in ferme of James Browne	iiii^{li}	xxxii^s
Mr. Murray of Wells in the ferme of Steedman	iii^{li}	xxiiii^s

Gunthorpe.

John Gallant, gent., in ferme of Willm. Dix	xx^s	viii^s

Morston.

fflaxman in the ferme of John Gouldsmith	xxx^s	xii^s
John Stileman in ferme of Wm. Armestead	xx^s	viii^s

Blakeney.

The Executors of James Calthorpe, esq., in the ferme of Tho. Youngman, and others $\}$ x^{li} iiii^{li}

Salthouse.

Christopher Mynns in ferme of Henry Parr, gen. $\}$ l^s xx^s

Will$^{m.}$ Watts, esq., in the ferme of diverse men $\}$ xl^s xvi^s

Augustine Palgrave, esq^r · in Salthouse and Kelling, Commissioner $\}$

Kellene.

Sam Foster, cler., in the ferme of diverse men in Kelling and Waborne $\}$ iii^{li} xxiiii^s

Waborne.

The Lord Cornewallis in the ferme of Mr. Wolton $\}$ ix^{li} iii^{li} xii^s

Bodham.

Mr.   Luckner in the ferme of Francis Roberts $\}$ iiii^{li} xxxii^s

Mr.   Watts in the ferme of Robert   Joynes $\}$ xl^s xvi^s

Mr. Denny in ferme of Francis Chesteny $\}$ xx^s viii^s ,

Langham.

The Duke of Westmoreland in ferme of severall men in Langham and Morston $\}$ xl^s xvi^s

William Nettleton of Wells in ferme of John Locksmith $\}$ lx^s xx^s

John Harvy, esq., in the ferme of William Mann $\}$ iii^{li} xxiiii^s

Hempstead.

Thomas Barney, esq., in the ferme of severall men in Hempstead and Bodham $\}$ xii^{li} iiii^{li} xvi^s

Edgfeild.

The Lady Jermin in the ferme of Mr. Tilney. $\}$ iiii^{li} xxxii^s

Mr.   Rowland in the ferme of severall men $\}$ iiii^{li} xxiiii^s

Captaine ffisher in the ferme of severall men of Edgfeild and Briston $\}$ iii^{li} xxiiii^s

Briston.

Thomas Homes, gent., in the ferme of severall men $\}$ iiii   xxxii^s

Mr. ffountaine in the ferme of Will. Boxer	xl^s	xvi^s
Mr. Langwood in the ferme of John Browne	xxx^s	xii^s
Mr. James Scambler in Briston, Edgfeild, and Hempsted	iii^{li}	xxiiii^s
Erasmus Earle, Serjeant-at-Law, Commissioner		
John Toke in ferme of Mr. Garrett, cler.	xx^s	viii^s
George Purton in the ferme of severall men in Briston, Holt, and Hempstead	xx^s	viii^s

Thornadge.

Sir Edmund Bacon, Commissioner

Sherington.

Mr. Warkhouse in Sherinton and Brinton in ferme of Thomas Copeman	iii^{li}	xxiiii^s
Will. Baley in the ferme of severall men in Sherington and Brinton	xl^s	xvi^s

Saxlingham.

Sir Thomas Guibon and Edmond de Gray, esq., Commissioners

Letheringsett.

James Ward, esq., in the ferme of Richard Richmon	v^{li}	xl^s
Samuel Lin in the ferme of Robert Peartree	xl^s	xvi^s

Summa Totalis 167^{li} 3^s 4^d

ESTREAT of ASSESSMENT to SUBSIDISE, NORTH GREENHOE, 1663.

The Assessment made the One and twentieth day of Sept · Anno Dom., 1663, upon the generall inhabitants in the said hundred for the two first of the foure intire subsidies granted to our most gratious soveraigne Lord King Charles the Second, by Act of Parliament made in the 15th yeare of His Majes^{tes} raigne of England &c. being rated and assessed by John Nabbs, Speller Tubbing, James Hawes, William Netleton, John Bond, William Framingham, gent., appoynted by the Commissioners hereof to assesse the same togeather with Robert Magnus and Philip Tubbing, cheef constables for the said hundred.

Binham.

LANDS.

Timothy Manne, sen.	xl^s	xvi^s
John Covy	xl^s	xvi^s
Elizabeth Money, widow of Richard Money	xl^s	xvi^s

Richard Cutting	xx^s	viii^s
Robert Olley	xx^s	viii^s
Martin Money, sen.	xx^s	viii^s

GOODS.

| Timothy Manne, jun. | lx^s | xvi^s |

Hinderingham.

LANDS.

Richard Godfrey, Esq., Commiss^r	v^li	ii^li
John Nabbes, gent., sessor	xx^s	viii^s
James Ward, esq.	iiii^li	i^li xii^s
William Maye, sen.	iii^li	i^li iiii^s
Peter Tubbing	iii^li	i^li iiii^s
Judith Tubbing, widd.	ii^li	xvi^s
Phillip Tubbing, sesser and chief constable	xxx^s	xii^s
Richard Bond	ii^li	xvi^s
William harnie	xx^s	viii^s
Stephen Lee	xx^s	viii^s
William Maye, jun.	xx^s	viii^s
George Stampe	xx^s	viii^s
Francis Browne	xx^s	viii^s
John Lovell	xx^s	viii^s
Lawrance Bond	xx^s	viii^s
James Sydall	xx^s	viii^s
Richard Page	xx^s	viii^s

GOODS.

| Dionis Bond | iii^li | xvi^s |

Houghton.

LANDS.

Nich^s ffenne	xx^s	viii^s
Nicholas Dagney	xl^s	xvi^s
Thomas Fenne	xx^s	viii^s
Charles fflight	xx^s	viii^s

Holkham.

LANDS.

John Cooke, esq., Commissioner	c^li	xl^li
John Spooner	xl^s	xvi^s
Tymothey Large	xx^s	viii^s

Cockthorpe.

LANDS.

| Thomas Swallowe, cler. | xx^s | viii^s |

GOODS.

| Barbara Hill, widd. | iiii^li | i^li i^s iiii^d |

feildawling.

LANDS.

John Stileman	xl^s	xvi^s
James Plane	xx^s	viii^s
William Betts	xx^s	viii^s
Robert Winne	xx^s	viii^s
John Olley	xx^s	viii^s
Mathew Loose	xx^s	viii^s
John Manne	xx^s	viii^s
Robert Barker	xx^s	viii^s

GOODS.

Christopher Ringer	iii^{li}	xvi^s

Stifkey.

LANDS.

Robert Framingham	v^{li}	ii^{li}
Speller Tubbing	iii^{li}	i^{li} iiii^s
John framingham	xl^s	xvi^s
Robert Read	xl^s	xvi^s
Thomas Read	xx^s	viii^s

GOODS.

William Michell, cler.	iii^{li}	xvi^s

Welles juxta Mare.

LANDS.

Mongoe Moray, cle.	xl^s	xvi^s
William Netleton, sessor	iii^{li}	i^{li} iiii^s
Thomas Curson	iiii^{li}	i^{li} xii^s
John Leech	xl^s	xvi^s
Robert Kinge	xx^s	viii^s
Robert Magnus, Sessor and Cheefe Constable	xx^s	viii^s
Richard Sporne	xx^s	viii^s
William Breame	xl^s	xvi^s
Roger Monsuer	iii^{li}	i^{li} iiii^s
William Wallett	xx^s	viii^s
Stephen Knappe	xx^s	viii^s
William Frayry	xx^s	viii^s
Alice Tidd, widd.	xx^s	viii^s
Thomas Reaer	xl^s	xvi^s
Henry Lawson	xx^s	viii^s
John Wasselkey	xx^s	viii^s
Elizabeth Leech, widd.	xx^s	viii^s
John Sporle	xl^s	xvi^s
George Rideout	xx^s	viii^s
Clement Magnus	xl^s	xvi^s
John Goldsmith	xl^s	xvi^s
Robert Buckler	xx^s	viii^s

GOODS.

Thomas Boult	v^{li}	i^{li} vi^s viii^d
Margaret Reeder	iii^{li}	xvi^s
Richard Driver	iiii^{li}	i^{li} i^s iiii^d

John Julyan	iii^{li}	xvi^s
Mathew Sporne	iii^{li}	xvi^s
John Clerke, late of Feakenham	iii^{li}	xvi^s
John Clerke, late of Hindringham	iii^{li}	xvi^s
Anne Barnard, wid.	iiii^{li}	i^{li} i^s iiii^d
Mary Tidd, jun., widd.	iii^{li}	xvi^s
Nicholas Wagstaffe	iii^{li}	xvi^s
James Wortley	iii^{li}	xvi^s
Alice Sporne, widd.	iii^{li}	xvi^s
Thomas Cullen	iiii^{li}	i^{li} i^s iiii^d

Warham.

LANDS.

Ambrose Money, cler.	iii^{li}	i^{li} iiii^s
Jeremiah Purland, sen.	iiii^{li}	i^{li} xii^s
Jeremiah Purland, jun.	xl^s	xvi^s
Alice Purland, widd.	xl^s	xvi^s
Henry Greene	xx^s	viii^s
Jonas Scott	iii^{li}	i^{li} iiii^s
Gregory Brewster	xx^s	viii^s
William Harnie	xx^s	viii^s
Robert Manne	xx^s	viii^s
John Tubbing, cler.	xl^s	xvi^s
Robert Purland, esq.	xl^s	xvi^s
Robert fisher, cler.	iii^{li}	i^{li} iiii^s

GOODS.

John Mantle	iiii^{li}	i^{li} i^s iiii^d

Snoring Magna.

LANDS.

John Smith	xl^s	xvi^s
Thomas Webb, jun.	xx^s	viii^s
Anne Barnes, widd.	xx^s	viii^s

GOODS.

Robert Pyle	iii^{li}	xvi^s

Egmore.

LANDS.

Dorothy Bacon, widd.	iiiii^{li}	ii^{li}

Walsingham Parva.

LANDS.

Edmund Smith, doctor of physick	xl^s	xvi^s
John Partington	xx^s	viii^s
William fairefax	iiii^{li}	i^{li} xii^s
William Leverington	xx^s	viii^s
John Bond, sessor	l^s	i^{li}
William Framingham, sessor	l^s	i^{li}
John Johnes	xx^s	viii^s
William Seaton	xx^s	viii^s

Thomas Salter	xl^s	xvi^s
Henry Willis	xx^s	viii^s
Anthoney Catts	iiii^{li}	i^{li} iiii^s
Anne Sherwood, widdow	xl^s	xvi^s
Elizabeth Dey, widd.	xl^s	xvi^s
Elizabeth Ford, widd.	ii^{li} x^s	i^{li}
George heblethwaite	xl^s	xvi^s
Robert Glennenney	xx^s	viii^s
Rob. Dix	xl^s	xvi^s
Francis Vincent	xx^s	viii^s
Thomas ffairefax	xx^s	viii^s

GOODS.

Mathew Blyfer	iiii^{li}	xvi^s
Sara Partington, widd.	iiii^{li}	xvi^s

Walsingham Magna.

LANDS.

Mathew Blyfer	v^{li}	ii^{li}
Roger Monsuer	xl^s	xvi^s
Henry Monsure	xl^s	xvi^s
Dennis Bucke	iiii^{li}	i^{li} iiii^s
Judith Gibson, widd.	xl^s	xvi^s
Anne Allen, widd.	iiii^{li}	i^{li} iiii^s
John Day	xx^s	viii^s
Henry Matles	xl^s	xvi^s
Robert Johnes	xx^s	viii^s

Thursford.

LANDS.

Sr Thomas Guybon, k$^{nt.}$ Com$^{sr.}$	xvi^{li}	vi^{li} viii^s
William Guybon, esq., Com$^{sr.}$	iiiii^{li}	ii^{li}
Humphrey Curson	xx^s	viii^s
John Comber	xx^s	viii^s
Robert Benington	xx^s	viii^s

Wyton.

LANDS.

Humphrey Bedingfeild, esq., Com^r	viii^{li}	iii^{li} iiii^s
Edmund Newgate	xl^s	xvi^s
henry Bedingfeild for goods	iii^{li}	xvi^s

GOODS.

Richard Myles	v^{li}	i^{li} vi^s viii^d
Robert Olley	iii^{li}	xvi^s

Berney.

LANDS.

James Hawes, sessor	xl^s	xvi^s
Robert Hastings	xx^s	viii^s

James Lynne	xx^s	viii^s
Henry Anderson	xx^s	viii^s

POPISH RECUSANTS

Barbara Suger, sen.	i^s iiii^d
Barbara Suger, jun.	i^s iiii^d
John Sugar	i^s iiii^d

The grosse and totals of this hundred is - - - } 163l. 11s. 00d.

SIR JOHN HOBART to THOMAS SKEET.

1665, Jan. 31.—Lease of Langley Abbey.

1667-1670.—Copies of Testimonials to one Captain William Mayden, "Commander of several Fireships," formerly a midshipman in H.M. Ships *Royal Charles* and *London*, by Prince Rupert, Admiral Spragge, Lord Albemarle, and Lord Sandwich.

SIR J. HOBART to SIR JOHN FOUNTAINE, S.L.

1670, May 2.—Mortgage of Langley (monastery, site, &c.).

December 21, 1672.—Rec^d then of Sir John Hobart, Bart., by the handes of John Breuster for a Perriwig £7, for mending of a Wigge £1 10^s and for 2 pounds of haire powder; 5^s in all - - - - - } £8 15s.

(S^d·) John Ringstead.

List of a Gentleman's Wardrobe, [SIR HENRY HOBART] 1673.

A particular of things delivered into Mr. Eagles charge in Sept., 1673.

Imprimis a dark coloured druggat coat and breeches with a flowered silk wastcoate.

Item a buttond and loopd coate and breeches of druggatt with a silk pink^t wastcoate.

Item a coate and a pair of sleeves of black cloath with black triming tagg^d and a black silk wastcoat.

Item a light coloured branched silk wastcoate which was worne with the camblet suite.

Item a coate and a paire of breeches of an Irish freese.

Item a coate and pair of breeches of a dear coloured clothe w^h a silke wastcoat of ye same colour.

Item a coate and a pair of breeches of a darke coloured searge loynd with flowrd silke and a wastcoate suitable to the lyning of ye coate and a pair of silke stockins suitable.

Item a light coloured druggate coat and breeches with a flowr^d silk wastcoate, the breeches were alterd at London beinge formerly Pantelloons.

Item a shagge white silke wastcoat.

Item a black bumbazine coate and breeches with a black silk wastcoate.

Item 2 muffles.

Item a capp of turbant fashion.

Item black ribeands made up in fashion of Pantelloons, which was formerly worne with the grey druggate suite, wth two Remnants of flowered silk suitable to the wastcoat belonging to the s^d grey druggat suite.

2. *Item* a sky coloured twylight with 2 boxes, 2 brushes, a glass cup, and a pair of slippers all of tabby laced with gold and silver lace.

Item an ash coloured silke wastcoat pink^d.

Item a large cotton wastcoate.

Belts.

Imprimis a wast Belt of buffe stitch^d with gold and silver and buckles of silver guilt.

Item a shoulder belt of black Spanish leather with silver buckles.

Item a shoulder belt with a dark coloured silk frienge and a silver twist about it.

Item twoe shoulder belts with black frienge.

Item a shoulder belt of a cynnamon colour cut and embroydered.

Item a black Spanish leather belt with gold frienge.

Item a wast belt stitch^d with silver and with silver buckles or clasps and belonging to the little sword.

Item a black Waste tabby belt stitched with black buckles.

Item a black cloath waste belt with black buckles.

Item a wast belt laced with a gold and silver lace and buckles of silver gilded.

Item a girdle or sash of silk and silver.

Item a buffe waste belt laid with a silver twist and ye buckles of silver.

Item a plaine Buffe wast belt with guilded buckles.

Item a black stitched tabby belt with buckles of silver.

3. Swordes.

Two rapiers with silver hilts.

Item a short walking rapier hatchd.

Item a scemytar hatcht with gold.

Item a walking sword with a damask^d hilt.

Item 3 pair of black stitch^d garters.

Item a pair of garters of black cloath.

Item 3 pairs of embroydred garters.

Item a pair of dark coloured Leather garters bound with gallowne.

Item a black Beaver hatt.

Item a coloured Beavour.

Item a black caster.

Item a coloured beaver with narrow verges.

Item a little black Cordiberk or riding hatt.

Item a longe Cordiberk or riding hatt.

Item a riding cap of black velvet.

Item a black mountere of velvet.

Stockings.

Imprimis 6 pair of cotton stirrup stockins.
Item tennè pair of pearle colour silk stockins.
Item six pair of old black silk stockins.
Item 3 pair of whole footed wollen stockins.
Item 2 pair of woolen stirrup stockins.
Item twoe pair of worstead stirrup stockings.
Item a pair of pink coloured silk stockins.
Item twoe pair of white wostead stockins with rigg^d topps.
Item a pair of black searge stockings.
Item 10 pair of old silk stockings.
Item a pair of grey wostead stockins with large topp.
Item twoe pair of cotton whole footed stockins.
Item a pair of thick gray with topp to ride in.

Buckles.

Imprimis twoe pair of diamond buckles.
Item one pair of gold buckles.
Item a pair of silver buckles, part of them gilded.
Item 4 other pair of silver buckles.
Item 3 pair of black buckles.
Perukes seaven and a new morning wigge.

Bootes.

Imprimis one pair square toed bootes of Rendall's make.
Item a pair of Paul's make not worne.
Item a pair of old bootes w^h large topps, square toes and narrow heles.
Item 3 pair of other round toed bootes.
Item 2 paire more made by Paul in present weareing.

Shooes.

New   *Imprimis* 6 pair of winter shoes.
worne.   *Item* 6 pair of summer shooes.
Item 3 pair of goloshaes.
Item 3 pair of black shooes of shamah dress.
Item 2 pair of dear colour cloath shooes.
Item 7 paire of other shooes worne.
A pair of leather buskins and gambadoes.

Wearing Lynnen.

Shirtes now in weare **11.**
Item 8 old shirtes.
Item 6 fine shirtes.
Item 6 wastcoates of single holland.
Item 3 wascoates of double holland.
Item 5 pair of drawers of single holland.
Item 5 pair of double drawers.
Item 3 pair of double holland sleves.
Item 2 pair of quilted sleeves.
Item twoe quilted breast cloaths.
Item 22 towells.

Item 15 pair fine holland sleves.
Item 2 diaper brest cloathes.
Item 3 quilted caps.
Item 4 double holland capps.
Item 7 single holland caps.
Item 3 laced caps.
Item 14 pair of socks.
Item 8 handkerchefes.
Item 6 plain crevatts.
Item 12 pair of plain cuffes.
Item a long laced crevat.
Item twoe plain crevats tied up with twist.
Item 4 long crevats.
Item 4 muslyn crevats made up.
Item 6 pair of little cuffes laced.
Item two pair of other little cuffes.
Item twoe point laces for ye forepart of a wastcoat or halfe shirte.
Item 5 point crevats.
Item 5 pair of point lace cuffes.
Item 2 muslyn stocks besides stocks tied to the crevats.
Item twoe laced crevats.
Item 5 pair of laced cuffes.

In the Cupress chest.

Imprimis a frieze coat lynd with searge.
Item a purple velvet coat.
Item a black cloath coate and breeches with a black silk wastcoate.
Item another black cloath coat and breeches with a blacke silk wastcoate.
Item a black cloath coat and vest of farendine with a pair of black cloath breeches.
Item a black cloath coate and a black silk wastcoate.
Item a black silk wastcoate lyned with white sasenet.
Item a Buff coate lyned with tabby.
Item a doublet of cloath of silver.
Item a pair of searge trousoes.
Item the body of a blacke farendine doublet with sleeves pin'd to it.
Item a parcel of black velvet being the loyning of a cloake.
Item a pair of knitt pantelloons of pearle coloured silke.
Item another pair of knitt pantelloons whip'd with riband of Philemot.
Item a pair of pantelloons whip^t with black ribeond.
Item twoe sweet bagges lined with gold lace.
Item two old morning Gownes.
Item a broad wast belt with silver frienge and silver buckles.
Item a waste belt belonging to the Buffe coate.
Item a shoulder belt w^h frienge of a pearle colour.
Item a black velvet shoulder belt.
Item a shoulder belt of white tabby and gilded buckles.

Item a grey frieze wast belt.
Item a narrow wast black belt with silver buckles.
Item a shoulder belt of black cloath.
Item a shoulder belt of black tabby.
Item a wast belt of black spanish Leather.
Item another shoulder belt of black cloath.
Item an old wastcoate of flowered silke.
Item one pair of riding gloves the inside fur'd.
Item one other pair of riding gloves.
Item a little girdle, blacke.
Item 3 pair of black shammy gloves.
Item a pair of other blacke Leather gloves.
Item a combrase laced of fillament colour.

Agreement for Purchase of Swans between SIR J. HOBART and JOHN SWAN, of Saxlingham, Norfolk.

1674, October 24.—That the said John Swan in consideration of the sum of tenne pounds of good money of England, five pounds part whereof the said John Swan doth hereby acknowledge to have received and had, hath and doth oblige himself his executors and administrators to deliver and cause to be delivered to the said Sir John Hobart or his assigns thirty and fower swans at Midsomer next or within 14 days following, upon the delivery whereof the said Sir John Hobart is to pay or cause to be paid to the said Jo. Swan or his assignes five pounds remaynder of the said tenne pounds. In witness whereof I have herewith set my hand the day and year above mentioned.

JOHN SWAN.

Witness: Thos. Seabourn.
Jo. Brewster.

A note of what swanes I marked that was boute of John Swane.

Imprimis at Langley marse one swane.
Item boute there a land birde.
Item at Hasingham Littel dike one swane.
Item at Harsinghame greete dike one swane.
Item at the diveles house one swane.
Item at Strumshote fen one cocke and one signete.
Item one swane more there.
Item at the Lower fene dike two swanes.
Item at Brindall house one swan.
Item at Sullingham fery one swane.
Item at Sullingham fene one cocke and three signetes.
Item at Possicke halle 2 swanes.
Item at Wickelingam one cocke and 3 signtes.

Robt. Kemp's note of Mr. Swans of Saxlingham. Swans upped in the year '75.

Imprimis at Bintry Common one swane.
Item at Grente Mille one swane.
Item against Beelowe church one swane.
Item at Linge mille one hene and one signett.

Item at Prates mille one swane.
Item at Warden medowes twòe ould swanes.
Item above White mille three swanes.
Item at Coosye blackewater 2 swanes.
Item at three briges one swane.

> Robert Kemp his accompt of the swanes bought of Wynter.

Manifesto of the Gentlemen of Norfolk for the Reduction of Expenses of High Sheriff.

1675, Jan. 12. Norff.—Wee whose names are hereunder written observing that notwithstanding a Statute made in the 14th yeare of the King for the preventing of the great and unnecessary charge of Sheriffs, yet such Persons as since that tyme have been Sheriffs in this County of Norff. have made great expenses contrary to the said Law which may be suposed to have proceeded from the apprehensions they might have had that those who should begin the reformation might be liable to censure as men more avaritious than those who preceded in the same office, soe that through want of good example the Law. is contemned and broken. And notwithstanding divers Statutes made prohibiting of Sheriffs letting their Bailliwicks to farme, which Law not being duly observed have tended more to the prejudice and oppression of the Country, wherefor to prevent the said unnecessary charge of Sheriffs and oppression of the Country

It is agreed by all the Persons whose names are here subscribed, that noe one of the Persons who shall subscribe to these Articles shall have more then forty men servants with Liveries attending upon him at the tyme of Assizes, nor under the number of twenty like attendants. Which Liverymen that are to be provided by such gentlemen as are subscribed to these articles shall be part.

That when any one of the said Subscribers shall be made Sheriff of the said County the Livery shall be a plain grey woosted camblet edged and loyned through with blew searge and trimd with bell mettall buttons, a black hatt edged with blew with a blew woosted hat band, and a plain shoulder belt of buffe, and a black leather saddle edged with blew, and shall as often as any Subscribers shall be made Sheriffs of the said County bee as near and as much alike both in colour, stufs, and otherwise as can be bought and made.

And every Liveryman shall likewise bring with him a javelyn suitable.

And when any of the Subscribers shall be made Sheriffs of the said County every other of the subscribers shall provide one man habited in such a livery as aforesaid to attend such Sheriff at the Assizes for the said County and shall beare the charges both of such Liveryman and his horse during the Assizes.

That when any of the said Subscribers shall be Sheriff of the said County he shall at the Assizes for the said County and during the tyme of such Assizes dine at an ordinary and make any Invitation of any Person whatsoever nor keep any undersheriff's table, which said ordinary shall not exceed fower shillings for meat, beer and ale, and all wine at that ordinary shall be paid for by those that call for it, and before it be used and spent, and the ordinary for the servants shall be eighteen pence and noe more.

That when any of the said Subscribers shall be made Sheriff of the said County every other of the said Subscribers in the first columne shall for ye better attendance of His Majesty's Judges personally accompany such Sheriff to introduce the Judges at the winter Assizes for the said County, and those in the second column at the Summer Assizes, and every one of the said Subscribers during the said Assizes shall dine at the same table with such Sheriff and pay for his own ordinary and proper chardges.

And in case by reason of any urgent or extraordinary occasion any one of the said Subscribers shall be hindered from coming in Person to accompany the said Sheriff in such manner as beforementioned that then he shall send some other gentleman to represent him and accompany the said Sheriff as himself ought to have done, and to pay as himself should doe if he were Personally present.

That for making such attendance on the Sheriff the more equall to all the Subscribers it is agreed that those who attend at the Winter Assizes the first year shall attend the Somer Assizes the next yeare and soe vice versa.

That noe persons shall be admitted to subscribe after the date hereof during the space of sixe weekes next after, unless such persons as shall be alowed by Sir John Hobart, Sir John Holland, Sir Ro. Kemp, Will. Windham, Ro. Longe, Roger Potts, Esq., Sir Christopher Calthorp, Rob. Walpoole, Roger Spelman, Christofer Bedingfeld, and John Pell, Esqres. or any 3 of them under their hands. Neyther shall any person after the said six weekes be admitted to subscribe unless he or they shall be alowed of by ye greater number of Subscribers.

It is further agreed that the subscriptions shall be made in a Parchment roll and kept by the present and succeeding Sheriffs of this County.

That every respective Sheriff shall return the default of the several Subscribers at the Assizes next following.

That the Subscribers shall hereby oblige themselves to take great care in the choice of their undersheriffs soe as they may be such persons as may not oppress the Country.

And that they shall not directly or indirectly take any profitt, reward or price eyther by themselves or undersheriffs for the Ballywick of the severall hundreds of this County.

John Hobart.	Willm Doyley, sen.
John Holland.	Willm Doyley, jun.
Robt Kemp.	Peter Glean.
Philip Woodhouse.	Ch^r Calthorp.

James Johnson.
Willm Rant.
Willm Windham.
Rob. Wallpoole.
Roger Spelman.
Nich. Wilton.
Th° Barnes.
ffra. Bickley.
Martyn Cobb. ·
Rich. Berney, jun.
Nich. Styleman.
Brampton Gourdon.
Ro. Suckling, jun.
John Berney.
John Herne.
Clement Spelman.

Christ. Crow.
Richer Browne.
Wm Tubbing.
Edm^d Pattrick.
Robt Longe.
Roger Potts.
Robt Wood.
Clement Herne.
Wm Branthwayt.
John Pell.
Edmund Brytiffe.
Gardner Hewet.
Christofer Bedingfield.
Robt Suckling, sen.
Willm Turner.
Gascoigne Weld.

JOURNAL of the LIEUTENANCY of the COUNTY OF NORFOLK.

1676, May 19.—Resolution at a meeting of the Deputy-Lieutenants :—

Thatt colours for the severall Regiments be as follows :—

The Regiment of Horse - - -	Blew
Sir Jacob Astley's Regiment of Foot - -	Blew
and the balls of distinction - -	White
Sir Wm Doyley's Regiment of Foot - -	White
and the balls of distinction - -	Red
Sir Christopher Calthorpe's Regiment of Foot-	Yellow
and the balls of distinction - -	Blew
Thomas Knyvett, Esq., his Regiment of Foot	Purple
and the balls of distinction - -	White

1676, July 11.—Mem. William Wyndham, a Deputy-Lieutenant for the County, did this day deliver in his certificate into the Court of SS for the peace for his having receyved the Sacrament according to the usage of the Church of England, and did take the oath of allegiance and supremacy as also the oath required by the Act for settling the Militia.

Ordered that in consequence of the great disservice done to His Majesty in the Militia of this county by admitting persons of small estates to be laid to the Horse by which means the number of the foot are very much diminished, that for the future no person having an estate under 200 pounds per annum shall be laid to the Horse but shall be charged to the Foot.

SOUTH ERPINGHAM HUNDRED.

1676, July 11.—A list of the hundred stores remaining in the Church porch in Aylsham, vizt. :—

Almost a barrel of powder.

16 pickaxes.	5 wooden beetles.
24 mattocks.	4 hatchets.
23 spades.	1000 yards of match.

About 2 bushells of muskett shott.

1677.—A LIST of DEPUTY LIEUTENANTS and MILITIA OFFICERS
for the COUNTY of NORFOLK.

Robert Lord Paston, Viscount Yarmouth,
Lord Lieutenant. :
Deputy-Lieutenants :—

William Paston. ⎫
Philipp Woodhouse. ⎪
Jacob Astley. ⎪
John Pettus. ⎪
William Doyly, sen. ⎬ Bts.
William Adams. ⎪
Thomas Garrard. ⎪
Edmund Bacon. ⎪
Francis Bickley. ⎭
Christopher Calthorpe, Knight
  of the Bath.

Sir Allen Appesley, Kt.
Sir Neville Catteline.
Sir W. Doyly, jun.
William Cooke, Esq.
Thomas Knyvett, Esq.
Robert Walpole, Esq.
Robert Coke, Esq.
Philip Harberd, Esq.
William Windham, Esq.
Edward Ward, Esq.
Robert Suckling, Esq.
William De Grey, Esq.

The First Foot Regiment.

Soldiers.

Sir Jacob Astley, Collonell.
W. Tubbing, gent., Capt.-
  Lieut.
Edward Astley, gent., En-
  signe.
Edward Lee, gent., Quar-
  termaster.
    Three Sergeants.   149

Philip Harberd, Esq., Lt.-
  Coll.
John Pollard, gent., Lieut.
Robt Nockold, gent., Ensigne.
    Three Sergeants.   112

Ed. De Grey, Esq., Major.
W. Wortes, gent., Lieut.
Roger Wiggot, gent., En-
  signe.
    Three Sergeants.   123

Symon Brytif, Esq., Capt.
Robert Chapman, gent.,
  Lieut.
Edward Benn, gent., En-
  signe.
    Three Sergeants.   157

Soldiers.

Jacob Preston, Esq., Capt.
John Symonds, Esq., Lieut.
Tho. Preston, gent., Ensigne.
    Two Sergeants.   151

John Harberd, Esq., Capt.
Hamond Thurston, gent.,
  Lieut.
John Starling, gent., En-
  signe.
    Two Sergeants.   131

Robert Doughty, Esq.,
  Capt.
Sam Gilpin, gent., Lieut.
Humphrey Carter, gent.,
  Ensigne.
    Three Sergeants   144

———
976

The Second Foot Regiment.

Soldiers.

Sir William Doyly, 112
Collonell.
John Harris, gent., Capt.-
Lieutenant.
Roger Reynolds, gent., En-
signe.
Robert London, gent., Quar-
termaster.
Three Sergeants.

Robert Suckling, Esq.,
Lieut.-Collonell.
Daniel Newton, Gent., Lieut.
Nicholas Sayer, gent., En-
signe.
Three Sergeants. 084

Thomas Gawdy, Esq., Major.
John Freeman, gent., Lieut.
Rob't Wrongrey, gent., En-
signe.
Two Sergeants. 107

Soldiers.

Anthony Freeston, Esq., Capt.
Henry Fenn, gent., Lieut.
Robert Game, gent., Ensigne.
Two Sergeants. 121

William Cooke, Esq., Capt.
Thomas Skeet, gent., Lieut.
Robert Grymmer, gent., En-
signe.
Three Sergeants. 081

Leonard Mapes, Esq., Capt.
Thomas Dengaine, gent.,
Lieut.
John Marston, gent., Ensigne.
Three Sergeants. 124

John Hyde, Esq., Captain.
Thomas Torey, Esq., Lieut.
Thomas Murrell, gent., En-
signe.
Three Sergeants. 113

In all 745

The Third Foot Regiment.

Soldiers.

Sir Christopher Calthorp,
Collonell.
Matthew Manning, gent.,
Capt.-Lieut.
Thomas Girling, gent., En-
signe.
Three Sergeants. 096

Laurence H. Oxburgh,
Lieut.-Collonell.
Richard Trice, gent.,
Lieut.
Geoffrey Colville, gent.,
Ensigne.
Three Sergeants. 116

Richard Godfrey, Esq.,
Major.
John Godfrey, gent.,
Lieut.
James Hawe, jun., gent.,
Ensigne.
Three Sergeants. 090

Soldiers.

Francis Bell, Esq., Capt.
W. Fisher, gent., Lieut.
Gregory Parlett, gent, En-
signe.
Three Sergeants. 148

Arthur Boteler, Esq., Capt.
Marten Cobb, Esq., Lieut.
Francis Bagg, gent., Ensigne.
Two Sergeants. 081

Thomas Hoogan, Esq., Capt.
Nicholas Parham, gent., Lieut.
Robert Hamond, gent., En-
signe.
Three Sergeants. 128

Edward Chamberlane,
Esq., Capt.
Wm Mason, gent., Lieut.
Edward Thorisby, gent.,
Ensigne.
Two Sergeants. 075

In all 784

The Fourth Foot Regiment.

Soldiers.

Thomas Knyvett, Esq., Collonell.
Capt.-Lieutenant Browne.
Robert Grey, gent., Ensigne.
Hen. Grey, gent., Quartermaster.
Three Sergeants. 140

Edward Woodhouse, Esq., Lieut.-Collonell.
Thomas Talbot, gent., Lieut.
William Browne, gent., Ensigne.
Three Sergeants. 132

W^m De Grey, Esq., Major.
Humphrey Futter, Esq., Lieut.
John Futter, gent., Ensigne.
Two Sergeants. 106

Soldiers.

Wm Rant, Esq., Captain.
Edward Denny, gent., Lieut.
Samuell Greeneway, gent., Ensigne.
Two Sergeants. 084

Wm Cropley, Esq., Capt.
John Gryme, gent., Lieut.
John Wade, gent., Ensigne.
Three Sergeants. 159

John Berney, Esq., Capt.
John Castle, gent., Lieut.
Clement Jermy, gent., Ensigne.
Three Sergeants. 094

John Knyvett, Esq., Captain.
Richard Mason, gent., Lieut.
Thomas Prettyman, gent., Ensigne.
Three Sergeants. 152

In all 867

The Regiment of Horse

Soldiers.

Wm Paston, Esq., Collonell
Thomas Weld, Esq., Capt.-Lieut.
Cornett.
James Couldham, gent., Quartermaster. 78

Sir Neville Catteline, K^nt. Major.
John Houghton, Esq., Lieut.
John Brereton, gent., Cornett.
Matthew Norgate, gent., Quartermaster. 59

Edward Ivard, Esq., Capt.
Rob. Payne, Esq., Lieut.
John Bringloe, jun., Cornett
Henry Harman, gent., Quartermaster. 49

Soldiers.

Sir W. Doyly, jun., K^t. Captain.
W. Barker, Esq., Lieutenant.
Francis Lane, Esq., Cornett.
Samuel Verdon, gent., Quartermaster. 70

Sir Thomas Garard, Bart., Capt.
Robert Thorowgood, gent., Lieutenant.
Edward Colborne, gen., Cornett.
John Parly, gent., Quartermaster. 58

Francis Guybon, Esq., Captain.
Charles Perkins, Esq., Lieut.
Hamond Claxton, Esq., Cornett.
Nathaniel Weld, gent., Quartermaster. 65

379

SIR HENRY BEDINGFIELD to LORD TOWNSHEND.

1677, July 20. Beckhall.—Being told yesterday by diverse of my acquaintance that came from the Sessions at Norwich that I was there made the publick discourse of the towne, occasioned by manie false and strange reflections that were made upon twoe letters written to your Lordship, one from my cousen Chr. Bedingfield, who had no commission from me to write, the other from my selfe, which they say were both shewn by you, which being a thing not used by other persons of Honor, I cannot believe it to be true, and have therefore sent this Bearer my Son to know how farre yor Lordship will owne this matter, and having suffered soe much prejudice by my cousin Chr. Bedingfield's letter I think I may justly require a sight of it, that I might knowe what he laies to my charge. As for what I said to him I will assure your Lordship I will neyther deny nor be ashamed of the discourse I had with him, tending only to the same end that I have discoursed with your Lordship this many yeares, which was to persuade you to keep friend to the King's interest, I believing that your reputation as well as your interest obliged you to it. But I doe nowe condemne myselfe for having been too zealous upon that point for which I crave your Lordship's pardon, although I think I can answer for it to the worlde before whom I have for this seaventeen or eighteen yeares declared a particular respect for your Person, and have upon all occasions stuck closse to you as you yourselfe will knowe, having no ends beside but to procure peace in these parts. There is certainly something more than ordinary in it that you should just now and never before make such sinister interpretations of an act of friendship, and wonder that I should be troubled at your publick appearing with those whom you yourselfe knowe have often declared to be no friends to His Majesty, and this is the sume of what you can take offence at, for whatsoever it is you have been pleased to say neyther you nor anybody can think me soe ignorant in good manners as upon any other account to take upon me to meddle in or prescribe your visitts, neyther did I offer any injury to your Lordship in lessning of mine, being a man inconsiderable, and finding all those visits I made prove to so little Purpose and this was the plaine right doune meaning of my letter to your Lordship when I said I could not hereafter so frequently appear at Raynham as I had done, all the rest of my letter I think was only such civilityes as is ordinarily paid to Persons of your quality from those that would shew their affections and respects, and it may be easily understood without the help of philosophy or double dealing that I may reserve an esteem for your Person yet not comply with your actions. Indeed I may possibly have good cause to be ashamed of the affectionate expressions I then made, unless I receyve something under your hand that may give me good reasons to subscribe myself as formerly I have done, my Lord,

Your Lordship's humble servant,
HENRY BEDINGFIELD.

My cousen Chris. Bedingfield coming to my house tooke occasion to exclayme against my Lord Townshend in the highest nature imaginable for his indiscretion in meeting Colonell Cock and others at Mr. Bullard's house. I replied that I was very sorry for it, both for my Lord's sake and my owne, for I should not think it fitt for me hereafter to appear so frequently at Raynham as I had done, though I could still remayne my Lord's humble servant, and I desired him as a friend to us both to tell him soe.

HENRY BEDINGFIELD.

(*Copy?*)

EXTRACTS OF PRICES, &c., from several ANNUAL ACCOUNTS of SIR J. and Sir H. HOBART.

1678.—20 milch cows at £3 10s. apiece.
8 bullocks at £2 5s. a piece.
Sold on an inventory taken for rent in arrear.

1689.—Bricks 12s. per thousand.

1696.—Harvest wages :—
For the whole harvest £1 17s. 6d.
John Berney for 7 weeks £2 9s.

A bill of many disbursements by Mr. Thomas Bell of Olton for severall things by him bought at Stirbridge ffaire in September, 1696, for the use of Sir Henry Hobart as followeth :—

	£	s.	d.
For 2 Cheshire cheeses weighing 29lb. and 14lb. at 35s. per hundred - - -	1	1	10
Item for 3 stone 4lb. of hoppes at £1 6s. per stone - - - - -	4	6	8
Item for carriage and porterage - -	0	3	0
	5	11	1

Various memoranda relating to the sale of timber, 17th cent.

1671-1698.—Accounts of the King's Bench and Marshalsea prisons, by Sir John Hobart and Sir Henry Hobart, respectively, treasurers.

1672-80.—Receipts, including receipts for chimney money.

1671-4.—Hevingham cum Marsham rent account.

1672-84.—Blickling Manor accounts.

1672-82.—Saxthorpe Manor accounts.

1664.—Horsham St. Faith's Manor accounts.

1679.—Election Expenses.

1679, May 6.—Received then of Sir John Hobart, Bart., by the hands of John Brewster the sum of twenty shillings for the hire of a horse to London at the hearing at the Barre of the house of Commons. I say rec.d

WILLIAM WOOLER.

1689, Feb. 25.—Twenty men from Upwell, Esning, Wisbech, and Walsoken. Left to pay att the Rampant Horse four pounds, sixteen shillings. S.d 20 men pold for Sir Henry Hubard.

1681.—Coach hire for the servants from Blickling to London cost £7.

17118

1682, Jan. 2.—Order of Privy Council allowing Sir Hen. Hobart to surrender his lease from His Majesty of the hundred of Mitford (Duchy of Lancaster).

(The same was much infringed by the Sheriff of the County of Norfolk where ye same lyes.)

1683, July 13.—Note of those armes taken from Blickling by Capt. Doughtey and Capt. Hauten on July 13th, 1683.

2 blunder busses	6 gonletts
2 carbins	8 gorgetts
8 roller of bandoleers	2 Buff coats
1 brass of pistles	4 pair of iron sleeves
2 buff belts	4 pair of cuishes
6 old swords	3 backes and breests
8 clubs with jukes	14 skirts
14 fourteen blacke bills	3 backe skirts.
5 halberts	
6 javelins	
1 Patison	
5 beavers	
3 head peices	

From Sir Hen. Hobart's Account Books.

1688, Nov. 1.—*Item.* To John Burritt and John Buttefant being the two soldiers that served in the armie for Chaplyfield estate in Norwich for one day's pay at 2s. 6d. a piece, 5s. ; and the muster master's fee for two yeares, 2s. ; and for powder and bullets, 2s. in all.

1688, Dec. 13.—*Item* more to the above said Warren for carrying a letter from Norwich to Blickling, then with a warrant from the Cheife Constable to send out a Light Horse for Wymondham estate to meet at Attlebridge. *Item* for orange riband for favours for the twoe soldiers that served in the armie for the Chaplyfield estate, the rest of the Company being all in the same colour.} 7s. 6d.

Certificate of Conformity with the Act of Uniformity.

1681, March 27. Intwood cum Keswick.—These may certify those whom it may concern that we whose names are underwritten did hear Ric. Clarke, Rector of Intwood in Keswick aforesaid, on the day and year above written, declare his assent and consent according to the Act of Uniformity and also read publiqly the thirty-nine Articles after divine service in the parish church aforesaid.

Witness our hands :—

Sd   Robert Hamond,
      Walter + Howard, church wardens.
            his mk.
      Roger Hamond.
      Willliam Howard.
      Francis Eagle.
      Henry H Bayes.
            his marke.

J^N COLLINGES to [SIR HENRY HOBART].

1683, Oct. 24. Norwich.—Answering his enquiry about a
Lease. " There did indeed a gentleman concerned write to me
about cataloguing and prizing Sir John's library, but I declined
it not onely in regard of my wofull distractions about my son's
busines, not yet issued, which ty me to this towne, but judging
my self no way fit, for tho as to Divinity bookes and ordinary
Philologicall bookes I could doe possibly as much as another, yet
I beleeved Sir John's Library consisted mostly of French bookes
and choice bookes of Philology, in which I had no skill at all. I
also told him this was no place to sell such bookes in, but if they
must be sold, the best way were to have them to London and
add the catalogue to some other libraryes in an auction, for as to
such bookes, a book of 20s. in this towne would not give 5s. I
also told him I had one of the bookes belonging to Sir J. H., viz.,
Davilas Fr. History, which I borrowed of him. As to yourself,
Sir, I remember nothing reflexive upon your Honour (I have bin
looking sometime for the l^r to have sent you the words in it, but
I cañot find where I have throwne it) all that was in it. He
seemed a little troubled that y^u would not please as yet
to be positive whether to take the goods as the house
stands furnished, which he thought might be acceptable
to any lady you should chuse, so as I concluded there
was some little discontent betwixt you and that he would
have been willing to be secured from trouble. And now, Sir,
that I have mentioned a lady I must tell you of the kindnes
of. a merchant in London to you, one Mr. Polluxfen (Brother
I think to the great Lawyer who told Mr. Dearsley that if a Lady
would be acceptable to you that had 5 or 6,000, and 700 per an.
at present, he would recommend such a one to you). Mr. Dearsley
wrote it to me either that week or the week following that wherin
your never to be forgotten father dyed, which made me not before
mention it, nor should I now, but that you might know the
respects of the gentleman. If the motion be beneath you, my
self know him not so much as *ore tenus*. Really, Sir, I cannot
tell who to recommend you if you desire the bookes should be
[*illegible*]. Mr. Haylett is the fittest I know, if he will catalogue
them and come to this town I will doe the best service I can to
affix prices. But I feare we shall both be out quickly, not understanding Frenche bookes, nor the choicer pieces of Philology.
Let Davila, Sir, I pray be set down with the rest. I have
waited an opportunity a long time to restore it to its place. And
now, Sir, I beseech the God of Heaven that y^r Noble Father's
and Lady Mother's prayers may be answered unto your bosom
and that y^r country might repay to you all your father's merits
of them and you may have many dayes to let them see that Sir
John liveth still in Sir Henry [Hobart] without Pythagorean
metempsuchosis.

Since I wrote what is above my sister Mitchel hath brought in
two pieces of newes, the one is of a murrain of horses in Essex.
M^r· Nightingale (M^{rs·} Cocks daughter) by a l^r to her mother this
day lets her know she hath lost her 4 coach horses of it. The

other is more strange, brought by one Gargrane, a good sober
fellow that collects the hearth money. Being last week at Acle
the Inkeeper told him the night before most of their houses were
filled with greate Toads so as he gathered them up with shovels
and threw them into fire till for the stench he could hardly
abide in the house, the rest he threw into a yard. Next morning
all were gone. They talk how that they came down in a shower.

John Brewster, [Steward,] to Sir Hen. Hobart.

1684.—Being sensible that your defensive armes would not be
returned tyme enough to get them cleansd and new colours
tyme enough to have them ready at the generall muster, I went
to Willm Smyth's where they were lodg'd and found there
twoe backs, one brest, and one headpiece, which together with
what was left at Blickling I made up 3 suits of armour (one headpiece excepted), and I must eyther borrow or els buy one against
this day. (I wanted one) sword and finding one at Willm Smyths
and brought it away and twoe case of new pistolls I have bought
and am promised another by Mr. Fountayn for the muster, the
coates and belts will be new drest against the tyme. I have
alsoe bespoke 3 new saddles, there being none at Blickling but
one and one not worth anything. My horse and rider are in
readiness in Claxton, and Mr. Britiffe will furnish you with the
other twoe and I think to send in the old Riders with Sir H^y R.
troope. Barney is one of them whoe though a little fellow yet
having formerly rode and being listed there I think may doe
better than another.

Extracts from the Journals of the Lieutenancy of the County of Norfolk.

Present, His Grace the Duke of Norfolk.

1688, Oct. 7.—Ordered that summons be sent to the Gentlemen
lately turned out of the Commission of the Peace to appear at the
Duke's Palace, Norwich, on Wednesday, the tenth of this
instant, and sent out to Sir John Holland, Sir Jacob Astley, ×Sir
Robert Kemp, ×Sir Thos. Ward, Sir W. Cook, B^ts.; Sir Neville
Catelyn, K^nt. Th^os. Knyvett, Robert Sucklyng, John Harbord, John
Knyvett, Robert Houghton, John Jay, Sir W. Rant, K^t ; Dr.
Robert Pepper, Rich. Wyth, Francis Gardiner, Leonard Mapes,
Abraham Castle, ×Francis Windham, Robert Daye, Charles le
Gros, Thomas Sotherton, Robert Day, John Richmond, John
Aide, John Repps and Hugh Hovell, Esqrs.
To whom his Majesty offered to reinstate them in their
commissions.

Reply of the Justices of the Peace who had been turned out of his Commission.

1688, October.—May it please your Grace,—When it was His
Majesty's pleasure to honour us with his Commission we served
him with loyalty and fidelity and as we were obliged by the
Church of England and our allegiance. And we are steadily

resolved to continue in all dutiful obedience to His Majesty and will be most willing and ready to serve His Majesty in all things which may consort with his Majesty's honour and our safety, which we cannot do by our acting in conjunction with Persons unqualified and incapacitated by the Laws of this Realm, especially by the statutes of the 25th of the late King.

The Lynn &c. Division met the Lord Lieutenant at the White Swan, Swaffham, and the like answer was given by those present (including) Sir Nicholas Le Strange, Sir Thomas Hare, Sir Thomas Gerard, B^{ts} ; Sir Christoph. Cathorpe, K.C.B., Sir Francis Guybon, Robert Walpole, Edmund Woodhouse, Henry Oxborough, Francis Cremer, Robert Wardell, Robert Coney, Lee Warner, ˣGabriell Armiger, Thos. Wright, Thomas Barber, Hatton Berners and Thomas Peirson.

N.B.—Those gentlemen who have this mark ˣ against their names did not appear being out of the county and Sir Thomas Garard appeared at Norwich and Sir Jacob Astley at Swaffham.

1688, Oct. 10.—Copy of an order of the Lord Lieutenant calling out the six militia troops of Horse upon four days' duty. Reciting an order of His Majesty of the 2nd October this instant requiring him to call together such part of the Militia Horse as he should think fit (who in case of Invasion might) "hinder evill disposed persons from joining with the Enemy."

Warrants were issued accordingly to His Grace's troop to meet at Swaffham upon Tuesday 16th October by ten of the clock and there to remain four days till further order.

Sir Francis Guybon's Troop to meet at Hempton Green upon Tuesday 16th October and to quarter at Fakenham and Hempton for four days till further order.

Capt. John Houghton's Troop to meet at Lingwood Heath upon Saturday 20th day of October and to quarter in Norwich for four days till further order.

Sir William Rant's Troop to meet at North Walsham upon Wednesday the 24th day of October and to quarter at North Walsham for four days till further order.

Capt. Phillip Bedingfield's Troop to meet at Mulbarton upon Monday the 29th of October and to quarter at Norwich for four days till further order.

Capt. Robert Long's Troop to meet at Totnell Heath upon Fryday the 2nd day of November and to quarter at Lin for four days till further order.

1688, Nov. 1.—Ordered by the Duke of Norfolk that summons be sent forthwith to the Deputy Lieutenants and Justices of the Peace in and about the Sea Coast to attend His Grace at his Palace at Norwich upon Saturday the 3rd this instant November by eleven of the clock in the forenoon (about watching the coast), &c.

1688, November 9.—Orders by the Duke of Norfolk, Lord Lieutenant, discharging the yellow regiment of Militia foot

under the command of Sir Nicholas L'Estrange which had
been ordered to muster at Lynn that day " by reason the small
pox is very much in in Lin Regis and that in quartering the said
Regiment there may be a means to dispers that Contagion about
the country" to be ready nevertheless to appear with their armes
compleat at an houres notice. An express sent to Lin forthwith.

1688, November 28th.—Pursuant to an order received from His
Grace the Duke of Norfolk summons were sent to the Deputy
Lieutenants and other gentlemen to attend His Grace at the
Palace in Norwich upon Saturday, the first of December, by 9 of
the clock in the forenoon.

1688, December 1. Norwich.—His Grace the Duke of Norfolk,
attended by his Deputy Lieutenants, Militia officers and several
other gentlemen, went into the Market Place, where the Mayor
and Aldermen met his Grace, to whom his Grace made the
following speech :—

Mr. Mayor,—Nothing doubting but you and the rest of the
Body as well as the whole Citty and County may be alarmed by
the great concourse of gentry with the numerous appearance of
their friends and tenants, as well as your owne Militia here this
morning, I have thought this the most proper place, as being the
most publick one, to give you an account of our intentions.

Out of the deep sense we had that in the present unhappy
position of affaires nothing we could think of was possible to
secure the Laws, Liberties, and Protestant Religion but a free
Parliament we are here met to declare that we will do our utmost
endeavour to defend them by declaring for such a free Parliament.

But since His Majesty has been pleased (by the news we have
this day) to order writs for a Parliament to sett upon the
15 January next, I can only ad in the name of myselfe and all
these gentlemen and others here met that we will ever be ready
to support your Laws and liberties and the Protestant religion.

And soe God save the King.

Upon which Mr. Mayor and Aldermen gave his Grace and
the rest of the gentlemen thanks for their good intentions, and
a numerous assembly did concur with his Grace and the rest of
the gentlemen.

His Grace being attended by great numbers of ordinary people
to His Grace's palace, he at his alighting called them to him and
told them he desired they would not take any occasion to commit
any disorder or outrages but goe quietly to their houses, and
acquainted them that the King had ordered a free Parliament to
be called, upon which they went away well satisfied.

1688, Dec. 3. Norwich.—Pursuant to orders from the Duke
of Norfolk the Deputy Lieutenants Militia Officers and other
Gentlemen were summoned to attend His Grace at Lin Regis
the 7th of this instant December by 9 of the clock in the forenoon
who appeared accordingly and accompanied him into the markett
place where the Mayor of Lin (being attended by the Aldermen and
a great number of people) made the following speech to His Grace.

My Lord,—The dayly allarums wee receive as well from forraigne as domestick Enemies give us just apprehensions of approaching dangers which press us to apply with all earnestness to your Grace as our great Patron in an humble confidence to succeed in our expectations that we may be put into such a posture by your Grace's direction and conduct as may make us appear as zealous as any in the defence of the protestant Religion, the Laws, and ancient Government of the Kingdome being the desire of many hundreds amongst us who most humbly challenge a right to your Grace's protection.

His Grace the Duke of Norfolk's Answer to the Mayor of Lin.

Mr. Mayor,—I am very much obleidged to you and the rest of the Body, and these here present for your good opinion of me and the Confidence you have that I will doo what in me lyes to supporte and defend your Laws and Liberties and the Protestant Religion which I will never deceive you in. And since the comeing of the Prince of Orange has given us an opportunity to declare for the defence of them ; I can only assure you that no man will venture his life more freely for the defence of the Laws Liberties and Protestant Religion than I will doe.

In which all these gentlemen here present and many more doe unanimously concur, and you shall see that all possible care shall be taken that such a Conjunction requires.

1689, September 7th. Norwich Castle.

Present :—Sir Henry Hobart.
Roger Pott. } B^ts.
W. Cooke. }
Fr^as Guybon, K.
John Harbord, Esq.

Order, to read the following letter of the Lord Lieutenant.

Gentlemen,—Whereas there are severall persons that have refused to take the oath mentioned and appointed to be taken by an Act of Parliament Intituled an Act for abrogating the Oath of Supremacy and Allegiance and appointing other oaths, &c., And others have refused or neglected to appear upon the summons that has been sent them (not giving a just excuse) I consider it necessary for His Majesty's service that you presently issue out orders or warrants to Disarme all such suspect Persons taking care that all arms so seized be secured and a just account thereof be returned to the office of His Majesty's ordnance.

Your servant,
Norfolke.

London, Aug. 29, 1689.

To the Deputy Lieutenants of the County of Norfolk or any three or more of them.

Ordered that our Clerk, M^r. Edmund L'Estrange, return the following answer to the Duke of Norfolk.

May it please your Grace,—In obedience to your Grace's command I have been to wait upon the Respective Deputy

Lieutenants in the several Divisions with the order received from your Grace bearing date the 29 of August for the disarming of such persons as have refused to take the oath mentioned and appointed to be taken by an Act of Parliament Intituted an Act for abrogating the Oaths of Supremacy and Allegiance, &c., and accordingly the Deputy Lieutenants following met at the Grand Jury room at the Castle at Norwich upon Saturday the 7th instant to consult about the best method for putting your Grace's order into execution, viz.: Sir Henry Hobart, Sir Roger Potts, Sir W. Cooke, Sir Francis Guybon, and Lt Coll. John Harbord, who having taken into consideration a late Act of Parliament Intituled an Act for the better securing of the Government by disarming Papists and reputed Papists, which as yet has not been put in execution (tho at the Sessions upon Saturday last held at Norwich by adjournment they were issuing out orders to proceed thereupon) they think that to putt in execution your Graces order against such as have refused to take the oaths (being Protestants) may be respited for some short time without any Prejudice to the Government, hoping that some who have refused to take the Oaths upon better consideration may take the said Oaths, however they resolve in case they doe not, to proceed against them with as much severity as the law will permit, pursuant to your Grace's order. And this they have commanded mee with the tendrance of their humble duty and service to give your Grace an account of with the assurance that they will ever be most ready to pay their obedience to your Grace's commands upon all occasions.

Norwich, Sept. 9, 1689.

1689, Sept. 30th Norwich Castle.

Present:—Sir Henry Hobart.

Sir Roger Potts ⎫
Sir Jacob Astley ⎬ Barts.
Sir Wm Cooke ⎭

Sir Francis Guybon, K^t

Thomas Knyvet ⎫
Robert Walpole ⎬ Esqs.
John Hudson ⎭

The Deputy Lieutenants took the oaths appointed to be taken by a late Act of Parliament intituled an Act for the abrogating of the Oaths of Supremacy and Allegiance and appointing other oaths.

Order, that the following Letter of His Grace the Duke of Norfolk be read:

1689, Sept. 19th London.— . . . If I remember right there was two objections against the disarming those that had refused the Oath, the one that it would look hard for them to be used so when the Roman Catholicks were not. To which I answer both the Roman Catholicks and they be used so now, at the same time, for if by their actions they so little distinguish themselves from them, pray let them fare alike in this particular only with this difference, that the Roman Catholicks' horses ought to be taken as well as their arms. And as for the 2nd that they may alter their minde to take them hereafter, I answer to that that whenever those that refuse them now shall take them I shall always fear there will be more of self interest in it than any affection to the present Government that can be relied on, for the taking those oaths or not is not so new a matter that any person can be unprepared or surprized in what he does, and tho' no man, I believe, has shewn himselfe less willing (ever since I have had any concern in Norfolk) to do a hard thing to any gentleman than I; and that I have always used these particular gentlemen with as much respect and friendship as any in the County, yet when it comes to the owning a Government which we must support or fall with it this is no jesting and I desire that the Deputy Lieutenants will doe effectually what I dare say they must not only think fit but necessary for the occasion.

Yr aff. friend,

[*Addressed*]　　　　　　　　　　　　　　　　Norfolk.

These for Mr Edmund l'Estrange of Horstead, Norfolk.

Ordered. That a warrant be drawn forthwith for the disarming of Sir Nicholas l'Estrange of Hunstanton, Bart., Sir Christopher Calthorpe of East Basham, Knight of the Bath, Capt. James Calthorpe of West Basham, Esq., and Charles Hastings of Wighton, Esq., as persons suspected to be dangerous to the peace of the Kingdom, and that the said warrants be directed to Gabriell Armiger, Esq., Capt. of a company of Militia presently in the Hundred of Gallow and Brothercross, for the execution thereof.

A warrant was signed accordingly.

1690, July 19.　Norwich Castle.

Present :—

Sir Francis Guybon, K^{t.}	Sir Roger Potts
Robert Walpole.	Sir John Pettus
John Harbord.	Sir John Astly
Edmund Wodehouse.	Sir Wm. Cooke

B^{ts.}

A letter was read from the Council dated 15 July. Reciting that " there is great reason by late intelligence to apprehend that the French may speedily attempt an invasion of this Kingdom " ordering the Ld Lieutenant to cause the several troops of Militia Horse within his Lieutenancy to be called together for a month's training.

English and Dutch Fleet against the French in the Year 1691.

Our Fleet in the year 1691.

Red Squadrons.

	Ships.	Captains	Men.	Guns.
1	Britannia	Edward Russell, Adm^{ll}	815	100
1	St. Andrew	Ld. Bartlett	730	96
2	Neptune	Geo. Rook, Rear Adm	660	90
2	Albemarle	Sr Fra Wheler	660	90
2	Sandwich	Anthony Hastings	660	90

	Ships.	Captains.	Men.	Guns.
2	Vantguard	Richard Carter	660	90
1	St. Michael	Tho[.] Hobson	660	90
2	Victory	S^{ir} Jo. Ashby, Vice Adm^{ll}	530	82
3	Royall Oake	Geo. Bing	470	70
3	Elizabeth	Prisman	460	70
3	Sterling Castle	Ben Waters	460	70
3	Essex	Bridges	460	70
3	Lenox	Richard Munden	460	70
3	Restauration	John Gothier	460	70
3	Exeter	George Mees	460	70
3	Hope	Prichard	460	70
3	Berwick	Richard Martyn	460	70
3	Burford	Hartlow	460	70
3	Eagle	John Leake	460	70
	Warr Spight	Stafford Fairborne	420	70
	Harwich	Robert Roberson	420	70
	Montague	Symon Foulkes	400	66
	Dreadnought	Basill Beaumont	355	62
8	Plymouth	Mayne	340	62

Blew.		Men	12380	1828

	Ships.	Captains.	Men.	Guns.
1	Souverayne	Sr. Ralp D'lavall, Vice Ad^{ll}	815	100
1	London	Sr. Cloudsley Shovell, Rear Adm^{ll}	780	100
2	Duke	Henry Killigrew, Adm"	660	90
2	Coronation	Charles Shelton	660	90
2	Duchess	Jo. Clements	660	90
2	Windsor Castle	Geo. Churchill	660	90
2	Ossery	Jo. Tyrrell	660	90
2	Katherine		540	82
3	Captaine	Danyell Jones	460	72
3	Edgar	Mathew Trophy	445	72
3	Suffolk	Ch^r Billop	460	70
3	Hampton Court	Thomas Traydon	460	70
3	York		460	70
3	Northumberland	Andrew Cotton	460	70
3	Expedition	Dover	460	70
3	Kent	John Nevill	460	70
3	Grafton	Wm. Boknham	460	70
3	Lyon	Robt. Wiseman	460	70
3	Reflection	Earle of Danby	420	70
3	Defyance	Gourney	420	70
3	Swiftsure	Clarke	420	70
3	Cambridge	Listock	420	70
3	Monmouth	Robert Reynolds	400	66
3	Monk	Ben Hoskins	340	60
			12440	1842

Convoys and out cruising.

		Commanders in chief.	Men.	Guns.
3	Rupert	Math Aylmer	400	70
4	Leopard		280	54
4	Oxford	Seth Thirston	280	54
4	Woollwich	Richard Kigwin	280	54
4	Happy Return	Monk	280	54
4	St. Albans	Richard ffittz Patrick	280	54
4	Deptford		280	54
5	Newcastle	David Lambert	280	54
4	Portland	Thomas Lee	240	50
4	Sampson	Hen. Robinson	240	50
4		John Glanvile	230	48
4	Reserve	J. Crawley	230	48
4	Crowne	Sillmott	230	48
4	Tyger Prize	James Barber	230	48
4	Dover		230	48
4	Bonaventure		230	48
4	Ruby	Frederick Froude	230	48
4	Bristoll	Horton	230	48
4	Antelope	Henry Wickham	230	48
4	Mordant	Batteler	230	48
4	Swallow	John Bridget	230	48
4	Assistance	Kegwin	230	48
4	Kingfisher	Thos. Johnson	220	48
4	Archangell	Jasper Hickes	200	48
4	Princess Anne	Richard Badford	200	48
4	Barkley Castle	Willm Talmash	200	48
4	George	Jo. Frankmore	200	48
4	Successe	Will. North	200	48
4	Coronation	Thomas Reyner	200	48
4	Phenixe	John George	180	48
4	Portsmouth	George St. Hue	220	46
4	Mary Galley	Danyell Dearing	200	44
4	Sam and Henr	Robt. Venner	180	44
6	Jerusalem	John Vepnell	180	44
4	Constant Warwick	Abr. Potter	180	42
4	Nonsuch	Rob. Synock	180	42
4	Haniball	John Waters	160	40
4	Scepter	Will Rogers	160	40
5	Smyrna Merchant	James Salmon	110	34
5	Supply	Wm. Harding	110	34
4	Charles Galley	Jer. Roach	220	32
5	Saphire	Chr. Mynns	135	32
5	Dartmouth	Young	135	32
5	Saphire	Roger Killigrew	135	32
4	James Galley		200	30
5	Garland	John Jenypher	130	30
5	Gernesey	Robt. Arthur	130	30
5	Pearle		130	30
6	Owner's Endeavour	Michaell Berry	100	30
5	Richmond		125	28

		Commanders in chief.	Men.	Guns.
6	Monmouth Yacht	W^m. Wright	030	18
6	Greyhound ˙	Thomas Gillan	075	16
6	Souldadaes	ffrancis Whuell	075	16

			10480	2274

	Ships.	Captains.	Men.	Guns.
5	Drake	Tho. Spragg	75	16
6	Stubbs Yacht	John Johnson	40	12
6	Dumbarton	Th°· Row	80	10
6	Deptford Ketch	Tho. Berry	50	10
6	Quaker Ketch	Austin Breswin	50	10
6	Sallamander	Jo. Votier	35	10
6	Mary Yacht	Henry Cullings	30	8
6	Catherine Yacht	Gabriell Mellison	30	8
6	Henrietta Yacht	W^m· Sanderson	30	8
6	Kingfisher Ketch	Edwd Boyne	25	8
6	ffanfare	Edw. Pattinger	30	4
6	Cleaveland Yacht	Rich. Byron	30	8

			00505	0112
Brought over	-	-	-	10480	2274

Men in Convoys and Cruisers	10985	2386

Men		
Shipps in the Redd Squadron	-	-	24
In the Blew Squadron	-	-	-	-	24
Convoys and Cruisers	-	-	-	-	65

English ships	-	-	113

Dutch ships	-	-	068
Fire ships	-	-	-	030

Ships in all	211

Men in the Redd Squadron	-	-	12380
Men in the Blew Squadron	-	-	-	12440
Men in the other ships	-	-	-	10985

Men in all	-	-	35805

Gunns in ye Redd Squadron	-	-	-	1828
In the Blew Squadron	-	-	-	1842
In the other ships	-	-	-	-	2386

Guns in all	-	-	6056

English	First Rate Ships -	-	-	-	05
	Second Rates	-	-	-	11
	Third Rates	-	-	-	33
	Fourth Rates	-	-	-	37
	ffifth Rates	-	-	-	10
	Sixth Rates	-	-	-	17
Dutch Ships	First Rate Ships and Second	-	-	-	09
	3rd Rates	-	-	-	21
	Fourth Rates	-	-	-	17
	ffifth Rates	-	-	-	11
	Gallyots and flutes	-	-	-	10

NORFOLK LIEUTENANCY JOURNALS.

1695[-6], March 2.—Norwich Castle. *Present* :—Sir Robert Potts, Sir William Cooke, Barts., Sir Neville Catelyn, Knight, Ash Windham and Edmond Wodehouse, Esquires.

The Copy of an order in Council for the seizing of the Persons and arms of all Papists and Persons disaffected to the Government having been read

And a letter from the Lord Lieutenant of the 25 February ordering the calling out of the Militia Horse and the Trained Bands of the County for the purpose

Ordered. That the respective Captains of the Militia Horse in the County doe seize and secure the persons and arms of Papists and Persons whom we in this conjuncture have reason to suspect to be disaffected to the present Government according to the directions following and that the seizure be made throughout this county upon Monday the 9th of this instant March 1695.

Ordered. That Capt. Erasmus Earle doe call together and march his Troop into Gt. Yarmouth upon Monday the 9th of this instant March and doe the same day seize and secure the persons and arms of Barnaby Wale of Aldbey, Robt. Brown, John Brown, and Robt. Spencer, all of S. Walsham, Samuell Young of Loddon, George Marsh of Aldbey, John Spencer of Wotton, Gawin Nash of Blofield, Thomas Huby of Topcroft, Wm. Pierce of Wotton, John Urwin of Gt. Yarmouth, Abraham Castle of Thrigbey, Welsh of Ludham Hall. All which persons are to be conveyed by him to the Corporation of Gt Yarmouth where he is also to receive and secure such prisoners as shall be sent to him at Great Yarmouth by any Commissioned Officer or his order and the said persones to keep in safe custody during his 4 days duty there. And that the said Capt. Earle be relieved by Sir Wm. Rant's Troope upon Thursday the 12th of this instant March by Two of the Clock in the afternoon of the same day to whome he is then to deliver such Prisoners as shall be in his custody at the same time.

Ordered. That Capt. Sir Wm. Rant do upon Munday the 9th of this instant March seize and secure the persons and armes of Edward Paston, Esq., James Weld of Sherringham, Ed. Fuller of North Walsham, Doctor Smith, Wm. Parker, Edmund Suffield, Christopher Layer of Booton, Wm. Lucar,   Lake of Sparham, Ck. and doe forthwith convey the said persons to the Corporation of G^t· Yarmouth . . . . and that Capt. Sir W. Rant do raise no more of his Troop at that time than the occasion will require. But that the said Sir Wm. Rant doe raise his whole Troop upon Thursday the 12th of this instant March (to relieve Capt. Earle).

Ordered. That Capt. Philip Bedingfield doe upon Monday the 9th of this instant March seize and secure the persons and arms of Sir Robert Yallop, Kt., Charles Yallop, Esq., Thomas Wood, Esq., Thomas Havers, Doctor Chitleburgh and Rob. Chitleburgh and convey them to Yarmouth. (To raise his whole Troop on the 15th instant and relieve Rant at Yarmouth.)

Ordered. Captain James Hoste to call together and march his troop into Swaffham on the 9th instant and the same day secure the person and arms of Geoffrey Cobbe of Appleton and convey him to Swaffham.

Ordered. That Lt. Col. Sir Francis Guybon do upon Monday 9th instant seize and secure the Persons and arms of Sir Henry Beddingfield, Bart., Beaumont Tasburgh, Esq., Edmund Black-bourne, Anthony Beddingfield, Henry Timperley, Charles Hastings, Charles Peyton, Jeoffrey Cobbs, Matthew Cuffin, John Catteway of Weston, Thomas Marwood steward to Sir Henry Beddingfield, Matthew Holcot of Lutcham (sic), (Thomas Duvall, John Clarke, Wm. Taylor, Wm. Bell, all of Swaffham),
Shaw of East Basham, Clk. (and convey them to Swaffham and deliver to Capt. James Hoste).

(Also to secure the persons and arms of Sir Nicholas l'Estrange, Bart., Sir Christopher Calthorpe, Knight of the Bath, and deliver them to the custody of Col. Edmond Wodehouse, and to raise his whole Troop and relieve Capt. Hoste on the 12th.)

Ordered. That Capt. Chas. Wright on Monday 9th instant do seize and secure the persons and arms of Sir Francis Jernegan, Bart., Sir Robert Yallop, Knt., Charles Yallop, Esq., and Giles Yallop, and convey them to Swaffham. (To raise his whole Troop on the 15th and relieve Capt. Sir Francis Guybon.)

1695[-6], March 8.—An order in Council dated 5 March being received this day discharging the previous order for assembling the militia horse. Notice was immediately given to discharge the troops on duty and to discharge such persons as should be in their custody.

1700–1751.—MISCELLANEOUS MEMORANDA AND LETTERS.

MARY COUNTESS OF SUFFOLK to

1702[-3], Feb. 2.—This comes to lett you know that to-morrow evening, Wensday, the corpes of M$^{rs.}$ Anne Hobart are carryed hence towards Norfolk, and wilbee at Norwich on Saturday night next. She is to be buried on Sunday immediately after

Sermon in Sir John Hobart's vault in Brickling Church. The body is not to go to Brickling house but directly to the church. I desier that youll take care to speake to the minister and clerk to be in readyness, &c.

The following gentlemen are desired to hold up the Pall:—

Mr. Thomas Herne.

The two Mr. Fleetewoods.

Mr. Jarmeys son of Bayfeild.

In case any of these cannot be had, then:—

Mr. Fountaine of Sall.

Mr. Parston, my L. Yarmouth's son.

There is but four designed for all.

You are to give ye Minister a guinea, and to ye Clarke and Sexton what you thinke propper, and amongst the poor twenty shillings. This is what Mr. Hobart hath desired me to write you, who am,

Your friend,
M. SUFFOLKE.

1703, Oct. 28.—A Schedule signed by W. Billing of 13 Pictures which, as appears from a Bill of Sale upon the same Paper, were sold to him by Sir Henry Hobert, late of Blickling, and were now (Oct. 28, 1703) bought back on behalf of Sir John Hobart,° Barronett, an Infant, son and heire of the late Sir Henry, by John Brewster, of Fundenhall, in Norfolk, for the sum of fifty pounds. (Receipted on the back.)

1. One piece of the Lord Chief Justice Hobart.

2. Sir John Hobart, his son.

3. Lady Frances, wife to the said Sir John Hobart. She was eldest daughter to the Earl of Bridgewater.

4. Mr. Myles Hobart, grandfather to the late Sir Henry Hobart.

5. The said Mr. Myles Hobart's Lady.

6. Sir John Hobart, grandfather to the present Sir John Hobart,° drawn when he was a young man and wore his owne haire.

7. Another piece of the said Sir John Hobart of later date drawn with a wigg.

8. The said Sir John Hobart's last lady, grandmother to the present Sir John Hobart.

9. Sir James Hobart, sometimes Attorney Generall, a piece of antiquity. He built Loddon Church.

10. Mrs Mary Trevor, sister to the present Lord Chief Justice of that name.

11. Lady Massey ⎱ Daughters to the Lady Hobart.
12. Mrs. Preston ⎰

13. Mrs. Elizabeth Hamond, grandmother to the present Sir John Hobart by Mr. Hamond her former husband (*sic*).

1703, Dec.—A receipt from Mary Countess of Suffolk for half a year's allowance for the six daughters of Sir Henry Hobart. [Anne, Elizabeth, Henrietta, Philippa, Dorothy and Catherine.]

° First Lord Hobart and Earl of Buckinghamshire.

1703[-4], Feb. 6, 7 and 8.—Note of expenses of Mrs. Anne Hobart's funeral at Blickling.

1704.—Memoranda relating to burial of Philippa Hobart.

1705.—A receipt for money "paid to the use of the poore of the parish of Blickling, being the penalty of an Act of Parliament for that M$^{rs.}$ Elizabeth Hobart who was buryed in the said parish church was not wound in woollen according to the direction of the said Act."

1705.—Marriage settlement of Henrietta Hobart and the Hon. Charles Howard.

1706-1710.—Receipts from the Countess of Stamford for allowances for the education and maintenance "of my two nieces M$^{rs.}$ Dorothy and Katherine° Hobart."

NORFOLK LIEUTENANCY JOURNALS.

1706, April 30.
Present :—Sir Ed. Ward, B$^{t.}$
John Harbord, Esq.
A copy of Order in Council of 4th April was received, ordering that the constables take a distinct and particular account of all Papists and reputed Papists with their respective qualities, estates and places of abode.

1707 [-8] March 16.—List of PAPISTS and NON-JURORS whose houses were to be searched for horses and arms by order of the Lieutenancy this day.

By Capt. Philip Beddingfield.
Papists or so reputed.
Charles Hastings of Wiveton, gent. (now of Studdy), Thomas Woods of Colekirke, Esq., Thomas Duvall of Swaffham, gent., William Taylor of Swaffham (dead), Richard Martin of Oxburgh, gent., Anthony Stockdale of Swanton Morly, John Jernegan, Esq., of Oxburgh.
Non-Jurors.
Sir Christopher Calthorpe of East Basham, Knight of the Bath, Thomas Wright of East Basham, clerk.

By Col. Horatio Walpole.
Papists or so reputed.
Edward Paston of Barningham, gent., Jervas Taylor of Billingford (dead), Edward Fuller of North Walsham, Thomas Reily, gent. of North Walsham, Richard Parkes of Aylsham (dead), Hamond Estgate of Brampton, George Bedell of Woodrising Esq.,   Dicks of Aylsham.
Non-Jurors.
Edward Edmund of Woodaling (dead), Richard Lake of Sparham, clerk,   Munsy of Booton, clerk.

---

* Afterwards wife of General Churchill.

By Capt. Jas. Hoste.

Papists or so reputed.

John Paston of Appleton, Esq., Geoffrey Cobbs of Appleton, gent., Charles Peyton of Grimston, (jurat) gent., Philip Bell of Wallington, gent., Sarah Hawkins of Downham, widow, Thomas Howse of Downham.

By Capt. Chas. Wright.

Papists or so reputed.

Sir Francis Jernegan of Costesy, Bart., John Jernegan of Costesy, Esq., George Jernegan of Costesy, gent., Edmund Blackbourne of Wymundham, gent., John Copping of Shropham, William Isaack of Ashill, Cuthbert Ridley of Ashill, William Ridley of Ashill.

By Capt. Thos. Berney.

Papists or so reputed.

John Spencer of Bowthorp Hall, gent.

Shottesham All Saints.

Robert Hemlinton of Earsham, Mrs. Elizabeth Havers of Thelveton, widow.

By Capt. Robert Suckling, jun.

Papists or so reputed.

Charles Yallop of Thorpe by Norwich, Esq., John Browne of Acle, gent., Robert Browne of South Walsham, gent., Dorothy Huby of Topcroft, widow, Henry Huby of Topcroft, chirurgeon, Thomas Huby of Topcroft, Coroner, Francis Cooke of Topcroft, farmer, William Price of Woodton, gent., George Marsh of Toft Monks, gent., Samuell Young of Gillingham All Saints, gent.

Non-Jurors.

Giles Yallop of Ludham, gent., John Walsh of Ormsby, gent.

1708, March 27.—The respective captains reported that they did not find any horse of five pounds value in the possession of any of the said papists or disaffected persons; nor arms excepting one musquet belonging to Mr. Richard Lake of Sparham, clerk, a non-juror, which with a belt of bandoliers was seized by Lieutenant Thomas Skottowe, which was ordered to remain in the custody of the said Mr. Skottowe till further order.

1707.—A receipt for half a year's board and schooling of Sir John Hobart from M. Tooke, Bishops Stortford.

1713-14.—Receipts, one for a silver punchbowl presented to Clare Hall, Cambridge, by Sir John Hobart.

1721.—Copy of Sir John Tyrel's will and his marriage settlement with Mrs. Elizabeth Cotton. Papers relating to the execution of his will.

1721-1769.—Five packets of letters and other documents relating to the property of the Hobarts in Cornwall—the Manors of Beer Ferris, Truro, Lanrake, etc. Relating also to elections at St. Ives in the years 1721, 1722, 1761, 1766, with lists of Voters. Letters of the 1st and 2nd Earls of Buckinghamshire in relation to these.

1723-1793.—Three packets of papers relating to Henrietta Countess of Suffolk, chiefly in connection with Marble Hill. Among these are :—

" A Schedule of writings relating to the Freehold, Copyhold and Leasehold Estate of the late Countess of Suffolk at Marble Hill, which were in the possession of the late Earl of Buckingham at the time of his decease " [in 1793].

A Letter from E. Budgell to the Countess of Suffolk, June 16, 1727, gives "an account of the Manor of Twickenham without any of that unintelligible cant we Lawyears often use to seem wise ourselves and keep others in the dark." . . . The Manor is at present possessed by three persons who bought it from the Commissioners. Two of these three present Lords want money very much, so that the thing will be sold, a great Penny worth. . . . . As 'tis held under his Majesty you will probably, Madam, be deny'd no reasonable favour you can ask." From another Paper it appears that " the whole or part of Twickenham was sold by the Trustees of Forfeited Estates as part of the late Viscount Bolingbroke's Estate.' N.D.

" A Particular in Rentall of the Manor of Twickenham in Middlesex as sett forth by the Commissioners of the forfeited Estates when purchased by the present owners in 1723."

A List of Freeholders, Leaseholders and Coppyholders in the the Estate. Among the freeholders and copyholders is Godfrey Kneller.

There are also bills of carpenters' and carvers' work, leases and business letters in connexion with the Marble Hill Estate, 1724-1753.

Business letters addressed to Lady Suffolk by John Earl of Buckinghamshire [her brother], Thomas Ryder and others, 1735.

The Will of George Berkeley, Esq.

A Copy of the Will of W. Plomer. 1742.

The Will of Henrietta Dowager Countess of Suffolk, widow of the Hon. George Berkeley, Esq. Sept. 27, 1758.

A packet of letters and other documents relating to a dispute as to right of way in Twickenham between Henrietta Countess of Suffolk and John Fridenberg, merchant, of the City of London. 1750-1755.

1727.—A copy of General George Wade's Report respecting the disarmament of the Highlands of Scotland, respecting also the recalcitrant clan of the late Earl of Seaforth, the repairing of the Castle of Inverness, the Exile of those attainted for High Treason and the riots on account of the Malt Tax.

1728[1729]-1735.—The will of Brigadier John Hobart of St. Giles in the Fields, Middlesex. [Brother of Sir Henry Hobart of Blickling]. Dated March 22, 1728[9].

Mar. 1734[5]-Nov. 1735.—Three letters addressed to Robert Britiffe from Mrs. Henrietta Bedingfield, [" daughter of the late Dame Dorothy Bedingfield"] relating to business in connection with John Hobart's death in 1734, she being his residuary legatee.

An account of all the plate, moneys, household goods, and of the books in the house of the late Brigadier Hobart. (An account of Family pictures is missing from this packet.)

1728-1739.—A packet of papers relating to the Gunnersbury (or Gunnaldsbury) Estate in N^th Ealing, late of Sergeant Maynard, sold by Lord Hobart to Mr. Henry Furnese in 1739. A survey of the estate describes the house as by Inigo Jones, "with Tapestry and hangings in the great room of the Cartoons, valued at 1,000l.; and likewise an Isle in the Parish Church of Ealing, the whole lately rented by the Duke of Queensborough at £300 per an."

A parcel of Letters from Robert Britiffe and W. Bristow to Lord Hobart relate to the sale of this estate and also to the purchase of Manington in Norfolk by the Walpoles.

1731.—Copy of Will of Sir George Walton.

1735.—Poll Books of Norfolk Election.

1740.—A List of the free burgesses of the borough of Malden in the County of Essex.

1749, May 12.—Order from the office of Ordnance to Calder, master gunner of Yarmouth, to receive the arms from Ld Hobart and take them to the Tower, viz. :—
" The armes of the Regiment raised by Lord Hobart at the late Rebellion."

Mem : Arms belonging to the County of Norfolk, 396 firelocks and bayonets.

Arms belonging to the City of Norwich, 198 firelocks and bayonets.

Sent back hyther in 1746 by order of Lord Buckinghamshire.

Recd of the R^t. Hon. Earl of Buckinghamshire the arms issued to his Lordship consisting of 399 firelocks and bayonets and 378 cartridge boxes which were delivered to him at the time of the late rebellion as Lord Lieutenant of the County of Norfolk.

SECTION III.

BUCKINGHAMSHIRE PAPERS.

Part I.—1740-1758.

Sir Thomas Drury's Correspondence.

Pedigree of Drury Family [of Overstone].

1740.—The Pedigree of the Drury family, by which it appears that Sir Thomas of this date was son to Joyce, daughter and sole heiress of Thomas Beacon, of Ilford, in Essex. Sir Thomas Drury married Martha, second daughter of Sir John Tyrel, of Heron, in Essex, Bart., by Mary, his first wife, daughter of Sir James Dolliffe, of Mitcham, in Surrey.

Joyce Drury to [her son] Sir Thomas Drury.

1744-[5], Jan. 26. Colne.—I send inclos'd the order for the East India Dividend. I had wrote last post, but have had a return of the gout in my right hand which has made me very ill again.

The letter that came by fryday's post the 10th instant was charged two shillings sixpence, weight two ounces $\frac{1}{2}$. I did not take it as I thought it was only news, I shall be glad to hear that you are well, and how both the children doe, with love to you and lady.

Order of Council to Lord Lieutenants.

1745, Sept. 5.—Reciting that the eldest son of the Pretender hath Presumed in open violation of the laws to land in the north-west part of Scotland, and ordering them forthwith to cause all arms belonging to Papists, non-jurors, or other persons that shall be judged dangerous to the peace of the kingdom within their Lieutenancy to be seized and secured according to the said Act, and to return an exact account to the Board.
Signed, Hardwick, Dorset, Pembroke, Cholmondley, Granville, Will. Yonge, T. Winnington.
Copy.

Samson Gideon to Sir Thomas Drury.

1745, Sept. 7. Garraways.—The D. of N. has wrote a Letter to the Lord Mayor to acquaint him by the King's order that the Pretender's son has set up his Standard in Scotland, which has caused a Common Council to be called who have agreed to a most Loyal Address. The Merchants have had a meeting and chose the Committy they did last year with addition of Mr. Selwin and our friend Mʳ· Janssen, who is the person that has promoted the whole and keeps up the spirit, and they resolved to address his Majesty and there are about 500 subscribed since yesterday, among whom are People of the greatest Fortunes in the City as well as merchants. We are to go to Kenzinton Wednesday next, after which above 200 have subscribed to dine together at Merchant Taylors or some other hall upon which we promise ourselves great aid in the present juncture. Ten of our Redgments are ordered from Flanders and part of the Dutch we judge are already arrived in Scotland. If the affair in these parts be not soon quelled it may prove of Evil consequence.

S. Sea 103.
Bank 143½.
India 173½.
Annu's 103.
Tickets 13.
3 Pᶜᵗˢ· 87⅝.
Salt 6½.

SAMSON GIDEON to SIR THOMAS DRURY.

1745, Sept. 13.—I am favoured with yours of the 11ᵗʰ Insᵗ· Am not at all surprised that you are alarmed, for by the Publick and privat accoⁿᵗˢ affairs seem to go in the North not to our wishes, and should any foreign force or forces land there or in any other part of the Kingdom it may prove of bad consequence, as we are at present provided, and we wish your Health would permit you to be in town at this Critical Juncture, for tho' a country Life may be preferable to the Continual dissatisfaction we labour under here still there are certain affairs not to be described at this distance and of which every man can only judge for himself. I would not willingly disturb you and still as you hold Stock on Loan if things do not cleare up you may suffer great inconveniences. Supose in Novʳ· next the present want of money or rather distrust &c. should increase or Continue, there is not any to be had even at 5% and E. India Bonds are not above 4 per cent. and should they come under parr so as to oblige the Company to give a greater Interest, you know what follows, for my part as I know not how to act for myself, much less can I advise; only thought proper to lay these considerations before you, on the other hand should the rebellion cease, affairs go well abroad by the appearance of a Peace, Every thing would take a different turne and stocks recover their former price, nay higher than Ever, and did you hold no more than what is in your name I should not have writt to you a line on the subject. Upon the whole I heartely wish you may resolve on what will tend most for your advantage.

S. Sea 102.
India 174 for the 30 instant and 175½ for the 12 Novr., which prolongation is after this rate of 7 pc. per annum.
3 pc. 87¼.
Annu' New 105¾.
Tickets 12.

CHAMPION BRANFILL to SIR THOMAS DRURY.

1745, Sept. 14. Upminster Hall.—We have Divers Reports as to the Strength and Success of the Rebels but there is not one to be depended on. 'Tis agreed that the Dutch must by this time be landed in Scotland so that we hope soon to hear of their being quelled. I don't believe the Ministers are in very great pain, for we have had no orders about the papists yet which you know we had when they talk[d] but of the Invasion sometime since.

SAMSON GIDEON to SIR THOMAS DRURY.

1745, Sept. 21. Garraway.—I congratulate you on the arrival of 14 E[t.] India Ships at Galloway in Ireland. They came without convoy; had not providence protected them we had been in a fine condition, as we are Elsewhere. The P. was proclaim'd last tuesday at Edinburgh, the People let the Rebels in without opposition, I can not express my thoughts this way but it looks as if we were betray'd or what is more neglected. The Dutch Troops are all arriv'd in the River Except 5 Transports to Burlington Bay in Yorkshire instead of Scotland. We may expect 6,000 of our forces next week, but still I must confess that people of Property being out of town at this juncture is not prudent. It is an indignity to ———— that 20 people should land above two months since and be suffer'd to put so many people in consternation, and if no more care is taken then what I perceive, the same fate may attend the City.

India 176.   Salt 6¼.
S. Sea 103.   Tickets 13.
Annuis 108.
3 pc. 11¼.

Enclosure :—
1745, Sept.—LIST OF SHIPS ARRIVED AT GALLOWAY.

Montague	-	Freeman	-	Mocha and Bombay
St. George	-	Robinson	-	Bengal
K. William	-	Phillips	-	Bombay
Winchelsea	-	Adair (dead)	-	Bengal
Winchester	-	Steward	-	Coast and Bay
Cæsar	-	Court	-	St. Helena and Bencoolen
York	-	Lafeectles ?	-	Fort St. George and China
Stafford	-	Baker		China
P. William	-	Langworth	-	Coast and Bay
Lapwing	-	Watts		Bengal and Bencoolen
D. Dorsett	-	Frognall		Coast and Bay
Beaufort	-	Stephens	-	Fort St. George
Godolphin	-	Jas. Stephens	-	Bengal
Dorrington	-	Crab	-	Do.

Arrived at Galloway on Monday last.

EARL OF HALIFAX to SIR THOMAS DRURY.

1745, Oct. 2. Audley Street, Wednesday night.—Tho' my hands are so full of business that I have not a moment to spare to anybody but you, I trouble you with this to acquaint you that I am informed the general meeting of our County to consider of proper measures to be taken in the present dangerous situation of our affairs is fixed for Friday next. I set out to-morrow morning and have a place in my Coach at your disposal.

EARL OF HALIFAX to SIR THOMAS DRURY.

1745, Oct. 7. Audeley Street, Monday night, 12 o'th Clock.—I take the earliest opportunity of informing you that His Majesty when I deliver'd the Association to him this morning with our Lord Lieutenant in his Closet (for his Grace's business made us too late for the Levée) express'd the utmost chearfullness and satisfaction at the procedings of his faithful servants in Northamptonshire. Before I had the Honour of seeing His Majesty he had given directions for my Commission as Colonel to be made out. I hope with your assistance (which I greatly depend upon, hearing how hearty a zeal animates you upon this occasion) and that of my other friends I shall soon compleat my Regiment. Never was there an occasion that called upon us to exert ourselves so strenuously as the present one, and that the safety of the whole depends upon the zeal and spirit of particulars.

P.S.—I am just now informed that Mr. Ward of Stoke, who has already some men, promises ten pence a day to all that will enlist over and above his Majesty's pay. This method I apprehend is a very unfortunate one for us, especially in the beginning of the affair ; and I heartily wish it may not get air in our Part of the Country. The Duke of Bedford gives no premium; those who engage with him have only the King's pay and yet his Regiment is almost compleat as I hear already.

CHAMPION BRANFILL to SIR THOMAS DRURY.

1745, Oct. 9. Chelmsford.—" We have just now signed here a most loyal Address with an offer of our Lives and Fortunes which you will say is no great Compliment from me and an Association, and tho' late we are come pretty Hearty. We had the Lords FitzWalter and Waldegrave and the greatest Appearance I ever saw at Sess. and almost Assizes." . . . . . .

SAMSON GIDEON to SIR THOMAS DRURY.

1745, Oct. 12. Garaways.—Our affairs relating to Stocks are somewhat better, tho' the great scarcity of money continues. I have been forced to pay after the rate of 12 cp. p. annum. We are aprehensive for Barwick and nothing but more regular Troops will put an end to our troubles. All things are in my opinion of no service but to hinder the King's Levees and cause discontent among his Troops.

SAMSON GIDEON to SIR THOMAS DRURY.

1745, Nov. 23.—There are sellers of [Lottery] Tickets at £9 14s. which shews you what such affairs are when left to their own course. The same would have happened last year had I not taken care to prevent it, which might have been done this year by buying about 2,000 Tickets, the want of which I wish may not be of fatal consequences in raising the next supplies.

HUGH MARRIOTT to SIR THOMAS DRURY.

1745, Nov. 19. Tooke's Court, near Chancery Lane.—I suppose you know that the City of Carlisle has been under a necessity of capitulating to admit the Rebels and pay 2,000l. to save them from Massacre. By the best accounts the Capitulation was made on Thursday night and the Rebels had a Gate given up to them on Friday morning. News of it was immediately sent to Marshal Wade, and the Letters which came from Newcastle to a friend of mine by yesterday's post mention the armys being advanced on their way to Carlisle by Hexham if practicable for the artillery, if not they must return and go round by Bernard Castle, and there is no hope that the Citadel of Carlisle can hold out till they arrive. The enclosed is from our steward in Cumberland written you will see before he knew what was passing about 16 m. further North. When I shall hear from him again God knows, for the enemy is no doubt at Penrith by this time or further and then all Posts will be stopped from thence as they were yesterday from Carlisle. When I pick up anything more than is in the newspapers on good authority I shall acquaint you with it directly and send you my letters if any, which be so good as to return by next post.

Since writing the above I find at the Rolls that it is not the citadel (which is an inconsiderable place) but the Castle that stands out, and that we have secured in it the artillery and military stores.

SAMSON GIDEON to SIR THOMAS DRURY.

1745, Nov. 30. Garraways.—Last Wednesday there was a Meeting at the Crown in order to endeavour to raise part of the Land Tax, and we adjourned till Tuesday next, am aprehensive it will be very difficult to compleat. However I will do on my part all that is in my power. The scarcity of money increases and the Exchange rises for Amsterdam, which proves that the Merchants are willing to give their assistance. The Lord Mayor has opened a subscription as you will find by the Papers. I contributed £100, and will give my assistance as I find it is not to be done from those it was expected. All the News (Except what is in the Papers) is that Stewart the Provost is in London and was taken into custody this morning.

PHILIPPA ISTED to SIR THOMAS DRURY.

1745, Dec. 5.—Mr. Neale of Wellingboro is just now come here, and brings word that a gentleman of that town whose authority may be depended on went this morning at three

o'clock to Leicester, where he stayed till several Officers belonging to the Rebel Army arrivid there to demand quarters for the
Army which was to be there this evening. Upon that unwell-
come news my Aunt desires me to give you this trouble, with her
best compliments, and begs the favour of you to send the four
horses (you were so good this morning) to offer her by the
bearer, with which we purpose setting out as early as possible
to-morrow morning. She desires to know which will be most
agreeable to you, either for her to return your horses as soon as
she gets to Town, or for her to keep them there; whichever you
chuse, she with pleasure will do.

Samson Gideon to Sir Thomas Drury.

1745, Dec. 5. Garraways.—We expected an account this
Evening of an action, but not hearing of any, fear they may have
slipt our Army which God forbid. As you are lame I cannot
expect you in Town. Otherwise no man would be absent with
your Concernes. If you have money in your hands that you
make no use of please to send me a drauft for £297 14s. . . .
The subscription in the City for the Land Tax amounted to
£503,000 and with much difficulty the S. Sea 40,000, London
Assurance 50m. and Royall 20,000 to compleat the Affair, but
what is that to the sum wanted? In short I am much discontented . . . .
P.S.—This is a crisis, if any thing turns in our favour there
will be money found.

Samson Gideon to Sir Thomas Drury.

1745, Dec. 7. Garraways.—I rec^d yours dated the 5th am
sorry you have been In such a Consternation and do assure you
the alarms of the Rebels aproaching had the same Effect here
but being informed that his Royal Highness the Duke would be
at Northampton this Evening we are in better spirits, there is a
perfect stagnation in our affaires here and nothing doing in Stocks
except 4 pc. annuis which are under parr.

Samson Gideon to Sir Thomas Drury.

1745, Dec. 10.—I hope your consternation has abated by finding the rebells are gone from you, at least it has in some
measure that effect here.
Coud you have Employd ten people I am perswaded they woud
not have spoke to more men who upon other Occasions are ready
to lend their money on Stocks &c. and still without effect, and
what helps to keep all Bankers Back is that one of them who
lives in the house that was Woodward has stoped payment, tho'
when they can buy India Bonds at £3 disco^t and demand the
money of the Company they make after the rate of 9 cp. per
annum with the best security, and Navy Bills at 10 cp. Disct. &c.
I do assure you had I the Cash none of these considerations
should be inducing to obstruct my advancing it to you at lawfull
Interest, but I am dubly unhappy in having mine Invested.

HUGH MARRIOTT to SIR THOMAS DRURY.

1745, Dec. 10. London.—I give you many thanks for your favour of the 7th. By the very false accounts you will perceive the News gave concerning the arrival of our Army at Northampton, you may see the value of a letter from the spot. It will be a singular satisfaction to me when you can continue me the favour of such. Rumours arise and are contradicted so very fast that I intend to trouble you with none. I will however let you know the truth of two matters about which I dare say you will be sollicitous. The first is that I have it from very good hands and it is universally agreed that the young Person in the Tower is not the Pretender's son. The other is about the *Law Regiment* which I fully thought on Sunday noon to have inlisted myself as a private centinel before night. The fact was represented to me thus, viz: that all the Regular Forces were to go as yesterday with his Majesty to encamp on Finchley Common and therefore as the guarding of the rest of the Royal Family remaining at St. James' must at all events be left to undisciplined men, none would be so proper for the purpose as persons of Fortune and publick character, and that as we Counsell who signed the Association and address (Note—none in the Law of inferior Rank to Counsell were allow[1] to sign it) had thereby offered our persons and were a known and considerable body His Majesty had been asked whether he would accept our service for that purpose, and had been pleased to say he would be much satisfied to leave his family in so good hands and that in fact most of the Counsell fit to bear arms who were of note either in their profession or for their families or estates had agreed to it. In this Light it was so honourable and gallant a Duty that I should have been excessively pleased to undertake it. But when I went on the Sunday evening to the general meeting at the Middle Temple Hall, I found there the Lord Chief Justice Willes, it is true, talking very floridly and averring he was to have his Commission as Colonel of this Regiment as soon as we had agreed upon a name for it: but instead of the honourable company I expected, there were not, that my glass could bring to my eye, 20 Counsell in the room that either had £200 per annum estate or business to that amount. Not 6 Counsell of any eminence (not one of the King's Counsell) and very few Attorneys or Solicitors of note, but the Assembly (except some young gentlemen students) was chiefly composed of the very low sort of Practitioners, not without a mixture of clerks and hackney writers, which last our colonel was unwilling to take out of the Muster Roll, and declared if we excluded them he would form them into independent Companies, but all under attorneys and solicitors were at last excluded. You may believe I would not inlist under these circumstances, when by His Majesty's message to us it appeared the cause of thinking of it was over. In short it was a mere job to make —— seem the head of the Law. Whether the truth got to Court or not I can't tell, but this morning the Colonel came in his Judge's habit and acquainted the Assembly that Lord Harrington had (instead of his expected commission, for that I assure you he never had, and so now owned) wrote him a letter by the King's order to acquaint the Gentlemen of the Law (with very gracious acknowledgements of the offer of their service) that he had now received certain advice that the Enemy were retreating into Scotland and that with so much precipitation that it was not expected even Wades army could get up with them, and as by this change of affairs there was no occasion to draw the forces out to Finchley, he desired they would put themselves to no further expence (for the uniform was really making) till further intimation of his pleasure. . . . . Thus ended this Project which promised so fairly and honourably at first, but by the impetuosity and selfintresstedness of‚ ————— grew into such ridicule that few gentlemen who in the zeal of their hearts and on account of the apparent immediate necessity signed on Saturday (which was the day it began) knew what to do with themselves or how with honour to go either on with it or from it.

AMBROSE ISTED to SIR THOMAS DRURY.

1745, Dec. 10. Ecton.—I have just recd. the accounts I send you from Mr. Rogers. Since he wrote Mrs. Rogers writes to my sister that a great part of the Duke of Kingston's Light Horse are arrivid at Northampton, and mentions an Article which he had not heard before, viz. that the Chief Officers of the Rebels lay at Mr. Binghams at Derby, and said there that they designed for North‚ton on Friday morning. But one of their chiefs went off in the night as they imagined to betray them to the Duke, and that was the reason of their returning in such a Hurry. A warrant has come hither to the same purpose as that to Overstone, and I find that such have been sent to all the Towns round as far as Yardley.

I propose to set out early tomorrow for the Regiment.

DENISON CUMBERLAND° to SIR THOMAS DRURY.

1745, Dec. 16. Stanwick,—Your news gave us great pleasure especially as it confirms a flying report we had here on Saturday from Leicester, that the Duke had demolished the rear of the Rebels and that they expected hourly to hear of their total destruction; which pray Heavens may be speedy and so general that not one, especially of their Chiefs, may escape.

S. GIDEON to SIR THOMAS DRURY.

1745, December 28. Garraways—The News of the Queen of Hungary having Concluded a Peace with the King of Prussia gave new Life to our friends and is indeed an affair that may produce good consequences. He is a Man of Extraordinary

---

* Denison Cumberland (1705-1774), Rector of Stanwick and later Dean of St. Paul's. He was Bishop of Clonfert, 1763-1772, and Bishop of Kilmore, 1772-1774. His son was Richard Cumberland, the dramatist.

Capacity, has upwards of 100 Thousand men Excelent troops and he aims much at Glory, and I hope will forward a general Peace in Europe. God send he may or by degrees we shall all be undone. Several rich merchants (of fortune in goods and beyond the Seas) have been oblig'd to stop payment. The scarcity of money being such that there is none to be raised at any rate and if it continues I cannot point out which way the Publick will be furnishe^d with the vast sums they must require. The Rebels are gone towards Edinburgh and Hally appointed generalissimo. Shall not enter into Politicks because I don't understand them. All I can lerne as a looker on is that we are in for the whole winter at least, unless some unforseen accident. Nothing doing in stock.

[REVD. NICHOLAS] LECHMERE to SIR THOMAS DRURY.

1745[-6], Jan, 14. [Warnford, near West Meon, Hants.]— The covers you was so kind as to frank are now near all used, and I would not presume to send you a fresh parcel without leave first obtained. I therefore beg a line or two to signify your pleasure herein. It is as I before told you the only amusement I have in a little country village consisting of Farmers only, and what I would be sorry to be without at any time, and especially at the present, which is the most critical that I can remember. I live about twelve miles from our coast between Chichester and Portsmouth, and it is impossible to express the terrors we have been in on account of the intended French invasion. Once in particular we had positive information that they were actually landing between Chichester and Arundel, the whole country was alarmed. Chichester-gates were shut and the People under arms, the same at Portsmouth, and several expresses actually sent up to London; when, Behold, the upshot of the whole affair was, some smuggling vessels landing their goods and a large party of armed smugglers on shore receiving them, which were taken for french troops just disembarkt. At the same time Admiral Vernon* with his fleet hovering over our coast, was at a distance interpreted to be a French squadron to cover their troops as they landed. I thank God we have by his good providence weathered the point so far, and I hope He will give such a blessing to the measures taken by the Government, as that they may defeat the machinations of our Enemys in all quarters. I heartily wish all happiness and prosperity to yself, my Lady and family.

JOYCE DRURY to SIR THOMAS DRURY.

1745-[6], Jan. 15. Colne.—I received your Letters and am very much concerned to hear that you have the gout so often. I sympathize with you. Since I wrote to you have had the gout very severe in my hands and feet, but thank God, I am better.

---

* Admiral Edward Vernon (1684-1757) created Admiral, 1745.

I fear the troublesome times wont be at an end soon, people this way have been very much frighted and hide their best effects. I desire you will send me a noat upon Mr. Owen for thirty pounds. I had rather have money then a Bank draught. I shall be glad to hear that you are well, with love to Lady Drury and the children.

Samson Gideon to Sir Thomas Drury.

1745[-6], Jan. 23. London.—At a General Court of the Directors (of South Sea Stock) proposed 1¾ per cent. for the 6 months due at Xmas and a Ballot demanded in favour of 2 per cent. Should the latter be resolved upon there will remain still a sinking fund to discharge the small debts due for dividend warrants, &c.

The fatal Bad news wee received yesterday from the North of which the papers abounds as stop'd the rise of our funds and sunk peoples Spirits considerably. H.R.H. the Duke is going down, and hope he will recover our shame, but it is pety he should go without ten Thousand men that he may run no risque.

Champion Branfill to Sir Thomas Drury.

1745[-6], Feb. 11. London.—We are in great Consternation. Yesterday the 2 Secretaries of State resigned. Lord Granville is appointed in the room of Lord Harrington, the other undisposed off. Too day Mr. Pelham, all the Admiralty, Lord Gower, Dukes of Richmund, Dorset, Devonshire, and too morrow the Chancellor and Attorney General, 'tis said the Attorney has refused the Seals as hath Willes ; his Reason was he did not care to part with a certainty for a place of so small Duration, as every body imagines they must soon come in again the Body they went out. . . . . .

I congratulate you as to the Flight of the Rebels, people are now very easy as to them.

Hugh Marriott to Sir Thomas Drury.

1745[-6], Feb. 11. Tooke's, near Chancery Lane.—I could not help accquainting you, lest other Correspondents should omit in this post that the whole Ministry you left in possession is or will be out before you receive this. D. of Newcastle and Ld Harrington resigned yesterday. L' Cobham's men all go out in a lump. It is expected Ld Can^e will give up the Seal to morrow. His successor is not known, but most People say the Attorney General has refused that high office, that L^d Ch. I. Willes is to be the man, and Sir Thos. Bootle to succeed him. Ld Granville is to be the Head of the new Ministry. It is said Ld Bath is to be a Secretary of State, and Ld Sandys again Chancellor of the Excheq^er. I think I never even out of the North writ you any thing more surprizing.

·CHAMPION BRANFILL to SIR THOMAS DRURY.

1745-[6], Feb. 13. London.—I wrote you last post of the great Revolutions in the Ministry. I now congratulate you on as speedy a Change to the Right as you were is the Word of Command all I hear is that everything is to be as it was. Lord Granville having continued sole Secretary for twenty-four hours the Secret History of the Affair I dont doubt you will have from better Hands. We have a Report of a Skirmish between some of the Rebels and some of our Troops to the loss of 400 of our Men but I know not the Truth.

HUGH MARRIOTT to SIR THOMAS DRURY.

1745-[6], Feb. 15. Tooke's Court, near Chancery Lane.—Till 3 o'clock on Wednesday (the last day of Term) It continued to be thought a fixed thing that Lord Chancellor was to resign, as many persons of the first quality had then actually done. But about that time He was sent for to Court off the Bench and all the Resigners of the first rank (the whole number that agreed to stand by one another in resigning was about 45) were that night at Court. We were told It was then agreed that Lord Granville should go out and the whole Ministry should be again as it was the week before: and it is said that the Intended New Ministry had before then been in the City to see what money they could get advanced on the Supplies and could not get a Farthing. Thursday evening It was thought all were to go out again and there was at least this foundation for it that the papers of seals (which you know used to be published the last day of Term) was not come to the Registers office on Thursday Night. And it is publicly said that those who had contracted with the old ministry to advance the money on the supplies granted for this present year had been to beg to be off their Contracts. On Thursday night the Chief Ministers assembled again. The paper of Seals is since come out and It is now universally believed that Lord Chancellor is quite safe again (to our great joy), and that the Ministry is to be just as it was before the change my last informed you to be intended.

WM. LISTER to SIR THOMAS DRURY, M.P.

1745[-6], March 15. Wellingboro'.—In December last I had the misfortune to break a Bone in my Leg and to displace my ancle joynt attended with imminent danger from mortification for sometime, which renders me unable to ride, otherwise I would have waited on your honour, having been concerned in raising some young fellows for Mr. Isted's company now lying at Carlisle and Lancaster. Their indigent condition through sickness and hardships being very deplorable obliges me to compassionate their sufferings, and frequently to exhort them to patience and steadfastness forces me most humbly to petition your honour to grant me the favour of some Franks, &c.

HENRY FOX to SIR THOMAS DRURY.

1746, March 31.—A 'whip' to attend the House "Wednesday se'ennight, when his Majesty's intentions with regard to foreign affairs will be opened and some opposition to what will be then proposed is expected."

CHAMPION BRANFILL to MR. THOMAS DRURY.

1746, April 17. Inner Temple.— . . . the News mends on us and stocks rise. I was just now told that there is an Express arrived that on the Duke's passing the Spey the rebels have actually fled and are dispersed. I wish it may be true; the Acc^t of another victory over the Spaniards and French by the Piedmontese and Austrians wants confirming. I believe we outdo you again in Hounds. Mr. Braund bought last Monday the widow Bennets (we have now 36 couple) who by the by has just been inoculated for the Smalls and is recovered, but has it very full in her Face, that Face which was the Admiration of one Sex and the envy of the other is no more.

CHAUNCY TOWNSEND° to SIR THOMAS DRURY.

1746, April 19.—I should most willingly give you the account why and who is togeather if in my power. The most I can make of it is all are togeather who have or can have places &c. for opposition seems to be only for and the only way to obtain their demands. Pitt seems the object and by what I hear the debate was not to the Question at all and but entirely personall and few spoke well, the best M^r· Lee† in behalf of the Question and his steady principles, blaming those who attempted so light and so mean a covering to the same last year, and those who now without new matter approved which last year disapproved.

HUGH MARRIOTT to SIR THOMAS DRURY.

1746, April 26. Tooke's Court, near Chancery Lane.—My fingers have itched to make you some amends of comfort by saying something to you on His Royal Highnesses glorious success. But as the Posts have happen'd I perceiv'd the Gazettes w^ld bring you Everything authentick about it as soon and as particularly as you c^ld receive any account of it from me. I shall only add that the firing of the Tower Guns on Thursday seemed to me the loveliest musick I ever heard and that that evening had the most universal Illumination save from great part of the Scotch People of Distinction and some Commoners whose sentiments have always been pretty well known. As the Gazette will probably come out to-night too late for the Post it may be a satisfaction to you to know (as I can assure you from good hands)

---

*Chauncy Townsend, a merchant in Austin Friars, died 1770. He was father to Joseph Townsend. geologist.

†Probably George, afterwards Sir George, Lee, D.C.L., M.P. for Devizes, 1742-1747.

that another Express came in to-day with still better accounts
of this great action but I have not particulars of credit enough
to send you.

CHAMPION BRANFILL to SIR THOMAS DRURY.

1746, April 27. Inner Temple.—I presume you have heard
before now of the entire Victory over the rebels, viz. 1,000 killed
and 600 taken prisoners. Ld Kilmarnock, the Secretary and
French Embassador, are among the last. Our private Accounts
make the number above as many again. They both agree that
our loss exceeds not 130 killed and wounded. There is no
mention of the Pretender's son. I reckon you will have a full
account to-night in the Gazette. . . .

CHAUNCY TOWNSEND to SIR THOMAS DRURY.

1746, May.—Your favour of the 6th I received and if had
answered it last post should have told you for a certainty that
Pitt had not overcome, but hear today Pitt is to be Paymaster.
Sir W^m. Yongue his Post and Fox the latter's, Arundell Sir J.
H. Cottons, and Legg for one at the Treasury and one at
the last gone at the Admiralty is what I don't hear who
succeeds to. I am sorry, I fear I see this cuts Pellham's throat,
for by this as in all late removes he gives into his Enemy's
hands. I am much better but Mrs. Townsend has had a return
of her fever very severe but now better in the Country. As to
our Court Marshall tis unnamable a great Expense to come at
nothing, they and the Court are the worst of a bad people.

WILLIAM HANBURY to SIR THOMAS DRURY.

1746, May 4. Harleston.—I congratulate you on the success
of our arms. The affair is now I hope finished.
I desired Butterfield, Mr. Isted's servant, to acquaint you that
George Briggs, late of his (now of Capt. Boisnegan's) company,
deserted from me at Lancaster, he is of Orlingbury. I wrote to
Mr. Isted concerning him but find he is gone to Bath. I must
therefore ask you to take him up and secure him in the County
Gaol of Northampton. . . . . .
I have herewith sent a printed pamphlet on the Clipston
hospital. It is in a very good way, much to the satisfaction of
the Visitor, and the Master has already 54 scholars, and is likely
to have many more. . . . . .

CHAMPION BRANFILL to SIR T. DRURY.

1746, May 29.—I take it that there must be something
arthritic in the air, for all the gentlemen in the Neighbourhood
are gouty, and their Horses are troubled with the same distemper.
. . . . . I am extremely glad to hear you continue in good
health and as a means to keep you so I am glad you write with
some pleasure about your Hounds, for I am satisfied that altho'

Hunting will not cure the Gout, yet that it will prevent a man's being a cripple with it in his younger time, for I have observed that the sportsman let his fit be severe, yet he recovers his strength and has no sensible remains if another fit attacks him, but the sedentary and sauntering man doth not recover his strength after the fit, before he's laid up with another, and in a few years is rendered a helpless, miserable object.

Hugh Marriott to Sir Thomas Drury.

1746, June 5. Tooke's Court, near Chancery Lane.—If you have a mind to put on solemnity indeed, Come up and be one of the managers ; for it seems the Speaker insists so strongly that while the Parliament is sitting, the Rebel Lords must be tryed by Impeachment that a Court is at last to be erected in West-minster Hall to that purpose, though it was hoped the Nation might have been spared that great expense. . . . . . .

Nathaniel Neal to Sir Thos. Drury.

1746, June 7. Million Bank.—We have had strong rumours of peace for several days, which have raised the Stocks, particularly French in India, but I am inclined to think the Commissions that have been lately sent hither from Holland for purchasing in those funds have been the chief occasion yet.

I presume you have heard Admiral Lestock[*] has been honour-ably acquitted by the Courts Marshall, and that he is soon to go to Sea with the command of a Fleet of Ships.

The secret Expedition for which the Troops were to have been embark'd at Portsmouth is now wholly laid aside. It is said that Admiral Martin[†] has block'd up the French fleet at Rochelle. The winter diversions as balls, plays, etc. are recommenced for the entertainment of the Prince of Hesse, but I suppose will not last above a week.

James Dolliffe to Sir Thomas Drury.

1746, Oct. 15. Hockston.— . . . I am very much concerned to hear we have been defeated in Flanders, from which I fear very ill consequences and particularly that it may occasion the Dutch to explain their long misterious conduct by coming to an agreement with France upon the terms they will prescribe under a pretence that they are not in a condition to make any further resistance. If this should happen and we are not included in the accommodation how are we to act ? And what are we to expect ?

---

* Richard Lestock, 1679 ?—1746 (December). This Court Martial related to the action in the battle off Toulon, 1743 [-4].

† Admiral William Martin (1696 ?-1756) had succeeded Admiral Vernon in the chief command, December 1745.

CHARLES COE to SIR THOMAS DRURY.

1746[7], Jan. 16. Maldon.—As nothing in my opinion is a greater proof of Friendship than a free and generous Behaviour, I am obliged upon that Principle to tell Sir Thomas Drury the Result of a Meeting on Tuesday last of five Aldermen and eleven Common Council men with your humble Servt as the only means to secure the Whig Interest at this Borough, vizt to support the joint Interest of Sir Richd Lloyd and Robert Colebrooke, Esqre at the next generall Election, and as I am never ashamed to assign the reasons of my Conduct, I will explain them and freely submitt them to your candid Judgment . . . by my last I am persuaded you were satisfied that I was zealously disposed to prevent the Tories imposing Mr. Edmund. Branston upon us at the next Election, tho' at the same time I, tho^t it quite unseasonable to come to a Nomination, notwithstanding I have been pressed hard by Gentlemen of very great figure. However as Mr. Bramston has not only rode the Country to Engage Votes, but made a personall application to all the Freemen inhabiting the Borough and as I am firmly perswaded some of the Tories have bragged that by this scheme they shall defeat the Coes, and as Sir Richard Lloyd has also made a very considerable Interest, the Whigs in Truth had no other Card to play in your Absence but to agree to this Junction, or let in a Friend of the Tories to break the Interest now and as a Naturall Consequence to be Master of the Corporation by another Parliament. I am sorry to tell you that everybody does not see the Bottom of this Contrivance so clearly as I wish they did, but as I have the most feasible Convictions of the Disguise I am obliged to join with the Corporation to support the nomination, and in this I hope you will not charge me with the lest Insinuation of Disrespect paid to your Character or Interest. Am sure I don't deserve such an accusation and had you appeared at the Sessions I would have shewn you my Regards. . . . . .

JAMES BIRCH to SIR THOMAS DRURY.

1746[7], Feb. 13. Chere Brocke [Cherbourg], Normandy.— This comes to aQuaint you of my onhapey misforton. Been taken for to France by a Privout Teare from Saint Mallow cald the Prince De Country on the Seaventh of December and brought here. But I hope good Serr you will sone Release me from this Ineymys Contrey or elsse I shall dy. I have got my Peroll of Honer, and the Commisarey has rote to Parriss for me to be Returned for a Captn of the Bockoncore of this plase Lately taken by the Porkeipine Man of War and carued in to plimouth his name is Capten Delamare of this Plase. So I hope good Ser, you will stand my Freind and Rite down to Plimouth for his Release and then I shall come home to serve you or your Intrast. he is at Tavistocke, and then I shall bee Bound to Pray for you all Days of my Life and will doe any thinge that Lyeth In my Power. I wold give you a Count of the afearis of this

contrey, but Duste not, for all Leaters are opend at Parjss. So
.deer Sir I remaine your most humbell servant to command,
JAMES BIRCH, of Maldon.

WILLIAM SMITH (Bailiff) to SIR THOMAS DRURY.

1746[-7], February 19.   Overstone.—Sir, the Distemper
amongst the Cattle is very little about us at present. The
nearest I no of is Honington. Mr. Knight I hear has lost nineteen very lately and saved very few, the other farmers most of
them had it some Time agone; I hear 'tis very much about
Market Harborough, and by all accounts more Die than ever.
I am informed that in some Parishes they Do not save two out
of Twenty. Sir, in our markets Wheat sells from 3s. 4d. to 4s.
per Bushell. Rie from 15s. to 17s. 6d. per Quarter. Barley
from 12s. 6d. to 14s. per Quarter. Old Beans from 13s. to 14s. 6d.
per Qr., and new Beans from 15s. to 17s. 6d. per Qr., and Oats
from 8s. to 10s. 6d. per Qr. The price of Meat is something
lower than it was. Beef and Mutton and Pork are from
2d. to 2½d. per lb. Veal that is good is 3d. and 3½d. per
pound.

CHAMPION BRANFILL to THE SAME.

1750, Nov. 13. London.—(Has just come up from Upminster)
We talk here of nothing but a Distemper which has got
amongst the Horses every where I can hear of, nor can I find one
that has missed it; they have violent coughs and most of them
run prodigiously at the nose. We have ten in our stables all
very ill, we have at present only let them blood and given them
mashes and warm water, but I call by and by on Dr. Tottergill for
further advice.

P.S.—You see in the Papers an account of a Colonel's Commission from the Pretender, found in the repairing an old house.
The Commission was to Holloway late Treasurer of Bedlam and
Bridewell, and it is imagined the dread of being found out was the
occasion of his shooting himself.

CHAMPION BRANFILL to THE SAME.

1750[-1], Jan. 29. London.—The sole conversation here is on
the House of Commons ordering Mr. Crowle, Mr. Murray,[*] a
brother of Lord Ellebank and one Gibson, an upholsterer, to
attend them on Thursday, Crowle for protracting the scrutiny at
the Westminster Election and boasting of it, calling the orders
of the house *bruta fulmina*, Murray for interrupting the High
Bailiff and using violent Threats, and the upholsterer for saying
that the Small Debts Bill was passed on purpose to corrupt the
High Bailiff; by the temper of the House yesterday it is sus-

---

[*] Honble. Alexander Murray, 4th son of 4th Lord Elibank (died 1777).

pected some of them will be sent to Newgate. I am told there are greater accusations against another person, but his name not mentioned.

Earl of Sussex to Sir Thomas Drury.

1758, Jan. 4. Euston.—I am informed that the parishioners of Bozeat are endeavouring to charge with the payment of levys to Bozeat, certain lands belonging to Caston which lay intermixed with the Bozeat lands. I would therefore beg the favour of you Sir that this affair may be postponed 'til I shall have an opportunity of getting my writings looked over, which I am informed will fully explain the matter.

John Hervey Thursby to the Same.

1758, Jan. 18. Abingdon.—I find in 'Burn' under Title 'Highway' an act made in the 22nd of Charles 2nd, Section 7 c. 8, laying a penalty on the owner of any wagon etc. travelling on any Highway with above five Horses; carrying any other goods than wheat are therein excepted; also in the 7th and 8th of Wm. 3rd, Cap 29, Sect. 2 the penalties are particularly mentioned how to be disposed of. As a certain person, Tenant to a great man, has been lately very insolent to me, on account of my speaking in a most civill manner to his servant for so often coming along our roads with vast loads with six horses, am resolved to punish him if I can; which by that law (as I doe not find it is repealed) I can doe by a conviction on my own view. (Asks his opinion whether the Act may now be enforced.)

Champion Branfill to the Same.

1758, Feb. 4. London—We have no news in Town, but that the Ministry draw together and some formidable Fleets are preparing for sea. Mr. Pitt is confined with the gout. Morton of Abingdon Aston and De Grey are called within the Bar—they took their seats yesterday. The World have made a match between the Duke of Bridgewater and the Duchess of Hamilton, which they say is to be soon. . . . Should this match take place and she bear him a son, she will have the only parsley Bed from whence two Dukes have been dug. . . .

Champion Branfill to the Same.

1758, Feb. 18. London.—I am very glad to hear that you can by any means lessen the Force of the Gout, that you may continue so to do is in my opinion the greatest Blessing I can wish you. I have steered quite clear this Winter, and I don't know what to impute it to unless it be the severity of last Winter's Attack. I drink as little Tea and Port Wine as I can, of neither of which I can entertain any great opinion. I suppose you have by this time seen the Account from India, notwithstanding which, I hear that our Officers will not allow that

either the King of Prussia or Clive know anything of Military
Affairs. I am told he will get for his own share (I mean Coll.
Clive) above £300,000, that he has sent by the sloop that brought
this Account £40,000, ten of which he has ordered to be distributed between three Sisters grown up, that he shall send
his Wife home by the Tyger with £120,000, and the rest he
will bring himself. I hear too that on Monday the Bill for
extending the Habeas Corpus is to be moved, and that Sir John
Glynne is to move to repeal the Septenniel Bill. . . . You
see that His Majesty put his hand into the wrong pocket for an
Essex Sheriff, he first pulled out Smart Lethuillier, but on
applying to the right pocket he has found one Mr. Hennekar,
who has bought the Estate of the Dyers about Dunmow. . . .

WILLIAM STRONG to SIR THOMAS DRURY.

1758, March 23. Peterborough.—I take the first opportunity
of acknowledging the receipt of your favour and am very sorry
upon several Accounts that I am under the necessity of joining
with the Rest of the Proprietors in opposing your Petition, but beg
you will be assured as the truth really is that it proceeds from ye
full conviction we are all under of the great injury and injustice
which would be done us by such an Act as is proposed to be
obtained. And I am persuaded that you would have put a stop
to this Scheme of draining your Lands if we could have had an
opportunity of waiting upon you, to have shown the unreasonableness of it.

The ancient and proper way of draining your Lands, Mr.
Askham's and the Rest is by Fenton Load and from the end of
Fenton Load next Chatteris by a 20 foot drain made for that
very purpose by the Corporation of Bedford Level into another
Drain which carries the Waters to Slade Load and so into the 40
foot. The mills upon your Lands have always thrown into Fenton Load and your Lands been embanked from any other outfall
which is nearer to sea by 3 or 4 miles than any other way.

BUCKINGHAMSHIRE PAPERS.

Part 2.— [1737]-1765.

THE PRIVATE LETTERS OF JOHN 2ND EARL OF
BUCKINGHAMSHIRE, TO HIS AUNT, HENRIETTA COUNTESS
OF SUFFOLK, AND OTHERS.

———————

N.D. [1737-1767.]—"The Late QUEEN's* CONVERSATION with
LADY SUFFOLK, upon her leaving Court."† [In 1734.]

LADY SUFFOLK: Madam, I believe your Majesty thinks I have
more assurance than ever any body had, to stay so long in your
family after the publick marks the King has given me of his displeasure. What occasioned my not waiting sooner upon your
Majesty you will not think was owing to assurance. I have ever
had, and hope I have ever shown it, the greatest duty and attention to everything that relates to you, and I could not think it
proper whilst you were indisposed to trouble you with anything
regarding me. I come now, Madam, to beg leave to retire.

QUEEN: You surprise me, what do you mean? I don't believe
the King is angry. How has he shown his displeasure? Did I
receive you as if you were under mine?

LADY S.: No, Madam, if your Majesty had treated me in the
same manner the King did, I could never again have appear'd in
your presence.

QUEEN: Child, you dream. Why, I saw the King speak to
you.

LADY S.: Yes, Madam, but those few words more sensibly
mark'd his displeasure than his silence either before or since.

QUEEN.: Tell me, has the King really never been down with
you since your return?

LADY S.: No, Madam.

QUEEN: Upon my word I did not know it.

LADY S.: Will your Majesty give me leave to tell you what has
past. (M.T.W.?)

QUEEN: I hope you take nothing ill of me. I would have seen
you.

———————

* Caroline of Anspach, d. 1737.
† This paper is endorsed by Lady Castlereagh :—" This was taken down by my
father [John 2nd Earl of Buckinghamshire] from Lady Suffolk's relation." Lady
Suffolk died July, 1767.

LADY S.: Your Majesty did.

Q.: Come, my dear Lady Suffolk, you are very warm, but believe me, I am your friend, your best friend. You don't know a Court.

S.: I am very sensible I do not, and feel at this time a most convincing proof of that ignorance. But I fear, Madam, if I have not acquir'd knowledge in twenty years I never shall now.

Q.: Why don't you talk to your friends? Indeed you cannot judge this for yourself. I always do so.

S.: If twenty years' service has not been able to defend me from falling a sacrifice to my enemys, would your Majesty have me, by calling in my friends, make them answerable for the measures I may take and involve them in my ruin?

Q.: Child, they are your enemys who want to get you out, and they will be the first to drop you. Oh, my dear Lady S., you do not know how differently, when you are out, people will behave.

S.: Madam, the first part of what you say I am very sure of, but really I do not understand the second, and that some people may show me it was the Courtier and not me that was liked, I cannot say that the keeping of such acquaintance will ·be an inducement to keep me at Court. Surely, Madam, such are better lost.

Q.: You are very warm.

LADY S.: Madam, I beg that if in talking to your Majesty I use any word that does not mark the greatest respect to the King, you will be pleas'd to tell me, for I come fully determined to take my leave with the same respect, submission and duty, with which I have behav'd for twenty years. Your Majesty has often told me that I have never fail'd in anything for your service in either of those places you have honour'd me with, and indeed, Madam, I don't know how far your Majetsy may think it respectfull to make this declaration but I beg it may be permitted me for a moment to speak of the King as of a man only who was my friend. He has been dearer to me than my own brother, so, Madam, as a friend I feel resentment at being ill-treated and sorrow to have lost his friendship, but as my King and master, I have the greatest submission to his pleasure, yet I wish I knew of what I am accus'd, tho' I know my innocence, as it must be some horrid crime.

Q.: Oh, fie! You commit a crime! Don't talk so.

S.: Madam, as I know his Majesty's justice and his warmth of friendship, I know he could not for anything less punish me so severely.

Q.: Lady Suffolk, I daresay if you will have a little patience the King will treat you as he do's the other Lady's, and I suppose that would satisfy you.

LADY S.: No, Madam.

Q.: Why, did you never see him show what you call Resentment to the Duchess of Richmond and Lady Albemarle?

Lady S.: Madam, I believe those ladys have more merit than I, and in every respect of greater consequence, but this case is very different; they have not lived twenty years conversing with his Majesty every day, nor had the same reason to think themselves honor'd with his friendship, nor has it been in his power to give so publick or remarkable instance of his displeasure to them. Consider, Madam, I have been absent seven weeks, return sooner than was proper for my health to do my duty in my place to your Majesty, and to show my respect to him upon his Birthday.

Q. : I heard when you was at the Bath that you did not design to come back, but I did not mind such reports.

LADY S. : I heard, too, Madam, that I was not to come back, for my business was done at Court; but I knew that I had a Mistress who had often told me that she was perfectly satisfyd with my services. I knew that I had a King and a Master and a friend whom I could not, nor ever will, suspect of any injustice, who would not punish me without I was guilty, and I know, Madam, I have done nothing, but still these reports must make me think his Majesty's publick neglect could not escape any of the standers-by, and I knew it was remarkd to my Brother* who came on Thursday morning and asked if it was true that the King had taken no notice of me since my return from Bath.

Q. : Well, Child, you know the King leaves it to me. I will answer for it, that all will be as well with you as with any of the Lady's, and I am sure you cannot leave my service then.

LADY S. : Really, Madam, I don't see any possibility of my continuing in it. I have lost what was dearer to me than anything in the world. I am to be upon the foot of the Duchess of Richmond and Lady Albemarle, so by the public thought to be forgiven some great offence, because I have been your servant twenty years. No! Madam! I never will be forgiven an offence I have not committed.

Q. : You won't be forgiven! This is indeed the 'Great Horse.'† Why, I am forgiven!

LADY S. : Madam, your Majesty and I cannot be named together. It's a play of words for your Majesty, but a serious thing for me.

Q. : Why, Child, I am the King's subject as well as you.

LADY S. : Madam, what I mean is that I cannot make your Majesty understand without you will be pleas'd to lay aside the Queen and to put yourself in my place. After five and twenty years to be ill-treated without knowing my crime and then to stay upon the foot of Lady Albemarle.

Q. : Upon my word, Lady S., you don't consider what the world will say. For God's sake, consider your character. You leave me because the King will not be more particular to you than to others.

LADY S. : Madam, as to my character the world must have settled that long ago, whether just or unjust. But, Madam, I believe I have never been suspected of betraying his Majesty, or of having done anything dishonest by any person whatsoever, and I

---

* John Hobart, 1st Earl of Buckinghamshire, d. 1756.
† "To be on the high horse"?

defy my greatest enemy (your Majesty owns I have such) to prove anything against me, and I cannot nor will not, submit to anything which may make that believ'd of me.

Q.: Oh, fie, Lady Suffolk, this is a very fine notion, a principle out of 'Clelia' or of some other Romance.

LADY S.: This may not be a Court principle, but I believe it is a just one and a proper one for me to have.

Q.: I will send you down one. Come, you love figures! Let me persuade you 2-3. Go down think of this (*sic*). There are people who want you out of Court, and they will be the first to drop you.

LADY S.: Madam, I consult nobody in this, there is no occasion.

Q.: But you cannot judge for yourself. Let me prevail, put yourself in somebody's hands and let them act for you. Indeed you are too warm. You are not fit to act for yourself.

LADY S.: (Repeated the same as before.)

Q.: No, indeed very respectfull; but you will repent it. I cannot give you leave to go.

LADY S.: When anybody can feel what I have and be so entirely me, as to be the only sufferer for the advice they give, I might follow the method your Majesty proposes, but as that is impossible I must beg leave to act for myself. I wish I might know what I have been accused of. It is in my absence that I have been ruined in his Majesty's favour. At the Bath I had a thousand witnesses to my behaviour. I know my own innocence. Nobody dares tell me that to their knowledge I have ever fail'd in my duty in any manner.

Q.: You are a very great Horse! Not dare to tell you you have been guilty!

LADY S.: No, Madam; for the Princess your daughter could justify my behaviour; Lord C——g, and many more. What I meant was no regard to myself that I cannot think any wretch so abandon'd to all shame as to stand in it, having the falsehood (pardon the word) shown them by such a number as was there.

Q.: Pray, Lady S., how did you live at the Bath?

LADY S.: (Here I told all. Who B. dined, and what happen'd to Ld. B.) No party's distinguish'd two to one (*sic*).

Q.: Lady S., pray consider! Be calm!

LADY S.: Madam, I beg your permission to retire; indeed Madam I have not slept since I came into your house, and believe I never shall under this suspicion of guilt. Madam, will you give me leave to mention my observation, and not think me impertinent? I am sure by your looks when I assert my innocence that your Majesty knows of what I am accus'd.

Q.: Oh, oh! Lady S. you want to get it out of me.

LADY S.: Madam, I do want to stand the accusation. I am not afraid. I know it would be to the confusion of my accusers.

Q.: I will not give you leave to go. I tell you plainly if you go to-day you go without my consent.

LADY S.: Madam, I beg you would reflect upon my unhappy situation. I own that after what past that the next time I saw his Majesty I should have dropt down if I had not gone out.

Q.: Well, Lady Suffolk. Will you refuse me this? Stay a week longer. Won't you stay a week at my request?

LADY S.: Yes, Madam, I will obey you, but as I am under his Majesty's Displeasure you will not expect my attendance, or that I come again to receive your commands.

Q.: Yes, I do, and I will see you again. Be sure you come again.

LADY S.: I will obey your Majesty.

Q.: Harkye, Lady Suffolk. You will come up as you used to do.

EARL OF BUCKINGHAMSHIRE to the COUNTESS OF SUFFOLK [his Aunt].

[1756.]—The Purchase money for the estate in Buckinghamshire, as far as we can judge, was about £35,000. Mr. Bristow says Lord Buckingham's* affairs are not yet settled enough to form a judgment of them exactly, but do's not seem to expect any money.

By my accounts from Norwich the Election will probably go there to my wish.† As the Duke of Newcastle has not been so explicite with regard to my affairs as I could wish, I wrote a letter to him yesterday in the afternoon, of which the following sentence was the principal part.

'I cannot possibly acquiesce under the Lieutenancys of Norfolk being given to another person, and I shall think any *favour your Grace may please to bestow upon a Norwich man during the time that this affair is pendent a breach of that friendship with which you have flatter'd me.*'

My behaviour at Kensington the other day was, I believe, very exactly what you advis'd. I was at the Levée yesterday, and the King was pleas'd to notice me. He enquir'd the day before as particularly into my affairs as you could have done. Lady Yarmouth receiv'd me with the greatest politeness. The Duke of Newcastle wrote me word before he saw me that he had laid my request in relation to the Lieutenancy before the King on Monday last. I wish I could be sure that he had represented it in the strong light in which I put it to him, or indeed mentioned it at all. George set out this morning at 1 o'clock for Cornwall. Lady Buckingham and Mr. Bristow‡ continue making the strongest professions that everything shall be settled to my satisfaction.

EARL OF BUCKINGHAMSHIRE to COUNTESS OF SUFFOLK.§

1762, Dec. 27. Moscow.—I am extremely sorry to hear from Lady Buckingham that you have had a return of that most disagreeable complaint, the gout in your eyes, but hope before this reaches them they will be well enough recover'd to make out

---

* The 1st Earl of Buckinghamshire died Sept., 1756.
† Harbord Harbord was elected for Norwich Dec., 1756.
‡ John 1st Earl of Buckinghamshire married Elizabeth Bristow as his second wife.
§ The Earl of Buckinghamshire was appointed Ambassador to Russia July, 1762.

this scrawl. Poor George,° who has for a long time been extremely out of spirits, is convinc'd that this climate will not agree with him and is therefore determin'd to ask leave to return to England. He has in every instance behav'd as well to me as possible, and would not now think of it without my approbation. As yet no mention has been made of it to Government, but the object of this letter is to desire your Ladyship (if you have no objection to it, and the plan should be agreeable to Col. Hotham) to use your interest with Lord Bute that he may succeed my brother.† I could not write to him myself as it was impossible for me to judge of Colonel Hotham's disposition, and was I to wait for an answer from him it would be near five months from the date of this letter before Lord Bute could receive my application.

I have just heard that the Address was voted in the House of Lords *nem. con.*, which gives me very great satisfaction, as I do most sincerely wish that all the animositys which the newspapers are full of may subside, as far as the nature of England may admit of it.

The EARL OF BUCKINGHAMSHIRE to the COUNTESS OF SUFFOLK.

1763, March 7. Moscow.— . . . Her Imperial Majesty‡ permitted me to attend her at the Court Manège, and I had the honour of seeing her ride. She was dresst in man's cloaths and it really is not flattery to say that few men ride better. She gave me leave some months ago to write to England for some horses for her and it is a great mortification to me not to have as yet received any answer from Col. Johnston to a letter I wrote to him upon that subject. My situation here grows every day more agreeable, as the Russians begin to treat me less upon the footing of a stranger than they treat the other foreigners. It is not that I believe my acquaintance with them will answer any particular purpose, but it contributes to my amusements and it certainly can be no disadvantage to a minister to be upon an easy footing with the people of distinction of that country where he resides. In a letter I yesterday received from Lady Buckingham she was pleased to depreciate the valuable presents I sent you and quotes Mr. Woranzow's§ authority. I shall not soon be guilty of such another act of extravagance.

I wait with great impatience for answers to letters I sent long since to England; all my packets by some mismanagement are sent round by Sweden, which makes a fortnight difference in the correspondence. The merchants have letters of the 1st of February from London. My last were dated the 19th of January. . . .

---

* George Hobart, afterwards 3rd Earl of Buckinghamshire.
† As Secretary to the Embassy at Moscow.
‡ Catherine II.
§ Alexander Romanovitch Woronzow, Russian Ambassador at St. James', 1762-1763.

You will have heard from Lady Buckingham that the Empress returns in May to Petersburg. I shall rejoice at it upon many accounts, though the neighbourhood of Moscow must be excessively pleasant in summer. As yet everything is cover'd with snow. The river has the appearance of a Broad Street and on Sunday is covered with thousands of people who resort there to see Sledge races and Boxing Matches.

The Earl of Buckinghamshire to Hans Stanley.

1763, March 28. Moscow.—I may regret my not hearing from you, lament your silence and expect a letter from you with an anxious degree of impatience. But believe me no delay of that sort can ever alter my feelings for my friend, or make me doubt of his partiality for me. Let me thank you for your account of the situation of the Great Man, and for your observations in consequence, which I am convinced are just. Your determination with regard to your remaining in the Admiralty unless you are offer'd an essential advance appears to me becoming of you.

It was generally suppos'd here, and the French Minister encourag'd those suppositions, that some difficultys having arisen in the conclusion of the definitive Treaty, you had been sent from England to settle them, as being much more Master of the the subject than the Duke of Bedford. You need not doubt of the letter to M. d'Alembert being the Empress' own composition. I will to-morrow acquaint her, as nearly as I am able to render the expression in French, with your opinion of it. . . .

Were you at Moscow you would prefer the Empress to every woman in the country, take her for all in all, tho' many of them are handsome and some very agreeable. In some of the Russian houses I am received not quite upon the footing of a stranger, but in every country it is a misfortune not to speak the language. You mention nothing of the Club, yet let me hope that it flourishes, and that the Evergreens vegetate around the genial Board. Remind them of their old Servant, whose next wish to that primary consideration of renewing the sacramental engagements on Friday night is to find himself with them on Saturday.

P.S.—You may have a most excellent lining of the Astracan lamb for about twenty pounds. Any of the others would be either excessively dear or very cumbersome.

Earl of Buckinghamshire to the Countess of Suffolk.

1763, April 13. Moscow.—Before this letter is finished George will be set out, his carriages and Horses are all nearly ready. At this moment he embraces his wife in thought and gallops an imaginary horse upon a visionary England. I send away a Courier to-morrow so that he will bring nothing from me but a repetition of my good wishes for you and a more regular account of what I am doing than it will be easy for you to trace in these rhapsodies, my letters. With this I send you a silver medal of the Empress. It is very like her and finely executed, the air of the face is in my opinion rather older than hers. You will also find a superficial, vague account of this country,° which I drew up for your amusement; I should be sorry to have it known here that anything of that sort had been sent by me. On Tuesday evening I had an entertainment at my house, nearly of the same kind with that which I mentioned in my former letters. The company was rather more numerous, but the Empress, who had given me leave to hope that she would come, was prevented by a violent headach. Upon the whole it passed off well and would have been thought a handsome entertainment in most countries. My uxorious Chaplain returns with my uxorious brother. I hope Erskine has not as much to confess to his wife as George with an indifferent memory could tell to his. Many of their sins have lodged at my door, but now they are removed I shall at least have the comfort to think that my virtue will be vindicated. If Colonel Hotham had no other reason for declining coming into this country but the state of his health it would be all-sufficient; this is no climate for a weak constitution. By the account you give me of the letters you have wrote to me, three are still wanting, and I should suppose the three last, though that is not sure, as I often receive a latter dated in January a fortnight after one dated in February. In a letter I wrote to Lord Bute upon the subject of the Secretary to the Embassy, I mentioned my wish that if Colonel Hotham did not come nobody might be sent whose connections being different from mine might make my situation here disagreeable. In a letter which I propose to send to his Lordship by this courier, I shall rather insinuate a desire that nobody may be sent at all. . . .

The EARL OF BUCKINGHAMSHIRE to the COUNTESS OF SUFFOLK.

1763, June 10. Petersburg.— . . . The Merchants' Newspapers (they always receive theirs a fortnight before me) mention that Col. Hotham is re-elected for St Ives without opposition. I wish to write both to him and Mr. Praed† upon the occasion, but am fearful until I have better authority than the Chronicle . . . . I see another article in the same paper which affects me very differently—the account of the most melancholy accident which has befallen Lady Molesworth and her family.‡ Such a calamity could not have fallen where it was less merited or where the consequences were more to be regretted. Life in general is a trifle, half of those who covet it, who grasp it most, can scarcely tell you why, but an amiable mother, with beautiful, engaging children, whose merit promised them many agreeable days, cut off at once—the idea is shocking, even to me, who do not think existence of very great importance.

---

* See for this 'Buckinghamshire Correspondence,' Vol. II., p. 283.
† Humphrey Mackworth Praed.
‡ A disastrous fire. (See Annual Register for this year, p. 75.)

Many are the unpleasant sensations which offer themselves to me upon that which is the present state of affairs in England. The first and strongest (to you I need not dissemble) is my concern for my gracious Master, and the reflection upon the uneasiness he must at this time feel, and which surely he has so little deserved. If there is a man, who from private interest or private spleen has raised this storm, may sorrow, disgrace and infamy attend him.º I have left many of my most intimate acquaintance at Moscow and find myself very much alone, though it is a very cheerful, very well furnished house. Some of them return with the Court, but the greatest part of them obtained leave to absent themselves for a year. . . . . . .

EARL OF BUCKINGHAMSHIRE to the COUNTESS OF SUFFOLK.

1763, July 12. Petersburg.— . . . . Lady Buckingham mentions her concern at your going to Marble Hill in the cold weather, but I will not dwell upon that, as I recollect my having reproved you for it in my very last letter. The Empress made her Publick entry on Saturday last. Fireworks were played off upon the River in consequence. They were very fine, but as it is now light here during the whole twenty-four hours, it greatly took off from their effect. . . . .

The weather has been so sultry for the last fortnight as to produce that state of relaxation which puts everybody out of humour and indeed disqualifies them for every sort of enjoyment, but that of drinking cool liquors and swallowing quantities of ice. One might imagine now that it never would be cold again, but probably within six weeks we shall have convincing proof to the contrary. In the account I sent you of my house I omitted to mention the quantities of fine china which adorn it, and consequently a circumstance which may possibly make you peevish—that in several instances very fine old Japan Jarrs have been cut and broke in order to make them fit the places. George sent me a letter from Berlin, containing several articles of news which he had read in the English papers, but not mentioning one word of the King of Prussia, his subjects or his dominions. . . . .

I have long expected a letter from Mr. Grenville,† till he writes it will not become me to trouble him again. He is certainly involved in very perplexing business, yet I am apt to believe he has disposed of some of his time in the last three months as unprofitably as in noticing me. Here I am and must expect to remain till next summer. What is to be next, I know not. Let it come in its own good day!

EARL OF BUCKINGHAMSHIRE to the COUNTESS OF SUFFOLK.

1763, July 18. Petersburg.— . . . Lady Buckingham in one of her last letters informed me that Lord Hallifax had

---

* The prosecution of Wilkes began on the 30th April, 1763. Ld. Bute resigned 8th April.

† George Grenville.

mention'd to her his having deliver'd the medal to the King, and speaking of her, let me thank you for your care as well as for the obliging solicitude you express upon her account. I am glad that Lady Harriet° meets with your approbation and that Mrs. Harriet approves of me. It distresses me to hear so melancholy an account of Lady Waldegrave. She has had no small share of my affection ever since her humane behaviour to Col. Johnston upon Lady Charlotte's death. . . . A few weeks ago I received a very particular and I believe a very true account of the political transactions of the last winter, the Person whose picture you draw† is mentioned in it and not greatly to his honor, he may be happy in himself and great in his own conceit, but I never knew the man whose connection I should so much wish to avoid. How he ever came to be in that rank in which he is plac'd is a wonder that it will cost me some time to get over. Every man who is the least cast into publick life wishes to be in some sort distinguish'd, yet I sometimes flatter myself that I have virtue enough if once I could see Government settled at Home agreeably to him who has a right to be pleas'd and upon that firm basis which may make England as respectable in peace as it has lately been in war to sit down contented with such a situation as may be allotted to me.

Earl of Buckinghamshire to the Countess of Suffolk.

1763, July 22. Petersburg.— . . . The Empress goes into the Country to-morrow, but I alas am left in town, yet the gales of the Neva refresh me and the passing bark delights my eye. I won't think you ill, because your letters are not mathematically correct; if you were to judge of health by writing, what a habit of body should I be in? You say not one word to me of Marble Hill, of Mr. Chetwynd, Mr. Walpole, Lady Blandford, and Mr. Cambridge, nor the least hint of the latter's opinion upon the case of Wilks and Secretarys; he must have been very ingenious, very busy, and ultimately a little tiresome upon that copious subject . . . .

Earl of Buckinghamshire to the Countess of Suffolk.

1763, Aug. 9. Petersburg.—I condole with you upon the death of poor Mr. Barlow, who was certainly a complaisant, inoffensive neighbour. Lady Buckingham writes me word that you are in good spirits, why indeed should you be otherwise? You act up to what your morality and your Religion tells you is right; the consciousness of that must make every occasional discomp-sure, every aylment which the frail nature of Man is liable to, of little import. I sometimes am a little deficient in faith upon matters of Religion, and more frequently of patience (or indurance, shall I call it?) in the affairs of this world; we must correct ourselves,

* His daughter. Mrs. Harriet was his niece, a daughter of Col. and Lady Dorothy Hotham.
† See Lady Suffolk's Letters, Vol. II., p. 275.

we must try to amend even constitutional errors—I was born
with a disposition to doubt and to fret—original punishment for
any sins I could probably commit. I could wish you would let
me know if you received a letter I wrote from Moscow in relation
to my returning to England etc., and in general if you have an
opportunity of mentioning what I then desir'd you. Lady
Buckingham informs me that Lady Dorothy has depatriated, and
has retired into the North, loaded with receipts for to make
marmalade, White Pot, Tanzy, Wet-your-whistles, Merry Downs,
Firmity and Almanzanis; and that in order to have everything
well regulated she has sent Nancy before and left her slippers
behind . . . . . . You don't mention Mr. Walpole, but
I hope you see him often as his company must be agreeable to
you. Do I pay a compliment to your taste when I take it for
granted that you prefer your Western to your Eastern Beau.
The latter is the more assiduous querist, yet I think I shall have
more pleasure in preventing the former's questions than in
answering his.

EARL OF BUCKINGHAMSHIRE to the COUNTESS OF SUFFOLK.

1763, Aug. 31. Petersburg.—The Empress has most
graciously received two English horses which she had permitted me to send for ; when she bestrides one of these English
horses with a French feather in her hat she carries the feather,
but the Horse carries her. Which will have the greatest influence,
horse or feather, the carrier or the carried ? Answer, for you
know your sex. Perhaps you may wish to know my opinion and
to prevent your wishes, tho' it is treating a political point, I will
say that in general I should give it for the feather, but in this
instance I hope and believe the horse will win. Her Imperial
Majesty really made me very happy yesterday in expressing how
much she was pleased with them. The present she ordered to
be made to my servants amounted to ninety pounds English. I
am sorry that publick affairs in England are not tending to a
system something nearer unanimity. It is a subject neither
agreeable nor proper to be entered into, especially in my very
uninformed situation. Yet I could wish some of my old friends
would recollect a sentence of Lord Bacon, quoted by Lord Haversham in the House of Lords in the year 1704. ' Let men
' beware how they neglect or suffer matters of trouble to be pre-
' pared, for no man can forbid the sparks that may set all on fire.'
I long to see your Spittle Fields weaver, Mr. Giles, in a dry
summer, it will not cost him much to cover his Lawn with green
watered Tabby. Compliments to Mr. Chetwynd, to Mr. Walpole,
to Lady Blandford, Lady Denbigh and Mrs. Harriet.

The EARL OF BUCKINGHAMSHIRE to the COUNTESS OF SUFFOLK.

1763, Sept. 13. Petersburg.—I find myself so much fatigued
this morning with dancing last night with the Maids of Honour,
that it is with difficulty I can undergo the fatigue of writing. Is

not this very much the stile an Ambassador should write in? But you must know that here the most venerable personages dance, that in Russia it would not appear extraordinary if Lord Ligonier led up a Polish dance, and Lord Henley and Lord Hardwicke quivered their fantastic toe to the tune of 'Buttered Pease.' The youth Buckingham however did not dance yesterday sufficiently to fatigue him, but as amusements are rare, he seizes all that offer, and perhaps it might be better for his friends and for himself if he danced more and wrote less. I hardly know how to take up again the subject, in which I was unfortunately interrupted the last post, the amours of the Marchioness of Blandford, and yet upon my word, the reflections which my regard for her suggest to me, have more than once broken my rest. That she will marry Count Woronzow, I no more doubt than that in consequence she will change her Religion, and attend him some few years hence to his mother country. You will therefore permit to make what certainly is far from an improbable supposition that she is at this moment his wife; and in that idea I should wish to convey through your channel to our common friend some advice which her husband's tenderness and delicacy for her will not in these early days when love is young and desires are new permit him to hint to her. She must learn Russ, eat mushrooms fryd in rape oil and pickled cucumbers in Lent; she must forget to courtesy and learn to bow, she must wear red without measure, dance Polish dances, and drink Chisterskij, Quash and Burton Ale, the nature of the two first her dear man will inform her of, the last she will know is the produce of England.

I hope tho' other countrys complain of the incessant rain, that the Marble Hill harvest has been fortunate, at the worst I comfort myself with thinking that you would cheerfully give up your prospect of wheat and barley for a green Meadow and a full River. . . . .

The EARL OF BUCKINGHAMSHIRE to LADY SUFFOLK.

1763, Sep. 23. Petersburg.— . . . Your connection with so many of his friends and relations must have made you take a sensible part with them in the loss they sustained by Lord Egremont's death. I am not a little impatient to hear who is to succeed him as Secretary of State. My letters only inform me that Mr. Pitt has absolutely declined the most gracious offers which were personally made him upon this occasion. There is a report that Sir Joseph Yorke is leaving the Hague, and that he is to be employ'd at home, if that should be the case no destination would make me more happy than being appointed to succeed him. I have mentioned in a former letter that I had wrote to entreat His Majesty's permission to return next spring, as by that time I flatter myself that the principal objects of my mission will be decided.

I had not heard a great while from Col. Hotham, but received a letter to-day seemingly wrote in great spirits, he appears very happy in a clear air, moderate exercise and a cheerful circle of friends and relations. I never could find out a satisfactory reason for it but undoubtedly the Country gentlemen live much more agreeably in the Northern parts of England than any of the others. I have been there very little as yet, but possibly some years hence may make the tour of Yorkshire and Durham in a Family Coach creeping on at the reverent rate of thirty miles a day.

1763, Sep.—1765, Jan.—A small bundle of private letters between the Earl of Sandwich and the Earl of Buckinghamshire are of no public interest.

The EARL OF BUCKINGHAMSHIRE to LADY SUFFOLK.

1763. Oct. 11. Petersburg.— . . . As no fresh scandal has lately reach'd me in relation to Lady Blandford and Count Woronzow, I am to take it for granted that either that affair is totally broke off or else so generally understood to be concluded as to be no longer the subject of conversation. You are always so properly upon the reserve that it will be difficult for me to draw any of the most interesting particulars from you, but I fancy at my return, between the Duchess of Argyle, Lady Denbigh, Lady Litchfield and Lady Seebright, I shall be acquainted at least with all that has passed. I hope however to hear something from you upon this and other important events when Michael returns, whom I expect every hour . . . .

It is probable that I shall have His Majesty's permission to leave this country about the end of next May, in which case I shall be in England some time in July.

The EARL OF BUCKINGHAMSHIRE to LADY SUFFOLK.

1763, Nov. 4. Petersburg.— . . . It is with some difficulty that I contrive to be cheerfull, partly owing to my having no opportunity of taking my accustomed exercise. It is a secret that I trust with you when I tell you that the only person here with whom I can possibly converse with any degree of confidence, that is to say, my secretary, is the most disagreeable, illiterate, underbred, wretch in the Universe. I am forced to do almost everything myself, tho' I pay him two hundred pounds per an. which is full double the usual stipend. He was recommended to me by Mr. Grenville at my own request, who said at the same time that he knew little of him except that he had been employed a short time at Warsaw. You will easily see the reasons which with the assistance of a little humanity have determined me to keep him during the term of my residence here. Two obligations I must confess I have to him, the one that he gives me a good deal of employment, the other that he properly humbles me with regard to my own performances, for that author must be very conceited indeed who could be vain of his works after having heard them read by him. I am sorry to hear my Cousin Hampden[o] has lost her lover, his will administered some consolation to her upon reflection, but I will do the justice to her good nature to believe that it did not diminish the just tribute of regret she owed him . . . . Not one word more of politicks except to enquire who you interest yourself for in the future election of the King of Poland. The libertys of that antient state cannot be in danger, as all the constables in the neighbourhood are hurrying together to preserve them. There is no surer way to prevent a Riot than by knocking those down first who might otherwise make it. The voters in Poland are rather more numerous than at St. Ives, otherwise I am convinced that the Election is as like the other tho' in minature as a Sprat is to a Herring. . . .

EARL OF BUCKINGHAMSHIRE to LADY SUFFOLK.

1763, Nov. 11. Petersburg.—Were it not for the information which I occasionally receive from that chaos of truth and falsehood, which composes the English newspapers, I should return to London as much a stranger to the customs, manners, ideas, and passions of my countrymen as well as to the names, merits, and qualifications of those eminent personages, who are distinguished by the applause of their fellow subjects upon the great theater of London, as if I had never seen my Lord Mayor, Nelly O'Brien, the Lions, Mr. Wilkes, or the Monument. Great and interesting intelligence I receive from the *Gazetteer*, the *Chronicle*, etc. Miss Elliot, Mr. Shuter, and Mr. Woodward exhibit at Covent Garden; Miss Pope, Mrs. Yates, and a nameless promising young gentleman display their merit at Drury Lane, some account is also given of the audience. Lord Granby was seen in a side box with Mr. Wilkes and the Rev[d.] Mr. Churchill, to the great satisfaction of the Pitt and Gallery. I have but lately heard of the consequences of those two worthy gentlemen who were placed so near my noble friend, they must therefore excuse me if I think they were most highly honoured in his company. I shall always, were it only in gratitude for former amusements, interest myself for the Theaters Royal. But there is another theater, other actors and other scenes nearly opening, an accurate description of which I am still more solicitous to receive. Is the season to begin with a Tragedy or a Comedy? If the former I hope the fifth act will be over before my return to England, and that I shall find all my friends laughing at the farce. . . .

I had destined my maiden widow cousin to the other Mr. Childe, but he is otherwise dispos'd, and therefore I think she may as well stay for me, for if any accident should befall poor Lady Buckingham, my cousin will certainly be young enough and sufficiently handsome for your ever affec[ate] Nephew.

---

* Maria Constantia, only daughter to Robert Trevor, who had assumed the name of Hampden, and became in 1776 Viscount Hampden. Her lover's name was Child. (See Lady Suffolk's Letters, Vol. II. p. 281.)

EARL OF BUCKINGHAMSHIRE to LADY SUFFOLK.

1764, Jan. 29. Petersburg.— . . . Amongst all the attempts which I have hitherto made to render my little Gazettes not totally uninteresting to you, I do not recollect having said anything of Count Orlow,° tho' a person who acts no inconsiderable part in the scene which is now before me. His appearance is noble and full as handsome as is consistent with a manly and rather athletic figure. His manner is surprisingly affable and easy, allowing for his most sudden rise to greatness and that excess of most obsequious adulation which is necessarily paid to his situation. In his early days when he had no great prospect of advancement he distinguished himself for his attach- to Her present Majesty, tho' her favor was not at that time the channel for preferment. He has not forgot his former state, and said to me lately, "Autrefois je me promenais beaucoup par nécessité; à cette heure, je me trouve Grand Seigneur et je roule en carosse."

His Sovereign considers him as ever watchfull over her safety and ready to lay down his life for her service. She has a pleasure each day in shewing him new marks of her favor. Her delight is to see him great. It is said and I believe with truth that he does not interfere in foreign affairs. The accounts which you send me of the altercations and animosity between the Grenvilles really give great uneasiness. It is the restless ambition of the eldest that has greatly contributed to the present publick and private feuds, yet surely at times when he is neither passion's nor indiscretion's slave, he is a well-intentioned, an amiable and very good humor'd man. My compliments to Mrs. Harriet, and desire her to attend to her French and her Dancing, as I probably before we meet shall have forgot my English, and am determined upon my return to dance the first minuet with her. . . .

EARL OF BUCKINGHAMSHIRE to LADY SUFFOLK.

1764, Feb. 7. Petersburg.—I receiv'd yesterday a letter from Lady Buckingham, in which she gives an account of your health, which is by no means agreeable to me. . . .

I believe it was mention'd in my last that I was invited to a Russian wedding. I was present at all the ceremonys of the day and some of those of the night, but the whole was conducted with so much dignity and solemnity that it were in vain to attempt making the description of it entertaining without deviating from the truth. I was admitted to the bride's toilet whilst she was dressing, she was in her stays, and several of her relations, women of the first distinction, were employ'd in adjust- ing her different ornaments. The toilet finish'd, the Company in about twenty coaches and six attended her to Court. Just before we set out the mother of the bride ordered us all to be seated and the doors of the room to be shut, as a prognostick of the future

---

* Grigori Grigorievitch Orlow, Catherine the Second's favourite.

tranquillity of the new marry'd couple, but unfortunately a child of the family who was offended at the prospects being intercepted, burst out into a most violent fit of roaring, which seem'd to me a much apter emblem of what might hereafter insue. Arrived at the Palace the bride was introduced to the Empress, who with her own hands ornamented her with the Crown jewels and pinn'd them on her tresses. The bride then proceeded to the Chappel, where the impatient bridegroom waited. He was crowned and she was crowned, he walk'd round the altar and she walk'd round the altar, he laugh'd and she cry'd. In the course of the ceremony the bride drop't her wedding ring, which, as a bad omen, gave great uneasiness to her mother. We then went home with them, sat down to a supper of sixty covers, undress'd the bride, who kiss'd every jewel of the Empress separately. We then kiss'd her and retir'd. . . . .

EARL OF BUCKINGHAMSHIRE to LADY SUFFOLK.

1764, March 23. Petersburg.—Just as I was beginning to write to you, I have received some letters from England by which I am not a little sorry to find that your health is not as yet re-establish'd, yet it may be hop'd that the approaching warm weather and a great deal of air and exercise, the best of all physicks, will have put an end to your complaints time enough for me to find you perfectly well at my return to England, whenever it shall happen.

The Russian spring is begun, that is to say, it freezes all night and thaws all day. Early in the morning you travel upon ice, but all the rest of the day the streets are canals. I know not what to make of my country by the accounts I receive of it, perhaps when I return my country will not know what to make of me, the Individual and the General in some respects resemble, they are both passionate, both capricious, and both unhappy. It is ridiculous what a trifling circumstance will sometimes influence my temper for a whole day. You will tell me it ought not, which is just what I tell myself, but our united remonstrances will have no effect. Don't you find by the disjointed sentences which compose these pages, the attempts at an idea which with difficulty stumble to the end of the period, that I am at this moment most delightfully dull? Indeed I cannot help it. Nature wants a fillip, but know not when it may be had. I often think of what Fontenelle, dying at the age of a hundred, said to his physician, who asked him if he felt any pain, '*Je sens le mal d'etre.*'

A fair lady was telling me my fortune last night, and informed me that I should live to be very old, "*Mais que cela ne'n vaudroit pas la peine, comme je deviendrois hypocondre et goutteux.*" *Voilà un bel horoscope!* . . . .

EARL OF BUCKINGHAMSHIRE to LADY SUFFOLK.

1764, March 30. Petersburg.— . . . By the great discretion and prudence with which my correspondents express themselves, I really believe that the method of proceeding against Mr. Wilkes has had a very bad effect, for they write as if they expected a Messenger every minute. The Russian Minister in England is not half so prudent, he writes and comments in a very free style, and I am once a week regularly mortified in not having it in my power to assert whether the marvels which he advances are true or false. I have this moment received letters from Ld Barrington and Col. Hotham, which give me a satisfactory account of some late transactions, and also one from Lady Buckingham, in which she mentions her fears in relation to the inoculation of her child. Why don't you govern her better? But I flatter myself it will all be over before you receive this. By the accounts given me of the moral Society in Albemarle Street, their existence cannot be of very long duration. Tho' it ought to be otherwise, and I am confident you wish it should, a little spirited vice is necessary to keep frail men together. I am not sorry that young ladys who engage themselves warmly in politicks should be taken with a little yellow jaundice. A comfortable time the poor Senator would have indeed, if after twelve Hours melancholy Parliamentary attendance, instead of finding at home some agreeable relaxation from more amusing and what is frequently as important dialogue, he is to be treated with a hash of the debates of the day introduced in a shrill. voice.

EARL OF BUCKINGHAMSHIRE to LADY SUFFOLK.

1764, April 27. Petersburg.—You will easily imagine that I wait with some degree of impatience to hear from Mr. Grenville, though it is rather in respect to my future views than my thinking there is any great probability of my staying here more than two months longer. Three posts are now due since I received Lady Buckinghamshire's letter, in which she mentioned mine of the 28th February. I feel every day more and more that the Russians are sensible of the pains I have taken to contribute to their amusement and grateful for the desire I have shewn to oblige them. It is at present my intention to have only two balls more, as though now we freeze with only sixteen hours sun, the weather will soon be too hot for such sort of amusements. The Assemblies on Tuesdays and Saturdays I shall continue as long as I stay here. The river has got loose from the ice and so far my prospect is improved, but bleak and most ungenial are the gales which waft the snow across it. The very concise summer of Petersburg will begin in about a month. What we call three seasons are in great measure united here—Spring, Summer and Autumn when the weather is particularly favourable will together make nearly four months. The vegetation of such things as will vegetate in such a soil and such a climate is performed almost with magick celerity, and reminds me of what in my early days I have seen exhibited by the dexterity of an ingenious artist, who produced a tree which budded, blossomed, bore ripe fruit, and withered in less than ten minutes. The depth of winter to those who can endure cold is the finest season, excellent roads, and a clear air which sharpens the appetite and enlivens the animal spirits. Lady Buckingham's letters overflow with her sensibility of your goodness to her and her child ; not being able to say enough upon the occasion, I shall desire you only to put a candid conjecture upon my feelings. . . .

EARL OF BUCKINGHAMSHIRE to LADY SUFFOLK.

1764, May 11. Petersburg.— . . . I am most particularly concerned that Mr. Grenville should have any reason to doubt of my taking the first opportunity to pay the proper acknowledgements for his kind attention to my wishes. Three Maids of Honour were marry'd on Sunday last. The foreign ministers were present and supped with them at the Palace that and the following evening. As two of the brides are my particular favourites and one my relation, I am tolerably well acquainted even with the most secret transactions· which passed upon the occasion; but it would not edify you greatly to receive a detail of events so like many events which have happened before. . . . It is a usage established from old times in Russia that the nearest relations of the bride and bridegroom after they are put to bed remain in the next room, and after a certain time—the length of which occasionally differs—the new-married couple pay them a visit and eat and drink with them. . . . You think this idle stuff, but you like I should write often and I like to write to you, and the unavoidable consequence of our two likings must be just such stuff as this. . . . I have a great deal to do, am in a hurry and very hungry. Must not your nephew at this moment be a most amiable existence ?

EARL OF BUCKINGHAMSHIRE to LADY SUFFOLK.

1764, May 28. Petersburg.— . . . The Empress and many of my acquaintance who attend have been in the country for some time and we have very little reason to expect to see more of the Court at Petersburg this summer, which will necessarily interrupt amusements and what is almost of as much consequence delay any business which I may have to transact. In another week I possibly may alter my opinion, but at present there appears to me a great probability of my being detained here another winter. Whenever I return it will give me great pleasure to see Lady Suffolk and my family. As to any other circumstances which may attend me I have no very favourable opinion of them. I am offered a little place in the country about a Marble Hill distance from Petersburg, where probably I may wander for a few days, but my Town House will be my chief residence as more agreeable than any country situation in this neighbourhood.

EARL OF BUCKINGHAMSHIRE to LADY SUFFOLK.

1764, June 8. Petersburg.— . . . I told Lady Buckingham in my last letter but one that I intended to give some prizes to be rowed for upon the King's birthday, and now I will tell you that they absolutely were rowed for. There were nine barges, seven of twelve and two of ten oars. Count Orloff's barge won the first heat, but lost the second and third, which were won by a boat belonging to the *Corps de Cadets*, a sort of Academy where all the young people of distinction are prepared for the Army and Navy. Count Orloff's barge won the second prize and the Hetman's the third. The day was fine and upon the whole everything went off to my satisfaction. . . .

I never depended much upon Townshend's friendship, but it has proved lighter in the scale than even I expected. You know too much of the world not to be sensible that *everything considered* it is impossible for any cordiality to subsist between Mr. Harbord and myself unless we act politically together. . . .

Earl of Buckinghamshire to Lady Suffolk.

1764, June 18. Petersburg.—I imagined to have sent you by this courier some positive account of myself, but my situation is in appearance as uncertain as every human event is in effect, yet it matters not much to me nor should it in effect to anybody. I cannot help thinking myself of that stock of men who will ever be most respected by their friends when in absence. Some of mine I will believe frequently recollect my desire to act in every instance with honour and humanity, my anxiety to please and oblige, my wish to contribute to their ease and amusement, without recollecting that absence of mind, that captiousness, that gloom contracted by an unfortunate disposition ever to ruminate on the dark side of my own story, which make me often a melancholy and sometimes a disagreeable companion.

It seems to me that I have lived long and that most of my days have passed as tediously as unprofitably. Necessity might have made your nephew good for something, but indolence and dissipation have ever prevented me from any useful application except when immediately call'd upon. In reviewing my past life and judging my actions by the loose rules of worldly morality I have neither done anything very wrong or very right. One unfortunate disposition, which I believe I picked from my nurse, has principally shaded my conduct ; guess it if you can, I am tired of my own reflections and undoubtedly so are you.

Earl of Buckinghamshire to Lady Suffolk.

1764, July 3. Petersburg.— . . . The Empress went last week to Cronstadt to view her fleet. It is an island situated in the Gulf of Finland about 15 miles from hence and is properly speaking the fort of Petersburg. During her stay here she made everyone happy who had the honour of attending her, and you will be flattered to hear she was particularly gracious to your nephew. When she went to dine on board the Admiral she took me with only three other persons in her barge. When she returned to Petersburg I was the only foreigner who was admitted into her yatch. The wind failing, she got into her barge and permitted me to attend her. When she arrived over against my house she told me that she knew I had no coach at the Palace, she would set me down at my own door. The next day though not a Court day I thought it incumbent upon me to appear at the Palace and to desire the Vice Chancellor to acquaint H.I.M. that I was there to express my sensibility of her goodness to me. He brought me for answer, "Que S.M. était extrêmement contente de mes attentions et que comme ma conduite était telle qu'elle m'envisageait plutôt comme un compatriote que comme un étranger, elle me priait de diner avec elle."

She set out on Sunday evening for Riga. She told me she should be absent three weeks. Just before her departure Count Orlow carried me into her private apartment that I might have an opportunity of making my Compliments to her. You will show this only to those who love me well enough not to laugh at any little vanity which may appear in the relation. Lady Buckingham writes me word that Mr. Grenville assured her I should hear from him very soon. It would really be a satisfaction to me if he could find leisure to send me a few lines. I very much approve of Lord Tavistock's marriage.[°] You may make compliments from me which are truly sincere to the Lady's family. Notwithstanding a person is fixed upon to succeed me at this Court, I cannot flatter myself with the hopes of seeing you sooner than Christmas.

EARL OF BUCKINGHAMSHIRE to LADY SUFFOLK.

1764, July 10. Petersburg.—There is no person but yourself to whom I can talk with confidence upon my situation, and therefore you must in some sort excuse my explaining to you some circumstances which give me great uneasiness. Your ladiship knows full well that Mr. Grenville is the only friend I can in the least depend upon in the present Administration. Lord Halifax has no longer any regard for me, and tho' Lord Sandwich ever since he came into office has behaved to me with the greatest civility and attention, I have no right to expect any particular support from his Lordship, the Duke of Bedford and Lord Holland. The manner in which His Majesty is pleased to recall me, leaving me at liberty with regard to the time, is most gracious, and I should have been thoroughly satisfy'd with it had not Mr. Grenville's silence upon that occasion most sensibly mortified me. I hardly dare tell you in my present temper how very little pleasure I promise myself in returning to England. Your Ladyship and Lady Buckingham will be glad to see me. I cannot answer for many more. . . . My Norfolk history sets heaviest upon me, and the thought that I must never expect to pass a cheerful day at Blickling. Lord Walpole, who tho' a worthy man, must from his connections ever act in opposition to me on the one side, and Mr. Harbord, who has taken the opportunity of absence to desert the man who essentially hurt himself

---

* To Lady Elizabeth Keppel.

to serve him, on the other ; I will, however, leave a door open for reconciliation as long as possible. I always doubted of General Townshend's real regard for me, he has been upon many occasions lavish in his professions of friendship, but ever avoided entering into any engagements relative to the affairs of Norfolk. As I have ever acted an open and candid part by him I had a right to make use of him if I could. Of that which he has acted I have no great reason to complain, tho' some circumstances which attended it will not be so easily forgot. The history of the receivers' place at Norwich is another unpleasant consequence of my being abroad as well as a further reason for my not wishing myself at home. Now I have said this much my heart is lighter, and upon reviewing my history bad as it is and drawn with a discontented pencil it does not absolutely amount to tragedy. Notwithstanding any peevish aversion I may have taken to England and the inordinate affection I have conceived for Russia, yet were it not for the hope that from a little delay I may return with more credit, I should humbly entreat that Mr. Macartney ' might set out immediately.

EARL OF BUCKINGHAMSHIRE to the COUNTESS OF SUFFOLK.

1764, July 31. Petersburg.—It is in the garden of the Summer Palace, a most pleasant and cheerful retirement, in which I pass three of four hours every morning, when my leisure will admit of it, that this letter is wrote. It is the third or fourth which might have been dated from thence, but at the other times it did not occur to me to mention the scene which stood before me. The garden is laid out in the old English, or rather in the Italian stile, shady walks, marble statues and fountains innumerable. The Palace is at one end, and a Terras which commands a very fine view of the river on the other. Distant thunder, dark clouds, and screaming Peacocks prepare me to expect a storm, but I shall write on in perfect tranquillity till the first drops reach me. Whether it is a change of temper, or the effect of advancing further in life, I know not, but I every day find that I contemplate every kind of storm with increasing tranquillity, or if any emotion arises it is more from general humanity, or particular regard to individuals than from my own fears or feelings.

Since my last I have past another four and twenty hours at Count Rosamowski's, and I return'd as before, with contrition to Ministerial conference and the consequences.

The Empress is expected this evening at Peterhoff, about twenty miles from hence, which I equally rejoice at both in my publick and private capacity, as I have sensibly felt in both the difference of her absence. Col. Hotham desires me at my return to England to bring a picture of her, but perhaps he will find a stronger resemblance than any I can obtain in Lady Dy. Clavering. Her Imp. Maj. is fairer and not so tall. I hear much of the new pavement, but am persuaded that is not the only alteration I shall experience in England, and tho' I may

---

* George Macartney, afterwards Sir George, and later Lord Macartney.

find it easier to glide along (Albemarle?) Street, yet there are other paths in which once I trod with pleasure, where should I venture to range I might meet rivals who would with reason mock at my stale pretensions. If I find you in health, and three or four, who, after three years' absence, I still esteem my friends, glad to see me, my reception in England will be equal to my wishes whenever I shall be in a situation to meet it.

EARL OF BUCKINGHAMSHIRE to LADY SUFFOLK.

1764, August 17. Petersburg.— . . . When you hear of my balls and assemblies and entertainments you must imagine my hours not only pass cheerfully but riotously gay, yet some day or other you shall learn how flimsy are my pleasures and how real my anxieties. I have often complained of the slender information with which my friends in England favour me, but never with the tenth part of the reason which I have now, in that, except deaths and marriages, I know nothing of my own country and am never able to contradict any idle report which the flippancy of a Gazette writer or the real or willfull misinformation of a foreign Minister prompts him to propagate. I am tempted to tear this paper as the contents may teaze you without availing me. Yet you are the only person to whom I fully open my heart and the only one who loves me in the manner I most wish to be loved. Of this sort however you shall never receive any more letters from me, and if facts must be mentioned they shall be mentioned without comments. . .

EARL OF BUCKINGHAMSHIRE to LADY SUFFOLK.

1764, Aug. 24.—(Complains of his own extremes in disposition.)

"I have lately had some letters from England. Lady Buckingham's are full of her sensibility of your goodness to her. Though she does not own it, I am persuaded you make her more than amends for the absence of her husband. Mr. Grenville has not as yet favoured me with a line, but I flatter myself daily with the hopes of hearing from him. He has certainly many most interesting occupations, but a letter is soon wrote." . . .

THE SAME to THE SAME.

1764, Sept. 7.—(Trivial recollections of his childhood.)

" Many, many thanks for your most kind letter which I have just receiv'd. I will upon the whole in obedience to your commands° make myself as easy as I can and confide in the good intentions of my friends. I have no other dissatisfaction in relation to Mr. Harbord but his having taken the opportunity of my absence to change his political conduct."

---

* See Lady Suffolk to Earl of Buckinghamshire of 9 August, 1764. (Lady Suffolk's Letters, Vol. II., p. 239.)

EARL OF BUCKINGHAMSHIRE to LADY SUFFOLK.

1764, Oct. 2. Petersburg.—By a letter I have lately received from Lord Sandwich Mr. Macartney will probably have left England before this arrives there. As soon as ever that gentleman comes to Petersburg I shall ask for my audience of leave, so that in all probability it will not now be many months before I embrace my good Aunt in Savile Row. It is very difficult to guess how long the journey will take me in that inclement season in which I am destined to travel. If, however, the sledge way is good, as I hope it will be, at the time I set out the first half-way will soon be despatched. The winter is already beginning, the Russians have got on their furs, but I remain in my autumn cloaths; if I took the same precautions they do I should not be able to live and dress like other people in England, as it is you will find me grown exceedingly chilly. Though it is not properly the subject of private correspondence I cannot help saying a little to you in relation to Mirovitz, a gentleman of whom lately you must have heard a great deal. He was a man of most profligate and debauched character, though since his rash attempt he has been devout to a degree of fanaticism. During his confinement and trial, and even at his execution, he behaved with the most becoming resolution. He acknowledged his errors and declared his readiness by laying down his life with the greatest resignation to atone for them. He owned he was informed of the incapacity of the unfortunate Prince[*] which excited him still more to the attempt, as had he succeeded he meant to govern through him. What seemed most to affect him was the punishment the unhappy soldiers were to suffer whom he had seduced. The particulars of the event were most theatrical, but not of a nature to give me pleasure to write or you to read. Let me till we meet guard you against the reports which the ill-natured, the prejudiced, the designing most assiduously propagate, lest you should censure those who from their feelings are greatly more the objects of compassion. The Empress since her return from Riga has been almost constantly in the country, where she saw very few people but those about her; now she is returned Petersburg will be the gayer. Yesterday there was a ball, as it was the Grand Duke's birthday. The nobility and foreign ministers supped with him, but the Empress retired early.

. . . Mirovitz's design was known only to two or three persons of no consequence.

THE SAME to THE SAME.

1764, Oct. 17. Petersburg.—In about six weeks I am to leave a country where I have now spent two years, and whatever pleasure a man may promise himself in breathing the air of his native soil and renewing his antient connections, yet the approach of a moment when you are to take an eternal leave of those with whom you have lived in an agreeable familiarity and

[*] Ivan, 1740-1764, the Infant Czar of 1740-1741.

a state of mutual benevolence, cannot but be painful to a feeling mind. The unwearied pains I have taken, the difficultys I have submitted to, and the unpleasant moments I have passed in order to attain my purpose makes the assertion that no foreigner ever lived upon that footing which I now do in Russia, scarcely liable to the censure of vanity. My situation has improved by degrees, but it is only within these few months that I have been quite satisfyed with it, to which the gracious distinctions which the sovereign has condescended to shew me have not a little contributed. What welcome I shall meet with in England except from my own family seems to me rather uncertain, as from the extreme negligence with which my friends have corresponded with me, I almost suspect I shall find myself a little upon the footing of a stranger. . . . So many alterations have happen'd in the interior of England that even at the best a new man cannot avoid some disagreeable embarassments. ˙ . . .

EARL OF BUCKINGHAMSHIRE to LADY SUFFOLK.

1764, Oct. 25. Petersburg.—Je vous écris si souvent que cela ne manquera pas de vous excéder. Cependant je fais mon devoir, je me livre à mon inclination; prenez patience, madame! Mercredi passé, le jour de nom du Comte Orloff, il donna bal à l'Impératrice. L'ambassadeur l'Angleterre eut l'honneur d'en être, et ne fut pas peu flatté, tant de s'y trouver l'unique étranger que de l'acceuil gracieux que la souveraine lui fit. Nulle gène, nulle contrainte, la soirée se passa agréablement au possible. Après souper, toute la compagnie sans exception, commença une danse polonaise. Nous n'étions pas touts du même âge, il s'y trouvait une fille d'honneur de 13 ans, et le Maréchal Múnnich qui approche de 84. Ce bon vieillard dont l'attachement respectueux pour le beau sexe donnerait un air de brusquerie à la tendre galanterie de notre cher Ligonier disait l'autre jour, en entendant raisonner sur la beauté, qu'il n'avait jamais vu de femme qui ne lui paraissait belle.

Un cas assez extraordinaire est arrivé ici et fait depuis quelques jours le sujet des raisonnements sages et frivoles de Petersbourg. La semaine passée, un soldat des gardes à cheval se maria. La cérémonie finie, on offrit du vin à la compagnie, tout le monde en prit, l'épouse excepté, car telle est la modestie des filles Russes, que le jour de leurs noces elles ne veulent absolûment rien prendre avant de se mettre au lit. Huit personnes donc prirent de ce vin, et un quart d'heure après six des dix s'avisèrent de jeter des éclats de rire des plus extraordinaires. En suite ils tombèrent en convulsions qui durèrent assez long tems. Le lendemain à la même heure mêmes éclats de rire, mêmes convulsions et cela durait encore le septième jour, quand l'Impératrice en fut informée. Les medécins en conséquence se sont assemblés en corps. On délibère encore sur les causes de ce phénomène, et quand on m'en dira quelque chose peutêtre je vous le communiquerai. . . .

L'envoie Turc doit avoir son audience publique ce matin et les dames travaillent furiensement à la toilette, quoique les Turcs sont des Mussulmans, ils sont aussi hommes, et il faut tâcher de leur plaire. C'est comme cela que pensent les femmes Russes, je crois que les Anglaises agiraient à peu près de même.

EARL OF BUCKINGHAMSHIRE to LADY SUFFOLK.

1764, Nov. 20. Petersburg.—"Not with a Highwayman, you sorry Slut!' says Mrs. Pechum to Miss Polly when after the discovery of her marriage with the seducing Captain she sweetly sings, ' Can love be controlled by advice?' Extraordinary as my letters usually are, the beginning of this will still surprise you, till you know that I am just informed that the sister of the M. of R. and the niece of the E. of W. has thrown herself into the arms of her Irish footman. As the lady is a full-grown child and has probably made her reflections the footman is the proper object of compassion. It is most amazing to me that the numberless instances of ruinous and disgraceful matches should not suggest some serious reflections to parents and guardians, and introduce a different mode of education. Yet what expedients can avail? How can you preserve and protect your child when the physician who feels her pulse, the surgeon who breathes (sic) the vein, every person whose profession or talents are essential to improve her, the footman who carrys the flambeau, and even the sprightly ostler, who expeditiously harnesses two miserable hacks to a post chaise are equally dangerous. . . .

Your extensive notions of liberty and the high prerogatives of the female world are well known to me and in a degree merit approbation, but will you not allow me to confine the daughters when I give it as my opinion that the mothers ought to know no controul—a doctrine which I preach by example. Mr. Prior says, " Clap your padlock on your mind." Agreed! But then there must be a mind to fix it on. If you fasten your padlock upon a sap of green wood can you expect it to hold? It may be said, Why should not young women have opportunitys of looking round the world, of seeing variety of men, of sifting their characters and choosing him whom their inclinations favour and their judgment approves? Because for obvious, if indeed for excusable reasons, nineteen times in twenty they will choose wrong. . . .

EXTRACT from a Small BUNDLE of PRIVATE LETTERS exchanged between the EARL OF BUCKINGHAMSHIRE, PRINCE BELASELSKI, and BARON CHERKASOW.

From the BARON CHERKASOW.

1765, February 15.—' Après d'exactes recherches j'ai trouvé que ce n'est pas ici la coutume ordinaire de donner de portraits, et que le dernier fut donné en conséquence d'une demande formelle,° et autant que j'en sais, vous n'en avez point fait. Mais vous pouvez comter que jamais ministre étranger n'a été aussi généralement estimé pendant son séjour ni autant regretté à son départ que vous. Vous avez vu la vérité de la première réflexion et je vais garantir celle de la seconde. On voit dans toutes les maisons des portraits de M. de Cappelmann, que l'on a décorés des quadres dorés à votre intention. Mais ce n'est rien. On vous tient pour un parfaitement honnête homme. Et c'est quelque chose.

Mardi le 1-12 de ce mois, l'on a representé chez le Grand Chambellan ' Le Philosophe marié et les Mœurs du Tems.' Les acteurs et les actrices furent applaudis et avec beaucoup de raison.

La Countesse Cheremeteff l'ainée et le Prince Belaselsky ont eu particulièrement mon approbation. Le Comte Cheremeteff, le Comte Orloff (Grégoire) le Comte Golowin, Monsieur Passek et ma femme m'ont chargé de vous présenter leurs complimens.

EARL OF BUCKINGHAMSHIRE to LADY SUFFOLK.

1765, Feb. 21. Koningsberg Brandenburg.—This letter will be sent you from Berlin, tho' probably without any addition to what is wrote this evening from the fair city of Koningsberg. I address'd Lady Buckingham yesterday and now it is my disposition to address you. If I delighted in repetitions or was lazily disposed, the copy of my letter to her with only the change of the date, would be an exact account of the transactions of the day and of my situation in the evening, two little circumstances excepted, that I have travelled without a tilt and am not within hearing of a crying child. It cannot but affect everyone who has a feeling heart, to trace the cruel effect of the war upon these unfortunate countries through which I am passing ; ruined villages, large and well-built towns absolutely depopulated are objects which continually meet the eye. I have suffered greatly all this day from cold and warm winds, the first came from the South, the most piercing I ever experienced from that quarter, the latter was a kind of subscription gale, for which I was obliged to the footman and the man who drove my cart. You know the Russians were long in possession of Pomerania, they have left their mark everywhere, but since the new connection between the Courts of Berlin and Petersburg, the unfortunate remains of the inhabitants are forbid throwing out any reflections of their calamities. A postmaster however ventured yesterday to whisper me that the Russians had given him the knout for sending intelligence to the King his master ; he was near dying under the hands of the executioner, and has never recovered his health since. But why should I distress your humanity with melancholy ideas ?—I have just burst out into an inordinate fit of laughter and I will tell you why—By way of a cheerful subject I was about to talk of the wild beast in

---

* This refers to the Empress' portrait.

Languedoc who eats virgins *par préférence*. Now if the existence
of that gentleman is not fabulous, and his feats are really true,
the story is extraordinary but by no means comical.

I am refreshing myself at an old Burgomaster's, and whilst a
room is warming for me, I have taken possession of his private
apartment. He has very much the air of an old Dutch soldier
that came over with King William, and he interrupts me every
moment to talk of the events of the War of Succession and of
other antient stories in most abominable Latin, to which I answer
in rather worse. For example—'Excellentissime Domine, si
bene mimini serenissimus Orangea Princeps Angliam invasit
Anno salutis 1689. Ego e contra, '1688.' But I forget that
you don't understand Latin. It is ten thousand pitys. You
may however intreat Lady Betty Germaine to explain the meaning of those few words to you. . . . . .

BUCKINGHAMSHIRE PAPERS.

Part 3.—1762-1765.

Papers relating to Poland and Courland, with Mr. Wroughton's
Letters.

Traduction du Polonais d'une Lettre à un Ami
du 6 Novembre, 1762.

Pour satisfaire votre curiosité sur les vraies causes et les
principales circonstances de ce qui vient d'arriver à Varsovie, il
faut prendre les choses d'un peu plus haut.

Au commencement du mois d'Aoûst le Comte de Brühl a écrit
au prince Zartoryski, palatin de Russie, qui alors se trouvait à la
campagne, que le Roi souhaitait de sçavoir son sentiment sur
la manière de remplir les grandes places alors vacantes.

Dans le principe que le meilleur moyen de rendre un pays heureux est d'en remplir les charges de gens vertueux et capables, le
prince palatin proposa le pisarz de Lithuanie Ogincki pour
palatin de Wilna, son beau frère le cadet Brzortouski pour petit

Général de Lithuanie, le palatin d'Inowraclaw, Zamoycki, pour vice-chancelier de la Couronne, le palatin de Mecistaw, Plater, pour vice-chancelier de Lithuanie. Le Comte de Bruhl répondit que le Roi avait vu la lettre du prince palatin avec plaisir. Malgrès cette expression favorable, de jour en jour on apprenait que les recherches du prince Radziwil, Miecznik de Lithuanie, et du palatin de Polock, Sapieha, gagnaient plus de terrain et la voix publique assure que Radziwil a employé pour cela 60,000 ducats et Sapieha 30,000. Quoique vous n'estes pas Lithuanois je crois cependant que vous scaviés que la loi donne au Palatin de Wilna le droit de légaliser le légitimité d'élection de chaque député ou juge au tribunal souverain de Lithuanie, de façon que quand le Palatin de Wilna est un homme violent et injuste, il dépend de lui de composer le tribunal presqu' à son grès de gens qui lui sont dévoués. Tout le Royaume sçait des injustices et des meurtres qui se sont commis sous la protection et même par les membres de ces tribunaux de la faction de Radziwil du vivant du défunt Prince Radziwil, que sera-ce à présent que la charge du palatin de Wilna est entre les mains de son fils ?—dont on connait le caractère et qui trouvait que son père le contraignait encore trop dans les persécutions sanguinaires qu'il exerçait dès lors contre tout ce qui n'était pas aveuglément soumis à ses volontés.

Il était du devoir des bons patriotes d'empêcher que la Lithuanie ne tombât entre pareilles mains. Pour contrebalancer l'argent du prince Radziwil le seul moyen que les princes Czartorycki crurent efficace fut de faire avertir le Comte de Bruhl que s'il donnait le palatinat de Wilna à Radziwil, ils seraient obligés de lui faire contester dans la Chambre des Nonces, la noblesse Polonaise.

Néanmoins le Palatinat et le petit généralat furent donnés à Radziwil et à Sapieha. Bruhl passa outre par deux raisons, la première parcequ'il s'imagina que les Czartorycki se laisseraient intimider par les satellites de Radziwil armés de pistolets et de cuirasses sous leurs habits, dont il a rempli la Chambre des Nonces, la seconde parcequ'il crut que les Czartorycki désireraient de faire élire un Maréchal de la Diète pour que Zamoycki peut devenir Vice-Chancelier, parceque selon l'esprit de la loi les sceaux ne peuvent être donnés qu'après un maréchal élu. Effectivement cette première raison fit que les Czartorycki n'éclatèrent pas le premier jour de la diette pour laisser encore du tems à tous ceux qui travaillaient pour Zamoycki, mais ce même jour-là au matin pendant que le Roi de sa bouche assurait le grand général Branicki qu'il donnerait le sceau à Zamoycki, Miecznik, Maréchal de la Cour, dit à Zamoycki même, "Vous ne pouvés monsieur estre chancelier car le Roy m'a déclaré il y a trois jours qu'il veut que je le sois, moi," et le soir lorsque le grand général en vertu de ce que le Roi avait dit le matin demanda la patente de chancelier signeé Zamoycki, Bruhl la lui refusa net. Alors voyant qu'il n'y avait plus d'apparence de faire avoir le sceau à ce digne et vertueux Zamoycki que toute la nation désirait pour chancelier, et qu'il y'avait tout à craindre que si le Maréchal le devenait, la Pologne ne fut sous le joug comme la Lithuanie, les Czartorycki se déterminèrent à parler. Enfin le second jour de la diette le Stolnik de Lithuanie⁰ dit dans la Chambre des Nonces, que ne pouvant connaître le Cte de Bruhl pour Polonais, il ne pouvait malgrès tous les égards et l'amitié qu'il lui portait personellement le laisser voter pour l'élection du Maréchal de la Diette. Apparemment on n'avait pas de bonnes raisons à lui apporter, car à ces mots, au lieu de répondre de paroles, les sabres tirés par des partisans de Radziwil qui se trouvaient les plus voisins du jeune Comte de Bruhl dans la Chambre des Nonces donnèrent le signal à tous les autres. S'il était possible de douter de la vérité notoire et publique de quel côté on a dégaîné le premier, la meilleure preuve se trouve dans un billet d'un ami de Bruhl écrit par un reste d'ancienne amitié, ou pour effrayer les Czartorycki, où il leur a mandé la veille de ce jour que si on parlait contre Bruhl dans la Chambre des Nonces, on s'exposerait au plus grand danger. Le même soir Szymakourki rompit la diette pour empêcher qu'on ne débattit plus cette matière incommode à Bruhl.

La preuve que cet homme a agi par instigation de ce ministre c'est que six semaines auparavant lorsqu'il fut élu nonce, le Maréchal Miecznik voulut l'engager à céder sa nonciature à un autre homme dont le Maréchal Miecznik et Bruhl se croyaient plus sûrs pour rompre la diette. Mais Szymakourki s'offrit à faire également cette fonction, pourvu qu'on le paya bien comme on a fait, à quoi on a ajouté tout récemment un consentement de cession ce qui est une grâce royale. Voilà l'exacte vérité des faits. Bruhl attribue à faux aux Czartorycki un mot vis-à-vis du Roy—'Tout ou rien!' Ils ne l'ont jamais dit ni pu dire, premièrement ils n'ont pas pu employer ce terme parceque jamais on n'a voulu leur promettre positivement même aucune partie des grâces qu'ils demandèrent en Lithuanie. Secondement lorsque le Primat au nom du Roi fit demander au Prince palatin une réponse finale sur les candidats aux charges, il la donna par écrit en disant ' que tant qu'il plaira au Roi de le consulter sur la distribution des vacances, il ne pouvait en proposer d'autres que ceux qu'il avait proposés avant deux mois parceque dans ce temps il n'avait consulté que le bien public, les talents et les circonstances personelles des sujets.' Jugez vous-même si dans tout ce que je viens de vous exposer il y a la moindre manque de respect au Roy ?

Si vous demandés pourquoi il y a plus de signatures aux mani-festes de Bruhl que ceux des Czartoryckis, je vous dirai que les 36 signatures de ceux-ci. se sont faites sans offres ni menaces, uniquement par amitié et par la conviction du mauvais droit de Bruhl, fondé sur les loix qui y sont énoncées, au lieu qu'on a em-ployé tout le pouvoir des promesses des grâces du Roy et des 4 généraux et des menaces les plus fortes du contraire pour faire signer les présens ; on a inséré les signatures des absens, témoin celle du neveu du grand Maréchal de Lithuanie ; on a fait signer

---

* Stanislas Poniatowski, afterwards King of Poland.

comme nonces des gens qui ne l'étaient pas, témoin,celui qui a signé comme nonce de Rozan et qui lui-même avait rompu la diettine de ce canton.

Dans ce manifeste Bruhl semble objecter aux Czartorycki qu'ils ont participé autrefois aux premiers actes où il est entré en jouissance des prérogatives de la Noblesse polonaise. Ils repondent qu'ils y ont connivé dans l'espérance que se croyant polonais il chérirait le bien-estre de cette patrie, mais que depuis qu'il a brisé tous les liens publics et particuliers qui les retenaient vis-à-vis de lui, depuis que la distribution vénale des charges et l'altération manifestement frauduleux des monnoyes fait le malheur de la patrie, ils ont fait parler les loix expresses.

Si l'on vous dit que les Czartorycki, jouant gros jeu, ils seront écrasés par la haine puissante du favori, là-dessus ils pensent premièrement qu'il faut faire son devoir à tout risque et qu'il se trouve encore chez nous des hommes intègres et courageux qui préfèrent l'honneur à tout, comme Wollowicz nonce de Sloninola bien fait voir en refusant mille ducats et une compagnie de gens d'armes que le Maréchal Miecznik lui offrait pour sa signature.
. . . . .

ᵃ Sur la MANIÈRE VIOLENTE avec laquelle de SIMOLIN, CONSEILLER D'ÉTAT de RUSSIE, a mis EN SÉQUESTRE toutes les terres et revenus de SON ALTESSE ROYALE le DUC DE COURLANDE.†

N.D. [1763, Jan.]—La veille de Noël, le 24ᵃ ᵐᵉ Décembre, 1762, M. de Simolin, Conseiller d'état de Russie, envoya le Lieutenant Colonel Schroeders mettre le Sceau Impérial sur les douanes au passage de la rivière, d'abord après le même Lieutenant-Colonel se rendit à la maison de poste pour défendre au Maitre de Poste de la part de M. de Simolin de ne donner de la part de qui que ce soit quelque argent de celui qu'il pourrait avoir en caisse. Le Maitre de Poste lui répondait qu'il n'en avait point pour le présent, et qu'étant engagé à son devoir par serment il n'avait d'autres ordres à suivre que ceux du Duc son maitre, sur quoi le Lieutenant-Colonel lui dit qu'il ne devait pas s'opposer à donner un revers comme quoi il ne donnerait aucun argent à qui que ce soit. Le Maitre de Poste lui répliqua qu'il ne pouvait pas y acquiescer. Le Lieutenant-Colonel lui dit alors que s'il s'y opposait, il le ferait jetter hors de la maison, et mettrait un autre Maitre de Poste à sa place, et il fit tout de suite mettre une sentinelle russe à sa porte. Sur l'avis que Son Altesse Royale en eut Elle fit venir M. M. les Oberraths ou Conseillers suprêmes, et après avoir écouté leur avis là-dessus, Elle députa M. M. le Landhofmeister de Hoven et le Chancelier de Kayserling à M. Simolin, les chargeant de lui témoigner de sa part sa surprise sur des démarches si contraires aux droits du Roi et de la

---

* See *Buckinghamshire Correspondence*, Vol. I., p. 191 (Wroughton to the Earl of Buckinghamshire of the 5th Jan., 1763). where this account is mentioned as having been received by him from the Ministers of Augustus III.

† Charles Christian of Saxony, son of Augustus III.

République, et aux siens propres, Elle le fit requérir de ne pas continuer à agir de cette sorte, et lui fit demander de quelle autorité il faisait tout cela, lui faisant dire, que si c'était par ordre de l'Impératrice,° lui, Duc, avait à tous égards tout le respect possible pour Elle, mais que n'ayant d'autres ordres à respecter que ceux du Roi son père et maitre, il protestait contre tout ce qui serait fait sans le consentement de sa Majesté le Roi, comme contre les démarches contraires aux droits du Roi, de la République et les siens. Les sus-dits Conseillers s'acquittèrent mot pour mot de cette commission et firent rapport que M. de Simolin leur répliqua avec beaucoup de vivacité et d'emportement, que tout ce qu'il faisait c'était selon l'ordre de l'Impératrice de mettre le séquestre sur tout ce qui avait apparence de revenu ; il a ajouté que tout cela ne serait pas arrivé, si l'on n'eut refusé les quartiers d'hyver aux trouppes russes. Les Conseillers lui répondaient que l'on n'avait jamais refusé ni quartiers, ni bois aux trouppes, mais qu'on n'avait pu se charger de faire des quartiers pour des trouppes étrangères, sans en faire le rapport au Roi, comme maitre direct de ce duché. M. Simolin leur dit à la fin que comme ils avaient tous deux des terres ducales en ferme, il leur notifierait par une lettre le même soir le séquestre ainsi qu'à tous les arrondateurs. M. M. les Conseillers lui répétèrent que le Duc leur Maitre aurait en toute occasion tout l'égard et respect dû à S. M. Impériale mais en ce qui regardait ces circonstances, il observerait ce que son devoir envers le Roi et la République exigeait de lui. M. M. les Conseillers après avoir fait leur rapport prirent le consentement du Duc pour aller insérer aux publiques une protestation contre tout ce qui pourrait être fait de contraire aux droits du Roi et de le République et de son Altesse Royale avec une relation fidèle de tout ce qui avait été jusqu'à présent dit et fait en cette rencontre.

Pendant ce tems M. de Simolin fit tenir une lettre de la teneur ci-jointe à tous les arrondateurs, leur intimant le séquestre Impérial des terres Ducales qu'ils tiennent en ferme. Un instant après il fit mettre une garde d'un bas officier et de huit hommes au magasin du bois que le Duc avait pour sa provision. La nuit du 24 au 25 il fit poster une sentinelle devant la maison où sont les archives, on a appris le matin que la même chose était arrivée au moulin du Duc, et que l'écrivain de ce moulin avait eu défense de rien donner de l'argent de ce produit. L'inspecteur des étangs qui doit fournir le poisson au Duc vint annoncer en même tems d'avoir reçu ordre de ne lui en point livrer. Le Bailli des deux Bailliages que S. A. Royale s'était réservés pour son économie et sa table reçut une même défense par un officier, qui fut placé avec quelques soldats dans ces bailliages de ne rien livrer pour la Cour. M. Simolin poussant enfin les choses à l'extrémité s'assura du magasin de foin et d'avoine, de la monnaie, de la brasserie et de la basse cour, où il y avait la volaille pour la table du Duc,

---

° The Czarina Catherine II.

n'oubliant rien pour lui couper tout moien de subsister. Suivant la raison que M. de Simolin allègue du séquestre c'est l'Impératrice qui l'ait ordonné, il est manifeste qu'elle l'a fait sur les faux rapports de ce Conseiller d'Etat qui dans ses relations envénimées, outre d'en avoir imposé à Sa Souveraine par un faux rapport que le Duc se soit opposé au quartier d'hyver que cinq Régimens russes ont pris en Courlande, doit avoir ajouté à ce prétendu refus et opposition, des circonstances les plus odieuses et même atroces, pour que cette Princesse se soit portée à une telle extrémité sans le moindre égard ni pour la personne de S. A. Royale, ni pour son rang et naissance, reconnu par tant de puissances et par la Russie même pour Duc Régnant, à qui Elle avait ci-devant accrédité ce même Simolin. Or que la raison que celui-ci a allégué soit destituée de toute vérité, cela est évidemment démontré puisqu'il dit que le Duc s'est opposé, et qu'il a refusé des quartiers d'hyver aux Trouppes Russes, pendant qui lui, Simolin, ne le reconnait pas pour Duc, qu'il ne lui a fait aucune réquisition (de quoi seul le Duc s'est plaint) que les trouppes ont pris leurs quartiers d'hyver selon la répartition arbitraire que lui Simolin en a faite, qu 'elles ont été pourvues du nécessaire, et que le Duc n'a point de trouppes pour s'opposer aux Russes.

Sur quoi Sa Majesté a pris la résolution d'expédier incessamment une personne distinguée dans la République à S. M. Impériale pour la rectifier sur les imputations de M. Simolin, et l'on espère que rectifiée, elle contremandera et révoquera des démarches si fort contraires aux principes de justice que cette Princesse a témoignés de vouloir exactement suivre dans son gouvernement, et qui sont si eloignées du bon voisinage et amitié que le Roi et la République se promettaient d'elle.

S. M. espère d'ailleurs de l'amitié de toutes les Puissances, ses amies et alliés, et de la République, et de la fidélité de sa nation, jalouse de son honneur et de sa liberté, d'être secondée à persuader la Cour de Russie de se prêter à des arrangemens plus conformes à la bonne intelligence, que de son côté tant sa Majesté et la République que le Prince Royal Duc Régnant de Courlande n'ont cessé de cultiver fort soigneusement aux yeux de toute l'Europe.

(1) *Exposé des motifs de Sa Majesté Impériale de toutes les Russies relativement aux affaires de la Courlande.

N.D. [1763, Jan. 4.]—L'Impératrice de toutes les Russies en montant sur le trône, croyait ne pouvoir donner des marques plus éclatantes du désir qu'elle a de cultiver l'amitié et le bon voisinage du Roi et de la République de Pologne, qu'en rendant la liberté à ceux pour qui le Roi et le Sénat l'avaient demandée tant de fois et si instamment sous le règne de l'Impératrice Elisabeth.

---

* Enclosed in a letter to the Earl of Buckinghamshire by Mr. Wroughton, English Minister at Warsaw, on the 5th of January, 1763 (see *Buckinghamshire Corresp.*, Vol. 1, p. 195).

C'était dans ces considérations que sa Majesté Impériale a accordé au Duc Ernest Jean de Courlande de pouvoir sortir librement, et qu'elle s'est interposée en même tems auprès Sa Majesté le Roi de Pologne pour qu'elle voulût restituer le dit Duc dans ses Duchés et lui rendre les domaines qu'en partie il avait dégagées lui-même, et qu'en partie lui ont été cédées de l'Impératrice Anne de glorieuse mémoire.

Plus ces demandes se fondaient sur tout ce qui est juste et équitable, d'autant moins Sa Majesté Impériale s'etait-Elle attendue, ni pouvait-Elle s'attendre qu'on l'expliquerait selon la réponse du Roi du 3 Septembre de l'année passée comme si Elle empiétait sur les droits suzérains du Roi et de la République

Mais peut-on dire avec fondement que celui qui sur l'affaire en question en fait la réquisition à ce Prince Suzerain même, empiète sur ses droits et les révoque en doute? Or, comment peut-on interpreter si peu amiablement ce qu'on a demandé de la part de la Russie avec autant de justice que d'équité? Qui peut ignorer la Constitution de la Diète de Pacification de l'année 1736, faite du consentement de tous les ordres de la République touchant les Duchés de Courlande et de Semgalle? On y a statué qu'après l'extinction de la famille de Kettler ces fiefs devaient être conférés à un autre pour lui et ses descendans mâles moyennant un Diplôme, en usage dans de pareils cas, et qu'on conviendrait avec lui des conditions féodales. La Commission de 1727, déléguée de la Diète de 1726 pour les affaires de Courlande, avait été prorogée jusqu'à cette époque; tout cela était observé et exécuté selon la dite constitution. Le Duc Ernest Jean reçut le Diplôme Royal. Les Commissaires nommés de la République convinrent avec lui des conditions féodales; il reçut l'Investiture selon la coutûme et le Diplôme de l'Investiture lui fut expédié solennellement sous les deux sceaux de la Couronne et du Grand Duché de Lituanie avec promesse au nouveau feudataire de la part de la République, de le protéger et le défendre, lui et ses descendans dans ses Duchés contre qui que ce soit; de manière que le dit Duc acquit par-là un plein et indubitable droit à ces Duchés pour lui et pour ses descendans mâles.

Or, si un Prince feudataire sans avoir commis un crime de félonie, ne peut être privé de ses fiefs acquis légalement, de quel droit veut-on soutenir que le dit Duc Ernest Jean soit privé de ses Duchés sans avoir été écouté sans jugement et sans crime contre le Roi et la République?

· Si dans le tems où l'on a songé à le priver de ses Duchés il y avait des raisons d'état pour l'en tenir éloigné, à présent les raisons d'état pour ne plus l'empêcher d'y retourner sont d'autant plus fortes qu'il est juste de rendre à un chacun ce qui lui appartient.

S'il est du devoir de la nature et du droit de voisinage d'assister et de protéger un Prince voisin opprimé contre la force et l'injustice, sa Majesté Impériale de toutes les Russies ne peut que maintenir le Duc et les états de Courlande et de Semgalle dans leurs droits, priviléges et prérogatives.

Il n'est pas inconnu à sa Majesté Impériale que ces Duchés sont un fief de la dépendance du Corps entier de la République et non pas du trône seul des Rois de Pologne selon la teneur du Diplôme de l'incorporation de l'année 1569, et selon la constitution de l'année 1736 statuée du consentement de tous les ordres de la République.

Par ces raisons sa Majesté Impériale de toutes les Russies ne veut ni ne peut jamais consentir que ce qui est statué par la République entière, soit renversé par une partie de cette même République, ni que les droits appartenants au corps entier de la République soient enfreints.

Par conséquent sa Majesté Impériale, éloignée comme elle l'est d'empiéter sur les droits de la République de Pologne sur les Duchés mentionnés, et elle n'est pas moins fermement resolue de les conserver constamment dans leurs dépendances féodales avec la République et ne reconnait ni ne reconnaîtra jamais nul autre pour Duc légitime des Duchés de Courlande et de Semgalle que le Duc Ernest Jean, investi légalement du consentement de toute la République.

Sa Majesté Impériale embrassant en cela ce que la justice et le droit du voisinage demandent ne fait que suivre les constitutions et les loix de toutes des Puissances de l'Europe, qui en vertu de ces constitutions ont reconnu Ernest Jean Duc légitime de Courlande.

(2) Billet du Vice Chancelier de la Courunne° pour accompagner la Réponse à l'Exposé Russe.

1763, Jan. 9.—Ne connaissant, Monseigneur, à votre Cour aucun droit sur la Courlande je ne sçaurai en chancelier convenir d'aucun motif que S. M. Impériale puisse avoir avec justice de disposer ainsi à force ouverte de cette Province. J'ai lu par conséquent avec beaucoup de surprise ceux que V. E. a allégués dans l'Exposé qu'Elle m'a fait tenir avec sa lettre du 4 d. c. Rien de plus contradictoire que S. M. Impériale ne consentira jamais que les droits appartenants au corps entier de la République soyent enfreints pendant qu'ils le sont en son nom, tout comme d'exiger du Roi que ce qu'Elle convient, selon l'Exposé, ne dépendra que de la décision de la République entière. Si la Russie forme quelque prétension sur la Courlande elle s'adressera à la République dont elle reconnait la souveraineté sur ce Fief et laissera le tems aux Etats de s'assembler et de connaitre les prétendus droits de Biron.

Supposant même le Roi et le Sénat responsable de quelque chose dans l'investiture donnée de la Courland au Prince Royal, ce n'est jamais envers la Russie qu'ils le soyent, mais envers la République entière. Les Etats, Monseigneur, n'ont fait aucune instance à Votre Cour de se mêler de la disposition de ce Fief ; de telles instances ne pourraient lui jamais être faits que par de mal intentionnés prêts à falsifier leur Patrie pour leurs intérêts et

---

* Of Poland.

avantage particuliers. J'espère donc que V. E. pour réaliser les assurances qu'Elle me donne des intentions constantes de sa Souveraine de ne vouloir empiéter en aucune façon sur les droits de la République ne manquera pas de l'informer de l'atteinte qu'on lui donne en son nom et l'assurer en même tems du cas infini que nous faisons de son amitié pour la République.

(3) Reponse° à l'exposé joint à la Lettre de Monseigneur le Comte de Keyserling, Ambassadeur de Russie du 4 Janvier, 1763. (*Enclosure.*)

1763, Jan. 10. Warsaw.—La justice est la base et le fondement des trônes des Rois ; ce n'est pas sa Majesté Polonaise, à qui l'on puisse reprocher d'y avoir manqué ; trop scrupuleuse même dans ses engagemens, on l'a toujours vue y sacrifier ses propres intérêts ; elle a donné un exemple de cette délicatesse extrême au sujet de la Courlande. Le fief de la dépendance de la République vaquait depuis l'an 1741, jusqu'a l'année 1758. (*a*) Le Comte Biron qui en avait été investi l'année 1739, *à la puissante recommendation de l'Impératrice Anne de glorieuse mémoire*, (*b*) au lieu de quitter un service étranger (*c*) pour aller remplir l'objet de son infeudation, continuant dans le même service pour son malheur, il y fut disgracié et comdamné avec ses fils à un exil perpétual, par un arrêt de l'Empereur Iwan du 17 *April* 1741. (*d*) L'on passe sous silence les circonstances du manifeste public contre lui en cette occasion par la dite Cour de Russie dans tout l'Empire, en Courlande même ainsi que dans toutes les Cours Etrangères ; l'intention du Roi n'ayant jamais été de lui faire quelque préjudice, mais de co-òperer à son bonheur s'il avait été possible à S. M. sans déroger aux droits de sa Couronne et à ceux de la République. Si d'ailleurs pour éclairer le public, le Ministère était obligé de relever des circonstances odieuses à Biron, il le ferait avec regrets, quoique ne devant rien épargner de ce qui peut servir à la justification de S. M. *contre les mêmes expressions peu ménagées* (*e*), de l'Exposé que l'Ambassadeur de Russie a joint à la lettre du 4ᵉᵐᵉ des motifs de S. M. L'Impératrice de Russie relativement aux affaires de Courlande. Cet Exposé *sans date et sans signature* (*f*) ne saurait jamais être avoué *de la Cour de Russie*, (*g*) étant trop éloigné de ce qu'une Puissance doit à une autre, et se doit à soi-même ; mais comme il a été accompagné d'une lettre de son Ambassadeur, soit que lui-même ait été surpris par ceux, qui dès longtems tiennent le même langage, se flattant de la protection de la Russie, ou que de bonne foi il pense ainsi ; et que par la manière inusitée de l'insinuer et de le répandre dans le public par des circulaires, on y fait connaître des intentions très-pernicieuses, le Ministre de S. M. chargé de veiller à l'intégrité des droits de sa couronne contre tout ce qui peut donner atteinte à son honneur et autorité, afin de réfuter une pièce écrite sans ménagement, se trouverait obligé

---

* Enclosed in a despatch of the Earl of Buckinghamshire to Lord Halifax, 26 March, 1763. (See *Buckinghamshire Corresp.*, Vol. I., p. 197.)

d'y répondre avec ressentiment; mais comme il ne saurait suivre d'autre exemple que celui de ses ancêtres, il ne sçaurait non plus parler directement ou indirectement d'une Puissance qu'avec tout les égards qui lui sont dûs, croyant fermement que sa Majesté Impériale dans tout ce que l'on fait en Courlande en son nom, ait été surprise par des interprétations sinistres, que l'on ait pu donner à la conduite du Roi et de son Ministere et à S.A. R. Mᵍʳ· le Duc de Courlande.,

Le premier article de l'Exposé fournit une preuve évidente que S. M. Impériale n'en a pas été prévenüe; il y est dit, que pour marquer son désir de cultiver l'amitié et le bon voisinage du Roi et de la République de Pologne, S. M. a rendu la liberté à ceux, pour qui le Roi et le Sénat l'avaient demandeé tant de fois sous le règne de l'Impératrice Elisabeth. Cependant il est connu à tout le monde, que ce n'est pas l'Impératrice d'aujourd'hui, qui a rendu la liberté aux Birons, de qui l'on parle, mais. l'Empereur Pierre III. (h) à condition qu'ils renonceraient en forme, comme ils ont fait, à tous leurs prétendus droits sur la Courlande, dans l'intention de se prévaloir de cette renonciation en faveur du Prince George de Holstein, ainsi que cet Empereur l'a fait connaitre . ouvertement, et par tant d'actes, nommément celui du séquestre sur les biens ducaux pour lequel il avait déjà donné ses ordres, et qui, après sa déposition furent révoqués par S. M. l'Impératrice par un effet de sa justice et équité naturelles.

La Cour de Russie conviendra de *cette renonciation faite par les Birons*, (i) et dont on en voit l'aveu dans la lettre de Pierre Biron au Baron Knigge son agent, et que celui-ci a publiée afin de prévenir les Courlandois, que l'acte de renonciation n'existait plus puisque l'Imperatrice l'avait rendu.

On ne s'arrête point ici sur les conséquences que l'on pourrait tirer contre les Birons sur une telle renonciation, la nullité de leur investiture étant démontrée suffisament ailleurs.

Ce qui *est encore plus remarquable* (k) dans ce 1ᶦᵉʳ article, est que l'on prouve l'amitié de l'Impératrice pour la République par l'attention qu'Elle a eu, en montant au trône, de satisfaire aux instances que le Roi et le Sénat ont faites à l'Impératrice défunte pour l'élargissement de Biron; et lors qu'il s'agit de ne point inquiéter le fils du Roi dans la possession de la Courlande, si légitimement acquise par l'investiture solennelle que le Roi lui en a donnée de l'avis du Sénat relativement à la constitution de 1736, l'on fait donner à S. M. Impériale une marque d'amitié pour la République tont à fait contraire à la première; Elle ne peut point consentir que les droits, appartenans au Corps de la République, soient enfreints par une partie de la République, savoir par le Roi et le Sénat (l) et Elle en fait revivre les instances faites sous le règne précédent. Si c'était l'intention de sa Majesté Impériale, elle aurait au moins attendu (m) qu'on lui renouvellât ces instances à Elle-même, et ne s'engagerait point à vouloir faire un plaisir, dont ni le Roi, ni le Sénat la prie, ni la République.

Ces instances ne sont encore point allées au delà des offices que la clémence a fait faire au Roi pour l'élargissement de Biron, *et on ne s'est jamais adressé à la Russie pour le rétablir*. (n)

Cet Exposé fait évidemment retomber tout le tort sur l'Impératrice Elisabeth de glorieuse mémoire, sur son Ministère et sur le Sénat même de Russie (*o*), de n'avoir jamais voulu donner seulement une réponse à tant d'instances, qu'elle avoue aujourd'hui lui avoir été faites consécutivement pendant tant d'années de la part du Roi et du Sénat pour l'élargissement de Biron ; jamais pour telles demandes que l'on ait faites du côté de la Pologne à la Russie, *on n'a pu obtenir la satisfaction qu'elle démentît les prétentions qu'Elle avait au fief, pour tenir ainsi qu'elle faisait la plupart des Terres Ducales en séquestre, et pour en tirer les revenus au profit de son trésor* (*p*).

La seule réponse enfin, qui a été donnée au sujet de ce Duché au Roi et au Sénat, ce fut l'année 1758, que S. M. l'Impératrice Elisabeth, par la voie de son Ministère fit déclarer solennellement, que par toute raison d'état de l'Empire ni Ernest Biron, ni ses enfans ne pourraient à jamais être élargis; que S. M. le Roi pourrait par conséquence conférer ce fief à un autre pour satisfaire à la justice et la continuelle demande des Courlandais d'être conservés sous le Gouvernement d'un Duc, et cette Princesse recommanda elle-même le Prince Royal Charles (*q*) pour être Duc de Courlande, faisant déclarer à Sa Majesté le Roi, qu'il serait chose utile à la République de conférer l'investiture de ce fief à S. A. Royale. Comment croire que les Etats de la République puissent jamais désapprouver une conduite si scrupuleuse de la part du Roi? Comment moins encore de la part de la Russie peut-on reprocher au Roi de l'injustice? *L'Impératrice Anne après la mort du Duc de Courlande Ferdinand sollicita le Roi* (*r*) qu'en vertu du pouvoir que la Constitution de 1736 lui avait donné en cas de mort du dit Duc d'investir un autre de ce Duché, S. M. daignât le conférer à *Jean Ernest Comte* de Biron. Comme la Constitution *n'avait faite aucune mention du dit* Biron (*s*) S. M. convoqua le Sénat, et ce n'est que de son avis qu'elle lui donna l'investiture, tout comme elle a été conférée au Prince Royal Charles, en vertu de la même Constitution; par laquelle on peut encore juger, que l'intention des Etats n'ait pas été exclusive de tout autre cas de vacance, vû que cette loi n'a été portée que pour révoquer le décret de la Commission de l'an 1727, d'incorporation de la Courlande à la Pologne pour être partagée en Palatinats, et pour conserver les Courlandais sous le Gouvernement d'un Duc ainsi qu'il y est exprimé. Par conséquence à cet égard encore on ne pourrait pas objecter le défaut de consentement de toute la République pour l'investiture du Prince Royal (*t*) le fief étant vacant, tant par la nullité de l'investiture de Biron que par sa mort civile ; mais où le consentement de toute la République était expressement requis, c'était pour dispenser Biron de se présenter en personne pour prendre l'investiture ; cependant il n'a été dispensé que par le Roi et le Sénat, (*u*) qui est cette partie de la République contre laquelle l'Exposé se récrie dans l'investiture du Prince Charles, qui cependant s'est présenté en personne pour satisfaire à la loi de toute la République. Biron ainsi investi en la personne de son plénipotentiaire, fut quelques années après par la sentence susmentionnée de l'Empereur Iwan III. portée par le Sénat, privé de l'honneur, de la liberté, de tous ses biens (v) et de ceux qui étaient administrés en son nom appartenants au domaine de la République, et fut confiné au fond de la Siberie. L'Impératrice Elisabeth le rappella à Taroslaw, en faisant connaître de son côté des intentions de le relâcher, S. M. remplie de clémence, pour seconder la bonne volonté de cette Impératrice, interposa ses instances pour le relâchement de ce Prisonnier d'Etat de la Russie; mais enfin son élargissement étant déclaré impossible par raison d'Etat, et en vertu de la sentence, qui avait été portée contre lui et ses fils d'exil perpétuel, n'étant plus à considérer que comme civilement morts, S. M. fut conseillée par le Senat de ne pas abandonner ce fief, mais d'en investir le Prince Royal Charles son fils, et d'adhérer ainsi aux instances que S. M. Impériale de glorieuse mémoire lui faisait (x) en sa faveur. Outre les raisons d'Etat et l'intérêt de la République qui obligeait S. M. d'y consentir, Elle s'y trouva autorisée par la République même par la constitution de 1736, que sur la nullité évidente de l'investiture que Biron avait reçue restait en entier comme si elle n'avait pas encore eu d'effet.

Sans répéter les motifs, qui sont allégués dans l'Exposé et mémoires précédens du Ministère pour prouver la nullité de l'investiture de Biron, celui d'avoir été investi sans être reconnu de la République et de n'avoir point eu son privilège muni du Sceau de la Couronne, suffirait pour la démontrer (y).

Mais quand tout cela ne serait point, quel droit la Russie acquiert-elle par-là sur la Courlande, fief incontestable de la République? Si c'est par droit de voisinage, droit nouveau que cet Exposé introduit, que S. M. Impériale prétendrait disposer de la Courlande, sur les motifs qu'il lui plaisait d'adopter, il n'y a pays, ni cour, qui n'ait des droits sur ses voisins. Le plus grand motif qui est allégué conformément à ce droit de voisinage (z) dans l'Exposé mentionné de la part de S. M. Impériale, se fonde à défendre un Prince voisin opprimé contre la force et l'injustice. Si c'est à Biron que cela se rapporte dès qu'il était innocent, *c'est la Russie qui lui a fait tout le tort et toute l'injustice*, (aa) de n'avoir jamais voulu le relâcher, et de le priver d'honneur, de biens, et de liberté; c'est à elle à le dédommager, mais pas aux dépens d'une autre Puissance, qui n'a eu aucune part à ses malheurs et ne lui a fait que du bien. Si au contraire Biron a été coupable, S. M. Impériale a tout le pouvoir de lui rendre dans son Empire l'honneur et la liberté, mais elle ne prétendra pas, de la façon qui'il a été traité, qu'il puisse être rétabli dans un Duché sans aucune formalité que celle des armes, et que simplement sur la grâce qu'elle lui accorde, le Roi, quoiqu'il le voulût, puisse sacrifier son fils qui est en possession de ce fief par une voye légale, et sans au moins ce consentement de la République en corps, que l'Exposé prétend avait été nécessaire pour lui donner l'investiture. L'honneur de S. A. Royale touche le Roi de trop près, et opprimer le Prince Royal pour soulager Biron, ce ne peut jamais être l'intention de l'Impératrice; car l'innocence du Prince est manifeste par toutes les raisons, qui ont été alléguées. L'honneur du Roi intéresse toute la République, et ce serait exiger qu'elle fût insensible, que de vouloir qu'elle regarde avec indifférence une puissance étrangère disposer d'une manière absoluë d'une Province qui lui appartient (*bb*) et cela par la raison de soutenir ses droits. C'est un malheur pour le Prince Royal Charles, si S.M. Impériale ne voudra pas le reconnaître pour Duc, ainsi qu'il a été reconnu dans les Gouvernmens précédens ; mais c'est un tort qui est *fait à toute la République, d'avoir à son insçu fait séquestrer par les trouppes Impériales tous les revenus du Domaine*, (*cc*) jusqu'à couper à ce Prince feudataire les moyens de subsister. Si S. M. Impériale reconnait la Suzaineté du Roi et de la République sur les Duchés de Courlande et de Semgalle, et qu'en bonne amie et voisine Elle ne veuille en aucune façon empiéter sur les droits dont la République est en possession, on la prie très-instamment de ne rien décider elle-même sur la Courlande, de suspendre les effets de la protection qu'elle accordé à Biron, et de laisser aux états de la République la liberté d'exercer les droits qu'elle leur reconnait de décider. On peut bien s'assurer de l'équité et délicatesse de sa Majesté le Roi, que quoique convaincuë de la validité et justice de ses démarches, loin de décliner la Diète, elle ne manquera pas de la convoquer le plûtôt qu'il lui sera possible, et d'informer les Etats tant des intentions de S.M.I. que des motifs qu'Elle a de s'intéresser pour le Comte Biron, comme si on lui avait fait de l'injustice en donnant l'investiture de la Courlande au Prince Royal de Pologne. La fidélité que les Etats doivent à leur Chef est inséparable de celle qu'ils doivent aux loix ; et le parti qui dans cette affaire de Courlande a jusqu'ici suscité des oppositions au Roi, aura toute la liberté d'y étaler ses argumens. S. M. Impériale par la constante intention qu'elle déclare avoir de ne donner aucune atteinte au bon voisinage et de prouver son amitié à la République, voudra bien en attendant retirer ses trouppes de la Courlande, conformément à l'article du Traité de perpétuelle Alliance, qui stipule à l'égard de la Russie *nullum in Curlandiam et Semigalliam jus sibi assumeret, nec bello eas infestaret ullave ratione vexaret* (*dd*), et voudra bien aussi recevoir en bonne amie et voisine les représentations, qui lui seront faites par ordre de S. M. par une personne distinguée* qu'elle lui envoie à ce sujet. S.M. Impériale sera convaincue que l'on n'a jamais disputé à Biron la possession de ses terres allodiales ; que S. A. Royale Mgr. le Duc de Courlande n'a pas seulement été dans le cas de pouvoir refuser des quartiers d'hiver aux trouppes Russes comme on lui a objecté ; que S. M. le Roi, le Prince Royal son fils, le Ministère et toute la Nation n'ont et n'auront rien de plus à cœur que de cultiver son amitié.

  F. Bielinski, G.M.

  M. Wodziecki, Evêque de Przemysl, Chancelier de la Couronne.

  T. Wessel, G.T. de la Couronne.

  Gl. de Mniszeck.

---

  * M. de Boroh.

(4) Réponse de S. E. Monseigneur le Comte de Keyserling, Ambassadeur de Russie à la lettre de S. E. le Vice-Chancelier de la Couronne accompagnée de la réponse à l'exposé du premier, en date du 4 Janvier, 1763.

1763, Jan. 10. Warsaw.—Il était superflu de mettre mon nom ou une datte à l'Exposé des motifs, puisqu'il était accompagné d'une lettre où il y avait l'une et l'autre. Ce n'était donc pas un écrit anonyme, ni fait dans l'intention de traiter cette affaire ministérialement, mais seulement pour prévenir les fausses insinuations qu'on a débitées tant ici que dans d'autres endroits, comme si la Russie avait dessein d'arracher les duchés de Courlande et de Semgalle à la République, et de se les approprier. C'a été dans cette vue qu'on a donné l'Exposé susdit, pour désabuser le Public et en donner part aux Sénateurs et aux Ministres de cette République. Mais comme dans la Réponse à cet Exposé, que V.É. m'a envoyée ce matin, il se trouve un nom qu'un Ambassadeur de Russie ne sçaurait reconnaître, et qu'il y est insinué que je devrais être désavoué au sujet du sus-dit Exposé, je déclare à V. E. ne pouvoir me charger d'envoyer à ma Cour une pièce conçue en termes si peu analogues aux égards qui lui sont düs, mais j'en garderai l'original pour servir de preuve en tems et lieu, etc. . .

(5) Réponse du Vice Chancelier de la Couronne à ce Billet du Comte de Keyserling.

1763, Jan. 12.—A cause de l'incommodité que me tient au lit je n'ai pas été en état de répondre plutôt à la lettre de V. E. que j'ai reçue le 11 de ce mois. Elle m'y apprend que dans la réponse que je lui ai envoyée ministérialement il y a un nom qu'un Ambassadeur de Russie ne sçaurait reconnaitre et qu'elle ne peut point se charger de l'envoyer à sa Cour. Comme l'intention du Ministère n'a été que d'alléguer historiquement tous les faits, motifs et raisons qui pouvaient servir à la justification de S. M. le Roi mon très gracieux Maitre, et à persuader la Cour de Russie, je prie V. E. de faire sousligner les noms qu'elle ne peut pas accepter et de me renvoyer la pièce. J'en conférerai avec mes collègues et elle sera convaincue de nos véritables sentiments de ne nous éloigner en rien des égards qui sont dus à un Ambassadeur et à sa Cour.

(6) Remarks⁰ upon the foregoing Réponse made by the Russian Minister for the use of the Empress Catherine II.

N.D. [1763].—(a) Si le fief de Courlande comme on le dit, a vaqué depuis l'an 1741, jusqu'à 1758, pourquoi a-t-on réclamé, l'an 1750, le Duc Ernest Jean comme Prince feudatoire de la

---

* Enclosed in a despatch of Ld. Buckinghamshire to Ld. Halifax, 26 Mar., 1763. The letters mark the corresponding paragraphs in the *Réponse*, see p. 200, which the Remarks profess to criticize.

République? Pourquoi n'a-t-il été que l'an 1758, qu'on a déclaré vacans ces fiefs? Il est notoire, que le dernier Duc Ferdinand de la maison de Kettler est mort l'année 1737. Si donc les fiefs de Courlande et de Semgalle n'ont vaqué que depuis 1737, jusqu'à 1741, ils n'ont pas vaqué. Le Duc Ernest Jean a donc été dans cet intervalle le Prince f udatoire de la République et Duc légitime de Courlande.

(b) Le rescript du Roi au Comte Lénard du 23 Septembre 1734 ; la lettre du Comte de Bruhl du 10 février 1736 ; les lettres du Roi, datées de Varsovie le 22 février 1736 et le 25 janvier 1737, démontrent assez évidemment que Jean Ernest ne devint pas Duc de Courlande par la puissante recommendation de l'Impératrice Anne de glorieuse mémoire, mais qu'il le devint par les offres que lui fit de ces Duchés la Cour de Pologne de son propre mouvement et par reconnoissance. Les originaux de ces lettres se trouvent entre les mains du Duc Ernest Jean. (c) On n'a jamais regardé comme crime de félonie l'engagement d'un vassal de servir un Prince Etranger. Le Roi et la République de Pologne n'ont jamais exigé que le nouveau Duc quittât les emplois, dont il étoit alors revêtu à la Cour Impériale de Russie. Bien loin de là on a été très-persuadé, qu'il y allait de l'intérêt du Roi et de la République de maintenir par sa présence la bonne amitié et le bon voisinage entre la Russie et la Pologne, si bien que le Roi même l'a félicité sur son avénement à la régence et a par cela même approuvé alors, ce qu'on prétend faire passer maintenant pour un crime de félonie.

(d) Il est bien surprenant que les quatre Ministres sous-signés se rapportent à un arrêt d'un Empereur de Russie, le nom duquel n'est pas reconnu, mais aboli, dans l'Empire de Russie, comme les manifestes de l'Impératrice Elisabeth de glorieuse mémoire le fait voir.

(e) Comme on n'a pas marqué les prétenduës expressions peu ménagées, qui doivent se trouver dans l'Exposé des motifs, il n'y a rien à dire là-dessus.

(f) Il était superflu de mettre le nom de l'Ambassadeur ou la date dans l'Exposé des motifs, puisqu'il était accompagné d'une lettre, où il y avait l'un et l'autre.

(g) Il est étrange de supposer que votre Majesté Impériale désavouera, non seulement ce qu'elle a ordonné, mais aussi ce qui s'est fait par son Ambassadeur puisqu'on prétend que tout se soit fait par surprise.

(h) Ce n'est pas l'Empereur Pierre III. mais l'Impératrice Catherine II. qui fait sortir librement hors de son Empire le Duc Ernest Jean et ses enfans. En verité! Cette circonstance n'entre pas dans les raisons de l'affaire en question.

(i) Cette prétenduë renonciation n'est jamais parvenuë à sa perfection ; supposé qu'elle eût été, elle n'aurait pas eu plus d'effet, que cet acte de renonciation, que le Roi de France, François Ier fut forcé de donner pendant sa captivité à Charles Quint, puisque ces sortes d'actes, extorqués par force, sont invalides et juridiquement nuls.

(k) L'amitié, que votre Majesté Impériale porte au Roi et à la République, se fait assez connáître en ce qu'elle souhaite que les prétendus droits du Prince Charles soient aussi bien fondés que ceux du Duc Ernest Jean; alors, elle serait charmée de faire pour le fils du Roi ce qu'elle fait pour le dernier, selon le beau commencement de la réponse à l'Exposé, que ' la justice est la base et le fondement des trônes des Souverains.'

(l) L'Exposé des motifs ne parle que d'une partie de la République, et non pas du Roi. Pourquoi donc faire une interpolation? N'est-ce pas le droit de s'expliquer, qui appartienne à un auteur?

(m) Si votre Majesté Impériale eût dû attendre jusqu'à ce que le Roi et le Sénat se fussent ïntéressés pour le Duc Ernest Jean, Votre Majesté l'aurait attendu en vain. Mais c'est la magnanimité et la justice qui font agir Votre Majesté pour des innocens et des opprimés.

(n) Il n'est pas dit dans l'Exposé des motifs, que le Roi et le Sénat de Pologne se soient adressés à la Russie pour relâcher le Duc Ernest Jean. Mais les propres mots en sont : " Que Votre " Majesté *Impériale a voulu rendre la liberté à ceux*, pour qui le " Roi et le Sénat l'avaient demandée tant de fois et si instamment sous le règne de l'Impératrice Elisabeth."

(o) Avec quelle justice et quelle vérité peut-on dire que l'Exposé des motifs fasse evidemment retomber tout le tort sur l'Impératrice Elisabeth de glorieuse mémoire, sur son Ministère et sur le Sénat même de Russie? Est-ce que ce tort s'ensuivrait de ce qu'on a dit des raisons d'Etat? Qui est assez peu savant pour ignorer que les raisons d'état se changent du vivant même des Souverains? Mais qui est-ce qui ne voit pas, encore plus évidemment, l'esprit de malignité caché, et qui ne tend qu'à faire révolter l'ancien mais pourtant fidèle Ministère contre la volonté de sa très gracieuse Souveraine?

(p) Mais c'est effectivement faire tort au souvenir de feuë l'Imperatrice Elisabeth de glorieuse mémoire, que de dire jamais on n'a pu obtenir "la satisfaction, qu'elle démentit les prétensions "qu'elle avait au fief, pour tenir, ainsi qu'elle faisait, la plupart "des terres Ducales en séquestre et pour en tirer les revenus au "profit de son trésor."

(q) Quoique feuë l'Impératrice Elisabeth de glorieuse mémoire a voulu beaucoup de bien au Prince Royal Charles, néanmoins le Grand Chancelier Comte Woronzow a fait connaître par ordre de Sa Souveraine, du mois de juin 1758 en réponse à la lettre du Roi du 15 Mai 1758 que, si pendant les conjonctures si délicates et guerrières alors, la matière de l'élection d'un nouveau Duc de Courlande fut mise sur le tapis, elle ne servirait qu'à donner occasion à des plus grands désordres, à des raisonnemens sinistres et à des soupçons dans la République même. Que l'exécution de ce dessein était un ouvrage, qui demande absolument la concurrence du Roi, aussi bien que celle de tous les Alliés. Que la négociation de la Paix future en pourrait fournir la matière désirée, d'autant plus qu'il n'est pas à douter, que les autres Puissances, qui y sont intéressées, ne

s'efforcent, à l'example de l'Impératrice, à contribuer officieuse-
ment á tout ce qui pourrait aboutir au contentement de
S. M. Polonaise et au bien de sa maison Royale. Par là, on voit
clairement que feüe l'Impératrice Elisabeth a été recherchée par
la Cour de Pologne, et qu'elle n'a pas voulu précipiter l'élection
d'un nouveau Duc.

(r) La fausseté, comme si l'Impératrice Anne eût sollicité après
la mort du Duc Ferdinand de donner ces Duchés en fief au Duc
Ernest Jean est démontrée par les quatre lettres, qu'on a déjà
alléguées *sub-littera*.

(s) Il est vrai, que la constitution de l'année 1736 n'exprime
pas explicitement le nom du Duc Ernest Jean, mais néanmoins
il y est nommé implicitement ; car la dite Constitution ordonne,
qu'après la mort de Ferdinand et l'extinction de la tige de Kettler,
ces fiefs soient conférés à un autre. Qui était donc cet autre ?
n'était ce pas le Duc Ernest Jean, à qui l'on a donné ces fiefs
more solito, selon l'ordonnance de cette loi publique ? Ou, en
voulant appliquer cette loi au Prince Royal Charles, il faudrait
soutenir que le Duc Ferdinand est mort deux fois, puisque la
Constitution de l'année 1736 ne parle que d'un seul cas de
vacance du fief ; qui est, qu'après l'extinction de la branche de
Kettler ce fief de Courlande soit donné à un autre, ce qui
s'exécuta en le conférant légalement au Duc Ernest Jean.

(t) Voilà un argument bien concluant ! La constitution de
1736 dit, de conserver les Courlandais sous le Gouvernment
d'une Duc ; et de là on conclut, qu'on peut disposer de ces fiefs
dans tous les cas sans le consentement ultérieur de la République,
de façon qu'on peut le prendre et le donner selon son bon
plaisir, quoique le Roi ait expressement promis dans le 58ème des
Pacta Conventa, qu'il emploïerait ses soins relativement à la
Courlande, conjointement avec la République, sans déroger aux
anciens droits de la Noblesse et des villes de ce Duché.

(u) La constitution de l'année 1683 dit, que la permission
accordée an Duc Fréderic Casimir de prêter hommage par des
plénipotentiaires ne servirait point d'exemple à l'avenir mais
cette constitution ne dit pas, que les Rois avec le Sénat n'en
puissent dispenser un Prince feudatoire par des raisons légales.
Posons qu'il y ait un manquement en ce que le Duc Ernest Jean
n'a pas prêté hommage en personne, à qui en attribuer la
faute ? Est-ce au Roi avec le Sénat, ou est-ce au Prince
feudatoire à veiller aux loix ? Tout ce qui en résulterait, ne
serait point de le priver des fiefs, mais au plus, de l'obliger à
venir prêter hommage en personne.

(v) Comment peut-on se rapporter à une sentence d'un
Empereur qui n'est pas connu parmi le nombre des Empereurs
de Russie, comme tout le monde le sait, par les manifestes
publiés de feuë l'Impératrice Elisabeth de glorieuse mémoire ?
N'est-ce pas sortir des égards qu'on doit à la branche régnante
de Pierre le Grand ?

(x) La fausseté de ce qu'on avance se fait voir par la lettre du
Grand Chancelier, Comte Woronzow, laquelle on a citée *sub
littera*. (q)

(*y*) La hardiesse d'une allégation aussi fausse est presqu' incroyable, puisque l'inspection seule des Actes de la République même fait voir, que non seulement le Sceau de la Couronne équivale à celui de la Lithuanie, mais même le Grand Sceau, appellé *Sigillum Magistaticum* par excellence a été apposé au Diplôme d'investiture du Duc Ernest Jean.

(*z*) Le droit de voisinage est fondé dans le droit de la nature et des gens, et si reconnu de tout tems dans le monde, qu'il serait superflu d'alléguer la foule d'exemples qui prouvent cette vérité. N'était-ce pas par ce droit de voisinage que la Russie soutint le Roi aujourdhui régnant sur le Trône de Pologne?

(*aa*) Si l'on a fait quelque tort au Duc Ernest Jean en Russie, elle tâche de le redresser. Il sera bon de suivre cet exemple.

(*bb*) Sa Majesté Impériale ne disposera aucunement du Duché de Courlande, mais Elle soutient seulement ce qui a été disposé de ce fiéf par la République entière.

(*cc*) Si le séquestre qu'on avait mis dans le tems passé sur les domaines en Courlande à l'insçu de la République; n'a pas été regardé comme un tort fait à la République, on ne s'attendait pas à l'explication, qu'on en a faite, d'autant moins que ce séquestre ne se fit pas pour faire tort à la République, mais pour soutenir le droit de toute la République.

(*dd*) Il n'y a point de traité ni article, où il se trouve ces mots: " Russia nullum in Courlandiam et Semigalliam jus sibi assumeret, nec bello eas infestaret, nullave ratione vexaret." Ce Traité de perpétuelle Alliance fut conclu l'année 1686. Dans ce tems-là la Livonie était dans la possession des Suédois, et par conséquence les Duchés de Courlande et Semigalle étaient voisins de la Suède et non pas de la Russie. Et alors il n'y avait ni lieu, ni raison de faire entrer la Courlande dans un Traité, que l'on faisait avec la Russie, on n'a qu'à lire le dit Traité de 1686. On n'y trouvera pas un mot de ce prétendu passage, ni en langue Russe, ni en Polonais et encore moins en Latin.

Thomas Wroughton[*] to the Earl of Buckinghamshire.

1764, May 9. Warsaw.—I have just time to inform you that our Diet assembled on Monday last; General Mokronoffsky delivered a manifest on the part of himself, several Senators and Nonces against the validity of the Diet, which had very near cost him his life; for several Arbiters endeavoured to massacre him, and would have effected it, without the immediate interposition of Prince Adam[†] and others of his friends. This alarm and confusion being over, the Chamber proceeded to the election of their Marshal, Prince Adam was unanimously chosen. Yesterday in the afternoon, the Great General,[‡] Prince Radzivil, the Palatin of Kiovia, and several others left the town; it is said that they will make a Confederation in the neighbourhood of Cracow, to be near at hand to receive support from Austria and Saxony; twenty-two

---

* British Envoy at Dresden and afterwards at Warsaw.
† Czartoryski. ‡ Branitzki or Branicki.

O

Senators and forty-nine Nonces have signed the Manifest, the major part of the Nonces are of contested elections.

The Bishop of Cracow has declared against the family,[*] and making a Manifest against the violence in the Chamber of Nonces and the precautions taken by the family of placing Guards in the streets about the Castle, leaves the town immediately and will probably carry off some friends from the family.

The Prussian Ambassador is arrived here.

NOTE on the part of the RUSSIAN GOVERNMENT in reply to that of M. DE BORCH.[†]

[1763,] April 4. Fait à Moscou.—Toute l'Europe voit et sans doute avec étonnement que la Cour de Saxe,après avoir formé un établissement des Duchés de Courland et de Semigalle pour un Prince de sa maison au mépris des droits d'un Duc auquel ils avaient été légitimement conférés de l'authorité des trois ordres de la République, ne se refuse à aucun moyen possible pour faire valoir une telle disposition toute illégale qu'elle est.

Loin de se rendre aux premières instances que S.M.I., sollicitée par son humanité et sa justice, s'était portée à lui faire en faveur d'un Prince malheureux et injustement dépouillé, sa réponse ne portait rien moins que l'anéantissement de tous les droits de la famille du Duc Jean Ernest en même tems qu'elle réclamait le droit de les juger. Ses démarches ultérieures, toujours guidées par la même partialité n'étaient dirigées qu'à forcer S.M.I. à abandonner un Prince qui n'a d'autre ressource que sa protection à qui elle est accordée et dont sa dignité l'engage à soutenir la juste cause.

Tel fut le dessein de la mission du Chambellan de Livonie S[r.] de Borch, et quoique S.M.I. ne pût l'ignorer elle ne voulut point luy refuser l'audience, persuadée qu'elle se devait à elle-même de convaincre le Roy de Pologne ainsi que les autres puissances que tout ce que S.M.I. faisait, elle n'y était déterminée par aucun autre motif que par celui de la plus exacte équité. Il présenta à l'Impératrice une lettre particulière du Roy qui ne portait aucun caractère et le recommandait seulement pour l'affaire de Courlande. Aux réprésentations qu'il fit sur cette affaire ainsi qu'il en était chargé, le Ministère eut ordre de luy communiquer la réponse de S.M.I. qui était telle qu'on ne pouvait manquer d'y reconnaître aussi évidemment la droiture de ses démarches et sa fermeté à les soutenir. Sans y avoir égard il revint à de nouvelles instances et les appuya avec un ton qui peut-être ne tenait que de l'entêtement mais dans le fait paraissait fort peu éloigné de celuy des menaces.

Il eut été contraire à la dignité de l'Impératrice d'y paraître indifférente, mais elle se contenta de faire déclarer une fois pour toutes au Chambellan de Borch qu'elle ne varierait point dans

---

[*] The Czartoryski.
[†] Jean de Borck or Borch, the informal envoy from Augustus III., sent to Catherine II. to represent the Polish view of the Courland question,

sa résolution qu'elle lui avait déjà fait communiquer que l'étant la dernière réponse qu'il avait à attendre elle luy fit indiquer un jour pour prendre congé.

Ce fut alors que le S^r· de Borch s'annonçait comme un homme revêtu du caractère d'envoyé du Roy de Pologne, prétendit qu'il ne pouvait prendre congé sans lettre de rappel, comme si celle dont il avait été porteur, qui n'était qu'une simple lettre particulière qui ne demandait de même qu'une simple réponse, avait été d'une nature et d'une forme à en avoir besoin.

Sans s'arrêter à cette fausse prétention S.M.I. ordonna à son Ministère de luy remettre sa lettre pour le Roy, de lui déclarer que sa mission était finie comme de fait elle l'était. Le Chambellan de Borch après l'avoir reçue, s'arrêta toujours icy, continua à vouloir faire le Ministre et quoiqu' averti qu'on ne l'écouterait plus, il n'en continua pas moins ses importunités soit par un zèle outré et mal entendu ou plutôt pour obéir à ses instructions qui tendaient visiblement à braver S.M.I. dans sa Cour.

De tels démarches pour forcer S.M.I. à rétracter une résolution qu'elle avait fait connaître si clairement, une conduite si opiniâtre et si inconséquente de la part d'une personne, qui n'avait aucun caractère et en affichait un ouvertement dans cette Résidence blessaient trop S.M.I. pour être souffertes plus longtems et elle ordonna à Son Ministère de signifier au Sr de Borch de partir dans deux fois 24 heures. Il y consentit mais ne voulant rien rabattre de ses premières prétentions de Ministre, dont il s'était entêté il voulut faire valoir la nouvelle qu'il avait reçue qu'un *Senatus Concilium* avait autorisé le Roy de Pologne à l'accréditer au nom de la République auprès de cette Cour, et il soutint qu'en se rendant à l'insinuation qui lui était faite de partir, il ne pouvait le faire que comme envoyé de la part du Roy et de la République. En vain lui a-t-on fait voir le néant d'une pareille prétention, en lui démontrant que sans lettre de créance, il n'y a point de caractère, que non seulement il ne luy en a point été envoyé, mais encore qu'il ne pourra luy en arriver de longtems jusqu'à l'arrangement pour le titre Impérial, non seulement il est parti dans cette idée, mais encore on apprend avec étonnement qu'il a envoyé à tous les ministres étrangers résidents ici, une note en forme de protestation rélative à son départ de cette Cour, où il se qualifie d'envoyé du Roy et de la République de Pologne.

Quoique l'Impératrice ne fasse nul doute qu'une pareille pièce ne soit appréciée comme elle le mérite, cependant pour détruire jusqu'aux moindres impressions qu'elle ne pourrait faire, S.M.I. a ordonné de communiquer à M.M. les Ambassadeurs et Ministres étrangers résidents à Sa Cour toutes les circonstances cy-dessus rélatives au départ du Sr Borch et les raisons qui le rendaient indispensable.

Ils y verront clairement le peu de solidité et l'inutilité de la Note du dit Chambellan qui s'arroge un titre qu'il n'a pas, qui réclame des droits qui ne sont pas faits pour luy et ne plaint que d'avoir eu ce que sa conduite et les instructions qui la dirigeaient luy ont mérité. Il sera aisé d'y reconnaitre que ce que S.M.I. a fait elle aurait été forcée de le faire même contre un Ministre accrédité, puisque le droit des gens ne peut s'étendre jusqu'à forcer un souverain à se voir offensé et bravé dans sa propre cour qu'à plus forte raison, ce qui a été fait vis à vis du Chambellan de Borch, qui ayant fini sa commission, ayant reçu sa réponse à une lettre que ne luy donnait aucun titre, s'obstinait à rester à Moscou, et n'y étant que comme particulier n'en continuait pas moins à faire le Ministre et à vouloir se communiquer avec le Ministére Impérial comme telle, contre les intentions et la volonté de S.M.—a été juste, tout à fait naturel et dans l'ordre.

Sa Majesté sera bien aise à cette occasion que les Cours étrangères voyent par les faits même, par la conduite du S^r. de Borch en Russié, par son obstination à vouloir être regardé comme ayant un caractère, enfin par sa prétention à vouloir qu'on le croye renvoyé de la Cour de Russie comme envoyé de la part de la République de Pologne, tandis qu'il ne l'est que comme un particulier qui a fini une Commission, à laquelle la République n'a jamais eu aucune part. Combien on cherche à faire illusion à la Pologne et à échauffer les esprits, au préjudice de la bonne union qui subsiste et doit subsister entre l'Empire de Russie et la République ; au lieu que tous les soins que Sa Majesté s'est donnés depuis le commencement de cette affaire, n'ont eu d'autre objet que de ne pas confondre une chose personelle à la Maison Royale de Pologne, avec ce qui concerne la République et qu'en soutenant les droits incontestables du Duc Ernest Jean sur les Duchés de Courlande, elle n'a fait que soutenir les droits mêmes de la République et a porté on ne pouvait plus loin la délicatesse et l'attention à aller au devant de tout ce qui pourrait faire naître des démêlés avec un état voisin, dont elle estime l'amitié et qu'elle est jalouse d'assurer de la sienne.

Thomas Wroughton to the Earl of Buckinghamshire. *

1763, July 16. Dresden.—They are busy here about the regulation of their army, which in four years is to be raised to 30,000 men. The difficulty is the settling a proper fund for the payment of it, which cannot be done but by the States assembled. The Diet is to commence the beginning of next month. I need not tell you that if an accident happens to the Count° it will produce as great a Revolution as the death of a monarch in an absolute country.

Lady Stormont has been here some weeks waiting for her husband, whose departure from London does not seem fixed.

Thomas Wroughton to the Same.

1763, Sept. 10. Dresden.—The entry of the Russian troops in Lithuania has filled us with the greatest apprehensions, but we have received per the last post from Warsaw the agreeable news of a pacification being made between the Russian

---

* Henri Comte de Bruhl.

Ambassador and the Primate of the Republic, by which means the Russians are to return to their own Country, and two very material points are gained by the family of Czartoryski.

It certainly gives me great pleasure that my friend Osten[*] has met with so gracious a reception, I thank your Lordship for this agreeable intelligence, and dare present my compliments to him thro' your Lordship's Channel.

Count Bruhl is in the most miserable situation a man can possibly be in, the Physician declaring it to be out of his power of saving him, that he may live some weeks or even months in this terrible anguish. He is one moment dying, and the next so much better as to write. He is visible only to his family, and his illness puts an entire interruption to all manner of business.

PROTOCOLLE DES CONFERENCES TENUES DANS LE PALAIS DU PRIMAT LE —— D'AOÛT.

N.D. [1763.]—(This relates to the proceedings which led to the pacification mentioned in Mr. Wroughton's of the 10th September, 1763, by which the Russian Ambassador agreed to the withdrawal of the Russian troops from Lithuania.) "Sachant le cas que sa très gracieuse souveraine fait de l'amitié et de la conservation de la tranquillité de la République."

(In return for which grace the Ambassador demands:—)

"1ème. Que le Prince Radziwil et le Tribunal de Wilna n'accablent ni poursuivent de décrets et de *Condemnatis* les amis de la Russie et ceux qui ont été contraires au dit tribunal.

2do. Que les Décrets et *Condemnata* dont l'exécution a été remise *ad tempus bene visum* n'aient point lieu. Par rapport au Tribunal de Petrikau il est notoire que c'est un Tribunal qui est uniquement du ressort de la Noblesse. C'est pour quoi il est juste qu'on lui laisse les mains libres, afin qu'elle puisse élire sans aucune contrainte les Députés et laisser juger à ceux à qui il appartient, de la légalité de l'élection et des Députés élus. Pour cet effet il est à propos qu'on éloigne toutes les trouppes du lieu du Tribunal et qu'on n'y envoye que le nombre accoutumé pour la garde." . . .

(A commission is also to be constituted of Polish and Russian representatives) "pour le réglement et la bonification des dommages causés par les trouppes Russes dans le Pays." . . .

En suite de quoi on a expédié des exemplaires signés de part et d'autre.—"Le 12. d'Août, Wolodkowicz a attaqué le logis du Sieur Sielicki, gentilhomme du Palatinat de Polock, Régent de la Chancellerie du Prince Czartoryski, a sabré plusieurs de ses gens et, entre autres, a emporté d'un coup le crâne d'un de ses gens. Le lendemain, Sielicki voulant porter plainte au Tribunal de cette violente attaque de son logis, à laquelle il n'avait donné aucune occasion que celle d'être ami de la maison Czartoryski, ne put trouver aucun avocat qui osa seulement plaider pour lui, tous disant qu'ils sçavaient combien il est dangereux d'être contre

---

* Adolf Siegfried von der Osten, Danish Envoy to Russia.

Wolodkowicz d'aucune façon. Sielicki fut donc forcé d'aller porter de ses propres mains le crâne sanglant de son domestique au Tribunal, qui le condemna encore à une amende en faveur de Wolodkowicz.

Le Sieur Piszezala, gentilhomme du Palatinat de Minsk, avait depuis plusieurs anneés une dispute de frontière avec le fameux Wolodkowicz. Celui-ci auquel le témoignage de plusieurs paysans, appelés comme témoins en justice, ne lui avait pas été favorable, les a enterrés tous vifs, a mis les corps dans un bois où leurs cris ont enfin attiré des gens à leurs secours. En suite par la protection armée de Radziwil, il a toujours empêché Piszezala de se mettre en possession de ce que plusieurs décrets de plusieurs Tribunaux consécutifs lui avaient adjugé. Enfin il avait épié un moment où Wolodkowicz, plus occupé ailleurs veillait moins sur cette terre et il s'y introduisait de bon droit, prouvé et confirmé par décrets. Peu après il est allé à Wilna pour y veiller à ce que dans ce Tribunal, favorable aux Haydenues (sic), Wolodkowicz ne regagna quelques avantages juridiques sur lui. Le 18 d'Août il soupait tranquillement dans son logis lorsqu'un coup de pistolet chargé de deux balles tiré de la rue lui a percé la poitrine et l'a tué raide mort.''

(Here follow accounts of other similar outrages and miscarriages of justice.)

''Voilà le Tribunal* dont il s'agit d'arrêter et contenir l'iniquité. . . . Or comme il est naturel que tous ceux qui ont signé les manifestes par les quels on ne reconnait pas ce Tribunal pour valide, refusent d'y plaider et se laissent contumacer, cela produira autant de bons patriotes appauvris, autant de richesses d'ajoutés à celles que les Radziviliens possèdent, mais ce qu'il y aura de pire c'est autant de prétextes de violences les plus sanglantes et de meurtres atroces, tous exercés contre des gens qui composaient le parti Russe.

Si du premier coup d'oeil on est étonné qu'une trouppe de Brigands puisse devenir terrible à tout un pays, on le sera moins en réfléchissant à l'enchaînement par lequel le moindre valet d'un Wolodkowicz par exemple, tel crime qu'il commette, est soutenu par son maître; celui-ci par le Tribunal de Lithuanie et le Palatin de Wilna; et ceux-ci par la faveur et l'approbation de la Cour, de façon qu'on se trouve seulement à quatre degrés depuis le malfaiteur le plus obscur, jusqu'à la Majesté du trône.''

From Stanislas Poniatowski to S. A. S. Mgr. le Duc Regnant de Courland and Semigalle.†

N.Y. [1764] A Varsovie, Mai le 31.—J'ai différé à dessein la réponse que je devais à la lettre dont V. A. S. m'a honoré le 7 du courant, pour avoir le tems de vous prouver par des souhaits la part que je prend à vos intérêts. Enfin grâce au ciel votre juste cause a triomphé. Hier les états de la République assemblés à cette Diète de Convocation ont reconnu pour nuls et invalides

---

* Of Wilna.
† John Ernest de Biren.

touts les actes qui étaient contraires à V. A. S. et ils confirment les droits incontestables que vous et vos descendants mâles ont aux Duchés de Courlande et Semgalle.

Je me trouve trop heureux d'avoir pu contribuer avec un zèle aussi véritable qu'heureux aux succès de vos désirs. (*Holograph.*)

Bil° concernant le Duc et le Duché de Courland.

N.D. [1764.]—La Constitution de 1607, Art. 20, sous le titre Curatelle a expressément défendu que sans le consentement de la Diète, le Roi ne dispose en aucune manière des Duchés appartenants à la République. Ce qui fut stipulé nommément pour les Duchés de Courlande et de Semigalle dans les *Pacta Conventa* d'Auguste III de glorieuse mémoire afin qu'il employât ses soins avec la République, elle donna peu de tems après à la Diète de Pacification de 1736 par une Constitution portée le pouvoir au feu roi Auguste III de disposer en faveur d'un autre des Duchés au décès du Prince Ferdinand pour lors en vie et de la famille de Kettler éteinte en sa personne. En vertu de cette Constitution Ernest Jean Comte de Biron obtint en fief pour lui et ses descendants mâles les Duchés de Courlande et de Semigalle, que les arrangements féodals, suivant la dite Constitution, devancèrent. C'est pour quoi nous conservons et maintenons le Duc Ernest Jean et sa lignée mâle dans ce droit et la possession du fief obtenu légitimement ainsi que la Noblesse de Courlande et de Semigalle dans ses droits, priviléges, pacte de sujettion et dans sa forme de gouvernement sauves les conditions auxquelles le Duc doit satisfaire, marqueés dans la Commission. Or comme en 1739 le Duc Ernest Jean ne prêta point hommage en personne mais bien par un Pleni-potentiaire contre la Constitution expresse de 1683, pour réparer en ce qu'il fut manqué à la loi et lui rendre sa première vigueur, statuons: que ce Duc en personne si la santé et l'âge peuvent lui permettre, ou son fils ainé devant succéder au Duché vienne rendre hommage à la fois pour lui et son Peré au futur Roi et à la Republique. De plus nous entendons que le Duc moderne Ernest Jean et ses descendants régnants, n'accepte aucun service étranger et que les Duchés de Courlande et Semigalle après que la branche masculine du Duc actuel Ernest Jean serait éteinte, retournent à la libre disposition de la République. Nous voulons que la Commission qui regarde les arrangements avec le Duc Ernest Jean vu la Constitution de 1736, effectuée le 12 Nov. 1737, à Danzig, soit insérée dans les Constitutions de la Diète présente.

Quant aux dispositions faites et le diplôme délivré, de même que sous les autres actes qui s'ensuivirent à l'insçu de l'Ordre Equestre et sans le consentement d'une Diète, uniquement par les derniers Résultats du Conseil des Sénateurs, comme elles sont contraires aux Loix et conséquemment invalides, déclarons :—Qu'elles ne sauraient causer aucun préjudice et obstacle au Duc Ernest Jean et à ses descendants mâles.

---

* Of the Polish Diet. (See *Buckinghamshire Correspondence*, Vol. II., p. 186.)

En outre, par l'autorité de la République nous enjoignons aux habitants de Courlande de telle condition qu'ils soient, d'être selon les loix des Duchés, fidèles et soumis en tout à leur légitime Duc Ernest Jean.

Comme il y a toute sorte de plaintes de la part des palatinats et districts du Duché de Lithuanie et de la Livonie même à l'égard des frontières, des frays onéreux, des douanes, des difficultés d'obtenir la justice et d'autres circonstances, nous aurons soin que le Roi futur expédie une commission à cet effet.

THOMAS WROUGHTON to the EARL OF BUCKINGHAMSHIRE.

1764, June 10. Warsaw.—I send your Lordship now two different relations of a scene that has passed between the Primate and the French Ambassador on the latter's waiting on him and informing him of the orders of his Court to quit this place ; the Ambassador has not delivered his ministerially, but I have received it from a third hand, and believe it to be as he relates it ; this story makes a great deal of noise here, and will probably make more in France, where the Primate dispatched yesterday a courier with the "exposé," and a letter to his Most Chn Majesty.

M. de Paulmy went from hence the day before yesterday, and it has been reported that he would soon be followed by the Imperial Ambassador, tho' I cannot learn from any word dropt from His Excellency, that he has as yet any such orders from his Court. I think this quarrel had better been avoided, as I do not see any good that can accrue from it in whatever point of view we regard it ; as to every thing else we remain in great tranquillity ; the great General is at a little town called "Sambour," and has already offered to capitulate, tho' upon conditions that have been judged unacceptable. We do not know if the corps that is sent after and is very near him, will think proper to attack him, or seeing the necessity to which he is drove, may not rather choose to make use of milder means and give him time to let his small army accede to the authority of the Prince Régimentaire.

The Diet will continue their session until the latter end of next week, when we expect a General Confederation of the King-dom of Poland, as there is already of the major part of the Dutchy of Lithuania.

RELATION de ce qui s'est passé chez le PRIMAT[a] le jeudi 7 Juni.

[1764.]—M. l'Ambassadeur s'est rendu chez le Primat avec le Sieur Hennin, Résident, vers les onze heures et demie. Il y a trouvé grand nombre des personnes, et entre autres le Prince Czartoryski, Palatin de Russie. Le Prince Primat sous prétexte d'incommodité n'a pas voulu s'asseoir et a demandé à M. l'Ambassadeur s'il avait quelque-chose à lui déclarer, ajoutant que

---

[a] Prince Ladislaus Lubienski, Archbishop of Gnesen and Primate of Poland.

S.E. pouvait dire ce qu'elle avait à dire ; M. l'Ambassadeur lui a
dit à voix basse qu'il venait lui faire part des derniers ordres
qu'il avait reçus de sa Cour, que Sa Majesté étant informée de tout
ce qui s'est passé en Pologne, lui avait ordonné de faire une visite
au Prince Primat et de lui dire (ici M. l'Ambassadeur a tiré son
original de la dépêche et lu,) que la République étant divisée et
la ville de Varsovie livrée aux Trouppes Etrangères (la depêche
portait *à la mercy*) de ces Trouppes, qu'ainsi le Roi lui avait
ordonné de ·se retirer jusqu'à ce que le calme et le bon ordre
soient rétablis en Pologne. M. l'Ambassadeur a ajouté "ce que
je désire qui soit bientôt, Sa Majesté ne cessant de prendre une
part sincère à la liberté et à la tranquillité de la République
comme elle a fait connaître par ses déclarations." Le Prince Primat
élevant sa voix a dit à M. l'Ambassadeur, " Vous ne reconnaissez
"donc pas la République ?" A quoi M. l'Ambassadeur a
répondu "Je reconnais la République divisée et la ville de
"Varsovie livrée à des Trouppes Etrangères, j'ai ordre de me
" retirer et je me retire." M. Henin a dit alors "Monsigr. le
" Primat répond à ce que M. l'Ambassadeur ne dit pas."

Le Prince Primat a dit en addressant la parole à M. l'Ambassadeur et regardant le Résident, " Puisque vous ne reconnaissez
"la République, vous pouvez aller la chercher, vous et tous les
"Ministres de France." M. l'Ambassadeur a répondu, " J'ai
"mes ordres, les autres exécuteront les leurs." M. Henin
s'avançant alors a dit au Prince Primat "Je rendrai compte à ma
"Cour, de ce que V.A. me déclare et j'attendrai ses ordres." Le
Prince Primat a repris parlant à M. l'Ambassadeur, " Si vous ne
" nous reconnaissez pas pour la République, vous pouvez d'aller
"chercher où il vous plaira." A quoi M. l'Ambassadeur réplique
de nouveau, "Je reconnais que la République est divisée et c'est
" parce qu'elle est divisée et que la ville est au pouvoir des
" Trouppes Etrangère que j'ai ordre de me retirer." Le Prince
Palatin de Russie a pris alors parole et dit " Il faut espérer que
quand le Roi de France sera mieux informé." .... M. l'Ambassadeur a répondu, " Le Roi est bien informé et j'exécute ses
"ordres." Alors le Prince Primat après avoir encore dit " Si vous
ne reconnaissez pas que nous sommes la République, allez la
chercher, et ajouta, "Adieu, M. le Marquis de Paulmy." M.
l'Ambassadeur a répondu " Adieu M. L'Archévêque" et s'est retiré
sans que personne l'ait reconduit. La garde a reçu ordre de ne
pas rendre à M. l'Ambassadeur les honneurs d'usage qu'il avait
reçu en entrant. C'est ainsi que s'est passé une scène dans laquelle
sans aucun fondement un Ambassadeur qui faisait par ordre un
compliment qui n'a rien de choquant a été brusqué d'une manière
qui l'a surpris au dernier point. L'article des honneurs
supprimés est hors de tout règle, puisque la guerre même étant
déclarée, un Ambassadeur rappellé, (et M. le Marquis de Paulmy
ne l'est point) jusqu'à sa sortie de sa résidence jouit de tous les
honneurs dus à son caractère.

(A second version of the scene giving a more favourable account
of the Polish attitude during the interview was also enclosed.)

THOMAS WROUGHTON to the EARL OF BUCKINGHAMSHIRE.

1764, June 24. Warsaw.—The Confederation in Lithuania joined by some Russian troops attacked a town and castle belonging to Prince Radzivil, defended by a considerable garrison (called Niedzwiesce) and after taking the town made an attempt upon the castle, but after firing some cannon shot against it, were obliged for that time to make a retreat. The Prince who was at *Bialla* in the Palatinat of *Brzese* with his little Army of about 5,000 men immediately marched to Count Flemming's house in the neighbourhood, took 200 men prisoners, a considerable quantity of ammunition, plundered a convent, burnt several houses in the village, and has done other great damages to the Count, and we were in pain for the seat of the Prince Chancellor Czartoryski, but we heard yesterday evening that he is marched to relieve *Niedzwiesce* and to fight the Russians, which is the step that his enemies had most to wish for.

We received also an account of a skirmish that has passed between the troops of the Great-General and those commanded against him by a M. Braniski, in which the advantage was on the side of the latter, who has taken about sixty prisoners.

Yesterday our Diet ended and was succeeded by a General Confederation of the Kingdom of Poland ; the Prince Palatin of Russia is chosen Marshal of it, and a Count Bzewieski, Great Notary of the Crown, departs in a few days for St. Petersburg to announce it to the Empress, and intreat the effect of her promises in the support of it and the laws and privileges of the Republic. The Diet of Election is postponed until the 27th of August. (*Cypher.*) I am very happy that your Lordship is likely to conclude the Treaty of Commerce and wish that of Alliance may soon follow. I executed the order I received from London upon this subject and am expecting to hear the issue of it.

THOMAS WROUGHTON to THE SAME.

1764, June 30. Warsaw.—We have received an account of all the troops that were with the Great-General having submitted to the Prince Palatin of Russia ; and the Great-General with the General Mokronoffski* being retired into Hungary, so that all is quiet on that side of the country.

We are anxiously expecting news of Prince Radzivil, who is marching to meet the Russians. Prince Repnin is gone from hence with all the Russian troops that were in this neighbourhood, and several other officers are sent by the Palatin of Russia

---

* General Mokronoffski a little later was deputed by the Grand General to approach Frederic with proposals.

1st. That he should guarantee the liberty of the Republic.

2nd. That he should mediate between themselves and the Russian party.

3rd. That certain Acts which tended to make the King's power despotic should not be made valid.

See *Polit. Corresp., Friedrich's des Zweitens*. Vol. 23, p. 448.

with private gentlemen's troops to attack him in the rear, or prevent his escape in case he should think proper to return this way.

The news from Constantinople is also very favourable to the family, the Porte declaring that they wish to see a natural-born Pole on the throne of Poland, agreeable to the views of the Courts of Berlin and Petersburg, and their having insinuated once more to the French Ambassador there, that they desire him not to give any more representations contrary to this resolution. You will be able to procure from the Vice-Chancellor,* or Panin,† a more authentic relation of this news, as I have not been able to get a sight of Keyserling, who has sent me a letter to Panin, which I have delivered to the messenger, and which your Lordship will be pleased to send to him immediately.

Thomas Wroughton to the Earl of Buckinghamshire.

1764, July 16. Warsaw.—Before yesterday a Courier arrived from France with an order for the French Resident to retire from hence as soon as possible, on account of the dispute between the Ambassador and the Primate; it is said that that Court is extreamly offended at that affair, but whither they intend to demand any satisfaction, or what kind they could ask, is utterly unknown to us here. The Imperial Ambassador and Resident are to quit the place in a few days, so that the intention of those two Courts seems to be not to recognize the election, on the pretext of foreign troops being entered and curbing the liberty of the electors.

We have no further news of Prince Radzivil, except his being in the Palatinate of Volhinia; as he must be almost surrounded with different corps of Russian troops, it cannot be long e'er we receive an account of something decisive in regard to him. Lieut.-Genl. Stöffel is entered with twelve thousand men in the Palatinat of Kiovia, and marched to Leopol to keep everything quiet in those parts. Since the accession of the troops that were with the Great-Genl. to the authority of the Prince Régimentaire, all is quiet in that quarter; the Great-Genl. himself is in Hungary.

Enclosed are 1st : " Copie du Billet de M. de Hennin, Resident de France, addressé a S. A. Mgr le Prince Primat de Varsouie le 16 Juillet 1764." 2nd : " Copie de la Dépêche écrite par Mgr le Duc de Praslin à M. Hennin, Résident de France en Pologne, de Compiègne le 30 Juin, 1764."

Thomas Wroughton to the Same.

1764, August 30. Warsaw.—The reconfederation of Halisch of which I informed you has been crushed, and the Mareshal with

---

* Prince Alexandre Galitzin.
† Nikita Ivanovitch Panin, 1718-1783. First Minister of Catherine II.

the most considerable people engaged in it taken prisoners in a town called "Stanislaw."

Our Diet of Election opened Monday last; as yet the Palatin of Kiovia, the Bishop of Cracow, and some others who had manifested against the legality of the Diet of Convocation have not been allowed to assist at it, as they have not thought proper to retract that protestation; but it is said that to-day all except the Bishop intend to join the Corps of the Republic. The two Chambers will make their junction this morning, that of the Nonces having chosen for their Mareshal a M. Sosnoffsky, Grand Notaire of Lithuania. Count Keyzerling's late illness will probably prevent the audience of the Ambassadors for this week; this Ceremony over, I imagine that in a few days after, our Election will follow, and that Count Poniatowski will be chosen in as peaceable and unanimous a manner as ever was known in this country.

Prince Dashkoff* died of a fever in this neighbourhood yesterday.

The KING OF PRUSSIA to the KING OF POLAND.†

1764, Nov. 29. Berlin.—Monsieur mon Frère C'est avec une véritable satisfaction que j'ai reçu la lettre de votre Majesté du 20 de Septembre et les nouveaux témoignages d'amitié que le Prince Czartoryski, Grand Veneur de la Couronne de Pologne, est venu me donner de sa part. Je lui ai en même tems une obligation infinie du choix qu'Elle a bien voulu faire en cette occasion d'une personne qui m'a été si agréable. On ne saurait être plus sensible que je le suis à la justice que Votre Majesté rend à ma façon de penser au sujet des désordres que pourraient avoir été commis à mon insu sur les frontières de la Pologne. Je puis me promettre que le compte que lui en rendra le Prince Czartoryski lui confirmera le désir que J'ai d'entretenir et de cultiver de tout mon pouvoir cette étroite intelligence avec la République de Pologne, si heureusement établie entre nous, et dont le maintien sera toujours un de mes soins les plus importants. Si j'ai eu le plaisir de donner à Votre Majesté des preuves évidentes des sentimens que je lui porte personellement, elles doivent lui répondre de tont le cas que je fais de ceux qu'Elle éprouve pour moi. Et la conformité de notre façon de penser nous doit être un garant réciproque de la solidité. Le Prince Czartoryski m'a si bien rendu compte de celle de Votre Majesté que je m'en rapporte à lui avec beaucoup de confiance sur les assurances qu'il lui donnera de mon amitié sincère et de la considération toute particulière avec laquelle je suis, Monsieur mon Frère, de Votre Majesté, le bon Frère, Ami et Voisin,

FRÉDERIC.

[*Copy.*]

---

* The husband of the celebrated Countess Dashkoff.
† This letter is not included in the published correspondence of Frederic II.

M. Woide to the Earl of Buckinghamshire.

[1765,] à Londres le 15ᵉᵐᵉ d'Août, chez M. Williams, Chymist at Galen's Head, Broad St., Soho.—Etant arrivé à Londres avant hiers je prends la liberté d'envoier à V.E. cyjoint la lettre de M. le Général de Goltz. Vous en serez instruit, Monseigneur, de la commission dont je suis chargé. Je suis parti de la Pologne au mois d'Avril. J'ai fait quelque séjour à Berlin, et je me suis arrêté plus de deux mois en Hollande. A la Haïe j'ai eu l'honneur de voir S. E. M. le Chevalier de Yorke, Ambassadeur de S.M. le Roi de la Grande Bretagne, j'ai de sa part une lettre de recommendation pour S.E. le Duc de Grafton, Secrétaire d'état et une pour Monseigneur l'Archévêque de Cambridge (sic) et son Aumônier. (Begs his protection and counsel.)

A. S. D. Baron de Goltz (Starost de Gaudentz) to the Earl of Buckinghamshire.

1765, Avril 6. En Grand Pologne.—C'est avec une confiance respectueuse que je prends la liberté de recommender à la gracieuse protection de V.E. le Sieur Charle Godfroi Woide Pasteur de la Communion Réformée en Grande Pologne que le Corp de la Noblesse Dissidente envoye en Angleterre pour porter leurs plaintes et très humbles prières au trône sacré de S.M. le Roy de la Grande Bretagne et implorer sa puissante protection pour ces infortunés. Les Dissidents auraient bien chargé de cette commission un homme de condition, mais l'état opprimé dans lequel ils se trouvent depuis la funeste Constitution de la dernière Diète de Convocation, il leur est même défendu de réclamer la protection des Puissances Protestantes comme guarantes de la Paix d'Olive, par conséquent de leurs droits et libertés; ils ont donc choisi le dit Pasteur Woide comme leur homme chargé d'affaire, qu'il puisse en secret en leur nom faire le récit de leurs souffrances et demander très humblement la haute protection de S.M. pour le maintien du libre exercise de religion, leurs droits et libertés.

Connaissant Monseigneur votre cœur généreux et vos sentimens Chrétiens pour protéger l'innocence et la vraie Religion je supplie V.E. de prendre dans sa protection le Pasteur Woide et de le vouloir gracieusement informer s'il doit rendre ses lettres de créance à V.E, ou à un autre Ministre du Roi, comme aussi de prévenir qu'il ne soit parlé de notre émissaire dans la Gazette.

BUCKINGHAMSHIRE PAPERS.

Part 4.—1762-1774.

Papers Relating to the Trade with Russia Collected by John, Earl of Buckinghamshire, during his Embassy to St. Petersburg (1762-1765).

'Traité de Commerce.'

A Paper described in a Report of the Lords of Trade, 11th Feb., 1763, as "A Particular Examination of the State of the British Commerce with Russia antecedent to the Treaty of 1734." ᵒ

N.D. [1762, May 18.]—En conséquence des ordres de votre Majesté nous avons examiné le projet d'un nouveau Traité de Commerce avec la Russie, qui a été dressé à St. Petersbourg et presenté à M. Keith, † l'envoyé de S.M. à cette cour, par l'ordre de S.M.I. Nous avons aussi considéré ce qui est détaillé dans la lettre de M. Keith à Milor Bute, qui lui est venu avec le dit Projet, et ayant, poursuivant les ordres consécutifs de S.M. communiqué cette proposition de la part de l'Impératrice ‡ des Russies à la Compagnie et aux marchands principaux, qui sont engagés dans notre commerce avec cet Empire, et demandé leurs observations and opinions làdessus, nous supplions très-humblement votre Majesté de nous permettre de lui exposer le plan cyjoint, ou contre-projet d'un Traité avec la Russie, que la dite Compagnie nous a présenté il y'a déjà quelque tems, contenant leurs sentiments en détail, et toutes les propositions qu'ils avaient à faire sur ce qui avait été offert de la part de l'Impératrice. Cependant comme quelque tems était échu depuis qu'on nous a remis ce papier, il nous a paru nécessaire avant d'offrir notre réprésentation finale sur une matière de telle importance, de consulter deréchef les messieurs qui sont intéressés dans cette Commerce, afin de pouvoir être informé s'ils avaient quelque chose d'ultérieure à nous offrir. Qui là-dessus nous ont donné la copie d'un Mémoire § cy jointe, addressé aux Seigneurs du Conseil de Votre Majesté, par les marchands Anglais résidents à Riga, dans laquelle les vexations et les empêchements dont le commerce des sujets de Votre Majesté dans cette ville est surchargé, par diverses procédés irreguliers et, à ce qu'ils disent, arbitraires des magistrats de la dite ville.

---

* See for this *Buckinghamshire Correspondence*, ed. Royal Hist. Sy., Vol. I 235.
† Ambassador to St. Peterburg 1758—Sep., 1762.
‡ Elizabeth Czarina, 1741—1762.
§ The gist of this is printed in *Buckinghamshire Corr.*, ed. R. Hist. Society, Vol. I, p. 90.

Mais avant d'entrer dans un examen précis ou de ce qui a été offert de la part de la feüe Impératrice, ou de ce qui nous a été remis par les marchands de la Compagnie et autres des sujets de Votre Majesté qui trafiquent dans ces pais, ou des idées qui nous surviennent sur le tout, en toute humilité nous supplions V. M. de vouloir bien nous permettre de constater aussi succinctement qu'il nous sera possible ce qu'il nous semble en général de la nature et de l'étendu de cette branche importante de notre commerce, les vexations et oppressions qu'elle a souffertes durant une longue correspondance commerciale avéc l'Empire Russien, et les propositions qu'on a faites pour remédier à ces vexations et oppressions qui donnèrent lieu au Traité de Commerce de 1734, par lequel V.M., pleinement informée des avantages qui résultent de ce commerce, non seulement aux sujets de Votre Majesté, mais aussi à l'Empire de Russie, des empêchements et des obstructions qu'il a essuyées, de l'effet des remèdes qu'on y a appliqués, sera plus à portée de juger de la convenance, de l'utilité ou de l'inutilité de ce qui a été offert de la part de la Russie pour la base d'un Traité de Commerce si bien pour ce qui regarde le commerce que la Marine de l'Angleterre.

Le Commerce des sujets de V. M. avec la Russie est principalement composé des denrées que nous faisons venir de ces pais, sçavoir le chanvre, le lin, la cire, le suif, le fer, les linges, du bois de charpente, du colle de poisson, de la rhubarbe, de la soye crue, du cuir, et de quelques autres Articles de peu d'importance; dont près des trois quarts est payé en or, ou en argent non monnoyé ou en Rixdalers, le reste leur est remis en draps et autres denrées de la production et de la manufacture d'Angleterre, et si on examinait la monteé des imports qui nous viennent de là Russie exactement sur chaque article, on trouverait que les Anglais achètent pour le moins autant des marchandises Russiennes qu'aucunes autres deux nations ensembles, et payent plus d'argent comptant à la Russie que tout le reste de l'Europe, et bien qu'on doit convenir qu'il est essentiellement nécessaire aux intérêts de l'Angleterre d'être pourvu régulièrement des munitions nécessaires à nos équippements maritimes, (ce qui fait une partie très considérable de notre commerce avec la Russie) cependant, en faisant une revue exacte de ce commerce en général, on trouvera que la balance, non seulement à l'égard du profit, mais des intérêts réels, penche beaucoup du côté de la Russie.

Et si on se rappelle touts les avantages et les privilèges accordés par les Empereurs de la Russie dans les premiers tems de ce commerce[a] aux marchands Anglais, on verra clairement que les Russiens eux-mêmes étaient de cette opinion. Et à dire la vérité la Couronne de Russie aurait péché essentiellement contre la politique, adoptée même par les états les moins versés dans les arts et les intérets du commerce, si elle avait d'abord poursuivi des mesures dont l'opération aurait pu mettre fin à un trafic si avantageux pour leur nation.

---

[a] In the years 1556, 1563, 1628. (See for this *Stow's Chronicle*, pp. 629, et seq. and 1044.

Comme pourtant ces priviléges étaient des actes purement volontaires, et qu'on pouvait de tems en tems les changer ou les abolir par ce même pouvoir qui les avaient accordés, on ne devait pas les considérer comme donnant un sûreté, un établisse. ment fixe et durable au Commerce des Sujets Britanniques; aussi en effet ne le donnèrent-ils pas, car, dans le cours de peu d'années, beaucoup d'inconvénients et d'empêchements suc. cédèrent, tant par l'intervention d'intérêts étrangers, que par des loix et des ordonnances d'état, fondées sur des préjugés locaux et partials qui ont lieu presque toujours dans l'enfance d'un état, quand on s'y trouve peu au fait de ses vrayes intérêts à l'égard de ses liaisons tant de politique que de commerce.

On verra plus au large quels furent ces empêchements et ces inconvénients dans un mémoire présenté au Gouvernement par la Compagnie dans l'année 1716,· quand on fit la proposition d'etablir le commerce des deux Nations sur un pied plus fixe et plus durable par un Traité.°

Nous n'entrerons pas à cette occasion dans le détail de cette négotiation, il suffira de dire qu'elle échoua, malheureusement, par l'intervention de propositions de politique, et d'intérêts tout-à-fait étrangers à cette considération; que tous les inconvénients et empêchements continuèrent sans remède, et conjointement avec d'autres causes produisirent des griefs encore plus onéreux; et comme ces griefs et ces inconvénients donnèrent lieu à cette négotiation qui établit le Traité de 1734, nous nous contenterons (comme ici dessus) de nous en rapporter aux mémoires où ils sont constatés, suppliants très humblement V.M. de nous permettre de lui exposer aussi succinctement qu'il nous sera possible la substance de ces griefs.

Nous avons déjà expliqué à V. M. qu'une partie du payement pour les denrées qu'on tirait de la Russie se faisait dans nos manufactures de laine, dont l'espèce la plus grossière servait pour habiller le soldat, et une grande partie de la plus fine, comme le drap large,† les aunes longues, les aunes impériales, et autres toiles différents, s'achetaient pour le commerce de la Perse par les marchands Russiens et Arméniens, qui trafiquaient à Shemakha, Ghilan, et autres villes sur la Mer Caspienne. On s'aperçoit pourtant par un mémoire de la factorerie Britannique à St. Petersbourg en l'année 1732, qu'en l'année 1724, la vente de nos manufactures par ces deux canaux se trouvait extrêmement interrompüe dans le premier, de ce que les Russiens achetaient le drap pour l'habillement de leurs soldats dans les territoires du Roi de Prusse où il se trouvait à raison de 15 à 20 pour cent à meilleur marché de ce que nous le pouvions vendre, quoiqu'il était évident que, comparant la valeur réele des deux, le drap Prussien était de beaucoup le plus cher; dans le second, en ce que les marchands Arméniens qui résidaient

---

* A draught of this projected Treaty is in Add. MSS. 28154, British Museum. (Townshend to H. Walpole, 3 August,1716.) See also Add. MS. 28155 for the negotiations in relation to it.

† Broadcloth.

en Russie avaient obtenu le privilége de traverser ce pais avec leurs marchandises, et ayant seulement 3 pour cent de droit de transport, tant pour les denrées Européennes qu'ils portaient en Perse, que pour la soye crue qu'ils en retiraient ; tandis que les Anglais trafiquant sous le même tarif, qui prit lieu à peu près en même tems qu'on accordait ce privilége aux Arméniens, étaient obligés de payer depuis 25 jusqu'a 75 pour cent sur plusieurs de leurs marchandises qui convenaient le plus au trafic Persien ; par cette inégalité dans les droits cette branche se trouvait absolument dans les mains des Arméniens, qui envoyèrent toute la soye crue et les autres productions de la Perse en Hollande, d'où ils faisaient venir toutes les manufactures de laine et autres marchandises qu'ils débitaient en Perse.

Les griefs pourtant qui étaient ceux qui nuisaient principalement au commerce des sujets de V.M. en Russie, ne se dérivaient pas ou de ce que nous n'avions point de Traité de Commerce, ou de la mauvaise disposition de la Cour de Russie, ils provenaient beaucoup plus des fraudes et des abus des *individus* particuliers dans la manufacture et la vente de nos draps, représentés et soigneusement exaggérés par les Prussiens (dans l'instance de l'habillement des soldats) dont l'intérêt à ce moment venait d'obtenir la supériorité, et nous nous trouvons plus disposés à faire cette remarque par raison que les griefs dont les marchands se sont plaignés ont eu lieu plus souvent des mauvais procédés et d'un manquement de probité dans les particuliers, que des restrictions injustes ou peu convenables de l'état où ils trafiquaient.

Ces griefs, bien que les principaux, n'étaient pas les uniques circonstances qui produisaient ces empêchements à l'égard de notre commerce en Russie. Les marchands Anglais résidents dans ce Pais avaient beaucoup souffert par l'augmentation des impôts sur toutes les denrées qui venaient d'Angleterre, mais particulièrement sur les manufactures de laine ; par les décisions partiales et irregulières des magistrats dans les démêles qu'ils avaient avec les sujets Russiens ; par la difficulté d'obtenir le payement de ce qui leur était dû de ceux d'entre les gens du pais qui avaient la mauvaise foi de vouloir l'esquiver ; par la méchanceté de ceux qui obligeaient leurs domestiques à trafiquer pour eux dans leurs propres noms ; de ce qu'il ne leur était permis d'acheter des maisons ou des magasins ; de ce qu'on leur refusait des passeports quand ils voudraient se retirer, à moins qu'ils ne donnassent des sûretés qu'il leur était presque impossible de prouver ; des fraudes et des abus dans le brack des marchandises, et d'une diversité d'autres défauts et actes d'oppression qui se trouvent pleinement détaillés dans un mémoire de la Compagnie en l'annee 1732. Il est vrai, que sur des rémonstrances qu'on a faites là-dessus, on offrit de remédier à quelques-uns de ces griefs par une ordonnance de sa Maj. Imp. mais comme elle aurait été, comme nous avons remarqué ci-dessus, sujette à être revoquée par la même autorité qui l'avait établie, et comme beaucoup des autres griefs étaient de nature à ne pouvoir se

remédier que par les engagements réciproques d'un Traité· de
Commerce, les deux nations convinrent amicalement d'entrer
dans une négotiation à cet effet.

En conséquence de cette Convention mutuelle, et de cette disposition amicale des deux Couronnes, le Lord Forbes,° qui était
alors Ministre Plen. de S.M. à Petersbourg, présenta le 8me
d'Aout, 1733, un mémoire contenant les propositions de la part
de l'Angleterre qu'on jugeait le mieux convenues à former la base
d'un Traité de Commerce.

Ces propositions qu'on avait rédigées en 29 Articles, contenaient
non seulement les stipulations pour la sûreté et la commodité
en général des marchands dans l'arrangement de leur commerce
sur les principes de l'équité, et des avantages réciproques, qu'on
trouve dans presque touts les Traités de Commerce ; mais
aussi on y̆ faisait provision pour remédiér à ces griefs qui
avaient donné touts ces empêchements à la vente de nos manufactures de laine, et de ces oppressions et de ces injustices qui
provenaient de la partialité des magistrats dans l'administration
des loix, et de ce qu'il leur manquait cette protection et ces
priviléges qui sont essentiellement nécessaires au commerce.

Pour remédier au premier de ces mals, on proposait que les
mêmes droits seraient payés *ad valorem* sur toutes les denrées
qu'on faisait entrer et qu'on déchargeait, qui se ne nuiseraient
pas aux productions et aux manufactures de la Russie, et que
quand le marchand n'aurait point de Rickdalers ou d'Ecus, il lui
serait loisible de payer les droits dans l'argent qui serait de mise,
à raison de tant de Copecks par Ecu ou Rickdaler, qu'il serait
permis aux Anglais de transporter toutes sortes de denrées par
les territoires de la Russie en aucun autre pais, payants un droit
de transit qui ne passerait par 3 pr Cent ad Valorem, donnants
aussi caution que ces denrées qu'on avait déclaré d'être de transit,
ne seraient pas consummées en Russie ; que les Anglais ne
payeraient pas plus de·droits d'entrée et de sortie des marchandises que les sujets d'aucune autre nation, et qu'on favoriserait
davantage l'entrée des marchandises de laine, pour mettre les
Anglais en état d'exporter, et de payer une plus grande quantité
des marchandises Russiennes.

Pour remédier aux griefs et aux oppressions dont les
marchands Anglais résidents en Russie se plaignaient, on propose que toutes les affaires mercantiles ne seraient jugées que
dans le Collége de Commerce, qu'il serait libre aux marchands
Anglais, et d'en disposer, et qu'ils seraient exempts de fournir
des quartiers pour Officiers, Soldats, ou autres dans leurs
maisons, qu'on donnerait des passeports aux marchands qui
seraient disposés à quitter le pais sans les obliger de prêter
caution, pourvu qu'ils notifiaient leurs intentions deux mois
auparavant ; que les marchands qui retenaient des domestiques
et les enregistraient au Police, ne seraient pas après responsables
aux seigneurs de tels domestiques, ni obligés de rien payer à ce
sujet à ces seigneurs, ou à d'autres, qu'ils ne seraient obligés de

---

* George Lord Forbes, afterwards 3rd Earl of Granard.

produire leurs livres de compte et papiers, si ce n'était pour faire preuve en justice, ni leurs effets ne seraient saisis, executés ou vendus, ormis en cas de banqueroute, et alors seulement par le jugement du Collége de Commerce; que touts esclaves Russes qui trafiquaient pour leurs maitres enregistreraient au Collége de Commerce les effets et les pouvoirs qu'ils auraient reçus de leurs maitres, et que leurs maitres seraient obligés de se tenir à leurs conventions, qu'on donnerait plein pouvoir au Collége de Commerce de faire arrêter les marchands Russes qui partiraient sans régler leurs comptes, ou qui ne se rendraient pas pour acquitter leurs dettes quand ils deviendraient dues, et de se saisir de leurs effets et de leurs personnes; que les marchands Russes seraient obligés en trois jours après l'arrivée de leurs marchandises à St. Petersbourg, d'en faire l'entrée tout à la fois, tant de ce qu'ils ont sous leurs propres noms, que ceux des autres; qu'ils seraient aussi obligés d'en marquer la quantité précise sans (réduction?) per Cent du poids actuel, ou de la mesure de telles marchandises; et qu'ils seraient sujets à payer les mêmes amendes que les étrangers, à l'égard des fausses entrées, en faisant entrer les marchandises qu'ils tirent des pais étrangers, que le brack sur toutes les marchandises serait le même qu'à Riga, et que les brackeurs seraient responsables pour touts les faux emballages, et qu'on trouverait quelque méthode pour remédier à la fausse mesure des linges, et qu'on ajugerait un échet égal au bandage sur les cuirs et la filasse, et que si quelque dispute survenait sur le déchet, l'acheteur serait en liberté de faire la taxe des marchandises.

En conséquence de ces propositions les Ministres de Russie donnèrent à Milor Forbes deux papiers séparés, l'un desquels contenait leurs observations sur les Articles différents qui se trouvaient constatés dans le mémoire qu'il avait présenté, l'autre contenait les demandes qu'ils contaient d'éxiger de leur côté.

En composant ces deux papiers V.M. s'apercevra que dans cette réponse pour ce qui regarde les demandes faites par les sujets de V.M. résidents en Russie, pour subvenir aux griefs dont ils se plaignaient, on en admet la justice, l'équité et la convenance, et bien qu'en dressant les Articles du Traité qui se rapportent à ces points, la mode de l'expression n'est pas précisement la même que celle des Articles proposés, et qu'en quelques instances le remède ne vise pas si juste et n'est pas si convenable ni si étendu que celui proposé par Milor Forbes, on n'en a retranché rien d'essentiel; aussi, depuis ce tems-là, n'y-a-t'il eu aucun fondement de plainte raisonable de part ou d'autre. Les difficultés principales qui se rencontrèrent dans le fil de cette négotiation naquaient de cette partie des Propositions de part et d'autre qui regardaient les droits exorbitants et autres désavantages auxquels l'importation de nos marchandises de laine se trouvait exposée, la liberté qu'on demandait de trafiquer en Perse en passant par la Russie, et les contredemandes de la Cour de Russie.

On voit dans le papier d'observations sur les 29 Articles proposés par Milor Forbes, que cette partie du quatrième Article, qui regarde le payement des droits *ad Valorem* sur les marchandises Anglaises est absolument rejettée, et quoique dans le cours de la négotiation on fit les plus grands efforts pour obtenir cette stipulation elle fut opposée avec la même rigueur, et absolument refusée. Aussi faut-il convenir que les raisonnements dont on se servit pour soutenir cette proposition ne nous paraissent pas de la première conséquence, et que nous ne sommes pas absolument au fait des avantages que les sujets de V.M. en auraient tiré.

On voit de plus dans ce papier d'observations que quoique la Cour de Russie accordait aux sujets de V.M. la liberté de trafiquer en Perse, cependant elle prétendait que ce ne serait que dans les marchandises de la crue et de la manufacture d'Angleterre, et de la crue de la Perse, que le droit de 3 pour cent ne serait qu'à l'égard de ce qu'on retirait de la Perse, que les droits se payeraient en Rickdalers, et que les marchandises Anglaises qu'on débiteraient en ce commerce, payeraient les droits dans le Port selon le Tarif.

Milor Forbes dans sa réponse remarque que les marchands le trouveraient extrêmement difficile de distinguer ce qui était de la crue de la Grande Bretagne et de la Perse, qu'à la vérité les Anglais transportait beaucoup de denrées qui n'étaient pas de la crue d'Angleterre en Perse, et qu'aussi ils en faisaient venir beaucoup de choses qui n'étaient pas de la production de la Perse, mais qu'ils ne pourraient jamais entretenir l'idée de passer en Perse par la Russie, si on exigeait plus de 3 pr cent pour le droit de transit, ce qui ajoute au dépense du transport de terre, monterait à plus que les frais de faire venir le marchandises de la Perse en Angleterre par mer. Il ajouta que l'avantage qui résulterait à la Russie de cette proposition était si grande, qu'on aurait pu s'attendre qu'on laisserait passer les marchandises en Perse par la Russie franches de touts droits, comme ce n'était pas un nouveau commerce pour l'Angleterre, qui le poursuivait de longtems par les états du Grand Seigneur, au grand avantage des Turcs.

Convaincus à la fin par ces raisonnements aussi clairs qu'équitables, ils consentirent à cette proposition dans sa forme originale comme on le trouvera dans le Traité de 1734.

A l'égard des propositions générales offertes par Milor Forbes qu'on devait donner plus de faveur et d'encouragement à l'importation de nos manufactures de laine, et que les Anglais ne payeraient pas plus de droits d'entrée que les sujets d'aucune autre nation sur les mêmes denrées, elles étaient en elles-mêmes si raisonnables et si justes, et l'équité en etait si bien soutenu par la considération des grandes avantages qui résultaient à la Russie de son commerce avec l'Angleterre, qu'il était difficile de s'ÿ opposer, aussi on verra que la dernière fut accordée dans les termes proposés par Milor Forbes, et que la Cour de Russie consentit à baisser et à fixer les droits sur certaines espèces de nos manufactures de laine, comme il est resté par le 27ᵐᵉ Art. du Traité en 1734.

Ayant ainsi constaté à V. M. ce qui se passa à l'égard des demandes offertes par la Gr. Bret., il conviendra de parler dè celles de sa Maj. Imp., comme elles se présentèrent sur les différents Articles du Projet de Milor Forbes.

Sur le premier, (qui stipulait une liberté de navigation et de commerce tant par eau que par terre dans toute la Russie et leš provinces qui ÿ appartiennent, où on permettait, ou on dorénavant permettrait, à aucune autre nation étrangère de trafiquer) la Cour de Petersbourg réclamait le même privilége pour leurs sujets qui trafiqueraient en Angleterre, si bien dans des vaisseaux construits en Russie ou en d'autres pais étrangers portants le pavillon Russien, que dans des vaisseaux Anglais, frétés par des Russes, et que ces vaisseaux et leurs commandants, et leur matelots, tant sujets de la Russie qu'étrangers, ainsi que les marchands et leurs domestiques seraient traités en Angleterre sur le pied de la nation la plus favorisée, et qu'il leur serait permis de passer partout sans empêchement. Sur le deuxième et le troisième Article du Projet de Milor Forbes (par lesquels on stipulait que les sujets de la Gr. Bret. auraient une communication libre dans toutes les Villes de la Russie, et la liberté de faire venir et de vendre toutes sortes de marchandises qui ne seraient pas de contrebande, et de se fournir de provisions et de tout ce qu'il leur serait nécessaire, et de se retirer sans empêchement quelconque) la Cour de Russie demandait une liberté pareille pour touts ses sujets, de passer dans touts les pais de la domination Britannique, non seulement avec des marchandises de la crue de Russie, ou qui étaient fabriquées de ce qui était de cette crue, mais aussi avec toutes les manufactures et productions qu'on pourraient faire venir en Russie d'aucun autre pais étranger sans exception. Ces Propositions étaient si évidemment contraires à toutes les loix de commerce et de navigation établies en Angleterre, et en effet visaient si directement à la racine de l'Acte de Navigation, le soutien principal du Commerce de cette Nation, que non seulement nous déclarâmes qu'elles étaient inadmissibles, mais aussi la Cour de Russie en convint, et en conséquence ils reduisirent leurs demandes de commerce et de communication réciproques à ces deux points. Premièrement, qu'il leur serait permis d'envoyer en Angleterre les marchandises des Tartares civilisés de l'autre côté de la Mer Caspienne, qui occupent ce vaste Pais qui s'étend entre la Sibérie, le Territoire du Mogol, les Frontières de la Perse, et la Mer Caspienne.

En second lieu, qu'ils pourraient envoyer les productions de leur Pais en Angleterre consignées à des sujets Russes à qui il serait permis de trafiquer en Angleterre.

Après avoir examiné le premier de ces points, on trouve qu'il était sujet à la même objection que la proposition originale, et il n'était pas possible de l'admettre dans cette forme, ... bien qu'il semblait un peu injuste d'exiger des Russes de nous permettre de poursuivre notre commerce en passant par leur pais, et en même tems de leur refuser ce même avantage.

Telle fut cependant la disposition équitable et modérée de la Cour de Russie à cet époque qu'elle ne se picqua pas du refus de

ce qu'il nous était impossible de céder, et se contenta de stipulations générales de liberté réciproque de faire venir dans les païs
respectifs des deux nations où il était permis de trafiquer *toutes
les manufactures des autres païs, dont la vente et l'entrée n'étaient
pas défendues.* A l'égard du second, (savoir la liberté d'envoyer
les productions de leur propre païs en Angleterre dans des
vaisseaux Anglais consignées à des sujets Russes,) la Compagnie Russie (qu'on avait consultée là-dessus,) consentit que les
Russiens trafiqueraient ici, pourvu que ils se conformeraient aux
règles, aux ordonnances, et aux statuts de la Compagnie, de la
même façon que ceux qui en sont libres, et aussi qu'ils payeraient
à la Compagnie un droit pour les marchandises qu'ils feraient
entrer égal à *l'excès payé par la Compagnie en Russie sur ce que
payaient les naturels du Païs*, pour mettre le Commerce sur un
pied égal. Dans le progrès pourtant de la négotiation sur cet
Article, on varia cette Proposition de la Compagnie, et il fut con-
venu par les deux partis, que pour établir cette égalité que la
Compagnie exigeait, les Russiens réduiraient les droits payés par
les Anglais sur la sortie des marchandises à ceux que payaient
leurs propres sujets.

Ceux-ci sont touts les Articles qui se sont présentés dans cette
négotiation qu'il nous a paru nécessaire de constater à V.M.,
quelques autres de moindre conséquence et d'un genre relatif aux
circonstances et à la situation particulière du commerce à cette
époque eurent lieu, mais comme ils ne nous semblent pas
essentiels à l'information de V.M. en cette occasion, V.M. nous
permettra de nous rapporter aux papiers eux-mêmes, dont des
copies sort ici jointes ; nous n'avons donc qu'à ajouter, qu'après
une pleine discussion de touts les points dont nous venons de
parler le Traité fut conclu et ratifié le 2me de Dec^{bre} 1734.

La conclusion de ce Traité, comme elle donna une sûreté et
une stabilité mutuelle au commerce des deux nations et opéra
à leurs avantages communs, donna aussi un essor et une
activité nouvelle à celui des sujets de V.M. La vente des manufactures de laine qui avait tant souffert auparavant s'étendit
beaucoup, on fit des contrats avec les sujets de V.M. pour le drap
pour l'habillement de l'armée Russiene, et la valeur annuelle de
nos manufactures de laine portées en Russie du Port de Londres
(prenant un milieu de l'année 1736 jusqu'a l'année 1745 inclusive)
monta jusqu'a 14,548*l.* 7*s.* 2*d.*, bien qu'avant la conclusion de ce
Traité prenant également un milieu de dix ans (viz. depuis
l'année 1725 jusqu'a l'année 1734 inclusive) elle ne produisit que
9,619*l.* 1*s.* 4*d.* On voit aussi que les marchands Anglais
encouragés par la permission donnée par le Traité de trafiquer en
Perse par la Russie, et portés par les représentations de Mr.
Elton qui venait d'être employé pour examiner la nature et les
sources de ce commerce et la manière et les facilités avec
lesquelles on pourrait le poursuivre, s'engagèrent avec chaleur
dans une entreprise qui promettait tant de profit aux particuliers
et tant d'avantage à la nation ; on s'addressa au Parlement pour
faire lever quelques difficultés qui se présentaient à l'égard de
l'Acte de Navigation, et en conséquence un Acte fut passé pour

cet éffet qui contenait aussi d'autres régulations pour l'avance-
ment de ce commerce, et bien que la conduite imprudente de Mr.
Elton en s'engageant dans la service du Schah de la Perse donna
beaucoup d'ombrage à la Cour de Russie, et que la confusion et
les désordres qui eurent lieu bientôt après par les grandes révolu-
tions de l'empire des Perses, empêchèrent nos marchands alors
aussi bien que depuis de poursuivre ce commerce, nous ne
laissons pas de nous flatter que, quand la confusion cessera, et
que les affaires de la Perse seront rétablies, la poursuite de cet
objet sera renouvellée, et que l'Angleterre en dérivera les plus
grands avantages.

Il est vrai que beaucoup de ces marchands qui sont principalement intéressés dans ce commerce avec la Russie, n'ont pas des
grandes ideés de cet objet et n'espérants pas de réussir sont assez
indifférents sur le succès de la proposition. Nous ne pouvons pas
pourtant convenir avec eux quand nous réfléchissons sur les circonstances et les avantages de ce commerce; combien aussi ne
devrions-nous pas cultiver toutes les branches nouvelles de notre
commerce, quand nous avons tant de rivaux qui s'efforcent de
nous enlever les vieilles ?

L'intention de cette répresentation ne nous permet pas
d'entrer dans un détail de touts les avantages qui résulteraient de
notre acquisition de cet objet, mais avec la permission de V.M.
nous nous en rapporterons à la copie cÿ-jointe de la lettre de
Mr. Burrish, datée de Petersbourg le 6me d'Oct^{bre} 1740, dans
laquelle ces avantages se trouvent pleinement exposés.

Ce que nous avons déjà constaté prouvera à V.M. quelques uns
de touts les avantages que le commerce de vos sujets a dérivés
du Traité de 1734, on n'a jamais nié que les avantages étaient
égals du côté de la Russie, aussi est-il assez clairement prouvé par
la continuation que la Gouvernement a bien voulu faire de ces
régulations longtems après l'expiration du Traité, dans des
tems et des situations très-peu favorables à l'intérêt de la Nation
Britannique.

Des trente Articles dont le Traité est composé le 4$^{m\circ}$, le 8$^{m\circ}$,
et le 27me sont les seuls par lesquels les sujets de V.M. dérivent
des avantages en commerce qui leur sont particuliers, distinctes
de ceux accordés aux autres Nations, aussi ne sont-ils pas au-delà
de ce que la raison et l'équité exigent, et de ce que la Grande
Bret. était en droit de demander en considération des griefs que
son commerce avait essuyé.

Quand nous réflechissons sur toutes ces circonstances, si bien
que de ce que la Russie dérive de son commerce avec l'Angleterre,
des avantages supérieurs à ceux que lui produise celui de presque
toutes les autres nations ensemble, et que bien que ce commerce
a subsisté si longtems on ne l'a jamais changé au préjudice de la
Russie en aucun point, mais au contraire, qu'il a eu tout
l'encouragement et touts les priviléges que les loix et la Constitution de notre Pais lui pouvaient céder, il nous est difficile de
diviner les motifs qui (à notre grand regret) ont déterminé la
Cour de Petersbourg d'offrir un Projet dont les principes et les
provisions nous sont si peu favorables, et si différentes de cette

équité et de cette modération qu'elle à témoignées en faisant ce
Traité de 1734, et qui auraient dû être soigneusement conservées
par les deux Nations par égard pour leurs intérêts mutuels.

[The rest of this Paper consists of criticisms upon the Articles
proposed by the Russian Government in the Treaty of Commerce,
which was finally concluded in 1767.]

" Extracts from the Petersburg Merchants' Petition to
the Empress, together with some Account of the
Proceedings relative thereto."

N.D. [1762.]—By an Ukase or Decree* from the high ruling
Senate, the Magistracy was ordered to summon the Merchants of
the different Citys throughout the Empire to debate on the
situation of their trade and represent whatever grievances or
hardships they labour'd under, in order that the same might be
removed and they in future be able to conduct their affairs with
more advantage to themselves and the benefit of Trade in
general.

Upon receipt of the above Ukase in Petersburg, instead
of the Merchants and Citizens being allowed to set forth what
they thought would conduce to the intention of the said
Ukase, a Petition was drawn up and not communicated to them
till they were cited to the Guild House, when after a hasty
perusal and without granting any time to consider on what it
contained, they were commanded to sign it, hereupon several of
them who are the most considerable traders declined signing
their names, objecting particularly to that Article which points
at the foreigner in general, and more especially at the libertys
granted to the British trading subjects, well knowing the fallacy
of what is therein set forth, and many of those who have under-
wrote the said Petition were compell'd to it by being retain'd in
the Guild House till they comply'd, tho' ⅔ths of them are people
of no capital or knowledge in trade.

It is further to be observ'd that the number of citizens here
amount to upwards of three thousand, who ought to have sign'd
the afore mention'd Petition had it been agreeable to their sentiments, whereas there are only eighty-eight merchants, and
fourteen mechanicks, barbers, and shoemakers, etc."

(Their names are appended.)

Extracts from the Petition above mentioned.

1. That all Foreign Merchants and especially the English
have nowhere such privileges and immunitys granted as here:—
1st, that they don't become vassals and citizens. 2nd, they
don't pay a single Copeck towards the charges the citizens are
at. 3rdly, they are exempted from City services, and write for
goods to this Port in their own name, keep the same in their
houses and retail them at high prices. Altho' some libertys
were granted to the English to the end that our credit in other

---

* [Of the 9th Decr., 1762, o.s.]

parts should be more generally established, yet by their learning the constitution of the country they became entire masters of the trade and cutt us off from all correspondence abroad. They sell their goods on time (*sic*) at high rates to People of no capitall, furnish them with ready money and bind them by contracts to deliver goods at low prices, by which the Russ Merchants are obliged to deliver their goods according to such Contracts, and if any remain over, they also retain them for payment of such debts as may be owing. They also know the quantity and growth of the products of this empire, they lessen the prices of Russ goods and keep their own at exorbitant rates. They export Russ goods in their own name, ship them in foreign Bottoms, notwithstanding the Parliament of England made an Act in Ann. 1600, that no goods should be brought in foreign Bottoms, except the products of that country to which the ships belong. They export from hence for about 4 Millions of Rubles in goods, and import for a much larger summ, whereon they get 10 per cent by commission and charges. They also get their clerks to be burghers to transport their goods and transact trade in their name.

2. Several who are no burghers erect fabricks, make deliverys, have saw mills, sell their goods in retail and export them to other countrys.

3. The principal Russ Burghers and Citizens of this place to free themselves from serving all offices and charges thereby accruing, solicit privileges, erect fabricks, and enter into farms.

5. All inland merchants and boors who bring goods to this market should not be allowed to retail.

7. Concerning all trading people and mechanicks and that the foreigners should be subject to a tax and subordination.

10. Lastly that all Brokers and Brankers, Notarys, Auctioneers and Gaugers and other inferior Custom House officers should be all Burghers.

SPECIFICATION of incoming and outgoing SHIPS out of the Russian Ports, 1762.

	Incoming.	Outgoing.
Cronstadt	387	234
Riga	957	872
Revall	223	218
Pernau	93	93
Arensburg	35	35
Narva	112	110
Wieburg	53	55
Friedrichsham	27	34
Archangel	42	48
Onega	7	10
Kolskoy	1	2
Hapsal	7	7
Termernikoff		3

AMOUNT of GOODS EXPORTED from ST. PETERSBURG in the
year 1762 by the undermentioned :—

			Roubles.	Copecks.
1762.—By the English	-	-	1,905,449	16
Russians	-	-	409,447	47
Hollanders	-	-	263,311	49½
Lubeckers	-	-	358,743	25½
Rostockers	-	-	71,051	37
Dantzigers	-	·	111,439	2
Hamburghers		-	265,126	50¼
French	-	-	73,169	89¼
Swisses	-	-	17,561	19¼
Saxons	-	-	7,370	46¼
Italians	-	-	45,109	33
Venetians	-	-	3,300	50
Imperials	-	-	141	34
Sweeds	-	-	45,669	2¾
Armenians	-	-	1,681	82¼
Sundry	-	-	52,903	91½
Total	-		3,631,475	77½

AMOUNT of GOODS IMPORTED to ST. PETERSBURG in the
year 1762 by the undermentioned :—

					Roubles.	Copecks.
By Russ Merchants		-	-	-	817,388	03½
English	,,	-	-	-	653,627	72
Hollands	,,	-	-	-	348,822	21¾
Lubeck	,,	-	-	-	257,667	71¾
Hamburg	,,	-	-	-	209,483	18
Dantzig	,,	-	-	-	46,677	1½
French	,,	-	-	-	56,608	87¾
Italian	,,	.-	-	-	16,023	43¾
Saxon	,,	-	-	-	89,916	8¼
Rostock	,,	-	-	-	18,810	52½
Sweedish	;,	-	-	-	12,984	28½
Swiss		-	-	-	82,556	87
Austrian	,,	-	-	- '	77,204	5¾
Armenians	,,	-	-	-	5,402	22½
Venetians	,,	-	-	-	6,578	24½
Court Factor	,,	-	-	-	25,052	29½
Sundry Passengers		-	-	-	140,963	48
Captains of Ships		-	-	-	68,788	48½
					2,934,554	74¾

SCHEME[∘] proposed by an ENGLISH MERCHANT as to
BRITISH TRADE with PERSIA.

N.D. [1763.]—The total subversion of laws and government
in Persia for so long a duration render it absolutely imprudent

* Made at Ld. Buckinghamshire's request, mentioned in his Despatch of the 7th
Feb., 1763.

to think of a Factory at Resht (even if the Russians were inclined to grant the former liberties to us) and I am convinced the Court of Russia will never consent thereto.

Therefore I propose that Russia permits one House of Trade or Factory to be established at Astrachan to consist of 2 or 3 persons, whose names are to constitute the Firm of the House, and that they may have 4 English clerks and 2 supercargoes.

That 2 small Snows or Ships of about 60 to 70 Tons each shall be ready and at the service of the British Factory every spring as soon as the ice is broke up in the Volga and the Port of Yarke (sic) free and open to carry such wares and marchandizes to Enzeli as the British factors shall chuse to ship; and that such snows or vessels shall be navigated by Russians, but be under the command of the British Factory's supercargoes as to their departure or return, and one of them with a clerk be permitted to go in the spring with each ship and return to Astrachan in the autumn; and that they depart from Enzeli on or before the 28th day of October for Astrachan. That the freight which the English are to pay for such vessels be agreed on and stipulated either by the month or for the season.

That no Russian subjects, Indians, Armenians, or Tartars or any but British subjects have liberty to ship any goods or go passengers in the two vessels referred to in order to prevent any quarrels or chicanes which that nation are but too apt to encourage. That whenever the Government of Ghilan or Resht may be so far settled that the Russian, Armenian, or other merchants may proceed to Resht to dispose of their merchandizes and purchase silk, the British supercargoes shall have that liberty also, leaving one supercargo and one clerk with the vessels in the mouth of the lake of Enzeli while the other with one clerk resorts to Perebazar or Resht or such convenient markets in Ghilan, as other merchants resort to.

By this method I apprehend all reasonable objections would be removed; for the Factory at Astrachan would be absolutely under their own power, the ships to be their own, navigated by their own subjects and the only command our people would have is that of their departure from Astrachan and returning from Enzeli to Astrachan, the latter being even limited; but there I shall anticipate one objection and it is the only one they can with any shadow of reason make, namely that these two supercargoes or their clerks may follow the example of Capt. Elton and enter into the Shaws' service and teach them the art of Shipbuilding, etc. To this objection I answer that Capt. Elton was certainly the most improper person in the universe to be sent into Persia by the English or suffered to go there by the Russians. He had been bred a mariner and a merchant; had even been employed in the Russian service where, I have heard him say, he had been ill-used. These circumstances together with an immoderate share of vanity and the instability of his mercantile situation which he saw declining daily, may probably have been the first motives for his taking the rash step of entering into the Shaws' service where he expected great honours would be conferred upon him and large profits arise to him and he have the satisfaction of revenging himself, not only on the Russians, but on Mr. Mungo Grame, for between two men never did greater animosity or hatred exist. Therefore care may be taken that none be employed in this new Plan but such as are mere merchants, and, should the Court of Russia desire it, security might even be given them that, in case of any irregularities or breach of any Article in the Treaty, the persons shall be forthcoming or the penalty paid.

But in the present confusion that reigns in Persia, an Empire without a head, there can be no fear that any attempt like that of Capt. Elton's will ever be made, for, if it could not succeed under Shah Nadir, what Emperor can ever make mariners of Persians who dread the water as much as cats.

I have as yet said nothing touching the advantages that would accrue to the British Nation in general as well as to every particular member in that trade and also the Factory in St. Petersburg; but there are arguments I fear we must be very cautious in explaining to the Russians, whose jealousy and even vanity would prompt them to refuse us, thinking themselves capable of carrying on that trade to the extent we should do; and therefore I would rather have them applyed on our side as a spur to accelerate the means for obtaining the liberties before recited.

I shall, before I conclude, observe that whatever advantages the Russians may propose from denying us and trading themselves to Persia, it is morally impossible that the silk they will or can bring as returns will ever be saleable here in England; for the greatest part of what they buy is of Georgians and Armenians, and greater thieves and villians there certainly are not in the world, and the Russians in their package of silk follow the same unfair methods. And as to the wollen and other goods they never can make the advantage of them that the English will, for the Russians send agents from Petersburg and Moscow into Persia, who rather than stay more than one season will sell cheap and buy dear in order to be gone, whereas the British Factory would support the market of European goods and keep down the price of silk; and, as a proof of this, let anyone who has had any tolerable knowledge of the Persia Trade deny if he can that the last three years, when I was at the head of the Factory, any Russians, Armenians, or others were able to make any figure in that trade,—nay they many of them complained they were starving and the trade not worth following. Yet the profits we obtained for our principals were more than would now amply satisfy them, and such as I dare not name; from whence it appears of what great consequence the obtaining of the liberty herein proposed would be to this nation.

Earl of Buckinghamshire to M. Panin.

1764, Avril 1er.—Voici à la fin le Papier que j'ai promis à V.E., qui n'a tardé si longtems que parcequ'on a voulu y travailler avec toute la précision possible.

Il convient de la prévenir que l'évaluation des Exports qu'elle trouvera ici est beaucoup plus forte que celle qui est enregistrée à la Douanne de Sa. Maj. Impériale, différence qui provient de ce que là, tout est apprécié sur l'ancien pied sans faire aucune attention à l'accroissement considérable qui s'est fait depuis quelques années sur le prix de toutes les denrées de la Russie. Il n'est pas nécessaire d'assurer V.E. que je suis persuadé que rien n'y est manqué au delà de ce qu'il aura actuellement coûté.

J'attens tous les jours une spécification pareille de Riga.

Il n'est impossible de laisser passer cette occasion sans lui témoigner une partie du chagrin que je ressens de l'état fatal où se trouvent les négotiations que je m'étais flatté avec quelque ombre de raison de conclure. Dans votre dernière conversation V.E. ne m'a que trop manifesté que pour le présent il n'ÿ a rien à espérer. Jusqu'à ce moment j'avais toujours cru que nous entrerions au moins dans le Traité de Commerce, supposant que la Russie était trop convaincu des avantages qu'elle retire du trafic de l'Angleterre pour vouloir nous laisser des doutes sur ces intentions de nous accorder les mêmes privilèges dont nos marchands ont depuis si longtems joui. V.E. me permettra de lui faire trois remarques sur les changemens qui sont arrivés dans cette commerce.

Que la Russie consume beaucoup moins de manufactures Anglaises. Que le prix des denrées que l'Angleterre retire de la Russie s'est accru sur presque touts les Articles d'un tiers, à l'égard d'autres, particulièrement le Col de Poisson, à l'infini. Et que le vivre à Petersbourg coûte le double au marchand de ce qu'il faisait dix ans passés.

Je suis sûr qu'elle conviendra avec moi le Traité d'Alliance est un objet qui, vue la situation critique des affaires de l'Europe, mérite toute l'attention des deux Nations ; qu'on ne peut envisager qu'avec regret les difficultés qui en retardent la conclusion. J'espére que V.E. me permettra de la voir aussi souvent qu'il lui sera possible durant le peu de tems qu'il me restera encore à passer en Russie, et qu'elle conservera toujours quelque amitié et quelque bienveillance pour celui qui a l'honneur, etc., etc.

EVIDENCE relating to RUSSIAN COMMERCE given before the HOUSE OF COMMONS.

1774, May 5.—Mr. Nicholas Cavanagh's evidence. (" Mr. Cavanagh is concerned in a merchant's house established at St. Petersburg and is lately arrived from thence. He resided there 32 years; he buys and sells and exports the linens of Russia.")

BUCKINGHAMSHIRE PAPERS.

PART 5. 1742-1793.

VICEROYALTY OF IRELAND—AMERICAN REBELLION AND OTHER PRIVATE CORRESPONDENCE.

W. PITT to THE COUNTESS OF SUFFOLK.

1742, July 6. London.—Just after I had received the honour of your letter yesterday, I had a second letter from my sister upon the same scheme, my answer to the first not having reached her, your Ladyship's being at Cheltenham when I made that answer, I was obliged to make it without troubling you upon it, though desired to take your opinion. My answer was (what I have again repeated) that I could not see the scheme proposed to her in any light that would let me think it fit for her ; that I thought Paris the most improper place for a single woman to live at, nor could I like her settling abroad any where, if her health did not make it necessary ; that I made no doubt but the society my Lady Bolingbrook's protection (which was the best in France) must place her in, would be, to all the world on that side the water, the most reputable advantageous thing imaginable; but that the world here would not know (and perhaps part of it not choose to know) any thing more of her situation, than that she was living at Paris a single woman, that I liked of all things her staying at Argeville, as long as my Lady Bolingbrook would give her leave but when that visit (which I hoped would be a very long one) was made, I advised her to come home. This, Madam, was the substance of my answer to her scheme, which I could by no means entertain a thought of.[*] I own, it afflicts me not to be able to agree with her in this project, which I see she has a great mind to, when I can only tell her what not to do with herself. I should have been very glad to have known your Ladyship's opinion before I gave my own ; if you think as I do of this matter, I shall be sure I think right, your friendship and goodness to my sister I think makes it unnecessary for me to make you an excuse for troubling you so long on her subject. I hope the waters agree with you, and with Mr. Berkley if he ventures to drink them.

GEORGE TOWNSHEND to the WORSHIPFUL MAYOR or RETURNING OFFICER of the Borough of Thirsk, Yorkshire.

(Endorsed, ' *Circular Militia Letter*.') `

1756, Aug. 6. Cranmore in Norfolk.—Enclosing the bill for constituting a general militia, which in the last, Sessions of

---

[*] *See* for this Mr. George Grenville to Lady Suffolk, Sep. 14, 1742, and Mrs. Anne Pitt to Lady Suffolk, July 10, 1757 (Vol. II. of Lady Suffolk's Letters, pp. 193 and 232) *See also* Walpole's version (Memoirs of the Reign of George III., p. 85) of Pitt's relations with his sister.

Parliament passed with unanimity. Great weight would be given to this bill if the approbation of Corporations were expressed in the form of petitions to the House of Commons.

"Every circumstance in the situation of this country which united the House of Commons in one sense of the necessity of passing such a bill as this has since the recess of Parliament increased upon us, for we have since that time lost Minorca, invited foreign troops and seen them called home, and found the war every day brought nearer to our doors, from whence nothing, in the opinion of the Commons of England, can keep the enemy, but a general, and to a certain degree, disciplined militia."

DUKE OF DEVONSHIRE to the EARL OF BUCKINGHAMSHIRE.

1757, Tuesday, June 14.—The Militia Bill having passed and there being consequently a necessity of having a Lord Lieutenant for the county of Norfolk, I have mentioned it to his Majesty, and at Lord Orford's request did recommend him to the King, who has consented to it. I am very sorry that in this instance I am under the necessity of taking a step that may not be agreeable to your inclinations, but my situation is such with the Walpole family as made it unavoidable; upon any other occasion I am sure I should be very glad to oblige your Lordship. I thought it a piece of respect due to you to give you the first information of it.

Extraits d'une lettre de M. DE MONTCALM* à M. DE BERNIER, Ministre de Marine.

1757, du 4 d'Août —Mes correspondences avec les colons Anglais subsistent toujours; même ouverture, même fidélité même candeur de leur part. Un peu de contrebande transporté habilement chez eux m'amène regulièrement leurs dépêches.

(*Extraits d'une Lettre de M. de ——— traduite par M. de Bougainville inclus dans l'autre.*)

"L'idée de cette lettre est de prouver que si les Français se donnèrent le soin d'encourager le commerce et les manufactures il ne dépendrait que d'eux de s'emparer de tout le commerce des Anglais avec leurs Colonies Amériquaines et que touts les efforts de l'Angleterre pour y mettre quelque empêchement seraient inutiles.—Elle dit "Pendant plus d'un siècle nos diverses Colonies ont eu très peu de correspondence entre elles; occupées à se former et s'établir, elles ne visaient qu'à elles-mêmes. Les Gouvernements d'ailleurs sont différents, les loix, la Religion souvent, & le commerce y contrastent. De là leur peu d'union; elles subsistaient l'une à côté de l'autre sans presque se connâitre.

Mais depuis cette guerre les colons se sont rapprochés de mœurs, d'intérêts, & de sentiments; obligés de fournir leurs contingents, ils se sont trouvés rangés sous le même pavillon; des liaisons, des correspondances se sont formées.

---

* Louis Joseph de Montcalm Gozon, Marquis de St. Véran (1712-1759) commander-in-chief of the French troops which defended the Colonies of France in North America He was killed at the siege of Quebec.

Coup décisif pour nous, parceque nous serons unis & que nous nous tiendrons par la main; on respectera nos droits, parcequ'il serait dangereux de les attaquer; le haut prix des denrées d'Angleterre surchargent si fort nos colonies qu'elles seront obligées à recourir à l'etranger, c'est-a-dire à ruiner l'Angleterre. Les pauvres prendront le devant, les riches suivront. J'espère que votre cour profitera de l'avis."

(Suite de la première Lettre.)

L'Article sur lequel mon correspondant s'est égaré c'est l'établissement des manufactures en Canada. Gardons-nous sur ce point d'imiter la folie de l'Anglais. Les Colons ne sont si indocils que parcequ'ils commencent à sentir qu'ils peuvent se passer de lui. Ils possèdent chez eux des manufactures de toute espèce & seront bientôt en état d'en vendre à la terre totale au lieu d'en faire venir. Pour les Natifs du pays laissons les à leur vie errante & laborieuse dans les bois avec les sauvages & leur exercise militaire, ils en seront plus braves, plus capables de servir l'état & plus fidèles à le vouloir.

Vers la fin de la lettre et parlant de la possibilité de la perte de Canada, il recommende à sa Cour de s'assurer par la Paix, de Louisbourg ou de quelque Isle voisine qui pouvait servir également pour la Pêche & pour entrepôt pour introduire les manufactures Françaises dans les Colonies Anglaises. Idée dont la France malheureusement ne s'est pas départie.

(Lettre 2me. M. de Montcalm à M. de Bernier.)

Les sentiments des Colonies Anglaises pour la Patrie sont si peu cimentés que si je le jugeais convenable à nos intérêts je me ferais fort dans peu de faire signer la neutralité à une partie d'entre elles.

Il s'appuie sur l'indiscrétion de l'Angleterre de n'avoir construit des forteresses que dans l'intérieur des Provinces.

Faute énorme de l'Angleterre de ne pas les taxier dès le commencement."

(Lettre 3me. Du même au même.)

Touts en général ne se soucient guère du Roi ni du Parlement d'Angleterre—aussi auraient-ils dès longtemps secoué le joug, si la crainte de la France n'eut été un frein pour les retenir, chaque Province serait devenue une petite République. Si l'ancienne Angleterre après avoir conquis la Canada scavait se l'attacher par la politique & les bienfaits, si elle la laissait à sa Religion, ses loix, sa langue, ses coutumes & son ancien Gouvernement; la Canada divisée dans touts ces points d'avec les autres Colonies, n'entrerait jamais dans leurs intérêts, ni dans leurs vues. Mais au contraire si elle veut la mettre sur le pied des autres, elle deviendrait bientôt la même à son égard.

(Remarque.)

Ces lettres sont en général si prophétiques qu'on les soupçonnerait en quelque façon d'avoir été écrites après coup.

CHARLES TOWNSHEND to the EARL OF BUCKINGHAMSHIRE.

1760, October 19. Adderbury.—If I had not been absent from
Adderbury when your letter came, your Lordship would have
heard from me by the return of the post, and if your letter had
not come so late in the year, and at a time when I am confined
by a multiplicity of business to this distance from London, I
should have brought you my answer to your summons myself;
as it is, I have lost the satisfaction of being of your party, which
mortified me exceedingly, as I know I should have passed my
time with the very people, in the very manner I mean and wish
to live. Lest you should think I make you a general excuse, I
must desire leave to tell you that Buccleugh being now fourteen,
I have been lately obliged to attend him at Eton, and lawyers in
town, several times, and that I have not yet the least command of
myself for two days; such a variety of forms has the preciseness
of ancient Scotch law created, and have the arts of modern
practice preserved, upon the appointment of a sole guardian in
that country; my attendance is the more necessary, as these
forms must be executed within a certain time fixed by law.
I beg your pardon for troubling you with such matters, but I
should be still more vexed if you did not believe it is not in my
power to be with you; which of our friends is with you? I hope
Vaughan, for Brickling will be excellent winter quarters for him
at the close of his Welsh campaign. Vernon is gathering berries
from Prince Ferdinand's laurels; and Stanley, I fear, is engaged
in launching the formidable expedition. My brother tells me
nothing is so magnificent as Brickling, nobody so popular as the
master of it. I foresaw it would be so. I knew you would bring
back the county to a sense of better things than political jealousy
and perpetual cabal, and that universal civility and a purer taste
in life would gain everybody. I read in the prints that Mr.
Harbord is married, and if his marriage pleases you, or, in your
judgment, strengthens his situation, I shall be pleased with it
also, let me take this opportunity of saying that I rejoice much in
your own late escape; the person would have disappointed you;
the fortune would to you have been no recompence; the manner
in which it went off proves you have no reason to lament it;
and you have acted throughout with sense and temper. I
should make another excuse for this topic; but I hope you will
make it for me, and that the hearty love I bear you will explain
and justify the liberty it takes.
I beg you will present my best affections to all our friends at
Brickling, my heart is wherever they are; for I have hung up my
arms at the St. Albans, whether it be in town or country; if Stanley
be with you, tell him Lord Lyttelton has just opened Haggley
House to the county of Worcester. The invitation was universal
to all ranks and all parties, and the plan really magnificent. The
county accepted. They all came in, and my Lord at last was the
only absent man. Some untoward accidents happened in the
execution: for in the first place my lord forgot to have the beds
aired; in the second, he classed the company according to their

birth and reputed estates into three divisions, and in the last place Mr. Lyttelton, destined to have opened the ball with the first person of the first class, mutinied, and would dance only with a smart girl he had brought in the morning from a neighbouring village unknown in her birth, equivocal in her character, and certainly at the very tail of my Lord's third division. Before the dinner was ended, everybody was talking of their private affairs and pedigree ; Bacchus's hall was turned into the Herald's office ; and the whole company become jealous and sulky. At the end of the three days my Lord's new palace was filled with disgust and complaints, and he is said to have confessed at last that distinctions are not prudent.

I hope we shall meet soon in town, I suppose at Newcastle House on the birthday.

HARBORD HARBORD[a] to the EARL OF BUCKINGHAMSHIRE.

1761, March 28. Norwich.—I doubt not you will be as much pleased as surprised to hear of the late transactions at Norwich. Mr. Bacon[†] and myself at our coming hither found all the Corporation, Quakers and principal manufacturers warm and hearty in our joint interest, many of the middling tradesmen disgusted with us both, but upon application nine out of ten promised to support me. Robt. Harvey and Preston were upon our first arrival talked of as candidates by many of the very low freemen, the former declared to us both he had no intentions of offering himself, the latter hesitated and ask'd the advice of the Gregorians assembled by notice in full chapter, who all declared they were engaged to support me, and much more than the majority said the same as to Mr. Bacon. Upon this Mr. Preston took all opportunitys of publickly and privately declaring he would support Mr. Bacon and myself. On Tuesday and the two following days, Alderman Thompson was a good deal talked of as a candidate, but his being one of the deputation from the Hall upon the 6th of November to invite Mr. Bacon and myself to represent that city, his public and private conversation from that time till within this week, made it appear impossible he should be so treacherous. However, on Thursday evening about seven, printed bills were dispersed all over the town requesting votes for Thompson and Robert Harvey, public houses open'd and they busy running about the town asking votes ; the managers who had canvassed the Town Quakers and all, Mr. Rogers, Tom Harvey, Ives, etc., were much alarm'd for Mr. Bacon, as many of their workmen had declared they would give only single votes, and Thompson had directed most of his people to vote for himself and me. On Friday morning when the Mayor, Mr. Bacon, etc., went down to St. Andrew's Hall, the other two candidates came with their mob up to the Town Hall and waited for Mr. Bacon and myself. A poll was directly demanded and our friends went to work. About

---

* Afterwards Sir Harbord Harbord and created Lord Suffield in 1786.
† Edward Bacon of Erleham (or Earlham), near Norwich.

five in the afternoon Harvey and Thompson proposed adjourning the poll till this day, but gentlemen prov'd so warm upon thus keeping the town in a flame, that at length they agreed to close the booths and upon the casting up the numbers they were for Harbord, 1,729; Bacon, 1,507; Thompson, 715; Harvey, 501. Not a gentleman that I know of will be found upon the poll of the two latter gentlemen, and we gave no money nor open'd any house, had no country votes, and Thompson had, as we have since discover'd, been picking them up for ten days to the number of, I fancy, 60 or 70. Mr. Lillington and some others were at first so alarm'd for B——n, that they refused some single votes and at length Crowe, Woods, Ives, Tom Harvey and others went down to the booths and used all their influence and interest with their respective workmen for the double votes, the steady and resolute and candid behaviour of the Sheriffs preventing any rioting, and I assure you I have seen more at this place when there was no opposition. The principal gentlemen are so exasperat'd at the behaviour of T——n that if he is already in the list of justices and is not struck out and if we can possibly do not get him (sic) out of his employment it will prejudice our interest here more than anything that I know of that can happen.

Charles Townshend to the Earl of Buckinghamshire.

1761, June 24. War Office.—I am sorry I was not in town when your Lordship's letter came to my house lest you should have found any inconvenience from the delay it has occasioned.

Your Lordship has only done me justice in your immediate contradiction of the reports of my having interfered upon the vacancy at Norwich and the competition of Mr. Gay and Mr. Thompson, for I very solemnly assure you that I have never heard the subject spoke of but occasionally by yourself and very lightly by my own family, and have never had the least or the most distant conversation upon it with the Duke of Newcastle or any other person in the Administration. May I in return beg the favour of you to put such of your Lordship's friends as have thus used my name so very positively and with such little justification upon naming when and from whom they have in fact ever heard such a report? I could add to this general representation of the truth of my conduct upon this occasion, how little my temper, situation or any passion I have lead me upon such contests to take any interest at all, much less would they suffer me to act an unfriendly part towards you, with whom I live, thank God, and ever have lived, in a degree of friendship against which matters of this nature, I fancy, will never by either of us be put in the ballance.

The Same to the Same.

1761, October 27. War Office.—As to Lord Buckinghamshire's letter of recommendation of Gardiner, whom he is unwilling to do anything for unless Lord Buckinghamshire is really desirous of serving him. On learning that he is, he gives him a commission. "The club meets on Saturday; it will meet with more pleasure if you are there. Times busy; war hot; opera thin; Pitt resigned; Vernon lame; Vaughan sanguine. I have given Bellenden a company at your desire."

GEORGE GRENVILLE to the EARL OF BUCKINGHAMSHIRE.

1762, April 13. Wotton.—Expressions of friendship. It is impossible to answer Lord Buckinghamshire's enquiry as to the time when the Prussian subsidy and the vòte of credit are likely to be considered in the House of Lords as no day has yet been fixed for their consideration in the House of Commons.

JOHN EARL OF HYNDFORD° to the SAME.

1762, August 1. Carmichael House.—"As his Majesty has been pleased to honour you with the Embassy to Russia I heartily congratulate your Lordship upon it, and I can make no doubt that you will acquit yourself in that office to the satisfaction of the King and of the Ministry and your friends, of which number I desire to be ranked as a sincere one.

As to the present politicks of the Court of Russia, your instructions must direct you how to act. But as to your domestic and economical affairs I must acquaint you in friendship that during five years of my Embassy I was out of pocket, for 'tis a very expensive Court, and, contrary to common sense, an ambassador must give great entertainments and make a vast show in equipage to be respected. As to your coaches, I would advise you to send them by sea from England, except what you want for the journey for yourself and servants which you may provide you in at Utrecht. But take care to avoid there a great rogue called Prichard, who takes upon himself the character of the King's Commissary, who has cheated many an English traveller and me in particular. You can't do without a German secretary, and if he understands the French language, it will save you a third, for I make no doubt you carry an English secretary with you. The next thing is servants, and I must begin with good cooks and a Maitre d'Hôtel, all which you may get at Hannover, and I would advise you to carry as few English servants as possible, except those about your own person, for they are sooner debauched at Petersbourg than at London (c'est beaucoup dire). This is very unconnected, but I must for your Lordship put down the articles as they occur to me at the distance of twelve years. Your Lordship may buy horses there of all kinds without being at the expense and risk of sending them thither. Mr. Keith, the King's Minister, will put you in the way of providing your family with all kind of wines and necessarys. I need not give you any caution as to wine or women, for I know your delicacy as to both, but you will be tempted. . . . . . .

° British Ambassador at St. Petersburg, 1744-1750.

I dare not desire to be remembered to Peter the 3rd, altho' I fancy he has not forgot me, at least he assured me he never would etc. He is a great lover of musick, and if you carry some good fiddles, he's very fond of them."   .   .   .

VISCOUNT BARRINGTON to the EARL OF BUCKINGHAMSHIRE.

1762, December 17. Cavendish Square.—Tho' you did not lay any injunctions on me to write to you, I think it my duty to inform you of the interesting transactions of your country: I ought to have done it sooner; but till last week I hoped by staying some time, I might send you more agreable news both to yourself and to me. The die is now cast, and opposition declared; nay actually begun. The Preliminaries have been opposed in both Houses of Parliament. In your House there was no division, tho' the Duke of Newcastle and Lord Hardwick spoke against them. Mr. Pitt came to the House of Commons on crutches and spoke (sometimes standing, sometimes sitting) for three hours and twenty-five minutes; after which he went away, amidst the acclamations of a mob, which had follow'd him even into the lobby. His speech was against the preliminaries, but without violence or personality; declaring he had no connections with any body. The House divided about midnight; 319 for the address approving the Peace, and 65 against it. The Attorney-General went away before the division; but he attended the next day on the report and spoke in favour of the Preliminaries in general, tho' he expressed doubts as to some articles, which he hoped might be altered in the definitive treaty: his brother Lord Royston voted with the Majority. The division the second day against the address was only 63, but if all had stay'd the day before, I believe instead of 65 they might have amounted to between four score and ninety. Such an eminent majority secures administration, and gives it credit as well as strength. Charles Townshend supported the Preliminaries soundly and well, tho' he had resigned his employment the day before. He says he shall continue to support Government till the end of the session, when he will be ready to accept the Board of Trade; but that he disliked the War Office. Stanley made an admirable speech for the Peace. You have heard that Strange is Chancellor of the Dutchy in the room of Lord Kinnoul, who resign'd (as he says) on acct. of the usage of his friend the Duke of Devonshire. It is said Ellis will succeed Townshend and Rigby succeed Ellis; and it is thought Lord Granby will be Master of the Ordnance when he comes home. It is expected that they who voted in the minority the other day will be turn'd out before the holydays.

Let me add a word about myself. I support Government, which I should do with the utmost satisfaction if the Duke of Newcastle did not oppose it. My motives in separating myself *politically* (personally I never can separate myself from his Grace) may be conscientious; they may be interested. I leave you to judge whence my conduct proceeds; you know me and

my actions for many years past. The Duke of N. continues to
treat me with friendship and kindness. I was very explicit with
him from the beginning; and he knows there never was a time,
when even *he* could make me do what I thought wrong. His
Grace had such offers several times in the summer, and particularly at the end of it, as I think he could not have refused, if he
had not been govern'd and flatter'd by the Duke of Cumberland,
who has undone him, and many of his best friends; but this is
intirely *inter nos.*

GEORGE GRENVILLE to the EARL OF BUCKINGHAMSHIRE.

1763, July 18. Downing Street.—Tho' the constant scenes
of busyness which I have been engaged in for some time pass'd
have scarcely allow'd me to perform the common offices of civility
to my friends, yet I trust that they know me too well to believe
that I can be wanting in those of friendship. Many changes
have happen'd in my own situation and that of the public since
we parted, but none can happen in my sincere regard for you or
in my desire to express it more effectually than by the
assurances contain'd in a letter. I had the pleasure of seeing
Mr. Hobart° as soon as he arrived in England and for the few
days that he staid here before he went into the country. The
account which he gave of himself made his return hither very
necessary, but I flatter myself that he will not be oblig'd to go to
Spaw to perfect his recovery. I rejoiced extremely to find from
him as well as from your own letters that the severity of
the winters in Russia has had no ill effect upon you. Your return
to Petersburg will, I hope, open a more agreeable and more active
scene to you and take away all complaint of want of occupation.
Such at least are the expectations that we form here, in consequence of the information which we receive. For my own part
I most sincerely wish it from the persuasion I have that whenever
you enter upon any busyness of importance you will in the
transaction of it do honour to yourself and service to the publick.
You was fully apprized of my sentiments upon that subject my
dear Lord, before you left England, and I can only say to you that
they still continue in all respects exactly the same. As you seem
not to wish to have any body appointed Secretary to the Embassy
in the room of Mr. Hobart, I believe I may assure you that no
body will, at least for the present. Indeed I perfectly agree with
you and enter into your reasons for not wishing it. I am
extremely sensible to the many kind expressions towards me in
both your letters, which I shall allways hope to deserve by every
means in my power. Adieu my dear Lord, there is no publick
news worth the sending you, and if there was you would receive
it by your publick dispatches, and as to anything of a private
nature relative to the interior of this country, as this letter will
probably go by the common post, it certainly would not be a
proper conveyance to send it by. . . .

°George Hobart, afterwards third Earl of Buckinghamshire.

LORD BARRINGTON to the EARL OF BUCKINGHAMSHIRE.

1763, November 17. Cavendish Square.—I have not time to
answer two very friendly and agreeable letters which I have lately
received from you, but which I shall acknowledge soon in the
manner I ought.

The paper herewith enclosed (which is an extract from a
letter I have just written) will inform you of the state of publick
matters here, which is much better than I expected it would be,
and bears a very favourable aspect. I will only add that the House
of Lords have come to very strong resolutions against a most
obscene and profane book called "An Essay on Woman," with
notes by Dr. Warburton, Bishop of Gloucester. For this breach
of the Bishop's privilege, Wilks the author will be in Newgate
after expulsion, if he does not run away, which in his present
state he can hardly do.

Inclosure.

1763, November 17. Cavendish Square.—Last Tuesday the
Parliament met, and the House of Commons, before the King's
speech was reported from the Chair, took into consideration a
Message from his Majesty, on the subject of Mr. Wilkes, stating
the impediments thrown in the way of his trial by the decision
of Westminster Hall, on the head of privilege. After long
debate on various points it was determined that the 'North Briton'
No. 45, was an infamous, seditious libel, etc. It was also resolved
to proceed further on the Message, next day, when the point of
privilege should be discussed, and enquiry made whether
Mr. Wilkes was the author of that paper, with intention, on proof
thereof, to expell him; but, just as the House was going to
proceed yesterday on this business, news came that he had been
shot thro' the body, in a duel, by Sam. Martin, late Secretary to
the Treasury. Martin had said in a speech, the day before (after
mentioning some virulent abuse thrown on him, in a former
North Britain) "that whoever was capable in a printed anony-
mous paper to asperse him by name, was a cowardly scoundrel."
Wilkes the next morning wrote a letter to Martin, acknowledging
himself the author of that paper, and they proceeded to Hyde
Park, where the duel was fought. The wound is not thought
dangerous; but it occasioned the putting off the consideration of
the Message, and we went on the Speech. The Address was
moved by Lord Carnarvon, and very well seconded by Lord
Frederick Campbell. Mr. Pitt spoke with great ability, and the
utmost degree of temper. He said he had not altered his
opinion of the Peace, which he still thought inadequate to our
situation and successes; but that being made and approved by
Parliament, nothing more unfortunate could happen than that
it should be broken. That it was every man's business to
contribute all he could, to make it lasting, and to improve it;
for which purpose he recommended union and abolition of
party distinctions as absolutely necessary. He spoke civilly
and not unfavourably of the Ministers; but of the King
he said every thing which duty and affection could inspire.

The effect of this was a vote for the Address Nemine Contradicente. I think if 50,000*l.* had been given for that speech,
it would have been well expended. It secures us a quiet Session ;
and with the help of a division of 300 to 111 the day before, will
give strength and reputation to Government, both at home and
abroad. I must return for a moment to Wilks, that you may
know more of Mr. Pitt's present temper, for which I cannot
account. He speaks as ill of him and his writings as anybody ;
he approved the resolution against his Paper No. 45, except one
word : but he is very warm on the affair of privilege, which he
insists to have been rightly determin'd by the Court of Common
Pleas, and violated by the Secretaries of State. He abused the
opinion given by the Crown Lawyers, and treated both the
Attorney and Solicitor-General very roughly tho' the former has
resigned, and was supposed to be politically connected with him.
I know not what to make of this, in all respects, most extraordinary man.

LORD BARRINGTON to the EARL OF BUCKINGHAMSHIRE.

1764, February 26. Cavendish Square.—You have probably
heard of some near divisions lately in the House of Commons,
but perhaps you are not inform'd exactly of the points which
occasion'd them. The following account will not be unacceptable
to you if you have not received a better.

Wilkes was taken up by Lord Halifax on a general warrant to
seize the printer, publisher or author of the "North Briton" No.
45, together with their papers. Of this he complain'd the first
day of the session as a violation of his privilege ; but the hearing of that complaint was postponed to the consideration of the
King's message concerning him. After Wilkes's expulsion, the
complaint was taken up (not in his name, but as regarding the
privilege of the *House*) by Sir Wm. Meredith and Sir George
Saville. On enquiry it was found that nothing had been done by
Lord Halifax or others concerned, but what was warranted by
the constant usage of office, from the earlyest times, particularly
when Lord Townshend, the Duke of Newcastle and Mr. Pitt were
Secretaries of State ; and therefore the House unanimously
agreed there was no ground of censure or blame on the present
occasion : but the opposition proposed a Resolution declaring
such general Warrants illegal, as in truth I believe them to be.
The Ministers would not consent to this declaration of the law
by one House of Parliament *only*, tho' they did not assert the
legality of the Warrants. They said Westminster Hall and the
judges there were the best interpreters of law ; or else an
Act of Parliament; and therefore proposed to adjoin the consideration of the matter for four months ; which was carry'd
at near seven in the morning by 232 against 218. There were in
the course of this proceeding several very long days, and near
divisions, many persons extremely well disposed to Government
and in employment, voting (in what they call'd a constitutional
point) with the opposition. I think they will most or all of them
come back to their friends : and if this point, greatly labour'd by

active opponents, does not raise more flame without doors than there is an appearance of at present, I hope it will not do Government any real or lasting mischief. As to change of administration, I dare say it will produce none; tho' perhaps the Court you are at may receive different information. Wilkes has been convicted on the indictments against him for writing the "North Briton" No. 45, and the "Essay on Woman," a most bawdy and blasphemous performance, so I think it impossible he can ever come over hither. He and his cause are already forgotten by the only friends he had, the mob; and we shall not soon have any similar writings.

Dull politicks, my dear Lord, are a very poor inadequate return for the charming letters you send me from Petersburgh, two of which remain unanswer'd; I mean those dated the 27th December and 10th January last. I have communicated them, or parts of them, where it was proper; and my communications were admired. The club is at your devotion, and goes as well as it can do without you. Strange and Stanley have had your messages, love you very much, and talk of writing to you. Our other club held on Sundays is in a very prosperous way, the vacancies have been well fill'd up, the meetings are well frequented, and our friend Johnston gets as many bumpers as he desires. There is an antiministerial club set up in Albemarle Street, at the house where poor Lord Waldegrave lived, on the footing of Whites; but I hear no amusement or vice going on there; so I conclude it will be soon abandon'd. Mrs. Welch lately return'd from Ireland with a fresh importation of beauty, was inform'd against and obliged to give security for her appearance; a bill of indictment was offer'd at the last sessions, but the grand jury had the good sense to return it ignoramus.

George Grenville to the Earl of Buckinghamshire.

1764, March 27. Downing Street.—Lady Suffolk has communicated to Mr. Grenville Lord Buckinghamshire's letter from which it would appear that he was desirous to have it at his option whether he should stay at St. Petersburg some time longer, or return immediately, as the situation of his affairs may render it desirable. Mr. Grenville has therefore applied to his Majesty and is able to inform Lord Buckinghamshire that nothing further will be done with regard to the appointment of any other person, or to his recall at the present.

"Lady Suffolk will always prefer Lord Buckinghamshire's credit and reputation even to the joy and comfort of seeing him.

Of Parliamentary transactions it would be difficult to say but a little, and improper to say a great deal."

Lord Barrington to the Same.

1764, May 9.—I did not intend writing any more to you, for by your letter of the 3rd of April I concluded you were soon to begin your journey hither, but I have since found reason to believe I was not so near the comfort of seeing you as I hoped and expected. Lord Sandwich tells me you may have your letters of recall whenever you shall desire them, and that you know you may. I am certain this paper will arrive at Petersburgh before those letters, not yet requested ; and therefore I send it, full of the most cordial and sincere assurances of my entire undiminished affection for your Excellency. You generally begin with a little politicks and I will (imitating your good example) do the same. ˌThe session of Parliament ended very well for the Administration, which has now in favour of its stability the publick opinion. You know how much that opinion will contribute to its stability. George Grenville has done admirably, indeed triumphantly, in the House of Commons. He gains ground every day in the city, a material place for the head of the Treasury. He has not indeed received any compliments *en corps* from the first commercial corporation in the kingdom ; but at Bristol, the second, he has been visited, complimented, feasted and honoured with his freedom. He went thither from Stoke with our friend Berkeley, now Lord Botetourt, fifth Baron of England ; and he visited his Lordship from Bath, where Mrs. Grenville has been sometime for her health. I wish you joy of Lord Halifax's Garter, an honour, in my opinion, well deserved and well timed. I hope my dear Lord to see it round your leg, while that leg is able to perform all the offices a true knight can require from it. Lord Bute came to town towards the end of the session. His Lordship and his most intimate friends declare he will never more have anything to do with ministry or even office ; and they add his perfect satisfaction in the administration now entrusted with the conduct of affairs. My old patron and friend the Duke of Newcastle is gone to Claremont for the summer in good health. I have seen him often this last winter, and Abdiel as I am, have always been kindly received. I believe he does not expect or even intend to be minister again, but he continues very restless. Mr. Pitt is almost worn out with gout, and except where Lord Chief Justice Pratt has been concern'd seems to me rather to have supported than opposed Government. By this time, the Court where you are probably knows how much it has been deceived by misrepresentations from home.

Have you seen a most curious collection of letters published here by M. D'Eon, secrétaire d'Ambassade to the Duc de Nivernois ? Wilkes is a child to him in abuse. M. de Guerchy, the Duc de Prâlin and others who are his objects have found him a most dangerous adversary, the more so for his being mad. Guerchy found out that he was visited by Lord Temple and expressed his surprise thereat to Lord Halifax, who made him this answer, "*Que voulez-vous que Milord Temple fasse ; il a perdu son propre Wilkes il faut qu'il se prenne au vôtre.*" We dare not send this gentleman out of the country, but the Attorney-General, by order, is prosecuting him for a libel against the French Ambassador.

The Earl of Pomfret has at last taken that deep laden rich aquapulca Miss Draycott. . . . . . You see what middle-aged Lords of the Bedchamber can do.

I must conclude this letter by informing you of poor Jack's
death at Paris the 2nd of last month, the heavyest affliction I
ever knew. He was seized with a sort of palsey, which ended in
an apoplexy. Water and matter were found in his head,
occasioned as the learned there believe by a shot when he was
unfortunately hit by David Hamilton in Norfolk. I cannot, like
old Farington, make a new friend at the Coffee House when I
have lost an old one. Come therefore my dear Lord and comfort
your ever affectionate Barrington.

Sir William Harbord to the Earl of Buckinghamshire.

1764, August 13.—(Regrets that he is staying another winter
as he now fears will be the case in so severe a climate and so
uncomfortable a situation. Details as to what he has done for
him on his Blickling estate.)

I can't indeed wonder that your Lordship should be a little
mortified at your friend Townshend's deserting you upon a late
occasion. However, tho' he carried his point, he gained no credit
by it, nor has your Lordship lost any. His breach of friendship to you, which is the light in which it is generally looked
upon, is condemned even by those who have no particular regard
for your Lordship, and many gentlemen of the first fortunes in
your country as well as most others are so dissatisfy'd with the
proceedings at the last election that your lordship before another
will have no great difficulty in overturning what has been done and
taking the lead out of the hands it is in at present, if you think
proper to exert yrself, but whether living upon easy terms with
all and treating friends and foes upon the same footing will have
the effect is a matter of some doubt.

Mr. and Mrs. Harbord who have been here since the adjournment of Parliament and your old friend Lady Harbord join in
compliments to your Lordship.

Lord Albermale (*sic*) has bought Quidenham and is to give
63,000*l.* for it.

Lord Barrington to the Earl of Buckinghamshire.

1764, September 24. Cavendish Square.—It being understood
that Mr. Macartney[*] is on the point of departure for Petersburgh,
I thought it useless to write to you any more; concluding that you
would not remain in Russia after the arrival of a person who
could take care of the King's affairs. But your letter of the
21st August acquainting me you shall not be here at soonest
before Christmas, I perceive that I have full time for another
letter. It shall be chiefly composed of politicks, for there is
nothing else stiring here.

I need not inform you that Monsieur Destaign[†], Governor of
St. Domingo (a man of great quality who deserved the gallows

---

[*] Afterwards Sir George Macartney.
[†] Charles Hector Comte d'Estaing. b. 1729. Guillotined 1794.

for having broken his parole when our prisoner of war in the East Indies) was pleased to seize Turks Island, one of the Bahamas; neither is it necessary I should acquaint your Excellency how completely the French Court has disavow'd that proceeding, and promised the most ample satisfaction; but possibly you may not authentically be informed that our Ministry have acted in this affair with the utmost spirit, and have been unanimous in so doing. A latter transaction perhaps may not yet have been communicated to you. Some French ships of war went to Newfoundland, where they met Captain Palliser, with a force not quite equal under his command. The French Commodore was preparing to visit the ports of the Island, in consequence as he said of orders for that purpose. This Palliser told him he must not permit, and should resist by force, notwithstanding his wish to proceed in the most amicable manner. The Frenchman at last declared he would not take any step that could violate the peace and every thing afterwards past with the utmost amity. Now it is thought here that in both these instances the French have a mind to feel our pulse, and that perceiving it beats high they have disavow'd their officers. It is thought we shall bring our negotiation with France concerning the money due for keeping prisoners of war, to a good issue; and that we shall receive a large ballance on that head.

I now come to home affairs, and have the satisfaction to assure you that every thing is very quiet both at Court, in the city, and in the country; except at Exeter, where there is a violent spirit of opposition headed by Mr. Heath the Town Clerk, and, as I am told, by our friend Vaughan; who has now some leisure moments from love, which he throws away on country politicks. Poor Legge[o] you know is dead, and the Duke of Devonshire who tho' very ill went abroad in hope of getting better, is much worse, has lost the use of part of one side by a stroke of palsey, and is thought in much danger. It is the general opinion both of them would be well at this time, if they had continued Chamberlain and Chancellor of the Exchequer. It is still thought Mr. Pitt will not oppose, Charles Townshend wants to make his peace, the minority have neither abilities nor union, and I verily believe they will not have numbers next Session. The Duke of Grafton who since you left us has commenced opposer and orator, lives incognito at Woodford in Essex with Nancy Parsons in a cottage, the only inhabitant of which besides themselves is a maid servant, and a shoemaker's boy comes in the morning to clean his Grace's shoes.

I have before inform'd you that poor Lady Barrington has been long in a declining way. I left her in no sort of immediate danger a week ago, and came hither for a few days, but last Friday she was rather worse and dyed in an hour after her danger was perceived. However it was known by every body but herself that she could not last long. I return to Beckett after her funeral."

* Henry Bilson Legge, d. 23 Aug. 1764. Chancellor of the Exchequer until 1762.

LORD BARRINGTON to the EARL OF BUCKINGHAMSHIRE.

1764, December 17. Cavendish Square.—In obedience to your
commands I again write to you, and I direct my letter to Berlin
with great pleasure, because your instruction to do so is a proof
that you are soon to return home. I have thought you too long
absent for some time, on your account and my own ; I hope I
shall never more have another uneasy thought about you.

I flatter myself from the flow of spirit and gayity in your
letter dated the 13th of last month, that you are well and happy.
It was reported here that you were ill at Petersburg. If that be
true, I hope you are intirely recovered. May you bring to
England all the health and vigour you carry'd abroad ; and may
you have good employment for both in your own country.

A sketch of the Carte du Pays to which you are coming may be
of some use and afford you some amusement. I will begin with
its politicks and be short on a dull subject.

Mr. Grenville's ability in the House of Commons last Session,
the firmness of the Court during the course of it, the spirit of
administration towards France and Spain since the recess,
the death of the Duke of Devonshire and Mr. Legge, the
outlawry of Wilkes, Mr. Yorke's acceptance of a favour from the
Crown and Mr. Pitt's supposed moderation, give the greatest
prospect of success, strength and perhaps unanimity in Parliament
this winter. You may be assured that the Ministers are perfectly
satisfy'd with their Royal Master, and intirely united in what
concerns his business. So much for publick affairs.

We have a most admirable first man on the opera stage,
Mansoli; our first woman is charming as to person, a good
actrice and a pleasing singer. Our tennor is much admired, and
Gardini conducts the orchestra. We hissed one set of dancers off
the stage the first night ; it is said a better set is coming.

Mrs. Cornelys has made Carlisle House the most elegant
place of publick entertainment that ever was in this, or perhaps
any country. The Duke of York returned from his travels and
the Duke of Gloucester emancipated from his Governor,
preceptors, etc., amuse themselves there constantly. The latter
of these Royal personages seems to have no dislike to the
Dowager Lady Waldegrave ; and she seems comforted for the loss
of our deceased friend, by the general homage pay'd her by the
living.

The Duke and Dutchess of Grafton are separated. . . She
has 4,000l. a year for herself and the children. The Duke has
declared he has no objection to her conduct, but chuses to live
alone, having found they could not live happily together. His
Grace passes his time with Nancy Parsons, and her Grace lives
in retreat. No court, no spectacle, no assemblies. Perhaps when
you arrive *antiche pene* may revive also. There is so much
similitude between the Duchess and Lady Buckingham that an
infidelity may be excused.

I do not recollect anything more worth your knowledge. The
opera club is very impatient for its dear president. Clubs put

me in mind of one lately established by the *Jeunesse* at Almacks call'd the *Macaroni*. It has demolish'd young Whites intirely, and old Whites is not without some apprehensions.

Adieu my dear Lord, make haste hither.

P.S.—The Primate of Ireland° is dead, and it is doubted a better Lord Northumberland will return to that country. Will you be a king?

The BARON J. B. DE CHERKASOFF to the EARL OF BUCKINGHAMSHIRE.

1765, Feb. 28 (N.S.). Petersburg.—Expressions of affectionate regret at his departure from St. Petersburg†—the Baronne Elizabeth de Czerkasoff adding a note to the same effect.

GEORGE GRENVILLE to the EARL OF BUCKINGHAMSHIRE.

1765, May 13. Downing Street.—Notwithstanding the great variety of busyness, in which I have been necessarily engaged, and which still continues to demand more hours than it is in my power to give, yet I cannot omitt expressing to you my warmest thanks for your very kind letter of the 25th of this month. You judge very truly, my dear Lord, that I cannot feel a more sensible joy at the reconciliation of every part of our family, nor more obliged to my friends there at the share which they take in it. As for the political situation and the many extraordinary circumstances which have passed relative to it since I saw you, it is not possible to write upon a subject which requires much more than a letter can or ought to contain, especially from me and therefore I reserve till I have the pleasure of seeing you all that I have to say upon it. In the meantime let me assure you my dear Lord that whatever that scene may be, I have received in the course of this transaction a comfort and satisfaction which I trust will only end with my life, the first part of it from that domestic union which you so kindly congratulate me upon, and the other from those testimonies of friendship and approbation which have so far exceeded, not my wishes indeed, but what I had a right to expect. Let me add too that amongst these none can give more pleasure than the proofs of your kindness and regard to, my dear Lord,

Your most faithfull and most affectionate
GEORGE GRENVILLE.

My best compliments attend Colonel Hotham.

The EARL of BUCKINGHAMSHIRE to the CAVALIERA MICHIETI.
(*In French.*)

1765, May 30.—Expressions of friendship and of condolence on the death of her husband.

"Après une absence assez longue dans un pais que les ignorants estiment un pais barbare, me voici de retour chez moi.

---

* Dr. George Stone, Archbishop of Armagh.
† Lord Buckinghamshire reached London from St. Petersburg 28 March, 1765.

Mon Séjour y a été assez agréable et vous êtes trop au dessus
des prejugés pour ne pas me croire quand je vous assure que le
genre humain y est à peu près comme ailleurs, les hommes n'ont
ni queux ni griffes et les femmes sont très-belles. Il est vrai
qu'il leur manque aussi bien qu'aux autres Européens la sensibilité
et la *morbidezza degli occhi Veneziani.*"

GEORGE GRENVILLE to the EARL OF BUCKINGHAMSHIRE.

1765, July 9th. Downing Street.—Though I have not been
able to acknowledge the honour of your Lordship's letter of the
27th of last month so soon as I ought and as I should have done
at any other time, yet I am convinced by the kindness of it that
you think me incapable of neglecting the first opportunity in my
power to do what you desire and recommend to my care. The
consequence of this I took the earliest and probably the only
occasion which I shall have of laying before the King that
article in your bill of extraordinaries which relates to your
travelling expenses and of representing to His Majesty the justice
and reasonableness of making some allowance on that head in
your particular case, notwithstanding the general rule and the
minute of the Treasury upon this subject. I have now the
pleasure to inform your Lordship that in consequence of this
representation his Majesty was pleased to signify to me his
directions that the sum of one thousand pounds should be allowed
to your Lordship for the expenses of your journey from St.
Petersburg to Moscow, but as I am informed that £200 has
been already allowed to you upon that occasion, if that is true,
no more than the sum of £800 can be paid to make up the sum
of one thousand pounds in the whole. I have given the necessary
orders to have that matter settled before I leave the Treasury
which I have reason to believe will be to-morrow or the next day,
as I should be glad if possible to have it completely done, that
you may have no further trouble about it.

I am extremely sorry, my dear Lord, for the uneasiness which
you express at your political situation and at the many disagreeable circumstances which have occured to you in the course of it.
I have felt them for you very sincerely and I hope I need not
say that my best wishes and utmost endeavours have at all times
been employed to remove or to diminish them. The change
which the King has been making for these two months
in his administration and which I understand will be declared
to-morrow, you will easily see makes it quite impossible for me
to be of any use at present to any of my friends. I know not
whether you have received any account of the intended arrangements from those who are to succeed me or how far your approbation and support of this new system has been desir'd and
applied for. I may possibly be a very improper judge of the
propriety of this measure, but I should be wanting to that friendship and openness with which I have always acted and shall
always act towards you if I did not say to you that I am thoroughly

persuaded that it will not tend to the honor and ease of the king, the safety and happiness of his people nor to the particular credit of those who are engaged in it.

The Plan after a great variety of unsuccessful attempts is now said to be as follows. Lord Rockingham, Mr. Dowdeswell, Lord John Cavendish, Mr. G. Onslow and Mr. Pelham to be Lords of the Treasury, and Mr. Dowdeswell to be Chancellor of the Exchequer. Duke of Grafton and General Conway to be Secretaries of State, Lord Winchelsea Lord President, Duke of Newcastle Lord Privy Seal, Duke of Portland Lord Chamberlain, Lord Egmont to continue First Lord of the Admiralty with four new Lords not yet settled who they are or in whose room. Lord Bessborough and Mr. W. Mellish to be the two Postmasters, instead of Lord Trevor and Lord Hyde, the younger Mr. Mellish, who is in Parliament, and Mr. J. Roberts to be the two Secretaries of the Treasury, instead of Mr. Jenkinson and Mr. Whateley. Lord Dartmouth to be at the Head of the Board of Trade instead of Lord Hillsborough. Many other arrangements are talked of, but not finally determined. I have now told your Lordship all that I know and make no comments, because I think them unnecessary. I will not even answer that all this will take effect, because if I am rightly enform'd, it has been chang'd every day and almost every hour. You will hear many other reports of support approbation, etc., but as most of them are false, to my own knowledge, I cannot but recommend to your Lordship to believe none of them till they are confirm'd in a manner which will admitt of no doubt.

George Grenville to the Earl of Buckinghamshire.

1765, July 16. Downing Street.—(Warmly acknowledges his kind expressions of friendship and good opinion.)

I set so high a value on the assurances which you give me of your affection to me as a private man and of your approbation of my conduct as a public man, that I shall certainly use my utmost endeavours to deserve both the one and the other. My best means for the continuance of the latter, must be to persevere in the same behaviour by which I have been so happy as to attain it, and my best title to the former is the sincerity of those sentiments which I have long borne to you.

P.S.—We go to Wotton on Fryday next where we shall be happy to see you whenever you can give us that pleasure, and we flatter ourselves from what you say at the end of your letter that you will find a time to do what will certainly be so infinitely agreeable to us. I beg you will make my best compliments to Mr. Nugent, if he is still with you.

Minutes for Mr. Tomlinson's Letter to Mr. Harbord.*

1765, August.—That Lord Buckinghamshire rather chuses to wave his own feelings and the facts upon which those feelings

---

* See for this political quarrel with the Harbords Lady Suffolk to Lord Buckingham-shire, 9 August, 1764. (*Lady Suffolk's Letters, Vol. II.*, p. 289.)

are founded, some of which Mr. Harbord may possibly not be fully acquainted with, as to mention them would be invidious and probably of no utility.

That if Mr. Harbord supposes that he has not already sufficiently prov'd his independency, he will possibly think it necessary to continue to act differently from Lord Buckinghamshire. In which case Lord Buckinghamshire will not readily submit to have it understood that of twelve members which Norfolk sends to Parliament, he do's not recommend one.

It may further be necessary to observe how unnatural it is for two persons who take different parts at Westminster to make a common political interest in the country. That if Mr. Harbord proposes in opposition to Mr. Grenville to support the present administration, in justice to Lord Buckinghamshire he ought to decline standing for Norwich at the next general election in consideration of which Lord Buckinghamshire will exert his influence to the utmost to bring him in for the county.

That the idea of a probable coolness with his neighbours at Gunton has given Lord Buckinghamshire more uneasiness than any misfortune he as yet has experienced.

That Mr. Harbord should consider the weight of property and of parliamentary interest his family together with the whole of Lord Buckingham's must have, when united together in a very short time ; and particularly how much their influence must operate both in Norfolk and Norwich, if living in a thorough good understanding they are not obliged to make any declaration prematurely, but offer either Mr. Harbord, or Mr. Hobart to the county, just as the then tempers of gentlemen lead.

That it is mutually for their honour and interest to give each other every publick and private support.

That no two persons can always be exactly of the same opinion and therefore for the sake of consistency it is indispensably necessary that upon such occasions one must give way to the other, upon which supposition it is submitted to Mr. Harbord, which of the two may best expect such a deference.

George Grenville to the Earl of Buckinghamshire.

1765, Oct. 21. Bath.—(Mrs. Grenville's ill health is his excuse for not writing earlier. Her painful and precarious situation fills him with the greatest uneasiness. Extremely sensible of Lord Buckinghamshire's solicitude.) I will certainly write to the Dean of Norwich, who is in Dorsetshire, by the cross post, which sets out from hence to-morrow night, and desire him to do all in his power to promote the change in the living of St. Giles' in Norwich between Dr. Gardener and Mr. Money, and to inform you of the steps which he is able to take in it, being fully persuaded of his hearty disposition to obey your commands as well from the real respects which he personally bears to you, as from the knowledge he has of the interest which I take in every wish of yours, which will make me feel extremely obliged to you for every opportunity of furthering them. As to Spanish Charles

Townshend's opinions which you inform me of, he will allow me to think that they partake a little of a Spanish Rodomontade; at least from the endeavours which it is universally believed have been us'd (though hitherto ineffectually) to dissolve the present Parliament, it does not seem that his superiors are of the same opinion. . . . .

The Earl of Buckinghamshire to Mr. Nugent.[*]

1765, Oct.—Your not having been well is a sort of apology, tho' the most disagreeable one you could have made, for not coming to Blickling. Nor does it seem totaly conclusive as your complaint was not of so acute a nature as to prevent your taking a journey to a house where you were well assured every possible care would have been taken of you. My wife and my daughter's officious attention would have vy'd to relieve you.

Lady Buckingham's partial friendship has long been known to you; partial I must call it as it seems even to exceed mine, nor can you doubt the preferential affection with which Lady Harriet regards you; which though in this instance it may prove her judgement and discernment, yet must make the heart of that parent feel some little degree of anxiety who considers how far such an early disposition to tenderness may hereafter lead her.

I have not heard anything material lately relative to our little masters, tho' general accounts of their divisions, irresolution and inability must reach even the remotest corners. Whatever face of triumph the second-rate politicians who have embarked in the frail green vessel, may display to the publick, I am well assur'd the leaders are fully conscious how little they are equal to their situation, and that they can never wear those new robes, which hang by a cobweb to their shoulders, with honor to themselves or utility to their country.

I have lately received a letter from Mr. Grenville. Reflection but the more convinces me of the calamity England has sustained by his being compelled to quit an office which he is not only the best but the only man in these times duly qualify'd to fill. The candid and the inform'd must lament his retreat, which can only please the interested and the ignorant, or those wretched merchants who living upon expedients make a lottery of trade, and would adopt the same miserable plan for the Publick, which in the end must prove equally ruinous to the General as to individuals.

When avarice or extravagance makes nineteen in twenty deaf to every other consideration but their own momentary advantage, surely the Treasury ought to be directed by a minister who acting from experience, knowledge and integrity, despises popular clamour, resists it with temper and firmness and whose measures, founded on true principles will best be justify'd by their consequences.

---

[*] Robert Nugent, successively Lord Nugent, Lord Clare and Earl Nugent,

This is only saying in worse terms what I am persuaded you would give as your opinion; and I know not why it found a place here except that in writing to a friend my pen is us'd to scrawl what first occurs to me.

(*Draft.*)

The Earl of Buckinghamshire to Mr. Nugent.

1765, November.—Lady Dorothy Hotham[1] intreats the favor of you to inform her particularly what method your father took to cure himself of the gravel, and how long it was before he found any benefit from it.

She would have wrote to you herself upon the subject, if she had not lately been mortify'd by having a letter return'd by a gentleman, and you will agree she ought to be cautious of again exposing herself to such a disgrace. I am glad my letter pleased you; you stile it 'elegant,' an epithet it ill deserves, unless the artless, yet decent, garb of truth may claim it. You injure me, however, by imagining that any part of it was wrote with an intention to check the career of your vanity in preventing the displaying of that tribute my complaisance paid to it in the account of that decided preference my wife and daughter gave you—fatal rivalship which may hereafter cool them in the performance of the reciprocal dutys of child and parent.

I judged of the election by the representative and could not imagine any merchant who voted for you could be offended at the sentiments you approv'd. I considered your city as a seat of commerce in the noblest and most extensive sense of the word, and that, excepting indeed the narrow circle of the White Lion Club, it would have been as difficult at this time to have found a mean, interested trader amongst the sons of Bristol as it was in the day of Queen Elizabeth to discover a beauty amongst the daughters.

Your account of Mrs. Grenville is but too disagreeably confirmed to me by Lady Suffolk, who has seen her since she came to town. Should the worst happen our friend's loss will be irreparable. As far as long study of that wayward sex has enabled me to analyse the intricate and indefinable qualitys by which their various natures charm and plague, she was the first prize in the marriage lottery of our century.

I love you and yours too well not to enter into all the anxiety you must have felt during your son's late absence in Ireland; he should for the future confine his gallantrys to England where he may be happy with twenty fine women upon easier terms than with one in that perverse country. You will see me in London in about a fortnight, but in the meantime let me give you one caution:—to insist upon my sister's not communicating your father's receipt to her friends (for she has some everywhere) in the New Ministry. Those gentlemen are certainly gravel'd and it is by no means your business to contribute to their present ease, much less to their radical cure.

(*Draft.*)

---

[1] Sister to the Earl of Buckinghamshire.

SIR. WM. HARBORD to the EARL OF BUCKINGHAMSHIRE.

1765, Dec. 16. Gunton.—Refuses to sell his Plumstead estate, but is not averse to an exchange.

The EARL OF BUCKINGHAMSHIRE to SIR WM. HARBORD.

1765, Dec. 21.—Explaining his reasons for having offered to buy Plumstead.

1766.—A packet of extracts from the North American Papers of the 24th Jan.

Short extracts from the following :—
1. Mr. Secretary Conway to General Gage of the 24th Oct., 1765.
2. The same to Governor Bernard of the same date.
3. Representation (dated Aug. 27, 1765) of the Board of Trade to Council relative to the Virginian Resolutions received in Governor Fauquier's letter of the 5th June, 1765.
4. Extract of a Representation (Oct. 1, 1765) of the Board of Trade to Council touching the proceedings of the House of Representatives of Massachusets Bay.
5. Report of Council, Oct. 3, 1765.
6. From Governor Bernard to Mr. Pownall, Oct. 1, 1765.
7. Governor Franklin's answer to Mr. Cox, Stamp Collector.
1765, Sept. 4. New Jersey.—"All with whom I have conversed seem to think they are as much bound to pay obedience to this Act, as to the Act of Dutys upon Trade and to those other Acts relative to the Colonys which they have heretofore obeyed, and that they ought not to make any opposition till they have first try'd all means of obtaining redress. These also seem to be the sentiments of the sober, discreet men of every province."

A Packet of Papers endorsed ' *Relative to North America and the Repeal of the Stamp Act.*'
1. America. (6) Intended Resolutions of the House of Peers, Jan., 1766.
2. North America. *Address.* (In consequence of the above Resolutions.)
3. Protest against the Repeal of the Stamp Act. 11 March, 1766. Signed· by the following Peers : Bedford, Coventry, Bridgwater, Dunk Halifax, Buckingham, Wentworth, Sandwich, Marlborough, Trevor, Ker, Leigh, J. Bangor, Waldegrave, Aylesford, Gower, Dudley and Ward, Powis, Weymouth, Scarsdale, Temple, Littleton, Eglintoun, Suffolk and Berkshire, Abercorn, Vere, Bolingbroke, W. Glouster, Thos. Bristol, Ferrers, Grosvenor, Townshend, Hyde, Charles Carlisle. *Copy.*
4. A Duplicate copy of the above.
5. 1766, 17 March. Protest against passing the Bill to repeal the American Stamp Act of last session. Signed by the

above with the exception of the following Peers : Bedford, Coventry, Wentworth, Waldegrave, Bolingbroke, Townshend. *Copy.*

6.   1768, Oct. 31.   Copy of a letter from Major-General Gage to the Earl of Hillsborough, dated Boston.

7.   1768, November 1.   Copy of a Letter from Governor Bernard to the Earl of Hillsborough.

8.   1768, November 1.   Copy.   Minutes of Council at Boston October 12, 1768.   (In Governor Bernard's.)

9.   Copy of the minutes of Council at Boston the 17th October, 1768.

10.   Copy.   Minutes of Council of 26th October, 1768.   (In Governor Bernard's to Mr. Pownall of 17 November, 1768.)

11.   Copy of the answer of the Justices of the Peace of Boston to the Governor.   (In Governor Bernard's of November 1, 1768.)

12.   Copy of Governor Bernard's order to Joseph Goldthwaite, esq.   (In Governor Bernard's of November 1st, 1768.)

GEORGE GRENVILLE to the EARL OF BUCKINGHAMSHIRE.

1766, June 23.   Wotton.—However indifferent I may be in general with respect both to the text and comment upon our present Political Situation, which can only be agreeable to those who can derive pleasure from the prospect of *Changes* founded upon the unhappy necessity of public distress, yet I feel very sensibly the proofs of your friendship in the information which you have given to me of the state of things and return you my sincerest thanks for every part of your letter.   I agree very much with you in the greater part of your opinions upon this subject, but I think you seem to over-rate the *little footing* which you suspect Lord Albermarle has gotten and his *Testament Politique* which, unless you have good grounds for it I should scarcely believe is ever likely to be adopted.   To be sure the present *Whig Administration* set up in opposition to the Tory and *Jacobite Families* who formed the last Ministry would furnish matter of observation to any curious enquirer into this species of their merit, who should find that they consisted of men descended from *Lord Strafford*, Sir Edward Seymour, King Charles the 2nd, Lord Nottingham, and Lord Dartmouth, with that *true Whig* the Chancellor of the Exchequer, and for their men of busyness and of confidence in the two great Offices of the Treasury and Secretary of State, the two Mr. Burkes, whose Whig pedigree, history and qualifications for this unlimited trust, may be learnt from those who have been lately in Ireland.   I should not have mention'd nor judg'd of any man by the Party merit or demerit of his ancestors if the *Whig Families* had not been impudently urg'd to make up for their notorious deficiency in all other circumstances.   But notwithstanding all this, and all that I hear from every quarter, I am of your opinion that the majority will not vary essentially till other things vary, or till those public difficulties, the seeds of which have been so liberally sown, shall begin to produce their harvest and in that case I pity the man whose fortune it shall be to reap them. What the event of it will be I know not. My only care must be to preserve my public opinions and my private honor inviolate that my friends may never be asham'd of me; and this I hope to accomplish because it depends upon myself. I am very much mortifyd to find by your letter, that you doubt whether you shall be able to call upon your friends in Buckinghamshire in your return from the West into Norfolk. Consider only that it is the nearest way and how extremely glad we shall be to see you here; the more so because I own after your kindness to me last year, we have no pretence to ask it, but must owe it entirely to your friendship and inclination. Believe me my dear Lord, these motives will be more than sufficient to carry me to Blickling even without my owing it to you (which I acknowledge with pleasure). I need not say that the hopes you give us of finding Lady Suffolk there would be the greatest additional inducement to us both if we could want any to come to you. But alas the returns of Mrs. Grenville's fits of pain are too frequent at present for us to reckon upon it. We have been at Shortgrove and at Petworth; she had a severe attack at both places notwithstanding which upon the whole she is satisfy'd that she has gained ground considerably, as she has certainly gained strength. Many of our friends have promised us to come here in the course of the summer; amongst others Mr. Nugent who wrote me word that he had seen you and how much oblig'd to you I was for your remembrance of me in your potations. Lord Lorne and Lord Frederick Campbell left us the day before yesterday and we expect Lord and Lady Aylesford and I believe Lord Trevor the day after tomorrow. We propose to go with them to Stowe in 5 or 6 days and I will certainly remember your invitation to Lord Temple, whose inclinations I am fully persuaded would lead him to Blickling, if after the excursions which he has already made and one more into another part of the world, which he has engag'd to make, he can again leave Stowe this summer, which I scarcely think possible, especially unless you can come into Buckinghamshire to tempt him.

GEORGE GRENVILLE to the EARL OF BUCKINGHAMSHIRE.

1766, July 1. Stowe.—(Acknowledging a letter from Lord Buckinghamshire at Bath.) I am extremely sensible of your kindness to me in the offer which you make me to bring in any friend of mine at a borough where there will be a great probability of success, but a considerable expense may be incur'd. I am persuaded that I know some friends of mine who will very willingly engage in a reasonable expense with a fair prospect of success, but as I see the impossibility of your writing more clearly and with a degree of certainty, so it is impossible for me till I can explain that matter more fully and in consequence receive an answer upon it, to give any certain answer to it, except to desire you by no means to postpone on my account any immediate arrangement which the situation of this affair may require, as I am sure what will be most advantageous to your interest will for every reason be most desirable and agreeable to me. . . . .

. . . . . .

P.S. We came hither yesterday and return to Wotton in 4 or 5 days. My wife still continues to have frequent returns of pain. She joins with Lord Temple in desiring their best compliments to you.

GEORGE GRENVILLE to the EARL OF BUCKINGHAMSHIRE.

1766, July 20. Wotton.—Tho' you will have seen from every newspaper and have heard from every correspondent in London that my brother, Lord Temple, returned to Stowe on Fryday and that he had declin'd accepting the office intended for him under the new arrangement, yet perhaps you may be glad to know the outlines of what was proposed to him, and I shall certainly be glad to give you the earliest intelligence which I received of this transaction. The modest proposal made to Lord Temple by Mr. Pitt, whom he saw but once during three days he was in town, was that he should stand as a capital cypher in the most responsible office in the kingdom unsupported by any of his friends, whilst Mr. Pitt, in the sine cure Office of Privy Seal without any risque or trouble, except what he chose, was to guide, nominate and form the whole. As a particular grace to him, he was to be consulted in naming to his own Board of the Treasury, care being taken that if any of Mr. Pitt's friends were left out of it, they should be otherwise as well provided for. There was no change of measures pretended, so that Lord Temple was to come in to support what he foresaw. He could not approve in contradiction to his declar'd sentiment of last session, and as to men, the only change was to bring in some of Mr. Pitt's immediate dependants, who with the rump of the last were to form the present plan of an able Administration. Lord Shelburne and Mr. Conway were to be the Secretaries of State and the Duke of Grafton Lord President. Lord Temple wish'd for *Union* for the sake of the King and of the kingdom, but not for *Obedience*, which he did not expect to have propos'd by one who well knew beforehand that he would not consent to it and to whom in the like case, he would not have proposed it, and as this could attain no public end, and was in itself utterly inadmissable, it put an immediate end to the whole idea. Lord Temple declined expressly to state me for any office whatever, knowing my sentiments, and that I thought it much more for my dignity and honour not to have my name mentioned ; so that it cannot be said that this was broken off by Lord Temple upon considerations for his own family. When he mentioned Lord Lyttelton for a Cabinet Council office it was receiv'd with scorn and at 'last as a particular favor to Lord Temple he might have had some office' for the present and have a Cabinet office on some future vacancy, but not now. The King receiv'd Lord Temple very graciously and favourably both the

days when he waited upon him, but you will not wonder that
whilst Lord Temple is thoroughly sensible of the King's goodness
to him that he should feel a treatment so unworthy and unexpected from Mr. Pitt. This my dear Lord is all that I can tell
you, what the further arrangements will now be, I know not, nor
can it be very material, as it must be very little different from
the former system with the addition of *wisdom, temper* and
moderation to the *ability* and *experience* of the former. Adieu
my dear Lord. Our friend Nugent who has been here these
3 days waits to carry this to town with him. (Assurances
of friendship. Mrs. Grenville's health still precarious but improving.)

George Grenville to the Earl of Buckinghamshire.

1766, July 29. Wotton.—(Nothing to add to the political intelligence of his last letter except what may be learnt from the
Gazettes.)

I now write only to thank you for your very kind offer to
bring in any friend of mine next Election for £1800,—if not
chose to cost him nothing—and to tell you my dear lord that ' I
greet your love not with vain thanks only, but with acceptance
bounteous.' I am convinced that two or three of my friends
will be at a loss whom this proposal will make very happy and
I suppose there will be no occasion to declare the name as yet
at least, and if not, I should wish not to do it for a little
while till I can see how their other endeavours are likely to turn
out, as I take it for granted whatever we may hear talked of,
that no ministry will put an end to the present well constituted
and happily dispos'd Parliament till pretty near its natural death.
Our friend Mr. Nugent seem'd to me not well when he was here,
and out of spirits, which is a bad sign for some, but I hope both
the one or the other will mend soon.

Richard Owen Cambridge to the Same.

1766, Aug. 2.—So far from the Center of Intelligence, I am
forced to delay writing till the last moment, that I may gain the
freshest news; the consequence of which is that I must write in
a hurry as the post is going and jumbling all things together.
'Tis well I did not tell you Lord Chatham was brought to bed
or a still greater personage, if such a one there be in these
parts.

I have this morning left Lord Suffolk and Col. Hotham. We
cannot all together furnish one paragraph of news for your use
or entertainment, and I only write to let your Lordship know that
I would amuse you if I could and since I can not I must insist
and will send you all our acknowledgements and repeat the
grateful sense we have of our entertainment in Norfolk.

It seems strange that a man within ten miles of London can
find nothing to write to one who is 120 miles distant, but for my
part, I live so much out of this sort of talk that I know no more

how these things are come about or what is to be next, than my
Lord Bute or any other person devoted to the most recluse
retirement. Not one of those whom I call my particular friends
have I happened to see.

It is at this instant thundering and raining, I hear Lord
Chatham is unpopular in the city already. He is certainly in
a very bad state of health. As soon as I know anything worth
your Lordship's hearing I will write.

GEORGE GRENVILLE to the EARL OF BUCKINGHAMSHIRE.

1766, August 5. Wotton.—As you desire to have an answer as
soon as possible upon that part of your letter which relates to
the Election at St. Ives, I would not omit writing to you
immediately after I have received it, tho' it is impossible for me
to do more than to refer myself entirely to you upon that
subject. I would upon no consideration put you to the least
extraordinary trouble or expense to show your kindness to me
by choosing any friend of mine there. I am fully satisfied of
your friendship towards me by the manner in which you made
me the offer—but if it suits you better upon account of the
fresh difficulties which I find by your letter are arising there, to
close with the proposals which Mr. Knile makes to you to fix
upon some other man, I earnestly desire that you will do so
without thinking a moment of what you have writ to me on this
subject, of which I shall only remember your obliging intentions.
On the other hand, if it were quite open to you and the election
could be sure for 2,500 as Mr. Knile states it to you, I believe I
could recommend a very good friend of mine who would accept
it with pleasure, provided he is not obliged to any further trouble
or canvas, except the appearing in the town if necessary a day
or two before the election.

I leave this matter therefore entirely to your decision, assuring
you that whatever is most advantageous to you cannot fail of
being most agreeable to me. As to the other part of your letter
I should flatter myself that your Lordship will congratulate me
upon *that Union* not taking place with our family on terms of the
utmost danger, servility and dishonor which I think would
have involved those who would have engag'd in such insolent
and insidious conditions in ruin and disgrace. I am very glad
you approve of what Lord Temple has done and of my sentiments
on this occasion and, I rejoice as an individual, tho' as a true friend
to the King and the Kingdom I lament the situation of both, and
am firmly of opinion that the event will show the folly and
instability of this interested weak and narrow system, on which
I will make no further comments, as you now know all that I do
about it and will see the rest from the Gazettes and your own
observation. . . . . . .

JOHN PATTESON, Mayor of Norwich, to THE SAME.

1766, Sept. 13.—Has the honour of transmitting to Lord
Buckinghamshire three petitions, relative to the dreaded scarcity

of wheat, which we are persuaded you will not, my Lord, think it a trouble to cause to be delivered, one to the Rt. Honble. the Earl of Northington, one to his Grace the Duke of Grafton, and one to the Rt. Honble. Ch. Townshend, Esq. I cannot but esteem it a most fortunate circumstance that these petitions will thus under your Lordship's countenance go with so much weight as I make no doubt but will obtain such relief as may be in the power of government to give.

John Patteson, Mayor of Norwich, to the Earl of Buckinghamshire.

1766, Sept. 24. Norwich.—(Thanking Lord Buckinghamshire for having enforced the petitions from this city.)

I have had a letter from the Treasury requiring the prices of wheat for three market days last past, which have accordingly been transmitted and this gives us hopes that the matter will again be brought under consideration of the privy council. (Encloses the Chancellor of the Exchequer's letters to Lord Buckinghamshire.[*])

C. Townshend[†] to the Same.

I have this moment received an express from the Duke of Grafton inclosing the representation from Norwich. His Grace will not be in town till Thursday morning. In this situation and from the anxiety of our friends, I doubt whether it would not be more prudent because more agreeable to them, if we were to send our answers this evening. In this, you will judge for us both, but I renew the subject least out of kindness to me, you should expose yourself to any supposition of delay. The Duke of Grafton has probably wrote to you, but in his letter to me, he only encloses the representation.

I have some idea that the lawyers have decided that the measure of an embargo would be unconstitutional, and I hear that the Secretary's of State have said in their letter to the city that the prohibition must wait the meeting of Parliament[‡], but you could easily learn this from the Lord Mayor who is a Norfolk man and a corn factor.

Gr. Sq. Tuesday morn. Sep. (otherwise undated [§]).

C. Townshend to the Same.

Gr. Sq. 11 o'clock. Having written you an ostensible letter give me leave now in our natural and more pleasant stile of friendship, to add this codicil, it is to whisper to you that the Council

---

[*] *See* Charles Townshend to Lord Buckinghamshire. (Dated Tuesday morning, Sept.)

[†] Chancellor of the Exchequer in July, 1766.

[‡] Parliament was prorogued from the 16th September to the 11th November, 1766. The Embargo upon the Export of Corn was proclaimed the 26th September.

[§] *See* following letter.

have met upon the subject. I was not present and I am told they decided against any interposition, probably they argued upon the sense of the two last acts taken together, and thought an embargo confined to corn and in time of peace, too bold a measure to advise. With this I have nothing to do, but I will suggest the necessity of another Council. I wish I may catch the sight of you before you return.

C. Townshend to the Earl of Buckinghamshire.

[Undated.]—Upon second thoughts, your Lordship would probably give more satisfaction to the City of Norwich, and I should like it better so far as relates to me, if you would be so good as to inform yourself of Mr. Conway's[*] public answer to the City of London, when they made the same application, in which I am told it is expressly said that the Privy Council cannot interfere. This would save me the necessity of seeming to discuss the reasons of that decision in a matter not within my office.

John Gay, Esq. to the Same.

(*Endorsed.*) September 1766, 5 o'clock.—We have perpetual alarms and informations of threats, thank God no further mischief has happened in the city. But some has been done in the neighbourhood at Trowse by almost demolishing the house of one Mr. Money there, and speeches given out with threats against Mr. Bacon's at Erleham etc.

Under our present circumstances it would have been happy for us if your Lordship was with us to advise and assist us and I do believe the knowledge of your presence amongst us would awe and restrain the mob, the apprehensions of many are great for this night. We do and will endeavour to do all we can to prevent further mischief. But we really want help, assistance and advice and the sooner we had your Lordship's the happier I think it would be for us all and might prevent further outrages.

Your Lordship's most faithful and most obedient,

J. G.

Hear a malthouse by Conisford Gates just now fired.

Lord Barrington to the Same.†

Cavendish Square, Sunday night.—I am this moment sending by express orders for two troops of dragoons to march from Colchester to Norwich to assist the civil magistrates there. It may be useful to acquaint you that let the call be ever so urgent I can send no further military aid into Norfolk, for the troops of the whole kingdom are employ'd and we have not enough by one

* General (Henry) Seymour Conway, Secretary of State.
† This letter is endorsed. *Norwich Riot*, September, 1766.

quarter. I know your weight, authority and spirit; I also know your discretion, my dear friend, and I am certain if this hint does no good, it can do no harm.

Adieu, in great haste, but great affection,

BARRINGTON.

I enclose this in my despatch to the Mayor of Norwich.

LORD BARRINGTON to the EARL OF BUCKINGHAMSHIRE.

1766, September 30. Cavendish Square.—It is fortunate that I wrote to your Lordship by my express to the Mayor last Sunday, for by that means you have the earlyest notice of my inability to send any more troops into Norfolk. All we have are disposed of, and we have occasion for 30,000 more at least to keep the mob of this country in order. I have foreseen and foretold the circumstances we are in above six weeks ago. I can blame nobody within that period; but God forgive and amend those who have contributed to our present anarchy; a charge from which no party or faction among us is exempt. I am happy to hear that you are going to Norwich, for I know how much good a man of your quality, spirit and discretion may do.

P.S. The troops have all had orders to obey the civil magistrate, so what there is may be disposed of where most wanted. I know how inadequate the force is to the need, and lament to the last degree that I can send no more. I need not desire you to keep our poverty unknown as much as possible consistent with the circumstances of your situation. The mob is up in my own neighbourhood. I have no troops to send, but I am going myself to see whether an English gentleman who has never injured his neighbours cannot influence them now in their madness.

JOHN NORRIS, High Sheriff of Norfolk, to the SAME.

[No date.]—I have but now finished my morning ride—just 3 o'clock—and am not able to mount my horse again and go as far as Blickling; were I to order my carriage at this late hour I know not when I should return; I mention this that your Lordship may see with me the impossibility of my waiting upon you. I think myself obliged to your Lordship for your friendly notice to me of a matter, the communication of which the Mayor seems to have alone entrusted to your Lordship.

Upon reading your letter I resolved upon the following scheme—to order the chief constables of my own hundred to despatch immediately their precepts to the several petty constables, commanding them to be at Lenwade bridge tomorrow morning before 7, there to join me, who with God's blessing will in person be at the Fair; they are to take their constable's staves. Since I formed my design I have recollected that this is the very measure prosecuted in London under similar circumstances, and it will be a high satisfaction to me to have my adoption of the same conduct approved by your Lordship and the gentlemen at your house. If the scheme is contrary to that formed by your Lordship and the gentlemen with you, I hope you will be kind enough to me to remember that I could not avail myself of your and their advice and yet that something was to be done forthwith.

Your Lordship and the gentlemen have, I presume, as magistrates, an unquestionable authority to direct the like kind of precept with mine to the chief constables of your respective divisions, on the supposition I mean of the measure itself appearing an eligible one. I could wish that we could all unite our warlike strength within two or three miles on that side of St. Faith, and if your Lordship can think of any plan convenient for us all I shall not fail to attend.

My wife's and my respects to Lady Buckingham.

W. W. Bulwer to the Earl of Buckinghamshire.

Heydon, Wednesday.—Upon my return home I was informed that a mob collected from the neighbouring parishes had assembled themselves at Cawston and that they intended to proceed to Marsham, where a large party from Norwich was to join them, that their intentions were afterwards to divide themselves into partys and to scour the country. I thought proper to give your Lordship this piece of intelligence, and I beg leave to know what steps your Lordship intends taking upon this occasion as I should be happy to concur therein.

(*Endorsed:* Oct. 1766.)

To the Lord Viscount Barrington.

1766, October 1. Norwich.—In addition to the facts we laid before your Lordship on Saturday, we beg leave to acquaint you that the mob, after destroying the corn mills, actuated with fresh fury, proceeded into many parts of the city, and both on Saturday night and Sunday broke open houses, destroyed furniture, fired a large granary, threw corn, flour, etc., into the river, and were guilty of every outrage which popular madness could suggest. During this time and in this extremity the magistrates and inhabitants exerted themselves to the utmost and have had the good fortune to disperse the rioters, near thirty of whom are apprehended and secured, who after disabling the engines which supply the inhabitants with water had threatened the destruction of the city by fire.

We beg your Lordship to accept our thanks for the honour of your letter to the Mayor. Nor can we with too much gratitude acknowledge the readiness with which your Lordship ordered us the assistance of the military. The inhabitants being nearly worn out with the fatigue of continually watching and patroling the city both by night and day and using every other means of preserving the public peace are this forenoon made very happy by the arrival of two troops of the Queen's Regiment of Dragoon Guards, commanded by Capt. Innis, who will now afford them a respite, and that quiet and tranquillity which with so much

difficulty they have recovered. At the same time we return your
Lordship our sincere thanks for this seasonable relief, it would
be extremely ungrateful in us to omit mentioning in the most
respectful manner the assistance and countenance which we have
received from the gentlemen of Norfolk, and particularly from
the Earl of Buckinghamshire, who on the first notice of this
unhappy affair instantly came hither and did us the honour
personally to assist us in putting a stop to the insolence and
madness of the daring multitude, and by his appearance and
counsel greatly contributed to restore peace and quiet amongst
us.

(Signed by about 40 of the magistrates and principal
inhabitants.)

John Patteson, Mayor of Norwich, to the Earl of Buckinghamshire.

1766, 1 October. Norwich. 2 o'clock, afternoon.—Is encouraged
by the eminent part which the Earl of Buckinghamshire has
taken in the suppressing of the late riots to beg his opinion as
to the propriety of the inhabitants of Norwich addressing
his Majesty with their thanks for his late Royal Proclamation
ordering an embargo. They are the more anxious to do
this as mention was made in the introduction to that
proclamation of an address for relief which went up from Norwich as well as London and Bristol. Two troops of dragoons are
this minute arrived. Thanks Lord B. for his undertaking to
recommend that Norwich be supplied with flour.

J. Gay to the Same.

Sunday morning.—The insurrection here began yesterday in
the afternoon between 1 and 2 in our Market Place by a tumul-
tuous assembly of disorderly persons driving the country people
away and overturning the provisions they brought. I had not
then left the Hall, where I had been with the Mayor, etc., at the
usual court, and with him, Sir T. Churchman, Harcourt, and one
of our sheriffs, who happened to be there, went immediately
amongst them to appease them and prevent further mischief,
but in vain. We were obliged for safety to retreat to the Hall.
We sent to others to come there to us, and immediately drew up,
printed and dispersed the enclosed. This had not the effect we
wished ; mob increased ; great threats. We had the proclamation
read in seven different places. The mills here (called the New
Mills) which supply us with flour were soon after attacked by the
mob. Bags and sacks of flour were cut and thrown into the
river, the buildings unroofed and greatly damaged. Most of the
bakers in town visited by the mob, their windows broke and
persons threatened. We have no military assistance. About 5
an express sent to Lord Barrington, Secretary at War, requesting
immediate assistance, as we know not where this will end, or
how it may cause disorderly people from the country to join the
mob here, who threaten the neighbourhood in the country. I

remained in the Hall with the Mayor, etc., and many of the principal inhabitants till near 1 this morning, where we planted a guard to preserve the Militia fire-arms lodged there. All our constables charged, and a double watch in the night, and the best precautions in our power used in this confusion. There has been no mischief in the night, but hear of many parties of mob in different places. Am just now going to the Hall to meet the Mayor, etc., and consider what best to do for the present. Mr. Addey holds his feast to-morrow. Could wish your Lordship might come, which may have good effect, his time of dineing apprehend to be between 2 and 3.

(*Endorsed*: Oct. 1766.)

Lord Barrington to the Earl of Buckinghamshire.

1766, Oct. 2. Cavendish Square.—I return you a thousand thanks for the early and good news you send me. · Norwich has the singular honour of reducing a mob without military aid, an example which I hope other places will endeavour to imitate. Though you ascribe all to the Mayor, forgive me if I suspect your spirit and good sense to have contributed the most to this event.

I go to Beckett next Saturday, but any commands of yours will be obeyed by Mr. D'Oyly, my deputy. I shall not go before a plan is begun which I think will soon put an end to these riots. They prevail in my neighbourhood and I intend to play the magistrate there.

The Same to the Same.

1766, Oct. 4. Cavendish Square.—I congratulate you most sincerely on the compleat victory obtained under fair auspices against the mob without military assistance. I carry'd the Mayor's letter to Court and shewed it to the King, who was much pleased with it and commended you. The hanging committee, as it is called, were in the ante-chamber, where I communicated the same letter to them all. They unanimously applauded what has been done, and I have at their desire furnished the Gazette with an article tending, I hope, to make others follow your example. Lord Mansfield was particularly your panegyrist. I think a plan has been found which will soon put an end to these riots in the counties of Wilts, Gloucester, Dorset and Somerset, where they have been most troublesome. Pray hang as many of your prisoners as possible.

P.S. The Duke of Northumberland stipulates to expect no place.

The Earl of Shelburne to the Same.

Hill Street, Saturday morning.—Desiring to see him. His motive " full of respect and regard." " I wish I may be able to give as good an account of the mobs in my part of the country as I hear your Lordship is of those in yours."

Endorsed: Spanish Embassy Office. Oct. 4. 1766.

GEORGE GRENVILLE to the EARL OF BUCKINGHAMSHIRE.

1766, Oct. 12. Wotton.—I do not at all wonder that the present Ministry should desire your concurrence and assistance, or that they should offer to you the Embassy at Madrid in the critical state of affairs in Spain; but I am surprised, considering the great importance of the object, after they had given the option of it to Mr. Stanley, as he informed me, so long ago as the month of July, that they should delay the making that offer to you till now. Your honorable conduct has convinced them of the falsehood of that opinion which has been so industriously propagated of late, that everybody is willing to treat with them, which is but a copy of the famous expression of Sir Robert Walpole's, that 'He knew every man's price.' They knew in many instances that this is not true, but if it were, the present patriot Minister has sufficiently manifested that he is ready to pay it. Your behaviour in stopping Lord Shelburne when he was entering into a dissertation upon the situation of the affairs in Spain is at once a proof of your own firmness and determination, and of your candour and fairness towards them. I reserve myself to talk to you more at large on this and many other subjects which are not proper for the post when I have the pleasure of meeting you in London, where I hope to find you a week before the Parliament assembles, as I propose to go to town the very beginning of next month. In the meantime I will only assure you that what you tell me upon that occasion can but confirm me in those opinions which I have long entertained of you and in those sentiments of the sincerest regard and friendship with which I am ever etc.

P.S. (Reports on Mrs. Grenville's health). . . . I take it for granted that your late address from Norwich to the King takes notice of the disorders which have happened there and which I fear are but too likely to continue all over the kingdom, as I do not see how provisions can be *low* whilest taxes are so *high*, or how they can buy *dear* and sell *cheap*.

THE SAME to THE SAME.

1766, Nov. 22. Bolton Street.—Though I take it for granted that you must have heard something of what has passed in the House of Commons since you left London, yet, as it is possible that you may not have been informed of it correctly, I send you the inclosed copy of what stands upon our Journals in consequence of my having directed some words of Mr. Alderman Beckford's to be taken down by the Clerk in order to their being censured if he did not retract them immediately. The second set of words contain his first explanation, and are, as I am told, exactly conformable to the doctrines laid down by those enlightened Whig Ministers, the Earls of Northington and Chatham, and Lord Chancellor Camden in the House of Peers the first day of the Session. To these words I likewise objected, and directed them also to be taken down as being, if possible, more criminal' than the former. Many arguments were used to palliate, but

not once to justify, these arbitrary and dangerous opinions, but
as I insisted that the words being taken down, and I ready to
make good my charge, the House was obliged either to censure
or approve them, and that if the latter was the case I should
think every man dishonoured who should ever set his foot
in that House after it unless it were to rescind it, and no one
venturing to stake his credit by supporting directly such odious
doctrines, Mr. A. Beckford, after three or four hours' debate,
thought it safer to give way, and to retract his opinion, and that
of his friends in the House of Peers, which you will see done by
his last explanation, with which as it contained my sense and
nearly my words, I acquiesced. We had not above 100 members
in the House, and my friends were all gone except two or three,
so that this great point was carried against the present minister
by those who act with the Court. Sir G. Elliot, Mr. Dyson and
that set of gentlemen spoke strongly against the legality and
the doctrine of a power in the King to dispense with
it, so did Mr. Burke, Lord Rockingham's late secretary, and
Mr. Dowdeswell, and for the necessity of a Bill of Indemnity
to *vindicate* the Constitution. What a disgrace is this at
the outset of an Administration calling themselves friends
to liberty, and what a triumph to you and the rest of our friends
in the House of Peers, particularly to Lord Mansfield, who feels
it to the utmost extent! Our Bill of Indemnity is to be presented
on Monday next, and it is said that the preamble is to admit the
illegality of the measure, and therefore the Act is to indemnify
all persons concerned in it, but I think we shall differ materially
with them in the Bill in the Committee. We hear that the
three Lords are extremely angry, and indeed I do not see how
they will get back with any tolerable degree of credit and of
honor when the Bill is brought to your House. There is in
general an air of great ferment and uneasyness, which was
augmented the same day that this event happened, by the
dismission of Lord Edgecumbe for Mr. J. Shelley. This
has produced a meeting of Lord Rockingham and his friends
where 'tis said that resignations were determined on and to take
effect on Monday, but, however positively they are asserted, I
always doubt of resignations till I see them. All I can say
therefore is that things appear to be in a critical and uncertain
situation in all quarters, the particulars of which it is not in my
power to explain in this manner and this distance, as they really
change from day to day. Whatever may be the event I would
not omit to apprize you of what has passed as far as I can, and
then to leave it to your own consideration and judgement. Lord
Temple proposes to be in town in five or six days, and so I am
told does Lord Suffolk, though I have not yet heard from him.
I flatter myself that Lady Buckinghamshire continues perfectly
well, and that you are now free from alarms of all sorts. I have
but barely room to add the assurances of that affectionate regard,
with which I am ever, etc.

Enclosure. Extract of Commons Journal of Nov. 18, 1766 (relating to Mr. Alderman Beckford's words 'that whenever the public is in danger the King has a dispensing power.' Also his explanation of these words).

George Grenville to the Earl of Buckinghamshire.

1766, Nov. 27. Bolton Street.—I have received your two letters of the 24th and 25th of this month, and in obedience to your directions write these few lines to inform you that the Indemnity Bill is to be read a second time in our House on Monday next. It cannot therefore be sent up to the House of Lords sooner than the Thursday or Fryday following, being the 4th or 5th of next month, and may probably be considered then at the second reading on the 8th, 9th, or 10th. I suppose the Commission at Norwich will be closed before the end of next week, and I know of no busyness likely to come on in the House of Lords before that time; as you therefore insist on my naming a day, I should imagine about Saturday the 6th of next month would answer all purposes. The Duke of Portland, Lord Scarborough, Lord Besborough, and Lord Monson have resigned to-day and more resignations are talked of to-morrow. The rest is all speculation, in a state of uncertainty as great as ever was known.

P.S. Lord Temple came to town on Monday last, and Lord Suffolk comes on Wednesday next.

John Patteson, Mayor of Norwich, to the Same.

1766, December 8. Norwich.—(Thanks for continual attention to the concerns of this city.) I have communicated Lord Buckinghamshire's application to the Secretary at War to some of my brethren, who all join with me in opinion that some additional troops would be very proper and very serviceable at this juncture, and particularly to have them here before the time of execution of the unhappy convicts.

We are at present perfectly quiet and much less murmuring than could be expected, which is to be attributed entirely to the exceeding great candour shewn by Sir Hen: Gould.

George Grenville to the Same.

1767, Jan. 27. Bolton Street.—I know not how it happened that your kind letter of the 19th of this month did not come to my hands till yesterday, a week after the date of it. I rejoice extremely to find by it that you and Lady Buckinghamshire are got back safe and well to Blickling, after an attempt, which I I should indeed have been very sorry (and notwithstanding my great partiality to everything you do, I must have thought you much to blame) if you had insisted in any longer. Lady Buckinghamshire's safety and your future happyness is of too much consequence to all those who love you for you to risk them upon any account, much less for an object so uncertain and contemptible as the political state has been, is and seems likely to continue for some time. I should imagine that notwithstanding that submission which at all other times you will do very right to pay, yet just now you are not bound to obey any decisions of my lady to send you to London one moment before she is perfectly safe and you perfectly easy and happy. You will I think, find nothing here worth your coming for, except the affection of your friends, who at this moment only can wish to be without you. Now for one word of politicks, according to your desire. The Earl of Chatham is still at Bath, and consequently the King's Administration has got the gout and hobbles terribly. Mr. C. Townshend indeed seems to wish to move a little more nimbly and to try to walk a little without crutches. We have had some general talk in the House about East India matters, in which Mr. Townshend has ventured to express his difference of opinion with Lord Chatham and his deputy Alderman Beckford. The committee for enquiring into that busyness is put off till next Fryday fortnight, in the meanwhile Mr. Townshend hopes to gain the E. India Company by kissing them, after the other great personage has kicked them. This negotiation has been on foot some time, and it is said by some will succeed, though others pretend to know that nothing can be done in it, as Lord Chatham is still absent and still in the clouds. Yesterday and to-day we have had some debates in the House of Commons on the estimates for the American troops, and the enormous expense attending them, amounting in the whole to above £400,000, or near a shilling in the pound on the land. This I proposed should be all defrayd by America and the West Indies, after having reduced it near one half by striking off the unnecessary articles. Mr. Townshend in answer to this, though he refused to consent to it, yet held a very strong language that America ought to pay that expense, and disclaimed in very strong terms almost every word of Lord Chatham's language on this subject, treating his Lordship's distinction between *Internal* and *External* Taxes with the same contempt as I did, and calling it *absurd*, *nonsensical* and *ridiculous* to the highest degree, determined, as he said, to assert his own opinions with regard to it, etc., etc. Nor did Mr. Conway, though he spoke on the same subject, say one word in support or vindication of Lord Chatham's sentiments or measures, nor any other person, though they were strongly censured by your humble servant, and though the division upon the question yesterday was 126 to 35, and to-day on the report 75 to 19. *Very empty Houses*, as you must perceive, on so interesting an occasion. This conduct furnishes many speculations, of which I own I am so weary that I wish myself out of the reach of them. I would not however omitt complying with your request, and, having done so, shall think myself well paid if this *long* account instead of a *succinct* one, gives you any amusement or satisfaction. As for Portugal, I know nothing but the daily lye of the newspapers. Mrs. Grenville continues perfectly well and is gone to the opera to-night. She joins with me in our best respects and sincere good wishes to Lady Buckinghamshire.

MR. JOHN ROGERS to the EARL OF BUCKINGHAMSHIRE.

1767, Feb. 5. Blackford.—I am requested to be a Petitioner to your Lordship in this most extraordinary time of dearness and scarcity of corn and other provisions on behalf of the poor of the Town of Plymouth, that you would be so good as to extend a part of Hele's Charity, which is at your disposal to the relief of the poor of said place. The Guardians of the Poor House have ordered a hundred pounds to be sunk out of their fund, to be laid out in the purchase of corn, etc., in order to be distributed at such a low rate as may be thought the Poor may very well afford from the fruits of their labour to give for the supply of their families. (Appeals to his well-known humane and innate disposition to compassionate the Distressed.)

The REV. MATTHEW WOODFORD to THE SAME.

1767, Feb. 8. Southampton.—Resigned the Rectory of Blickling on the 2nd inst. Proposes the terms of money arrangement to be made with his successor, that he should pay Mr. Gordon, who has served the cure since the 16th of November last, etc.

SIR HORACE MANN to THE SAME.

1767, June 6. Florence.—(As to a Commission Lord Buckinghamshire has entrusted him with.)

I have found a young fellow who I hope will in every respect answer your Lordship's expectations. My first chief point was to be assured of his abilities, for which purpose, not trusting totally to my judgement, I desired Lord Cowper to let him play at his house where the best performers of this place often meet, and they have assured me he is a very good and ready player in concert, that he understands music well, if they may judge by the composition which he produced, though he owned that they had to be retouched by his master, and that the only defect he has which is common to all young men, that of attempting in solos too much and what is more difficult than pleasing. His name is Luigi Fanti, a native of Imola, of about 24 years of age, a scholar of Paolo Alberghi, a noted player there who was a scholar of Tartini° and is a good figure. Before I had heard of him, I had proposed the commission to two or three Florentines of much less abilities than he has, but they rejected the conditions as being much too low, whereas this young man hardly enquired into them, his sole ambition being to get into the world. I could indeed have wished to have had the power of making some addition to those conditions, particularly in regard to cloaths, as it is usual here, not only to young fellows of this sort, but to all upper servants, to give them two suits of cloaths a year besides their wages, but I have stuck literally to the conditions which your Lordship prescribed, assuring him only in general terms that he would meet with encouragement from you according to

---

* Guiseppe Tartini (1692-1770).

his abilities and good behaviour. He wished much to have the
liberty of playing at the theaters, but this too I told him must
entirely depend upon your Lordship. He is as impatient to set
out as you can be to have him, and contrary to most of his
profession who raise difficulties about everything he has consented to go by sea which will not cost one-third of what must
have been allowed him for the journey by land. I will therefore
write tomorrow to Leghorne to dispose everything for his
departure, and I enclose to your Lordship the paper that he has
signed, of which he has a copy . . . Besides the violin, he
plays on the base, and french horn, and is in every respect very
decent and well-behaved.

I am much obliged to the Prince of Brunswick for his kind
interpretation of the marks of respect which I endeavoured to
show him; he was adored by everybody and if any opportunity
should offer, pray mention how gratefull I am for the honour
he condescended to do me here. . . . .

Sir Horace Mann to the Earl of Buckinghamshire.

1767, June 30. Florence.—As to the arrangements he has
made for the journey of Luigi Fanti to London.

George Grenville to the Same.

1767, July 14. Wotton.—You will certainly have heard before
this can reach you of the negotiation opened with Lord
Rockingham by a message delivered to him from the King by the
Duke of Grafton on Tuesday last, and that Lord Rockingham
communicated this to the Duke of Bedford and his friends at
Woburn, who refused to give any answer till they had apprized
me of it, for which purpose Mr. Rigby came here on Friday last
and Lord Temple, and I saw him again at Stowe on Sunday.
The particulars of what has passed cannot easily be comprized
in a letter. I have therefore desired Mr. Charles Lloyd, who you
know was my private secretary when I was in the Treasury and
who was with Lord Temple and me when Mr. Rigby came to us,
to relate them to you more fully than I can do by letter. I
understand from some of my friends that you was in town, and I
have directed him to take the earliest opportunity of waiting
upon you that you may not be ignorant of anything I know or of
my sentiments upon that subject. You will not be surprized at
my having insisted with Mr. Rigby that my name should not be
mentioned for any office whatsoever, notwithstanding which, if
the measures—and particularly that of asserting and establishing
the sovereignty of Great Britain over the Colonies, are such as I
can approve, no pretensions of mine shall be a bar to any
arrangement for the public benefit in which my friends may be
honorably placed. On the contrary I shall rejoice extremely at
it and support it in that case out of all office more chearfully than
I could in office, and shall be happy if by waving everything of
that sort for myself, I may be justified in throwing whatever

weight I may have into the scale of my friends. Every motive has determined me in this resolution in the present circumstances. I have often told you that I would not be forced upon the King by anybody whatever, and that even if I were called into his service, I must judge for myself whether I could engage in it. As I mean to refer to Mr. Lloyd to explain to you the whole of this situation I will only add that my brother Lord Temple agrees most perfectly with me in every part of it, and that I have every reason to be satisfied with the Duke of Bedford and his friends on this occasion, as they have given me the strongest assurances of their regard and good opinion. Everything is in a state of the greatest uncertainty, nor does it seem clear to me to what degree the King means to authorize Lord Rockingham. A week has already elapsed, and not only nothing is done but he has not even seen the King which, if it is intended to succeed, is surely very extraordinary. I will make no more comments, but wait the event, which must soon be determined.

Charles Lloyd to the Earl of Buckinghamshire.

1767, July. York Buildings, Wednesday night, 9 o'clock.—I arrived about an hour ago from Wotton, where I received a letter of introduction to your Lordship from Mr. Grenville, together with his commands to wait upon you and give you an account of the late very extraordinary scene of politicks, which I was the more enabled to do, as I received from him and Lord Temple at Stowe an accurate information of the several particulars. Upon calling at your door all that I could learn with any degree of certainty, was that your Lordship is at Blickling. I trouble you, my Lord, with this one word, to acquaint you that, in conformity to Mr. Grenville's desire, I shall inclose in a packet directed for your Lordship, by the Norwich Post Coach which will set out to-morrow evening, the best narrative I can give, and shall order the parcel to be left till called for at the King's Head in Norwich. I was particularly charged not to trust either any narrative of the late transactions, or even the letter of introduction (which contains some general outlines), to the post. I have recourse to the above method as the only one I know, pressed in time as I am, that can acquaint you both speedily and securely of what Mr. Grenville was extremely desirous should be communicated to you. As soon, therefore, as your Lordship receives this letter you may send for the parcel, as I take it for granted it will be left at the King's Head in Norwich on Friday evening next.

1767, July 16. *Enclosure.*—On Tuesday, the seventh of this month, a negotiation was opened with Lord Rockingham by a message from the King through the Duke of Grafton which was delivered at a meeting held at General Conway's house. After some previous compliments the Duke of Grafton told Lord Rockingham that the King wished that Lord Rockingham and his friends might form his Administration, and that he intended his Lordship should resume the office of First Lord of the Treasury. Lord Rockingham having asked whether he was at liberty to communicate this to others besides his own friends was answered that the question had been foreseen, and that he might communicate it, but it seemed intended that this was meant to the Duke of Bedford and his friends only. The Duke of Grafton made an offer of himself to serve under Lord Rockingham, and expressed some hopes that the *remains* of Lord Chatham's friends might be treated with some indulgence. Upon being desired to explain himself he mentioned *the Chancellor*. Lord Rockingham in the account of this conference which he gave by letter to Lord Albemarle, speaking of this intimation concerning the Chancellor, says: "But your Lordship knows my sentiments so well upon this point, that my determination is taken though I did not then enter into the detail of it." Lord Albemarle, who was then at Woburn, shewed Lord Rockingham's letter (by his Lordship's desire) to the Duke of Bedford, in the conclusion of which was a proposition from Lord Rockingham to come to Woburn if the Duke of Bedford and his friends were disposed to act with them in Administration. The answer given was that the Duke of Bedford and Mr. Grenville were one, and that he would not proceed without consulting Mr. Grenville. The intended visit was therefore postponed till that was done, and Mr. Rigby (who, as well as Lord Gower, was then at Woburn) proposed to go to London to enquire whether Mr. Grenville was returned from the west, and to give Lord Rockingham the meeting that evening, which he did accordingly, and repeated to him their resolution not to do anything without consulting Mr. Grenville and that they were determined not to be separated. In consequence of this Mr. Rigby went to Wotton on Friday the 10th, and assured Mr. Grenville in the strongest terms of the Duke of Bedford's regard and union with him both in system and in principles, and his own determination to cultivate it to the utmost. He said he had told Lord Rockingham that neither the Duke of Bedford himself, nor he as an individual, would ever depart from the ground taken to assert and establish the entire Sovereignty of Great Britain over her Colonies. That he was told in answer, that he, Lord Rockingham, hoped that might be settled to their satisfaction. Mr. Rigby added that Lord Rockingham declared for a wide and comprehensive system, but it is not known that anything, either with regard to measures or men, has been talked of in detail, nor is it certain to what degree Lord Rockingham is authorized. Mr. Grenville, after acknowledging the sense which he had of the behaviour of the Duke of Bedford and his friends towards him, answered, that as to measures his opinions were well known, especially with regard to the capital one of asserting and establishing the Sovereignity of Great Britain over America, in which he was happy to find that the Duke of Bedford and his friends so perfectly agreed with him, that as to arrangement of offices, as no message was sent to him, so he had no answer to give, nor if there had would he have given one without Lord Temple. That he entirely approved of a wide and comprehensive plan for an administration as the likeliest to produce vigor and permanency, without which no system for the public good could be pursued. That upon these principles he should be extremely glad to see his friends honorably placed in the King's Government and would chearfully support an administration formed upon them, but that he would support it out of office, and Mr. Grenville insisted that his name should not be mentioned for any office whatever, as it had long been his determination not to be obtruded upon the King. Mr. Rigby went on Saturday the 11th to meet Lord Rockingham at Woburn, Mr. Grenville went the same day to Stowe, on Sunday the 12th Mr. Rigby came over to Stowe and told Mr. Grenville that the Duke of Bedford and Lord Gower were extremely satisfied with his answer, to which Lord Temple agreed in every particular ; and Mr. Grenville and Lord Temple both assured Mr. Rigby that no factious or interested views of theirs should stand in the way of any public settlement, which if possible they sincerely wished to see made upon those principles in which Mr. Rigby assured them that they all concurred. Mr. Rigby's language in both visits was as open and as amicable as could be. Mr. Grenville's real wish on this occasion is that his friends could be honourably placed in the King's Government upon principles, which he can neither depart from himself or advise others to leave, and will be happy if, by waving any pretensions of his to office, he might contribute to that great purpose instead of getting an office for himself, which might give jealousy and must lessen his claims for provisions for his friends.

It must be observed that neither Lord Temple nor Mr. Grenville *bound or pledged* themselves to anything. They spoke their opinions upon the two propositions as stated by Lord Rockingham to the Duke of Bedford—the one of a broad, wide bottom of government, the other of adopting proper measures, and particularly respecting America.

THOMAS WHATELEY to the EARL OF BUCKINGHAMSHIRE.

1767, July 23. Parliament Street,—I have this moment received a letter by a private hand from Mr. Grenville, in which he desires me to acquaint your Lordship with the particulars of the late transactions in town, the account of which he had but just received at Wotton, and had not then time to transmit to his friends. That which I therefore send to your Lordship will not I hope differ materially from his, as I have been told it by the same person as has wrote to him, and whose relation to me is, that the Duke of Bedford, Lord Sandwich, Lord Weymouth, and Mr. Rigby met the Dukes of Portland and Richmond, Lord Rockingham and Mr. Dowdeswell, by appointment, at the Duke of Newcastle's, on Monday evening. In the beginning of the conference Mr. Rigby read a letter from Mr. Grenville to him, in which he states, as he has always stated, his and Lord Temple's concurrence in the intended comprehensive plan, to be founded on the condition that the measures to be adopted, and particularly the capital measure of asserting and establishing the Sovereignty of Great Britain over the Colonies should be such as they could approve of. This occasioned some difficulty and altercation in the outset, but the discussion of the subject was at last postponed for the present; and they were proceeding in the business on which they had met when Mr. Conway, being named for an office of nomination, was objected to by the Duke of Bedford, who said he understood that Mr. Conway himself professed the military line ; and that continuing him in a civil employment was contrary to the general idea upon which the new arrangement was founded. The conversation ended here that night ; and Lord Rockingham desiring the next day to have a second meeting less numerous than the former, it consisted only of his Lordship, the Duke of Newcastle and Mr. Dowdeswell, the Duke of Bedford and Mr. Rigby. Then Lord Rockingham mentioned Mr. Conway to be Secretary of State and Minister in the House of Commons. The same objections were renewed and urged more strongly ; his Grace besides complaining that so material a part of the arrangement had never been hinted before, and absolutely refusing on every consideration to consent to the placing Mr. Conway in such a situation. Lord Rockingham has positively insisted upon it, and therefore, without going any further, it was found necessary to put an end to the negotiation, each party declaring the other as free from all engagements whatever, as if nothing had passed between them. The Duke of Bedford and Mr. Rigby carried on the conference with the utmost temper and firmness, and acted throughout with the highest spirit, and yet the greatest moderation. Since this conclusion of the affair Lord Rockingham has had a short audience, of the particulars of which your Lordship knows I am not confidentially informed ; but, to judge by appearances, the whole affair seems now to be at an end, and speculations upon what is to follow are again as uncertain as ever.

C. LLOYD to the EARL OF BUCKINGHAMSHIRE.

1767, July 23. York Buildings, Thursday.—I was extremely concerned to find by your Lordship's letter which came to my hands yesterday that I had omitted inserting Mr. Grenville's letter in the packet sent to Norwich. Lord Lyttelton, to whom it was enclosed by mistake, is moving about at present from place to place. I have wrote to him at Bristol, where he is expected the latter end of this week, and in the meantime take the liberty of sending you a copy; as your Lordship will already have seen the contents of it in the narrative, I am in hopes that delay will not be of much consequence, especially as you are well satisfied of Mr. Grenville's intention that the earliest communications should be made to you of the late transactions. As your Lordship will have undoubtedly authentic information from other quarters, I will only mention in the general that yesterday Lord Rockingham acquainted the King that he could not undertake to form an Administration. This was the result of two conferences held at

Newcastle House on Monday and Tuesday last, where, after a discussion of the American question, which Lord Rockingham and his friends seemed inclined to leave to the Duke of Bedford's arbitration, they differed on the nomination of the person who was to take the lead in the House of Commons; Lord Rockingham insisted it should be Mr. Conway, whereas the Duke of Bedford contended that he ought to return to his military line. The idea of yesterday was that General Conway would resign immediately. The persons distinguished at the levée were Lord Rockingham, Mr. Conway and Lord Hertford.

Lord Bute's people are in high spirits. Nobody pretends to guess at the event.

Persons present at the First Conference. Duke of Bedford, Mr. Rigby, Lord Sandwich, Duke of Newcastle, Lord Weymouth, Mr. Dowdeswell, Lord Rockingham, Duke of Richmond.

At the Second. Duke of Richmond, Lord Sandwich, Lord Weymouth were not present.

PRINCE of COURLAND⁰ (PIERRE S. H.) to the EARL OF BUCKINGHAMSHIRE.

Mittau, ce 30 Juillet, 1767.—Expressions of gratitude for the dogs sent him by the Earl.

(*In French.*)

BARON KLOPMANN to THE SAME.

1767, July 30. Mittau.—For fear of troubling your Lordship too often with mine, I waited till the staghounds were arrived, which I hope will make an apology for not having sooner acknowledged your most obliging favour.

The hounds are very fine, and a great present to the Duke and the Prince, who both return their best thanks to your Lordship, desiring only to find opportunitys of their acknowledgment for it.

Since the departure of our most aimable Princess, who went to Pirmont about three weeks ago, in order to make use of the waters, our Court seems to be very dull and tedious. We are chiefly in the country, and to repair the hopes of the best company, enjoie the pleasures of the season.

The Polish news will become soon more interesting. The 5th of October the diet of pacification is to begin. In the meantime things are just in such an order, and so far settled, that nothing is to fear any more. The persuasive measures Prussia has taken to explain the disputes of the dissidents to the holy order of the bishops and their party, have had the best effect. The King is in high spirits, more so than he was last winter.

Prince Razivill makes now a quite different figure. He has money, sense and spirits to be at the head of the Confederation, while he had none two years ago. In short he'll enter in all the schemes of the Court, not to forget himself.

---

* Peter, elected in 1766, Prince of Courland, during the lifetime of his father, John Ernest de Biren, Duke of Courland and Semigalle.

Her Impl. Majesty this most gracious Princess, the wonder and admiration of her age, is come back from her journey. She resides 16 werst from Moscov, called Columna, and according the last advises is gone for a few days to Troitzka, 60 werst from thence.

Now I am at an end of all my politicks. Pray when do you think Mr. Hans Stanly will travell away? or who is to be nominated in his place, for I should be extremely glad to know beforehand something about his coming this way, as well as be much pleased to shew him all possible services and politeness in my power.

Supposing Sir George* being returned by this time, I must beg as a most particular favour of your Lordship to assure him of my duty and regard, wishing to be soon favoured with his.

Fearing now to tire too long your Lordship's patience, I beg leave to assure you of my most humble regard and sinceer attachment, and desire not to forget,

Your Lordship's, etc.

CHARLES LLOYD to the EARL OF BUCKINGHAMSHIRE.

1767, August 18. York Buildings, Tuesday.—Your Lordship's letter of the 28th of last month was sent after me to Derby, whither I was gone upon an excursion into the north, and from whence I am just returned. Mr. Grenville, I find, received information on Saturday last that the Duke of Bedford had that day told the Duke of Marlborough at Blenheim that the Duke of Newcastle had very lately informed him that the present Parliament would certainly be dissolved, and that the time fixed for declaring it was at the next prorogation on the 31st of this month. The Duke of Newcastle was certainly not unlikely to have early intelligence of such a measure if intended, and yet I do not find this report current here; I heard it indeed to-day from a person to whom Lord Vere mentioned it, quoting Lord Charles Spencer for his authority, which your Lordship sees is derived from the source of intelligence already mentioned. As you desired to know what passed, I thought it not improper to state to you the degree of information received, and you will from hence give it its proper weight. I shall go to Mr. Grenville's on Sunday, if in the mean time any thing material comes to my knowledge, I shall not fail to transmit an account of it to your Lordship.

P.S. Lord Frederick Campbell is certainly to go to Ireland as first Secretary to the Lord Lieutenant.†

THOMAS WHATELEY to THE SAME.

1767, August 18. Parliament Street.—Your Lordship's commands to me upon a former occasion to send you any news which

---

* Sir George Macartney, British Ambassador to St. Petersburg, 1765-1768, in succession to the Earl of Buckinghamshire.
† George, Lord Viscount Townshend, appointed August 12, 1767.

was material, is the reason of my troubling you now with a piece of intelligence which may be important if it should prove true, and of the credibility of which your Lordship will judge when I have informed you of the authority on which I repeat it. It is a letter from the Duke of Newcastle to the Duke of Bedford, informing him that the Parliament will certainly be dissolved, and that the dissolution will probably be notified at the next Prorogation, which must be before the 31st of this month. It is probable that such a measure should be adopted ; it will certainly be kept as secret as it can be ; the Duke of Newcastle may very possibly have early notice of it; he is a good judge of the authenticity of his information, and he is absolutely positive; but on the other hand, I can learn no trace of it from any other quarter. It rests therefore solely on that authority, but that is generally in these affairs so good, that I would not defer apprizing your Lordship of the intelligence such as it is by the only opportunity I shall have, as I am just now going out of town, and it will not be in my power by another post either to confirm or contradict the news.

P.S. It is the more singular that nobody has yet heard of this news, as the Duke's letter was written so long ago as last Wednesday.

Thomas Whateley to the Earl of Buckinghamshire.

1767, August 21. Nonsuch Park.—As I have very accidentally had an opportunity, tho' in the country, to learn the grounds upon which the Duke of Newcastle gave that intelligence to the Duke of Bedford, which I took the liberty to communicate to your Lordship by last Tuesday's post, I think it incumbent upon me to trouble you with a few lines to inform you that his Grace did not write that letter upon any information which he had received, but merely upon speculation. That speculation, however, seems so well founded to some, for whose judgment I have the highest deference, that they are firmly persuaded the measure will be adopted, but as yet no positive facts are known upon which to support this opinion. The reasons they alledge incline me to expect it, but as I had given your Lordship a more positive information, I thought it necessary to apprize you that the noble Duke in his assertion intended only to convey an opinion not to affirm a fact!

C. Lloyd to the Same.

1767, Sep. 10. Yorkbuildings. Thursday.—Lord North came to town yesterday, saw the D. of Grafton and was at the King's Levée. It is generally said that he has refused the Chancellorship of the Exchequer and as generally known that he will accept, if compelled by the alternative of taking that office or of having none at all. Lord Guilford is in a dangerous state of health, this may possibly operate on Lord North's present conduct. Lord Mansfield was in the Closet yesterday an hour and an half. The King did not set out till seven this evening for Richmond, the Princess of Wales was with him till the instant of his leaving the Queen's house. Lord Bute it is said is come to Town so ill as to be attended by three physicians. The Duke of Bedford and Mr. Rigby dined at Clermont on Monday last. I left Mr. Grenville very well at Wotton on Saturday, he is now at Lord Lyttelton's.

PHILIP LLOYD, Dean of Norwich, to the EARL OF BUCKINGHAMSHIRE.

1767, Oct. 17. Deanery, Norwich.—Will have pleasure in doing all that depends on him to serve Mr. Tilson, whom Lord Buckinghamshire recommends, when the vacancy of Hempstead happens.

The EARL OF HUNTINGDON to THE SAME.
(Endorsed by the latter Letter of Dismission.)

1767, Nov. 5.—The King has commanded me to acquaint your Lordship that he appointed the Duke of Roxburgh to be one of the Gentlemen of the Bedchamber in your Lordship's Room. I flatter myself your Lordship will forgive me the disagreeable necessity of executing the duty of my office.

The EARL OF BUCKINGHAMSHIRE to the EARL OF HUNTINGDON.

1767, Nov. 8.—I have receiv'd your Lordship's favor of the 5th of this month and should think very ill of myself if I was not prepared upon all occasions and in every situation to submit becomingly to his Majesty's pleasure.

It is incumbent upon me to express a proper sense of the obliging manner in which you have made the communication, and to assure you, etc. (*Draft.*)

GEORGE GRENVILLE to the EARL OF BUCKINGHAMSHIRE.

1767, Nov. 14. Wotton.—I have writ to Sir Richard Bampfylde according to your desire informing him of your intentions that Mr. Hobart should offer himself as a candidate for the City of Exeter at the next General Election in case of Mr. Tuckfield's death or of his declining to stand again on account of the bad state of his health. I have apply'd to Sir Richard Bampfylde for his interest in favor of Mr. Hobart, and have explain'd to him that it is not your intentions to make any opposition to the two present members. I am told that Sir Richard Bampfylde is to be attack'd in the county of Devon, if so, I suppose that your Lordship is well dispos'd towards him, as there cannot otherwise be any reasonable prospect of success in the present application to him. I heartily wish it may succeed but whether it does or no, I shall at least have had the pleasure of complying with your request, and of showing my regard for Mr. Hobart, in return for that which he has frequently expressed towards me. I was very sorry to find by your letter that His Majesty had been prevail'd upon to appoint another gentleman of the Bed Chamber in your place. Has any expression or cause of his displeasure been ever signifyd to you, or is it to be holden forth as a mark of the displeasure of his Ministers and avowd upon that principle? When I have the pleasure of seeing you in Town, you will perhaps be better able to answer these questions than you are by letter. Mrs. Grenville and I propose to be in London on Saturday the 21st of this month. She is upon the whole considerably better this year that the last, and has had no return of her former pains for some months.

Hans Stanley to the Earl of Buckinghamshire.

1768, Oct. 29. Paultons.—Warm expressions of friendship and of his hope to visit Blickling. The occupations in which he passes his time described.

Richard Owen Cambridge to the Same.

1766, July —. —Having been all the morning in London, it is now so near the going out of the post that I have not time to put in all our thanks to your Lsp. and Lady Buckingham, nor to mention Lady Suffolk, nor Mme. Perrier's being brought to bed of a boy, nor anything but the very little which is known for certain. All that is, that the D. of Grafton has the Treasury, and Mr. Townshend is Chanc. Exchequer. In his room to be two pay-masters. Ld. Shelbourne, Secretary of State with Conway. So far *I am sure* is *settled* and they kiss hands on Wednesday. The *talk* is that Lord Camden is to be Chancellor, Northing[ton] Pres: Councill. The D. of Rutland to be laid on a bed of roses (that is —'s expression) that Ld. Bristol may have his place. I'll write no more hearsay. Hume has Salisbury and Litchfield the Deanery of St. Paul's.

Earl of Buckinghamshire to George Grenville.

1769, July.—I hope Mrs. Grenville and the young gentleman are now so well recovered that you can with pleasure give an answer to the inquisitive sollicitude of a distant friend. Thus far is the object of my letter, but as my pen is in hand I will send you some little account of our Norfolk Politicks.

The Norwich Assizes is usually a very general Meeting of the County and upon our arrival there we found all the Townshend and Walpole Party drawn up ready to resist a petition in consequence of an alarm given in the news-papers, by what authority as yet has not been traced.

The foresight of the High Sheriff had secured them a majority upon the Grand Jury, and the Foreman, tho' our friend, has unfortunately one of those undeciding characters who are very often greatly embarassing to a party and scarcely ever essentially useful.

Mr. Mills, Mr. Harbord, Sir Wm. Wiseman, my brother and many other gentlemen of distinction were absent, and tho' several of our zealous patriots were even angrily urgent, it was judged more eligible not to make the attempt than to risque the incurring a disgrace. I am sorry this conduct was advisable as the Petition would probably not have been in the wild diffuse stile but confin'd simply to the merits of the Middlesex Election, at least such were the idea's of Sr Edward Astley, Mr. Coke and Sir Wm. Harbord and of several others. Tho' the Court influences many persons of distinction in this Country, the majority of the freeholders are greatly dissatisfy'd with the present Government, some to a very intemperate degree; and there is great reason to believe that they will try at the Michaelmas Sessions to have a Petition.

The worthy Bishop of Norwich° has left us, insensibly attracted into the vortex of Cambridge. He was initiated into the disinterested mystery's of that pious body and adores with them their new Apis.

Notwithstanding the frequent reports of his Grace's wishes and intentions to retire from publick business, I cannot think he will quit the Closet till he is thrust out, yet were he wise, surely he would wrap himself up in poor Lord Winchelsea's Blue Ribbond, nor venture the meeting of a Parliament, who if they are in any degree influenc'd by the temper of the Nation will make his situation as disagreeable to him as hitherto it has been disgracefull.

Sir Wm. Harbord to the Duke of Newcastle.

[1769], Sep. 30. Norwich.—(*Copy.*) Explanatory of his conduct in relation to the Petition referred to in the preceding letter.

George Grenville to the Earl of Buckinghamshire.

1769, Augst. 16. Wotton.—I should have answered your kind enquiry after us as soon as I received it, if I had not been prevented by having so much company in the house as not to allow me one moment's leisure. We are now almost alone except the Count and Countess de Welderen, the former of whom has been confin'd to his bed here for this fortnight by a very bad bilious fever. He has been attended by two Physicians from Oxford, one of whom is now in the house and tells me that he hopes the danger is over tho' he has still a return of fever and is extremely reduced. Mrs. Grenville has had some returns of her complaint but they have been much slighter, and I hope that upon the whole she is much better than she was. I am much obliged to you for the account of your Norfolk Politicks. If the body of the freeholders are dissatisfy'd and think that their rights and those of all the Electors in England are violated by the late determination in the House of Commons they may

---

* Philip Yonge, or Young, Bishop, 1761-1783,

certainly remonstrate against it in a proper manner, and I take it for granted will do so whatever means are employed to prevent it, because they always have it in their power. If they do, they will give weight to the resistance which has been made to that measure in the House of Commons and prevent the like measure for the future ; if they do not, those who think of it as I have done must content themselves with having done their duty in the proper place by opposing a resolution which appeared to them to be a direct breach of the Constitution. You will have seen by the News-Papers and probably have heard I have met Lord and Lady Chatham at Howe, and that they have since come over to us at Wotton and stay'd with us two or three days. Every thing passed extremely well in all respects, and whatever effect it may have in the political world, where it may possibly occasion much speculation, I am persuaded that our friends will be glad of an event which will contribute so much to our domestic happyness by healing the wounds which have so long prevented the union and peace of our family. As to Politicks I hear nothing but what tends to render the state of them more and more uncertain. I heartily lament the situation of the King and Kingdom, but I think it cannot be cured, till both or at least till one of them shall be fully convinced of the danger. I agree with you that the D. of G. will not quit the Closet till he is forced to it whatever reports may be given out of his wishes and intentions, nor do I think his wishes or intentions will be any remedy to the evil either one way or the other. I have long thought so, and my public sentiments continue unaltered and so, I trust, will my private friendships particularly that which I have long had the pleasure to cultivate with you.

GEORGE GRENVILLE to the EARL OF BUCKINGHAMSHIRE.

1770, July 14. Charleton.—(Referring to Marble hill and trusts of Lady Suffolk's will.) I should be very sorry to be depriv'd of the pleasure which I flatter'd myself with of meeting you here if I had not heard from Lord Suffolk that you was more agreeably and better employ'd in Staffordshire.[o] May that employment (the best in which you can be engag'd) turn out as much to your happyness as your own wishes or those of your warmest friends can desire. Nothing my dear Lord, could give me a more cordial satisfaction than to be a witness of it, but I am engag'd in the Autumn to make another excursion to Packington and Hagley, and afterwards to receive some company at home, which I fear will make it impossible, but my desire to do it is so sincere that if I can I certainly would come to you at Blickling. I shall stay here till Fryday next, the 19th of this month, when I shall return to Wotton. I am obliged to you for the news which you send to me about the Colonies. I hear that there is much talk about them, but I am

---

* The Earl of Buckinghamshire was married for the second time on the 24th September, 1770, to Miss Caroline Conolly, of Stratton in Staffordshire, a grand-daughter of the Earl of Strafford.

still persuaded that there will be nothing done, which I am sure in the present crisis cannot be right. Every fool can find fault, but it requires wisdom and ability to act with firmness and discretion after a series of the greatest folly and weakness which ever disgraced a country. Lord Suffolk joins with me in our kindest wishes and best compliments to you.

A PACKET OF PAPERS endorsed :—" PROCEEDINGS IN COUNCIL delivered by the EARL OF BUCKINGHAMSHIRE :—Papers from the Council Office, 1770."

No. 1. (*Copy.*) Minutes of the Lords of the Committee of Council for plantation affairs, upon considering the state of disorder, confusion and misgovernment in the province of Massachusetts Bay. Dated 26 June, 1770.

No. 2. (*Copy.*) Minutes of the Lords of the Committee of Council. Dated 27 June, 1770.

No. 3. (*Copy.*) Minutes of the Lords of the Committee of Council. Dated 4 July, 1770.

No. 4. (*Copy.*) Report of the Lords of the Committee of Council. Dated 4 July, 1770.

No. 5. (*Copy.*) Order of His Majesty in Council. 6 July, 1770.

No. 6. (*Copy.*) Order of His Majesty in Council. 6 July, 1770.

A list of the above Papers.

J. SNOW to the EARL OF BUCKINGHAMSHIRE.

1771, May 1 (by the Almanack, by the weather Xmas Day). The Chantry.—The embanking the Tavy and Tamar I shou'd realy think very practicable and would answer very well. Mr. Heywood is going to experiment this summer in his marshes, and I think your Lordship might advantageous make a trial under Gnatam, where are many acres of shallow muddy grounds hardly cover'd but in spring tides and which lay much skreen'd both from strong tides and currents. Heywood mention'd the very thing to me as he pass'd lately thro' here and he will give your Lordship full accounts both of the charges and manner of doing of it by the same undertaker as Parker employs and Eliot has successfully employ'd. Hang politicks, I detest them ! K., Lds. and the Commons are the only Government I know. If they are all in the wrong, I hope they will mend without recourse to swords, pistols and levelling republican principles. I can't help very sincerely condoling with your late disappointment in family hopes, but let not, my dearest Lord, your noble courage be cast down. I hope and trust your pious endeavours will succeed better next time. *Tu ne cede malis, at contra audentius ito.* .

I quite approve and congratulate you of preferring private social happiness to noisy dependent concernment in publick affairs, at present in such confusion. . . I remember a french

Harlequin once giving a description of our Countrey said, " Pour l'Angleterre, c'est une grande bête, dont le cul est devenu la tête," which I realy think was a just as well as drole Harlequinade.

Adieu, my dear Lord, I have rubb'd through this long winter pretty well and hope when I hear of two or three swallows flying about, to crawl out of my long imprisonment in my old residentiary Castle. My wife and family join in every grateful wish to you and yours with your ever faithfull and obliged, etc.

LORD CRAGGS CLARE[*] to the EARL OF BUCKINGHAMSHIRE.

1771, June 1. Kensington.—Warm expressions of gratitude to Lord and Lady Buckinghamshire for having undertaken the trust in relation to his daughter. Can now fill up with heartfelt joy a blank in his Will, which without their assistance he wou'd never have been able to do with any comfort or satisfaction.

THE SAME to THE SAME.

1773, Feb. 19. Bath.—If ever I coud have had a moment's doubt of the tender attention which my daughter woud experience from your friendly and good heart, the earnest which you have given me in the last letter with which your Lordship honoured me, wou'd convince me that my death wou'd only produce a change of one loving father for another, as willing and more able to protect and serve her. In my impatience to be in London at a time when I considered absence as a crime in every public man, I set out from hence on my way thither, after a confinement of seven weeks to my house, and at the end of seventeen miles stopt at Lord Shelburn's house, fatigued, but in other respects feeling rather better for my journey. There I rested next day, and in the following night had a return of fever worse than at my first seizure. When it had abated a little, I prefer'd returning to my Physician here rather than remain at so great a distance, where he coud afford me but few and short attendances.

MINUTES OF CONVERSATION with LORD DARTMOUTH.[†]

1774, March 2.—The first idea to have removed the Customs and Trade from Boston to some other Port in the Province, objected to by the Lawyers because the Captains of ships producing their clearance are legally entitled to require that a Custom House officer should attend them to any particular port.

Second. To have prosecuted the leaders at the Town Meeting viz. Williams, Hancock, Molineux, for High Treason for the opinions they gave at that meeting, and the guard plac'd upon the ships in consequence. The Solicitor-General coincided with this, but the Attorney-General objected as Hancock assigned as a

---

[*] Created Earl Nugent in 1776.
[†] Apparently between Lord Dartmouth and the Earl of Buckinghamshire.

reason for placing the guard that it was only to prevent others from destroying the Tea who might do it with an idea of afterwards throwing the odium upon their party.

A Bill to be brought into Parliament to enact the removal of the Custom House, Assembly, etc., from Boston; to make it a high crime and misdemeanour at any Public Meeting to dispute the Sovereign Legislative authority of Great Britain; and to enforce the payment of an indemnification to the East India Company for the Tea destroyed; also to regulate the Justices of the Peace whose general remissness has encouraged these Riots. (Obs. Not the Province or the Town, but the Leaders at the Meeting previous to the Riot.)

I proposed that the persons of whose active part at the Town Meeting the Council have evidence upon oath, should be declared incapable of holding any post of trust, honour or profit in the Province.

COMMENCEMENT OF THE AMERICAN REBELLION.[*]

It is evident that our present situation with the Colonys is so critical that no effectual middle term can be found; we must either insist upon their submission to the authority of the Legislature or give them up intirely to their own indiscretion. The first seems the lesser evil but it is by no means easy to determine the measures necessary for carrying it into execution and yet the decision upon those measures must be immediate. It would have become the wisdom of the Nation from the very infancy of the Colonys to have attended to the growth of them and to have introduc'd new regulations as the increase of cultivation, commerce, opulence and population made new regulations necessary. But above all this fatal spirit of independency should have been check'd in its very first appearence which on the contrary has been foster'd and cherish'd by measures which it were vain to dwell upon, tho' the painfull recollection cannot but be suggested by their consequences. This necessary policy too long defer'd will now admit of no delay, it is the duty of a good citizen strenuously to attempt that which, if difficult now, will in a very short space be impracticable.

Tho' the other Colonys are but too deeply engag'd in this business, yet as that of the Massachusets Bay has taken the lead, it were better perhaps to suppose that they acted from the instigations and example of the disaffected there, and consider the town of Boston as the immediate object of the resentment of this country. I have been inform'd that there is evidence upon oath against several of the leaders at the Meeting previous to the destruction of the tea. They should be declar'd incapable of holding any office of trust, honor or profit in the Province, and if their effects can answer the damage sustained by the East India Company they should be condemn'd to make it good. It appears to me that for the future no person should be admitted into the

* This is in Lord Buckinghamshire's handwriting, but is unsigned. But *see* p. 295, Lord Hardwicke's letter of Dec. 26.

assembly or council or suffer'd to act as a justice of peace who do's not acknowledge a supreme power of Legislation in the Parlt. of England. This was, however, thought of before and great objections made to it. The removal of the Custom House from Boston and in consequence carrying the trade of the Province to another Port might also be expedient, and some regulations are necessary for preventing fraudulent bankruptcy and facilitating for recovering the just debts of our merchants. The determinations of Government should be sent with five or six Frigates with orders if there did not appear a disposition to submit to intercept their trade. This will be called Making War upon your Colonys but is it not evident that in their present temper nothing but an appearance of this Country's being resolved to support its authority at all events can prevent their throwing off even the appearence of allegiance? It would perhaps be advisable immediately to withdraw all the troops from the interior of the Country and to bring them to the Sea Ports. The Canadians also should be attended to who, if they already are not, might easily be made, the best subjects of the Crown in North America, their disposition is military and the idea of the force which might be brought from there would not a little contribute to keep the disaffected within bounds. From such accounts as have reach'd me it may be presum'd that there is no real love or true spirit in these people, and that they will submit to the superiority of this Country if they think it will be exerted. But even supposing they should successfully resist, they would only obtain that situation where a very few years longer of the languor and inattention of Great Britain would place them. *When they have submitted* for the present no further taxation should be thought of, but the Act of Navigation should be kept up in the utmost strictness, every step taken to discourage their manufactures and above all things some method thought of to stop the migration of the inhabitants of England and Ireland as far as possible and to prevent the further population of the inland parts of America.

EARL OF HARDWICKE to the EARL OF BUCKINGHAMSHIRE.

1773, March 17. St. James's Square.—After thanking you for the good company you placed me in last night at the Opera, I take the liberty to transcribe for your amusement what my brother[o] writes of the situation of affairs in the North. " The " Situation of Europe does not clear up. On one side it is " universally supposed that Peace will not be concluded between " the Turcks and Russians ; on the other, that there is more " reason to apprehend a rupture in the North than to expect " tranquillity. Certain it is, that in Russia, Sweden and Denmark " preparations are making by sea and land, and the French give " out that they will send all their German regiments from Dantzick " to Sweden, whilst a report is propagated from St. Petersburg " that the Porte has promised a large subsidy to Sweden, a sum of

---

[o] Sir Joseph Yorke, Minister at the Hague, created Lord Dover, 1788

"which is already committed; if these two last articles (which I "give as uncertain) should be verified, I think his Swedish Majesty[*] "may be tempted to try his fortune, for the leaven of Aristocracy "in the old Government which smoulders under the ashes might "break out if a popular object in that Country (such as a war "with Russia) was not started to give another turn to the national "spirit. I believe I have said before that I have not the least "idea of the part Austria would take in the *Turckish* quarrel, but "it is positively said she has declared to France that she will be "neuter in any Swedish quarrel. We can but lament over the fate "of Poland in general and of Dantzick in particular, which City "will probably be sacrificed to the momentary interests of Russia "against her essential and fundamental duty. The Empress of "Russia feels that the K. of Prussia is in the wrong, but he is in "the possession of directing her Councils," etc.

I am afraid I have tired your lordship with my diplomatick prose, but then I have quoted a better authority in those matters than my "*Ipse dixit*" would be.

It looks to me that we *here* only wait for events and have taken no decisive party.

Très-assurément nous ne faisons pas grande figure.

J. M. Heywood to the Earl of Buckinghamshire.

1774, June 21. Manston.—(As to "Pike's tenement" in Beer, "one of the prettiest estates in the parish and worth about £40 a year."

A resident steward is necessary on Lord Buckinghamshire's estate in these parishes.)

You may depend upon my getting the best intelligence I can of your Rector's conduct respecting what you mention'd to me, but have no reason as yet to think he has done anything oppressive. I think your L[d]ship said you would write to him about the wood which you imagined had not been disposed of to the greatest advantage to yourself, etc., etc.

Roger Kerrison to the Same.

1775, Jan. 17. Norwich.—Lord Buckinghamshire has so often (since he ceased to represent the City of Norwich in Parliament) distinguished himself not only as a benefactor to distressed Indigence but a liberal encourager of public Institutions that the Parishioners of St. Peter Mancroft are emboldened to sollicit his name to a subscription lately set on foot for having a Peal of Twelve Bells in that Tower.

(Congratulations on the birth of an heir.) . . .

Earl of Buckinghamshire to Roger Kerrison.

No Date.—Promising ten guineas towards St. Peter's Bells. *Draft.*

---

* Gustavus III, 1771-1792.

His having given lately £100 towards the Discharge of Debtors confined in the City and County Gaols, added to the expense of inclosing the Norfolk and Norwich Hospital from the road, amounting to near £400, will in some sort apologise for his not being a larger contributor. "It will ever be the pride and glory of my family to merit the approbation and countenance of the Citizens of Norwich," etc.

Draft.

BARON CHERKASOW to the EARL OF BUCKINGHAMSHIRE.

1775, August 31. Moscow.—Acknowledging the receipt of some engravings sent by the Earl to the Empress of Russia, he has been ordered by her to request his L dship to forward her the Act of Parliament called "The Act declaring the rights and liberties of the subject and of establishing the succession to the Crown," W. and M. I., Session 2, Cap. 2. Asking also for a good French translation of the same.

ROBERT FELLOWES to the SAME.

1775, Nov. 29. Shotesham.—Acknowledging a letter, enclosing a draft for two hundred and fifty pounds upon Messrs. Drummond, a mark of his "boundless liberality" to the Hospital [the Norfolk and Norwich]. "I entirely agree with your Lordship that a close wall was a proper enclosure for the Hospital, and so I always thought, but the Majority were of a different opinion and gave directions accordingly."

LORD NUGENT to the SAME.

1775, Nov. 11. Stoke.—You have very naturally supposed that I coud not without much time and blotting answer the best written and most elegant letter I ever yet received; and have accounted for my long silence from this consideration. But, be not so vain! It has travel'd from Blickling to Bristol, from Bristol to London, from London to Bath, and from Bath to Bristol. Now, compute the distance and compare them with dates, you will find I coud not answer you a day sooner. After meeting Lady Dorothy on the road, I found at my arrival in London that my son was set out for Ireland, only to cut throats with a certain Col. Gabbet, who, he had been inform'd, misrepresented what he had said of Mrs. Bunbury to her husband when they met upon the same laudable business.

I felt a little uneasy upon the subject as you will readily believe, and instead of proceeding to Bristol returned to Gosfield, where I was some time after released from my apprehension by my son's return from Ireland with a letter from the said Col. Gabbet which, with reason, thoro'ly satisfied him.

I am now eating Turtle and drinking Punch. I shew'd your letter to George Grenville and his Lady; they wanted comfort and they had it. Poor woman! She is, I fear, in a desperate way; and they both set out this day for London without having receiv'd any benefit from Bath.

They desire their love to you, and feel, as they ought, what you say. You have used a device which has succeeded to keep Lady Buckingham's and your daughter's partiality for me a secret from my constituents.

Such reflections upon Merchants! I fear your interest declines at Norwich. I am sure I could ruin it by communicating your letter there. But I will keep your secret, provided you promise not to interrupt my happiness by any peevish fit of jealousy. You will by this bargain retain the love of thousands and I possess the goodwill of one whom I woud prefer to millions. God bless you all.

Mr. Alderman Durbin waits.

(Note at the head of this letter.) Woud to God you cou'd share the happiness I am enjoying by the cheerful society of a certain gentleman who shall be nameless.

Affectionately yrs, Botetourt.*

EARL OF HARDWICKE to the EARL OF BUCKINGHAMSHIRE.

[17]75, Dec. 26. St. James's Square.—I take the liberty to send you in confidence the last letter I received from my brother at the Hague, thinking it will amuse you, and put you a little *au fait*, not only of his negotiations but of the general state of Foreign Affairs. Your Lordship may repost it any time in the course of the morrow. We make here at present a great mystery of common things; how the Russian affair has slipped out of our fingers, I know not.† Sir Joseph‡ was not in that secret, I believe.

Your Lordship made me not only *happy* but *vain* by approving my crude idea about America. I am sensible of the delicacy and difficulty of it, and till we can strike them by an *Appareil de Force*, it cannot be attempted with a prospect of success. I am very sure that the sooner we can end that business *quo-cunque modo* the better. When I say that, I do not exclude the idea of doing it with dignity and decorum, but I see difficultys in carrying it thro' *à la rigueur* which my poor conceptions cannot get over.

I hope when I come to Town after the holy-days, if nothing else mend, we shall at least have better operas.

GENERAL HOWE to THE SAME.

1776, July 8. Staten Island.—It was not without the deepest concern that I heard of the late calamitous state of your family,§ being sensible both your Lordship and Lady Buckingham must

---

* Narbonne Berkeley. created Baron Botetourt April, 1764. a title which had been extinct since 1406. He died s.p. 1776.

† This probably refers to a negociation on the part of the Government to procure Russian Auxiliary troops in the American war. (See *Recueil des Instructions données aux ambassadeurs et ministres de France.* Vol. II. 329.)

‡ Sir Joseph Yorke.

§ The Earl of Buckinghamshire lost two infant sons in 1775 and 1776.

have suffered infinite pain. But as I have understood from Fanny her Ladyship bore her misfortunes with a calmness and resignation that was much admired, and which arising from the purest principles no doubt it must have softened the affliction.

The Halifax Armament got into Sandy Hook on the 29th last past, and the army is now cantoned in this island with every necessary refreshment to be wisht, and what is not frequently seen, to the great joy of the inhabitants who have been long oppressed by the Rebels for their unremitting attachment to H. M's Government.

It is reported that the Canada army is upon Lake Champlain, and a rebel Newspaper mentions an army being before Charlestown which had been summoned to surrender and rejected without any further particulars; and in the same paper the Congress has formally declared the Colonies to be free States.

We impatiently look for the Hessian reenforcements which we have reason to expect hourly from advice being had that they sailed from Portsmouth six weeks past and I hope Lord Howe will not be long after them.

The Enemy is numerous, and strongly entrenched upon York and Long Islands, with a respectable artillery both for the field and defences of the harbours.

But many of the inhabitants of this neighbourhood have declared their resolution of joining us, and taking up arms against Rebellion, and the measure of independency is by no means popular.

Sir Horace Mann to the Earl of Buckinghamshire.

1776, Oct. 19. Florence.—Every mark of Your Lordship's kind remembrance gives me the greatest satisfaction and recalls to mine the great goodness you formerly honoured me with. I seize therefore this first opportunity to express my acknowledgements for your letter by Mr. Giles, who delivered it to me a few days ago. I endeavoured to convince him by every attention in my power of the respect I shall always shew to your Lordship's recommendations and how happy your commands of this or of any other nature will always make me.

⁕　　⁕　　⁕　　⁕　　⁕　.　⁕　　⁕

The Lady who so long ago attracted your attention here is in perfect good health and seemed much obliged by your Lordship's remembrance of her. She is a widow, a 'Dama di Corte,' and has where withall to live comfortably though with frugality, *mi ha incaricato con molta premura di presentarle i suoi piu teneri saluti e di dirle che ella conserra encora perlei la piu cara e sincera rimembranza.* Had she have been as tender when your Lordship was here as those expressions denote you would not now complain of her past severity, though you must give me leave to say that neither I nor many others here then thought her so insensible to your addresses.

EDMUND SEXTEN PERY^a to the EARL OF BUCKINGHAMSHIRE.

1776, Nov. 30. Dublin.—Congratulations on his appointment to the Govt. of Ireland. It will be his duty as well as his inclination to assist him to the utmost.

GENERAL [JAMES] JOHNSTON to THE SAME.

1776, Dec. 5. Dublin, Henrietta Street.—I have found it necessary to agree with Lord Harcourt for the two setts of horses, they wou'd have been sold for more money in separates and the servants all dispers'd. You had better have the Chariot and the Berlin, and if you tell me you will leave this extent of business to me, I will take care of it all. If you can be at some expense to enlarge St. Woolston's, that and another house for your young family may hold you.

By all means direct for the yacht to wait for you at Holly Head. You may otherwise be detain'd at Parkgate frequently a fortnight and have a long and dangerous passage afterwards. . .

I can gett all manner of men servants here for you except cooks. Lord Harcourt had four. In short the fewer horses and servants you are at the expense of transporting the better. Two or three very fine black light leg'd stone horses with long tails and no whites will finish this business. . . .

JOHN HELY HUTCHINSON,† [Provost,] to THE SAME.

1776, Dec. 5. Trinity College, Dublin.—Congratulations on Lord Buckinghamshire's appointment and offers of support.

DAVID GARRICK to THE SAME.

[1776 ?] Dec. 12. Adelphi.—Tho' I have for near forty years fac'd the most formidable criticks yet I could not till this moment have resolution enough to write and send this letter to your Lordship. Nothing indeed ought to distress a man of sensibility more than giving trouble without the least right or pretence for it. Thus, my Lord, having no excuse for my presumption, I must necessarily appeal to your goodness for my pardon. I have a nephew, my namesake, whose dangerous state of health oblig'd him some time ago to sell out of Lord Pembroke's Dragoons. We never expected that he would have got the better of his disorder. He is now quite recover'd, is a young man with a tolerable person and his character a good one. Lord Pembroke and the officers of the Regiment speak of him with great partiality. His situation at present is very disagreeable to him, and if your Lordship would take pity on him and honour him with your commands to attend your suite in any capacity you should think proper, he would think himself most particularly happy, and I, my Lord, should never forget the obligation. I

---

* Speaker to the Irish House of Commons. *See* for Edmund Pery's Correspondence, 14th Report Hist. MSS. Commission 1895, *p.* 155 *et seq.*
† *See p.* 159 of the same Report.

might have procur'd a more powerful interest for this solicitation, but I was resolv'd to owe any favour I might receive to Lord Buckingham alone, so that he might have no difficulty in refusing

His Lordship's most humble, etc.,

D. Garrick.

GENERAL [JAMES] JOHNSTON to the EARL OF BUCKINGHAMSHIRE.

1776, Dec. 24. Dublin.—As to the arrangements for Lord Buckinghamshire's arrival in Ireland.

THE SAME to THE SAME.

1776, Christmas Day.—The same, with estimates of carriages taken of Ld. Harcourt.

			£
The Harness for eight	-	-	105
The Berlin	-	-	135
The Chasse Marine	-	-	30
The Chariot (probably)	-	-	330 (first cost)

etc. . . . . .

THE SAME to THE SAME.

1776, Dec. 28.—Estimates a new chasse marine at £60. The State Horses are exercised in it.

EARL OF HILLSBOROUGH to THE SAME.

1777, Jan. 20.— . . . Perhaps if I had met you we might have had some conversation concerning your kingdom,° but I know of nothing particular to trouble you with. I certainly should not have omitted to mention the Primate to you as one of the best men living. He is a man of very sound judgement and what is better of a very sound heart, a true friend to the dignity and interest of Government, and has effected more for the civilization and improvement of Ireland than any ten men for these hundred years. He hates and despises a job, and whatever information he gives you I will venture to say you may depend upon. It has surprized me that his Grace, who is at the head of the first linnen county in Ireland, and of the province in which it flourishes, should not be a member of the Linnen Board. It was my intention to have offered him the first vacancy, had I been Lord Lieutenant, as his predecessors have always had a seat at that Board. I mention all this to your Lordship by way of just tribute to most distinguished and remarkable merits. As to myself, none of your humble servants will be less troublesome to you, or more sincerely attached to the support of your Administration than I shall be. I hope you will not think the prayer of the humble petition enclosed of very grave and serious

---

* The Earl of Buckinghamshire arrived in Dublin as Viceroy of Ireland, 25 Jan., 1777

consequence, and that you will grant the petitioner's request. I heartily wish you a safe and pleasant journey and voyage, and that you will be as well satisfied and pleased with your people as I am sure they ought to be with you.

Sir John Irwine[*] to the Earl of Buckinghamshire.

1777, Feb.—He has received a letter from Ld. George Germain, of a private nature, telling him that the King desires to see him. He therefore asks leave of the Ld. Lieutenant to go to England, etc. . . .

M. le Marques de Noailles, French Ambassador in London, to the Same.

1777, Mars 3. Londres.—Requesting his good offices in the forwarding of a box which Mr. Dickson, an apothecary in Dublin, wishes to convey to the Ambassador for M. de Sartine, Minister of the Marine in France. It contains a remedy said to be very efficacious against a species of ant, from which the French colony of Martinique has suffered much.
(*French*.)

Hans Stanley to the Same.

1777, March 20. Privy Garden.—I am very sure you must be sensible that if you have not before heard from me my silence has not certainly arisen from inattention or indifference. I have indeed restrained my own inclination from an idea that one ought not without an absolute necessity to break into the first hours of people that are arriving to new situations and important affairs. I conceive, that wanting neither method nor diligence, you are at present able to command that leisure which is the fruit of them, and that I therefore may now and then remind you of my very faithful and affectionate attachment without being too troublesome. My own inclination must render these sentiments a very principal part of my correspondence, with regard to other articles of it your Lordship may depend upon my obeying any commands I receive from you, and endeavouring to inform you of what perhaps you are less likely to learn from other letters. I should possibly have broke thro' the rule I set out with if the House of Commons had afforded me an excuse, but that assembly has been very near annihilated ever since you left England, and Lord North's illness has for very near a month past prevented any propositions of business coming before it. The attack has been a very serious one, and his recovery for some time but slow. He went, however, on Sunday last, to Bushy Park ; and C. Townshend, whom I saw yesterday just arriving from him, assures me that he is now able to take the air, and that he mends apace. We suppose, in consequence, that the Civil List and

[*] Created May, 1775, Commander-in-Chief of all Land Forces in Ireland, Governor of Londonderry and Culmore Fort, and a little later, a Member of the Privy Council.

other subsidiary points will be moved soon after the Easter Holy days. My knowledge of these latter transactions must be very imperfect. I am, however, from report afraid that they do not go on either as to numbers or as to terms so well as we wish ; this assistance is, however, extreamly wanted, for success has always depended much upon opinion, and by all accounts the late unhappy defeat of the Hessians has extremely revived the spirit of the Rebels. It has appeared to me that tho' some local resistance might still remain in parts, the business would have been accomplished from the time that they had no subsisting army to oppose to you, and I verily think, that without this unfortunate accident, the time of the men already listed being then expiring, Mr. Washington would have been left without any military force. What increases my regret is that the blow might have been avoided as far as appears from circumstances as they are stated, if that Corps had not been too far advanced, or if they would have retreated about eight miles, or if in short they had not left a strong post they were in possession of, to come into the open field, and even then if they had acted with more vigor.

General Robinson arrived here yesterday evening from N. York, and I happen'd afterwards to see Ld. G. Germaine, who has received no material intelligence. Robinson sailed the 13th of February, on which day Sir Wm. Howe was setting out upon an expedition to the Jerseys. There has been some small skirmishes, in all which we had the superiority. The plan of the Americans has been to beat up and straighten our winter quarters, judging that our loss is much more difficult to repair than their own. Earlier letters from that country had said that Washington was declar'd Protector, the title is not such ; he is named by the Congress Dictator of America for six months ; and they certainly have by this step adopted a form of Government much more adequate to the conjuncture. The alteration is said to have arisen from the complaints of the General as to bad choice of officers, delays, &c., &c. Three French Officers are coming over prisoners here. How ought you to treat them? As their own Sovereign has not acknowledged the Colonies for a State, neutrals cannot serve with them as volunteers, and therefore I fancy that Grotius and Puffendorf would consider them as no better than *Praedones*.

You will undoubtedly know better than I can all the probabilities for and against a French war ; our continuance here was so short that I could hardly impart to you my own crude remarks and conclusions made in the last summer. I in general thought their Ministry not dispos'd to the measure, but the crisis is so delicate that both nations may probably be involved in it without much premeditation by some act of petulance. Their conduct in receiving the American Privateers and their prizes may be overlooked. I understand that these latter were never condemned, but the purchaser took the title along with the effects such as it was ; but if it be true that they have refused to restore the Lisbon Packett claimed as a vessel belonging to the King, the affront is certainly of the grossest kind. What is at the same time very extraordinary, I am told from tolerable good authority that letters from Dr. Franklin to the Congress have been intercepted, saying that he despairs of engaging that Court in hostilities against us.

I doubt all this is but an unchearful sort of correspondence, we go on, however, feasting, dancing, marrying, and giving in marriage like our ante-diluvian predecessors ; as to which particulars I refer you to Lady Buckingham, adding what I know must be to you the best consolation, when public prospects are gloomy, that I have never seen her Ladyship enjoy a better share of health and beauty.

I set out in about a week for my anniversary at Paultons, which will be very full this year of your friends, and where you are most certain of being often remember'd. If there remains a *liber commeatus* I shall go soon after the Birthday, if not before, to Paris, and from thence to Spa, being determin'd to return again to those waters from which I received last year so great and so permanent a benefit. I flatter myself that a third journey thither will be unnecessary, and that I shall be able next summer to execute what I have so much at heart as the paying my respects to your Excellency at Dublin, for tho' I think nothing can have been so proper and so judicious for you as the acceptance of your present commission, I am as an individual a very principal sufferer by your absence ; you know with how much sincerity I express myself in saying that I have met with very few men in my life with whom I have liked to pass it so well as with yourself, and at the present period of it, tho' I enjoy very good health, three or four years is a great defalcation. I must however comfort myself that your services will probably be the cause of your finding yourself for the future, whenever you return, in the situation I have long wished you, and that I meanwhile have the satisfaction of hearing from all hands that you are gaining respect and approbation of which indeed I had no doubt, having as you know formerly had the means of studying you in one of those predicaments, *quae indicant virum.*

Having thus, my dear Lord, renew'd, I hope, not too inopportunely my correspondence with your Excellency, I have nothing to add but that I desire it may on your part be carried on only when it entirely suits your leisure and convenience ; for if anything occurs that I think you will wish to be apprized of, I need not say that I shall not wait the regular and formal return of an answer from you. I beg my best compliments to Sir John Irwin.

Lord Fitzwilliam to the Earl of Buckinghamshire.

1777, April 10. Mount Merrion.—Is unable to let Mountmerrion to the Earl of Buckinghamshire as he had hoped.

Statement on Irish Trade by S[ackville] H[amilton.*]

1777, April 17.—It may be thought improper to propose at this juncture any alteration in the system of American trade, and it

---

* *See* 14th Report of the Hist. MSS. Commission, *p.* 165. Sackville Hamilton was in this year Chief Secretary for the Inland Department of the Commissioners of Custom.

may be in vain to suggest it untill that country be settled. But if we should be at the eve of such an event, this may possibly be a proper time to take up the matter; to unite with the settlement of that country the consideration of enlarging our trade with the islands in order to extend the manufacture and commerce of Ireland, a country which from its situation and the connections and disposition of the people can never create a jealousy or be suspected of wishing for any interests separate from England.

It is not amiss in the first place to state the progress of the laws respecting the Plantation trade in order to show the foundation of this observation. That the Irish trade with America stood formerly upon the same footing as the English. That the restrictions laid on it were prejudicial to the interests of the Empire and that by a partial restoration of the trade we have recovered what little wealth or industry we can boast of. If these good effects have followed without any prejudice to the trade of Great Britain the argument and we hope the indulgence may be extended.

The Act of Navigation (the bulwark of British Commerce) considers England and Ireland as one country, and lays no restraint on the Irish trade with the Plantations. (12 Chas. 2nd, Eng.)

The Wool Act of the same year (12 Chas. 2nd, Eng.), and that which passed two years after (14 Chas. 2nd, Eng.), affect Ireland only as they affect England.

In the first Irish Parliament which was called after the Restoration, the several Acts granting an hereditary revenue to the Crown were passed; among others the Act of Tonnage and Poundage, whereby a revenue of 5 per cent. was granted on the exports of Ireland, and the duties of custom on the produce of the Plantations were rated at only one half when the commodities should be imported from England. (14 and 15 Chas. 2nd, Irish, see the proviso at the latter end of the Statute.) This was immediately followed by an English Act (15 Chas. 2nd, Eng.) prohibiting any exportation from Ireland to the Plantations but of servants, horses and victual.

Several laws were afterwards enacted in England to limit the Plantation trade, but as the limitations and restrictions (so far as they concerned this Kingdom) were binding only in the Plantations, some trade was still carried on directly to Ireland. But in the year 1695 an English Act (7 and 8 Wm. 3rd, Eng.) prohibited the importation of any goods to Ireland from the Plantations on any pretence, so that even stranded goods cannot be disposed of here. Thus the Plantation trade both of export and import was totally taken away and remained so for some years.

This discouragement to settlers threw the Protestant interest into decline. (See the Preamble of 3 and 4 Anne, Eng.) Something was necessary to be done for its support. Our linen was permitted to America, and in some years it was allowed to go duty free (3 Geo. 1st, Eng.), to continue so long as British linens should be imported free into Ireland. Industry now began to shew some signs of life. In the succeeding reign it was discovered that the entire restriction of our imports from the Plantations was a prejudice to the navigation and trade of Great Britain and of the Colonies. (See the Preamble to 4 Geo. 2nd, Eng.) We were then permitted to import goods of the Plantations, except sugar, tobacco, cotton-wool, indico, ginger, speclewood, dying woods, rice, melasses, furs, copper ore, pitch, tar, turpentine, masts, yards and bowsprits. Confined as these benefits were, they were nevertheless of infinite importance to a country so confined in trade. And the wealth of Ireland increased with its population insomuch that during the last war she supplied these kingdoms with near an hundred thousand men for their fleets and armies, and maintained forty regiments in pay. Ireland is as yet far below that state to which encouragement would raise her. The whole kingdom does not fit out so many merchant ships as belong to any one of the considerable ports of England or America. Industry does but crawl through the land. In many parts of the south and west the country is open, waste and uninhabited. Even within a small distance of the Metropolis the want of improvement is too obvious. Should the system of commercial politicks in England admit of further attention to this country; should the opinion be avowed that as the riches and inhabitants of Ireland increase, the amount of Irish estates spent in England and of English luxuries consumed in Ireland will find a proportional increase, and should this truth be acknowledged that the wealth of Ireland, however acquired, must ultimately center and accumulate in England, *that* wealth may be in some measure increased by admitting a direct importation from the American Islands of sugar, cotton-wool, dying stuffs and dying woods.

Sugar.—At present it is difficult to make up a cargo for Ireland without this article, and as it must first be landed in England, that circumstance increases the freight, insurance, delay and hazard, and gives a double opportunity of smuggling upon the coasts.

Cotton Wool.—Quantities are spun in Ireland for the use of the English manufactures. Such as is of American growth must be sent from England, which enhances the cost to the English factor. A direct importation would in this article be of importance to England as well as Ireland.

Dying Stuffs and Woods.—The injury to our manufactures by any difficulty or needless expense in the importation of these articles does not require any comment.

Our exports to the Plantations are restrained in every article of the manufacture or produce of Ireland except plain linen, victual, horses and human creatures. An indulgence to export thither the following goods, or any of them, would be highly acceptable :—Broad, narrow, fine or coarse cloths, serges, poplins, camlets, ratteens, frizes, flannels, blankets, stockings, shoes, boots, saddles, painted or stained linens, bottles containing wine or beer, subject no doubt to the like duties or regulations as the same articles are subject to upon exportation from Great

Britain. If we quit the Plantation trade. to consider of improvements for the trade of Ireland, to which no objection will arise in Great Britain, our difficulties increase. The produce and manufactures of both countries are so much alike that if encouragement be proposed for any particular article in Ireland some town in England will immediately complain, and the representatives will be instructed to oppose it. So long as local regards prevail every such project will be defeated. But considering the mutual advantage of both countries nationally, see whether any objection lies to the general plan. Put the intercourse of commerce between the two countries upon an equal footing, so far as is consistent with the public revenue of each, and open the importation of every produce and manufacture of Ireland into England. The effect of this must be that Ireland will become as one great factory to England. The profits of every manufacture will equally circulate through London, the supply of foreign marketts will be increased and at a cheaper rate by the price of labor being reduced, or provisions being cheaper to the manufacturer.

But if so general a plan be not proper to launch into, and it must be confined to one article, let it be the woolen trade, continue the prohibitory laws as to foreign countries, but open the export free to England. It may be the means of recovering that trade which France has of late years taken into her hands. If this be too much, open it at least for coarse cloths and frizes.

Contrary to sound policy, a part of the hereditary revenue has been placed upon our exports, continue it as to foreign countries, but let it be given up on the exports to Britain. Let the law be in force from two years to two years to keep pace with the Money Bills, and let Parliament make it good in the Biennial Supplies. In order to prevent fraud by exportation to other countries under colour of an export to Britain it may be done by way of drawback upon a certificate of the landing in Britain.

EARL OF SCARBOROUGH to the EARL OF BUCKINGHAMSHIRE.

1777, April 17. London.—As to help which he hopes for (apparently pecuniary) in the " winning of a colliery, which would be of infinite advantage" to himself and his successors.

M. LE MARQUIS DE NOAILLES to THE SAME.

1777, April 25. Londres.—Asking for his good offices with respect to a memorial which he encloses, addressed to him by the administrators of the General Hospital at Paris. (The memorial not here.) " Il y est question d'une créance qui est devenue le patrimoine des Vaurzes."

EARL OF SUFFOLK to the LORD LIEUTENANT OF IRELAND.

1777, May 14. Duke St., Westminster.—Has conveyed Ld. Buckinghamshire's thanks to his Majesty for his late act of grace and goodness to his family.

" The last accounts from America are tolerably good. I make no doubt the next will be still better ; and trust in God that we are in a fair way to subdue the Rebellion notwithstanding all the difficulties and embarrassments attending it."

LORD GEORGE GERMAIN to the LORD LIEUTENANT OF IRELAND.

1777, June 9. Pall Mall.—You will hear by this post that Lord Percy is arrived from Rhode Island, an event I endeavoured to prevent. He will not be in town till Saturday. The packet in which he came brought letters from Sir Wm. Howe. They seldom contain anything but the facts that may have happened since he last wrote. He gives an account of a success gained by Lord Cornwallis in surprising a post of the Rebels within six or seven miles of Brunswick, in which he killed about 30 and took several prisoners, with three pieces of brass cannon. Private letters state this advantage in a stronger light, but you know there is a little affectation of modesty in all the accounts he sends. He tells us likewise of an expedition sent into Connecticut under Tryon's command consisting of 1,000 men and six pieces of cannon. Sir Wm. Erskine and Brigadier-General Agnew were likewise employed, and the object was to destroy a large magazine at Danbury, about twenty miles from the coast. At the same time we learn from Lord Howe (but not a word from the General) that three frigates and 12 transports with soldiers sail'd up the North River, their object was likewise to attack magazines, and by the enclosed extract of a letter from Sir Peter Parker you will see that both attacks met with success. Several prizes have been lately made, as we learn by the New York Gazette, and by the same authority I suspect that the Amphitrite, which carried officers and stores from France, was blown up in an action at the entrance of the Delawar. The article says that Captain Hammond had engaged a French ship with 27 guns, loaded with military stores from France, and that after a short attack the French ship blew up and everyone on board was lost. General Howe says the camp equipage was not then arrived, April 27th, which I suppose means to convey that he cannot begin his campaign till he receives them. I hope he will not be long detained on that account, as the ship sailed on the 27th of March from Spithead. I thought these particulars might be satisfactory to your Lordship, that you might be informed how far the many reports you will hear upon the arrival of this packet may be depended upon. Thank God, our session ends to-morrow. We continue to receive the most friendly assurances from France. I cannot say their actions correspond with their professions, which may make it prudent to say nothing about them in the Speech.

SACKVILLE HAMILTON to the EARL OF BUCKINGHAMSHIRE.

1777, June 21. Custom House, Dublin.—Upon examining the books I do not find any entry of the exportation of Cotton Yarn

U

from hence to England, and in the English Book of Rates the reason appears : a duty of about threepence a pound on the importation in Great Britain.

I humbly submit to your Excellency's consideration whether a free importation there of Cotton Yarn from hence may not be of advantage to the weavers at Manchester, &c., while the unembarrassed exportation from hence joined to the direct importation of the Cotton Wool from the Plantations would be an acceptable grace to this kingdom.

I propose to take the advantage of your Excellency's indulgence to go to the county of Down, from whence I hope to return on Thursday to receive any commands your Excellency may be pleased to honor me with, than which few things can gratify me more.

Lord Cadogan to the Earl of Buckinghamshire.

1777, July 2.—Hoping to pay his duty as "one of Lord Buckinghamshire's Irish subjects" in November. Has great pleasure in hearing "that Irish affairs carry so good an appearance under his administration."

°The Exports from Ireland to the Plantations are confin'd to victuals† and to white and brown linen cloth, the manufacture of Ireland.‡

Chequered, striped, printed, painted, stained or dyed linens are excluded from those markets, as they are from the British markets by two subsequent Acts,§ in violation of a solemn compact between the Parliaments of England and Ireland‖ in consequence of which compact the Parliament of Ireland laid an additional duty of 4s. on every 20s. value of broadcloth exported out of Ireland, and 2s. on every 20s. value of other woolen manufacture, which are in effect a prohibition. Altho' white and brown linens may be sent directly from Ireland to the West Indies, yet very few are so sent, as there is little consumption there of fine linens, and as coarse, white and brown linens of the manufacture of Great Britain and Ireland, exported from Great Britain and being the property of some persons residing in Great Britain or in some of the British Colonies of America, receive a bounty in Britain from which the resident in Ireland is excluded, those linens are all exported from hence.

---

* This MS. is unsigned.
† 3 and 4 Queen Anne, chap. 8.
‡ 6 Geo. II, chap. 13. s. 4, 13.
§ 9, 10 11, 12 Queen Anne.
‖ Vide Journals of the H. of Commons of England, Jovis 30 Die Junii, 1698. Address to the King: "That you will make it your Royal care and enjoin all those you employ in Ireland to make it their care and use their utmost diligence to hinder the exportation of wool from Ireland except to be imported hither and for discouraging the woolen manufacture and encouraging the linen manufacture in Ireland, *to which we shall always be ready to give our utmost assistance.*"

While Ireland is thus confined in her exports to the Plantations, her imports from the West Indies are restrained by law to Rum.[*] Every other West India produce must be first unloaded in some British port; by which Britain gains no revenue, as there is a drawback of the duties upon re-exportation, while the cargoes intended for the Irish market are exposed to more hazards in their passage from England to Ireland than in a voyage from the West Indies to Europe, beside the increase of expense by demurrage to the Irish.

These hazards and expenses are often doubled, as it often happens that vessels loaded with West India cargoes for the Irish market touch first at some fresh port to unload their rum, or being driven on the Irish coast proceed after to a British port to unload and reload for the ultimate place of their destination. As a cargoe of rum is but nearly equal in value to a cargoe of victuals, and as more victuals are consumed in the West Indies than rum in Ireland, the Irish ships confined to barter for one article only, exceeding in quantity the demand of the Irish market and which may be raised in the West Indies to an unmarketable price by those who take advantage of their necessity, must be obliged to return to Ireland loaded only in part or dead freighted, or take other produce to a British port to be after exported in the whole or in part to Ireland, with all the risk and expence already mentioned, or if the whole of the cargo be to remain in Britain, the Irish vessel must trust to the precarious chance of being freighted with other merchandize for Ireland at the port where it arrives. All these grievances imposed upon Ireland affect the West India planters in the price of victuals with which they might be supplied from Ireland at a cheaper rate, and of chequered, striped, painted, printed, stained or dyed linens, which their sailors, negroes, and the low ranks of their people wear, and with which they are now intirely supplied by foreign linens exported with a drawback from England, which operates as a bounty deny'd to British and Irish linens.

They also supply the Colonies of other nations to which the Irish would extend that manufacture if they were allowed to export it to the West Indies, and if the same allowance were granted to Irish duck sail cloth and cordage, Holland would no longer engross that trade as it now does in a great degree already from St. Eustatia.

If the West Indies are not to be taxed in aid of the revenue of Gt. Britain, it is absurd and inconsistent that they should be deprived of the liberty of sending their produce directly to Ireland, by an exclusion which, bringing no increase of revenue to Gt. Britian, is virtually a tax upon their imports from Ireland, as that exclusion inhances their price. By opening the market of the West Indies directly to Ireland more of their produce would be consumed there, and by consequence more would be produced, for quantity increases with demand.

---

* 6 George II. chap. xiii. s. 4, 19. 12 George II. chap. 30, s. 5, 16, 31. 31 George II. chap 35, s. 1.

There are still great tracts of land uncultivated in Jamaica and very little of the ceded Islands is as yet cleared.

Opening the Irish market would therefore be a premium upon West India cultivation, and by the increase of produce in the West Indies, altho' Ireland should have a share of that increase, England would have incomparably a greater, as Ireland could receive no more than the value of its confined exports to the West Indies.

Under the present restraint upon Irish export a cargo of provisions is not equal to a third of sugars, and if by a relaxation of that restraint Ireland should be enabled to purchase the whole of a cargo, it is clear from experience in other instances such as glass° and woolen goods,† the materials of which are all produced in Ireland, that where manufacture is permitted but exportation is prohibited, as would be the case of sugar there,‡ Ireland would not be able to supply a quantity equal to her own consumption.

The remainder must therefore be had from England, that great market of the staple commodities of Ireland, which possesses four fifths of her trade and is the centre of exchange for the remaining fifth.

The decrease of export from Great Britain to Ireland of West India produce would by an increase of produce in the West Indies in a considerable degree be compensated by an increase of export to foreign markets of those articles which by law can be exported ; and every such increase would diminish the French exports to the same markets, giving to Great Britain an advantage over our rivals in trade.

Every gain to Ireland by lowering the price of West India produce for home consumption would enable the inhabitants to purchase more of manufactures importable by law only from Britain, such as woollen goods and many others which are composed of British materials and employ incomparably a greater number of hands in their production and manufacture, not above 30 men being employed in a large sugar house, and by consequence an increase in the consumption of such manufactures would be of greater advantage to the community in general and to the landed interest of Britain in particular, than the consumption of manufactures whose materials are imported. It is evident from the Custom House accounts compared with the Statutes relating to Irish Trade that every advantage given to the trade of Ireland has increased the quantity of British manufactures exported thither, and of the materials of manufactures imported here from thence.

Experience also proves that the number of Irish spending their fortunes in England has increased in a still greater proportion.

The sugars should be cheaper in Ireland than in Great Britain, they cannot interfere with us in foreign markets as their exportation is prohibited. But if it were not, tho' the duties upon importation there are lower than here, yet as there is a drawback

---

* 19 George II., chap. 12, s 24-25.
† 3 and 4, Anne, chap. 8, s. 2-3.
‡ 5 George I., chap. 21, s. 1.

upon the duties here upon exportation, the situation of Great Britain with respect to Holland, Germany, the East Countries and Russia, to which alone sugars are exported in Europe, rendering the passage from Britain nearer and less subject to risk, would make it impossible for Ireland to meet us at those markets, even if she had a capital in trade equal to the purchase of more than she wants for her own consumption. If it be objected that sugars imported under a high duty into Ireland may be smuggled into Great Britain, it is clear from experience that they cannot; as there are few or no complaints of such practices with relation to French sugars, which are cheaper than British or to sugars imported from hence to foreign markets with a drawback of the duty without any security by certificates or otherwise of their being delivered at the ports for which they are cleared out.

The security will be still greater with respect to Irish sugars, as they must be smuggled with the Irish duty upon them.

It is a bad policy to impoverish our best customer, and the quantities of British manufactures consumed in Ireland and the quickness of returns to England render Ireland the best customer that England deals with. A capital of one thousand pounds upon which returns are made once a year is of more advantage in trade than a capital of 3,000l. upon which returns are made only once in three years; as the profits of each year becomes an additional capital, which is precisely the case of the trade to Ireland, compared with that to America.

It is said that Ireland is not taxt for the benefit of Great Britain, but the fact is clearly otherwise.

It is tax't for a Peace Establishment of 15,000 men, 3,000 of whom are at all times employed out of Ireland for the service of Great Britain.º

It is tax't for pensions given to Brittons, an improper application of which does not lessen the burden upon Ireland, and it is taxt for Irish place men and military officers residing in Britain.

It pays a grievous tho' a voluntary tax of above £500,000 per annum to other absentees possessing fortunes in Ireland. But the heaviest of its burdens is composed of exorbitant taxes in Customs and Excise upon foreign necessary imports and native exports and productions to which it is necessitated by exempting British imports from all additional duties, an exemption which operates as a premium upon the trade of Great Britain to Ireland. To supply this exemption, beef amongst innumerable other articles is taxed upon exportation, and the duties of excise upon home-made beer are so high that English porter is drunk as cheap in Ireland, to the utter ruin of the brewery there.

Ireland from its proximity can never become independent of Britain in any possible state of prosperity while emigrations from thence occasioned by oppression, and which can only be

---

* In war that establishment becomes much higher.

prevented by indulgences, have enabled America to aspire to independence and may exalt her to an empire formidable to Britain.

If a direct exportation should be allowed from the West Indies to Ireland, the same law[o] which prevents the produce of foreign islands from being smuggled into Great Britain must no doubt be extended to Ireland, where the Board of Revenue is absolutely under the control of an English Lord Lieutenant and every officer of Customs and Excise is appointed by him.

The Commissioners of that Board and the Under Commissioners of Excise, who have now a power of proceeding in a summary way and of giving judgment and laying penalties and forfeitures in all cases of Excise, may have the same authority[†] in the execution of this Act for prohibiting the importation of all foreign glass, which is effectually prevented.

The West India planter will therefore be as secure in Ireland as in Great Britian against smuggling in foreign sugars. But it is not improbable that some planters who before the war with America repined at our conquest of the French Islands as the acquisition of the ceded Islands obstructed the means of their improvements, and complained of the low price of British sugars for home consumption and exportation, should under various pretences object to a plan conferring a general benefit upon Great Britain, Ireland, and the West Indies, but which at the same time would destroy a monopoly affording greater gains to a few from a stinted improvement of the Islands and a more limited importation of produce into Great Britian and Ireland.

If the local interest of a few, whether in Britain or the West Indies, or a combination of those interests prejudicial to both Countries, continue to defeat every proposition for the advantage of Ireland, no time will be ever thought favourable for the relief of that opprest Country, and no future period can ever be so proper as the present, when Ireland in common with the West Indies has been ruined by a war (in the causes of which they had no share) merely because they belonged to Great Britain. The Americans mourned over Ireland while they captured her miserable trade, and took those to their bosoms who would join in their cause as fellow sufferers under one common oppressor.

LT.-COL. P. THOS. DE BURGH to RICHARD CUMBERLAND.

1777 (?) June 25. Mount Street, Friday.—The improbability of finding you at home induces me to trouble you thus. The determination to accept of some offers to raise regiments here, may possibly soon be extended to Ireland. From your situation as well as intimacy with Sir. R. Heron, I conclude any such resolution must soon reach your knowledge. 1 am going to-morrow into Hampshire for about a month, and if any

---

[*] 4 George III. chap. 15, s. 20.

[†] As has been given to them by a British Act of Parliament, 19 George II., chap. 12 and 25.

occasion should offer to make a renewal of my former proposals
on that subject proper, you will oblige me extremely by giving
me intimation of it. I have breathed the air of St. James's too
long not to be convinced how little is to be obtained for once
asking, but on the other hand wish to avoid giving myself as
well as others unnecessary trouble where success does not
appear probable.

ROBERT GORDON [Commissioner of Provisions] to the
RIGHT HONOURABLE RICHARD HERON.[*]

1777, July 7. Cork.—I have this moment received the
following account from New York by letters dated 10th June,
and from Brunswick the 7th June last, that Washington had
decamped with his army about ten thousand men, and retreated
towards the Delawar; that our people had followed and that
General Sir William Howe had left New York with most of the
troops in and about it on the tenth June, in the evening, for
Ambay; that four thousand troops, Germans and British, had
arrived a few days before and had joined the army. All which
was then in motion after Washington.

The EARL OF HARDWICKE to the EARL OF BUCKINGHAMSHIRE.

1777, July 19. London.—When I look at the date of your
last letter (June the 7th) I am ashamed at not having answered
it sooner—when I consider the insignificance of my correspondence, I flatter myself you will hold me excused.

Your Excellency seems to intend the turning over a new *leaf*
in Ireland, by getting *rid* of King James' Robes; if you had not
told me so, I should have had no notion that any chief Governor
would have worn them after the battle of the Boyne. I wish all
rags in church and state as well disposed of; I shall be happy
to hear when your Parliament meets that the Lord-Lieutenant
novo splendore resurgit.

As to our public *notions*, we are waiting for decisive accounts
from America; the army must be now in *activity*, Howe or Lord
Cornwallis on the Jersey side—Burgoyne on that of the Lakes;
an expedition is intended by sea against Philadelphia which
Lord Howe commands, and I suppose his brother accompanys it
as events arise in the Jerseys. Lord Howe has a great fleet and
several frigates, &c., which we should be glad of just *now* against
the privateers. Washington's Army (Militia included) is said to
be all 11,000 men; there is a force at Philadelphia under Lord
Stirling. Gates commands at Ticonderoga and there is a strong
post at Mount Independence between Canada and New Hampshire which it is thought Burgoyne will make his post if he
succeeds at Ticonderoga. Washington is said to be dissatisfied
with the Northern Colonys, for not sending him greater
reinforcements.

---

[*] Chief Secretary to the Earl of Buckinghamshire, Member for Lisburn and a
Privy Councillor in Ireland. See 14th Report Hist. MSS. Commission, p. 157. He
was created a Baronet in 1778.

Sir Joseph [*] expects that Silas Deane will make them a visit
in Holland. He has prepared the Regent there for it and will
obey any orders he receives about him. It is certain that many
foreign adventurers have gone into the American Service and
some who have asked commissions in the French, under leave of
absence for two years. I am told, however, from good authority,
that Cunningham is embargoed at Dunkirk, and that circular
orders have been sent to the French Ports not to permit any
American Privateers or their prizes to remain there above
24 hours. I can only wish that this last order may be observed.
It is a problem with me whether very good success in America
will make the French take a more open part or not. I lay on
the side of success. I mean that very great on our side would
discourage them, but if the ballance hangs even, or our advantages are inconsiderable, one cannot answer for what they may
do.

I thank your Excy. for the verses, I am sure I much approve
and subscribe to the first and last. I really believe that the
Emperor had no other idea in his French excursion but to amuse
himself; he has visited every body, seen every thing, and
committed himself in nothing.

My physician sends me to Brighthelmstone for sea bathing.
When I am tired of this country and my connections fall off, you
will allow me to hope for a hospitable reception in Dublin Castle.

P.S. Shall I beg my best compts. to Sr. Jn. Irwin?

J. Gay to the Earl of Buckinghamshire.

1777, July 30. Norwich.—I have in obedience to your
Excellency's commands, enquired of the present state of the
Norwich Manufactory, and the present comparative price of the
English and Irish yarn.

Those from whom I have information are Messrs. Ives's,
Harvey, Addey, Maltby, Thurlow, Gurney and Partridge.

They nearly agree in giving me account :—

"That now and for some time past the trade and business
here in their Manufactory is brisk, their orders large, and full
employment for the journeymen."

And the inclosed[†] is a comparative view of prices between the
Irish Bay yarn and the English oiled or half scoured yarn from
1771 to 1777.

Earl of Hillsborough to the Same.

1777, August 3. Hillsborough.—When I left London I was
fully resolved to go soon after my arrival at this place, to Dublin
to wait upon your Excellency; but found my little village
crowded with all the gentlemen of the county at our races,
which prevented me from having that honour and pleasure, and
now I find our Assizes, which I must attend, come on so soon as

---

* Yorke.
† Enclosure lost.

to put it out of my power to leave the country. I therefore take
the liberty to trouble your Excellency with a line to express how
highly honoured I shall think myself if you should intend to
take a view of this part of the Island, that you will be pleased
to destine a few days to my cottage; the contrast between it and
the palaces of Norfolk may perhaps amuse you, at all events the
landlord will endeavour to make it agreeable. If I should be
disappointed in my wish of seeing your Excellency, I will
trouble you with a line or two upon public affairs.

EARL OF HILLSBOROUGH to the EARL OF BUCKINGHAMSHIRE.

1777, August 9. Hillsborough.—I return you my best thanks
for the polite and partial sentiments your Excellency expresses
of my poor endeavours to be of some service to this part of the
country. I have great expectations of the benefits it will derive
from your Administration. The dignity, decency and propriety of
your setting out, very sufficiently warrant those expectations, and
clearly evinced to me (and I have the pleasure to add, to all I
converse with) that your real objects are the honour and support
of the Crown, and the true interests of the country, objects so
entirely connected and so mutually dependent on each other that
they cannot be separated. You do me too much honour in supposing that I can offer any thoughts that can be of use to the general
system of government, but in a little time I will venture a line or
two for your Excellency's consideration, in regard to certain
interior regulations ; but not 'till I lose the hope of waiting upon
you, which is not yet absolutely my case.
At the same time that I received the honour of your Excellency's
letter, I got one from the present Lord Inchiquin, who knowing
that I am happy in your acquaintance, desires me to mention to
you the Lieutenancy of the County Clare, vacant by the death of
his uncle the late Lord ; I can presume to say no more to your
Excellency upon that subject than I shall say to him in my
answer to his letter, that it is probable his attachment to
Government, his antient family and nobility, and his large
property in that County, may induce your Excellency to think
him the most proper person to succeed his uncle, which should
it be the case, will ensure the succession to him. I have a small
favour to ask of you, my dear Lord, and *par parenthèse*, will say
that no person in this country that pretends to the least consequence shall trouble you less with applications than I will, tho'
no one will be more steadily attached to the support of your
administration. When you left London Lady Hillsborough and I
applied to your Excellency in favour of a Mr. Boyd in case the
Collector of Donaghadee should be promoted. Poor Boyd is dying
if not dead, he is surveyor of Donaghadee, £70 per annum or thereabouts, not more ; the favour I would request is that Mr. William
Hull, now a Revenue Officer in a lower employment may succeed
him ; I should consider this as a particular mark of kindness to
me. Your Excellency knows by your Norfolk and Norwich
affairs how usefull and indeed necessary to one's importance in

one's country the favour and countenance of Government are ;
I should therefore hope that in what relates to the County of
Downe you will permitt me from time to time to lay my wishes
before you, and to receive them with as much indulgence as
circumstances and engagements may allow.

EARL OF HILLSBOROUGH to the EARL OF BUCKINGHAMSHIRE.

1777, August 15. Hillsborough.—Warm expressions of friendship and promises of support.
Thanks for his kind provision for Mr. William Hull.

SAME TO THE SAME.

1777, Aug. 26. Hillsborough.—As to an affidavit enclosed for
his consideration (not preserved) whether a proclamation should
not be issued upon it. " The atrociousness and barbarity of the
crime are abominable.''

EARL OF BELVEDERE to THE SAME.

1777, Aug. 31. Spa.—Hoping that his acceptance of £800 a
year pension, instead of the Muster office, which had been so
solemnly promised him in succession ; as well as his late offer to
the King to raise a regiment of 500 men, together with his steady
and constant support of government for nineteen years without
any personal reward, will stand in the way of his being superseded (on account of his enforced absence) by those who have
been a thorn in the sides of Government, while his family have
been spending their lives and fortunes in support of it.
Etc., etc. . . .

SIR JOHN IRWINE to the EARL OF BUCKINGHAMSHIRE.

1777, Sept. 23. Jermyn Street.—I have not heard from my
Lord Suffolk to-day ; but it comes into my head to mention to
your Excellency my wish, that if Mr. Boscawen's relations agree
with Capt. Vyse for his troop, that your Excy. would please to
recommend Lieut. Vereeker of the 5th Dragoons (who has been
13 years a Lieutenant, and is the eldest of that rank in the
Regiment) to be Captain Lieutenant to the 1st Horse (supposing
Captain Cummin to be dead) ; the officer commanding the 1st
Horse having determined not to recommend the eldest Lieutenant.
Then the 5th Dragoons can have no reason to complain as the
Lieutenants will get a step notwithstanding Mr. Boscawen
purchases into the Regiment. I should then humbly desire your
Excy. to recommend Cornet Marilla of the Carabineers to be
Lieutenant of Dragoons in the room of Lt. Vereeker. He is the
eldest cornet of the Carabineers, and was put by on the last pro-
motion in that Regiment ; by which means your Excy. will have
the giving of a Cornetcy of horse to the young gentleman you
were pleased to mention to me, and seemed so interested about.

I trouble your Excy. with these lines merely for you to turn this arrangement in your thoughts, and as soon as I hear from Lord Suffolk about Vyse's business, shall take the liberty to send you a state of the succession in the manner I used to do when I had the happiness to be near you, which will point it out clearer.

Not a word yet from Sir Wm. Howe, the wind is fair, so we expect to hear every moment. General Haldiman is set out for his Government of Canada. I hear no news, when I do I shall trouble your Excy. with a letter.

SIR JOHN IRWINE to the LORD LIEUTENANT.

1777, Sept. 25. Jermyn Street.—I have seen General Burgoyne's dispatch to Lord George Germain which came in this day, dated 30th *July, near Fort Edward on the Hudson's river.* He says after a most disagreeable march, attended with many difficulties, he is arrived there, that the rebels, who abandoned every post, cut down trees and threw every obstruction in his way; that they kept continually firing upon him, but without killing a single man; that they had not even touched a man of the King's troops, but had wounded some irregulars and some Indians. He adds that the troops are in perfect health and excellent spirits. The rebel army is retired to Saratoga, where it is said they mean to make a stand. By other accounts I find Genl. Schuyler has quitted the army intended to oppose Mr. Burgoyne, that Arnold has joined it with 12 pieces of brass cannon, and has taken the command, declaring he will defend Saratoga. I forgot to mention that Burgoyne says, on his march he killed and took 300 of the rebels. In a postscript to the letter to the Admiralty from Capt. Pearson, who commands the naval force with Burgoyne, he says it was resolved to march on the 5th August to attack the rebels at Saratoga.

I think this is the substance of the letters; and as no gazette will be published till Saturday, I would not omit giving your Excellency the earliest intelligence of what I knew. It is a good thing to have secured a post on the Hudson's river.

No news from Sir Wm. Howe.

Lord Suffolk still continues ill. He cannot write and I cannot see him.

GENERAL R. PEIRSON to SIR J. IRWINE.*

1777, Sept. 27. Troushill Lodge.—Has just received a letter from his regiment informing him that Capt. Chester, of the 36th Regt., in direct violation of the King's regulations, has agreed with Lt. Molyneux, of the 12th Dragoons, to sell him his Company for 1,800 guineas. The shortness of Lt. Molyneux's service, compared with that of some of the lieutenants of the 36th Regt., who are as old as most in H.M.'s service, and the

---

* Enclosed in the following letter.

sum offered, so much beyond H.M.'s regulations, makes the transaction a most unsuitable one, which he hopes will not be authorized by Sir J. Irwine. . . .

SIR JOHN IRWINE to the EARL OF BUCKINGHAMSHIRE.

1777, Sept. 30. Jermyn Street.—I am this moment come from Kew. Letters are come from Quebec, from merchants and gentlemen of the council there, dated the 9th August mentioning that they had heard from the Army on the 4th of that month. That Genl. Burgoyne was preparing his cannon, &c., to attack the rebels at Saratoga, but that they had fallen back to Half Moon, a post where the Mohawk river runs into the Hudson's river ; where they now profess to make their stand. Genl. Burgoyne will not let time slip away, and the troops are in good health and spirits.

I spent two days with Lord Suffolk at Blackheath. He asked a thousand questions, and desired a thousand compliments to your Excellency. He is much better, and I hope in a few days will be able to go about as usual. He is most exceedingly grateful to your Excellency for your kindness to Mr. Boscawen. He has wrote into Monmouthshire to him to write without loss of time to Capt. Vyse and settle matters with him.

I have received this day the letter I take the liberty to inclose, that I may take up less of your time. I have wrote to Genl. Peirson, and have told him that it is very true Sir Capel Molyneux did sollicite your Excy. that his son might have leave to purchase a company, but that I did not understand that you had given him any hopes that it was a thing to be done soon, and certainly not to the prejudice of senior officers of service ; and from what I know of your way of proceeding I did not believe it would take place, you had such care of the service of officers ; that it was also true Sir Capel had spoke to me, but I had not given him any encouragement ; so that he might see the apprehensions of his officers was without foundation. However if your Excellency would do me the honour to write me three or four words of comfort which I might either read or repeat to the general when I see him, with great submission, I think it would be adviseable.

Not a word from Sir Wm. Howe. I need not add that our impatience is great. I am afraid a Jamaica packet is taken.

P.S. The King is impatient for the review reports of the general officers. Perhaps your Excy. will think proper to quicken their being sent over.

TO LORD VISCOUNT WEYMOUTH from the EARL OF BUCKINGHAMSHIRE.

1777, Oct. 30. Dublin Castle.—I had the honor of transmitting to your Lordship, the latter end of last June a Petition from the Merchants and Traders of the City of Cork, representing that altho' the season was then so far advanced, several thousand barrels of beef and pork remained upon hand, over and above the supplies wanted for the use of His Majesty's Army and Navy and of the several settlements, garrisons and forts abroad, as well as for the East India Company, and that being restrained by the then subsisting embargo from exporting the said provisions which are of a perishable nature to foreign markets, and being apprehensive, not only of the immediate loss, but of exposing this principal branch of trade to the danger of being diverted into other hands ; they prayed for a removal or suspension of the said embargo. Your Lordship immediately returned for answer, that my letter with the petition inclosed had been sent to my Lord President, to be laid before His Majesty in Council. I also transmitted to your Lordship in July last, a petition from the Merchants of this City upon the same subject. But not having been informed of His Majesty's determination upon these petitions, I concluded that the circumstances of public affairs would not then admit either of the removal or the suspension of the embargo. I have lately been informed by different persons, that not only the Merchants and Traders but the Landholders and gentlemen of the country have expressed the strongest apprehensions, that by this restraint from exportation, so large a quantity of provisions, and especially of that inferior kind, which has usually been taken by the French, is continued upon hand, that there is danger of its being lost; and that the landholders will scarcely be able to get for their cattle the prices they paid for them when laid in to fatten. And tho' the present difficulty may have been in part occasioned by combinations amongst the graziers, and by their giving extravagant prices for their stock in the prospect of much greater exports than there was any reason to expect ; yet it has been very particularly represented to me of late, that at fairs where great numbers of fat cattle used to be sold, the sales this year have been so inconsiderable, proceeding from the causes already mentioned, that the country gentlemen find great difficulty in obtaining their rents.

There has been a further meeting of the Merchants and Traders of the City of Cork who have sent up to their representatives in Parliament a petition addressed to the House of Commons, stating the general distress, as they term it, arising from the embargo, and praying the interposition of the House therein. And I understand a similar petition is preparing from the Merchants of the City of Dublin, and will perhaps be followed from other places.

It was proposed that the Cork petition should have been laid before the House yesterday, but as I should wish that the matter in question might first be submitted to his Majesty's consideration, hoping that there may be such alteration in public affairs, as will now admit of some relaxation of the embargo, either that it might be wholly taken off or for a certain limited time, so as to give an opportunity of exposing the stock on hand which it is stated will otherwise perish, or that the embargo might be confined to the provisions of a certain quality, so that the inferior kind, which is not taken by our contractors but sold to the French, as is represented for the use of their negroes and other such purposes, might be exported. I have prevailed upon the gentlemen who were to have introduced the petition (of which I inclose a copy) to defer the presenting it for the present. It appears to me that as the rents in many parts of this Kingdom are made up and paid from the export trade, if some relaxation of the embargo could be allowed it would tend greatly to quiet the minds of the people in general, and would be a very gracious measure to this Country.

I hope therefore I may express my wishes, that it may be consistent with his Majesty's measures at this time, to give them some relief; but if reasons of state do not admit of it, I shall use my utmost endeavours to prevent any resolution upon the subject which may be disagreeable to his Majesty.

P.S. Since writing the above Mr. Daly, member for Galway gave notice that he should on Saturday next, move to take into consideration the subject of the present embargo. His Majesty's servants will endeavour to put off this motion till I shall be honoured with his Majesty's commands upon the subject, which I would therefore humbly request to receive as soon as may be convenient.

(*Copy.*)

Lord Barrington to the Earl of Buckinghamshire.

1777, Nov. 1. Cavendish Square.—We are full of anxious expectation of news from Howe and Burgoyne. . . . . . .

Earl of Hillsborough to the Same.

1777, November 1. Hillsborough.—Your Excellency's obliging indulgence to my intrusions engages me to continue them, and I am particularly led at present to give you this trouble by having received the letter I had the honour to mention to you. I now take the liberty to enclose to you an extract from that letter, it comes from a gentleman of very good understanding, and contains very just information and sound sense tho' cloathed in plain language. I have conversed with several judicious persons upon his proposal of making every distiller contract for the whole duty which his still ought to pay if constantly worked, and they are unanimously of opinion that nothing could tend more to the encrease of the revenue and to the stopping of those abominable frauds that are committed every where, both by the corrupt connivance of gaugers and surveyers, and sometimes of higher officers, and by the fraudulent small stills. In England I understand imported spirits pay 5s. per gallon, in Ireland only 2s. 6d. I humbly think the English duty ought to be adopted here, and a proportional encrease upon the distilling at home. I know the objection, that an encrease upon the importation would prove a bounty upon running; true, but not any way adequate to the encrease of the revenue, and the advantage that would arise to the public from enhancing the price of spirits. And if the licences were raised to 6*l.*, and put under the direction of the magistrate, I am confident that end which your Excellency does me the honour to concur with me in wishing might be in great measure attained; if the contracting as in the enclosed should be adopted. As to what I took the liberty to mention to your Excellency concerning the Absentee-tax paid by members of the British Parliament, I think it unjust and impolitic; but not proper that any alteration in it should move from your Excellency. I must now take the liberty to mention to you the pier at Donaghadee. In my Lord Harcourt's Lieutenancy I prevailed to obtain 1,000*l.* towards that necessary work, which has been carefully and judiciously laid out; and I take leave to assure your Excellency that this work is of very great importance to both kingdoms. I understand that to complete this work, which Mr. Heron viewed as he passed, it will upon estimate take near £1,700 more than they have already laid out. I pray you, my dear Lord, to favour this work, as I assure you it is not a job, and so soon as I know your resolution concerning it, the gentleman who has the conduct of it will go to Dublin to pass his accounts before the House of Commons, and to get a petition preferred if your Excellency approves of it.

I cannot help (tho' not desired) laying another matter of this kind before your Excellency. Some years ago, Mr. Hall, who was then member for this County, procured from Parliament part of a sum towards building a pier at Warren's Point, of great consequence to the preservation of vessels trading to Newry, and entering into the Bay of Carlingford. The work is in great forwardness, and the gentleman (Mr. Hall) would contract and give security for the completion of it for £500, tho' it would cost him two or three hundred additional; but as it would advantage his estate, he would willingly do it. This I also assure your Excellency is no job, but a truly public work, and I should hope your Excellency will approve of it; there is, I think, somewhat of disgrace attending works unfinished, especially when so small a sum as £500 will complete them. I feel quite ashamed at taking up so much of your time.

JOHN THOMLINSON to the EARL OF BUCKINGHAMSHIRE.

1777, Nov. 6. Holkem.[*]—So long a silence is a very ill requital to that compliment you were pleased to pay to a late effort of my pen, but having no public county news worth your perusal, I was willing to wait till I could at least speak agreeably upon your Lordship's private affairs which have for some time worn rather a gloomy aspect on account of poor Copeman's inability to dispose of your sheep. However it was a very general case, and I dare say the disappointment has not affected you so much as it has done your steward. But it gave me great pleasure last week to find that at Harlston Fair he had luckily

---

[*] Holkham in Norfolk.

ridded such a part of the *refuse* as to bring the best within the possibility of a wintering, on which account he had just scouted a Jew butcher's offer of 5s. 9d. per head for his lambs, upon the expectation that the present high price of Scots might extort the other 3d., which is the height of his hopes. To give your Lordship some idea of the cheapness at Cawston, very tolerable lambs were sold for 3s. 6d., so that upon the whole you have escap'd well, and when you receive the account of the present crop of corn, I have not the least doubt of the year's turning out well upon the farming line.

Copeman would not let me be satisfied with his narrative (which was not less diffuse than usual), he insisted upon my being an eye witness of your riches. In the barns I found wheat and barley up to the roofs, which were prognosticated to be made too large by some late alterations and two stacks of barley and one of prodigious fine beans in the yards besides, and such a crop of wheat upon the Aylsham Lawne as will fill them all again next harvest, so that tho' you have received a check in your sheep, it is likely to be repaid in your crops.

I made this excursion from Heydon whist-party, which was enlivened by Tom Bell's coming over to offer his attendance in the Lease Grounds to Mr. Bulwer and me, which he of course accepted, and begs leave to thank your Lordship for a good days diversion; in which two brace of pheasants fell by my twigg and one by his Wuship's. A brace of woodcocks we attacked, but in vain ; they were left, I believe, untouch'd. Pheasants are extremely scarce except in such repositorys as Blickling, which induc'd me to transgress the usual stint of a brace, and may probably be the reason why these gallants with great apparatus of dogs and servants have travell'd to most of them in this country. They even attacked your Lordship's nursery by the ice house and shot very often before Tom Bell cou'd get up with them. However, tho' he drove them off, they threatened to come again next day, which they accordingly did, but Tom was ready to receive them with his gun and spaniels, and swore they should not enter the premises till some of them *died upon the spot*, which vigorous measure drove them off, but they have visited Gunton and Holt, and were coming here, but luckily have chang'd their road.

They travel without horses, and no person as yet has made them out.

The News Papers give us a happy presage of your Excellency's reign, which we pray may end as auspiciously as it has begun. Among your courtiers you will find a Mr. Roper, a son of the late Mr. Duttons, and brother to Mrs. Coke, who has changed his name for a large estate, and also a Colonel Roberts, uncle to Mr. Coke. You will also soon hear of a young divine of the name of Roberts, who is at present Chaplain to this family, but intends to visit the said Colonel, his father, upon the family's removal to town next week, when I hope their expectations will be blessed by Mrs. Coke's bringing a son, in which great work she advances rapidly.

I have had the honour of spending much of my time this summer in this house, and can justly say that though it has been constantly crowded, the honours never could have been better done. Mr. Coke still pursues his plan of ornamenting this place in the highest manner, and seems in no danger of erring upon the rock of too strict an economy like the person you mention.

By the death of his mother Sir Harbord seems determin'd to push the building of his house next summer which Dick Gardiner's compassion for Lady Harbord seems inclin'd to permit him to accomplish—for on that account it seems he did not challenge him at Swaffham Races, tho' fully determin'd then to take up the matter afresh—however Mr. Coke has got fairly quit of him, and I hope he is better advis'd than to proceed to further hostilities.

As I premis'd in my last your Lordship has nothing to regret on the score of sporting—in both pheasants and partridges it has been a lamentable year; nor have the woodcocks as yet made us any amends. I hope that amusement has been more compleat in Ireland, and that your gun has perform'd its usual feats.

The neighbourhood of Aylsham are much alarmed with a report that Lord Hobart was in a very ill state of health, which your Lordship's last letter to Copeman happily contradicted—you seem to have received as erroneous an account of Mr. Gay's health, who seems to be much better than usual – Mr. Coke has given him the (Wighton?) Courts, tho' much pressed to give them to Jones. It seems at last settled that all matters with Mr. Caudwell are to be amicably adjusted, he retaining his £400 per ann., but relinquishing all trust and interference—the contracts for the leases under value I hear will be quietly given up by all the tenants except Mallet, who vows he will stand a law suit.

I have already encrouch'd too much on your Lordship's patience—*ne in publica commoda peccem*, I must conclude with my best wishes for your political and private happiness and with my respects to Lady Buckingham, Lady Harriet, Henry, and Mr. and Mrs. Herne.

I go to town next week.

EARL OF HILLSBOROUGH to the EARL OF BUCKINGHAMSHIRE.

1777, November 10. Hillsborough.—I set out to-morrow for London, and give your Excellency the trouble of a line only to say that if you should have any commands on the other side of the water, which I can execute, I shall be happy to receive and obey them. I can not omitt at the same time, renewing my earnest application to obtain some remedy against the inordinate use of spirits among common people. I have allready troubled your Excellency with much upon the subject. I beg leave to add that it would be a good regulation to make the gauger pay half of the fine, upon conviction by any one else. I am confident most frauds are committed in conjunction with those gentlemen.

R. MARSHAM to the EARL OF BUCKINGHAMSHIRE.

1777, Nov. 12. Stratton.—Favors from great men, like those from fine ladys are augumented and doubled, when they are confer'd at a time, when the granter has good reason to withold them entirely. Such I esteem the honour of your Excellency's very obliging and entertaining letter, just after the meeting of your Parliament; when beside that important and great business, you must be weary'd with abundance of avocations and attentions. My Lord I was very impatient to see your Excellency's speech to your Parliament; which fully answer'd my raised expectation, and to prove I do not flatter, I will venture to say, I wish one article had been omitted: viz.: you say the King might have found many more able Ministers. I will not make an apology for disagreeing with your Excellency in this: for I believe myself right, and the Lord Lieutenant mistaken. Your Excellency sees I find faults from principle and conscience. I wish the opposition both in your Excellency's and the British Parlt. could say as much for themselves. But as I hate to differ with your Excellency, I will drop the subject, as I cannot give up my judgement. I am very glad things go on smoothly in Dublin, and hope they will continue in the same tràct, that your Excellency may enjoy without allay a tour round a country abounding with natural beauties, which I shall enjoy again from your Lordship's pen.

When I have the honour of writing to your Excellency, I wish for some provincial news. But I know of none; only that Twiss of Norwich dy'd last week; and report says has left his large fortune equally divided amongst his children. So the traveller that made so conspicuous a figure in so many kingdoms of Europe is now reduc'd to the size of a plump Norwich weaver. News, however, may be without reaching my ears, as I am rooted down here like my trees: with this difference only, that the spring gives no new life to me. I have been removing some of the dead trees by the road side, between Blickling and Norwich, and when you return, "to join the dignity of life with ease," I hope growing plants will show themselves. My Lord it is not confin'd to Ireland that trees grow too thick. I never yet knew any man that planted the grove, that could thin it enough. I feel it for my self, and see it in all others. I remember a very large and fine wood in the High-land of Scotland (I think Lord Kinnoul's) so thick as to deprive them of heads, and the Duke of Portland's (according to the new Evelyn) must be all spoiled.

As your Lordship did not mention the contrary, I hope Lady Buckingham and all your young family are well, and the Black Rod also. I forgot whether 'tis since I wrote that I feasted on your Excellency's venison, or whether I sent my thanks which I certainly ought to have done. My wife and son desire their best respects.

An odd circumstance attended your Excellency's Letter to me. The Dublin post-mark was the same as the date, viz., 27 Oct., the London post-mark was 3 Nov.: and wrote thus by the

Norwich Post-Master. '*This Letter was dropt into the Norwich Box this 8th of Nov., 77, at 10 o'clock in the forenoon.*' It did not appear to have been open'd. The Label under the Arms is smooth without the Motto. The Seal is the Arms of Hobart single.

R. Marsham to the Earl of Buckinghamshire.

(Fragment undated.)—I know trees ought to be removed as soon as they whip each other with a moderate gale: but I love them as my children, and I cannot act with my own judgement. So I have taken a method of my own. If a tree is 50 feet high, I take off 6, 8, 10, or 12 feet: and then leave the uppermost branches a foot from the stem: the next floor of branches I leave half a yard or 2 feet long, and so downwards, leaving them longer. By this means I leave the headed tree in its natural shape, and inable it to receive the same advantage from the rains and dews as it had before. This prevents its whipping its neighbours which should be the better tree: and I flatter myself, the headed oaks may stand till they are worth 2 guineas a tree, with very little harm to the grove. They also threw out thick heads, which I hope will prevent the best trees from throwing out a great many lateral shoots, the common consequence of thinning too much at once by letting in too much air amongst them. Let me recommend this method to your Excellency. The only reason I know against it is, the headed trees will not increase so much in the stem as those untouch'd. But I had one that gained an inch this summer, and I hope every year they will suffer less than the first, and if they may stand till they are worth 2 guineas, instead of 5s., and the grove appear much thicker at a distance, I am a great gainer. But 'tis at present such a favourite hobby horse that I believe the headed trees will become in time both as good and handsom as if they were left to nature. My wife and son join in most respectful compliments to your Excellency.

P.S. My Lord, an oak I planted in 1720 is this autumn 83 feet and $\frac{1}{2}$ of timber in the body: measuring bark as timber. I believe very few under 70 years old can say so much; but I wish your Excellency may say it in time.

Sir John Irwine to the Same.

1777, Dec. 1. Jermyn Street.—This moment Major Keyler is arrived from Sir Wm. Howe, he left him on the 28th Octr. and Sir William's letters are dated the 26th October. The accounts formerly received are confirmed of the several actions between Sir William and the rebels. He got possession of Philadelphia on the 26th Septr since which there has been another action, the rebels were drove sixteen miles: our troops have behaved remarkably well in all these affairs. We have lost Brigr. Agnew and Lt.-Col. Bird, both very good men. I have not learned any other names yet, and write in great hurry, but as I know that there cannot be a gazette to-night I was resolved to give your

Excellency this confused account as better than none. The bad part of the news is, that Washington has still a *Corps d' Armée en force*, it is true that Sir W. Howe is within four miles of him, and was to attack him the first moment he could. In trying to take a fort which commands the river Delawarr, the Augusta man of war of 64 guns was run aground and could not be got off, so that our people took everything out of her and blew her up. Our grenadiers took a 32 gun frigate of the rebels. On the other hand Sir Hen. Clinton has opened the communication of the Hudson's river by taking two Forts, in which the bravery and coolness of the troops was most extraordinary. They had a march of 12 miles, at the end of which they stormed the two forts, having four hundred yards of abattis to go through defended by 40 pieces of canon loaded with grape; they never fired a shot till they got within the works. There we lost Lt.-Col. Campbell of the 52nd, and Major Sill of the 63rd.

There are bad reports, however they are but reports, about Genl. Burgoyne. I find Howe knows nothing more of him than we do.

Lord Barrington to the Earl of Antrim.

1777, Dec. 18. Cavendish Square.—The present situation of our affairs having induced the Ministers to think of raising some new corps, I took the earliest opportunity of communicating to them for consideration your Lordship's proposal for that purpose contained in a letter with which you honoured me last March. Augmenting the forces is purely a matter of State, and the functions of the War Office do not begin till both the measure and the manner of executing it, have been settled in the Cabinet.

Sir John Irwine to the Earl of Buckinghamshire.

1777, Dec. 20. Jermyn Street.—. . . We have several reports here from France that are favourable to our arms, but they are as yet only reports. In the mean time the spirit of the people seems to be raised, and we hear of offers from different places for new levies; what will most surprise you is, that there is a reason to expect an offer of that sort from London. It is certainly true (perhaps for the first time in the history of England) that the present ministers are popular. Genl. Burgoyne's letter does him harm in the publick. His charge against ministers with regard to his orders, is thought unfair; and those who are in the secret of them say it is unjust; however the ministers are determined to let the blame lie at their doors till his return, before they expose his orders to the publick view. You will I presume be astonished to know that Genl. Burgoyne sent a duplicate of his letter to Lord George to Lord Derby, and that his Lordship was actually reading to the company at Almack's that letter, much about the time Lord George sent the original to the King at the Queen's house. This makes much conversation.

At the desire of Lord Pembroke I trouble your Excellency with the inclosed. It is in favour of his near relation Mr. Evans, whose case is a hard one. I understand Lord North will also write to your Excy. on the subject. By what I hear, the poor man, his wife and children are actually starving.

EARL OF HILLSBOROUGH to the EARL OF BUCKINGHAMSHIRE.

1777, Dec. 21. Hanover Square.— . . . . I need not tell you what has been said on this side concerning your speech, and a certain committee; I fear a degree of dissatisfaction took place *every where* but I am glad to observe that it subsides; and I assure your Excellency that I have not been idle in endeavouring to soften and to justifie. Lord Carmarthen is Chamberlain to the Queen, Winchelsea and Aylesford Lords of the Bedchamber, the other vacancy being made by the dismission of Jersey. Young West is Equerry. This intelligence may be as early as from anybody. Onslow Comptroller, Palmerston Treasury, Mulgrave Admiralty, and Worsley, in place of Hopkins dismissed, Greencloth, is no news. You have something else to do than to read my small talk, I shall therefore once more entreat you to think about correcting the intolerable drunkenness of the north.

LORD BARRINGTON to THE SAME.

1777, Dec. (?)—The error in payment of Regiments lent by Ireland, and found by Mr. Barry Barry, has been rectify'd in the Committee of Supplies. I cannot write or talk about the dreadful catastrophe of Burgoyne's army,* and I wish I could think of any other thing.

SIR JOHN IRWINE to THE SAME.

1777, Dec. 31. Jermyn Street.—The King was perfectly aware of your Excy.'s wish to gratifie the Duke of Leinster, but his Majesty seems determined that the post of Quarter Master General shall be filled by one conversant in, and bred 'up to, that particular branch of the service, which H.M. says Col. Sandford has not been. H.M. was pleased to say that a sensible officer might make out routes and a distribution of quarters, but that it required another sort of education to mark camps, take up posts, &c., which might perhaps unfortunately become necessary for us in Ireland, and it was therefore of the greatest consequence that the person to execute that office should by no means be new in the business. I think the King had also some idea that Col. Sandford's health, he being sometimes afflicted with the gout, might render him less active than might be necessary for such an officer as the Quarter Master General in the time of actual service.

---

* His surrender had taken place on the 13th October.

COLONEL LELAND* to the EARL OF BUCKINGHAMSHIRE.

1778, Jan. 2.—(As to his not having obtained the appointment of Deputy Quarter Master General for Ireland, although recommended for it by Lord Buckinghamshire. Among other reasons his situation as an officer in the Guards would not admit of his residence in Ireland.) For they give out that in case of a war in Europe, your Excellency's kingdom is to be the seat of it and you are to be saved from destruction by your Quarter Master General. That I am mortify'd is very true, and not the less so that your recommendation should not take the place of every other predilection though it is the fashion to say that the (King) in military matters will be his own minister; but consequences ought to be looked to, particularly in this case, for it should not reach to Ireland.

As to American affairs, they are it is believed in a most deplorable state; Clinton very judiciously dispatch'd his Aide-de-Camp, Drummond, to make good his ground here in case of any disaster happening at New York, which is even now said to be taken, tho' not believed. He meant likewise to prepare the way for his own coming, not wishing to remain in America, things being now, there, in a state of the greatest confusion. The force he has with him does not exceed five thousand men, half of which are provincials, very few British, and the rest foreignors. He has communicated his plan of defence should he be attack'd, and the world are of our opinion—" that Clinton "will make them pay dear for the attempt—that the most "brilliant enterprize of the whole war was effected by him, and "that it was to Clinton Burgoyne was indebted for the favourable "terms granted him by Gates, who did not know how soon he "might be at Albany." Notwithstanding Mr. Burgoyne says he *dictated* to Mr. Gates, he by no means aspires to the command of the Army, forseeing it might probably devolve upon him, from the impossibility of matters continuing in their present channel. The above is pretty much the sum total of Drummond's mission.

Much is conjectured about the future command in America, and many are named; but nothing I should imagine will be determin'd upon, till further accounts are receiv'd from thence.

The Scotch Corps are all fix'd, some of which it is thought will be raised, others not; the whole meant to be rais'd will be raw undisciplin'd men, and not fit for service the ensuing campaign.

I saw Lord G[eorge] G[ermaine] this morning, who seems quite serene and in good spirits, he told me that the late defection in your House of Commons has proved the strength of your Government, as you were so strong without them; and has given your Excellency the best and fairest ground here with all the Ministers. Whenever anything reaches my knowledge worth communicating to you, I shall not omitt giving you the earliest intelligence.

* John Leland, Lieut.-Col. of the Foot Guards, 1772, and in 1781 Deputy Governor of Cork Fort.

LORD CHANCELLOR (LIFFORD°) to the EARL OF BUCKINGHAMSHIRE.

1778, March 12.—This day the Dowager Lady Viscountess How surrender'd before me her pension of seven hundred and fifty pounds per annum upon this establishment, which she held under a grant by letters patent under the great seal of this kingdom for her life. . . . . The deed of surrender, etc., remains with the Deputy Keeper of the Rolls here.

ROBERT MURRAY KEITH to THE SAME.

1778, March 20. Vienna.—I embrace with great pleasure the opportunity of obeying your Lordship's commands and of expressing my gratitude for the very obliging proofs of kind remembrance with which your Lordship honour'd me in your letter of the 13th February.

I have for many months past offer'd my best services to the sons of Lord Fingal. Your Lordship's recommendation makes me doubly zealous in my endeavours to be useful to these young gentlemen. I shall present them at Court as soon as Lent is over, and if the youngest, who I am told is desirous of entering into the Austrian Service, obtains the King's leave for that purpose, he may be assured of any little assistance I can give him in his advancement. I have desired the Abbé who is their governour to convey the same assurances to Lord and Lady Fingal, together with my best compliments.

I am here in the midst of the most extensive and formidable warlike preparations that can be conceived, tho' the moment of explosion may still be at some distance.

The Bourbon Treaty with the Rebel Colonies which the French Ambassador has just now made public here, will before this letter reaches your Lordship, have given to Great Britain the fairest opportunity of exerting her national strength, and her indignant spirit in the best and most meritorious of all causes I can have no doubt of her success, nor of that share in the honour of it which will justly fall to your Lordship in fulfilling the important duties of the high employment his Majesty has entrusted to your approved zeal and distinguished abilities. No man living can be more interested than I am in every circumstance of this decisive crisis.

JAMES FORTESCUE† to THE SAME.

1778, April 1. Dundalk Grand Jury Room.—(Introducing to him the Rev. Mr. Woolsey, who has been requested by the principal Roman Catholics of this county to deliver their address to his Excellency.)

They have done it in the most ready and cordial manner, and as I know personally many of the subscribers I do believe they

---

* James Hewitt, Ld. Chancellor of Ireland, created Ld. Lifford, 1767.
† The Rt. Hon. James Fortescue, M.P. for Louth and a Privy Councillor for Ireland.

are sincere. Anyhow we ought to believe them, and as a real friend to Govt. I wish the same was done in every county in Ireland. I should think it right to have it published in all the papers as an example to the other parts of Ireland. Such an event will alter the opinions of the French, etc., etc., on the continent and we should make the most of it. . . .

LORD BEAUCHAMP* to the EARL OF BUCKINGHAMSHIRE.

1778, April 9. London.—(Takes the liberty of recommending to Lord Buckinghamshire's notice the resolutions which the House of Commons has come unto in favour of the Trade of Ireland.) Though the House seemed almost unanimous in the first stage of the business, I forsee some symptons of opposition from Lancashire and a part of Scotland, which makes me vastly anxious that before the House meets again after the Easter Recess your Excellency should (if the subject strikes you in the same light) assist our endeavours in the House of Commons by your representation of the necessity of gratifying the people of Ireland at this critical moment, to which they seem particularly entitled from their late very generous and handsome conduct. . . . . I think your Excellency's interposition in the present instance essentially necessary to turn the scale in favour of Ireland against the combination which I see forming against the propositions which Lord Nugent and I have brought forward.

The EARL OF HILLSBOROUGH to THE SAME.

1778, April 18.—I take the liberty to enclose to your Excellency a letter I have received from a Councellor Maffet. You will see that it relates to a convict at Downpatrick. The man condemned is a young fellow of Hillsborough and hitherto has borne, as I hear, a good character. In his present case it does not appear to me that anything can be said in his favour, but that the act was committed in a riot. Whether that circumstance may induce your Excellency to respite him till you can have the Judge's Report I can not tell, but I hope he will meet the fate he deserves, and the Judge is the fittest person to determine what that may be. This unhappy accident is one among many others, produced by the cursed drinking of spirits; I believe the rioters, on both sides, were intoxicated almost to madness with them. I have not troubled your Excellency with my remarks upon the report you was pleased to send me. It appears to me not to be of consequence at present, but I will not omitt it all together, for I think it is easy to shew that both reasoning and facts are ill founded. I understand the convict is to suffer next Saturday.

* Rt. Hon. Francis Seymour Conway Viscount Beauchamp, M P. for Antrim Co., and for Oxford in England. A member also both of the English and Irish Privy Council.

HUGH MAFFETT to the EARL OF HILLSBOROUGH:

1778, April 10. Carrickfergus. On circuit, in Dublin, Bolton Street.—My business is of an urgent nature and I cannot waste time in apology—my application is to save the life of a fellow creature, who was yesterday condemned to die. Francis Bulger is the name of this unfortunate man, and the crime of which he has been convicted, was the murder of one Gray, upon your Lordship's course of Hillsborough, about seven months ago. The attorney employed for the convict was young in business, rash, and ignorant—had he made due preparation for the trial the verdict must I think, have been manslaughter, but he was every way unqualified for managing the defence, and his miserable client stands now upon the verge of life. I was one of the counsel and I will tell your Lordship what we proved. The people of Broomhedge and Trumney were noted as rioters, and from this latter place came Gray. They had conceived malice against the inhabitants of Hillsborough and publickly denounced vengeance, on which account the alarmed people resolved to be upon their guard. On the day of the bloodshed, when both parties seemed to menace deadly mischief Counsr. Smith and a Mr. Lethun addressed the people of Hillsborough and prevailed on them to disperse. They even promised they would not strike unless they should be first assaulted, but this provocation was not a moment withheld. Lethun declared that immediately on their dispersal, the Broomhedge and Trumney mob came on, hurraing, hooting, at the people of Hillsborough and cursing them as cowards, and by another witness we showed that they *first* came to blows. We showed further, by the witnesses produced on the side of the prosecution, that the deceased had been very active in the riot, and that he had knocked down, at least, eight men with his own hand. In the progress of the unhappy difference he was beat, however, from the field, and pursued by Bulger, who seized him as he was mounting a ditch, and stabbed him in the kidneys, with a bayonet, which had been fastened on a pole, of which wound he shortly died. It did appear indeed that Bulger had boasted, *on the moment,* that he had thrust the weapon six inches into the body of Gray, who had only a cudgel in his hand, but still this expression was clearly used in heat of blood, and we accounted for the bayonet by showing, *satisfactorily,* that Mr. Gawen Hamilton, late governor of the Corporation, had ordered a number of those weapons into the hands of the Hillsborough people, to awe disorder, and terrify the unruly into peace. In a word, my Lord, it seems undoubtedly a *Jury* Case of Manslaughter, and since the character of the unhappy prisoner is such as must recommend him, I do most earnestly beseech your Lordship to interfere with government in his behalf. His execution is fixed for this day fortnight at Down, so that, if your compassion can be interested, a minute must not be lost. My abrupt manner will be accounted for from the particularity of the occasion, and your noble mind will excuse me for any violation of decorum.

I ought to have mentioned to your Lordship that Counsr. Smith did not attend to give his testimony, nor had he been summoned for that purpose. We therefore moved to put off the trial but our motion was refused. His testimony would have changed the complexion of this affair.

Earl of Sandwich to the Earl of Buckinghamshire.

1778, May 4th. *Private.*—Upon the notice we received of a rebel privateer being in St. George's Channel we sent the Stag frigate of 28 guns in pursuit of her, and she sailed on that service from Spithead the 22nd of last month, the Thetis of 32 guns is sailed from the Clyde on the same errand, and the Heart of Oak armed vessel of 20 guns and the Boston of 28 are also in pursuit of her. Your Excellency may be assured that every possible attention will be paid by the Admiralty to the security of the coasting trade of Ireland, and it is not want of inclination but want of means of doing it that prevents our having a larger number of ships stationed for that purpose ; but till we have a larger supply of frigates from abroad, or can procure men enough for the ships we have ready to receive them all our exertions will come far short of our wishes.

If the towns upon the coast of Ireland could be prevailed on to furnish us a number of good seamen we should be much better enabled to give them proper protection ; this has been done with good effect in many parts of England, and I hope that the example will be followed on your side of the water; but at the same time it is necessary for me to add that ships alone cannot protect any coast entirely without there are troops and batteries on shore.

The Earl of Hillsborough to the Same.

1778, May 11. Hanover Square.—I am much obliged to your Excellency for the favour of the letter I have this moment received. I think you quite right in not shewing mercy to the unfortunate convict, as there was no foundation for it. Such mercy is cruelty to the public.

The Irish Bills are now before the House of Commons here, but to say the truth, I think the success doubtful. If they fail, possibly your Session will not conclude so happily as is to be wished. The best way is to forward business as much as you can, so as to hasten the Prorogation.

I should be glad to know how you stand with regard to Ensigns' commissions, raising men, perhaps I would recommend one or two.

The Duke of Atholl to the Same.

1778, May 15. Greenock.—Recommending to his notice the officers of the Atholl Highlanders, especially the commanding officer, Major Dalrymple. By the King's permission the Duke has kept the Lieut.-Colonelcy and two of the Companies open for the present. The Corps has been raised but a short time, and unfortunately are at present without colours and caps.

EDWARD BACON[*] to the EARL OF BUCKINGHAMSHIRE.

1778, June 4. Bruton Street.— . . . I hope the Exportation Act for Ireland will give satisfaction there.

I am sorry that the advocates for that and the other Bills gave an expectation to the Irish of many things, that were impossible for England to grant.

The over zeal of some gentlemen was very injudicious, as you very wisely observe, on the outset, in the first resolutions of the committee, and rais'd such a storm as augur'd very bad consequences on this side of the water.

However wisdom prevail'd, and only one of the resolutions passed with great amendments into an Act of Parliament. But I cannot help observing a little on the shape in which it was brought in. The title was for exportation of *certain* goods from Ireland, and the enacting clause, all goods. Wool and woollen goods only are excepted. In the preamble, the Act of the 12th of C. II., entitled "An Act for the encouragement of Trade," &c., is inserted, which was a gross mistake, for the relief desir'd was from the Act of the 15th C. II. Your Lordship, I am sure, have the Bill as it was brought in and the Act as it now stands, to which I refer you for the truth of my observation. In the two divisions in the course of this business I voted in the favour of it. In the debates there was a great deal said about the compact between the two kingdoms in King William's time that England should have the woollen manufactures and Ireland sho'd have the linen.

Earl Nugent has given notice that in the beginning of the next Session of Parliamt. he will move for a Bill to allow the exportation from Ireland of a certain kind of woollen manufactures, and if he should persist in it I apprehend that all the different parts of G^t Britain any ways concerned in the produce of wool or woollen manufactures will warmly oppose and join the cotton manufacturers who are very much hurt with what has already been done for Ireland.

My constituents wrote very earnestly to me that it was absolutely necessary to prohibit the sending the woollen manufactures of G$^t.$ Britain out of Ireland for if that was to be permitted the Irish wou'd have an opportunity of exporting large quantities of their own woollen manufactures along with and under colour or denomination of being British. This was what was their opinion after mature deliberation.

I am extreamly concerned at the distress of both Kingdoms, but will not trouble your Lordship with the particulars as you certainly know from your high situation the state of one, and the

---

[*] M.P. for Norwich, 1756-1784, one of the Commissioners of the Board of Trade in 1760.

other from the accounts you must receive of the scarcity of
money, the low price of the funds, and that no merchants can
get any bankers to discount bills either foreign or domestic.

I shall go into Norfolk in a few days, where I intend to stay
till next winter, and if I can be of any service to your Lordship
I shall with pleasure receive your commands.

The Norfolk Militia I hear are to go into Warwickshire.

W. W. Bulwer to the Earl of Buckinghamshire.

1778, July 2. Heydon.—Is happy in the thoughts of his son
being under his Lordship's protection. . . . . .

Sir Francis Drake to the Same.

1778, July 18. Nutwell.— . . . You were pleased last
year to grant me a reversionary lease of the moiety of the Fishery
of the River Tavy in the parish of Beer Ferris. In May last I
was informed by my servants that Mr. Short had let a fishery
of the River Tavy in Beer Ferris to some men of that parish. In
a few days after I saw Mr. Gullet your steward here and represented to him what had been done by Mr. Short and that though
it was a temporary injury to me, as your tenant, it was more
materially injurious to your Lordship, who had a permanent
interest. I likewise particularly stated to him the manner in
which Mr. Snow acted on a similar occasion. . . .

(These representations having been ineffectual, Sir Francis
Drake applies directly to Lord Buckinghamshire, at the same
time enclosing a letter from his late steward, Mr. John Edgecombe, which throws a further light on the question.)

(*Enclosure.*)

John Edgecombe to Sir Francis Drake.

1752, June 5.—Mr. Snow has been with me. He said the
information you have had of his authorizing any person to fish
this season is false. He owns that he fished last year too far in
your right, not knowing then the extent of the lease, on sight of
which he is now satisfied you have all Lord Buckingham's right
to the fishery, but he saith that the liberty of landing fish on that
Lord's land is not exclusive of the like liberty granted or which
may be given to others. Mr. Snow saith he pays yearly to the
Prince of Wales (as Mr. Hurrel did) 1s. for the liberty of fishing
in the River Tavy, that the Corporation of Saltash claim the like
right, but that he has prevented their having any benefits of such
right by forbidding them to land on Beer-side, and prevailing on
Mr. Heywood to deny any landing on his side. In this he thinks
he is not your enemy, but rather may be esteemed a friend.
After all he will do nothing to affront you, but he hopes you will
excuse him in preserving the *right of his parsonage* by exerting
his right of fishing under the Prince, which he will make no other
use of than for diversion.

Rev. Mr. Short to the Earl of Buckinghamshire.

N.D.—(Begging for the rest of his Donation (100*l.*) to the Exmouth Chapel, which has already been built) and " finished as handsomely as the money subscribed would permit, and indeed if your Lordship had not given so generously it never would have been built, by which you have much obliged the inhabitants of Exmouth, and it is to be hoped will greatly promote the cause of Religion."

Sir John Irwine to the Same.

1778, July 27. Head Quarters, Clonmel Camp.—I have the honour to acquaint your Excellency that I found the camp here in good order and more regular than I could have expected (considering the number of young men and officers) owing to the great care of Lt.-General Cuningham's and the attention of the Major Generals. The weather being extremely bad, I am in great pain for the health of the troops, and for the horses of the cavalry. All possible care has been, and will be, taken to prevent as far as can be the bad effects of it.

I must entreat that your Excellency will be pleased to send me Lt.-Colonel Vallancy's map of the South of this country. I find it will be impossible for me to carry on the service without it. If your Excellency would order it to be sent to me to the Camp at Kinsale, whither I am going immediately, it will be of great use.

The Same to the Same.

1778, Aug. 1. Innishannon.—Early this morning I received the map, for which I return your Excellency my humble thanks. Great care shall be taken of it.

I have found this camp in tolerable order, the troops are straightened in room, but they are healthy, have had good dry weather, and I hear of no complaints as to provisions or behaviour.

There being no field officer with the 18th Regt. of Dragoons (Col. Lyon being sick in quarters), is not only very improper, but very inconvenient, and the eldest captain of that Regiment (Walmsley) being major of Brigade, adds to the inconveniency. I should therefore hope your Excellency would think it right to order Major Vyse to join his regiment during the encampment. I mention it also for his sake, lest the King should be displeased with him; and though his Majesty should say nothing about it at present, yet when the time came to do Major Vyse some good, an objection might then be made to him on this account. The post of major is so very essential, especially at this time, that if your Excellency could spare both him and Major Southwell,* for some little time, it would be both beneficial to the Service, and to the gentlemen concerned.

---

* Both Major Vyse and Major Southwell were A.D.C. to the Ld. Lieutenant.

SIR JOHN IRWINE to the EARL OF BUCKINGHAMSHIRE.

1778, Aug. 2. Head Quarters, Innishannon.—. . . I am extremely sorry that your Excellency has thought fit to recommend the captain-lieutenant of the 30th regiment for the vacant company, it will be a distressing blow to a great many people; for the capt.-lieut. was so distressed that he could not shew his head and would have been thrown into jail, if your Excellency had not consented to his selling his commission (which he bought) and after that consent was given, he would have been arrested, if the lieutenant who was to buy of him, had not advanced him the greatest part of the purchase money to stop the mouths of his creditors, and he had leave given him to leave the regiment; now how to recover that money so advanced to captain Gibbs, I cannot see, but I forsee many disagreeable circumstances which may arise from overturning the arrangement already made, both in point of rank and other circumstances. I should therefore most humbly suggest for your consideration, that your Excellency would let the purchase of the captain-lieutenantcy go on as originally proposed ; that you should be pleased to recommend captain-lieutenant Jacob of the 11th Regt. for the vacant company in the 30th Regt., and Mr. Hobart for the captain-lieutenantcy in the 11th Regt. I mention Capt. Jacob because he is the eldest capt.-lieut. in the army here, except Capt. Haste of the 68th, but he is so old a captain that he prefers remaining in the 68th because whenever he gets a company in that Regt. he will take rank of half the captains. If your Excellency will adopt this proposal no harm will be done ; a capt.-lieut. will be gratified, and I forsee no inconvenience that can happen, whereas I forsee many if you do not. I therefore most humbly recommend this matter to your Excellency.

I propose leaving this camp for that at Clonmell to morrow. I hope to get there in two days (for it is slow travelling in this country) and there I must remain some days, having many things to arrange, and not having once been able to see the troops perform any one thing, from the incessant bad weather we had during the two days I was there; after which I shall pay my duty to your Excy. at Dublin.

Something must be thought of to prevent the desertion, and some way fallen upon to try to fill up the augmentation, which I do not find as successful as I could wish. On both these matters I shall be glad to hear your Excellency's sentiments, and receive your commands.

Fresh disputes and complaints about the 18th Regt. of Dragoons, which make me repeat my wish that Major Vyse might be sent down during the encampment.

The EARL OF CLANBRASSIL to THE SAME.

1778, August 7. Dundalk.—Was so persuaded of the expediency of the Popery Bill, that he had already sent his proxy to Lord Clermont before he received his Excellency's letter.

Sir John Irwine to the Earl of Buckinghamshire.

1778, August 10. Clonmel.—I am honoured with your Excellency's letter of the 7th and own that I am not much pleased with the account of our fleet; being persuaded that the French will make out a very favourable story for themselves; however I hope we may not hear more disagreeable accounts from sea.

In the arrangement which I had humbly the honour to submit to your Excellency I protest I had nothing in view but to prevent confusion and trouble, both which must now inevitably happen. I know nothing of the parties, hardly by sight; but if your Excy. had pleased to let the purchase go on in the 30th Regiment, and have recommended your nephew for another captain-lieutenantcy totally distinct from that, there could have been no confusion, nor no one could have been dissatisfied; whereas now, many will be dissatisfied in point of rank, and distressed in point of money, and I do not see how the money can be got back which has been advanced to Captain Gibbs. Col. Goold (the Commanding officer of the Regiment) tells me that the lieutenant and ensign who had advanced the money must sell their commissions, and he says they are both very deserving officers.

I propose putting this corps in motion to-morrow as if they were going towards an enemy, to teach them what they must carry, and, as far as possible to prevent confusion if that event was to happen, to accustom them to being moved: I shall march in two columns towards a place called Fethard, where we can easily draw up: I hope this may be executed without hurry and the loss of any of our things.

The Same to the Same.

1778, August 15. Head Quarters, Clonmel.—I should be glad to know the sort of intelligence Lord Weymouth has sent your Excellency with regard to the threats of the enemy against our coasts by their privateers, because perhaps it may be necessary to make some change in the disposition of our troops. Your Excellency does not say whether they are French or American privateers.

I must entreat your Excellency to refuse sending two companies from the troops in Ireland to defend the Isle of Man. It is true that ever since that Island has been taken from the Duke of Atholl, while troops were wanted there, they were sent from hence; but it must be considered we did not want troops here at that time, and that there were few in England, now that we want troops, and that there are so many in England the case is far different. Added to what your Excellency was pleased to say to Lord Weymouth respecting numbers here, give me leave to say that besides what we want to complete, many of those we have are not fit to join their regiments, so that of our real fighting men our number is very low. If you take them from

any of the regiments in camp, you will break the regiments
from whence they shall be taken all to pieces, especially
their light companies being taken from them, as their
Grenadiers must also, if we come to have any thing to
do; and I think they cannot be spared from the present
garrison of Dublin. Whereas in England they have a
large body of Militia, and several companies of Invalids,
who are idle, and can be easily spared from that part of
England which is as near the Isle of Man as Ireland is. I am
fully persuaded that the sole reason for applying to your Excy.
was, because troops formerly went from Ireland to the Isle
of Man and that upon a proper representation from your
Excellency (the face of things being so totally changed since
that was the practice) the idea of it will be dropped on the other
side of the water. With regard to numbers who join, I had but
too strong a proof of it the other day, when I drew out this army
here to perform some manœuvres, and I found the number of
fighting men infinitely short of the numbers in my returns;
that is, the men were present, but forced to be turned out of the
ranks when we began to fire, &c. I shall not be more particular on that head now because I hope to have the honour of
making my bow to your Excy. in eight or ten days' time,
when I shall have an opportunity of conversing with your
Excy. And the less we talk of our weakness the better, except
to those who must know it.

The SPANISH AMBASSADOR [LE MARQUIS D'ALMADOVAR] to the
EARL OF BUCKINGHAMSHIRE.

1778. Londres ce 18me Août.—Expressions of friendship
towards Lord Buckinghamshire and towards the English
nation. (*French.*)

LORD TOWNSHEND to THE SAME.

1778, August 21. Portman Square.—You observe very justly
that the Ministers when they write only on great official points,
omit interesting circumstances unconnected with the dispatch.
I am happy to inform your Excellency that the two hulks are
sailed with the Field Artillery. One man on board them who is
to remain is as gallant and as distinguished a man in the Delawar
as ever dealt in this matter. I shall soon send the light guns—
which have been cast and perfected since the order came, and
could not in our vast expenditure be ready before the 1st week of
next month.

The artillery men from Ireland have been instructed by Capt.
Congreve, an officer of great merit and service in the application
both of his and Genl. Desagulier's guns, and the men have been
very attentive and are very clever.

I inclose your Excellency what I believe to be very good
intelligence. It is from a great patriot in opposition, who has

failed in no information he has given the Houses. It is very formidable, and if not defeated, Ireland, I fear, will soon have Spain as well as France to look to.

Our best compliments to Mr. Conolly when you see him.

(*Enclosure.*)

The French Fleet were certainly to sail from Brest, August the 20th, 1778. Their force were 38 ships of the line, 28 frigates, 5 fire ships. Admiral Keppel expected to sail the 20th also.

The EARL OF HUNTINGDON to the EARL OF BUCKINGHAMSHIRE.

1778, August 21. London.—A letter of introduction to be delivered by Col. Murray of the Guards, uncle to the Duke of Athole.

" I hear from every quarter that the prediction I made to Lady Buckingham and to everyone else *that she would play the part of a Queen better than any,* is fully verified."

The EARL OF HILLSBOROUGH to THE SAME.

1778, August 22. Hill Park.—I think I may now congratulate your Excellency upon your having gotten through the longest and most difficult Session of Parliament I ever remember in Ireland. Your success in it is very much to your own honour, and gives very great pleasure to your friends, I am heartily sorry that I cannot conveniently go over to Hillsborough this year, to express mine to you in person, but I hope your Excellency will give me full credit for it, when I assure you I yield to none of them in that respect. If however the Militia is to be embodied, I apprehend that I must contrive to slip over for a few weeks, for as I am Lieutenant of Downe, I would not wish the Militia of that great protestant County should be regulated without me; I therefore request the favour of your Excellency to let me know your intentions with regard to it, that I may regulate myself accordingly. I know Barrington is a constant intelligence to you, I therefore do not pretend to send you news, indeed my situation hardly enables me to hear any before it may have reached the Castle of Dublin. The Duke of Ancaster's successor is not yet named, nor does it that I can learn yet transpire who is likely to succeed him. I am going into Staffordshire to visit my daughter Charlotte, if therefore your Excellency should have leisure to honour me with a line, I pray you to direct at John Chetwynd Talbot's, Esquire, Ingestrie, near Litchfield.

LORD TOWNSHEND to the LORD LIEUTENANT.

1778, August 29th. Portman Square.—You observe in one of your letters to me, if I do not mistake, that the political occurences which do not relate to your department are not considered as matters of communication; I know it to be so, and have felt the awkwardness of that circumstance when in Ireland,

and it is upon this ground alone that I presume to trouble you with the inclosed, which is the intelligence of this day. I have it from Mr. Agar, who has it from office. It affords a better prospect as to our American affairs altho' very bad. Ld. Howe's abilities and the confidence of the sailors there may yet do great things.

We may expect in a few days very deciding events from Mr. Keppel if the French will meet him again, probably they may steer for the Spanish Coast, as they may not be so strong as he is, and endeavour a junction with their Toulon ships.

I hope the hulks with the medium guns will soon arrive in Dublin Bay, as they sail'd under convoy from Plymouth, and I shall send the light field guns very soon, which I believe are well calculated for that service, and the sooner they go the better, as I find they now are likely to be in fashion here, General Keppel having desired four of them for Coxheath. They shall be replaced as soon as possible.

DUKE OF GORDON to the EARL OF BUCKINGHAMSHIRE.

1778, Sept. 1. Gordon Castle.—I hope your Lordship will excuse me for giving you this trouble—it is at the earnest request of Mr. Shaw who is very desirous to have the honour of being introduced to your Lordship—he is the person who lately published an analysis of the Galic or Erse language, since which he has made a tour thro' the Highlands and Western Islands of Scotland in order to pick up materials for a dictionary to which is to be added fragments of ancient poetry of Fingal, songs, &c.— he is now going to Ireland to collect every thing that may be of use to him before his publication and to get as many subscribers to this work in that country as he can—if your Lordship will honor him with your name as a subscriber I am persuaded it will be of the utmost consequence to him, and will be very obliging to me—I have taken the liberty to enclose his proposals.

I have been very busy since I came to this country in recruiting and hope very soon to have my regiment compleat as we are now about 900 strong.—I hope Lady Buckingham and your Lordship enjoy perfect health. I should be really very happy to take a trip over with Lady Westmorland to pay my court at the Castle, but I am now a kind of a prisoner having the command of part of this coast to watch for the French privateers.

EARL OF ALDBOROUGH to THE SAME.

1778, October 15. Belan.—(Expostulating with great irritation at having been addressed *thro' a third Hand* in answer to a confidential letter.)

"Noblemen will not like being classed with the canaile, or " relish letters wrote by clerks in office, or in truth by any but " the Person they address," etc., etc.

Sir John Irwine to the Earl of Buckinghamshire.

1778, October 23. Royal Hospital.—Lieutenant Doughty of the 32nd having been returned absent without leave since the month of March last, and it having been reported to me by Lieutenant-General Cunninghame, as well as by Lieutenant-Colonel Fletcher, the Commanding Officer of that regiment (two of whose letters on that subject I have already had the honour to lay before your Excellency) that though Lieutenant Doughty has been repeatedly ordered to his post he has not joined the regiment, I therefore think it my duty to represent the same to your Excellency and to submit, whether in order to preserve discipline, it may not be proper to lay this very extraordinary conduct of Lieutenant Doughty before his Majesty.

Earl of Thanet to the Same.

1778, October 28. Bath.—Has been very bad. Warm thanks for kind letter and for remembering him in the midst of business.

Earl of Drogheda* to the Same.

1778, November 3. Aix in Provence.—Had obtained leave from his Majesty to come abroad for his health. Two winters have not been enough to reestablish it, and he has to beg for a further extension.

Though convinced that the business of his Department will not suffer in the hands of so able an officer as Mr. Ward, yet he is miserable at his enforced absence.

Earl of Suffolk to the Same.

(*Private.*)

1778, Nov. 7. Duke St., Westminster.—(Recommending to his notice the Reverend Mr. Champayne, a brother of Lady Paget.)

It is a mortifying circumstance that we are to meet Parliament without having beaten the French fleet in Europe or America! But we have been more fortunate in the arrivals of our trade and the captures made upon that enemy. I trust however we shall not be only commercially successfull hereafter.

Francis Matthew† to the Same.

1778, November 17. Dublin.—A petition in favour of the unfortunate Mr. Baker, under sentence of death. Knows that it is his Excellency's established rule to take the report only from the Judge, &c., &c.

---

* Major-General Charles, Earl of Drogheda, Master-General of Ordnance in Dublin.
† M.P. for Tipperary, and created Baron Llandaff of Thomastown in 1783.

EARL OF ALDBOROUGH to the EARL OF BUCKINGHAMSHIRE.

1778, November 20, Friday noon.—I called at my Lord Chancellor's this morning and his Lordship's opinion is that you may at pleasure appoint Governors to Counties in the room of others without any criminal process, that it has been done, and he would tell your Excellency so, whenever you mentioned the affair to him.

I am the better pleased at this, because it saves me the delay and trouble of such process which I had determined upon if necessary, for which the affidavits against him in King's Bench for disturbing instead of preserving the peace and good order of the country and the mandamus's and informations granted against him afford sufficient grounds, and as your Excellency was pleased to say you approved of me in his room, I shall be extremely obliged to you for the appointment soon as may be, the officer on whom I called (when I missed finding your Excellency either time at home) at the Secretary's office having informed me, it is a business quickly done, there being blank commissions ready for filling up soon as your Lordship pleased to give the orders.

I believe it will be sufficient to say therein that you have been pleased to appoint Edward Earl of Aldborough Governor of the County Wicklow in the room of the Honble Benjn. O'Neal Stratford, and indeed in my application, and your Excellency's complying therewith it was understood by me and I believe the county in general, that he was only as my locum tenens.

I shall call at the Secretary's office to-morrow, when I suppose the commission will be made out.

JOHN HELY HUTCHINSON (Provost), to THE SAME.

1778, November 29.—I had the honour of your Excellency's Letter, and submit in all things with the most cheerful resignation to his Majesty's pleasure. From the obliging expressions in your Excellency's letter, from the promise of Sir John Heron that his Majesty shou'd be acquainted with the constant support which I had given to the measures of Government during the last session, and from your Excellency's kind acceptance of my services at the conclusion of it, I must flatter myself that I have not, thro' any fault of mine, been depriv'd of the favour which I have had the honour of receiving from your Excellency.

I have, my Lord, unconnected with any party in many different administrations and in many different conjunctures, steadily and uniformly supported the measures of his Majesty's Government in this country during the whole course of his reign, and I am happy in the hopes that, under the administration of Lord Buckingham, the countenance and support of Government will not be withdrawn from an old and faithful servant of the King.

RICHD. OWEN CAMBRIDGE to the EARL OF BUCKINGHAM-
SHIRE.

1778, Dec. 3. Twickenham.—I rejoice to hear Lady
Buckinghamshire is arrived well. I do not forget that your
Lordship required of me, at parting, that I should give you a
letter when there was anything to be said from hence. It is a
very strange thing that the whole of this summer should have
past in expectation, and not one event should have happen'd to
decide on any councils, but a long state of sameness should leave
us still in the same anxiety. The proof of this is the King's
speech. I am of opinion that could we sleep away the winter, as
we have the summer, we must gain our point, for America can
neither hold out with ability or unanimity without some event of
éclat in its favour or such as may be held out to the deluded
people as seeming so. That we are not in the best state of
ability is certain, but comparatively with America or even France
we are certainly best able. Great honor is done to your friend
Stanley in that admirable piece of ridicule 'the Anticipation,' by
giving him a speech so true, so argumentative and yet so short,
by merely showing that France is quite at a stand; and however
some people in Holland may be troublesome, I am assured the
Dutch will not lend France a penny.

Your Lordship gave me another thing in charge :— to watch
the Navigation and by no means to relax in what we have
obtained by the clause in the Act to have no horses. I have
never used your Lordship's name but firmly taken on my self to
refuse them, proving that it would be the inevitable ruin of our
much admired walk and, besides that the banks which are not
secured by wood work are continually worn away by the last
hindmost horse, it is confest there can be no way found to
prevent its being the common and crowded ride of the whole
country. Whatever I have said to prevent horses here I have
never proposed (to save our side) to send 'em over to the t'other,
but to go on still with *men*. The Committee of Navigation
determine to have horses and to *embank* on the other side,
offering at their own expense to raise the gardens so that they
may overlook and not be overlook'd by the towing path beneath,
and to pass the Duke of Montagu's by a long line, and at the
end of his garden change horses, and ballast the river to go on
that side. I have nothing to do with this, but the Richmond
people have been moving to throw it on us, and even offer'd to
let the horses pass the bridge toll free. They have made parties
in the town and declared to the Committee they were sure of
gaining your Lordship's consent. I suppose they mean to
importune Mr. Hobart, who will hardly throw an evil (if it was
one) from Richmond upon Marble Hill, especially as he knows it
would be of no avail without *my* consent. I am afraid I have
been long, but I was willing your Lordship should not have an
imperfect account of this, or any affair : and now to be short, I
recommend your Lordship to write to me that you hear there
are who wish to ask your Lordship a very unreasonable request

which you cannot grant: and if this be done soon it may prevent
a great deal of trouble, which I have but just learnt has been
brewing a great while, though the Committee assured them they
will make so handsome a terrass walk without their gardens,
that the people of Richmond shall be gainers of a walk on their
side without spoiling their walk on this, and the Duke of Montagu
assures me he dreads to have it on this side, and has no objection
to the way proposed, and Lady Cooper acquiesces for her terrass
which is to be widen'd for the path. I have taken the liberty to
write to your Lordship with the freedom and shortness of business,
and shall receive the shortest line from your Lordship with due
acknowledgement.

General R. Pearson to the Earl of Buckinghamshire.

1778, Dec. 4. Southampton.—Communicating to him his
appointment to the command of the 13th Regt. of Dragoons, a
mark of the King's approbation " to the commander of the Camp
at Warley." Some further personal honours which have been
paid him are reported in the *Morning Post* of October 26, 1778
(here also related).

Sir John Irwine to the Same.

1778, December 29. Royal Hospital.—I am much concerned
to find from Mr. Hamilton's letter of the 27th that some expression
in mine of the 26th to your Excellency had given you offence,
which I most assuredly did not, nor certainly could not, mean,
otherwise than so far as I had the misfortune to differ in my
opinion of the measure from your Excellency and as my protest
against it.

I beg leave to assure your Excellency, and I hope you are persuaded, that there is no person more desirous upon every occasion
to shew every respect to your Excy., and (I repeat it once more)
a ready obedience to your commands, than I.

Account of Taking St. Lucia.[a]

1778.—On the 9th of December Commodore Hotham with the
troops arrived at Barbadoes, joined Admiral Barrington and
sailed the 12th for St. Lucia, landed the troops the 14th on. that
island. D'Estaing appeared with 10 sail of the Line and a
number of Frigates, having 5,000 men on board, landed them,
attacked the British troops in their entrenchments on the 18th
in three columns, the 1st led by himself, the 2nd by Count de
Bonillé were received on the point of the bayonet and repulsed
with the loss of 405 killed and 900 wounded. About 140 British
killed and wounded. Attempted to attack the Fleet without
success, sailed with all his force for Martinique the 29th, leaving
the English in possession of the Island, which capitulated in

---

* The source of this account is not given.

sight of the French fleet. It is supposed this sudden movement was occasioned by intelligence of Admiral Byron's squadron approaching. Brigadier Meadows slightly wounded in the arm.

Earl of Buckinghamshire to Lord George Germain.

1779, Jan. 4.—Is unable to satisfy Ld. Carlow as to an application he has made for a particular living for his son.

The Same to the Same.

(*Private*.)

1779, Jan. 14. Dublin Castle.—In the last letters which I received from Sir Rd. Heron previous to Lord North's leaving London, he gave me reason to hope that there was was an intention of relieving Ireland from the expense of the three thousand men upon this establishment now serving abroad, and one of His Lordship's Cabinet has communicated it as a matter determin'd to our Attorney General. I should rather think this information premature, as Lord North would scarcely absolutely decide upon a measure of such moment without in some degree consulting the other servants of the Crown. There is nothing new to offer upon the State of this Kingdom, the whole has been represented in the fullest and fairest light, that those who have the care of the whole Empire may determine upon such regulations as, consistent with the general good, may be adopted for this detach'd part.

It is said that the friends of the Agar family express their dissatisfaction upon the promotion of Dr. Fowler° with a warmth bordering upon resentment. Yet it appears to me that the favors of Government have rather been lavish'd upon them. The Bishop of Cloyne, discontented as he may be, is morally sure of being recommended to the Archbishoprick of Cashell, † Lord Clifden ‡ has just been created a Peer and is a Commissioner of the Revenue. As he sold his seats in Parliament he has no influence in the House of Commons, and I should suppose that Mr. Ellys holding a Capital Office in England is not intitled to advance claims here. He had however weight sufficient at Westminster to prevent the removal of the Dublin Custom House, which evidently, besides great inconvenience to trade, loses many thousand pounds to the Revenue. In this and in some other instances English Ministers are most amazingly mistaken with respect to the consequence of individuals here.

The Roman Catholicks are in the highest good humor, the outrageous and illiberal conduct of the American Congress has greatly cool'd the ardour of many of their reputed friends in Ireland, and upon the fullest enquiry I am realy of opinion that the country has at no period been in general better dispos'd.

---

* Dr. Fowler, Bishop of Killaloe, was made Archbishop of Dublin in December, 1778.

† The Right Rev. Charles Agar, Bishop of Cloyne, was made Archbishop of Cashell, in August, 1779.

‡ James Agar was created Baron Clifden (in Kilkenny), July, 1776.

They will struggle with any difficultys they find themselves equal to, but the wisdom of England must cautiously prevent those difficultyes from increasing beyond their strength.

In a letter from Mr. Jenkinson he mentions the improbability of any further indulgence being given to the Irish trade. I do not deem myself competent to decide upon the species of indulgence which England should hold out to this kingdom; yet something should necessarily be done and that with little delay.

BISHOP OF NORWICH [a] to the EARL OF BUCKINGHAMSHIRE.

1779, Feb. 2. London.—Must trouble his Excellency with a few lines relative to a person who by his many and great faults has render'd his family (I fear not render'd himself) very unhappy. I allude to Mr. Greene, the chancel of whose church Hunworth or Stody, has been entirely demolish'd by the high wind on the 1st of January. It has been represented to me that the maintenance of five children depends upon the receipts from these livings, and I am requested to permit his manager to wall up the east end of the chancel instead of rebuilding it, so as to leave convenient room for the communion table. And I am so well satisfied with the reasonableness of the request, considering the great distress of the poor children, that I am very ready to comply with it if it meets with your Excellency's approbation.

EARL OF ALDBOROUGH to THE SAME.

1779, Feb. 12. Nassau Street.—Mr. Saunders has chearfully taken the office of Sheriff upon him this year to accommodate your Excellency, tho' very injurious to his affairs to be detained a second year from England. The last year he was prevented from going by his successful endeavours to suppress at the risque of his life civil disturbances and by a villainous prosecution against him for murder, which he purposely put off for two assizes, he was most honourably acquitted of, and I believe there are few gentlemen in the Queen's County and other neighbouring ones, who do not in a great measure owe the peaceable possession of their estates to his spirited yet temperate conduct against those outlawed pests of society. I hope your Lordship will agree with me that his troubles, crosses and great losses on those occasions merit your Excellency's good opinion and the notice of his Majesty. I had applied to your Lordship formerly to confer an honour upon him. My applications to your Excellency have not been of a pecuniary or mercenary nature, attended with no expense to Government but as rewards to merit and the well-wishers to administration. His paternal ancestry have had many orders of chivalry both among the Morleys and Saunders and enobled maternally. He has made the Tour of Europe as extensively and with as much reputation as any young gentleman ever did, as our Ambassadors in Italy and France can testify, and, if

---

* Philip Yonge (or Young), Bishop of Norwich, 1761-1783.

not thus detained, he had e'er now in all probability have been allyed to a young lady of most amiable accomplishments, ample fortune, and very good connections as most in Great Britain. She is still unmarried, and I wish to repay her constancy by procuring what both so well merit, a Peerage. I have therefore to request that among such Commoners as your Excellency may think fit hereafter to recommend to his Majesty to be so distinguished that my nephew Morley Saunders, of Saunders Grove, in the County of Wicklow, may be one by the stile and title of Baron Roscommon.

EARL OF BUCKINGHAMSHIRE to LORD GEORGE GERMAIN.

(*Private.*)

1779, Feb. 15. Dublin Castle.—Many thanks for the good news contained in your Lordship's Letter of the 10th.

The numbers of the associated companys greatly exceed my expectation, they have grown up insensibly, but none of the servants of the Crown seem to think them dangerous.

Upon the rumor of the Provincial Regiments many Gentlemen daily offer to raise corps to form them, but I doubt they would not chose foreign service. Most of those gentlemen belong to the companys above mentioned.

I keep the packet waiting jûst in three words to repeat, that any plan his Majesty adopts for the raising men shall be pushd to the utmost.

THE SAME to THE SAME.

1779, Feb. 15. Dublin Castle.—(The bearer of these letters is from the African coast, sent by Mr. Lacy, who solicits some advance for him in consequence of the deaths in that country. He has experienced many hardships.) I am distrest beyond measure for Church preferment, which must at present plead my excuse to Lord Carlow.

LORD CHANCELLOR (LIFFORD) to the EARL OF BUCKINGHAMSHIRE.

1779, Thursday 18. Chancery Chamber.—The Chancellor presents his best respects to His Excellency the Lord Lieutenant. Has been much out of order for some days, and tho' he sat all day yesterday and to-day in the Court of Chancery, he is not well enough to dine at a full table and in company to-day, and hopes that his Excellency will permit him to beg his Excellency's permission to eat a chicken at home. Begs leave to mention to him a matter that he should have mentioned if he had seen his Excellency before dinner, viz :— There was presented to him for the Great Seal the grant of the Deanery of Cork and the presentations to two livings to Mr. Erskine. One of the livings is the present of the Crown *in pleno jure*, the other is the gift of the Crown as vacant by the advancement of the last incumbent to the Bishoprick of Killaloe. I inquired whether Mr. Erskine had compleatly got rid of his English preferments, but could receive no answer or satisfaction. The Chancellor therefore thought fit to suspend putting the Great Seal to these instruments, for that by a Statute of this Kingdom of the 17th and 18th C. II., the Deanery and the livings would be vacant in case Mr. Erskine at the time had spiritual preferment in England. This happened in the case of the present Bishop of Kilmore[*] who had not surrendered his livings in England at the time his patent for the Bishoprick passed the Seal, and he was obliged afterwards to have a new patent when he had his English preferment. In the present case there is something more, for this Act says that upon a presentation becoming so void the true and real patron may present, as if the person so presented having at the time English preferment had resign'd or had dyed.

Now possibly under this part of the Statute your Excellency might lose the presentation and the patron possibly would say the Crown's turn, by making the incumbent a Bishop, has been served by the presentation of Mr. E. which is become void, and I am now to present as if the person presented by the Crown had resigned or had dyed.

The Chancellor was willing to communicate this to his Excellency, and therefore troubles him with this long scrawl.

J. M. HEYWOOD to the EARL OF BUCKINGHAMSHIRE.

1779, Feb. 27. Grosvenor Street.—As Sir Francis Drake is going to write to your Lordship on the subjects of the fishery in the River Tavy and his dispute with Mr. Short, I trouble you with a few lines just to say what passed between the latter and myself the last time I saw him, which may serve to show you his sentiments, may point out to you in what manner to act and prevent any misrepresentation of the facts. Last spring Mr. Short enter'd into an association with several of the lowest people of the Parish of Beer who were so indefatigable in this lucrative pursuit that they not only alarm'd Sir Francis Drake by prejudicing his fishery, but by employing a number of people took very unfair advantages over my tenant, who had agreed with them for the sake of peace and quietness to fish alternately, viz., three days in the week each. In the autumn I spoke to Mr. Short on the subject, in the hopes of settling the matter so as to prevent all disputes and asked him if Sir Francis had not forbid his fishing, and if he fished in your Lordship's right or as Rector of Beer. His answer I confess astonished me. He said "*that you had no exclusive right*, that it did not signify by what rights he fished, it was by the same right which his predecessors had exercised." These words he more than once repeated. It is of little consequence to me whether the rights of fishery on your side the river is reserved in your Lordship's family or granted

---

[*] Dr. George Lewis Jones.

by lease to Sir Francis; but was I even less interested than I am
in this business, I cannot refrain from informing you of anything which may materially concern your property in that
neighbourhood. . . .

"Quaker Treffry to Parson Short."

2d day, morning. Beer.—Roger Treffry's respects to his friend
Short, and as he hath been informed by John Harris that he is
ordered to level a heap of earth on the green, that I have cast up
on my right, I think it necessary to say it hath been a matter of
surprise that the Earl of Bucks. or any person under him should
give away them pollard trees which grew on that part of the
green, but as they were given to the poor and done perhaps thro'
inadvertency I do not much regard it; but I claim both soil and
trees from the Parish Steble to the Water as an *appurtenance*
belonging to my estate and as much my right as either field
thereon which I can prove without a doubt.

If thou hast any desire to have it removed to *please thy eye*, as
soon as I have leisure I intend to do it, but must beg no other
person may meddle with it.

Earl of Hillsborough to the Earl of Buckinghamshire.

1779, March 4. London.—I know not how to express my
sense of your Excellency's kindness to me. The matter of what
is in agitation is trifling, but the manner of your granting my
request is infinitely pleasing and obliging to me. The contents
of Mr. Meredyth's letter adds if possible to this. I pray your
Excellency to let Mr. John Marshall be appointed to the hearth
money collection of Hillsborough, and I will be answerable for
his conduct. He will give ample and indisputable security, and
is a very proper person in every respect, and will answer all my
wishes.

The latter part of your Excellency's letter, in which you
mention in the most obliging manner my entering again into
public business, is founded I imagine only upon reports, for I have
heard nothing otherwise about it. I am sorry to tell you that
matters hobble on but unpleasantly, and yet nothing is more to
be feared than the breaking up of the present Administration,
for there is not anything half so good to replace it. I therefore
do most heartily wish its continuance. Poor Lord Suffolk is gone
extremely ill to Bath, most people think not to return. Should
this be the case he will be a very great loss, but I think his youth
gives him a chance of recovery. Various conjectures have been
thrown out of a successor, your Excellency, Lord Rochford, Lord
Sandwich and myself have been mentioned, but I believe without
any foundation. I have made my letter a little longer than
usual because Barrington, who I know sends your Excellency all
the news, is gone out of town.

SIR JOHN IRWINE to the EARL OF BUCKINGHAMSHIRE.

1779, March 10. Jermyn Street.—I return your Excellency many thanks for the honour of yours of the third instant, but should not have troubled you with a letter which can give your Excellency no entertainment had it not been for the death of Captain Graham, of the Athol Highlanders, who died at Naples, whither he went for the recovery of his health on the 31st of January last. The Duke of Athol and Colonel Murray have been with me to desire I would recommend to your Excellency Captain Lieutenant James Menzies for the Company; the eldest Lieutenant, Charles Murray, for the Captain-Lieutenantcy; the eldest Ensign, John Mackay, to be Lieutenant; and Volunteer Thomas McPhail to be Ensign. The peculiar circumstances of that regiment, especially with respect to the language spoke in it, induces me to hope that your Excy. will comply with the requests of the Duke of Athol and Col. Murray.

Mr. Hobart, knowing I was to have the honour to write to your Excellency, has desired me to mention that to-night on a motion of Lord Newhaven's (after a division of 47 to 42) leave is given to bring in a bill for permitting the importation of sugar into Ireland. I need not mention that Mr. Hobart was in the majority. I was not in the division; Mr. Stuart McKensie and I being both engaged to dinner, with Lord Newhaven's leave, went off together.

I most sincerely condole with your Excy. on the loss of our friend, poor Lord Suffolk, though his death was fortunate for him, as he was in a miserable way. Two or three people (Lord Carlisle, Lord Hillsborough, Lord Stormount and Lord Rochford) are talked of to be his successor, but nothing is yet fixed. The Duke of Beaufort had an audience to-day, and as is believed asked for the Garter. I never saw Lady Buckingham look better.

P.S. My stay here must be some days longer than I proposed, as a question or two of some importance will come on in the House of Commons.*

COUNTESS OF KILDARE to THE SAME.

1779, March 25.—Your reasons for disencumbering this poor Nation of adding or renewing pensions I must applaud, tho' unsuccessful in my application in regard of my neice Lady Burdett's children, and her small pension the chief support of them, and dyeing with her. They and their father have lived since I may say upon charity, by donations of money from their relations both of Sir William Burdett and hers; yet their distress is such as Sir William is under the necessity of disposing of some moveables to provide food for the family as alsoe clothing to prevent starving with hunger and cold. I beg pardon for trobling your Excellencie with these particulars of their misery, but in hopes to move your pitty to these wretched infants, and from

* Sir John Irwine was M.P. for E. Grinstead

your benevolence grant their father some small employ that
might prevent them all from perishing. I don't mean a place of
trust of money ; Board of Works or any not unbecoming a gentle--
man to execute. If Lady Buckingham was here I shou'd hope
for her suporting this request by her influence with your
Excellencie, but as I can have no prospect of that protection, I
venture, and flatter myself you will excuse this, which nothing
but the daily scenes of indigence I am, and have long been, too
well acquainted with, cou'd have prevail'd with me to trouble
your Excellencie with the deplorable case, and from whose com-
passionat tender feelings I depend that I have not laid it before
you in vain.

EARL OF BUCKINGHAMSHIRE to LORD GEORGE GERMAIN.

(*Private.*)

1779, March 31. Dublin Castle.—The intelligence of our most
brilliant successes as well in the East as in the West Indies has
give me a long inexperienced flow of spirits. But Lord Suffolk's
death both in a publick and in a private light is a thorn in my
pillow which will not easily be removed.

The mode in which the measures favourable to Ireland have
been press'd in Parliament has been equaly injudicious and
improper ; till Lord North had expressly signifyd that nothing
should be done, the specifick propositions ought to have been
submitted to him. I cannot but be persuaded of its being
unnecessary to declare that Lord Newhaven's taking such a lead
has neither been directly or indirectly encouraged by me. Your
Lordship well knows that my wish has been uniformly that
English Government should form their determination upon the
state which it was my duty fairly and fully to exhibit. The
relieving Ireland from the expense of the troops serving abroad
is a concession of the first magnitude and of the most immediate
operation, a lottery *sub modo* will also mitigate the usurious contracts, without which otherwise our money could not be obtain'd,
the separation of the Post Office, if England sets the example of
abolishing the privilege of franking, may become a material
article of revenue, and if the indulgence of exporting cottons and
linnens mix'd was added to these, all complainings and additional
requisitions may be deemed most unreasonable.

A most painfull reflection too frequently occurs to me that my
Administration should exist at a period when of all others
England was the most oppressed with difficultys, which this
country instead of relieving was necessarily oblig'd to increase.
The most my best endeavors can expect is a mitigation of general
censure and that the very few candid will give me credit for
difficultys which they have not leisure to investigate. You will
deem me, however, the vainest of men for declaring that in my
own deliberate, let me hope, dispassionate judgment, events have
not hitherto led me to wish to have held a different line of conduct. When the days of tranquillity return you shall indulge me
in expatiating a little upon that subject.

As some of my letters to Sir H. Clinton have miscarry'd you will forgive my requesting that directions may be given for transmitting the inclosed.

Lady Buckingham expresses her being particularly happy in Lady Crosby's society.

EARL OF HILLSBOROUGH to the EARL OF BUCKINGHAMSHIRE.

1779, April 26. Hanover Square.—I have been so furiously attacked by a cold and sore throat that I have not been able to hold my head down long enough to write a letter for these ten days. This has prevented my paying my duty to your Excellency, and returning you my thanks for my Hillsborough hearthmoney collection, which is, I presume, by this time in possession of Mr. John Marshall.

You will laugh, and yet I am sure be sorry to hear that our friend Barrington has got a smart fit of the gout. I fancy he swears a little, but our respective complaints keep us asunder. Your Excellency will expect to hear from *me* who is to be Secretary of State. And perhaps you will be surprized when I assure you I know nothing of the matter. I have put my mark under (*me*) because for ten or twelve days past everybody seemed to agree it would be offered to me. My private opinion and indeed hope has been, and still is, that it will not come to me. I say my hope, because I think I should be weak enough to accept it, tho' indubitably much happyer as I am, ' *Armis Herculis ad Postem fixis*,' when I quitted the Colonies. So much for me and Secretary of State. I do assure you my dear Lord, I have most cordially and actively obeyed your Excellency, in stating the deplorable condition of poor Ireland, and soliciting relief. The payment of the troops is all that could be got. My patience is severely tried by those two foolish Bills, the Tobacco and the Stamp. The first is an insult to the misery of that country, the other an Irish Relief indeed! By way of support, a Bounty totally to destroy the small remains of sailcloth and the cordage manufactures. All this I represented to our friend, Nugent, but your Excellency knows he abounds considerably more in wit and obstinacy than in prudence and judgment. I shall not be surprised if these two *encouragements* should produce a good deal of clamour on your side. Upon the motion made by Lord Bristol the other day to remove Lord Sandwich, Lord Lyttleton and Lord Pembroke voted with the minority, and the first made a furious anti-ministerial speech. I am told Lord Stormount (*sic*) spoke very well indeed; this is the second time he has distinguished himself this sessions.

We are under apprehensions about the Ramillies 74 Gun Ship of War, and news from the West Indies is impatiently expected. I have this instant got a note from Barrington to tell me he has the gout in the other foot. What a rich fellow he will be. I have been so long confined that I do not know whether Lady Buckingham is with you; if she is I beg your Excellency will present my most respectfull compliments to her.

LORD CHANCELLOR (LIFFORD) to MR. WAITE.°

1779, May.—Illness will prevent me from attending his Excellency's levée.

I don't wonder that the people of England grow serious about the foolish and mad associations here. I am sure they make me very uneasy, as I am sure that they must if they have any effect work to the prejudice of this country, especially if seriously taken up on the other side of the water.

LORD BARRINGTON to the EARL OF BUCKINGHAMSHIRE.

1779, May 17. Cavendish Square.—In your letter of the 7th instant you bid me account for Mr. Rigby's conduct in the House of Commons and for the disagreements which appear in Parliament among the Ministers now in office, etc. I am ever desirous, my dear friend, to assist your wishes; but in truth I know nothing but what *meets the eye* in the political world. No wonder, however, that an Administration which has no system, no steadiness and little concert should appear sometimes to differ. I am apt to believe the Bloomsbury's are in no plot, and have no object but to keep what they possess. I am told Lord North and Lord George Germain managed the debate to which you allude so unfortunately, that even their warmest and best friends supported them with great reluctance, and openly blamed their conduct. Happily for the Ministry the opposition is so universally detested and feared, that they find a support in the nation to which they are not entitled but from *comparison*.

I am happy to read in one of your letters that your subjects in Ireland are growing more moderate. I really cannot blame their associations. The English nation and it's Parliament wish to assist the Irish trade, both from policy and gratitude; but are prevented by the clamours raised by local manufactories. Are such monopolists entitled to any favour from a nation which they oppress? I hope next Session of Parliament the right thing will be done in spight of clamour. Lord Nugent has been very absurd, and has carry'd thro' the Houses two Bills which can neither benefit or quiet the country where he is a candidate for popularity.

There are some ugly rumours about our fleet in the West Indies, but void of all foundation.

Sir James Wallace with a 50 gunship and two small ships of war follow'd to Cancalle Bay the sea-force which attack'd Jersey. He silenced a battery on shore, took a fine frigate of 34 guns, destroy'd two other frigates and a sloop, in short, as I am told, everything which he found there; and this in spight of the French artillery and many thousand troops under arms who were near spectators.

---

* Probably Thomas Waite, appointed a Privy Councillor in Ireland, 1777.

The Spanish Ambassador (M. le Marquis d'Almodovar)
to the Earl of Buckinghamshire.

1779, May 29. Londres.—Taking the liberty of sending him
some specimens of Spanish wine which are much appreciated
here, and acknowledging with gratitude " deux pièces d' Irlande"
sent him by the Viceroy.

Earl of Buckinghamshire to Lord George Germain.

1779, June 28. Dublin Castle.—Your Irish friends flatter
themselves that the report of your indisposition is not founded.
Your Lordship must know of the Order, receiv'd here yesterday,
to encamp the Army immediately, and you cannot be a stranger
to the inability of our Treasury to answer the consequential
expence. The notification of His Majesty's pleasure to augment
the staff came at the same time, and I fear the very material
additional charge which in the course of a twelvemonth has been
introduc'd under that head, will occasion great dissatisfaction,
and very unpleasing Parliamentary animadversion, especially as
we have only two regiments of infantry more than we had under
the old staff (July the 1st). I was interrupted here and have not
had leisure to continue till now when I am to express my
particular thanks for two letters since receiv'd, the latter of
which gave me as much pleasure in reading as your Lordship
seems to have experienc'd from the circumstance upon which it
treats. The military gentlemen are tearing me to pieces for the
money which they know I have not, and the appearance of their
embracing too many ideas at once concerns me. A large sum
ought to be remitted from England, or no defence can be made.
Proposals for raising corps crowd in upon me from every side,
which, very, very few instances excepted, are dictated by idea's
of military rank, county influence, or emolument. The same
publick spirit in no degree prevails in this kingdom, which so
generaly pervades England, that of contributing uncompelled to
the exigencys of the State. Yet candor should allow that this
possibly may proceed from a circumstance which influences disagreeably in many instances, that excess of expense which, in
Ireland, distresses every order of men. This, however, cannot
apply to the great absentee proprietors who, I understand, are
alarmed at a rumour of my having submitted to the Cabinet an
idea of taxing them. Their not offering at this moment in some
shape or other to assist a country where they possess such valuable stake's is certainly impolitick. I have nothing material to
mention which you will not see in my official dispatches, except
that since my last to Ld. Weymouth, fresh assurances have been
given by several principal Roman Catholicks of their attachment
to His Majesty and their cordial disposition, if call'd upon,
actively to assist him. Your Lordship's account of His Majesty's
late deportment in the Cabinet was most gratefull to me, tho'
the communications with which he has occasionally honor'd me,
left me no doubt of the extent of his ability's.

This letter, which was begun on the 28th of June, is concluded the 4th of July, you will conceive that the interruptions have been occasion'd by business and that, possibly, the business was not of a most agreeable cast.

JOHN TOMLINSON to the EARL OF BUCKINGHAMSHIRE.

1779, July 9. Cley.—(Concerning an offer made to Mr. Weg for the purchase of his estate for £900.) He is not inclin'd to take less than £1,000 for it, tho' I have represented the increased difference between money and land since the offer was made. However his distresses are not less than they were, and Mr. Copeman has promis'd to continue the mortgage for a larger period (upon his own account, I understand from Mr. Gay, if inconvenient to your Lordship). (Reports the death of a Major Lacy.)

The part Spain has taken has made us not only extremely anxious for the safety of your Lordship's Kingdom of Ireland, but even *pro Aris et Focis* in Norfolk, where you may possibly be surpris'd to hear of no small apprehensions of an invasion from a privateer's crew at least, and tho' Parliament seems averse to increasing the militia by ballot, yet I verily believe some volunteer corps will be rais'd at the Assizes.

While the Bill was depending Mr. Coke went over to Lord Orford at the Camp at Alborough in Suffolk to offer his service, if an additional Battalion was rais'd, or if not, to ask permission to raise some few companies among his friends; and mentioned Sir E. Astley's and Sir Harbord's intentions of serving, but yet steer'd clear of offering to serve under his Lordship's immediate command, as at least he may be said to be military mad, so much so that Mr. Coke is extremely fearfull that his brother, and Mr. Bulwer, that his son, may be brought into some danger or disagreable situation by his Lordship's attacking the Smuglers, against whom he vows vengeance for their resistance last year. As a proof of his Lordship's not being in his sober senses he wants to promote Capt. Alderman Gobbet to the Majority in case it should be vacant either by Col. Barker's being broke by an intended Court Martial, or by Mr. Windham's resignation on account of health, which, however, is so far re-establish'd as to be thought quite out of danger, tho' he cannot join the corps this summer.

Lord de Ferrers also wants to have the command of a Battalion or indeed any less body distinct from Lord Orford's commands.

I came down early this summer to fix my sisters at Yarmouth and on my farming matters, by which means I was at the Norwich Guild. Sir Harbord made his entry into the country that day, but did not appear to be received with great applause by the court, and will be less so by the vulgar on account of the inclosure of *free* Mousehold Heath, which is now depending, and at a meeting on which account Mr. Lens was wounded by a brick bat and others discomfited, which has produc'd certain warrants and actions that will not much increase his popularity ; and it is the general opinion that if he represents Norwich again it must be by Mr. Bacon's good offices and the desire of preserving the peace of the city. There is also an opinion that Bacon will join young Ives, but that I can scarce think will be the case. There are certain Gregs° of the name of Day very strenuous for Mr. Hobart's offering himself, but in these times unanimity is much to be wish'd for. Exclusive of foreign enemies we are much distress'd here and thro' England in general by the poverty of our farmers and what they call the low price of things. The fact is I cannot let my farm now in hand to its value and therefore seem likely to hold it another year, and unfortunately my great farm comes out of lease at Mich⁸· 1780, for which I have not yet been bid near its value, so that event which I have been longing for with so much ardor may now happen too soon.

Our farmers cannot sell any sheep at the fairs, and unless the late fine rains ensure a good turnip crop, I do not know how they can keep them, for the drought has been so great in these parts that they lately ask'd £5 for a waggon load of new hay. At the same time that I feel and lament these unfortunate circumstances, yet the mentioning them may be some consolation to those under your Lordship's Government that know only their own grievances, which seem to spread too rapidly over the whole empire.

The Assizes on the 26th will certainly produce some resolutions about increasing the Militia or forming companies in the different districts. I shall then do myself the honour of communicating them.

CHARLES JENKINSON to the EARL OF BUCKINGHAMSHIRE.

(*Private.*)

1779, July 17. London.—Has this day spoken to Lord Hertford desiring that no step may be taken to bring forward a measure which you say in the present moment would lay you under difficulties.

SIR JOHN IRWINE to the EARL OF BUCKINGHAMSHIRE.

1779, Aug. 7. Head Quarters, Ardfinnan Camp.—I had the honour to receive your Excellency's letter whilst I was on the road to Corke. Ever since, I have been in such constant motion, and so taken up with business that I have not been able to return your Excy. my humble thanks for it.

With all submission to your Excy., give me leave to say, that if Colonel Sandford, or whoever your Excy. destined for the place of Inspector of recruits, meant to make it a sinecure your Excy. would do perfectly right to suppress that employment, but as such an officer is at this time more necessary than ever, I sincerely hope your Excy. will reconsider that matter ; for now that we expect the gentlemen of the country will raise men for us, it will be very proper those men should be inspected, and at

* *See* Mr. Harbord to the Earl of Bucks., p. 242, March 28, 1761.

this time no General or field officer can be spared to attend such a duty. My intention therefore was to propose to your Excy. the establishing the Inspector at some particular place, where he should examine all the recruits, somewhere between this and Corke, by which he might see the recruits for the army near that city as well as this encamped here. I therefore beseech your Excy. to once more think of this affair.

With respect to the post of Constable of Carrickfergus I have less to say; I only take the liberty to observe that though the late Colonel Browne was the first who enjoyed that place, and therefore it may be said to be created for him, yet it was not intended the place should be put an end to with his life; for if your Excy. will please to consider there is not a Prince in Europe who has so few favours of that nature to give away to old and deserving officers as the King our Master has, and which he has often regretted, which I confess makes me wish that your Excy. would not suppress that post.

I will not take up more of your Excy.'s time at present than to tell you that we have a great many sick in this Camp, which makes me earnest to have some better way of taking care of them than we at present have, which can only be done by establishing a general hospital for that purpose.

Sir John Irwine to the Earl of Buckinghamshire.

1779, Aug. 15. Ardfinnan Camp.—I had the honour this day to receive your Excellency's letter of the 13th. If the united fleets are entering the channel I take for granted we shall soon hear of an action, and that the consequence of it will decide whether we shall or shall not be invaded.

His Majesty having determined as to the late Col. Browne's employments, it is unnecessary to say any thing on that subject. I lament very much that such a number of recruiting parties are sent over to this country, when we have so great occasion for men to defend ourselves ; perhaps if your Excy. would be pleased to represent this matter to his Majesty it might be put a stop to, or at least restrained in some degree, or they might send us over some recruits from thence, which method I should like best of all. I can assure your Excy. the gentlemen of the country with whom I have conversed complain very bitterly of England for this very measure of recruiting their troops in this Kingdom ; say they are ill-treated and neglected, and it is their opinion that England wishes to see Ireland invaded, in the hope it would prevent an invasion of England.

I rejoyce that the augmentation of the artillery is consented to. There is a great want of officers in that corps, we have not near sufficient for the common duty.

I propose leaving this, to pay my respects to your Excy., about this day se-night, unless you are pleased to order me sooner. I shall make Col. Luttrell very happy by letting him know your Excy.'s approbation.

Give me leave to return you my best thanks for the honour of
your letter of the 10th. By that it does not appear (from
Governor Johnston's intelligence) as if all we read and hear of
embarking troops on the French coast was true. I am very
thankful to your Excy. for the kind concern you are pleased to
express about my health. I am pretty well of the disorder in my
stomach, but have got a most severe cold.

I proposed sending this letter by post, but have this moment
received an application from Maj^r Ross of the 81st Regt. to lay
before your Excy. a proposal for raising 700 Highlanders, which
proposal (according to the present mode though it is not to relate
to Ireland) is to go through your Excy. to be transmitted to be
laid before the King. He flatters himself H.M. will accept his
proposal, and desires leave to go to London for a few days, which,
he being a deserving officer, I hope your Excy. will please to
permit him to do.

The EARL OF SHANNON to the EARL OF BUCKINGHAMSHIRE
(Lord Lieutenant).

1779, Sept. 16. Castle Martyr.—I am sorry to inform your
Excellency that the plan for reducing the arm'd societies in this
country into a legal and regular form has not yet met with the
success which I hoped for, or which it deserved. It was so
model'd by Col. Luttrell as in my opinion not only to obviate all
objection, but to make it in every light desirable. An alarm,
however, respecting it had been rapidly and successfully spread
the moment it transpired that such a scheme was in agitation,
and men's minds were so strongly prepossessed against the
measure that it was received with every symptom of jealousy
and distrust, and seem'd to be condemn'd by almost all, before
it had been well explained to any.

I trust, however, that gentlemen's suspicions may be yet
removed, and they may yet be convinced, that nothing is meant
but to promote the general good, and that the only object of the
scheme is that their own protection, and that of the kingdom
should go hand in hand. Your Excellency may be satisfied that
I shall take every opportunity, where it can be done with effect,
of recommending and promoting in this, as I flatter myself I
have been instrumental in doing in a neighbouring county, a
scheme which in my conscience I think at this critical time so
necessary, and so much for the honor and advantage of the
kingdom.

EARL OF BUCKINGHAMSHIRE to LORD GEORGE GERMAIN.

1779, Sept. 16. Dublin Castle.—It may be necessary to
observe to your Lordship that the draft of the Lord Lieutenant's
Speech,* which is conveyed to Lord Weymouth by this

---

* See for the form in which it was finally delivered the 12th October, the Annual
Register for 1779, p. 352.

messenger, is not precisely such, as, but from the particular circumstances of the time, I should have wish'd to have submitted.

Many alterations have been made by the several gentlemen consulted, which are acquiesc'd in from the consideration that the loss of a question upon the Address would not only influence upon the whole conduct of the Sessions but might branch out into numberless disagreeable political consequences in other respects. All my friends assure me that any attempt to prevent the Parliament's entering into the commercial subject would be equally injudicious and unavailing.

—In a juncture like the present your discernment will see the propriety of my requesting the assistance and instructions of his Majesty's English servants. (*Draft.*)

EARL OF BUCKINGHAMSHIRE to LORD GEORGE GERMAIN.

(*Private.*)

1779, October 19. Dublin Castle.—Tho' I cannot risque any sanguine assertions, yet there is a degree of satisfaction in observing that discreet men seem terribly alarmed and wish for for their own sakes to prevent that ruin and confusion which seems to threaten their country. I hope to be able to send an official letter to-morrow to Lord North with a state of my future prospect, which, however tho' time presses, cannot be wrote without great deliberation. (*Draft.*)

THE SAME to THE SAME.

(*Private.*)

1779, October 24.—Last night's post brought the London Gazette in which the Lord Lieutenant's Speech is inserted. This is the only intelligence which hitherto has reached me of my very disagreeable, and, indeed, alarming dispatches having been receiv'd. Suspence is a most unpleasing circumstance to an anxious mind, but in this instance is very sufficiently accounted for by the peculiar difficulty which must attend the framing any determination upon them. No man who has the least glimmering of information will presume to advance that the King can pledge himself for the conduct of Parliament, and yet there prevails a degree of universal impatience for his answer as if the wording of it was finaly to decide upon the hopes of this Kingdom.

The Duke of Leinster and Mr. Conolly* tho' at first disinclin'd to the armed societys at least so far as not to engage in them are now become their great promoters. In the course of the summer upon its being rumor'd that his Majesty might possibly be induc'd to grant commissions to the officers, they both express'd a desire to be honor'd with those of Colonel. Mr. Conolly went

---

* The Rt. Hon. Thomas Conolly was M.P. for Londonderry County and a Privy Councillor for Ireland.

into the North, from whence he was to transmit me a list of gentlemen desirous of having inferior commissions, and the Duke said he would speak to his friends upon the same line. From that time his Grace has been totaly silent with respect to the measure, and Mr. Conolly wrote me a letter from the North declining the idea. During his residence there he engag'd in those societys and contributed very much to give them some systematical military regulations.

I have been assur'd that in different parts of Ireland several have taken the oaths and that more are inclin'd to it, but also that there are some companies whose principles are determindly republican.

It concerns me to hear from every quarter that more corps are forming, as whatever may be their professions and avow'd principles they are in general so independent of their ostensible leaders, that tho' sober people reluctantly speak out, they are in fact very uneasy respecting the line of conduct which the spirit of the moment may induce them to adopt.

One very serious regulation is introducing in some of them, that of appointing their officers by rotation. (*Draft.*)

EARL OF BUCKINGHAMSHIRE to LORD GEORGE GERMAIN.

(*Private.*)

1779, November 18.—I should rather judge that your Lordship's information with respect to the Prime Serjeant's° having assign'd my want of plan as a reason for his retreat was not strictly founded. But if he drop'd any expression of that tendency, it must have alluded to England's not holding out any specifick plan of commercial concessions, &c. He hinted his intention of retiring about the 20th July, just at the moment of Sir R. Heron's return, previous to which no system for the opening of the sessions could have been fix'd, and with respect to that system the Prime Serjeant would have been with reason disgusted if he had not been principaly concern'd in the digesting of it. He had long been alarm'd at the difficultys with which Government was surrounded, and did not feel his resolution equal to the resisting popular clamour and Parliamentary abuse. I do not recollect the mentioning to your Lordship his having advis'd me so long as May last to sollicit my recall. Some of the Irish Gentlemen, who profess attachment to Government either are or affect to be frightened at the general distraction and mutinous disposition of the times, and are politically inclin'd to justify their unsteadiness at my expence, that when publick tranquillity is restor'd they may preserve a claim of basking in the sunshine of a new Government.

The Attorney General † and Mr. Foster ‡ remain firm, the Provost, with whom they cannot be prevail'd upon frankly to

---

* Rt. Hon. Walter Hussy Burgh, M.P. for University of Dublin.

† John Scott, Attorney General for Ireland since 1777, and Privy Councillor, afterwards Ld. Clonmell, and Chief Justice.

‡ John Foster, M.P. for Louth and made a Privy Councillor in this year. (*See* 14th Report, Hist. MSS. p. 160.)

communicate is disgusted, and seems to be angling for popularity.
Three most important dispatches remain unnotic'd, and a letter
this morning receiv'd, mentions that Lord North and Mr. Robinson
were both in the country upon the 13th. If within two days no
instructions are sent me, it will become necessary to form some
decision with the best advice I can obtain to prevent a confusion
which otherwise may become irremediable. The Attorney
General has a guard still at his house, but every means is taken
to give the most immediate check to any disturbance. In justice
to Mr. Beresford and several others, their disposition to co-
operate with the measures of Government should be notic'd,
but I fear the number is most inconsiderable compared with
those who avow an intention of espousing the measure of a
Short Money Bill. (*Draft*.)

EARL OF BUCKINGHAMSHIRE to LORD GEORGE GERMAIN.

(*Private*.)

1780, Jan^ry 10.—During my three years Irish residence, in the
number of letters with which your indulgence has favord me, I
never trac'd one line which, to my conviction, was not dictated
by friendship. Before the receipt of your last, I had in a most
secret dispatch stated to Lord North my sentiments with respect
to what measures might be most expedient for securing the
immediate objects of Government. At a crisis when not only a
majority but something bordering upon unanimity in Parliament
is called for to overawe turbulent spirits without doors, I could
not risque sending a plan to be generaly communicated to his
Majesty's servants. It is my duty at this instant to muzzle if
practicable the illhumor of every individual.

There are of those here and from hence holding a different
language who are not totaly unattended to in England. Could I
have two hours deliberate conversation with your Lordship and
Lord North, I would undertake to convince you of the indiscretion
of their ideas and the interested motives which dictate them.
When this sessions is expir'd, which I am of opinion may end
happily, and the day comes when a more peaceable situation will
allow leisure to those in whose hands his Majesty's Government
may be trusted to form an Administration upon an extensive
plan, business may be conducted with more certainty, yet
increasing as the claims of individuals are upon Government, I
scarcely can conceive how it will be possible to secure a decided
majority by that best tie, their own emolument.

If assurances are to be depended upon the business of Government will be carryd through, and any peevish questions parryd
by respectable numbers; as however it is not possible for me to
form a conclusive judgment, my mind does not know a moment's
tranquillity.

You scarcely can conceive the various torments which I
experience from jealousy, incredulity, confidence abus'd, distrust,
and inconsistency, the divisions and sub-divisions of connection;
a gentleman will act in concert with one man as to a particular

object, but oppose him and co-operate with his adversary in another. Two or three letters from England have mention'd an intention to let our Test Bill pass. I know not the circumstance which would so much contribute to quiet the spirit of the most dangerous body in this Kingdom as that measure's being fairly understood. You will see from authentic minutes of speeches in Parliament deliver'd when the resolutions were voted, that many of the respectable country gentlemen have held very temperate language. You cannot but as much approve of the sentiments of Mr. H. Burgh upon that occasion as you may justly have arraigned them upon others. Lord Macartney has just left me, he returns in two days to England where he will deliver his ideas respecting the present state of this Kingdom. (*Draft.*)

Welbore Ellis[*] to the Earl of Buckinghamshire.

1780, January 15.—(Informing him of the death of Hans Stanley.[†]) I know how deeply this event will affect you, as I well know the sincere friendship which subsisted between you, Lord Cadogan, Mr. d'Oyly, and myself. Yesterday we opened his Will, wherein we found, that he has appointed your Lordship, Mr. Brathwaite, and an attorney of Southampton, Trustees.

. . . . . .

I beg leave to congratulate your Excellency on the happy effects of the late measures in Ireland. I am not, however, I must confess, without some fears, while I observe such heavy clouds on the horizon which portend a storm. I persuade myself, that your Excellency is too experienced a State pilot to be lulled into security by the present fallacious appearance.

Lord. Cadogan to the Same.

1780, Jany. 15. Whitehall.—It is a most painfull task to disturb your present happiness with an account of one of the most shocking events in private life that ever happened. Our poor friend Stanley has follow'd his father's example and is no more. I thought it doubly my duty to write to your Lordship not only as one of his most intimate friends, but as I find your name as one of his trustees for carrying his will into execution. He has left everything to his sisters for their lives and after both their deaths he has given his moity of our joint Chelsea property to me ; his moity of his Welch estate to Mr. Rice, who stood in the same predicament with him there (but being dead is, I conclude, a lapse legacy) and has given Sloane all his Hampshire and other properties, who is to take the name and arms of Stanley when the contingency takes place. He has left some legacies and among them £200 to your Lordship, and has provided for a natural son of his now at sea. His personal estate

* Welbore Ellis, M.P. for Weymouth and Melcombe Regis, and a Privy Councillor, was brother-in-law to Hans Stanley.
† The Rt. Honble. Hans Stanley, Cofferer of the Household, Governor of the Isle of Wight and M.P. for Southampton, etc.

will about answer the demands upon it but rather deficient for that purpose. There are no Executors so that Mrs. Ellis and Mrs. D'Oyly must take out administration.

I really, my dear Lord, have not yet recover'd myself enough to add much more except that all parties seem satisfied with the distribution of his affairs. His loss you will deplore as much as any of us. He died at Althorp and left me at Caversham but a few days ago in the greatest appearance of health and tranquillity of mind I ever saw.

Lord Macartney to the Earl of Buckinghamshire.

1780, January 21. Charles Street, Berkeley Square.—As far as I can observe, it appears to me that the Administration here expect an absolute certainty of your Excellency's being able to finish the Session with honour and success. They are fully persuaded, I believe, that you will do every thing that you possibly can for that purpose, but I don't think they will be satisfied, if after all that has been done for Ireland, there should now seem the smallest chance of any defeat or miscarriage in your Parliament. As your Excellency did me the honor of talking to me very confidentially I shou'd ill repay your goodness, if I did not give you my sincere opinion in return. If you venture to meet the Parliament and any constitutional question should be carried against you, they will never forgive you for risking it, they will consider it as a dissolution of Government and every mischief and ill consequence that follow from it will be laid at your Excellency's door. Therefore, my dear Lord, put nothing to the hazard. Get a majority to pledge themselves to you and to one another, or don't meet them. You have been deceived once already, and you will not be excused, if deceived a second time. I must entreat you to pardon me for taking this liberty, it can proceed from no possible motive but my regard for your Excellency and my wishes for your ease and reputation. I have not had the good fortune of finding Lord George Germain at home altho' I called twice at his door. I have seen Lord North and Lord Hillsborough but once, being obliged to confine myself for these three days past with a severe cold and sore throat. Lord N. and Lord H. told me that they had fully answered the letters which you mentioned to me. Should your Excellency have any commands for me I shall be happy to execute them to the best of my power.

Welbore Ellis to the Same.

1780, Jany. 27.—(Referring further to the death and testamentary dispositions of Hans Stanley.)

I beg leave to congratulate your Excellency on the very important success of Sir G. Rodney by the capture made of the Spanish sixty-four gun ship, five frigates and nine other transports loaded with victual and naval stores. Three of them are as I understand arrived at Plymouth, the rest are said to have been left off the Lizard, but the wind blowing still fresh at last they have not been able to come up the Channel. Sir George has taken the Spanish man-of-war and some of the victuallers with him; those with naval stores are the ships which are expected.

[COLONEL the HON^BLE.] WILLIAM GORDON to the EARL OF BUCKINGHAMSHIRE.

1780, Jan^ry 29. London.—I had the honor to receive your Lordship's most obliding letters, and can assure you that in whatever rank I may return to Ireland, it shall be my constant study to do everything in my power to forward his Majesty's service. It makes me extreemely happy to hear the 81st do their duty in such a manner as to deserve your approbation. Good news is expected soon from Sir Henry Clinton, he is gone with a large body of troops to Charlestown, and General Leslie with another corps is gone to James's River, so that if Lord Cornwallis can keep Washington at bay, we have reason to expect success. It is not certain that Pensacola is taken. As I know much of your Lordship's time must be at present taken up with business of importance, I beg you would not think of giving yourself the trouble of answering my letter, I beg to present my respects to Lady Buckingham. In the name of my Highlanders, I return her Ladyship a thousand thanks for the favourable opinion she is pleased to have of them.

HANS SLOANE° to THE SAME.

1780, March 12. London.—I am satisfied no one of Mr. Stanley's friends has felt more deeply the great loss we have all had in his decease, than your Lordship. It has broke in upon that centre of union in Privy Garden, which having been so long a sure place of frequent meetings of mutual friends, makes his loss irreparable to us all. Such a multitude of affairs arising from this misfortune has fallen to my lot to attend and arrange, that knowing at the same time the alarming intricacy of all political matters on your side the water, made me postpone breaking in one moment on your time so fully engaged as it has lately been. Happy I am, as one of your Irish subjects, to flatter myself, that I begin now to see some hope of a calm, which I was afraid was so endangered in Ireland, as to threaten more dreadful consequences to the State than any foreign foe. Your Lordship's wise and prudent administration during this critical period, has given some warm Irish Patriots time to reflect, that it were better to rest satisfied with the advantages allready secured to their commerce, than pursue other points, which might draw on great objections in future. It is time for Ireland to repose from all her own internal commotions, and look at this country, where a plan originally and undoubtedly commencing on ideas of a job for the General Election, may

---

* M.P. for Southampton and a Commissioner of the Board of Trade.

probably grow to such a magnitude, that none but the most desperate would wish for, and that the great independent country gentlemen should by their interposition prevent. These considerable individuals do however at this moment of expectation of a dissolution of Parliament, stand on such tender ground from the popular meetings in their respective counties, as to leave the great body of them no choice as to their immediate conduct in the House. It becomes therefore a doubt what parts of Burke's bill may, or may not pass in the Committee.

Our foreign enemies are the least of any to be dreaded. France, by what I hear, is not likely to make any great figure in the Channell. Her present preparations at Brest indicate great and distant detachments, one of which of no small magnitude with a considerable body of troops is conjectured to be destined for North America, and is expected to sail soon.

Every account which has been so lately brought by our fleet from Gibraltar, confirm the detestation of the Spaniards to the war, which prevails universally but in the Cabinet at Madrid.

(Concludes with a request for patronage for a Mr. McGuire.)

Earl of Buckinghamshire to Lord George Germain.

(*Private.*)

1780, April 22.—My several dispatches to Lord Hillsborough will have stated our late Parliamentary transactions, the meritorious zeal of the Attorney General whose situation particularly requir'd his refuting the doctrines advanced by Mr. Grattan produc'd many disagreeable declarations which gave time for the suggestion of Mr. Burgh's insidious amendment and tended to lessen a majority which otherwise might have been more decided.

Mr. Burgh is supposed to have taken his amendment from a hint which fell from Mr. Flood. The Provost and his sons with some others under obligations to Government voted in the minority. The merit and the gratitude of the two gentlemen mentioned is so conspicuous that it would be derogatory to the conspicuous propriety of their conduct to couple them with meaner delinquents.

The question of the Mutiny Bill is in its consequences the most serious which could have been brought forward. It was incumbent upon me to submit the opinions deliver'd at our select meeting, but I do not feel myself in any degree equal to the forming a decided judgment of my own.

Several gentlemen who had formaly pledged themselves to support Government voted in the minority last Wednesday, which, together with the circumstance of many individuals concealing their sentiments makes it difficult for me to assert what may be the event of the attack upon Poyning's Law. How can the Lord Lieutenant speak with confidence upon any point at a period when no fix'd principle directs, no obligations attach and no assurances can bind? Every inconvenience must necessarily be increased from the distracted state of the Mother Country;

the doubts of the stability of the English Administration cannot but lessen the authority of those who act under them. I this morning put my name to a dispatch which, from the different people consulted who each suggested some new hint or variation in terms, appears to me a most disgracefull performance ; to have digested it would have caused some delay and indeed the essentialy varying expressions offer'd upon so nice a subject might have been taking too much upon myself. I think it clearly conveyed the transaction of the meeting and the necessity of my receiving immediate instructions.

The delay of determination with respect to the Irish Commercial business keeps back our supplys which, otherwise, are going on very well. No letters come to me from England, so that my conjectures from the newspapers and the communications from persons who affect to receive regular details of ministerial secrets, are my only documents for the forming any judgment of the situation of English Administration, my country and my Sovereign. I cannot help selecting from many circumstances which tend to weaken my situation in Parliament that of my having receiv'd private information of the Provost's having asserted that a modification of Poyning's Law would not be disagreeable in England.

(*Draft.*)

EARL OF BUCKINGHAMSHIRE to LORD GEORGE GERMAIN.

(*Private.*)

1780, May 22ᵈ· [Dublin.]—My official dispatch to Lord Hillsborough upon the subject of the Mutiny Bill was in a great measure drawn from the sentiments of those gentlemen whom I deem'd it incumbent upon me to consult. But so far from having shewn any disposition or the least inclination to transmit a proposition of that tendency, I have not omitted any opportunity of inforcing the inexpediency of it and the very fatal consequences which might attend the pressing forward so material a constitutional innovation. At a general meeting yesterday of the principal officers of the crown and the gentlemen of most distinguish'd influence, I stated my last instructions from Lord Hillsborough, express'd in the most forcible terms my wish to oppose a Mutiny Bill, and, after earnestly requesting the support of all the friends of English Government, immediately withdrew, as conceiving that no further deliberation was admissible. Indeed, your Lordship will receive the copy of a letter which I this morning sent to the Speaker, it may convince you that there is no remissness on my part.

There is scarcely a doubt of the Bills being admitted, but possibly the remonstrances which have been inforced, and the apprehensions which have been express'd, may determine its being model'd into something not very exceptionable. Tho' it has not been particularly mark'd to me except through Mr. Sackville Hamilton, the late conduct of the Irish Nation must be so deservedly reprobated in England, that private correspondence will necessarily have circulated it pretty generally here.

There exists that indisposition in all the men of abilities to act in cordial concert, that every proceeding in Parliament is in a degree uncertain. I am also oblig'd continualy to conceal re-sentment, for the purpose of carrying the business of Government through the session; when it is concluded, divested from any resentment of my own, or any apprehension of that of others, I shall state the merits and misconduct of gentlemen in and out of office, and recommend with firmness and impartiality such arrangements as may give a more consistent strength to H. M. Irish Government than the particular fatality of the times and the insanity of individuals has lately admitted of.

(*Draft*.)

Sir J. Irwine to the Earl of Buckinghamshire.

1780, May 23. Jermyn St. . . .—I should have made the best use I could of the succession you proposed to have made on the vacancy occasioned by Col. Lascelles' removal, but it was settled before I last wrote. I fancy I forgot to say that Col. Lascelles sold his Lieut.-Colonelcy and the whole succession goes by purchase. Your Excellency will perceive by various ways that this country is at last returning to its senses, and business going on in the House of Commons in the old way. I believe we shall conclude Mr. Bushe's bill today, and I take for granted Mr. Dunning's Committee will be closed on Friday next.

H. T. Clements[*] to the Same.

1780, May 26.—Is persuaded " that every well wisher to H. M.'s Government, your Excellency's administration and the welfare and the happiness of the two Kingdoms must ardently contribute to obtain the Bill for Mutiny and Desertion, now to be framed."

William Burton [†] to the Same.

1780, May 26. Treasury.—From the time that the question of a Mutiny Bill has been agitated I have had but one opinion, that of the necessity of passing it, from this obvious reason, that the execution of every part of the British Act subjects those concerned to the prosecution and trial by Jury. The shape that may be deemed most admissible is certainly that which will be adopted by every well-wisher to the wellfare of Great Britain and Ireland. My wishes to assist Your Excellency's Administration (if there could be any additional incentive) induce me to act upon that principle.

---

[*] Henry Theophilus Clements, M.P. for Leitrim, Deputy Vice-Treasurer of Ireland and Privy Councillor since 1777. He was also Deputy Constable of Dublin Castle.

[†] The Rt. Hon. William Burton, M.P. for Ennis, and a Privy Councillor. He held also the office of Teller of the Exchequer.

EARL OF GRANARD to the EARL OF BUCKINGHAMSHIRE.

1780, June 2.—I esteem myself extremely fortunate that I have it in my power to give so early a proof of my respect and attachment to His Majesty and His Government, and I feel myself much indebted to Your Excellency for pointing out that method which enables me to express by my present conduct those sentiments. Since your Excellency thinks it desirable for His Majesty's service that Mr. S. Hamilton should be in Parliament at this juncture I shall delay gratifying the dictate of private friendship to return him for the now vacant seat in my Borough of St. Johnstown. . . .

(*Copy.*)

SIR FRANCIS DRAKE to THE SAME.

1780, June 3. London.—Relating to his having parted with his estates at Beeralston, and to his having long brought into Parliament " a gentleman of Lord Buckinghamshire's recommendation."

EARL OF BUCKINGHAMSHIRE to LORD GEORGE GERMAIN.

· (*Private.*)

1780, June 8.—(Desiring an answer to his despatch which accompanies the Heads of a Bill respecting the regulation of the Army in Ireland, which were brought up from the House of Commons.)

No new occurrence deserving particular communication has happen'd since my last, the appointment, however, of Lord Charlemont by many of the Northern Volunteer Companys to act as their Reviewing General, do's not imply a very affectionate disposition to Government, as it was not possible for them to have made a more offensive choice. This circumstance will be far from pleasing to Mr. Conolly, but he prudentialy means to decline shewing any dissatisfaction, and purposes to be present at the Derry Races as usual.

The delay of intelligence from Charlestown, the general disapprobation signifyd by Sir G. Rodney relative to the conduct of his Fleet (which seems indeed to be so general as to prove too much), the imperfect rumors which have reached me of the Riot raised by that madman G. Gordon, added to my feelings with respect to those material Irish Measures which still remain undecided, keep my spirits in unceasing agitation. If the Protestant tumult was as serious as some letters received here represent, I cannot but imagine that either the English Messenger who arriv'd yesterday, or the post would have brought me a line upon the subject. Lady Crosby seems in great health and spirits, my daughter is happy in enjoying a considerable proportion of her society.

(*Draft.*)

GEORGE BYNG [*] to the EARL OF BUCKINGHAMSHIRE.

1780, June 9. Wrotham Park.—Tho' I received your very kind letter on Tuesday, I have not felt my mind at rest sufficient even to return you my grateful thanks. The miserable situation of the town, the irresolution of the Many, the indecision of those in power, left every body at the mercy of the Mob, not formidable in my opinion from their numbers, but from the want of knowing what to do in those with whom the power was lodged.

You will have heard from other hands the damages done, they are great, but to one who thinks the whole might have been prevented by the least prudential forsight, I am wild to think that so much weakness should have been discovered to the people with so much real strength at hand. Lord Rockingham's house was threatened, I set up both Tuesday and Wednesday night as one of its weak defenders, had they come there as they threatened instead of going to Lord Mansfield's, I believe they would in some measure have been quieted, by meeting such a resistance as would have marked out to them how easily a house may be defended. The House of Commons adjourning yesterday, and a considerable military force marching in to town made my presence no longer necessary so I returned here, mortified to the greatest degree at the sight of the two most detestable extremes, a lawless mob, and a Military Government.

Tho' I was the first in the House to attack Lord G. Gordon, yet I have not heard the least intimation of any attack on my house, it would have fell an easy, undefended prey as I thought more of my friends than for myself.

Do give my love to Lady Buckingham, accept my unfeigned thanks.

EARL OF HILLSBOROUGH to THE SAME.

(*Private and Secret.*)

1780, June 11. St. James's.—I should not have failed to have given your Excellency constant accounts of the dreadful and unaccountable Insurrection which for four days together has made such devastation in this town, and threatened not less than the total destruction of it, and even the subversion of the Government, but that I really have not had time sufficient to write any letter but such as were absolutely necessary, and I have been the less uneasy on this head, because I knew that our friend Lord Barrington wrote to you every night the accounts he had received from me. He is gone out of town today, and I therefore acquaint your Excellency that this day has been quiet and has been employed in stating the evidence against Lord George Gordon, who, your Excellency knows was yesterday committed to the Tower, and against many other prisoners, and in discovering and taking many of the rioters. I most sincerely hope, and have reason to believe that the military have at last put an end to this disturbance. The Parliament is adjourned to

* M.P. for Middlesex.

Monday se'ennight, till which time I believe we shall remain on our guard. I think it fit to inform your Excellency that Lord George Gordon, in the course of his examination yesterday, informed us that he had received a letter from the Protestants in and near Killarney in Ireland, desiring his Lordship's advice how they should behave, as they were under great apprehensions from the Papists in that part. This I believe his Lordship disclosed without consideration, and it is very probable he has correspondents in different parts of that kingdom, which will make it necessary for your Excellency to be very attentive to this subject, lest disturbances should also break out on your side, for I apprehend it would totally destroy poor Ireland to have a contest about Religion, superadded to those with which we are threatened about the Constitution.

Earl of Hillsborough to the Earl of Buckinghamshire.

1780, June 15. St. James's.—I have the pleasure to inform your Excellency that since my last the riots and disturbances that had almost threatened the dissolution of Government and the destruction of this city have happily subsided. Our jails are full of criminals, but they are all of the lowest rank of the people, except Lord G. Gordon, who will probably suffer. The King goes to the House on Monday to give us a speech upon these matters.

I congratulate your Excellency with all my heart upon the very important and decisive success of Sir H. Clinton, the Extraordinary Gazette I have the honour to enclose will relate it to you. During our commotions no business but what related to them could go on, we shall now resume our attention.

Sir John Irwine to the Same.

1780, June 15. Jermyn Street.—I most sincerely congratulate your Excellency on the important news brought this morning by Lord Lincoln of the taking Charlestown with 7,000 men prisoners by Sir Henry Clinton, suffering no more than two officers killed, very few wounded, and under 200 killed and wounded private. Lord George, who is gone to the Cabinet, has left orders for a Gazette to be sent to your Excy. as soon as it can be printed. I hope it will come out before the post goes off. This news has thrown a great damp on the dissaffected, and was proclaimed by the guns and *feu de joye* of all the troops in the camps and several parts of the town.

Charles Town.

Taken :—

7 Ships and 3 French Frigates.
500 Pieces of Cannon.
1 General.
6 Brigadier Generals.
16 Colonels.

22 Lt.-Colonels.
25 Majors.
114 Captains.
250 Subalterns.
120 Staff.
4,200 Rank and File.
900 Sailors.
900 Militia.

6,554 in all surrender'd at discretion.
12th May, loss of 200 British.
All the Continental Troops released on parole.
7 Privateers carried into New York.
8,000 Rations were issued daily.⁕

[MAJOR] RICHARD VYSE to the EARL OF BUCKINGHAMSHIRE.

1780, June 16. Lichfield.—I left London on Tuesday evening, and have the satisfaction to inform your Excellency that everything was at that time perfectly quiet. As I take it for granted you have received the most authentic intelligence with respect to everything that has lately happened at that place, I will not trouble you with a detail of circumstances as execrable as extraordinary, and which never could have happened at all but for the pusillanimity or design of two or three blundering or treacherous magistrates. If proper enquiries are made, much good may arise out of evil ; if they are not made, or an ill-timed lenity arrests the course of justice, the confusion which has happened is but the beginning of misfortune. I am happy to have it in my power to inform your Excellency that all the reports which have been most industriously circulated in this country of insurrections and riots in many different counties, are entirely, except Bath, without foundation. It is true that a riot has happened at Nottingham, and that a detachment of the Blue Horse marched this morning from hence to that place in consequence of it, but this was entirely owing to a drunken quarrel between the soldiers quartered there and the people of the town, which happened so long ago as the fourth of June, and has no connection at all with anything that has happened at any other place. All the trading towns in this part of England have orders for more business than they can possibly execute, and are at present in the most perfect state of tranquillity. Give me leave to congratulate your Excellency on the success of our arms at Charles Town. The enclosed is an account which I have just received from London. As no Gazette was published when it left that place, you possibly may not yet have seen it. The following is part of a letter which I received some days ago from my friend Sir. Jos. Yorke, dated Hague May 26th, and which is of too comfortable a nature for me to omit transcribing it to your Excellency. " The last

---

⁕ Enclosed in the following letter.

twelve months have been so full of remarkable events that one's head has been ready to turn every minute. I have had, and still have, my share of the bustle, but as I never ceased to think and say, so I have now the satisfaction to see, that England is equal to it all, and that in spite of foreign and domestick foes, she has a fair chance of rising superior to all her difficulties, with the hopes of which I am not a little happy. I can assure you that our reputation rises every day in Europe, whilst our enemies grow sick of the contest. My friend Lord Buckingham's task has been a very difficult one, he has conducted himself nobly, and will I still think see his labours crowned with success; nobody honours him more, or wishes him better than I do."

I did myself the honour of calling upon the young ladies in Bond Street the morning I left London, in hopes that I might have had the pleasure of informing your Excellency that I had seen them well, but I was disappointed by their being in the country.

Wm. Short to the Earl of Buckinghamshire.

1780, June 21.—Referring to a dispute between Lord Buckinghamshire and Sir Francis Drake.

Earl of Hillsborough to the Earl of Buckinghamshire (Lord Lieutenant).

1780, July 5. St. James's.—I most sincerely congratulate with your Excellency upon the good news in the Extraordinary Gazette I have the honour to enclose to you. I trust the rebellion and war draws to a conclusion. Nine of our rioters are this day ordered for execution, and many more will be convicted. Lord George Gordon is I understand to be indicted and tryed in Surrey before the special commission, but I can't tell when.

Earl of Buckinghamshire to Lord George Germain.

(Private.)

1780, July 8.—The late scenes of confusion and the important events in America, tho' of a very different cast, will fully account for your having omitted rather longer than usual giving me those flattering proofs of that obliging attention, which is one of my most essential comforts in a situation requiring many.

My expectations with respect to the Sugar Bill never went further than that middle term which your letter gives me reason to expect and I would willingly persuade myself that it will give satisfaction at least to such as any concessions can satisfy.

The Bill for the Regulation of the Army, &c., has amongst my many difficultys been the heaviest. During the time of its agitation in the House of Commons, my letters from Office treated the subject very generaly, and to my understanding, not very explicitly. Nor has any most distant hint of specify'd Amendment reach'd me, except that the Cabinet had objected to the words *during the continuance of this Act.* In consequence of that hint an unavailing attempt to remove the difficulty was made in the Privy Council. Your Lordship must, however, understand that any alteration tending to make the Bill perpetual would never be admitted in the Irish Parliament; such at least is the opinion of all those who have come within the scope of my consultation. If other material amendments had occur'd to me which could have been rendered palatable, they would certainly have been propos'd. This will naturaly account for my not suggesting any to his Majesty's Ministers in a measure upon the decision of which the tranquillity of this Kingdom and the existence of his Majesty's Army in Ireland may ultimately depend. It would be extreme rashness to pledge myself for the conduct of a House of Commons where there prevails so much suspicion, so much uncertainty, and such a particular capacity of eccentrical distinction. The general cast of the foreign intelligence with which you favour me is most agreeable, and I derive no little degree of satisfaction from the mortification of his Prussian Majesty whom I have ever dislik'd, not only as a determin'd enemy to England, but as a character equaly detestable in political and in private life. Whoever investigates the whole tenor of his conduct will scarcely discover any one act which indicated the most distant feelings of humanity. If the old connection between the House of Austria and the Court of Petersburg could be renewed, and England, as formerly, stood the bond of that connection, the adventitious strength which Russia has obtain'd since the accession of the present Empress, would enable such a union completely to chèck the restless ambition of France back'd by the insidious enmity of Frederick the 3rd (*sic*). The idea of Russia never offers itself without my lamenting the oeconomy of the English Treasury during the year 1764; as it render'd ineffectual a negotiation, which, most honourable to me, would have prov'd materially usefull to my country.[*] It could not indeed but have given a different cast to every political transaction in which England has since that time been engag'd. The House of Commons was this day further adjourn'd to Monday the 24th.

(*Draft.*)

EARL OF BUCKINGHAMSHIRE to LORD GEORGE GERMAIN.

(*Private.*)

1780, Aug. 1.—When you look at the date of this letter you will not wonder at my being rather mortify'd from the circumstance of my not having receiv'd a single line respecting the important Irish business (as yet undetermin'd) since your Lordship's of the first of the last month.

A letter from Mr. Cotterel to Sir Richard Heron, signifying that the remainder of the Irish business was defer'd without fixing

---

[*] Lord Buckinghamshire failed in that year to carry a Treaty of Alliance with Russia, which was proposed by the English Government to Catherine II.

any particular day, has made it necessary for me to dispatch a messenger with official letters to Lord Hillsborough and Lord North.

I am persuaded that the reasons which determin'd the Cabinet to this delay were sufficiently cogent, but the circumstance distresses me for the present and alarms me for the future.

A feverish attack has sensibly affected me for the last two or three days, which the actual situation of my mind is by no means calculated to remedy.

(*Draft.*)

LORD LOUGHBOROUGH[*] to the EARL OF BUCKINGHAMSHIRE.

1780, Augt. 27. Lancaster.—Your goodness for me will have suggested the only reason that could excuse my delaying to express the strong sense I have of your kind remembrance of me. The change of my situation took place at a moment so singular that I found myself at once engaged in business to which I was so totally unaccustomed, that the anxiety if not the occupation of it never left me one moment. The first prospect I have perceiv'd at this place (the last upon my circuit) of being disengaged, I have taken up the pen to assure your Lordship how much your favourable opinion exalts me in my own, and how much I prize every testimony of your esteem. I trust I may congratulate you upon the happy conclusion of a Session in the beginning of which it was impossible that your friends should not feel great anxiety for the uncommon difficultys of your Lordship's situation, in the progress of which they have found much more room for congratulation to your Lordship and by your means to the publick.

EARL OF BUCKINGHAMSHIRE to LORD GEORGE GERMAIN.

1780, Sep. 16. Dublin Castle.—As your Lordship cannot entertain a doubt of the weight of your applications with me, I may with less scruple declare that from old acquaintance and friendship the recommendation of Lord Townshend could not want any adventitious interposition. But the number of gentlemen whose names I already stand pledg'd to submit to his Majesty upon the list of Peerage is so considerable as very possibly may be disapprov'd; and the adding a gentleman, however honourable and respectable, whose claims were all long prior to my connection with this Kingdom, may embarrass the whole, and would, with reason, disgust many to whom I have refus'd that favor, tho' I stand personaly oblig'd to them for supporting his Majesty's Government through the late difficultys.

* Alexander Wedderburne, H.M.'s Attorney General, was created Lord Chief Justice of the Court of Common Pleas in June, 1780, and immediately afterwards Lord Loughborough, Baron of Loughborough.

EARL OF BUCKINGHAMSHIRE to LORD GEORGE GERMAIN.

(*Private.*)

1780, Sep'. 16.—Your two letters of the 11th were receiv'd this morning. From your not mentioning mine of the 2d and 5th they probably had not then reach'd you, which obviously arises from the easterly winds, which of late have been very prevalent. My most affectionate attachment to your Lordship has made the omission with respect to Col. Tonson a distressing weight upon my heart; that business must be settled, at any rate, to your satisfaction.

My latest informations tell me that the disposition to tumult in Dublin daily subsides, some foolish resolutions may be publish'd, but they will be counteracted by every man of discretion and property. If they reach England they should only be consider'd as the fermentation of a wretched faction supported by a few interested individuals and an abandon'd rabble.

The numbers of applications, remonstrances and representations which have been shower'd upon me from the idea of my immediate recall, has prevented me from enjoying one moment's tranquillity since the Prorogation, but I will now hope that the great brunt is nearly over.

To speak confidentialy with respect to Lord Townshend, he has not the least claim upon me. We have liv'd upon very good terms in society, but our county politicks have ever been most adverse.

The idea of his Lordship carry's me into Norfolk, and induces me to mention that the uniform determination of every Administration without exception for these last thirty years to depress my family and to exalt the Townshends and Walpoles has produc'd the present situation. Repeated slights determin'd me to shew that I did not deserve them and was the occasion of their having two enemies Members for that County instead of two friends;[*] an evil which at this time their efforts could not remedy nor could I, unprovok'd, oppose those whom I had encourag'd originaly to stand a contest. With respect to Norwich there scarcely exist the man whom I less esteem than Sir H——— H———, his situation at Norwich was my act, and he has repaid me by accumulated ingratitude, it is unnecessary to add my indifference respecting his election.

Mr. Thurlow[†] in my opinion, may stand a worse chance from his sudden attack than if he had proceeded more regularly. Had I been in Norfolk my brother might have profited by the confusion.

(*Draft.*)

THE SAME to THE SAME.

(*Private.*)

1780, Oct' 7.—The receiving his Majesty's commands to order the 3d, 19th and 30th Regiments to be immediately prepar'd for

---

* Astley, De Grey and Coke had represented the county in Parliament from March. 1768, to the date of this letter.

† Mr. John Thurlow was an unsuccessful candidate for the representation of Norwich in 1780.

foreign service most seriously alarm'd me. Mature reflection and communication with the very few whom at this time there is an opportunity of seeing, has rather increas'd than lessened my apprehensions. Sir John Irvine, who last night return'd from our little encampment, feels more strongly upon the subject than myself, and your Lordship must be sensible of the consequences which may arise from the withdrawing three form'd regiments, one of which consists almost entirely of Englishmen, to be replac'd by three nominal corps to be recruited here, and who perhaps may not altogether in the course of a twelve-month amount to half an effective batallion. Possibly these considerations may not have suggested themselves to his Majesty's Ministers from the multiplicity of objects under their deliberation, and the immediate exigencys which may have arisen from the circumstances of the war. As in my local situation I stand in some degree responsible for any measure which may affect that part of his Majesty's Dominions committed to my care, I hope my having submitted ideas similar to the above in a private official letter to Lord Hillsborough will not be thought officious or unbecoming.

EDWARD TIGHE[a] to the EARL OF BUCKINGHAMSHIRE.

1780, Oct. 19. Bath.—Congratulations on his release from a most arduous situation in which however his conduct has merited and obtained universal applause and has astonished those who were in any degree acquainted with the nature of his labours.
. . . .

REVD. JOHN ERSKINE[b] to THE SAME.

1780, Oct. 26. Cork.— . . . You are now about to be delivered from a very turbulent scene, in which you have so prudently and worthily perform'd your part; and if I may judge of the sentiments of the nation, from what I hear in this quarter of it, none who have held the reins of Empire for so many years have ever left it with so much solid applause without the shadow of reproach. This will crown you with honour in the sight of all good men, and what is still more valuable, will be a lasting and homefelt comfort in your own breast. . . .

[CAPTAIN] A. CORBETT to THE SAME.

1780, October 31. London.—I received your Excellency's letter of the 24th last night. I did imagine that my Lord Hillsborough had informed your Excellency of the King's pleasure that Lord Carlisle should set out for Ireland the 5th of December, which prevented my giving you more early intelligence. I had the honor of writing to your Excellency last

---

* M.P. for the Borough of Athboy. He had an office in the Irish Court of Exchequer, that of Comptroller of the Pipe.
† Dean of Cork.

night and to Mr. Sackville Hamilton. I dined to-day *tête-à-tête*
with my Lord Carlisle,* and stated to him as from myself the
almost impossibility of your Excellency's arranging your affairs
by the tenth of December, as you had had no answer from Lord
North the 24th of this month.

He told me it was the King's pleasure that he should set out
the 4th of December, Sir George Cornwall is chosen Speaker,
the division was 203 to 134. There is no public news in town,
From what I foresee I take it Mr. Storer will be Lord of Trade in
the room of Mr. Eden, but it is only my conjecture. I am very
glad your Excellency was well entertained in the County of
Wicklow. Mr. George Hobart, I believe, will be in England in
ten days or a fortnight's time.

EARL OF BUCKINGHAMSHIRE to LORD GEORGE GERMAIN.

(*Private.*)

1780, Novr 2.—One short word will fully express my present
feelings, *despair.*

Lord North seem's determin'd upon no measure but that of
expelling me with humiliation and disgrace from this kingdom.

If the next mail do's not bring me a letter from him (as the
hurry of Parliamentary business will after that put his noticing
me entirely out of the question) I shall transmit every part of
the business officially to Lord Hillsborough to be laid before his
Majesty, appealing in some degree to him as a slighted and
insulted servant.

Your favour of the 28th is received and acknowledg'd as a
further testimony of your good will.

(*Draft.*)

A. CORBETT to the EARL OF BUCKINGHAMSHIRE.

1780, Nov. 3. London.—I am sorry to perceive by your
Excellency's letter of the 26th of last month that you think me
wanting in attention in not informing you sooner of Lord
Carlisle's intention of setting out the 5th of December. I took
it for granted that Lord Hillsborough had informed your
Excellency of it, and was much surprised to hear yesterday from
Sir Stanier Porten that they knew nothing at their office of what
time Lord Carlisle was to set out. I feel exceedingly for the
very disagreeable situation your Excellency must be in, in not
hearing from Lord North. He is now exceedingly ill. Mr.
Foster leaves London in a day or two, and I hope he will be able
to give your Excellency some satisfactory information concerning
your arrangements. As your Excellency wishes me to return I
should set out immediately had not Lord Carlisle written to beg
your leave for me to stay with him. . . .

---

* The Earl of Carlisle was appointed in September, 1780, to succeed the Earl of
Buckinghamshire in Ireland. Captain Andrew Corbett was one of his A.D.C.

Sir John Irwine to the Earl of Buckinghamshire.

1780, Nov. 8. Piccadilly.—I have obeyed your Excy's commands to the best of my power by saying every where how extremely distressful it will be to you if on so short notice you should be obliged to leave Ireland, but I fear with very little effect, for I understand it is the King's order to Lord Carlisle that he should be in Ireland as early in December as possible; however my private opinion is that his Lordship will not leave this place so soon as the 5th (as is given out), if he does it will be the greatest inconvenience to him, as he himself told me.

By what Lord George tells me he has observed, I find he thinks your Excy. will find a gracious reception here. Lord North continues confined, so whatever business was in his hands, there it will remain till he is able to go to St. James's. Every body pities you for this delay, but I do not find any body active in endeavouring to relieve you from this disagreeable situation.

Earl of Buckinghamshire to Lord George Germain.
(*Private.*)

1780, Novr. 12.—Five mails which arriv'd together on Friday brought me no information with respect to my arrangements. Mr. Forster has been expected these three days, but in vain, his return will be some species of consolation to me. Rumor insinuates that four of the gentlemen upon my list of New Peers will be rejected; my engagements were fulfill'd in transmitting the recommendations to his Majesty who is the best judge of the propriety of them. A dispatch was sent some few days since to Lord Hillsborough requesting the King's approbation that Lord Carlisle's journey might be postpon'd for a few days till my business could be settled. If this is rejected it will give me the fullest conviction that my slender credit in the closet is ruin'd. Disagreeable truths with respect to the situations and opinions of this Kingdom it has been my unfortunate duty to state, it was not within my ability to induce the Irish to think with me or generaly to adopt that conduct which as a dutifull subject and a good citizen I wish'd to recommend. The conclusion of my administration has however been judg'd to be honourable and meritorious by the world at large, and with every prospect of confusion the tranquility of this Kingdom has been preserv'd. At the moment of my writing those few lines of the 2^d of November, the agitation of my mind had greatly warped my understanding, calmer moments induc'd me to adopt a more temperate conduct as you will observe from my official dispatches. But tho' the warmth of my feelings is smother'd by discretion, yet the interior ferment is still the same. May you, my dear Lord, never experience any thing similar.

P.S. You may have seen in the newspapers that the Volunteers propos'd to escort me at my departure, an offer which I have politely declin'd as I have any marks of their attention upon every occasion.

(*Draft.*)

ROBERT GAMBLE[*] to the EARL OF BUCKINGHAMSHIRE.

1780, Nov. 22. Sackville Street.—(Mr. Secretary Hamilton had communicated to him his Excellency's intention of recommending him and his family to His Majesty.) I cannot conclude this letter without assuring your Excellency that mixing a great deal with the world I receive the most inexpressible pleasure in hearing your Excellency the subject of praise and affection among all ranks of men. When you shall be remov'd to the Royal Presence you will carry with you the most honorable testimony and reward of your virtuous administration, the hearts and affections of a truly grateful people, who will not fail to publish to Europe that your Excellency has been the real friend and patron of Ireland. I shall ever be proud that your Excellency has been pleas'd to think me not unworthy of your attention for speaking the language of my heart.

SIR JOHN IRWINE to THE SAME.

1780, Decr. 2. Piccadilly.— . . . . I do not pretend to enter into the subject of your situation at present. I can only assure your Excy. that no man can feel more about it, and I believe no man has said so much on that head in all places, than I have.

Give me leave to trouble your Excy. with two proposals of Colonel Burgoyne, one for raising, the other for getting together a Regiment of light Dragoons. He has desired me to transmit them to your Excy., which I could not refuse doing; besides I am of opinion that the first of the two proposals (if it was thought necessary) might be useful with some little alteration.

. . . .

As soon as the parliament adjourns, I propose going to the Bath for two or three weeks, where I hope to put my stomach into better repair.

A Packet of 24 Papers relating to the period of Lord Buckinghamshire's Vice-Royalty, Jan. 1777—Dec. 1780, contains the following :—

An address from the Merchants, Traders and others, inhabitants of Dublin upon his arrival.

An address from the Roman Catholics of Ireland on the same occasion.

The Quakers' address, ibid.

The Protestant Dissenters' address, ibid.

Lord Buckinghamshire's enrolment as a Freeman of the City of Cork.

1777, April 11.—Presentation of the Freedom of the City of Dublin conferred on the Earl of Buckinghamshire.

1777, Feb. 20.—Honorary Degree of Doctor of Trinity College, Dublin, conferred 20 February, 1777. Signed by John Hely Hutchinson, Provost.

---

* M.P. for the Borough of Newcastle in Dublin in 1781.

1777, Nov. 19.—Lord Mayor's address.

1778, Feb.—An address praying for Royal Protection to the Fisheries of Ireland.

Division Lists for the years 1777 and 1778. (Errata List).

1778, Feb.—Address from the Trustees of the Linen Manufacture.

1778, Mar. 7.—Address of the Mayor, Sheriffs, etc., of Cork to the Lord Lieutenant.

1778, March 26.—An address praying for preferment for the Rev. Mr. Dean Pery.

A petition against the taxes about to be levied for paving, cleansing and lighting the city of Dublin.

The address of the Lords Spiritual and Temporal on the occasion of war being declared against France.

The election of Lord Buckinghamshire as President to the Lying-In Hospital.

An address from the High Sheriff and Grand Jury of the County of Leytrim.

An address from the Merchants of the City of Dublin, with thanks for Protection from American Privateers.

The Humble Petition of Mary Ann D'Arcy, spinster (attested by Charles Elphin).

1780.—Address of the Freemen and Grand Jury etc. of the County and City of Dublin—(on the occasion of Lord Buckinghamshire's departure).

May, 1776 to 1791.—To the period also of the Earl of Buckinghamshire's Vice-royalty belongs a large correspondence in relation to patronage, and even as late as 1791, eleven years after he had left Ireland, applications were still made to him to use his supposed influence with successive Ministers or Lord Lieutenants. The letters are from the following :—

1776.—Lord Howe (in reply to Lord Buckinghamshire's recommendation of Lt. Drury), the Earl of Suffolk, Mr. Edward Stopford, Earl Ludlow, the Lord Chancellor of Ireland [Lifford,] the Earl of Courtown, Lord Desart, Earl of Cavan, Mr. Caulfield, W. Maxwell, J. Staples, Charles Churchill, the Earl of Clanbrassil, M. O'Bryen [Taplow Court,] the Earl of Radnor.

1777.—Lord Clifford, J. Hatsell, Sir John Irwine, Earl of Coventry, R. Vernon Sadleir, Lord Inchiquin, Capt. E. Fuller, Francis Matthew, Viscount Glerawly, Lord Erne, Lord Glandore, the Earl of Ely, Mrs. Grenville, Viscount Barrington, W. Tonson, the Earl of Oxford, General R. Pierson, Earl of Denbigh.

1778.—Lord Brownlow, R. Worsley, Edward Eliot of Port Eliot, the Earl of Rochford, Lt.-General J. Johnston, the Countess of Kildare, Mr. James Fortescue, Lord Ravensworth, the Archbishop of Dublin, Dr. John Craddock, the Duke of Marlborough, Hans Sloane, Sir John Goodricke, the Archbishop of Cashel, [Dr. Michael Cox,] Sir William Draper, J. Heywood, G. Thornton, the Earl of Clanricarde, the Earl of Lanesborough, R. Rochfort, the Earl of Belvedere, the Marquis of Hertford, the Earl of Guilford, Lord Marchmont, Lord Cadogan, Robert Gamble (to Sir Richard Heron), the Earl of Hardwicke, Mr. Wedderburn, the Bishop of Cork, Sir Wm. Osborne, R. Fitzgerald, the Earl of Shannon, the Duke of Queensbury, the Earl of Bective, the Earl of Ross, Robert Clements, Rev. John Erskine, Sir Michael Cromie, Lord Inniskillen.

1779.—Lord de Vesci, Countess of Massareene, Arthur Pomeroy, "The humble Memorial of Lady Mary and Lady Katherine Butler on behalf of themselves and their four Infant Sisters," Edmund Pery, Col. Brown, Viscount Carlow, Bishop of Killaloe (Dr. Chinnery), Sir Wm. Howe, Mr. Thomas Nesbitt, Earl of Tyrone, Earl of Granard, Lord Amherst, Count de Welderen, C. Turner, the Archbishop of York, Lord Clifden, Major Vyse, Captain Wm. Elliot, Hugh Hill, Col. Sandford, the Earl of Tyrone, the Duke of Leinster, Lord Annaly, the Bishop of Ossory (Newcome).

(1780.)—Edward Hamilton, the Earl of Altamont, Lord Bangor, Thomas Mahon, Lord Crosbie, Robert Jephson, the Countess of Granard, Rt. Hon. W. Brownlow, Lady E. Ponsonby, Lord Walpole, Lt.-Gen. Cunningham, Hon. James Browne, Lord Westport, Dean Woodward [of Clogher], Alderman Henry Bevan, Col. Wm. Burton, Charles Coote (Dean of Kilsenora), Earl of Inchiquin, Lord Chief Baron Ducie, Lord Farnham, Lord Naas, Mr. John O'Niel, Lord Doneraile, Sir Robert Deane, Edward Hunt.

1781.—The Lord Primate of Ireland (Dr. Richard Robinson, of Armagh), Lt. Bolton, Earl of Carlisle, Sir A. Schomberg, Count O'Rourke (to Ld. North), Mr. Paul Canning, Sir R. Palmer, the Rt. Hon. Wm. Eden, the Earl of Sandwich, Lady Roche, James Shiel, Godfrey Green, Sir James Browne, Sir Charles Douglas.

1782.—Capt. (Richard Vere) Drury.

1784.—Capt. H. W. Lacey, (1785) Luke Gardiner, (1786) Anthony King.

1788.—Capt. Sweetman.

1790.—Sir Boyle Roche.

Between 1781 and 1791.—There are draught letters also on this same subject of patronage from the Earl of Buckingham-shire to (1781) Earl of Carlisle, Rt. Hon. W. Eden, Mr. Edward Tighe, the Archbishop of Cashel, Mr. Green, Sir J. Brown, (1783) Lord Altamont, (1785) Luke Gardiner, (1788) Earl Nugent, (1791) P. Tottenham.

DEAN RICHARD WOODWARD° to the EARL OF BUCKINGHAMSHIRE.

1781, Jan. 3. Dublin.—(Reference to some Church patronage.) Nothing new has occurred since you left this kingdom but the phœnomenon of public thanks following a departed Lord Lieutenant, and our newspapers filled with applause instead of abuse. Lord Carlisle was prevented by the gout from making a visit to Castletown on Monday.

---

* Dean of Clogher—made Bishop of Cloyne, 1781, Jan. 20.

LORD HILLSBOROUGH to the EARL OF BUCKINGHAMSHIRE.

1781, Jan. 3. Hanover Square.—Acknowledges his obliging letter, informing him of his safe arrival. Congratulations on his return. "If my Lady Buckingham looks as beautiful as she did on New Year's Day, I pity you."

The EARL OF BUCKINGHAMSHIRE to SIR H. CLINTON.

1781, Jan. 5. London.—I almost doubt if all my letters have reached you, but your candor will attribute it to the circumstances which necessarily render the correspondence between America and the British Islands very uncertain.

The account that we have respecting the situation of the war damp'd those hopes which of late have been too sanguinely entertained in Ireland. It concerns me very seriously that the resources of the Empire cannot supply you with means adequate to the exigencys of the service and your acknowledged ability of exerting them.

Two days only have elapsed since my return to England, and not having as yet seen either my Master or his Ministers you must not expect any authentick information. It has been my good fortune to leave Ireland in peace and prosperity, the goodwill of the Nation attended me to the yatch, and there has been some reason to think that my indefatigable attention may have contributed to dispell that illusion which might possibly have produced events too nearly resembling your unhappy American— write when you can—if Phillips is near you assure him of that affectionate regard which has frequently felt his calamity's.—This will be delivered to you by Wm. Ludlow, son of Lord Ludlow. and nephew of Lord Scarborough; it is without reluctance that I obey Lady Buckingham's command in recommending him to your protection. She is not less your friend than my dear General, yours, etc.

(*Draft.*)

MAJOR RICHARD VYSE to the EARL OF BUCKINGHAMSHIRE.

1781, Jan. 12. Dublin Castle.—Congratulations on his return to his native land after the troubles and fatigues he has suffered. M$^r.$ and M$^{rs.}$ Vyse are about to leave their habitation in the Castle where they had received so much kindness from Lord Buckinghamshire and his family.

THOMAS CONOLLY to THE SAME.

1781, Jany 13. --By your silence about your passage and journey I conclude them both as void of novelty as possible, except that you had been near falling in with the *Royal Chace* on the latter. I have often wish'd myself present at your interview last Wednesday, your prudence might be greater than mine, but certain I am that no truth should escape the King's knowledge that could in any shape give him a right idea of this kingdom, of which I am persuaded he has but a faint one. You owe this to your own character and to both these country's, who I am persuaded will always go hand in hand, unless separated by artful or misinformed servants of the Crown.

Our new Lieutenant came here (his first visit, being confined since you left him with the gout) on fryday and left us this morning. He is very well bred, and easy in his manner, tho' very slack of conversation, not only at his levée, but everywhere. Blaquire° I hear and believe is to have a great share of Mr. Eden's† confidence and is to be a *second Minister*. This will not do, nor ought it, I see it big with evils of all kinds, but I fear Government here will soon be too far enlisted to go back. If anything could warp my principles about supporting Government this would, but I will endeavour to make the best of it, and parry as much mischief as I can. Our gallery is full, some singing, some playing at chess, others at cards, in short making so much noise that I must conclude this with an apology for not digesting its contents better, but as you have excused much nonsense from me before, you will forgive me now.

P.S. Loves to Caroline and dear little Emily.

John Foster to the Earl of Buckinghamshire.

1781, Jan. 21. Collon.—Had great pleasure in hearing from Lord Buckinghamshire that his reception at St. James' was entirely to his satisfaction. "The labours of a difficult administration involved with the subjects of the greatest nicety and embarrassed with every distress peculiar to the times are now rewarded in the approbation of His Majesty joined with the grateful applause of a whole nation."

Sir Henry Clinton to the Same.

1781, Jan. 15 and 22.—Your Lordship may possibly read in our newspapers that the whole Rebel army has revolted. Not so, my dear Lord, but 'tis true that the Pensilvanians have, and I think it likely it will not stop there ; they demand arrears of pay, &c., &c., and to be discharged. I, of course, offer more than Congress can or will give. My offer reached them a day before theirs, General Wayne, etc., were admitted to a Conference with them, but as yet I have received no answer that I can depend upon ; though the army is in motion, I dare not for the present do more than favour the revolt and offer an asylum. One step beyond that might before I know their sentiments alarm their jealousy, mar all, and reunite them to their late tyrants. My situation is critical, W . . n's not less so. I have however all to hope. He, all to fear.

---

*Sir John de Blaquiere, formerly Chief Secretary to Lord Harcourt. The spelling varies.

† William Eden, afterwards Lord Auckland, 1789, Principal Secretary to the Earl of Carlisle, the new Lord Lieutenant, appointed October, 1780.

‡ Wayne, General in command of the Pennsylvanian Line at Morristown.

All will, I doubt not, go well to the southward this winter, as Lord Cornwallis is in great force by the detachments I have made from this army.

Tis said, and I believe it that E. Allen and his Vermonters has joined the Canadian Army. *Enfin* if we are properly reinforced, if we remain superior at sea, and have an active *co-operating* Naval commander, I think rebellion will be staggered in the course of next campaign, without the French should be reinforced also, or these people subsidized with money, but if we are starved, all our golden dreams will vanish. I beg my best respects to the Countess.

22 Jan.—I refer your Lordship to E. Dalrymple. The revolters have been cajolled, they have however carried their point respecting discharge, two thirds have got it. Jersey claims the same and must have it, they are to receive their arrears of pay, etc., in continental bills, 75 for 1. There are now sitting at Trentown three members of Congress, and three sergeants of the Revolters settling matters together.

Your Lordship will conceive the moment is critical. I shall watch it. I rejoice at your return from Ireland after so honourable an administration.

The packet this instant under sail.

(Enclosed with the above are the following printed slips:— I. and II.)

I. 1781, Jan. 7.—'Proposals made to the non-commissioned officers and soldiers of the Pennsylvania Line at Princeton.'

His Excellency, Joseph Reed, Esquire, President, and the Honourable Brigadier General Potter, of the Council of Pennsylvania, having heard the complaints of the soldiers, as represented by the sergeants, inform them, that they are fully authorized to redress reasonable grievances, and they have the fullest disposition to make them as easy as possible ; for which end they propose :—

First. That no non-commissioned officer shall be detained beyond the time for which he freely and voluntarily engaged, but where they appear to have been in any respect compelled to enter or sign, such enlistments to be deemed void and the soldier discharged.

Secondly. To settle who are and who are not, bound to stay, three persons to be appointed by the President and the Council, who are to examine into the terms of enlistment ;——where the original enlistments cannot be found, the soldier's oath to be admitted to prove the time and terms of enlistment, and the soldier to be discharged upon his oath of the condition of the enlistment.

Thirdly. Wherever any soldier has enlisted for three years or during the war, he is to be discharged unless he shall appear afterwards to have re-inlisted voluntarily and freely. . . . The gratuity of *one hundred dollars* given by Congress not to be reckoned as a bounty, or any men detained in consequence of that gratuity. The Commissioners to be appointed by the President and Council, to adjust any difficulties which may arise on this article, also

Fourthly. The Auditors to attend as soon as possible, to settle the depreciation with the soldiers and give them certificates. ––Their arrearages of pay to be made up as soon as circumstances will admit.

Fifthly. A pair of shoes, overalls and shirts will be delivered to each soldier in a few days, as they are already purchased and ready to be sent forward whenever the line shall be settled.— Those who are discharged, to receive the above articles at Trenton, producing the General's discharge.

The Governor hopes that no soldier of the Pennsylvania Line will break his bargain, or go from the contract made with the public—and they may depend upon it, that the utmost care shall be taken to furnish them with every necessary fitting for a soldier.

The Governor will recommend to the State to take some favourable notice of those who engaged for the war.

The Commissioners will attend at Trenton where the clothing and the stores will be immediately brought, and the regiments to be settled with in their order. A field officer of each regiment to attend during the settlement of his regiment.

Pursuant to General Wayne's orders of the 2nd instant, no man to be brought to any trial or censure for what has happened on or since New Year's day, but all matters to be buried in oblivion.

Jos. Reed.
James Potter.

(*Enclosure.*)

II. 1781, Jan. 8.—His Excellency's proposals being communicated to the different regiments at Troop Beating this morning, they do voluntarily agree in conjunction that all the soldiers that were enlisted for the term of three years or during the war, excepting those whose terms of enlistment are not expired, ought to be discharged immediately with as little delay as circumstances will allow—except such soldiers as have voluntarily re-enlisted. In case that any soldier should dispute his enlistment, it is to be settled by a committee and the soldier's oath.

The remainder of his Excellency's and the Honourable Board of Committee's Proposals is founded upon honour and justice, but in regard to the Honourable the Board setting forth that there will be appointed three persons to sit as a Committee to redress our grievances. It is therefore the general demand of the line and the Board of Sergeants, that we shall appoint as many members as of the opposite, to sit as a Committee to determine jointly upon our unhappy affairs. As the path we tread is justice and our footsteps founded upon honour, therefore we unanimously do agree that there would be something done towards a speedy redress of our present circumstances.

Signed by order of the Board,
Wm. Bowzer, Secretary.

Pursuant to your Excellency's demand concerning the two Emissaries from the British, the Board of Committee resolved that those men should be delivered up to the supreme authority in order to shew that we should remove every doubt of suspicion and jealousy.

Also that the men may disperse upon being discharged, the delivering up their arms, etc.

Signed by the Board in the President's absence,

Daniel Connel, Member.

Trenton, 1781, Jan. 10.

PETER HOLMES,° Esq., to the EARL OF BUCKINGHAMSHIRE.

1781, Jan. 21. Winagh.—This letter will be delivered to your Lordship by Mr. Bayly, son of a gentleman of large property in this neighbourhood with whom I am connected by the nearest ties of friendship and of blood. He has been called to the barr here, but is now determined to go over to Charlestown, South Carolina, to vindicate and assert his rights to a very extensive property that his family have long enjoyed in that country, but in the possession of which they have been disturbed by the late troubles that have desolated that country.

The regret you were pleased to express at not having had an opportunity during your residence here of confering on me some mark of your favour induces me to hope that your Lordship will readily embrace this opportunity of serving me thro' my friend, and that you will give or procure for this gentleman such letters of recommendation to persons in office at Carolina, as may enable him to present his just claims with vigour and effect.

I should think that a gentleman of profession educated in those principles of loyalty and attachment to his Majesty's Government so universally prevalent here, not absolutely unworthy the notice of American Administration when going there on such an errand, especially when those principles are likely to receive energy and effect from that influence which is inseparably annexed to extensive property.

CAPTAIN BURGH to THE SAME.

1781, Feb. 17. Dublin.—(Personal news and various preferments.) The Deanery of Derry† I understand is to be manufactured with an English Prebend, who is to resign to Dr. Aikin. . . . . The event of the English Mutiny Bill has given very general satisfaction and has destroyed all pretence for the revival of the declaratory resolution. Lord Carlisle has taken Mr. Beresford's country house, but still lives in town.

SIR LUCIUS O'BRIEN‡ to THE SAME.

1781, Feb. 20. Dublin.—Asks for the letter or a copy of the letter in which Lord North had expressed his appreciation of the

---

* M.P. for the Borough of Banagher in King's County.
† The Revd. Edward Emily, A.M., was appointed Dean of Derry on the 3rd April, 1781, in succession to the Revd. W. Cecil Pery.
‡ Of Dromolen, County Clare, and M.P. for that county.

service which he had rendered to the trade of Ireland in 1778 before the Parliament of Great Britain. "It was a testimony which I thought I had reason to be proud of, and which I could wish even to transmit to my children."

BISHOP OF CLOYNE to the EARL OF BUCKINGHAMSHIRE.

1781, February 23. Dublin.—My actual appointment to the See of Cloyne would have occasioned your Lordship the trouble of receiving my thanks again, had I known to what place to address them, which I did not till I had the honour of your letter yesterday. The childishness of the measures taken at first to defeat your Lordship's recommendation, and afterwards to transfer a part of the obligation to your successor comes the nearest to an apology for the shabbyness of them. It looks as if the author of them knew no better. Your Lordship will be diverted at the last expedient. It was found out (after five months scrutiny) that I was a popular seditious man, and would prove a Napper-Tandy in Lawn. I laughed at the accusation, but it is a serious matter if Lord Carlisle (who is a man of honour) is to receive his ideas of men and things in this country from the ingenious and worthy gentlemen who described my character.

It will give me a most sincere pleasure to have an opportunity of expressing in more than words my gratitude to your Lordship. I can explain (I think) clearly the arrangement proposed by Sir R. Heron to me. It was that I should as soon as I had it in my power give a living of £500 a year to Mr. Ogle, to advance his preferment between £200 and £300 or rather £300 a year; Mr. Ogle in that case resigning his living of Castle Bellingham (with £220) to Mr. Maunsel. Our conversation was so explicit that I mentioned it to Mr. Ogle and his friend Mr. Leigh, but shall be silent for the future till I receive your Lordship's commands.

Mr. Conolly must be delighted to find all his friends rejoicing at his newspaper honours. I don't think I shall venture to mention the circumstance to Lady Louisa. The most distant hint of an Irish peerage makes her look grave.

EARL OF BUCKINGHAMSHIRE to F. NESBIT.

1781, March 15.—The very unexpected and mortifying disappointment which I experienced with respect to many projected arrangements at the close of my Administration have prevented me from seeking for any particular communication upon Irish affairs with the Ministry since my return to England.

Lord North told me at St. James's that the first day of my appearance these pensions recommended by me were going over and it is my firm opinion that the delay arises from the dilatoriness of office and the multiplicity of important business at this time in agitation. It has never been suggested to me that there was any difficulty relative to the pension in which you are interested.

(*Draft.*)

The Archbishop of Dublin[*] to the Earl of Buckinghamshire.

1781, Mar. 19. The Palace.—I cannot omit this joyfull occasion of congratulating your Lordship on the glorious event of taking St. Eustatia, St. Martin and Saba, together with 240 ships, an infinite quantity of naval stores, provisions, merchandise, &c., and that too without the loss of almost a man, which at all times must greatly enhance the value of the conquests, but in our present critical situation renders them doubly valuable. Every one must rejoice to find that this immense loss in ships, stores, &c., falls almost entirely on the merchants of Amsterdam, a punishment strictly due to their notorious perfidy.

Mr. Keating's promotion to the Deanery of Clogher has enabled me to comply fully with your Lordship's wishes. (Has therefore collated Mr. Bourne, the Duke of Leinster's friend, to the Chancellorship of St. Patrick's and St. Werburg's, and Mr. Champagne to the prebend and living of Castle Dermot.

Hopes to be able shortly to express his gratitude to Lord Buckinghamshire in person in London.)

Thomas Conolly to the Same.

1781, March 19. Castletown.—It was very kind of you to send me so much good news at its first arrival in London and I already anticipate a further account in about a year hence of the taking of the Spice Islands, and if worth while Batavia, so that the Mynheers by their treachery will help to make us amends for what we have lost by that of others. Peace, however, is what we must all wish for, this kingdom to make money and yours to save it, to prevent a national bankruptcy.

Tell Caroline that I believe she will loose her chaperon for Kensington Gardens for this Spring, as our climate here is *too fine* to leave it, and a journey or two to the north this summer will break in so much upon my time that I shall give up London and the fine world and rest contented with those pleasures and amusements this poor kingdom produces.

I have seen our new Viceroy but seldom, once here, and two or three times, to pay my respects at Levée, Drawing Room, etc. I have likewise seen Eden here and in Dublin ; he is very alert in examining and stating the different accounts of the different Boards. He has struck the ballances, and has ask'd where they were ; by the by, he has had a very lame account of several of them. Knox's debt, instead of £16,000 has turned out 40 thousand, eight hundred. Tom Shepherd of Drogheda has received the thanks of the Board for his assiduity and regularity. Our loves to Caroline.

P.S. . Lord Carlisle has taken *Beresford's* country house and Eden, Blaquiere's. You must guess the consequences.

---

[*] Dr. Robert Fowler, Bishop of Killaloe, promoted to the Archbishopric in Dec. 1778.

CAPT. A. CORBETT to the EARL OF BUCKINGHAMSHIRE.

1781, March 25. Dublin Castle.— . . . Let the enemies of Ireland say what they will. I must differ from all such and do justice to the character of the Irish in saying that they entertain the most grateful sense of the many advantages they obtained in the course of your Lordship's Viceroyalty.

The news of the taking of St. Eustatia has been received with every demonstration of joy, and the country in general I am told continues everywhere in the same peaceful disposition as when you left it. . . .

The EARL OF BUCKINGHAMSHIRE to the ARCHBISHOP OF DUBLIN.

1781, March 30.—Your Grace will read with pleasure that his Majesty has honor'd me with a most gracious reception. As to those of his Ministers whose illiberal and injudicious conduct cast a shade upon the close of my Administration, you certainly will applaud, in anxious times like the present, my treating rather with coolness and reserve, rather than intemperate resentment.

(Draft. Extract.)

SIR HENRY CLINTON to the EARL OF BUCKINGHAMSHIRE.

1781, May 15.—Your Lordship has finished *all your* campaigns most honorably. If not relieved from the disagreeable embarassments under which I have laboured these many months, I too shall close my campaigning in this continent I hope without disgrace.

I would have written to your Lordship a long letter, but beg leave to refer you to our friend G. Leland with whom I have had most confidential conversation.

I will show your Lordship a letter I have written to the Duke of Brunswick with a short account of the operations of this campaign.

From Col. Leland your Lordship will know my griefs.

SAME to COLONEL LELAND.

1781, May 20.—You will observe what our situation is, if Lord Cornwallis should unfortunately decide upon a junction with Phillips. I must not say what will happen to the southward, nor what might have been prevented if his Lordship naturally jealous of Green (had) either fallen back into the Carolinas from Guildford Court House, from Cross Creek, or even from Wilmington, either by sea or land to George Town, for you will observe in Lord Cornwallis's letter of the 10th of April he says that Green was still at Deep River, which I have reason to believe is still further from Camden than Wilmington is. But these are only private opinions.

(Copy in Lord Buckinghamshire's handwriting. Endorsed " Extract.")

SIR HENRY CLINTON to COLONEL LELAND.

1781, May 23.—The same sanguine opinions still prevail in England, and amongst other things they look upon Allen as actually in arms with us, whereas all I have said is that he has separated himself from the Congress; but private letters will ruin us, they acquaint the Minister, likewise, that I can spare 10,000 men from 12,000. All my private letters say that the old Admiral is recall'd. I hope the next accounts from the Fleet will confirm it; should they not, I wait another packet from Europe and if not made easy in that respect I must quit a command which you will bear me witness cannot be honorable connected with such a naval chief. Accounts from Lord Cornwallis notwithstanding Lord Rawdon's victory, are unfavourable; a general spirit of revolt shows itself. I heartily wish that Lord Rawdon, whilst it is in his power, may move to the southward of Santee. Lord Cornwallis seems much inclined in the absence of Green to attempt a junction with Phillips, and his principal motive seems to be to avoid, as he terms it, the disgrace of going by sea to Charlestown. What a reason for making a move which must be fatal to the Carolinas and may be so to his own army, and even to that of Phillips, if the reinforcement I have sent does not arrive in time, in short, should his Lordship have made this move, *il sera, selon moi, impossible de rétablir une campagne si mal commencée et à plus forte raison, je me retirerai du jeu.* In the temper I am in, if I knew where to find his Lordship, I should do it immediately, for notwithstanding I am free to own if we are properly reinforced, the French, not, and we remain superior at sea and don't blunder, much may be done in the course of this campaign, yet if by our false move we lose the Carolinas we are undone. To this hour I know not the force Lord Cornwallis entered the Carolinas with. No returns but what he had in the action by which the Guards, who joined his Lordship 800 fit for duty are reduced to 422 ; Bose° from 480 to 256, and all the rest in proportion.

(Copy of extract in Lord Buckinghamshire's handwriting.)

THE SAME to THE SAME.

1781, May 26.—The more I ponder upon our situation in the Carolinas the more I am alarmed at it. Lord Rawdon's success will have saved it for the present and I hope if Green is likely to remain in force, and he is not reinforced, that his Lordship will quit Camden.

General A. is arrived, he says that one of the reasons of the reduced numbers before Guildford was the great number of soldiers worn down with fatigue. He hints at desertion, which such a march must of course have occasioned. I have been comparing the returns fit for duty of those I last year left with

---

° A Hessian Regiment whose commander was De Bose.

his Lordship, the reinforcements I have since sent him and his last returns, and I find the deficiency nearly 2,445 men at a much healthier season than when I left him.

(*Copy of extract in Lord Buckinghamshire's writing.*)

LT.-COL. VYSE to the EARL OF BUCKINGHAMSHIRE.

1781, June 6. Dublin.—(Delayed writing till the 4th and 5th of this month should be over.)

The former being the Birthday and the latter a general Field day of the Volunteers, between them both I had flattered myself with the hopes of being able to pick up something that might have contributed for a moment to your entertainment.

On Monday there was an Ode and Dinner at the Castle as usual, and on Tuesday morning his Excellency returned again to the country. There was much about the usual number of men at the Castle in the morning, but our shew of ladies was not indeed very brilliant; for excepting Lady Carlisle and her sister, Mrs. Towler and Mrs. Sackville Hamilton were our only beauties. Lord Charlemont, Reviewing General of the Volunteers, has had a guard at his house ever since they assembled, and had a levée on the morning of the Birthday, about the same time that there was one at the Castle.

So great a number of the inhabitants of this place never, I believe, were collected together before as were assembled yesterday morning in the Phœnix Park. The number of Volunteers was not near so great as I expected to have seen. They did not, I think, exceed above eighteen hundred in all, but these were very well appointed and armed, and would, I dare say, have performed all their business with much more regularity had not a heavy rain began just as their General came upon the ground. The papers have swelled their numbers to between three and four thousand. Your Lordship may therefore upon this occasion believe about half what they tell you, which is giving them a much more ample credit than they often deserve. My calculation I believe is tolerably exact, as I compared it with several others made by persons who had been at the trouble of counting them.

I send your Lordship enclosed a plan of a Review which is to take place on the 20th July next. With respect to our own military operations for the summer, nothing is to be determined till Sir John Irwine returns to us. Whether any of us are to take the field or what disposition is to be made of us we are at present totally ignorant.

It is rumoured that an arrangement in the law-line is soon to take place, in consequence of the Lord Chancellor's wishing to retire. . . .

Since I troubled your Lordship with my last letter I have myself been a very great traveller, at least almost as great a one as this island would allow me to be, having spent above two months at the different quarters of my new regiment, at Ballinrobe, Dunmore, Castlebar and Sligo. Farther to the west I could not go. I found my regiment much in the situation I expected, but I knew, in some degree at least, the state of it before I joined it, and therefore did not suffer any mortification from disappointment. I have endeavoured all in my power to convince both the officers and men that I have no object but their happiness and interest, and I make no doubts but we shall agree extremely well. I wish to interest them in every measure that I take, by pointing out to them the advantages of that order and regularity it is intended to establish. My journey round the quarters of my regiment was a very long one, and great part of it thro' the wildest country I ever saw, and which is, I think, less improved within these twenty years than any other part of Ireland. . . .

Edward Tighe to the Earl of Buckinghamshire.

1781, July 17. Waltrim, near Bray.—Mr. Hamilton, I understand, is somewhat better. He is drinking water in the North of Ireland, which Dr. Quin believes will be of great service to his health. I wish he had taken a trip to Spa, or at least to Bath. . . .

The Lord Lieutenant appears to pass almost the whole of his time at his little Fingalian Villa, where I understand there is not room even for Corbet. There is an audience, however, every Thursday at the Castle.

Eden is most active, punctual and cheerfull. He is rummaging all the offices, and inforcing residence and attendance. Very good employ, before more pressing business arises. The losses to the public by Knox and others are attributed to the ill state of the office of the Accountant General. Such failures naturally awaken attention.

The Volunteer forces appear in great splendour at field days, reviews, &c., in several parts of the kingdom. There had been one in the Phœnix Park the day before I landed, and the men were for three days billeted upon the inhabitants of Dublin. Yet I much doubt whether the numbers are increas'd. While the war lasts they probably will flourish. Peace so earnestly to be wished for must effectualy put an end to them. The wild ideas of independence and separation, &c., I am told are spread far and wide. I cannot refrain exclaiming :—

" Curse on the innovating hand attempts it !
" Whose damn'd Ambition would get.''   (*sic.*)

I know your Lordship will pardon my warmth.

The Same to the Same.

1781, July 31. Waltrim, near Bray.— . . . My time is chiefly occupied by bathing, medicine, exercise, and some degree of study. I see no politicians, but by accident, but have the pleasure to hear your name always mention'd with the highest respect and gratitude.

His Excellency I have seen only once. He lately pass'd very near me in a tour to General Cuninghame, Powerscourt, &c.

I have had two private days with Eden in the Park. We have been intimate for many years, and I wish to give him all the little assistance in my power. He seems to think that the moment Flood shew'd himself determinedly hostile you should have insisted upon his dismission from office, and not have consented to wait for the *conclusion of the Session*. This was said in a tête-à-tête. I find that he has been receiv'd very cooly and as he tells his friends, with insolence; has not receiv'd the least satisfaction or even encouragement as to any of his points, and has been fairly told that he had a narrow escape, which he did not deserve.

The having made any request in the least degree improper would hurt me exceedingly, but a view of the rough loose sheets of your Irish History,° to refresh my memory in case of questions, would I think, be usefull. Your Lordship is very well assured that the use which I should make of any extracts or memoranda would and indeed must be for the honor of your Government.

Reviews of the Volunteers are still going on, and Government are still busy in correcting abuses of office and regulating the revenues. I hear, however, that several of the Northern corps (and Mr. Brownlow in particular) have refused to enter into violent resolutions at Belfast in imitation of the lawyers and some other bodies. I hear we are reasonably strong in the Channel, but I tremble for the East and West Indies.

The King's last speech is a very good one. I hope his next will contain something to cheer us.

EARL OF BUCKINGHAMSHIRE to SIR H. CLINTON.

1781, August 19.—Leland has just left me after a friendly visit of ten days, during which time our conversation repeatedly turned upon the general situation of America and the circumstances which more particularly affected yourself.

It concerns me very seriously that you should experience other uneasiness than what must necessarily rise from the most critical and anxious trust committed to your care, but if as you suspect Ministers have paid attention to private correspondence (rather) than to the information immediately received from you, it is a misfortune which the writer of this letter has shared in the fullest extent.

During the tedious series of my last turbulent sessions, when difficulty every hour multiplyd upon me, my commendations were little depended upon, but there was every reason to apprehend that the assertions and insinuations of my open and secret enemies were received with predilection. Positive proof cannot be given of this; at the close however of my Government even after every difficulty had been most decidedly surmounted Ministers refused to dismiss those who, tho' loaded with accumulated favours, had strenuously opposed me, nay promoted one who stood in that predicament in preference to an honourable

---

* Lord Buckinghamshire writes later that this was no longer in his own hands.

and steady friend particularly patronised by me. Is it not then natural to doubt as well of the candor as of the cordiality of the Cabinet? The surest way by which a little man may rise to second-rate greatness is by furnishing intelligence agreeable to the wishes, passions and prejudices of his superiors.

The news of Admiral Arbuthnot's return was most gratefull to me, as well as the idea which now universally prevails that ample justice is done to your merit, and that you will have no cause to withdraw those services from your country which are so essential to her.

Nothing can be more private than my present situation—scarcely any communication with Ministers and none with the opposition, tho' I do not implicitly swear by the conduct of the first, I most cordialy abjure the measures of the latter. Leland told me of the notice taken by the Royal family of your son, which could not but be, as it was intended, flattering to you; the idea of seeing the young gentleman hereafter with his father at Blickling gives me sensible pleasure.

Lady Buckingham regards you most cordialy.

The Earl of Buckinghamshire to Edward Tighe.

1781, Aug. 21.--Some apprehensions insinuated in your last letter respecting the political dispositions of many of your countrymen have painfully dwelt upon my recollection, should they prove so wild as, instead of availing themselves of their lately acquired advantages, to quarrel with Great Britain, the Nation will commit a more disgraceful blunder than invention ever attributed to any Irish individual. Their conduct during the last sessions (some factious flights excepted) bought them golden opinions,—which should be worn in the gloss—and the exchange of good-will they claim in addition to any publick feelings would induce me vainly to hope—*alios animos in contentione Libertatis et honoris, alios secundum deposita certamina in incorrupto judicio fore.*

Upon the whole it is my most cordial wish that success may attend your present Government, and I should think their steadiness and abilitys, together with the support they are sure of from home, will easily surmount any difficultys with which they may be threatened.

It is not in my power to send you any flattering news, some accounts of the state of America have lately been given me by men fresh from the spot who must have possessed diffusive intelligence; the campaign seems to be wasting without any of those decided events which can alone prevent the ruinous continuation of the war.

The reception given to Mr. Flood at the Castle was truly becoming. When Mr. Eden says I ought to have insisted upon that gentleman's immediate dismission, he do's not recollect, for he could not but have known, the very slender favor I possess'd in the English Cabinet, you were no stranger to my apprehensions at some critical periods, when the perverseness of some men, the duplicity of others, and the consequential accumulated embarassaments provoked me to suspect that there were not wanting those in either Kingdom who wish'd my disgrace almost at the expence of publick calamity.

Indeed, tho' ideas of this tendency might be admitted in the peevish moment of distress, calm reflection must convince us such abominable absurdity could not realy exist.

My retreat from London was very early, and no material information has reached me in these shades, but in the beginning of June cordiality and concert did not prevail amongst the great men. You will, however, as an honorable politician hear with pleasure, that the English American Patriots daily lose ground in the national esteem. Many of them possess abilitys and private virtues, had they been totally inestimable, the destruction their suggestions have produced would have been less extensive. Let them prosper in their private situations, yet never attain that ministerial dignity their ambition has so ruinously emulated.

" Nor reap the Harvest tho' they've spoil'd the feild."

(*Draft.*)

EDWARD TIGHE to the EARL OF BUCKINGHAMSHIRE.

1781, Sept. 3. Waltrim, near Bray.—Your very obliging favour of Aug. 21st was most flattering. The sentiments so exactly correspond with my own, that I cannot consider myself as of that country, which, in such a time, and under such circumstances of obligation, has the folly and wickedness to seek for a rupture with the elder sister.

I am in truth a mix'd subject, and I feel myself to be an impartial one. My birth, as well as my parents, my education, and habits are English; my fortune, prospects and Parliamentary connexions Irish.

Still it may be hoped that my apprehension with respect to any present hatching of wicked politicks are not founded. I mean so far as to include any considerable numbers. Spirits there are, and ever will be, who are nothing if not mischievous ; from them, questions in Parliament of the worst tendency are to be expected. Indeed the newspapers sufficiently shew the intentions of several individuals and of some bodies. For these, the real friends of the Constitution should be prepared, and I shall esteem myself much honor'd, if when you have half an hour to bestow upon such a subject, you will favor me with a few sentences, detach'd or otherwise, which you would wish to have pronounc'd at College Green. Supported by your opinion and assistance, I shall feel myself embolden'd more than I have ever done. Diffidence, arising from several causes, and ill-health have in general kept me upon my seat, but ' I own the glorious subject fires my breast.'

That some vote tending to a separation will be proposed there can, I fear, be little doubt. To meet it with argument, force and resolution should be one of the first objects of Government.

I believe the Lord Lieutenant and Secretary have very nearly the same opinion of individuals that your Lordship entertain'd. The idea of a quondam Secretary having much weight does not appear to me to be well founded. He probably has been listen'd to as well as several others, but by no means with peculiar confidence. Mr. E. seems to think (and as far as my judgment and experience goes, thinks wisely, and I remember it was your Lordship's opinion) that many of what are called constitutional questions, particularly Poyning's, have no real or intrinsic importance, and that the House of Commons contains such a variety of different sentiments upon that subject that it might safely be indulg'd in the framing almost any propositions arising from it. If he can satisfy the King's Cabinet of this truth perhaps the doctrine may be usefull in these times.

Lord Loughborough is now at Eden's in the Park and I hear is to stay in Ireland some time. Just at this juncture an invasion has started up. Your Lordship had many of them, but this is *the first appearance this season.*

I understand that Mr. Foster and those few who deserve to be confided in, will have their full weight when the curtain is drawn up. Hitherto Mr. E. has been peeping through the slits, and has had the management, I believe, to conceal not only from the audience, as is the case at the French Comedy, but even from the actors, *who* are to perform the principal characters.

Upon this day month the Parliament of Ireland is to meet, *bonis avibus,* I trust.

The EARL OF BUCKINGHAMSHIRE to ED. TIGHE.

1781, Sept. 25.—The idea of any votes being formaly propos'd tending to a dissolution of the connection between the two Kingdom's or at least of such a vote's being countenanc'd by any respectable characters, go's much beyond any parliamentary proceeding which my apprehensions had suggested, they had scarcely gone further than the probability of some proposition to modify Poyning's Law, and to render the Mutiny Bill biennial. Not that I am prepared to set bounds to the absurdity or wickedness of a few individuals, and indeed it is for the advantage of Government that a violent measure should be started if decidedly reprobated at the first blush. The arguments against Ireland's attempting a separation are equally forcible and obvious, but it must be in an hour of very particular vanity that I can encourage the conceit of adding any thing material to those which must occur to your own good judgement.

Did it fall to my task to treat this subject, my great difficulty would be the rendering the home truths call'd upon by the occasion palatable to the prejudices and the heated imaginations of a popular Assembly. Spacious as the field is, the reasoning perhaps may be reduc'd to the three following Heads :—

The present enviable situation of Ireland in contradistinction to that of any other State.

The physical impossibility as Europe is now constituted of Ireland's existing an independent Government.

And the certainty of the Roman Catholicks becoming the ruling religion in consequence of her separation from Gt. Britain.

You are not to learn the advantageous ground upon which your Country now stands or that it is only problematical from a most humiliating doubt whether the Irish are capable of that persevering industry necessary for the availing themselves of the happiness and prosperity which awaits them, and whether persons of moderate property will by vesting it in trade prefer the situation of an opulent merchant to that of a distressed gentleman? However the spirit of England may be depressed by ingratitude and treachery abroad and domestick faction, she is not as yet so far humiliated as to give up her authority in Ireland without a serious struggle, and even should her opposition prove unavailing, some material inconveniencys must be apprehended from her resentment. But, for argument sake we will suppose the emancipation to have been accomplish'd.

It is scarcely to be presum'd that the current expense of the nation could in consequence be reduc'd, the contrary is by far more probable.

The interest of her present debt, trifling as it is comparatively with ours, and the expences of any rational system of Government which she can establish, cannot long be paid without adventitious resources which are only to be obtained by commercial exertions. Her trade can never become a material object but by the acquiring a preference over the manufactures of other nations whose interest must determine them to extinguish that rivalry in the bud if not respectably protected. Such protection should be deriv'd from a maritime force. But can that force be easily established in a Country where the building an additional Revenue Cruiser is almost a deliberation of State?

It will be argued that the military expence may be reduc'd by the Volunteers being substituted for the Regular forces. Will any man soberly contend that those bodys rais'd in the fever of the times, in most instances indeed upon the spur of the occasion from a meritorious spirit of self-defence, but in others by faction and the vanity and emulation of individuals, constituted as they are, can become formidable to an invading enemy, inforce the execution of the laws, and check the thousands of profligate beggars who watch the opportunity of pillage in the interior of the Kingdom. It is indeed most certain that the cordial protection of the disinterested House of Bourbon would officiously meet your wishes, and as certain that such protection must lead to a subjection, to the which her absolute sovereignty would be preferable. The territorial value of Ireland, her proportional inability of resistance and her locality with respect to England and France, render her decidedly dependent upon either the one or the other.

If that assertion is founded, those who wish to enjoy liberty under law and who profess the Protestant Religion will have no great difficulty in determining their election.

That great drain of Irish treasure, the number of absentees, would rather increase than diminish by a change of Government, and every argument which at this time militates against the taxing them would still continue equaly conclusive.

As to the third point I should scarcely think it possible to maintain seriously that a connection with France would not sooner or later give lead in Ireland to the Roman Catholicks. Every political reasoning must determine that ambitious Nation to encourage religious tenets and principles of Government congenial to her own. Equity also would justify the preference given to the opinions of so decided a majority of the inhabitants.

But let us suppose Ireland establish'd as an independent State, treating upon an equal footing with foreign Nations and not courting any protection. The interior strength of the country could be as nothing, and civil war must be hourly apprehended, if some terms were not made with the Catholicks. Conscious of the superiority of their numbers, would they be satisfyd without some share in the government, and when once possess'd of that share, would not those numbers actuated by the acknowleg'd genius of their religion grasp at the whole?

Tho' this is already but too long I must still add a few words. Were any inference to be drawn with respect to the possible independence of Ireland from the existence of the lesser States of Europe such as Venice, Naples, Switzerland, Genoa, Tuscany, &c., it may be obviously answered that some of them are only nominally so, others owe their situation to their insignificance, some to the rivality of neighbouring Powers, who would not allow the other to make the acquisition, some also to the great policy of Europe.

It is unnecessary to insinuate to an enlightened understanding like yours that if in discussing great national systems full and judicious allowance is not made to the specifick genius of the individuals and every distinguish'd local and relative circumstance of each country, the reasoning will be very erroneous.

(*Draft.*)

Sir H. Clinton, Kt., to Lord J. P. Clinton.

1781, Oct. 3 to 11.—That you may understand nearly what Lord Cornwallis's situation has been and is now, I give you a short journal of events as they have turned up.

On the last of August, suspecting Washington's intention of detaching to the southward, I sent information to his Lordship.

On the 2nd September having reason to believe it was certain, I sent messengers with a promise of reinforcement, whenever the Admiral shou'd tell me it cou'd proceed, or if it cou'd not proceed, to make the best diversion I cou'd.

On the 6th received his Lordship's of the 29th, saying that Le Grasse had arrived in the Chesapeak with about 25 sail of the line from the West Indies.

On the same day, sent to his Lordship to inform him that the best way to assist him, was to go to him. That I should do so with 4,000 already embarked, as soon as the Admiral informed me it was practicable; acquainting his Lordship that the Admiral had 19 sail of the line, and that, by accounts from Europe, Admiral Digby was hourly expected.

On the 13th received information of the action of the 5th.

On the 14th determined in a Council of War that the only way to succour Lord Cornwallis was to go to him, for that nothing cou'd turn Washington from such an object.

On the 17th received the Admiral's letter of the 15th saying that the enemy were masters of the Chesapeak; that he intended to return to York with his shattered Fleet to avoid the Equinox; that he knew nothing of Admiral Digby officially, but hoped that his arrival wou'd enable him to look at the French Fleet.

On the 23rd determined in a Council of Generals that it was their opinion that Lord Cornwallis required immediate succour; that it shou'd be attempted even with risk to fleet and army; and agreed to request a conference with the Admirals on the subject.

On the 23rd received a letter from Lord Cornwallis of the 16th and 17th: in the first he had little to apprehend before the end of October, but in that of the 17th he changes his tone; probably upon hearing that Barras,° not having joined before, had now joined Le Grasse.† And together they were 36 sail of the line: and said if not very soon relieved, I might be prepared for the worst.

On the 24th the Council met and unanimously agreed as soon as the Fleet cou'd be repaired, by joint exertions to endeavour to succour his Lordship, and afterwards to co-operate with him.

While in Council, Admiral Digby arrived with three ships of the Line. As the surest and best means of conveying us, and not being separated from the Fleet, I proposed that the navy should take us on board; which they readily consented to. Upon which messengers were dispatched to Lord Cornwallis, and the greatest probability that we shou'd start on the 5th of October.

On the 29th, finding the Fleet not so forward, I requested another conference. It was there determined amongst other things, that the Fleet wou'd be ready by the 12th, to take us on board. Of this little alteration I informed his Lordship, and let him know that if by accident, the Fleet shou'd be still delayed a little longer, I wou'd start the instant I cou'd. But shou'd he judge that we cou'd not arrive in time, he was at liberty to do any thing he cou'd, to save his Army. I requested his ideas, how he thought we cou'd best form a junction, and gave him mine and the General Officers' if I did not receive his opinion which would of course, determine us.

On the 3rd sent an Officer to Lord Cornwallis to explain.

On the 4th heard from Lord Cornwallis, that he had received mine of the 24th, with great satisfaction, and that if we cou'd arrive in a reasonable time, he cou'd hold out: and that his works were in a tolerable state.

---

* Louis Comte de Barras. † François Comte de Grasse, 1723-1788.

On the 11th two Line of Battle Ships arrived from the West Indies, which makes our Fleet 25 sail of the line, and two fifties, with a number of Frigates. 'Tis not a move of choice, but of necessity. If Lord Cornwallis's Army falls, I shou'd have little hopes of seeing British Dominion reestablished in America, as our Country cannot replace that Army. If we do not try to save it, we cannot succeed; if we do we may. Lord Cornwallis is of opinion with us, that the only way to do it, is to go to him, and having formed a junction with him, we shall, if possible attack Washington; or if that is thought impracticable, we shall save as much of Lord Cornwallis's corps as we can, shou'd it be thought right to keep the post of York. I of course go myself, and, if I succeed, I shall resign the command to his Lordship.

When operation in Chesapeak was ordered, I layed before Government the danger I thought it was exposed to, without a permanent superiority at sea. I was promised, if not a superiority, an equality, " to secure those operations." If that is not the case, let Lord Sandwich, Sir George Rodney, and the Minister answer it. Lord Cornwallis was compleatly invested on the York side on the 3rd. He has provisions, with economy, I hope, to the middle of November at least.

11th. A cruel wind stopt us yesterday; we are however all ready to start the first favourable moment. This journal is tolerably correct, your Lordship will shew it to such friends as you judge proper.

EDWARD TIGHE to the EARL OF BUCKINGHAMSHIRE.

1781, Oct. 8. Dublin.—When I considered it as probable that questions hostile to the connexion between the two Kingdoms might arise, I judg'd chiefly from those votes and resolutions and addresses which of late have fill'd the newspapers, and from the attempt of last Session by what was call'd the declaratory vote. I had no other grounds. Certainly there have existed for some years past a few short-sighted politicians who affect to consider Ireland merely as a country under the same King with Great Britain, and connected no otherwise than Hanover, &c. To such I alluded. Your few but striking arguments are a sufficient refutation of such silly and unfounded doctrine.

Eden is in great spirits upon this eve of his campain. He has very good assurances, and as far as can be seen at present, very good prospects. Mr. O'Neil is to move the address to the King. Lord C. Fitzgerald to the Lord Lieutenant.

With respect to the pensions of the last year I am convinc'd that they are perfectly understood and exactly discriminated. Not one of them, in my opinion, will be laid to your account. But if any matter shall arise upon that subject which appears to me to reflect in any degree upon your Lordship's conduct, I trust I cannot sit silent unless more able and impartial tongues prevent me, which I am confident will be the case.

My most sincere acknowledgments are due for the paper containing most judicious objections to the idea of Irish independence,

As to Poyning's it is really nothing but a good tub, and therefore should not be parted with. My arm is much out of order and I fear my scrawl is difficult.

SIR H. CLINTON to the EARL OF BUCKINGHAMSHIRE.

1781, October 10. New York.—I am honored with your Lordship's letter; in my last I informed you that Le Grasse with 36 sail of the line had taken possession of Chesapeak Bay, and that Washington march'd towards Lord Cornwallis; his Lordship has about 8,000, including sailors, marines, etc.; the 8,000 French, 4 or 5,000 Continentals, and a numerous Militia. Washington broke ground on the 2nd. The only way (in the opinion of *all*) to succour Lord C. is to go to him, his provisions will I hope last till the middle of November with care, his works by the delays of the enemy, he says, are in tolerable good order, his position I believe an exceeding strong one. Admiral Graves has now 25 sail of the line and two fifties. These with 5,000 troops on board will start in a day or two to try by joint exertion to succour Lord Cornwallis by York river (which by the bye the enemy's fleet masks). If the Navy succeed (of the probability of which they of course are the only judges) in their part, ours will I hope not fail.

This is not a move of choice my dear Lord as you will see, but of necessity; if Lord Cornwallis's army falls, I shall have little hope of seeing British dominion re-established in America, as our country cannot replace him and his army. If I succeed in saving his Lordship, I shall if possible bring W. to action, and then resign a command I have long since determined to do the instant it could be done with propriety; the treatment I have *till of late* met with, and the insinuations thrown out by his ministers, some of them published in a rebel paper, are such as no man will submit to serve under; my Lord ———'s approbation of my conduct has been witheld from me too long, it now comes to late. When I was *directed* to hold the Chesapeak and carry on operations there with *all* I could spare from other stations, I observed to the Minister, that if the enemy should be superior for only a few weeks the Corps in Chesapeak would run the greatest risk, I was in answer promised that "Sir G. Rodney should have positive orders to watch La Grasse and to follow him to this coast in time sufficient to cover our operations in Chesapeak," instead of which Sir S. Hood has brought only 13 sail, 3 arrived with Admiral Digby, two this day from Jamaica. If therefore we are reduced to an inferiority of 25 to 36, if the Corps in Chesapeak is risked, nay lost, *il faut vous addresser* to Lord S——h, Sir G. R——y or the M——r. I know nothing of sea moves. If the conflict tho' an unequal one happens at sea, which most think it will, I have all to hope from the *savoir faire* of our Naval Chiefs and our better sailing, if we attempt to force them in any position they may take to cover York river, though we may suffer a little; but there are many circumstances that may give us every hope of success; the army 'tis true may be crippled in either case a little, with what remains however I will do the best when I am put ashore. I show you, my dear Lord, both sides of our prospect, till we sail of course we look at both, once started only at one. We go in proper good humour with each other, and each determin'd to do his best. I beg my best respects to the Countess. I have enclosed my last letter to Lord C———, either Lord John or Leland will shew it your Lordship.

I hope to pay my respects to you in December. If I save Lord C. you may expect me, if he falls I must wait my fate here. Lt.-Col. Eyre of the 59th, who commanded at the attack on Fort Griswold goes home wounded, and if possible will have the honor to deliver this to your Lordship.

SIR H. CLINTON to the EARL OF BUCKINGHAMSHIRE.

1781, Oct. 29. South of Chesapeak.—A thousand thanks for your kind letters. Your Lordship will find by my last that we did not sail from New York till the 19th nor arrive off this till the 24th, almost a fortnight too late as Lord Cornwallis I fear capitulated the 17th. His Lordship was lost for want of the naval support under Sir G. Rodney, who we were told was ordered to watch Le Grasse's motions and follow him here to cover our operations in Chesapeak ; such has been Lord Cornwallis's fate, and such, my dear Lord, will be the fate, as I have repeatedly told the Minister, of every port if the enemy remains superior at sea.

The French fleet is at anchor in our sight, for such an object as Lord Cornwallis and his corps we should have risked an attack altho' we are only 25 to 36, but having *now* two such objects 'tis not perhaps our business to risk an action, but if the enemy comes out and attacks, which as the wind is fair he may do this day, "*nous ferons notre mieux.*"

EDWARD TIGHE to THE SAME.

1781, November 2. Dublin.—Nothing worthy of being mention'd to your Lordship occur'd in the H. of C., until yesterday when Sir Lucius O'Brien brought forward the Portugal business in spite of the engagement made by Mr. Eden.

Sir Lucius spoke and read treaties, &c., for hours, and then a smart debate came on, upon a question to appoint a Committee to enquire into the trade between Ireland and Portugal.

Isaac Corry⁰ and Fitzgibbon† were the two first that oppos'd this motion. Corry made a speech of eulogium upon Lord Hillsboro. Grattan, Yelverton‡, Bushe§, Ogle, Hussey Burgh and Flood supported the motion. Daly and Brownlow‖ were absent.

* Isaac Corry, M.P. for the Borough of Newry.
† John Fitzgibbon, Attorney General in 1783, and afterwards Lord Fitzgibbon and Earl of Clare, and Chancellor.
‡ Barry Yelverton, M.P. for Carrickfergus, afterwards Lord Chief Baron and Lord Avonmore.
§ Gervase Bushe, M.P. for Kilkenny.
‖ Rt. Hon. Wm. Brownlow, M.P. for Armagh (City) Co., and a Privy Councillor.

Flood spoke decisively as to measures and himself. Call'd upon the House to support their free trade, and used every means to persuade and to inflame, digress'd upon the Perpetual Mutiny Act and curs'd the authors of it and the Legislature that pass'd it, spoke much of himself and of his office and call'd upon members situated like himself to risque every thing for the sake of establishing that free trade which their resolution and steadiness had obtained.

Eden, tho' highly provok'd by Grattan, was temperate, pertinent and steady.

A little before midnight the house divided.

Ayes for a Committee   44.
Noes   117.

My arm is not in order, and I scrawl abominably which I hope your indulgence will excuse.

Having for some time a habit of giving your Lordship a summary account of such matters I have chosen this opportunity in particular as the question was strong and Mr. Flood very conspicious.

The business is getting forward in the Committee of Accounts &c. Nothing more has been said as yet upon the subject of Pensions.

The Provost spoke, rather heavily, with the Majority.

Sir H. Clinton to the Earl of Buckinghamshire.

1781, November 9. New York.—In my last off Chesapeak I told your Lordship my apprehensions for Lord Cornwallis, alas! they were too well founded, could we have arrived in time we are of opinion we should have succour'd his Lordship by entering York river, at all events by James; we should have saved part of of his Lordships' Corps perhaps with the loss of part of that under my immediate orders. If the Navy remain superior in these seas, Charlestown tho' it can stand a siege must finally fall, and tho' perhaps the season is too far advanced to attempt this plan at this season, we must have our turn, if the French remain in this country in such naval and land force, and we are not reinforced in proportion, and covered by a fleet. I refer your Lordship to Lords Lincoln and Dalrymple.

The Same to the Same.

1781, November 30. New York.—If Lords Lincoln and Dalrymple should have arrived safe it will be unnecessary for me to say more upon our late misfortune than my letters by them and their information will give your Lordship, but if they should be taken it may be necessary for me to say a few words in answer to Lord Cornwallis' letter of the 20th of October, which, before I had seen his Lordship, out of delicacy I did not chuse to do.

There is but one cause, my dear Lord, perhaps to impute our late great misfortune, the want of promised naval superiority under Sir G. Rodney, but there are certain implications (to call them by no other name) in Lord Cornwallis' letter which I must take some notice of; from that letter it may be supposed that his Lordship had been compelled by me to take the post at York, that he had represented the defects of the ground, and that of course it was not his Lordship's preference that he was detained there contrary to his own judgement; and that I had likewise *promised* the exertions of the Navy before I was justified in doing so by the resolution of Flag and General officers on the 24th September, which his Lordship received the 29th (many days after General Washington's troops arrived at Williamsburg), that I had promised the Fleet would sail about the 5th of October. Before I ordered the letter to be printed, in a conversation with his Lordship he did not deny that York was his own preference; he owns he never represented any defects in the ground till his letter of the 20th October, written after the capitulation; that I had never promised him the joint exertions of navy and army, till I did so in my letter of the 24th of September; and that in speaking of the probable sailing of the fleet to his succour, he ought to have given my own words, " we have every reason to hope the fleet will start about the 5th of October." As to intrenching tools I have sent to Chesapeak with the different detachments above 3,000, a very great proportion indeed in 6 months; the instant I received a requisition for more I ordered them, but at the time I received it the enemy were in possession of Chesapeak.

Should his Lordship's letter of the 20th of October have made an unfavourable impression in Europe, I shall expect from his Lordship's candour a formal avowal of his sentiments on the above points, for if that shall not be the case I shall depend on my friends to publish such parts of our correspondence as shall set this matter in a proper view.

P.S. His Lordship tells me his letter of the 20th of October was written under great agitation of mind and in great hurry; no man can have felt more for him and his gallant army than their humble servant, no man would have gone greater lengths to have preserved them, and God forbid I should give his Lordship any unnecessary trouble at this time.

EDWARD TIGHE to the EARL OF BUCKINGHAMSHIRE.

1781, November 14. Dublin.—The House rose at four o'clock this morning having negativ'd a motion to bring in heads of a bill to amend, explain, and limit the Army Act.

It is understood that Daly, Bushe and Fitzgibbon are friendly to the Castle. Yet they voted in favor of the motion, and spoke. Ayes 77. Noes 133.

Flood and Burgh seem to be in determin'd opposition. Neither Mr. Conolly nor Mr. Brownlow said any thing, but both, I believe, voted with the Majority.

To-morrow the sugar duties come on and will I conclude take up some time, yet the business of Supply and Ways and Means is more forward by eight or ten days than I have in general known it to be.

Not one word has fallen upon the subject of pensions since the recess of October.

EDWARD TIGHE to the EARL OF BUCKINGHAMSHIRE.

1781, Nov. 23. Dublin.—The House of Commons rose between four and five this morning having settled the Sugar duties in the Committee of Ways and Means agreeably to the duties of last Session by 144 to 163.

Mr. Flood, Grattan and Forbes as spiteful as possible, every body else both in and out of the house seemingly in great good humour and reasonable content. I see, both the 'Hibernian' and 'Freeman' give tolerable accounts of the proceedings, therefore I need not attempt to inlarge upon them; suffice it to say that matters go off much more easily than I expected, that the complexion of Parliament is very fair, and the accounts from the Country good and promising.

The cold water thrown in the north upon the resolution framed by the Lawyers' Corps, and carried down in August by Lord C. &c. added to the loyal spirit exhibited upon a rumor of invasion has been of the greatest service to Government. They have now friendly to their measures not only every family of consequence, but almost every individual worth obtaining. The Ponsonbys, Daly and Bushe are among the last who have flock'd to the standard. It is said that his Grace of L. is to succeed to the Ordnance very soon. Daly is certainly to succeed Lord G. and I know not what is to be done for the Ponsonbys or for Bushe. The bottom seems to be too large.

Jack Hamilton is very well. We often speak of your Lordship with true regard and gratitude. He writes well and he promises me to send you a full budget whenever the recess commences, which is expected a week before Christmas. Mr. Conolly is seldom in the House, I saw him there the day before yesterday for a short time and had the pleasure of conversing with him.

The EARL OF BUCKINGHAMSHIRE to SIR H. CLINTON.

1781, December 8.—Your letters and the several communications which you so obligingly directed to be made, have reached me. You could not doubt of my being persuaded that your attention to the publick service had been equal to your ability. Tho' every man will form some opinion upon critical events, yet my information is not so general or so compleat as to justify my risquing any opinion with respect to the whole of the land operations to the southward. But with less scruple it may be asserted that the delay of our Fleet in coming upon your coast was unpardonable and the primary cause of the present calamity. Your return to England must now necessarily be delayed.

The preserving some Port in America, particularly the most important one which is your immediate charge, and a greater marine exertion is our only chance for salvation.

If America (especialy connected with France) becomes independent, we may possibly be allow'd to eat bread and beef in our little island; but imperial sway, national dignity, ostentation, and luxury must with our commerce be annihilated.

I attended the opening of the Parliament and immediately after returned to Blickling. London you will conceive could not be very agreeable, tho' despondency in the city, circumstances considered, was far short of my expectation. The interposition of the Courts of Vienna and Petersburg to produce a pacification with Holland and some probability of its being successful has kept up the spirits of the money'd and mercantile men, and the stocks are consequently much higher than might have been presumed.

I have received no authentick intelligence since my leaving Town. Mr. C. Thompson was not then arrived; when we meet we cannot but speak of you with esteem and affection. I flatter myself that this place will, hereafter, be most familiar to you. Leland will probably be with me at Christmas, it is almost certain, as a lady who has inspired him with a most profound sentimental passion will be of my party.

(*Draft.*)

Lord G. Germain to the Earl of Buckinghamshire.

1781, Dec. 10. Patishall.—I shall take care to obey your commands by the first opportunity by sending your Lordship's letter to Sir H. Clinton.

I do not wonder that you should prefer residing in the country to the living in town, when the distress of the public and the triumph of the factions can create no pleasing ideas in a liberal mind like your Lordship's. On Wednesday the Opposition make their great effort when the army estimates came under consideration, what support Administration may meet with I know not, but I am very sure that your ideas for the carrying on the war in America are the most proper to be adopted under our present circumstances, but the misfortune is that it is impracticable to explain in publick what must be confined to the executive power, but I hope the measure may be so convey'd to individuals as to influence their conduct.

Much conversation about changes, if any negotiation of that sort is carrying on it is unknown to me, but as I never enquire about it, I may be late in my intelligence. The mediation of Russia is accepted here, and I conclude it will be received in Holland with equal satisfaction, tho' the forms of their Government may delay their answer.

The Brest Fleet had not sail'd the 29th of November. Letters from Paris of the 3rd of this month say it was expected the fleet had sail'd on the 1st of December, tho' no account could have then arrived, I have heard from others that it was not in such forwardness. I hope the last account may be true that

Admiral Kempenfeldt may have a chance of falling in with them, and that Sir G. Rodney may arrive at the Leeward Islands before them. All accounts from Ireland agree that the publick business and the encouragement of trade, particularly of the Fisheries are carrying on with dispatch and with a most respectable majority notwithstanding the violence of your friend Mr. Flood; it must be some satisfaction to your Lordship to see your plans adopted, and that you represented the merit and demerit of individuals in the true light, tho' the awards and punishments were left to be distributed by your successor. Your attention to me upon all occasions demands my sincere thanks, it is certain however pleased I may be in seeing my daughter marry'd to a man of her own choice, yet it would have been an additional satisfaction to me if Mr. Herbert's residence had been in England.

Sir C. Thompson is very well, but his ideas upon our present situation do not give me much encouragement.

The EARL OF BUCKINGHAMSHIRE to the BISHOP OF CLOYNE.

1781, Dec. 10. Blickling.—A just tribute of gratitude ought to have been earlier paid for the interesting information so agreeably conveyed in your favour of the 14th of November, but I delayed acknowledging it till I could write from London in order to give you in return some English intelligence. A very material event indeed met my arrival there, but it was of such a calamitous magnitude as for a time incapacitaty'd me and every feeling man from any power of digested reasoning. After having paid my duty to his Majesty and to Parliament which in our House (before Christmas) is usually confined to the first day, I return'd to this place, the tranquillity of which has restor'd me to some composure, tho' nothing can prevent most painfull reflection upon the future prospects of this Empire but a partial removal, at least, of that gloom which now looms upon us from every quarter. As to the scene in London, the distress was really universal at the fashionable end of the town. The countenances of Ministers, Maccaronis, tradesmen, artisans, and painted ladys all expressed it; his Majesty however, and it became him, appeared compos'd and it was asserted that some Patriots amidst their lamentations for the ruin of their country and their execrations of the authors could not from discerning eyes conceal a latent satisfaction. This observation is not my own.

The city had just before receiv'd intelligence of a pacification with Holland, at which they were so greatly elated that notwithstanding Lord Cornwallis's misfortune the Stocks are at least two *per cent.* higher than they were a month since. This rumor has since gain'd ground. There certainly is something in agitation with the Dutch, to whom Catherine the 2'd has offered rather a peremptory mediation. Our Ministers seem to have determined upon one judicious measure, that of increasing our Navy to the utmost, such efforts may do much, but we shall scarcely extricate ourselves with any degree of dignity from our distress, unless the other Powers of Europe will see the most self evident of all propositions that the destruction of the British Empire must ultimately place universal Monarchy in the House of Bourbon.

I do not mean that the French will overrun the Continent, but the Empire of the Ocean and all commercial superiority must be theirs. It will inevitably rivet those chains with which the pride of Spain has submitted to be bound.

I speak without authentick authority but there is an appearance as if the Courts of Vienna and Petersburg would not suffer England to be completely undone. What an humiliating consolation, and how different from my feelings when I set out on the Russian Embassy* and the name of an Englishman commanded deference in every quarter of the globe.

Probably as we no longer are equal to an offensive land war in America we shall content ourselves with labouring to preserve the most material ports. ·If the colonys are completely emancipated, and remain connected with France, there needs no particular spirit of divination to forsee, that our West and East Indies, Newfoundland, fishery commerce and naval power must be lost. But having suggested the worst there is a becoming and usefull spirit in hoping the best. Some reports prevail with respect to a partial change of Ministry, such ideas will ever arise from publick distress. There has been however lately a mildness in the mode of some members of opposition which might be construed into their thinking they saw right. The times require that his Majesty should have a Minister who, supreme over every department, should plan and be responsible for the whole.

I am most happy to hear that the charitable institution to the which your better judgment led me to contribute go's on well.

(*Draft.*)

COLONEL LELAND to the EARL OF BUCKINGHAMSHIRE.

1781, Dec. 15. The Tower.—   .   .   .   The place where I date my letter announces my present situation, and will apologize to your Lordship for my not being able to accept of your hospitable and friendly invitation. It would have given me sincere pleasure to have added to the Christmas party at Blickling, and partaking of its *agrémens.* Here I am to be confin'd till the 29th instant at 10 o'clock in the morning, after my release some domestic business will oblige me to return into Sussex for a short time ; but I shall with great pleasure drink the Queen's health in Bond Street on the 10th of January. Had I wanted any inducement to carry me to Blickling, the object you mention being there upon whom my eyes have so long dwelt with pleasure and will still do so, would certainly have been a great one. I beg your Lordship will assure that object of my most kind and sincere good wishes, and how sorry I am I cannot be the bearer of them myself.

---

* In 1762.

Lord Rawdon was at the Levée yesterday, where I saw him ; nothing in particular transpir'd but that no officers of note fell during the siege of York Town ; a Major Cochrane was killed, who had escaped thro' the French Fleet in the night and arriv'd safe with his dispatches from Sir Henry Clinton to Lord Cornwallis, together with two engineers. Two hours after he landed he received his doom by a cannon shot taking his head off. An eligible mode when such an event is decreed.

Lord C. is hourly expected, any news that reaches me you may depend upon hearing, and in return I shall be happy to be inform'd that the circle at Blickling are as happy as I know they have the means of being.

P.S. General Rainsford a few days embark'd for the Continent *à la sourdine* in order to proceed to Leghorn from whence he is to throw himself into St. Phillips—it is said the other three don't accord together—and to remove the possibility still further of the command devolving upon a foreigner.

Sir H. Clinton to the Earl of Buckinghamshire.

1781, Dec. 29.—As I had the honor to write to your Lordship by the ' Robust,' I have now only to request you will read two pamphlets, which Mr. Carter will send you. I do not wish that the contents of these pamphlets should be made publick, Lord Cornwallis' conduct on his arrival in England will I hope make that unnecessary, otherwise I shall depend on my friends to do me that justice they, I am sure, must think I deserve ; from the Minister I am I fear to expect nothing but *illtreatment.* Lord Cornwallis tells me his letter was written in a hurry and under great agitation of mind, I felt for him and his gallant army, and had also my moments of agitation when I embarked my little army on board an inferior fleet, and put the fate of this war upon so very unequal a conflict as it must have been in every respect, at least till I had formed a junction with Lord Cornwallis. I expect to be attacked early in the Spring, and tho' I do not ambition this command more than I did, as your Lordship will believe, I should be sorry to abandon this army at a time tis reduced so low and threaten'd, but the instant that it is properly reinforced, I hope to have leave to resign it. This command my dear Lord is sufficiently arduous with all the support that a Minister can give me, what must it be when I am neglected, and illtreated, every opinion but mine taken, any plan but mine adopted, I am forced into operation planned by others. promised support, and unfortunate from that being wantonly withheld from me. I am sure my good Lord you will forgive me if I still harp upon that letter of Lord Cornwallis, he says " that his intrenching tools did not much exceed 400 when he began his works the latter end of August," whereas by a formal return of his chief engineer he had on the 23rd of August *992,* but if he had not 20 *ce n'était pas ma faute* for I had sent to Chesapeak this year above 3,000. His Lordship did not hint at the least want till the 23rd of August, which I received the 31st, two days after the

French were in Chesapeak. I should not have been surprised if his Lordship or his engineer had not known how many there were at the close of the siege, but at the beginning of his works he certainly must; why he was so incorrect I cannot guess, I ought not to suppose, he had in that or any other part of his letter, any intention of casting blame upon the innocent, and yet by implications and misstating of some facts it may I fear have that appearance. I fear I shall not have time to write to my good friend Sir Charles Tompson, pray give him the pamphlets to read, altho' his friend A——s does not appear to have been quite so consistent as for the sake of my country, and myself indeed I wish he had, but we have nothing to blame but 75 (*sic*).

Colonel Leland to the Earl of Buckinghamshire.

1781, Dec. 30th.—It may be no news for you to hear that the Duke of Newcastle has resigned for Sir Henry Clinton, being able no longer to withstand the calumnious insinuations thrown out (and cruelly encouraged) against his conduct. He demands a public enquiry, which I am sure will end in his justification— an enquiry, the usual stigma (at least meant as such) that has obscured the pretensions of every Commander-in-Chief in that unhappy country to military fame !—that of our friend is secure from danger. The *ton* of the Court I find is *not* to applaud him ; I have seen your relation and neighbour but once (very lately), and consider him as an unerring barometer. I have seen and known so much within the few years that have passed, that, with the sensibility of mind which I very much suffer under, a very little would compel me to renounce public society. But these are times that call upon every individual to lend a hand—and mine, if worthy of acceptance, shall not be wanting. I find from Mr. Tomlinson, whom I met to-day, that you have wanted an American general to repell the enemy from your woods; a few riflemen would do more good than the justices' warrants. I am released from the Tower and shall go into Sussex for a few days. Allow me to request that you will accept of my sincere good wishes and also present them to the party at Blickling, regretting that I cannot make one. . . . .

Before I quitted the Tower, your friend V. had been often with Laurens° and his release was daily expected to take place from his very infirm state of health.

Archbishop of Dublin† to the Same.

1782, Jan. 18. The Palace.—(On Lord Buckinghamshire's recommendation has collated Mr. St. Lawrence, Lord Howth's son to the Union of Timolin.) I condole with your Lordship

---

* Late President of Congress in America, and taken prisoner in September, 1781, on his way to Europe to conclude a treaty with Holland. (*See* Annual Register for 1781, *p.* 142.)

† Dr. Robert Fowler, created Bishop of Killaloe in 1771, Archbishop of Dublin in 1778.

most sincerely on our fatal losses in America, on our more recent ones of St. Eustatia and St. Martin, and on the very gloomy prospect of our national affairs. How happy ought we of this kingdom to think ourselves and how thankfull to Providence for having as yet scarce felt the least calamity of war! . . . Old Dr. Clements° was buried this day with great parades. The city has not yet fixed on a successor, but doubtless they will endeavour to choose one who will invariably oppose (as usual) the measures of Government.

. . . I shall rejoice most sincerely to hear . . . . " that your Lordship's important services here have at length been amply rewarded. . . .

SIR H. CLINTON to the EARL OF BUCKINGHAMSHIRE.

[1782] Jan. 25. New York.—My letters by the *Robust* and *Europe* will have said all I shall say upon our late great misfortune. By every symptom from every intelligence we are to expect a foreign armament here early in the spring, should it be so and we are not timely relieved our situation may become critical, *mais nous ferons notre mieux*. I have desired Mr. Carter to send your Lordship two pamphlets. I do not wish to attack any body, but I must not be wantonly attacked. Pray read my correspondence with the two admirals, recollect what has been said in publick, and then tell me, my good Lord, if that has not been the case. The 10th article of Lord Cornwallis's Capitulation has occasioned great discontent among the loyalists, the principle of discrimination is certainly unwise in such a war. The word *punish*, too, implies guilt, but as all the world must do Lord Cornwallis the justice to say he has on every occasion protected the loyalists, and that very article was framed to excuse their persons and property, I am surprised so much is said of it. I have been obliged to send very full instructions to the different ports, and General Leslie's Proclamation shews what is necessary to be done there, I hope these will have the effect we wish for. The defection of the militia and loyalists in general as well within our ports as without will be most injurious to the King's affairs. Your Lordship will believe I am not more in love with command than I was, but I have not the least idea of quitting it in the threaten'd state of these ports. My line is very inadequate to the defence of them, even against a rebel force, and we were masters of the sea. The Minister, forgetting the great detachments I have sent to the southward, often overrates my numbers here altho' I send him regular returns. That my friends may have it in their power to set him right I have sent duplicates of those returns to them. Your Lordship no doubt has seen a letter of Lord G. G. to me published in a rebel Paper, I should have quitted the command immediately on receipt of that letter and some others of the same tenor about that time, but I could not then with propriety do it, and altho' the Minister changed his

° W. Clements, M.D., was M.P. for the city of Dublin and King's Professor of Physick for Trinity College.

tone soon after, I had resolved if I had succeeded in my attempt to succor Lord Cornwallis to have resigned the command to him, nor can I serve with honor or satisfaction under such a M——r.

The *Hermione* is arrived in Chesapeak with £350,000 for W———.

Captain Sage of the Royal Artillery will have the honor of delivering this; he was with Lord C. at York and has the only survey of the ground.

Sir H. Clinton to the Earl of Buckinghamshire.

1782, February 16.—Altho' I am almost blind I will not employ the hand of a friend. Sir G. Rodney is a bold man to say he wrote to me, he had not even the good manners to acknowledge the receipt of my letters on service; he informed Admiral Graves, 'tis true, that his suspicions agreed with ours, that La Grasse intended to visit us in the hurricane months, and he faithfully promised to come before him, or at least follow him to this coast, why he did not he can best tell. When Lord G. Germain and Lord Cornwallis forced me into operation in Chesapeak the Minister told me that Sir G. Rodney had most precise orders to come to this coast the instant La Grasse left the Leeward Islands, which was 1 believe the 4th of July, instead of which Sir George brushed this coast about the 8th September with 4 sail, and sent 4 sail more to Jamaica, and 14 here with Sir S. Flood, convinced, 'tis presumed (as Sir Samuel was), that La Grasse could not bring more than 16 sail. Unfortunate campaign! If the West India fleet had not been wantonly witheld from us, it would have terminated at least without disgrace, but no more of that.

Bishop of Cloyne to the Same.

1782, Feb. 20. Dublin.—As the enclosed Resolutions of the Volunteers assembled at Dungannon made à good deal of impression on my mind, I thought they might engage tho' not *gratify* your curiosity. The paper will speak for itself. The few I have heard mention it think it calm and moderate. For myself, I like it the less for that reason If it had more of violence and passion, I should fear it less. It partakes the coolness of my late acquaintance, Dr. Franklin, and I am persuaded was not penned at Dungannon. The resolutions relative to Papists never originated there; but any allies are welcome to strengthen the party. Grattan and Flood (particularly the former) are foremost in support of Gardiner's Bill which comes on this evening for repeal of the Penal Laws. Great as our majorities are within doors these Congresses without will probably give employment to Administration not of the most pleasing kind. If any further progress is made by these Volunteer Legislators, your Lordship may depend on hearing the earliest account of it, as I know how deeply you must feel interested in the welfare of this kingdom to which you have so eminently contributed.

Mr. Conolly, to whom I shewed the enclosed, looked very cross and foretold mischief which yet I hope will never happen.

Lady Louisa has lately met with an accident by a fall, which might have broke her leg, but has only left her a little lame.

Lord Townshend to the Earl of Buckinghamshire.

1782, Feb. 21. House of Lords, past three.—I came to town to-day to meet Lord Cornwallis, his Lordship having requested me to move for copies of four letters from him to Sir Henry Clinton, which he finds are not received at the Secretary of State's Office, and which he thinks are very material to him, of which he has copies and can authenticate.

As your Lordship is very justly attentive to Sir Henry Clinton, I thought it right to acquaint your Lordship of this request of my relation. Lord Cornwallis has already mentioned the business to Mr. Knox. The Chancellor is not yet come down to the House, and it will probably be some time before I shall make this motion.

The Same to the Same.

1782, Feb. 26. Blackheath.—The letters required, which are declared by Lord Cornwallis not to be before the House, are :—

1. From Lord Cornwallis to Sir Henry Clinton, dated Portsmouth, 24 July, 1781.

2nd. York Town, 16 August, 1781.

3rd. Do. 20 August, 1781.

4th. Do. 22 August, 1781.

That from Portsmouth was acknowledged by Sir Henry Clinton in a letter of 2nd August.

The Same to the Same.

1782, Feb. 21. "Peers," near 5.—The motion for the Papers Lord Cornwallis wished for is put off, another mode of bringing them before the House being suggested, of which I daresay Lord Cornwallis will with pleasure give you notice.

Notes on the Clinton–Cornwallis Controversy. By Sir Henry Clinton. "The enclosures are to be made use of or not, as my friends shall judge proper."

A printed pamphlet (referred to in Sir Henry Clinton's of the 25th Jan., 1782) containing " Correspondence between his Excellency, General Sir Henry Clinton, K.B., and Lt.-General Earl Cornwallis."* This is annotated in MS. by Sir H. Clinton. The first letter is from Sir Henry Clinton, dated 8 July, 1781, New York. The last is also by him of the 2nd and 10th of December, 1781, New York.

"Annotations for Lord Cornwallis's Correspondence." This contains 33 MS. notes on the above controversy.

---

* This correspondence is elsewhere published.

The EARL OF BUCKINGHAMSHIRE to SIR H. CLINTON.

1782, March 4.—Your letters and several interesting communications have been delivered to me. Tho' you may have thought me lately rather an inattentive correspondent, your friends must have informed you that I have been in no degree unmindfull of any circumstance here which might in the least affect you. To the best of my judgment the present enquiry will end in nothing, but whatever turn it may take the investigation of that part of the business in which you are implicated cannot but lend to your honor. The opinion of the publick in general seems to be, that, as well some of your friends as those of Lord Cornwallis have marked too much sollicitude. The real object of the enquiry is deem'd to be an attack upon the Admiralty. The present interior confusion of this country is equal to the multiplyd calamitys of the war. The nation have no confidence in the Administration and full as little, perhaps less, in the Opposition. Unhappily England bankrupt in genius as well as other resources do's not offer one man (we have been ruined by distinct Department Ministers) capable of preserving the Empire. An exuberancy of declamatory eloquence is to be found in either House of Parliament. But an individual where experience, judgment, integrity, sound discretion unite is not the produce of this season.

You ought to felicitate yourself upon the appointment of a successor. I think well of Sir Guy Carleton, yet should in every light have lamented the exchange had there existed any longer a probability of your being supported by a force equal to your spirit and ability. Lady Buckingham will rejoice in seeing you. Nor can there be a doubt of your reception being in general such as the man can claim who has exerted himself in all which depended upon him to maintain the honour, dignity, and authority of his country.

(*Draft.*)

THOMAS CONOLLY to the EARL OF BUCKINGHAMSHIRE.

1782, March 10. Castletown.—You could not have disposed of "Runner" in a better manner than you have done and I make no doubt but that he will carry Lady Howe very well. I am only sorry that by Louisa and me forgetting to answer your letters upon his subject you have kept a useless horse so long.

I know you do not like to hear unpleasant news and I could send you none from hence that would have pleased a person of your quick feelings and anxiety for those you love, I have therefore on purpose been silent. I shall only say that the expenses of this Administration as far as promises go, for we have not yet got the Bill, has not produced a better effect with the Nation, the Parliament, and the Volunteers than the more honourable and economical system adopted by yourself ; and I much fear that Government to-morrow will think themselves obliged to give way and concur with Mr. Yelverton's motion for " quieting possessions held under English Acts of Parliament," which will lead to declaratory resolutions after the recess, which they will then not be able to stop, as the instructions from Grand Juries and Volunteers will be so numerous and compulsory. The natural consequences of this you can foresee as well as any man, Poyning's, Mutiny Bill, etc., must be given up, and all will be sett down to the Mutiny of Dungannon, a mutiny that has been fostered by the Patriots, by professors of patriotism in both kingdoms, and which would never have existed had the resolutions of the House of Commons in your time and the Address to the Lord Lieutenant been complied with.

This is an engine that for the future will always be made use of here till Great Britain is strong enough to support this Government and her own, and God knows when that day will come.

We propose being in London if the Congress at Dungannon and the Parliament will permit me in first week in May, and I will attend Caroline as a chaperon in Kensington Gardens when she is not more agreeably provided with one. Loves to her saucy face and likewise to dear little Emily whom it is impossible to forget.

The EARL OF BUCKINGHAMSHIRE to the BISHOP OF CLOYNE.

1782, March 27.—Neither indolence nor the want of leisure have prevented my writing, but the train of melancholy ideas relative to this devoted Empire which still succeeding in my mind must unavailingly flow from my pen, rendering my letters equaly unpleasing to the composer and the reader.

It is not enough that France, Spain, Holland and America should unnaturaly unite for the annihilation of England, that the shortsighted Court of Petersburg and the ungratefull House of Austria should persevere in the coldest neutrality. But Ireland also, tho' now oblig'd in the extreme, must augment her embarrassments and aggravate her distress. Yet let your patriots indulge what flattering day dreams they may, experience will fully prove that independence cannot be maintained with a most limited revenue, or unrestrained commerce asserted without a frigate. Can they suppose that when they got rid of the remaining phantom of English shackles (it is no more) and that the triumphant fleet of the House of Bourbon sails unmolested through either channel, that the Western Ports of Ireland will be permitted to meet the trade of French America, or that the infant fishery which it was my cordial wish to cherish can either be carry'd to material effect with exclusive advantage to their countrymen?

If hereafter England, Ireland and Scotland should become provinces to France, an idea scarcely now so improbable as our present situation was a very short period since, Ireland will scarcely prove the object of predilection, and when the political insinuation and old connection of your Northern neighbour are consider'd, possibly 'La Garde Ecossaise' will be prefer'd to

'La Brigade d'Irlande.' This reasoning may appear superficial and trivial yet it flows from a heart warmly zealous for the interests of England and Ireland.

The change of ministry has made no alteration in our fortune and the intelligence from the West Indies, tho' arising from no error of theirs, has tarnished the trappings of our new Governors.

Being neither in the councils of the setting or of the rising suns my information cannot be deem'd sterling, but it is surmis'd that you will have a new Lord Lieutenant, and that the Duke of Portland, if such is his inclination, will have the preference. Poor Irwine is reckon'd amongst those who are to retire, the loss of his Irish emoluments will be a severe blow to that liberal and most well tempered man. Mr. Conolly's intended English journey is a pleasing reflection to me. I wish you were of the party, as it will ever be a satisfactfon to me, either in a publick or a private light, to avail myself of your excellent understanding.

(*Draft.*)

JOHN FOSTER[*] to the EARL OF BUCKINGHAMSHIRE.

1782, May 27.—Our House met to-day. The Duke of Portland came in state as on the opening of a session and made the enclosed speech.

Mr. Grattan, seconded by Mr. Brownlow, moved the enclosed Resolution for an address to his Majesty. Mr. Ogle, seconded by Mr. James Stewart, moved an address of thanks to his Grace.

On Mr. Grattan's Motion the Recorder objected to the paragraph, stating that when "gratified at these particulars, no constitutional question between the two nations will exist which can interrupt their harmony,"—as it pledged the House against ever agitating any constitutional question. Mr. Flood and Mr. David Walsh supported him. On the other side it was contended that an explicit declaration of our perfect content, and a final adjustment of every constitutional question was necessary; that the paragraph did not extend to questions not existing, etc. Finding all the house against them, Mr. Flood declared he would not interrupt unanimity. Mr. Walsh said the same, and the Recorder persisted; but on many entreaties being used to him and Mr. Fitzpatrick rising to hope that if they did not feel and mean themselves to be pledged they would divide, as he could not otherwise tell the real sense of the house and his object was a final settlement and compact. Walsh declared he would divide. Mr. Flood retired, and on the division there were 24 'Ayes,' and the Tellers—*i.e.* Mr. Walsh and the Recorder—were the only ' Noes.'

After the addresses Mr. Grattan moved a Vote of Credit for £100,000 to raise seamen. He stated it sufficient for 20,000, and it was referred. I wished it to be a resolution for 20,000 seamen specifically; and then to have voted the sum necessary.

---

[*] In 1785 Chancellor of the Exchequer in Ireland.

Never was a nation more apparently satisfied and content, and I trust the wisdom of Britain will meet its just reward in our perfect affection and support. Mr. Bagnal is to move on Wednesday to have an estate purchased and house built for Mr. Grattan, the great deliverer, benefactor, etc. Invidious suggestions would insinuate that the Recorder is disappointed of being a Judge and Mr. Walsh of being Solicitor General.

Mr. Grattan, Yelverton, Burgh and the Chancellor are the private confidential men. . . . As it was near eleven when we broke I fear being late for the post.

JAMES BROWNE[a] to the EARL OF BUCKINGHAMSHIRE.

1782, June 27. Sackville St., Dublin.—After the kindness with which you were pleased to honour me during your Administration in this kingdom, I should feel myself unpardonable if I could be guilty of any want of attention to you upon any occasion ; and I fear I might be thought neglectful if I failed to communicate to you the manner of my losing the office of Prime Serjeant which you had been pleased to confer on me.

Immediately on the arrival of the Duke of Portland in this kingdom, rumour gave out that our new Lord Lieutenant would make vast changes here, would proscribe pretty generally all who had been attached to former Governments, would throw himself wholly into the hands of what was called the Opposition. Accordingly soon after, as it were one of the first acts of his Grace's Administration, I (amongst others) without any kind of previous notice received an official letter acquainting me that my office was granted to another and that his Majesty had no further immediate occasion for my service. I acquiesced, made no reply.

But my nephew, Lord Altamont, making my cause his own, directly wrote to his Grace and requested to know what offence or fault could have given cause for this treatment of his nearest relation. The Duke was pleased to answer him that he knew not of any offence given by or fault alledged against me, but that it had been thought necessary for his Majesty's service to restore Mr. Burgh to that office which he had formerly filled with such ability, and it was not at all meant thereby to throw any slight on me or on him or on his family.

Lord Altamont replied that I had never sought for that office till Mr. Burgh had resigned it, and that my removal without any fault even alledged against me was so evident an injury as he could not be insensible of or patient under and therefore he must beg leave to resign his Government of the County of Mayo.

Since that time the Chief Baron of the Exchequer died and I am very well assured that the intention of Government here is to make Mr. Burgh, Chief Baron, and Counsellor Thos. Kelly (a gentleman of great eminence of the Bar, but not in Parliament) Prime Serjeant in his room.

---

[a] Hon. James Browne, M.P. for Borough of Tuam,

How such conduct can be for his Majesty's service is beyond my sagacity to discover. Here are two very high offices in the Law disposed of and what strength is acquired? Mr. Burgh's vote and abilities (to gain which one change was made) are lost in the House of Commons, nothing gained there in his room; on the contrary any little weight of my family in Parliament there has been very uncommon pains taken to lose. It consists only of one vote in the Lords and at present only two in the Commons, but at the next election to rise to its usual number of three in that House; whence one might compute that this change might on any division make the difference of seven voices in the Commons and two in the House of Lords against Government.

Whether the other changes lately made in the law will have the same effect, I shall not take upon me to say; but I think I might aver with some confidence that a few more *such* changes would overturn any Government I remember in Ireland.

Your Lordship will I am sure excuse the trouble I thus presume to give you, since it really proceeds only from that regard and attention which I shall ever pay to one whom I am so highly indebted to, that no changes can ever make me forget the esteem and attachment with which I am, etc., etc.

The EARL OF BUCKINGHAMSHIRE to the HONOURABLE J. BROWNE.

1782, July 7. Exeter.—Your letter reached me at this place, where I have stopped for four and twenty hours in my road to an estate which my Irish residence and other circumstances have prevented my visiting for several years.

My concern for your late disappointment is in some small degree alleviated by a selfish satisfaction in finding you do justice to my lasting regard to those gentlemen whose support gave strength and credit to my Administration. My good wishes to the late Ministry of this country could not but be sensibly affected by the disappointments of my engagements to many meritorious Irish gentlemen, by which they disgraced and clouded my retreat. With the present Administration I have no connection. These circumstances must evidently deprive me of all confidential political communications, and the motives which determine measures either abroad or at home must in consequence be unknown to me.

But it is impossible for me to learn without surprise, that however it might have been deemed expedient to change his Majesty's Law-Servants in Ireland, the arrangement was not settled in a mode to avoid the disobliging so able and meritorious a gentleman as yourself and so respectable a family as Lord Altamont's.

(Draft.)

MR. CONOLLY to the EARL OF BUCKINGHAMSHIRE.

1783, April 17. Castletown.—Although this kingdom at present affords no news except riots at Kilkenny and other parts in respect to the admition (*sic*) of fencible regiments, as they are christen'd, into their towns, and that I shall, I hope, be in London by this day fortnight to kiss your hands, yet I cannot help expressing an earnest wish that you may return here to us as our Viceroy, for stay our present Chief Governor will not, being so incensed at the coalition between North and Fox.

I asked him the other day whether he would have thought himself bound to resign if Lord Melbourne had succeeded in his flirtation with Lord North before Christmas and had brought him in. To this I could get no reply, tho' it is evident to everyone that the separation of the Whigs upon my Lord Rockingham's death created the necessity of a Coalition between two of the three contending parties.

I was always, as you know, a croaker, but the affairs of England have turned out more desperate than I ever imagined; nothing but a very strong, wise and upright Administration can preserve you from troubles which if once begun on your side will immediately kindle here, tho' Paddy has got everything he has asked, and more I am certain than is good for him, as I think it will be some time before his new Constitution will begin to work to his expectation. We shall want a man of business, prudence and experience, and as I think you perfectly answer in all these points and I can see no other person half so fitt that has any chance of coming, I must wish for the good of both kingdoms that you may be the man. Our loves to Caroline and saucy Emily.

LUKE GARDINER to the EARL OF BUCKINGHAMSHIRE.

1788, April 27. Phœnix Park.—(Has received so many civilities from him that he makes no apologies for troubling him now.) The General Election approaches and the Archbishop of Dublin has a very strong interest in this county. I have perceived of late that his Grace has treated me with some degree of coolness, the cause of which it is not necessary to mention to your Lordship, but can only assure you that it did not proceed from any improper conduct on my part. If your Lordship should think proper to write to him on this subject in my favour, I think it would have the greatest weight and it would confer an additional obligation on me.

The EARL OF BUCKINGHAMSHIRE to the ARCHBISHOP OF DUBLIN.

1788, May 5.—His friendship for Mr. Gardiner and his opinion of his deservings urge him to mention that Lord Buckinghamshire's wishes are earnest for Mr. Gardiner's success. . . .

THE SAME to MR. GARDINER.

1788, May 5.—Communicating to him the gist of the contents of the preceding letter, with his own wishes for his success.

The ARCHBISHOP OF DUBLIN to the EARL OF BUCKINGHAMSHIRE.

(*Private and confidential.*)

1783, May —. The Palace.—I had last week the honour of your Lordship's very obliging letter desiring me to interest myself in favour of a man who has not the least pretention to any civility from me, he having shewn me none, but on the contrary disrespect, and in some instances marked it very strongly. He is besides considered by many of the Clergy as the avowed promoter of every project which can injure the rights of our Established Church, or advance those of any (other) religious persuasion. Such a man therefore, your Lordship may be sure, cannot be countenanced either by me or my friends. And his soliciting your Lordship to apply to me in his favour, without any previous application to me, can be considered by me in no other light than looking on me as a cypher, and thus adding a fresh insult to those he has repeatedly shewn me ; it plainly avowing that altho' he was conscious his behaviour to me did not entitle him to the most distant hopes of my countenance, yet being armed with Irish effrontery he wou'd wrest it from me by applying to your Lordship, whom he hoped I wou'd not refuse. Nor wou'd I refuse your request cou'd I consistently with the feelings of a gentleman and man of honour grant it. But his behaviour having been so flagrant I flatter myself your Lordship will highly approve of my determination to assist his opponents. At the same time allow me to assure you that I shall be happy to oblige you (as I have always) whenever I can do it consistently with honour. I shou'd have immediately done myself the honour of answering your Lordship's very obliging letter had I not been fully employed in my troublesome Visitation. My best wishes attend all your Lordship's family. Lord Temple is very impatient to leave us ; he told me this day Lord Northington was to set out for Ireland on the 26th, and he hoped to be released from his shackles on the 1st of June.

The EARL OF BUCKINGHAMSHIRE to the REV. MR. ELLIOT.

1783, ——.—I do not live in such habits with your new Lord Lieutenant as to render the solliciting any favour of him however trivial either natural or easy to me. He is generaly deemed a man of sense ; the gentleman appointed to be his secretary is highly esteem'd, and from my own observation seems able and well-informed.

They are both of them new in business, but if my Irish intelligence will have early opportunitys of acquiring experience. Lord Temple is thought by those who know him well to be particularly fortunate in his recall,[o] as in a twelvemonth those flowers might have faded which now will strew the path of his retreat.

---

* The Earl of Northington was appointed to succeed Earl Temple in the Viceroyalty on the 3rd May. 1783.

Ireland in my opinion sustained a loss in the Duke of Portland. Without any apparent brilliancy, his understanding is sound and direct, his principles most honourable and his intentions excellent. Peace has in no degree remov'd the anxiety of thinking men. Connections have been so much broken, faith and professions violated, public character so invidiously analysed, every species of subordination so industriously reprobated and the minds of the multitude so decidedly vitiated that the establishing an administration to govern steadily at home and to negotiate respectably with foreign powers cannot be the operation of a short period.

(*Draft.*)

The EARL OF ALTAMONT to the EARL OF BUCKINGHAMSHIRE.

1783, June 6. Westport House.—(Requesting Lord Buckinghamshire's intercession with Lord North to further his claims to the Ribband of the new Irish Order.[a])

The stigma thrown upon my nearest friends by the Duke of Portland avowedly for their support of Lord North's Administration gives me a claim upon his Lordship.

The EARL OF BUCKINGHAMSHIRE to the EARL OF ALTAMONT.

1783, June 20.—(Is obliged to refuse his request.) Since my return to England I have had no communication with Lord North excepting an exchange of the most distant civility.

Lord Altamont's letter to Lord North was therefore sealed unread and delivered at Lord North's house.

The BISHOP OF CLOYNE to the EARL OF BUCKINGHAMSHIRE.

1783, Sept. 21. Cloyne.—If Mr. Conolly has not undertaken to explain to your Lordship the circumstances which prevented me from writing for so long a time, I could scarcely have mustered up resolution to write even now, but from the mere awkwardness of breaking, should have protracted a silence, at the recollection of which I am equally amazed and ashamed. As he has mentioned, I will not dwell on the several severe accidents which affected my body and mind to such a degree as disqualified me to think on business the most necessary, or to enjoy what at another time would have been most pleasurable. I could not otherwise have permitted a correspondence to be interrupted from which I derived so much honour as well as pleasure. More than once I was in hopes of having it in my power to begin a letter with an account of my having obeyed your Lordship's commands in favour of Mr. Ogle, but the clergy appear to me as long lived as I do to some of them; the effect I flatter myself of our regularity.

This week produces no events, or worse than none; for your Lordship will be sorry to hear that your friend, Lord Shannon's, general interest is nearly overset by the democratical spirit now

---

* That of St. Patrick. (*See Annual Register*, Vol. XXVI, 280.)

prevailing. Longfield, who is monstrously ungrateful, has beat him in the City of Cork, and he is in great danger in the county. His borough interest remains, and indeed is increased by Lord Midleton's complimenting him and Mr. Ponsonby with the borough of Midleton, but still the dignity of the Shannon family *is shorn of its beams* by the loss of a general influence over so great a county. Your Lordship sees the proceedings of the *Dungannon Parliament,* and can foresee its consequences better than I can. If the Bishop of Derry° mends the State and Lord Charlemont the Church, our Constitution will soon be a curious one. For my part I am content with the present with all its faults, and hope Government will resist any further innovation.

The EARL OF BUCKINGHAMSHIRE to the BISHOP OF CLOYNE.

1783, Oct. 5. Blickling.—Your Lordship cannot have forgotten how much it was my wish in every reasonable instance to further the prosperity of Ireland and must consequently do justice to my feelings at the ruin and confusion which the wickedness of some, the absurdity of many, and the folly and ignorance of more is bringing forward.

If English Government is discreet they will not interfere unless call'd upon by the most respectable individuals of the country, and if those individuals are wise, such a call with the strongest assurances of effectual co-operation will not be long delay'd. It is scarcely to be conceiv'd how much the hearts even of the most liberal-minded Englishmen are ulcerated at the return made to their benevolence, and, indeed, to their submission. The Bishop of Derry seems to have thoughts of becoming a Right Revd. O. Cromwell, and if his cassock was to be searched possibly a breviaire similar to that of Cardinal de Retz might be found.

Happy at all times to hear from you, a letter at this interesting period will be more particularly agreeable.

The English Treasury has scarcely ever been placed in more honourable hands than the present; they ought, and I cordially hope that they will be supported.

Lord Shannon's disappointment gives me real uneasiness.
(*Draft.*)

LORD ROSS to the EARL OF BUCKINGHAMSHIRE.

1783, Oct. 15. Dublin.—I received the honour of your letter of the 2d, and am very happy that I have it in my power to acquaint your Lordship that this day the disagreeable business which was between Mr. Conolly and Mr. Montgomery has been settled. Yesterday Mr. Montgomery came to town. The moment I heard of it I went to him with a message from Mr. Conolly, but before I could see him the Chief Justice had bound him over, and the moment Mr. Conolly appeared he was also bound over. This day two of Mr. Montgomery's friends, a Mr. Brooks

---

° Frederic Hervey, since 1779 4th Earl of Bristol. He had been made Bishop of Cloyne in 1767 and translated to Derry in 1768.

and a Mr. Boyd, met Mr. Staples and me and it was agreed that upon Mr. Montgomery allowing he had misconceived Mr. Conolly everything should end there. Accordingly they both met in the Speaker's Chamber and parted reconciled.

I need not tell your Lordship how very uneasy this business has made me and how happy I am to have it over. As I was certain that you must have the same feeling upon this occasion, I would not delay one moment in letting you know the event.

The BISHOP OF CLOYNE to the EARL OF BUCKINGHAMSHIRE.

1783, Oct. 18. Cloyne.—The very particular pleasure which I received from your Lordship's last kind letter occasions you the trouble of this with hardly another idea in it. In this remote corner I have scarce any medium of information but the newspapers, which hitherto have told lies only on one side. I am glad, however, to see in the last "Freeman's Journal" a tolerable paper in answer to the two first resolutions of the Dungannon meeting. They are so easily reduced *ad absurdum* that there is no great merit in doing it. Nor indeed any great use, for an Irish Presbyterian Volunteer is above human reason. But the author has taken what to me appears a better line. He proves that those resolutions carried into execution must put all government and property into the hands of the Papists. This, which was intuitively clear to every understanding but that of a demagogue, may probably disunite the heterogeneous body of reformers and give to Government its proper superiority. However proper it may be for English Administration to wait till they are called upon by the great men of this country as the best means of securing their co-operation, I could wish they would not delay sending over our complement of troops. I think it but *respectful* in Parliament to have their guards ready to return the salute of armed petitioners. Mr. Conolly croaks as usual. He is very apt to guess right, but I hope will prove a false prophet. Our friend the Dean of Cork who has inlivened a few days of my retirement, begs your Lordship's acceptance of his best compliments with mine. I must again repeat my thanks for your letter of forgiveness. Your Lordship is a better Christian than I am, for I have not yet forgiven myself for the appearance of inattention.

The BISHOP OF CLOGHER[*] to the EARL OF BUCKINGHAMSHIRE.

1783, Nov. 7. Dublin.—Your Lordship I fear will be ready to conclude from the length of a silence which cannot be defended, and for which I most seriously condemn myself, that you once in your life at least conferred very solid favors on a very undeserving man ; and that he who had the honor of being considered your first chaplain during the greatest part of your residence in this country, has turned out a very ungrateful and good for

---

* The Right Revd. Dr. John Hotham, Bishop of Ossory, was made Bishop of Clogher in April, 1782.

nothing fellow. Yet this, my Lord, I will venture to say, is not yet the case. I have, and shall ever retain, the warmest sense of all your goodness to me, and with your Lordship's permission will venture to hope, notwithstanding all interruptions in the line of correspondence, that your favourable opinion of your old servant will continue during your life ; as my gratitude to, and sincere friendship for, my noble master and benefactor most certainly will to the last hour of mine. Your Lordship cannot be a stranger to the general situation of this country ; I will not, therefore, attempt to describe it. It is indeed beyond description, and if I be not more mistaken than ever I was in my life, the Island must be fought for in a much shorter time than is commonly imagined. Palliations will not do ; we impute to timidity and political impotence every expression of friendship from your side of the water, and insolently rise in our expressions and demands on every concession. On Monday next is to be the meeting of the delegates from each province in the heart of the metropolis, for which purpose the Bishop of Derry arrived in town this day, escorted by a squadron of Derry Volunteers. I narrowly missed seeing his public entry, but am told that the Right Reverend Father in God wore a purple coat faced with white, and on his head a gold laced hat with a cockade. He was received at Lord Charlemont's by different corps of Volunteers under arms, and takes up his residence at Mr. Fitzgerald's, who went out to meet him this morning about a couple of miles, in great pomp and splendor of equipage, &c. I am, as I believe your Lordship will do me the justice to allow, far, far indeed, from a man of blood. But should I live to see the day when all authority is lost, when armed associations prevail in every part, when treason is publicly spoken, written, printed and avowed, when rebellion seems popular and meritorious, when the people of principal property and consideration in a country dare not speak their sentiments or take a part towards its preservation, when its national assemblies sit in silent and tremulous expectation of the resolutions of a self-constituted and illegal one to decide perhaps on the expedience or necessity of their further existence and its Government stirs not a finger towards their support, should it be my misfortune to live to see an Island in so deplorable a predicament, I should almost if not altogether be of opinion that a thousand good troops stationed in each of its provinces, and a dozen or twenty frigates hovering about its coasts would be the most expeditious and effectual way of bringing its infatuated inhabitants to reason. *Mais changeons de matière, et de plume.* If Lady Buckingham and Lady Emily have not entirely forgotten me, they will perhaps think it is high time that I should enquire after and present my best compliments to them both, which with your Lordship's permission I take this opportunity of doing very cordially and earnestly. I might even add some expressions of love, but whether they would come so decently (even from an old Ecclesiastic) thro' the channel of a father and a husband I am not so certain ; it might be thought rather too much upon the brogue.

I have the pleasure to assure your Lordship that your two centurions (to wit, Mrs. St. George and Mrs. Molyneux) are both in good health, and for aught I know as handsome as ever. The same may be said of Lady Brandon. *Elle va toujours son train*, and Queen Ann's motto (or Queen Elizabeth's) will suit her Ladyship admirably, "*Semper eadem*," which a wicked wag once put into English thus "worse and worse." My old flame Harriet Fitzgerald, now Mrs. Grattan,[*] hath produced unto her husband a daughter, and I am told (for I have not seen her this winter) looks most deplorably. Messrs. Grattan and Flood are still both alive. Their quarrel it is said is at an end, but how it can be so according to the code of honour, as it is called, I confess, tho' a dealer in mysteries, I cannot comprehend. Mrs. Elliot gave also a daughter to her spouse not long since, and they say seems not the worse for it. As to Elliot himself, it gives me very singular and real pleasure to be able to acquaint your Lordship that a more steady and exemplary clergyman does not exist in his Majesty's dominions. He is entirely clerical from head to foot; attaches himself closely to his parish and according to every account I can procure is really a credit to the gown. But no wonder, for Elliot is a good man at heart, and has more than a common share of understanding. He very sincerely lamented to me his not being able to pay his duty to your Lordship at Blickling, when in England last year, and the more so as Mrs. Elliot does not every day see so noble a country seat. Whilst on the subject of ladies producing daughters, I am really sorry to add that my landlord's wife, Mrs. Gardiner in this street, was also brought to bed some time ago, but is I believe at this moment breathing her last. Mrs. Hotham sent to enquire after her half-an-hour ago and the answer was returned that her strength was exhausted and that she could not live an hour. Were it not for this last piece of intelligence, which is certainly of the melancholy cast, I should now wind up this interruption to your Lordship by observing that I have proceeded in this letter as might naturally be expected from a man who has just hired a very tolerable man cook, as I have done this fortnight. I have given your Lordship two courses. In the first you found I believe something to *chew* upon ; the second produced, according to the rules of cookery, the Volaile, or as we have it in the Hebrew, the Volatile, the light, airy, delectable and picquant. But alas I have not as yet a confectioner, so that in the article of dessert I must fall short. But I think I know my man and that I have to deal with a practical one, &c.

P.S.—What says your Lordship to the petition lodged in form against the city of Clogher for an undue election ? Such I assure you is the case, and in these times I will not pretend to say what may be the consequence, but I do venture to affirm that the election was, perhaps, the most constitutional one in the kingdom. It has not yet disturbed, nor shall it disturb, my rest for five minutes. I take the liberty of troubling your Lordship

---

[*] Henry Grattan m. Miss Fitzgerald in 1782.

with two more packets by this mail. The one is a letter for my
friend Harry, who informs me he is now at Blickling; the other
is a pamphlet sent from the Press, which promises to make a
noise, and may serve to show your Lordship that my gloom in
the first sheet of this letter was not wholly without foundation.

Mrs. Gardiner has just expired.

The Bishop of Cloyne to the Earl of Buckinghamshire.

1783, Nov. 22. Dublin.—The inclosed paper will give your
Lordship an idea of the object of our *National Convention;*
though you will have more trouble in reading it than I intended,
by the mistake of the person who cut it out of the "Dublin
Evening Post" of this date. If I could have formed any judgment of the probable event of this extraordinary meeting, I
should before this time have communicated it to your Lordship.
At present the conjectures are various. Mine, on which I do not
much rely, is that all who have any thing to lose, sincerely wish
that they had never engaged, and would be happy to see the
Convention closed. The division of the Popish interest has
produced what appears to me a happy effect. Had they all
supported Lord Kenmare *and counterfeited* an indifference with
regard to the right of voting, there would have been no check on
the demands of the Presbyterians, to extend it *to all Protestants*
in the several Counties possessed of a certain freehold right to
vote with all the Borough Towns. But the weaker part of them
under the guidance of Sir Patrick Bellew (an intimate of the
Bishop of Derry) *honestly* declared their wishes to enjoy a right
of voting, alarmed the Presbyterians and made them narrow
their claims, to avoid, on one side the danger of admitting
Papists to vote and of course by their numbers gaining the
Government of the kingdom, and on the other, the risk of
alienating their popish allies by excluding them only. This
confusion of schemes will I hope disperse the Babel-Consultation,
and send them back to their several homes to talk a variety of
unnecessary nonsense.

Everything depends on the firmness of Government. If our
ministers have good nerves, they have, I think, nothing to fear,
but a few more regiments would do us no harm. Mr. Conolly
was the only delegate who did not attend the meeting, or make
any apology for non-attendance. It would be well for this
country, that there were more men of equal decision.

S[ackville] Hamilton* to the Earl of Buckinghamshire.

1783, November 27. Dublin Castle.—The condition of Ireland,
though singular and in a certain degree critical, is, I hope, not
yet so serious as it appears upon paper, and I trust there is more
than sufficient good sense and moderation to balance the
absurdity of a few. The Right Reverend Oliver is by no means

* Secretary to the Lord Lieutenant. *See also* Ed. Tighe to the Ear' of Buckinghamshire, 26 Jan., 1764.

an object of apprehension, the ridicule which so justly strikes your Lordship is much stronger in the eyes of every one upon the spot, where a thousand additional circumstances heighten it and make him the jest of every company. If he goes no further than calling some of our knights and esquires drunkards and whoremasters, his preaching will have the usual effect; but if he attempts to take away Mr. Pery's bauble I think he will meet with a stiff resistance and possibly find a cracked skull. No; a much abler man is the Phlogiston that keeps the metal of the convention together, without whom they would speedily crumble into dust. The Volunteer of Derry is of no consequence. He of Winchester is, but not sufficiently so, to make us all forget the happy state of our Constitution or to hazard the fate which your Italian epitaph records. This with the determined firmness of Government to support the Constitution, will not suffer me to have the slightest despondency upon the event.

The BISHOP OF CLOYNE to the EARL OF BUCKINGHAMSHIRE.

1783, Nov. 9. Dublin.—The interest your Lordship takes in the welfare of this kingdom must make you solicitous to know the event of (what is called) the National Convention.

This evening Mr. Flood moved for leave to bring in a Bill for a *more equal representation in Parliament*. The motion alarmed our *sleeping* Administration; who expected (if they thought about it) such a motion to come in two months after Christmas. Being alarmed they came to a resolution (inspired by Mr. C—y) to oppose the motion, *originating from an armed body convened for the purpose of aweing Parliament*. Yelverton, Attorney General, took this ground and maintained it well. Flood in his answer was so tiresome and spoke so little to the point that I own (perhaps I should blush for it) I was tired and came home to dinner before I heard the decision. Your Lordship will excuse my giving my ideas of the transaction. If Flood had intended the success of the measure, in my opinion, he would have sent down the plan fixed on by the Convention to the Country, to get it confirmed and recommended by the several counties convened by the Sheriffs. Which recommendation might be conceived by those who have known nothing of Country meetings, to contain the senses of the people. But this would not answer his purpose, who is immediately going off to England, and hopes to carry with him an importance derived from having all *Ireland at his back* to shake the present ministry in England, which was the *real* object of the late meeting at Dungannon, originated like the former from English parties who chose to fight their battles on Irish ground. At present Government and *all* the great men of the country are united and bear a firm countenance, and therefore for one I have not the least fear of insurrection.

To talk nonsense costs nothing to fools; but to act, that is to risk life and property, will make even fools consider. If they were to rise they are unprepared, disunited, have neither money, magazines or anything to render them formidable.

I wish we had a few more regiments. Your Lordship knows it is too much the system (if it can be called *the system*) of English Ministers to be neglectful of this country. The House of Commons is still sitting. If it sits too late to give you the division, *I promise* you a triumphant majority. To-morrow you shall have the division.

The BISHOP OF CLOYNE to the EARL OF BUCKINGHAMSHIRE.

1783, Nov. 30. Dublin.—I am happy to be able to make good my prophecy, by last night's post, that there would be a triumphant majority against Flood's motion for leave to bring in a Bill of Reform of Parliament. It was negatived, 157 to 78. The House then came to the following resolutions :—

Resolved, that it is now become indispensably necessary for this House to declare that they will maintain the rights and privileges of Parliament against all encroachments whatsoever.

Ayes 150 ; Noes under 70 ; several members being gone away.

Resolved (on a motion by Mr. Conolly), that an humble address be presented to his Majesty to assure him of our attachment to his royal person and government, thoroughly sensible of the blessings we enjoy and determined to preserve the present happy constitution inviolate at the risk of our lives and fortunes.

Mr. Flood, Brownlow, and about thirty of the opposition (after a little whispering) seceded and the resolution passed without a division. One *No* by Grattan, who is now the contempt of all parties, and the disgrace of them too, by having an unanimous grant of £50,000.

Resolved, that a message be sent to the Lords on Monday to request their concurrence in the address. House broke up between 3 and 4 this morning.

As I have the resolutions only from Mr. C—'s memory, they may not be exact verbatim, but your Lordship has the meaning and principal expressions. I sincerely congratulate your Lordship on this transaction, which, by its decision, will in my apprehension restore quiet to this Country—and I the more warmly congratulate you from the important share our friend Mr. Conolly had in it. Everybody now applauds his wisdom as well as firmness, in never attending the illegal Convention.

Had the moderate men of property and character absented themselves, the few violent men of rank would have been ashamed of their shabby companions and the meeting would have become ridiculous. Their presence gave it dignity and made it formidable. Adminstration were timid, misled by Grattan, Ogle, and Lord Carysfort, a *wonderful* choice of ministers. Yelverton too had been deeply engaged by his former conduct to support the volunteer importance. Government strongly urged Mr. C—— to attend the Convention. He saw deeper, and obstinately refused. They now see he was right. Still I wish for a few more regiments. The appearance of them would possibly prevent a few rash block-heads from being knocked on the head —who at present may presume on the weakness of our military force.

EDWARD TIGHE to the EARL OF BUCKINGHAMSHIRE.

1784, Jan. 26. Dublin.—An unwillingness to break in upon your Lordship in such times as the present has hitherto prevented me from acknowledging the very valuable lines addressed to me from Marble Hill. The picture is admirably drawn, and I must grieve to think that it is too just.

This day the House of Commons met, and after some hours passed in ordinary business, Mr. Molyneux, who is a new member and rises upon every occasion, proposed an address to the King, approving of the overturn of the Coalition. Mr. Fitzgibbon moved an adjournment to Feb. 9th, and professed a dislike to entering into the Parties of the other country.

Mr. Conolly did the same in his short manner, and this last motion in the end was carried without a division.

As there were not forty members present when the question was proposed, if Mr. M——— had understood Parliament he might have prevented an adjournment to Feb. 9th, by making it necessary to adjourn to to-morrow.

I understand that the Lord Lieutenant ° is as easy as any man can be in his situation. Your old friend and servant, Mr. Sackville Hamilton, speaks of him with great respect. I could not refrain from reading your Lordship's favor to him and Mr. Foster, and both were as much pleased with the description as the subject would allow.

My little boy has undergone two fevers since September last. During December he was twice in extreme danger, from whence Quin and Sir Nathaniel Barry and Dr. Charles Quin have at last restored him.

SIR THOMAS DURRANT† to the EARL OF BUCKINGHAMSHIRE.

1784, Feb. 25. London.—Your attentions to me have been so frequently repeated as to render it difficult to vary the terms of expressing my acknowledgement.

The very novel political scene now before us cannot but be extremely embarassing to those whose opinions are form'd upon the principles of the Revolution. The important part of the question is not whether Mr. Fox or Mr. Pitt are to be Ministers, but whether the Crown is to support an Administration in opposition to a majority in the House of Commons.

The House of Lords have indeed step'd forth, yet there was every reason to believe, previous to the assiduous circulation of the Crown's abhorrence of the East India Bill, that it would have pass'd by a majority of at least one third.

That Bill is generally conceiv'd to have occasion'd the disgrace of the Duke of Portland, yet it is somewhat whimsical that the first of the Cabinet who received his dismission was Lord Stormont, tho' he and his unkle, Lord Mansfield, had both voted in opposition to it. It is also confidently asserted that when the

---

* The Duke of Rutland was appointed to succeed Ld. Northington Feb., 1784
† Of Scottowe in Norfolk.

Bill was submitted to his Majesty's deliberation, previous to the introduction of it in Parliament, he never hinted even his disapprobation. If Mr. Pitt can firmly establish himself he stands forth Minister of the Prerogative and the immediate creature of the Crown, triumphant over the House of Commons, and with a tolerable foundation for depending upon the complaisance of the other House. Mr. Pitt's disinterested disposal of the Office of Clerk of the Rolls commands the general applause,— it was a noble flight of young ambition. At his age with such abilitys, with such expectations, the pinnacle of political greatness almost within his reach, it might also be deem'd a measure of the most judicious foresight and the most deliberate wisdom.

The friends of the present Ministers are fond of contrasting the virtues of Mr. Pitt's private character with the excesses of Mr. Fox. Mr. Pitt is undoubtedly not accused of gaming, extravagance, or any other particular vice. It is rather problematical whether a man will make the better Minister for having uniformly kept the ten commandments, and would not it be possible to find in history instances of those who, apparently correct in their private conduct, have atchiev'd the most capital publick mischiefs? With respect to the immediate subject of your letter, I shall only mention, tho' without presuming to dictate to a better judgment than my own, that it is my determination to omit no opportunity of manifesting my attachment to the constitution on the principles of the Revolution, which words begin and conclude my letter. There is a report of a conciliation between the contending partys, but the difficultys seem insurmountable.

The BISHOP OF CLOYNE to the EARL OF BUCKINGHAMSHIRE.

1784, May 16. Dublin.—Our suspense is at end, I wish I could say comfortably, but the minds of the lower people are distracted, and Administration seems bewildered and irresolute. The volunteer spirit has worn out in people of rank and fortune, who feel that they had gone too far ; and is transferred to such as have nothing to lose. Numbers of the mere mob of Dublin, in absolute rags but provided with arms, are constantly drilled, sometimes late in the night. It can scarcely be doubted but that some foreign money is circulated amongst them, but unless they are countenanced by people of property I should hope our good neighbours the French would not take on themselves the entire support of this ragged army. The associations to purchase Irish manufactures have set our looms in motion for the present, but without greater frugality in the master and industry in the workman the relief will be only temporary, and I despair of reformation whilst the manufactures are carried on in Dublin. Your Lordship will wish to know the operation of our new judicial polity in respect to appeals. Nothing can be worse, it surpasses even our apprehensions. At the beginning we had some hopes, but the Ely cause extinguished them. Before it began, the judgement of many, very many of our Peers was anticipated by those who speculated on the sure standard principles of kindred and county influence. Those of the Judges who had been advocates for the parties continued so, and gave the same opinions with the same warmth as they had formerly at the Bar.

The *only* Law Lord in the House did not shine on this occasion in *any particular*. Many peers voted who had not given any attention to the pleadings ; some who had scarce ever been in the House during the trial. What added to the distress of those who were anxious for justice was the difference of opinion amongst the judges, on the sole point of law In point of numbers there was a balance on the side of Hume ; but after considering in the best manner that I could the comparative experience and the manifest partiality of individuals, the real weight of authority was to my apprehension in favour of Loftus, and after studying the case with a degree of labour beyond any I ever exerted in so short a time, I was and am convinced that justice was on that side. I committed my arguments to writing and submitted them to some judicious friends, who were of opinion that I *ought* to deliver them, which I did without deviation. I mention this detail to your Lordship to account for the conduct of a Bishop of your making, in not following *the* Law Lord. Indeed, his Lordship's opinion was unfortunate with regard to its influence on our benches, as out of nine present not one was convinced by him. In the last appeal from him he was equally unlucky with regard to the Judges, who were unanimous in reversing a material part of his Decree ; which was in truth so obviously contrary to justice (in the adjustment of an account) that a merchants' clerk could have corrected it. I was too sick of the Ely Cause to attend any other—Lord Bristol has been for some time quiet and sick—perhaps for that reason—quiet does not agree with his constitution. I should apologise for not having wrote before, and now for having wrote a letter of such unreasonable length. In my next I shall give some account of the situation of Buckingham Hospital, which from the distressed state of this country has not gone on in the manner I could wish, though no exertions of mine have been wanting.

I set off for Cloyne to-morrow.

The EARL OF BUCKINGHAMSHIRE to the DUKE OF NORTHUMBERLAND.

1785, Jan. 27.—Sir Richard Heron has lately informed him that the Duke of Bedford had expressed a wish in relation to the donative of Werrington. His answer however was that Werrington was at this time in the possession of the Duke of Northumberland and that he could enter into no negociation upon the subject. Thinks it right to inform the Duke of this. . . .

The DUKE OF NORTHUMBERLAND to the EARL OF BUCKINGHAMSHIRE.

1785, Jan 27. Northumberland House.—Is very much obliged to Lord Buckinghamshire for having communicated to him the application made to him concerning the donative of Werrington, and for the appointment to that preferment of the Duke's friend. The Duke would be glad to buy that living, if Lord Buckinghamshire is inclined to sell it, as it is so immediately adjoining his property as to make it a very desirable object to him.

The EARL OF BUCKINGHAMSHIRE to the DUKE OF NORTHUMBERLAND.

1785, Jan. 29.—Has no thoughts at this time of disposing of Werrington, but the Duke may depend upon its remaining in its present situation as long as he shall wish it should.

Draft.

The BISHOP OF CLOYNE to the EARL OF BUCKINGHAMSHIRE.

1785, March 28. Dublin.—A series of distressing circumstances in my family have prevented my writing to your Lordship for a long time. I had nothing of a publick nature to communicate, having been shut up in the country; nothing private that was not calculated to distress my friends.

On my coming to town, a month ago, I had the mortification to find that partly from the want of money, partly from want of zeal to follow your Lordship's good example, Buckingham Hospital, though completed and partly furnished, is yet unapplied and stands a monument how ill the nation diserved your bounty.

It has been the object of my attention, if it should be found impracticable to apply it to inoculation, how to convert it to some charitable use, and preserve to the founder the credit due to him. Two modes have occurred to me, either to transfer it to the Governor of the House of Industry, as a place to receive and educate the children of beggars who ought to be separated from the vagrants; or make it a Lock Hospital for venereal patients. The latter is most popular, most easily practicable and by being a separate charity would make your foundation stand single and not merge and of course be as it were lost, in a more expensive establishment. But I cannot think of taking any step without your Lordship's previous approbation.

As I propose visiting England in less than a month's time, I should wish to be favoured, as early as it is convenient, with your Lordship's commands.

It will be a particular pleasure to me to pay my duty to your Lordship, but as the health and spirits of my family and other business determine me first to Bath and Bristol, I must defer that honour till my revolution brings me towards London.

JEREMIAH IVES to THE SAME.

1786, Sept. 12. Norwich — . . . Your Lordship in confidence is pleased to ask my opinion relative to the ensuing election. . . . A very good friend of your brother's has given me an accurate account of the state of the canvas; and allowing all the doubtful and neutral votes to be in favour of Sir Thomas Beevor there will then remain a considerable majority in favour of your brother.° So much depends on the management on the day of election . . .

Your family interest is now at stake, it must now be established or it will receive such a check as will not be easily recover'd.

The REVD. JOHN STRACHEY to the EARL OF BUCKINGHAMSHIRE.

1786, Oct. 26. Newman Street.—The Parsonage House and other buildings upon his glebe at Erpingham† being compleated, he desires, as he is required by Act of Parliament to "insure the "same against accidents by fire at such sum of money as shall "be agreed upon by Ordinary, Patron and Incumbent," to submit to Lord Buckinghamshire a description and estimate of the premises.

EARL OF EXETER to the EARL OF BUCKINGHAMSHIRE.

1786, Dec. 25. Burghly.—Is commissioned by Mr. Walsingham and Lord Vernon to enquire whether he will do them the honour of belonging to the Sunday Evening Concert Society. Their entertainments have met with general approbation.

E. B. HERNE to THE SAME.

1786, Dec. 30. 32, Edward Street, Manchester Sqr.—Requesting the favour of a wild turkey to give a friend. Has not now the opportunity he had when he lived in Norfolk to get one.

The DEAN OF NORWICH [PHILIP LLOYD] to EARL OF BUCKINGHAMSHIRE.

1787, Jan.—Mr. Gay has, I trust, acquainted your Lordship that it was impossible for me to obey your Lordship's commands in respect to Hempstead. That living was disposed of at the General Chapter, which is the regular manner of doing all businesses of that kind. The Chapter was held on the 16th of December last, and the living of Hempstead given with the Vicarage of Wighton, which was also vacant, both together they make a very inadequate provision for a very worthy clergyman whose name is Tickell; he is brother to Mr. Tickell, a Commissioner of Stamps and author of the pamphlet "Anticipation;" and his character and behaviour are such that I flatter myself your Lordship will not disapprove of the nomination.

BISHOP OF CLOYNE to the EARL OF BUCKINGHAMSHIRE.

1787, Jan. 23. Dublin.—Before this letter comes to your Lordship's hands, I hope you will have received from my printer,

---

*The Hon. H. Hobart was returned M.P. for Norwich, Sept. 1786, in succession to Sir Harbord Harbord, created Lord Suffield.

†In Norfolk.

Mr. Cadell, a copy of a pamphlet of mine on the state of the Irish Church. The anxiety in which I passed the summer in the midst of outrage, and the unremitting labour of attending to the distemper of our clergy, and at the same time preparing to state their rights to the publick, must apologize for my not communicating to your Lordship a detail of those enormities which filled the newspapers and yet were not fully stated. Nothing could be more disgraceful or more full of public dangers than the situation of the entire province of Munster for eight months past. Yet in Dublin the tone was *all is peace*. In this situation, convinced fully of the contrary, I came forward, a forlorn hope, and this day four weeks past produced boldly the real state of the Church and country. Hasty as the composition was, the subject bore it up, and the sixth edition is this day exhausted. Till Parliament met my nerves were on the strain, but the sanction which my state received from the Lord Lieutenant's Speech and the Addresses of the two Houses relieved me from apprehension of being thought rash in giving the alarm. The motives for reprinting the pamphlet in England are stated in the preface. Much could I have wished to tell your Lordship all my fears, which perhaps your better knowledge would have dispelled, but they could not all be safely committed to the post. At present as the danger is seen it therefore grows much less, and the friends of the Protestant interest are somewhat easier. Whatever may be your Lordship's judgement on my reasoning, you will, I flatter myself, find in my little tract a zeal and a spirit to fill that station which I owe to your Lordship's goodness. It will not bear your critical eye ; but your biass to the constitution in Church and State may make you favourable.

EDWARD TIGHE to the EARL OF BUCKINGHAMSHIRE.

1787, Feb. 21. Dublin.—In spite of the low state of this wretched country your Lordship's kind permission ought to have been sooner attended to.

I have been here three months and during the whole of that time new calamities and new outrages have been brought from many parts of the Island by almost every post. If I should transcribe the feeling, well-wrought speech of Ross from the fourth act of Macbeth it would scarcely be too much.

The Bishop of Cloyne's book as he himself declared is soft, cool and mild in comparison of the real distresses not only of the Clergy but of all good subjects.

At length, however, I hope and believe the reign of this devil is almost finished, as the leaders of Parliament and indeed every person concerned in or connected with the State or Property of the Country feel it necessary, as well they may, to express almost unanimity and to exert a very strong hand. The Government appears to be firm, able and resolved; and opposition is so exceedingly trifling, in all senses of the word, that it is little more than " *exceptio probat regulam.*" I fear the consequences of the concessions to P. . . . of 1778 and 1780 were not fully weighed, and I am sure all the concessions and proceedings which tended to disunite these realms were highly mischievous to property, to energy, to safety. But it was the madness and, I think, the folly of the day.

The Parliaments have four great subjects—a Riot Bill, a further Police Bill, Commerce, Education. The last is, I think, the greatest of all.

Till people of all sorts are brought up with some sort of principles there cannot be any hope of security, and lying, thieving, dirt, laziness and spirituous liquor will carry the day. The first Bill has been under discussion three days and Dr. Quin would not allow me to stir from my chamber, for I had a real fever, though, thank God, but a slight one; and the account from Parliament of only thirty opponents to the principle of the great measure has restored me. (192, v. 30.)

There have not been any private plays since I arrived, but the Attic Theatre (Lady Ely's) are getting up "Every man in his Humour," "King Lear," "The Miser," with your Lordship's good suggestions, and "The Fairies." I do not hear of any more.

I must not conclude without assuring you that I entirely concur with your sentiments with regard to the drama communicated in your last favour of November, particularly in regard to the false taste of the old writers in many particulars, especially in punning.

P.S. My love to Lady Emily if you please.

MAJOR THE HON. ROBERT HOBART to (his Uncle) the EARL OF BUCKINGHAMSHIRE.

1788, Jan. 25. Dublin.—Everything proceeds so smoothly in the political line of this country at present, that was it not some time since I wrote I should not think myself justified in troubling your Lordship with a letter. Next to politics, scandal is the most productive source of literary correspondence; but the troops have scarcely taken the field, nothing hitherto has arisen worthy of communication. However I am confidently of opinion that, notwithstanding appearances, things before long both in the political and scandalous line will be in such a state as to render the word "smooth" inapplicable.

The gentlemen, styled patriots in the newspapers, availing themselves of the popular prejudices have, I believe, to a man (except Conolly and Grattan) offered their services to my Lord Lieutenant; but his unfortunate adherence to economy has prov'd incompatible with their views, and they already begin to murmur. They cannot desert the interests of their country gratis, and so many are in pay that it is impossible to add to the number.

Your Lordship's experience in this country must have convinc'd you that a patriot selling his vote is like a girl selling her maidenhead; the first deviation from virtue can only be obtained by love or money. No man can love the Marquis of Buckingham, consequently he must pay largely.

2 E

The Duke of Leinster and the Lord Lieutenant have had
several interviews. Their politics suited to a hair, but the
substantial consideration, I understand, has failed. *" Tam
frustra comprensa manus effugit imago."*
One of his Grace's followers in the House of Commons was
hostile yesterday, Longfield held by fair words, Corry (and he
influences O'Neil, I might have said directs his political conduct)
is not yet satisfied, nor is he likely to be. The curious part of
the history of these gentlemen is that they at all times profess'd
the greatest personal regard and good opinion of the Duke of
Portland, but oppos'd him on principles of English Party, and
now that the most obnoxious man in England to that party is
sent over Lord Lieutenant they consider themselves as acting
with perfect consistency in offering him their support. His
Excellency was wonderfully civil to me, but as he makes use of
the same words to everybody else, I do not think much of them.

Vicomte de la Herreria to the Earl of Buckinghamshire.

1788, Jan. 30. Turin.—Since he last saw Lord Buckinghamshire
he has represented Spain at various Courts in Holland, Naples,
and now at Turin, which he will leave in May for Lisbon. He
was three years in Paris, under M. D'Aranda—"Mais cette deten-
"tion n'est pas eteé (*sic*) tout-à-fait infructueuse, car j'ai eu
"l'honneur d'y connaître la belle et aimable Miladi Belmor, qui
"à titre de sa beauté, de ses belles qualités, et de fille de Milord
"Buckingham faisait pour moi une très précieuse connaissance."
(Commissioning Lord Buckinghamshire also to procure for him
various pieces of Irish linen, both for sheets, shirts, and the
table.)

The Earl of Buckinghamshire to Vicomte de la Herrerea.

1788, Feb. 28.—Is not surprised at the mistake which has
caused the Vicomte to address him as the Viceroy of Ireland.
He is so no longer. It is the Marquis of Buckingham, formerly
Lord Temple, who now holds that post.
Lady Belmore has often spoken of him, and takes the
opportunity of assuring him of her friendship.

Sir Henry Clinton to the Earl of Buckinghamshire.

1788, Aug. 4. Spa.—Had I had anything worthy your Lordship's notice to communicate you would have heard from me
sooner. A letter from Romanshoff's army which I have seen
gives some particulars of the naval action at the entrance of
Lake Liman. The Capt. Bashaw seems to have conducted
himself like a blockhead; he grounded his fleet on the sands in
the entrance, and gallies, gunboats and armed vessels (for there
was not a single Russian line of battle ship there) nearly compleated his destruction, he himself, however, escaped with a few
ships to Varna. Altho' the Swedes have certainly struck a blow
in Finland by this time, unless the Danes join them, which I for

one do not think they will, or the Prussians, or French interfere, I am convinced the Turks will sue for peace by October, not that I expect that the Emperor[*] will have great success (perhaps the contrary) till the Turks risking an action on the Pruth to save Bender are beat and retire *à la débandade* over the Danube, where M. De Romanshoff will probably besiege Bender ; he is too wise to undertake it till he has beaten the Serasquier, tho' 'tis the fashion to say here that he will. The news of the districts nearer home your Lordship has as soon and probably better authenticated than we have here. The spirit of liberty stalks abroad, everything seems to rest upon what may be the close of the contest in F(rance). I leave this about the 20th Sept., and after visiting Brunswic shall return to England about November.

SIR HENRY CLINTON to the EARL OF BUCKINGHAMSHIRE.

1788, Sept. 28. Spa.—When I wrote to your Lordship last it was from appearances as they then presented themselves. I really thought from exaggerated accounts of Russian naval victories, that Romanshoff would have advanced into Moldavia and Wallachia, and opened the door to the Emperor's offensive, and that the Turk would have sued for peace behind Mount Hæmus and Rhodophe before November; I now believe that the Capt. Bashaw has relieved Ocsikoff, and that the garrison has probably made a successful sortie, and Romanshoff has repassed the Neister to prevent Potemkin's being between the Corps of Oxicoff and Bender, or how account for the tardiness of the Russians ? 'Tis probable the Grand Visir knowing all this has wisely made his greatest efforts against the Emperor in hopes of bringing him to terms he cannot expect from the Russians ; with whom 'tis very unlikely they can make any, as each contends not for the *independence* but for the *dependence* of Crimea. The Emperor having failed in his attempt on Belgrade at the opening of the Campaign is now blamed for the attempt and the failure ; 'tis pity (I now speak only professionally) he could not afterwards have made an offensive move, besieged Belgrade in form, and covered it by a Corps either at Hassan Massa, or on the Morava, that perhaps would have been the best way of covering Bannat and Transilvania, but as it was not done, it no doubt was not practicable. The Grand Visir in his present move has assumed the appearance of offensive (so necessary to fill his buletin at Constantinople) without the danger generally attending it, unless he is unwise enough to commit himself in the open part of Bannat. His operation as far as it has gone tho' it might possibly have met with greater obstruction could not have been prevented even by a Eugene (on the defensive behind the Save) ; the Turks by spirited exertion and perseverence and *great loss* have gained the principall debouchées into Bannat and Transilvania. I do not, however, think they will advance into the open country, much less do I

---

* Joseph II.

think that the Emperor will attack them unless they do or should they retire, nor do I suppose H. I. Majesty will retire over any of the branches of the Tamiseh, for if he does 'tis probable he will lose Transilvania and his short communication with the Danube by Pan Zova. The Grand Visir will probably repass the Danube with his Guards to prevent Landon's[9] undertaking the siege of Belgrade, which I am apt to think he meditates.[†] As the Emperor did not find it expedient to attack the Turk in the Defilées, and before he had secured them by possession of Mehadia[‡], in my humble opinion he has acted very judiciously in not attacking him since, but in trying rather to draw him into a country where defeat may be more decisive, but I suppose the Turk will be satisfied with holding the Debouchées of Bannat and Transilvania, which will oblige the Emperor to keep a considerable army in each, instead of a small corps which was all that was necessary in either before he lost the Debouchées.

If the Grand Visir, now that he has drawn the Emperor into the Bannat, does not immediately make some attempt on the right of the Danube, or Landon does not do something at Belgrade, or in Bosnia, or on the Morava at Nissa, or Semendria, things will probably remain as they are till Romansoff, *enabled* to advance into Moldavia and Wallachia, relieves the Emperor ; no direct move of his own can do it I apprehend. Oct. 1st.—By a Vienna Gazette of the 20th Sept. it appears probable as they say that an action happened at Slatina on the 14th. I cannot believe it. The Turk will not surely attack the Emperor in the open country, or even advance into it, nor will the Emperor attack him unless he does—or that by Romansoff's advancing in Wallachia, or Landon's threatening Belgrade or something else shall oblige the Turk to retreat, and if he does I do not conceive that the Emperor can press him much.

When the two Imperials met at Cherson they determined on measures probably, but they do not seem to have considered the means also ; the R. army has certainly been ill provided. I have not the least doubt but that the siege of Oxicoff will be hurried into a blockade, and the great effort will be to save the Emperor, who can't now extricate himself by any direct move, unless the G. Visir blunders on the left as the Capt. Bashaw did on the right.

The DUKE OF PORTLAND to the EARL OF BUCKINGHAMSHIRE.

1788, Nov. 17. London.—The importance of the subject which has overcome the difficulties which the uncertainty of the time it may come under our consideration had opposed to my submitting it to your Lordship's attention, will I hope and believe induce you to forgive the anxiety I feel for your presence in the House of Lords on next Thursday ; at the same time

---

* Gédéon Ernest, Baron de Landon (1716-1790), Field Marshal of the Austrian armies.
† Belgrade fell before Landon the 6th Oct., 1788.
‡ *Or* Meadia.

that I must acknowledge the little probability there seems to be of any measure being then proposed in consequence of the calamitous and I believe desperate state of the King's mind. The moment when such a proposition may be offered is so uncertain that I cannot help risking the danger of being thought importunate rather than subject myself to the hazard of appearing wanting in the attention and sincere respect I possess for your Lordship by suppressing my wishes for its not being brought forward in any shape without your being a party to the deliberations it must undergo. A business so perfectly and happily novel, so new a phenomenon in the Constitution, an occasion so connected and interwoven with the very essence of it appears to me to be entitled to the consideration of every man and to require the determination of it to be made under the sanction of the first and most respectable characters of the kingdom. This opinion makes me bold in soliciting your Lordship's attendance. . . . . .

DUKE OF PORTLAND to the EARL OF BUCKINGHAMSHIRE.

1788, Dec. 19.—(Acknowledging the important communications Lord Buckinghamshire has made to him.)
"I anxiously wish you to believe that I do not regret the injunctions you have been laid under respecting the statement of the reasons and that the impression they have made upon your Lordship is to me a sufficient proof of their weight." . . . Is anxious to see him "upon this very important and awefull subject."

EARL OF BUCKINGHAMSHIRE to the DUKE OF PORTLAND.

(*Draught. Undated.*)—Though I feel justly sensible of your Grace's attention in expressing a desire to see me, yet it is most sincerely my wish to decline that honour, as your time might be much better spent. You may, however, command me at any hour this morning or to-morrow before 1 of clock. Your Grace will understand that however strong my opinion may be for his Royal Highness rather to accept the Regency under restrictions than to risque the consequences of declining, yet my vote will be very frankly given for his not being laid under any.
. . . .

HORACE WALPOLE to the EARL OF BUCKINGHAMSHIRE.

1788, Dec. 14. Berkely Square.—I am quite confounded by your Lordship's goodness and by the honour you have done me which I esteem as much as the great curiosity your Lordship has been pleased to send me; and I beg leave to return you my most grateful thanks for both. I should bring them myself to your Lordship's door were I not confined to my house by a great cold, but I shall have that honour the first moment I am able. . .

The letter will be very valuable in my little collection tho'
certainly it was more worthily placed in such a seat as Blickling;
but as your Lordship is more pleased in conferring favours than
in possessing curiosities, I will only say that you could not have
honoured any man with such a present who would be more
sensible of such a distinction and who is more proud of being
with the greatest respect and gratitude, etc. . . .

GEORGE SELWYN to the EARL OF BUCKINGHAMSHIRE.

1790, Jan. 22. Cleveland Court.—You should not be surprised
if you find me, as I am, a little vain upon being able to assist
your recollection of anything that is ingenious, either in an
antient or modern writer. The passage in Pliny, which dropt in
our conversation the other day, was one which struck my fancy,
it is now more than fifty years since, when I first read Mr.
Rollin's work, called "La Manière d'Enseigner et d'Etudier les
Belles Lettres." I read it for the second time not a month ago.
What made me remember it, was a remark of Mr. Rollins', which
says that " *Ob unam hanc culpam*," seems as if Pliny had some
idea of original sin. Of that and of other parts of Sacred
History they had some imperfect knowledge no doubt. Only
they regarded *that* as fabulous, which we are instructed to believe
is not so.

It is the preface to the Seventh Book which I wish your Lordship to read over again, and then you may, if you please, cast
your eye over some of the subsequent chapters, which will entertain and surprise you. I have long wish'd to have an edition of
Pliny with copperplates, because, after I have found the name of
a fish, bird, beast or plant, in three or four languages, I am still
at a loss to get a precise idea of it.

Squilla is call'd a Shrimp, and is so I believe ; but when
Juvenal speaks of a *Squilla* being serv'd up in a dish which
would hold a Turtle, it cannot be the same. Yet those on the
coast of Africa and near Alexandria were certainly of a greater
size than some, and brought at a great price, for those at Rome
who kept expensive tables.

Pliny's account of the alliance, offensive and defensive, between
this fish and the *Nacre de Perle* is very amusing.

But to return to that passage which was first mentioned, can
there be so admirable a picture drawn as that of a new-born
infant ? And how beautiful is his remark upon that helpless
state ! There is another in Juvenal which I admire equally :—

" *Primos incipientem.*
Edere vagitus et adhuc a matre subentem."

I have been too often in a nursery at this early period, since
my acquaintance with Lord Carlisle, not to be struck with this
description.

P.S. The first time I ever saw your Lordship was in Lady
Suffolk's appartment at Leicester House in King George 1st'
time, and there used to be Dr. Arthburnot (*sic*) (Arbuthnot ?),
whom perhaps you may still have some remembrance of.

How happy he would be and how able to explain some of
Pliny's Natural History, which, as extraordinary and improbable
as his accounts may be of some things, is to this day very
valuable and full of great learning.   .

There is a French translation, as I am told, not ill done, and
I have seen one in English by an old Doctor, but it is not worth
the money asked for it.

EXTRACT of a LETTER from "a very intelligent man" enclosed
by LORD BUCKINGHAMSHIRE to LORD HAWKESBURY.

1792, Oct. 14.—Not having the honour of being personally
known either to Mr. Pitt, Lord Grenville or Mr. Dundas, your
Lordship will excuse my taking this liberty of troubling you
upon a subject of publick import.

In this part of England, and it is said in many other Countys
the crop of wheat has been very indifferent, so bad also in
quality that the millers assert they cannot manufacture it without a mixture of old corn.   A very disagreeable spirit prevails
amongst the common people, which in this neighbourhood is most
assiduously fomented and if in addition to the increasing price of
every necessary consumption, bread was to become dear, the consequential dissatisfaction may produce very serious mischief.   The
only preventive measure is an immediate stop to the exportation.
This is stated merely to do justice to my own feelings, not with
a presumption that my judgment can have any material weight.

LORD HAWKESBURY to the EARL OF BUCKINGHAMSHIRE.

1792, Oct 15. Addiscombe Place.—Acknowledging his letter of
the 14th and will not fail immediately to communicate it to the
rest of His Majesty's servants.

DUCHESSE DE BIRON to THE SAME.

1792, Oct. 18. Richmond.—(Thanking him for a basket of
game.)

"Elle a bien du regret qu'il n'habite pas dans ce moment sa
maison dans le voisinage de Richmond, le temps n'aurait pas été
favorable aux promenades sur l'eau, et il aurait été difficile de
répéter celle de Twicknam, mais elle se serait flattée d'avoir
d'autres occasions de le rencontrer."

LORD WALPOLE to THE SAME.

1792, Dec. 23.—Enclosing a letter from Mr. Aufrere which
describes the good effects which have been attained in the two
Hundreds of Happing and Tunstead in having requested the
assistance of the farmers, etc., in those two Hundreds. " I hope
I may flatter myself that in conjunction with your Lordship, Mr.
Bulwer and other friends we might have equal interest with the
farmers, etc., in this Hundred to act in like manner and with
equal good effect. Perhaps it might be worth your Lordship's

attention how far it might be advisable to connect the two Hundreds of N. and S. Erpingham, that they may act together. By this means the number would be more formidable in all times and in all events of any riot whatever, on pretence of the high price of provisions, etc. . . . .

Lord Hawkesbury to the Earl of Buckinghamshire.

1792, Oct. 28. Addiscombe Place.—I defer'd acknowledging the receipt of your Lordship's letter of the 19th till I had been in Town, to attend several meetings expressly appointed for taking into consideration the propriety of prohibiting the exportation of wheat; upon duely weighing the information received from all parts of the kingdom, the King's servants do not yet think themselves justified in taking the measure; but I conceive that the circumstances on which they mean to found their advice to his Majesty in this respect are likely soon to occur; in which case the exportation of wheat from the kingdom will be prohibited by order in council.

MISCELLANEOUS ADDENDA.

Subsidy Roll for Norfolk on the occasion of the Knighthood of the Black Prince.

[1347] 20 Edw. III.—Assessment of subsidies for the county of Norfolk made by Nicholas de Castello, Edmund de Baconsthorpe, William att Park, Roger de Dersyngham, "collectores auxilii xl sol. de singuilis feod. militum domino Regi concessi in comitatu predicto ad filium suum primogenitum militem faciendum."

Will of Henry Catte, of Hevingham.

[1439] 17 Henry VI. Wednesday, St. Agnes.—Testamentary Deed of this date, reciting a feoffment (inter alia) of manors, &c., in twelve parishes and elsewhere in Norfolk, to William, Bishop of Salisbury, by name of Master William Askewe, clerk, William Yelverton and others, to the use of his will. Declares his will to be (inter alia) Sale of certain lands for payment of debts and legacies (his wife to have Skernyng manor for life on condition of releasing her dower therein). An enquiry to be made as to what lands in Hevingham, &c., were held in fee and not entailed. These to be held by his wife Dionysia for life, and the reversion (with the reversion of Skernyng) to be sold and the proceeds " per executores meos pro anima mea et animabus eorum quibus teneor fiant in missis et aliis piis operibus caritationis." The entailed lands are to be confirmed to the tenants in tail by deeds indented, security being taken that the tenants in tail do not impeach the rest of his will. He gives to Dionysia, his wife, the custody and use of his best missal and at her death he desires that it be delivered to the churchwardens of Hevingham (propositis ecclesie de Hevingham predicta) "ad deserviendum ibidem in capello beatæ Mariæ in ecclesia predicta in perpetuum et dum durare poterit." A hundred marks from the sale of the "Crown" in Norwich left him by his late wife, Katherine, is to supply remuneration for his servants and distributions among the poor and celebrating masses at the executors' discretion. There is to be no general 'roga' or distribution at his funeral. (*Seal.*)

1562, 3 Eliz., 8 July.—Charter from the Queen to Sir Nicholas Bacon's free school at Redgrave, Suffolk. Finely illuminated. Fragment of seal.

N.D.—From Mr. Buller. "Armes."

A shield.

> 1st and 4th Quarters, Hobart.
> 2nd, Lyhart. Arg. A Bull passant.
> Sab. armed and unguled or, in a border sable bezanté.
> 3rd, Hare. Gu, 2 bars or, a chief indented of the 2nd.

The arms on the stone chimney-piece (at Blickling) are the famous Sir John Fastolf's, impaling those of Tibtoft or Tibtot, whose daughter and co-heiress he married.

Fastolf: Quarterly or, and az; a bend gules; 3 cross crossletts, or,

Tibtot: Arg. a saltire ingrailed gules.

A packet of private letters on business addressed to the 2nd Earl of Buckinghamshire during the period 1760-1791, for the most part relating to his estates at Blickling, Beer Ferris, Marble Hill, and a house in Bond Street.—(1745) A letter from John Hobart to his grandfather, W. Britiffe, mentions his father Lord Hobart's permission to him " to goe abroad," and his refusal to allow him more than £400 a year.—A draught letter from the 2nd Earl of Buckinghamshire to Miss H. Pitt, with her answer (both undated) apparently relating to a proposal of marriage.—An address to the Norwich electors (undated). The conditions attached to the marriage portions given by the 2nd Earl of Buckinghamshire to five young women of Norwich. (See Annual Register for 1762, *p.* 71.)

There is a plan for roofing over with a dome the outer court at Blickling (1785); with an estimate (£137 13s. 7d.) "for the stucco work of the ceiling and entablature intended to be done in the great room at Blickling," (27 April, 1779) William Ivory being the designer, and William Wilkins of Norwich proposing to execute by hand the ornamental parts. In the same year Wm. Ivory furnishes designs for the frieze and cornice of the State Dressing-room at Blickling.—In March, 1767, according to accounts furnished by Wm. Bailey to the Earl, ten workmen are employed at Blickling in pulling down the 'old Hall' for at least a fortnight, under the directions of Mr. Ivory. Bailey relates that he is selling sheep at a guinea a head, and that the butcher is supplying the house with meat at 4s. a stone.

A packet of letters (1764-1788), of too trivial or indefinite nature to be separately catalogued, from the following:—

Harbord Harbord, E. Bacon, of Erleham (or Earlham), Sir John Turner, the Earl of Eglingtoun, the Marquis of Tavistock, Charles Yorke, Dr. Lloyd (Dean of Norwich), W. H. Cavendish, Robert Fellowes (of Shottisham), the Earl of Rochford, the Prince de Masserano (Ambassador from Spain in 1777), the Earl of Suffolk, the Earl of Hillsborough, Lord Ludlow, Viscount Barrington, Mr. John Carter, the Earl of Ely, Lord Lifford (Lord Chancellor of Ireland), Capt. William Elliot, Mr. Thomas Johns (of Exeter), Mr. (afterwards Sir Thomas) Durrant (of Scottowe), the Earl of Clanbrassil, the Earl of Sandwich, Mr. Thomas de Grey, Mr. Edward Tighe, the Marquis of Buckingham, Mr. Gay, Mr. Sweetman.

Draught letters from the Earl of Buckinghamshire to the Duke of Northumberland, Lord Carberry, Lord Orford, Mr. C. D'Oyley, Lord Howe, Luke Gardiner, Mr. Crowe, the Bishop of Cloyne.

Fragments of Letters (copies) from the Marquis de la Fayette to Sir Henry Clinton, and also from the latter to the Marquis.

Chapel Field House.

1574.—Corporation of Norwich to Sir Thomas Cornwallis. Conveyance of the wall between his garden and the orchyard.

1609, 24 Feb.—Corporation of Norwich to my Lord Hobart. Feoffment of the orchard called the Chery Yard near Chapel Field House.

1670, Feb. 24.—Corporation of Norwich to Sir John Hobart. Lease of Chapel Field Croft with all the land within the wall and the Tower next St. Giles Gates, for 50 years at £16 p.a. Reserving right for the citizens of ingress &c. as often as the case should require for taking musters and mustering men and horses and exercising them in military discipline. Also for pitching tents, &c. for such musters; and for the erecting of butts of the earth to be there had, and for shooting at the said butts and twelve score mark.

1670, May 4.—Order of the Mayoralty Court of Norwich to the churchwardens and overseers of St. Peter Mancroft, and St. Giles, not to put any persons into the towers in Chappell a field, without consent of Court.

INDEX.

A

A . . . . General, in North America, 388.

Abbes :
John, of Buxton, 44.
Richard, of Aylmerton, 99.

Abbot, George, Archbishop of Canterbury, 83.

Abdiel, Lord Barrington an, 250.

Abell, John, of Lyng, 93.

Abercorn, Earl of. *See* Hamilton.

Abingdon :
letter dated, 164.
Aston, 164.

Abraham, Thomas, of Blakeney, 107.

Absentee Tax. *See* Ireland.

Accounts, annual, of Sir J. and Sir H. Hobart (1678-1696), 129, 130.

Acle (Norfolk) : 132.
an abuttal of, 72.
the "*Pounds,*" a piece of water at, 57.
Papists at, 145.

Acts of Parliament :
for abrogating Oaths of Supremacy, &c., 135, 136.
army (Irish), 402.
relating to burial in wool, 144.
for disarming Papists, 136.
Church preferment (Irish), 346.
Highway (Charles II., 22), 164.
exportation for Ireland, 331.
of Navigation :
   in relation to Russia, 229, 230, 233.
   in relation to America, 292, 302.
for settling the militia, 124.
relating to navigation of Thames, 341.
relating to Parsonage Houses, &c., 431.
Perpetual mutiny (Ireland), 401.
relating to Plantation Trade, 302, 303, 306, 307, 308, 310.
Septennial, proposal to repeal, 165.
Stamp (American), repeal of, 260.

Acts of Parliament—*cont.*
of Tonnage and Poundage, (Irish), 302.
of Uniformity, certificate of compliance with, 130.
Wool, 302, 331.

Adair, Captain of ship *Winchelsea,* 150.

Adam :
"*nepos episcopi,*" 40.
Prince. *See* Czartoryski.
Richard son of, 26.
le Schipper, 18.

Adams, Sir William, 125.

Adderbury, letter dated, 241.
Charles Townshend at, 241.

Addey, Mr., at Norwich, 271, 312.

Addiscombe Place, letters dated, 439, 440.

Addresses to the Lord Lieutenant (Ireland) (1777-1780), 377-378.

Adelphi. *See* London.

Admiralty, the, 157, 160, 172, 256, 325, 330.
an attack on, 412.
letter to, 315.

Adyolf, John son of Roger, 27.

Æluric, Emma daughter of, 17.

African coast :
deaths on the, 345.
turtles on the, 438.

Agar :
Charles, Bishop of Cloyne, Archbishop of Cashell (1779), 343, 379.
James, created Lord Clifden, 343, 379.
family, dissatisfaction of, 343.
Mr., 338.

Agnew, Brigadier-General, 305, 323.

Aide, John, 132.

Aikin, Dr., 384.

Ailesham *or* Ailsham. *See* Aylsham.

Ailmer son of Godwin, 13.

Aix (in Provence), letter dated, 339.

Alan :
son of John de Reinham, grant of villeins by, 18.
seal of, 4, 19.
—— Simon son of, 47.
Will. son of, 10.

Alan, *armiger,* 11.

Albany (North America), 326.

Albemarle, Earl of, &c. *See* Keppel.
Lord. *See* Monk, George.
Lady, 167, 168.

Albemarle, H.M.S., 137.

Alberghi, Paolo, a noted player, 276.

Alborough, William, of Sharrington, 109.
Alborough (Norfolk), landowners in, 99.
Alby (Aldbey), (Norfolk), 101.
landowners in, 141.
Alcocke or Altcocke:
Katherine, 91.
Martha, of Foulsham, 92.
Philip, of Knapton, 97.
Aldborough, Edward, Earl of. See Stratford.
Aldeburgh (Suffolk), camp at, 353.
Alderford (Aldreford), (Norfolk), landowners in, 90.
Alderford, Bartholomew de, 19.
Aldman, William, 41.
Alexander:
filius Eluuriz, 12.
the porter, 13.
Capellanus de Sancta Fide, 17.
Alexander, William, Earl of Stirling, in America, 311.
Alexandria, 438.
Alger, William, 17.
Allen:
Anne, of Walsingham, 116.
E., and his Vermonters, 382.
——, separates himself from Congress, 388.
James, of Aylsham, 101.
John, of Swannington, 94.
——, of Lammas, 104.
Stephen, of Holt, 106, 110.
Thomas, of Great Witchingham, 96.
——, of Saxthorpe, 104.
Almacks', 324.
the Macaroni at, 254.
"Almanzanis," a recipe for, 176.
Alnwick, William, Bishop of Norwich, Manorial Court of, 31.
Alquen, a messuage, 41.
Altamont, Earl of. See Browne.
Altcocke. See Alcocke.
Altholf:
John son of Robert, 28.
——, his brothers Thomas and Ralph, 28.
Althorp, 361.
Alvechirche, John de, Archdeacon of Suffolk, 16.
Alvered, Stephan, de Ryveshale, 16.
Alvington (Alvingetun):
Thomas de, 37.
William, 54.
Alyett, Ralph, 41.
Alyngton, William, Esq., of Cambridgeshire, 54, 55.
Ambay (North America), 311.
America:
260, 261, 275, 280, 291, 292, 295, 300, 302, 303, 305, 306, 310, 311, 312, 326, 339, 341, 363, 391-3, 396, 399, 408, 413.
British policy towards, criticized, 239, 240, 280, 292.
French, 413

America—*cont.*
North, British Colonies in.
——, an *appareil de force* necessary in, 292, 295.
——, aspire to independence, 310.
——, British dominion threatened in, 398, 399, 404, 406.
——, command of the forces in, 326.
——, emigration to, discouraged, 292.
——, sovereignty asserted over, 277, 279, 281, 291, 292.
——, French Colonies in, 239, 413.
——, French fleet in, 305, 339, 397, 400, 401, 407.
——, French policy towards, 239, 240, 300, 301, 312, 327, 363.
——, lists and extracts of papers relating to, 260, 261.
——, signatures to protest against repeal of Stamp Act for, 260.
——, trade with, 239, 240, 301, 302, 303, 304, 306, 307, 309, 310, 413.
——, war in, 295, 296, 300, 305, 311, 312, 315, 316, 323, 324, 326, 342, 362, 368-9, 381-2, 386, 387, 388, 389, 396-410.
American:
administration, 384.
Islands, importation from, 303.
patriots, English, 393.
privateers, 300, 312, 378.
question, the, discussed, 282.
rebellion, 238, 296, 305.
——, notes on the commencement of, 291-292.
service, adventurers in, 312.
taxation, George Grenville on, 275.
troops, expenses of, 275.
Americans, the, their plan of campaign, 300.
policy towards Ireland, 310, 343.
Amherst, [Jeffery], Lord (1779), 379.
Amicius, Master, 12.
Amphitrite, French convoy, 305.
Ampleford, Henry, of Holt, 106.
Amsterdam, 152.
Ancaster, Duke of. See Bertie.
Anderson, Henry, of Berney, 117.
Andrew, son of William, 42.
Andrews:
Christopher, landowner, 91.
Ralph, of Great Witchingham, landowner, 96.
Thomas, of Weston, landowner, 95.
Anketell, Robert, 55.
Annaly, Lord. See Gore, John.

Anne:
  Queen, 306, 308, 423.
  the Czarina, 198, 200, 202, 206, 208.
  of Cleves (Cleevys), property at West Somerton, 74.
Annes, William, churchwarden at Blickling, 29.
Annesley, Francis, Viscount Glerawly, 378.
Antelope, H.M.S., 139.
Anticipation, " a piece of ridicule," 341.
  the author of, 431.
Anti-Ministerial Club in Aibemarle Street, 249.
Antingham (Norfolk), 81, 97.
Antrim, Earl of. *See* Macdonnel.
Anwyta, 9.
Apedall, Thomas de, 49.
Apis, ' the new,' at Cambridge, 287.
Apoditch, James, of Morston, 106.
Appesley, Sir Allen, Deputy Lieutenant for Norfolk, 125.
Appleby, Walter de, clerk, 50.
Appleton (Norfolk), 142.
  Papists at, 145.
Aquitaine, Edward II., Duke of, 50.
Arbuthnot:
  Admiral, 392.
  Dr., 438.
Archangel, 233.
Archangell, H.M.S., 139.
Archbishop of Armagh. *See* Stone *and* Robinson.
  of Canterbury. *See* Abbot *and* Stafford.
  of Cashell. *See* Agar *and* Cox.
  of Dublin. *See* Fowler.
  of York. *See* Kemp *and* Markham.
Ardfinnan Camp, letters dated, 354-5.
Arensburg (Russia), 233.
Argeville (France), Lady Bolingbroke at, 238.
Argyll, Duchess of (1763), 178.
Arlston, Joseph, 93.
Armagh:
  Archbishop of. *See* Archbishop.
  M.P. for (1781), 400.
Armenian trade:
  with Persia, 224, 225, 235, 236.
  with Russia, 225, 234, 235, 236.
Armenians, " thieves and villains," 236.
Armestead, William, of Morston, 110.
Armestrong, Thomas, of Holt, 110.
Armiger, Gabriell, 133.
  Captain of Militia, 137.
Armine *or* Ayermine, W., Bishop of Norwich, 31.
Arms in Norfolk, 130, 132, 144, 145.
  taken to the Tower, 147.
Arnald, Roger son of, 47.
  ——, Gervase and John his sons, *ibid.*

Arnold [Benedict], in America, 315.
  Richard, witness, 44.
  Walter, attorney, 54.
Arragon, the Lady Catherine of, her tenants ot the Honour ot Clare, 74.
Arthur, Robert, naval commander 139.
Artnburnot. *See* Arbuthnot.
Artillery:
  in Ireland, 355.
  held for the American war, 336, 338.
Arundel, my lord of. *See* Howard, Thomas.
Arundel, reports of landing near (1746), 156.
Arundell, —, 160.
Ashby, Sir John, Vice-Admiral, 138.
Ashill (Norfolk), Papists at, 145.
Askew *or* Askewe, William, Bishop of Salisbury, 43, 440.
Askham, Mr., 165.
Aslacton (Norfolk), deed relating to, 71.
Asshly, Isaacke (Guestwick), 92.
Assistance, H.M.S., 139.
Assize:
  breaking the, punishment for, 3.
  record of (for wrongful disseisin), 52.
Assizes:
  regulations for (Norfolk), 122, 123.
  Norwich, 286, 354.
Assurance Company. *See* London.
Astle, Thomas, 53.
Astley, Astly, Asteley:
  Mrs. Dorothy, 96.
  Edward, Ensign in Norfo'k Militia, 125.
  Sir E., 353.
  Edward, of Guist, 92.
  Sir Edward, 287.
  Sir Jacob, of Melton Constable, 108, 124, 132, 133, 136, 137.
  ——, Deputy-Lieutenant for Norfolk, 125.
  ——, his regiment of foot, 124.
  ——, reinstated on the Commission for the Peace, 132, 133.
  Sir John, 137.
Astrachan:
  an English factory at, 235.
  lambs wool, 172.
Atchurch (*ad ecclesiam*):
  Walter son of John, 22.
  William, 22, 37, 42.
Athboy (Ireland), M.P. for, 374.
Athill *or* Atthill:
  Andrew, of Saxlingham, 110.
  William, landowner, 91.
Atholl *or* Athole, Duke of. *See* Murray.
Atholl Highlanders, 330, 348, 362.
  want colours, 330.

Athow, Richard, of Briston, 109.
Atilia, rent of, 73.
Attic Theatre, plays at the, 433.
Attlebridge (Norfolk), 130.
Attorney General, the (1745), 157.
    (1762), 245.
    (1763), 248.
    (1774), his opinion on Boston riot, 290.
    (Ireland) (1779), 343; refutes Grattan, 363.
    (1783), 400, 425.
Attwode *or* Attewode, John, 22, 24.
Audeley, Philip, 63.
Auckland, Lord. *See* Eden.
Aufrere, Mr., on Norfolk politics, 439.
Augusta, man-of-war, 324.
Augustus III., King of Poland and Elector of Saxony, 192-208, 210, 211, 215.
Aula, Adam de, witness, 47.
Auncell, Edmund, 'husbondman,' 44.
Austin Friars, 159.
Austorgius, prior of Horsham St. Faith's, 2, 10, 16.
Austria, 209.
    House of, 371, 413.
    policy of, 371.
    —— (in 1773), 293.
    —— (in 1782), 413.
Austrian:
    army, 435, 436.
    service, the, 327.
    trade with St. Petersburg, 234.
Austrians, the (1746), 159.
Auteyn, Robert. *See* Hautaine.
Averagium, 61.
Averas, Sir Roland de, witness, 47.
Aviz, Walter, de Einford, 16.
Avonmore, Lord. *See* Yelverton.
Ayermine. *See* Armine.
Aylesford:
    Earl of. *See* Finch.
    Lady, 262.
Aylmer, Matth., 139.
Aylmerton (Norfolk), landowners in, 99.
Aylsham (Ailsham, Aylesham, Aylysham), 35, 67, 81, 101, 144, 321.
    'bruery' at, 76.
    Duchy gaol. *See* Lancaster, Duchy of.
    landowners in,
    lawne, the, at Blickling, 320.
    manor of, 35.
    military stores in church porch of, 124.
    Papists at, 144.
    vicar of, distrained, 21.
    ——, presented, 27.
Aynse, William, of Hevingham, 44.

B

'Babel Consultation,' a, 424.
'Bacchus Hall,' at Hagley, 242.
Bacon:
    Sir Edmund, 112, 125.
    Edward, of Earlham, M.P., 242, 243, 267, 354, 442.
    ——, commissioner of the Board of Trade, 331.
    Dorothy, 115.
    Lord, quoted, 176.
    Sir Nicholas, his free school at Redgrave, 441.
    Samuel, 106.
    William, 102.
Baconsthorpe (Bakenesthorpe, Bakunsthorpe), 53, 102.
    Edmund de, 440.
Bacton *or* Backton, Norfolk, 94.
Bafield-cum-Glandford, landowners in, 106.
Bagg, Francis, 126.
Bagnal, —, M.P., in Ireland, 415.
Bahamas, the, 252.
Bailey, William, 442.
Bailiwick, the:
    of Duchy of Lancaster, 81.
    of hundreds in Norfolk, *ibid.*
Bainard, William, 47.
Baker:
    Captain, 150.
    Mr., under sentence of death, 339.
Bakunsthorpe. *See* Baconsthorpe.
Baldewyne, John, 22.
Bale (Bathely *or* Bately), 106, 110.
Baley, William, 112.
Balls, Richard, 107.
Ballinrobe (Ireland), 389.
Bamfylde, Sir Richard, 285.
Banagher (King's County), 384.
Bande, John, 105.
Bangor, Lord. *See* Ward.
Bangor, J. bishop of. *See* Egerton.
Baningham (Norfolk), 102.
Banat *or* Bannat (Hungary), 435-436.
Barbadoes, Commodore Hotham at, 342.
Barber:
    James, Commander - in - Chief (Navy), 139.
    Thomas, 133.
Barbour, John, 94.
Bardolf:
    Sir Thomas, 18, 42.
    Thomas, 11.
Bardolf Fen, 85.
Baret, Simon, 52, 53.

Barker:
    Colonel, 353.
    John, 54.
    Robert, 114.
    Roger, of Irmingland, 68.
    Thomas, 54, 101.
    William, a prisoner, 86.
    W., 127.
Barkley Castle, H.M.S., 139.
Barlow, —, 175.
Barnak, manor of. *See* Wymondham.
Barnard (Bernard) Castle, 152.
Barnard:
    Anne, 115.
    family, pedigree of. 65.
Barneingham Parva. *See* Barningham.
Barnes:
    Anne, 115.
    Jeremy, 102.
    Thomas, 124.
Barney, —, 132.
Barney (Norfolk). *See* Berney.
Barningham (Norfolk): 144.
    Norwood, landowners in, 99.
    Parva *or* Stafford, 52, 54, 102
    Towne, 99.
Barras, Louis Comte de (Admiral), in West Indies, 397.
Barrington:
    Admiral, at St. Lucia, 342.
    Lady, death of, 252.
    William Wildman, 2nd Viscount, Secretary at War, 182, 270, 337, 347, 350, 367, 378, 442.
    ——, letters from, 245-254, 267, 268, 271, 318, 324, 325, 351.
    ——, letters to, 269.
Barron, William, 96.
Barry:
    Barry, 325.
    Sir Nathaniel, physician, 427.
Barsham *or* Basham:
    East, 137, 142, 144.
    West, deed relating to, 52, 74.
Bartlett, Ld. (*sic*), Commander R.N. (1691), 137.
Barwick. *See* Berwick.
Basham, East (Norfolk). *See* Barsham.
Bashaw, the Captain, in Russo-Turkish war, 434, 435, 436.
Basseth, William, 17.
Bassett, Henry, 107.
Bassingham (Bessingham, Basingham): 100.
    Robert de, 13.
    Walter, son of Robert de, confirms a grant of salt, 13.
    William de, witness, 48, 49, 50.
Bataille, William, witness, 19.
Batavia, 386.
Batch, Elizabeth, at Sparham, 94.
Bate, Luke, of Saxthorpe, 48, 51.
Bateman:
    Adam, 25.
    Robert, 48.
    William, 98.
    W., bishop of Norwich, 32.

Bates, William, 99.
Bath, Lord. *See* Pulteney.
Bath, 160, 168, 169, 250, 262, 275, 294, 347, 390, 430.
    letters dated, 262, 290, 339, 374.
Bathely *or* Bately (Norfolk). *See* Bale.
Batteler, commander - in - chief (Navy), 139.
Bawdswell *or* Baudswell (Norfolk), landowners in, 90.
Baxter *or* Baxtere:
    Thomas, 97.
    John, 53.
Bayes, Henry, 130.
Bayfield, William, 93.
Bayly, Mr., 384.
Bay-yarn, English and Irish compared, 312.
Beacon:
    Elizabeth, 91.
    Joyce, 148.
    Thomas, 148.
Beare:
    Richard, 104.
    Robert, 102.
Beauchamp:
    Viscount. *See* Conway.
    John, Lord (1442), 54.
Beaufort, Duke of (1779). *See* Somerset.
Beaufort, ship, 150.
Beaumont, Basil, 138.
Beck, Geoffrey de, 47.
Becke, Mrs., 93.
Beckett (Berkshire), Lord Barrington at, 271.
Beckford, W., Alderman, in House of Commons, 272-275.
Beckhall (Norfolk), letter dated, 128.
Beckham:
    East (Norfolk), 100.
    West, 102.
Beckham, Samuel, 106.
Bective, Earl of (1778). *See* Taylour.
Bedell, George, 144.
Bede Roll, 2, 20.
Bedford, Duke of (1745). *See* Russell.
    my Lord of (1634-1637). *See* Russell, Francis, 4th Earl of.
Bedford Level, 165.
Bedingfeld, Beddingfeld, Beddingfield, Bedyngteld:
    Anthony, 142.
    Adam, 11.
    Christopher, 123, 124, 128, 129.
    Dame Dorothy, 147.
    Dame Frances, her contract of marriage, 82.
    Henry, 90, 99, 116.
    Sir Henry, 99, 128, 129, 142.
    ——, letter from, 128.
    Mrs. Henrietta, 147.
    Humphrey, 116.
    Philip, 144.
    Robert, 56.
    Thomas, 93.
Bedlam, 163.

Beer (Devonshire), 293.
  fishing rights in, 346.
  letter dated, 347.
  Pyke's tenement in. 293.
  rector of. *See* Short, Wm.
  Alston, 366.
  Feris, manor of, 146, 441.
  ——, fishery in, 332.
  ——, Lord Buckinghamshire's right in, 332, 346.
Beeston (*or* Beston):
  John, 18.
  Ralph, 52.
  Thomas, *ibid.*
Beeston Regis (Norfolk), 100.
Beevor, Sir Thomas, a candidate for Norwich, 431.
Beggars:
  expenses of, 79.
  Irish. *See* Irish.
  licensed, 78.
  transportation of, 79.
  whipping of, *ibid.*
Begvyles, a manor in Winterton, 54.
Bek, Anthony, Bishop of Norwich, 31.
Belache. *See* Belaugh.
Belagh, *ibid.*
Belan (Ireland), letter dated, 338.
Belaselski, Prince, 190, 191.
Belaugh (Belough, Belache, Belagh), (Norfolk), 102.
  Henry de, 42.
  William de, 17.
Bele, Hervey, entry of, into homage of Horsham St. Faith's, 6.
Belfast, 391.
Belgrade, siege of, 435, 436.
Belhus, Theobald de, 12.
Bell, Belle:
  Edmund, 104.
  Francis, 126.
  John, 96, 104.
  Philip, 145.
  Ralph, 37.
  Richard, 86.
  ——, of Wood Dawling, 96.
  Sir Robert, letters from, 84, 85.
  Thomas, 24.
  ——, of Oulton, 129.
  Tom., at Blickling, 320.
  William, 96, 104, 142.
Bellenden, ——, a company given to, 244.
Bellers, John, 55.
Bellew, Sir Patrick, a friend of Bishop of Derry, 424.
Belmore, Lady, 434.
Belvedere, Earl of. *See* Rochfort.
Bemund, John. Headborgh of Blickling, 24.
Bencoolen (Sumatra), 150.
Bender (Bessarabia), 435.
Bendish, John, 90, 99.
Benetingesker, 17.
Bengal, 150.
Benington, Robert, 116.
Benn, Edward, 125.
Bennet, the widow, 159.

Bentinck, William Henry Cavendish, 3rd Duke of Portland, 274, 427, 434, 436, 437.
  character of, 419.
  Viceroy of Ireland, 414, 415.
  letters from, 436, 437.
  letter to, 436.
Berengarius, Prior of Horsham St. Faith's, 2, 7, 13.
Beresford:
  George de la Poer, Earl of Tyrone, 379.
  Mr., 359, 384.
  ——, his country house taken by Lord Carlisle, 386.
Berkeley:
  Hon. George, 238.
  ——, will of, 146.
  Narbonne, Lord Botetourt, 250, 295.
'Berlin,' Lord Harcourt's, 297, 298.
Berlin, 174, 221, 253.
  Court of, 191, 219.
  letter dated, 220.
Bernard Castle. *See* Barnard.
Bernard, Governor, letters from and to, 260, 261.
Bernes, Richard, 55.
Berners, Hatton, 133.
Berney (Norfolk), 116.
Berney (Barney *or* Berneye):
  Henry de, 28.
  John de, 43, 60.
  ——, Katherine wife of, 60.
  John, 124, 127, 129.
  Richard, 59, 124.
  Sir Richard, sells Langley Abbey, 5.
  Robert, 53.
  Roger, 61, 62.
  Sir Thomas de, 60.
  Thomas, 111, 145.
Bernier, M. de, Minister of Marines, letter to, 239.
Berningham, Sir Nicolas de, 48.
Berningham *or* Bernyngham. *See* Barningham.
Berry:
  Michael, 139.
  Thomas, 140.
Bert *or* Berte:
  John, 46, 56.
  Robert, 28.
Bertie, Robert, 4th Duke of Ancaster, 337.
Berwick (Barwick), 151.
Berwick, H.M.S., 138.
Bery, John de, 52.
Bessborough, Lord. *See* Ponsonby.
Betrothal without licence, presentment for, 6.
Betts, William, 114.
Bevan, Alderman Henry, 379.
Bialla (Galicia), 218.
Bickley, Sir Francis, 124, 125.
Bielinski, F., 204.
Bigge, John, 14.

Bigot, Thomas, 60.
Bills in Parliament:
  Army (Ireland), 366, 370.
  East India, 427.
  Education, 433.
  Establishment (Burke's), 363.
  for extending Habeas Corpus, 165.
  of Indemnity (1766), 273, 274.
  Mutiny:
    (English), 384.
    (Irish), 363-366, 370, 371, 394, 401, 413.
  Police (Ireland), 433.
  Popery, 334.
  re Possessions held in Ireland, &c., 413.
  Reform of Irish Parliament, 426.
  Riot (Ireland), 433.
  Septennial, 165.
  Short Money (Ireland), 359.
  Small Debts, 163.
  Stamp (Irish), 350, 351.
  Sugar (Ireland), 370.
  Test, 364.
  Tobacco (Irish), 350, 351.
Billingford (Norfolk), 91, 144.
Billington, Robert, 100.
Billop, Christopher, 138.
Bilney, Reginald de, 51.
Bing. See Byng.
Bingham, Mr., 155.
Binham (Norfolk), 112.
Bintry (Bintrye, Bynetre), 9, 49, 121.
Birch, James, his letter from Cherbourg, 162.
Bird:
  George, 96.
  Lieut.-Colonel, 323.
Biren or Biron:
  Duchesse de, letter from, 439.
  Ernest John, Comte de, Duc de Courland XV., 198-212, 214, 215, 216, 282.
  ——, —— invested with Duchy, 198-202, 206, 214, 215.
  ——, ——, renounces it, 201.
  ——, exile of, 200, 202, 203.
  ——, recalled by Peter III., 201.
  Pierre de, Prince de Courland, 201, 282.
  ——, letter from, 282.
Birston, Birstonne, Birstoun. See Briston.
Birton, William, 20.
Biscop, Herbert, 8.
Bishop's Stortford, Tooke's school at, 145.
Blackbourne, Edmund, 142, 145.
Black Death, the, 3, 33.
Black Prince, the. See Edward.
Blacke, Christopher, 101.
Blackett, John, 86.
Blackford, letter dated, 276.
Blackheath, letter dated, 411.
Bladwell, William, 95.
Blafer, Hugh de, 40.
Blakeney (Norfolk), 111.

Blandford, Marchioness of, 175, 176, 177, 178.
Blaquiere, Sir John, in Ireland, 381.
  his country house taken by W. Eden, 386.
Blaxter, Nathaniel, 103.
Blenheim (Oxfordshire), 283.
Blennerhasset:
  John, 57.
  William, 57.
Blickling, Blycling, Blyclyng, Brickling:
  1-3, 5, 20-30, 71, 82, 102, 130, 132, 143, 144, 185, 241, 251, 258, 262, 268, 274, 276, 278, 286, 288, 294, 320, 404, 406, 407, 408, 423, 424, 441, 442.
  arms taken at, 130, 132.
  Borghs, Head, 24.
  Bertrams, a messuage in, 29.
  customary of Manor Court, 22-24.
  Dygardes, a messuage in, 29.
  Hall (old), pulled down, 442.
  House, accounts of, 87, 88.
  ——, improvements in, 441, 442.
  Hundred, roll of Edward I. relating to, 1.
  Kirkegap at, 29.
  Leet Rolls, list of, 21-22.
  letters dated, 405, 420.
  —— relating to, 441.
  levy for church at, 27.
  Manor, 1-3, 20-30.
  ——, Court Rolls, 21-22.
  manorial documents, 1-3, 20-29.
  mausoleum at, XVIII.
  mill, 29.
  muniments at, 1-3.
  owners of, 1, 2, 3, 21, 28-30, 102, 103.
  rectory of, 276.
  rental of, 22.
Blofeld, Blofield or Blofeyld:
  Jeremy, 101.
  Jerome, 100.
  Leonard, 101.
  William, 100.
Blofield (Norfolk), 141.
Blomfield's History of Norfolk, 2, 4, 18.
"Bloomsburys," the, 351.
Blue Horse. See Regiments.
Blue Squadron, 138.
Blunde, Mirylda la, 39.
Blunt:
  Henry le, 35, 36, 39.
  Simon le, 39.
Blycling or Blyclyng. See Blickling.
Blyfer, Mathew, 116.
Boar and Bull, free, 29, 35.
Board of Conciliation (American), in relation to revolted regiments, 382, 383, 384.
Board of Trade: 245, 256, 331, 362.
  representation to Council on American affairs, 260.
  report on commerce with Russia, 222-232.

2 F

Board of Works, 349.
Boat race on the Neva, 183-184.
Boddy, William, 91.
Bodham (Norfolk), landowners in, 108, 111.
Bohun (Buun), Humfrey de, 2, 12.
Boise:
  John, 108.
  George, 108.
Boisnegan, Captain, 160.
Bokenham or Bukenham Castle. *See* Buckenham.
Bokenham, William, 138.
Bolewik, Robert de, 42.
Boleyn or Bulleyn:
  Bridget, 106.
  Elizabeth, 29, 44.
  ——, family of, at Blickling, 2.
  Sir Geoffrey, 3, 29, 30.
  ——, Alderman of London, 30.
  George, 105, 106.
  James, 106.
  Sir James, 29, 31, 44.
  Thomas, 29.
  William, knight, his will, 29.
  ——, at Marlingforth, 70.
  William (1469), 55.
Bolingbroke (Bullingbrooke):
  Lord. *See* St. John.
  Lady, at Argeville, 238.
Bolton, Lieutenant, 379.
Bombay, 150.
Bonaventure, H.M.S., 139.
Bond or Bonde:
  Dionis, 113.
  John le, 42.
  John, 112, 115.
  Laurence, 113.
  Ralph, 36.
  Richard, 113.
Bondeker, Adam de, 24.
Bondes:
  Wulmere, 36.
  Wlvive, 38, 39.
Bonpaign, Agnes, 34.
Book of hours, at Blickling, 1.
Book of rates, English, 306.
Bootle, Sir Thomas, 157.
Booton or Boton (Norfolk), 102 144.
  church at, 43.
Borch, Jean de, envoy from Augustus III., 204, 210, 211, 212.
Borghs, Head, 24.
  See also Capital Pledges.
Boscawen, Mr., purchases troop, 314.
Bose, General de, commanding Hessian Regiment, 388.
Bosnia, 436.
Boson, John, 53.
Bosons manor, 54.
Boston:
  (Lincolnshire), sluice at, 84.
  (North America), Custom House at, 290-292.
  ——, J.P.s of, 261.
  ——, Minutes of Council at, 261.
  ——, proposals relating to, 290-292.
  ——, riot at, 291, 292.

Boston, H.M. Ship, 330.
Boteler:
  Arthur, 126.
  Henry, 55.
  Ralph, Lord Sudley, 54.
Botetourt, Lord. *See* Berkeley.
Botheby, Christopher de, 42.
Bougainville, M. de, 239.
Bouillé, Count de, at St. Lucia, 342.
Boult, Thomas, 114.
Bourbon, House of:
  protection by, of Ireland, 395.
  their treaty with the Rebel Colonies, 327.
  triumphant, 406, 413.
Bourgchier (Bourchier, Bouchier):
  Cardinal, Lord Chancellor, 29.
  Lord, 65.
  ——, Humfrey son of, 65.
  ——, ——, his indenture relating to Wymondham, 65.
  Johane, wife of Humfrey, 65.
Bourke, John, 1st Baron Naas, 379.
Bourne, Mr., Chancellor of St. Patrick's, 386.
Bowthorp Hall (Norfolk), 145.
Bowzer, William, 383.
Boxer, William, 112.
Boyd:
  Mr., at Dublin, 421.
  ——, surveyor of Donaghadee, 313.
  William, Earl of Kilmarnock, taken prisoner, 160.
Boyle, Richard, 2nd Earl of Shannon, 419, 420.
  letters from, 356, 379.
  family of, 420.
Boyne, battle of the, 311.
Boyne, Edward, Commander-in-Chief (Navy), 140.
Boyton, 'manor of,' 54.
Bozeat (Northamptonshire), letter in relation to lands at, 164.
Bozoun, Simon, prior of Holy Trinity, Norwich, 70.
Bradfeud, Henry de, porter to Horsham St. Faith's Priory; release by, of a messuage to the Priory, 16.
Bradfield, Edward, 97.
Bradie or Brady:
  Elizabeth, 101.
  John, 101.
Brakne, extent of manor of, 72.
Brame, James, 106.
Brampton or Bramton (Norfolk), 44, 102, 144.
  deed relating to, 72.
Brampton:
  Andrew de, 34, 35, 42.
  Robert, 44, 74.
  Thomas, 55.
Bramston, Edmund, 162.
Brandeston (Norfolk), 90.
Brandeston, Godfrey de, 49.
Brandon, Lady, at Dublin, 423.
Branfill, Champion, letters from, 150, 151, 157, 158, 159, 160, 163.

Branicki or Branitzki, the Great General of Poland, 193, 209, 216, 218.
Braniski, M., 218.
Branteston, Henry de, 38.
Branthwayt, William, 124.
Branton (Norfolk), manor of, 35.
Brathwaite, Mr., at Southampton, 360.
Braunche, John, 54.
Braunde, Mr., 159.
Braunthonne or Branton, Andrew de, 42.
Bray (Ireland), 390, 393.
Braybroke:
    Robert de, Bishop of London, 69.
    Roger Mallory de, at Matlask, 69.
Breame, William, 114.
Breese or Brese:
    Augustin, 96.
    Martha, 105.
    Thomas, 93.
    William, 37.
Breinter, Gregory, 115.
Brekes, Roger, 29.
Brennecat, Walter, 19.
Brereton, John, 127.
Brest, 363.
    French fleet at, 337, 404.
Breswin, Austin, 140.
Bretiff, Edmund. See Britiffe.
Breton, William, owner of manor of Stratton, 73.
Brett:
    Anthony, 95.
    Nathaniel, 94.
Brettenham, Clement de, 52.
Brewers, presentment of, 7.
Brewes:
    Robert, 56.
    Thomas, 56.
Brewse, Dominus de, 46.
Brewster:
    Gregory, 115.
    John, 89, 117, 121, 129, 132, 143.
Brickling. See Blickling.
Bridewell, 163.
Bridges, Captain, 138.
Bridget, John, 139.
Bridgewater:
    Earl of, Frances daughter of. See Egerton.
    Duke of, ibid.
Brie, Robert de, 9.
'Brigade d'Irlande,' 414.
Briggs, George, 160.
Brighmer, John, 102, 108.
Brighton (Brighthelmstone), 312.
Brindall. See Brundall.
Bringloe, John, 127.
Briningham, landowners in, 108.
Brinton, landowners in, 110, 112.
Brisstune. See Briston.
Bristol: 281, 294, 430.
    address from, relating to export of corn, 270.
    election at, 259.
    Queen Elizabeth at, 259.
    George Grenville at, 250.
    White Lion Club at, 259.

Bristol, Earl of. See Hervey.
Bristol, Thomas, Bishop of. See Newton.
Bristoll, H.M.S., 139.
Briston (Birston, Brisstune, Bristone, Birstoun, Byrston, Burston, Byrsten) (Norfolk): 45, 48, 49, 50, 52, 54, 109-112.
    landowners in, 109.
    Manor Rolls of, 45.
Briston, Roger de, 47.
    ——, Simon son of, 47.
    Simon de, 48, 49, 50.
Bristow:
    Elizabeth, afterwards Countess of Buckinghamshire, 170.
    W., 147.
    Mr., 170.
Britannia, H.M.S., 137.
Britiffe, Britaff, Brytif, Brytiffe, Bretiff:
    Anne, 100, 101.
    Clement, 108.
    Edmund, 100, 102, 104, 108, 124.
    Mr., 132.
    Philip, 108.
    Robert, 147.
    Simon, 110, 125.
    William, 441.
British Empire, destruction of, a menace to Europe, 405-406.
Brockdish or Brokedis, Reginaldus de, 17.
Brockdish, grant of land in, to St. Faith's monastery, 17.
Brodrick, George, 4th Lord Midleton, in Ireland, 420.
Bromholm (Norfolk): 74.
    Clement, the prior of, 73.
    seal of, 73.
    —— convent and church of, 73.
    deeds relating to, 73.
Broomhedge (Ireland), 329.
Brothercross Hundred (Norfolk), 81, 137.
Brown, Browne, Broun:
    Sir Anthony, his swan marke, 83.
    ——, property at Boston, 84.
    Capt. Lieutenant, 127.
    Colonel, 355, 379.
    Daniel, 93.
    Francis, 113.
    Sir J., 379.
    Hon. James, 379.
    ——, M.P. for Tuam, letter from, 415.
    ——, letter to, 416.
    James, 110.
    John, 109, 112, 141, 145.
    John, Lord Westport, 379.
    John Denis, 3rd Earl of Altamont, 379, 415, 416.
    ——, letter from, 419.
    ——, letter to, 419.
    Peter, 87.
    Richer, 98, 124.
    Robert, 141, 145.
    Roger, 98.
    Simon, 87.

Brown—*cont.*
  Thomas, 91, 101.
  Thomas, Bishop of Norwich, 31.
  William, ensign, 110, 127.
  William, sheriff of Norwich, 81.
Brownlow:
  Lord. *See* Cust.
  Right Hon. William, M.P., in Irish Parliament, 391, 400, 402, 414, 426.
Brudenell, George, Duke of Montagu, 341.
  his garden on the Thames, 341, 342.
Bruhl, Comte de, 192, 193, 194, 195, 206, 212, 213.
  his claim to Polish nobility contested, 193, 194.
Brun, Walter le, 16.
Brundall (Brindall), 121.
Brunham, Robert, 53.
Brunville, Ysabell, entry of, into the homage of Horsham St. Faith's, 6.
Brunswick (America), 311.
  action at, 305.
Brunswick (Germany), 435.
Brunswick:
  Duke of (1781), 389.
  Prince of (1767), 277.
Brus, Ralph de, 47.
Brydges, James, Earl of Carnarvon, 247.
Brygg, William, 53.
Brytiffe, Brytif. *See* Britiffe.
Brzese, Palatinate of Poland, 218.
Brzortouski, General, 192.
Buccleugh, Duke of. *See* Scott.
Bucke:
  Dennis, 116.
  Robert, 90.
Buckenham (Bokenham), Old, Castle, 63, 64.
Buckenham, pedigree relating to the title of, 5.
Buckingham, Marquis of. *See* Grenville.
Buckingham Hospital, at Dublin, 429, 430.
Buckinghamshire:
  Caroline, Countess of, 288, 295, 301, 321, 322, 341, 348, 349, 350, 362, 367, 413, 417.
  Elizabeth, Countess of, 170.
  Mary Ann, Countess of, 170, 171, 172, 174, 175, 176, 179, 182, 183, 185, 187, 191, 253, 258, 269, 273, 274, 275.
  Earl of. *See* Hobart.
  ——, his papers, 148-442.
Buckinghamshire, 69, 262.
  estate in, 170.
  Grenvilles in, 262.
Buckler, Robert, 114.
Budgell, E., 146.
Buis, Nicholas, 19.
Bukeskin, Walter, 42.
Buleman, Joceline, 39.
Bulger, convicted of murder, 329.
Bullard, Mr., 129.

Bulley, Robert, 44.
Bulleyn. *See* Boleyn.
Bullingbrooke. *See* St. John.
Bulwer:
  Edward, High Collector for Eynsford, 90, 92.
  Mr., 320.
  Roger, 92.
  Thomas, 102.
  W. W., 300.
  ——, letters from, 269, 332.
  William, 92.
Bun *or* Bunn:
  Charles, 95.
  Elizabeth, 95.
  William, 95.
Bunbury, Mrs., cause of a duel, 294.
Burbage (Leicestershire), 55.
Burdett:
  Lady, niece of Countess of Kildare, 348.
  Sir William, distress of, 348.
Burel:
  Agnes, 20.
  Andrew, 43.
  family, 20.
  Hervey, 19, 20.
  Hervey, son of William, 20.
  Peter, brother to William, 18.
  William, 18, 20, 43.
  William, son of Hervey, 20.
Burford, H.M.S., 138.
Burgh:
  Captain, letter from, 384.
  Hussey, Right Hon. Walter, M.P., 358, 360, 363, 400, 402, 415, 416.
  Thos. de (Colonel), letter from, 310.
Burgh (Burrough, Burrow) (Norfolk), landowners in, 102.
  Castle Church, 62.
  Parva (Norfolk), landowners in, 108.
Burghe, Robert, Proctor-General of the Consistory of Norwich, 57.
Burghly (Northamptonshire), letter dated, 431.
Burgoyne:
  Colonel, proposal of, for raising a regiment, 377.
  General, in America, 311, 316, 318, 324, 325, 326.
  ——, despatch from, 315.
Burke, Edmund, 273, 363.
Burkes, the two Mr., 261.
Burlingham, Thomas, 108.
Burlington Bay, transports in (1745), 150.
Burnham: 33.
  Thorp, Bailiff's account for, 70.
Burr, Burre:
  Edmund, 102.
  Richard, 88.
  Robert, 101.
Burritt, John, 130.
Burrish, Mr., letter of (1740), 231.
Burrough. *See* Burgh.
Burrow, *ibid.*

Burston, Simon de. *See* Briston.
Burton:
  Anne, 92.
  James, 91.
  Richard, 55.
  Robert, 110.
  William (Right Hon.), 365.
  —— (Colonel), 379.
Burwode, John, 20.
Bus, Nicolas, 10.
Bushe:
  Gervase, M.P. for Kilkenny, 400, 402, 403.
  Mr., 365.
Bushop, Robert, 32.
Bushy Park, Lord North at, 299.
Bute, Lord. *See* Stuart.
Butler:
  Brinsley, 2nd Earl of Lanesborough, 378.
  Lady Katherine, 379.
  Lady Mary, 379.
  Michael, 105, 110.
  Robert, 109.
  Sam., 105.
  Simon, 92.
Butley (Buttele), St. Mary of, deed relating to, 74.
Buttefant, John, 130.
Butterfield, 160.
"*Buttered Pease*," tune of, 177.
Butts, Mr., vicar of Langley, 62.
Buun. *See* Bohun.
Buxton (Norfolk), 29, 44, 73, 102.
  deed relating to, 71.
Buxton, John, 109.
"Byhofful," 43.
Bylaugh, Beelowe, 90, 121.
Bylling [Thomas], Recorder of London, 30.
Bynetre. *See* Bintry.
Byng *or* Bing:
  George, afterwards Baron Byng, 138.
  George, M.P. for Middlesex, letter from, 367.
Byngbury, tithing of, 79.
Bynks:
  Alice, 88.
  Richard, 140.
Byron, Admiral, in West Indies, 343.
Byrston. *See* Briston.
Bzewieski, Count, 218.

C

Cadell, Mr., a printer, 432.
Cadogan, Charles Sloane, 3rd Baron, (1778), 379.
  letter from, 306.
Cæsar, ship, 150.
Cailly, Thomas de, 63.
Caineto, Sibyll de. *See* Cheyney.

Caistor (Castre), 54.
Caldecotys, manor of, 54.
Calder, master gunner at Yarmouth, 147.
Caldewelle Mill, near Thurning, 15.
Caldewode, Robert de, 22.
Calthorpe *or* Calthorp:
  landowners in, 103.
  manor of, 64.
Calthorpe *or* Calthorp (Calethorp):
  Sir Christopher, of East Basham, 123, 124, 125, 133, 137, 142, 144.
  Capt. James, of West Basham, 137.
  James, 111.
  Roger de, 24.
  William, 55.
Calys, Margaret, sister to Henry Catte, 44.
Cambridge: 287.
  "*Archévêque de*," 221
  Clare Hall, 145.
  St. Peter's College, 27, 54.
Cambridge:
  Mr., 175.
  Richard Owen, letters from, 264, 286, 341.
Cambridge, H.M.S., 138.
Camden (North America), 387, 388.
Camden, Lord Chancellor. *See* Pratt.
Camera, John de, 16.
Camp, Benedict, 75.
Campbell:
  John, Lord Lorn, *afterwards* 5th Duke of Argyll, 262.
  Lord Frederick, 247, 283.
  Colonel, of the 52nd, 324.
Canada: 240, 315.
  French criticism on English policy towards, 240.
Canadian Army, 296, 382.
Canadians, the, best subjects of the Crown in America, 292.
Cancalle Bay, France, action in, 351.
Candler, James, a Popish Recusant, 100.
Cankewelle, Baudwine de, 50.
Canterbury:
  George, Archbishop of. *See* Abbot.
  John, Archbishop of. *See* Stafford.
"Capital Pledges":
  at Blickling, 26.
  at Horsham St. Faith's, 7, 9.
  See also Borghs, Head.
Capon:
  John, 87.
  William, 88.
Capon rent, a, 7.
Cappe:
  Agnes, 8.
  Nicholas, 48, 49, 50.
  Ralph, 38.
Cappelmann, M. de, 191.
Captain, H.M.S., 138.
Carberry, Lord. *See* Evans.

Carbonel, Berengarius, steward of the manor of St. Faith's, 7, 10.
Carbrook (Kerebrok), '*Domus de*,' 36.
Cardeston. *See* Kerdiston.
Cardwell, Mr., 321.
"Cardynal, my Lord," the Chancellor. *See* Bourgchier.
Careter, John le, 16.
Carleton (Carletune, Karletune): 59, 61.
    Banyards, Manor Rolls, of, 62.
    Bastwyk, Manor Rolls of, 59, 62.
Carleton:
    Sir Guy, succeeds Sir H. Clinton, 407, 409.
    Walter de, 14.
Carlingford, Bay of, 319.
Carlisle, city of, 152, 158.
Carlisle, Charles, Bishop of. *See* Lyttelton.
    Earl of. *See* Howard.
Cariisle House, an elegant place of public entertainment, 253.
Carlow, Lord. *See* Dawson.
Carmarthen, Marquis of. *See* Godolphin.
Carmichael, John, 3rd Earl of Hyndford, ambassador to Russia, 244.
    letter from, 244.
Carmichael House, letter dated, 244.
Carnarvon, Lord. *See* Brydges.
Carolina, South, 384.
Carolinas, the, North America, 387, 388.
Caroline:
    See Buckinghamshire, Countess of.
    of Anspach, Queen of George II, conversation with Lady Suffolk, 166-170.
Carpenter:
    Edward, 22.
    William, the, 14.
Carr *or* Carre:
    Nicholas, 98.
    William, 106.
Carrickfergus, constable for, 355.
Carrow Abbey (Norfolk):
    Cellarer's accounts for, 70.
    deed relating to, 71.
Carryer, John, 100.
Carter:
    Dawn *or* Daun, John, 58-59.
    Helen, will and probate of, 2, 58.
    Humphrey, 102, 125.
    John, 442.
    Richard, 138.
    Mr., a messenger from Sir Henry Clinton, 407, 409.
Carteret, John, Earl Granville, 148, 157, 158.
Carysfort, Lord (1783). *See* Proby.
Cashell: 343, 379.
    Archbishop of. *See* Cox *and* Agar.
    Archbishopric of, 343.
Caspian Sea, the, 224, 229.

Castello, Nicholas de, 440.
Castle:
    Abraham, 132, 141.
    John, 127.
Castle Dermot, Mr. Champayne presented to, 386.
Castlebar, 389.
Castle Guard, 22, 37.
Castle Martyr, letter dated, 356.
Castlereagh [Emily], Lady, 166. *See also* Hobart.
Castleton:
    Elizabeth, 90.
    William, Prior of St. Faith's, 20.
Castletown, letters dated, 386, 412, 416.
Castlety, W., at Horsham St. Faith's, 5.
Caston (Northamptonshire), 164.
Castor:
    John, 106.
    Robert, 109.
Castre, in Flegg. *See* Caistor.
Catelyn *or* Catteline, Sir Neville, 125, 127, 132, 141.
Caterine, Nicholas, 25.
Cates:
    John, 109.
    widow, 109.
Catesby, Sir William, 55.
Catherine II., Empress of Russia, 171-220 *passim*, 232, 237, 293, 294, 371.
    asks for English Act of Parliament, 294.
    description of, 171.
    offers mediation to Dutch (1781), 405.
    policy in Courland, 195-212.
    reviews her fleet, 184.
Catherine yacht, the, 140.
Catholics, Roman. *See* Papists.
Catte *or* Cat, Catt, Chat, Kat:
    Dionysia wife of Henry, 440.
    Henry, 32, 43, 44, 440.
    Henry le, 37, 42.
    Herbert, 40.
    ——, Alda wife of, 3, 40.
    ——, will of, at Hevingham, 3.
    Katherine, 43.
    Margaret, 43.
    Peter le, 41.
    William, 40.
    ——, Lauretta wife of, 41, 42.
    William le, 34-36, 38, 39, 41, 42, 43.
Cattes Manor:
    in Horsted, 44.
    in Hevingham, 3, 30, 31, 32, 43.
    customaries of, and rentals, 32.
    Book of Demesne Lands of, 32.
Catteway, John, 142.
Catton *or* Cattone, 16.
Catton:
    Roger *fil. sacerdotis de*, 16.
    Ralph de, 18.
Catts, Anthony, 116.
Caudwell, Mr., 321.

Caulfield:
James, 4th Viscount Charlemont, 389.
——, "mends the church," 420.
Mr., 378.
Cavan, Earl of. *See* Lambart.
Cavanagh, Nicholas, evidence of relating to Russian commerce, 237.
Cavendish:
Lord John, Lord of the Treasury, 256.
W. H., 442.
William, 3rd Duke of Devonshire, 157.
William, 4th Duke, 245, 252.
——, letter from, 239.
——, relations with the Walpoles, 239.
——, death of, 253.
Caversham (Oxfordshire), 361.
Cawsey, John, 96.
Cawston (Causton) (Norfolk), 35, 42, 44, 103.
Court Rolls of, 70.
landowners in, 103.
manor of, 35.
rioters at, 269.
Cawston, John de, 25.
Cecil:
Brownlow, 9th Earl of Exeter, letter from, 431.
William, 2nd Earl, 85.
William, 75.
Cecily, relict of Richard the baker of St. Faith's, 18.
Chaineto, Ralph de. *See* Cheyney.
Chambers, Richard, of Bawdswell, 90.
Chamberlayne:
Edward, 126.
Richard, of Hackford, 93, 100.
Champayne, Rev. Mr., brother to Lady Paget, 339, 386.
Champlain, Lake, 296.
Chancellorship of St. Patrick (Dublin), Mr. Bourne appointed to, 386.
Chancellor:
the Lord (1745). *See* Yorke, Philip, Earl of Hardwicke.
(of Ireland). *See* Hewitt, James.
Chancery, order in, relating to Sir John Fastolf and Sir Geoffrey Boleyn, 3.
Chantry, the, letter dated, 289.
Chanu, Stephan le, 18.
Chaplain:
Turold, the, 40.
William, the, 39.
Chaplains of the parson of Blickling (Richard), accused of usury, 26.
(Richard and Robert), prosecuted for assault, 25.
Chapelfield *or* Chaplyfield. *See* Norwich.

Chapman:
Edmond, 104.
Henry, 92.
John, 92.
Nicholas, 90.
Robert, 92, 104, 125.
Seth, of Foulsham, 91.
Spencer, of Weston, 95.
Thomas, 109.
Charlemont, Lord (1781). *See* Caulfield.
Charles V. of Germany, 206.
Charles Christian, of Saxony, 195-7, 199.
his claim to Courland, 201-7.
his property in Courland sequestered by Russia, 195-7, 204.
Charles Edward, 'the young Pretender,' 148, 154, 160.
Charles, galley, H.M.S., 139.
Charlestown, 388, 401.
summoned to surrender, 296.
capture of, 368.
Charleton, letter dated, 288.
Charlotte, daughter of Earl of Hillsborough. *See* Hill.
"*Chasse Marine,*" Lord Harcourt's, 298.
Chat. *See* Catte.
Chategrave. *See* Chetgrave.
Chatham:
Lord. *See* Pitt, William.
Countess of, 288.
Chatteris, Fen drainage near, 165.
Chaungedelond, land called, 18.
Cheavely *or* Chevely:
Elizabeth, 110.
Robert, 110.
Chelmsford, letter dated, 151.
Chelsea, Cadogan and Stanley property at, 360.
Cheltenham, 238.
Chent. *See* Kent.
Cheny. *See* Cheyney.
Cherbourg, letter dated, 162.
Cheremeteff, Count and Countess, 191.
Cherkasoff *or* Cherkasow:
Baron J. B. de, letter from, 254.
Baroness Elizabeth de, 254.
Baron, letters from, 190, 294.
Cherlton *or* Cherletone:
Robert de, 52.
Thomas de, 51.
Cherson, 436.
Chesapeak River, the (North America), 396, 400, 402, 407-8.
Chesapeak Bay, 399, 401, 410.
Chesapeak, 399.
letter dated, 400-401.
Cheshire cheeses, price of, 210.
Chesneto. *See* Cheyney.
Chesney. *Ibid.*
Chesteny, Francis, 111.
Chester, Capt. (of 36th Regiment), 315.
Chetgrave *or* Chategrave *or* Chattgrave, extents of, 61, 73.

Chetwynd, Mr., 176.
Chever, Richard, 29.
Cheyney (Cheny, de Cheyny, de
    Chaineto, de Chesneto, de
    Caineto, de Kaneto, de
    Chesney):
    family of, 1, 2, 3, 10, 11.
    Margaret de, 2, 11.
    Sybil de, 2.
    Turgys de, 11.
Chichester, in arms (1746), 156.
Chief Justice, Lord, of England.
    See Coke, Hobart, and Popham.
Child, Mr., 179.
China, 150.
Chinnery, Dr. (Bishop of Killaloe),
    379.
Chitleburgh:
    Dr., 142.
    Robert, warrant against (1696),
    142.
Cholmondeley, George, 3rd Earl
    of Cholmondeley, signs Order of
    Council (1745), 148.
Christiana, William son of, 34.
Christine, daughter of William Bas-
    set, 17.
Church ales, 20.
Churchill:
    Charles, 378.
    George, 138.
    George, 4th Duke of Marl-
    borough, 283, 378.
    ——, protests against Repeal of
    Stamp Act, 260.
    Rev., ——, 179.
Churchman, Sir T., at Norwich, 270.
Chusser, John le, 24, 26.
Circular Letter, with Bede Roll, 20.
Clanbrassil, Earl of (1771—1778).
    See Hamilton.
Clanricarde, Earl of. See De Burgh.
Clare:
    County, 384.
    ——, Lieutenancy of, 313.
    Hall. See Cambridge.
    Honour of, 74.
Clare, Earl of. See Fitzgibbon,
    John.
    Lord. See Nugent, Robert.
Claremont, Duke of Newcastle at
    250.
Clark, Clarke or Clerk:
    Captain of the Swiftsure, 138.
    John the, 38, 41, 42.
    John son of the, 34, 36, 38, 41.
    John, 115, 142.
    Richard, rector of Intwood, 102,
    130.
    Walter, of Newton, 19.
    William, 98, 102.
Clavering, Lady Diana, 186.
Claxton, 132.
Claxton, Hamond, 127.
Claybourne:
    Henry, "Cater," 88.
    James, of Hindolveston, 93.
Cleaveland, yacht, 140.
Clelia, romance of, 169.

Clements:
    John, 138.
    Right Hon. H. T., letter from,
    365.
    Robert, 374.
Clere:
    Dionicia, 73.
    the family of, 147.
    ——, at Blickling, 2.
    Edward, 29, 65.
    Sir E., sells Blickling, 82.
    Sir John de, 2.
    Sir John, 29.
    ——, advowson of Blickling con-
    veyed to, 29.
    Sir Ralph de, 47.
    Ralph, 47.
    Robert, 73.
    William, 73.
    William de, 43.
Clerk:
    of the Market, office of, 81.
    of the Pells (office of), 428.
Clermont, Lord (1778). See Fortes-
    cue.
Cleveland Court, letter dated, 438.
Cleves (Cleevys), Anne of. See Anne.
Cley, Cleye (Norfolk), 110.
    landowners in, 110.
    letter dated, 353.
Cleyton, Dame, of Thorpe Market,
    99.
Clifden (Kilkenny), 343.
Clifden, Lord. See Agar, James.
Clifford, Lord, 378.
Clinton-Cornwallis controversy, 401,
    402, 407, 408, 409, 410, 411, 412.
Clinton:
    Lord, J.P., letter to, 396.
    Sir Henry, 324, 326, 350, 362,
    368, 404, 407-8, 411, 434-5, 442.
    ——, letters from, 381, 387,
    388, 396-398, 399-400, 401, 407,
    409, 410, 411, 434, 435.
    ——, letters to, 380, 391, 403,
    411, 412.
    ——, pamphlet and notes by,
    411.
    Thomas, Earl of Lincoln, 368, 401.
Clinton (Edward), Sir E. Fynes and
    Lord Clinton and Saye, Lord High
    Admiral of England, 74.
Clipston (Northamptonshire), the
    hospital at, 160.
Clive, Col., sends wife and treasure
    home, 165.
    ——, English officers' opinion of,
    164, 165.
Clogher: 379, 421.
    Bishop of. See Hotham.
    Dean of. See Woodward.
Clogher, Deanery of, presented to
    Mr. Keating, 386.
    city of, a disputed election at,
    423.
Clonfert, 155.
    Bishop of. See Cumberland.
Clonmel Camp, 334.
    letter dated, 333, 335.

Clonmell, Lord. *See* Scott, John.
Clopton ——, 69.
Cloyne, Bishop of. *See* Agar, Woodward *and* Hervey.
Cloyne, 343, 379, 429.
  letters dated, 419, 421.
  see of, 385.
Clucke, Edmund, 102.
Clyde, the, 330.
Clyfton:
  Constantine de, 63, 64.
  Elizabeth, 65.
  John de, 64.
  Sir John, 63, 65.
  Margaret wife of Constantine, 63.
Clynton and Saye, Lord (1552). *See* Clinton, Edward.
Clypesby, Edmund de, 52.
Cobb *or* Cobbe:
  Martyn, 124, 126.
  Geoffrey, 142, 145.
Cobham, Lord (1745). *See* Temple.
Cochrane, Major, killed at York Town, 407.
Cock:
  Colonel, 129.
  Mrs., 131.
Cockthorpe (Norfolk), landowners in, 113.
Cocus. *See* Cook.
Coduham, John, 44.
Coe, Charles, letter from, 162.
Coes, the, 162.
Cæsar, ship, 150.
Coke:
  Lord Chief Justice, ix.
  John, Sheriff of Norfolk, letter from, 86.
  Mr., 287, 321, 353.
  Mr. and Mrs., at Holkham, 320.
  Robert, 125.
  See also Cook.
Cokefeld, Sir John de, witness, 49.
Colbert:
  John, 8.
  Sibilla, at Horsham St. Faith's, 6-9.
Colby (Norfolk), 68, 103.
Colby:
  Henry de, 26.
  Henry, son of John de, 24.
  John de, 24, 28, 29.
Colborne, Edward, Norfolk Militia, 127.
Colchester, dragoons ordered from, to Norwich, 267.
Cole:
  Alan, 7.
  Matilda and Sibyll, 7.
Colebrooke, Robert, candidate for Maldon, 162.
Colkirk (Colekirke), (Norfolk), 144.
Coli, Robert, 48.
Collett, John, 58.
Collinges:
  Dr. John, biographer of Lady Frances Hobart, xii
  letter from, 131.

Collon (Ireland), letter dated, 381.
Colne (Essex), letters dated, 148, 156.
Colne, Stephen de, 18.
Colonies, British, in America. *See* America *and* Plantations.
Coltishall (Coulteshall), landowners in, 103.
Columna, near Moscow, 283.
Colville, Geoffrey, 126.
Comber, John, of Thursford, 116.
Combes, manor rolls of, 72.
Committee:
  of Safety, letter to the (1659), 89.
  Standing, at Norwich, petition to, 86.
  to adjust dispute of the Pennsylvanian line, 381.
Common rights, 59, 76, 80.
Common Council, called (1745), 148.
Commons, House of (England), 237, 239, 244, 245, 247, 248, 250, 253, 275, 281, 282, 287, 288, 328, 330, 348, 351, 365, 367, 370.
  Beckford in, 272.
  hearing at Bar of, 129.
  Journals of, quoted, 272, 306.
  and Mr. Pitt, 245, 428.
  prospects of, in 1784, 427-8.
  privilege of members, 247, 248.
  in Ireland. *See* Ireland.
Compiègne, despatch dated, 219.
Compounding an assault, 10.
Compton, Lady Elizabeth, her report of Lady Suffolk, xiv.
Conches, Abbey of, in Normandy, 2, 11.
Coney, Robert, 133.
Confederation, the general, in Poland, 216, 282.
Congham (Norfolk), Court Roll for, 70.
Congress (American): 343, 382, 388, 408.
  declares colonies to be free states, 296.
  influence of, in Ireland, 343.
  and the Pennsylvanian line, 283.
Congreve, Capt., 336.
Connecticut, expedition to, 305.
Connel, Daniel, of the Pennsylvanian line, 384.
Conolly:
  Caroline, afterwards Countess of Buckinghamshire. *See* Buckinghamshire.
  Right Hon. Thomas, 337, 357, 358, 366, 402, 403, 411, 414, 419, 420, 421, 424-7, 433.
  ——, hints of an Irish peerage for, 385.
  ——, M.P. for Londonderry, 357.
  ——, letter from, 380, 386, 412, 416.
  Lady Louisa, 385, 411, 412.

Constables of the Hundreds, 105, 112.

Constant Warwick, H.M.S., 139.

Constantinople, 219, 435.

Conteshale, John, 54.

Conti, Prince de, a privateer called, 162.

Convention, National, a, for Ireland, 422, 424-6.

Convocation, Diet of (Poland), 220.

Convoys and Cruisers in the English fleet (1691), 140.

Conway:
  Right Hon. Francis Seymour, Viscount Beauchamp, Earl, and afterwards, Marquis of Hertford, 282, 354, 379.
  ——, letter from, 328.
  Henry Seymour, General, Secretary of State, 256, 263, 267, 275, 278, 281, 282, 286.
  ——, letter to General Gage, 260.

Cony, John, a prisoner, 86.

Cooe, Mr., parson of Burrough Castle, 62.

Cook, Cooke *or* Coke (Cocus, Coqus):
  Alan, 7.
  Alexander, 9.
  Anthony, 91.
  Edmond, 101, 110.
  Francis, 145.
  John, 107, 110, 113.
  Mary, 104.
  Ralph, 40.
  Richard, 102.
  Robert, 102.
  Rodbert, 40.
  Roger, 15.
  Thomas, 101.
  Walter, 17.
  ——, Robert son of. 17.
  William, 12, 101, 125, 126.
  Sir W., 132.
  Sir William, 132, 135, 136, 137, 141.

Cooper:
  Edward, of Thimblethorp, 95.
  William, 104.
  Lady, her "Terrass" on the Thames, 342.

Coote, Charles, Dean of Kilfenora, 379.

Copeman:
  Robert, of Barton, 92.
  Thomas, of Great Yarmouth, 95, 112.
  Thomas, agent to Lord Buckinghamshire, 319, 320, 321, 353.

Copland, Bridget, of Elsing, 91.

Copping, John, of Shropham, 145.

Coqus. *See* Cook.

Corbett:
  Capt. A[ndrew], 374, 375, 390.
  ——, letters from, 374, 375, 387.
  John, account of sheep of, 74.

Cordel, Bartholomew, 16.

Cordiberk, a, 118.

Cork *or* Córke: 326, 355.
  Deanery of, 345.
  M.P. for city, 420.
  freedom of, conferred on Earl of Buckinghamshire, 377.
  petitions from merchants and traders of, 316, 317.
  letters dated, 311, 374.

Cork:
  Bishop of. *See* Mann.
  Dean of. *See* Erskine.

Cornelys, Mrs., at Carlisle House, 253.

Cornwall, Sir George (*sic*), 375.

Cornwall, Hobart property in, 146.

Cornwallis, Cornewallis:
  Lord (1663), 111.
  Charles, Marquess, in America, 305, 311, 362, 382, 387, 388, 389, 396-9.
  ——, capitulation of, 400, 401, 402, 405, 407, 409, 410.
  and Clinton Controversy. *See* Clinton.
  Sir Thomas, 442.

Coronation, H.M.S., 138, 139.

Corpusty (Corpesti): 4, 18, 46, 51, 52.
  Adam de, 47, 48.
  Hugh de, 46, 47, 48, 51, 52.
  John de, 49.
  Richard, the baker of, 47, 49.
  Robert son of Adam de, 47.
  Roger de, 48.
  Steingrim de, 47.

Corpusty cum Irmingland, landowners in, 103.

Corry, Isaac, M.P. for Newry, 400.

Cory, Thomas, sheriff, 81.

Cosenage, 66.

Costessy, Cossey (Coosye) (Norfolk):
  swans at Blackwater, 122.
  Papists at, 145.

Cotarii, in Hevingham, 34.

Cotterell, Mr., 371.

Cotton:
  Andrew, Captain, 138.
  Mrs. Elizabeth, marriage settlement of, 145.
  Sir J. H., 160.

Cotts, Thomas, of Bawdswell, 90.

Couldham, James, 127.

Couldwell, William, clerk, 93.

Coulsen, William, 104.

Coulteshall. *See* Coltishall.

Council, order of. *See* Privy Council.

Courland, Duchy of: 195-212, 215, 216.
  Bill concerning, 215-216.
  and the commission of 1727, 198, 202.
  constitutions of, 198, 199, 202, 203, 208, 209, 210, 215.
  a fief of the whole Polish Republic, 199, 201, 203, 204, 208, 209, 210, 212, 215.

Courland, Duchy of—*cont.*
 protest of Augustus III., concerning Russian action in, in December, 1762, 195-197.
 ——, Russian *exposé* relating to, 197-199.
 ——, ——, Polish ministers' reply to, 1763, January 10, 200-204.
 ——, ——, Polish Vice-Chancellor's note accompanying the reply of 10 January, 199-200.
 ——, ——, Keyserling's reply, 205.
 ——, ——, Polish Vice-Chancellor's reply to this, 205.
 ——, Russian ministers' remarks on Polish reply, 205-209.
 Russian policy towards, 195-212.
Courland, Duke of :
 Charles Christian. *See* Charles Christian, of Saxony.
 Ernest John. *See* Biren.
 Ferdinand. *See* Kettler.
 Frederic Casimir. *See* Kettler.
 Prince Pierre of. *See* Biren.
Court, Captain, 150.
Court Christian :
 at Blickling, 26, 28.
 presentment for pleading in a, 3, 25, 26, 28.
Court of Common Pleas, 248.
Courtenay, Richard, Bishop of Norwich, 31.
Courtown, Earl of (1776). *See* Stopford.
Cove, Charles, groom, 87.
Covele, Walter de, 19.
Coventry (Coventre *or* Covyntre) :
 George William, 6th Earl of Coventry, 378.
 ——, protests against repeal of Stamp Act, 260, 261.
 Beatrice, daughter of Lucy de, 49.
 John de, 48.
 John, son of Lucy, of, 49.
 Lucy de, 48, 49.
 Robert son of Lucy de, 48.
Covy, John, 112.
Cowper, George, 3rd Earl Cowper, 276.
Cox :
 Dr. Michael, Archbishop of Cashell, 378.
 Mr., stamp collector, 260.
Coxheath, field guns at, 338.
Coxper, Elizabeth, of Hackford, 93.
Crab (ship), 150.
Crabgate, Dalling, 46.
Cracow, 209.
Cracow, Bishop of, 210, 220.
Craddock, Dr. John, 378.
Craggs Clare. *See* Nugent, Robert.
Oranmore (Norfolk), letter dated, 238.

Cras *or* Cres :
 Geoffrey le, 46.
 Roger le, 49.
Craske, Geoffrey, 34.
Crass, Robert, 41.
Crawley, J., 139.
Creighton, John, 2nd Baron Erne, 378.
Cremer, Francis, 133.
Crepping, Creppyng *or* Oreppingge :
 Margaret, 49, 51.
 Richard de, 50, 51.
 Sir Richard de, 49, 50, 51.
 Simon, pardon to, 50, 51, 52.
 Sir Simon de, at Saxthorp, 4.
 Simon de, 50, 51.
Cressy *or* Cressey :
 Family, viii.
 John, 107.
 Hugh de, 2.
 Roger de, 15.
Creyke, Richard, 52, 53.
Cricketots. *See* Critoft.
Crimea, the, 435.
Critoft manor. *See* Hevingham.
Critoft :
 Peter, 106.
 Robert, 107.
Crobert, William, witness, 6, 8, 68.
Crockley, William, 110.
Croft :
 Richard de la, 47, 48, 49.
 Roger de, 46.
 Thomas de, 48, 49, 50.
Croket, Avise, 8.
Crome, John, 98.
Cromer, landowners in, 97.
Cromie, Sir Michael, 379.
Cromwell (Crumbwell, Crunqwelle) :
 Lady Matilda, 64.
 Oliver, will granted in name of, 87.
 ——, his Upper House, ix.
 "a right Reverend Oliver," 420.
 "Oliverian" swords confiscated xii.
 Ralph, Lord, 4, 54, 64, 65.
 Sir Ralph, 52, 65, 74.
 manors in Wymondham, 64, 65.
Cronstadt, 184, 233.
Cropley, William, Norfolk Militia, 127.
Crosbie *or* Crosby :
 (John) Lord (1780), 379.
 William, Earl of Glandore, 378.
 Edward, 100.
 Lady, 350, 366.
Crosdale :
 Roger de, 50.
 Simon de, 46, 47, 48, 50.
 Simon, son of, 49.
Cross Creek, N. America, 387.
Crow *or* Crowe :
 Christopher, 124.
 Mr., 243, 442.
Crowle, Mr., 163.
Crown Lawyers, the, attacked by Mr. Pitt, 248.
Crowne, H.M.S., 139.

Cubitt:
  John, 91, 98.
  William, 78.
Cublesden, William Trussel de,
  letter from, 75.
Cucuk:
  Henry, 37.
  John, 37.
  Richard, 35.
  William, 37.
Cuffe, Otway, 3rd Baron Desart,
  378.
Cuffin, Matthew, 142.
Cullen, Thomas, of Wells juxta
  mare, 115.
Cullings, Henry, captain, 140.
Culmore Fort (Ireland), 299.
Cumberland, 152.
Cumberland (William Augustus),
  Duke of, 153, 155, 157. 159, 246.
Cumberland:
  Denison, Bishop of Clonfert and
    of Kilmore, 155.
  ——, letter from, 155.
  Richard, 155, 310.
Cummin, Captain, 314.
Cunningham:
  —, embargoed at Dunkirk, 31!
  Lieutenant-General, 379.
  General, in Ireland, 390.
Curson:
  Humphrey, 116.
  Richard, of Brampton, 102.
  Thomas, 114.
  William, 43.
Curtays, Curtis, Curtys or Curteis:
  Francis, clerk, 101.
  Richard, 101.
  Richard, a husbandman, 88.
  William le, 16.
  William, 18.
Curzon, Nathaniel, 1st Lord Scars-
  dale, 260.
Cust, Brownlow, Baron Brownlow,
  378.
Custody of an infant under
  manorial law, 8.
Custom House:
  accounts, 309.
  at Boston, N.A., 291, 292.
  in Russia, 233.
Customs and Excise (Ireland), 309,
  310.
Customary:
  of the manor of Blickling, 21-24.
  —— Hevingham Cattes, 32.
  —— Hevingham Critofts, 32.
  —— Parkhalle, 32.
  —— Rippon Hall, 32.
  —— Saxthorp Loundhall, 4.
  —— Wymondham Cromwell, 65.
  —— Wymondham Grisaugh,
    65.
  —— Wymondham Rokels Lytte-
    bar, 65.
Cut, William, 9.
Cutting, Richard, of Binham, 113.

Czartoryski, Czartorycki or Zar-
  toryski:
  Prince Adam, 209.
  Augustus Alexander, Prince
    Régimentaire, 216, 219.
  family, the, 193-195, 210, 213.
  (Michael), Great Chancellor of
    Lithuania, 213, 218.
  Prince, Grand Veneur of the
    Crown of Poland, 220.
  Prince, Palatin of Russia, 192,
    216, 218.

D

Dacke:
  Mary, of Reepham, 94.
  William, ibid.
Daco, Adam, 19.
Dacre, Elizabeth, Lady (1456), 74.
Dagney, Nicholas, 113.
Dagworth:
  family of, 2.
  manor at Blickling, vi., viii., 2.
  Sir Nicholas, 21, 28.
  ——, Eleanor, relict of, 21.
Dalbini, the title of Buckenham de-
  rived from, 5.
D'Alembert, M., 172.
Dalling Hall Monceux, manor roll
  of, 70.
D'Almadovar, Marquis de, Spanish
  Ambassador, letters from, 336,
  352.
Dalrymple:
  Major (Atholl Highlanders), 330.
  Lord (1781), brings despatches
    from Clinton, 401.
Daly, Mr., M.P. for Galway, 400,
  402, 403.
Dama di Corte, an Italian, at
  Florence, 296.
Danbury, N.A., magazine at, 305.
Danby, Earl of (1691). See Osborne.
Dancers hissed from the stage, 253.
Daniel or Daniell:
  Abbot of Hulme, 40.
  Richard, 41.
  Robert, of Hindolveston, 93.
Dantzick or Danzig, 215, 292, 293.
  trade of with St. Petersburg,
    234.
  sacrificed to Russia, 293.
Danube, the, 435-6.
Danvers:
  Thomas, 55.
  William, 55.
Dapifer:
  Adam, 40, 41.
  episcopi, John, 40.
  Peter, 41.
D'Aranda, M., 434.
D'Arcy:
  alias Richard Southwell, 5, 74.
  Mary Ann, petition of, 378.

Dartmouth (1st) Lord. *See* Legge.
William, 2nd Earl of, *ibid.*
Dartmouth, H.M.S., 139.
Dashkoff:
Princess (Catherine), 220.
Prince, 220.
Daubeni, Hugh, 17.
Daunger, Nicholas, of Irmingland, 68.
Dautre, Dawtre *or* Dawtery:
Leonell, 52.
William, 52, 53.
Dawson, William Henry, 1st Viscount Carlow, 343, 345, 379.
Davies, Thomas, 106.
Davila's French History, 131.
Davy:
Richard, clerk, 29.
Robert, 29.
Dawney, Edward, clerk, 107.
Day *or* Daye. *See also* Dey.
family (in Norwich), 354.
Edmond, 107.
J., 33.
John, 116.
Robert, 102, 132.
Daynes, Thomas, 99.
Deane:
Sir Robert, 379.
Silas, expected in Holland, 312.
Dearing, Daniel, 139.
Dearsley, Mr., 131.
Dedham (Suffolk), 54.
Deeds:
ancient, at Blickling, v., 2-75.
dates of miscellaneous, 57, 61, 62, 64, 65, 67, 68, 69, 71-75.
summaries of, 46-57.
Deedes, Thomas, of Sidestrand, 98.
Deep River, N. America, 387.
Deeping Fenn, 84.
Defyance, H.M.S., 138.
De Burgh, John Smith, 11th Earl of Clanricarde, 378.
De Grasse, Comte. *See* Le Grasse.
De Grey:
Edmond, of Antingham, 97.
—, called to the Bar, 164.
Ed., Major, Norfolk Militia, commissioner of assessment, 112, 125.
Thomas, 442.
William, deputy lieutenant (Norfolk), 125, 127.
Delamere, Captain, at Tavistock, 162.
Delavall, Sir Ralph, Vice-Admiral, 138.
Delawarr, River, 305, 311, 324.
Demund, Robert, son of John, 25.
Denbigh, Earl of (1777). *See* Feilding.
Lady (1763), 176, 172.
Dene, William le, 14.
Dengaine, Thomas, 126.

Denmark, preparing for war (1773), 292.
Denney *or* Denny, Edward, 104, 109.
Dennis, John, of Reepham, 94.
Denstone, Clement, 54.
D'Eon, M., secretary to the French Embassy, compared with Wilkes, 250.
De Pree, *alias* Duningham, 92.
Deptford, H.M.S., 139.
Deptford, Ketch, H.M.S., 140.
Deputy Lieutenants for County of Norfolk. *See* Norfolk.
Deputy Lieutenant, his certificate of having received the sacrament according to the usage of the Church of England, 124.
Derby:
Edward, Earl of (1777). *See* Stanley.
Hugh de, 51.
Derby: 283.
rebel army at (1745), 155.
Dereham (Derham), Thomas de, 16.
Derling (in Horsham St. Faith's), 19.
Derry:
Bishop of (Earl of Bristol). *See* Hervey.
Dean of. *See* Emily.
Derry:
Deanery of, to be " manufactured," 384.
races, 266.
volunteers, 422.
Dersingham (Dersyngham):
Dame Frances Bedingfeld of, 82
Roger de, 440.
Desagulier, General, his guns, 336.
Desart, Lord (1776). *See* Cuffe.
D'Estaing, Charles Hector, Comte, Governor of St. Domingo, 251, 252.
in command of French Fleet at St. Lucia, 342.
Despencer, Henry le. *See* Spenser.
Devizes, 159.
Devon, county of, 85, 285.
Devonshire:
William, 3rd Duke of. *See* Cavendish.
William, 4th Duke of, *ibid.*
Dewing:
Edward, Norfolk Militia, 127.
Henry, of Hackford, 93.
Stephen, of Great Witchingham, 96.
Dey:
Elizabeth, 116.
John, 104, 105, 108.
Mary, 104.
Mr., 87.
Robert, of Foulsham, 91.
Robert, of Sall, 94.
Diatson, John, Prior of Romburgh, 57.
Dickleburgh (Dickleburch), Roger de, 16.

Dickson, Mr., an apothecary in Dublin, 299.
Diem clausit extremum, 65.
Digby, Admiral, in American war, 397.
Dionisio, Hugo de Sancto, 15.
Dispensation to Sir John Hobart to eat flesh in Lent (1632), 83.
Dispensator, Roger, 12.
Dispensing power, the, of the King, 273.
Division lists (1777-8), Irish Parliament, 378.
Dix:
  of Aylsham, 144.
  James, 109.
  John, 109.
  Robert, 116.
  William, 110.
Dolch:
  Robert, 24.
  ——, Maud *or* Matillida, wife of, 24, 25.
Dolliffe:
  Mary, 148.
  Sir James, of Mitcham, 148.
  ——, letter from, 161.
Donaghadee:
  collector of, 313.
  Pier at, 319.
Doneraile, Lord. *See* St. Leger.
Donne, Thomas, 106.
Doo:
  Godwin le, 22.
  Valentine le, 22.
Dorothy, Lady. *See* Hotham.
Dorrington, ship, 150.
Dorset:
  Earl of. *See* Sackville.
  Duke of (1745), *ibid*.
Dorset, Duke of, ship, 150.
Dorsetshire, 257.
  corn riots in, 271.
Douglas:
  Sir Charles, 379.
  Charles, 3rd Duke of Queensberry, 147, 379.
Doughty *or* Doughtey:
  Captain, 130.
  Lieutenant of the 32nd, 339.
  Frances, 97.
  Richard, 98.
  Robert, 97, 101, 125.
  William, 101.
Dover, Captain, 138.
Dover, H.M.S., 139.
Dover, Lord. *See* Yorke, Sir Joseph.
Dowdeswell, Mr., Chancellor of the Exchequer and Lord of the Treasury, 256, 273, 280, 281, 282.
Down, 329.
  County, 306, 314, 319.
  ——, Lord Lieutenant of, 337.
Downham (Norfolk), 145.
Downpatrick, 328.
Downs, William, 63.

D'Oyley:
  Chancery Case relating to, 75 (*temp.* James I.)
  Mrs., 439.
  Sir William, deputy lieutenant for Norfolk, 123-126.
  William, jnr., *ibid*, 123, 125, 127.
  Mr., 360.
  Mrs., administers Hans Stanley's will, 361.
  Mr., Lord Barrington's deputy, 271.
Dragoons. *See* Regiments.
Drake, Sir Francis, 332, 366.
  dispute of fishery rights with, 346-7, 370.
  letters from, 332, 366.
  letter to, 332.
Drake, H.M.S., 140.
Draper, Sir William, 378.
Drappitt, John, 93.
Draycott, Miss, marries the Earl of Pomfret, 250.
Drayton (Norfolk), 54, 94.
Dreadnaught, H.M.S., 138.
Dreit, Richard de, 12.
Dresden, 209.
  letters dated, 212.
Drew *or* Drewe:
  John, parson of Harpelee, 53, 73.
  Roger, 53.
Driby, Joan de, Lady of the Manor in Wymondham, 63.
Driver, Richard, 114.
Drogheda, 386.
Drogheda, Charles, Earl of. *See* Moore.
Dromolen, 384.
Dromore, Bishop of. *See* Scroope.
Drummond:
  Clinton's A.D.C., 326.
  Messrs., bankers, 294.
Drury, Druery *or* Drewry:
  Dr., 378.
  family, pedigree of, 148.
  John, clerk, 53.
  Joyce, letters from, 148, 156.
  Martha, Lady, 148, 157.
  Mary Ann, afterwards Countess of Buckinghamshire, xiv. *See* Buckinghamshire.
  Richard Vere (Captain), 379.
  Roger, 53.
  Sir Thomas, M.P., letters addressed to, 148-165, *passim*.
  ——, his mother and wife. 148.
  William, 101.
Dublin: 298, 312, 319, 322, 329, 334, 336, 339, 372, 373, 378, 386, 387, 390, 409, 428, 432.
  Accountant General's office at, 390.
  Archbishop of. *See* Fowler, Dr.

Dublin, addresses from, 377, 378.
Provost of. *See* Hely Hutchinson.
Bay, 338.
Bolton Street, letter dated, 329.
Castle, 312, 316, 357, 365, 389.
——, letters dated, 343, 345, 349, 352, 356-7, 372, 380, 382, 387, 389, 390, 424.
Chancery Chamber, letter dated, 345.
Chancery, Court of, 345.
civil disturbances in, 373.
College Green, 393.
Custom House, 343.
——, letter dated, 305.
freedom of city conferred on Lord Buckinghamshire, 377.
Henrietta Street, letter dated, 297.
Hospital, 378.
letters dated, 297, 298, 339, 364, 379, 384, 385, 389, 398, 400, 402, 403, 410, 420, 421, 424-8, 430-3.
manufactures in, 428.
merchants, 378.
mob of, drilled, 428.
Mount Street, letter dated, 310.
M.P. for, 409.
Muster office, 314.
Nassau Street, letter dated, **344.**
the Palace, letters dated, 386, 408, 418.
petition from, 317.
Phœnix Park, a review in, 389, 390.
——, letter dated, 417.
Royal Hospital, letters dated, 339, 342.
Sackville Street, letters dated, 377, 415.
Saint Woolston's, 297.
Treasury, letter dated, 365.
Trinity College, 377, 409.
——, letter dated, 297.
Volunteers billeted in, 390.
Duchess, H.M.S., 138.
Ducie, Lord Chief Baron (1780). *See* Moreton.
Dudewik, Norfolk, '*campus de*,' 41.
Dudley and Ward, Earl of. *See* Ward.
Dugdale's Monasticon, quoted, 2, 73.
Duke, H.M.S., 138.
Dumbarton, H.M.S., 140.
Dundalk, letters dated from, 327, **334.**
Dundas, Mr., 439.
Dungannon:
Congress at, 413, 425, 426.
mutiny of, 413.
"Parliament" of, 420.
volunteers assembled at, 410.
Dunham, Alexander de, witness, 19.
Dunich, Anabele, 14.

Duningham, John, *alias* De Pree, 92.
Dunkirk, 312.
Dunleys, in Southwark, 55.
Dunmore (Ireland), 389.
Dunmow (Essex), 165.
Dunning, Mr., 365.
Durbin, Mr. Alderman, at Stoke, 295.
Durham: 178.
Bishop of. *See* Langlee.
Durrant:
John, 101.
Sir Thomas, of Scottowe, in Norfolk, 427, 442.
——, letter from, 427.
William, 105.
Dutch, the, 341, 405.
their relations with France, (1746), 161, 341.
ships in the British fleet (1691), 140, 141.
troops in Scotland (1745), 149, 150.
Dutton, Mr., at Dublin, 320.
Duvall, Thomas, of Swaffham, 142, 144.
Dyer's Estate at Dunmow (Essex), 165.
Dyson, Mr., 272.

E

Eagle, H.M.S., 138.
Eagle:
Francis, 130.
Mr., 117.
Ealing:
parish church at, 147.
North, 147.
Earle:
Erasmus, 103, 112, 141, 142.
John, 103.
N., 84.
Thomas, 108.
Earlham *or* Erleham, near Norwich, 10, 242, 267.
Earsham, 145, 442.
East India Company:
Committee for considering the affairs of (1766-7), 275.
Bonds, 148, 149, 153.
proposed indemnification to, 291.
trade with city of Cork, 317.
Eborall, Thomas, 30.
Eborard *or* Eberard, Bishop of Norwich, 2, 39, 40.
Ecclesia, William de, 35, 36, 38, 40.
Ecclesiam, ad. *See* Atchurch.
Ecton, letter dated, 155.

Eden, Mr. (Rt. Hon. William, afterwards Lord Auckland), 375, 379, 381, 386, 390, 392, 394, 400, 401.
   character of, 390, 401.
   discussion with, 391.
Edes, Margaret, 25.
Edgar, H.M.S., 138.
Edgecombe, John, steward, 332.
Edgcumbe, Richard, 2nd Lord Edgcumbe (1766), 273.
Edgfield (Eggefeld) (Norfolk), 52, 109.
   landowners in, 111.
Edinburgh, Pretender's Army at, 150, 156.
Edmund:
   the carpenter, 27.
   Edward, 144.
Edmunds, Isadora, 104.
Edridg, Thomas, of Buxton, 102.
Edward the Black Prince, knighthood of, 440.
Edward, Fort, on the Hudson River, 315.
Edwards, Bridgett, 105.
Egelunde, 14.
Egerton:
   Lady Alice, viii.
   Lady Frances. *See* Hobart.
   Francis, Duke of Bridgewater, 164, 260.
   John, Earl of Bridgewater, viii., 143.
   John, Bishop of Bangor, protests against repeal of Stamp Act, 260.
   Peter, 85.
Eggefeld. *See* Edgfield.
Eglinton, Henry, landowner, Bawdswell, 90.
Eglintoun, Earl of. *See* Montgomerie.
Egmont, Lord (1765). *See* Perceval.
Egmore (Norfolk), 115.
Egremont, Earl of. *See* Wyndham.
Einford, Walter Avis de, 16.
Elden, Edmund, 98.
Election expenses in Norfolk, 129.
Elibank (Ellibank), Lord (1751). *See* Murray.
Eliot:
   Edward, of Port Eliot, 378.
   Mr., embanks Rivers Tamar and Tavy, 289.
Elizabeth:
   Czarina, 197, 201, 202, 203, 206, 207, 208, 222, 223.
   ——, supports Prince Charles of Saxony, 202, 203.
   Lady *or* Princess, 29, 44.
   Queen, her opinion of Bristol, 259.
Elizabeth, H.M.S., 138.
Elliot:
   Mrs., 423.
   Miss, at Covent Garden, 179.
   Rev. —., letter to, 418.
   ——, character, 423.
   Sir G., 273.
   William (Captain), 379, 442.

Ellis:
   John, Dean Prideaux's letter to, x.
   John, 98, 101.
   Mrs. (executrix to Hans Stanley), 361.
   Welbore, 245.
   ——, letter from, 360, 361.
Ellys, Mr., 343.
Elmham, William de, 52.
Elmham, South (Suthelmham), 43.
Elphin, Charles, 378.
Elsing *or* Elsinge (Norfolk), landowners in, 83, 91, 99.
Elton, Captain, in Persia, his history, 230, 231, 235, 236.
Eluuriz, a witness, 12.
Elwin:
   Thomas, of Thurning, 95.
   Peter, sen. and jun., of Thurning, 95.
Ely:
   cause, the, 428, 429.
   Earl of. *See* Loftus.
   Lady, her theatre, 433.
Elys, John de, 74.
Embargo:
   upon export of corn:
   ——, by Royal proclamation, 266, 270.
   ——, by order in Council, 440.
   upon export of provisions, 317, 318.
Emerson, John, of Northrepps, 98.
Emily:
   (Lady). *See* Hobart.
   Rev. Edward, Dean of Derry, 384.
Emperor, the (Joseph II.), 312, 435, 436.
Empire of the Ocean, the, prophecy as to, 406.
Empson:
   Henry, 103, 105.
   William, miller, 56.
Engayne:
   family, at Blickling, 2.
   John, 22, 24.
   ——, Elene, his wife, 24.
Engelram, William son of, 12.
England, 181, 189, 370, 385, 395, 403, 407, 413, 414, 425, 430.
   "bankrupt in genius," 412.
   migration from, to America, 292.
   oppressed with difficulties, 349, 417.
   public spirit in, 352.
   relations of, with Ireland, 351, 361-365, 393, 395, 396, 413.
   ruin of, prophesied, 404, 406, 413.
English:
   Channel, 362, 363.
   and Dutch fleets in 1691, 140, 141.
   parties in Ireland, 425.
Ennis, 365.

Enzeli, lake of (Caspian Sea), 235.
Erlham, Ralph de, 10.
Ermylaunde. *See* Irmingland.
Erne, Lord. *See* Creighton.
Ernest John *or* John Ernest, Duke. *See* Biren.
Erpingham (Erpyngham):
(Norfolk), landowners in, 103.
deed relating to, 68.
Manor Rolls of, 29.
North, Hundred of, 81, 97, 440.
parsonage house and glebe in, 431.
South, Hundred of, 81, 101, 440.
view of frankpledge for, 68.
Erpingham:
John de, 26.
Sir Thomas, landowner in Saxthorpe, 4, 21, 53.
family of, at Blickling, 2.
Erse *or* Gaelic dictionary, scheme for, 338.
Erskine:
chaplain to Earl of Buckinghamshire, 173.
Rev. John, 374, 379.
——, two livings presented to, 345, 346.
——, Dean of Cork, 374, 421.
Sir William, in American war, 305.
Escole. *See* Scule.
Esning, 129.
Essay on "Woman," 247, 249.
Essex, vii., 54, 73, 131, 147, 148, 165, 252².
Essex, H.M.S., 138.
Estgate, Hamond, 144.
Estreat of the assessment for subsidies in the Hundred of N. Erpingham, 97-101.
——, S. Erpingham, 101-105.
——, Eynsford, 89-97.
——, N. Greenhœ, 112-117.
——, Holt, 105-112.
Estrin:
John de, 18.
William Hamund de, 18.
Eton, 241.
Eudo, *Clericus*, 17.
Eugene, Prince, 435.
Europe, 237, 370, 397, 408.
French fleet in, 339, 404.
independence of America in relation to, 405, 406.
independence of Ireland in relation to, 395, 396.
situation of, in 1773, 292.
trade in, 307, 309.
Europe, the ship, 409.
Euston, letter dated, 164.
Evans:
Mr., 325.
George, 3rd Baron Carberry, 442.
Evelyn, John, his notice of the Duke of Norfolk, xiii.

Everard:
son of Hugh, 47.
son of Steingrim, 47.
Thomas, of Knapton, 97.
brother of the lord Tedbald, 12.
Evered, William, 106.
"Every man in his humour,' acted at the Attic Theatre, 433.
Exchange of land (13th century), 19.
Exeter, 442.
election at, 285.
letter dated, 416.
opposition to the Government, at, 252.
Exeter:
Earl of. *See* Cecil.
Lady, sister of Lady Frances Hobart, 89.
Exeter, H.M.S., 138.
"Exiter, my lord of " (1638). *See* Cecil.
Exmouth Chapel built, 333.
Exorcist, taking order of, without Lord's license, 3, 27.
Expedition, H.M.S., 138.
Exneye, William, 74.
Export of corn, 266, 267, 439, 440.
addresses for relief relating to, 265, 266, 270.
embargo upon. *See* Embargo.
riots in Norfolk relating to, 267-272, 274.
Eynsford (Norfolk), Hundred of, 89-97.
Eyre, King's Commissioners in, 3.
Eyre:
John, of Sculthorpe, 53.
Lt.-Colonel of the 59th regiment, 400.
Eyward, Robert, witness, 7.

F

Faber:
John, 19.
Ralf, 19, 42.
Richard, 34, 37.
Robert, 38.
Thomas, 35, 36.
Fairborne, Stafford, Captain, 138.
Fairefax:
Thomas, 116.
William, 115.
"*Fairies*," the, performed at the Attic Theatre, 433.
Fakenham (Norfolk), 52, 133.
Fanfare, H.M.S., 140.
Fanmakere, Robert, 28.
Fanti, Luigi (violin player), 276-277.
Farington, "old," 251.
Farnham, Lord. *See* Maxwell.
Farthing, Peter, 88.

Fastolf *or* Fastolfe:
　family of, at Blickling, 2.
　Sir John, 3, 4, 29, 30, 45, 46,
　　54, 55, 56, 57.
　——, his coat of arms, 441.
　——, covenant of, with his
　　bailiff for farming the manor,
　　temp. Henry VI., 56.
　——, suit of, with Geoffrey
　　Boleyn, 29.
　John, Esq., 54.
　Richard, 74.
Fauquier, Governor, letter relative
　to the Virginian resolutions, 260.
Fawcett, Henry, sheriff of Norwich,
　81.
Fayette, Marquis de la, 442.
Feake, Philip, 106.
Feazer, Robert, 107.
Fecsor, James, 102.
Feilding, Basil, 6th Earl of Den-
　bigh, 378.
Felbrigg (Felbridge):
　landowners in, 100.
　letter dated, 87.
Felbrigg:
　John, 43.
　Robert, 43.
　Simon de, 53, 73.
Feletorp *or* Feltorp. *See* Felthorp.
Fellowes, Robert, 442.
　letter from, 294.
Feltham, Robert, 100.
Felthorp (Feletorp, Feltorp): 16,
　54.
　Alexander de, 39.
　Roger de, 16, 19.
Felton:
　Hamon de, 52.
　Thomas, 110.
　Timothy, 110.
Fen, John atte, 37.
Fen drainage, 84, 85, 165.
　letter on, 84, 165.
Fenn *or* Fenne:
　Henry, Lieut., Norfolk Militia,
　　126.
　Hugh, 55, 56.
　Nicholas, 113.
　Thomas, 113.
Fenton Load, 165.
Ferdinand:
　Duke. *See* Kettler.
　Prince [of Brunswick] (1760),
　　241.
Fermor, George, 2nd Earl of Pom-
　fret, *m.* Miss Draycott, 250.
Ferreris, Richard de, 40.
Ferrers:
　Lord de (1779). *See* Townshend.
　Earl (1766). *See* Shirley.
Ferrys, Christopher, cook, 87.
Fethard (Ireland), 335.
Figge, William, 25.
Field Dalling *or* Dawling, land-
　owners in, 114.
Fildyngs *or* Fyldyngs:
　Everard, 55.
　William, 55.

Finch:
　Heneage, 1st Earl of Notting-
　　ham, 261.
　Heneage (3rd Earl of Aylesford),
　　protests against Repeal of
　　Stamp Act, 260.
　——, visits George Grenville,
　　262.
　——, Lord of the Bedchamber,
　　325.
　Daniel, 8th Earl of Winchelsea,
　　President of the Council, 256,
　　287.
　George, 9th Earl of Winchelsea,
　　Lord of the Bedchamber, 325.
Fincham, John, 108.
Finchley Common, camp at, 154,
　155.
Fingal, ancient poetry of, collected,
　338.
"Fingalian villa" of the Lord Lieu-
　tenant, 390.
Fingall, Lord. *See* Plunkett.
Finland:
　Gulf of, 184.
　war in, 434.
Fire ships (1691) in the English
　fleet, 140.
Firmary, Mary, 100.
Fisher (Fyssher):
　Captain W., Norfolk Militia,
　　111, 126.
　Robert, 101, 115.
Fishmongers, the Company of, land-
　owners in Holt, 110.
"Fisshus" a, at Gt. Yarmouth, 74.
Fitts, Richard, 109.
Fitzgerald:
　Lord C., moves Address (Dublin),
　　398.
　Harriet, marries Henry Grat-
　　ton, 423.
　Mr., in Dublin, 422.
　R., 379.
　William, 2nd Duke of Leinster,
　　325, 357, 358, 379, 386, 434.
Fitzgibbon, John (afterwards Lord
　and Earl of Clare), in House of
　Commons, Dublin, 400, 402, 427.
Fitzpatrick:
　Mr., in Irish House of
　　Commons, 414.
　Richard, Captain, 139.
Fitz-Robert, Ranulph, Lord of
　Lound, 47.
Fitz-Roger, Robert, 5, 11, 15, 19.
FitzRoy, Augustus Henry, 3rd
　　Duke of Grafton, 221, 252,
　　253, 266, 277-279, 284-286-288.
　his appointment as First Lord
　　of the Treasury, 286.
Fitz-Simon, Henry, grant of land
　by, 41.
Fitzwalter:
　Lord. *See* Mildmay.
　Robert, founder of St. Faith's,
　　Norwich, 1, 2, 10.
　——, charter of, 10.
　Sibyll, 2, 10.

Fitzwarin, Richard, 47.
Fitzwilliam, Richard, 7th Viscount Fitzwilliam, 301.
'Flaggs,' the digging of, an offence, 80.
Flanders:
    defeat in (1746), 161.
    troops ordered from (1745), 149.
Flatman, John, a husbandman,' 88.
Flaxman, Richard, 110.
Fleet, British, 146, 164.
    in 1691, 139-140.
    in American war, 342, 383, 396-398, 399, 400, 402, 403, 410.
Fleetwoods, the two Mr., 143.
Fleg, Roger de, 40.
Flegge, near Yarmouth, 54.
Flemming, Count, 218.
Fletcher, Lt.-Col., commanding the 32nd regiment, 339.
Flight:
    Charles, of Houghton, 113.
    John, 97.
    Robert, 98, 99.
Flint, Roger, 100.
Flood:
    Rt. Hon. H., 363, 400-403, 405, 410, 414, 423, 425, 426.
    ——, hostile to Lord Buckinghamshire, 391, 392.
    Sir S., 410.
Florence, letters dated, 276, 277, 296.
Florindune, Geoffrey de, 14.
Flowerdew, John, of Hethersett, 65.
Foldage, liberty of, 29.
Fold Course, 37.
Fontenelle, saying of, 181.
Footman, Richard, 87.
Footpaths, presentment as to, 9.
Forbes:
    George, 3rd Earl of Granard, 226, 227, 228, 229.
    George, 5th Earl, 379.
    George, 6th Earl, letter from, 366.
    ——, Irish M.P., 403.
Ford, Elizabeth, 116.
Forester, William le, witness, 6.
Forster, Mr., 376.
Fortescue:
    Rt. Hon. James, M.P., 1st Earl of Clermont, 327, 334, 378.
    John, Chief Justice, 54.
Foster:
    John, later Chancellor of the Exchequer, Ireland, letters from, 381, 414.
    ——, M.P. for Louth,' 358.
    Mr., 394.
    ——, at Dublin, 427.
    . Sam, of Kelling, 111.
Foulkes, Captain Simon, 139.
Foulsham, Norfolk, landowners in, 91.

Fountaine (Fountayn, Fountayne):
    Mr., of Sall, 143.
    Mr., 112, 132.
    Sir John, S.L., 117.
    James, of Sall, 94.
Fowle, T., witness, 18.
Fowler, Dr. Robert, Bishop of Killaloe, afterwards Archbishop of Dublin (1778), 343, 386, 408, 417.
    letters from, 386, 408, 418.
    letters to, 387, 417.
Fox:
    Charles James (1783), coalition with North, 417, 427, 428.
    Henry, 160.
    Henry, Lord Holland, 160, 185.
    ——, letter from, 159.
    Reginald, 51.
Foxley (Norfolk), 92.
Framingham:
    John, 114.
    Robert, 114.
    William, 112, 115.
France, 161, 216, 217, 219, 238, 239, 240, 252, 253, 305, 337, 341, 344, 378.
    and America, 363, 404, 406, 413.
    contest in, 435.
    King of. See Francis I. and Louis XV.
    policy of, towards English Colonies in America, 239-240, 305, 388.
    relations of, with Ireland, 395, 413.
    war news from (1777), 324.
Francis I. of France, his captivity, 206.
Franck, Thomas, 108.
Franckling, Edward, 108.
Franklin:
    Governor, letter to Mr. Cox, 260.
    Dr., 410.
    ——, letter of, intercepted, 301.
Frankmore, John, Captain, 139.
Fransham, Agneta, at Blickling, 21.
Frayry, William, 114.
Fraunceis or Fraunceys:
    Alexander, the Chaplain, 17.
    William, 18.
    John de Spykesworthe, 16.
    Simon le, 18.
Fre, Nicholas, 25.
Frederic Casimir, Duke of Courland See Kettler.
Frederic II., King of Prussia, xv., 155, 165, 174, 218, 220, 224, 293.
    character of, 155, 371.
    letter from, 220.
Freedom, presentment as to, 8.
Freeman:
    Capt. of the ship Montague, 150.
    John, Lieut. Norfolk Militia, 126.
Freeman, villain claiming to be a, 9.
Freeston, Anthony, Capt., Norfolk Militia, 126.

Freethorp Manor in Keswick (Norfolk), rolls, 66.
French:
the, 159, 406, 435.
Ambassador, the, taken prisoner (1746), 160.
at Chesapeak, 408.
at Dantzick, 292.
at Newfoundland, 252.
fleet, 161, 252, 337, 339, 351, 396, 400.
——, in America, 342, 396, 397, 399, 400, 404, 407.
frigates, &c., capture of, 368.
invasion apprehended, 137.
Islands in West Indies, 172.
Minister, the, in Russia, 172.
naval engagement with (1777), 305.
naval tactics, 338.
privateers, 338.
prophesy as to the, 406.
sugars, 309.
trade, 234, 239, 240, 308-310, 317, 318.
Frere le, William, presented for making and selling a rein, 7.
Freysell, John, 26.
Fridenberg, John, merchant, 146.
Friedrichsham, incoming and outgoing ships from, 233.
Frier, Capt., 71.
Frognall (Captain), 150.
Froude, Frederick, commanding H.M.S. Ruby, 139.
Froysel, Robert son of John, 28.
Fryer, Thomas, 95.
Fulcher, Richard, 103.
Fulham, 30.
Fuller:
Captain E., 378.
Edward, 142, 144.
Geoffrey, of Sparham, 94.
Henry, of Brandeston, 90.
Zachariah, of Wood Dalling, 96.
Fundenhall (Norfolk), 143.
Funnell, Ralph, 90.
Furnese, Henry, buys Gunnersbury, 147.
Futter:
Humphrey, 127.
John, 127.
Fygge, Robert, son of Simon, 28.
Fyn, Simon, 25.
Fyncham, John, 55.
Fynes, Sir E., Knight (1552). See Clinton, Edward.
Fynderne, William, esquire, 54.
Fyssher. See Fisher.

G

Gabbet, Colonel, a duel with, 294.
Gage, General, letter to, 260.
letter from, 261.
Gaifer, Bishop's chaplain, 40.
"Galen's Head," 221.
Galfridus. See Geoffrey.
Galitzin, Prince (Alexander Michael-ovitz), Vice-Chancellor of Russia, 185, 219.
Gall, Edmund, 104.
Gallant, John, 96, 110.
Gallow, Hundred of, 137.
Gallyots and Flutes, Dutch ships, 141.
Galway, Galloway, 150, 318.
Game, Robert (Norfolk Militia), 126.
Gamble, Robert, letters from, 377, 379.
Gappe, Robert atte, 74.
Garard or Garrard:
Elizabeth, 104.
Sir Thomas, 125, 127, 133.
"Garde Ecossaise," la, 413.
Gardener, Dr., exchanges Norwich living, 257.
Gardiner:
——, given a commission, 243, 244.
Francis, 132.
Luke, 379, 417, 418, 442.
——, his bill in the Irish House of Commons, 410.
——, letter from, 417.
——, letter to, 417.
Mrs., 423.
——, death of, 424.
Richard, 321.
Gardini conducts orchestra, 253.
Gargrane, —, 132.
Garland, ship, 139.
Garraways. See London.
Garrett:
Mr., 112.
Thomas, 109.
Garrick, David, letter from, 297, 298.
Garter, the, Duke of Beaufort asks for, 348.
Gates, General, grants favourable terms to Burgoyne, 326.
——, at Ticonderoga, 311.
Gaudentz (Poland), 221.
Gawdy, Thomas, 57, 126.
Gay:
Mr. (John), 243, 321, 353, 431, 442.
——, contests Norwich, 243.
——, letters from, 267, 270, 312.
Edward, of Wood Dalling, 96.
John, 100.
Robert, 100.
William, 99.

Gedge, Edmond, "Fermer," of Ravenshall, 62.
Geistwicke. *See* Guestwick.
General warrants, 248.
Genneye, Genney *or* Genny:
William, 54.
the elder, 30.
William, Sergeant at Law, 55·
Genoa, 396.
Geoffrey (Galfridus, Gaufridus):
chaplain to the Bishop (Turbeville), 12.
son of Peter, 41.
de Hicheligge, 12.
de Lodnes, 16.
the smith, 47, 48, 49.
Thomas son of, 35.
George I., King of England, 308, 438.
George II., King of England, 151, 166-170, 176, 227-230, 306-8, 310, 317, 318.
George III., King of England, 238, 244, 255, 256, 263, 264, 277-278, 280-282, 284-286, 288, 310, 339, 340, 352, 407, 414, 423.
contented with no ministers, 253.
Regency under, 437.
George:
Prince, of Holstein, 201.
John, Captain, 139.
Lord. *See* Germain.
George, H.M.S., 139.
Georgetown, North America, 387.
Georgians, "thieves and villains," 236.
Gerard, land called, 41.
Germain:
Lord George, 299, 300, 315, 324, 326, 351, 357-359, 361, 363, 366, 368, 370-372, 373, 375, 376, 409, 410.
——, letters from, 305, 404.
——, letters to, 343, 345, 349, 352, 356, 357, 358, 359, 363, 364, 366, 370, 371, 372, 373, 375, 376.
Lady Betty, 192.
German troops in America, 311.
Germany, British trade with, 309.
Gernesey, H.M.S., 139.
Gervase (Gervas, Gerveys)
Sir Thomas, bart., 133.
Ralph, 51.
son of Richer Hare, 49.
merchant of Scottowe, 15.
son of Roger, 47.
Geyst. *See* Guist.
Ghilan (Persia), 224, 235.
Gibbs, Captain, 334, 335.
Gibbes' stables, in Salisbury Lane, 89.
Gibny:
Nicholas, 48, 50.
Sibilla, 48.
Gibraltar, 363.

Gibson, Judith, 116.
Gideon, Samson, letters from, 148-153, 155, 157.
Gilbert, Anne, 107.
Giles:
Mr., a Spitalfields' weaver, 176.
Mr., an emissary to Sir Horace Mann, 296.
Gillens, Thomas, 140.
Gillingham (Norfolk), 145.
Gilpin, Sam., 125.
Gimingham, Gymingham:
landowners in, 97.
manor rolls of, 69.
Girdleston, Thomas, 109.
Girling, Thomas, Norfolk Militia, 126.
Gislabert, witness, 12.
Gisnei, William de, 15.
Glandford, 106.
Glandore, Lord. *See* Crosbie.
Glanville, John, 139.
Glean, Peter, 123.
Glennenney, Robert, 116.
Glerawly, Viscount. *See* Annesley.
Gloresdale:
Adam de, 48, 50.
Stephen, son of Adam, 48, 50.
Glosdale, John de, 48.
Gloucester: 247.
corn riots in, 271.
Gloucester:
[William Henry], Duke of, courts Lady Waldgrave, 253.
Earl of, 35, 36.
Bishop of. *See* Warburton.
Glynne, Sir John, 165.
Gnatam (Devonshire), 289.
Gnesen (Poland), 216.
Gobbet, Captain, Alderman, 353.
Gochop, John, 14.
Godfrey:
John, Norfolk Militia, 126.
the Chaplain, 47.
Richard, 113, 126.
son of Alan, 10.
son of John, 10.
Godes, Ralph, 49.
Goding, Ralph, 39.
Godolphin, Francis, Marquis of Carmarthen. 325.
appointed Chamberlain of the Queen, 325.
Godolphin, ship, 150.
Godsone, Adam, 25.
Godwin, Ailmer son of, 13.
Gogle:
John, 99.
Thomas, 97.
Goldsmith *or* Gouldsmith, John, 110, 114.
Goldthwaite, Joseph, 261.
Golowin, Count, 191.
Goltz, Baron de, Polish General, letter from, 221.
Goodricke, Sir John, 378.
Goodwyne, widow, of Wood Norton, 96.

Goold, Colonel, of the 30th, 335.
Gordon:
    Alexander, 4th Duke of (1778), letter from, 338.
    Lord George, 366-368, 370.
    Col., the Hon. William, letter from, 362.
    (Rev.) Mr., 276.
    Robert, a commissioner of provisions, letter from, 311.
Gordon Castle, letter dated, 338.
Gore:
    John, 1st Baron Annaly, 379.
    Ralph, Earl of Ross, 379.
    ——, letter from, 420.
Gosfield, Lord Nugent at, 294.
Goslinge, Edmund, 103.
Gosnald, Anne, 103.
Gostling:
    Thomas, 88.
    widow, 88.
Gothier, John, Captain, 138.
Gotts, Nicholas, 107.
Gould, Sir Henry, 274.
Goulding, John, 107.
Gouthorp (Gowthorp), 67.
Gourdon, Brampton, 124.
Gourney, Capt., 138.
Gower:
    Granville, 2nd Earl Gower, 279, 280.
    ——, protests against repeal of Stamp Act, 260.
    John, 2nd Lord (1745), 157.
Grafton:
    Duchess of, 253.
    Duke of. See FitzRoy.
Grafton, H.M.S., 138.
Graham, Capt., Atholl Highlanders, 348.
Grame, Mungo, 226.
Granard:
    Countess of, 379.
    George, 3rd Earl. See Forbes.
    George, 5th Earl of, ibid.
    George, 6th Earl of, ibid.
Granby, Lord. See Manners, John.
Grand, Agnes, 25.
Grange, John, 90.
Granville, Lord (1745). See Carteret.
Grattan:
    Rt. Hon. Henry, 363, 400, 401, 403, 410, 414, 415, 423, 426, 433.
    ——, address proposed by, 378, 414.
    ——, an estate to be purchased for, 415.
    Mrs. (Harriet Fitz Gerald), 423.
Gray or Graye. See Grey.
Grave lights, expense of, 59.
Graves, Admiral, 410.
Green or Greene (Grene):
    of Norwich, 110.
    Bartholomew, 109.
    Elizabeth, 107.
    Godfrey, 379.
    General, in North America, 387, 388.

Green—cont.
    Henry, 115.
    Mr., 344, 379.
    John, 53.
    Richard, 100.
    Thomas, 54.
    William, of Whitwell, 96.
Greencloth, Board of, 325.
Greeneway, Samuel, 127.
Greenhoe:
    North, Hundred of (Norfolk), 81, 112-117.
    South, Hundred of, 81.
Greenock, letter dated, 330.
"Gregorians," the society of, at Norwich, 242, 354.
Grenville:
    George, 174, 178, 181-183, 185, 187, 238, 244, 249, 250, 253, 254, 257, 258, 274, 277-281, 283, 285-288, 294.
    ——, letters from, 244, 246, 249, 254, 255, 256, 257, 261-265, 272, 274, 277, 285, 287, 288.
    ——, letter to, 286.
    ——, at Bristol, 250.
    ——, his Colonial policy, 275-277.
    ——, his opinions of Grafton ministry, 263, 264, 265.
    ——, ——, of Rockingham ministry, 261.
    ——, superseded, 255, 258.
    ——, triumphs in the House of Commons, 250, 253.
    Mrs. George, 250, 257, 275, 286, 287.
    ——, her illhealth, 259, 262, 264, 272, 294.
    family, 180.
    ——, reconciled, 254.
    Lord (1792), 439.
    Mr., 181.
    Richard, 2nd Earl Temple, 180, 250, 260, 262, 265, 273, 274, 277, 278, 279, 280, 434.
    ——, negotiations of. with Pitt, 263-5.
    George, 3rd Earl Temple and Marquess of Buckingham, Viceroy of Ireland, 417, 418, 433, 434, 442.
Gresham:
    ——, 4.
    William, at Intwood, 68.
Gresham, landowners in, 100.
Greshaugh or Greisheighe Manor. See Wymondham.
Gressenhall (Norfolk), 83.
Greswold, Fort, North America, 400.
Greville, Mrs., 378.
Grey, Greye, Gray or Graye:
    ——, death at Hillsborough, 329.
    Edward, of Mickelhalle, Saxthorp, 46.
    Christopher, 102.
    Edmund, Earl of Kent, 55.

Grey—*cont.*
  Edmund, Lord de Hastyngs, Creysford and Ruthyn, 4, 55.
  George, 101.
  Giles, of Sidestrand, 98.
  Henry, 127.
  Humfrey, 55.
  John, gent., 20.
  Philip, 102.
  Robert, 55, 127.
Greyhound, H.M S., 140.
Griel, Geoffrey, a "five-akering," his service to Langley Abbey (1288), 60.
Grimbald's land in Ripetune (Rippon), 40.
Grimston, 145.
Grinstead, East, Sir John Irwine, M.P. for, 348.
Grisius, Robert, 41.
Grisaugh. *See* Wymondham.
Gros:
  Charles le, 132.
  Geoffrey le, 19.
Grossus, Gocelin, 40.
Grosvenor, Richard 1st Lord, 260.
Grotius, his authority quoted, 300.
Gryme:
  George, 97.
  John, 127.
  Richard, 97.
  Robert, 97.
  Thomas, 97.
Grymmer, Robert, Norfolk Militia, 126.
Grys:
  Henry, 24.
  Margaret, daughter of Richard, 26.
Grysheigh. *See* Greshaugh.
Guards, the, in N. America, reduced in numbers, 388.
Guarinus. *See* Warin.
Guerchy, M. de, 250.
Guestwick (Geistwick), (Norfolk), 92.
Guet. *See* Wayte.
Guibon. *See* Guybon.
Guildford, N. America, 388.
——, court house, 387.
Guild of St. Andrew, Horsham, 20.
Guildhouse, grant of a, from Prior and Convent of St. Faith's, Horsham, to John Greye and others, 20.
Guilford:
  Earl of. *See* North.
  Lord Keeper, *ibid.*
Guist, Geyst (Norfolk), 92.
Gula Augusti, 61.
Gullet, Mr., in Devonshire, 332.
Gundolf, William, 17.
Guns in the English and Dutch fleets (1691), 140.
Gunnersbury or Gunnaldsbury, Estate in North Ealing, 147.
Gunny, 11.
Gunnysmede or Gunnyldesmedwe, in Horsham, 11.
Gunthorp, William de, 52.

Gunthorpe (Norfolk), landowners in, 106, 110.
Gunton (Norfolk): 257.
  landowner in, 97.
  letters dated, 260, 320.
Gunton, Henry, 99, 105.
Gunvile manor. *See* Wymondham.
Gurnay or Gurney:
  Alice, 53.
  Edmund, Lord of the Manor of Saxthorpe, 45, 52.
  Edward, 52.
  Esmon or Osman, 52, 74.
  Mr., a Norwich manufacturer, 312.
  John, 52, 53.
  William, 56.
Gurnays, in Wotton, manor of, 52.
Gurnel, William, 16.
Gurquant, Gurwhant or Gurwhan, Simon, Chaplain, 52.
Gustavus III., King of Sweden, 293.
Guton, in Brandeston, Norfolk, 54.
Guybon or Guibon:
  Francis, 127.
  Sir Francis, xiii., 133, 135-137, 142.
  Sir Thomas, 112, 116.
Guyet. *See* Wayte.
Gwydo, 9.
Gyfford, William, clerk, 55.
Gymingham. *See* Gimingham.
Gyrlyngton, 54.
Gyslingham, the Prior of, 36.
Gyssing, Gysinghe:
  Thomas, knight, at Blickling, 20.
  Will. de, 16.

H

Hackford (Norfolk), landowners in, 93.
Haemus, Mount, 435.
Hagley or Haggley (Worcestershire), 288.
  entertainment at, 241-242.
Hagon, Haghene, or Hacun:
  John, 24.
  John 54, 57.
  William (presentment for damage (Horsham)), 7, 8.
Hague, the, 221.
  letter from, 369.
  Embassy at, 177.
  Sir Joseph Yorke at, 295, 369.
Haldiman, General Frederic, Governor of Canada, 315.
Half Moon, N. America, 316.
Halifax, Lord. *See* Montague.
Halifax armament, the, in Sandy Hook, 296.
Halisch (Poland), reconfederation of, 219.

Hall:
　John, 44.
　Robert, 101.
　Mr. (Roger), M.P. for County Down, 319.
　Thomas, of Alderford, 90.
Hallman, Thomas, of Hindolveston, 93.
Halteyn or Haltein. See Hautaine.
Halton, Sir Thomas, 84.
Hally (or Hawley), Generalissimo of English Army (1745), 156.
Hamburg, trade of, with St. Peters-burg, 234.
Hamilton:
　David, 251.
　Duchess of, 164.
　Edward, 379.
　Gawin, 329.
　Mr., 342, 390.
　Jack, at Dublin, 403.
　James, 8th Earl of Abercorn, protests against Repeal of Stamp Act, 260.
　James, 2nd Earl of Clanbrassil, 334, 378, 442.
　——, letter from, 334.
　Sackville, 364, 366, 375, 427.
　——, Secretary to the Lord Lieutenant, 377, 424.
　——, letters from, 305, 424.
　——, statement on Irish trade by, xvii., 301.
Hammond, Captain, engages French ships, 305.
Hamon, brother of Walter, 12.
Hamond or Hamund:
　Mrs. Elizabeth, 143.
　Francis, of Sparham, 94.
　John, 103, 107.
　Mary, marriage certificate of, 87.
　Mr., 143.
　Robert, 130.
　——, of Roughton, 98.
　——, ensign (Norfolk) Militia, 126.
　Roger, 130.
　William, de Estrin, 18.
Hampden:
　Robert, Viscount Hampden (1776), 179.
　Mary Constantia, 179.
Hampshire: 156, 310.
　New, N. America, 311.
Hampton Court, H.M.S., 138.
Hanbury, William, letter from, 160.
Hancock, a leader at Boston town meeting, 290.
Haniball, H.M.S., 139.
Hankes, Sarah, 90.
Hanover, 244.
　and Great Britain, 398.
Hanworth (Norfolk), 97.
Hanworth, Richard de, 61.
Happing, Hundred of, 439.
Happy Return, ship, 139.

Hapsal (Russia), 233.
Harbord or Harberd:
　Sir Harbord, 185, 187, 242, 243, 251, 256, 257, 287, 321, 353, 373, 442.
　——, letter from, 242.
　——, marriage, 241.
　——, created Lord Suffield, 242 431.
　John, 125, 132, 135, 136, 137, 144.
　Lady, 251, 321.
　Mr. See Harbord, Sir Harbord.
　Philip, Lieut.-Col. Norfolk Militia, 125.
　Sir William, 251, 287.
　——, letters from, 251, 260.
　——, letter to, 260.
Harbords, the, 256.
Harch, Peter de, 12.
Harcourt:
　Lord, 381.
　——, establishment as Viceroy in Ireland, 319.
　Mr., at Norwich, 270.
Hardekin, Roger, 14.
Hardenheth, John, messor at Wy-mondham, 64.
Hardhend, Nicholas, 60.
Harding, William, 139.
Hardley (Hardeley, Hardele), 60.
　Cartulary for, 61.
　an extent of manor, 73.
Hardwick (Herdewyc), 73.
Hardwicke, Lord. See Yorke.
Hare, arms of, 441.
Hare:
　Edric, 13.
　John, of Bawdswell, 90.
　Richer, 49.
　Sir Thomas, 133.
"Harlequinade, a droll," 290.
Harleston or Harlston (Norfolk):
　letter dated, 160.
Harleston fair, 319.
Harleton, John, 54.
Harley, Edward, Earl of Oxford, 378
Harman, Henry, Quarter-Master Horse Regiment, 127.
Harmer:
　John, 97, 110.
　Robert, of Trunch and Anting-ham, 97, 99.
　Thomas, 98.
　William, 86.
Harnie or Harnye:
　John, of Twyford, 95.
　William, of Hinderingham, 113.
　William, of Warham, 115.
Harold (King), 1.
　his house at Blickling, 1.
Harpley (Harpelee), 73.
　church of, 52, 53.
Harriet:
　Lady. See Hobart.
　Mrs. See Hotham.
Harrington, Lord. See Stanhope.

Harris :
  John, Capt.-Lieut. (Norfolk) Militia, 126.
  ——, at Beer, 347.
Harsingham. *See* Hassingham.
Hartlow, Captain of H.M.S. *Burford*, 138.
Hartston, John, of Reepham, 94.
Harvey, Harvy :
  ——, a Norwich manufacturer, 312.
  John, 111.
  Robert, 242, 243.
  Tom, 242, 243.
Harwich (H.M.S.), 138.
Hase, John, of Billingford, 91.
Hassan Massa, near Belgrade, 435.
Hassingham (Harsingham) Dyke, 121.
Haste, Captain, 334.
Hastings (Hastinges, Hastyngs) :
  Anthony, Capt. H.M.S. *Sandwich*, 137.
  Charles, a reputed Papist, warrant against, 137, 142, 144.
  Edmund, Lord de. *See* Grey.
  Elizabeth, of Stodey, 107.
  family, formerly Lords of Gressenhall and Elsing, 83.
  Francis, 10th Earl of Huntingdon, letters from, 285, 337.
  ——, letters to, 285.
  Martin, 107.
  Robert, de, 73.
  Robert, of Berney, 116.
  William de, 75.
Hatsell, J., 378.
Hautaine, Hauten, Autayn, Haltane, Halthein, Haltein, Halteyn :
  Agnes, 12.
  Captain, 130.
  Robert, 15, 16.
  Theobald, his expedition to Jerusalem, 12.
  ——, grant by, 11.
  Walter, 12.
Hautbois, Houtebys or Houteboys :
  Magna (Norfolk), 104.
  Parva, 104.
Haveringland, Heverland, 6, 10, 93.
Havers :
  Mrs. Elizabeth, a reputed Papist, 145.
  Thomas, 142.
Haversham, Lord. *See* Thompson.
Hawe, James, ensign (Norfolk) Militia, 126.
Hawes :
  James, 112, 116.
  Thomas, of Erpingham, 103.
Hawkesbury, Lord (1792). *See* Jenkinson.
Hawkins, Sarah, a reputed Papist, 145.

Hay :
  Henry, of Bylaugh, 90.
  Thomas, 8th Earl of Kinnoul, 245.
Haydon, ——, 30.
Haylett :
  Mr., can catalogue Sir Henry Hobart's books, 131.
  William, 104.
Haynes, John, servant, 87.
Haynford (Heinford), 16, 55.
Heacham or Hecham (Norfolk), 53.
Heart of Oak, H.M.S., 330.
Hearth money, 132, 347, 350.
Heath, Mr., Town Clerk of Exeter, 252.
Heblethwaite, George, 116.
Heckingham, Hekyngham, 60.
Hekingham, Roger de, 16.
Heles' charity to relieve the poor of Plymouth, 276.
Hele, Sir John, of Wembury, 85.
Helesdhon. *See* Hellesdon.
Helhoughton (Heletune, Helgheton, Hegletune), 10, 18.
Hellesdon (Heylesdon, Helesdhon, Heylisdune), 12, 54.
  deed relating to, 15.
Helwyn, John, 32.
Hely Hutchinson, John, Provost of Trinity College (Dublin), 297, 358, 363, 364, 377, 401.
  letter from, 340.
Helyas, Prior, 40.
Hemerus, presbyter, 40.
Hemesby. *See* Hemsby.
Hemlington, Hemlyngton, deed relating to, 71.
Hemlinton, Robert, a reputed Papist, 145.
Hempstead (Norfolk), 107, 111, 112.
  vicarage of, 285, 431.
  landed proprietors in, 107, 111.
Hempton Green (Norfolk), 133.
Hemsby, Hemesby, 28, 54.
Henin, M., French Resident at Warsaw, his interview with the Primate of Poland, 216, 217.
  letters from, and to, 219.
Henley :
  Robert, Lord, 1st Earl of Northington, 177, 266, 286.
  ——, an enlightened whig minister, 272.
  Robert, 2nd Earl, Viceroy of Ireland, 418.
  ——, retires, 427.
Henniker (Hennekar), Mr., has bought the Dyer's estate near Dunmow, 165.
Henrietta Yacht, 140.
Henry, janitor, 16.
Henry I., confirmation by, of Blickling manor to Bishop Herbert, 1.
Henry, Beatrice, daughter of Alice, building lease by, 8.

Herbert:
  Bishop. *See* Losinga.
  Mr., marries daughter of Lord
    G. Germain, 405.
  Henry, 9th Earl of Pembroke,
    148.
  ——, 10th Earl of Pembroke,
    325, 350.
  ——, ——, his dragoons, 297.
  Roger, son of, 12.
  William, 3rd Earl of Powis, 260.
Herciator, 33.
Herdewyc, Vill of. *See* Hardwick.
Hereford, John, Bishop of. *See*
  Trevenant.
Herford, Warin de, 38.
Hering, Walter, 8.
Herlynge, John de, 43.
Hermione, ship, brings specie for
  " W," 410.
Herne *or* Hyrne:
  Ann, 93.
  Clement, 93, 124.
  E. B., letter from, 431.
  Emma, 14.
  Francis, 103.
  John, 124.
  Mr. & Mrs., 321.
  Thomas, 143.
  Thomas, mayor of Norwich, 81.
  ——, letter from, 81.
Heron, in Essex, 148.
Heron:
  Mr., 319. *See also* Sir Richard.
  Sir John, 340.
  Sir Richard, 310, 343, 358, 371,
    379, 385, 429.
  ——, letter to, 311.
  ——, M.P. for Lisburn, 311.
Herreria, Vicomte de la, letter from,
  434.
Hertford:
  Lord. *See* Conway.
  Joanna, Countess of, 46.
  Richard de, 50.
  ——, rector of Parish Church
    of Saxthorp, 4.
Hervey *or* Hervy:
  Augustus John, 3rd Earl of
    Bristol, 286, 350.
  Frederic, 4th Earl of Bristol,
    Bishop of Cloyne and of
    Derry, 420, 422, 424, 429.
  ——, described, 422.
  ——, a volunteer of Derry, 425.
  camerarius, 40.
  parson of Stratton, 73.
  son of Henry de London, 41.
  Thomas, 28.
  William, 64.
Herward, Clement, 53.
Heselholt, 33.
Hesse, the Prince of (1746), 161.
Hessian reinforcements for America,
  296, 388.
  defeated in America. 300.
Hethersett, 65, 72.

Hetman, the. *See* Rozamowsky.
Heveningham. *See* Hevingham.
Heverland. *See* Haveringland.
Hevingham *or* Heveningham (Norfolk): 3, 5, 29, 30-44, 73, 104,
    129, 440, 441.
  abuttal of Andrew Thetford's
    land in, 32.
  'Brodlande,' 41.
  Church, 43, 44.
  extent of manor of, *temp.* Hen.
    III., 3, 33-39.
  extract from account roll of
    (1347-1348), 33.
  deeds relating to, 39-44.
  Hevidlonde in, 41.
  manor rolls of, 30-33.
  Catts' manor in, 30, 31, 32, 35,
    43.
  book of demesne lands in, 32.
  landowners in, 104.
  rentals and customaries of, 32.
  Critoft *or* Keritoft in, 31, 32,
    ——, Manor Court rolls, 31.
  cum Marsham, manor, 31.
  abuttal, 32.
  Park Hall manor in, 31, 32, 43,
    44.
  Regis, 31, 32.
  Rippon Hall manor in, 31, 32,
    39, 40, 43, 44.
Hewett, Hewet *or* Hewitt:
  Gardner, 124.
  James, Lord Lifford, 327, 340.
  ——, Lord Chancellor, 442.
  ——, letter from, 345, 351.
  Thomas, of Elsing, 91.
  William, 95, 103.
Hexham, 152.
Heydon *or* Heidone (Norfolk), 46, 52,
  320.
  landowners in, 103.
  letters dated, 269, 332.
Heydon:
  Christopher, esquire and knight,
    45, 46, 56.
  Henry, 55, 56.
  John, 55, 56.
  Mary, servant, 88.
  Richard, 56.
  Suzan, servant, 88.
Heyles, Robert, 29.
Heylisdune, Heylesdon. *See* Helles-
  don.
Heynford, Heynesford, 54.
  deeds relating to, 71.
Heyward, Francis, of Ringland, 94.
Heywood, Mr., at Beer, 289, 332.
  J. M., letters from. 293, 346.
Hickes, Jasper, 139.
Hickling (Hicheligge), Priory, 54.
Hickling, Geoffrey de, 12.
Highlands of Scotland:
  Mr. Shaw's tour in, 338.
  trees in, 322.

Hikelyng, Sir Thomas, Canon of Wayburn, 75.
Hil, Hugo del, 41.
Hill:
  Barbara, of Cockthorpe, 113.
  Charlotte, daughter of Earl of Hillsborough, 337.
  Hugh, 379.
  Wills, 1st Earl of Hillsborough, 321, 325, 329, 330, 348, 361, 363, 364, 367, 368, 372, 374-376, 400, 442.
  ——, superseded in Board of Trade, 256.
  ——, letters to, 261.
  ——, letters from, 298, 312-314, 318, 321, 325, 328, 330, 337, 347, 350, 368, 370, 380.
  Lady, 313.
Hill Park, letter dated, 337.
Hillsborough (Ireland), 328, 329, 337.
  hearth money at, 347, 350.
  letters dated, 312-14, 318, 321.
Hinderingham (Norfolk), landed proprietors in, 113.
Hindolveston (Hyndolveston), Norfolk, 93.
Hinks, John, of Bintrye, 91.
Hipeton, John, son of Adam de, 34.
Hirmingiond. See Irmingland.
Hobart (Hubard or Hubbart):
  Ann, of Edgfield, 109.
  Anne, her funeral (1703), 142, 143, 144.
  Brigadier John, 147.
  Catherine, afterwards Mrs. Churchill, 143, 144.
  Dorothy, daughter of Sir Henry, 143, 144.
  ——, daughter of Sir John, 85.
  Lady Dorothy, sister of 2nd Earl of Buckinghamshire. See Hotham.
  Edmund, assessor of Holt, 105.
  Edward, who died beyond seas, 84.
  Lady Emily, afterwards Lady Castlereagh, 381, 413, 417, 422.
  Elizabeth, her burial, 143, 144.
  family, miscellaneous memoranda relating to, 3, 142-144.
  ——, arms of, 441.
  ——, portraits of, 143.
  ——, property of in Cornwall, 146.
  Frances, Lady, 63, 143.
  ——, conveyance of Langley by, 87.
  ——, letter from, 89.
  ——, her manor at Wymondham, 63.
  ——, portrait of, 143.
  George, Hon. (3rd Earl of Buckinghamshire), 246, 285, 375.
  ——, secretary to Embassy at St. Petersburg, 171-173, 246.

Hobart—*cont.*
  Henrietta, afterwards Countess of Suffolk, xiv., 116, 143, 144, 146, 166-192, 238, 247, 256, 258, 262, 286, 288, 438.
  ——, her conversation with Caroline of Anspach, 166-170.
  ——, letters to, 146, 170-192, 238.
  ——, her published letters, 238.
  ——, marriage settlement, 144.
  ——, writings relating to her estate at Marble Hill, 146.
  ——, her will, 146, 288.
  Lady Henrietta (*or* Harriet), afterwards Lady Ancram, 1, 175-188, 258, 321.
  Sir Henry, Kt. and 1st Bart., Chief Justice of England, v., vi., 3, 31, 45, 59, 68, 75, 81, 82, 143, 442.
  ——, character of, v.
  ——, letters to, 81, 82.
  ——, purchase of Blickling by, 81-82.
  ——, portrait of, 143.
  Sir Henry, knight and 4th Bart., 89, 117, 129-132, 135, 136, 143, 147.
  ——, his duel, xiii-xiv.
  ——, letter to, 131.
  ——, list of his wardrobe (1673), 117-121.
  ——, regiment raised by, 147.
  Henry, Ketteringham rectory conveyed to, 72.
  ——, of South Pickenham, will of, 85.
  Hon. H., M.P. for Norwich, 431.
  James, 85.
  Sir James, Attorney General, 143.
  ——, his portrait, 143.
  Sir John, 2nd Bart., 84, 85, 143, 442.
  ——, dispensation granted to, 83.
  ——, letters to, 83, 84, 85.
  ——, his portrait, 143.
  ——, his wife's (Lady Frances) portrait, 143.
  John, brother of Henry, of South Pickenham, 85.
  Sir John, 3rd Bart., 87, 89, 102, 117, 121, 123, 129, 131, 143.
  ——, letter to, 83.
  ——, marriage certificate of, 87.
  ——, his house in Petty France, 89.
  ——, two portraits of, 143.
  ——, Waborne released to, 69.
  Sir John, 5th Bart., afterwards 1st Earl of Buckinghamshire, 145-147, 168, 170, 441.
  ——, his portrait, 143.
  ——, letters to, 146.
  ——, presents punch bowl to Clare Hall, 145.

Hobart—*cont.*
John, 2nd Earl of Buckinghamshire, 146, 288, 311, 332, 347,
375, 391.
——, correspondence of, 170-
192, 239-382, 384-442.
——, death of his sons, 295.
——, his embassy to Russia,
170-254, *passim*, 371.
——, proposed embassy of, to
Spain, 272.
——, dismissal of, from office of
Gentleman of the Bedchamber,
285.
——, helps to put down riot at
Norwich, 270.
——, his Irish history, 391.
——, M.P. for Norwich, 293.
——, his opinion of George
Grenville, 258.
——, ——, of the Rockingham
ministry, 258-259.
——, ——, of Russians, 255.
——, political quarrel of, with
the Harbords, 184, 185, 187,
256, 257, 373.
——, presentations and ad-
dresses to, 377-378.
——, protests against repeal of
Stamp Act, 260.
——, his review of Irish affairs,
376, 391-396, 416, 419.
——, ——, of results of American war, 404-406, 413, 414.
——, sends engravings to
Catherine II., 294.
——, his viceroyalty of Ireland,
297-381 *passim*, 385.
John, farmer's boy, 88.
Lord, infant son of 2nd Earl, 321.
Miles *or* Myles, 143.
——, contract on marriage of,
82.
——, his portrait, 143.
——, his wife's portrait, 143.
Mr., 143, 334, 341, 348, 354.
Nathaniel, 85.
Philippa, 143.
——, her burial, 144.
——, probate of will, 87.
Robert, letter from, 433.
Hobart papers, the, 76-147.
Hobson, Thomas, Capt., H.M.S. *St.
Michael*, 138.
Hockston, letter dated, 161.
Hogan:
John, servant, 87.
Robert, 97.
Holcot:
Matthew, 142.
W., witness, 7, 8.
Holdinge, John, "his mark," 89.
Holebeche, John de; 16.
Holkham *or* Holkem (Norfolk), 319.
letter dated, 319.
landed proprietors in, 113.

Holland: 161, 221, 225, 312, 341, 404,
408, 413, 434.
peace with, 405.
trade with Great Britain, 309.
—— St. Petersburg, 234.
—— West Indies, 307.
Holland:
Lord. *See* Fox.
Sir John, ix., 123, 132.
Holloway, —, a Jacobite, 163.
Holy Head (Holyhead), 297.
Holme, Daniel, abbot of, 40.
Holmes, Peter, letter from, 384.
Holstein, 201.
Holt:
Hundred of, 105, 110, 112.
——, the estreat of subsidies for
(1663), 105-112.
landed proprietors in, 105.
Holt, William de, at Blickling, 26.
Holveston:
family at Blickling, 2.
Sir James, 28, 29.
the Lady Joan, 21, 28.
Homage, entry into, 6, 8.
Home, Hugh, 3rd Earl of March-
mont, 379.
Homes, Thomas, of Briston, 111.
Honeworth. *See* Hunworth.
Honington, 163.
Honing *or* Honying (Norfolk), 53.
Hoo, Thomas, Lord of Manor of Ing-
worth, 68.
Hood, Sir Samuel, in American war,
399.
Hoogan, Thomas, Capt. (Norfolk)
Militia, 126.
Hooke, Edmond, of Beeston, 100.
Hope, H.M.S., 138.
Horning, Alfred de, 73.
Horses and cattle, distemper among,
131, 160, 163.
Horses, English, in Russia, 176.
Horseydown. *See* Horsleydown.
Horsford:
Geoffrey, 33.
Hugh *serviens* de, 18.
Horsford (Horsseford) (Norfolk): 57.
deed relating to, 72.
road to, 12.
Horsham St. Faiths':
manor of, 2, 5-20, 129.
Chirchecroft in, 14.
cross in churchyard of, 2.
church of St. Andrew, 20.
——, a cleyme of wood from, 81.
——, Priory of, 2, 3, 5-20.
——, extent of Priory lands of,
6.
Richard, Lord Prior of, 5.
John Stokes, Lord Prior of, 3,
20.
history of Priory, 2.
Manor accounts of, 5, 6, 129.
rolls and deeds relating to, 5-20.
Horsleydown (Surrey), 55.
Horsseford. *See* Horsford.

Horstead (Horsted), 44, 137.
Horton, Captain, H.M.S. *Bristoll*, 139.
Hosa, Henry de, 11.
Hoskins, Ben., Captain, H.M.S. *Monk*, 138.
Hospital, master of the, 26.
Hoste, Captain James, 142, 145.
Hotham:
  Commander at Barbadoes, 342.
  Dr. John, Bishop of Ossory and of Clogher, 421.
  ——, letter from, 421.
  Lady Dorothy, sister to the 2nd Earl of Buckinghamshire, 175, 176, 259, 294.
  Colonel, 171, 172, 173, 175, 177, 182, 186, 254.
  Mrs. Harriet, 175, 176, 180.
  Mrs., 423.
Houghton (Norfolk), landed proprietors in, 113.
Houghton:
  Alice, 106.
  Captain John, Norfolk Militia, 133.
  Elizabeth, 106.
  John, 106, 127.
  Judah, 106.
  Robert, 132.
Houteboys parva. *See* Hautbois.
Houtebys, Magna, *ibid.*
Hovell, Hugh, 132.
Hoven, Landhofmeister of, 195.
How, Dowager Lady, 327.
Howard:
  Hon. Charles, marriage settlement of, 144.
  Henry, 7th Duke of Norfolk, Lord Lieutenant of Norfolk, XIII., 132-137, 141.
  ——, his Palace at Norwich, 133, 134.
  Henry, 12th Earl of Suffolk [and Berkshire], 260, 264, 273, 274, 288, 289, 314, 315, 316, 378, 442.
  ——, death of, 348, 349.
  ——, ill at Bath, 347.
  ——, letters from, 304, 339.
  Frederick, 5th Earl of Carlisle, 374-376, 379, 384, 386, 438.
  ——, Viceroy of Ireland, 374-376, 381.
  Henry, conveys Verdon to London, 89.
  Sir John, Lord Howard, 55.
  Richard, 37.
  Thomas, 14th Earl of Arundel, 83.
  Walter, 130.
  William, 130.
  William, 1st Viscount Stafford, 261.

Howe, General Sir William, 329.
  ——, in America, 300, 305, 311, 315, 316, 318, 323, 324.
  ——, letter from, 295.
  Lady (1782), 412.
  Richard, Lord Howe, 296, 305, 311, 338, 378, 442.
Howes, Howse, *or* House:
  Richard, 86.
  Robert, 102.
  Samuel, 99.
  Thomas, a reputed Papist, 145.
Howlett, Anthony, of Foxley, 92.
Howlyn, William, clerk, 53.
  parson of Plumstede, 73.
Howth, Lord. *See* St. Laurence.
Howys, Thomas, 54.
Huberd:
  Andrew, 43.
  John, 42.
Hubert, "*serviens*" of St. Faith's, 13.
Huby:
  Dorothy, a reputed Papist, 145.
  Henry, *ibid*, 145.
  Thomas, *ibid*, 141, 145.
Hudson, John, 136.
Hudson's River, the, 315, 316, 324.
Huggemayden, William, 16.
Hugh:
  chaplain of St. Faiths', 13, 29.
  Medicus, 19.
  Nepos Bertrandi Prioris, 12.
  Nepos Prioris, 12.
  Nicholas, son of, 26.
  Robert, son of, 12.
Hull, William, a revenue officer, 313, 314.
Hullerd, Roger, 25, 26.
Hulm. *See* Holme.
Humbleyard, Hundred of, Escheat Roll of, 72.
Hume [John], Bishop of Salisbury, 286.
  trial relating to, at Dublin, 429.
Hundred Roll of Edward I., relating to Blickling, 1.
Hunewyne, Robert, 48.
Hungary, 218, 219.
  the Queen of (Maria Theresa), 155.
Hunnolwesbrom, a field called, 14.
Hunstanton (Norfolk), 137.
Hunt:
  Edward, 379.
  Robert, bailiff, 88.
  Robert, assessor of Hempstead, 105, 107.
  Thomas, of Sharrington, 109.
  William, 109.
Huntingdon, 85.
Huntingdon, Earl of. *See* Hastings.
Hunworth (Honeworthe), (Norfolk), 52.
  landowners in, 108.
Hurrel, Mr., 332.
Hurton, John, 102.
Husbandry *and* Huswiefrye, lack of apprentices to, 76.

Husbond, David, 55.
"Husbond" of a tenement, 8.
Hutchinson:
    John Hely. *See* Hely Hutchinson.
    Richard, 99.
Huuitewelle. *See* Whitwell.
Hyde:
    John, Captain (Norfolk) Militia, 126.
    Thomas Villiers, 1st Lord, superseded as Postmaster, 256.
    ——, protests against repeal of Stamp Act, 260.
Hylingtune, William de, 14.
Hyndford, Earl of. *See* Carmichael.
Hyndolveston. *See* Hindolveston.
Hyntewode. *See* Intwood.
Hyrne. *See* Herne.

I

Ilchester (Somerset), a House of Correction at, 79.
Ilminster (Ilmyster), (Somerset), orders relating to the relief of the poor made at, 77.
    relating to rogues at, 78.
Ilford (Essex), 148.
Imola (Italy), 276.
Impe:
    John, 24, 26, 27.
    Robert, 26.
Impeachment of rebels (1746), 161.
Inchiquin, Lord. *See* O'Brien.
Indians:
    trade regulations relating to, 235.
    in American war, 315.
Indies:
    East, 252, 391, 406.
    West, 275, 306-310, 349, 350, 351, 391, 398, 406, 410, 414.
Ingestre (Staffordshire), 337.
Inglose *or* Ynglose:
    Henry, 60.
    Sir Henry, 29, 54, 55.
Ingoldsthorpe, John, of Blickling, 21.
Ingworth (Ingeworthe), (Norfolk), 22, 104.
    Manor Rolls of, 68.
    landowners in, 104.
Innis, Captain, commanding Queen's Dragoons, 269.
Innishannon, letters dated, 333, 334.
Inniskillen, Lord (1778). 379.
Inowraclaw (Poland), the palatin of, 193.
Intwood (Intwode, Hyntewode): 130.
    Manor Court rolls and deeds relating to, 68.
    parson of, 14.
    Vill of, 14.

Inverness, repairing the Castle of, 147.
Ireland: 238, 254, 283, 298, 299, 310, 321, 325, 326-331, 333-340, 343-346, 349, 350, 351, 352, 355, 356, 362, 368, 371, 374, 376, 382, 413, 414, 416, 418, 419, 420, 425.
    Absentee Tax for, 319.
    Board of Revenue in, 310.
    coast defences of, 330, 335.
    coasting trade of, 330.
    Commander in Chief in. *See* Irwine.
    compared with Hanover, 398.
    Constitution for, a new, 417.
    customs and excise in, 309-310, 318.
    Deputy Keeper of the Rolls for, 327.
    Deputy Quarter Master General for, 326.
    duel in, 294.
    Earl of Buckinghamshire appointed to, 297-298.
    House of Commons in, 297, 343, 394, 400-403, 410, 413, 414, 416, 426, 427, 432, 434.
    ——, petitions to, 316-318.
    ——, speaker to, 297.
    mobilisation in, 335, 336, 374.
    migration from, to America, 292.
    Parliament of, 306, 343, 361, 363, 366, 371, 381, 393, 394, 412, 413, 416, 421, 425, 426, 427, 432, 433.
    pensions for, 309, 314, 385, 401.
    Post Office in, 349.
    Primate of. *See* Stone *and* Robinson.
    Prime sergeant in, office of, 415.
    Quarter-Master General for, 325.
    relations with England, 392-396, 398.
    Roman Catholics in, 327, 343, 352, 368, 377, 395, 396, 421, 424.
    taxation in, 309, 310.
    timber in, 322.
    trade of, 301-304, 306-310, 317, 318, 328, 330, 331, 344, 350, 351, 362, 364, 385, 395, 400, 401, 405, 413, 433.
    troops in, 330, 335, 336, 352, 355, 421.
    Viceroys of. *See* Lords Lieutenant.
Irish:
    absentees, 308, 352, 396.
    Acts of Parliament, 302-306, 346.
    armed associations, 351, 356, 357, 358, 422.
    beggars, 79.
    ——, not to be allowed to land, 80.

Irish—*cont.*
  Bills before the House of Commons, 330.
  Church, 418, 420, 432.
  fisheries, 378, 405, 406, 413.
  House of Lords, 416, 429, 432.
  industry, 395.
  Militia, 337.
  Order, a new, 419.
  patriots, 362, 413, 433.
  Presbyterians, 421, 424.
  treason, 422.
  Volunteers, 366, 376, 389, 390, 391, 395, 410, 412, 413, 421, 422, 425, 428.
Irmingland (Irminglond, Hirminglond, Irmyngland, Ermylaund) (Norfolk):
  Arnold de, 47.
  Geoffrey de, 47, 48.
  Godfrey de, 47, 48, 49.
  ——, Bartholomew, his brother, 47.
  John de, 24, 28, 48, 49, 50.
  Ralph de, 24, 47, 48, 49, 50.
  Ralph, son of John de, 28.
  Roger de, 47.
  Simon de, 47.
Irmingland: 49, 50, 51, 52, 56.
  deeds relating to, 68.
  house at, formerly "Symneles," 68.
  manor rolls of, 68.
  rental of, 68.
Irwine *or* Irwin, Sir John, Commander in Chief in Ireland, 301, 312, 374.
  letters to, 315.
  letters from, 299, 314, 315, 316, 323, 324, 325, 333-335, 339, 342, 348, 354, 355, 368, 376, 377, 378.
Isaac, William, 145.
Isted:
  Ambrose, letter from, 155.
  Mr., 160.
  ——, his company, 158.
  Philippa, letter from, 152.
Italy, 344.
Italian trade with St. Petersburg, 234.
Itteringham *or* Iteringham: 47, 49, 52, 104.
  deed relating to, 71.
  landowners in, 104.
Ivard, Edward, 127.
Ives
  ——, at Norwich, 242, 243, 312.
  Jeremiah, letter from, 430.
  John, of Foulsham, 91.
  Mr., 354.
Ivory:
  Robert, of Sparham, 94.
  William, designs stucco work at Blickling, 441, 442.
Iwan III., Czar, 188, 200, 203.

J

" Jack's " death, at Paris, 251.
Jacob:
  an infant alien, 100.
  Captain-Lieutenant, 334.
Jamaica, 308.
  packet, a, 316, 399, 410.
James Galley, H.M.S., 139.
James River, North America, 362, 401.
James II., his robes, at Dublin, 311.
James Francis Edward, the "Pretender," 7, 148, 150, 154, 160, 163.
  his son. *See* Charles Edward.
Janssen, Mr., 149.
Japan jars, 174.
Jay, John, 132.
Jealous, William, of Swannington, 94.
Jeckes :
  John, of Haverland, 93.
  Robert, 86.
Jeffreys, Judge, xi.
Jell, Robert, 97.
Jempson, John, 90.
Jenkins, Judge, his comparison of Hobart and Coke, viii.
Jenkinson, Charles, *afterwards* Lord Hawkesbury, 344.
  superseded as Secretary to the Treasury, 256.
  letters from, 439, 440.
Jenny :
  Catherine, of Intwood, 68.
  William, of Intwood, 68.
Jenypher, John, 139.
Jennys :
  Richard, 101.
  Samuel, 101.
Jeoffrey, Robert, 109.
Jephson, Robert, 379.
Jermin, the Lady, 111.
Jermy *or* Jermie
  Mr., 143.
  Anne, 97.
  Clement, 127.
  John, 92.
  Robert, 106.
Jermyn Street. *See* London.
Jernegan:
  Sir Francis, 142, 145.
  George, 145.
  John, 144, 145.
Jersey :
  attacked by French, 351.
  New, 311.
  ——, army of, 382.
Jerseys, the (America), 300, 311.

Jerusalem:
  Hospital of, 12.
  temple of, 47.
  Theobald Halteyn's expedition to, 12.
Jerusalem, H.M.S., 139.
Jervis, William, 109.
Jewell, Edmund, 93.
Joceline, brother of William, the Archdeacon, 41.
John:
  Capellanus, 16, 19.
  the clerk, son of Robert, 41.
  son of the clerk, 34, 41, 42..
  son of Beatrice, 26.
  Dapifer episcopi, 40.
  parson of Massingham, 53.
  and Thomas, servants of the Lady at Blickling, 25.
Johnes or Johns:
  John, 115.
  Robert, 116.
  Thomas, 442.
Johnson or Johnsons:
  Henry, 100.
  John, 140.
  James, 124.
  Richard, 97.
  Robert, 96.
  Thomas, of Hyndolveston, 93.
  ——, Captain, 139.
  William, 99.
Johnston:
  Colonel, later General, James, 171, 175, 249.
  ——, letters from, 297, 298, 378.
  Governor, 356.
Jolle, Simon, 9.
Jones:
  Daniel, 138.
  George Lewis, Bishop of Kilmore, 346.
  Inigo, 147.
  Mr., 321.
Jordan, 40.
Josep or Joseph, John, 47, 48, 49, 50.
Joyce, Roger, of Wood Dawling, 96.
Joynes, Robert, 111.
Julyan, John, 115.
Jurdon:
  Thomas, 36.
  James, 44.
Justices of the Peace turned out of the Commission (1688), 132, 133.
Juvenal cited, 438.

K

Kaneto, W. de. See Cheyney.
Karletune, Walter de. See Carleton.
Kat or Katt. See Catte.
Katherine, H.M.S., 138.
Keating, Mr., Dean of Clogher, 386.
Keeling:
  R., 75.
  William, of Foulsham, 91.

Kegwin or Kigwin:
  [Captain] H.M.S. 'Assistance,' 139.
  Richard, commanding H.M.S. 'Woolwich,' 139.
Keith:
  Mr. [Robert], minister at St. Petersburg, 222, 244.
  Robert Murray, minister at Vienna, letter from, 327.
Kelling or Kellene:
  landowners in, 107, 111.
  deed relating to, 72.
Kelly, Thomas, counsellor, 415.
Keltham, Thomas, of Saxlingham, 110.
Kemp or Kempe:
  John, Cardinal Archbishop of York, 54.
  Charles, of Wood Dawling, 96.
  Edmund, of Irmingland, 68.
  Robert, his account of swans, 121, 122.
  Sir Robert, 123, 132.
Kempenfeldt, Admiral, 405.
Keninge:
  Elviva, 25.
  Robert, 22.
Kenmare, Lord (1783), 424.
Kent (Chent):
  Earl of. See Grey.
  Robert de, 12, 13, 19, 46.
Kent, H.M.S., 138.
Keppel:
  Admiral, 337.
  General, 338.
  George, 3rd Earl of Albemarle, 251, 279.
  ——, buys Quidenham, 251.
  ——, his "Testament Politique," 261.
  Mr., 338.
  Lady Elizabeth, 185.
Ker:
  John, 3rd Duke of Roxburgh, appointed Gentleman of the Bedchamber, 285.
  William, 3rd Marquis of Lothian, protests against repeal of Stamp Act, 260.
Kerdestun, Roger de, witness, 15.
Kerdiston (or Cardeston), 44, 94.
  landowners in, 94.
Kerebrok. See Carbrook.
Keritoft or Kerytoft. See Critoft.
Kerrison, Roger, letter from, 293.
  letter to, ibid.
Kesewic, Simon de, 14.
Keswick (Kestwyk or Keswyk), manor rolls of, 66, 67, 130.
Ketchod, Kethod, Kythod or Kytot: 24.
  John, son of John, 27.
  ——, son of Nicholas, 27.
  Nicholas, son of Richard, 27.
  William, 24, 26.
Ketelleye, Roger de, 17.
Kett or Kette:
  Hugh, Provost of Wymondham manor, 64.
  Richard, 64, 90,
  Thomas, of Ringland, 94.

Ketteringham :
    manor rolls of, 72.
    rectory of, 72.
Kettler :
    the family of, in Courland, xv.,
        198, 206, 208, 215.
    Duke Ferdinand, 202, 208, 215.
    ——, his death, 206, 208, 215.
    Duke Frederic Casimir, 208.
Kew, 316.
Keye :
    Richard, " Head Borgh," 24.
    Robert, at Blickling, 27.
Keyler, Major, a messenger from
    Sir Wm. Howe, 323.
Keyserling, Count Hermann Karl
        de, the Chancellor, Russian
        Ambassador, 195, 200, 205,
        219, 220.
    replies to Polish Vice-Chan_
        cellor, 205.
Kide :
    Elgar, 46.
    ——, Elviva, wife of, 46.
Kilbie, Joane, of Oxnett. 104.
Kildare, Countess of, letter from,
    348, 378.
Kilfenora, Dean of. See Coote.
Kilkenny : 343.
    M.P. for (1781), 400.
    riots at, 416.
Killaloe :
    Bishop of. See Fowler and
        Chinnery.
    bishopric of, 345.
Killarney, Protestants of, alleged
    communications of, with Lord G.
    Gordon, 368.
Killigrew :
    Admiral Henry, 138.
    Roger, commanding H.M.S.
        Saphire, 139.
Kilmarnock, Lord. See Boyd.
Kilmore, Bishop of. See Cumber-
    land and Jones.
King, Kinge or Kynge :
    Anthony, 379.
    Robert, 90, 114.
    Thomas, sen. and jun., of Lyng,
        93.
    W., 54.
King William, ship, 150.
" King Lear," at the Attic Theatre,
    433.
King's Bench : 340.
    prison accounts of, 129.
King's County, 384.
King's Professor of Physic for
    Trinity College, 409.
Kingfisher, H.M.S., 139.
Kingfisher Ketch, H.M.S., 140.
Kingston or Kyngston :
    Duke of (1745), his Light Horse,
        155.
    Sir Thomas, 54.
Kinnoul, Lord, his woods in the
    Highlands, 322. See also Hay.
Kinsale, camp at, 333.

Kiovia :
    Palatin of, 209, 220.
    Palatinate of, 219.
Kirtling, John, 54.
Knappe, Stephen, of Wells-juxta
    mare, 114.
Knapton (Norfolk), landowners in,
    97.
Kneller, Godfrey, a freeholder at
    Twickenham, 146.
Knigge, Baron, agent of Pierre
    Biren, 201.
Knight, Mr., 163.
Kniht, Robert le, 41.
Knile, Mr., reports upon election at
    St. Ives, 265.
Knox's debt of £40,000 in Ireland,
    386, 390.
Knox, Mr., 411.
Knut, Adam, 37.
Knyvett or Knivet :
    Joan, daughter of Humphrey,
        Duke of Gloucester, 63.
    John, 65, 66, 127, 132.
    Katherine, 63.
    Thomas, 63, 102, 124, 125, 127,
        132, 136.
    Philip, 63.
    William, 63.
    ——, pedigree of, 5.
Knyvett's manor. See Wymondham.
Kolskoy, Russian Port, 233.
Koningsberg, Brandenberg, letter
    dated, 191.
Kritoft. See Hevingham, Critoft.
Kythod. See Kethod.
Kytot, ibid.

L

L——, His Grace of, 403.
Lacey, Lacy :
    Capt. H. W., 379.
    Mr., 345.
Lafeectles (Capt.), commanding ship
    York, 150.
La Grasse, French Admiral in the
    Chesapeak, 396, 397, 399, 400, 410.
Lake, Richard, of Sparham, 142,
    144, 145.
Lambart, Richard, 6th Earl of
    Cavan, 378.
Lambe or Lamb :
    Peniston, Lord Melbourne, his
        " flirtation " with Lord North,
        417.
    William, of Weston, 95.
Lambert :
    David, commanding H.M.S.
        Newcastle, 139.
    General, his order as to Lady
        F. Hobart's horses, viii., 89.
    ——, letter to, 89.
Lambert, Camerarius, 11.

Lammas cum Hautebois parva, land-owners in, 104.
Lammesse:
  Benedict de, 15.
  Rudolf de, *ibid.*
Lampitlond, 14.
Lancashire, opposition in, to free-dom of Irish trade, 328.
Lancaster, 158, 160.
  Duchy of: 67, 76, 81, 86, 130.
  ——, account rolls of, 69.
  ——, gaol, at Aylsham, petition from prisoners, 86.
  ——, the liberty within the Hundreds of North and South Erpingham, North and South Greenhoe, Smythdon, and Brothercross leased to Sir Henry Hobart, 81.
  ——, list of officers belonging to, 81.
  ——, Order of the Court of, 76.
  letter dated, 372.
Landon, Gédéon Ernest, Baron de, Field Marshal of the Austrian forces (1788), 436.
Land tax, 152, 153.
Lane:
  Francis, 127.
  Robert, 26.
Lanesborough, Earl of. *See* Butler.
Langcroft, Richard de, 47.
Langfurlong, 41.
Langham, landowners in, 108, 111.
Langle. *See* Langley.
Langlee, Thomas, Bishop of Dur-ham, 21.
Langley (Langle, Langlee, Laun-gele): 5, 59-61, 62, 121.
  Abbey, 5, 59-61, 117.
  ——, founded by Robert Fitz Roger, 5.
  ——, bought by Chief Justice Hobart, 5.
  ——, lease of, 117.
  Manor: 87.
  ——, Rolls of, 5, 59, 61.
  ——, extents and rentals of, 60, 61-62.
  ——, cartulary of, 61.
  ——, deeds relating to, 61-62.
  map of manor, 62.
  "marse," swans kept at, 121.
Languedoc, 192.
Langwade:
  Elizabeth, 99.
  Samuel, 99.
  William, of Thorp Market, *ibid.*
Langwood:
  Mr., of Briston, 112.
  William, of Alby, 101.
Langworth, Captain, 150.
Lanke:
  Godwin, 19.
  Margaret, 8.
  Simon, 6, 7.
  William, 8.
Lanrake (Cornwall), 146.

Lante, Henry, 39.
Lanyon, Thomas, 29.
Lapwing, ship, 150.
Large, Timothy, of Holkham, 113.
Larke, Edmund, 25.
Larkebat, a field called, 14.
Larwood, Amy, of Wickmere, 105.
Lascelles, Colonel, 365.
Laurens (Henry), in the Tower, 408.
Laverocke, Barnard, of Ringland, 94.
Lawes, Thomas, of Aylsham, 101.
Lawson, Henry, of Wells, 114.
Lawyers' Corps, the, in North Ire-land, 403.
Layer, Christopher, of Booton, taken prisoner 1695, 142.
Leake:
  John, commanding H.M.S *Eagle*, 138.
  William, of Holt, 106.
Leces, Mariota, 39.
Leche, Mary, wife of Robert, 6.
Lechmere, Rev. Nicholas, letter from, 156.
Lee:
  Edward, 125.
  Sir George, M.P. for Devizes, 159.
  John, of Burrow parva, 108.
  Stephen, of Hinderingham, 113.
  Thomas, commanding H.M.S. *Portland*, 139.
  Mr., 159.
Leech:
  Elizabeth, 114.
  John, of Wells, 114.
"Leéd querns," a grant of land with, 72.
Leem *or* Lem, John de, 38, 42.
Leet *or* Lete:
  Jury, a, questions to be refer-red to, 80.
  Rolls, 5, 21, 31, 45, 63, 64, 67, 70.
Leeward Isles, La Grasse at, 410.
Legard, Edmund, at Blickling, 87.
Legge:
  George, 1st Lord Dartmouth, 261.
  Henry Bilson, 160, 252.
  ——, death, 252, 253.
  William, 2nd Earl of Dartmouth, Head of the Board of Trade, 256.
  ——, conversation with, 290.
Legh, Thomas, 85.
Leghorne, 277, 407.
Leicester, 55.
  rebel army at, 153, 155.
Leigh:
  Edward, 5th Lord Leigh, pro-tests against repeal of Stamp Act, 260.
  Mr., 385.
Leinster, Duke of. *See* FitzGerald.
Leitrim (Leytrim), 365, **378.**

Leland, Colonel, 387, 391, 392, 400, 404.
    letter from, 326, 406, 408.
    letter to, 387, 388.
Lem. *See* Leem.
Leman, Thomas, of Bawdswell, 90.
Lenard, Comte, 206.
Lennox, Charles, 3rd Duke of Richmond, 280-282.
Lenox, H.M.S., 138.
Lenwade Bridge, on road to Norwich, 268.
Lens, Mr., 303.
Leopard, H.M.S., 139.
Leopol (Poland), 219.
Leslie, General, 362.
    proclamation by, 409.
Lestock, Admiral Richard, court martial on, 161.
Le Strange:
    Edmund, clerk to Lieutenancy of Norfolk, 135, 137.
    Hamon, letter from, 82, 83.
    Sir Nicholas, 133, 134, 137, 142.
Letheringsett, landowners in, 109, 112.
Lethuillier, Smart, 165.
Lethun, Mr., 329.
Leverington:
    Robert of Salthouse, 107.
    William, of Walsingham, 115.
Levishaye *or* Leveshaye:
    Andrew de, 41.
    Henry de, 42.
    William de, 41, 42, 73.
Levota, fil. Will., piscatoris de Thaverham, 6.
Lewyn, Simnel, 25.
Lexham, West, 52.
Ley:
    Constantine de, 19.
    Vill of, 73.
Library belonging to the Hobarts, 131.
Lichfield, letter dated, 369.
Lichfield, Lady, 178.
Liddell, Henry, 1st Lord Ravensworth, 378.
Lieutenancy of Norfolk. *See* Norfolk.
Lifford, Lord Chancellor. *See* Hewitt, James.
Liggons, Thomas, 100.
Ligonier, Lord (1763), 177, 189.
Lillington, Mr., at Norwich, 243.
Liman Lake, naval action at, 434.
Lin, Samuel, of Letheringsett, 112.
Lin *or* Lynn. *See* Lynn.
Lincoln, Lord. *See* Clinton.
Lincolne, Nicholas, 44.
"Lincolns," in Middlesex, 82.
Linen:
    Board, the (Ireland), 298.
    manufacture, address by Trustees of, 378.
    trade, Irish, 302, 306 307, 434.
Linge. *See* Lyng.
Lings, Robert *Capellanus de,* 19.
Lingwood Heath (Norfolk), 133.

Lisbon, 434.
Lisbon packett, French seizure of the, 300.
Lisburn (Ireland), 311.
Lister, William, letter from, 158.
Listock (Captain), commanding H.M.S. *Cambridge,* 138.
Litcham (Lutcham) (Norfolk), 142.
Litchfield, —, Dean of St. Paul's, 286.
Litchfield (Staffordshire), 337.
Litester's rebellion, note on, 4, 31.
Lithuania: 192, 193, 194, 198, 209, 212-214, 216, 218, 220.
    Stolnik of. *See* Poniatowski.
Littleton, Thomas, a Justice of the King's Common Bench, 55.
    See also Lyttelton.
Livelode, the recovery of a, 65.
Livonia:
    xv., 209, 216.
    Chamberlain of, 210.
Lizard, The, Cape, 362.
Llandaff, Baron, of Thomastown. *See* Matthew, Francis.
Lloyd:
    Charles, 277.
    ——, letters from, 278, 281, 282, 284.
    Philip, Dean of Norwich, 257.
    ——, letters from, 285, 431, 442.
    Sir Richard, 162.
Loades, John, of Wiveton, 107.
Locke:
    Edmund, 100.
    Elizabeth, 93.
Locksmith, John, of Longham, 108, 111.
Lockton, Thomas, of Scottowe, 105.
Loddon (Lodnes): 141.
    cartulary for, 61.
    church, 143.
    deed relating to rectory of, 72.
Loddon, Geoffrey de, 16.
Loftus, Henry, 1st Earl of Ely, 378, 442.
Lomb *or* Lombe:
    Edward, of Causton, 193.
    Elizabeth, of Beeston Regis, 100.
    John, 19.
    John, of Cawston, 103.
    William, of Oulton, 104.
Lomnour, Elward, 44.
London: 75, 82, 89, 129, 131, 146, 157, 159, 164, 171, 179, 212, 241, 244, 268, 272, 294, 299, 304, 313, 336, 337, 352, 367-370, 413.
    address from, for relief, relating to export of corn, 167, 270.
    Adelphi, letter dated, 297.
    Albemarle Street, 187.
    ——, an Anti-Ministerial Club in, 249.
    ——, the "moral society" in, 182.
    Assurance, 153.

London—cont.
Audley Street, letters dated, 150, 151.
Berkeley Square, letters dated, 361, 437.
Bolton Street, letter dated, 272, 274.
Bond Street, Lord Buckingham-shire's house in, 441.
——, letter dated, 406.
Broad Street, Soho, at Galen's Head, letter dated, 221.
Bruton Street, letter dated, 331.
Cathedral Church of St. Paul's, repaired, 81.
Cavendish Square, letters dated, 245, 247, 248, 251, 253, 267, 268, 271, 318, 324, 351.
Chancery Lane, letters dated, 152, 157, 158, 159.
Charles Street, Berkeley Square, letter dated, 361.
Covent Garden, 89, 179.
"Crown," The, 152.
Downing Street, letters dated, 246, 249, 254, 255, 256.
Drury Lane, 179.
Edward Street, Manchester Square, letter dated, 431.
"Garraways," letters dated, 148, 150, 151, 152, 153, 155.
Grosvenor Street, letters dated, 346.
Hanover Square, letter dated, 325, 330, 350, 380.
Hill Street, letter dated, 271.
Hyde Park, 247.
——, duel in, 247.
illuminations in (1745), 159.
Inner Temple, letter dated, 159, 160.
Jermyn Street, letters dated, 314, 315, 316, 323, 324, 325, 348, 365, 368.
Kensington, 149, 170.
——, letter dated, 290.
——, gardens, a chaperon for, 386, 413.
Leicester House, Lady Suffolk's apartments at, 438.
letters dated, 136, 157, 158, 163, 164, 238, 304, 311, 328, 335, 337, 344, 347, 349, 354, 362, 366, 374, 375, 380, 427, 436.
Merchant Taylors' Hall, 149.
Merchants, address from, 148.
Middle Temple Hall, 154.
Million Bank, letter dated, 161.
Newcastle House, 242, 282.
Newgate Prison, 164, 247.
Newman Street, letter dated, 431.
Northumberland House, letter dated, 429.
Pall Mall, letter dated, 305.
Parliament Street, letter dated, 280, 283.

London—cont.
Piccadilly, letter dated, 376, 377.
Port of, 230.
Portman Square, letter dated, 336-337.
Privy Garden, 362.
——, letter dated, 299.
reception of American reverses in, 405.
Saint James, 154, 311.
——, letters dated, 367, 368, 370, 376, 381, 385.
St. James' Square, letter dated, 292, 295.
Savile Row, 188.
Spitalfields, 176.
Tooke's Court, letters dated, 152, 157, 158, 159, 161.
Tower, the, 154, 159, 367, 408.
——, letter dated, 406.
War Office, letter dated, 243.
York Buildings, letters dated, 278, 281, 283, 284.
London or Lundune:
Bishop of. See Braybroke.
Henry de, 34, 36, 41, 42.
Henry son of Simon de, 41.
John de, 28.
Reginald de, 16, 19.
Robert, 125.
Simon de, 41.
London, H.M.S., 138.
Londonderry, Governor of, 299.
Long Island, Colonial forces at, 296.
Long, Longe:
Captain Robert, his troop to quarter at Lynn, 133.
John, 57.
Robert, 123, 124.
Mrs. Susan, 102.
Longfer, widow, 102.
Longfield, —, M.P. for Cork city, 420, 434.
Loose, Matthew, of Feilddawling, 114.
Lords Lieutenant of Ireland. See Bentinck, Grenville, Harcourt, Henley, Hobart, Howard, Manners.
Lord Mayor [of London], 148, 152, 179.
a Norfolk corn-factor, 266.
his address, 378.
Lords, House of, 171, 175, 176, 244, 247, 260, 272, 273, 274, 436.
letter dated, 411.
(Ireland), address on the war with France, 378.
Lorewen, Sibilla, 14.
Lorne, Lord (1766). See Campbell.
Losinga, Herbert, Bishop of Norwich, 40.
Lothian:
family, the, v.
Marquis of. See Kerr.
Constance, Marchioness of, i.
Lottery Ticket, price of (1745), 151.

Loughborough, Lord (1781). *See* Wedderburne.
Louis XV. of France, 216, 217.
Louisa, Lady. *See* Conolly.
Louisbourg, 240.
Lound Mill. *See* Saxthorpe.
Loundhall *or* Loundhalle, *ibid.*
Louth, 327, 358.
Love, Luve:
    Edward, 29.
    John, John servant of, 28.
    —, 38.
    Robert, 26.
    Thomas, of Hanworth, 97.
Lovell, John, of Hinderingham, 113.
Lovesae, W. de, 38.
Lubbocke *or* Lubbock:
    Elizabeth, of Aylsham, 101.
    Martha, of Scottowe, 105.
    Richard, 103.
    Robert, of Wickmere, 105.
    Thomas, of Erpingham, 103.
    William, of Erpingham, 103.
Lubeck, trade with Petersburg, 234.
Lubienski, Ladislaus, Primate of Poland, 194, 213, 216, 217, 219.
Lucar, William, taken prisoner (1695), 142.
Luckner, Mr., 111.
Ludham, 141, 145.
Ludham, Thomas, 54.
Ludlow:
    Peter, Earl, 378, 380, 442.
    William, 380.
Lumley, Richard, 4th Earl of Scarborough, 274, 380.
    letter from, 304.
Lund, Eda de, 48.
Lundres, John de, 73.
    ——, Alicia, wife of, 73.
    Richard de, 73.
Lupell, Hernald, 40.
Lutcham. *See* Litcham.
Luttrell, Colonel, 355-356.
Luve. *See* Love.
Lyhert *or* Lyhart:
    arms of, 441.
    Walter, bishop of Norwich, 31.
Lynes, marsh at, 60.
Lynford, John, 29, 54.
Lyng, Lynge *or* Linge, Norfolk, landowners in, 93.
    swans kept at, 121.
Lynn (Lin):
    Episcopi, 53.
    Regis, 83, 133, 134, 135.
    ——, mayor of, 134, 135.
    ——, smallpox at (1688), 134.
Lynn *or* Lynne:
    Henry, of Twyford, 95.
    James, of Berney, 117.
    John, 93.
    Samuel, of Hindolveston, 93.
    William, of Bintrye, 91.
    ——, of Hindolveston, 93.
Lyon, Colonel, of 18th Dragoons, 333.
Lyon, H.M.S., 138.

Lytot, William, 26.
Lyttelton:
    Charles, Bishop of Carlisle, 260.
    George, 1st Lord, 241, 263, 281, 350.
    ——, banquet at Hagley, 241, 242.
    ——, protests against Repeal of Stamp Act, 260.
    Mr., 242.

M

Macaroni Club, the, at Almacks, 254.
Macartney, Sir George (afterwards Lord), 186, 188, 360, 361.
    British Ambassador to St. Petersburg, 283.
    letter from, 361.
Mackay, John, ensign of the Athol Highlanders, 348.
MacDonnel, Ronald William, 6th Earl of Antrim, 310.
    letter to, 324.
Mackenzie, William, 5th Earl of Seaforth, his recalcitrant clan, 147.
Madrid, Cabinet at, 363.
    embassy at, xvi., 272.
Maffet, Counsellor, 328-329.
    letter from, 329.
Magnus:
    Clement, 114.
    Robert, chief constable, 112-114.
Mahon, Thomas, 379.
Maldon (Essex): 163.
    election at, 162.
    list of free burgesses of borough of, 147.
    letter dated, 162.
Malham, Catherine, of Booton, 102.
Malherb, Andrew, 11.
Mallard, Peter de, 40.
Mallet, —, 321.
Malling, —, at Holt, 110.
Malt tax, riots on account of, 147.
Maltby, —, Norwich manufacturer, 311.
Maltebi. *See* Mautby.
Man, the Isle of, garrison for, 335, 336.
Managrene *or* Mangrene, a vil, 14, 15.
Manchester, Lord. *See* Montagu.
Manchester, weavers at, 306.
Mannington (Manyngton): 49, 50, 54.
    deeds relating to, 71.
    landowners in, 104.
    purchased by the Walpoles, 147.

Mann *or* Manne:
  Sir Horace, 276-277.
  ——, letter from, 295.
  Dr. Isaac, Bishop of Cork, 379.
  John, 114.
  John, of Weston, 95.
  Nicholas, 53.
  Robert, of Warham, 115.
  Timothy, 112, 113.
  William, 108, 111.
Manners, John, Marquess of Granby
  and 3rd Duke of Rutland,
  179, 245, 286.
  Charles, 4th Duke, Lord
  Lieutenant of Ireland, 427.
Manning, *or* Manninge:
  Matthew, Capt.-Lieut., Norfolk
  Militia, 126.
  John, of Overstrand, clerk, 98.
Mansfield, Lord. *See* Murray.
Mansoli, operatic singer, 253.
Manston, letter dated, 293.
Mantle, John, 115.
Mapes, Leonard, Capt., Norfolk
  Militia, 126.
Marble Hill (Twickenham), 146, 174,
  175, 177, 183, 288, 341, 427, 441.
Marchmont, Lord. *See* Home.
Mareschal *or* Marchal:
  Aileen le, VIII.
  J. le, 36, 37, 38, 39.
  William, 41.
Margatson, Thomas, of Sall, 94.
Marham, 17.
Mariners, wandering, how to deal
  with, 79.
Mariot, Richard, 37.
Marker, Thomas, of Sall, 94.
Market Court Rolls, 6, 64.
Market Harborough, 163.
Markham, William, Archbishop of
  York, 379.
Markshall (Merceshalle, Merkes-
  hafle), William de, 42, 73.
Marlborough, Duke of. *See*
  Churchill.
Marlepitlond, 50.
Marlesford, 17.
Marlingforth, Manor Roll of, 70.
Marriage, entry in homage on, 8.
Marriott, Hugh, letters from, 152,
  154, 157, 158, 159, 161.
Marsh, George, 141, 145.
Marshall, John, 347, 350.
Marshalsea *or* Marshalsye prison,
  accounts of, 77, 129.
Marsham (Norfolk): 29, 40, 41, 42,
  43, 44, 104.
  deed and extent relating to, 72.
  landowner in, 104.
  cum Hevingham, 31.
  Regis, *ibid.*
  rioters at, 269.

Marsham:
  Mrs. Anne, 105.
  Henry, 105.
  ——, at Stratton Strayless, XII.
  Robert, 44.
  Robert, letters from, 322-323.
  Robert de, grant of a villain by,
  17.
  William, 105.
Marston, John, ensign, Norfolk
  Militia, 126.
Martham, manor roll of, 70.
Martham:
  Philip de, 40.
  Robert de, 52, 53.
Martin *or* Martyn:
  the clerk of Saxthorp, 49.
  John, 32.
  ——, will of, 44.
  Richard, Captain, 138.
  Richard, 144.
  Robert, will of, 44.
  Robert, 109.
  Samuel, his duel with Wilkes,
  247.
  Admiral William, 161.
  widow, 109.
Marting, James, clerk, 109.
Martinique, D'Estaing at, 342.
  devastations of a species of ant
  in, 299.
Marwood, Thomas, 142.
Mary:
  Galley, H.M.S., 139.
  yacht, 140.
Marys, Richard, 100.
Mason:
  John, 29.
  Richard, Norfolk Militia, 127.
  William, of Trunch, 99.
  William, 126.
Massachusetts Bay Province:
  House of Representatives of,
  260.
  Port of (Boston), 292.
  in rebellion, 289, 291.
Massareene, Countess of (1779), 379.
Masserano, Prince of, Ambassador
  from Spain, 442.
Massey:
  Lady, daughter to Lady Hobart,
  143.
  Leonard, 132.
Massingham (Norfolk), 53.
Matchett, John, of Gimingham, 97.
Matelask, Margaret, daughter of
  Agnes of, 25.
Matlask (Norfolk):
  manor roll of, 69.
  landowners in, 100.
Matles, Henry, of Walsingham, 116.
Matteshale, Robert de, 75.
Matthew, parson of the church of
  Little Rackheath, 52.
Matthew, Francis, afterwards Lord
  Llandaff, 339, 378.
  letter from, 339.
Maunsell, Mr., and the living of
  Castle Bellingham, 385.

Mausoleum at Blickling, xviii.
Mautby (Maltebi):
    Salt works at, 13.
    Robert, *persona* de, 13.
    Simon, *prepositus* de, 13.
Mauteby, Robert, 43, 53.
Maxwell:
    Barry, Lord Farnham, 379.
    W., 378.
May *or* Maye, Mai, Meye, Mey:
    Henry le, 8.
    Matilda le, 10.
    Payn, 26.
    William de, 19.
    William, 113.
Mayden, Capt. William, copy of a testimonial to, 117.
Maynard, Serjeant, his estate in North Ealing, 147.
Mayne:
    Captain, 138.
    William, Lord Newhaven, in Ireland, 379.
    ——, his motion in the House relating to sugar, 348.
Mayo, Government of, 415.
McGuire, Mr., 363.
McKensie, Mr. Stuart. *See* Stuart-Mackenzie.
McPhail, Thomas (Volunteer), of the Athol Highlanders, 348.
Mead, brewed, 26; sold, 3.
Meadows, Brigadier, wounded at St. Lucia, 343.
Mecistaw (Poland), the palatin of. *See* Plater.
Mees, Captain George, 138.
Mehadia (Hungary), 436.
Melbourne, Lord. *See* Lamb.
Melcombe Regis (Dorset), 360.
Melior, John, 28.
Melleson, Gabriel, 140.
Mellish
    Mr. W., Postmaster-General, 256.
    the younger, a Secretary to the Treasury, 256.
Melton Constable (Norfolk), landowners in, 108.
Mendham, Walter de, 41.
Menzies, James, lieutenant of the Atholl Highlanders, 348.
Mercator, Henry, 17.
Merchant, Robert, the, 47.
Meredith, Sir William, 248.
Meredyth, Mr., 347.
Mereworth, Marjory *or* Margaret, 51, 52, 74.
    Sir John de, 51, 52, 74.
Merrion (Mount), (Ireland), Lord Fitzwilliam at, 301.
Messenger
    Augustin, of Hackford, 93.
    Edward, of Wood Dawling, 96.
Metcalfe, Geofrey, ·· bearer of a circular letter with bede roll from St. Faith's Priory, 20.
Methwolde, manor roll of, 70.
Metton, landowners in, 100.

Mey, le Meye. *See* May.
Michell, William, clerk, 114.
Mickelhall *or* Micklehall. *See* Saxthorpe.
Michiet:, the Cavaliera, letter of condolence to, 254.
Middleton, Middelton, Midilton:
    Philip de, 37.
    Thomas de, 33.
    [William], Bishop of Norwich, 3
Middlesex: 82, 147, 367.
    election, 286, 287.
Midleton:
    borough of, in Ireland, 420.
    a vill, 73.
Midleton, Lord. *See* Brodrick.
Miecznik of Lithuania. *See* Radzivill.
Might:
    Jeffrey, of Gunthorpe, 106.
    Thomas, 106.
Mildmay, Henry, Lord Fitzwalter, 151.
Miliariis, William de, 17.
Militia: 336, 337, 399.
    arms, 271.
    Bill, 239.
    circular letter as to, 238.
    the Norfolk, (1677) 124-127; (1688) 133, 134, 137; (1695) 141-142; (1778) 332, 354.
    colours of the several regiments, 124.
    estates of under £200 a year to be charged to the foot and not to the horse, 124.
    list of officers of, in Norfolk, ix., 125-127.
    Horse, 137, 141, 142.
Miller:
    Elizabeth, of Hanworth, 97.
    Henry, of Wickmere, 105.
    John, 99, 100.
    Robert, 97, 99.
    Robert and Walter (millers of Horsham St. Faiths' presented for bad milling), 36.
    Thomas, of Matlask, 100.
    William (Willelmus *molendarius*), 9, 10.
Mills, 6, 15, 21, 23, 29, 33, 34, 39, 47, 50, 54-56, 72, 196.
Mills, Mr., at Norwich, 287.
Million Bank, the. *See* London.
Millner, John, 106.
Milverton (Somerset), Hundred of, 79.
Minere, le:
    Adam, 38.
    John, 38.
Mingay, John, of Gimingham, 97.
Ministry, the (of 1777), popularity of, 324.
Minorca, 239.
Minsk (Russian Poland), 214.
Mirovitz, his attempt upon Ivan, 188.
"Miser," the, at the Attic Theatre, 433.

Mitcham (Surrey), 148.
Mitchel, —, sister to Dr. Collinges, 131.
Mitford (Norfolk), Hundred of, 130.
Mittau (Courland), 282.
   letter dated, 282.
Mniszeck Gl. de, Marshall of the Polish Court, 193, 194, 195, 204.
Mocha, 150.
Mogul, territory of the, 229.
Mohawk River (North America), 316.
Mokronoffski, General, 209.
   retired into Hungary, 218.
   approaches Frederick II. with proposals, 218, note.
Moldavia, 435, 436.
Molesworth, Lady, 173.
Molineux or Molyneux:
   Sir Capel, 316.
   Lieutenant, of 12th Dragoons, 315.
   Mr., a new M.P. in Irish House of Commons, 427.
   Mrs., a beauty at Dublin, 423.
Molendarius. See Miller.
Monasteries, dissolution of, 3, 5, 60.
Monasterio, William de, 41, 42.
Money (Munne, Mune, Muyne, Moyne):
   Ambrose, clerk, 115.
   Elizabeth, 112.
   Hugh le, 26.
   John le, 24.
   Martin, 113.
   Richard, 112.
   Richard le, exchanges land with Prior of St. Faiths, 13, 14.
   William, of Foulsham, 91.
   Mr., at St. Giles', Norwich, 257.
   ——, his house at Trowse attacked by mob, 267.
Monk:
   George, 1st Duke of Albemarle, testimonials from, 117.
   Captain, 139.
   William le, 67.
Monk, H.M.S., 138.
Monmouth, H.M.S., 138.
Monmouth Yacht, H.M.S., 140.
Monmouthshire, 316.
Monsey (Munsy, Munsey):
   Robert, 144.
   Thomas of Hackford, 93.
Monson, John, Lord Monson, resignation of. 274.
Monsuer, Roger, 114, 116.
Monsure, Henry, 116.
Montagu, Duke of. See Brudenell.
Montagu:
   Edward: 2nd Earl of Manchester, 88.
   ——, 1st Earl of Sandwich, 117.
   John, 4th Earl of Sandwich, 178, 185, 188, 250, 282, 347, 350, 379, 442.
   —— letter from, 330.
   ——, protests against Repeal of Stamp Act, 260.

Montagu-Dunk, George, 2nd Earl of Halifax, 185, 200, 205, 248, 250.
   letters of, 150, 151.
   protests against Repeal of Stamp Act, 260.
Montague, ship, 138.
Montcalm de St. Véran, Louis Joseph. Marquis de, 239
   French commander in chief in America, letters of, 239, 240.
   relations of, with English Colonies in America, 239, 240.
Montgomerie, Alexander, 10th Earl of Eglintoun, 260, 442.
Montgomery, Mr., his quarrel with Mr. Conolly, 420, 421.
Monyman, Nicholas, of Aylmerton, 99.
Moore, Charles, 6th Earl of Drogheda, Master-General of Ordnance, Dublin, 339.
   letter from, ibid.
Morava, the, 435, 436.
Moray. See Murray.
Mordant, H.M.S., 139.
More, John, 109.
Morel:
   Nicholas, 47, 48, 49, 50.
   William, 53.
Moris, Roger, 86.
Morle, Sir Robert, knight, 53.
Morley family, 344.
Moreton, Thomas Reynolds, 2nd Baron Ducie, 379.
Morristown, 381.
Morston, landowners in, 106, 110.
Mort, Henry, 24.
Mortimer or Mortymer:
   Constantine, 33.
   Robert, 43.
Morton (Norfolk), 94.
Morton:
   —, of Abingdon Aston, 164.
   John, 55, 56.
   Sir John, 55.
Moscow, 170-172, 174, 176, 210, 212, 236, 255, 283.
   letters dated, 170-173, 294.
Moseley:
   Sir Edward, 85.
   Dame Mary, 85.
Motte, John, 56.
Moughton, 57.
Mount Independence, North America, 311
Mousehold Heath. See Norwich.
Mowting, Thomas, 95.
Moy, William, of Swannington, 94.
Moyne. See Money.
Muddyshift, James, 90.
Mulbarton (Norfolk):
   extent of, 72.
   manor roll of, 68.
   militia at, 133.
Muletune, Mylo de. 14.
Mulgrave, Lord. See Phipps.
Mullers, William de, son of Hugh de Mulers, 15.

Multon, W. (clerk), Blickling, 29.
Munden, Richard, 138.
Mundesley, landowners in, 97.
Mundham, church and manor of, 54.
Munford, John, of Wayborne, 107.
Mune or Munne. See Money.
Munnich, Marshal, 189.
Munsey or Munsy. See Monsey.
Munster, Province of, in disorder, 432.
Muntford, Alice, of Calthorpe, 103.
Murray (Moray):
  Hon. Alexander, 163.
  Charles, a lieutenant in the Atholl Highlanders, 348.
  Colonel, of the Atholl Highlanders, 348.
  ——, uncle to the Duke of Atholl, 337.
  David, 7th Viscount Stormont, 348, 350, 427.
  John, 3rd Duke of Atholl, 335.
  John, 4th Duke, 330, 348.
  Mr., 110.
  Mongoe, of Wells, clerk, 114.
  Patrick, 5th Baron Elibank, 163.
  William, 1st Earl of Mansfield, 271, 273, 284.
  ——, attack on his house, 367.
Murrell:
  Hugh, of Morton, 94.
  Thomas, ensign Norfolk militia, 48.
Mus, Ralph, 48, 50.
Muster Office. See Dublin.
Muyne. See Money.
Myles, Richard, 116.
Mylverton. See Milverton.
Mynn or Mynns:
  Christopher, 92.
  Christopher, of Salthouse, 111.
  ——, commanding H.M.S. Saphire, 139.
  Henry, of Guist, 92.

N

N., the D. of. See Newcastle.
Naas, Lord (1780). See Bourke.
Nabbs, John, 112, 113.
Nally, Robert, of Irmingland, 68.
Naples, 396, 434.
Narva, 233.
Nash, Gawin, 141.
Nassau de Zulestein, William Henry, Earl of Rochford, 347, 348, 378.
Navigation, Committee of (Thames), 341, 342.
Neal, Nathaniel, letter from, 161.
Neale, Mr. (of Wellingborough), 152.
Neister, the, 435.
Nele, John, 55.

Neptune, H.M.S., 137.
Nes:
  Bartolomew de, 13.
  Osmund de, ibid.
Nesbit or Nesbitt:
  E., letter to, 385.
  Thomas, 379.
Netherhall manor, in Essex, 54.
Netleton, William, 111, 112, 114.
Neuman. See Newman.
Neva, the, 175.
Neve:
  Adam le, 14.
  Henry le, 16.
  Oliver, 96.
  Thomas, a ward, 75.
Nevill, John, 138.
New Jersey, letter dated from, 260.
Newcastle, 152.
Newcastle, Duke of. See Pelham-Holles.
Newcastle, borough of, in county Dublin, 377.
Newcastle, H.M.S., 139.
Newcastle House. See London.
Newcome, Wm., Bishop of Ossory, 379.
Newfoundland: 406.
  French attempt upon, 252.
Newgate, Edmund, 116.
Newhaven, Lord. See Mayne.
Newman, Neweman or Neuman:
  Henry le, 38, 39.
  John le, 48, 51.
  Nicholas, 48, 49, 50.
  Robert, shepereve, 74.
  Thomas, 103.
  William, 108.
Newry:
  M.P. for (1781), 400.
  vessel trading to, 319.
Newspapers:
  Evening Post (Dublin), 424.
  Freeman, 403.
  Freeman's Journal, 421.
  Hiberniam, 403.
  Morning Post, 342.
  New York Gazette, 305.
Newton (Newtune):
  Daniel, lieutenant, Norfolk militia, 126.
  Thomas, Bishop of Bristol, 260.
  Walter the clerk, son of William of, 19.
Nicholas:
  Master, 12, 41.
  parson of the church of Booton, 43.
  Richard, son of, 47.
  Thomas, son of, 15.
  son of Henry de London, 41.
  the tanner, 48.
Nicholls:
  Will., of Foulsham, 92.
  Richard, ibid., 92.
Niedzwiesce, a castle belonging to Prince Radzivil, 218.
Nightingale, Mrs., 131.
Nissa (Servia), 436.

Nivernois, Louis Jules Barbon Mancini Mazarini, Duc de, 250.
ambassador in London, 250.
Noailles, M. le Marquis de, ambassador to London, 299, 304.
Nockold, Robert, 125.
Noel, Edward, 1st Viscount Wentworth, signs protest against Stamp Act, 260, 261.
Noers, Ralph de, 11.
Nonces, chamber of. See Poland.
Nonjurors, 136, 144, 145.
Nonsuch Park, letter dated, 284.
Nonsuch, H.M.S., 139.
Norfolk, IX., 1-75, 132-137, 142, 147, 185, 186, 238, 239, 251, 262, 266-270, 313, 353, 427, 431.
Committee for (1656), 88.
declares for a free Parliament, 134.
election, Poll Books (1735), 147.
gentlemen of, manifesto by, for reducing the expenses of the office of High Sheriff (1675), X., 122-124.
Deputy Lieutenants for (1677), IX., 124, 125; (1688-9), 134-137.
High Sheriff of, X., 122-124, 268.
insurrection in, temp. Ric. II.; 31.
Lieutenancy of : 170, 239.
——, journals of, IX., XII., XIII., 124, 132-137, 141-142, 144, 145.
Lord Lieutenant of X., XI., XII., XIII., 125, 239.
Militia for. See Militia.
petition dated, 86.
politics in, VIII., IX., 257, 286-287, 373, 375.
riots in, 267-271.
shrievalty of, 86.
subsidy roll for, 20 Edw. III., VII., 440.
swanneries in, 83, 121, 122.
Norfolk, Henry 7th Duke of. See Howard.
Norgate, 14.
Normandy, 2, 162.
Norreys, Roger, 18.
Norris, John, High Sheriff of Norfolk, letter from, 268.
North :
Edward, Lord (1554), 29.
Francis, 1st Earl of Guilford, 378.
Frederic, Lord, 284, 325, 343, 349, 351, 357, 359, 361, 372, 375, 376, 379, 384, 385.
——, coalition of with Fox, 417, 419.
——, illness of, 299.
William, 139.
North's Memorials of Lord Keeper Guilford, XI.
North Briton, the, 247-249.
North Repps, landowners in, 98.
North River, North America, 305.

North Walsham, 3, 133.
Northampton, VII., 153, 155, 160.
Northamptonshire, 151.
Lord Lieutenant of. ibid.
Northington, Earl of. See Henley.
Northous, Robert atte, of Ormesby, 73, 442.
Northumberland, Duke of. See Percy.
Northumberland, H.M.S., 138.
Norton, Thomas, 93.
Norton (by Langley), 60, 61.
Norwich (Norwyche):
X., XI., 3, 14, 20, 39, 40, 41, 42, 43, 54, 57, 67' 86, 89, 110, 128, 130, 133, 134, 141, 142, 147, 186, 242, 243, 265- 271, 281, 286, 293, 295, 322, 323, 353, 354, 373.
address from, for relief in relation to export of corn, 265, 267, 270, 272.
arms belonging to, 147.
assizes at, at time of Wilkes agitation, 286.
Berstreet, 10.
Castle, 37, 135, 136, 137, 141.
Chapelfield or Chaplyfield : town house of the Hobarts, 89, 130, 442.
——, soldiers serving for, 130.
City gaol, 294.
Commission at, 274.
Convent of the Holy Trinity, 40, 70.
Conisford gates fired by mob, 267.
'Crown,' the, 441.
deanery, letter dated, 285.
diocese of, 20, 57.
Duke of Norfolk's palace at, 132, 133, 134.
elections at, 170, 242, 243, 430, 431.
hospital, enclosure for, 294.
"King's Head" at, 274.
letters dated, 42, 81, 86, 131, 242, 266, 269, 270, 274, 287, 293, 312.
manufacturers of yarn at, 312.
mayor of, 266, 268-271, 274.
mayor and aldermen of, Duke of Norfolk's speech to (1688), 134.
militia firearms at, 271.
Mousehold Heath, proposed enclosure of, 353.
politics, 242, 243, 257, 274, 373.
post coach, 278.
quakers at, 242.
riots at, 267-271, 274.
Saint :
—— Andrew's Hall, 242.
—— Giles-gates, 257, 442.
—— Martin le Bailey, 10.
—— Michael, Berstreet, 10.
—— Olave's, 58.
—— Peter Mancroft, 293, 442.

Norwich:
  Bishop of, 22, 27, 33, 34, 39, 40, 57.
  ——, barony of, 34.
  ——, manors of, 3, 30-35.
  ——, presented for making a water-course, 27.
  See also Bishops Alnwick, Armine, Bateman, Bec, Brown, Courtenay, Eborard, Lyhert, Losinga, Middleton, Skerning, Spenser, Turbus, Wakering, Walpole, Yonge.
  dean of. *See* Lloyd.
Norwich, Richard de, 47.
Nottingham, the King at, 51.
  riot at, 369.
Nottingham, Lord. *See* Finch.
Nougoun. *See* Nugun.
Nuers, Symon de, 40.
Nugent, Robert, afterwards Lord Nugent, Viscount Clare and Earl Nugent, 256, 258, 262, 264, 290, 294, 328, 331, 350, 351, 379.
  at Bristol, 294.
  letters from, 290, 294.
  letters to, 258, 259.
  his son's quarrel with Col. Gabbet, 294.
Nugun *or* Nougoun:
  Ralph de, 46, 47, 49.
  ——, Nicholas son of, 46.
  Richard de, 46, 47.
Nuiun. *See* Nugun.
Nutwell, letter dated, 332.

O

Oats, price of (1746), 163.
Oath:
  of Supremacy and Allegiance, Act for abrogating, 135, 136.
  "tactis sacrosanctis Evangeliis," 18.
  against revocation of grant, 18.
O'Brien:
  Sir Lucius, letter from, 384.
  ——, in Irish House of Commons, 400.
  Murrough, 5th Earl of Inchiquin, 378, 379.
  ——, in County Clare, 313.
  Nelly, 179.
  Mr., 378.
Ode:
  Matilda, 50.
  Robert, 48, 49, 50.
  William son of Robert, 49, 50.
"Odes," a tenement called, in Saxthorp, 54.
Ogincki, Pisarz of Lithuania, 192.

Ogle, Mr., 414, 419, 426.
  is to resign Castle Bellingham, 385.
  in Irish House of Commons, 400.
Oldhall *or* Oldhalle:
  Edmund, 53, 69, 73.
  ——, manor court of, at Saxthorpe, 45.
  ——, seal of, 54.
  Sir W., 4.
  William, 54.
  Sir William, releases land in Blickling to co-feoffees, 29.
Oliva, peace of, 221.
Olley *or* Ollye:
  John, of Fieldawling, 114.
  Rice, 93.
  Robert, 113, 116.
Olok, William, 34.
Onega, Russian port, 233.
O'Neil:
  Mr., moves address in Irish House of Commons, 398, 434.
  John, 379.
Onslow:
  George, Lord (4th Baron), 325.
  Mr. G., Lord of the Treasury, 256.
Opera Club, the, 253.
Orange ribbon for the soldiers (1688), 130.
Orange, the Prince of, Norfolk declares for (1688), 135.
Orders in Council:
  for seizing the arms of Papists and disaffected persons (1696), 141.
  ibid. (1745), 148.
  for discharging the same (1696), 142.
  for an account of Papists and reputed Papists, 144.
Orford, Earl of. *See* Russell and Walpole.
Orlingbury, 160.
Orlow *or* Orloff, Grigori Grigorievitch, 180, 184, 189, 191.
  character of, 180.
Ormesby *or* Ormsby, Great, 54, 73, 145.
O'Rourke, Count, 379.
Osborne:
  Sir William, 379.
  Thomas, Earl of Danby, 138.
Osmund, a witness, 41.
Ossory, Bishop of. *See* Hotham *and* Newcome.
Ossory, H.M.S., 138.
Osten, Adolf Siegfried von der, 213.
Oulton (Olton, Ouletone, Oweltune), 47, 48, 49, 104, 129.
  landowners in, 104.
Oulton (Ouletone, Oweltune):
  Robert, 58.
  Sigar de, 47.
Outlacke, Thomas, 98.
Outlaw:
  Ralph, clerk, 94, 97.
  Thomas, 97.
Overhall manor, in Essex, 54.

Overstone (Northamptonshire), 148, 155, 163.
   letter dated, 163.
Overstrand (Norfolk) landowners in, 98.
Oweltune. *See* Oulton.
Owen, Mr., 157.
Owners' Endeavour, ship, 139.
Oxborough, Henry, 133.
Oxburgh (Norfolk), 144.
Oxburgh, Lt.-Col., Norfolk militia, 126.
Oxnead (Oxenede, Oxnett), Walter, priest of, 12.
   landowners in, 104.
Oxford, VII.
Oxford, H.M.S., 139.
Oxford, Earl of (1527). *See* Vere.
—— (1777). *See* Harley.
Oxicoff, 435-436.
Oxnett. *See* Oxnead.
Oyard, Andrew, at Wymondham, 63.

P

Packington, 288.
Page:
   Christopher, of Barningham Parva, 102.
   John, of Saxthorpe, 104.
   Richard, 113.
   Thomas, 102.
Paget, Lady, 339.
Pagrave *or* Palgrave:
   Sir Augustin, his manor at Wymondham, 80.
   Augustin, 99, 111.
   Sir John, Kt., Bart., of Norwood Barn'ngham, 99.
   Richard de, 34, 35, 36, 37, 39.
Palliser, Captain, in Newfoundland, 252.
Palmer *or* Palmere:
   Edward, of Wytton, 74.
   Geoffrey, of Marlesford, 17.
   ——, John and William, sons of, grant by, 17.
   Henry, 57, 104.
   Margaret, prioress of Carrow, 70.
   Owen, chief constable, 105, 107.
   Reginald le, 25.
   Richard le, 24, 25.
   Roger, 26.
   Sir R., 379.
   William le, de Catton, 16.
   ——, Juetta, wife of, presented for usury, 27.
Palmerston, Lord. *See* Temple.
Pan Zova, Austrian frontier, 426.
Panbroch. *See* Pembroke.
Pane, Henry, 105, 107.
Panin, Nikita Ivanovitch, first minister at St. Petersburg, 219.
   letter to, 236.

Papists and disaffected persons, order in Council for seizing their arms and persons, 141, 142, 144, 148.
Papists:
   or so reputed, in Norfolk, lists of, 136, 144, 145.
   in Ireland. *See* Ireland.
Parc. *See* Park.
Pardon to Simon Crepping, on a conviction for deceit, 50-51.
Parfitt, John, of Ringland, 94.
Parham, Nicholas, Norfolk militia, 125.
Paris, 238, 251, 301, 404, 434.
   hospital at, 304.
   Peace of, 245, 247.
Parish overseers, duties of in 16th century, 77-78.
Parish Church, rogues to be conveyed to the, to be whipt, 80.
Park, Parke *or* Parkes (Parc):
   Peter atte, 36.
   Richard, 144.
   Sir William de, 49, 50.
   William de, 34, 39, 41, 42, 93, 101.
   William atte, assessor of subsidies, 440.
Parker:
   Alice, 59.
   J., 64.
   Mr., 289.
   Sir Peter, in America, 305.
   Robert, 47.
   Richard, 144.
   William, 102, 142.
   Wulvive, 39.
Parkgate, 297.
Parkin *or* Parkine:
   Christopher, of Wickmere, 105.
   John, 109.
Parkings, William, of Coltishall, 103.
Parlene, Hugh de, 50.
Parlett:
   Gregory, 3rd Militia Foot, 126.
   William, 91.
Parliamentary pay, 86, 88.
Parmenter, Thomas, petition of, 88.
Parly, John, Norfolk militia, 127.
Parr, Henry, 111.
Parre:
   Henry, 107.
   Robert, of Trimingham, 99.
Parsons, Nancy, 252, 253.
Partington:
   John, of Walsingham, 115.
   Sara, 116.
Partriches and fesaunts within the waryn of Eynford and Saxthorp, 57.
Partridge, —, a Norwich manufacturer, 312.
Parys:
   John, 35.
   Joanna, 28.
Passe:
   Adam, 24.
   Nicholas, 22.
Passek, M., 191.

Paston (Parston):
Clement, of Marlingforth, 70.
——, of Towne Barningham, 99.
Dorothy, relict of Clement, 99.
Edward, 142, 144.
Mr., 143.
Mrs. Frances, 90.
John, 70, 145.
Sir John, 55.
Robert Lord, Viscount Yarmouth, x., 125, 143.
Sir Robert, of Oxnett, 104.
William, 55, 127, 143.
Sir William, 69, 125.
Pateshall, letter dated, 404.
Patronage in Ireland, list of letters relating to, 378-379.
Patteson, John, mayor of Norwich, letters from, 265, 266, 270, 274.
Pattinger, Edward, Captain R.N., 140.
Pattrick, Edmund, 124.
Paul, Grand Duke of Russia, 188.
Paul, a bootmaker, 119.
Paulmy, M. le Marquis de, French Ambassador at Warsaw, 216, 217, 219.
Paultons (Hampshire), Hans Stanley at, 301.
letters dated, 286.
Pawle:
Edmund, 99.
Mary, 103.
Phillip, 100.
Richard, 99, 100.
Pay, Christopher, 95.
Payn or Payne:
John, 25, 26, 103.
Robert, Norfolk militia, 127.
Thomas, 44.
William, 98.
Peace establishment for Ireland, 309.
Peace of mayhem, the consideration for a grant, 3, 41.
Pearle, H.M.S., 139.
Pearetree, Robert, of Letheringsett, 109, 112.
Pearson, Captain, naval commander, 315.
Peche, William, 11.
Pechum, Mrs., 190.
Peddersty. See Saxthorp.
Pedham Hall, a manor of Boyton, 54.
Peers, new Irish, 372.
Peirson, Pierson:
General Richard, 316.
——, in command of 13th Dragoons, 342.
——, letters from, 315, 378.
Thomas, 133.
Peitevin, Richard, witness, 15.
Peletot:
Odo de, 48.
William de, 48, 50.
Pelham:
Henry, 157, 160.
——, Lord of the Treasury, 256.
John, at Blickling, 21.

Pelham-Holles, Thomas, Duke of Newcastle, 148, 157, 170, 243, 245, 246, 248, 250, 281, 282.
Lord Privy Seal, 256.
resigns (1745), 157.
—— (1781), 408.
Pell, John, 123, 124.
Pembroke:
Earl of. See Herbert.
(Panbroch) Dominus. See Valence.
Pennsylvania, president and council of, 382, 383.
Pennsylvanian line, the xviii., 381-383.
Penrith, 152.
Pensacola (Alabama, N.A.), 362.
Pensions:
Irish, 385.
on Irish establishment, 309.
Pepper, Dr. Robert, 132.
Perceval, John, 2nd Earl of Egmont, First Lord of the Admiralty, 256.
Percy:
Lord, arrived from Rhode Island, 305.
Hugh, 2nd Earl and 1st Duke of Northumberland, 254, 271.
——, letters from, 429.
——, letters to, 429, 430.
Perebazar (Persia), 235.
Perkins, Charles, 127.
Pernau (Esthonia), 233.
Perrier, Madame, 286.
Perriwig, price of a (1672), 117.
Persia, 229-231, 234-236.
confusion in, 236.
Shah Nadir of, his relations with Russia, 236.
——, protects Elton,, 231, 235, 236.
scheme of trade with, 234, 235, 236.
trade with, 224, 225, 227, 228, 230, 231.
Persian dread of water, 236.
Person, John, 53.
Pery:
Dean, 378, 384.
Edmund Sexton, 379.
——, letter from, 297.
Pesche, William, 15.
Peter:
constabularius, 40.
the third (Czar), xv., xvi., 201, 206, 245.
the Great (Czar), 208.
dapifer, 41.
William the son of, 19.
Peterborough, letter dated, 165.
Peterhoff, 186.
Petersburg. See St. Petersburg.
Petition, fine for false, 9.
Petitions, 86, 88, 232, 265, 266, 287, 378
Petrikau (Poland), tribunal of, 213
Pettus:
John, of Thurgarton, 101.
Sir John, 125, 137.
Thomas, 81.

Petty, William, 3rd Earl of Shelburne, 290.
  his interview with Lord Buckinghamshire, 272.
  letter from, 271.
  Secretary of State, 263, 286.
Petty France. *See* Westminster.
Petworth, George Grenville's visit to, 262.
Peyton:
  Charles, 142. 145.
  Sir John, letter from, 83.
Pheasants, 57, 321.
Phenixe, H.M.S., 139.
Philadelphia, expedition against, 311.
Phileby, Adam de, abbot, 61.
Philip, the bishop's officer, 39, 40.
Philip, Chaplain de Sancta Fide, 17.
Philipes *or* Phillips:
  Robert, 90.
  General, in North America, 380, 387, 388.
  Captain, 150.
Phipps, Constantine John, 2nd Lord Mulgrave, 325.
"Phlogiston" of the Convention, the, 425.
Pickenham, South, 85.
Picroft, Thomas, of Scottowe, 105.
Piedmontese, the, reported victory of, over Spaniards, 159.
Pierce, William, 141.
Piers, grants in aid of building, 319.
Pierson. *See* Peirson.
Pikarell, John, 95.
Pillecrowe. *See* Pyllecrowe.
Pillemere, John le, 26.
Pillory, the, as a punishment, 25.
Pilyng, Edmund, 48.
Pirmont, waters of, 282.
Piszezala, *le sieur*, a gentleman of Minsk, 215.
  murdered, 214.
Pitans:
  Alice, 9.
  Geoffrey, 9.
  Robert, 9.
Pitt:
  Mrs. Anne, her stay in France, 238.
  Miss H., 441.
  William, 1st Lord Chatham, 159, 160, 164, 177, 244, 245, 247, 248, 250, 252, 253, 263, 264, 265, 275, 287, 288.
  ——, letter from, 238.
  ——, on privilege, 248.
  ——, his proposals with respect to the Grafton ministry, 263, **264**.
  ——, speech on the Preliminaries, 245, 247.
  ——, unpopular in the city, 265.
  William (the younger), 427, 439.
  ——, private character of, 428.

Plan of government (July, 1765), 256.
Plane, James, of Fieldawling, 114.
Plantations, the:
  minutes and report of Committee of Council upon, 289.
  order of H.M. in Council relating to, 289.
  trade with England and Ireland, 301-304, 306-310.
Plater, Palatin of Mecistaw, 193.
Playford, Henry, of Northrepps, 98.
Pleydell Bouverie, Jacob, 2nd Earl of Radnor, 378.
Pliny's *Natural History*, 438, 439.
Plomer:
  John le, will of, 49.
  ——, Agatha, his wife, 49.
  W., will of, 146.
Ploughman, Henry, 88.
Pluket, Richard, 19.
Plumpstead, Bartholomew, 100, 103.
Plumpstead *or* Plumstede: 52, 73.
  landowners in, 100.
  Sir William Harbord's estate in, 260.
  deeds relating to, 71.
Plunkett, Arthur James, 7th Earl of Fingall, 327.
  his sons at Vienna, 327.
Plymouth, H.M.S., 138.
Plymouth, 162, 338, 361.
  dearth at, 276.
Poachers at Blickling, 28, 320.
Pokoc, John, 7.
Poland, xv., 192-221, *passim*.
  Chamber of Nonces, 193, 194, 209, 210. 220.
  constitution of, 199. 215.
  dissidents in, 221, 282.
  election to the crown of, xv., 179, 218. 219, 220.
  fate of, 293.
  France quarrels with, 216-217, 219.
  general confederation of, 216, 218.
  King of. *See* Augustus III. and Poniatowski.
  papers relating to, xv., 192-221, 282.
  primate of. *See* Lubienski, Ladislas.
  relations of, with Courland, 195-212, 215, 216, 282.
  Senatus concilium of, 211.
  Sigillum Magestraticum of, 209.
Pole, De la (William), Earl of Suffolk, vii.
Poles, De la, the, vii.
Poley, William, prior of St. Mary of Buttele, 74.
Polish:
  dances, 177.
  nobility, Count Bruhl's claim to, disputed, 193-195.
  Republic, the, 196-208, 211, 215.

Pollard :
  John, 125.
  Reginald, 17.
Polluxfen, Mr., a merchant in London, 131.
Polock, Palatinate of, 193, 213.
Pomerania, 191.
Pomeroy, Arthur, 379.
Pomfret, Earl of (1764). *See* Fermor.
Poniatowski, Stanislas, Stolnik of Lithuania, 194.
  and King of Poland, xv., xvi., 194, 214, 220, 282.
  letter from, xv., 214.
  letter to, 220.
Ponyng, Edward, of Marlingforth, 70.
Ponsonby
  Lady E., 379.
  Mr., "complimented" with the borough of Middleton, 420.
  Rt. Hon. William, 2nd Earl of Bessborough, 274.
  ——, Postmaster-General, 280.
  ——, resignation of, 274.
Ponsonbys, the, 403.
Poor, resolutions and advice upon a statute touching the relief of the, 76-78.
Pope :
  Adam, receiver for Duchy of Lancaster, 69.
  Alexander, xiv.
  Cecilia, 42.
  Miss, at Drury Lane, 179.
  John, 42.
  Seyhiva, 42.
Popham, Sir John, Lord Chief Justice, 76.
Popish recusants, 100, 117, 141.
"Porcarius," 33.
Porcupine, H.M.S., 162.
Poroditch, Thomas, of Batheley, 106.
Porte, the Sublime, 219.
  promises subsidy to Sweden, 292.
Porten, Sir Stanier, 375.
Porter :
  Frances, 92.
  Henry le, 7, 9, 16.
  ——, Alicia, wife of, 7.
  John, of Suffield, 98.
  ——, of Bylaugh, 91.
  Thomas, 92.
  William, of Foxley, 92.
Portland, Duke of. *See* Bentinck.
Portland, H.M.S., 139.
Portsmouth, 156, 161.
  Hessians sail from, 296.
  letters dated, 411.
Portsmouth, H.M.S., 139.
Portugal, trade with Ireland, 400.
Possicke, Possewyk *or* Posswic : 50.
  swans at, 121.
  John de, 11.
  John, *clericus* de, 13.
Post letters, 148, 163, 171, 173.
Potemkin, Prince, 435.

Potter (Pottere, Potere) :
  Abraham, 139.
  Brigadier-General James, his proposals to the soldiers of the Pennsylvanian line, 382, 383.
  Ralph le, 38.
  Robert le, 38.
Potts :
  John, of Mannington, 104.
  Sir John, *ibid.*, 104.
  Sir Robert, 141.
  Roger, 123, 124.
  Sir Roger, 135, 136, 137.
Pounde, Thomas, 55.
Povere, John le, 49.
Powell, Elizabeth, 98.
Powerscourt, 390.
Powis, Earl of. *See* Herbert.
Pownall, Mr., 260, 261.
Poyning's Law, 363, 364, 394, 399, 413.
  "a good tub," 399.
Poynter, Andrew, of Bintry, 91.
Praed, Humphry Mackworth, 173.
Praedones, French officers in the service of the Colonies called, 300.
Praslin (Prâlin), Duc de, 219, 250.
"Prate's Mill," swan kept at, 122.
Pratt :
  Charles, 1st Baron Camden, Lord Chancellor, 272, 288.
  ——, Lord Chief Justice, 250.
  William, of Gt. Witchingham, 96.
Prattant, Humphry, of Lammas, 104.
Prayd, Robert, 24.
Preist. *See* Priest.
Prente, Henry, 37.
Pres (the tenement), 60.
Presbyterians in Ireland, 421, 424.
Presentments to manor courts, specimens of, 6-10, 21-28.
Prestcroft, at Horsham, 7.
Preston :
  ——, proposed candidate for Norwich, 242.
  Jacob, Capt. 1st (militia) Foot, 125.
  Mrs., dau. to Lady Hobart, 143.
  Thomas, Ensign, 1st (militia) Foot, 125.
Pretender, the. *See* James Francis Edward.
  his son. *See* Charles Edward.
Prettyman, Thomas, Norfolk Militia, 127.
Price, William, 145.
Prices, lists of, 129, 163.
Prichard, a great rogue, at Utrecht, 244.
Prideaux, Dean, x., *note.*
Priest *or* Preist :
  Giles, of Wayborne, 107.
  Martha, of Hempstead, 107.
  Robert of Roughton, 98.
Prigge :
  Beatrice, 24.
  Estrilda, 26.

Primrose, Robert, of Southrepps, 98.
Prince Palatin of Russia. *See*
    Czartoryski.
Prince *Régimentaire*. *See* Czartoryski.
Prince William (ship), 150.
Princesse Anne, H.M.S., 139.
Princeton, 382.
Prior, Matthew, quoted, 190.
Prisman, Captain, 138.
Pritchard, Captain, 138.
Privateers:
    American, 300, 378.
    French, 338.
Privilege:
    of Parliament, 247, 248.
    of bishops infringed, 247.
Privy Council:
    action of. in relation to the em-
        bargo of corn, 266, 267.
    ——, order of (1745), 148.
    ——, —— (1770), 289.
    in Ireland, 371.
Privy Garden. *See* London.
Privy Seal Office, "a sinecure for
    Mr. Pitt," 263.
Proby, John Joshua, 2nd Baron
    Carysfort, an Irish minister, 426.
Protestant Dissenters, address to the
    Lord Lieutenant, 377.
Protestants in Ireland, 395, 424, 432.
Provence, Aix in, 339.
Provost [of Edinburgh], Stewart,
    the, taken prisoner, 152.
Prussia: 435.
    alliance of. with Russia, xv.
    King of. *See* Frederic II.
    and Poland, 282, 293, 435.
Prussian:
    Ambassador, 210.
    cloth in Russia, 224, 225.
    subsidy, 244.
Pruth, the river, 435.
Przemysl (Poland), 204.
Puffendorf, 300.
Pulteney, William, Earl of Bath, 157.
Purland:
    Alice, of Warham, 115.
    Jeremiah, 115.
    Robert, 115.
Purton, George, 112.
Puttocke:
    Agnes, 14.
    Edward, of Belough, 102.
Pyam, William, 18.
Pycot, Richard, 21.
Pye, Thomas, 81.
Pygotte, Margaret, Prioress of
    Carrow, 70.
Pyke, John, 109.
Pyle, Robert, 115.
Pyllecrowe *or* Pillecrowe:
    Myles, 17.
    Nicholas, 17.
    William, 17.
Pynkeney:
    William de, 10.
    ——, Hugh, son of, 10.

Q

Quakers in Ireland, address from,
    377.
    at Norwich, politics of, 242.
Quaker Ketch, ship, 140.
Qualissal, William de, 28.
Quebec: 316.
    siege of, 239.
Queen's County, sheriff of, 344.
Queensberry (Queensborough), Duke
    of. *See* Douglas.
Quidenham (Norfolk), bought by
    Lord Albemarle, 251.
    Sir John Holland of, ix.
Quin:
    Dr., in Ireland, 390, 427, 433.
    Dr. Charles, in Ireland, 427.
Quyit:
    John, 48.
    le, John, 48.

R

Rackheath (Rakheythe), (Norfolk):
    Great, church of, 52.
    Little, *ibid*, 52.
Radnor, Earl of 1(776). *See* Pleydell-
    Bouverie.
Radziwil, Prince Miecznik of Lithu-
    ania, Palatin of Wilna, 192,
    193, 194, 209, 213, 214, 218,
    219, 282.
    opposes the Czartoryski, 193,
    194.
Rainsford, General, embarks for Leg-
    horn, 407.
Rake, Henry, 36.
Rakheythe. *See* Rackheath.
Ralph:
    abbot of Langley, 160.
    the baker, 26.
    rector of Keswick, 67.
    son of Lady Ulviva de Itering-
        ham, 49.
    William, son of, 17.
Ramilies, 74, gun ship, 350.
"*Rampant Horse*" (inn), the, 129.
Ramsey, John, 105.
Randolph:
    the cook, 40.
    John, 33.
Ransome, ——, a candidate for the
    mastership of Wymondham school
    (1653), 87.

Rant:
    Sir Thomas, of Thorpe Market, 99.
    Sir William, 124, 127, 132, 133, 141, 142.
    ——, raises troop (1696), 142.
    William, of Thorpe Market, 99.
Ravenshall (Norfolk), 62.
Ravensworth, Lord (1778). *See* Liddell.
Rawdon, Lord (1781), 407.
    in North America, 388.
Rawlyns manor, in Suffolk, 73.
Raylye, William, of Twyford, 95.
Raymer, Thomas, of Bylaugh, 91.
Raymond *or* Raimond:
    Nephew of Bertram the Prior, 12.
    Prior of St. Faith's, 11, 19.
Rayner, Thomas, 110.
Raynesthorp manor of, Keswich, 66.
Raynham (Norfolk), 128, 129.
Read:
    Robert, of Stiffkey, 114.
    Thomas, *ibid,* 114.
Reaver, Thomas, 114.
Rebellion:
    (Scots) of 1639, 85.
    the, of 1745, 148-161.
    ——, news of the battle of Falkirk, 157.
Recruits, Inspector of (Ireland), 354.
Red Squadron, 137.
Redgrave, free school at, charter of, 441.
Redham Hall, manor of, 54.
Redmayne, Dr. Robert, letter from, 62.
Reed, Joseph, President of the Council of Pennsylvania, 382-383.
Reeder, Margaret, 114.
Reedham, Geoffrey de, 19.
Reepham (Refham, Ryffeham) cum Kerdeston (Cardeston) (Norfolk): 95.
    landowners in, 94.
    manor of, 44.
Reepham:
    John de, 42, 73.
    Reginald de, 42.
    Roger de, 42.
Reflection, H.M.S., 138.
Regency, the, under George III., 437.
Regiments:
    Athol Highlanders, 330, 331, 348.
    Carabineers, 314.
    Duke of Bedford's, 151.
    Blue Horse, 369.
    1st Horse, 314.
    Bose's Hessian, 338.
    Dragoons:
        ——, Lord Pembroke's, 297.
        ——, Queen's, at Norwich, 269.
        ——, 5th, 314.
        ——, 12th, 305.
        ——, 13th 342.
        ——, 18th, 300, 324, 333, 334.

Regiments—*cont.*
    Grenadiers, 336.
    Earl of Halifax's, 151.
    Militia. *See* Militia.
    "The Law," 154.
    3rd, 373.
    11th, 334.
    19th, 373.
    30th, 334, 335, 373.
    32nd, 339.
    36th, 315.
    52nd, 324.
    63rd, 324.
    68th, 334.
    81st, 356, 362.
Regiments, proposals for raising, 310, 314, 377.
Reginald, son of Walter, 26.
Regrating, crime of, 28.
Reily, Thomas, 144.
Reinham:
    Alan de, 18.
    John de, 18.
Rendall, 119.
Rendle, John de, 74.
Rendlesham, Robert chaplain of, 13.
Rente, Robert, 24.
Repnin, Prince, 218.
Repps, John, 132.
Repton. *See* Rippon Hall.
Rescht (Persia), 235.
Reserve, H.M.S., 139.
Restauration, H.M.S., 138.
Retz, Cardinal de, 420.
Revall (Esthonia), 233.
Reveshale. *See* Ryveshale.
Revolution, the, of 1688, 132, *et seq.*
Reymer, John, 92, 98.
    ——, widow of, 98.
    William, 92, 98.
Reyner, Thomas, Naval Commander, 139.
Reynolds:
    John, clerk, 98.
    Robert, captain, 138.
    Roger, Norfolk Militia, 126.
Reynor, Thomas, clerk, 108.
Rhode Island, 305.
Rhodope, 435.
Rice:
    Mr., 360.
    Sara, 98.
    Symson, 98.
Richard:
    the parson of Blickling, 26.
    Lord Prior of Horsham, 5.
    the parson's servant, 38.
    Robert son of, 12.
    son of Adam, Thomas and Ralph, sons of, 26.
    son of Henry Fitz-Simon de London, 41.
    de Marsham, 41.
    son of Simon, 39.
Richards, John, 132.
Richardson, his chancery suit, 75.
Riches, Nicholas, 95.
Richmon, Richard, 112.

Richmond: 205.
    in relation to Thames naviga-
        tion, 341, 342.
    letters dated from, 439.
Richmond:
    Duchess of, 167, 168.
    Duke of. *See* Lennox.
Richmond, H.M.S., 139.
Rideont, George, 114.
Ridgwell, Godfrey, of Sparham, 94.
Ridley:
    Cuthbert, 145.
    William, 145.
Riga, 185, 188, 222.
    trade with, 227, 233, 237.
Rigby:
    Mr., conduct in House of Com-
        mons, 351.
    Richard, 277, 279-282, 285.
    ——, succeeds Ellis, 245.
Right, little writ of (close), 23.
Rikhill, William, 52.
Ringall, widow, 110.
Ringer, Christopher, 114.
Ringland, landowners in, 94.
Ringstead, John, 117.
Riots:
    at Bath, 369.
    at Boston (N.A.), 291.
    the Gordon, 336-369.
    at Nottingham, 369.
    Norwich (corn), 267-271.
    on account of the malt tax, 147.
Rippon *or* Ripton Hall (Ripetuna).
    See Hevingham.
Risbrough, Thomas, 101.
Riveshal *or* Rivyshall. *See* Ryves-
    hale.
Roach, Jeremiah, 139.
Roberson, Robert, captain, 138.
Robert:
    the cook, 40.
    parson of the church of Great
        Rakheythe, 52.
    pincerna, 41.
    Ralph, son of, 37.
    Sacerdos de Tirnigges, 17.
    the parson's servant, 37.
    the tanner, 48.
Roberts:
    Francis, 108, 111.
    Colonel, at Dublin, 320.
    Mr. J., a secretary of the
        Treasury, 256.
    Mr., chaplain to Coke family,
        320.
Robins:
    Richard, 103, 104.
    Thomas, 103.
Robinson:
    Captain, 150.
    General, returns from New
        York, 300.
    Henry, captain, 139.
    John, 91.
    Mr., 359.
    Dr. Richard, archbishop of
        Armagh, Lord Primate of
        Ireland, 298, 379.

Robust, the, ship, 407, 409.
Robyn, John, 49.
Robyns, Thomas, 54.
Rocelin, William, son of, 17.
Roche:
    Sir Boyle, 379.
    Lady, 379.
Rochelle [La], 161.
Rochford, Lord (1779). *See* Nassau
    de Zulestein.
Rochfort, George, 2nd Earl of Bel-
        vedere, 378, 442.
    letter from, 314, 378.
Rockingham, Marquis of. *See* Went-
    worth.
Rodney, Admiral Sir G., 361, 362,
    366, 396-400, 402, 405, 410.
Roger:
    Archdeacon, 40.
    bishop of Norwich. *See* Sker-
        ning.
    Master, 12.
    Robert son of, 15.
    Robert son of, Lord of Wark-
        worth, 11.
    son of Simon de Birston, 49.
Rogers:
    John, 110.
    Mr. and Mrs. 155, 242.
    Robert, 108.
    William, Alderman of Norwich,
        6.
    William, 139.
Rogues, Statute of, orders under,
    made at Ilmynster the 11th of
    April (1600 *circ.*) to be confirmed
    at the sessions, &c., 78.
Rokels Lyttebar, manor of, 65.
Roland, son of William the priest;
    10.
Rolfe, Mrs. Mary, of Tuttington,
    105.
Rollesby:
    Robert de, 74.
    John son of, 74.
Rollin, M., his work on literature,
    438.
Rolls, the, 152.
Roman Catholics:
    See Papists.
    in Ireland. *See* Ireland.
Romanshoff, General, 434-436.
Romburge Priory, a cell of St.
    Mary's at York, 57.
Rome, 438.
Rook, Rear-Admiral George, 137.
Rookwood
    Margaret, of Weston, 95.
    Thomas, 95.
Roper:
    Mr., a brother of Mr. Coke, at
        Dublin, 320.
    Richard, 109.
    William, 109.
Roscommon, Baron, title of, re-
    quested, 345.

Rose:
    Andrew, of Antingham, 97.
    Roger, 25.
Ross, Earl of (1778). *See* Gore.
Ross, Major, of the 81st, 356.
Rostock (Mecklenburg), 234.
Roughton (Norfolk), landowners in, 98, 99.
Rounce, Dennis, of Cromer, 97.
Row, Thomas, captain, 140.
Rowland, Mr., at Edgfeild, 111.
Roxburgh, Duke of (1767). *Se(* Ker.
Royal Charles, H.M.S., 117.
Royal Oak, H.M.S., 138.
Royston, Lord. *See* Yorke.
Rozamowsky, Alexis Grigorievitch Count, 186.
    Cyril Grigorievitch, Hetman of the Cossacks, 184.
Rozan (Poland), nuncio of, 195.
Ruby, H.M.S., 139.
Rudham:
    Ralf de, *capellanus*, 16.
    Geoffrey de, 19.
Ruellennus, 46.
Ruffus:
    Osmund, 40.
    Richard, 41.
    Stephan, *ibid.*
Rugge, Thomas, 98.
Rum from West Indies, 307.
Rungeton, the vill of, 73.
Runham, manor, 54.
Rupert, H.M.S., 139.
Running dogs, liberties to keep, 29.
Runseye, Roger, 81.
Runton, landowners in, 100.
Rupert, H.M.S., 139.
Rupert, Prince, a testimonial by, 117.
Russel *or* Russell:
    Admiral Edward, afterwards Earl of Orford, 137.
    Elizabeth, 108.
    Francis, 4th Earl of Bedford, 84, 85.
    Francis, Marquis of Tavistock, afterwards 5th Duke of Bedford, 429, 442.
    Francis, Marquis of Tavistock, married Lady Elizabeth Keppel, 185.
    John, 4th Duke of Bedford, 151, 172, 185, 277-285.
    ——, protests against repeal of Stamp Act, 260, 261.
    ——, his regiment, 151.
    Thomas, 107.
    William, a citizen of Norwich, 20.
    William, 18, 19.
Russelis, Robert, 101.
Russia: 170-237 (*passim*), 246, 250, 292, 293, 371.
    "Adventitious strength" of, 371.
    company. 222-231.
    college of commerce, 226, 227.

Russia—*cont.*
    Court of, ambassadors' expenses at, 244, 255.
    Czar of. *See* Iwan and Peter.
    Embassy to, Lord Buckinghamshire's, 170-192, 246, 371, 406.
    Empress of. *See* Anne, Catherine II., Elizabeth.
    English treaty of alliance with, 218, 237, 371.
    ——, treaty of commerce with, 218, 222-232, 237.
    ——, ——, of 1716 (projected), 224.
    ——, ——, of 1734, 222, 223. 224, 226-232.
    ——, ——, of 1767, 232.
    Grand Duke of. *See* Paul.
    grievances of English merchants in, 223-228, 237.
    ——, in 1732, 225.
    mediation of, 404-406.
    negotiations of, with Poland, 197-199, 205-209, 213-214.
    Prince Palatin of (in Warsaw), 218.
    preparing for war (1773), 292.
    senate of, 202.
    trade with, XIV., XV., 222-237, 309.
    ——, Lord Buckinghamshire's papers relating to, 222-237.
    trade grievances of, against England, 232, 233.
    Vice-chancellor of. *See* Galitzin.
Russian:
    auxiliary troops proposed for American war, 295.
    customs, 177.
    exports to Britain, 223, 234, 237.
    policy in Poland and Courland, 195-212.
    ports, list of ships at (1762), 233.
    troops refused quarter in Poland, 196, 197.
    ——, in Lithuania, 212.
    uniforms, cloth for, 224, 230.
    weddings, descriptions of, 180-183, 189, 213.
Russians, the: 171, 178.
    at war with Turks, 292.
    exaggerated victories of, 435.
    in Pomerania, 191.
Rust, Will, 6, 8.
Rustens *or* Rusteyns (manor). *See* Wymondham.
Rut, Henry, 39.
Ruthyn, Lord de. *See* Grey.
Rutland, Duke of. *See* Mannors.
Rye (Ry), honour of, 36, 37.
Rydel, Geoffrey, 16.
Ryder, Thomas, 146.
Ryffeham. *See* Reepham.
Rygeday, Margaret, 16.
Rynouse, Robert, 20.
Ryptonhall. *See* Rippon Hall.

Ryssley, Prior John, 20.
Rystone, Thomas de, 22.
Ryther:
    Joanna wife of John, 44.
    John, 44.
    William, 44.
Ryveshale *or* Reveshale, Riveshal
    (Suffolk):
    deeds relating to, 16, 73.
    Henry de, *miles*, 16.
    John, his son, 16.
    John de, 17.
    Sir John, 60.
Ryvishallmerke, 17.

S

Saba (West Indies), taken 386.
Sackville *or* Sakeville:
    Jordan de, 49.
    Lionel Cranfield, 1st Duke of
    Dorset, 148, 157.
    Sir Richard, P.C., 57.
    Thomas, Earl of Dorset, 57.
Sade, Thomas, 38.
Sadleir, R. Vernon, 378.
Sadler, Thomas, 104.
Sage, Captain, R.A., 410.
Saint:
    Albans, H.M.S., 139.
    Andrew's Hall. *See* Norwich.
    Audomerus. *See* Omer.
    Benedict, order of, 20.
    Botolph, vill, 28.
    Domingo, 251.
    Dunstan's. *See* Saxthorpe.
    Edmunds, sacrist of, 26.
    Eustatia (West Indies), 307.
    ——, taken, 386, 387.
    Faith's: 13.
        (*See also* Horsham St.
        Faith's.)
        near Norwich, 269.
        Alexander, chaplain of, 17.
        Hugh, *ibid*, 19.
        John, *ibid*.
        Philip, *ibid*, 17.
    George, Mrs., a beauty at
    Dublin, 423.
    George's channel, 330.
    George, fort (Calcutta), 150.
    George (ship), 150.
    Giles. *See* Norwich.
    Giles in the Fields, Middlesex,
    147.
    Helena, 150.
    Hue, George, 139.
    Ives (Cornwall), 146, 179.
    ——, election at, 179, 265.
    James'. (*See* London.)

Saint—*cont.*
    John, Lord, 84.
    ——, Oliver, Earl of Boling-
    broke (Bullingbroke), 83.
    ——, Frederick, 2nd Viscount
    Bolingbroke, 260, 261.
    ——, ——, at Bath xiv., his pro-
    perty at Twickenham, 146.
    ——, Ranulph de, 47.
    Johnstown (Wexford), borough
    of, 366.
    Laurence:
        Thomas, Lord Howth, 408.
    ——, his son, 408.
    Leger, St. Leger Aldworth,
    Lord Doneraile, 379.
    Lucia (West Indies), taking of,
    342.
    Malo, privateer from, 162.
    Martin:
        le Bailey. *See* Norwich.
        William de, 10.
    Martin (West Indies), 386.
    ——, taken, 409.
    Mary's. *See* Tintern *and* York.
    Michael, H.M.S., 138.
    Michael, Berstreet. *See* Nor-
    wich.
    Olave's:
        Southwark, a messuage in,
        55.
        Norwich. *See* Norwich.
    Omer, Thomas, 11.
    Patrick:
        new order of, 419.
    ——, chancellorship of, 386.
    Paul's:
        Cathedral, repair of, (1632),
        84.
        Dean of. *See* Cumberland
        and Litchfield.
    Paul, Henry de, 16.
    Petersburg, vi., xiv., 172, 218,
    222-237, *passim*, 244, 246,
    249-251, 253, 255, 292, 404,
    406, 413.
    ——, Earl of Buckingham-
    shire's embassy at, xiv.,
    xvi.
    ——, Consul General at,
    xvi., 192.
    ——, court of, 174, 180,
    183, 219, 371.
    ——, connection of, with
    Berlin, 191.
    ——, exports in 1762, from,
    234.
    ——, imports, 234.
    ——, letters dated, 173-190,
    254.
    ——, merchants' petition
    from, 232-233.
    ——, Seasons at, 181, 182,
    188.
    ——, summer palace at, 186.
    Phillip's (Minorca), 407.
    Werburg's (Ireland), chancellor-
    ship of, 386.
    Woolston's. *See* Dublin.

Sakcr, *alias* Parker, Alice, 58.
Sakeville. *See* Sackville.
Salisbury: 43, 89.
    Bishop of. *See* Askew *and* Hume.
Sall (Saule *or* Salle) (Norfolk): 28, 143.
    church at, vii.
    landowners in, 94.
    Robert de, 75.
    Roger de, 46.
    John de, 18.
    Warin de, 47.
Sallamander, H.M.S., 140.
Salmon, James, 139.
Salt, grant of, at Malteby, 13.
Saltash, corporation of, 332.
Salter, Thomas, 116.
Salthouse (Salthausen), landowners in, 107, 111.
Salve:
    Agnes, 25.
    Cecily, 25.
Salway, Carrickfergus, letter dated, 329.
Salwey, Richard, 89.
Sam and Henry, H.M.S., 139.
Sambour (Poland), 216.
Sampson, H.M.S., 139.
Sandford, Colonel, 325, 354, 379.
Sandwich, Earl of. *Soe* Montagu.
Sandwich, H.M.S., 137.
Sandy Hook, the Halifax armament at, 296.
Sandys, Samuel, 1st Lord of Ombersley (1745), 157.
Santee, R., North America, 388.
Saphire, H.M.S., 139.
Sapieha, Palatin of Polock, elected '*petit général*' of Poland, 193.
Saratoga, 315, 316.
Sartine, M. de, French minister of the Marine, 299.
Saule. *See* Sall.
Saunders:
    family of, 344.
    Grove (co. Wicklow), 345.
    Morley, sheriff of Queen's County, peerage solicited for, 344, 345.
Saunterson, Captain, 140.
Savere, Ralph le, 6, 9.
Savile, Sir George, 248.
Saxlingham (Norfolk), 121.
    landowners in, 110.
Saxony, xv., 209.
    Augustus III. of. *See* Augustus III. King of Poland.
    Charles Christian of. *See* Charles Christian.
    court of, 210.
    and Courland. *See* Courland.
    trade of, with St. Petersburg, 234.
Saxthorpe, vii., 4, 45, 57, 69, 129.
    deeds relating to, 4, 46-57.
    free chapel of St. Dunstan's at, 4, 55, 56.
    " Gate Mille " in, 50.

Saxthorpe—*cont.*
    landowners in, 104.
    Legate mill in, 47.
    Lound mill in, 47.
    manors in:
        Lound hall, 45, 46, 52, 56.
        Mickelhalle *or* Micklehall, 45, 46, 56.
        rolls of, 45-46.
        Muccelond in, 47.
        " peddersty " in, 4, 54.
        private chapel at, 4, 50.
        rentals of, 46.
    view of frankpledge in, 45·
Saxtorp, William de, chaplain, 49.
Say:
    Sir John, 55.
    Roger, Lord, at Wymondham, 63.
Sayer, Nicholas, Norfolk militia, 126.
Sayers, Thomas, 103.
Schade, Thomas, 39.
Scales, Lord, Chief Steward of the manor of Aylsham Lancaster, 67.
Scambler *or* Scamler:
    James, 105, 112.
    Mr., at Wolterton, xii.
    Thomas, 104.
Scarborough, Earl of. *See* Lumley.
Scarning (Skerning), 440.
Scarsdale, Lord. *See* Curzon.
Scatclyn, Geoffrey, 49.
Sceget. *See* Schechet.
Scepter, H.M.S., 139.
Scethich, the vill of. *See* Setchey.
Schade:
    Elvida, 37.
    Thomas, 37, 39, 41.
Schechet (*or* Sceget), Ralph de, 12, 13.
Schet *or* Sceth. *See* Sket.
Schipper, Adam le, 18.
Schirlok, Mariota, wife of William, 26.
Schomberg, Sir A., 379.
Schroeders, Lt.-Colonel, envoy of Russia in Courland, 195.
Schuyler, General, in America, 315.
Sconce, Edmund, 93.
Scotch corps to be raised (1778), 326.
Scothoch. *See* Scottowe.
Scotland: 147, 148, 149, 150, 155, 338.
    treeplanting in the Highlands of, 322.
    attitude of, towards Irish trade, 328.
Scott:
    Henry, 3rd Duke of Buccleugh, 241.
    John, Attorney General of Ireland, afterwards Lord Clonmell, 358, 359, 363.
    Jonas, 115.
Scottowe (Skottowe, Skothowe, Skothoch *or* Scothoch (Norfolk), 44, 427, 442.
    deeds relating to, 72.
    landowners in, 105.

Scottowe:
Gervase, merchant of, 15.
Robert, the clerk of, 17.
Stephen de, 24.
Thomas, 145.
William, 103.
W., 45.
Scots, "advance money" to the (1656), 88.
Scroope, Thomas, bishop of Dromore, 44.
Scroutby (Norfolk), 54.
Scule (or Escole): 13.
John, 16.
Robert, son of, 13, 15, 17, 19.
Simon, 16, 19.
Walter, 19.
William, son of, 13. 15, 17.
Sculthorpe (Skulthorpe), 53.
Scyet, Richard, 42.
Seabourn, Thomas, 121.
Seaforth, Earl of. See Mackenzie.
Sealth:
Robert, of Wood Dawling, 96.
William, ibid., 96.
Seaton, William, of Walsingham, 115.
Secheford, Geofrey de, 19.
Sedley, Thomas, of Bacton, 94.
Seebright, Lady, 178.
Sefred, Robert son of, 13.
Selot, John, 55, 56.
Selwyn:
George, letter from, 438.
Mr., 148.
Semann:
the smith, Beatrice wife of, 25.
Thomas, clerk, of Blickling, 29.
Semendria (Servia), 436.
Semigalle or Semgalle (with Courland), Duchy of, 198, 199, 204, 205, 206, 209, 215. See also Courland.
Serasquier, the, in command of Turkish army, 435.
Setchey (Scethich), deed relating to, 73.
Seugham, Ralph de, 10.
Severn, River, 80.
Seymour, Sir Edward, 261.
Shackle, Thomas, of Great Witchingham, 96.
Shah Nadir. See Persia.
Shakerley, Rowland, 56.
Shannon, Earl of. See Boyle.
Sharrington, landowners in, 109.
Shaxton, Lucy, 106.
Shaw:
Mr., his proposals for a Gaelic Dictionary, 338.
Mr., of East Barsham, 142.
Richard, a Popish recusant, 100.
Shelburne, Earl of. See Petty.
Shelley, Mr. J., 273.
Shelton:
Charles, Captain, 138.
Ralph de, 52, 53.
Shemakha (Caucasia), 224.

Shepereve, a, 74.
Shepheard, Robert, 106.
Shepherd, Tom, of Drogheda, 386.
Sheringham (Norfolk), 142.
landowners in, 100, 101.
Sherinton, 112.
Sherwood, Anne, 100, 116.
Shiel, James, 379.
Shillinge, William, 102.
Shinkwyn, Margaret, 93.
Shirley, Washington, 5th Earl Ferrers, 260.
Short, [William], 332.
rector of Beer, 346.
letter to, 347.
letters from, 333, 370.
Shortgrove, George Grenville's visit at, 262.
Shorting:
Widow, 108.
Thomas, 106.
Shotesham or Shottisham (Norfolk), 442.
letter dated, 294.
All Saints, 145.
Shovell, Sir Cloudesley, 138.
Shropham (Norfolk), 145.
Shuter, Mr., at Covent-Garden, 179.
Siberia, 203, 263.
Sidestrand (Norfolk), landowners in, 98.
Sielicki, a Pole, attack upon, 213, 214.
Sigar, Siger, Syger:
of Oulton, 47.
——, Robert son of, 47, 49.
Thomas, 50.
Sill, Major, 324.
Sillmott, Captain, 139.
Simenel, Robert, 50.
Simolin, M. de, Russian Counsellor of State, sequestrates lands and revenues of the Duke of Courland. 195-197.
Simon, Richard the son of, 39.
Skeet, Thomas, Norfolk militia, 117, 126.
Skerning, Roger de, Bishop of Norwich, 42.
See also Scarning.
Skerret, Myles, 57.
Sket (Schet, Sceth):
Richard, 18. 19.
Robert, de Erpingham, 22.
William, de Einford, 16.
Skeyton, landowners in, 105.
Skilling, Edmond, of Reepham, 94.
Skippon, Philip, of Foulsham, noted as "ultra mare," ix., 91.
Skothowe or Skottowe. See Scottowe.
Skut, of Iteringham, 47.
Skyppyng, John, 24, 25, 26.
Slade load, in the Fen Country, 165.
Slatina (Slavonia), 436.
Sligo, 389.
Sloane, Hans, 360, 362, 378.
letter from, 362.

Sloninola (Poland), 195.
Smallpox, the, called the 'Smalls,' 159, 182.
Smith, Smyth or Smythe:
  Andrew le, 43.
  Dame Alice, of Corpusty cum Irmingland, 103.
  Counseilor, 329, 330.
  Dr., 142.
  Edmund, doctor of physick, of Walsingham, 115.
  Geoffrey, the, 49.
  John, clerk, of Runton 100.
  ——, of Snpring, 115.
  ——, of Antingham, 81, 82.
  Martha, 101.
  Ralph, the, 42.
  Richard, 103.
  Robert, 103, 104.
  Sarra, 42.
  Thomas, 35, 36, 100, 102, 108.
  William, 103, 132.
  William, letter from, 163.
  See also Faber.
Smyrna Merchant, H.M.S., 139.
Smythdon, Hundred of, 81.
Snetesham, William de, 53.
Snoring, Great (Norfolk), landowner in, 115.
Snow, J., 332.
  ——, letter from, 289.
  Joseph, 98.
Soame, Some:
  Henry, 101.
  Samuel, 101.
Somerset:
  corn riots in, 271.
  Poor Law in, 77-80..
Somerset, Henry, 5th Duke of Beaufort, 348.
Somerton, West, deed relating to, 74.
Sorrell, John, chief constable, 105, 106.
Sosnoffsky, Grand Notary of Lithuania, 220.
Soukis, William, 33.
Souldadaes, H.M.S., 140.
South Sea stock, 149, 150, 153, 157.
Southampton, 276, 360.
  letters dated, 276, 342, 360, 362.
Southerton, Thomas, 132.
Southgate, Anne, of Elsing, 91.
Southrepps, landowners in, 98.
Southwark (Surrey), 54, 55.
Southwell:
  Major, A.D.C. to the Lord Lieutenant, 333.
  Sir Richard, 57, 74.
  ——, the flocks of, 74.
  Richard, 55, 56.
  ——, alias D'Arcy, 74.
Southwood or Suthwode, deed relating to, 71.
Souverayne, H.M.S., 138.
Spa, 246, 301, 390.
  letters dated, 314, 434, 435.
  Hans Stanley at, 301.

Spain, 253, 337, 406, 413, 434.
  critical state of affairs in, 272.
Spaniards, defeat of, 159.
  attitude of, in 1780, 363.
Spanish:
  Ambassador (Marquis D'Almadovar), 352.
  coast, 338.
  embassy, 271, 272.
  man of war taken, 362.
  "Spanish Charles." See Townshend.
Sparham (Norfolk), arms seized at, XIII., 142, 145.
  landowners in, 94.
Sparrow, Robert, of Foulsham, 92.
Speclewood, 303.
Spelman, Spilman:
  Clement, 124.
  John, of Northrepps, 98.
  Roger, 123, 124.
Spencer:
  John, 31, 141, 145.
  Lord Charles, 283.
  Robert, 141.
Spendlowe or Spendluue:
  Edmund, 105.
  John, 105.
  William, 41.
Spenser (Despenser, Spencer), Henry le, Bishop of Norwich, 4, 21, 31.
Spey, the, 159.
Spice Islands (East Indies), 386.
Spirall, William, 103.
Spirits, English and Irish duty on, 318.
Spitlehowses, parishes rated for, 77.
Spithead, 305, 330.
Spixworth (Spykeswth), Norfolk, 16.
Spole, Matilda, 9.
Spooner, John, of Holkham, 113.
Sporell. See Spurrell.
Sporle, John, 114.
Sporne:
  Alice, 115.
  Matthew, 115.
  Richard, 114.
Spurrell (Sporell or Spural):
  Elizabeth, of Wymondham, 64.
  George, 106.
  Robert, 108.
  William, 101, 103, 166.
Spragge:
  Admiral, 117.
  Thomas, Captain, 140.
Spratt, John, 86.
Springall, Richard, 91, 96.
Spye, Margaret, daughter of Simon, 25.
Spykeswth. See Spixworth.
Squilla, a dissertation on the, 438.
Stafford:
  Lord. See Howard.
  John, Archbishop of Canterbury, 54.
Stafford, ship, 150.
Staffordshire, 288, 337.
Stag, The, H.M.S., 330.

Staingrim, Staingrin, Taingrin or Steingrim:
Archdeacon of Norwich, 41.
—— of Corpusty, 47.
——, Edward, son of, 47.
——, Roger, son of, 47.
Stallam:
Roger de, 13.
William de, 15.
Stamford, Countess of (1706), 144.
Stampe, George, 113.
Standforth, Henry, 107.
Stanford, John de, 19.
Stanhope, William, 1st Earl of Harrington, 148, 155-157.
Staninghall (Stanighale):
William de, 16.
Ralph de, 18.
Stanislaw (Poland), 220.
Stanley:
Edward, 12th Earl of Derby, 324.
Hans, 172, 241, 245, 249, 283, 360, 361, 362.
——, in "Anticipation," 341.
——, his estates, 360.
——, letters from, 286, 299.
——, letter to, 172.
——, offer of Spanish Embassy to, 272.
——, dies at Althorp, 361.
James Smith, Lord Strange, 249.
——, Chancellor of Duchy of Lancaster, 245.
Stanwick (Northamptonshire), letter dated, 15.
Staples:
J., 378.
Mr., at Dublin, 421.
Starling:
John, Norfolk militia, 125.
Robert, 96.
Starre, John, 99.
Staten Island, letter dated, 295.
Statutes. See Acts.
'Steble,' the parish, at Beer, 347.
Steedman, —, 110.
Steingrim or Stengrim. See Staingrim.
Stephens:
Captain, 150.
Captain James, 150.
Sterling Castle, H.M.S., 138.
Steward:
Captain, 150.
Michael, 88.
Stewart:
James, in Irish House of Commons, 414.
William, of Sall, 94.
——, the Provost, in custody in London, 152.
Stifkey (Norfolk), landowners in, 114.
Stileman or Styleman:
John, 110, 114.
Nicholas, 124.
Stirling, Lord (1777). See Alexander.

Stock Exchange, movements of, 149, 150, 153, 157, 161.
Stockdale, Anthony, 144.
Stody or Hunworth, church (Norfolk), 344.
Stody or Studdy, 144.
landowners in, 107.
Stöffel, Lieut.-General, 219.
Stoke, 151, 250.
letter dated, 294.
Stokes, John, Prior of St. Faiths, 20.
Stone, Dr. George, Archbishop of Armagh, Primate of Ireland, 254.
Stopford:
Edward, 378.
James, 2nd Earl of Courtown, 378.
Storer, Mr., 375.
Storh, Matthew de, 47.
Stormont or Stourmont:
Lady, 212.
Lord Viscount. See Murray.
Stotton, Timothy, 93.
Stoughton, Thomas, of Lyng, 93.
Stourbridge (Stirbridge), Cambridgeshire, expenses at Fair, 129.
Stowe, 262, 263, 277, 278, 280.
letters dated, 262.
Strachey, Rev. John, letter from, 431.
Strafford, Earl of. See Wentworth.
Strange [Lord]. See Stanley.
Strangers, presentment for entertaining, 6.
Stratford:
Benjamin O'Neal, process designed against, in the King's Bench, 340.
Edward, Earl of Aldborough, 340.
——, letters from, 338, 340, 344.
Stratton (Strathonne, Straton):
(Norfolk), 42, 43, 44, 73.
church of, 73.
deeds relating to, 73.
letter dated, 322.
manor of, 73.
(Strawless or Strayless, Norfolk), xii.
landowners in, 105.
(Staffordshire), Miss Conolly, of, 288.
Stratton:
John, son of Philip de, 42.
John Phillip, of, 73.
Stred, Matthew de, 17.
Streit or Streyt:
Richer, 42.
Ralph, 38.
Strong, William, letter from, 165.
Strumshote fen, swans at, 121.
Strus, Dominus Johannis de, 19.
Stuart:
John, 3rd Earl of Bute, 171, 173, 174, 250, 265, 285.
Mackenzie (McKensie), James, 348.
Stubbs, yacht, 140.

Studdy. *See* Stody.
Sturmer *or* Sturman, Henry, 54.
Styleman. *See* Stileman.
Styntone, manor of, 47.
Styth:
    Roger, 71.
    Thomas, of Witchingham, 96.
Subsidy men, 77.
Subsidies, estreats of, 89-117.
Successe, H.M.S., 139.
Sucke. *See* Sukke.
Suckling:
    Robert, 124, 125, 132, 145.
    Lieut.-Col. Robert, Norfolk
      Militia, 126.
Sudbury (Suffolk), 41.
Sudbury, William, clerk, 98.
Sudley, Ralph, Lord (1442). *See*
    Boteler.
Suffield (Norfolk), landowners in, 98.
Suffield *or* Suffeild:
    Catherine, of Burrough, 102.
    Edmund, 142.
    Lord. *See* Harbord.
Suffolk, 16, 41, 54, 353.
    Earl of. *See* De la Pole.
    Henrietta, Countess of. *See*
      Hobart.
    Mary, Countess of, letters from,
      142, 143.
Suffolk [and Berkshire]:
    Earl of. *See* Howard.
Suffolk, H.M.S., 138.
Sugar duties, 403.
Sugar *or* Suger:
    Barbara, 117.
    John, 117.
Suggate, Elizabeth, 100.
Sukke *or* Sucke:
    Nicholas, 24.
    Robert, Reginald son of, 24.
Sunday:
    Club, 249.
    Evening Concert Society, 431.
Sundlond, William de, 12.
Supplies, Committee of, 325.
Supply, H.M.S., 139.
Surlingham *or* Sullingham fen and
    ferry, swans at, 121.
Surrey, 55, 148, 370.
Sussex, 406, 408.
Sussex, Earl of (1758). *See* Yelver-
    ton.
Sustead (Norfolk), landowners in,
    101.
Suthelmham. *See* Elmham, South.
Suthwode. *See* Southwood.
Sutton, Blyth, 88.
Svein, Geoffrey le, 19.
Swaffham (Norfolk), 133, 142, 144.
    races, 321·
Swaine, Robert, 100.
Swallow, H.M.S., 139.
Swallow, Thomas, 96, 113.
Swan, John, purchase of swans of,
    121.
Swanington (Norfolk), landowners
    in, 94.

Swans, 83, 121.
Swanton:
    landowners in, 104.
    Morley, 144.
    Novers, landowner in, 108.
Swardeston (Swerdeston) (Norfolk),
    account roll of, 70.
    rectory of, leased, 71.
Sweden: 171, 192.
    aristocracy in, 293.
    old Government of, 293.
    preparing for war (1773), 292.
Swedes, the:
    Livonia in the possession of, 209.
    strategy of, 434.
Swedish Majesty, His. *See* Gustavus
    III.
Swedish:
    quarrel, the, 293.
    trade with St. Petersburgh, 234.
Sweetman:
    Captain, 379.
    Mr., 442.
Swerdeston. *See* Swardeston.
Sweyne, Brice, 22.
Swift *or* Swyft:
    Jonathan, xiv.
    Peter, 8.
Swiftsure, H.M.S., 138.
Swiss trade with St. Petersburg, 234.
Switzerland, 396.
Sydall, James, 113.
Sydenham, Richard, 52.
Sydney, Robert [Lord], viii.
Syger. *See* Sigar.
'Symneles,' a house in Irmingland,
    68.
Symonds *or* Symons:
    Henry, 98.
    John, of Suffield, 98.
    John (Norfolk militia), 125.
    Joseph, 92.
    Robert, 37.
    Thomas, clerk, 98.
    William, assessor, of Stodey,
      105, 107.
Sympson, William, 103.
Synock, Robert, 139.
Syrer, Ralph le, 7.
Szymakourki, —, bribed to break
    the Polish diet, 194.

T

'Tabby' silk, 118, 120, 176.
Tacolneston (Norfolk):
    deeds relating to, 72.
    manor rolls of, 66.
Talbot:
    Gilbert, 64.
    John Chetwynd, of Ingestre
      337.
    Thomas (Norfolk militia), 127.
Tailage, 23.

Talmash, William, 139.
Tamar River, the, scheme for embanking, 289.
Tamiseh R. [or Temes], the (Hungary), 436.
Tanner:
  Nicholas, the, 48.
  Robert, the, 48.
  William, the, 48, 49, 50.
Taplow Court, 378.
Taroslaw, 203.
Tartars, trade with, 229, 235.
Tartini, Guiseppe, musician, 276.
Tasburgh:
  Beaumont, 142.
  Thomas, 53.
Taseburg, Ralph de, 15.
Tateshall, Joan de, 63.
Tatishall, 64.
Taunton (Somersetshire), 79.
Taverham or Thaverham (Norfolk), 6, 12, 21, 54.
Taverham:
  Augustine de, 12.
  Baldwin de, 21.
  William, 21.
Tavistock, 162.
Tavistock, Marquis of. See Russell.
Tavy, River, the, 322.
  fishing rights in, 346.
  scheme for embanking, 289.
Taylor:
  Jervas, 144.
  Katherine, 109.
  William, 142, 144.
  W., a husbandman, 88.
Taylour, Thomas, 1st Earl of Bective, 379.
Tea destroyed at Boston, 291.
Tebard, William, 55.
Templars, suppression of, 72.
Temple:
  Anthony, 56.
  Henry, Viscount Palmerston, at the Treasury (1777), 325.
  Lord. See Grenville.
  Richard, 1st Lord Cobham, 157.
Templum Gerosolomitani. See Jerusalem.
Tennant, James, of Roughton, 98.
Termernikoff (Russia), 233.
Thanet, Earl of. See Tufton.
Thasher, Richard, 106.
Thaverham. See Taverham.
Thelveton, 145.
Themelthorp (Thimblethorp), landowners in, 95.
Thetford (Norfolk), 67.
Thetford:
  Andrew, 32.
  John, will of, VII., 44.
Thetfords, the, 3.
Thetis, H.M.S., 330.
Theobald:
  "Dominus," 12.
  ——, Edward and Henry, his brothers, 12.
  Walter, 12.
Thirning. See Thurning.

Thirsk (Yorkshire), mayor of, 238.
Thirston, Seth, 139.
Thomas, abbot of Tintern and convent of St. Mary, grant by, 57.
Thomastown (Ireland), 339.
Thompson or Tompson:
  Alderman, candidate for Norwich, 242, 243.
  Mr. C., 404.
  Sir C., 405.
  John, 1st Lord Haversham, quotation by, 176.
  ——, Newswriter, 9.
  Nicholas, 97.
  Robert, 87.
Thorisby, Edward, ensign Norfolk militia, 126.
Thornage (Norfolk), landowners in, 109, 112.
Thornton, G., 378.
Thorowgood, Robert (Norfolk militia), 127.
Thorp or Thorpe:
  John de, 26.
  Richard de, 24.
  William de, 42.
Thorpe:
  near Norwich, Papists at, 145.
  exchanged for a manor at Blickling, 1.
  Market, landowners in, 99.
Thorpgate, Agnes de, 24.
Threxton or Threkeston, deed relating to, 71.
Throckmorton, Bass., 81.
Thrigby (Norfolk), 141.
Thumereil, franchise of, 34.
Thurgarton (Norfolk), landowners in, 101.
Thurlow, John, stands for Norwich, 373.
  reports on Norwich manufactures, 312.
Thurning (Thirnyng, Tirninge, Tirninges or Tirnigges) (Norfolk): 15, 17.
  landowners in, 95.
  Alexander, persona de, 17.
  Humfrey de, 17.
  William, 52.
  William, priest of, 17.
Thursby, John Hervey, letter from, 164.
Thursford, landowners in, 116.
Thurston:
  Alexander, 81.
  Hamond, Lieut. (Norfolk militia), 125.
  ——, of Drayton, 94.
Thurtone, 61.
Thwayt or Twayet (Norfolk), landowners in, 105.
Thynne, Thomas, 3rd Viscount Weymouth, 260, 280, 282, 335, 352, 356.
  letter to, 316.
Tibenham, Stephen de, 18.
Tibtot or Tibtoft, arms of, 441.
Titchwell (Tichewell), 54.

Tickell, Mr., author of "Anticipation," 431.
Ticonderoga, N. America, 311.
Tidd:
  Alice, 114.
  Mary, 115.
Tighe, Edward, 374, 379, 442.
  letters from, 390, 393, 398, 400, 402, 403, 427, 432.
  letters to, 392, 394.
  a "mixed subject," 393.
Tilney, Tileny, Tylney:
  Frederic, 103.
  Mr., 111.
  Widow, 109.
Tilson, Mr., 285.
Timber, growth of, 322, 323.
Timolin, Union of, 408.
Timperley, Henry, 142.
Tintern:
  Abbey, 57.
  convent of St. Mary of, 57.
Tipperary, M.P. for, 339.
Tirel:
  Robert, 46.
  Walter, 48.
Tithebi:
  Benedict de, 47.
  Warin de, 47.
Tithings, swearing-in to, 27.
Tithing men, 78, 79.
Toads, shower of, 132.
Todinam, Thomas, witness, 55.
Toft Monks (Norfolk), 145.
Toke, John, 112.
Tolke, John, 104.
Tolye, William, 54.
Tomlinson or Thomlinson, 408.
  John, letters from, 319, 353.
  ——, minutes for a letter to Mr. Harbord from, 256.
Tompson. See Thompson.
Tonson:
  Colonel, 373.
  W., 378.
Tooke, Mr., of Bishop Stortford, 145.
Topcroft (Norfolk), 141, 145.
Toppais, Eudo, 42.
Toppesfield, Robert de, 13.
Torald or Turold, —, bishop's chaplain, 40.
Torey, Thomas, Lieut. Norfolk militia, 126.
Totinger:
  Godfrey, 49.
  Ralph, 49.
Tottenham, P., 379.
Tottenhill (Totnell Heath) (Norfolk), 133.
Tottergill, Dr., 163.
Toulon:
  French navy at, 338.
  battle of, 161.
Tower, the. See London.
Tower, James, 102.
Towler, Mrs., at Dublin, 389.

Townshend:
  Charles (2nd Viscount), 224, 248.
  Hon. Charles, 241, 243, 245, 251, 252, 266, 275, 286, 299.
  ——, Chancellor of Exchequer, 266, 286.
  ——, guardian of Duke of Buccleugh, 241.
  ——, letters from, 241, 243, 266, 267.
  Charles, called "Spanish Charles," afterwards Baron Bayning, 257, 258.
  Chauncy, letters from, 159, 160.
  Mrs., 160.
  family, 373.
  ——, politics of the, 286.
  George (1st Marquess), 372, 373.
  ——, protests against repeal of Stamp Act, 260, 261.
  ——, letters from, 238, 239, 336, 337.
  ——, Viceroy of Ireland, 283.
  George, Lord Ferrers de Chartley, 2nd Marquis Townshend, 353.
  General, 184, 186.
  Horatio (1st Viscount), 129.
  ——, letter to, 128.
  Joseph, 159.
Trade:
  American. See America.
  Armenian. See Armenian.
  French. See French.
  Irish. See Ireland.
  ——, Sackville Hamilton on, 301-304.
  Lords of, 222, 375.
  Persian. See Persia.
  Prussian. See Prussian.
  Russian. See Russia.
  Tartar. See Tartars.
Transilvania, 435, 436.
Traydon, Thomas, Captain, 138.
Trees, pruning of, 323.
Treffrey, Roger, quaker, letter from, 347.
Trentall, foundation for singing, 2, 58.
Trenton, 382.
  letter dated, 384.
Tresham, Thomas, 55.
Trevenant, John, Bishop of Hereford, feoffee, 69.
Trevor:
  Mrs. Mary, portrait of, 143.
  Lord Chief Justice, 143.
Trevor-Hampden:
  Robert, 4th Lord Trevor and Viscount Hampden, 179, 262.
  ——, protests against repeal of Stamp Act, 260.
  ——, superseded as Postmaster-General, 256.
  Mary Constantia, 179.
Trice, Richard, Lieut. Norfolk militia, 126.
Trimingham, landowners in, 99.

Troitzka (Russia), 283.
Troushill Lodge, letter dated, 315.
Trowse (near Norwich), riots at, 267.
Trophy, Matthew, 138.
Trumney (Ireland), 329.
Trunch (Norfolk), landowners in, 70, 99.
Trunch, John, forfeits for treason, 69.
Truro (Cornwall), 146.
Trussel:
    Edward, 74.
    William, 74.
    ——, letter from, VII., 75.
Trussels, the, at Weybourne, VII.
Trustees of forfeited estates, 146.
Tryon, Major-Gen. W., 305.
Tuam, M.P. for (1782), 415.
Tubbing or Tubbinge:
    John, clerk, 103, 115.
    Judith, 113.
    Peter, 113.
    Philip, chief constable, 112, 113.
    Roger, 14.
    Speller, 112, 114.
    William, 124.
    ——, Capt. - Lieut.   Norfolk militia, 125.
Tuckfield, Mr., 285.
Tudeham, John de, 42.
Tufton, Sackville, 8th Earl of Thanet, letters from, 339.
Tukeby, William de, 16.
Tungate, Benedict de, 16.
Tunstead, Hundred of, 439.
    manor roll of, 70.
Turbary, right of, 47.
Turbus, William, Bishop of Norwich, 3, 40.
"Turckish quarrel," the, 293.
Turkill, the sons of, 49.
Turkish envoy to Russia, 190.
Turks:
    trade advantages of, 228.
    at war with Russians, 292, 435.
    —— with Austrians (1788), 434, 435, 436.
Turk's Island, 252.
Turner:
    C., 379.
    Sir John, 442.
    Ralph, 58.
    Thomas, a prisoner in Aylsham gaol, 89.
    William, 124.
Turin, letter dated, 434.
Tuscany, 396.
Tuttington, landowners in, 105.
    view of frankpledge for, 68.
Twayet. See Thwayt.
Twickenham: 146, 439.
    letters dated, 341.
    Lady Suffolk's estate in, 146.
    manor of, 146.
    ——, list of freeholders, etc., of, 146.
    river banks at, 341.
Twiss (of Norwich), 322.

Twyford (Norfolk), landowners in, 95
Tyger, ship, 165.
Tyger Prize, H.M.S., 139.
Tyler:
    Stephen, 55.
    Thomas, 44.
    Wat, 4.
Tylney. See Tilney.
Tynkeby, R. de, 18.
Tyrel or Tyrrell:
    Hugh, 50.
    John, 138.
    Sir John, his will and marriage settlement, 145.
    ——, Martha, daughter of, m. Sir Thomas Drury, 148.
    Juliana, daughter of Robert, 50.
    Matilda, 50.
    Robert, 50.
    Walter, of Mannington, 48-50.
Tyrone, Earl of (1779).   See Beresford.
Tyvile or Tyvill, Ralph de, 14, 67.

U

Ufford, Robert de, 63.
Ukase relating to trade (1762), 232.
Ulfe, Elizabeth, 100.
Upminster, 163.
    Hall, letter dated, 150.
Upwell, 129.
Ursewyk, Sir Thomas, Chief Baron of the Exchequer, 55.
Urwin, John, 141.
Utbard, Barnard, 105.
Uther, Roger, of Cley, 110.
Utrecht, 244.

V

Vagrants, laws relating to, 76.
Vahan, John, clerk, 104.
Valence:
    Dominus de, 46.
    William, Earl of Pembroke (Panbroch), 4, 49.
    Sir William de, 48.
Vallancy, Colonel, his map, 333.
Vantguard, H.M.S., 138.
Varna, 434.
Varsovie. See Warsaw.
Vathecke, Anne, 102.
Vaughan, ——, 241, 244, 252.
    his "Welsh campaign," 241.
Vaurzes, the, a memorial in relation to, 304.

Vaux (Waus, Vallibus, Wallibus): 14.
  Alexander de, 14, 67.
  ——, Alexander, son of, 14, 67.
  John de, 67.
  Ralph de, 67.
Vawle, Mary, 103.
Veer. See Vere.
Venables-Vernon, George, 2nd Baron
  Vernon, 431.
Vendeval. See Wendenval.
Venice, 396.
Venetian:
  eyes, "morbidezza," of, 255.
  trade with St. Petersburg, 234.
Venner, Robert, 139.
Vepnell, John, 139.
Verdon, Samuel, Norfolk militia,
  127.
  under sheriff, XI., 89.
Vere or Veer:
  de, Earl of Oxford, at Waborne,
    69.
  John, knight, manors of, 74.
  John de, Earl of Oxford, manors
    of, 74.
  ——, Elizabeth, wife of, 74.
  Lady de, 69.
  (Vere Beauclerk), Lord (1766),
    260, 283.
Vereeker, Lieut. of the 5th Dra-
  goons, 314.
Vergeons, William, 44.
Verlt, Philip de, 13.
Vermonters, the, 382.
Verney, Sir Thomas de, 60.
Vernon:
  Admiral, 156, 161.
  —, 241, 244.
  Lord (1786).   See Venables-
    Vernon.
Vesey, Thomas, 1st Viscount de
  Vesci, 379.
Veys, William, 38.
Victory, H.M.S., 138.
Viellas, Garcifer, 7.
  his house in Upgate, Horsham, 8.
Vienna, 404, 406, 436.
  letter dated, 327.
Villeins, grant of, in Hegletun, to
  St. Faith's priory, 18.
Vincent, Francis, 116.
Virginian "Resolutions" in 1765,
  260.
Visir, the Grand, 435, 436.
Volga, R., 235.
Volhinia (Poland), 219.
Volunteer, character of an Irish
  Presbyterian, 421.
Volunteers: 356, 357, 366, 376.
  as legislators, 410.
  review of Irish, 389.
Votier, John, Captain, 140.
Vrary, John, 103.
Vyse:
  Captain, sells his troop, 314,
    315, 316.
  Lieut.-Col., letter from, 389.
  Major, 333, 334.
  ——, letters from, 369, 379, 380.

W

Wabourne (Waborne, Wayborne),
  VII., 69.
  abuttal of manor in, by peram-
    bulation of bounds, 69.
  canon of, 75.
  manor rolls of, 69.
  landowners in, 107, 111.
Wade:
  General George, 147, 152, 155.
  Gilbert, 11.
  John, 127.
Wadham, John, 52.
Wages, harvest (1696), 129.
Wagstaffe, Nicholas, 115.
Waite, Thomas, Privy Councillor in
  Ireland, 351.
Wakering (John), Bishop of Nor-
  wich, 31.
Waldegrave:
  Lady, 175.
  Dowager Lady, 253.
  Lord (James 2nd Earl Walde-
    grave), 151, 249.
  John, 3rd Earl (1766), signs
    protest against repeal of
    Stamp Act, 260, 261.
Wale, Barnaby, imprisoned, 141.
Waler, John le, 24.
Wales, Princess of (Augusta), 285.
Waleys:
  Henry le, 14, 15.
  Nicholas le, 15.
Walker, Richard, 92.
Walkerel, a witness, 40.
Wallace, Sir James, in command at
  Cancalle Bay, 351.
Wallachia, 435, 436.
Waller, Richard, 26, 54.
Wallett, William, 114.
Wallibus, Alexander de. See Vaux.
Wallington, 145.
Walmoden, Amelia de, Countess of
  Yarmouth, 170.
Walmsley, Brigade-Major, 333.
Walpole or Walpoole:
  George, 3rd Earl of Orford, 353.
  ——, Lord Lieutenant of Nor-
    folk, 239.
  Colonel Horatio, 144.
  family, and the Lord Lieuten-
    ancy of Norfolk, 239.
  ——, exalted in Norfolk, 373.
  ——, purchase Mannington, 147.
  Horace [afterwards 4th Earl of
    Orford], 175, 176, 238, 442.
  ——, letter from, 437.
  H[oratio] (afterwards 1st Baron
    Walpole, of Wolterton), 224.
  Lord (Horatio 2nd Baron, of
    Wolterton), 185.
  ——, letters from, 319, 439.

Walpole—*cont.*
   and Townshend party in Norfolk, 286.
   R[alph], Bishop of Norwich, 30.
   Robert (1675), 123, 124.
   ——, deputy lieutenant of Norfolk, 125, 133, 136, 137.
   Sir Robert, 272.
Walsh':
   John, 145.
   Dr., in Irish House of Commons, 414, 415.
Walsham:
   North, 4, 133, 142, 144.
   South, 72, 141, 145.
Walsingham:
   Great, landowners in, 116.
   Little, landowners in, 115.
   Waye, the, 54.
Walsingham, Mr., 431.
Walsoken, 129.
Walter, William son of, 35, 36.
Walter, *nepos Episcopi*, 40.
Walton, Sir George, will of, 147.
Waitrim near Bray (Ireland), letters dated, 390, 393.
Wandelard, Robert, 40.
Wangford, William, 54.
Warburton, Dr. [William], Bishop of Gloucester, 260.
   breach of his privilege, 247.
Ward:
   Alderman, 98.
   Bernard, 1st Baron Bangor, 379.
   Edward, 125.
   Sir Edward, 144.
   James, 110, 112, 113.
   John, 1st Viscount Dudley and Ward, 260.
   Mr., of Stoke, 151.
   W., officer in Ordnance Department, Dublin, 339.
   Sir W., 132.
Wardell, Robert, 133.
Warden, Robert, "worstedman," 20, 58, 59.
Warden Meadows, 122.
Wardeyn, Andrew, 27.
Wardrobe, list of a gentleman's (1673), 117-121.
Wardship:
   conveyance of, 75.
   grant of a, 52.
Warham (Norfolk), landowners in, 115.
Warin (Guarinus) *hostiarius*, 40.
Warkhouse, —, 112.
Warley, military camp at, 342.
Warner:
   John, 103, 105.
   Lee, 133.
Warnes:
   Edmund, 102.
   Edward, 104.
   John, 105.
Warnford (Hants), 156.
Warr Spight, H.M.S., 138.
Warrants, General, 248.

Warren, 130.
Warren's Point (Ireland) pier at, 319.
Warsaw (Varsovie), xvi., 178, 192, 197, 200, 205, 206, 209, 212.
   letters dated, 200, 205, 209, 212, 214, 216, 218, 219.
Warwickshire, 332.
Washington, General George, 324, 362, 399.
   "Dictator of America," 300.
   in command of army, 311, 396, 399, 402.
Wasselkey, John, of Wells, 114.
Waters:
   Ben, Captain R.N., 138.
   John, Captain, 139.
Watker, John, 102.
Watson, Robert, clerk, 108.
Watts (Wattys): 150.
   John, son of Thomas, 28.
   William, 111.
Waus. *See* Vaux.
Waxham, 56, 74.
Wayborne. *See* Waborne.
Wayegrave, Thomas, 37.
Wayne, General, in command of Pennsylvanian line at Morristown 381-383.
Wayneflete, Will, Bishop of Winchester, 4, 54, 55.
Wayt *or* Wayte (Guet, Guyet):
   Alice, 39.
   Matilda, 39.
   Peter, 37.
   Roger, 41, 42.
   Thomas, 36.
   William, 56.
Webb, Thomas, 115.
Webster:
   John, 87.
   William, 103.
Wedderburne, Alexander, Lord Loughborough, 379, 394.
   letter from, 372.
Wederall, Robert son of John, 28.
Weg, Mr., 353.
Wekythyll, John, 73.
Welch, Mrs., indicted, 249.
Weld:
   Gascoigne, 124.
   James, of Sherringham, 142.
   Nathaniel, 127.
   Thomas, 127.
Welderen, Count and Countess de, 287, 379.
Wellingborough, Northamptonshire, 152.
   letter dated, 158.
Wellington (Willington) (Somersetshire), House of Correction at, 79.
Wells, William, 90.
Wells:
   Somersetshire, 79.
   juxta mare (Welles) (Norfolk), 110, 111.
   landowners in, 114.
Welsh, —, of Ludham Hall, 141.
Wembury (Devon), 85.

Wendenval or Wendeval:
  family, 4.
  Avelisa or Helvisa de, 4, 46, 48, 50.
  Sir Robert, 48, 50.
Wendlinge, William de, 16.
Wentworth:
  Charles Watson, 2nd Marquis of Rockingham, 256, 273, 277, 280, 281, 367.
  ——, his ministry, 256, 279.
  John, 99.
  Thomas, Earl of Strafford, 288.
  Viscount. See Noel.
Werkworth, Robert Fitz-Roger, Lord of, 11.
Werrington, donative of. 429, 430.
Werthe, Reyner de, chaplain, 16.
Wessel, T., Grand Treasurer of Polish Crown, 204.
West:
  Mr., 322.
  Sicilya, 88.
  Thomas, 54.
West Meon (Hants), 156.
Westaker, 18.
Westcote, Nicholas, 55.
Westfeld, 18.
Westminster: x., 257, 343.
  Duke Street, letters dated, 304, 339.
  election of 1750, 163.
  Hall, 161, 247, 248.
  Petty France, 89.
  Whitehall, letters dated, 89, 360.
Westmor, John, 91.
Westmorland, Lady, 338.
Westmoreland, Duke of (1663) (sic), 111.
Weston: 142.
  landowners in, 95.
Westport, Lord (1780). See Browne.
Westport House, letter dated, 419.
Westwinch, 73.
Weymouth, 360.
Weymouth, Lord. See Thynne.
Whalley, Edward, abbot of St. Mary, York, 57.
Whateley, Thomas, superseded as a secretary to the Treasury, 256.
  ——, letters from, 280, 283-284.
Wheler, Sir Francis, Captain R.N., 137.
Whipping of rogues to be conducted by advice of minister, &c., 80.
Whiteacre, Richard, 103.
White, James, 103.
White Mill, 122.
  Swan, Swaffham, 133.
Whitehall or Whytehall. See Westminster.
White's Club, 249.
  "young and old," 254.
Whiteacre, Richard, 103.
Whitlingham, swans at, 121.
Whittlesey, the king's acres in, 84.
Whitwell [Huuitewelle] (Norfolk), landowners in, 96.

Whitwell:
  Henry, 103.
  Richard de, 17.
  Sir William de, 42.
Whuell, Francis, commander, 140.
Wichingham, Bertrand de. See Witchingham.
Wickelingham (Whitlingham ?), 121.
Wickes, Rice, 92.
Wickham, Henry, commander, 139.
Wicklow, 345, 375.
  governor of, 340.
Wickmere (Wikemere, Wickmer, Wykmer), 46.
  landowners in, 105.
Wieburg, a Russian port, 233.
Wife, plaint against, of husband (Horsham), 7.
Wiggett or Wiggot:
  Edward, 97.
  Francis, 102.
  Roger, 125.
Wight, Isle of, 360.
Wighton (Wyton), 137, 144.
  landowners in, 116.
  vicarage, of, 431.
Wikemere. See Wickmere.
Wilbraham, Sir Thomas, 85.
Wild:
  Edward, 92.
  John, 91.
  Nicholas, 109.
Wildgos, Nicholas, 74.
Wildun, William, 25.
Wilkes [John], 174, 175, 179, 181, 182, 247-249.
  arrest of, 248.
  compared with D'Eon, 250.
  his duel with Martin, 247.
  essay on "Woman," 247, 249.
  and the North Briton, 247-249.
  outlawry of, 248, 253.
Wilkins, William, carver, 441.
Wilkinson, Thomas, will of, 29.
William, Roger son of, 19.
Willes, Chief Justice, 154, 157.
William:
  Archdeacon, the, 41.
  Bishop of Norwich. See Turbus.
  Chaplain, 46.
  the priest of Heletun, 10.
  Pistor, 40.
  priest of Tirniggos, 17.
  prior of Holy Trinity, Norwich, 40.
  son of Baldwin de Thaverham, 21.
  son of Ralph, 17.
  son of Roger, 19.
  son of Simon, 34.
William III., King, 192, 331.
Williams
  a leader in the Boston town meeting, 290.
  John, 29.
Williamsburg, Washington at, 402.
Willins, William, 441.
Willington. See Wellington.

Willis, Henry, 116.
Wilmington (North America), 387.
Wilna, 192.
    Palatin of. *See* Radziwill.
    tribunal of, 213, 214.
Wilson :
    Nicholas, 100.
    William, 101.
Wiltam, Peter, 37.
Wilton, Nicholas, 124.
Wiltshire, corn riots in, 271.
Winagh (Ireland), letter dated, 384.
Winchelsea, ship, 150.
Winchelsea, Earl of. *See* Finch.
Winchester :
    (Winton), 425.
    W., Bishop of. *See* Wainflete.
Winchester (ship), 150.
Windham *or* Wyndham, 353.
    Ash, 141.
    Charles, 2nd Earl of Egremont,
      his death, 177.
    Francis, 132.
    Sir George, of Cromer, 97.
    John, of Felbrigge, 100.
    Thomas, letter from, 87.
    William, 123, 125.
    and Norfolk politics, x., xi.
Windsor Castle, H.M.S., 138.
Winne, Robert, 114.
Winnington, T., 148.
Winpou, William de, 13.
Winterton *or* Wynterton, Norfolk,
    54.
Winton. *See* Winchester.
Wisbeach, 129.
Wise, Edmund, 87.
Wiseman :
    Robert, Captain R.N., 138.
    Sir William, 287.
Witchingham (Wychingham) :
    Bertrand de, 13, 15.
    Sir William de, 43.
Witchingham, Great, xiii.
    ——, landowners in, 96.
    Little, *ibid*, 97.
Witham, deed relating to, 71.
Withers, Robert, 98.
Witton, Wytton : 71, 72, 74.
    Richard de, 16.
Wiveton, 144.
Wlviva de Iteringham, the Lady,
    49.
Woburn (Bedfordshire), 277, 279, 280.
Wodehouse. *See* Woodhouse.
Wodeman, John, 25.
Wodrow, Henry, 109.
Wodziecki M., Bishop of Przemysl,
    204.
Woide, M., Charles Godfrey, envoy
    of the dissident nobility in Poland,
    letter from, 221.
Wolcy. *See* Wolsey.
Wollowiez, nuncio of Sloninola, 195.
Wolodkowitz, 213, 214.

Wolsey, Woolsey, Wolcy :
    Bridget, of Ingworth, 104.
    Rev. M., 327.
    John, of Thwayt, 105.
    Thomas, of Erpingham, 103.
    William, 20.
Wolterton (Woltertone), landowners
    in, 105.
Wolterton, Roger de, 24, 49.
Wolton, Mr., 111.
Wood :
    Robert, 124.
    Thomas, 142.
Wood Dalling *or* Dawling, land-
    owners in, 96.
    manor roll of, 70.
    non-jurors in, 144.
Wood Norton (Norfolk), landowners
    in, 96.
    Priory lands in, 73.
Wood Rising, 144.
Woodford, Rev. Matthew, letter
    from, 276.
Woodford (Essex), 252.
Woodhouse *or* Wodehouse :
    Edmund, 133, 137, 141-142.
    Edward, 127.
    Francis, 63.
    John, 74.
    Philip, 123, 125.
    Roger, 63.
    Sir Thomas, 56, 74.
Woodrow, John, 100.
Woods :
    ——, 243.
    Thomas, 141.
Woodton, 141, 145.
Woodward :
    Dr. Richard, Dean of St. Ma-
      cartin Clogher, and Bishop of
      Cloyne (1781), 379, 432.
    ——, letters to, 405, 413, 420.
    ——, letters from, 379, 410,
      419, 421, 424-426, 428, 430,
      431, 442.
    ——, his book on Ireland, 432.
    ——, "a Napper Tandy in
      Lawn," 385.
    Mr., 153.
    ——, at Covent Garden, 179.
Wool trade in relation to Ireland,
    306, 331.
Wooler, William, 129.
Woolsey. *See* Wolsey.
Woolwich, H.M.S., 139.
Worcester, 241.
Woronzow :
    Count, Grand Chancellor of
      Russia, 207, 208.
    Alexander Romanovitch, Rus-
      sian Ambassador to St. James',
      171, 177, 178, 182.
Worsley :
    Edward, 109.
    R., 378.
    Sir Richard, 378.

Wortes *or* Worts :
  John, 97.
  Richard, 99.
  William, 99, 107.
  W., 125.
Wortley, James, 115.
Wotelond, 41.
Wotton (*sic*) (Norfolk), 52.
Wotton (Buckinghamshire), 256, 263,
    264, 277-280, 285, 288.
  letters dated, 244, 261, 263-265,
    272, 277, 285, 287.
Wotton :
  John, 44.
  Thomas, of Waborne, 107.
Wrantham, Simon, clerk, 42.
Wrchipe, Thomas, 24.
Wright :
  Captain Charles, 142, 145.
  Thomas, 105, 133, 144.
  William, commander, 140.
Wrongrey, Robert, 126.
Wrotham Park, letter dated, 367.
Wroughton, Thomas, 192, 195.
  British envoy to Elector of
    Saxony, xv.
  resident at Warsaw, xvi., 209.
  letters from, 195, 197, 209, 212,
    216, 218, 219.
Wychingham, William de. *See*
  Witchingham.
Wydo, *rector ecclesiæ de* Corpesti,
  18.
Wygate, 17.
Wykmere. *See* Wickmere.
Wylles, Dennis, 60.
Wymondham, 5, 63-66, 80, 130, 145.
  abuttal of lands in, 65.
  Barnak, Calthorp, Crunquelle,
    Cromuell, Cromwell *or* Crom-
    welle, Gresaugh, Greisheighe,
    Grisaugh *or* Grysheigh, Gun-
    vile, Rusteyns, Sutton, Nor-
    ton, Silfield, Wattlefield
    Knyvetts, *and* Grisaugh
    Knyvetts, manors in, 63-65.
  common rights at, 65.
  leet jury of, 80.
  Regis, 63.
  Rentals, extents and custom-
    aries for, 64-65.
  (Windham) school, master of,
    87.
Wyndham. *See* Windham.
Wyngfield, Sir Robert, 56.
Wyniston, John de, 18.
Wynter : 122.
  Alienora, 53, 55.
  Edmund, 53, 54.
  John, 52-53.
  Robert, 53, 73.
  William, 52.
Wynterton. *See* Winterton.
Wyth, Richard, 132.
Wytlok, Thomas, 24.
Wyton. *See* Wighton.
Wytton. *See* Witton.

Y

Yallop :
  Charles, 142, 145.
  Giles, 142, 145.
  Robert, 98.
  Sir Robert, 142.
Yardley, 155.
Yarke (on the Caspian), 235.
Yarmouth, Great (Yernemouth *or*
  Yarmuth), 54, 60, 74, 141, 142, 147,
  353.
Yarmouth :
  Henry de, 22.
  Lady. *See* Walmoden.
  Lord. *See* Paston.
Yates, Mrs., at Drury Lane, 179.
Yaxley :
  Richard, 107.
  Robert, 101.
  Samuel, 107.
  Walter, of Hevingham, 31.
Yelverton : 4.
  Barry, M.P. for Carrickfergus,
    400, 412, 415.
  ——, Attorney - General, 425,
    426.
  Ela wife of Sir William de, 56.
  Henry, Earl of Sussex, letter
    from, 164.
  John de, 52, 53.
  Margaret de, 52.
  William, 43, 55, 440.
  William, Justice C.P., 54, 55, 56.
Yernemouth (*or* Yermuth), Great.
  See Yarmouth.
Yevele, Henry, of Southwark, 55.
Ynglose. *See* Inglose.
Yvinus de Sudgate de Hegletune et
  Isabella, grant of, to priory of
  St. Faith's, 18.
Yonge. *See* Young.
York :
  Edward Augustus, Duke of, 253.
  John, Cardinal Archbishop of.
    See Kemp.
  William, Archbishop of. *See*
    Markham.
York :
  Abbey of St. Mary's at, 57.
  Colonial forces at, 296.
  Island, 397.
York :
  New, 300, 311, 326, 369, 398,
    400, 401.
  ——, letters dated, 401, 409, 411.
  River, 399, 401.
  town, 402.
  ——, siege of, 407, 410.
  ——, letters dated, 411.
York, ship, 138, 150.

2 K

Yorke :
    Hon. Charles, Attorney General,
        245, 442.
    Mr., 253.
    Sir Joseph, Ambassador at the
        Hague, 177, 221, 292, 295,
        312, 369.
    ——, his review of situation in
        1773, 292, 293.
    Philip, 1st Earl of Hardwicke,
        148.
    ——, as Lord Chancellor, 157,
        158.
    Philip, Lord Royston, 245.
    ——, and 2nd Earl, letters from,
        177, 292, 295, 311, 379.
    ——, his review of situation in
        1777, 311.
Yorkshire, 150, 178, 238.

Young, Yonge or Yongue :
    [Captain], 139.
    Philip, Bishop of Norwich, 287,
        344.
    Samuel, 141, 145.
    William, 148.
    Sir William, 160.
Youngman, Thomas, 106, 111.
Yve, Robert, 8.

Z

Zamoycki, Palatin of Inowraclaw,
    193.
Zartoryski. See Czartoryski.

CIRCULAR OF THE COMMISSION.

HISTORICAL MANUSCRIPTS COMMISSION.

PUBLIC RECORD OFFICE,
CHANCERY LANE,
LONDON, W.C.

HIS MAJESTY THE KING has been pleased to ratify and confirm the terms of the Commission issued by Her late Majesty, appointing certain Commissioners to ascertain what unpublished MSS. are extant in the collections of private persons and in institutions which are calculated to throw light upon subjects connected with the Civil, Ecclesiastical, Literary, or Scientific History of this country; and to appoint certain additional Commissioners for the same purposes. The present Commissioners are:—

> Sir R. Henn Collins, Master of the Rolls; the Marquess of Ripon, K.G., the Earl of Crawford, K.T., the Earl of Rosebery, K.G., the Earl of Dartmouth, Lord Edmond Fitzmaurice, M.P., Lord Alverstone, G.C.M.G., Lord Hawkesbury, Lord Lindley, Lord Stanmore, G.C.M.G., Sir Edward Fry, Mr. John Morley, O.M., M.P., Sir H. C. Maxwell-Lyte, K.C.B., and Prof. C. H. Firth, LL.D.

The Commissioners think it probable that you may feel an interest in this object, and be willing to assist in the attainment of it; and with that view they desire to lay before you an outline of the course which they usually follow.

If any nobleman or gentleman express his willingness to submit any unprinted book, or collection of documents in his possession or custody, to the Commissioners, they will cause an inspection to be made by some competent person, and should the MSS. appear to come within the scope of their enquiry, the owner will be asked to consent to the publication of copies or abstracts of them in the reports of the Commission, which are presented to Parliament every Session.

To avoid any possible apprehension that the examination of papers by the Commissioners may extend to title-deeds or other documents of present legal value, positive instructions are given to every person who inspects MSS. on their behalf that nothing relating to the titles of existing owners is to be divulged, and that if in the course of his work any modern title-deeds or papers of a private character chance to come before him, they are to be instantly put aside, and are not to be examined or calendared under any pretence whatever.

The object of the Commission is the discovery of unpublished historical and literary materials, and in all their proceedings the Commissioners will direct their attention to that object exclusively.

In practice it has been found more satisfactory, when the collection of manuscripts is a large one, for the inspector to make a selection therefrom at the place of deposit and to obtain the owner's consent to remove the selected papers to the Public Record Office in London or in Dublin, or to the General Register House in Edinburgh, where they can be more fully dealt with, and where they are preserved with the same care as if they formed part of the muniments of the realm, during the term of their examination. Among the numerous owners of MSS. who have allowed their family papers of historical interest to be temporarily removed from their muniment rooms and lent to the Commissioners to facilitate the preparation of a report may be named :—His Majesty the King, the Duke of Rutland, the Duke of Portland, the Marquess of Salisbury, the Marquess Townshend, the Marquess of Ailesbury, the Marquess of Bath, the Earl of Dartmouth, the Earl of Carlisle, the Earl of Egmont, the Earl of Lindsey, the Earl of Ancaster, the Earl of Lonsdale, Lord Braye, Lord Hothfield, Lord Kenyon, Mrs. Stopford Sackville, the Right Hon. F. J. Savile Foljambe, Sir George Wombwell, Mr. le Fleming, of Rydal, Mr. Leyborne Popham, of Littlecote, and Mr. Fortescue, of Dropmore.

The cost of inspections, reports, and calendars, and the conveyance of documents, will be defrayed at the public expense, without any charge to the owners.

The Commissioners will also, if so requested, give their advice as to the best means of repairing and preserving any interesting papers or MSS. which may be in a state of decay.

The Commissioners will feel much obliged if you will communicate to them the names of any gentlemen who may be able and willing to assist in obtaining the objects for which this Commission has been issued.

R. A. ROBERTS, *Secretary.*

HISTORICAL MANUSCRIPTS COMMISSION.

REPORTS OF THE ROYAL COMMISSIONERS APPOINTED TO INQUIRE WHAT PAPERS AND MANUSCRIPTS BELONGING TO PRIVATE FAMILIES AND INSTITUTIONS ARE EXTANT WHICH WOULD BE OF UTILITY IN THE ILLUSTRATION OF HISTORY, CONSTITUTIONAL LAW, SCIENCE, AND GENERAL LITERATURE.

Date.	—	Size	Sessional No.	Price.
				s. d.
1870 (Re-printed 1874.)	FIRST REPORT, WITH APPENDIX - - Contents :- - ENGLAND. House of Lords; Cambridge Colleges; Abingdon and other Corporations, &c. SCOTLAND. Advocates' Library, Glasgow Corporation, &c. IRELAND. Dublin, Cork, and other Corporations, &c.	f'cap	[C. 55]	1 6
1871	SECOND REPORT WITH APPENDIX AND INDEX TO THE FIRST AND SECOND REPORTS - - - - - Contents :— ENGLAND. House of Lords; Cambridge Colleges; Oxford Colleges; Monastery of Dominican Friars at Woodchester, Duke of Bedford, Earl Spencer, &c. SCOTLAND. Aberdeen and St. Andrew's Universities, &c. IRELAND. Marquis of Ormonde; Dr. Lyons, &c.	,,	[C. 441]	3 10
1872 (Re-printed 1895.)	THIRD REPORT WITH APPENDIX AND INDEX - - - - - Contents :— ENGLAND. House of Lords; Cambridge Colleges; Stonyhurst College; Bridgwater and other Corporations; Duke of Northumberland, Marquis of Lansdowne, Marquis of Bath, &c. SCOTLAND. University of Glasgow Duke of Montrose, &c. IRELAND. Marquis of Ormonde; Black Book of Limerick, &c.	,,	[C. 673]	6 0
1873	FOURTH REPORT, WITH APPENDIX. PART I. - - - - Contents :— ENGLAND. House of Lords. Westminster Abbey; Cambridge and Oxford Colleges; Cinque Ports, Hythe, and other Corporations, Marquis of Bath, Earl of Denbigh, &c. SCOTLAND. Duke of Argyll, &c. IRELAND. Trinity College, Dublin; Marquis of Ormonde.	,,	[C. 857]	6 8

Date.	—	Size.	Sessional No.	Price.
				s. d.
1873	FOURTH REPORT. PART II. INDEX - -	f'cap	[C. 857 i.]	2 6
1876	FIFTH REPORT, WITH APPENDIX. PART I. - Contents :— ENGLAND. House of Lords ; Oxford and Cambridge Colleges; Dean and Chapter of Canterbury ; Rye, Lydd, and other Corporations. Duke of Sutherland, Marquis of Lansdowne, Reginald Cholmondeley, Esq., &c. SCOTLAND. Earl of Aberdeen, &c.	,,	[C.1432]	7 0
,,	DITTO. PART II. INDEX - - -	,,	[C.1432 i.]	3 6
1877	SIXTH REPORT, WITH APPENDIX. PART I. - Contents : – ENGLAND. House of Lords : Oxford and Cambridge Colleges ; Lambeth Palace ; Black Book of the Archdeacon of Canterbury ; Bridport, Wallingford, and other Corporations ; Lord Leconfield, Sir Reginald Graham, Sir Henry Ingilby, &c. SCOTLAND. Duke of Argyll, Earl of Moray, &c. IRELAND. Marquis of Ormonde.	,,	[C.1745]	8 6
(Reprinted 1893.)	DITTO. PART II. INDEX - - -	,,	[C.2102]	1 10
1879 (Reprinted 1895.)	SEVENTH REPORT, WITH APPENDIX. PART I. Contents :— House of Lords ; County of Somerset ; Earl of Egmont, Sir Frederick Graham, Sir Harry Verney, &c.	,,	[C.2340]	7 6
(Reprinted 1895.)	DITTO. PART II. APPENDIX AND INDEX - Contents :— Duke of Athole, Marquis of Ormonde, S. F. Livingstone, Esq., &c.	,,	[C. 2340 i.]	3 6
1881	EIGHTH REPORT, WITH APPENDIX AND INDEX. PART I. Contents :— List of collections examined, 1869-1880. ENGLAND. House of Lords ; Duke of Marlborough; Magdalen College, Oxford; Royal College of Physicians; Queen Anne's Bounty Office ; Corporations of Chester, Leicester, &c. IRELAND. Marquis of Ormonde, Lord Emly, The O'Conor Don, Trinity College, Dublin, &c.	,,	[C.3040]	[Out of print.]
1881	DITTO. PART II. APPENDIX AND INDEX - Contents :— Duke of Manchester.	,,	[C. 3040 i.]	[Out of print.]
1881	DITTO. PART III. APPENDIX AND INDEX - Contents :— Earl of Ashburnham.	,,	[C. 3040 ii.]	[Out of print.]

Date.	—	Size.	Sessional No.	Price.
				s. d.
1883 (Re-printed 1895.)	NINTH REPORT, WITH APPENDIX AND INDEX. PART I. - - - - - Contents :— St. Paul's and Canterbury Cathedrals; Eton College; Carlisle, Yarmouth, Canterbury, and Barnstaple Corporations, &c.	f'cap	[C.3773]	5 2
1884 (Re-printed 1895.)	DITTO. PART II. APPENDIX AND INDEX - Contents :— ENGLAND. House of Lords. Earl of Leicester ; C. Pole Gell, Alfred Morrison, Esqs., &c. SCOTLAND. Lord Elphinstone, H. C. Maxwell Stuart, Esq., &c. IRELAND. Duke of Leinster, Marquis of Drogheda, &c.	,,	[C.3773 i.]	6 3
1884	DITTO. PART III. APPENDIX AND INDEX - - - - Contents :— Mrs. Stopford Sackville [re-issued, revised and extended as [Cd. 1892].	,,	[C. 3773 ii.]	[Out of print.]
1883 (Re-printed 1895.)	CALENDAR OF THE MANUSCRIPTS OF THE MARQUIS OF SALISBURY, K.G. (or CECIL MSS.). PART I. 1306-1571. -	8vo.	[C.3777]	3 5
1888	DITTO. PART II. 1572-1582. -	,,	[C.5463]	3 5
1889	DITTO. PART III. 1583-1589. -	,,	[C.5889 v.]	2 1
1892	DITTO. PART IV. 1590-1594. -	,,	[C.6823]	2 11
1894	DITTO. PART V. 1594-1596. -	,,	[C.7574]	2 6
1896	DITTO. PART VI. 1596. -	,,	[C.7884]	2 8
1899	DITTO. PART VII. 1597. -	,,	[C.9246]	2 8
1899	DITTO. PART VIII. 1598. -	,,	[C.9467]	2 8
1902	DITTO. PART IX. 1599. -	,,	[Cd.928]	2 3
1904	DITTO. PART X. 1600. -	,,	[Cd.2052]	2 3
1885	TENTH REPORT - - - - This is introductory to the following :—	,	[C.4548]	[Out of print.]
1885 (Re-printed 1895.)	(1.) APPENDIX AND INDEX - - - Earl of Eglinton, Sir J. S. Maxwell, Bart., and C. S. H. D. Moray, C. F. Weston Underwood, G. W. Digby, Esqs.	,,	[C.4575]	3 7
1885	(2.) APPENDIX AND INDEX - - - The Family of Gawdy.	,,	[C.4576 iii.]	1 4
1885	(3.) APPENDIX AND INDEX - - - Wells Cathedral.	,,	[C.4576 ii.]	[Out of print.]
1885	(4.) APPENDIX AND INDEX - - - Earl of Westmorland ; Capt. Stewart; Lord Stafford ; Sir N. W. Throckmorton ; Sir P. T. Mainwaring, Lord Muncaster, M.P., Capt. J. F. Bagot, Earl of Kilmorey, Earl of Powis, and others, the Corporations of Kendal, Wenlock, Bridgnorth, Eye, Plymouth, and the County of Essex ; and Stonyhurst College.	,,	[C.4576]	[Out of print.]
1885 (Re-printed 1895.)	(5.) APPENDIX AND INDEX - - - Marquis of Ormonde, Earl of Fingall, Corporations of Galway, Waterford, the Sees of Dublin and Ossory, the Jesuits in Ireland.	,,	[4576 i.]	2 10

Date.	—	Size.	Sessional No.	Price.
				s. d.
1887	(6.) APPENDIX AND INDEX - - - Marquis of Abergavenny; Lord Braye; G. F. Luttrell; P. P. Bouverie; W. Bromley Davenport; R. T. Balfour, Esquires.	8vo.	[C.5242]	1 7
1887	ELEVENTH REPORT - - This is introductory to the following :—	,,	[C.5060 vi.]	0 3
1887	(1.) APPENDIX AND INDEX - - - H. D. Skrine, Esq., Salvetti Correspondence.	,,	[C.5060]	1 1
1887	(2.) APPENDIX AND INDEX - - - House of Lords. 1678-1688.	,,	[C.5060 i.]	2 0
1887	(3.) APPENDIX AND INDEX - - - Corporations of Southampton and Lynn.	,,	[C.5060 ii.]	1 8
1887	(4.) APPENDIX AND INDEX - - - Marquess Townshend.	,,	[C.5060 iii.]	2 6
1887	(5.) APPENDIX AND INDEX - - - Earl of Dartmouth.	,,	[C.5060 iv.]	2 8
1887	(6.) APPENDIX AND INDEX - - - Duke of Hamilton.	,,	[C.5060 v.]	1 6
1888	(7.) APPENDIX AND INDEX - - - Duke of Leeds, Marchioness of Waterford, Lord Hothfield, &c.; Bridgwater Trust Office, Reading Corporation, Inner Temple Library.	,,	[C.5612]	2 0
1890	TWELFTH REPORT - - - - This is introductory to the following :—	,,	[C.5889]	0 3
1888	(1.) APPENDIX - - - - Earl Cowper, K.G. (Coke MSS., at Melbourne Hall, Derby). Vol. I.	,,	[C.5472]	2 7
1888	(2.) APPENDIX - - - - Ditto. Vol. II	,,	[C.5613]	2 5
1889	(3.) APPENDIX AND INDEX - - - Ditto. Vol. III.	,,	[C.5889 i.]	1 4
1888	(4. APPENDIX - - - Duke of Rutland, G.C.B. Vol. I.	,,	[C.5614]	[Out of print.]
1891	(5.) APPENDIX AND INDEX - - - Ditto. Vol. II.	,,	[C.5889 ii.]	2 0
1889	(6.) APPENDIX AND INDEX - - - House of Lords, 1689-1690.	,,	[C.5889 iii.]	2 1
1890	(7.) APPENDIX AND INDEX - - - S. H. le Fleming, Esq., of Rydal.	,,	[C.5889 iv.]	1 11
1891	(8.) APPENDIX AND INDEX - - - Duke of Athole, K.T., and Earl of Home.	,,	[C.6338]	1 0
1891	(9.) APPENDIX AND INDEX - - - Duke of Beaufort, K.G., Earl of Donoughmore, J. H. Gurney, W. W. B. Hulton, R. W. Ketton, G. A. Aitken, P. V. Smith, Esqs.; Bishop of Ely; Cathedrals of Ely, Gloucester, Lincoln, and Peterborough, Corporations of Gloucester, Higham Ferrers, and Newark; Southwell Minster; Lincoln District Registry.	,,	[C.6338 i.]	2 6

Date.	—	Size.	Sessional No.	Price.
				s. d.
1891	(10.) APPENDIX - - - - - The First Earl of Charlemont. Vol. I.	8vo.	[C. 6338 ii.]	1 11
1892	THIRTEENTH REPORT - - - - - This is introductory to the following:—	,,	[C.6827]	0 8
1891	(1.) APPENDIX - - - - - Duke of Portland. Vol. I.	,,	[C.6474]	3 0
	(2.) APPENDIX AND INDEX. Ditto. Vol. II. - - - -	,,	[C. 6827 i.]	2 0
1892	(3.) APPENDIX. J. B. Fortescue, Esq., of Dropmore. Vol. I. - - - - -	,,	[C.6660]	2 7
1892	(4.) APPENDIX AND INDEX - - - Corporations of Rye, Hastings, and Hereford. Capt. F. C. Loder-Symonds, E. R. Wodehouse, M.P., J. Dovaston, Esqs., Sir T. B. Lennard, Bart., Rev. W. D. Macray, and Earl of Dartmouth (Supplementary Report).	,,	[C.6810]	2 4
1892	(5.) APPENDIX AND INDEX. House of Lords, 1690-1691 - - -	,,	[C.6822]	2 4
1893	(6.) APPENDIX AND INDEX. Sir W. Fitzherbert, Bart.; The Delaval Family, of Seaton Delaval; Earl of Ancaster; and Gen. Lyttelton-Annesley.	,,	[C.7166]	1 4
1893	(7.) APPENDIX AND INDEX. Earl of Lonsdale - - - - -	,,	[C.7241]	1 3
1893	(8.) APPENDIX AND INDEX. The First Earl of Charlemont. Vol. II.	,,	[C.7424]	1 11
1896	FOURTEENTH REPORT - - - - This is introductory to the following:—	,,	[C.7983]	0 8
1894	(1.) APPENDIX AND INDEX. Duke of Rutland, G.C.B. Vol. III. -	,,	[C.7476]	1 11
1894	(2.) APPENDIX. Duke of Portland. Vol. III. - -	,,	[C.7569]	2 8
1894	(3.) APPENDIX AND INDEX. Duke of Roxburghe; Sir H. H. Campbell, Bart.; Earl of Strathmore; and Countess Dowager of Seafield.	,,	[C.7570]	1 2
1894	(4.) APPENDIX AND INDEX. Lord Kenyon - - - - -	,,	[C.7571]	2 10
1896	(5.) APPENDIX. J. B. Fortescue, Esq., of Dropmore. Vol. II.	,,	[C.7572]	2 8
1895	(6.) APPENDIX AND INDEX. House of Lords, 1692-1693 - - -	,,	[C.7573]	1 11
	(*Manuscripts of the House of Lords, 1693-1695, Vol. I. (New Series.) See H.L. No. 5 of 1900. Price 2/9). Ditto. 1695-1697. Vol. II. See H.L. No. 18. 1903. Price 2/9.*			
1895	(7) APPENDIX. Marquis of Ormonde - - - -	,,	[C.7678]	1 10

2 L

Date.	—	Size.	Sessional No.	Price.
				s. d.
1895	(8.) APPENDIX AND INDEX. Lincoln, Bury St. Edmunds, Hertford, and Great Grimsby Corporations; The Dean and Chapter of Worcester, and of Lichfield; The Bishop's Registry of Worcester.	8vo.	[C.7881]	1 5
1896	(9.) APPENDIX AND INDEX. Earl of Buckinghamshire; Earl of Lindsey; Earl of Onslow; Lord Emly; T. J. Hare, Esq.; and J. Round, Esq., M.P.	,,	[C.7882]	2 6
1895	(10.) APPENDIX AND INDEX. Earl of Dartmouth. Vol. II. American Papers.	,,	[C.7883]	2 9
1899	FIFTEENTH REPORT - - - - - This is introductory to the following :—	,,	[C.9295]	0 4
1896	(1.) APPENDIX AND INDEX. Earl of Dartmouth. Vol. III. - -	,,	[C.8156]	1 5
1897	(2.) APPENDIX. J. Eliot Hodgkin, Esq. - - -	,,	[C.8327]	1 8
1897	(3.) APPENDIX AND INDEX. Charles Haliday, Esq., of Dublin; Acts of the Privy Council in Ireland, 1556-1571; Sir William Ussher's Table to the Council Book; Table to the Red Council Book.	,,	[C.8364]	1 4
1897	(4.) APPENDIX. Duke of Portland. Vol. IV. - -	,,	[C.8497]	2 11
1897	(5.) APPENDIX AND INDEX. The Right Hon. F. J. Savile Foljambe -	,,	[C.8550]	0 10
1897	(6.) APPENDIX AND INDEX. Earl of Carlisle, Castle Howard -	,,	[C.8551]	3 6
1897	(7.) APPENDIX AND INDEX. Duke of Somerset; Marquis of Ailesbury; and Sir F.G. Puleston, Bart.	,,	[C.8552]	1 9
1897	(8.) APPENDIX AND INDEX. Duke of Buccleuch and Queensberry, at Drumlanrig. Vol. I.	,,	[C.8553]	1 4
1897	(9.) APPENDIX AND INDEX. J. J. Hope Johnstone, Esq., of Annandale	,,	[C.8554]	1 0
1899	(10.) Shrewsbury and Coventry Corporations; Sir H. O. Corbet, Bart., Earl of Radnor, P.T. Tillard; J. R. Carr-Ellison; Andrew Kingsmill, Esqrs.	,,	[C.9472]	1 0
1898	MANUSCRIPTS IN THE WELSH LANGUAGE. Vol. I.—Lord Mostyn, at Mostyn Hall.	,,	[C.8829]	1 4
1899	Vol. I. Part II.—W. R. M. Wynne, Esq. of Peniarth.	..	[C.9468]	2 11
1905	Vol. I. Part III.—Peniarth. Sir T. Wiliams; John Jones; Robert Vaughan.	.,	[Cd.2443]	0 8
1902	Vol. II. Part I.—Jesus College, Oxford; Free Library, Cardiff; Havod; Wrexham; Llanwrin; Merthyr; Aberdâr.	,,	[Cd.1100]	1 9
1903	Vol. II. Part II.—Plas Llan Stephan; Free Library, Cardiff.	,,	[Cd.1692]	1 8
1905	Vol. II. Part III.—Panton; Cwrtmawr.	,,	[Cd.2444]	0 8

Date.	—	Size.	Sessional No.	Price.
				s. d.
1899	Manuscripts of the Duke of Buccleuch and Queensberry, K.G., K.T., at Montagu House, Whitehall. Vol. I.	8vo.	[C.9244]	2 7
1903	Ditto. Vol. II. (Part I.) - - -	..	[Cd.930]	1 10
1903	Ditto. Vol. II. (Part II.) - - -	.,	[Cd.930-i]	1 11
1903	Ditto at Drumlanrig Castle. Vol. II. -	,.	[Cd.1827]	1 1
1899	Ditto Marquess of Ormonde, K.P., at Kilkenny Castle. Vol. II.	,,	[C.9245]	2 0
1902	Ditto. New Series. Vol. I. - -	,.	[Cd.929]	1 7
1903	Ditto. Vol. II. - - - -	,,	[Cd.1691]	1 10
1904	Ditto. Vol. III. - - - -	,.	[Cd.1963]	2 0
1904	Ditto Mrs.Stopford-Sackville. Vol. I. -	,,	[Cd.1892]	1 10
1899	Ditto Duke of Portland, K.G. Vol. V. -	,,	[C.9466]	2 9
1901	Ditto. Vol. VI., with Index to Vols. III.-VI.	,,	[Cd.676]	1 9
1901	Ditto. Vol. VII. - - - -	,,	[Cd.783]	2 3
1899	Ditto J. M. Heathcote, Esq. - -	.,	[C.9469]	1 3
1899	Ditto J. B. Fortescue, Esq., of Dropmore. Vol. III.	,,	[C.9470]	3 1
1899	Ditto F. W. Leyborne-Popham, Esq. -	,,	[C.9471]	1 6
1900	Ditto Mrs. Frankland-Russell-Astley -	. ,,	[Cd.282]	2 0
1900	Ditto Lord Montagu of Beaulieu - -	,,	[Cd.283]	1 1
1900	Ditto Beverley Corporation - - -	,,	[Cd.284]	1 0
1901	Ditto Various Collections. Vol. I. - Corporations of Berwick-on-Tweed, Burford and Lostwithiel; the Counties of Wilts and Worcester; the Bishop of Chichester; and the Dean and Chapters of Chichester, Canterbury and Salisbury.	,,	[Cd.784]	2 0
1903	Ditto. Vol. II. - - - - Sir Geo. Wombwell; the Duke of Norfolk; Lord Edmund Talbot (the Shrewsbury papers); Miss Buxton, Mrs. Harford and Mrs. Wentworth of Woolley.	.,	[Cd.932]	2 4
1904	Ditto. Vol III. - - - - T. B. Clarke-Thornhill, Esq.; Sir T. Barrett-Lennard, Bart.; Pelham R. Papillon, Esq.; W. Cleverly Alexander, Esq.	,,	[Cd.1964]	1 6
1902	Calendar of the Stuart Manuscripts at Windsor Castle, belonging to His Majesty the King. Vol. I.	,,	[Cd.927]	2 11
1904	Ditto. Vol. II. - - - -	,,	[Cd.2189]	. 2 9
1902	Manuscripts Colonel David Milne-Home of Wedderburn Castle, N.B.	,,	[Cd.931]	1 4

Date.	—	Size.	Sessional No.	Price.	
				s.	*d.*
1904	Manuscripts Marquess of Bath at Longleat, Wiltshire. Vol. I.	8vo.	[Cd.2048]	1	9
1904	American Manuscripts in the Royal Institution of Great Britain. Vol. I.	,,	[Cd.2201]	2	3
1904	SIXTEENTH REPORT (containing a list of the owners of Manuscripts upon whose collections Reports have been made to July, 1904).	,,	[Cd.2209]	0	9
1904	Manuscripts of the Earl of Mar and Kellie at Alloa House, N.B.	,,	[Cd.2190]	2	7
1905	Ditto J. B. Fortescue, Esq., of Dropmore. Vol. IV.	,,	[Cd.2233]	2	6
1905	Ditto Lady Du Cane	,,	[Cd.2367]	2	6
1905	Ditto Marquess of Lothian, at Blickling Hall.	,,	[Cd.2319]	2	2
	Ditto Dean and Chapter of Wells	,,		[*In the press.*]	
	Ditto Marquess of Ormonde. New Series. Vol. IV.	,,		[*In the press.*]	
	Ditto Earl of Verulam	,,		[*In the press.*]	
	Ditto Earl of Egmont. Vol. I.	,,		[*In the press.*]	
	Ditto. Ditto. Vol. I. Part II.	,,		[*In the press.*]	

HISTORICAL MANUSCRIPTS COMMISSION.

THE

M A N U S C R I P T S

OF

J. M. HEATHCOTE, Esq.,

CONINGTON CASTLE.

Presented to both Houses of Parliament by Command of Her Majesty.

NORWICH:

PRINTED FOR HER MAJESTY'S STATIONERY OFFICE,

BY THE "NORFOLK CHRONICLE" COMPANY, LTD.

And to be purchased, either directly or through any Bookseller, from
EYRE AND SPOTTISWOODE, EAST HARDING STREET, FLEET STREET, E.C., AND
32, ABINGDON STREET, WESTMINSTER, S.W.; or
JOHN MENZIES & Co., 12, HANOVER STREET, EDINBURGH; and
90, WEST NILE STREET, GLASGOW; or
HODGES, FIGGIS, & CO., LIMITED, 104, GRAFTON STREET, DUBLIN.

1899.

[C.—9469.]   Price 1s. 3d.

INTRODUCTION.

THE collection reported on in this volume consists almost entirely of the correspondence of Sir Richard Fanshaw, Bart., ambassador from Charles II. to the Courts of Portugal and Spain. The papers mostly belong to the years of his embassies, *i.e.*, 1661-1666, and throw much light upon the relations of England with the Peninsula and especially upon the history of the little English army there, sent out under the Earl of Inchiquin, and afterwards commanded by Count Schonberg.* They are rendered additionally valuable by the fact that they form a companion series to the Spanish, Portuguese and Tangier correspondence at the Public Record Office and to Vol. 7,010 of the Harley MSS. at the British Museum. Fanshaw usually kept the drafts of his letters, and there is also an excellent letter-book for the period of the Portugal embassy, so that the collection is much richer in "out" letters than is often the case. This is particularly fortunate, as the letters actually sent are in very many cases missing from the Foreign Office papers.

The later part of the collection, relating to the embassy to Spain, is by no means so complete, there being very little purely diplomatic correspondence found in it, but although separated from the other papers, this correspondence is not lost. The letters from January, 1664, to February, 1665, are printed in the volume of "*Original Letters of his Excellency Sir Richard Fanshaw*," published in 1702, whilst those of a later date are to be found in the Harley volume at the British Museum, mentioned above, having been apparently selected with the idea of forming a second series.

The Calendar opens with the instructions given by Charles I. to Fanshaw as his ambassador to Spain [*p.* 1], signed by the King on October 9th, 1647, just after he had been allowed to gather his Council round him for the last time. There is a pathetic ring about this—perhaps one of the last diplomatic acts of the King. No funds were forthcoming for the enter-

---

* This is his own spelling of his name.

tainment of the ambassador from his Majesty of England, and the means proposed for his maintenance were only the proceeds of some fish sent over to Bilbao from Ireland in Lord Strafford's time. A month later the King fled to Carisbrooke, and although Fanshaw went abroad and his wife mentions in her "*Memoirs*" his credentials to Spain, he did not go further than France.

Two years later Fanshaw again received "instructions" to repair to Spain [*p.* 3]—this time at the bidding of the young King, now at St. Germain's—to meet Hyde and Cottington, "ambassadors extraordinary" there. He went accordingly, but in July the ambassadors extraordinary wrote that he had pressing occasions to return to England, and they saw no use in keeping him any longer; that nothing could be got from Spain but good words and professions, nor was anything else like to be got, the Spaniards finding "their own necessities every day increasing upon them, and putting them to all the shifts imaginable to furnish themselves with ready money" [*p.* 4].

The King was now in Scotland, and Hyde and Cottington were anxiously waiting for news of his reception there. A little later his sister Mary, Princess of Orange, writes to him about her portion money, and the Duke of York asks for his directions [*pp.* 4, 5], and is, as his godmother, the Queen of Bohemia, assures the King "most truly obedient and affectionate" to his brother [*p.* 6]. The Queen also sends her nephew scraps of news from foreign parts. The German Princes and deputies assembled at Frankfurt have "congratulated his crowning," the Duke of Würtemberg has burned the book in which Dr. Seifrid of Tübingen declared the late King's murder lawful, and has gone near to burning the Professor also, and her son "Ned" has been calling the "pretended ambassadors" from England to the Hague by their true names. All these letters are holograph.

One more trace of Charles in Scotland is here—a recommendation of one Edward Whitney to the Governor of Virginia, signed by the King [*p.* 6], and then there is a break of eight years in the papers.

Belonging to the year 1659, there is a little group of interesting autograph letters from Sir Edward Hyde [*pp.* 7-15].

For some years before, Fanshaw had been a prisoner upon parole in England, and unable to communicate with his friends abroad, but the Protector's death having set him free, he went to Paris with the young Lord Herbert. This was William, son of the Earl of Pembroke, not to be confused with Henry, son of the Marquis of Worcester, who was at this time a prisoner in the Tower.

Hyde, who was without doubt (in spite of Lady Fanshaw's strong belief to the contrary) a steadfast friend to Fanshaw, was desirous to find some fitting employment for him, in the parcelling out of places caused by the rising hopes of the Royalist party.

He had already been named as Latin Secretary, but Hyde considered this post, if "not dignified by the person" who held it, as of but little importance. There was no signet belonging to it, it was entirely under the direction of the Secretary of State, and the fee was only 100*l.* a year, for which reasons it had always fallen to inconsiderable men [*p.* 9]. Probably neither Hyde nor Fanshaw gave a thought to the present holder of the office in England, or could have realized (if they did) that by its connexion with his name it would be "dignified" for all time.

The post which Hyde chose for his friend—to be held with the other—was that of Master of Requests, whose position he declares to be only second to that of Secretary of State, he having the King's ear for three months in the year, and being able easily to make six or seven hundred per annum, even if he never offered any suit for himself.

These two offices were accordingly conferred upon Fanshaw, and held by him until his death, although both duties and emoluments were often interfered with by his absences from England.

The long letter concerning offices is much of it in cipher, which seems, from divers allusions by himself and his friends, to have been always rather a trouble to Fanshaw. There are many pages of decipher amongst his papers, evidently sent to him from England in answer to a confession to Arlington (in a letter in the Spanish Correspondence at the Public Record Office) that he thought he must have taken out the wrong key, as he could not make out above five words in the despatches, and those five did not cohere.

It seems doubtful whether he ever read the letter here printed at all, for an attempt (in his own handwriting) to unravel the first sentence, in which the words, "for the wrong he has done you," take the remarkable form of "from they wara onga ha here divide gaine," cannot have helped him much to grasp the contents, although it has proved a very useful clue in discovering the key of the cipher.

In November, Hyde wrote, sympathizing with his friend in a sorrow which we know from Lady Fanshaw's *Memoirs* to have been the death of their son [*p.* 15].

Her ladyship states that her husband went to the King in December, but her dates are not very trustworthy, and from Hyde's letter of January 14, 1660, it would appear that Fanshaw was then still in Paris.

Hyde asks very affectionately about Fanshaw's studies and pursuits, longs to see his translation of *Querer por solo querer*,* and urges him, if he must needs confine himself to translations, which he thinks is a pity, to make a collection of Spanish letters of the best writers [*p.* 11]. These letters from Brussels contain of course many allusions to affairs in England. In the August of this year, 1659, the Royalists were depressed and disappointed that the army had not dissolved the Parliament, and Hyde confesses that he does not understand matters there, nor does he know either what Montague and the fleet mean to do, or what is the temper of Monck and his army. Then comes his outburst of dismay at the treachery of Sir Richard Willis, in whose loyalty he had believed, so long as belief was possible. "Would you ever have thought it possible," he writes, "that Sir Richard Willis could prove false?" The Knot, too, he thinks, have not done their part, and the risers with Sir George Booth in Lancashire and Cheshire, "left to contend alone," have failed. His chief comfort is that the conquerors scarce know what to do with their victory, and that the army will probably once more break up the form of government. Meanwhile, the King's servants were in a truly miserable condition, "above two years in arrear of their board wages, which God knows, if paid, would but give them bread."

At the beginning of November, the little Court at Brussels was hungry for news; having heard nothing since Parliament was dissolved. Hyde believes that "the confusion there is very

---

* A play by the Spanish dramatist, Hurtado de Mendoza.

high, and yet that there is some governing power that is well obeyed," for no letters are allowed to be sent over, "which kind of restraint hath never been practiced since the beginning of these troubles." The treaty of the Pyrenees, too, was giving cause for anxiety, the ministers at Brussels "censuring the method very much." When the letters did come, Hyde was more perplexed than ever. The turns in England, he says, quite turn his head, and he knows not what to think of them. "Nothing more extravagant than that the Rump should sit and govern three kingdoms, yet nothing to come can appear more impossible than that which they have passed through." If his next letters do not tell of some fresh broils, he will be melancholic [*p*. 16]. This is the end of the group of letters, which form a very pleasant addition to Hyde's correspondence at this time.

Other letters of his are scattered throughout the volume. There are courtly little notes to the Queen Regent of Portugal and to Queen Catherine [*pp*. 16, 27], upon whose arrival in England he writes, apologising for not being at the port to welcome her on the ground of "lack of health and excess of business," and also the strict veto of the King—"the most indulgent master in the world." These letters were apparently done into Spanish by Fanshaw, as what are here are drafts in his hand. In August, 1662, he writes in evident dismay to the Queen Regent of Portugal on hearing that the young King is taking the reins into his own hands, and urges her not to entirely free herself of her burden, as by so doing she will deprive her son "of the most faithful, the most experienced, and the most devoted counsellor that his Majesty can ever have or hope for" [*p*. 31]. In April, 1663, when barely recovered, as he says, from the fiercest fit of gout he ever had in his life, he assures Fanshaw that in spite of ill-health he has been as solicitous for the cause of Portugal as he possibly could be; but "could endeavour nothing effectually but by secret and underhand treating with France," for which he has had a good opportunity, and which he hopes will have good effects [*p*. 75]. His protest concerning the succours demanded by Portugal is quoted elsewhere. As regards home news, he hopes the Parliament mean to give the King supplies, which will prevent inconveniences in the three kingdoms, "in which there remain yet many restless spirits." A month later, he writes indignantly of the refusal of the Vice-King of Goa to deliver Bombay into Marlborough's hands. " The act is so foul that less than the head of the man cannot satisfy for the indignity, and for the damage his Majesty will expect and exact notable repara- tion." If this is not given, there will be an end to the alliance with Portugal [*p.* 89]. This is the last of Clarendon's letters in this collection. Those written to Spain must be looked for in the published letters and at the British Museum.

Next in order is a series of royal letters [*pp.* 16-31], includ- ing the " love-letters " of Charles II. and the Infanta Catherine, which are somewhat less formal and perfunctory than Royal letters were wont to be. Those of the King have here and there a touch of individuality about them, as when he recalls the joy with which, after long years of exile, he returned to his kingdom and was welcomed by his people [*p.* 17]. His belief, too, in the personal power of Kings was no doubt very sincere [*p.* 30]. But those of the young princess, assuring her unknown husband that her one desire in life is for the winds to waft her quickly to him, and of her mother, declaring that her new son is as dear to her as her own child, are more complimentary than convinc- ing. It is evident that Charles wrote his letters in English, while the two Queens and the young King of Portugal wrote theirs in Portuguese. They passed through Fanshaw's hands and he translated them. His master's letters, with his own Spanish translations of them, were no doubt duly presented by him at the Court of Lisbon, but of those given him in return he often did not trouble to send the originals to England at all, as they are here, amongst his papers. We fear that Prof. Ranke's pretty picture of King Charles talking to his bride in her native tongue must go, but he knew some Spanish (though apparently not very much), and perhaps made that serve his turn. Fanshaw sends Spanish papers to England, saying to Bennet that he believes the King will be " fully appre- hensive of them " if Bennet reads them to him distinctly, " with never so little of explanation thereupon " [*p.* 50]. The Portu- guese papers he always translates, either into Spanish or English.

When Fanshaw reached Portugal in the summer of 1661, that kingdom was in the midst of its struggle with Spain. The independence won in 1640 had never been acknowledged, and the old suzerainty was claimed and in danger of being regained. King John had died in 1656, and his wife, Luisa

de Guzman, ruled on behalf of her son Alfonso. D'Ablancourt
says of her, " C'etait une princesse d'une grande esprit, et qui
eut porté la gloire de sa regence bien loin, si elle avoit eu
de conseillers qui eussent secondé son habilité, et surtout un
fils ainé qui fut digne d'elle." Clarendon, Fanshaw, and Inchiquin all bear their testimony in her favour [*pp.* 31, 48, 61].
By arranging a marriage with Charles II. for her daughter, she
enlisted the sympathy of England, and while she offered Bombay and Tangier as part of Catherine's dowry, the English
King, on his part, promised to send a body of English troops
to assist Portugal against Spain. But neither the marriage
nor the presence of the heretic troops seems to have pleased the
Portuguese, and at the time of her downfall the Queen was
accused of having " exhausted the wealth and aliened the flowers
of the Crown " in order to advance this one child [*p.* 69].

It had been intended that Fanshaw should either accompany
the Infanta to England or remain behind her [*p.* 17], but her
journey was postponed, and he returned before her.

In January, 1662, his secretary and cousin, Lionel Fanshaw,
tells him what had happened since his departure. The Spaniards
were now preparing for their next campaign, and were already
drawing towards the frontiers, whilst the nobles of Portugal,
on their side, were making ready to take the field [*p.* 25].

In April, 1662, the young Queen started for England, under
the escort of the Earl of Sandwich and his fleet, and, at first, made
such good progress that a "light vessel," sent after her by her
anxious mother, failed to overtake the English ships, and had
to return without news [*p.* 26]. After this, however, she was
delayed by storms and did not reach England until May 14th.
One cannot but think that her reception at Portsmouth must
have seemed to her discourteous and cold. The King was not
there to meet her; indeed, excepting her ladies and the Duke
of York (*see Pepys'* Diary *and Lister's* Life of Clarendon),
it is difficult to say who was there, for Clarendon and Fanshaw, who might be expected to be amongst the first to go,
both sent excuses [*p.* 27]. However, after proroguing his
Parliament, Charles repaired to " the happiest meeting which
has ever taken place," and whatever his feelings about his
bride may have been, he was at any rate polite enough to
praise her to her mother and brother, while, if her mother's

assurances are to be believed, she was more than satisfied with her reception by the King.

After this there are only casual notices of the Queen. We read of her poor health, her visits to various waters, and the hopes of the people that she will give them an heir to the throne; and Sir Philip Warwick gives a description of her costume as she went to take the air "in a scarlet coat, richly laced, and trimmed with sky-coloured ribbon" [*p.* 149].

Hardly had the Queen landed in England, before a change took place in Portugal, which seriously affected the relations of the two countries. In a letter dated July 1st, 1662, n.s., Alfonso announces that in consideration of the state of the kingdom, and to relieve his mother of the burden resting upon her, he has taken upon himself the government [*p.* 29]. The news was received with dismay in England. True, Charles sends flattering words to his royal brother, assuring him that the troubles in Portugal may now be said to be almost ended, "*tanto puede la assistencia personal de los reyes,*" but he goes on to give him a broad hint that he will do well to rely upon the experience of his mother, "the nursing mother of the renewed liberties of Portugal" [*p.* 30], while Clarendon, as we have seen, writes to the Queen in the same strain. How far she herself wished to retire it is difficult to say. She says so, of course, and her courtly correspondents are far too polite to suggest any other reason, but she probably made a virtue of necessity, and Fanshaw, writing to his brother-in-law, Sir Philip Warwick, tells him that she was removed "with many particular disgusts heaped upon herself and all those her Majesty employed in greatest trusts" [*p.* 69]. No wonder the friends of Portugal were alarmed. The Queen had courage and experience. Alfonso, a youth of nineteen years of age, had nothing but his vices. He dismissed his mother's counsellors and placed the government in the hands of a young favourite of his own, the Conde de Castelmelhor, making him *Secretario de la Puridad,* an office, Fanshaw says, found "nowhere but in Portugal, even here rarely taken up, and once (by Don Sebastian) abolished, as too much to be put into any one hand" [*p.* 36]. And yet from that moment fortune turned.

Castelmelhor found the country on the verge of ruin. So soon as he took the reins, victory declared itself on the side of Portugal, the soldiers were better paid, the people less hardly taxed. He was very popular, for the reasons, Fanshaw writes, that he was of noble birth, which was more than could be said of many of Alfonso's associates, and that he was poor and remained poor, a fact which in itself spoke volumes [*p.* 96].

The other minister who is prominent in these pages is Antonio de Sousa de Macedo, Secretary of State, who had formerly been in England on behalf of his government. Lady Fanshaw tells us that Charles I. had made his son a baron, and this fact receives some confirmation from the announcement that "Antonio de Sousa hath lately married the young Baron, his son—by proxy—to a very beautiful young lady of high birth." Unfortunately, the beautiful young lady did not apparently appreciate the honour, or her friends either, for we read that she was in a monastery and would not come out, and that a band of young nobles stopped De Sousa on his way to fetch her, and would not let him proceed further, for which some of them were put in prison [*p.* 25].

The Earl of Inchiquin had by this time arrived with the English troops, as also some ships, and the design was to send the troops to succour Alentejo, while the ships made a diversion in Galicia [*p.* 29]. The party who had wished for English help being now banished or degraded, the English soldiers were but coldly received, and very soon it was reported that they could get no money, were every day in an uproar, and that the officers were already demanding passes and hurrying back to England [*p.* 32].

In September, 1662, Sir Richard Fanshaw returned to Lisbon as permanent ambassador from the Court of England. His wife and little ones were with him, and at first they were housed in the *Quinta de Alleyro*. There was talk of a grand supper to be given there, but partly from want of room, and also because he found that the feminine members of his family would be severed from him and "driven into a corner" Sir Richard declined the honour [*p.* 34]. They afterwards went to a house of their own, with a fine view over the beautiful bay [*p.* 41].

Negotiations were still afloat between Spain and Portugal. The King of Spain—or of Castile, as the Portuguese were careful to call him—would not acknowledge the right of Alfonso to sign as King of Portugal, but was inclined to agree that each might sign merely *yo, el rey* [*p.* 36]. When Fanshaw con-

gratulated Castelmelhor upon this concession, the favourite
replied that Castile had never scrupled to acknowledge his
master as King of Brazil, which answer led the ambassador
to fear that Portugal was not so firm but that Spain might
yet "either beat him or treat him out of his dominions"
[*p.* 38]. Fanshaw was also much perturbed by the intrigues
of France [*pp.* 41, 63], but Clarendon characteristically made
very light of them, and was not at all troubled by the apprehension that France would get the better of England [*p.* 89].

Meanwhile the English troops were becoming more and more
dissatisfied [*pp.* 42, 44], and in November declared that they
could no longer serve the Crown of Portugal, "by reason of
the unsupportable wants and injuries which they groan under"
[*p.* 45]. These papers are full of their complaints, but they
struggled on month after month. Sometimes the Portuguese
ministers were induced to send them a little money, and sometimes to hand over further portions of the Queen's dowry, which
King Charles agreed should be so used, probably thinking
that there was little chance of his ever getting it at all in
any other way. Fanshaw told him plainly that he did not
believe Portugal had the money to send, and that the Secretary,
making him a visit, as he suspected for that very purpose, had
incidentally observed that "after payments of Queen's portions
are not usually exacted with rigour," and that he believed the
Queen Mother's of England was never all paid, or not till very
late [*p.* 53].

In April, 1663, Count Schonberg, who had, by the influence
of Turenne, brought some French troops to Portugal, was
appointed commander of the English "strangers" also, and
was received with acclamation by the soldiers [*p.* 74].

The treaty with Spain was in its death pangs, the Spanish
armies were advancing, and England could do little to help.
"I do freely confess to you," Clarendon writes in answer to
Fanshaw's grievance, "that the prospect you presented to us
was very dismal, and the expedients you proposed very
impracticable. . . . Alas, my lord, we have no money to
send fleets or troops upon adventures, nor can anybody imagine
that the burden of a war of Portugal can be sustained upon the
weak shoulders of the Crown of England." The King has, he
continues, with difficulty enough, fitted out a fleet, but if the re-

mainder of the Queen's portion is not paid he will not be able to continue the expense. The treatment of the English troops offers no encouragement to send more, and to imagine that he can send troops from England and then pay them in Portugal "is indeed ridiculous." For the present, out of compassion for his poor soldiers, he is willing to allow them a further payment from the dowry, and then if the ministers of Portugal cannot make effectual provision for them, they must come home [*p.* 75].

In May, 1663, the campaign with Spain had begun, and there are some very interesting and lively letters from Schonberg. He was far from contented with the management of affairs, and had the utmost contempt for the two Generals, the Conde de Villa Flor and Marialva. However, they did not ask his advice, and would not take it when he offered it, so he relieved his conscience by writing his views on the matter to Castelmelhor, and then prepared to do his best [*p.* 84].

On May 12-22 the city of Evora yielded to the Spaniards under Don Juan of Austria, after a very slight resistance, and the arrival of the news at Lisbon was the signal for a rising there—a rising for the King, not against him; but such, Fanshaw writes, "as if, beginning strangely in the morning, the storm had not as strangely ceased towards night, might have done Don Juan's business as well as if they had risen for him." The people marched to the Palace, shouting *Viva el rey y mueran los traidores*; the King appeared at a window and tried to quiet them, but a woman in the crowd, spying Marialva near his Majesty, "cried out that traitor would throw the King out at window," whereon a rumour ran through the city that "so horrid an act was already perpetrated." After saluting the King, the populace fell "to the second part of their acclamation, namely *mueran los traidores*," sacking the palaces of the Archbishop, Marialva and others, and killing many people; but towards evening "the friars, coming out of several convents in solemn procession, and bringing with them church buckets of excommunication," managed to quench the flame of sedition and quiet was restored. The people's desire was to hurry away the King into the field, but the effect of the tumult was "point blank contrary," for Alfonso, who, up to this time, had resolved on going, now seemed as resolved to stay at home, on the ground that if he were absent worse tumults might occur [*pp.* 92-96].

On May 20-30, Schonberg writes that the army was on the
march to relieve Evora when the news of its yielding arrived,
those who defended it not giving anyone time to help them.
The cowardice with which the commanders have acted, is, he
declares, beyond anything he has ever seen in any war, and they
ought all to be hanged. He does not approve of the orders
sent from Lisbon for an immediate battle, and says he "never
saw a Council so bent upon ruining themselves without delay,"
and as to his Generals, he cannot get them to make up their
mind to anything [*pp.* 97-98]. But he disposed his own troops
as advantageously as he could, and on June 4th. (new style)
had a skirmish with the Spaniards, of which he himself "makes
little more than a facing of the enemy," whereas at Lisbon
"it is cried up for a great battle and no small victory"
[*pp.* 99, 105].

On June 8th the great battle of Ameixial or Canal was
fought, and we have some interesting accounts of the victory,
one written under Schonberg's supervision [*p.* 107], and another
by Col. James Apsley [*p.* 101], younger son of Sir Alan and
brother of Lucy Hutchinson, who, having been under a cloud
in England, was now redeeming his character by his valour,
much to the satisfaction of his family [*pp.* 112, 124]. Schonberg was warm in his praise of the conduct both of the French
and English troops, but the victory over, he was again confronted
by the same difficulties. The commanders, he writes, "after
having done so well, think of nothing but of resting themselves,
instead of making use of their victory. They understand
nothing about war. The soldiers are brave enough, but the
chiefs carefully avoid all risks, and as to him who ought to have
led us, no one saw him during the battle at all" [*p.* 106].
This great personage spent two days in "labouring to compose his chronicle," but Schonberg evidently did not trust him,
and thought it safer to send his own version [*p.* 109]. The
official account gave the number of English slain as fifty, but
Apsley says about fifty were killed in each regiment of foot,
with about forty or fifty wounded; and that the loss of the
horse was far greater. Six English commissioned officers were
among the slain. [For the behaviour of the English in this
battle and the jealousy of the Portuguese, see Schäfer's "*Ges-
chichte von Portugal,*" pp. 656-658.] Schonberg sent Don Juan's
carriage and his standard, taken by one of the French officers,

to Lisbon, to be presented to the King. For himself, he says, he has taken no booty, but has to lament the loss of his old cloak, lent to his trumpeter, who was shot as they were scaling the heights [*p.* 109].

The Portuguese army now invested Evora, and Schonberg was eager for an immediate attack, but again he had to tell the old tale. "There is not a commander who does anything unless he is obliged. Messieurs de Villa Flor and Marialva set them the example, for their only care is to write letters and to ask what is going on in the siege. Neither one nor the other has been nearer to the town than the quarter where they are lodged, and they do not even know on which side we have opened the trenches" [*p.* 114]. However, after the storming of Fort St. Antonio—by an equal number of English and Portuguese, as Secretary Sousa says [*p.* 115]; by two hundred Englishmen alone, according to Col. Apsley [*p.* 116]—Evora capitulated on June 25, and the Spaniards were permitted to depart with much better terms than Schonberg thought necessary [*p.* 115]. He was especially troubled that they were allowed to take their horses, Portugal having much need thereof, but the Portuguese chiefs assured him that they should manage to evade that part of the agreement, "and this answer," as Fanshaw remarks, "troubles the Count ten times more" [*p.* 119].

The hot weather having now begun, the campaign was considered at an end, and people might well imagine, writes d'Ablancourt to Turenne, that Portugal was saved; but there were still great rocks ahead, not the least being the indifference of the Portuguese themselves. "There is here no question," he says, "of an enemy foreign in religion, manners or language, or who has done such injury to this nation as to make reconciliation impossible." The correspondence with the Portuguese towns found in Don Juan's cabinet showed how ready the people would be to go over to Spain if Spain proved the stronger, and what in other places would be called betraying their country or siding with the stronger party, would here pass as a return to their duty [*p.* 124].

One tangible result was gained by Portugal from the battle of Ameixial, *i.e.*, the possession of many Spanish notables as prisoners, the two most important being the Marquis de Liche, son of Don Luis de Haro, and Don Añelo de Guzman, son of the Duke of Medina de las Torres. Charles II. did his best afterwards to procure their liberation, but Castelmelhor courteously reminded him that these prisoners were the fruit which Portugal enjoyed from the battle in which she risked so much, and that their detention afforded the best ground to hope for peace, from the desire of Spain for their liberation [p. 141].

The English forces in Portugal continued to add to their reputation, and especially distinguished themselves at Valença, where they alone responded to an order to attack the town, and stormed a breach whilst the rest of the army looked idly on, losing eleven commissioned officers in half an hour, and nearly half their men [p. 160].

On June 17th, 1665, they had their share in gaining the great victory of Villa Viçiosa or Monte Claros, when the Spaniards were totally routed by Marialva, which made them "look very blue," as Consul Westcombe observes [p. 197].

The last mention of the English troops is in January, 1666, when Maynard writes from Lisbon that they were now so few that no considerable service could be expected of them, but that there was a good understanding between them and the Court, and they had but four months' pay due to them [p. 223].

More than two years before this, in August, 1663, Fanshaw had returned to England, taking with him an earnest request from the King of Portugal that he might be allowed to go to Spain, and there once more try to arrange a peace with Portugal [p. 131].

On January 31st, 1664, he and his family again left England and journeyed to Madrid, which, however, they did not reach until June 8th, new style. The details of their journey are well known from Lady Fanshaw's *Memoirs*. The new ambassador had his first audience on June 18, the arrangements for it involving much discussion of various points of etiquette [p. 155]. As already stated, the diplomatic correspondence of this mission must be mostly looked for in the printed volume and the Harley MSS.,* but the letters still remaining here show how many other matters Fanshaw had to take in hand. We find him trying to procure justice for the English consuls, liberty for the English prisoners, access to the Spanish ports for the English ships, and free intercourse with Tangier, his

---

* Some cipher letters to Bennet of the summer of 1664 are in this collection, but they are all given in the printed volume, and the originals of them are at the Record Office.

complaints to the Spanish Court being, he says, almost as constant as the occasion for them [*p.* 213]. In August, 1665, he interested himself in favour of Don Francisco de Alarçon, a Spanish nobleman, prisoner in Portugal, not only writing himself to Castelmelhor and the secretary, but allowing his wife, at the instance of the prisoner's mother, to write to De Sousa's wife [*p.* 199]. The secretary replies that the King is anxious to gratify his Excellency so far as is possible, but cannot interfere with the laws, and, "in matters which may be said to belong to the public," is accustomed to let things run their course without using his royal power [*p.* 203]. His wife reminds Lady Fanshaw that "we women are apt to give more weight to feelings of pity than to reasons of state," but promises that her husband will not fail to act if an opportunity should occur [*p.* 204].

In September, 1665, the King of Spain died, and his young son, Charles II., was proclaimed [*pp.* 205, 207].

During this year, Fanshaw engaged in the ill-fated negotiation with Spain, which brought about his recall [*p.* 222]. He agreed with the Spanish Court upon a treaty, with the proviso that it was to be ratified at a certain date, unless protested against by England. Lady Fanshaw believed Clarendon's (supposed) hatred of her husband, and his anxiety to find a place for his "cast Condé," as she calls Sandwich [*p.* 230], to have been the cause of his disgrace, asserting that the English ministers had had the papers in their hands five months; that far from making any demur, they had said that it infinitely concerned them to make an end of the matter, and that "room was left in the league" to add anything his Majesty thought fit [*p.* 226]. Moreover, a paper written and formally signed by Lionel Fanshaw and apparently (from its watermark) drawn up after their return to England, gives a statement of the various dates, and declares that ample time was allowed for an answer from England [*p.* 255], but as, according to the showing of this document, the express was not despatched until November 1st and the treaty was signed on December 17th, it can hardly be thought that a very sufficient margin was left for the possible delays and accidents of the double journey, to say nothing of the time needed for deliberation in England.

Lady Fanshaw's idea that her husband's disgrace was the result of an intrigue in England, is, however, strongly supported by other evidence. Lister points out that (as appears from Pepys' *Diary*) Lord Sandwich's embassy to Spain was already resolved upon on December 6th, ten days before the treaty was signed in Madrid, and that Lord Clarendon speaks of this treaty as if it had been signed before the death of Philip IV. (which occurred on September 17th), saying that Fanshaw's recall was then decided on, but that the resolution was not acted upon, by reason of the plague driving the King from London and dispersing the Council; "that is, the recall of Fanshaw, in consequence of his having signed a treaty in December, was resolved on before July." (*Life of Clarendon, Vol. II., p.* 359.) It may perhaps be possible to disentangle this skein a little. Lister declares that Clarendon's anachronisms deprive his statement of all credit, but this is putting the matter rather too strongly. It is true that he wrote his *Life* (as Mr. Firth reminds us in his article in the *Dictionary of National Biography*) when separated from his friends and his papers, and relied on his memory, which often confused events, yet he would hardly invent all that he says here, nor is it likely that an ambassador who was giving perfect satisfaction would be turned out simply to find Lord Sandwich an employment where he would be out of the way. Madrid was not the only place in the world for honourable banishment. In the first place, Clarendon relates with considerable precision what took place in the Council some few weeks before the death of the King of Spain; and it will be seen that this exactly tallies with Lady Fanshaw's statement that the papers had been in the hands of the English ministers for five months. The inference therefore is that the treaty had been negotiated in Spain and sent to England as Clarendon describes (although he is mistaken in thinking that it was signed *), and that in some way it created dissatisfaction—unjust dissatisfaction—at Court. Clarendon himself evidently thought that Fanshaw was hardly used, and so far from having any hand in it, says that " besides the gentleman's absence, who would with greater abilities have defended himself than any of those who reproached him, it was no advantage to him to be known to be in the Chancellor's confidence, and therefore the more pain was taken to persuade the King that he was a weak man (which the King himself knew him not to be), and they

---

* No doubt it contained the proviso for its speedy signature, on the ground of the King's critical state, quoted by Clarendon.

put such a gloss upon many of the articles and rejected others
as unprofitable, which were thought to contain matters of great
moment, that they would not consent that a trade to the West
Indies could be any advantage to England, and the like."
Fanshaw's recall was resolved upon, but, owing to the plague,
nothing was done, until, as Clarendon plainly says, " the business
of the Earl of Sandwich made it thought on as a good expedient."
Probably the death of the King of Spain was looked upon as
putting an end to the treaty, and apparently no remonstrance
was sent to Fanshaw; thus, as his wife argues, he might well
believe that he had a free hand in the matter, when, after the
confusion attendant on the accession of the young King was
over, the matter was taken up again in Spain.

In January, 1666, Fanshaw started on his mission to Lisbon,
there to meet Sir Robert Southwell and, with him, to try once
more to arrange terms of peace between Portugal and Spain,
and the volume fitly draws to a close with the correspondence
between the husband and wife during their brief separation
[*pp.* 224-240]. These last letters of Fanshaw's are very
characteristic. He writes loving words to his wife, bids his
girls make ready to act his play before Sir Robert Southwell,
whilst his little boy Dick may "lug his puppy by the ears
quite unconcerned" [*p.* 237], and urges strongly upon his
friends at the Spanish Court—who openly resented another ambassador being sent to supersede him—his desire that they should
offer to Lord Sandwich a reception no less cordial than that
which they had given to himself [*p.* 236].

Lady Fanshaw's letters are exactly what we should expect—
loving, unaffected, and impetuous. Her mind was evidently
sorely exercised concerning the view taken in England of her
husband's proceedings in the matter of the treaty, and the coming of the Earl of Sandwich distressed her greatly, her only
comfort being that the Spanish ministers had as good as said
that they would have nothing to do with him if he did come.
She urges her husband to hasten back as soon as may be, as
he will see [we give her words in her own rather eccentric
spelling] "by Ld. Ar: that in his cantin languadg he wold
fane have his cast jenerall reape the frute" which Fanshaw
has sown [*p.* 225]. She relates with much satisfaction all that
the Duke of Medina de las Torres has said to her, and her own
demure answer, that she was very sorry she was not capacitated

to understand things of state and that she knew nothing of Lord Sandwich's coming but through the news letters. Having thus declared her entire ignorance of the subject, she proceeds to unravel for her husband's benefit the intrigues which she believes to lie at the bottom of the business—intrigues of Molina, Arlington, and her pet abomination, Clarendon.

"But lord," she says, "what a loud laugh it will make when ther pittefull desines are known." The truth will surely come to light, and so her beloved must be cheerful and remember that as he has always had God and honour before his eyes, so he will never want a blessing. He is to take care of his health and safety, to correct her in anything she does amiss, and she will try to mend it (for indeed she is very diffident, as he knows, of her carriage in this place), and not to fail to put a proper value on himself, seeing that however foolish this might be in a young man (though now the English fashion) he has warrant for it not only in his natural parts, but in his long experience. She longs to know how his business is progressing, but if it will not do—either public or private—he must not be troubled, but leave it to God, as he has always done hitherto. "Liquies prithy" she implores him, "send me word when thou thingest thou shalt be backe agaene in gras of God." In spite of her pious resignation, she is much pleased that they at Madrid are "raging mad" with the Conde and in great heat at the coming of the Earl, the Duke declaring him to be a Cromwellist, "wich will not go down heare" [*p*. 227, 228]. Also there is good news from England. "I have been shown severall letters," she writes, "that upon the receat of thyn of the 20 of the last, nu stile, the King did express openley a very great joy of the worke of thy hands, and pertikelerly spoke much in thy prays with great estime, and soe did the Duke of Yorke with the Secretary, Ld. Ar: and all the hole Corte, but ouer dear frent Ld. Ch: sayd truly he did not expect this work to be so fineshed and shoed himselfe very malincoley, at wich the King lafed and soe doth maney a one, and wright that now he will be much trubled how to provide for his cast Cundey, but I heare that he will make him Governor of Tanger." Mixed with her talk about state affairs are fragments of news and gossip. "The Quine Mother of France is ded, and departed this life with thes blessed words in her mouth to the King, her son, love pease and make pease with all the world that you may have eternall pease." The Hollander is in a very ill condition and the Prince of Munster in a very good one. "The last newes of the plage from Ingland was seventy in all, but fourteene in the sittey." Also a play has been acted before the King, "in wich maney nationens mett, and the Frenchman mayd them all afrayd," until an Englishman came by and got much the best of it. To come nearer home, "The Markis de Lichey this day sent me a littell grahound pupey, so fine a cretuer a never saw in my life, wich I take care of much for thee, but Dick luces [lugs] her by ·the eares. . . . He groues a lovely fine boy and all the carles [girls] are verey well and soe am I, but wish thee with me a thousand times. . . . Never was any bepell so thurstay as thes are for good nues from thee, wich God of his marcy send" [*pp*. 230, 231, 234].

Finally, she sends her "dearest life" a little good advice as to his behaviour on his return. He is to take great care what he says to Father Patrick—telling him as much of the business as will stay his stomach and no more, he must be "respective" to the Duke, and above all he must keep up his own dignity, as having spent time and money and toil on behalf of Spain, and must show them that he deserves and expects thanks, however things may go.

On Thursday, March the 8th, new style, the loving couple were re-united in health and safety [*p*. 240]. Lord Sandwich arrived at Madrid in April, and the Fanshaws began to make their arrangements to return home.

No letter here records the blow which fell before that journey was begun, but it may perhaps be permissible to borrow a few lines from a despatch of Sandwich's to Arlington, in the Spanish Correspondence. "The conclusion of this letter," he writes, "must be tragical, it having pleased God to take my Lord Ambassador Fanshaw out of this life on Saturday last, the 16-26 inst. [June] about eleven of the clock at night. I was in his embraces in the evening, when his hands were cold and life hastening to expire, yet had he perfect sense. He most Christianly submitted to God's will, expressed great love and fidelity for his Prince, and resisted temptations from the people of this religion, who did press upon him more than was fitting in that hour of parting. He is universally lamented here as a good and worthy person."

Next in importance to the papers connected with Spain and Portugal are the letters written from or relating to the British garrison at Tangier, which form a very valuable supplement to those at the Public Record Office. The first notices of it occur just when Lord Peterborough, its first governor, was returning home, Lord Rutherford, created Earl of Teviot, taking the command in his place. He held it "in very good posture" [*pp.* 119, 148], confronting the Moorish chief, Gayland, who, having seized part of the dominions of another chief, Benbowcar, had made his headquarters at Arzilla, and prowled with his wild followers round the little English garrison. All went well until the sad tragedy of May the 3rd, 1664, when Lord Teviot and his gallant party were surprised and slain. The original of Col. Bridge's letter to Fanshaw, announcing the disaster, is here [*p.* 152], but it has been already printed from the Record Office copy. More interesting therefore is a long letter [*p.* 154] from "stout" Col. Alsop, another of Cromwell's old officers, who was now doing the King good service, with due sorrow expressed for the sins of his youth [*p.* 164]. He gives a vivid account of what happened when the sad fact was known, taking good care to explain that the command of the garrison by right devolved upon himself, and was only given to Col. Bridge upon his own refusal and at his desire. Under Bridge's care the little handful of English daily faced the Moors, and could boast that they had not lost an inch of ground nor a single man since the Earl's death [*p.* 158]. Sir John Lawson hastened with his fleet to their help, and on July 24th writes that Col. Fitzgerald had arrived as Deputy-Governor and that all was well. In August there are cheery letters from Fitzgerald, and Alsop writes that the garrison is paid up to the end of Lord Teviot's time, that the redoubts are nearly finished, and the Mole only waits for Cholmeley to arrive with materials. Commissioners had been sent to interview Gayland, without, however, accomplishing anything, and Alsop believes that the next they see of him will be in hostility, but that if they stand to their business bravely, his flag of truce will be sent in the same day, and he will get little but knocks [*p.* 164].

In March, 1665, Lord Belasyse went out to Tangier, and Fanshaw wrote that his arrival would, he hoped, cure the world of an error which had prevailed for many months, that his Majesty had sold the place. The new Governor soon reported

that they were in a more prosperous condition than ever, and
that the ominous 3rd of May had passed without any appearance
of the enemy.

In June, Consul Westcombe at Cadiz mentions rumours of a
peace with Gayland, but doubts not that Lord Belasyse will
observe the Spanish maxim, *"In paes o en guerra, guarda
bien tu tierra"* [*p.* 197].

One thing troubled Lord Belasyse greatly, and this was the
need for him to defend the Moors of Algiers against the claims
of the Spaniards and Dutch concerning prizes. It goes against
his conscience, he writes, "to contribute to serve Turks against
Christians" [*pp.* 201, 209], and yet he is obliged to do it, to
preserve peace with these people.

In October, 1665, he had to confess that Gayland was no ways
inclined to peace, "being courted by the Duke of Medina Celi
and the Dutch to the contrary," and that if it were not for
Benbowcar's diversion (that chief being now engaged in an
attempt to get back his former possessions) they would probably
hear more of him. They were, however, strong enough to oppose
any attempts either by land or sea, and if only supplies were
sent from England, he had no doubt but that the place would
become every day more important [*p.* 210]. Unhappily the
next news was that these much wished for supplies had been
intercepted by the Dutch and that two provision ships and
the *Merlin* frigate had been captured [*p.* 210]. The captain
of the frigate, Charles Howard, writes to Westcombe that he
had to surrender, after a fight of five or six hours, in which,
Westcombe assures Fanshaw, he "behaved himself bravely with
his twelve guns" [*p.* 211]. This misfortune was like to put the
little garrison in straits for want of supplies, but they struggled
bravely on, aided by the fact that in spite of Medina Celi's
orders, Spanish boats constantly put across and sold them provisions [*p.* 210], and much protected from attack by the
contests of the Moorish chiefs against each other, the King of
Tafilet having come down upon Gayland, firing and destroying
all "the stately gardens and vineyards about Fez," taking
divers castles and killing many men, and he in his turn being
pursued by the "Saint" Benbowcar, who seized upon Fez and
left his son in possession there while he went to look after
the said King [*p.* 212].

Closely connected with the affairs of Tangier are the letters
from Sir John Lawson, Admiral Thomas Allin, and other commanders, giving us many interesting details concerning the
English fleet. The captains had much difficulty in getting free
access to the Spanish ports, owing to the unfriendly feelings
of the Duque de Medina Celi, Governor of Andalusia, towards
the English, and the difficulty increased when the great out-
break of the plague in England gave the Spanish authorities
a valid reason for refusing to admit English ships which had
come from home, and a plausible excuse for keeping them out,
even if they had not. On December 17, 1664, poor Admiral
Allin wrote to tell Fanshaw of the night of dismal rain and darkness, in which his own and four other ships had gone ashore, with
the loss of the *Phœnix* and *Nonsuch*; a calamity which had
half broken his heart [*p.* 172]. On the heels of this news,
however, came the good tidings that he had had an encounter
with the Dutch, had taken two of their ships and sunk two
more, so that Fanshaw was able to write him a letter rather
of congratulation than of condolence, suggesting that the shipwrecked men can be "recruited with Dutch ships," while the
Mole at Tangier may be "supplied with Dutch workmen upon
liberal and Christian terms" [*p.* 173].

Between the English and the Dutch in Spain there was
continual friction, and it seems to have made very little difference
whether the two nations were in amity or at enmity with each
other. There are perpetual complaints of the high and mighty
ways and the vainglorious boastings of the Hollanders, and great
accordingly was the joy when the news of the battle off Sole
Bay [June 3rd, 1665] arrived,* sent first by Williamson, with a
message from Arlington that he hopes the enclosed will content
Fanshaw in point of news for one week [*p.* 194]. The rejoicing
was all the greater as there had been disturbing rumours—spread
by the Dutch—that England had been defeated; indeed Fanshaw had heard from Holland that even there attempts were made
to conceal the truth, and that thanks were actually offered up
in one of the churches, only an hour or two before the real
facts were known, which quickly turned their joy into mourning [*p.* 198]. In December, 1665, Westcombe sends a list
of the English ships taken by the Dutch during the past year,

---

* This is not, of course, the battle usually known by that name, fought in May,
1672, when the Earl of Sandwich was killed.

with a rather amusing calculation to prove that the Dutch
had spent 540,000 pieces of eight in making captures worth
only 332,000 pieces, "and therefore they need not brag much
of the profit" [*p.* 220].

On *p.* 34 is an interesting account of the taking of St. Iago
upon Cuba by an English fleet, under command of Capt. Chris.
Mines or Myngs, sent for that purpose from Jamaica by Lord
Windsor. The copyist has misread his dates, but a few words in
the minutes of the Council of Jamaica preserved amongst the
Colonial State Papers, show that the expedition started in
September. The town was captured, the shipping seized, and
the great castle commanding the harbour, with "houses sufficient
for a thousand men," blown up with gunpowder.* The King of
Spain sent to Charles II., asking whether he countenanced Lord
Windsor's action, but Consul Rumbold says confidently that
nothing will come of this, as the Spaniards are always easiest
to manage "when best beaten" [*p.* 71].

In connection with the West Indies, attention may be drawn
to a number of curious depositions relating to the unfortunate
Prince Maurice, his shipwreck and imprisonment and the
supposed manner of his death; concerning which there are only
one or two slight rumours recorded in the Colonial State Papers.
One account even professes (though in a very confused fashion)
to give the words spoken by him to a chance fellow prisoner
[*pp.* 117, 134-139].

Scattered throughout the volume are many interesting
allusions to events in England, only a few of which can be
noticed here.

In November, 1662, there is mention of the "treasonable
plot among the Anabaptists," an inconsiderate design, got up
by inconsiderable persons; "imprudent, restless spirits, attempting to their own ruin" [*p.* 48.]

A month later, Lord Inchiquin relates the manner of Sir
Edward Nicholas' enforced resignation of his secretaryship,
"Jack" Ashburnham being sent to him to explain that
"the practices of ill-spirits" in the kingdom required more
activity than his years could undergo, and to offer him 10,000*l.*
and the title of a baron. Nicholas appealed to Clarendon, but
he had been informed by the King of his intentions "in so

---

* Since this report went to press, Captain Myng's letter has been printed in
the English Historical Review, July, 1899, from another copy, in the Bodleian
Library.   c

brisk and short terms" that he dared not interfere, and Sir
Edward accordingly resigned, accepting the money, but declining the honour [p. 54]. Sir Henry Bennet took his place,
and, as Inchiquin tells Fanshaw, in words which recall
Macaulay's celebrated comparison between Pitt and Newcastle,
is like to be a very powerful man in this kingdom, where
my Lord Chancellor meddles only "with the matters relating
to his office and the affairs of State, but does not speak in the
behalf of any man for place or employment." Bennet would
assuredly never hesitate to "speak" if it suited his views and
if the applicant made it worth his while. Fanshaw writes
to congratulate the new secretary, and while acknowledging
his obligations to Nicholas, says, no doubt honestly enough,
that it will be a great advantage to have to do with a "patron"
who understands the Spanish tongue [p. 50]. Lister, in his
Life of Clarendon, observes that Fanshaw's letter of February
7th, 1663 (January 28th, old style), to Sir Henry Bennet, complaining that for the five months he has been in Portugal, he has
not had a word from any Minister of State, "reflects severely
upon the conduct of our foreign affairs under that secretary";
but he fails to note that Bennet was only appointed in November,
1662, and that Fanshaw is speaking of the previous *régime*.
In his answer to this letter, the new secretary says that he
perceives with much resentment how Fanshaw has wanted a
punctual correspondence, and that it falling to his lot to make
this good for the future (owing to the re-arrangement of the
work of the two secretaries), he will not fail to send a letter
upon every occasion [p. 65].

Congratulations are also offered to Williamson, on his retention
of his office, but one feels that these ought rather to have been
addressed to his Chief, for his good fortune in securing one of
the most loyal, zealous, and capable Under-Secretaries whom the
world has ever known. Many news-letters were sent to Fanshaw
by this indefatigable collector, who, while gathering materials
from far and wide for his *Gazette*, was always willing to provide
entertainment for his friends, and who gives many items of
gossip not mentioned by either Pepys or Evelyn [pp. 144, 148,
150, 175].

In March, 1663, Morice writes of the King's futile attempt to
obtain some toleration in religion. The House of Commons
would have none of it, being "fond of the Act of Uniformity;

in other things apt to comply with the King, though not with that prowess of affection which they carried down with them" [*p.* 74]. But although they were not apt to comply in this matter, they said so very civilly, and carried their point with much prudence and respect to the King, and "as much mastery of their passions as a philosopher" [*p.* 77].

On *p.* 127 is a notice by Lord Inchiquin of the charges brought against Clarendon by Bristol, which he believes "certainly had hurt only the latter, and been laid aside had not the matter been kept in suspense by two accidents. The one was too early and too earnest expressing from his Majesty and the Duke, showing their desire and intention to punish my Lord of Bristol, and how severely was doubtful. And the other was the timorousness of my Lord Chancellor, who gave advantage to his adversary by the consenting to the giving of time," Lord Bristol having named Lord Ormond and Lord Lauderdale as two of his witnesses, of whom one was in Ireland and the other in Scotland.

There are many allusions to the great plague, especially in regard to the difficulties occasioned thereby to the fleet and the maritime trade of England. Consul Westcombe would like it to be kept more quiet, but Fanshaw reminds him that it would be of little purpose to prohibit the merchants in London writing of it to their factors in Spain, unless the bills of mortality were suppressed, and the Spanish Ambassador and his followers in England persuaded not to mention it, which clearly would be impossible [*p.* 201]. Dr. Ryves gives a vivid picture of the panic caused by it. "Truly, my lord," he says, "we have been afraid one of another, as if the curse of Cain had been upon us, to fear every man that met us would slay us. The highways have been unoccupied, all intercourse of letters obstructed. and no man thought himself secure in his closest retirements" [*p.* 216]. *See also* letters of Bulteel, Sir Thomas Beverley, and Sir Andrew King [*pp.* 217-219].

In conclusion, it must be noted that the dating of letters written by Englishmen abroad at this period offers peculiar difficulties, as the practice was extremely uncertain. For instance, Hyde and the other Royalists in exile always dated new style, but Sir George Downing, whilst at the Hague, used the old. By means of endorsements of the date of receipt, mention of the day of the week, and allusions to current events, it is however generally possible to ascertain the true date. Fanshaw and his wife, when abroad, invariably used new style, unless the contrary is stated, to which fact is due much confusion in the dates of their published papers. The little series of letters from Lady Fanshaw, here given, was a quite unexpected "find," as they were tied up in a bundle of papers of the year 1667, many months after the death of him to whom they were addressed. The consuls and merchants in Spain and Portugal usually dated new style, but the garrison at Tangier kept to the English fashion, probably because their chief intercourse with the world was by means of English ships.

All letters of any importance, or containing matter of general interest, in the Fanshaw collection, are here calendared, but of the numerous letters (nearly always of complaint) from consuls, merchants, and ships' commanders, and of the mass of official documents, mostly in Spanish or Portuguese, only a selection has been given.

In the spelling of the family name, the form Fanshaw rather than Fanshawe has been adopted, as Sir Richard himself seems always to have used it, as did his cousin and secretary; also it is that given in the volume of printed letters.

Other proper names are printed as spelt by the writers (except in the case of a few very eccentric spellers), the ordinary form being added in the Index. The terms Spanish, Portugal, or Tangier Correspondence have reference, in all cases, to the Foreign Office and Colonial Papers at the Public Record Office.

The Report on these papers and this Introduction have been prepared by Mrs. Lomas.

THE

MANUSCRIPTS OF JOHN M. HEATHCOTE, ESQ.,

OF CONINGTON CASTLE, HUNTS.

CHARLES I. to RICHARD FANSHAW.

1647, October 9. Hampton Court. "Instructions for our trusty, and well-beloved Richard Fanshaw, Esq., our Remembrancer of our Court of Exchequer, employed by us as our resident with the King of Spain.*

1. You shall repair into Spain.

ERRATUM.

Page 6, line 15, *for* Leifrid *read* Seifrid; also in Index.

.... in our name all such sums of money and other proceed [*sic*] of the said fish which shall be found due unto us by the said account.

3. If what you shall by virtue thereof receive from Jackson, shall be by you upon the place judged sufficient to support you in the quality of our resident in that Court until you may be further supplied by us, you shall then present your letters of credence—herewith likewise delivered you—unto our brother of Spain, expressing in our name the high and particular value we have of his Majesty's person and friendship, and our earnest desire to continue the peace and good correspondence established betwixt the two crowns.

4. You shall retain the said sums and other proceed of the goods aforesaid to your own use, upon account towards the satisfying unto yourself all and every such sum and sums as are and shall be due and accruing unto you for the said employment by virtue of our Privy Seal, bearing date the seventh day of February in the twentieth year of our reign—whereof a copy attested by our Chancellor and Under-Treasurer of our Exchequer is hereunto annexed—and of any other allowance which we shall make to you for your service in that kingdom, for which this shall be your warrant, unto which we do hereby engage ourself to add at your request hereafter such further and other warrant and discharge as by your counsel learned in the law shall be advised,

---

* Lady Fanshaw mentions the "Credentials to Spain" given by the King to her husband; but, although he left England at this time, he d'd not go further than France.

possible to ascertain the true date. Fanshaw and his wife, when abroad, invariably used new style, unless the contrary is stated, to which fact is due much confusion in the dates of their published papers. The little series of letters from ʟady Fanshaw, here given, was a quite unexpected "find," as they were tied up in a bundle of papers of the year 1667, many months after the death of him to whom they were addressed. The consuls and merchants in Spain and Portugal usually dated new style, but the garrison at Tangier kept to the English fashion, probably because their chief intercourse with the world was by means of English ships.

All letters of any importance, or containing matter of general interest, in the Fanshaw collection, are here calendared, but of the numerous letters (nearly always of complaint) from consuls, merchants, and ships' commanders, and of the mass of official documents, mostly in Spanish or Port---------
bee
I
tha
alw
it i
O _____ .... .p... .y ...e writers (except in the case of a few very eccentric spellers), the ordinary form being added in the Index. The terms Spanish, Portugal, or Tangier Correspondence have reference, in all cases, to the Foreign Office and Colonial Papers at the Public Record Office.

The Report on these papers and this Introduction have been prepared by Mrs. Lomas.

THE

MANUSCRIPTS OF JOHN M. HEATHCOTE, ESQ.,

OF CONINGTON CASTLE, HUNTS.

CHARLES I. to RICHARD FANSHAW.

1647, October 9. Hampton Court. "Instructions for our trusty, and well-beloved Richard Fanshaw, Esq., our Remembrancer of our Court of Exchequer, employed by us as our resident with the King of Spain.*

1. You shall repair into Spain.

2. You shall, by virtue of our warrant to Philip Jackson, an English merchant usually residing at Bilbao (herewith delivered you), require from the said Jackson a true and faithful account of certain quantities of Irish fish, formerly consigned unto him by the late Earl of Strafford in the time of his government of our kingdom of Ireland, to be sold in Spain for our use, and you shall, by virtue of the same warrant, demand and receive from him in our name all such sums of money and other proceed [*sic*] of the said fish which shall be found due unto us by the said account.

3. If what you shall by virtue thereof receive from Jackson, shall be by you upon the place judged sufficient to support you in the quality of our resident in that Court until you may be further supplied by us, you shall then present your letters of credence—herewith likewise delivered you—unto our brother of Spain, expressing in our name the high and particular value we have of his Majesty's person and friendship, and our earnest desire to continue the peace and good correspondence established betwixt the two crowns.

4. You shall retain the said sums and other proceed of the goods aforesaid to your own use, upon account towards the satisfying unto yourself all and every such sum and sums as are and shall be due and accruing unto you for the said employment by virtue of our Privy Seal, bearing date the seventh day of February in the twentieth year of our reign—whereof a copy attested by our Chancellor and Under-Treasurer of our Exchequer is hereunto annexed—and of any other allowance which we shall make to you for your service in that kingdom, for which this shall be your warrant, unto which we do hereby engage ourself to add at your request hereafter such further and other warrant and discharge as by your counsel learned in the law shall be advised,

---

* Lady Fanshaw mentions the "Credentials to Spain" given by the King to her husband; but, although he left England at this time, he did not go further than France.

A

when the strict forms of business may be observed, you passing your account and rendering unto us the surplusage, in case any should be.

5. Or if you upon your own credit and upon the credit of the said assignment upon Jackson and our Privy Seal above-mentioned—our own present disabilities together with the causes thereof being notoriously known—can procure, either in England or of any of our subjects abroad, so much money as you in your discretion shall think sufficient to venture upon the employment withal, you may in this case likewise present our letters of credence, and we shall account the procuring and furnishing of the same for such a purpose a testimony of great zeal to our service both in you and in any that shall so assist you therewith. And—if you shall fail of money from Jackson whereby to disengage yourself and satisfy such person or persons—you may confidently depend upon our favour and justice for the enabling you thereunto by the due payment of you hereafter—when the same shall be seasonably desired from us on your behalf—according to the tenor of our said Privy Seal, as also for the advancing your ordinary entertainment from forty shillings—which sum only is expressed in the said Privy Seal—to three pound per diem, being that proportion which we have given to others whom we have formerly employed there in that quality, whereof we were not at that time sufficiently informed when we granted that Privy Seal, it having been never in our intention to allow you less than we had done to other men for the same service. Which particulars—when the times will permit—we shall be always ready to confirm, at your humble desire, by due form of Privy Seal for the additional twenty shillings per diem apart, or by a new Privy Seal—comprehending the whole—in lieu of the former.

6. Yet—to leave nothing untried in the meantime for your more speedy reimbursement and satisfaction of such person or persons as may help to furnish you as aforesaid for our service, and for your further and better support therein—if, when you are upon the place and shall have taken upon you the employment upon the terms expressed in the last foregoing instruction, it shall sufficiently appear—by Jackson's own confession or otherwise—that there are really moneys owing to us from him, and yet that either he refuseth or is backward to account for and to deliver the same unto you in obedience to our said warrant, so that you shall conceive he takes advantage of the times—wherein they cannot possibly be had—to stand upon strict formalities, whereby to defraud us of—or at least to keep from us at a time when we have most need thereof—our proper due, you shall then, as in your discretion you shall find fit, either to his Catholic Majesty himself or to some of his ministers, apply yourself in our name for justice, and by all just ways and means constrain the said Jackson to do us right by delivering to you what belongs to us as aforesaid, or at least by depositing the same in safe and indifferent hands.

7. But if when you come upon the place you shall see for the present no certain way whereby to support yourself in that our

service, neither as in the third nor as in the fifth preceding instruction, you may in this case, either totally or until you shall be otherwise supplied by us or by your own further endeavours as in the fifth, suppress our said letters of credence, provided you present the same—if at all—within eight months after the date hereof, unless you shall receive other express directions from us.

8. You shall—in case you enter into the employment—from time to time, and upon all occasions that shall be offered, endeavour and negotiate in our name the observation of the peace betwixt the two crowns, and that our merchants and other subjects may enjoy the full fruit and benefit thereof in their trade and other lawful intercourse with that nation.

9. If whilst you are in the said employment you shall judge it necessary to repair into England, either for the better understanding of our pleasure and directions concerning your negotiation and deportment in that Court upon your personal representation unto us what you have observed upon the place appliable to our service, or for the better settling your own private concernments in reference to your pay for the said employment or to your proper estate at home—now suffering amongst others under the success of the late unhappy war—you have hereby our free leave so to do, without attending our particular pleasure therein—in respect of the distance of the place—we leaving it to your discretion to make choice of such a time wherein your attendance here will be most advantageous, or your absence from thence least prejudicial, to the service you are employed in, and to your care, to return into Spain with such diligence as our affairs shall require.

10. You shall pursue such further instructions as you shall from time to time receive from us, or from whom we shall appoint to signify our commands to you, with whom likewise you are to hold frequent correspondency of letters in what concerns our service. Given under our signet at our honor of Hampton Court this 9th day of October, 1647, and in the 23rd year of our reign." *Sign Manual. Sealed.* $4\frac{1}{2}$ *pp.*

CHARLES II. TO RICHARD FANSHAW.

1649, August [20-]30. St. Germains—" Trusty and well beloved, we greet you well. Our will and pleasure is that you immediately repair *to St. Sebastians to meet my Lord Cottington and Sir Edward Hyde, our ambassadors extraordinary to Spain. And* if they are past from thence before you arrive, then to pursue such directions as they shall leave there for you. But if you come thither before them, then you are to stay till they arrive, provided that your absence from *Ireland be dispensed with by the Marquis of Ormond, whose leave you* are to have, and to govern yourself entirely in this matter according to such directions as you shall receive from him."

With note: " This is in your own cipher." *Sign Manual.* 1 *p.* [*The passages in italics are in cipher, deciphered in the margin, but not apparently very exactly.*]

LORD COTTINGTON and SIR EDWARD HYDE to CHARLES II.

1650, July [17-]27. Madrid—" Mr. Fanshaw hath deferred his journey from hence for some weeks longer than he intended, in hope that we might send by him such account of our service to your Majesty as might make us appear successful, as well as diligent, in your commands, but now his own pressing occasions and his desire to enable himself to wait on your Majesty as soon as may be, which in regard of the distance will require other provisions than he before apprehended, makes him unwilling to stay longer here, nor can we reasonably advise him, since we do not find it easy, with all the diligence and importunity we can use, to bring this people particularly to express what offices of friendship they do intend to perform to your Majesty and by what degrees, their own necessities every day increasing upon them and putting them to all the shifts imaginable to furnish themselves with ready money, from the present disbursement whereof they hope to put a good end to that war, of which they are most weary; and if it had not been for these accidents, we do believe that we should before this time have received some earnest of their kind purposes towards your Majesty, for the manifestation whereof we have yet only had good words and professions, which they still continue with the same solemnity. We have given Mr. Fanshaw so particular information of all we know or believe here with reference to your Majesty's service and to our own ill-condition, that we shall not trouble your Majesty further than to beseech you to hear him, whose integrity and devotion to your service, and his great ability to serve you, your Majesty well knows, and, therefore, we doubt not but your Majesty will give him likewise such a dispatch in what concerns himself as may testify your grace and favour towards him. It will be of great importance to your service that we know here, as soon as may be, of the good reception your Majesty hath found in that kingdom [Scotland], and of any other access of good fortune which may advance your service, in which no men can labour with more duty and affection how unprofitably soever, than we." Signed. 1¼ pp.

MARY [PRINCESS OF ORANGE], to her brother, CHARLES II.

1651, March [19-]29. The Hague—" I formerly desired Monsieur Heenvliet to acquaint your Majesty how much I was concerned in the business of Amboyna, the proceed thereof having been by the King my father assigned to the Prince of Orange in satisfaction to my portion, and the three acts under the Great Seal—by which only the business can be concluded—were delivered into Monsieur Heenvliet's hands for the Prince's use, which acts were after delivered to Mr. Long and by him to Sir William Boswell by the consent of the Prince, with an intention to have advanced money for your Majesty's assistance, but that failing, the acts should have been redelivered to Monsieur Heenvliet, but they were, after Sir William Boswell's death, taken out of his study by

Humfry Boswell and put into the keeping of Mr. Webster. Now, understanding that your Majesty, not rightly apprehending what was desired by me in Monsieur Heenvliet's letter aforesaid, directed Mr. Long to give Monsieur Heenvliet the treaty of marriage at Beverley, and the papers of Amboyna to the Queen of Bohemia, in this necessity, my very jointure being in danger to be shaken in case the portion appear not to have been paid, I was bold to make use of a blank I had of your Majesty by Seamor to command Mr. Webster to deliver me those acts, but how he hath refused that your Majesty will find by a particular relation sent along now, whereto I refer, beseeching your Majesty to allow what I have thus done, and to sign the warrants herewith sent for Webster's and Mr. Long's putting me into possession of the said acts and papers, whereby your Majesty will lay a very important obligation upon me. I will only add this, to desire your Majesty to pardon the length of this letter and to believe that it's not in my power to express to your Majesty the real kindness I have for you, as being with all my heart, my dearest brother, your Majesty's most obedient and humble, most affectionate sister and subject Marie." *Holograph.* 3½ *pp.*

JAMES, DUKE OF YORK, to CHARLES II.

1651, [March 25-]April 4. Breda—"Since I received your Majesty's commands for my return into France I have omitted nothing that might enable me to put them in execution, both by my endeavours to furnish myself with money for the expense of my journey, wherein yet I cannot prevail—that which your Majesty assigned me upon my Lord Culpeper being almost [all] of it expended before it was received—and by frequent solicitations to the Queen to procure me an invitation into France, and an establishment when I should come there. In answer to which I have only received one letter from her Majesty by Harry Seamor, which I sent your Majesty enclosed in the letter I writ by his servant. By Harry Bennett—who I now daily expect from Paris—I hope to know what resolution will be taken concerning me, there being nothing more tedious and displeasing to me than to be forced to delay the performance of what your Majesty commands me to do, but, when the Queen shall inform your Majesty of the reasons that have occasioned this delay, I hope you will not think there hath been any backwardness on my side, and though no reasons were alleged, yet the assurance your Majesty hath in my duty and obedience and readiness to obey all your orders will sufficiently answer for me. I am now by the arrival of those the rebels call their ambassadors at the Hague forced to stay here, which adds extremely to my trouble, being at the same time neither able to obey your Majesty as I would, nor to enjoy the comfort of being with my sister. But I hope the next letters I shall trouble your Majesty with will be dated from Paris, if not, your Majesty shall know the fault is not in me, and in case the disorders in France should grow to that height that the Queen should not think it fit to send for me, I shall then humbly desire your Majesty's orders what I am to do in the next place, and to be confident that I will never take up any resolutions but such as shall be conformable to your Majesty's commands."

Postscript.—" I most humbly beseech your Majesty let Richard Fanshaw come that I may find my rest, and your Majesty shall then see I have much cause to ask for help from your goodness to repair me against some that would ruin me and do your Majesty no good." *Holograph.* 1½ *pp.*

ELIZABETH, QUEEN OF BOHEMIA, to her nephew, CHARLES II.

[1651, March 29-]April 8. The Hague—"Since my last to your Majesty, I have received a letter from Curtius, that at Francfort all the Princes' deputies assembled there did come to him to congratulate your coronation; that one Dr. Leifrid, professor at Tubing[en] in the Duke of Wirtemberg's country, having writ a base book to prove the King's murder lawful, the Duke put him into close prison, and had the book burnt by the hangman's hands; and condemned the author to the fire, but he was saved by great intercession, and banished for ever the country. The Electors of Cleves and Collein [Cologne] show much affection to you also, and all the princes and towns, especially Francfort. Curtius thinks it would do your Majesty much service to give him command and letters to thank them for their congratulating your crowning. I believe Secretary Nicholas doth write more fully of it to you by Broughton. You will hear of the high business betwixt my son and their pretended ambassadors, whom Ned called by their true names. I dare trouble you no further at this time, having just reason to ask your pardon for doing it so much now by so many letters. This bearer comes from my dear godson [the Duke of York], who is most truly affectionate and obedient to you." *Holograph. Seal with crown and arms.* 2 *pp.*

CHARLES II. to SIR WILLIAM BERKELY, Governor of Virginia.

1651, May 20. Camp at Stirling—Our deceased servant, Charles Murray, having died indebted to the bearer, Edward Whitney, in the sum of £460, which, from our care for the credit and memory of our servant we have promised to pay; " and for that through the continued troubles and disorders in all our kingdoms, we have not hitherto found the way to do it as we intended," we desire you to satisfy to him the said sum, which we shall take as a special testimony of your affection, and shall be ready to make good " whenever the present exigencies of our affairs shall be a little over." We further recommend the said Edward Whitney to your favour in the plantation, where he intends to spend his stock and the remainder of his days, this being " not a superficial recommendation, but a thing we very much desire, in regard of the approved honesty and old relations of the man." *Sign manual. Duplicate. Seal impressed.* 1 *p.*

[Sir Edward Hyde] to Richard Francis [Sir Richard Fanshaw.]

[1659, April 30-]May 10. Brussels—"Now I have leave to write to you I will use my old freedom, and if you scape chiding before I have done you will have better luck than you have been used to, but I will first tell you why I proceeded with so much ceremony as to ask your leave to write before I would do it, when I knew you were to be at Paris. I could not imagine it possible that you could have been so long out of England—though I knew well the unlawfulness of the correspondence whilst you were there—without one letter to this court, where you have two such friends besides your master, if you were not restrained—for I never doubted your affection—by some contract from such commerce. And I was the more confirmed in that apprehension, when about a month since, (that is the most,) Harry Coventry sent me a packet from the Hague, which he had received the day before, after Sir Edward Brett, who is a very honest man, had refused to receive it, not giving enough credit to the messenger—though he had been his officer—who had brought such a superscription out of England, which he thought few honest men would have the courage to avow. As I found my own title on the outside, so, when I had opened it, I saw your name in as legible characters, in a letter of the 4 October, which if it had been intercepted, as it might have been as well in all that time, would have put an end to your voyage, but the messenger had been very faithful in all but the speed, the seals were unviolated and all is now safe. But upon the reading it, I was, I say, again confirmed that you had taken that liberty before you entered upon your charge, and that you were bound by your articles not to write afterwards to me, though you were in other cases at liberty if called upon, for I could not imagine otherwise but that you would rather have chosen to have sent the same dispatch after you came out of England, however that you would have made some enquiry after it as you passed by Paris, from whence you sent a civil remembrance only to me by Church. I enlarge myself the more upon this, because by that omission, and for want of your friends knowing your mind and your right, one thing hath passed to your prejudice to the old resident here, and when I read your letter to the King, he was the most out of countenance I ever saw him, and had as absolutely forgot, indeed remembered no more of his engagement to you, than of anything was done the day he was born; and I must again tell you, it cannot be enough wondered at that you would not, during the time of your stay in England, when you had frequent opportunities, or at your first coming over, be sure that the King should be put in mind of your pretence, which had determined all other.

" Your master is as kind to you as you can wish, and what is at present gone will quickly again be to be yours; all the rest you have for asking, though nothing shall be done in it till we meet, because I think we have somewhat better in view for you. I am very ready to give you counsel in what you propose, which is not to be loose until we can call you away to your advantage, at least not to a starving condition, which upon my credit we are all at present. I like your stay at Paris, for methinks we have no unpleasant prospect about us, and if you think this correspondence safe, send me a cipher, and I will offer you some consideration which I cannot well without a disguise. What I say for myself, I say for my Lord Lieutenant* that you shall be very happy if it be ever in my power to serve you." *Holograph.* 1½ *pp.*

The SAME to the SAME.

[1659], May [7-]17. Brussels—" I have yours of the 7th, and if mine of this day seven-night be come to your hands, I need answer little to the greatest part of it, and I continue still of the same mind, that you were to blame in not giving your friends seasonable notice of all your concernments, which were not to be presumed to be safe in that single memory, which could never have committed a fault against you but by forgetting. I believe in a little time you may have reparation in that particular, I mean in kind, I am sure you will in weight, if I can judge aright, but I will not enlarge upon that or anything else of moment till you send me a cipher, and then you shall know what I think in all things; and if you leave orders with Church how to send my letters to you, you shall not fail of them, and of all necessary advertisements which may concern you and your interest. Nothing you write to me shall be mentioned to any but between the King, my Lord Lieutenant* and myself, nor have I ever mentioned your name to anybody as if I heard of you, but casually to Mr. Heath, who spoke to me as from you, but I acquainted him not with anything you had said to me, but only that a letter you had long since sent out of England came not to me till within this month. You cannot wish your friends kinder to you, and I do assure you I will make that kindness as useful as I can; either write to my Lord Lieutenant* yourself, or mention him in mine, as he deserves from you."

Postscript.—" What will your young man come to ? " *Holograph. Seal with crest.* 1 *p.*

The SAME to the SAME.

[1659], May [21-]31. Brussels—I have deferred acknowledging yours of the 15th till I may reasonably presume you are returned and that this will find you at Paris, nor will I retract one word of my chiding in the former, which, notwithstanding all you say in defence, and the delay in the delivery of yours from England, which was not your fault, you do very richly deserve, for without doubt you ought, and had opportunity enough to have done so, let your friends know what you had in justice to expect, and which you could not reasonably presume would be

---

* This word is a mere scrawl, but may be read Lt. Ormond arrived at Brussels just at this time, and was Fanshaw's chief patron.

enough remembered, and yet I must tell you the forgetful person is more severe to himself than you could be, if you gave your mind to it.

I send you herewith a cipher, and then we may talk freely what is of concernment, and I shall when I know you have it, tell you all that I think may concern yourself, but you must give me leave—for I am not ashamed to tell you that my eyes are not so good as you have known them, and I find wonderful ease in dictating—sometimes, especially when there is much use of cipher, that I write by another hand that is more legible, and you shall have the less reason to fear it in point of secrecy, when I promise you that I will in my letters to you use the help of no other hand. but of one of my sons, I having two with me, very capable of the service. God keep you." *Holograph Seal.* 1 *p.*

The SAME to the SAME.

[1659], June [4-]14. Brussels.—I have yours of the 6th, and will now discourse with you concerning yourself, and will in the first place tell you that *your master* will make you all the recompense he can *for the wrong he has done you*, and yet I must say to you again that you were to blame not to help his memory in these catching times *by letting us know your right.** The conclusion is, as soon *as that place falls, which it will do* ere long, it shall infallibly *be yours.*

You are the secretary of the Latin tongue, and I will mend the warrant you sent, and have it dispatched as soon as I hear again from you, but I must tell you, *the place in itself*, if it be not dignified by the person, who hath some other qualification, is not to be valued. *There is no signet belongs to it*, which can be only *kept by a Secretary of State, from whom the Latin Secretary* always receives orders and prepares no dispatches without his direction, and hath only a fee of a hundred pound a year. And therefore, except it hath been in the hands of a person who hath had some other employment, it hath fallen to the fortune of inconsiderable men, as Wakerly [Weckerlin] was the last.

I have long thought *upon a fit place for you, to which both the other being united, you might* appear with lustre enough and a very competent support, *and if you were of my mind, you would think* it the finest *place about the court*, as in truth it is, *and for a place of action** inferior *only to the Secretary of State, and from whence to be secretary is a very natural step, and that is Master of Requests, by which you have the King's ear* three months in [the] year, as much *as the secretary, and in which you would very* honestly get six or seven hundred pound a year though *you should never make any suit for yourself.* It is a proper qualification *for any body and a road** *to anything your friends can propose** *for you.* *This place the King has promised Ormond** *and me for you, and that you shall be the first who* shall *be sworn in it;* and as I said before, *this place, with the other two.* will be both ornament and profit, and I confess to you

_____
* Doubtful words.

neither of the other two alone is worthy *of you*. As soon as I know your mind in this, I will see everything done that is necessary. I cannot propose anything reasonably to you or for you *about the interview upon the frontiers*,† for besides that I do not wish that you should sustain any present loss by a relation *to the King's cause** before it can be profitable to you, the Cardinal** will be there*, and there are other reasons which you shall know hereafter, and this is all I can think of to say with relation to yourself.

Tell me now all that occurs to you as fit to be known by us both with reference to persons and things in England.

Is my *Lord of Pembroke** so mad or so foolish that he can never be made of any use** to the King?* Since all your friends, and all to whom you have now any relation, *do very well know your affections, can they not be* persuaded *through you to convey any information to us, or anything else that may be most necessary?*

Tell me in the last place upon what your studies are at present fixed, what books you have written and printed since I saw you, and why you never sent me those books. I hope you will think this a large despatch, and like it better than if it were in the proper handwriting of your most affectionate servant. *In the handwriting of his son; the last few words only by himself.* 1½ *pp.* [*The parts in italics are in cipher, undeciphered.*]

The SAME to the SAME.

[1659, June 25], July 5. Brussels—"I excused myself the last week by Church, for not answering yours of the 20th, and I have since by the last post, yours of the 27th and but the last night your other of the 21st, for Mr. Heath having been out of the town, and not returning until yesterday, I could not receive it sooner. If you had not directed me otherwise I had sent your concernments by the post, as I think I might well have done with security enough, and in my own judgment better than the other way, but you shall be obeyed: and at this by me receive no further trouble—for I have so much to do by this post that I can very hardly despatch it—than the assurance" of my constant affection. *Holograph.* ½ *p.*

The SAME to the SAME.

[1659], July [9-]19. Brussels—I have yours of the 11th, and, if it had not come in the very article, your former prescription had been obeyed, the good lord departing from this town on Thursday; yet I am still of opinion this is the better conveyance; if you have not enclosed all the instruments you expect, it is for want of skill in preparing them. The patent for Master of Requests I shall see despatched, being I think better able to get the form than you can, and indeed it had been done by this time, if my directions to Breda, where a patent of a friend of mine is, had been observed or better understood, but I have not

† The treaty of the Pyrenees.   * Doubtful words.

been yet able so well to describe the place where it is as to lead Dr. Morley to find it; I shall within few days recover it, the other for the Latin Secretary you must retain yourself, for the secretary nor I do know whether it be by patent or warrant, only I am sure the old form is to be observed, because the fee is contained in it. When you write next to me, say somewhat of kindness to the good secretary that I may show him, who is much your friend: I believe I shall say somewhat to you in my next in cipher, and methinks if your friends in England use any freedom towards you, you should have many things to impart which would need that disguise. I will say no more at present than that I wish you in entire possession of all you desire, and that we may spend the rest of our time together, and that I may have frequent opportunities to express to you how very heartily I am, your most affectionate servant."

Postscript.—" You will have no cause to use Mr. Heath's service in any of the particulars, and, therefore, you need not let him know anything, for which I have a reason." *Holograph.* 1 *p.*

The SAME to the SAME.

[1659], July [16-]26. Brussels—I have yours of the 18th, and I hope you have mine of the day after, and when I writ that, I did believe I should have had occasion to have enlarged in this upon many particulars, but yet all things are as they were, by which you may perceive there are many idle discourses abroad in the world, and truly if those discourses do not harm, it is a great miracle. I have told you heretofore, that till we can do you good, we will do you no harm, and the ease and quiet you are in shall be preserved, but *if the King were once in England, I should think it necessary you should make haste to him, though you broke some covenants, which in that case I believe would not be taken ill.* I thank you for your poetry, which I see you refresh yourself in both languages. I do very much long to see your *Querer por solo querer,* both in the translation and the original, I have heard it much commended, but could not procure it whilst I was in Spain. If you will needs exercise yourself in translations, which methinks you should not choose to do, when you can so well digest your own thoughts upon many subjects, I wish you would collect a parcel of Spanish letters, which though you will not find together in any one volume, at least that I have seen, you may out of several authors bring together such a collection of letters, both serious and light, which will appear better in English than any volume of letters that I ever saw in any language. God send us into a place where we may spend our time better, and bring us well together." *Holograph.* 1 *p.* [*The sentence in italics is underlined in the letter.*]

The SAME to the SAME.

[1659, July 22-]August 1. Brussels—I have yours of the 25th, and have delivered your compliments to the persons concerned. I

shall take care to procure you anything out of the stores you
mention, which may be useful to you, and if you and I can once
bring ourselves together, you shall be well enough informed of
all that is necessary, but I must now tell you, with some trouble,
that after a full search for the patent at Breda, it is evident that
it is not to be found, it being left in a trunk in England, therefore, you shall do well to send to some friend to send you a copy
from thence, which is very easy to be done without the least
notice. I am afraid your letters from England are not so cheerful
as they were, for it is a wonderful thing to see how our friends
are cast down upon the acts of this last week, though there
appears no other ground for it than that they are not together
by the ears, and because they are disappointed in their expectation of the dissolution of the Parliament by the army. I do
confess to you I do not like my own letters, nor do enough
understand the temper and resolutions there; I wish I were
sure there is no foul play amongst people who are trusted, and
if a man prove faulty, of whom you and I have always had a very
good opinion, we shall not hereafter know upon whom to depend
in point of integrity. There is one comfort, that many days
cannot pass, before we shall be able to make a reasonable judgment which is like to come to pass. We do not understand
anything of the Sound, or what Montague resolves to do, nor
is the temper of Monck and his army sufficiently understood by
us. I wish you all happiness." *Holograph.* 1 *p.*

The SAME to the SAME.

[1659, July 30-]August 9. Brussels—"I thank you very
heartily for yours of the 1st, and have some reason to believe that
your letters from England of this day seven-night brought you
nothing to allay your hopes from thence. I wish with all my heart
that those of this day bring you no other tidings, for there is so
much discourse of plots and of treachery that I cannot be without
apprehension for a little time more. If nothing fall amiss, I
hope we may write cheerfully to each other shortly, and I pray
fail not to let me know what letters inform you. You can expect
nothing of news from this place, but the health of your friends,
which generally is good; mine at present interrupted by a little
indisposition." *Holograph.* ½ *p.*

The SAME to the SAME.

[1659], August 30. Brussels.—I was very glad to receive
yours of the 23rd, and to find that no misfortune should then
have befallen any of your friends, and yet I cannot but wonder
that so long after the day none of them were in arms, when in
so many other places there was encouragement enough. I have
long told you that there was a false brother amongst our friends
who did infinite mischief, but I never named him because I
thought you would never believe it, as I myself was very unwilling to do. Would you ever have thought it possible that

Sir Richard Willis could prove false and treacherous, and to correspond with Thurlow? I know not what may be the issue, hitherto our hopes are fair, but I do believe if that Knot upon which you and I have so much depended, and which I am persuaded have failed only by the craft of him whom they never suspected nor it may be do yet, had done their part, very few had miscarried, and little blood had been spilt in the quarrel. I hope the other parts of the kingdom will not look on and leave our Cheshire and Lancashire friends to contend alone. I look our next letters shall bring us much good, be sure you tell me particularly what yours bring, it is pity you have not a way of communicating more freely with your friends. God send us a good meeting." *Holograph.* 1 *p.*

The Same to the Same.

[1659], September [10-]20. Brussels—I excused myself to you by Church for not writing the last post, when besides the impression the common tale made upon my spirits, I was really very sick, nor am I yet well recovered. I have since yours of the 12th, and when I signified my expectation of a long letter from you, it was upon the news of your wife's arrival, who I presumed would be able to inform you of many important particulars. I do tell you, and to the end you may warn all such of your friends who are not yet undone and may be in danger by the same friendship, that all this hopeful design hath been ruined by the treachery of Sir Richard Willis, of whom I had so good an opinion that I would have put my life into his hand, as I did the life of him whom I love as well. I did not depart from this confidence till the King received such clear evidence of his treachery as left no room for doubt, and yet I believe few men believe it, nor can evidence of that kind be published, but men must take the King's word, who could not be moved in the point till there remained no room for doubt. I should be glad you would take the pains to inform me of as many particulars concerning persons and things as you can, for in this dispersion of our friends we know little more than the prints inform us. We have yet reason to hope well of Spain, of which I presume our master can by this time better judge, for I should be much troubled if I did not believe his Majesty to be at this present with Don Lewis,* though I have not heard one word from him, or any about him, since he received the ill news. My service to your wife." *Holograph.* 1 *p.*

The Same to the Same.

[1659], October [1-]11. Brussels—I have yours of the 4th, and will say no more of that wicked, false brother than that you are to warn all your friends to take heed of him, for all yet do not believe him false. You see the conquerors scarce yet know how

* Don Luis Mendez de Haro, &c., Conde-Duque de Olivares, Marques del Carpio y de Liche, chief minister of the King of Spain. Ob. 1661.

to use their victory, nor do the prisoners look on them with any reverence, it is probable the army may by this time have once more broken their form of government. Church is a very honest man and my particular friend, and if I do at any time say anything that troubles him, it is without any purpose to do so, for I know his fidelity and diligence to be exemplary, and if I do not give him cause to believe that I think so, it is only want of skill in me. I must not give over the consideration of my poor sister and discoursing it with you, though you tell me that you know not what to contribute to her service. I knew not so many particulars of her condition as you tell me, having not heard word from her above this twelve months, and I do with great indignation hear the carriage of her son towards her, who if he be in the same distemper, ought not to have the tuition of her. What is become of her brothers, is there none of them who can or will protect her from oppression? I do again desire you, if it be possible, to engage some friend to speak with her son from me, that he may know I desire to have an account of the true state of the business between them, and expect that he should use her with the duty that is due to her; I know it is not easy to get such a message delivered, yet if it be possible I wish it done, she deserves all the offices from me I can perform towards her. God keep you and yours." *Holograph.* 1 *p.*

The Same to the Same.

[1659], October [15-]25. Brussels—I have yours of the 17th, and though I know not what to reply to what you have said of my poor sister, I do heartily beg you to think of somebody that may so speak to her son of her that I may know what he says; for I am willing to think he may not be without some civility towards me. I must now ask you a question which I am sure you will answer me very frankly, knowing that I cannot ask it to any ill purpose. Tell me then of what age is your pupil Ld. . . . * and what are his faculties and disposition, and is he more like father or mother.

You took great care kindly in one of your letters to mention honest Church to me, as a man very fit to be cherished, and I am so much of your mind that I do heartily desire to do him a very good turn, and doubt not to live to compass it, but I cannot but complain to you of him, of which you must take no notice, that he is too solicitous to have money given him by the King, and notwithstanding I do truly inform him of the miserable condition all the King's servants are in, above two years in arrear of their board wages, which God knows, if paid, would but give them bread, he still thinks he ought to be supplied and makes great moan of being ready to starve, when it is very strange that family can be in want; I have often told him that when the King is able to spare it, I will remember him, as I have done formerly, yet he is not satisfied. You must not take notice that I complain of him, but find some such way to talk of

---

* Fanshaw was with the eldest son of the Earl of Pembroke, but the word, which is carefully cancelled, does not appear to be Herbert.

the necessities of this place, which in truth can hardly be imagined, that he may not think it reasonable to continue that importunity. The King was not at the frontiers the 14th, which makes me mad. God keep you." *Holograph.* 1 *p.*

The SAME to the SAME.

[1659, October 29-]November 8. Brussels—I have yours of the 31st of the last, and do thank you for the character you give of the young man, which is a very good one, and you shall hereafter know the reason why I ask it; I have no more to say upon that argument but to know whether there be any thought of his being called home. We know nothing of the affairs of England since the very day that the Parliament was dissolved, and the extraordinary and unusual care that is taken to keep us from knowing what passed makes us believe that the confusion there is very high, and yet that there is some governing power that is well obeyed, for we have not only any letters from thence, now these two last post days, but our packet boat is not suffered to go to shore nor to send the letters, but is forced to return to Ostend, which kind of restraint hath never been practiced since the beginning of these troubles. I should be glad to find that all the proceedings of the Parliament were so totally condemned that all our friends were at liberty, as having justly opposed a power that had no dominion over them. I know not what to say of our Spanish friends, if they have in truth pursued their journey to Madrid and left Don Lewis behind them, they may have cause to be sorry for it, and the ministers here censure the method very much. I do confess the whole journey hath been so conducted and so contrary to former resolutions, that I am not a little troubled at it. I hope the next week will bring me some satisfaction, and that the King will find so quick a dispatch in all he desires that he will not stay long in those parts. I wish you heartily all happiness." *Holograph.* 1 *p.*

The SAME to the SAME.

[1659], November [5-]15. Brussels—" I have received yours of the 7th, which hath renewed very much my trouble and sorrow for you, which was before in some degree abated out of the hope that the foundation of it was not true, for Church, writing in a postscript as a thing he only feared, and in the next letter saying nothing of it, I entertained a faint hope that God Almighty had withdrawn that affliction from you and so I forbore condoling in my own letter with you the last week. I know not what to say but to refer you to your own good spirit and ratiocination. Your friends in England hold up their heads again, and I hope we may once more meet there." *Holograph.* ½ *p.*

The SAME to the SAME.

[1660], January [14-]24. Brussels—I have yours of the 16th, but the letter of the former, as all that were directed to me by that post, are miscarried, and lost to me; therefore, recollect yourself, if anything were in it for my information, and renew it in your next.

I presume you hear from my Lord Lieutenant all that concerns yourself. That which I do indeed take unkindly, *both from the King and Ormond,** as* I have told them, is *that they would* put off and defer the answer till they came hither, when the resolution was taken there, and never so much as consulted here. *The King has offered the place indeed to one who* upon my conscience will never deserve it, *yet,* in the interval, it will not be fit to *fill* * *it*. I will say no more to you of myself, than that there is nothing I desire more, and hope one day to see it, and without *money* * *which should* never have tempted me.

Indeed the turns in England turn my head, that I know not what to say or think of them. Nothing more extravagant than that the Rump should sit and govern three kingdoms, yet nothing to come can appear more impossible than that which they have passed through, and if our next letters do not tell us of some new broils, I shall be melancholic. God keep you.

Postscript.—I look you should thank me in your next for the books I sent you. *Holograph.* [*The words in italics are in cipher, undeciphered.*] 1 *p.*†

ALFONSO, KING OF PORTUGAL, to KING CHARLES II.

1661 [January 24-] February 3. Lisbon—Recommending Consul Thomas Maynard, who has shown great care, zeal, and love in his Majesty's service. *Signed by the Queen Regent. Portuguese. Seal impressed.* ½ *p.*

LORD CHANCELLOR CLARENDON to the QUEEN OF PORTUGAL.

1661, July 9. London—This will be placed in your royal hands by the Ambassador of Portugal, who is returning to Lisbon by desire of the King, my master, to arrange for the speedy arrival of the Queen, my mistress, whom may God conduct safely; this being the thing in all the world most desired by my master, and after him by all his subjects. For myself, this alliance more than fulfils my ambition to serve the Crown of Portugal and your Majesty, whose august person may God guard, granting you the long life, which is so needful to both kings for the augmenting of their greatness and mutual friendship by the counsels and care of so great a Queen and so prudent a mother. *Spanish. Draft by Fanshaw.* 1 *p.*

CHARLES II. to his wife, QUEEN CATHERINE, Infanta of Portugal.

1661, July [9?] Palace in London—The good Conde de Ponte‡ —who has been very useful to me—is now starting for Portugal,

---

* Doubtful words. † These letters from Hyde to Fanshaw are almost all addressed "For Mr. Francis," and most of them have a note (written below the address) from Percy Church to Fanshaw, requesting him to have them delivered. ‡ Francisco de Melo, Conde de Ponte and, in 1662, Marques de Sando.

the marriage contract being signed; and I am also sending after him a servant of my own, to assure you of my inexpressible pleasure at this happy conclusion. I am now about to make a progress in my dominions, whilst awaiting the arrival from hers of my supreme good. I cannot rest anywhere, and vainly seek relief from my inquietude, longing to see her beloved person in my kingdom as anxiously as I desired, after long exile, to see myself there, or as my subjects desired to see me, the which was shown to all the world by their demonstrations on my arrival. May you have the peace which comes from the protection of God, with all the health and happiness that I can desire. *Spanish. Draft by Fanshaw.* 1 *p.*

CHARLES II. to his Mother [in law], the QUEEN OF PORTUGAL.

1661, August 21. London—The bearer of this, Sir Richard Fanshaw, a trusty and well-beloved gentleman of my household, is dispatched by me as ambassador extraordinary to the Queen, my wife, to tell her of my daily increasing desire to see her hasten her arrival with my ambassador, and of the arrangements made for her service on the journey here. I beg you to grant to this my servant all the license and orders that may be needful on the part of your court, and that you yourself will aid your royal daughter to forget that for my sake she must leave the court of so good a brother, and the embraces of so tender and affectionate a mother. *Spanish. Draft by Fanshaw.* 1 *p.*

CHARLES II. to his wife, QUEEN CATHERINE.

1661 [August 21?]. London—The bearer, of this, Sir Richard Fanshaw, who has served me for many years faithfully and honourably, is the same whom I recommended to you in my last letter, sent by the Conde de Ponte. He is going as ambassador extraordinary to yourself, to assure you of my infinite affection and to arrange for your arrival here with all possible speed. He would attend you on your journey, were it not that being appointed to our common service, he must, as matters now stand. fit himself at once for the office of resident ambassador at the court of Lisbon, when he has, with all due respect, seen you embark and under sail in my fleet, which the Earl of Sandwich will soon bring to anchor in your port. He is the bearer of orders and all that is needful for the performance of my wishes with regard to the marriage ceremonies deemed necessary before we see each other, as also in regard to your coming hither, and I pray you to give entire faith and credit to what he says in my behalf, especially as touching the assurance of my devoted love, which goes on increasing as the joy of seeing you and the right to call you mine draw nearer, and will do so more and more when you are my own. May God guard you and grant long life to you, whom I long for every day and every hour. *Spanish. Draft by Fanshaw.* 1 *p.*

CHARLES II. to SIR RICHARD FANSHAW.

1661, August 23. Whitehall—Instructions for our trusty and well-beloved Sir Richard Fanshaw, knight and baronet, employed by us into Portugal.

Since you understand by the treaty between us and Portugal how much we have obliged ourself to support the interest of that crown, you will easily believe that we are very much concerned to have a clear information of the state of affairs there, of the Government, of the factions in court and state, of the humour of the people amongst themselves, and of their inclination to return to the Government of Spain; therefore, you will use all your diligence and dexterity to inform yourself as exactly as is possible in all those particulars, and to that purpose in the first place—

1. You shall use your utmost diligence and dexterity to make a friendship with those ministers who are most entrusted in the management of the affairs of that crown, and shall upon all occasions assure them of our resolution to assist and support that crown, and of our particular kindness to them, which we shall manifest upon any occasion, and you shall by them and all other ways inform yourself of the strength of their armies, of the greatness of their fleets, of the revenue of the crown, by which it is enabled to support that great expense.

2. Since you know one of the principal advantages we propose to ourself by this entire conjunction with Portugal is the advancement of the trade of this nation and the enlargement of our own territories and dominions, in order thereunto you shall use all diligence to inform yourself of the true interest by trade between this kingdom and Portugal itself and how the same may be improved; and to that purpose you must be sure to conserve all the privileges already granted to our merchants there, and to improve the same as there shall be occasion.

3. You shall prepare all things in readiness for the delivery of the Island of Bombaim in the East Indies into our hands against the month of November, when our fleet shall be ready to set sail for the receiving thereof and shall call at Lisbon for all necessary orders thereunto; and you shall very earnestly press that Bassine may likewise be put into our hands, which we insisted on in our demand, and understood by the answer made to us that the Ambassador had had power committed to him to have consented to the same, but he protesting against having any such power prevailed with us to leave the same out of the treaty. Therefore you shall confer freely with him upon it and let him know that we depend upon him still to assist us in the procuring thereof; and in the managing those instances you shall govern yourself by his advice, and if he doth wish that you should for the present suspend any such demand, as presuming that it cannot be reasonable or effectual, you shall forbear it accordingly.

4. You shall inform yourself the best you can of the true present condition of the Portuguese in the East Indies, and what their returns from thence are; and if you find that Goa is so

besieged by the Dutch that Portugal receives no benefit from thence, nor is able to have a trade with it, you may easily represent how impossible it is for their own subjects there long to acquiesce under such a restraint, and that if the same were likewise put into our hands, it would be presently freed from the Dutch, and then Portugal would have all the benefit of trade from thence as if it were in their own hands: and if they shall desire that we would take Goa into our possession by setting up our standard there, it may be done in such a manner, and with so small a garrison, as can be no bridle to that populous city from paying their allegiance to the King of Portugal. Toward this and all arguments of this nature, their weakness to withstand the Dutch and the danger of having all those dominions fall into their hands must be the principal motives, and therefore must be carefully understood by all the means you can use, in the meantime you are to prosecute all that is necessary for the settling the English factories there according to the treaty.

5. You shall take all the ways you can to inform yourself of the power of Portugal in Brazil and the West Indies, what their dominions are in those parts, how possessed and how governed, how the trade is settled between that and Portugal, and then how those commodities which come from thence to Portugal are afterwards distributed over the world. You shall inform yourself what quantity of sugars are yearly brought from thence into Portugal, what duties it pays there, how much is spent within that kingdom, and whither the rest is sent and in what ships, whether the trade be driven from thence only by Portuguese, or by whom else, and in what bottoms; in a word the chief end of this particular enquiry and disquisition is that you may thereby discern whether it may be practicable that the English may engross to themselves the sole trade of sugar, taking the whole commodity at a price, and we being bound to send our fleet to Brazil, and therewith to convoy such a proportion of sugar to Portugal as shall every year be assigned to that consumption, and may then transport the rest whither shall seem best. You have had so much said to you upon this argument by those who manage that design that there need be no more enlargement upon it in this place.

6. You are well informed of the carriage of the Portugal Ambassador in Holland, who having done us as much hurt as he could there is now gone to Lisbon with a resolution to do us as much more as he can; and, therefore, you shall do all you can to discredit him with the King and Queen-mother, and let them know that we look upon him as a person of manifest disaffection to us; that he did not only neglect complying with us in all we desired, but we are sure showed our letters to De Witt, and imparted to him whatever we sent to him, and therefore we neglected to answer his last letter. That for the peace with Holland, we are free from wishing that Portugal should omit the making such a peace as they find necessary for their preservation, but we cannot be pleased that ever Holland shall be admitted to enjoy the same privileges in trade with our subjects,

since we are sure the alliance we make with Portugal and the hazard we run thereby merits that there should be some distinction between us in those concessions; and, therefore, you shall use all your diligence, and call in the Ambassador the Conde de Ponte to your aid, that such an equality between us and our subjects and the Dutch be not accepted and confirmed by the King of Portugal, but that by virtue of that article whereby it is provided that nothing in this treaty with the Dutch shall contradict anything that is agreed with the English, that preference and privilege to our subjects in trade may be preserved: and you shall use all your credit, and desire the Queen-mother and even our wife to appear avowedly in it if there be cause, that the Count of Miranda be not suffered to return Ambassador into Holland, as a person we look upon as disaffected to us and consequently not fit for that employment. Given at our court at Whitehall the 23rd day of August, 1661, in the thirteenth year of our reign.

You shall recommend in our name to the Queen Regent our good mother as occasions shall be offered the interests of Russell in that court. *Sign Manual, countersigned by Secretary Morice. Copy.* 3½ *pp.*

CHARLES II. to SIR RICHARD FANSHAW.

1661 [August]—Instructions for our trusty and well-beloved servant, Sir R[ichard] F[anshaw], Knight, presently dispatched by us in quality of our envoy extraordinary to Portugal the [   ] of [   ], 1661.

1. You shall speedily repair to Lisbon—winds and weather favouring—in our good ship the *Princess*, under the command of Captain Hall, who hathp received orders from our dearest brother, the Duke of York, to transport you thither.

2. After you have presented our credentials—herewith delivered to you—we will that you shall use such speech to the King of Portugal our good brother, and to our good mother the Queen Regent there, as may testify our high transport of joy for the marriage we have lately concluded, with a firm purpose and desire on our part not only to conserve the good amity that is betwixt us and him our said brother, and consequently to preserve concord and mutual intercourse betwixt the subjects of both crowns, according to the good treaties that remain betwixt us for that intent, but to improve the same from time to time as occasion shall be offered, requesting their license for you to address yourself unto our dearest consort in that dutiful and reverential posture which is permitted to subjects and servants by a Queen of England, with our letter—herewith likewise delivered to you for her—and with what else you have in command from us.

3. You shall acquaint our said dear wife—our never to be doubted love and affection to her person being first expressed—that our intent in sending you at this present thus qualified with our authority is principally and only in order to her more

speedy embarkation and honourable conveyance to these her kingdoms by your preparing there for the Earl of Sandwich, and by your soliciting her royal brother and mother to dispose her will to endure an absence of so dear and excellent relations, and to apply the concurrent authority of that crown to expedite all things that shall be on their part necessary and conducing to the prosperity and lustre of this voyage.

4. You shall present unto our dear wife from us [as] a small earnest of our love the particulars following, viz.: [*particulars not filled in*].

5. You shall—with all due respects and deference to his person and quality—communicate and co-operate with the Earl of Sandwich in all matters of our service, particularly as to the speedily conducting our dear wife, where with great impatience we shall expect her.

6. As to the monies and goods—part of our wife's dowry—which are by virtue of the marriage treaty to be delivered on board before her embarkation, you are to do as followeth, viz.: [*blank space*].

7. You shall, in this same quality of our Envoy Extraordinary, with all dutiful observance and diligence imaginable attend the service of our dear wife in the Admiral's ship with her, and so until her arrival in our presence, unless the necessity of our service—which will be hers likewise—shall oblige you to stay behind in the quality of our ambassador resident in that court, in which case it shall suffice that having first been presented with that character by the Earl of Sandwich at his parting audience, you attend our said wife on board until she be under sail.

8. In case you shall—as in the next foregoing instruction—stay behind with the character of our ambassador resident with that King, you are hereby authorised to receive and detain in your hands, out of the dowry monies in the 6th foregoing article mentioned, the sum or value of ———*l.* sterling by way of advance for the ordinary allowance of the first half-year of your Embassy at 6*l. per diem* to be reckoned from the day you shall be presented in that quality as aforesaid, in discharge of so much to grow due to you out of our Exchequer by virtue of your privy seal upon that account.

9. You shall deliver to our right trusty and right well-beloved cousin and Councillor the Earl of Sandwich—our Ambassador Extraordinary to Portugal—at your first meeting our credentials and instructions herewith delivered unto you for him, advertising him thereof by letter, as also of what else you shall conceive requisite for our service that he know, by such opportunities of conveyance to him as you may happen upon in the interim.

10. You shall deliver unto our good brother, the King of Portugal, the treaty between us, bearing date the — of ——— 1661; and herewith delivered unto you likewise for that purpose ratified by ourself under our hand and Great Seal of England.

And you are to see the counterpart thereof ratified there in like manner by our said brother, and transmitted to us, if not done before your arrival." *Draft in Fanshaw's hand. 4 pp.*

KING CHARLES II. to the KING OF PORTUGAL.

1661, August 30. Hampton Court—Announcing the appointment as ordinary ambassador for the time being of Sir Richard Fanshaw, Latin Secretary and Master of Requests, late Ambassador Extraordinary to the Court of his Portuguese Majesty. *Signed. Latin. 1 p.*

EARL OF SANDWICH to SIR RICHARD FANSHAW.

1661, September 22. Aboard the *Royal James*—Stating that his ships will be in readiness to sail on Tuesday next, and mentioning a "bull-running," which he hopes to see. *Torn. Holograph. ½ p.*

CHARLES II. to SIR RICHARD FANSHAW.

1661, October 11. Whitehall—The plenipotentiary Extraordinary of the King of Sweden here, the Lord John Frederick Van Friesendorff, has a cause at law depending in Lisbon, and as the King, his master, has no resident there, we desire you to confer with the Lord Ambassador Francisco de Melo, the Earl of Ponte, and to do what you can to bring the business to a happy issue. *Noted by Fanshaw :* "True copy, the original remaining with me, and upon it the impression of his Majesty's royal signet." *1 p.*

EARL OF SANDWICH to SIR RICHARD FANSHAW, Envoy Extraordinary to the King of Portugal.

1661, November 7-17. Tangier Bay—"This is only that no ship should come from hence but that you should have some advice of our station. I continue riding here for the same ends as before, but as yet we have not discovered over here any news of the fleet from England. We hear the Prince of Spain is dead, and that the Queen is lately brought to bed of another Prince, which hath caused great joy in the Spanish parts hereabouts." The ships are in haste to be gone, so I can add no more. *Holograph, Seal of arms. ½ p.*

QUEEN CATHERINE to CHARLES II.

1661, November [18-]28. Lisbon—Stating that she takes advantage of Sir Richard Fanshaw's return to England to procure news of his Majesty, for which she is so anxious that the voyage of the Envoy might seem rather the contrivance of her passion than to negotiate the affairs of Portugal. *Draft translation in Fanshaw's hand. 1¼ pp.*

Queen Catherine to Charles II.

[1661, November 18?]—"My lord and husband, I shall take it for a particular favour that your Majesty for my sake would be pleased to bestow upon the bearer hereof, Sir Richard Fanshaw, some considerable office in my household, the which he himself may propose unto your Majesty, being such as your Majesty shall find him capable of, for the well (*sic*) that his deportment hath appeared to this court, and the cheerfulness wherewith he undertakes this voyage at my command for the service of this crown. And likewise that your Majesty would be pleased to grant unto his wife, Donna Anna, the office to be that woman of my bedchamber, unto whom it belongs also to be Lady of the Jewels, and that this favour may be granted her, as well for the services of her husband, whom your Majesty doth so graciously own, as for her much virtue and particular qualifications, which, I am informed, are found in her person for the discharge of that employment." *Translation in Fanshaw's hand.* 1 *p.*

The Earl of Clarendon to Sir Richard Fanshaw.

[1661], December 6. Worcester House—" I have little to add to what I wrote by Mr. Church [the which?] you will easily believe when I tell you that from the minute I gave him my letters I was carried to my bed, and have ever since lived in that torment that I cannot yet stand more upon my feet than upon my head. We all promise ourselves that we shall shortly see our royal mistress here, concerning whom I know you will entertain me at large when we meet, which your friends say will be speedily and that you are resolved to come away with the Queen. I will not be so unkind as to dissuade you from anything you think good for yourself, nor will you take it ill of me for not thinking as you do, so I do not hinder you from doing as you desire, only I pray think of some person fit to be sent thither as soon as you come away, for it will be absolutely necessary always to have a minister in that court, and we shall want one there when our fleet for the East Indies passes by in February next. I pray consult with my Lord Sandwich—which I have forgot to mention in my letter to him—about explaining, or rather improving those articles in the treaty which concern our freedom of trade to the Brazil and West Indies. We did press some liberty in the point of license and conduct money, which though not yielded to *in terminis*, the Queen of Portugal did send the King word that there should be such a private allowance another way in that affair, which should be equivalent to what we proposed. The ambassador will inform you (and so will the Bishop Russell) more exactly in this, and then I would be glad you could so state our privileges with reference to that trade that we might engage a company here to that undertaking, which I find easy to do, upon a little more encouragement. You are enough instructed in the business of the sugar to make at least

such approaches to it as to discover what is practicable in that
kind, and I must tell you I do expect to find you marvellously
learned in that whole trade of the East and West Indies, how to
make both of more use to us, and particularly how a constant
trade to Goa may be advantageous.

I am so tormented with pain and business that it is not possible
for me to remember all I should say.

I have written to my Lord Sandwich to settle all differences
there amongst the merchants, that they may submit to the
Consul in all that is just; the man,—Mr. Maynard—hath
deserved well of the King, and was first sent thither in Cromwell's time, by his Majesty's leave and direction, therefore,
nothing upon that account ought to be a reproach to him. Say
all things from me of ceremony and kindness to the ambassador,
who is a worthy man, I think. To yourself, I say no more than
what I dare swear you believe, that I am unalterably your most
affectionate servant.

Postscript.—I perceive I have forgot to say anything of this
good bearer, Mr. Montague, who is sworn Master of the Horse
to our royal mistress. I am sure I need not recommend him to
your friendship, and you will take all occasions to insinuate the
quality and right of that office whenever the In[fanta] walks
abroad." *Holograph.* 3 *pp.*

Frey Domingo del Rosario * to the Duke of Ormond.

1661—December [7-]17. Lisbon—" Noething is soe wellcome
unto me as the honnor of your Excellency his commaunds, for I
doe love and worship extreamely your person, and generallie all
your highly-renowned howse and familie." I have presented your
request to both Queens, and they answered with civility that
nothing shall be denied to you if the King does not mislike it,
but they cannot resolve anything without his approbation.
" I pray pardon my bouldnes in presenting soe smale a thing as
them twoe leetle barels of aranges to soe high a personage; it is
but a token of love." I dare not write to the Duchess, but I
shall always be her passionate servitor and yours. *Seal of arms.*
1 *p.*

Queen Catherine to Charles II.

1661, December [12-]22. Lisbon—Very dear husband and
lord, only the pleasure of receiving a letter from you can com-
pensate me for the pain which the lack of it has cost me, for
as I know not how to live without this solace any delay is very
distressing to me. I need not tell you how much I value it, nor
the joy with which I have greeted the arrival of Mr. Hugh
Cholmeley, whose commission is the best guarantee for his welcome. Not to delay my gratitude for your kindness, I send this
reply by Sir Richard Fanshaw,—who is setting out very shortly,
I know not whether stimulated more by my wishes or by the
importance of the business on which he goes—so that, as I cannot
have the happiness of myself assuring you of my affection, he may

* Confessor of the Queen-Regent. By birth an Irishman, of the name of O'Daly.

testify to you my solicitude, and be the means of alleviating it by begging you to let me hear from you as continually as I pray to God to bring the fleet quickly to carry me to your presence, when, seeing you, my longings will be at an end. Meanwhile I beg God to give prosperity to your life, upon which all my happiness depends. *Portuguese. Holograph? 1 p. With translation into Spanish by Fanshaw.*

LYONELL FANSHAW to SIR RICHARD FANSHAW.

1661[-2], January 8-18. Lisbon—I hope your Honour is safe in England by this time, in spite of contrary winds, and that you have found her ladyship and the little ladies in perfect health. After you left I went to the Quinta and paid off the lacqueys, excepting the two whom you gave me leave to keep. I am allowing them 80 reals a day, which is the same that the Condé de Ponte allows to his. I have not yet got your litter into my custody, but have seen the currier about it. Thomas de Cruce and Mr. Bird went with me, and we think the gilding overhead looks very well. Mr. Halbord has gone from Cadiz to Tangier. His business in Cadiz was with a letter from the Earl of Sandwich to desire the release of one Major Stephens,—taken by the Spaniards near Jamaica,—which he obtained. We hear that " the Governor of Tituan's brother comes often on board my Lord of Sandwich to desire a friendly commerce with the English, and offers twenty miles distance round about Tangier to be at their disposal." Sir John Lawson, Sir Richard Stainer and others are said to have made great purchases of houses at Tangier.

"Antonio de Sousa * hath lately married the young Baron, his son—by proxy—to a very beautiful young lady of high birth, himself being proxy for his son," but Mrs. Fitzgerald told me " that the young lady was in a monastery and would not come out till they had granted her some things which were not included in the agreement before marriage, but since that I hear that some young nobles, accompanied with the Condé de Thore, stood in his way when he went to receive her, and would not suffer him to go any further, giving him very reproachful language, for which it is said some are put in prison."

It is reported that the Spaniards are drawing towards the borders with sixteen or twenty thousand men, and that the Marques de Marialva,† the Marques de Nice,‡ the Condé de Thore and other nobles are preparing for the field.

On the 14th Mr. Cholmeley and the Consul had audience of both the Queens, and after dinner they went to visit some persons of quality, who are in prison at Bellyne for threatening revenge on each other for the death of a gentleman killed in a tennis court. The Duke de Carevall ‖ is banished the court for refusing

* Antonio de Sousa de Macedo, Secretary of State, formerly Resident in England.

† Dom Antonio Luis de Ménésés, Conde de Cantanhede; created Marques de Marialva in 1660, and generalissimo in Alentejo in 1662.

‡ Don Luis Vasco de Gama, Condé de Vidiguiera, Marques de Niza.

‖ Nuño Alvarès Pereira, Duque de Cadavall, Marques de Fereira, ambassador extraordinary from Portugal to France in 1667.

to apprehend them and answering the King that it was not his office. I heard yesterday that the Count de Schonberg is ordered here from the frontiers, but do not know why. Mr. Price and I are sensibly advanced in the language of this country and hope to do you service with it hereafter. 4 *pp.*

ALFONSO, KING OF PORTUGAL, to his brother, CHARLES II.

1662 [March 24-]April 3rd. Lisbon—Stating that in 1657 he had promised Mr. John Roche,—an Irish gentleman, who for some years had assisted Frey Domingo del Rosario, elected Bishop of Cimbre, in negotiations with the Crown of France—a place in the service of the Infanta Catherine when she married; and praying the King therefore to admit him to a fitting post about the now Queen of England, making him page of the Back-stairs until a better place is vacant. *Signed by the Queen Mother. Translation.* 1 *p.*

The QUEEN OF PORTUGAL to her much loved cousin, the EARL OF CLARENDON.

1662, April [11-]21. Lisbon—In my letter to the Queen I sent greetings to your Excellency. The Conde de Ponte, Marques de Sande, is now going to your court as ambassador extraordinary, and as the affairs of this kingdom always meet with your support and favour—for which I owe, give, and always shall give thanks to your Excellency—I beg and hope that the matters of which he has to treat may receive the same, he having orders to do nothing without your approbation and directions. I entreat your Excellency to be good enough to listen to and direct him, assuring you that my son will always be very grateful for your kindness. *Portuguese. Signed.* ½ *p.*

The QUEEN OF PORTUGAL to her son [in-law], CHARLES II.

[1662, April]—These last days have passed sorrowfully enough, with two enemies, the absence of the Queen and my anxiety concerning her safety on the sea. For the first only God can comfort me, but as to the second I implore your Majesty to tell me that she has arrived safely and how your Majesty likes her. How she likes your Majesty I do not ask, for I know it without hearing. These last days of her voyage the winds have been so strong that a light vessel, which I sent after her the day following her departure, has returned without seeing anything of the fleet. All difficulties and dangers will be easily overcome for the pleasure of your Majesty's company. *Spanish. Holograph.* ½ *p.*

QUEEN CATHERINE to LORD CHANCELLOR CLARENDON.

1662, May 6. The Admiral's ship—Having resolved to send M. de Montague, my master of the horse, to enquire after the health of my lord the King and to give an account of my voyage

I take the opportunity of sending this letter to you, to assure you of my esteem and of my hope soon to see you in restored health. *Portuguese. Copy by Fanshaw.* ½ *p.*

SIR RICHARD FANSHAW to [the MARQUES DE SANDE?].

1662, May 8. London—I pray you not to impute it to lack of loyalty or zeal that I and my wife are not amongst the first to kiss our Queen's hands upon her landing. I am comforted for this by the hope that we shall both have the honour of doing so before we leave for Portugal, and also that the Queen will retain us amongst the number of her servants, although about this I do not know what to say, as I find all places occupied and to my wife's pretensions the King has not answered either yes or no. If the Queen will be pleased of her great kindness to repeat by word of mouth the request which she made in writing, no doubt our ambition will be gratified, as everything depends upon her Majesty and your Excellency. *Spanish. Draft.* 1 *p.*

LORD CHANCELLOR CLARENDON to QUEEN CATHERINE.

1662, May 9. London—The news of your Majesty, brought by Mr. Montague, together with a letter from your royal hand for me have caused me the utmost content, only exceeded by that of the King, my master, and of the entire kingdom. I should immediately have started for the port to be amongst the first to do homage to you, but for lack of health and excess of business. Nevertheless, I shall encourage myself with the hope that I may not be the last of this court who will enjoy that pleasure and comply with the obligation which all—and none more than myself—have to your Majesty, whom God has brought safely to this your kingdom. *Spanish. Draft in Fanshaw's hand.* ½ *p.*

The SAME to the SAME.

1662, May 17—Your Majesty's letter would have sufficed to bring me to life if I were dead, how much more then to comfort me when ill. Indeed I should at once have set out slowly for Portsmouth had I not been detained both by the commands and the affairs of the King, who—being the most indulgent master in the world,—strictly forbids my accompanying him after the dissolution of Parliament to be a witness of the happiest interview which has ever taken place. Fortunately his Majesty permits me all that you command, namely, to be present at your arrival at Hampton Court, where already, by his royal orders, all is ready for your Majesty's reception, at which I shall not fail, for all that I am worth. I say nothing of my desire to serve you, for the bearer, Sir Richard Fanshaw, is a man of known veracity, and he will stand sponsor for this. *Spanish. Draft by Fanshaw.* 1 *p.*

CHARLES II. to his brother [in-law], the KING OF PORTUGAL.

1662, May 23. Portsmouth—Your Majesty's of the 21st of last month has come to my hands. Having robbed you of the brightest jewel of your crown to adorn my own I must employ all my powers in defence thereof, and so you will have gained a brother without losing a sister, who, although lost to your sight, will never lose you from her memory. We both pray that God may grant long life to your Majesty. *Spanish. Draft by Fanshaw. ⅓ p.*

CHARLES II. to his mother [in-law], the QUEEN OF PORTUGAL.

1662, May 23. Portsmouth—Being now freed from dread of the sea and enjoying in this spring time the company of my dearest wife I am the happiest man in the world and the most enamoured, seeing close at hand the loveliness of her person and her virtues, not only those which your Majesty mentioned in your letter—simplicity, gentleness and prudence,—but many others also. These things oblige me to think of the interests and procure the tranquillity of her beloved country, as will be seen by my deeds and by the orders and powers which I give to my ambassador, whom, on arriving at Hampton Court, I shall dispatch to that of Portugal. And I wish to say of my wife that I cannot sufficiently either look at her or talk to her. May the good God preserve her to me and grant your Majesty long years of life, in which to be a comfort to us both. *Spanish. Draft by Fanshaw. ⅔ p.*

LUISA, QUEEN OF PORTUGAL, to her son [in-law], CHARLES II.

1662, June [20-]30. Lisbon—This evening there has come to my hands a letter from your Majesty of November 15th of last year, but why did I not receive another by this ship which has brought me so much pleasure and still more in the news which the Queen, my dearly loved and precious daughter gives me of the health of your Majesty and of the happiness which, thanks be to God, she enjoys in your company, with which she is so content that if she were not so sober she would believe she was going mad, so well does your Majesty know how to make a wife happy. To see her so greatly consoles me for her absence, but you owe it to me to comfort me by your letters, which I beg for as the best remedy for my sorrow.

The treaty did not fail on our part, for we did all we could, as we always shall do in your Majesty's service, my subjects desiring heartily to assist me therein. I have no more to say save that I cannot tell which of the two is more my child, the Queen or your Majesty, to whom may God grant many years of life. *Spanish. Holograph. 1 p.*

ALFONSO, KING OF PORTUGAL, to KING CHARLES II.

1662, [June 21-]July 1. Lisbon—Announcing that in consideration of the state of the kingdoms and to relieve the burden resting upon his mother the Queen, he has taken upon himself the government, that his frontiers are invaded by three powerful armies of the enemy, and that it would be very well if the English ships could make a diversion in Galicia while the troops succoured Alentejo under the Earl of Inchiquin, in whose experience and valour he has every confidence. Also praying that the succours which have not yet arrived may be sent, as even all is not as much as his kingdoms have need of to resist so powerful an invasion. *Portuguese. Signed.* 1 *p.*

The SAME to the SAME.

1662 [June 21-]July 1. Lisbon—Rejoicing over his sister's happiness, stating that the promised succours are very much needed, in consequence of the invasion of three armies of the enemy, and expressing the hope that with their help he may have the success which has always attended English arms in Portugal. *Portuguese. Signed. Endorsed by Clarendon,* " King of Portugal," *and by Fanshaw, with notes of the contents.* 1 *p.*

LUISA, QUEEN OF PORTUGAL, to CHARLES II.

1662 [June 22-]July 2. Lisbon—The Earl of Inchiquin has arrived with four hundred horse, besides a hundred and fifty which had arrived before. The infantry has not yet come, but we hear that it will be here in a few days. They come at a very opportune time, for most people declare that the enemy will go to war this year as they have done in all former ones. Some ships have also arrived. May your Majesty live a thousand years for your remembrance of me and the troubles of these kingdoms. The Earl, the troops and the ships shall all have good entertainment, not only as regards the payments which you demanded, but in everything, as the ministers of the King, my son, will not be wanting in anything which they believe to be for the service and pleasure of your Majesty. That God may guard you is the earnest desire of your mother. *Spanish. Holograph. Endorsed by Clarendon,* " The Queen of Portugal." ¾ *p.*

CHARLES II. to PHILIP IV., King of Spain.

1662, July 14. Hampton Court—Letter of credence for Sir Richard Fanshaw, Bart., Master of Requests, Secretary of the Latin tongue and member of the Council of State. *Latin. Signed by the King and countersigned by Secretary Morice.* 1½ *pp.*

QUEEN'S DOWRY.

1662, July 19-29. Statement by Duerte da Silva—The King of Portugal obliged himself to give two millions of Portuguese crowns to King Charles II. as the Queen's dowry; the first million to be delivered on board the navy royal coming for England either in specie or, if that were wanting, in sugar, diamonds or other effects. "And in regard it did not accommodate the King of Portugal to send all in moneys he sent jewels, sugars, diamonds, gold and silver, credit bills of exchange and the customs of four ships which unladed in this kingdom that came from Brazil directly, contrary to order." On account of this first million I have paid 218,785 crowns, partly in money, partly in ammunition for the navy going to Algiers, and for the remainder the King of Portugal sent me to England with the effects mentioned to sell them and give satisfaction to his Majesty, who representing his present need of some of the money, I paid 35,250*l.* sterling; viz.: Sir Thomas Vyner, 22,000*l.*; the Gentlemen of the Bedchamber, 8,250*l.*; the Commissioners for Ireland, 4,000*l.*, and his Majesty, 1,000*l.*; and obliged myself to pay the Duke of York 20,000*l.*, of which this week I shall make up 10,000*l.*, "and have told my Lord Ashley that I will give satisfaction to the 34,000*l.*, which Alderman Backwell, Sir Thomas Vyner and Meynell is to have, all which makes up the sum of 89,250*l.* [and] with what was paid in Portugal will be in value worth more than 760,000 crowns, with which I am not able to understand what I am told, that I pay nothing, being that I have to this sum assisted with my credit a great parcel of moneys, so that till the jewels be not [*sic*] sold and the duties of the Brazil ships be not recovered I cannot anticipate myself with more payments. But at the same instant that I shall sell any of them shall deliver in the moneys, for I do not use to traffic with what is not my own. And as touching the reduction of the Portugal crowns in sterling moneys" I conceive that they should be received at their value as the current money of Portugal. *Copy in Fanshaw's letter book. 2½ pp.*

CHARLES II. to his brother [in-law], the KING OF PORTUGAL.

1662, August 7. Hampton Court—I have received two of yours, both of the 1st ult. and a duplicate of one of them. The one replies, by way of congratulation, to what I wrote to your Majesty of the happiness of my life with my beloved wife, and the other speaks of the present troubles of Portugal, which, now that you have taken the sceptre into your own hands, I consider to be already almost remedied, so much is done by the personal intervention of Kings, and the more so, as your Majesty will be able to avail yourself—as I gather from the same letter that you will do—of the experience of our most prudent mother, who, it appears to me, neither ought nor will wish, as the natural mother of your Majesty and the nursing mother of the renewed liberty of Portugal, to prefer her own ease to such just obligations. I,

for my part, will not fail in my promised succours, so that if one
thing fails the other will be more than sufficient. Those which
were lacking when your Majesty wrote · have now—as I am
assured by letters of more recent date which came in the same
ship—duly arrived, and I cannot fear either that they will fail
to imitate the valour of *their* ancestors in the service of your
crown or your Majesty the generosity of *yours* in your treatment
and rewarding of them, the bearer of this, my ambassador, Sir
Richard Fanshaw, serving as a reminder for both and giving
himself entirely to your royal service. God grant you many years
of life. *Spanish. Two drafts by Fanshaw. 1 p*

LORD CHANCELLOR CLARENDON to ALFONSO VI., King of
Portugal.

1662, August 7. Hampton Court—This goes by the hand of
the ambassador, Sir Richard Fanshaw, for whom I will be surety
that he is a gentleman devoted both to your Majesty and to the
Portuguese nation—his knowledge of which induces the King,
my master, to send him to that Court—and I am persuaded that
he would be surety for me in the same way, nor can there be
any doubt whatever that according to our power, when occasion
offered, I should redeem his pledge and he mine. I will say
no more now save may God guard and give prosperity to your
royal person and to all that belong to you. *Spanish. Copy by
Fanshaw. ½ p.*

LORD CHANCELLOR CLARENDON to the QUEEN OF PORTUGAL.

1662, August 7. Hampton Court—The bearer of this, the
ambassador Sir Richard Fanshaw, a gentleman who knows me
well, and who is not unknown to your Majesty, excuses all expression here of my sincerity in soliciting and from time to time
urging on the advancement and satisfaction of the Crown of
Portugal, and of your royal person and that of the Queen, my
mistress. But I am anxious with regard to those kingdoms, on
the one hand from what I have seen in a letter from the King
of Portugal to the King, my master, his Majesty commencing to
manage personally the government thereof, no doubt with the
design of easing in part the burden which your Majesty has
carried, and on the other hand because they tell me that you
mean entirely to free yourself from that weight, which if true
and if it continues, will not only deprive the King, your son,
of the most faithful, the most experienced and the most devoted
counsellor that his Majesty can ever have or hope for; but all
those, wheresoever they may be, who are zealous for the good
of Portugal. It will greatly conduce to the soothing of my mind
if your Majesty can relieve me of this anxiety. That God may
grant long life to your Majesty is the humble prayer of your
devoted servant. *Spanish. Draft by Fanshaw. 1 p.*

CHARLES II. to his mother [in-law], the QUEEN OF PORTUGAL.

1662, August 9. Hampton Court—I have received three
letters from your Majesty—two of the 30th of June and one of

the 1st of July—almost at the same time, so that I can only pay you little for much. This goes by the hand of Sir Richard Fanshaw, who is as well known to you to be a good Portuguese as he is to us to be a man of worth and my trusty servant, and who has been strictly charged to do his utmost both for the Crown of Portugal and for your Majesty. I beg you to excuse my saying more now, except that I pray God to grant you the very happy years which I and my much loved wife desire for you. *Spanish. Copy in Fanshaw's hand.* ½ *p.*

LIEUTENANT COLONEL FITZGERALD to SIR THOMAS FANSHAW.

1662, August [19-]29. Tangier—I enclose a copy of Mr. Rumbold's letter, which is well worth your consideration. If it had come before Sir John Lawson's departure for Toulon he would hardly have left us, though indeed he could not well have stayed, for want of provisions. He left me the *Mermaid* and *Greyhound*, and the *Norwich* is now at Sallee, "to countenance the affairs of Ben- bucar,* upon which have come these results of the Spaniards, and have forced Guylan to ask these succours mentioned in Mr. Rumbold's letter." When they know Sir John is gone they may make some attempt upon us with their ships, but our garrison is in a very good posture, our men in good health and heart, and with provisions sufficient for a considerable time. 1¼ *pp.*

EDWARD BRIDGEWOOD to JOHN CREED, Secretary to the Earl of Sandwich.

1662 [August 28-]September 7. Lisbon—I have been ill almost ever since you left with the fleet and am not yet well, but to keep up our friendship I will give you some information of what has been passing here. "Our young King, Dom Alfonso, finding himself 'agravar'd' with some of his old counsellors, has taken the regiment of his kingdom into his own hands, placing and dis- placing, banishing and degrading several of his nobility and principal officers, which gives very much discontent to the gentry and has been the occasion that our soldiery have been received so coldly, who although they are yet in the King of England's pay, yet the money cannot be gotten in, which causes the soldiers every day to be in an uproar, all being weary of the service, wishing themselves at home again," and indeed they have reason, for the misery they are like to go through will be very great. My Lord Inchiquin gives passes to all officers who desire them but not to any of the soldiers. Many commanders are gone or going, and I could wish that his Majesty would be pleased to preserve so many gallant men from the ruin which seems to await them. Sir Richard Stayner is here with three or four great ships. He has had a sore fit of sickness, but is now recovered. "It is strange to me there should be so much neglect in the gentle-

---

* Ben Buker or Ben Bowcar (Cidi Mahumet Ben-el Hadge Ben Bowcar), a Moor- ish chief, who had made himself master of Fez, Tetuan &c., but had been partly con- quered in his turn by Gaylan or Gayland, another chief, whose head quarters were now at Arzilla.

men in England about victualling the fleet, not to take care to supply them here with money or pay their bills in England." Mr. Maynard is able to carry on his business with the 20,000 crowns the general left him to receive, but there are many differences between him and Mr. Robert Cocke as to the supply of the fleets, for two victuallers never do well together. My bill of 3,000*l.* is paid at last, but it made my heart ache to see the account of charges, spent in bribing great persons at Court, "not so much for the money as to see our courtiers will do nothing without such excessive bribes, in never so just a cause." 2 *pp.*

Sir George Carteret to Sir Richard Fanshaw.

1662, September 3rd. London—The bearer, Monsieur Arson, is the person of whom I spoke to you at Hampton Court, and is going to Portugal to try to recover some debts. "He was very kind unto all his Majesty's friends abroad; and especially unto me during my durance in the Bastile," and you cannot therefore oblige me more than by helping him to recover his right in a country where he is altogether a stranger. 1 *p.*

Sir Henry Bennet to Sir Richard Fanshaw.

1662, September 8. London—"I willingly embrace any occasion of assuring you of my humble service, which you may freely command here or anywhere else when you have any use of it. This goes to you by the bearer, Fray Domingo del Rosario, who hath prevailed with me to get the King to recommend him to the Secretary of State, and will not be content unless I also do the like myself for him to you. If what he asks of you be reasonable I should be content he found my entreaties have credit with you. With this occasion many of the inferior sort of the Portuguese are dispatched, in appearance to their satisfaction. I wish you may find it so there. Amongst the rest there goes one Don Gasper de Sevila, who came lately hither. He saith he shall have occasion of offering something to you when he is at Lisboa, relating to the good of that kingdom. The King desires you should hear him if he do so, and that you would acquaint him with it here particularly, and, if you think the matter requires it, apart from your ordinary despatch." I make use of the father's letter to tell you this, and if the King do not forget, you will also have a word of it from him. *Holograph.* 2½ *pp.*

Sir Richard Fanshaw to Consul [Maynard].

1662, September [18-]28. I have just received the letter which Mr. Secretary wrote to you last night, and therein the best news I have had since I arrived. I have been much pained "that three days' ceremonies of public entertainment and reception (for so many were then understood necessary), must interpose to suspend me from the honour of kissing his Majesty's hand,"

and entering upon the pressing affairs of State, and as I now understand that "for the treating with meals there is no such custom in this Court as to ordinary ambassadors" I pray earnestly though gratefully that I may be excused as to the intended supper. The truth is I am unfit to receive that honour in the Quinta de Alleyro, the reception rooms there being disfurnished and encumbered with my own goods in packs until I remove to a more convenient house of my own. Also, as I told you yesterday, "I never intended the female part of my family should eat upon this account, by which means they would be severed from me and driven into a corner, so upon the whole matter I adhere to my suit that the intended supper may be excused." *Draft.* 1¼ *p.*

EARL OF SOUTHAMPTON and LORD ASHLEY to the COUNCIL OF STATE.

1662, September—Reporting the business of the four ships trading to Brazil—viz., the *Concord,* Mr. John Rand; the *Hector,* Mr. Andrew Rand; the *Sampson,* Mr. Hans Crowder; and the *Little Lewis,* Mr. Anthony Maynard;—which had returned to England without paying their dues at Lisbon; and advising that the Portuguese Ambassador be moved for the speedy payment of the balance of the million crusadoes, the first part of her Majesty's portion, which, reckoning the crusado at 3s. 6d.—whereas it has been proved that his Excellency himself received 3s. 7d.—amounts to 47,637l., the time allowed having long elapsed and the bankers in London, who have advanced the money for his Majesty's public services, "being much disappointed by their so long attending for the same." *Copy.* 2½ *pp.*

BRAZIL SHIPS.

[1662, September?]—Statement to the Portuguese Ambassador that his Majesty and his ministers had at first determined to remand to Lisbon the four Brazil ships which came into the port of London, but the accredited agent of the King of Portugal, Sir [Augustine] Colonel, requested that the duties might be received here, in which he was joined by the ambassador's brother. If the ambassador desires any order to the Commissioners of his Majesty's customs, the Lord High Treasurer of England will give his warrant accordingly. *Copy in Fanshaw's letter book.*

ANTONIO DE SOUSA DE MACEDO to SIR RICHARD FANSHAW.

1662, October [2-]12—Requesting a meeting with him at ten o'clock the following morning at the Palace to confer upon the business of the two Crowns. *Portuguese.* ½ *p.*

[CAPT. CHRIS.] MINES* to [LORD WINDSOR].

1662 [October] 19—Aboard the *Centurion* athwart the harbour of St. Iago. According to your Excellency's commands of the

---

* There are two letters of his amongst the State Papers, both signed Chris. Myngs. See *Cal. of S.P. Dom. Chas. II., Vols. LXVII., No. 28, and XCVIII., No. 126.*

21st of 5 bre [7 ber] we set sail from Point Cagaway [Jamaica] on the 22nd, but it was the 5th of October before we got sight of the Castle of St. Iago upon Cuba. We decided to land under a platform two miles to windward of the harbour, the only place possible to land and march upon the town on all that rocky coast. We found no resistance, the enemy expecting us at the fort, and the people flying before us. Before we were all landed it was night. We were forced to advance into a wood, and the way was so narrow and difficult and the night so dark that our guides had to go with brands in their hands to beat a path. By daybreak we reached a plantation by a river's side, some six miles from our landing and three miles from the town, "where being refreshed with water, daylight and a better way, we very cheerfully advanced for the town" surprizing the enemy, who hearing of our late landing, did not expect us so soon. At the entrance of the town the Governor, Don Pedro de Moralis, with two hundred men and two pieces of ordnance, stood to receive us, Don Christopher, the old Governor of Jamaica (and a good friend to the English), with five hundred more, being his reserve. We soon beat them from their station, and with the help of Don Christopher, "who fairly ran away," we routed the rest. Having mastered the town we took possession of the vessels in the harbour, and next day I dispatched parties in pursuit of the enemy and sent orders to the fleet to attack the harbour, which was successfully done, the enemy deserting the great castle after firing but two muskets. From the 9th to the 14th we spent our time in pursuing the enemy, which proved not very advantageous, their riches being drawn off so far we could not reach it. "The ill offices that town had done to Jamaica had so exasperated the soldiers that I had much ado to keep them from firing the churches." From the 15th to the 19th we employed ourselves in demolishing the forts. We found great stores of powder, 700 barrels of which we spent in blowing up the castle and "the rest in country houses and platforms." The castle mostly lies level with the ground. "It was built upon a rocky precipice, the walls on a mountain side some sixty feet high; there was in it a chapel and houses sufficient for a thousand men." We are now in safety in the harbour on our return to Cagaway. *Copy by Lionel Fanshaw.* 3 *pp.* [*Dated* 7 *bre* 19*th by mistake.* *See Col. Cal.* 1661-1668, *p.* 109.]

EARL OF INCHIQUIN to SIR RICHARD FANSHAW.

1662, October 20. Lisbon—"Sir Robert Leech, now come [from] England, telling me that orders are come to continue the fleet here this winter under Captain Allin's command," and that letters are come for you, I pray you not to communicate anything "to these people till we know by their instructions what they would be at and that we have our money," lest they change their resolutions. *Holograph.* $\frac{1}{2}$ *p.*

SIR RICHARD FANSHAW to LORD CHANCELLOR CLARENDON.

1662, October [20-]30. Lisbon—Since sending my last
of the 10-20 by Col. Roscarrock I have received the King
of Portugal's propositions in reference to the succours
from England. The original being in Portuguese, I transmit
it in English, but papers in other languages I shall leave
in the original, " his Majesty and your Lordship understanding
them all perfectly well between you." At an audience to which I
was summoned, the King said he thanked the King, his brother,
for his offer of mediation between him and Spain, and meant to
make use of it, to which end the Conde Castelmelhor * (Secretary
de la puridad), would inform me of what had passed and was
passing in order to the said treaty. [*Margin*, " Sir H. B.—
El Conde de Castelmelhor. Secretario de la puridad; an office
nowhere but in Portugal, even here rarely taken up, and once
(by Don Sebastian) abolished, as too much to be put into any
one hand."] That evening the Count came to my house and
told me the following :—

In the time of the Regency of the Queen Mother, there arose
between Juan Nuñez de Acuna in the Portuguese army, and Don
Luys de Meneses, [*Margin*, " Sir H. B.—His father (Conde de
Tarroro) was by King John upon his acclamation to govern
Tangier; carried his family with him, but landed in Andalusia,"] a Portuguese by birth, but now general of horse
in Galicia for Spain (and created by the King of Spain Marques de Panalva), something of kindness, " as between enemies
there were not so to one another's persons," and from this " they
fell to wish a peace," and tried to bring it about, but without
any authority from their Kings. They arranged four preliminaries :—

1. That the treaty should be between the two Kings of Portugal and Castile.

2. That the King of England should be mediator.

3. Cessation of arms.

4. Plenipotentiaries to treat on either side at some place on the
borders ; and with these propositions Nuñez has now returned.

The Spaniards, however, objected to the first, urging that " by
a preliminary " it brings in all that the Portuguese hoped for;
and as to the second, they desired the Pope, but did not decline the
King of England. The third and fourth would follow as a
matter of course. Nuñez is being sent back with orders to insist
on all four points, excepting that each King may sign *Yo, el
Rey*, without other title. Don Luys told him in confidence that
the desire for peace " proceeds originally from the Queen of
Spain,† with those that adhere to her, as the Duke of Medina de las
Torres,‡ Conde de Castrillo, Lon Luys de Angoren (now Secre-

---

* Don Luis de Souza Vasconcellos.
† Marie-Anne of Austria, second wife of Philip IV., and regent during the minority of her son, Charles II.
‡ Don Ramiro Nuñez Felipez de Guzman, Marques de Toral and Duque de Medina de las Torres, chief minister of Spain.

tary of State, sometimes of war, always a great negotiant with strangers), who,—considering how old and infirm her husband is, how young and infirm her son; on the other side the high and just jealousies which run upon Don Juan of Austria,* especially if continuing at the head of a great army," who may pretend to the tutorship of the infant King, and moreover that the King of France may also "stickle for the tutorship of him, and in case he fail, for the inheritance before her daughter,"—is anxious to secure the friendship of Portugal. As to the mediation of the King of England, the Portuguese will do nothing without it, hoping that by tenders of friendship to them and menaces of open hostility to Spain his Majesty will both facilitate the peace and mend the condition of Portugal, they knowing that "whatsoever accord they made, Spain would make no scruple of breaking it the next day if he saw an advantage, alleging that faith was not to be kept with his rebels."

As to the state of Tangier I refer you to a packet which I am sending to Secretary Nicholas from Lord Peterborough. *Draft by Fanshaw in letter book. 4 pp. [Extracts from this and the following letter, as also of those dated November 16 and 29, made by Fanshaw for Sir Henry Bennet, are in the Portugal Correspondence at the Public Record Office.]*

SIR RICHARD FANSHAW to LORD CHANCELLOR CLARENDON.

1662, October [21-]31. Lisbon—I beg that only his Majesty and yourself may see this, as if it came to the ears of the Portuguese that I was so diffident of their strength and of their management either of the war or the treaty without his Majesty's help, *aut re, aut opere aut consilio bono,* and they should hear my complaints of the unkind and unskilful usage of our troops they would never believe in my unfeigned zeal for their service. The King of Portugal, in his propositions, plainly says that without money from the King of England he cannot maintain the troops, and yet offers no ports, "either as pawns for repayment or as safe retreats and landing places for our men." At present, to their great peril, they are scattered in distant quarters, and some have already lost their lives by the hands of those whom they come to serve. Moreover, they must be independent of any foreign command, except in specified cases. "If this Crown would come roundly to such like terms as I have newly hinted at here, after the example of the Hollanders in Queen Elizabeth's time, who were not then lower than Portugal is now in the judgment of all that I can speak with but themselves, his Majesty might haply consider of assisting them, as the Queen did the others, even to a breach or hazard of a breach with Spain—which is one of this King's propositions, especially if those particulars should be clearly made out in proof, which I presume my Lord of Peterborough's despatch herewith to Secretary Nicholas imports" that

* Son of Philip IV. and the actress Maria Calderon.
Countries, now commander of the army of Estramadura. · Late governor of the Low

Spain is leagued with Guylan, and had an armada at Cadiz to
block up Tangier, if Sir John Lawson had not come opportunely
to prevent it. I conceive that the discourse of Cardinal D'Ossatı,
in his printed letters to the French King from Rome, on the
taking of Cadiz by the English, is very pertinent to the present
occasion, concluding that it is now in the power of England, by
alliance with Portugal and the accession of Tangier, to work
much more woe to Spain than " when the Earl of Essex possessed
himself of Cadiz; and more than I judge it to be his Majesty's
either inclination or interest to do at this day, unless in defence
of his own," or securing his present rights and future possibilities.
For his present rights, the remainder of the Queen's portion is
still due, and for future possibilities, in case this King and his
brother should fail, the Crown of Portugal would, in right of the
Queen, " devolve to his Majesty and their issue, and although
even when it came to that it might cost hot water to get it, yet
the same forecast which Philip II. used in as remote a possibility
might do much towards it, especially as English forces may remain here in number upon account of the Portugal King's
service, and perform it faithfully too, as long as either brother
should live or have posterity, without so much as secretly wishing the male line should determine till the end of the world,"
although with England's power by sea the outlying dominions
of Portugal would be of more consequence to us than to this
Crown and nation. Now, if Spain " either beat or treat this King
out of his dominions in the whole or a part, besides the exchange of a brother in the throne for an enemy . . . and
besides the possible burden of royal guests at home, where will
be the rest of the portion, and that contingency I have mentioned?" I assure your Lordship I see no hopes of effecting
anything unless the Spaniard be either treated or beaten into a
peace. As to this King being treated out of his kingdom, I must
tell your Majesty that when I said to the Conde de Castelmelhor
that it seemed to me no small thing that the King of Spain
agreed that this King should sign *Yo, el Rey*, he replied "that
the said King doth not scruple to suppose this, King of Brazil,"
but I could not " get out of him whether there is the least inclination on the Portuguese part to consent thereunto." If so, it can
only be from utter inability to hold out another summer, and
it would then be for our King to consider whether he should
exert his strength to prevent it. It is to be observed that in
these propositions the succours are only to be in case peace does
not follow, but even if Spain be now in favour of a treaty, I am
sure she would change her mind if the English troops were withdrawn, whereas, if they were augmented, she " would then be in
very good earnest, especially if our English were possessed, by
way of pawns or for retreat, of St. Uvall, Lagos, Faro and Oporto,
more or less, as should be agreed." A peace would be so unpopular in Spain that if the Queen and her adherents really wish
for it they would be glad of such an English power " visibly
hanging over their heads, as might seem to force them to consent to what they most desire." I think his Majesty might send

here certain provisional propositions, as to 1, the advantageous peace which Holland enjoys with the Spaniard, who would have said in times past, am I a dead dog that I should do this thing; 2, what conditions Baron de Bataville offered the King to divert the marriage with Portugal; and 3, what other conditions England has been offered from Spain, " not excepting the private tamperings between Spain and Cromwell." I know many wise men think it would be better for our King to await the death of the King of Spain and then do what we like in the West Indies while the Spaniards are at broils amongst themselves, but before that Portugal might be overrun or have her hands tied by a peace. News has just come that an armada with the Duke of Abburquerque is setting forth from Cadiz. If this is to block up Tangier " there is the war made to our hands. If they take it, one of the best cards for ours is trumped. If they aim at or should snap the Brazil fleet or some of the towns of Portugal, here were our friend lamed . . . when lulled asleep with overtures of a treaty. If your Lordship will please to look back upon the time when the Duke of Alva overran these kingdoms in the space of a few days, the Portugals were then as confident and as much despisers of the Castilians, even when they were masters of the field to the gates of Lisbon, as now they are or can possibly be, and then, too, there was a secret treaty disposing by one Diego de Carcamo, authorized by both sides and by King Philip, really intended as to the giving conditions to Don Antonio and the kingdom rather than drive both into despair, but the Duke, who found it feasible and more honour for him to conquer than to make any accord whatsoever, handled the matter so that the said Antonio did or seemed himself to decline it until he was absolutely undone. All which—taking their measures right—had been prevented if Portugal had then in due time desired from England upon the like terms, and Queen Elizabeth afforded them, such succours as she did to Holland in the like distress, and what her Majesty gave Antonio afterwards in vain—the Spaniard being prepossessed of all—under the command of Sir John Norris, when—the tradition says—the Earl of Essex stuck his dagger in Lisbon gates and hung his gold chain upon it.

Thus have I presumed to shake out before your Lordship a world of rubbish, amongst which nevertheless, to my eye, even upon a review, some few things do glister like reason, which therefore I bring to the touch of your Lordship's judgment. I beat a hundred bushes to start one hare, I vent a hundred follies of my own to draw one *acierto* from your Lordship, this being I am certain an honester project than to tell a lie to find a truth." *Copy in letter book.* 8 *pp.*

SIR RICHARD FANSHAW to LORD CHANCELLOR CLARENDON.

1662, [October 28-]November 7. Lisbon—You will remember that on the 31st ult. I spoke of the King of Spain's consenting to this King's signing *Yo, el Rey*, and my suspicions thereupon. " Now for unriddling of all this, it is not two hours since the Secretary of State told me that Castile would not stick to leave to this King not only all the other dominions of this Crown, but even Portugal itself, only with the title of *Señor* de Portugal—I should rather believe *Conde*, because of the first erection of it by that title, into a sovereignty holding in fee of Castile—because his Catholic Majesty would not at any rate admit of any King within Spain but himself, much less to treat one henceforward *de magistad*—but this I understand not neither if he would allow him King anywhere—whom he hath formerly treated *de vos*," but that this they would never consent to, preferring if needs be to purchase their peace by a money payment to Castile. One useful argument we may draw from this, that if Portugal can pay Castile she can also pay our Queen's dowry and reimburse the King for what he spends in a quarrel in which he has no personal concern. I cannot venture " to make myself an undertaker in these matters, well knowing that things are not rational because I judge them so, nor feasible here because they are rational. These are a people—in the opinion of much wiser men than I—so singularly jealous of their interests as to destroy very often their interests by their jealousies. However, attempts of this kind for the common good of England and Portugal " must not be omitted " since he that aims at the moon, though he shall never hit her, shall shoot higher than he that levels at a bush." *Draft by Fanshaw in letter book. 2 pp.*

SIR RICHARD FANSHAW to CAPTAIN [THOMAS] ALLIN.

1662 [October 29-]November 8. Lisbon—Having obtained leave from the King of Portugal for the squadron under your command to return to England, I pray you to proceed homeward without delay. And as you and Capt. Spragg have consented, at my request, to convey a quantity of sugar for the Earl of Inchiquin in the *Portland*, I hereby avow that it is done by my encouragement, " first, that the fleet is immediately homeward bound together, without expectation of any fight; secondly, though these are merchandise yet they are not merchants' goods, which the instructions forbid; thirdly, the Earl of Inchiquin could not possibly procure his own and the soldiers' pay here in any other kind; fourthly, this pay was upon the account of the King, our master, and of the Queen's portion," and so may be transported in the King's ships. God send you a speedy and happy voyage. I hope we may see you with your flag here again in the spring. *Copy in letter book. 1 p.*

SIR RICHARD FANSHAW to LORD CHANCELLOR CLARENDON.

1662, November [6-]16. Lisbon—"On Sunday last a great man of the Court, though none of the Council, giving me a visit told me amongst other discourse that a gentleman, who had been a secretary to Cardinal Masserin, was lately arrived from France, lodging privately in Count de Chomberg's house, and that he brings an offer of twenty thousand men to serve this King *in case he will forbear concluding a peace with Castile*, with other assistances, I presume he meant *money.*

I have since taken occasion to visit the Conde de Castelmelhor, Archbishop of Lisbon and Secretary, to see if any of them would take notice to me of such a thing, being a matter that related to the treaty, but none of them did.

This very day the Count de Chomberg, who had never come at me before since this incognito arrived, though till then hardly a day escaped him, brought the Monsieur to dinner to me, being forthwith bound for France by the way of the Downs. A smart young man he is, and one whose face I think I have seen before, but it is not that secretary of the Cardinal's who appeared so active the last winter at Whitehall, unless he be much altered since. The Court calls him Monsieur de Carneton; but I presume that is not so like to discipher him, as the letting your Lordship know that is the same who coming into England presently after I left the Court—as himself tells me—would have had Mr. Coventry's letter to embark with me at Plymouth, but was advised by him rather to take that passage when the Conde de Ponteval came, which he did, and by that account hath been here privately treating and discovering ever since the 19th of the last.

To apply which, though twenty thousand men be too great a number to believe at once, either for the French to spare or much less for Portugal to accept, considering that whenever the French King could have a title to the Crown of Spain he would consequently have a pretence to this of Portugal, and in truth me thought this gentleman looked to-day so wistly upon and talked so concernedly of the great beauty and commodiousness of this desert port—of which I have a perfect and close view from my house—as if he thought his master—if it were his—could find money enough in France to people it with ships; yet something considerable of that kind is undoubtedly either intended or pretended by the French to stop their proceedings in the peace. For Monsieur le Comte de Chomberg was absolutely going, until this person came—as my Lord Insiquin can certify—and now stays, although this person is going.

Whilst I am writing, comes in to visit me a French sea captain of my acquaintance, a person well versed here and of good observation. He tells me Monsieur de Carneton is Monsieur Colbert,* sometimes Intendent de Finances a Brecage, and great confident of the late Cardinal; his brother—a greater—at this time one of the two or three of greatest credit about the French King, especially in the matter of revenue. That this gentleman brought with him hither bills for sixty thousand crusadoes, which were well answered, yet that he carries nothing away of any moment; that he goes away very well satisfied of this Court, and—as the relator conceives—will return very shortly, indeed, Count de Chomberg told me the gentleman was come upon some private encouragement from Monsieur de Turene to discover

---

* Mons. Charles Colbert du Terron, Marquis de Bourbonne, Intendant of the Marine and Counsellor of State. The statement that he was a brother of the great minister is a mistake.

the state of things and inclinations here, with intimation that when he came home with an account thereof he should be owned as occasion should require.

All these particulars put together with what is there further known of the present interests and designs of several Princes and States than can be to me here, I could humbly wish that his Majesty and your Lordship would be at the trouble [to] read over again upon this occasion Cardinal Bentivoglio's brief narrative in print *del Trattato della Tregua di Fiandra*. The which gave me a light to foresee in my last despatches what I see already acted in part whilst they are now upon their way.

1. There and here, a King of Spain the invader.
2. There and here, the invaded, a people whom he challengeth for his subjects.
3. There and here, France straightly allied with the invaded, yet making his own peace with Spain upon terms of high advantage to himself, leaving his allies totally out.
4. There and here, the Crown of England protecting and assisting the deserted allies of France, bringing them thereby into a capacity of treating with Spain upon honourable terms. If it be doubted as to Portugal, I must vouch the Archbishop of Lisbon, who took an occasion to tell me not three days since that Spain would never hear of treating with them till this alliance with England.
5. There and here, France—uncalled—interposing himsel in the treaty; here to frustrate it, there to reap to himself from England the principal honour and advantage of making it, and so I do suspect here, too, if he shall see he cannot frustrate it.

I must confess, his Majesty being advertised whereby to make his own uses thereof, I discern no harm in what the French are doing, *this being such a rub to the treaty as I believe would make it stumble on faster on the other side if there could be a way found out to assure oneself first and then Spain of a real and timely assistance from France, though but to the half of what is spoken of, and if on this side it should stop upon that account—provided their confidence thereof proved not vain—yet Portugal would subsist, and so the miracle being done the less matter who did it, there being respite to obviate such ill consequences as might come of that by laying hold of other good opportunities which that might minister in the interim.*

But—as I feared in my last—our English troops are already actually breaking, and that the worst way, a party being run over to the Spaniard with six hundred crowns which they were convoying to their fellows, unto whither all the rest are like to follow, and which is worst of all—if we may believe a word spoken in haste by a great minister, with very colourable reasons to back it—their doing so, if not desired here as an ease, yet not at all apprehended as a mischief to this Crown.

I am so much of the contrary opinion, as to tell them daily as plain as I can speak it to themselves that I do believe, how real soever the Spaniard may be now—which I much doubt, too, when I read of a treaty by the same Crown with Queen Elizabeth's Commissioners at Ostend and Burborough in the very year of 88 whilst their great armada was getting ready—yet the running over of such and so many men would so change the case as might make them take up quite contrary resolutions, and the rather for these *underminings of France,* which are not so secret neither but that in a hot comparison not long since at Madrid about the right of precedency between those two Crowns, the Conde de Castrillo telling the French Ambassador there—who urged the submission at Paris upon that which happened in England—that the King of Spain would speak with his master farther concerning that matter when he should have finished the conquest of Portugal, the ambassador—who is a fiery Archbishop *— replied, the King, his master, would find the way to defend that kingdom well enough from his; and it is said that this repartee being very well relished by the young King and people, too, at Paris, is not without a train after it, of which this private negotiation of Monsieur Colbert is one.　Whereunto nevertheless I shall easily yield, there is much the less credit to be given, and consequently my consent the rather to the demolishing of those castles I have here built in the air, if your Lordship shall find that he is not a person so allied and qualified as is represented, whereby to estimate the consequence of his errand by the confidence which the French Court reposes in his person.　[*Margin,* " Sir H. B.　This only difference appears now at last from my first advertisement of his true name, that he is not brother but cousin german to the powerful minister Colbert."]　To the frontiers I find he hath made a step since his arrival here, and of the kingdom a survey—as his own words are.

Herewith enclosed is a copy of my last memorial to this King concerning the troops; that his Majesty there and your Lordship may read the very words in Spanish which my zeal transports me to try as my utmost diligence for the keeping these troops yet together, if it be possible, because of those irremediable mischiefs which I apprehend from the contrary, much greater to Portugal than any fault I intend by this complaint to charge it with, for really this Crown hath, since our people's arrival here, disbursed upon them very great sums, whereof I cannot give a particular till I get it from these ministers, because I found at my coming here that his Majesty's Latin letter by my Lord Insiquin made all the three months upon account of the Queen's portion immediately payable to his Lordship, whether I were arrived or not, differing in that one point from his Majesty's Spanish letter at the same time, being indeed of my own drawing, but not without order, so that there remains at this time only six weeks due to the troops, and a month of this six weeks they say—and I believe—they will pay within a very few days, as also another within a matter of a fortnight after. But this is not according to their promises, which were to advance every month's pay beforehand, being convinced that our men being strangers in a dear country, where no credit is, could not

* Georges d'Aubusson de la Feuillade, archbishop of Embrun.

otherwise possibly subsist, but must fall into such desperate disorders as now break out. And this it is which troubles me the
more for them, to see that when they have drained themselves so
low as undoubtedly they have, to comply with our troops as to
the advance of the three months out of the Queen's portion—
which, not being expected by them, hath come from them like
their hearts' blood—they should now in the most unhappy conjuncture for it imaginable lose the fruit and thanks of all that, for
want of squeezing out a few drops more in time, doing it, too,
afterwards when it is too late, which timely payment would likewise—with some exemplary justice to boot—qualify what is past
as to the murder of some of our men and prevent it for the
future, the same being another part of my complaint in this
memorial and must ever be where there is cause for it, without
intention nevertheless, to fix it as a particular scandal to this
nation, where much fewer of ours in proportion have been lost
in that kind than by the French and Flemish Boors in the
business of Dunkirk.

Upon the whole, my Lord, here appears to me no cement
at all in our troops, being admirable individuals but the worst
body that ever was, only because they are none; the reason
whereof appertains unto the martial officers alone to give; as
little cement between ours and this nation, who were anciently
quite of another temper and disposition one towards another
than now they are on either side. To remedy which—finding
that part in a great measure incumbent upon my duty—I have
employed all the dear experience I have got for the space of
thirty years in the humours of both, and assembled all my
nerves—besides something of singular alacrity I have always
found in myself as to the matter of reconciling where there was
any room for it—as his Majesty and your Lordship may clearly
see by all my papers of this negotiation remitted into England,
if I am not sufficiently understood before by so many years' service. In fine, break I see these troops will at a most unlucky
hour—without a miracle—in a thousand pieces; if in fewer, the
worse, but that must be either by marching in bodies to the
enemy—which they have begun—or, in the same manner hither,
by way of mutiny or for embarkation, which cannot be in any
shipping belonging to this Crown—that is not—or of England—
that is not here, no more than orders from his Majesty for their
transportation if there were—and yet this extravagance they have
in their heads, too, and in agitation amongst themselves, as
their superiors inform me.

To return now in a word to Monsieur Colbert—for, with submission, I humbly hope I resve [rêve] not in mingling often these
two things together—I am told, whilst I am writing this, that he
hath proposed *a match to this King with a daughter of the Duke
of Orleans, I suppose Mademoiselle*, because my author says a
succour of *six thousand men from France is to be maintained here
upon the account of her dowry*—so the French King not the war
maker—this is *vox populi*; and then in such case a like
body of English, upon good terms, to back and counterpoise the

French, seems no ill provision for England and Portugal both, but then there must be a new model from head to foot. For conclusion of all, because it appears to me—and I think will to your Lordship—more than possible that I may speedily see a French Ambassador in this Court, and most certainly—if I go thither, which seems also probable—one in that of Spain, as also others from other sovereigns, I pray your Lordship's favour that I may insert here the very words of Mr. Walsingham—then entering upon his Embassy in France—among other queries to which he humbly desired the Queen's resolution, viz.:

How I shall behave myself in any public assembly towards the ambassador, as well of Spain as Portugal, either in taking or giving place.

I thinking it no shame at all for me to be ignorant of what so renowned a minister of state as that was; and therefore hereby, most humbly begging, by your Lordship's representation, a resolving instruction to the like question *mutatis mutandis* propoundable by me at this time.

These ministers tell me they expect now every day Juan de Nuñez back from the frontiers with a final answer to the four proposals he carried from hence in order to the treaty, and with the names also of the Commissioners from the Catholic King."

Postscript.—" My dispatch by this same conveyance to Mr. Secretary Maurice doth more at large discover—as to matter of fact, without any descant of my own thereupon—the despairing condition, resolutions, and inclinations of the troops." *Draft, partly by Fanshaw, in letter book.* 6½ *pp.*

Sir Richard Fanshaw to the Duke of York.

1662, November 8[-18]. Lisbon—" A point of honour having been stirred by this Crown, when Capt. Allin was now lastly here, concerning his bearing a flag in this river, I have herewith enclosed the letter from the Secretary of State which stirred it before the Captain's departure, and my answer after; both of them copied in the several languages wherein they were written, lest translating them should occasion any mistake. Which account I thought proper and my duty to render unto your Royal Highness, not knowing whether this court doth finally acquiesce in my answer, or whether the pretence will be renewed by the Portugal ambassador in England. And this I do the rather presume and hold myself obliged to do as he that may with better right than everybody pretend the quality of your Royal Highness's servant." *Copy in letter book.* ½ *p.*

Sir Richard Fanshaw to Secretary Morice.

1662, November [8-]18. Lisbon—States that soon after Capt. Allin's departure with the despatches, there came more of Job's messengers from the English troops, bringing a remonstrance from the English officers to the King of Portugal, declaring that they cannot any longer serve this Crown, " by reason of the unsupportable wants and injuries which they groan under," and that Colonel Molesmouth writes in utter despair " plainly affirming that in his opinion these troops for the future are never likely to do honour to their country or service to this, in respect of their usage and necessities." *Copy in letter book.* 1 *p.*

EARL OF INCHIQUIN to SIR RICHARD FANSHAW.

1662, November 8. Bay of Oyeres [Oieras]—I have not received the license promised me. Possibly the Secretary of State may be more dilatory in sending it than may stand with Mr. Jacob's convenience, and I beg your assistance, as until he has the license I cannot have my money. I wish you and your worthy lady all happiness. *Holograph.* ¾ *p.*

SIR PHILIP WARWICK to his brother [in-law], SIR RICHARD FANSHAW.

1662, November 12—I am heartily glad to hear of your good health and settlement. "Trouble we are all born for, and in proportion to the strength of every man providence loads him, so as you know why I pity you not, though I know how much you undergo. That your great wheel turns, I hope it will be for the good of us and all Christendom." As regards my own sphere, Da Silva, failing so long of his payments of the first part of the portion, has been arrested, which may make some noise with you. The ambassador having put in a memorial to the King, the Council referred it to the Lord Treasurer and Lord Ashley, who have returned this answer, by which you will see " how moderately we have valued the crusado, how justly we proceeded in the Brazil duties, and that by the Portugals' disowning the contracts and bonds taken by Colonel we were disabled by our law to force our merchants to make payment of a foreign prince's duty.

" Here have been imprudent restless spirits attempting to their own ruin, for it had no great depth their plot, but believing purchasers and discontented persons would have joined with them ; they were adding number to their malice, which some principal men will by a legal conviction ere long have strangled in them. The King is very observant and kind to the Queen, and her faint fits, which she is now and then troubled with, we take a symptom of breeding, which is not so plainly averred as I can say it is so, but ladies say it is more than a hope. I stand engaged and shall be indebted for a time to my sister for her letter, and I pray God bless all the babies. My wife subscribes with as much affection as a sister can do." *Copy in letter book.* 1 *p.*

The enclosure.

Statement that a million crusadoes at 3s. 6d.—which is three half-pence less than their value according to the Mint—come to 175,000l., of which 127,362l. has been paid and 47,637l. is still owing.* Signor Silva mentions the consignation of the

---

* The exact calculation would be 127,362*l.* 7*s.* 6*d* paid, and 47,637*l.* 12*s.* 6*d.* still owing.

Brazil ships hither as if it had been to make up part of the portion, whereas it was an accident or a fraudulent design by the interested parties; and his Majesty would have sent them back to Lisbon if Sir Augustine Colonel had not interposed, and therefore cannot take them as any concern of his own. Nevertheless he would have guided it so that the English merchants should have given bond to pay the duties here had not Bishop Russell disowned Colonel in the affair, whereon the merchants gave up Colonel's bond and resumed their own. It is very unreasonable to argue that payment should be made in worse coin or in money raised above its value, and the commodities were sent that the King of England might be paid in money within two months, so that "now to argue he must attend until the proceed of those commodities is no good and natural consequence." Copy in Fanshaw's letter book. 2¼ *pp.*

Juan Nunez da Cunha to the King of Portugal.

1662, November [13-]23—I had yesterday an interview with Don Luis de Men[eses], and as the beginning of our consultations we have settled a truce for one month, during which time we may go on with the treaty of peace. I declared to him that the first and an indispensable article of our treaty was the mediation of the King of Great Britain, whose interests are so bound up with your Majesty's that you cannot act without him. He said, although with reluctance, that no doubt that King might come in as mediator, by persons satisfactory to your Majesty. I have heard that the King of Castile is doing all he can to disunite you and the King of Great Britain by deceiving the English ambassador and by means of his confidential agents in England. As these deceits may disturb the harmony between us and England, your Majesty should order them to be prevented, and above all we must get what is necessary to arm the frontiers, as thus only we can make peace and be in safety. *Portuguese. Copy in letter book.* ½ *p.*

Annexed,
  Copies of the confirmation of the cessation in Spanish and Portuguese, signed respectively by Don Balthazar de Roixas Pantoja * *and Juan Nuñez da Cunha. Dated November 22.* 1 *p.*

Bishop R. Russell to Sir Richard Fanshaw.

1662, November 14. London—"This is to kiss your Excellency's hands and wish you much joy in your title and employment, the trouble of both will come fast enough upon you without wishing in a time abounding with little else and a country destitute almost of all things that should alleviate those cares which wants and disgusts must inevitably cause, only thus much for your comfort I dare affirm, that if you agree not with Portugal

---

* Governor of the army of Galizia.

no Englishman living shall ever agree with it, and if Portugal agrees not with you it shall agree less with any Englishman living. My Lord of Inchiquin is come to Court, where he vents himself furiously against the Conde de Castelmelhor and Antonio De Souça. *Cætera* he is more moderate, very large in the eulogiums of the Queen and zealous for the conservation of the country. From thence the characters we have of him are just like those he gives of Antonio de Souça and the Conde; where the fault is, you who were upon the place can best judge. Here by the more serious t'is thought that fault was not wanting on both sides. His Lordship does you the justice to acknowledge your prudent, candid and cordial assistance, and all our letters speak so much in your commendation that now I begin to see it is possible to be impartially cordial and yet be beloved of both parties. Things here are much at the same pitch you left them except a new secretary and the sale of Dunkirk, which you must persuade them there, and with truth, t'was done with an eye towards the future assistance of them by both Crowns; else it will make an ill noise there as it hath done here, and I fear will more when the Parliament comes to sit. I should be very glad you, your lady and little ones live there with health and content. A tender of my most humble service to her ladyship and her three sweet little ladies, and if any friends of mine there can be any ways serviceable to you or them t'will be very much " to my satisfaction.

Endorsed by Fanshaw :—" Received at Lisbon 9th of February, 63, *stylo loci,* by the hands of the President of the College." *Seal of arms.* 1 *p.*

Secretary Morice to Sir Richard Fanshaw.

1662, November 19. Whitehall—I have received both your packets, and abridged the first sixteen pages for his Majesty, " who else would never have had the patience or given the time to have heard one quarter thereof." Your intelligence and the propositions of the King of Portugal were the subject of a long debate before the King and a select Council, the result whereof was to invite the Portuguese ambassador to an explanation. " The things propounded carry their denial in the face thereof, and we think strange of the counsel whereby they were offered, yet somewhat I presume his Majesty will do toward payment of the auxiliar force which he sent over. It may perhaps be news to tell you that Sir Edward Nicholas is removed from his place, and hath the recompense of 10,000*l.* and 100*l.* per annum in fee, and Sir Henry Bennet succeeds him. Dunkirk is sold to the French for 5,000 pistoles. Here hath been a treasonable plot amongst the Anabaptists to attack Whitehall, secure the King, seize the Tower and surprize Windsor Castle; but it was an inconsiderate design, not formed nor any determinate way agreed on to execute it," got up by inconsiderable persons, without means to carry it on, who therefore, after some debates, gave it up in despair, "but the very thought and design and debate will forfeit the lives of seven or eight of them, which are taken, unto justice; many of them are fled." ¾ *p.*

Endorsed by Fanshaw : —" Whitehall, from Secretary Moris, 19 of November, 62. Received at Lisbon from Col. Appesley 26 of February, 63, *stylo loci.* That from Lord Insiquin [*see p.* 54 *below*] was of the 29th of December, after his Lordship had been there kept five weeks in suspense·"

Sir Richard Fanshaw to Lord Chancellor Clarendon.

1662, November [19-]29. Lisbon—Stating that he has just come from the Palace, where the Secretary of State told him that Don Luys and Nuñez have met again upon the frontiers of Minio; that Don Luys took notice of the French incognito's having been at Lisbon to prevent their proceeding by great offers; that they both concluded that the French were using arts to deceive both kingdoms, and therefore they should the rather agree with each other; and that the Spaniard offered to proceed immediately, but the other said that he had instructions to press for more Commissioners, whereupon they severed for that time. *Copy in letter book.* $\frac{1}{2}$ *p.*

Marques de Sande to Sir Richard Fanshaw.

1662, November 20. London—Congratulating him upon his own and his wife's safe arrival at Lisbon and upon the estimation in which he is held by the Court there; and begging him to try to obtain from the King, his master, a further delay in the time for paying the Queen's dowry, and also permission to include in it the 40,000 crusadoes due from the four Brazil ships which failed in their obligations to Portugal. *Portuguese. Signed.* 1 *p.*

Sir Richard Fanshaw to Lord Chancellor Clarendon.

1662, [November 28-]December 8. Lisbon—" Upon the first of this instant December, being the solemn anniversary of the proclaiming the King in Lisbon, having had leave for it the day before, I went to the Palace in as good equipage as I could to congratulate his present Majesty in the King my master's name, the birthday of the liberty of Portugal. Coming a little of the soonest, the Conde de Castelmelhor entertained me in his lodgings with a letter which his Majesty had that very morning received from Juan Nunez, which perusal gave me occasion, when the King was ready for me, to observe unto his Majesty how that same day which twenty-two years past restored his royal family, proved now a second time auspicious to it and to Portugal in this news of an owning their right in some measure by a suspension of arms and beginning of a treaty *de rey a rey,* either of which is more than ever the King of Castile would be brought to in that whole twenty-two years. All which was particularly well taken by his Majesty and the whole Court, who celebrated the festival with some increase of joy and hope upon this very account. The festival is the Immaculate Conception of our Lady. which mystery from that time was made by the last King

24. D

and continued ever since the new patron of Portugal, without exclusion of the old which is our St. George, our Lady being rather qualified their defendress." I send a copy of the cessation for a month, by which you will see that it is "restrained to that frontier where the Portuguese is at this time superior, leaving all hands at liberty on the Alentejo side, where the Spaniard is master of the field," which makes us think there may not be much in it, however a cessation here is *de igual a igual,* which—if no more should come of it—seems a very considerable advantage to Portugal in point of reputation." The Secretary of State assures me that in the spring I shall see such forces of their own as never were yet. *Copy in letter book. 2 pp.*

SIR RICHARD FANSHAW to LORD CHANCELLOR CLARENDON.

1662, December [5-]15. Lisbon—Stating that he has applied for an audience, to deliver a petition from some English merchants and a memorial concerning the second payment of the Queen's portion, but has not yet obtained one; and also that he has had a letter from the Secretary of State in relation to the purchase of the houses lately inhabited by Portuguese in Tangier, which he advises his Majesty to give him power to bargain for if needful. *Copy in letter book.* 1¼ *pp.*

SIR RICHARD FANSHAW to SIR HENRY BENNET.

1662, December [9-]19. Lisbon—I only had notice yesterday of your being made Secretary of State, and wish you much good and long enjoyment of it. "I shall be a gainer by the change as well as you, for although your predecessor was a person very obliging to me—which I shall ever with thankfulness acknowledge—yet the nature and scene of my present negotiation requires a Spanish patron; *i.e.,* a minister in that place who is a master of the language," as many important documents pass in it, which lose much by translation, "and this of the kingdom in which I now am would lose its force and sense if translated into any other but that; whereof his Majesty himself also will be fully apprehensive, when you shall only read the papers therein distinctly unto his Majesty with never so little of explanation thereupon." I much prefer to have my dispatches disapproved than not taken notice of, since I may mend my faults by proper directions, and failing thereof ought to be called home. In my last I sent a copy of the cessation for a month, restrained to the frontiers of Galicia. What is meant by it "you may sooner guess, at that distance, from your late experience of Spain and your better intelligence of the present temper or distemper of that Court, with what they may fear of a new breach by France, or suspect at home among themselves than I can do in their enemy's country, though but at next door. . . . I might fear it ominous to us both if I should begin my addresses to you with tiring your patience, therefore I rest your most faithful and ever most devoted humble servant." *Copy in letter book.* 1 *p.*

Sir Richard Fanshaw to Secretary Morice.

1662, December [11-]21. Lisbon—The English troops "are yet together by reason of one month's pay at this present counting unto them in the frontiers, but in such a mouldering, perishing, discontented fashion as gives me no confidence of their continuing so a fortnight longer," especially since it is now well known that Col. Roscarrock and the Earl of Insiquin have arrived in England with despatches representing their distressed condition and yet no answer comes to them, neither have I received a line from any minister of state in England since my arrival here. The Brazil [Company] is dissolved "and this King takes the stock and management into his hands, having established a Council to manage it, whereof the Conde de Outoguia is made president." Unfortunately, news has come that the Brazil fleet will not return home this season, in respect of preparing for their spring *campaña*, "though expect it excedingly rich about May." His Majesty hath raised the gold here, but only time will show whether the effect thereof is good or bad. The Ostend men-of-war commit daily piracies upon our English on this coast. Sir John Lawson is at Malaga, having concluded a peace with Tripoli and Tunis like to that with Algiers. A carvel from Tangier, bought by Sir John Mennes for his Majesty, has been cast away in this port but almost all the men saved. I had an order from this King to secure her four guns for his Majesty, "and to keep what else is saved from land-shipwreck, too usual in such cases by the *canalla* in all countries, who pick up God's goods in the devil's name." *Copy in letter book.* 1½ *pp.*

Sir Richard Fanshaw to Lord Chancellor Clarendon.

1662, December [14-]24. Lisbon—I am told that the Queen's physician has brought despatches of great importance from England, but what they are I know not, "for neither do they communicate to me anything of it, neither have I from any minister of state in England, either at this or any other time since my arrival, received one word to this moment, though the matters which have been represented thither by me with Col. Roscarrock, Capt. Allin, Sir Peter Wyche and Capt. Robinson were of [the] greatest—in my humble opinion—this scene could be capable of." The treaty is so far forward that a cessation for one month upon one frontier is actually concluded, "in order to a further cessation and treaty in all the forms by several commissioners to be nominated by each King, and full authorities from Madrid to this purpose are expected here daily." Presently the grand treaty will begin, and "this King—as the Conde de Castelmelhor hath told me—is likely to nominate me to appear amongst his [commissioners] in the name of the King of England. Then shall I be in such a dilemma, whether to go or stay, or how to carry myself if I do go, as I have in my former discoursed to your Lordship, having commission and credential to the King of Spain sufficient, but no instructions thereupon." Nor am I less in the dark about the English troops here, whose necessities are such that I scarcely hold their keeping together possible. As regards the treaty "no clocks in a great city do differ so much from one end to the other as opinions concerning a peace do here in several frontiers." In that of Minio, it is in that forwardness that the old regiments there are credibly reported to be re-embarking from Galicia for Flanders; "on Alentejo-side—where Don Juan of Austria is—not so much as that matter of fact believed of the one month's cessation in Minio, nothing but preparations for an early *campaña*, nothing but swallowing of all Portugal in expectation by a direct march to Setuval with the first of the spring, fresh throwing out of billets amongst our English with higher offers than the former, to debauch them over from the service, all which I have both from Major-General O'Brien and from the consul, who are newly returned from that frontier, by which it may be imagined how much more confident that enemy would be if our men, in utter despair, should actually run over to them." The Count de Chomberg, who understands this war better than any man living, assures me that of themselves "the Portuguese can no more be prepared in point of time for Don Juan, than they can plant timber in the space of a year," so that if the King of Spain proceeds to a treaty, it will be owing partly to the French King, partly to Don Juan, and partly to the supposed resolution of our master to support Portugal. The Portuguese would never forgive me this language, and yet I sincerely desire to serve them and to persuade his Majesty to help them, "it being honour enough for them—to add unto their ancient stock of glory—that they—a small nation—have withstood the Spanish monarchy two and twenty years, having at some time had both England and Holland upon their backs to boot, and yet what most warms me in the case is, that after all this, they may not now perish, when Spain and the world look upon them as in his Majesty's arms and protection; for if this were not, I could see the companions of my youth triumphant, even in Lisbon, without breaking my heart. His Majesty's interest in the succession to this Crown and in the remainder of the Queen's portion I have not mentioned now, having descanted thereupon to your Lordship elsewhere, but there appears to me still as little possibility of the latter as of the former, should the Spaniard prevail by arms." I have had an audience of the King "with a high compliment over and above, as to free admittances in the future unto his royal person without the ceremony of asking leave beforehand, but the scent of portion to my nostril no warmer than it was, nor yet of performing articles with the then petitioning merchants."

Postscript.—Since finishing the above I have had a visit from the Secretary of State, who said that his master wished me to thank mine for his care of Portugal, as narrated by the Marques de Sande, and that he wished also to thank me "for the good offices which the said Marques certified I had done to this Crown by my representations into England. He then proceeded to the case of Duarte de Sylva," now a prisoner in London with a serjeant-at-arms, begging me to recommend him to our King in two points; "the one, the money, instead of the jewels, which de Sylva would have to be instead of the money; that his Majesty would be pleased to accept it with some respite for the payment of it . . . the other the rate of the crusado, which de Sylva would pay at 3*s*. 3*d*. and his Majesty's ministers require 3*s*. 6*d*., that his Majesty would cause it to be moderated in some reasonable way, and de Sylva upon these terms to be set at liberty." 1 cannot think these things "were the real scope of so solemn a message, and do rather imagine that the principal verb of the secretary's discourse lay in an expression which he slided over in the midst thereof—by way of parenthesis—to induce his Majesty's indulgence to Sylva, that after-payments of Queens' portions are not usually exacted with rigour in all points, for that he thought the Queen Mother's of England was never all paid, or not till very late." The cessation expired, I find, on the 21st, and I hear nothing of any renewal of it. "The Queen of Portugal hath now declared her resolution to turn recluse, of which more by my next." *Copy in letter book.* 4 *pp.*

SIR RICHARD FANSHAW to his brother [in-law], SIR PHILIP WARWICK.

1662, December [14-]24. Lisbon—"Yours of the 12th of the last I have, and therein, though not much of light in my affairs, for want of my having given you more, yet all I have received since my leaving England. There is the trouble, which of all I undergo puts me most to my bearing. There is but one that can put me more to it, and is indeed the only one unsupportable to my broad shoulders, *i.e.*, if I should be reduced to a necessitous condition in a public employment in a foreign country, my royal master—whom I have the honour to represent—flourishing at the same time. All these ingredients must go into it to make the potion too bitter for me to swallow; and even so, I could have digested it, too, if either I had been ambitious of the employment for the title's sake, or covetous of the preferment I believed would, or passionately desired should follow it. In all which points you very well know my mind and my case." You will see by the enclosed the danger I run of this necessitous condition unless by my Lord Treasurer's abundant goodness I am succoured from the Exchequer, my father [in-law], Sir John Harrison, having full powers to receive and give discharges on my behalf for all that is due to me by virtue of my privy seal. "The said enclosed will further give you a summary account of my day's work, as it is fit I should do where I ask my wages and counsel too.

One thing I assure you, I take as much pains and thought as
those whose workmanship deserves much better, possibly a great
deal more, too, like travellers that ride faster when they are out of
the way." My wife joins me in service "to yourself, my dear
sister, and both yours." *Copy in letter book.* 1 *p.*

Annexed,

　　Account of moneys due to Sir Richard Fanshaw as
　ambassador, Latin Secretary and Master of Requests, amount-
　ing to 1,260l. ½ *p.*

EARL OF INCHIQUIN to SIR RICHARD FANSHAW.

1662, December 29. London—"I have been now five weeks
kept in suspense what to write touching the business of Portugal
by reason of my Lord Chancellor having the gout, which has
occasioned the Council to decline meddling therewith, but by the
discourse I have had with the King I find no money can be had
here, only a letter will be sent to pay 6,000l. more on the account
of the portion, but I hope France will send money suddenly. and
that by that means our men will be maintained there, if not I
know not what will become of them, for I see no hope that
shipping can be had to bring them off so soon as they are like
to be in distress there.

I have told the King and my Lord Chancellor how troublesome an employment your Excellency's was like to be, and how
difficult a thing it would be for you to give a satisfactory account
of the affairs you should transact in during the continuation of
the present Government, whose principles are quite different from
those that this Court took their measures by, and they are both
so fully possessed of the unsteadiness and weakness of those
ministers that your Excellency may be most confident no miscarriage there will be imputed to your want of conduct, and
indeed I find cause to believe that wherever you were they would
likely have that opinion of you.

The manner of Sir Edward Nicholas's being eased of the burden
of his secretaryship was thus: Jack Aspernam [Ashburnham]
was sent to him to let him know that the practices of ill spirits
throughout this kingdom did require more labour and activity
at this time than his years and infirmities could undergo and
that therefore it was requisite his Majesty should put in another,
but that he would give him 10,000l. and make him a baron in
recompense of his place. This message being delivered, the secretary declared himself to be very much surprised with the thing
and desired time till next day to give an answer. In the interim
he goes to acquaint my Lord Chancellor with it, believing that
his Lordship would give him both advice and protection, but the
King had told my Lord Chancellor his resolution in so brisk
and short terms, quitting him without staying for his opinion
on the matter, that his Lordship did not think fit to give any
advice, nor to meddle in the matter, telling only to Sir Edward,
that he need not quit his place if he pleased, which he durst
not rely on as a sufficient encouragement to insist on keeping it,

seeing his Lordship did decline interposing in it, and therefore he accepted the 10,000*l.*, but declined the honour, in lieu whereof a thing worth about 2,000*l.* more was given him. Thus I had the story from his own mouth.

Sir Henry Bennet does give much satisfaction in his office, and is like to be a very powerful man in this kingdom, where my Lord Chancellor does now meddle only with the matters relating to his office and the affairs of state, but does not speak in the behalf of any man for any place or employment.

The lady you wot of is still very much in credit.

The King of France, notwithstanding his great preparations, is like to agree with the Pope, but on what conditions we do not yet know, for his Majesty keeps Avignon yet.

I do send the letter to acquit us of repaying the eight days, the King allowing them out of his portion.

The public news is shown by the printed papers herewith sent your Excellency.

The Ambassador here has given me many thanks for the earnestness I have shown in serving the King of Portugal here to the utmost of my power, how unsuccessful soever my endeavours have been, and he says he has written thereof to the King and the ministers there. If it be so I hope it will be a means to facilitate the license, if it stick still as it seems it did when the *Ruby* came away. And I beg your Lordship's assistance in that business.

The Earl of Chesterfield is gone into the country of purpose to remove his lady from the court thither, being jealous of some addresses made to her by his Royal Highness, but I am most confident the blow he fears has not been at all given, though there want not censurers on this occasion. I kiss my lady's hands." *Signed.* 2 *pp.*

Endorsed by Fanshaw:—" From the Earl of Insiquin. Dated at London 29th of December, 62. Rec. at Lisbon 27th of January, old style, by Mrs. Maynard, who then landed at Cascays, having been at sea from Saturday was a sennight, which added unto the five weeks there mentioned makes above seven weeks from the time Lord Insiquin and Capt. Trelawny had been soliciting in London unto the time that this ship, the *Unicorn*, left the Downs. With a letter from his Majesty to the King of Portugal."

MAJOR LAURENCE DEMPSY to [SIR RICHARD FANSHAW?]

1663, January [4-]14. Lisbon—By a letter from the Sieur Denys de Melo, general of artillery and now commanding the armies in Alentejo, where the English troops are, and the discourse held with me by the Secretary of State, I see that his Majesty and his ministers are very much misinformed concerning the said troops, and judge that malicious persons have given false informations both to the generals and to the ministers. Having received orders from the Earl of Inchiquin and others to assist with five troops in the city of Beze and other places from the first of last July until now, and having served with them both in quarters and on the march, I declare that both in the cities of Beze, Cuba, Portalegre, Casteladavida or elsewhere in all that time, and whether in quarters or on the march, if they committed any disorders I had them punished; and to prove the falseness of the informations against us and the good carriage of the English troops I offer as witnesses of the truth the Chamber of Beze, Sir Manuel Geneiro of Cuba, the Governor of Auyz, the Governors of the towns where we were and the Commissary General Juan de Crato. And for the further manifestation of the good fame of our troops I beg you to demand an audience for me from the Secretary of State that I may represent the truth to him. *Spanish. Copy in letter book.* 1¼ *pp.*

SIR RICHARD FANSHAW to KING CHARLES II.

1663 [January 27-]February 6. Lisbon—Long letter on the affairs of Portugal, of which the original is amongst the Portugal Correspondence at the Public Record Offiec. *Copy in letter book.* 4 *pp.*

SIR RICHARD FANSHAW to SIR HENRY BENNET.

1663 [January 28-]February 7. Lisbon—Stating that about a fortnight ago he met a friar, one of the Queen's preachers, who said he had a letter for him from Sir Henry, which however he has never received. Regrets this the more as he has not had a word from any minister of State during the five months he has been in Portugal, which makes him "so blank and out of countenance" that he is ashamed to show his head in the Court, especially as many dispatches have come from the Marquis of Sande, showing that there are ways to hear from the Court of England, though none for him. *Copy in letter book.* 1 *p.* [*Original amongst the Portugal Correspondence.*]

SIR RICHARD FANSHAW to the MARQUES DE SANDE.

1663, January 29-February 8. Lisbon—I have received your Excellency's letter of the 20th of November, that and no other since I have been at this Court, which I say, not as undervaluing it, but because Mr. Bere, an English merchant, lately arrived at this Court, tells me that many have been written to me. In what you say of the regard shown me by the King here and all the court—much beyond my merit—and also of the good offices which I am always ready to do for the Portuguese crown and nation with the King, my master, and his ministers, you neither deceive yourself nor me, as the employments given me here and my accounts sent home can witness for me. As to your request that I will urge the King, my master, to include in the dowry the 40,000 crusadoes due from the four ships from Brazil, I have heard that already that business is settled to your satisfaction, but in regard to your Excellency's view that Portugal ought to have a further respite in time for the payment of the dowry, to speak plainly, as is my wont, I cannot agree with you without disowning my own opinion and breaking my orders, which are to urge payment in conformity with the treaty. The King and ministers here show themselves willing to comply with this, acknowledging their delay, still I have done what I can for you by representing the state in which Portugal is at present. May God remedy it ere long. *Spanish. Copy in letter book.* 1 *p.*

Sir Richard Fanshaw to Charles II.

1663 [January 31-]February 10. Lisbon—Since my former of the 6th instant to your Majesty two great packets have arrived in this court from the Marquis of Sande, yet I remain still without a line of intimation of your pleasure concerning Portugal from any minister of State in England whatsoever. "But by oblique ways I do understand as followeth, which hath occasioned this second and yet higher presumption than the other : —

1. *From my Lord Insiquin,* of 29th of December, that his Lordship had then been five weeks kept in suspense what to write touching the business of Portugal, by reason of my Lord Chancellor's having the gout, which occasioned the Council to decline meddling therewith. To the same effect these ministers tell me their letters speak, to their and my very great affliction, both for his Lordship's person and for the danger which this sinking kingdom runs by the loss of so much precious time, the date of mine having been a fortnight and two days before the ship which brought it left the Downs, so, added to the other, it makes above seven weeks, but that by the discourse he, the said Lord Insiquin, had had with your Majesty he found no money can be had there, unless by an intended letter from your Majesty for one 6,000*l.* more on account of the portion, which—besides the inconsiderableness of such a sum among so many mouths— is such an uncertain and dilatory way of satisfying soldiers as hath already almost broke the hearts of them and of these ministers, and my Lord Insiquin's and mine : but his Lordship hoped France would send money suddenly, and that by that means our troops will be maintained here, if not, he knew not what would become of them, for he saw no hope that shipping could be had to bring them off so soon as they were like to be in distress here ; withal that his Lordship had done me the right to tell both your Majesty and my Lord Chancellor how difficult a thing it would be for me to give a satisfactory account of the affairs I should transact in, during the continuation of the present government, whereupon I might be most confident no miscarriage here would be imputed to my want of conduct ; his Lordship farther adding that indeed he found cause to believe that wherever I were both your Majesty and my Lord Chancellor were likely to have the same opinion of me ; this latter part being in truth an obligement of supererogation, whereas the former— as both your Majesty and my Lord Chancellor may well remember—is only a fulfilling of my own prophecy, even though the Queen Mother's regency—which yet was superseded before

I left the court of England—had continued, not for lack of good-will or of large and spreading views of reverence to this crown, but because the same are totally upon the matter employed in and obstructed by their wars and the effects thereof, unless—for so I explained myself—through a peace with Spain by your Majesty's mediation.

2. *From Bishop Russell*, that I must persuade these here, and with truth, that the sale of Dunkirk was done with an eye towards the future assistance of Portugal by both crowns.

3. *From the Conde de Castelmelhor*, coming to my house yesterday, as to the treaty of peace with Spain, *que aun esta verde*, the English whereof is all the doubts which my dispatches ever since I arrived in this court have imported concerning the same; war—as it is the worst, so—being the first fruit that is ripe in any country, and of which there never was so forward and promising a spring in Castile since it brake out between these neighbouring kingdoms as this present year; and yet I do not yet hold the treaty to be stark dead neither, withal believing that none but your Majesty can fetch life in it again, and that by a high hand.

4. *From the same Conde de Castelmelhor*, at the same time, that your Majesty's speedy and effectual succours are most earnestly implored by this King and his ministers, in whose name he requested me to represent as much to your Majesty with the most earnest language I could use, added to my former despatches, knowing I had already written to your Majesty on their behalf by this very conveyance.

5. *From the Count de Chomberg*, the herewith enclosed state of the war and preparations in these kingdoms on both sides—or rather on one side only—whereby your Majesty will see from a person whom your Majesty knows much better than I pretend to do, and who by his profession ought not to know what fear is—assuring myself also that he does not—I am certain hath more reason to know the depths and shelves of this war than any stranger living, and the sad, indeed desperate condition, this kingdom is in without your Majesty.

6. *From the same Count de Chomberg*, that by letters he hath newly received out of France the French King hath sent his ambassador, Monsieur de Cominges,* fully instructed to offer to your Majesty his master's effectual concurrence under hand in your Majesty's name and under your royal conduct of the affair to preserve this labouring crown.

7. *From the English Consul here*, that by his letters from England your Majesty doth very much lay to heart the improvement and enlargement of your new sovereignty in Barbary, having for the same purpose nominated Lord Rutterford for Governor of Tangier, allotting withal 30,000*l.* per annum for a royal mould till finished; and constituted an extraordinary committee, headed by his royal highness the Duke of York, to manage that affair at home, whilst the said Lord Rutterford

---

* Gaston Jean Baptiste de Cominges-Guitant, Lieutenant-General and Captain-of the guard to the Queen Mother, ambassador to Portugal in 1657, and to England in 1663.

passes thither with such a body of horse, foot and appurtenances as may be termed a small army, so consequently with such a strength of shipping as may pretend to the name of a royal fleet."

These premises considered it is a question whether your Majesty may not think it fit—

1. To dispatch Lord Rutterford somewhat earlier and stronger for Tangier.

2. With orders to anchor on his way, either here or in the Bay of Cascayes.

3. With further orders to serve this crown, taking the auxiliaries here, with their old officers if possible, especially Sir Thomas Morgan.

4. With express condition that this little army is to be dependent only on their own commanders.

5. With like condition to be possessed of some strong place on this coast, as a retreat for the forces and caution for payment of your Majesty's charges and the Queen's dowry; the said forces finally proceeding to Barbary.

6. With orders to your ambassador here to declare that if this court refuses these terms your Majesty will be discharged of further brotherly protection of this crown, for "when Spanish bullets and pistols shall at once fly thick about the ears of the Portuguese, it may not be in your Majesty's power at that time of day to protect them against themselves, much less against the Castilians, or your Majesty's own people, in that case, against both, without such holds."

7. With further orders to your general, in case of refusal, to sail straight to Africa and for the troops here to retire.

8. Finally, with orders to your ambassador here in such case to retire also, "unless your Majesty shall think it fit that he stay to see the last man borne, if peradventure the successful approach of the Spaniards should fright this nation into their wits by frighting it out of them."

These rough and wild notions may provoke your Majesty to laughter, but I hope not to indignation. In the twenty years I have served you "your Majesty did never take me to be romantic in business till I tasted this air where I am, being likewise not insensible that this very excuse—if your Majesty should discover me to any that should report it back to this court—may prove worse than the fault excused and turn to my greater condemnation here, where I have hitherto the fortune to be a piece of a favourite." *Draft.* 6 *pp.* [*The letter itself is amongst the Portugal Correspondence, but it is calendared here as throwing light upon the sequence of events.*]

SIR RICHARD FANSHAW to the EARL OF INCHIQUIN.

1663 [January 31-]February 10. Lisbon—I have received yours of December 29th by the consul's wife, "esteeming it for a great rarity as a letter from England, though no rarity as it is a favour from your Lordship." It gave me more light as to what may be relied on here as to our present troops and as regards

further succours for this besieged kingdom than ever I had
before, and yet I am still in the dark. To my wonder our troops
are yet in being and I use all my arts to keep them so, as does
also your brother, the major-general, " who sticks close to them
and their interests in the frontiers personally." I thank your
Lordship for your favourable reports of me and also for " your
interludes of something of recreative between the acts of more
serious affairs." *Copy in letter book.* 1 *p.*

SIR RICHARD FANSHAW to LORD CHANCELLOR CLARENDON.

1663 [January 31-]February 10. Lisbon—Expressing his
regret at learning by letters from the Marquis of Sande that his
Lordship has been long laid up with the gout—in consequence
of which the debates upon Portuguese affairs have had to be postponed—and hoping to hear of his happy recovery. *Copy in
letter book.* ½ *p.*

SIR RICHARD FANSHAW to SECRETARY MORICE·

1663 [January 31-]February 10. Lisbon—Renewing his complaints at receiving no letters from the ministers of state, which
he imputes rather to miscarriage than only to the multiplicity
of other affairs, and expressing his longing " for that happy hour
which will both unriddle this mystery" and give him some light
as to what his Majesty's pleasure is concerning Portugal. ½ *p.*

SIR RICHARD FANSHAW to R. RUSSELL, Lord Bishop of Port Alegre.

1663, February [1-]11. Lisbon—" Your Lordship's of the 14th
of November from London I received here 9th instant by the
hands of the president of the English college, by the contents
whereof I find our court there hath taught your Lordship to
say many kind and obliging things, though true cordial kindness
I presume you are not now to learn of anybody, particularly
towards myself, who have always found it from your Lordship.
As to what your Lordship writes in reference to the mutual
characters the Earl of Insiquin and some ministers of this court
give one of another, that faults were on both sides according to
the opinion of the more serious there—I suppose you mean the
more wise—I, who for the most differ from the opinions of the
wisest, do it in this, too, that I think the fault was in neither, but
in the builders of Babel, who brought in the division of tongues,
and in the great architect thereof—the devil—who to hinder the
progress of good works—as God did of that which was a bad
one—never wants arts to create misunderstandings even in such
as from the tongue outward understand one another perfectly,
and would go on hand in hand together if they knew each other's
minds as well [as they do their dialects]. I must add withal
that really there were not assets here to comply with my Lord
Insiquin's just desires on behalf of our troops, and these

ministers' own engagements oftentimes to boot, which I am unwilling to call a fault on either side, but a misfortune on both, * as in the case of assets which one justly claims, and the other as justly pleads [want of] them in excuse.

For the point of my agreeing with Portugal and Portugal with me, it is hitherto fully as much as your Lordship can expect or wish, and will always be so on my part. But I do much fear it will not continue so with them, if ever it should come to be discovered unto them how much in all my despatches for England ever since I arrived in this kingdom [I compare] the strength, wealth, forecast and military discipline thereof comparatively to those of their enemy. Their invincible courage *more majoris* I deny not, but that it must necessarily make them invincible I do deny; no cowardice being so excusable as to fear for others, yet this I only whisper to such friends of Portugal as yourself, who may contribute their help to it at a dead lift, *aut re, aut opere, aut consilio bono.*

Therefore, finally—in reference to what your Lordship adds that the sale of Dunkirk was done with an eye towards the future assistance of Portugal by both crowns—I do conjure your Lordship—whether you write yourself English or Portuguese, and so, in this case, both is best—to solicit succours hither, with the same speed and proportion as if the ship of this state were infallibly to sink this very next summer without them." *Draft. 2 pp. Copy, with some variations, from which the words in brackets are taken, in letter book.*

SIR RICHARD FANSHAW to WILLIAM COVENTRY, Secretary to the Duke of York.

1663, February [3-]13. Lisbon—The bearer, Captain Holmes, has been detained here for three weeks waiting for despatches, the King being on a hunting journey at some distance from the city. "The time now approacheth"—being when Kings go forth to battle—that I hope for further testimonies of his Highness' royal favour . . . by your mediation, this kingdom being in effect a perfect isle with these wars, to and from and by which there is not now any safe correspondency left of letters or trade " without the help of his Majesty's frigates, by reason of the pillaging by Biscay and Ostend men-of-war. *Copy in letter book.* ¾ *p.*

SIR RICHARD FANSHAW to MAJOR ROBERT HOLMES.

1663 [February 3-]13. Lisbon—" Now, I hope you may truly report to any friends in England who shall ask after us both that all danger of my wife's present indisposition is over; [if] you had happened to set sail yesterday you must either have

---

* The letter book has " as in the case of executors, where a creditor or legatee puts in a just claim or demand and the others as justly plead they want assets to perform. In one thing I am sure your Lordship will confess my Lord Inchiquin clearly in the right, namely in his high eulogiums of the Queen-Mother, and all that are of a contrary opinion in a gross error." The last two paragraphs of the draft are not in the copy.

said nothing thereof, which was then desired, or told quite another story, which, coming to her father's ears, might have caused misgiving apprehensions in him, which, I must confess, I myself, present, was not wholly free from. But God be thanked.

The enclosed to Mr. Chiffinch is the warning I give him of you, and this present is my letter of attorney to you to solicit him daily for a thing he wots of. . . . I have considered this night in my bed—having my mind more at ease than before—of what you started in discourse yesterday, occasioned by the prospect of the Tagus from my house, concerning how acceptable and useful a yacht for a present from his Majesty to this King might be, as also how commodious and honourable a principal barge as a boon from his Majesty to myself." I should be glad if you could throw out a hint of it, when you give his Majesty the draught of this incomparable post, but I dare not presume to give you any commission therein. *Copy in letter book.* 1 *p.*

SIR RICHARD FANSHAW to his "ancient good friend," TOM CHIFFINCH.

1663, February [3-]13. Lisbon—"Having not received a word to this hour concerning my picture of our master in a jewel, pursuant to his Majesty's reiterated directions and your promises to see it done and sent away after me, . . . I have given to the bearer hereof, Captain Holmes, my letter of attorney to arrest you for it, that is to say, never to leave haunting you until it be got" and sent to me. I should not so impudently urge this were it not that I think the grace shown to his ambassador would do his Majesty service here " the nature of princes and states being to value, not only a messenger, but his errand, too, at the rate his master appears to value him, neither more nor less. And now, before I part from this subject of pictures—being your own element—let me request you to bespeak and remit to me with some convenient speed a copy of that you have of the King's tutor in his robes of prelate of the garter. I wish it no better copied than that of his Majesty in great by Mr. Stone, which is the honour of my house here. When it is finished my father, Sir John Harrison, will pay for it upon my account." *Copy in letter book.* 1 *p.*

SIR RICHARD FANSHAW to the MARQUES DE SANDE.

1663, February [3-]13. Lisbon—Has been charged with the enclosed for the Queen and his Excellency, in behalf of the Queen-Mother, and begs to hear as soon as may be that they have been received. *Spanish.* ½ *p. Copy in letter book.*

Enclosing,

1. *The King of France to the Pope.*

1662, *August* [20-]30. *St. Germains—Complaining of the attack made upon the Duc de Créqui, his ambassador extraordinary, the ambassadress and other French in the streets of Rome by the Corsican guard, and demanding satisfaction. Copy. Translated into Portuguese. ¾ p.*

2. *The King of France to the Cardinals.*
Same date and to the same effect. Copy in Portuguese. ¾ p.

3. *King Louis XIV.*

1661, *February* [16-]26. *Vincennes—His Majesty having received a complaint from the Comte de Fuensaldague [Fuensaldaña], ambassador from his Catholic Majesty, that certain Frenchmen have taken service in Portugal in contravention of the treaty between France and Spain, this is to order all such his subjects to leave Portugal and return into their own country within three months. French. Copy in Sir Richard Fanshaw's letter book.*

Sir Richard Fanshaw to Lord Chancellor Clarendon.

1663, March [2-]12. Lisbon—I have already told your Lordship of the great eagerness with which the present ministers of this court, since the change of government, received the suggestion that our King might be willing to assist in procuring a peace with Spain and their insistance that he should enter as mediator into the treaty. This continued "until the arrival from France of Mons. Colbert, by the name of Mons. Carneton, with intimations of underhand assistances from that crown by means of a marriage of this King to Mademoiselle, upon condition nevertheless—as I was afterwards told by no inconsiderable person—that they should conclude nothing with Castile." My suspicion was that the French King meant either to frustrate all endeavours of peace or to supplant our master in the honour of being the mediator therein "by his Majesty's wedding the cause as well as the daughter of Portugal, when the French had utterly abandoned it. . . . I have since my last discovered the following instance, which I take to be very pregnant in the case" :—On the 12th of January last, this style, the Conde de Castelmelhor—doing me the honour to visit me at my house—asked me to recommend him to some English ship with a trustworthy master, to take an *incognito* to Barcelona and bring back another person, for the special service of this court. I next day recommended a ship, but "less than the *Royal Catherine,* a merchant ship, but of great force and excellent accommodation, would not serve the turn." With the good will of the owner—Mr. Abraham Jacob—this ship was had, and on the 20th of January set sail with an *incognito,* apparently not of high quality, who told Mr. Jacob that on reaching Barcelona road a person would immediately embark and come for Portugal, while he that went from hence remained in Spain. What I have newly discovered is that this *incognito* was by name Joseph Jardin, secretary of the French embassy in Madrid, and his father, the French Queen's jeweller. A brother of his was sent here as agent before, but taken by the Turks, and he or another of the brothers had relation to Mons. Cominges, now ambassador

in England. Add to this the choice this court has made of the
Count de Chomberg to command the English here, under the title
of General of foreign auxiliaries,—whereas when the Earl of
Insiquin recommended him as his successor they rejected the
motion, desiring to be rid of him—it being a question "whether
of the two crowns of England and France will have more influence
upon them so commanded and especially if recruits of men and
money shall come from France," and add also the fact that when
Cominges had been here as ambassador he reported very meanly
of this nation on his return to France—for which the Portuguese
ambassador there, the Conde de Souvre,* sent him a challenge—
and "I am apt to infer that he looks upon Portugal either as a
present prey to the Spaniard, or a future windfall to the English,
both of which he would prevent by his activity. Add lastly that
the Marquis of Sande,—who was not long since ready to be ex-
ploded this court for his good service both to it and ours in negotiating the marriage,—is said to be gone or going ambassador for
France," Don Francisco de Melo succeeding him in the business
of England. Count Chomberg, in "several winding discourses,"
has tried to gain my concurrence with his appointment, but I have
told him clearly that if his Majesty should send another from
England to command the troops I should have myself to present
such person to this King. This I said in regard of my proposals
to his Majesty concerning the new modelling of the English
auxiliaries, "these cautions being in no sort contradictory to what
I have several times formerly written that I took Mons. Chomberg, in regard of his particular long experience here, and knowledge of the language, to be the ablest commander as to this war
and kingdom of any stranger, but rather in part proceeding from
this very consideration. For conclusion of all I hope before
this comes to hand to receive from your Lordship his
Majesty's sense upon the matter thereof, not contenting
yourself with showing me my folly—as hitherto—by silence
only, because the wise man—upon second thoughts—advises to
answer a fool according to his folly, lest he be wise in his own
conceit; there being till then something of just excuse for these
hot vapours of mine from a heart passionately concerned for my
King and country, namely, that I am but as the schoolmen who
were said to be wild with dark keeping, whereas if I had the least
light from authority that the Marquis of Sande and Mons. de
Cominges there have been opener to his Majesty than this Court
is here to me" and that his Majesty and the French King have
the same design and interest, I would do my utmost to promote
the endeavours of both. In the meantime I may be pardoned
if I continue my jealousy of French influence, especially if the
Royal Catherine should bring back from Barcelona some person
out of France—by the way of Madrid—of great quality, abilities
or both, who may have the power though not the title of an
ambassador. The commissioners for the treaty are shortly to
meet upon the borders, with little enough expectation, I confess,
on either side. The ministers here, although they tell me

---

* Juan da Costa, Conde de Souvre or Soure.

nothing, treat me with great civility and express all the confidence imaginable in my good affections to this crown. "If I have not talked idly ever since I began—which was my first fear—yet now I find myself plainly coming to it by talking long, and therefore make haste" to say farewell. *Draft, very much corrected. 7 pp.*

SIR HENRY BENNET to SIR RICHARD FANSHAW.

1662-3, March 6. Whitehall—"Your Lordship's of the 7th past—new style—was the first I have ever been honoured with from you, wherein I did with much resentment on your Lordship's behalf perceive with how much disconsolation you have been left in that employment for want of a punctual correspondence from hence, which it falling into my lot to make good for the future, I beseech your Lordship to rely upon the promise I make you herein that no occasion shall pass wherein you shall not either receive letters from me or an humble excuse for the want of them, with all the news here that may relate either to your employment or satisfaction.

Having said this I am to give your Lordship account that I obtained of his Majesty to hear your two letters of the 6th and 10th February read to him by me in the presence of his Royal Highness, the Lord Chancellor, Lord Treasurer, Lord General, Lord Chamberlain and my Lord Ashley, at which meeting the matters your Lordship proposed in the said letters were debated, and I commanded to make this return to them. In the first place that his Majesty values much your Lordship's care and application to all things that concern his service and satisfaction in the promotion of the affairs of that kingdom, which he hath taken particularly into his thoughts, with an intention and purpose to contribute all the advantages he can possibly thereunto. Towards which his Majesty would have been very glad that his royal mediation might have been worth something in the treaty of peace or suspension of arms which it is conceived hath been kept on foot this last winter between his Catholic Majesty and them, but finding himself not called upon therein by either side he could not properly take notice of it.

As to the proposition your Lordship makes of having my Lord Rutherford sent into those ports in his way to Tangier with a strength to succour that kingdom, they rendering some cautionary towns to secure to his Majesty the repayment of his charges and securing his men, it is not held a practicable thing upon them, they showing such an aversion to the admittance of strangers.

Upon the observation of this and many others in the like nature his Majesty is infinitely troubled to see how little that kingdom is likely to contribute to its own preservation, notwithstanding which he is resolved to leave nothing undone which may depend on him, according to which his Majesty commands me to let you know that by the end of this month at the farthest there shall be in the river of Lisbon at least seven of his best men-of-war,

E

victualled from their parting hence for eight months, to give countenance to all the undertakings of the King of Portugal this summer, by securing their ports from being blocked up and the return of their fleet from Brazil. In fine with orders to do all things that shall be for the benefit of that kingdom, except only the breaking downright the peace with Spain. And that moreover, by the time aforesaid, there shall be paid to his Majesty of Portugal's orders two hundred thousand crowns for the benefit of his affairs, which they will understand to whom they shall be beholding for it.

As for what concerned the miserable condition in which his Majesty's troops are there he looks upon it with infinite perplexity of mind, as not seeing any way before him by which to give them ease, nor thinking it fit to add any new ones for their recruit, unless he could see some better assurance for their entertainment. As for the six thousand pounds you mention to be raised from the remainder of the portion, it was ordered by his Majesty to make up the deduction of the Portugal pay from what the English was before, as a pure effect of his goodness and commiseration of the troops. To encourage which his Majesty hath commanded me to write by this occasion a kind letter for him to the said troops, which I hope will be ready to accompany this. With which, having told you the Parliament sits now again, that our affairs are in the same state you left them, that the King and Queen are both in good health—God be thanked—and that we feel the spring growing hastily upon us, I have no more but to offer you my humble services." [*In Williamson's handwriting, signed by Bennet.*] 3½ *pp.*

Sir Richard Fanshaw to Colonel Molesworth.

1663, March [7-]17. Lisbon—Concerning the complaints made against him (Molesworth) by Major-General O'Brien that he had inveighed in all companies against his brother, the Earl of Inchiquin, and against himself, the said Major-General, as having designed to pass over with the English troops to the Spaniards. *Draft.* [*There is a copy of this, undated, in the Portugal Correspondence.*]

Robert Cocke to his Excellency [Sir Richard Fanshaw].

1662-3, March 15. Lisbon—" A demonstration to show your Excellency how the Consul [Maynard] do follow the steps of his old master Cromwell, the great traitor and usurper.

" 1. He first, under colour of religion and zeal to the good old cause, with great humility did so far insinuate himself with the merchants that they named him consul and procured his confirmation by Cromwell, then he began to act, and immediately thrust out Consul Robinson, authorised to serve by virtue of his Majesty's patent, trampling all respect and loyalty to his Majesty under feet, pretending zeal to the cause.

" 2. Wherein he did not only abuse his Majesty's favour bestowed on the said Robinson, but usurped the consulship and place of a worthy gentleman, Colonel Thomas Rawdon, who for the loyalty and good service done his Majesty of blessed memory by Sir Marmaduke, his father, and himself, being employed hither to King John of Portugal as agent from his Majesty, then in Oxford, not having else to bestow on him gave him the patent of this place, which by reason of the persecution the poor royalists lay under by that tyrant Cromwell, especially the active persons in the service of his Majesty, were forced to fly away to save their lives when they had lost their estates by Cromwell and unjust sequestration, and in the absence of the said Colonel, then being in the Barbadoes, procured the place belonging to the said Colonel, keeping it violently from him, which is the highest degree of usurpation.

"3. The place of consulship was augmented to half per cent., which formerly was but a quarter, in consideration that the nation might maintain a minister, which out of the consulship should be paid 300 *mil reis* a year, for some time did enjoy an able honest minister, his life and conversation agreeable to his doctrine, but the ill treating of him by the consul in words and not paying him according to promise made him forsake the place, to the great grief of all the nation, which the consul did to defraud the ministry and usurp the 300 *mil reis* to himself as he hath done for the space of three years.

"4. He hath likewise defrauded and usurped the place of Paymaster General from Sir Peter Weich [Wyche], which place was bestowed on him by his Majesty and came over with the soldiers to that purpose, and did execute the place with loyalty, but such was the subtle dealing of the consul, he possessed himself of the place.

"5. He likewise hath by a false and sinister way, in raising scandals against the person and ability of Robert Cocke, not only to the usurping of his place, but endeavouring to take away his good name, reputation and life, which place was given him by his gracious Majesty in recompense of good and loyal service done his Majesty of blessed memory, and his sacred Majesty, whom God preserve, and give him victory against his enemies and true knowledge of those fained friends which pretends loyalty, which if occasion should present, as God forbid, would be the first to execute the malice and then pretend service for persecuting his Majesty's loyal subjects, as the consul now doth in a wicked and malicious way, accusing of honest men and royalists under title of fanatics and some criminally for their lives, as he did Mr. Edward Bridgwood, Mr. William Peach, and Mr. Roger Bradall, all honest men and loyal subjects to his Majesty. Many specified in this paper were great sufferers for his Majesty's cause, when he the said consul was an active rebel in the service of Cromwell, though his impudence permits him to name them under the notion of fanatics.

"6. He makes nothing of breach of patent, giving himself titles and styles never allowed him, naming himself agent and giving his two votes in elections, as if [he] were an absolute prince, whose spiring mind and ambitious heart suits no subject, much

B 2

less to so mean a quality, for to reckon up other particulars
would be too tedious and troublesome, but I give God thanks
that it hath pleased his Majesty to provide so wise and judicious
a minister in chief as your Excellency, on whom myself and the
greatest part of the nation relies for justice, not suffering him
to execute further violence on his Majesty's loyal subjects." 2
pp.

SIR RICHARD FANSHAW to [MAJOR-GENERAL] CHRISTOPHER
O'BRIEN.

1663 [March 18-]28—Hearing from the Palace that the King
has determined to send you to England—together with the informations from Madrid which have been the cause of your imprisonment—by the frigate which will presently go for London from
the Tower of Belen, I replied that I believed you had accounts
to settle with the ministers here first, and that you ought to
have permission for your friends and servants to come and go
freely.   To this they have answered that the said accounts
shall be settled to-morrow and that the request as regards your
friends and servants is reasonable.   *Spanish.   Copy in letter
book.* ½ *p.*
    Annexed,
        1. *Don Antonio de Sousa de Macedo to Sir Richard
        Fanshaw.*
        1663, *March* [20-]30 [*sic*].   *The Palace—Stating that the
    King has resolved to send O'Brien to England, and that his
    accounts will be arranged at once. Portuguese. Copy.* ⅓ *p.*
        2. *The Same to the Same.*
        1663, *March* [21-]31.   *The Palace—Stating that he has
    given orders for the admission to Major-General O'Brien
    of all those bearing the ambassador's pass. Portuguese.
    Copy.* ½ *p.*
        3. *The Same to the Same.*
        1663, *March* [16-]26—*Stating that, as regards the business
    of Dom Christopher O'Brien, they have received intelligence
    from persons of credit in Castile that the Earl of Inchiquin
    was in treaty in England with the Castilian minister Moledi,
    for the passing over to Spain of his brother Christopher,
    with all his troops. Portuguese. Copy.* ½ *p.*

SIR RICHARD FANSHAW to his brother [in-law], SIR PHILIP
WARWICK.

1663, March [20-]30. Lisbon—I could not have thought it
possible for me to have subsisted so long without any of the
moneys due to me from the Exchequer, which I see no chance
of your getting when I consider that the warrants which my
Lord Treasurer and the Chancellor of the Exchequer signed for
me upon the customs, where we do not want friends, are still
unsatisfied.

"Between you and me I suppose I may adventure to say that when I was named to this embassy neither the English nor Portugal ministers that concluded the match did expect to receive sufficient to defray it upon account of the after payments of our Queen's portion; much less, as things have gone since in this Court, by removing the Queen Mother from the Government, with many particular disgusts heaped upon herself and all those her Majesty employed in greatest trusts, upon this very score, say they, that she exhausted the wealth and aliened the flowers of the crown for the advancement of that one child; but what [sic] talk of them, succeeding ministers and governments being always ready. enough to speak and hear things to the disadvantage of their predecessors. To return where I was. Did not Bishop Russell at Hampton Court, to my face, make a mockery of peoples talking of second payments of the portions of Queens, especially in reference to Portugal, so wasted and oppressed as it is with wars? Did not the Marquis of Sande—I have noted it to you heretofore—in a letter to myself, pleading for Duarte de Sylva, affirm that, the portion being so great, more than longer days of payment might be expected in favour of Portugal," yet at the lowest ebb of my hopes, "not making it my particular case at all or abating one jot of my manly countenance, I obtained lately so much of our gracious Queen's portion as will satisfy near half my arrears, not dispairing, now the ice is broke, of exempting myself from a necessity of troubling your Exchequer again upon the account of this pilgrimage." I may well fail to receive the whole, for the little time which I hope I shall be continued abroad, no great sums "being possibly to be had here in the present most exhausted condition of this crown and kingdom, a potent monarch and nation at full leisure pressing them within their gates. This pass, by God's blessing, I have happily brought it to, that the King . . . hath expressly owned and given earnest for the whole remainder of the portion, with many obliging expressions to boot in reference thereunto, which I have to shew in black and white." Of one thing, however, I must warn you, viz. :—That this King having raised the value of gold and intending to raise that of silver will probably wish to pay it at the raised value, which would defraud us of a fourth, to which I shall never consent without his Majesty's express orders. "I do assure you without vanity, if either a rougher or a tamer fellow than myself had had the soliciting of this matter he might well have been a great while longer at it without any token either of earnest or acknowledgment: how I have gained ground by degrees may make a story apart, one of these days." *Copy in letter book.* 3 *pp.*

SIR RICHARD FANSHAW to SECRETARY MORICE.

1663, March [21-]31. Lisbon—I have only just received yours [*of November* 19. *See above, p.* 48], acknowledging my despatches, and I thank you for "reducing their tedious length to a compass supportable by his Majesty." This is the only letter

from any minister of state which has come to my hands, "excepting two from Mr. Secretary Bennet, both of them of very
high civility to my person, but neither of them containing anything in reference to my employment, his honour not having,
at the writing thereof, received any particular light concerning
it. Those proposals which went from this crown with my Lord
Inchiquin your honour and the Council there had very great
reason to judge extravagant, if the Marquis of Sande, when he
was so properly called by the Board to explain thereupon, had
nothing either out of old or new instructions to say beyond the
letter. To him the original was sent from his master to manage
it, the secretary only giving me a copy." *Copy in letter book.*
1 *p.*

SIR RICHARD FANSHAW to SIR JOHN MENNES.

1663, March [21-]31. Lisbon—"The inclosed is from your
old fellow traitor, Mr. Cock, who yet—for a man of your way—
hath been always held honest." He says, and I believe it, that
his victualling accounts to the Commissioners of the Navy are
so also and that he has remitted them duly from time to time.
"If both these things are true the man hath very ill-luck,
which is another sign of an honest man as well as of a proper
one." Pray get his bills answered for him if you can that he
may lose nothing but his place. If I had not interposed with
the landlord he would now have been in gaol for the rent of the
store-house.
"I and all mine present our very affectionate services to you
and to your new lady when you have her; wishing you better
health than the soundest of us have been able to boast of since
we came here; the Menessian air not greatly agreeing with any
of us." I hope you will soon be sending a trim squadron to
defend us from the Spaniards. I pray you let the Captains have
instructions to pick up the pirating Ostenders and Biscayers,
who pillage "friend and foe with and without pretence. Not
so much as a letter can come hither secure without a frigate,
and therefore I pardon the having received but one from you
in the space of eight months that I have now been here, provided
you put forth lustily in the spring. But you will not write a
man any news then neither, though as ignorant of all things
there as those need to be that are in Japan, and moreover your
old friend and servant." *Copy in letter book.* 1¼ *pp.*

SIR RICHARD FANSHAW to LORD VISCOUNT CORNBURY.

1663, March [21-]31. Lisbon—On the 15th December I sent
you a letter for our gracious Queen from her mother, which I
hope came safe to hand. I now send what will be less welcome,
"a written plain relation, containing only matter of fact, of the
manner of the Queen Mother's retreat here to a house which her
Majesty intends to found into a nunnery; and then some prints,
stating the present condition of the affairs of Portugal, ecclesi-

astical, civil and military; upon which poles—one more than the heavens turn upon—will move all that I have occasion to advertise your Lordship hereafter." *Copy in letter book.* $\frac{3}{4}$ *p.*

SIR RICHARD FANSHAW to SIR KENELM DIGBY.

1663, March [21-]31. Lisbon—I am sorry I cannot send you either the seed-pearls or the honey of Algarves which you desire. The first, I find after long and diligent inquiry, are no longer to be got in this country for money, by reason of deadness of trade, and for the latter, we only arrived here when all the honey was taken and mixed with bean-meal, as is the custom, so that we bought none for our own use. When we do I will not forget your orders. "This is my wife's account, who joins with me, as in services to yourself, so in a petition that you would cast us both and all ours at the feet of our gracious Queen. . . . We beg likewise our most humble services at Bristol House to my Lord and my lady. When I have seen all the spring and the Brazil fleet produce here, I shall not forget his Lordship's commands neither, as to flowers and birds. Till then any letter of mine would be too empty a thing to put into a hand whereto I owe my primitive obligations. I am sorry that this to you comes so." *Copy in letter book.* 1 *p.*

HENRY RUMBOLD, English Consul at Cadiz, to [SIR RICHARD FANSHAW].

1663, March [21-]31. Cadiz—Letter of intelligence, of which the original, sent by Fanshaw to Sir Henry Bennet, is in the Spanish Correspondence at the Public Record Office. Amongst the items of news it is stated that two thousand soldiers have arrived from Italy in Dutch ships under the command of Espinosa, a Catalan much affected to the French, and also seventeen hundred men from the Canaries, sent at the islands' own charge, to fight against Portugal; that the King of Spain has sent to England to know if that King will own Lord Windsor's action in Cuba,* but will probably be easily answered, as experience shows that "the Spaniard is most pliable when best beaten;" and that there are hopes that the match of Portugal with France will proceed, as a post has come to the Duke of Medina Celi that the King of France has sent the Duc de Créqui to the frontiers and that he and the Pope are, by their Commissioners, fully agreed.

In the margin is an abstract of the contents in Spanish, as sent to the Portuguese Secretary of State, and against one paragraph—which states that five hundred run-away English soldiers have arrived from Portugal—is written, "In the extract hereof, which I sent to the secretary, I left out this part, being a thing not to boast of." *Copy in letter book.* 2 *pp.*

SIR RICHARD FANSHAW to SIR JOHN HARRISON.

1663 [March 25-]April 4. Lisbon—Requesting him to "deliver and distribute" all the packets which he sends him sealed

---

* *See* p. 34 above.

up in a bag of green serge, and of which he encloses a list signed by Capt. Hodges. For news begs to refer him to his wife's letters, as his necessary despatches have quite tired him out. *Copy in letter book.* $\frac{3}{4}$ *p.*

The enclosure.

Captain Richard Hodges.

1663, [*March 25-*]*April* 4. *Lisbon—Acknowledgment by Richard Hodges, Commander of H.M. frigate, the* Wester-gate, *that he has received the following packets and letters, viz.:—*

Packets for Sir Henry Bennet, Sir William Morice, the Marquess of Sande, Viscount Cornbury and Mr. Samuel Boothhouse;

Letters for the Lord Chancellor, Secretary Morice, Sir Philip Warwick, Sir John Mennes, the Earl of Insiquin, the Earl of Portland, Sir Kenelm Digbie, Ferdinando Marsham, Esq., and Sir John Harrison;

And two printed papers in Latin, touching the want of confirmation of Bishops in Portugal for each of the following:—

The Vice-Chancellor of Cambridge, Sir John Harrison, the Bishops of London, Lincoln, Salisbury and Winchester, the Archbishop of Canterbury, Dr. Earle, Dean of West-minster, Dr. Creighton, Dean of Wells, Dr. Heavers, Pre-bendary of Windsor, Dr. Hich [Hickes?] in Yorkshire and Sir Philip Warwick. Copy in letter book. 1 *p.*

Sir Richard Fanshaw to Major-General O'Brien.

1663 [March 29-]April 8. Lisbon—" Since I parted from you I have ruminated how I might turn some discourses you held to me yesterday in the Tower of Belem to your best advantage," and have sent my secretary to you, " being really myself not in condition of health to repeat that journey and small voyage to boot." If you will trust me with the letters from my Lord your brother and your answers, I promise you, on the word of a gentleman, to return them speedily, to make use of anything in them that I can for your service, and to wrest nothing in them to your prejudice. *Copy in letter book.* $\frac{3}{4}$ *p.*

Antonio de Sousa de Macedo to Sir Richard Fanshaw.

1663 [March 29-]April 8. The Palace—Thanking him for certain papers received and stating that he now sends the order to the Governor of Belem to deliver up Dom Christopher O'Brien to his Excellency's order. *Portuguese. Copy in letter book.* $\frac{1}{2}$ *p.*

Sir Richard Fanshaw to Don Antonio de Sousa de Macedo.

1663 [March 29-]April 8—Having understood that the King of Portugal had finally resolved that Major-General Christopher O'Brien should be embarked immediately in the English frigate, the Governor of Belem now informs him that he has had no orders to that effect. If it had not been for lack of a favourable wind the frigate would have already sailed. *Spanish. Copy.* ½ p.

Sir Richard Fanshaw to Señor Miguel Bravo, Governor of Belem.

1663 [March 30-]April 9. Lisbon—Stating that the order for the embarkation of Major-General O'Brien comes from the King of Portugal, and that the "security and gratitude" are given by Sir Richard himself. *Spanish. Copy.* ½ p.

Sir Richard Fanshaw to Major General O'Brien.

1663 [March 30-]April 9. Lisbon—I yesterday had a letter from the Secretary, with one for the Governor of Belem, both importing that the said Governor was to deliver you to my orders, that you might pass to England in H.M. frigate *Westergate,* Captain Richard Hodges, commander, I being surety that you would, on your arrival there, render yourself to Sir Henry Bennet. But the Governor now tells me that as you were committed to his custody by a *decreto* of the King, he can only deliver you up on a like *decreto*; and as I do not think it my business to urge it at this time, I must, if the frigate goes without you, try to serve you in some other way. In case they should yet dispatch you, I beg you give the enclosed to Secretary Bennet. *Copy in letter book.* 1 p.

The enclosure,
Sir Richard Fanshaw to Sir Henry Bennet.

1663 [March 29-]April 8—Certificate, in Spanish and in English, that Major-General Christopher O'Brien is a prisoner on parole, and "as free a passenger as any on board" the Westergate, *but promises to render himself to Sir Henry Bennet, to answer the charges preferred against him by the King and ministers of Portugal. Copies. Each ½ p. [The original, in Spanish, is in the Portugal Correspondence, but without the superscription.]*

Secretary Morice to Sir Richard Fanshaw.

1663, March 31—I have received several letters from you, but none of my replies seem to have come to your hands. You will have an account of the debates in Council concerning Portugal from another hand, "for since the laying down of Mr. Secretary Nicholas and the stepping up of Sir Henry Bennet into his place, by a new partition of provinces betwixt us, Portugal is fallen to his lot." The King is willing to give six months' pay to the English troops there, to be paid by the King of Portugal out of our Queen's dowry. "His Majesty, before the Parliament, set forth a declaration holding out some liberty and indulgence to all different parties in religion, but the House of Commons resented [*sic*] it not, and after much debate and sundry traverses between both Houses they jointly agreed to petition the King to make proclamation for the proscribing all popish priests and Jesuits except such as by contract of marriage were to attend both the Queens, and by the law of nations to wait on ambassadors. The House of Commons is fond of the Act of Uniformity; in other things apt to comply with the King, though not with that prowess of affection which they carried down with them." *Copy in letter book.* 1 *p.*

English Officers in Portugal to Sir Richard Fanshaw.

1663, April [1-]11. Ellvas—Announcing that the appointment of Count Schumberg to command the regiment had been received by the troops with joy and cries of "a Schumberg, a Schumberg," assuring him of their fidelity, and acquainting him that their late Lieutenant-Colonel * has been tried by a Council of War and sentenced to be shot, from which only his Excellency's clemency can save him. Twenty-six signatures. *Copy in letter book.*

Captain Richard Hodges to Sir Richard Fanshaw.

1663, April 4. H.M. ship *Westergate*—Complaining that being come as low as St. Julian's, in the Bay of Wares [Oieras] and forced to anchor there, several guns were fired at them, so that they were obliged to anchor amongst the rocks. *Copy in letter book.* ½ *p.*

Sir Richard Fanshaw to Don Antonio de Sousa de Macedo.

1663, April [5-]15—Complaining of the conduct of the Governor of the Castle of St. Julian in firing upon one of his Majesty's ships, and demanding an explanation. *Spanish. Copy in letter book.* ½ *p.*

Sir Richard Fanshaw to the Conde de Castelmelhor.

1663, April [7-]17—States that he has received a letter from Sir Henry Bennet, Secretary of State, who is charged with the affairs of Portugal. The King of England thanks the Count for his good offices, hopes to send six of his great ships to the river of Lisbon before the end of the month, and offers his assurances that he will do everything possible for the good of Portugal, short of an actual rupture with Spain. *Spanish. Copy in letter book.* 1½ *pp.*

---

* This is Col. Guy Molesworth. *See* a letter of Consul Maynard's, dated March 21-31, in the Portugal Correspondence.

SIR RICHARD FANSHAW to the KING OF PORTUGAL.

1663, April [11-]21—Certifying the titles of honour and laws of precedence in use in the English nation. *Spanish. Copy in letter book. 2 pp.*

SIR RICHARD FANSHAW to SIR HENRY BENNET.

1663, April [11-]21. Lisbon—Rough draft and two copies of letter in Spanish concerning the proposed treaty between Spain and Portugal, the letter actually sent being in the Portugal Correspondence at the Public Record Office.

Annexed,
> *Copy of the "Mercurio Portuguez" for March, 1663, a small pamphlet, endorsed by Fanshaw: "This gazette speaks something of the Treaty between Spain and Portugal, as I presume everyone will do more or less as long as any show of life shall remain therein. For Mr. Secretary Bennet." 4½ printed pages.*

EARL OF CLARENDON to SIR RICHARD FANSHAW.

1663, April 12. Worcester House—"I will make no excuse to you for my long silence, nor for having been so many months without acknowledging the many letters I have received, much less will I make any excuse for those whose province it is to keep a constant correspondence with you, and I hope the new secretary who hath drawn Portugal into his partition will be more particular with you, for I do know by very sad experience how melancholy a thing it is to be an ambassador and not receive frequent advertisements from his master and his ministers. When I have told you that I was thrown into my bed, in the middle of November, by the fiercest fit of the gout I ever underwent, insomuch that I scarce writ a letter in four months, nor am yet—in truth—recovered to any good state of health, you will easily excuse my omissions; but I assure you I have been as solicitous both in sickness and in health for the good of Portugal as I could possibly be, and I could endeavour nothing effectually but by secret and underhand treating with France, for which I have had a good opportunity and of which you will find very good effects. I do very freely confess to you that the prospect you presented to us was very dismal, and the expedients you proposed very unpracticable. We never had the least imagination that there could be any reality in the treaty from Spain, and had all moral assurance to the contrary, and by this time I hope you are all undeceived. All the overtures made by you did suppose us to be in a condition very different from what ours is, and from what I did conceive you could imagine it possible to be. Alas, my Lord, we have no money to send fleets or troops upon adventures, nor can anybody imagine that the burden of a war of Portugal can be sustained upon the weak shoulders of the Crown of England. The King hath—with difficulty enough—been able to set out a fleet now to assist that kingdom, but if care be not taken there for payment of the remainder of the portion, the King will have little encouragement or—in truth—ability to continue that expense, and if Portugal doth not manage their war—in the order and conduct of it—more to the satisfaction of their neighbours they will not long be able to draw help from them. I hope they will gain more reputation this next campaign than they have done; you will easily believe the news of the treatment our English troops have had there is very small encouragement to make new levies here, and to imagine that the King can send troops from hence and take care for the payment of them there is indeed ridiculous, so that they must either resolve to have no need of foreign troops or to provide to have means to pay them punctually; for the present the King is contented, out of compassion to his poor troops, that out of the money due to him you do procure so much as may make up the pay allowed there to amount to our own establishment, which we suppose is a third part more than they allow there, so that you must press for so much of the King's money as may raise the payment of Portugal to our own establishment for three months, and if in that time they do not take care to make effectual provision for the troops the King must provide to bring them away, which will put an end to all possible expectation of ever raising a man for that service; in the meantime and whilst the troops shall continue there the King is very well contented that they be all put under the command of Monsieur Shombergh, who being a Protestant and speaking English well, it is presumed will be very grateful to the soldiers, who will receive much protection and advantage from him.

There were three hundred horse wanting of the one thousand horse which should have been sent over, and which were therefore not sent then only for want of ships for their transportation; but the horse were ready in Ireland, and the ships which transported the other to Lisbon were hired and paid to go from Portugal to Ireland to take them aboard, but upon the Queen's arrival here it was desired that the sending of those horse might be suspended, and so all that charge was lost, and the ambassador now desires that those horse may be forthwith provided only with saddles and arms without riders, and we are doing all we can to provide accordingly. There is nothing afflicts me more than the very sad condition our English troops are in, to which it is not in the King's power to apply any other remedy than he hath done, money being every jot as scarce here as it was at your departure. I suppose you will have by this time received some letter or declaration of the King to the officers and soldiers for their encouragement. I do not know whether the Secretary hath sent you the copy of the King's answer to the formal memorial sent from Portugal, which is now again given to the ambassador upon his desire, and therefore I send it again to you, and I cannot but tell you that I look upon the ambassador as a very worthy honest gentleman and in truth a man that distinguishes as well between what is to be hoped and what is to be wished as any man can do who is so much troubled with the spleen, and so hypochondriac. I know I need not bespeak you to live with all possible kindness and confidence towards him. He hath had his patience exercised enough here by some wranglings and ill-offices by those of his own country, who no doubt will use the same endeavours to dishonour him at home and bring disadvantages upon him there, which I am sure he does not deserve, being (in truth) a man of as great integrity, zeal and affection for his King and country as lives, and I think in real ability and wisdom to serve them superior to most of that nation, at least to any I have known. I must likewise recommend very heartily to you the Bishop, who hath not been so kindly treated here as he hath deserved, some men having been able to do him very ill offices, who if they were his friends would do him little good. I do very particularly recommend him to your kindness to do him all the good offices and to give him all the fair testimonies and vindication from all reproaches as can be in your power, industry, and dexterity to do and express towards him.

I shall give you no account of news here, which I hope some other of your friends take care to do. I hope the Parliament will assist the King with supplies, that all inconvenience may be prevented in the three kingdoms, in which there remain yet many restless spirits. God keep you and me." [*The last paragraph only in Clarendon's own hand.*] 3½ pp

SIR PHILIP WARWICK to his brother [in-law], SIR RICHARD FANSHAW.

1663, April 12—" It is sufficient occasion to keep up an intercourse of letters that carry little with them—as mine must in relation to your affairs—by what you last hinted that you had received so few from those ministers of state from whom you might expect them. What fell out in my province I gave you a full account of in my Lord Treasurer's answer to the memorial of the Portugal ambassador, which hath fallen heavy on Don da Sylva, who hath been in restraint ever since and was but within these two or three days released. He wanted his liberty, we our money, and upon the whole matter *Pamphilus symbolum dedit*, we pay the reckoning. I do assure you I walk within my own circle, and perchance as conjurers do it would not be safe to tread without it, and therefore, lest I mistake, I must refer you to the Major to describe the posture of our affairs, and to assure you, though the Houses of Parliament complied not with that trust in respect of dissenters from our Church which we might have safely lodged in the King,—because we would keep him often from importunity, sometimes from misrepresentations—yet it was carried with that prudence and moderation, duty and respect to the King that you would have said the House of Commons had as much mastery of their passions as a philosopher hath of his, and the intelligence betwixt the King and them—believe me in this—is very firm. And had not the

Roman Catholics' pretensions been too rife, our countenancing the laws against them had not been so pressing. I believe you have some correspondent sends you all our prints; for our declarations, reasons upon them, proclamations and gazettes is as much as any of us can inform you that are of the wrong side of the curtain. If we could have one of the long walks you and I were wont to make when my sister grudged us being so oft and so long together we might find discourse, but since that is denied you see to what grave authors I refer you. At this time we hear Queen Mother of France is very ill, and Mons. Hamilton is dispatched to express our condolement, but it will make more stir in the world when we hear her brother hath finished his course; so many posts, so many years almost have told us of his being nigh the goal that now I believe he hath found some place of repose. And as old Archbishop Mathews said to my Lord Lincoln, he was glad he was a young man that expected the advantage of his death, for he might tarry for it. Our potent wealthy neighbour will not embark in any design that may interrupt that expectation. Methinks you should make the Prince you are with and his great neighbour friends, for naturally I am of the Spanish faction—or love that trade—and then we might be the less embarked. My sister and babies shall have never less respect that they have the less paper, but by this length you may see how willing I should be to say somewhat, if I knew what." *Copy in letter book.* 1¼ *pp.*

Samuel Boothhouse to Sir Richard Fanshaw

1663, April 12. Whitehall—Your many friends and servants at Whitehall and Westminster doubtless send you all the news, so I will only tell you "that the great care and pains which your Lordship took to rectify the Office of Requests hath not found such good effects as undoubtedly would have succeeded had yourself continued here to see the-administration of it; for this day Sir Ralph Freeman told me they were at the old pass with the Secretaries, and is hopeless of better till your Lordship returns, which would be ere long if the many wishes thereof could effect it."

I lent your lodgings to Sir Ralph Freeman for the last three months "to accommodate his daughter, who desired to see the Court entertainments, as balls and plays, which have been frequent this last winter." 1 *p.*

Duke of York to Sir Richard Fanshaw.

1663, April 15. Whitehall—"The opportunities of writing to Portugal have of late so seldom offered themselves that you will not wonder that I have not let you know how well satisfied I am with the letters which I received from you." I have directed the principal officers and Commissioners of the Navy to write to you concerning a debt due to the King from one

Bridgewood, and turned over to Mr. Cocke. "Your very loving friend, James." *Seal of the royal arms in garter, with coronet, impressed.* [*The last words in the Duke's own hand.*] ½ *p.*

Sir John Mennes to Sir Richard Fanshaw.

1663, April 17. Good Friday—"I writ by Major Holmes so late that I have little to say more than what I then gave you; the Parliament being adjourned until the Monday after Easter week everyone is retired, I hope to their devotions, and we are in a great stillness. His Majesty keeps St. George's Day, Thursday in Easter week." I pray you let Mr. Cocke have a fair hearing when his business is examined. He has always been faithful to the King, and did and suffered more for him when Prince Rupert was at Lisbon than the whole body of merchants. The difficulty in his accounts is merely the want of some petty vouchers. ½ *p.*

Duke of York to Sir Richard Fanshaw.

1663, April 18. Whitehall—"Although I wrote to you few days since, yet in regard that was committed to the hands of a person some ways concerned in the subject matter of it, I have thought fit by this also to let you know that I took very well the letters which you have written me since your residing at Lisbon, and likewise to recommend to your care the management of a proposal lately made to me, the particulars whereof you shall receive from my secretary." *Copy in letter book.* ½ *p*

Secretary Morice to Sir Richard Fanshaw.

1663, April 19—Repeating the information contained in his former letter [*see p. 73 above*], which he fears has never reached the ambassador's hands. *Copy in letter book.* 1 *p.*

E[dward] Montague to Lord [Ambassador Fanshaw].

[1663], April 19. London—"I give your Excellency a thousand thanks for your last favour, and because I would lose no opportunity of expressing my service to you I lay hold of this, though I have but just the time to write these few lines, and therefore I beg of you not to mention me to her Excellency Señora Maria de la Cruz till I send you an answer to the favour she did me, which shall be by the first opportunity. We have little news at present but such as your Excellency will meet with in the news books concerning the Parliamentary affairs. I made your compliment to her Majesty, who received [it] with all the testimony of kindness, and commanded me to assure of it. Her Majesty's house and service is now settling, and will be established I believe about midsummer, at which

time her Majesty goes to Tunbridge to take the waters. I have
no more at present, but to assure your Lordship of my being
in all things" your most humble servant.
Postscript.—"I beg the favour of your Excellency to represent me to the Queen Mother as her most faithful and obedient
servant." 2¼ *pp.*

Sir Henry Bennet to Sir Richard Fanshaw.

1663, April 20. Whitehall—Our fleet is now ready for Lisbon,
as also the ships to transport the French regiment, consisting
of twelve hundred men, with many experienced officers. There
also goes in specie one of the two hundred thousand crowns
that were promised, and the other will be ready shortly.
I send you the Portugal ambassador's memorial and his
Majesty's answers thereunto. "It would be a very great comfort
to me to be able to send you with this the news of our Queen's
being with child, but yet God Almighty hath not made us so
happy. Her Majesty talks of going this spring to Tunbridge
and to the Bath, but I think none of these remedies will do
her so much good as the falling heartily to our English meat.
For news I have to tell your Lordship that this day the Duke
of Monmouth was married to the young Countess of Buccleuch,
and at the instant I am writing this I suppose his Majesty is
putting them to bed together, but with resolution to part
them presently.* After to-morrow both their Majesties go to
Windsor for the celebration of St. George's Feast, at their
return from whence we must to the Parliament again, to see
whether they will be as hearty in the revenue as they have been
keen in settling the Act of Uniformity and securing us against
popery. My Lord Rutherford, now Earl of Teviot, is ready
to set sail for Tangier, where we hope his experience, activity
and industry will contribute much to the improvement of that
place."
I long to hear what is going to be done in Portugal this
summer in reference to the war, and what possibility there is of
an accommodation with Spain. "I should not hold it impracticable if it were well handled, but the humour of both
those nations renders it difficult enough." I send you a cipher
which we may mutually make use of, as occasion serves. *Copy
in letter book.* 1½ *pp.*
Enclosing,

    1. *Portugal Ambassador to King Charles II.*
    [1663, *April*]—*Memorial praying (1) that he will send
the rest of the horse; (2) that he will call upon the Lord
Treasurer and Lord Ashley to take course with John Grun
and John Parker that they may pay the duties owed to the
King of Portugal upon the ships from Brazil; (3) that
they will also put an end to the business of Duarte de Silva;
(4) that the Portuguese put out of their houses at Tangier
by Lord Peterborough may have satisfaction. Copy.* ¾ *p.*

---

* They were both children, he having been born in 1649, and she in 1651.

2. *Charles II. to the Portuguese Ambassador.*

[1663, *April*]—*Answer to the above memorial. His Majesty has taken the affairs of Portugal much to heart, but it is impossible for England alone "not yet recovered from the distractions it hath lately endured in the times of license" to assist, and he is therefore trying to persuade the King of France to interpose also. His Majesty is very sorry that the succours which, upon earnest entreaty, he has already sent—instead of being so profitable as by their courage and experience he knows they might be—are alleged to have been a considerable damage to that kingdom, and therefore he will send no more, especially as if they do not receive their accustomed pay they can do no good service, but will transport these home again as soon as the King of Portugal signifies his pleasure to that purpose. Meanwhile he has ordered his ambassador in Portugal to give them three months' pay out of what he receives of the Queen's portion. What encouragement the King of Portugal has from Castile, concerning the Treaty, his Majesty knows not, but suspects all overtures of that kind not to have much sincerity, never having found the least inclination thereunto in that King, who has done his best to persuade his Majesty to abandon Portugal. A fleet is now being sent to defend Portugal from attacks by sea, and do all other services for that kingdom, "which shall not amount to a manifest declaration of war against Castile, which in all respects would not be seasonable." Copy.* 1¾ *pp.*

SIR RICHARD FANSHAW to the BISHOP OF LONDON.

1663 [April 21-]May 1. Lisbon—"Your Lordship will herewith receive the copies of settlement of a preacher here to the English merchants after a long vacancy. Part of the reasons why I guess it was so long are expressed in the same papers, to explain which a little further and clearer your Lordship may be pleased to take notice that according to the literal constitution thereof the advowson and gift of this cure of souls is in the English merchants at London trading to Lisbon. Those that immediately pay the tithes or maintenance are the English trading here, factors for the most part to the other. The collector or paymaster the consul, with this difference from common collectors or paymasters, that without anything to the contrary in the letter of his patent,—and further he will not be bound,—during all vacancies, the money goes into his own purse. Meantime the merchants here resident pretend such mean profits ought to be applied to the common stock for charitable uses whereby to ease them, and consequently their principals at London, that is to say, to the use of the patron of the church and of them that pay tithes. If it were so in England and no law for lapses, how many livings would be filled?

Now in this place the present mischief is remedied for once without any exceptions on behalf of those in London who might claim the right of presentation, since, having omitted it for three

24.   F

years, the strictest laws of England would give it the King *pro hac vice*, especially to prevent the losing of so great a spiritual privilege as this by not usage.

Possibly for the future some middling course may be found out to save both rights without the one prejudicing the other; as, that the King by the Bishop of London there or by his Majesty's public minister here for the time being, may present in case of so many months vacancy as may be limited, and not otherwise, unless, by Act of Council preceding this institution, the gift of this place amongst other foreign cures ought still to remain in the Bishop, and that all mesne profits should be in reserve to the next incumbent, the more to invite one hither the longer there shall be a vacancy. Certainly without censuring this or that, these or those individual persons, but speaking as to succeeding times in general, if either the Lisbon consuls or merchants shall be savers or gainers by a vacancy, a preaching minister here—taking it one time with another—is likely either not to be placed or after he is to be worried out." *Copy in letter book.* 1⅓ *pp.*

WILLIAM COVENTRY to SIR RICHARD FANSHAW.

1633, April 22—A proposal has been made to his royal Highness that if he should "obtain from his Majesty a permission to employ three of his Dutch prize ships to Brazil—his royal Highness paying the men and victuals—and likewise obtain from the King of Portugal leave for them to go and return to Lisbon, it is supposed his royal Highness might make an advantage of ten thousand pounds upon the voyage, or well towards that sum." There is no doubt as to obtaining the ships. As to the leave for them to go, you can best speak who are on the spot. The chief doubt is concerning the probability of profit. I am told that if they go under the West India Company they must wait for the return of the fleet, which is often long, and so eats up the profits, while if they are freighted by private persons a license must be bought at a considerable rate; also that in Brazil, the Governors, unless very well feed, will not allow them to lade, "which how great a share of the profit it may devour I know not," and "that the owners of the ships often make very bad voyages thither." These arguments are discouraging, but on the other hand the security of the King's ships, carrying the King's colours, might induce the merchants to give a greater freight than usual. His royal Highness would like you to consult with Sir John Lawson and Capt. Holmes and give them your opinions in the matter. *Copy in letter book.* 1¼ *pp.*

COMTE DE SCHONBERG to SIR RICHARD FANSHAW.

1663, May [3-]13. Estremos—I could not write to you before, as for four days I have been almost entirely on horseback. The enemy, having marched this way, camped yesterday by the stream of the Terra. To-day they have continued their march towards Rioles, but I expect that they will turn to the left towards Evora. They yesterday summoned the Castle of Evora-Monte to surrender, and I am anxious about Evora. These people will not believe that the enemy will dare to advance so far into their country, but they will presently see the truth of what I have often said to your Excellency. The garrison consists of three thousand men and five hundred horses, and I doubt the enemy attacking it, but believe they will go to Villa Viciosa, a place which the Portuguese have neglected to fortify, although it could have been done in a fortnight. Our people will not understand the danger which threatens them. The enemy may have about a hundred squadrons, making at least six thousand horse, and eighteen battalions, making nine thousand foot soldiers, while we have nothing like the number of soldiers that they in Lisbon show upon paper. Some money has come for the English troops, but not enough to make a month's pay. You should represent strongly to the Count of Castelmelhor how important it is at the beginning of the campaign that they should have some money. *French. Copy in letter book. 1 p.*

SIR HENRY BENNET to SIR RICHARD FANSHAW.

1663, May 7. Whitehall—Your letters have given me much light on what you have done in Portugal, which I knew but very obscurely before. As regards the agreement with Spain, I see much to discourage me, especially in the number of French agents resorting to the Portuguese Court, whose movements I beg you to observe and report.

Mons. de Cominges has been here many months, but deferred his public entry from his desire to have revoked the order of Council, forbidding other ambassadors' coaches to attend it. "We were fain to send an express to France about it, where we prevailed to hold our point, with which he made his entry according to our rule." Commissioners are named to treat with him, but he makes such difficulties that we are sending Lord Holles to France to begin a treaty there. Sir George Downing is also to be immediately dispatched to Holland. Mr. Beling has returned from Rome, and, it is said, has brought no letters for either Queen in answer to theirs. "The sum is, they are not indulgent to us either as English or Portuguese. For the former, we are pretty well quit with them, and for the latter, if you can behave yourselves well this campaign, I make no doubt but you shall have both King and Bishop with you by their acknowledgment." I send you a paper concerning the English officers' petition. "We are now in great debates in the House of Commons relating to a final establishment of his Majesty's revenue and the Militia, before the conclusion in which it seems earnestly to be desired that inquiry may be made into the hitherto management of the revenue and the sale of offices, which, though it seem to be a froward beginning, will I hope end well, and I make no question of it, if we have time enough before the hot weather comes upon us, for 'tis certain this Parliament is composed of persons entirely affected to the Crown, and though sometimes froward and out of humour, do yet ever return to their duty to him."

My Lord General and myself have examined Major-General O'Brien, and I do not so far " see enough to make me conclude him actually guilty of any treaty with the Spaniards. To-morrow we shall make our report to his Majesty, and whatsoever the conclusion be in it see it performed with all the respect and decency which ought to be " towards the Portuguese Court. The Major-General is at present only a prisoner in his chamber. *Copy in letter book. 2 pp.*

COMTE DE SCHONBERG to SIR RICHARD FANSHAW.

1663, May [7-]17. Estremos—Four days ago I told you how I had urged our general to send a strong garrison, and that I had obtained a party and four pieces of cannon, but mostly just to please me, as he assured me that I need not be anxious about Evora, for the enemy would never venture a siege so far in the country. You know what my apprehensions in this matter have been, and now they are fulfilled. Two days ago Don John of Austria put a battery into the Convent de Carmes, which stands two hundred paces from the wall, and a Frenchman who has surrendered, valet to the Engineer Detangres, says that his master, talking with Jocquet, said that the place could hold out eight days. Jocquet said that Don John had asked what fortifications they were beginning at St. Antoine, and being told that I had wished to make a citadel, but was stopped by the Court, he replied, " When I have taken Evora, I will go on with it." By the letters which I have seen from the King to the Conde de Villa Flor, I perceive that they order him to relieve Evora, even if it brings on a battle, and they give me to understand that they hope I shall make no difficulty about it. As to that the King's will is enough for me, as they do not ask my advice. I have relieved my conscience by writing to the Conde de Castelmelhor what twenty-five years' experience of war has taught me, that we have only raw troops and raw officers, that we can hardly put as much infantry together as the enemy, and have only three thousand horse to their six, that the four hundred horse from Bera cannot arrive in time, that from Minho none comes at all, and that if they wish to hazard the kingdom upon one battle it would only be right to send from Lisbon all the nobility, all the infantry, and all the horse. But there seems to be some fate which closes the ears of the Council to all salutary advice. There are in Evora at least five thousand armed men and six hundred horses, and if they only had commanders who knew how to defend a place, the enemy might despair of taking it. Our English troops would be on a very good footing if they were paid with some regularity, and would do very good service. Lieutenant Crook has gone over to the enemy with his valet, but the loss is not great. I am waiting impatiently to hear that the frigates have arrived and brought us more troops. *French. Copy in letter book.* 1½ *pp.*

Sir Richard Fanshaw to the Conde de Castelmelhor.

1663, May [9-]19—Stating his desire to accompany the King upon his proposed expedition. *Spanish. Copy in letter book.* ½ *p.*

Conde de Castelmelhor to Sir Richard Fanshaw.

1663, May [9-]19. The Palace—I have shown the King the letter in which you desire to accompany him to Alentejo, and he orders me to tell you that he much values your zeal and will esteem your company, remembering that—as our chronicles relate—the then ambassador of England was present at the famous battle of Algibarrota, when King John I. of glorious memory vanquished the King of Castile of the same name. *Portuguese. Copy in letter book.* ½ *p.*

Don Antonio de Sousa de Macedo to Sir Richard Fanshaw.

1663, May [9-]19. The Palace—We have received two dispatches from Alentejo, and know that your Excellency will be pleased to hear that they are very cheering. Letters from Estremos and Evora say that the people of that city are in good heart, and that the enemy has received heavy losses from our attacks. Our cavalry have occupied the highways, and so the Spaniards neither have nor hope for succours, and have little food. Their soldiers begin to despair, saying that they are lost, and the inhabitants and soldiers of the city and our cavalry outside have taken many horses and killed others. Don Juan of Austria, to encourage his men, has proclaimed that they will be allowed to sack Evora, and that they shall have from the country what will pay all their arrears, but nothing he says consoles them. Our army have abundance of food, and are longing to go in search of the enemy, and we hope by God's blessing to have a glorious victory. If Don Juan escapes it will be as much as he can count on. *Portuguese. Copy in letter book.* ¾ *p.*

Sir Richard Fanshaw to Don Antonio de Sousa de Macedo.

1663, May [10-]20—Expressing his joy at the good news from Alentejo and especially from Evora, which he hopes may be followed by still better from day to day "until the end crown the work;" and requesting to be told, if possible a day beforehand, when his Majesty intends to cross the river. *Spanish. Copy in letter book.* ½ *p.*

DON ANTONIO DE SOUSA DE MACEDO to SIR RICHARD FANSHAW.

1663, May [10-]20. Lisbon—Requesting him to transmit certain papers for the Portuguese ambassador in London, and stating that further letters relate attacks made on Evora by the Spaniards, in which they lost five hundred men. *Portuguese. Copy in letter book.* ½ *p.*

SIR RICHARD FANSHAW to SIR HENRY BENNET.

1663 [May 11-]21. Lisbon—Giving him an account of the siege of Evora and the prospects of the war. *Copy in letter book.* 2¼ *pp.* [*Original amongst the Portugal Correspondence.*]

SIR HENRY BENNET to SIR RICHARD FANSHAW.

1663, May 12. Whitehall—You will receive by Captain Trelawny his Majesty's reference to you of the petition of the English officers and soldiers brought hither by him, "which his Majesty desires you should make valuable towards them the best you can, and also this gentleman," who would have carried them a better and speedier dispatch if he could. I pray you also "to favour my old acquaintance, Colonel Michael Dongan, in his pretence to succeed Major-General O'Brien in his regiment of horse, whose immediate officer he was." The Lord General and myself have made our report concerning the said Major-General, to the effect that "there was not much ground in either the Council's or Colonel Molesworth's accusation of him, not enough to punish him here or indeed enough to detain him any longer prisoner, but the Portugal ambassador not being of our mind, he is yet detained upon his word in his own lodging." *Copy in letter book.* ¾ *p.*

Annexed,

1. *Petition of the officers and soldiers sent to Portugal under the Earl of Inchiquin to the King, complaining that they cannot get their pay from the Portuguese ministers, and praying for relief, as they are almost starved to death, and have had to sell their very clothes to keep themselves alive. Copy.* 1 *p.*

2. *His Majesty's answer, stating that he has referred the petition to his ambassador in Portugal, with orders to give them three months' pay from the moneys due to him by the King of Portugal, and that if he cannot procure better conditions for them in the future they shall be brought home; but desiring them in the meantime to serve under the Comte de Schonberg (who being a Protestant and much affected to his Majesty's service will take all possible care of them), with such fidelity, courage and patience as may be for the honour of his Majesty and the nation. Whitehall, May 11, 1663. Copy.* 1 *p.*

The Duke of York to Sir Richard Fanshaw.

1663, May 12. St. James—You will receive this by Sir John Lawson, whom his Majesty hath sent with a fleet to Portugal, and I suppose you will have advices from the Secretary of State about it, " only one thing I shall add, which is to desire you to use all the means you can to get the fleet dismissed as soon as may be, in regard of the great expense it is to the King." I will only now recommend Sir John Lawson to you, and request you to consult with him and Captain Holmes concerning the proposition for sending ships to Brazil, of which I wrote to you before. *Copy in letter book.* ¾ *p.*

William Coventry to Sir Richard Fanshaw.

1663, May 14. St. James—The bearer, Sir John Lawson, will instruct you concerning all the naval business. He is engaged in a contract to build the Mole at Tangier, and the sooner you can obtain liberty for him to go there the better. Letters from the Earl of Marlborough "tell us the Portugals have refused to deliver Bombaim, which you may believe hath put those to some shifts which went to receive it. . . . The Parliament hath of late been in some ill-humour, but I hope when they have pleased themselves with inspection of the revenue and some other things with which they seem to be offended at, as selling offices and the like, that they will take care for the King's support. I beseech you hasten our fleet home, as much as may be, for the charge is great." His royal Highness has written to you about the ships for Brazil. "I am sure you will be cautious to proceed on very solid foundations, or else to lay it aside, that so catching at a shadow we lose not the substance, of which his royal Highness hath no superfluity." *Copy in letter book.* 1 *p.*

Sir Henry Bennet to Lord Ambassador Fanshaw.

1663, May 14. Whitehall—"Since the writing my former I have received your Lordship's of the 1st instant, together with an enclosed copy of his Majesty of Portugal's letter to the King, our master, of 29th April, which I have read to him, his Majesty, contrary to his accustomed temper, having scarce patience to hear it through. Whether the Portugal ambassador have delivered the original or no I cannot tell; but when he does it is certain he will make the same observation I do to you now, and it is that the King, our master, could not in anything be more dissatisfied than he is in the letters he hath lately received from my Lord Marlborough, acquainting him that the Viceroy at Bombaim hath flatly refused his Lordship to give him possession of the place, excusing himself upon the insufficiency of my Lord's power to receive it, which had no less [*sic*] the Broad Seal to authorize it. In fine the dishonour and disappointment of such a thing and the expense his Majesty hath been at to send for it hath left him in the last resentments against this usage that can be imagined. I am told the ambassador here hath endeavoured to put his Majesty upon the sending over land into those countries, which is looked upon as a very poor expedient in such a case, and I am bid to tell your Lordship that less than the Viceroy's head and satisfaction for all the damages and expense his Majesty is exposed to by this disappointment will not suffice to pay his Majesty for this affront, it being expected that what be done of this kind and the possessing us of the foresaid island—which by the way is found to be far inferior to what it was represented—come from Portugal itself, without the concurrence of any demands or diligences on our side." Notwithstanding this his Majesty will not divest himself of his concern for Portugal, and is willing to accept the part the King offers him in the intended treaty, being content that you should act in his name if the King of Spain consents. "Whatever these overtures may produce in the winter, the strength with which both sides are in the field, and the application with which France is like to foment the quarrel, makes me suspect there will be small fruit of them for the present." Meanwhile, I shall let you clearly know how we stand with Spain, as you cannot do anything in the negotiation which is likely to be ticklish enough, and amongst people very reserved, unless you have all manner of lights to direct you." Last November, an Irish gentleman arrived from Spain "casually—as he said—in his way towards Flanders, who, having been known to his Majesty there, to my Lord Chancellor and myself, more particularly in Madrid, he upon several occasions bewailed to his Majesty and to both us, the ill intelligence in which we lived towards Spain," and being pleased with our replies returned to Madrid with a letter from the king to his Catholic Majesty, and to the Duke of Medina de las Torres from my Lord Chancellor and myself. Thence he writes to us that the letters were kindly accepted, that he himself is returning to England shortly, and that they desire that an ambassador may be sent to Spain. *Copy in letter book. 2¼ pp.*

Joseph Williamson to Sir Richard Fanshaw

1663, May 14—I am proud to be encouraged to address you, though I can add little to the account of affairs of state, which you receive fully from Mr. Secretary's own hand. We hear from Leghorn that "they of Algiers have resolved absolutely to break with the Dutch, as well to gratify the mutineers among themselves as from the pretended exceptions they take to the Dutch, viz. :—1, their not redeeming their slaves; 2, their not furnishing them with provisions capitulated for, &c.; 3, their protecting Hamburgers, &c." Letters from Cadiz say they are much dejected there at hearing from the West Indies of our hostile carriage towards them, which has wholly ruined their trade.

Postscript.—No new Governor of Jamaica is yet resolved on. Lord Craven is talked of for the office and name, with Col.

Mostyn to be his Lieut.-Governor, and go to the island. Meanwhile the King has ordered Sir Chr. Littleton to " desist those hostilities upon the Spaniards or other neighbours, as much disturbing the settlement of that plantation." 1½ *pp*.

EARL OF CLARENDON to SIR RICHARD FANSHAW.

1663, May 16. Worcester House—Since I writ last to you I have received yours of the last of March, which is the only letter I have of yours upon my hands unacknowledged or unanswered, though Mr. Secretary shewed me the copies of two long material letters, which you writ him word you had sent to me; and he rceived those copies by the same conveyance which brought me mine of the last of March, but the originals I never received; I suppose he will answer the contents, I shall therefore only say that I am not at all troubled with the apprehension that France will get the better of us by supporting Portugal more efficaciously than we can do, or by being the mediator and umpire of the peace between Spain and them. I am very well content they shall do the first to what degree they please and to rob us of the glory of it; so Portugal be supported, I am satisfied, and for the other of the peace I do as little suspect it. We shall still have as much benefit from Portugal by trade as we desire, let Spain or France do what they will, and so it be still kept severed from the Crown of Castile, we have our end. But I perceive the business of the treaty is now more *opiniatred* than ever, the King of Portugal having himself writ to the King of England, our master, to accept of the office of mediator in their treaty, and that you may be present at the treaty upon the frontiers, so that I perceive they think the matter more real than it is in my power to do, and they say the King of Spain hath accepted the mediation. This letter from the King of Portugal would have met with a more cheerful reception and answer if it had arrived three days sooner, but it was brought to the King the very next day after we received the news from my Lord Marlborough of the very unworthy carriage of the Vice-King of Goa, in refusing to deliver the Island of Bombay into the King's hands according to the treaty. The act is so foul that less than the head of the man cannot satisfy for the indignity, and for the damage his Majesty will expect and exact notable reparation; and if some sudden satisfaction be not given there will be an end of our alliance with Portugal, for the King hath no patience in the consideration of it, and must conclude that this Viceroy, transported in our own ships from Lisbon, must carry the instructions with him which produced this foul act, for which the excuses are so childish: (1) That the King's letter to him for the delivery of it was not attested by the secretary; that the King's hand was not to the instrument under the Great Seal, &c. Sir Abraham Shipman, who was to have the command of the island, stays with his men in a little desolate island twelve leagues from Goa, expecting when the Vice-King will come into his wits. There is nothing more to be done from hence. If the King of Portugal be in truth offended with what is done he will immediately send away and take care that the first news we hear from thence is that Sir Abraham Shipman is in possession of the island. If this be not done with all the circumstances of reparation, farewell the friendship with Portugal, and they are not to wonder if they hear that we and the Dutch are united in the East Indies, and that we do all else to their prejudice. This intelligence kept the King from writing himself to the King of Portugal till he knows his resentment of this high affront, but after you have expostulated highly upon this affair you are—as I suppose Mr. Secretary will instruct you at large—to let the King of Portugal know that though the King, your master, is highly affected with this affront, yet, in confidence that he shall receive speedy justice and reparation, he will not suddenly withdraw his care and protection from Portugal, and therefore he doth accept the mediation between them and will do what he can to procure an advantageous peace between the two crowns, and in order thereunto is well pleased that you are present at the treaty, provided that you adjust all things in that manner with the Spaniard that your reception and treatment by them may be such as is suitable to your master's honour and the quality you hold in his service, and of this I need say no more, the Secretary having undertaken to give you full instructions to the purposes aforesaid. I shall conclude with recommending the bearer, Captain Trelawny, to your particular care and protection, that he may not in any degree suffer in the retrenchment of his pay or undergo any other disadvantage by his absence from hence, whilst he hath been soliciting their service here. He is a very good young man, and his brothers are much my friends. God keep you and yours." *Holograph. 3 pp.*

EARL OF TEVIOT to SIR RICHARD FANSHAW.

1663, May 17-27. Aboard the *Reserve*, near Lisbon Road— Though my indisposition at sea might obtain pardon for my silence, "yet the high respect I owe your merits and the passion I have to be honoured with your Excellency's commands engageth me to offer your Excellency by this undigested piece my most humble respects and obedience, and to beg of you some light and instructions about Tangier." Will the Portuguese send some one to estimate the houses abandoned by them and do you think their pretensions just? *Copy in letter book. ½ p.*

MAJOR ROBERT HOLMES to SIR RICHARD FANSHAW.

1663, May 17. H.M.S. *Reserve*, off Cascales—I am sorry I cannot wait on your Excellency, "by reason my Lord Rutherford is in such haste for Tangier." I got all your letters except Mr. Chiffinch's, who said he was ashamed to write because he could not get the jewel for the small picture. The great one I send by this bearer, Mr. Duncum, a kinsman of Lord Rutherford's.

Should you have any despatches for England I can send them by the ship which is to take back Lord Peterborough. If there is no King's ship to be met with I am to carry him back myself, and in that case will try to persuade him to touch at Cascales that I may see you. Sir John Lawson is to be at Lisbon very soon. My most humble service to my lady and your daughters. 1½ *pp.*

SIR RICHARD FANSHAW to the CONDE DE CASTELMELHOR.

1663, May [18-]28—I heard from England by the Secretary's letter, dated 30th ult., this style, that his Majesty's fleet was setting out for Lisbon, as also the ships with the twelve hundred French soldiers and many experienced officers,—another letter calls them the regiment of Marshal Turenne,—and that there was moreover coming one of the two hundred thousand crowns promised, with assurance that the other will be ready in a short time. In confirmation of this Captain Holmes wrote to me yesterday that General Lawson will shortly be here with the squadron assigned for this coast; that the twelve hundred French are at Plymouth, ready to be sent over in merchant ships, with two of his Majesty's to convoy them, and that he thought they might be already on their way. To which I add that London, from which the body of the squadron comes, being so distant from Plymouth, they will not wait for each other, and if they arrive at the same time it will be quite by chance. Further I judge that the money will come with the body of the squadron. Having touched on this I cannot but inform your Excellency that the Lord Chancellor and the two Secretaries of State have straitly charged me to take much care concerning that money for the English troops of which the Marquis of Sande's letter spoke, and of which the Council gave me a part the other day, it being part of the money given them by the King, my master, from the dowry of the Queen, our mistress. I have already written to them that since that time the Council has given me every satisfaction as to their compliance in this matter, and I now thank your Excellency for telling me what the King has determined concerning the money, which will enable me to encourage the soldiers. *Spanish. Copy in letter book.* 1½ *pp.*

SIR RICHARD FANSHAW to LORD CHANCELLOR CLARENDON.

1663, May 20-30. Lisbon—Wishes that anything rather than illness had been the cause of his Lordship's silence—even his displeasure—as the temper of his mind so far excels that of his body that this might have been weathered by submission more easily than so obstinate a sickness by the help of doctors. Refers him to Sir Henry Bennet's letter for " the present state of this distracted kingdom." *Copy in letter book.* 1 *p.* [*The original is in the Portugal Correspondence.*]

SIR RICHARD FANSHAW to SIR HENRY BENNET.

1663, May 20-30. Lisbon—My last dispatch to you "left Don Juan before Evora, with such opposition from the city and such hopes within the city of being speedily relieved by the Portugal army, as I do believe afforded much matter of triumph to a Portugal packet which accompanied mine of a less sanguine complexion, who am not in my nature much apt to sing before the victory, and therefore I do not yet boast of the ruin which Don John hath run himself under by this bold advance, leaving the Portugal army and garrisons untouched behind him, with time for all Portugal to gather about him and no place for recruits out of Castile to come to him. In the interim, matter of fact is, that the very next day, namely, 12-22 instant—as appeared since—the city was delivered to Don John upon conditions of safety of lives and estates to the inhabitants, which, although some discourses run here to the contrary, are hitherto in all reasonable conjecture observed with great punctuality, with advantage over and above—as is said—by burning of taxbooks and much gracious and compassionate language in the ears of that clergy and people, which he desires not to have made a secret to the rest of the kingdom, whereby to invite no less than force the whole to the Spanish Government, both which had equally co-operated in the snatching up of Evora whilst the Portugal army was close upon their march to relieve it.

The one and the other, upon the first publication of the news, which was 15-25, day after Corpus Christi, which this King and Court had passed in such universal and joyful procession as you know—by the example of Madrid in great—did work a quite contrary effect in the common people of this city—who are *finissimos* Portugueses—yet such a one as if, beginning strangely in the morning the storm had not as strangely ceased towards night, might have done Don John's business as well as if they had risen for him.

Rise they did, but it was for the King and kingdom they said, and so really intended. The occasion this:—Some soldiers being mustering in the palace yard in order to marching for Alentejo, a small officer of theirs came up to the door of the *Secretaria*, where some ministers were in *junta*, and expostulated there with more than ordinary heat and noise the fresh loss of Evora, that the King and kingdom is betrayed in every place; that they were sent to the butchery when they should be led to the war; and for this—the King going in person—every man in this city was in readiness to follow and serve him with the last drop in their veins. He was answered by one of the Council at the door that all men well knew how the King had already proclaimed his resolution for going in his royal person forthwith, and that all things were in a visible preparation thereunto, that therefore he, the said officer, would better show his zeal below by making a line in the broad place for all to pass that would wait upon the King to the war. This immediately he put in execution, in great fury of affection to his King and not without some indignation at the errand he was sent upon. Many passed the line for that purpose, others for company, and multitudes of men and women rushed into the place like a deluge from all parts of the city of the meanest of the people, and after the small officer they marched to the palace stairs with *Viva el Rey, y mueran los Traidores.* There, after some principal ministers coming down to pacify them without effect, the King himself with his brother and Lords appeared in the *Terrero de Palacio,* and the reverence to their King, who spoke to them, but most with his hand, to be gone, did in some measure qualify, but could not appease or persuade them to love him with more respect to his laws and less danger to his affairs, which yet his Majesty might have brought them to in the end; but a beggarly woman in the crowd, spying near the King the Marques de Marialva—Conde de Castañeda that was, and hath the battle of Elvas to justify him a good Portuguese—cried out that traitor would throw the King out at window; presently some of them took a fancy that the King's speaking to the people from above with his voice and hand was for help; this was not generally believed upon the place, where the signs were better understood, but in the city it was, and more, that so horrid an act was already perpetrated.

Those upon the place, having saluted the King in such manner as hath been here related, fall to the second part of their acclamation, namely, *mueran los Traidores.* They divide themselves into several bodies, consisting of men, women, and children; now not so much as the first or any small officer to head them, nor any above the rank of a butcher. Part plunder the Archbishop of Lisbon's palace of all that was in it to a very great value. Another part do the like to the Marquess of Marialva's house, where his own goods and his brother's, the *Regidor's,* were reputed of yet very much higher value than the Bishop's. In both places great and rich curiosities, which they could not remove whole, they broke in pieces out of the windows, as also the glass windows and as much of the materials of the house as their skill could attain to, which is not so much as that of the French when such a madness takes them in the head. In the house of the Marquess between thirty and forty persons lost their lives, most of them of the invaders, and the most of them again, women and men, crowded to death or drowned in a kind of a well or heap of water, which the defendants left open on purpose—say some—for haste of getting away—say others. In the interim the ladies of the house, of great blood, bred in high plenty, fortified—if I may so say—with the weakness of their sex and eminent amongst the eminent in virtue and good works to their church and poor, necessitated in a discomposed dress to take their flight through a back door to a monastery of nuns, where they remain to this day, and will until a quarter appointed within the purlieus of the palace be made ready to receive them, as having no security elsewhere; nor in Lisbon a house of their own to put their heads in. About two miles out of town they have a *Casa de Campo*—the Portugal word is a *Quinta*—which hath hitherto scaped the fury of the people, partly by being out of the way, and partly because such of the rabble as thought it worth their while to go half a league to do a mischief arrived there and beginning their pranks found themselves too weak for some honest neighbours, to whom the Marquess was better known than to them, and such of the Queen's people as her Majesty—whose place of retirement is thereby—was most graciously and piously pleased to send thither before, hearing what had passed at Lisbon, to prevent their violence. It is absolutely the noblest place of recreation by estimation of all men within this kingdom, and one of the finest in itself that ever I saw anywhere belonging to a private man, the gardens and vineyards extending to this river or sea of Tagus.

The last house plundered that dismal day by a third party was of Luis Mendez de Elvas, whom they miscalled a Jew and the author of many projects to enrich himself and impoverish them, namely, taxes and raising of the value of their coin, as well gold as silver. It pleased him who bridles the sea with a rope of sand to put here bounds to the fury of the people; the friars coming out of several convents in solemn procession, and bringing with them church buckets of excommunications— over and above those of the lay magistrates—to quench the flame of sedition, which, had night come on first, might have proved as unquenchable as those from whence it was kindled; and yet the first actors, all the while, thinking they did nothing but what was very well and commendable. The owners of the houses had they been at home would have fared no better than their goods, but, happening to be at that time in the palace, they have there remained ever since. This day the Marquess of Nysa—a person whose house was threatened, too, by some of the rabble—is gone for the army with new recruits from these parts; and to-morrow the Marquess of Marialva follows, not yet discouraged from the public service.

One effect that day's tumult seems to have had point blank contrary to the very particular end whereat the people most aimed, which was to hurry away the King into the field; for, whereas his Majesty till that instant was absolutely resolved of going in person, it is now generally supposed that resolution is altered, and upon this very ground that if the *Canalla*, out of an excess of loyalty and courage, did those outrages in the presence of their King, in his Majesty's absence what might the middling sort of people bring to pass, out of a desire to put an end to a long war now brought to their door—love to the Castilians will never do it with them—especially if they shall be strongly possessed that they are bought and sold by the Grandees, or if any new blow should follow the loss of Evora, or if, as the rascality was quenched that day with buckets from the church, so these of higher stomach and concern should be kindled into a higher mutiny with a coal from the altar, nothing of all which is held impossible in this conjuncture. I had almost forgotten a fourth, not the least material or possible among them, namely, if their Brazil fleet—which according to advice is now daily expected upon the coast—or any considerable part thereof should fall into the mouths of their enemies. On the contrary his Majesty's ships—so long expected—with what they bring, would come very seasonably and usefully at this time towards the quieting the apprehensions of the many and preventing the underhand designs of some, as in more cases than this of Portugal, when a tide of times seems ready to turn.

17-27th instant Captain Holmes in the *Reserve*, passing on for Tangier with the Earl of Teviot, set a kinsman of his Lordship's ashore at Cascays, who brought me yours of the 20th of the last. In obedience whereunto, as to that part where you pleased to express a longing to hear what they are like to do or suffer in this country this summer in relation to the war, I do refer you not only to what is here above written, but to all that ever I wrote or said since I had the honour to be called to this work, unless extraordinary powerfully or at least very timely supported from abroad. Brave men at arms they are, but weak. This is and hath been my single opinion, though now I begin to have some company in it even of Portingals, who fall into the account that strangers and that in greater numbers and that hitherto would be of more use to them than they were aware of. For though in general words by their paper, when my Lord Inchiquin went, they did desire more, yet it was not in such a manner or upon any such caution—suitable to the proceedings of other ages and nations—as if they either expected, or indeed wished, to have them; which in case they had done—as I might hope their ambassador had with all instructions in that behalf— the proposals might be as impossible, but not so unreasonable as they appeared.

As to what immediately follows in your letter, that you long especially to hear what opinion I have of the possibility of an accommodement between this kingdom and Spain, for that you should not hold it unpracticable if it were well handled, though the humour of both these nations renders it difficult enough, I must humbly refer you to my former despatches likewise from the time of my first arrival here, which I presume may before this have come to your hands, wherein, as on the one side I did more than concur with your sense of the difficulties, by shaping to myself more obstructions than perhaps were true and real, so, on the other side, I endeavoured to demonstrate by good precedent that, in the very like case, at least as great difficulties and obstructions as the utmost I fancied, had been heretofore overcome and removed. True it is that the mediating King or Kings took very good care at that time that neither party should have his humour or all his will, and yet did not so much as threaten either with a downright breach, only menacing the one that he or they should defend his adversaries more vigorously and justifiably for the future if the treaty brake off by his default, and assuring the other that he or they would withdraw all manner of assistance from them if it brake off by theirs. This was the manner of flourishing the *montante* in those days, which were not so long ago as those of King Arthur, when knight errantry was set·up. Something my former papers offered to consideration of conveniences as well as honour which might accrue to his Majesty by such an effectual mediatorship, and somewhat of inconveniency in case an overrunning should happen by the sword whilst his Majesty doth own this cause to the world, by his troops, by his royal ships, and by having an ambassador here. But then was then, and now is now. In the meantime you have by your opinion, at the time you wrote that letter, that an accommodement was not then utterly unpracticable, put me into some degree of countenance as to mine—of which really I began to be very much ashamed—that a year ago it was possible, and much more the last winter, when the season gave time, and the overtures and condescensions from Spain—with what feigned or fallacious purpose soever—opportunity unto his Majesty to give the rule therein as to his princely wisdom and equity should appear meet and necessary. You have farther by that expression given me matter of encouragement to proceed upon the same theme—which I had absolutely laid down—hereafter, if the fortune of Don John permit, to which end I shall reserve the favour of the cipher you sent me for that purpose, rendering you my most humble thanks for it. The formality of the treaty is still on foot upon the frontiers of Galizia." *Copy in letter book. 7 pp.*

Postscript to the foregoing letter :—" By way of key to this letter, in reference to the tumult only and the jealousies which either caused or inflamed it, I crave leave to inform your honour, as upon the place :—First, that the people do not suspect either the Marquess of Marialva or his brother, the Regidor, of disloyalty to King or country, having plundered them, say they, *por traidores, no; por ladrones, si;* because after eminent service to both they were grown excessively rich upon public receipts and offices.

Secondly, the grand favourite—Conde de Castelmelhor, secretario de la puridad—though a young man for so exorbitant a trust, especially in such a storm as now bloweth, and in his general carriage high enough upon the insteps, yet because nobly born, without much of wealth to this day to bear it out, never once murmured at by the rabble; on the contrary, one among the rout crying they ought to plunder all but him—some say it was a domestic of his own, however it proved no ill-luck for him to be beloved by those—all the people cried, Amen.

Thirdly, a general acclamation in another fit of the Conde de Atougia, as a minister not only nobly born and clean handed, but who had already passed his purgatory, as to corruption, in the quality of Viceroy in the Indies.

Fourthly, some and the most—whether present or absent, lay or clergy—the fury of their language would give no quarter to, who, having been marked by the late King of dear memory with a black coal, have, notwithstanding that (say all) for that very reason (some suggest), been called out of banishment and prisons to the greatest trusts about the person and affairs of this; of whom the Dean of Evora one, who headed with an eloquent speech the surrender of that city; on the contrary, excluding and banishing to this day such as the late King, and by his example and precepts the Queen Regent, had most experience of and confidence in. These are the words of those whose actions I have above related.[*]

One mistake in my last despatch to your honour by the *Bristol Merchant* I am very willing to recant in this. Among the horse I there mentioned to have got into Evora there were no English—the common command of the auxiliaries of both nations in Count de Schomberg caused the mistake—they were all French; one Monsieur Chouet, a very gallant, tried commander, their leader; himself made prisoner, the rest, to the number of about a hundred, no more—for part could not make their way through when he was hurt and taken, but were forced to retire to the Portugal army—temporary prisoners of war together with those of the garrison, upon the articles of the city such as they were. For I must, as unwillingly, retract another error of mine in that despatch, if it were mine, having taken it up upon very authentical certificates. The truth is there was nothing like that slaughter of Spaniards by those of the city, which is there modestly reported after the copy that was sent me, neither any considerable defence made thereof. The Dean of the church, when notice came that the Portugal army was upon their march to relieve the town and Don John thereupon doubled his menaces, made an eloquent harangue to surrender, which put a quick end to the business.

It is here said that Monsieur Marcyn [†] is to come to command for the King of Spain under Don John, and to hang a tuson [toison] upon his garter. Really they report he is to have that order [*i.e.*, the Golden Fleece], and I presume he is better read in story than for it to relinquish the other, though this latter is also reported. That he should be to serve on that side, I take to be the worst news for Portugal that have come a great while, except this which Don John himself hath brought. R. F."
$1\frac{3}{4}$ *pp.*

COMTE DE SCHONBERG to SIR RICHARD FANSHAW.

1663, May [20-]30. Camp at Landroal—I received your Excellency's letter of the 19th just as we were beginning our march to relieve Evora, but those who defended it did not give us time enough. The cowardice with which the commanders have acted is beyond anything I ever saw in any war, and they ought to be hanged. I hear that Manuel de Miranda,[‡] who was at their head, fearing that he might meet with the treatment which he deserved at Court, although his brother, Henri Henriques de Miranda is very powerful there, turned back half way and returned to Evora. Truly, I do not find the grand valour in the officers of this army of which Antonio Sousa de Macedo boasts, and I think the cause is the very slight punishment for their poor defence of Jeruminhe last year. The hearts

---

[*] This first part of the postscript is cancelled.
[†] John Gaspar Ferdinand de Marcin, Marquis of Claremont d'Antrague, Knight of the Garter.
[‡] Governor of Evora; his brother Henri, gentleman of the Bedchamber.

of the Castilians are so lifted up that they think they will be
able to beat us without much danger. They certainly have a
great advantage over us in having double our cavalry. When we
marched to relieve Evora we had only two thousand five hundred
horses, but three days ago four hundred more came up. Every
day letters arrive in which the King orders Don Sancho * to give
battle. I never saw a Council so bent upon ruining their kingdom
without delay. They have followed my advice to post ourselves
upon the road, so that the enemy's convoys cannot pass without
our having time to join in and have a fight, since they wish
it so greatly at Lisbon. To post ourselves, as they write,
in sight of the enemy would not be much good unless the enemy
would fight, and on the other hand to send in search of the convoys, in order to run after them with our infantry, would be very
difficult. The enemy will have hard work to keep his garrison
in Evora without taking a post either at Rodonde or Terena.
I have done my utmost to persuade the Comte de Villa Flor to
have some fortifications made there, but they do not listen to what
one says to them. They would not put their troops in order
during the winter before the enemy came, when I, yet ill in bed,
begged them to send for their troops at Menho and Tras los
Montes, but now that their affairs are all in disorder they are
sending. In a word one can do nothing with these people, for
they do not know what is best for them. The day before yesterday
I offered to go myself with fifteen hundred horse to surprise
Xeres and pillage the surrounding country, returning in three
days, before the enemy had time to do anything, but they cannot
make up their minds. To-day I have sent sixty English and
French towards Evora and Monte Mor to prevent the peasants
carrying provisions into the place. Don John of Austria has
for the last two days been working at a fortification on the model
of that which I began at St. Anthoene. I am sorry that at the
Court of Lisbon they will see, by its use to the enemy, that the
advice which I gave them was good. We are expecting some
troops from la Beia and from Lisbon, with which we shall march
towards Evora. If the Court does not pay them something
the troops will be very feeble a month hence. This war
is not like previous ones ; it will last a long time, only the foreign
troops can be relied on, and if they are paid so badly they will
not stay. The English are in great need, and the Comte de
Castelmelhor must do something for them. I have lent them
what money I had, but this sort of thing cannot go on. So far
not a single soldier has given up, which I think is very good.
I have cashiered Lieutenant Cruck, who had greatly neglected
Trelawny's company, and he has gone over to the enemy. He is
not a great loss. I am very impatient for news from England,
and shall be beholden to your Excellency when you can give
me some.

Postscript.—I have just got a letter from Sir Henry Bennet,
saying that a regiment of infantry is coming, with picked officers,
but that the Portuguese ambassador has not asked for any

---

* Don Sancho Manoel, Conde de Villa Flor.

English troops. Judging by their treatment of those which they have got they do not appear to wish for any more. I hope the Conde de Castelmelhor will send us some money. *French. Copy in letter book.* 2¼ *pp.*

SIR RICHARD FANSHAW to the EARL OF TEVIOT, Governor of Tangier.

1663 [May 23-]June 2. Lisbon—I received your Lordship's from aboard the *Reserve*, my obligation for which is increased by your bodily indisposition when you wrote it, but the comfort I took in it diminished. I hope, however, that the indisposition has ended with the voyage, and "give your Lordship hereby, with a very good public heart as to our King and country and with a very good private one as to your Lordship's person. the joy of your Lordship's arrival in Tangier, from which I prophecy in time, by your conduct and endeavours, a fair extent of the British pale, with the primitive blessing of *crescite et multiplicamini*; the rather because your Lordship is a person likely to lay your foundation in arts as well as in arms, of both which you are a master." As regards the Portuguese houses I believe it would be best and safest for those who shall possess them hereafter, for you to purchase them for the King, and told him so when I was in England as also by letter since. The ground on which they stand might be useful for erecting magazines and the like. Our merchants wish much that there were some "commodious structure there—somewhat in the nature of a statehouse, I think they mean—where they might deposit their goods" under a guard of soldiers, paying a consideration for its use. *Copy in letter book.* 1½ *pp.*

SIR RICHARD FANSHAW to COMTE DE SCHONBERG.

1663 [May 25-]June 4. Lisbon—Your Lordship's of the 30th ult. came just when I had received a query from Secretary Bennet concerning the doings of the Portuguese this summer in relation to the war, and I have therefore sent it to him for his Majesty to see. I am told that Don John has marched towards Beja with four thousand horse, and the Portugal army after him, so "your Lordship may now very speedily make a judgment of the whole issue of this summer's work, having accustomed yourself to see events much longer beforehand." When you have done so I beg you to give me particulars of what you think should be done by the Kings of France and England to prevent the ruin of this crown, which, even if the three Kings do not accept your suggestions, cannot fail to be useful. *Copy in letter book.* 1 *p.*

COMTE DE SCHONBERG to SIR RICHARD FANSHAW.

1663 [May 27-]June 6. Country near Evora—I have been glad to hear of your well-being in a letter from Mons. Fremont.*

* Nicholas de Fremont, Sieur D'Ablancourt, author of the *Mémoires.*

He could not give me news of anyone in whom I take more interest. Five days ago we left our camp at Landraol to cut off two thousand cavalry and as many infantry going towards Alcasser da Sal, not an easy matter when an army goes after a light body of soldiers, very superior to ours in cavalry. The day before yesterday, having taken up our quarters half a league from here in the Val de Palme, the enemy took up his on the other side of the stream of Eugebe, and the next day marched towards the stream, where our infantry, in the avant-garde of which were two hundred English musketeers, engaged with theirs and, after an hour's fighting, forced them to retire. They then marched along the stream towards Evora, and we, in order to prevent their taking the post which we now hold, marched alongside of them. Having taken some heights I placed cannon on them, which disturbed the enemy at a bridge where they quitted the high road. In the evening we saw them passing the stream, protected by the vines and wood near the convent *dos Pinheros*, where they camped that night, while we made our camp half a quarter of a mile away, where we have made some slight entrenchments. *French. Copy in letter book.* 1 *p*

ANTONIO DE SOUSA DE MACEDO to SIR RICHARD FANSHAW.

1663 [May 28-]June 7. The Palace—Stating that his Majesty has received notice of the arrival of the English ships, bringing the regiment of French infantry, but that they are not to disembark until quarters have been prepared for them, which will be on the morrow. *Portuguese. Copy in letter book.* ½ *p.*

SIR RICHARD FANSHAW to [the COMMANDERS OF THE SHIPS?].

1663, May 28-June 7. Lisbon—Informing them of the receipt of the above letter, postponing the landing of the troops, congratulating them upon their happy arrival, and inviting them both to dinner on the morrow to celebrate his Majesty's birthday. *Copy in letter book.* ½ *p.*

ANTONIO DE SOUSA DE MACEDO to SIR RICHARD FANSHAW.

1663 [May 28-]June 7. The Palace—Last night there came news that the day before our army, half a league from Evora, engaged with the enemy, and forced them to retire with much loss, and that the two armies are now in posture to renew the attack. *Portuguese. Copy in letter book.* ½ *p.*
Annexed :—A list of those killed and taken prisoner. ½ *p.*

SIR RICHARD FANSHAW to SECRETARY ANTONIO DE SOUSA DE MACEDO.

1663, May 29-June 8. Lisbon—This being the birthday of the King, my master, and also the day when, after long persecutions, he re-entered London—the greatest festival ever seen there since the world began—and being moreover the day when he led the Queen, his wife, into his royal palace, I hope, seeing that the two Kings are brothers, that in the future it may also be counted a happy day for Portugal, as it already brings us very good news from the army. *Spanish. Copy in letter book.* ¾ *p.*

DON ANTONIO DE SOUSA DE MACEDO to SIR RICHARD FANSHAW.

1663 [May 29-]June 8. The Palace—On this, the birthday of the King of Great Britain, we have received letters from our army, confirming the news from Evora concerning the great loss of the enemy, including two noblemen of very high degree, and the valour shown by the English troops, for which his Majesty has ordered letters of thanks to be written to Don Michael Dongan and James Apsley, on behalf of all. *Portuguese. Copy in letter book.* ½ *p.*

SIR RICHARD FANSHAW to DON ANTONIO DE SOUSA DE MACEDO.

1663, May 29, English style. Lisbon—Yours serves as a reply to one which I had just sent to you. I will say no more, having many festivities on hand on this, my master's birthday. I hope that the birthday of the King of Portugal may bring very good news for this kingdom. *Spanish. Copy in letter book.* ¼ *p.*

ENGLISH ARMY in Portugal.

1663 [May 29-]June 8— A relation [by Col. James Apsley] of what passed in the armies of Portugal and Castile from the 7th of May till the 8th of June in this present year, 1663, *stylo loci.*

Don John of Austria having passed the Guadiana over the bridge of Badajos the 7th of May with all his army, composed of about ten thousand foot and six thousand horse and eighteen pieces of cannon, with a very fair equipage and large train of waggons and carriage horses, being charged with provisions for six weeks, marched directly towards Evora, the very heart and capital city of the province of Alemtejo, taking his way half a league from Estremos, where our General lodged with those troops which remained after the reinforcing of the frontier garrisons. The army of the enemy were all together, but our troops were separated and in divers places, and some other regiments of ours had not at that time joined with our body, wherefore we suffered the enemy to pass by us within our sight without adventuring any hazard by engaging. All that his Excellency the Earl of Schonberg could do in this occasion was to oblige the gentlemen of Portugal to send into the city of Evora— where at that time there was no garrison—two thousand five hundred foot and seven hundred horse. His Excellency also ordered some other troops which were to join with the army to put themselves into the city, insomuch that before the enemy's army could get down before the city there were within it four thousand foot and seven hundred horse, besides three thousand inhabitants who took up arms for the defence of themselves and the city. This formidable number of men did not terrify Don John in his intended enterprise, but he confidently attacked the city, though he made no near approaches to it. Partly through the ignorance of those who should have defended it and partly through their treachery, Don John had persuaded those gentlemen and citizens to surrender it, and to render themselves prisoners of war, when they had not been besieged above five days.

We hearing of this sudden capitulation, it caused us to make up an army which was fully resolved for to hazard itself for the relief of that city, but in our march the news met us that it was surrendered, wherefore, after the debate of a council of war, it was not thought convenient to attack the enemy, who was reinforced with seven hundred of our horse, under the walls of their new conquest. Whereupon, according to the advice of his Excellency the Earl of Schonberg, it was agreed we should lodge at Landroal, six leagues from the enemy, where we might easily hinder any convoys of provision which might come to the enemy either from Jerumania or Aruntias [Aronches].

This fell out so luckily that on the 30th of May the enemy was forced to send out two thousand horse and some foot mounted on mules to march as far as Alcacevas, Porto del Rey and Alcacer de Sal, to bring in a supply of provision—for which they were much necessitated—and to gather in all the corn and meal which they did believe they should have found in the storehouses of this province. Upon the first advice of the marching of this party we removed from Landroal with all speed and diligence to use our endeavour to have cut off those troops, but they having understood what we were endeavouring they took a great compass about to shun us, insomuch as it was impossible for us to hinder their joining. We kept on our way by the plain to pass the river Eudigby [Digebe], upon the side of which we encamped a little league from the place. The same night the army of the enemy came to encamp on the mountains over against us—the river of Eudigbe being between us and them—they played their cannon very furiously all night within our camp, but to little or no effect. In the morning early Don John had ordered his army in *batalia* over against the river, as if they had intended to have fallen upon us, for he sent some commanded foot with five or six battalions to second them, to endeavour the forcing of a pass which was defended with one hundred and fifty English commanded musketeers, who suffered the enemy to come within musket shot, lightly skirmishing with them, but reserving the most part of their fire for a better opportunity. At last the enemy adventuring to approach nigher, the English poured in all their shot upon them at once, and with a small party of horse passed the river and routed those commanded foot, together with the battalions which were to second them, and caused them to retreat in disorder. In the meantime our cannon were placed very dexterously and advantageously to endamage the enemy, for they killed very many officers of quality and missed but little of the person of Don John.

This great effect of our artillery, with the little appearance of our power to put them in disorder before us, did at last force Don John of Austria to march off on his left wing, mounting the hills on that side the river, which made us do the same thing on our side of the river, still removing our cannon from one hill to another with great effect, till at last they insensibly parted from us, so that we lost the sight of their march for above three or four hours; towards evening they passed over the river of Eudigby, about half a league above our camp.

This made his Excellency the Earl of Schonberg believe that infallibly next morning Don John would take his opportunity to give us battle, keeping us within the plain, they having six thousand horse against three thousand, besides the succour of the troops in Evora, which they could have commanded, it being but a little league from them, therefore the whole night we laboured hard to entrench ourselves, especially on our right hand, our left being defended by the river. The enemy finding it a long way to come to us, he spent the whole next day in sending back his baggage—which then lay under the walls of Evora—and to order the garrison which he had resolved to leave in that city, and to take care for the convoy of the prisoners which were taken at Evora. And when it was night he caused all his equipages to march to Vinda de Duque [Venta del Duque] by the same way which he came to Evora, and by this his diligence he came to encamp on this side the river Bera. We had notice of this his march before it was day, which made us take our right way to Evora-monte over the mountains, so that we came to encamp on the other side of the said river, three quarters of a league higher than the camp of the enemy.

Next morning, being the 8th of this present June, we understood by divers parties that the baggage of the enemy was marched towards Estremos, and that the army of Don John was drawn up in *batalia* upon the plain to cover and hide that march. Upon that advice we made very great haste to possess ourselves of the mountains which were a little league from Estremos. The enemy did the same with his foot, and planted them cannon shot from us on the top of two mountains, of which one of them was possessed by the right wing, the other by the left wing of their foot. At the bottom of the mountains the horse were drawn up upon the plain in the way they were to march in two lines, by this order of *batalia* their baggage lay under a good covert and they had leisure enough to draw off by the sides of the two hills. About evening his Excellency the Earl of Schonberg, having observed the left wing of the enemy's army to be without horse, the foot keeping the tops of the mountains which they possessed on that side, after many irresolutions of the Portuguese Generals, his Excellency the Earl of Schonberg persuaded them at last to attack the enemy's horse which were in the plains with all our horse, strengthened with a good quantity of foot, and that our foot, who were in two lines as the enemy's were, should attack the enemy's foot on the tops of the two mountains, and in the valley between them.

On this manner we gave the onset an hour before sunset, and the English foot with much pains climbed up the highest mountain, which was possessed by the right wing of the enemy's army and guarded with five pieces of cannon. The English marched on, shouting as if victorious, but discharged no shot till they came within push of pike of the enemy, and then they poured in their shot so thick upon them that made them quit their ground and fly towards the left wing, leaving their cannon behind them, which were afterwards turned upon them, much to their prejudice. Notwithstanding the rich baggages and coaches and wealthy plunder which were on the top of the hill—the English seeing the field not cleared—there was not one man of them stirred out of his rank, but kept close serried together to prevent any second onset, which immediately followed, for they were assaulted front, flank and rear by divers of the enemy's troops of horse, but having their fire ready at all hands they quickly quitted themselves of those troops. This was performed rather with an absolute resolution than any conduct or order, for after soldiers had serried themselves close no officer's voice could be heard, but each soldier would give the word of command either as they saw or feared their enemy, bu all this while a man could not but joy to see so vivid a courage and so firm a resolution as was in every common soldier to die by one another. The Portuguese Generals, having not been accustomed so see so close an approach before firing, did give the English for lost, and did believe they all had intended to have joined with the Castilians, but when they saw their thick firing and the good success the English obtained thereupon, they called us comrades and good Christians. Our horse in the plains had not so good success, for the English horse were too forward in charging, and were not at all seconded by the reserves of Portuguese, which was the loss of Colonel Dongham [Dongan], Captain Paulinge and many other gallant Englishmen. Our cavalry, though not seconded by their reserves, rallied and charged three or four times, and at their last repulse they were able to charge no more. The two English regiments of foot joined together and marched down in the valley for the relief of their horse, where they were met by his Excellency the Earl of Schonberg, drawn up by a woodside. His Excellency caused them to face to the left, and marched them through the wood. The enemy's horse, which remained firm, had no sooner espied the foot but they cried, "There comes the English redcoats, who give no quarter," and so they betook themselves to flight just at the entrance of the night, and left us absolute masters of the field.

That night we kept guard within the wood, but the next morning we perceived the field was clear and that it was an absolute victory on our party. The enemy had an inestimable damage, having lost his cannon and train of artillery and generally all the baggage of his army; there were fourteen coaches taken of several Princes, Dukes and Earls. It is such a loss that the Castilians cannot repair in a short time. The foot were all entirely routed, a good part of them being fallen into the hands of the peasants, who used no kindness towards them. Most part of their colonels and chief officers were either killed or taken, as also the general officers of the horse. But that which is most remarkable is that after so great a victory the enemy were too many for us.

We lost out of the two English regiments not above forty in each regiment, and no officers killed but Captain Atkinson and Captain Goudinge, both of Colonel Apsley's regiment, and we had not above forty or fifty in both regiments who were wounded. The loss of the horse was greater, for besides the loss of Colonel Dongham and Captain Paulinge, who died in the field, and Cornet Meakinge and Cornet Wharton, who were mortally wounded, they had above an hundred killed and wounded in those five troops.

To this I have added a list of such officers and soldiers with ordnance and such other necessary as belonged to their train, according as it was given into the Viador's Office by the soldiers and countrymen after the fight, and as it stands there recorded. Prisoners:

The Marquess of Lixe [Liche].

Mre. de Campo Don Juan Henriques.

Mre. de Campo Marques de Faisco [Conde Luis de Fiesco].

Mre. de Campo Daniel de Gusman.

Mre. de Campo Colonel Conde D[e But?].

Mre. de Campo Stephen de Aquella [Estevan de Angulo].

Mre. de Campo Conde de Escalante.

Mre. de Campo Conde de Ferexqui [Fresqui?]. 8 *small pps.*

SIR RICHARD FANSHAW to COMTE DE SCHONBERG.

1663 [May 30-]June 9. Lisbon—I have to-day received yours of the 6th inst. For my part "I shall implicitly hang my belief upon no relations so much as your Lordship's, as a person not only upon the place and acting so eminent a part in the present scene, but the most indifferent imaginable as to those relations which are wont to tempt men to partiality. The only fear is that your Lordship may in your reports undervalue those successes in which your proper conduct might justly claim the greatest share; for example, that last by Evora, of which your Lordship makes little more than a facing the enemy, whereas, in this Court, it is cried up for a great battle and no small victory, as the enclosed copies will let your Lordship see, though I doubt not but fame hath done as much before this can arrive; and yet at what time these things were first written and spread abroad, to the high joy and reviving of this place, the news of Don John's departure homeward and the Portugal army's pursuit of him at the heels was not come. However, then, and much more since, the action by Evora is celebrated at all hands; these ministers and people extolling to the French, when they meet them here, the things which your Lordship and the French wrought that day, and to us, when they meet us, what your Lordship and the English; but still it is the Conde de Schomberg. We, on the other side, of the two nations, agree well enough among ourselves to share you between us, a virtue which we owe to necessity, as having neither of us a total right in you. Meantime, as to those thanks Monsieur de Fremond hath been pleased to give your Lordship for the now acquaintance between him and me, he hath taken upon him a debt of mine, which I will faithfully discharge him of. I love and honour him for many things, but most for loving and honouring your Lordship so truly and zealously as I perceive he doth, which is a very good quality, though it be mine too." *Copy in letter book.* 1½ *pp.*

DON ANTONIO DE SOUSA DE MACEDO to SIR RICHARD FANSHAW.

1663 [May 31-]June 10—Announcing the defeat of Don John's army with very small loss on the Portuguese side. *Portuguese. Copy.*

Annexed :—Information to the King of Portugal that his army had routed that of Don Juan, with great loss of foot, horse, baggage and artillery. and that amongst the prisoners were the Marques de Liche and the Conde de Escalante. Masiel [May 30-]June 9. *Portuguese. Copy in letter book.* ½ *p.*

COMTE DE SCHONBERG to SIR RICHARD FANSHAW.

1663 [May 31-]June 10. Estremos—Four days ago I informed you of the state of the war, since which God has given us so great a victory over the enemy that all are surprised at our success. I send you a hasty account of it which I have drawn up. If you were here you would agree with me that we should consider it *"un bienfait bien plus grand"* on account of the good commanders which they have, while we have not four who know how to put three regiments into battle array, nor how to make them fight. I always feared their horse, and I was not mistaken, for ours had hard work to stand against it until we had defeated their foot. Everyone is pleased here with the behaviour of the English troops. We lost about fifty of our horse, but few of the foot, although more than eighty were wounded. Colonel Dongan was killed, and I intend to give his place to Major Demsy, who behaved very well. I send this express chiefly to procure money for the English troops. Pray speak to the Comte de Castelmelhor about it. Although we have won this battle, there will be enough for them to do, as the enemy still have four thousand horse. I want to attack Evora, but our commanders here, after having done so well, think of nothing but of resting themselves, instead of making use of their victory. They understand nothing about war. The soldiers are brave enough, but the chiefs carefully avoid all risks, and as to him who ought to have led us, no one saw him during the battle at all. *French. Copy in letter book.* 1 *p.*

Annexed,

Account of the battle [*of Ameixial or el Canal*].

Don Juan of Austria having begun his campaign by the taking of Evora and (by the cowardice and ignorance of the commanders there) having in five days taken prisoner more than four thousand foot and seven hundred horse who were defending it, we were deprived of the chance of relieving it. The Count of Schonberg then wished our army to be posted near Landroal to prevent the passage of any convoys by Jerumena or Aronches and to watch the proceedings of the enemy, the need of provisions having obliged Don Juan to detach two thousand horse and some foot (mounted upon mules) to go to Alcacevas, Porto del Rey and Alcacer da Sal in search of corn.

Our army started from Landroal to cut off these troops, but upon the first news of our march they were ordered to retire quickly and to abandon their booty. We continued our march along the plain, but finding that we could not hinder their joining, we turned to cross the river Zigebe [Digebe], encamping upon its banks for the night, while the enemy camped upon the heights on the other side of the stream, facing us. The next morning they marched down in battle array, as if to attack us, and advanced their foot to within musket shot, our cannon annoying them all the time, killing several officers of note, and only just missing Don Juan himself. Finally they turned on their left wing, re-ascending the stream, and we did the like, firing upon them until they were lost to sight for three or four hours amongst the vines and olives, when they crossed the river about half a league from us. This made the Count of Schonberg believe that Don Juan intended to give battle next day, seeing us in the plain, and being so near Evora that he could make use of all his troops, and we worked all night throwing up entrenchments. The enemy spent the next day in fetching up their baggage from near Evora, ordering the garrison left there, and arranging for the convoy of the prisoners. That night they camped upon the river Tera, of which we had no notice until day, when we took the road to Evora-Monte, across the mountains, and encamped on the same river, three quarters of a league higher up. Next day, the 8th inst., we heard that Don Juan was sending away his baggage between Estremos and Suzel, his army remaining in order of battle upon the plain to cover their march, whereupon we hastened to occupy the heights near Estremos. The enemy did the like, posting their foot upon two high mountains, and drawing up their horse in two lines below, thus giving good cover to the baggage. After much irresolution on the part of the Portuguese Generals, the Count of Schonberg persuaded them to attack the enemy's horse upon the plain with all ours,

*for this purpose passing all from our right wing to the left,
while the foot passed upon the right to the two mountains
and the valley between them. This succeeded so well that
our foot easily forced back the enemy, having attacked with
more resolution than skill—good officers being more rare in
this country than in any part of the world. Our horse
had not such good success, as the Count of Schonberg had
always feared, so, seeing that we were masters of all the
heights, he put in order some regiments which he met of the
second line and commanded them to stand firm, while he went
to join our two English regiments. These he advanced
towards the plain to assist the horse, which had been beaten
back and dared not renew the attack, but when the enemy
saw our foot advancing, they took to flight at nightfall,
and our victory was complete. The enemy lost all their
baggage, and many persons of quality were killed or made
prisoners, of whom the following is a list :—*

Mestres de Campo, prisoners.

Marques de Liche, son of Don Luis de Haro.

*Don Añelo de Guzman, son of the Duke of Medina de las
Torres.*

Conde de Escalante.

Conde de Lodestein.

Conde Luis de Fiesque.

Don Estevan de Angulo, reformado.

Gaspart Martines, Lieutenant-Colonel.

Horse.

Don Juan Nobales.

Don Antonio de Montenegro } *Commissaries General.*
Don Francisco Valador.

Conde Boito, commanding two troops of horse.

Conde de Fiasetri, Captain of horse.

Don Garcia Sarmento.

Captains of foot	22
Ensigns ,, ,,	20
Adjutants in charge	2.
Serjeants major	2.
Quarter-masters major	7.
Serjeants	19.
Soldiers, prisoners, unwounded	1,000.
Soldiers, taken, wounded	2,000.

*The General of artillery with two mestres de campo
and other officers of note were killed.*

French. 2¾ *pp.*

[Comte de Schonberg] to [M. de Fremont?].

1663, [May 31-]June 10—I believe that after the Comte de
Castelmelhor, you are the person in all Portugal most relieved
by our victory; for as for the Secretary of State, he did not believe in the possibility of failure. If you had seen, as I have done,
how our affair has been managed, you would be thankful that we

have got out of it so well, for hardly any of those at the head of it know what they are doing. If the Comte de Castelmelhor understood matters he would not be so ready with his orders for us to give battle. I have a headache to-day, and can only write hurriedly. I am sending a note to M. de Turenne, to whom you must give all particulars, " puisque le Comte de Villa Flor, qui depuis deux jours travaille à faire la cronique n'y aura rien oublié." I send M. de Baubigny, in the first place to get some money from the Comte de Castelmelhor for the English soldiers, whose good services the day before yesterday merit better treatment than they receive, and secondly, to say that the *Viador* will not make proper payment for Mons. de la Plesse, who was killed in the battle. The foreign cavalry lost more men than all the other horse put together. My own regiment opposed Don John himself. Most of his squadron were killed on the spot and his standard taken by M. de Baubignis [*sic*], to whom I have given charge to carry it to the Count of Castelmelhor that it may be presented from me to the King. Mons. de Saussay and Des Fontaines wish to be recommended to you. We have got Don John's carriage at your service. I took no other booty in the battle, but have lost an old cloak which my trumpeter had on, who was shot through the head as we were climbing to where the regiments of Cherny and Keiserstein were. We there found some silver dishes of Don John's, who had had his collation at that place. I hope our French have arrived. We shall still be able to show them some sparks of war at Evora, and we hope to see you with M. Carneton at the siege. I have not time to finish my gazette, but M. de Cleran has taken the substance of it from my draft, and you will be able to polish it up to send to M. de Turenne. I pray you to give my letter to the ambassador. I hope some vessel will be going for France, which will take the news. *French. Copy in letter book. 2 pp.*

FRENCH ACCOUNT of the battle.

1663 [May 31-]June 10. Estremos—If my letter of the 3rd from Beja has made you doubt whether I was at the battle I now inform you that the noise of the cannon near Evora reached me at Serpa, and I started at once, joining our army the night before we started to follow the enemy. [*Here follows an account of the battle, in which, however, there is no mention of the English troops.*] The Count's [Schonberg's] regiment was badly enough treated, but had the honour to beat Don Juan's guards and to capture his standard, which has been sent to the King. Of all our friends, only poor La Plece was killed. I hope that as soon as the roads are free M. de Carneton will come to rejoice with our Count over a success which redounds so much to his glory, and has made such a noise in the world. *French. Copy in Fanshaw's letter book. 1 p.*

SIR RICHARD FANSHAW to SIR HENRY BENNET.

1663, June 5-15. Lisbon—"Upon the ever to us happy and often superlatively joyful 29th of May," it has pleased God to give his Majesty's nearest ally an absolute victory, not without the assistance of our English troops, under the excellent conduct of the Count de Schomberg. I refer you to the enclosed relations of those "who were both eye-witnesses and actors in the battle, and of them principally to the testimony of strangers . . . whose business it was not to tell our tale only, but the management and success of that day in the gross." The battle really began two days before in the brush near Evora, when the English vanguard showed the Portuguese "that the Spanish Armada was not invincible, and taught the Spaniard on the other hand that the Portugal army was not contemptible." I am not ashamed of my former fear or indeed despair of the fortune of Portugal, seeing that it was shared by the Comte de Schomberg himself, nor do I see the error of my conjecture that without a powerful help from England Portugal was lost, but "I did not discern that powerful succour to be already here whilst I was soliciting for it," or believe it possible that a beheaded remnant, with so many discouragements to boot, could have proved such instruments of good, "for which infidelity of mine I humbly crave his Majesty's pardon and theirs." *Copy in letter book.* 2½ *pp.*

ANTONIO DE SOUSA DE MACEDO to SIR RICHARD FANSHAW.

1663, June [5-]15. Palace—Stating that the plague is very severe in Algiers, and begging his Excellency to use all precautions as regards the English ships. *Portuguese. Copy in letter book.* ¼ *p.*

SIR RICHARD FANSHAW to SIR HENRY BENNET.

1663, June 7-17. Lisbon—On Sunday, the 10th, Captain Utbert, commander of H.M.S. *Phœnix*, arrived here from Havre de Grace with a new French incognito, who has brought a hundred thousand crowns for the use of the King of Portugal. On Tuesday, the 13th, Major Holmes came from Tangier, where he left the Earl of Teviot highly contented with the place. Captain Smith remains there, to carry home the Earl of Peterborough. On Thursday, the 14th, I was invited to a conference with the ministers here, who told me that Francisco Fereira was being sent to England, Holland and France to announce the late victory and stir up the allies to send further help of men and money to enable this crown "to follow their blow smartly." I told them plainly that the report in England of the treatment of our men would make it impossible to persuade any more to follow them, but that as to ships, some had already arrived, and the rest were hourly expected. As regards France and Holland I could say nothing at all, being a stranger to the arrangements between Portugal and them, " whereof nevertheless I happened to know a little more than any minister here had told me. The Secretary replied, no, no, there was nothing concealed from me," and upon their requesting my good offices with my master, which in general I promised, the conference broke up.

As soon as the news of the victory arrived, M. Carneton, *alias* Colbert, resolved to return to France, saying that the case was so altered that he must seek fresh instructions. The twelve hundred French are daily expected and " may come time enough to have their share in the re-siege of Evora—this day, as I suppose, begun—which, though it remain *aislada* [isolated], may cost very hot work to get, being commanded by an old Biscay soldier, who—they here say—fears neither God nor man." *Copy in letter book. 3 pp.*

CAPTAIN B. GILPIN to SIR RICHARD FANSHAW.

1663, June 8. H.M.S. *Hector*, near the bar of Faeror [Faro]— Stating that Admiral Smith is preparing to sail for home with the Earl of Peterborough, staying only for the Earl of Teviot's commission ; that two new redoubts have been built at Tangier, and that there are provisions of all sorts for fourteen months in the town, besides a hundred and twenty tons of oatmeal come lately and more coming. *Copy in letter book. 1 p.*

SIR RICHARD FANSHAW to the CONDE DE CASTELMELHOR.

1663, June [8-]18—As the non-cession to England of the island of Bombay is the chief point which he wishes to discuss with the Council, he thinks it best, for avoiding of either exaggeration or suppression, to send the letters concerning it, which he has had copied in English—a language which the Secretary of State understands well—seeing that if in translations the words are offensive the deeds are apt to be so also. *Spanish. Copy in letter book. 1¼ pp.*

SIR RICHARD FANSHAW to COMTE DE SCHONBERG.

1663, June 9-19. Lisbon—I send you his Majesty's answer to the officers' petition, a copy of my warrant, ordering me to distribute the first 6,000*l.* obtained from the Queen's portion amongst our forces, and also a copy of a letter from Mr. Secretary Bennet, recommending Captain Trelawny, " as also with singular kindness our renowned Colonel Michael Dongan, who is now beyond the sphere of human activity to serve him, save only by doing justice to his fame, in which all the world here doth unanimously concur, English, French and Portugueses." I could heartily wish that " a list were made out of the muster-rolls of all the strangers, to the meanest common soldier, with the particular places of their birth," for though I presume that the Portuguese will do justice to their merits in that famous battle, and in what they have already written are no niggards in their just commendations of the strangers, yet " we have an English verse somewhere as common as a proverb : In the way of love and glory, Each tongue best tells his own story." Secretary Bennet's letter also recites the issue of Major-General O'Brien's examination, " which I wish were known to the soldiery there with you for the better clearing of his honour and innocency amongst them, whilst I shall be as industrious in this court to obtain his *quietus est* from hence," which I expect to be able to do, because I believe they never really thought him guilty. I hope the soldiers will understand how difficult it will be for me to obtain the 6,000*l.* for them from this court. I know the ministers here will wish to count it as part of their arrears, instead of a donative from our own King, but to that I shall never agree. " Major Dempsey, now Lieut.-Colonel by your Excellency's favour, desires me by letter to render your Lordship thanks for his preferment, and prays withal a lift for his countryman, Captain Bryn," who "performed signally in the day of battle." *Copy in letter book.* 2½ *pp.*

SIR RICHARD FANSHAW to LORD CHANCELLOR CLARENDON.

1663, June [10-]20. Lisbon—" For the great favour of your Lordship's of the 12th of April I rendered my most humble thanks by mine dated the 20-30th of May.

" Your Lordship's second by Captain Trelawny, more particularly entering into the marrow of the negotiations under my hand, hath yet farther obliged me and shall to follow and perform as near as I can all your Lordship's lights and commands therein.

" I do not here tell your Lordship for news the great victory obtained against Don John, because fame, which seems to fly through the air, uses to carry such extraordinary successes faster than human observation, either ship by sea or post by land. Only I would inform your Lordship, the best I can on the sudden, particulars how and by whom it was gained, enclosing herewith, by way of patterns, the Portugal relation in Spanish *—which will shortly come forth here in Latin likewise—as also a summary account of what the King our master's subjects acted that day from Colonel James Apsley,† whose name is now deservedly high in this kingdom since the battle, having before lain under much obloquy, but not in reference to courage, after which—as your Lordship will there see—a relation at large will come with an English bias, if any at all, of which I accuse neither English nor Portuguese ; but must rationally conclude that the truth will be found in the mouth of two or three witnesses, leaving—for one—an ear for the French relations too ; all which put and compared together, that nation of the three which gets the plurality of votes for the second place in merit seems to me to

---

* Probably that of which there is a copy in the British Museum, " Relacion de la famosa y memorable vitoria, &c." (9195, c. 25.)   † *See* p. 101 above.

have a right to the first; or else let the Spaniard judge for all. But I hope they will agree among themselves for the laurel, as they did in the battle." *Copy in letter book.* 1 *p.*

SIR RICHARD FANSHAW to the LORD BISHOP OF LONDON.

1663, June [10-]20.   Lisbon—" Your Lordship's I have received, which tells me where you can do me no good, and certainly I ought to rest very well satisfied without your Lordship's obliging me by the benefits of another, who have so much already obliged be by your own, and would yet more have done it had the importunities of another given your Lordship leave to dispose of what is your own.   It were a good deed to do it yet to anger him, but that your Lordship is no ways revengeful, and besides— according to what I hear out of England—it is both my fear and my hope that before this come to hand your Lordship will have changed your station."

Postscript.—" I give not your Lordship a relation of the great victory here against the Spaniard because you meddle not with blood, but it will sound so loud there, as well as in other parts of the world, that your Lordship must hear it however, unless you stop your ears very close." *Copy in letter book.* $\frac{3}{4}$ *p.*

SIR RICHARD FANSHAW to the BISHOP OF WINCHESTER.

1663, June [10-]20.   Lisbon—I have received your last letter but the one sent in Lord Cornbury's cover miscarried, as nearly all my letters have done unless sent by a frigate.   " From my Lord Chancellor I have received two, both of them as to quantity of a bountiful length and as to quality very obliging in their contents, by which means that of your Lordship's which is missing proves the less loss to me, though still a great one because I take a delight in being often told how much I am in his Lordship's favour and yours.   The news of this country I need not tell your Lordship.   All Christendom will be full of it before this can arrive." *Copy in letter book.* $\frac{1}{2}$ *p.*

CONDE DE CASTELMELHOR to SIR RICHARD FANSHAW.

1663, June [10-]20.   The Palace—Regretting that the orders given for the delivery of the Island of Bombay have not been carried out, and requesting his Excellency to point out what he conceives necessary to be done. *Portuguese. Copy in letter book.* $1\frac{1}{4}$ *pp.*

COMTE DE SCHONBERG to SIR RICHARD FANSHAW.

1663, June [12-]22.   Camp before Evora—If the Conde de Castelmelhor will send some money, as he promised me, the troops here will have nothing to grumble at.   My regiment of foot lacks goo officers, and so is rather insubordinate, but I shall

24. d   H

remedy this with a little care and patience. I have made Demsy Lieutenant-Colonel. Captain Sutton, persuaded by his lieutenant, wishes to retire from the service, but I do not know whether I shall do well to give him his *congé* after the campaign. The officers here do not take sufficient care of their cavalry horses. In the dearth of good officers I have some idea of making my eldest son colonel of the regiment. If we had some good old officer I should not do it, my son being yet very young, and in any case I shall decide nothing until you tell me that you will help me to make my excuses for so bad a choice. The day before yesterday four hundred men, of whom the two hundred forming the vanguard were commanded by our young Major Bellasis, carried the fort of St. Antonio with the loss of three soldiers. I hope that to-night we shall attach *le mineur* to the wall, behind which I do not doubt that the enemy has made some entrenchments. The Comte de Satirani [Santirena] does not show any such capacity in his defence of the place as the Spanish prisoners in Lisbon led us to expect. Those who have given themselves up here say that their horse mean to come out to-night and withdraw into their own country. I have sent twenty squadrons to stop their way. Don John is said to be gathering troops to relieve this place. I hope he is, and then we will march against him. A fortnight after a victory, the soldiers who have been beaten remember it. My belief is that in four or five days the enemy must capitulate, and I think we ought to treat them as they treated our side. When Evora is taken we might, for the reputation of the arms of Portugal, advance into the enemy's country, if it were not that our men are fatigued and that it is beginning to be very hot, so that it is to be feared that the rest of the auxiliaries would desert and that the troops, especially the foreigners, would perish. These people here are already tired of the fatigues of the campaign; they are naturally lazy, and there is not a commander who does anything unless he is obliged. Messieurs de Villa Flor and Marialva set them the example, for their only care is to write letters and to ask what is going on in the siege. Neither one nor the other has been nearer to the town than the quarter where they are lodged and they do not even know on which side we have opened the trenches. It is pitiable that a King should not have a single commander in his kingdom. The result is that affairs go on so slowly that one is disgusted, doing all one can and yet accomplishing nothing.

Mr. Trelawny has just brought me his packet. I have seen all the papers and entirely agree with what you say.

I will have a roll drawn up of the soldiers and their birthplaces, and will tell them of the good will of the King. Mr. Trelawny will be made Major of the regiment. The 6,000*l.* must certainly be only distributed, as you say, according to the orders which you receive from the King.

Postscript.—The Sieur de la Ples, my lieutenant, has been killed. He has left me his harriers, which he told me he bought from a German Colonel when they were very young, six months ago. They tell me here that they were taken from you. I do not know whether they are bad or good, and I hear that they have not been run yet. You may dispose of them as you will, seeing that you are the master of all that I have, whether acquired well or ill. I think the officers and soldiers killed in the battle ought to have their arrears paid up and have written to the Conde de Castelmelhor, with whom you might confer on the matter.

June [15-]25—The consul has been delayed by business until to-day, when the enemy has capitulated. Our Generals were so tired of the siege and so apprehensive that Don John would send succours that they wished to grant all that was asked, and without my seal and against all reason they have given in on the article concerning the horses. All the soldiers, both horse and foot, remain prisoners of war until October 15. I should think that there are about three thousand five hundred men. *French. Copy in letter book.* 2½ *pp.*

Antonio de Sousa de Macedo to Sir Richard Fanshaw.

1663, June [13-]23. The Palace—Announcing that the fort of St. Antonio at Evora has been stormed and taken by two hundred English and two hundred Portuguese, each under command of their Major, with great loss to the enemy; and that the English behaved with much valour and determination. *Portuguese. Copy in letter book.* ½ *p.*

The Same to the Same.

1663, June [15-]25. The Palace—Announcing that God has been pleased to restore to them the city of Evora, which, after two breaches had been made in the fortifications, capitulated, the commanders, with two pieces of artillery, being allowed to leave, but all the horse and foot, ten pieces of artillery and all the baggage falling into the victors' hands; and congratulating his Excellency upon this success, in which the English troops had a great share. *Portuguese. Copy in letter book.* ½ *p.*

Colonel J[ames] Apsley to [Sir Richard Fanshaw].

1663, June [15-]25. Camp before Evora—"I have sent your Excellency a full relation of our proceedings in the camp till the 8th of June. I am much afraid I have been too busy in imposing any intelligence upon your Excellency, who must of necessity be far better advised of all passages by the letters of our General, but since his care and trouble is much, I had reason to believe he had forgot the merits of our countrymen by a French relation I saw composed by Monsieur Claran by the command of the Earl of Sumbergh [Schonberg], wherein we are only nominated as assistants when indeed we were the sole victors. I hope a soldier may be excused from vanity in the relation of a truth, for my Lord Bacon teaches me that vainglory in

H 2

them is a virtue, *in Ducibus et viris militaribus gloriosum esse non inutile est; sicut enim ferrum acuit ferrum, ita per gloriam hanc animi etiam acuuntur invicem et excitantur.*[*] We rested six days after the battle at Estremos to furnish ourselves with battering-pieces, powder, sale [*sic*], scaling-ladders and whatever else was necessary for the siege or storming of a town. We came to Evora about the 14th of June, where we joined with the army of the Marquess of Marialva, which came from Lisbon and consisted of five thousand foot and five hundred horse. The first two days we did nothing but cut down fagots; when we had enough we began our approaches. The Earl of Sumbergh and the Generals were all lodged in a garden and convent near to the fort of St. Anthony, which was built upon their water work; part of the convent was within half-musket shot of the fort, where his Excellency had placed some cannon, but his Excellency espied a quicker way of taking of it than by battery, and when he had well surveyed the place, about the 22nd of June, I having the guard, he sent to me to send him two hundred musketeers under the command of a major and two captains, which was performed according to command, and I sent Major Bellases with two hundred musketeers. About twelve of the clock at night the fort was stormed and taken by those few men; we only had one captain wounded and three soldiers killed. The next day they offered to capitulate, but presently broke off. Our approaches went on very fast. Some two days after the Lieutenant-General who commanded our approaches, emulous of the honour was gotten by the storming of the fort of St. Anthony, did command out two hundred musketeers also. which I sent him under the command of Captain Roach and Captain More. The Lieutenant-General was resolved we should storm, though he had not judgment to know what, when or where, so he gave command that these two hundred men should storm a half moon of the enemy's and that they should kill all that were found in the ditch between that and the wall. His command was obeyed, though we were sensible of the unreasonableness of it, and there was only one man found there, the rest having got into town, though they ran in with that fear they had not time to shut the port; we lost three men and had four wounded; next morning the treaty was finished, but what the articles are I know not." *Endorsed by Lady Fanshaw:* "Sir Allan [*sic*] Apsley's letter." 2 *pp.*

Sir Richard Fanshaw to the Conde de Castelmelhor.

1663, June [16-]26—Stating, in reply to his Excellency's of the 20th, that he cannot draw back from any of the demands of the King, his master, for the punishment of and recompense for the affront offered him by the non-delivery of Bombay, and that moreover it would be well that the city of Bazaim should also be given into his hands; with further demands for the

---

[*] *See the Essay, De Vana Gloria.*

payment of the English troops and regulation of naval commerce. *Spanish. Copy in letter book.* 4 *pp.*

Annexed,
> *Five papers of extracts from instructions, &c., relating to the above matters.* 3 *pp.*

FEDRIC [*sic*] DE SCHAMPS to PRINCE RUPERT.

1663, June [16-]26. Isle of la Tortue [or Tortuga]—Captain Fernes having arrived in the port of la Tortue, where I command for my uncle, the Governor, and having told me that he belonged to you and that you had sent him expressly to learn tidings of the illustrious Prince Maurice, I have done all in my power to obtain intelligence, but am grieved to have to give you the sad news, of which there seems no doubt, that he is dead, as you will see by the deposition which I send you of one of my townspeople, who was then a prisoner in St. Domingo. Also another resident here has told me that he long lived at Porto Rico and had often heard it said that Prince Maurice was dead.

Some time ago there was a man here who was at Porto Rico when this noble Prince was lost, who assured me that he was dead, and a Spaniard, coming from Malacre, had a very handsome *chevelure* fastened on his hat, which was believed to have been that of the Prince himself. This is all the news I can learn. I wish I had better to send you, for although I have not the honour of being known to your Highness, I have heard so much in your praise in the houses of Boulion and of Duras that I ardently desire to offer you my services. I pray you to forgive a young scholar if there are any faults in this letter and if he does not offer you all the respect and the titles due to you. *French. Copy.* 1¾ *pp.*

Addressed :—" À tres-haut et tres-illustre Prince Robert et Prince du Palatin, Duc du Bavary et Duc Combrelant " [Cumberland].

On the same sheet.

1663, June [16-]26—Deposition of William Beaucham, Frenchman, that having been captured by the Spaniards he was taken prisoner to the town of St. Domingo, where, after his release, he heard some mariners of a ship from Porto Rico talking to those of St. Domingo upon the shore. Seeing a great Flemish ship in the port the Porto Rico men said it was like the English ship which was lost on the coast of Porto Rico. Those of St. Domingo asked if many had been saved, to which the others replied that not a man was saved, as those that escaped the sea were all massacred, and that Prince Maurice was lost.

The men of St. Domingo asked if they had massacred him, too, and one of them replied no, but that they had made him drink a cup of chocolate, which was as much as to say that they had poisoned him.

June [16-]26—Being at the Spanish island of Saveana there
was one Martin Roubinet, master of a shalop, who had met a
priest who told him that Prince Maurice was at Porto Rico,
but a Spanish ensign bade him be silent and he heard nothing
more. *French. Copy.* 1¼ *pp.*

SIR RICHARD FANSHAW to SIR HENRY BENNET.

1663, June 19-29. Lisbon—" My last despatch concluded with
the arrival here of the twelve hundred French from Plymouth
after the battle, but time enough, as I then thought, for the re-
siege of Evora, but I was deceived, for the said French, having
sickness among them by their very long lying on shipboard,
were thereby so discomposed as that they could not reach to be
of any use there until that upon the 23rd instant a party of
four hundred of the Portuguese army, whereof two hundred
which made the vanguard were English commanded by Major
Bellasis, a most gallant young man, brother to my Lord of
Faulconbridge, did carry the fort of St. Antonio, suburban to
Evora, with the loss of only three soldiers of ours, but of a matter
of three hundred Spaniards of six hundred which were the
defenders, being the medium of eight hundred which some report
were therein and others four hundred. This prodigious action
I relate with very great modesty in reference to our English
and their commander, for there are that do affirm that of the
other two hundred of the party, which should have seconded
them, not a man was come up until ours had finished the
work, and that then ours would not suffer them to enter for a
share of the honour, the booty not being worth the wrangling
for; all I have heard named was a Capuchin's robe, which one
of our common soldiers plundered from the owner's back; and
to the great merriment of himself and the beholders—of which
the friar himself had his part in that he had scaped so well with
the loss of his upper skin only—put it upon his own, cowl and
all upon his head, saying he would be clad in summer, though
he had gone naked all the winter. Many other comical passages
in this campaign the Portuguese tell here of our countrymen,
but many more tragical ones—I do believe—the Castilians will
tell of them by way of complaint into England. Sure it is
that so few men—I will not now endear the matter by the circumstances of their discouragements as I have done heretofore—
absolutely speaking did never act more great and daring things
in any part of the world. In fine, to return to fort St. Antonio,
where I left two hundred of them lacking three, the stupendous-
ness of that action was such that the Portugal army preparing
for a general assault, the surrender of the city followed not
long after, the news thereof arriving here at Lisbon together
with the Brazil fleet, to complete the joy of this Court, upon the
15-25 instant. The conditions were that the Spaniard should
march out with bullet in mouth, colours flying and two pieces
of ordnance, the rest, which were ten pieces and their other
baggage, should remain, that the Spanish officers should march

quite away, all the soldiers as well horse as foot to the number of above three thousand five hundred to remain prisoners until the 15th day of October. The condition as to the horses themselves is the same as to their riders, a thing which troubled Comte de Schonberg very much, knowing the very great want this kingdom hath of those necessary creatures, but the Portugal chiefs answered him they would find an evasion for that, the Castilians having broken the same article with them at the late surrender of the city to Don John, and this answer troubles the Comte ten times more.

This being in substance all of note which hath happened here since my last, it remains to observe whether there will be anything more attempted this season, the heats now growing near their height. The issue will be subject for my next, which your honour may expect not long after this, though not so soon as I imagined unless by some emergent opportunity of writing, the matters upon which I did and yet do intend to dispatch an express for England—as requiring no less by the weight thereof—lying under debate, but, as all business, not ripening so fast in these Spanish climes as fruits do; and now I am resolved to put home for very clear resolutions in all particulars which are commanded me by our royal master, most especially as to what may be absolutely relied upon in reference to these incomparable troops—so many of them as remain, which may be about half the number which came the last year—that either they may be well secured of their future good pay and treatment in this kingdom or his Majesty seasonably informed of the uncertainty thereof—*which would be as much as to say the improbability*—whereby not to lose the opportunity of his Majesty's fleet whilst it remains in these seas, for transporting them elsewhere, there being certainly no country in the world that hath or apprehends war, which would not be most joyful to entertain them as friends and as troubled to see them their enemies. But I trust, whenever they leave this service and not by their own default—whereby to disoblige his Majesty that way—they shall never serve any other again but himself whilst his Majesty hath a soldier in England and so many royal plantations abroad, of which Tangier is not the least hopeful and lies excellently to their hand with constant pay and provisions, and where—as I apprehend it—the more their numbers shall be the more they will have to live upon. My Lord of Peterborough can inform his Majesty better for the taking of true measures herein, so will the successive despatches and addresses from his indefatigable successor, the Earl of Teviot.

The latter had already—according to a letter I have newly received from his Lordship by the way of Algarve, whither he had sent Captain Gilpin with a frigate for some necessaries—in a fortnight space hooked in a little piece of country by two new-erected forts and a circular trench to the town, and I do verily believe that in process of time he will add as many skins to it, one without another, as there are of an onion. His Lordship writes me he hath as good hopes of the mole, if there want not Exchequer supplies: and truly—methinks—it were great pity that those should be failing to a work which may one day help to supply the Exchequer. This letter was brought me by an express from Faro, where Captain Gilpin lies with the frigate making his provisions by assistance of an English merchant there—one Mr. Johnson, whom the Earl employs therein,—and in expectation of an effectual letter from this King to his ministers in that kingdom for the shipping off now and from time to time such necessaries of all sorts as shall be bought for the use of the garrison at Tangier, whether for building, fortification or provision, which letter from his Portugal Majesty —being promised it in very ample manner—I attend here hourly to despatch the express back, and in case I should find it short as to all occasions which the Governor of Tangier may have in other parts of these dominions, I shall solicit that afterwards when I go to the palace in person, being at present restrained by something of private disaster in my family. A sort of disaster mine is whereunto your honour is not as yet liable, and when you may be, that it never betide you to mix water with your joys is the wish of yours, &c. *Copy in letter book.* 3½ *pp.*

SIR RICHARD FANSHAW to the EARL OF PETERBOROUGH.

1663, June [19-]29. Lisbon—"The last night I received the report of your Lordship's arrival upon this coast at Cascays, immediately whereupon or most undoubtedly this morning early I had speeded to wait upon your Lordship there, had not the good news surprised me at a time when my pores were shut with the sense of a loss of something dear to me newly received, and the fear of another, in a nearer degree of dearness, perpendicular. In fine that night, which was a critical one, is past, not without eminent effects of the danger it uses to bring along with it and the danger itself—as I do now most confidently hope—with it, so that if this present day and following night pass according to expectation without new alarms, I have no more of cloud left by to-morrow's sun than that and the first sight of my Lord of Peterborough will totally disperse. To which end—God willing—I will then take coach to wait upon your Lordship at your ship, and thence hither, unless my friend Captain Halbord have so discredited to your Lordship the town of Ulysses as that your Lordship will not think it worthy so much as of a short survey." The bearer of this, my kinsman and secretary, will send me your Lordship's resolution by express to-night. *Copy in letter book.* 1 *p.*

MONS. DE FREMONT to SIR RICHARD FANSHAW.

1663, June [19-]29—Regretting that business with the Condé de Castelmelhor prevents his coming in person, and stating that the Comte de Schomberg, whom he had left in good health, would be that same evening with his army at Estremos, having been obliged to go thither to stop the proceedings of the enemy in the neighbourhood of Terena and Landroal. *French.* 1 *p.*

CONDE DE CASTELMELHOR to SIR RICHARD FANSHAW.

1663, June [20-]30. The Palace—Stating that the King has ordered him to reply upon those points concerning which his Excellency wrote to himself and to the Secretary of State—that as to the supply of necessaries for Tangier from Algarve they wrote to the Governor last September, but if a fresh letter is necessary it shall be sent; that in regard to Bombay fresh orders are being sent with all speed, but that the King cannot understand the demand for the cession of Baçaim, and as in such matters it is not possible to act without consulting the treaties and the public convenience he can make no reply until he has seen the documents on which the claim is founded—with further matters concerning the English troops and commerce. *Portuguese. Copy in letter book.* 1¾ *pp.*

SIR RICHARD FANSHAW to the EARL OF TEVIOT.

1663 [June 21-]July 1. Lisbon—The ministers here tell me that what Mr. Johnson asks, "namely, a letter from the King of Portugal to the Governor of Algarve in favour of Tangier" was sent long since, but I now enclose another to the same effect, and also several attested copies of an extract from a letter of the Conde de Castelmelhor, which you may find useful, presuming that "credit will be given to my attestation and reverence to the Conde's name. . . . I will commend your Lordship and the hopefulness of [your] plantation no more unto you, because I see you apt to construe it as a compliment. It is a fairer way of proceeding to let you know what I say of both to others," so I send you a copy of what I have written to Secretary Bennet by the Earl of Peterborough. I confess that I wish you the reversion of the English troops in Portugal, "and so I should do were they recruited to ten thousand and all of the same kidney, supposing room can never be wanting for them who are so good at making of room. I say where there is continent enough in the hands of not the most warlike people in the world without disparagement, knowing very well what the Africans have been in ages past, and therefore what they [may] be again in the future, nor yet at all looking upon them as contemptible in the present. But to return to our countrymen. This copy gives your Lordship only the fag-end of their exploits here this summer. The enclosed print in Spanish * relates particularly the very great victory obtained by this Crown over Don Juan of Austria, to which, even according to this Portugal's relation, [they] contributed very eminently. There are—and nations unconcerned

See note on p. 112 above.

too—that attribute exceedingly much more to their valour than this speaks of." *Copy in letter book.* 1¾ *pp.*

Annexed,

> *Copy of extract from Conde de Castelmelhor's letter of June 20-30, relating to Tangier.*

SIR RICHARD FANSHAW to CONDE [DE CASTELMELHOR], Secretario de la puridad.

1663 [June 22-]July 2—Stating that he has resolved to go to England to obtain fresh instructions from the King and his ministers. *Spanish. Copy in letter book.* 1¼ *pp.*

The SAME to the SAME.

1663 [June 26-]July 6—Reiterating his views concerning Bombay, Bazaim, the English troops, &c., and stating that, having resolved to send an express to obtain full information as to the views of the King of Great Britain and his ministers, he has come to the conclusion that the only way of obtaining satisfaction will be to go himself. *Spanish. Copy in letter book.* 2½ *pp.*

LIEUT.-COLONEL LAURENCE DEMPSEY to SIR RICHARD FANSHAW.

1663 [June]—I have not hitherto been able to give your Excellency an account of our victory " by reason of the great care I had to look after the slain and wounded men " of our regiment. The valour and gallantry of our English was beyond what I can express, but I must briefly say " that both our horse and foot gained that victory, and in the open field and occasion the Generals all did acknowledge the same, and I do not doubt but that our own General, Count Schonberg, and Conde Villa Flor will inform your Excellency of this to be true." I send you enclosed a list of our slain and wounded and also of the enemy's losses, so far as I can learn them. We sadly need accommodation for our wounded and money for our present subsistence, for our officers are in great want and our soldiers ready to perish, although Count Schonberg does all he can for our relief. We lost seventy horses in the battle, and are told that our own King has to remount us, " which was a very sad answer in my opinion." To-morrow we begin our march to Evora. Count Schonberg has made me Lieut.-Colonel of the regiment of horse. 3 *pp.*

Enclosing,

> 1. *List of killed and wounded in the General's regiment of horse :—Lieut.-Colonel Dongan, Lieutenant Pollen and seventy-five soldiers " killed outright," and nine other officers and about a hundred soldiers wounded, some of whom have since died. The troops mentioned are those of the General, Lieut.-Colonel Dongan, Major Dempsey, and Captains Trelawny, Sutton and Sharpe.* 1 *p.*

2. " A relation of all the prisoners belonging to the Spanish army," agreeing for the most part with that given by the Comte de Schonberg. 1½ pp.

DUKE OF YORK.

[1663, June?]—Statement by Sir John Lawson that when the King of Portugal has granted license to the Duke of York to send three ships to Brazil, Mr. Jacob, merchant of Lisbon, will undertake to freight the *Mathias*, *Great Charity* and *Augustine* on the following terms, viz.:—That if the Duke of York man the three ships with two hundred able seamen, fit and victual them for twelve months and pay the wages, Mr. Jacob will pay him 14,000*l.*, of which 2,000*l.* will be paid at their setting sail and the rest on their return, and will also provide wages and victuals for any term over the twelve months. *Copy in letter book.* ½ *p.*

DUKE OF YORK.

1663, July [1-]11—Statement that his Britannic Majesty has lent his brother, the Duke of York, three of the royal ships to trade to Brazil, which will go as merchant ships, paying all dues and giving the usual security. *Superscribed by Fanshaw:* "Proposition of the Duke of York, begging license from the King of Portugal to send three ships to Brazil, lent him by the King, his brother, by way of Lisbon, giving security for the same and paying all rights to the Exchequer." *Spanish. Copy in letter book.* ½ *p.*

SIR RICHARD FANSHAW to SIR HENRY BENNETT.

1663, July 3-13. Lisbon—Giving news of the present state of affairs, and stating his resolve to sail a month hence for England. *Copy.* 2¼ *pp.* [*Original in the Portugal Correspondence.*]

SIR RICHARD FANSHAW to WILLIAM COVENTRY.

1663, July 3-13. Lisbon—I received the Duke's letters with joy and pride, and believe that the most dutiful way of answering them will be a diligent execution on my part. I have satisfied myself that if the license be given "the clear gains to his Royal Highness will probably amount to six or seven thousand pounds, without disbursing anything considerable beforehand, as Sir John Lawson hath contrived the bargain," and I have put the business of the license into the hands of the King's favourite, whose answer I expect in a few days. The matter has to be laid before the Council, who of late have objected to granting such licenses, even though paid for, believing them to be detrimental to Portugal in the end, " how useful soever to stop a present gap or accommodate a particular person." Sir John Lawson means to send Major Holmes back to England, but meanwhile has despatched him to Tangier that he may carry home the latest news from that garrison. *Copy in letter book.* 1 *p*

SIR ALLAN APSLEY to LORD [AMBASSADOR] FANSHAW, in Portugal.

[1663], July 6. St. James'—I thank you for your generous kindness to my brother, and beseech you " to continue your charity to him and to afford him your kind advice to preserve the reputation you have given him. To give a man a good fame is more than to give him riches, and I am afraid my brother was poor throughout." I wish I could be of service to you here, but I believe your own virtues will prevent you from having occasion for so mean a help. I pray you present my humblest duty to your excellent lady. 1 *p*. *Seal of arms.*

M. DE FREMONT to S[ON] A[LTESSE] M[ONSIEUR] L[E] P[RINCE] D[E] T[URENNE].

1663, July [13-]23. Lisbon—As the Comte de Schomberg tells me that he has written at length to your Highness concerning the regiment which has been sent I will confine myself to the affairs of Portugal. I fear that the noise of the victory gained by this people over the Castilians may somewhat diminish the desire to help them or at any rate retard its effects, from the idea that they are quite strong enough and that there is no wish for them to be conquerors, but only good defenders of their country. Truly those who hear of this battle without understanding the humours and ways of the Portuguese might with reason conclude that the kingdom is saved after the happy success of this campaign, and yet I assure your Highness that it has as much need of help as ever and that the assistance cannot be too speedy or too effective, for this crown has been this spring in the greatest difficulties, not to say upon the verge of ruin, seeing that they might have lost the battle instead of winning it, and if so there would have been a general revolt and a blind following of the party of the conquerors. It may seem strange to you to hear me talk after such a fashion, but I beg you to consider that there is no question here of an enemy foreign in religion, manners or language, or who has done such injury to this nation as to make reconciliation impossible. When they meet they dispute the ground foot by foot and fight obstinately about the streams and passages of the smallest importance. But it is simply one part of a country rising up against the other, and is rather a civil than a foreign war. Both parties have the same religion, the same customs, the same language, and if there is any essential difference between them it is that in the slightest

adversity the weaker remembers that it was less burdened with
taxes under the stronger and, beneath their rule, enjoyed
many other advantages besides that of peace. This does not
appear much in the present state of affairs, but the people will
only remain faithful while fortune is doubtful, and if it once
declares for the first master nothing will stop its progress. And
this, which in other places would be called betraying their country
or taking sides with the stronger party, would pass here for the
action of people who voluntarily return to their duty, and, avoiding an evil, accept what is good. The riot in Lisbon after the taking of Evora is a good example, and if this is not enough, the various dealings of the principal ministers here with Spain and the
correspondence of many towns of this kingdom which have come
to light amongst Don Juan's papers, only confirm too much the
private views of these people. Triumphs and fanfaronades would
be no guarantee after the loss of a considerable town or the
winning [sic] of a battle, for the enemy knows better than they
do how to profit by such advantages. After the day of Cano [el
Canal] all one could obtain from the Portuguese was to retake
Evora, and although fortune offered them the best opportunity
in the world to retake Aronches,—having set fire to the powder,
razed the castle and killed or wounded twelve hundred men,—
yet they were so faint-hearted that they dared not attempt it,
and these same people, who, after the defeat of the Spaniards,
ought to have made three sieges at the same time, did not find
themselves, three weeks afterwards, in a position to take even
one place which was already half surrendered. If the Portuguese were certain of beating their enemies every year they
could not relax more than they are doing now, each one thinking only of resting after their victory rather than of taking
advantage of it, and preferring the pleasure of going home and
talking about it to that of profiting by it at the expense of the
enemy. At present there only remain in the body of the army
the few foreigners who are here, but it is to be hoped they are
enough to repair all the faults that are being committed. This,
however, they cannot do unless the King of England sends men
and your Highness endeavours to make a fund for their subsistence. When I remember what was given, when we were very short
of money, to our allies of Holland, Sweden, &c., to make a simple
diversion, which was often more profitable to themselves than
to us, it seems to me that there ought to be no difficulty in
granting this Crown eight or nine hundred thousand pounds
since, besides the expenses of the war and the results of the peace
with the Low Countries, they have to bear the costs of a marriage
for which the embassy alone cost them three hundred thousand
crowns. Moreover the assistance they demand need not be for
long, as it can be stopped at the first change of affairs in Spain,
and meanwhile we shall prevent a number of kingdoms, countries and towns in Africa, America and the Indies from falling,
for a second time under the power of the House of Austria. I
have already sent your Highness an account of the foreign troops
here, and if you think the King may agree to pay something you

cannot speak to him too soon about it. *French. Copy in letter book. 3 pp.*
Annexed,

1. *Letter from M. de Fremont to Mons. Hasset, London, requesting him to see Sir Richard Fanshaw and discuss with him the question of the succours designed for Portugal. French. Copy. ½ p.*
2. *Papers concerning the expenses of the foreign troops in Portugal. French. Copy. 4 pp.*

SIR RICHARD FANSHAW to the CONDE DE CASTELMELHOR.

1663 [July 22-]August 1—In the first place, I beg your Excellency to assist me to express my gratitude to the King for the great favour which he has shown me in sending to enquire after my health, an honour which would suffice to cure a much greater evil than that from which I was suffering. It was never so great as to prevent my seeking you at the palace if that had been necessary, but I had already represented everything clearly on paper, which I know by experience is enough for your Excellency without my interfering with other business by my visits, and also I knew that you could not discuss matters with much profit before the arrival of the frigate, which, as I hear from an officer sent by the Captain, is now just entering this port. *Spanish. Copy in letter book. ½ p.*

SIR RICHARD FANSHAW to the COMTE DE SCHONBERG.

1663 [July 24-]August 3. Lisbon—It is not in my power to alter the resolutions of Princes, but I endeavour that their brotherly intentions may be brought to execution and that things may not be depended upon which are not practicable. I desire as much as anybody the service of Portugal, but I cannot hope that the English will stay here and still less that recruits will come, without more certainty as regards money. Some very gallant officers here have expressed a fear that when our troops know that I am leaving the country, they will ask my leave to return to England also; but to this I have answered that "they came not hither because I was here, for I was then not here, why then should they quit because I went, especially since it was to serve them better." Moreover, not one of those who have gone asked my leave, knowing that I had no authority to give it.

Capt. Travers is here, ill of a fever, as is also his wife. I find him a very good man, and hear that he is also a very good officer. Those here extol and love him very much. *Copy in letter book. 2½ pp.*

SIR RICHARD FANSHAW to SQUIRE NORWOOD and MAJOR HOLMES, on board H.M.S. *Reserve.*

1663 [July 29-]August 8—"I presume you were yesterday so well satisfied with the message and re-invitation from this King

to you as well as to me, to see their bulls, that you will give the Court the opportunity to put themselves in countenance by seeing whatsoever was of negligence towards you the last day amended and repaired, in confidence whereof I request you to dine with me to-day somewhat the earlier, because I would have time to wait upon you, and who else you please to bring, till I see all placed, and then send my coach back for my family."
Copy in letter book. ⅓ *p.*

EARL OF INCHIQUIN to [SIR RICHARD FANSHAW].

1663, July 29. London—"I know you have an account of the heads of the charge brought in against my Lord Chancellor by my Lord of Bristol, which certainly had hurt only the latter and been laid aside had not the matter been kept in suspense by two accidents. The one was too early and too earnest expressions from his Majesty and the Duke, showing their desire and intention to punish my Lord of Bristol, and how severely was doubtful, and the other was the timorousness of my Lord Chancellor, who gave advantage to his adversary by consenting to the giving of time for the examination of the matter, which the House I believe would not have voted had it been put to the question, though some of the Lords were led to be for it by a subtilty of my Lord of Bristol's, who for that end named my Lord of Ormond and my Lord of Latterdale [Lauderdale] for two of his witnesses, the one being in Ireland and the other in Scotland. Thus it came to pass that the hearing of the matter should be remitted to the next session and witnesses examined in the meantime.

Since then the Houses were busy on the Subsidy Bill, which they have passed, and on two others, against Conventicles and Papists, which admitted of so much dispute as that neither of them have passed, only the speaker of the House of Commons has desired his Majesty would by proclamation cause the laws in force to be effectually put in execution against them, and so the Parliament was on the 27th prorogued till the 16th of March, and that night the King went to the Queen at Tunbridge, where he stayed till this morning, and now he is come back hither, where I believe he will be stayed by a bill that my Lord of Anglesey has brought from Ireland, whereby new ways are to be taken for the settlement of that kingdom, which cannot be effected by those already prescribed. Thus I believe the progress for this year will be laid aside, though all things be in a readiness for it.

We find that the King of France is marching his troops to a place in Lorraine, called Marsall, which that Duke has strongly garrisoned and victualled, and here we believe the war will again begin between the house of Austria and France. My son is cashiered in France and my pension there taken away by means of the Portuguese, who have employed Monsieur de Turenne to assure them of my intention to serve the Spaniard and draw my brother thither, for which indeed there was some colour, because I had some propositions from the Spaniard to invite me to it, but I protest to you that even those propositions had not a syllable in them tending to the prejudice of the Portuguese, Mollery [Moledi?], that was here, knowing well—without speaking to me—that there would be no hopes of getting me to consent to any such proposition. And I do protest to you again that I never had any capitulation with him of any sort whatsoever, all that ever passed being bare proposition. Yet I have suffered much by it in point of interest and reputation both, for though it had been free for me to deal with the Spaniards or any other, having then no obligation on me to the King of Portugal, yet people did not know but that I had still a command there and believed that I betrayed a trust. This is so much the more severe as that I protest before God I have endeavoured to serve the Portuguese with my credit and industry, and that I owe so much to the two Queens that my hands are tied up, if I had a mind or power to revenge myself." I am infinitely obliged for your goodness to my brother and myself. *Holograph.* 1¾ *pp.*

Consul Thomas Maynard to Sir Richard Fanshaw.

1663 [July 30-]August 9. Lisbon—"I was this forenoon at the palace, where as soon as the Condé de Castelmelhor saw me, he told me in a very high voice that I endeavoured to make a breach between the two crowns, and that Cromwell was dead, and that we had now a King in England, to whom he would give an account of my actions. I told him I did bless God we had a King in England, and did beseech the Lord to give him a long and prosperous reign, but what he meant by the other expressions I did not understand . . . to which he replied that your Excellency told him that I was the cause of the disgust that happened Monday last at the palace, by exasperating Colonel Norwood and Major Holmes against the Court, and I told your Excellency what then had happened to them in a worse sense than the nature of the business deserved." I understood it was your desire that this business should be forgotten and therefore was willing to pass by the affronts I received, and I made the best of it to the Conde and the Secretary of State, but if the two Kings are to be troubled in the business I must beg that his Majesty may know the whole truth, and if I declared the affront to those gentlemen in a worse sense than it deserved I shall beg no favour to shelter me from the censure of any man. I shall make bold to wait on you this afternoon, when Colonel Norwood and Major Holmes are with you to tell you themselves the truth of what happened, but meanwhile I have said nothing to them about the business. *Copy in letter book.* 1 *p.*

Sir Richard Fanshaw to Consul [Maynard].

1663 [July 30-]August 9. Lisbon—"In answer to yours of this day, I am sorry the matter of Monday last hath rankled so far when I wished and hoped it quite forgotten," but I can only say ".what you know already, namely, that you having acquainted me that these gentlemen were turned out of the palace in an affronting way, I declared to you and to his Majesty's officers there that I would not come again to the Bulls, or within the palace gates, but only to take leave of the King; which I would not nor durst have said, but upon supposition that they were turned out, not only not placed, or not well placed, which yet I should have taken very unkindly, but not so high." *Copy in letter book.* ½ *p.*

ALFONSO, KING OF PORTUGAL, to his sister, QUEEN CATHERINE.

1663, August [5-]15. Lisbon—I have enjoined Sir Richard Fanshaw, ambassador of the King my brother, who is returning to England, to assure you of the pleasure which it will give me to be of service to his Majesty and of my willingness to satisfy my obligations, for many reasons, and especially for the great love which he shows to his Queen, my sister and mistress. I confide so much in Sir Richard's judgment that I know he will acquit himself of this office as I desire, and I need not beg you to give him credit on my behalf. *Spanish. Copy.* ½ *p.*

ALFONSO, KING OF PORTUGAL, to the DUKE OF YORK.

1663, August [7-]17. Lisbon—Stating that he has desired Sir Richard Fanshaw—who is now returning to his own country, and whom he highly values for his many excellent qualities— to express his gratitude to his Royal Highness for the particular kindness which he has always shown towards the affairs of Portugal. *Latin. Copy.* ½ *p.*

ALFONSO, KING OF PORTUGAL, to LORD CHANCELLOR CLARENDON.

1663, August [7-]17. Lisbon—Expressing the satisfaction which Sir Richard Fanshaw, now returning to England, has given as ambassador to the Court of Portugal. *Latin. Copy.* ½ *p.*

SECRETARY ANTONIO DE SOUSA DE MACEDO.

1663, August [10-]20—Certifying that there has been paid to Sir Richard Fanshaw no more than 20,000 crusadoes of the Queen of England's portion. *Portuguese. Copy.* ¾ *p.*

SECRETARY ANTONIO DE SOUSA to SIR RICHARD FANSHAW.

1663, August [11-]21—Requesting him to come and speak to his Majesty at once, as news has arrived that the King of Spain is dead. *Portuguese. Signed.* ¼ *p.*

LIONEL FANSHAW to SIR RICHARD FANSHAW.

1663, September 6-16. Lisbon—Lord Teviot arrived here last Friday, and this morning I attended him to the palace, where he went to kiss the King's hand. After he had been with the King, the Conde de Castelmelhor and the Secretary of State discoursed with him and showed him drafts of fortifications whilst the Infante was at Mass, whose hands he likewise went to kiss. He tells me he had a pass to go through Spain, "but by reason of some late unhandsome actions of the Spaniards would not make use thereof, but sent it back to the Duke de Medina Torres." 1¾ *pp.*

SIR RICHARD FANSHAW to SIR HENRY BENNETT, Secretary of State.

1663, September 20. London—I received your Honour's from Bath last Tuesday night at Cirencester, in my way to Cornbury, which I made my way to London. My warrant, mentioned as enclosed, was left out. I pray you to send it by the next, and I will enquire for it at Mr. Williamson's. The enclosures for my Lord Chancellor and Dr. Fell I have delivered, the one into his Lordship's own hands, the other—in absence of the Dean—to Dr. Allestree, at the Dean's lodgings. *Seal of arms.* ½ *p.*

KING OF SPAIN to the DUKE OF MEDINA CELI, at St. Mary Port.

1663 [September 22-]October 2. Madrid—Authorizing him to take into his service and pay the engineer, Martin Bechtman, who lately served in the fort of Tangier, and offers to assist "*en la reputacion d'esta plaça a mi corona*," but desiring him to commit himself to nothing further, until they hear from Gaylan, and determine what is to be done in the matter. *Endorsed as being a true copy. Spanish.* ¾ *p.*

LIONEL FANSHAW to SIR RICHARD FANSHAW.

1663, [September 25-]October 5. Lisbon—An old French minister has arrived from London, who was formerly chaplain to the Comte de Schomberg, and since that to the Earl of Teviot at Dunkirk. Now he has come to tender his service to the Comte de Schomberg again. "On Tuesday last save one, Monsieur Fremont desired my permission that the aforesaid minister might the next day preach to himself and others in your Lordship's house, and likewise preach and administer the sacrament of the Lord's Supper there upon the Sunday following; telling me that the Conde de Castelmelhor said it would be most convenient for them to be there, where Protestant sermons used to be; wherefore, presuming that if your Lordship had been here they would not have had your denial, they had not mine."

The Marques de Liche lately tried to escape in woman's clothes, but was discovered, some say by those who had promised to help him.

A Mr. Haddock from London has brought news of your arrival there, but in so short a time that I could not credit it. The Consul tells me that he hears from Whitehall that you will certainly shortly return here. 2 *pp.*

Sir Richard Fanshaw to Charles II.

1663 [September?]—"If my yesterday's papers—as I humbly hope they did—have satisfied your Majesty that my above twelfth instruction is a good license for my personal resort at this time to your royal presence, I may almost presume that these now will qualify it a command," as they import an earnest request from the King of Portugal that your Majesty will appoint me to negotiate an accommodation between Spain and Portugal in your name and by your mediation, that King "throwing himself entirely upon your Majesty's counsels, after that he hath prospered to so great a degree by your arms," and courting you "alone in his mended condition who courted him in his desertion, his deserter at the same time courting him passionately under the shape of assistance." If your Majesty embraces this overture and accepts my services therein, I pray that my payments may be as large and punctual as the weight of the negotiations require, "since if I am not well paid I am ruined, whereas if I am, I am not enriched, being obliged, for your Majesty's honour and service, to live up to it. And to live splendidly in a remote country, whilst I am representing my master, can only serve me—without God's mercy—to endanger me to a habit or expectation of spending beyond a slender estate another day, creating in me a vanity just enough, but which will no more feed me hereafter than I have done that hitherto; my present fortune in the meantime lying fallow and neglected, and my domestic relations perhaps either dying away or forgetting me, or at least the present comfort of them—and above all, that of your Majesty's presence—denied me." And finally I pray to be allowed to address summary accounts of my transactions direct to your royal person, at the same time that I shall constantly remit larger despatches to your ministers. *Draft.* 4 *pp.*

Prewritten.—Copy of the 12th article of Fanshaw's Instructions, giving him permission to repair to the King's presence if weighty emergencies arise. ½ *p.*

Enclosing,

1. *The King of Portugal to Charles II.*

1663, *August* 15. *Lisbon—Regretting that the state of affairs in his kingdom does not permit him to send the rest of his sister's portion, praising the talents and prudence of Sir Richard Fanshaw, and praying that he may be employed to negotiate a peace with Spain, his Britannic Majesty being the mediator therein. Spanish. Copy.* 1¼ *pp.*

2. *The King of Portugal to Queen Catherine.*

1663, *August* 15. *Lisbon—To the same effect as the preceding, praying her to intercede with her husband that Fanshaw may be sent ambassador to Spain to conduct the negotiations, he having all necessary qualifications—zeal, prudence, fidelity, and an intimate knowledge of the affairs of those kingdoms. Spanish. Copy. ⅔ p.*

SIR HENRY BENNETT to SIR RICHARD FANSHAW.

1663, October 22. Kirkhouse—"My Lord Dongan was with me this day, and is preparing to go to Spain through France, and afterwards into Andalusia, and because I thought no man could more properly than he bespeak you either a house or other things fit for you, I put you in mind of it, that either by himself or others, to whom he may speak in my name, many things may be provided you before you come. In fine, 'tis an occasion you may make very good use of." [*In Williamson's writing, signed by Bennett.*]

Margin.—Copy of Fanshaw's letter of thanks in reply. 1 *p.*

The KING OF SPAIN to FRANCISCO SALMON, Accountant of the Navy, &c.

1663 [October 26-]November 5. Madrid—Giving orders that he is to allow the hundred and twenty-eight negro slaves on board the English ship *Charles*—master, William Crawford— to be brought into Cadiz and there sold; the proceeds to be deposited in the hands of the said Francisco Salmon, who is to take care that no other contraband goods are brought in with them. *Spanish. Copy.* 1¼ *pp.*

SIR RICHARD FANSHAW to SIR HENRY BENNETT.

1663, November 12—"Finding you already in business within the Council chamber, when I thought to have moved you this morning touching a blank left by my Lord Treasurer for his Majesty to fill up in the warrant prepared for my privy seal," I presume to represent to you that I understood that my entertainment was to "look back" thirty days, in imitation of Sir Arthur Hopton's warrant. The extracts from the Signet Office show several others which look further back, viz.:—Sir H. Wotton, ambassador to the Emperor, in 1620; Sir John Digby, for Spain, in 1622, and Sir Fras. Cottington in 1629; also Sir Thomas Rowe, for Germany, in 1641; not to speak of Lord Holles the other day. His Majesty, however, "appearing unsatisfied that any such thing at all should be done at this time and in my case, hastening also to others that attended" before I could explain the matter to him, I beg you to represent my case to him, which is that some of my family are yet in Lisbon, and that, being nominated to another and larger embassy, I have not only kept together my servants, but have added more, so that I humbly hope that by your mediation my warrant may look back to the said time, which was the 12th of September last. *Draft. 2 pp.*

SIR RICHARD FANSHAW to SIR HENRY BENNETT.

1663, November 22—Memorandum recommending his secretary, Lionel Fanshaw, to be Secretary of the Embassy at Lisbon, the said Lionel Fanshaw having been in this service two years and a half, and proved himself trustworthy therein. With note that according to "the signet extracts of former times, lately collected by my Lord Treasurer's command, Mr. Dickenson there had in two several embassies 40s. per diem to each as secretary of the embassy, even when there was table and house of an ambassador present to ease his expense." *Draft. 2 pp.*

EARL OF MANCHESTER to EDWARD, EARL OF SANDWICH, Master of the Wardrobe.

1663, December 2—Warrant for delivery of "one crimson damask estate, with his Majesty's arms and badges embroidered thereon, with a chair of estate" and other things, for the use of Sir Richard Fanshaw, Lord Ambassador for his Majesty to the King of Spain. *Copy. ½ p.*

The SAME to the SAME.

1663, December 2—Warrant to provide and deliver for the use of Sir Richard Fanshaw, "one large Bible of Imperial paper, with all the sculps, bound richly in two volumes, two Common Prayer books in folio, six in quarto, twenty ells of fine diaper for the Communion table, and ten ells of fine diaper for towels for the Communion." *Copy. ⅓ p.*

The SAME to SIR GILBERT TALBOT, Master of the Jewel House.

1663, December 2—Warrant for delivery to Sir Richard Fanshaw of four thousand four hundred and twenty ounces of silver plate, for his service as ambassador. *Copy. ⅓ p.*

MASTER and FELLOWS OF JESUS COLLEGE, Cambridge, to SIR RICHARD FANSHAW.

1663, December 10—Reciting the evils which had afflicted them in the late troublous times, when the detestable zeal of furious men had invaded their chapel and banished the liturgy, the same fate presently befalling the furniture of the Lord's table, hangings, wind-organ, sacred books, pavement, windows and all things which did not please the profane taste of their new masters; lamenting that when, to their great joy, orders were given that the liturgy should be resumed, they found to their sorrow that their buildings were in no fit state to receive so pleasing a guest, and appealing to Sir Richard's generosity to help them. Dated, " *Quarto idibus* Dec." *Latin. Seal with the College arms.* 1 *p.*

LORD TREASURER SOUTHAMPTON to the FARMERS OF THE CUSTOM HOUSE.

1663, December 28—Requesting them to have 1,000*l.* ready for Sir Richard Fanshaw, as soon as he shall have struck his tally, that there may be no delay caused to his journey. *Copy.* 1 *p.*

PRINCE MAURICE.

1663—"Relations concerning his Highness Prince Maurice," 1662, 1663 :—

" The information of Margaret Hazard of Gosport, near Portsmouth, who by her letter of the 4th of January, 1661, to her husband, Captain Robert Hazard, then in London, and since by another letter of the 8th of January, 1661, writ that one Thomas Masters of Godshill in the Isle of Wight told her—Richard Bushell and his wife being present—that he came from the Caraccas in the West Indies, where he saw Joshua Clarke—a person that was in the same ship with his highness Prince Maurice—and left him well there, which Joshua Clarke informed him that their ship was wrecked, and that he with two more were saved on an island in the West Indies, and how the Spaniards coming thither to water took them prisoners and carried them to the Caraccas, where an English surgeon, taking good liking to this Clarke, preserved him.

This Thomas Masters was since brought to Mr. Coventry to give him relation concerning this business, who told him that he was twice with this Joshua Clarke after his escape in the West Indies, and that he told him the ship which Prince Maurice was in was wrecked on the Virgin's Islands, and that on a piece of the wreck he with two others were saved, and afterwards were taken by the Spaniards as above related, where he is still a prisoner."

" The information of Robert Gildersleeve of Ipswich, who, with four more, were taken prisoners in the West Indies by the Spaniards and carried to Havanna in Cuba, where in the same prison he found six Frenchmen prisoners, who had made an escape from Porta Rica [Porto Rico], and afterwards were retaken and brought thither. These Frenchmen told him that when they were prisoners in Porta Rica they heard one make moan in a room next to them, which occasioned them to use means by a cleft or hole in the wall to discover who it was, who speaking very good English and French, and by his relation of being wrecked and cast upon an island in the West Indies and brought thither prisoner by the Spaniards, and other circumstances, they believed him to be some person of quality."

" Captain Fearns relates that one Powell, a prisoner at Havanna, taken at the same time with the aforesaid Robert Gildersleeve by the Spaniard, informed Mr. Benisfield, then Governor of St. Christofers, in the presence of this Fearns, that those Frenchmen before mentioned by Gildersleeve told him that they spoke to Prince Maurice, who was in a dungeon next wall to them where they were imprisoned in Porta Rica, and that the Prince desired them to make known his sad condition to his friends by the first opportunity that some means might be used for his release."

" A relation of John Couper, Englishman born, saith that in the year 1655 and in the month of June was at the island called Birque [Bieque], otherwise Crab Island, and was there fishing for *tortuga* [turtle], and was there surprised in our boat by a Spanish barque, and was carried to the town of St. John the [de?] Porta Rica, and was there examined very strictly if you know of any English frigates about the coast, we declared all that we knew not of any shipping upon the coast, but being examined what countrymen we were it was found that I was an Englishman. There was eight persons of us, and all Dutch but myself and a boy; the boy was examined and threatened, and out of fear told the Governor that I knew what shipping was upon the coast, whereupon I was taken and put upon the rack and threatened to be racked if I would not confess the truth. I told them they might do their pleasure, where upon better consideration took me off the rack and put me into the dungeon, and when I was there one quarter of an hour after they were gone there was one spoke to me in the dungeon in Dutch and asked me what I was. I told him I was an Englishman. I saw nobody, being dark, but at last we come to one another and took me by the hand, asked me whence I came. I told him in Dutch, then he declared to me in English that he was cast away on this coast in a hurricane and brought to the town, and when the Governor examined me and I told him I was cast away in one of the ships that belonged to Prince Rupert and five men more were saved, he asked where they were. I told the Governor the people in the country that took us carried them away, and that I had not seen them since, the rest told the people that I was Commander of the ship, so they took me away from the rest, yet I desired them when I was saved that they would not tell what I was, but there is no trust in man. I shall desire you to keep in mind what I say, and if the Governor should examine you not to confess anything, but when you get liberty pray if it be your fortune to meet with any that has any Spaniards prisoners to tell them my condition, for I am of English parentage, and it may be I may be released. Presently after this relation came people to take me out, so that I could not have any more conference with him, but bid me remember what he said to me; he sighed, and so the guard of soldiers carried me away to the Governor, and there examined again upon the former business, and cleared me and the rest, and I was told the next day that the

Governor was angry with the Adjutant for carrying me into the dungeon, it seems that it was a mistake of the Adjutant. This Malato [? mulatto] speaks good Dutch and English. We kept at this Malato's house fourteen days, and then had liberty to come away. I have related this to several people, but nobody took any notice of it; this I declare as truth, being aboard the *Briar* frigate of the King's, May the 28th, 1663, and at anchor under St. Peter's Island and against Tortolea [Tortola], as witness my hand."

Witnesses—

RICHARD HADDOCK.   *Signed by mark,*
THO. WHITEHEAD.   JOHN COUPER.

"The relation of Captain Anthony Dee Pee of the city of Nantes in Brittany saith that twelve months since he, being master of the pink called the *Turtugo* (*sic*), belonging to the Governor of the Island of Turtugo [Tortuga], saith that he took some prisoners on the south side of Cuba, in the port called Porto Prince, and one of these prisoners, being a white man, a Spaniard born, I examined all the prisoners upon several things, but this Spaniard gave me a particular relation of Prince Maurice, that it was the general report at the city of the Havanna that Prince Maurice was a prisoner at Porta Rica in the castle called the More. In testimony to which has been related to me by this aforesaid Spaniard, I have thereunto set my hand this 13th of June, 1663, in the island of Turtugo."

Witnesses—

RICHARD HADDOCK.   *Signed by mark.*
THOMAS ROW.   ANTHONY DEE PEE.
THO. WHITEHEAD.

"Captain William Pride and Thomas Row, being in the Governor's house of the Island of Tortuga, and hearing the Governor examine some people concerning his highness Prince Maurice there, being then there in company a Spaniard, which Spaniard heard one give a relation to the Governor that Prince Maurice was dead, the Spaniard shook his head and made answer that Prince Maurice to his knowledge was living five years ago, and a prisoner in the castle of Porta Rica, and the said Spaniard belongeth to Porta Rica, and was taken prisoner. We whose names are hereunder written were ear witnesses to what we do declare." June 15th, 1663.

Witnesses—

NICHOLAS GARNER.   WM. PRIDE.
THO. WHITEHEAD.   THOMAS ROW.

"Extract out of Captain Henry Fern's journal, March 13th, 1662."

"Captain Ferns, being becalmed under the Island Domanico, [Dominica?], spoke with a Frenchman, who had been at sea with his highness Prince Rupert under the command of Captain Coavans in the *Honest Seaman*, came out of Toulon in her, was in her when she was cast away

on the north side of Hispaniola, and has been in the West
Indies ever since. Concerning Prince Maurice he told him
that he had heard several people say that his highness was
cast away on the Island of St. German's, and that he was a
prisoner at Porta Rica, that he knew the Frenchmen that were
prisoners at Porta Rica when his highness was there, and heard
them speak of his highness being prisoner, and that he believed
one of them was then in the Island of Turtugeo, that he was
at the taking of St. Ageo, a league on the north side of Hispaniola
three and a half years since, where there were two Irishmen.
One of them knew that he belonged to the *Honest Seaman*,
and in discourse of their former voyage told him that he wondered his highness Prince Rupert would not get his brother
Prince Maurice out of prison at Porta Rica, for there he was
kept close in the castle called the More. This Frenchman, whose
name was Conge, asked him how he knew it. The Irishman
told him that it was generally reported at St. Domingo by the
chiefest of the Spaniards that Prince Rupert's brother was
a prisoner at Porta Rica, and how Don Whan Morfoue
[Col. Murphy ?], an Irishman in great esteem with the
Spaniards, who wore the habit of St. Ageo and is
Captain of the fort of St. Jeronymo at St. Domingo,
told this Conge several times that if he could tell how to
convey a letter to Prince Rupert he would, to inform him
what condition his brother was in. Once the Irishman told this
Conge that Don Whan Morfue said that if he knew where to
find Prince Rupert he would send him with a letter, but about
that time Don Whan Morfue and the President of St. Domingo
had a falling out, so that the design was laid aside.

25 March, 1663.—Captain Ferns, being at St. Christophers, the
Governor there told him how several persons, French and Dutch,
reported that in the castle called the More at Porta Rica had
been a gentleman prisoner a long time, and the most of them
said that he was a German, and this he has been told by several
French gentlemen.

Abraham Abrahamson told the Governor of St. Christophers
and Captain Ferns that about eighteen months past he was at
Porta Rica, and then there was but one prisoner in the castle
called the More, and as he understood by a moletta [*mulatto ? see
above*], one that kept a tavern where he lodged, and had lived at
Stashous with the Hollanders, that there was a gentleman in
prison in the More, how the soldiers told him he was a German
and had been long a prisoner before this man came to dwell
at Porta Rica.

April 12.—At Tortolea the Deputy-Governor told Captain
Ferns that there was a gentleman, a German, in prison at Porta
Rica in the castle called the More, and kept there a long time
close prisoner. He was at Porta Rica about ten months since.

April 30.—At the Virgins came to the harbour a French
sloop with ten men, who had been at Hispaniola; they were
bound for St. Christopher's. The master and most of the company assured Captain Ferns that a great English ship lay

wrecked seven leagues to the eastwards of Porta Rica. Matte Jacous, one of them, told him that he was at Porta Rica three years since a prisoner, there were then eight prisoners, three French and three English [*sic*], who had run away with a boat from Barbadoes and put in at Porta Rica. The Governor sent them aboard of a Spanish barque and of a great Dutch sloop, and came to anchor by the wreck. When they returned to Porta Rica he heard the Spaniards say it was a ship of Prince Rupert's, that they had taken out of her forty guns besides other things. The master told him that he had heard the Spaniards say it was a ship of Prince Rupert's fleet. This master had been trading with the Spaniards on the south side of St. German's, and heard the people of the village of Quama say that one of Prince Rupert's ships was cast away on their coast of St. German.

May 19.—Being at St. Christopher's, Frederick. Gorer, master of a sloop, who had been several times at Porta Rica, told him that there he heard the people say that one of Prince Rupert's ships was cast away on the coast, but the men were all drowned. Captain Ferns replied that it was strange all should be drowned, seeing the wreck lay above water two years. He answered perhaps some might come ashore, but none were brought to town. The Couckelers [cowkillers] were cruel and would kill them, for the King of Spain commands all to be slain that come upon the coast. And asking of him if he had seen anything that was saved of the wreck, he answered that he saw English guns and several other things driven ashore in the bay.

June 14.—Captain Ferns went ashore to the Governor of Tartugeo, who had with him a Spaniard, prisoner, an inhabitant of Porta Rica twelve years; has been five years from thence, left his wife and two children there; he said Prince Maurice was cast away on the north side of St. German's, and six leagues to windward of Porta Rica. When he came from Porta Rica his highness was a prisoner in the castle, the More; there were none suffered to see or speak to him. This was talked privately amongst the people. He heard of none brought to the town besides. The Governor sent several boats to the wreck, and brought away many things, ropes, a great anchor, a mast laid by his house. He heard the people say those things were brought from the Prince's ship." 4 *pp.*

Annexed,

1. "A Spaniard of Porta Rica, who was taken at Port de la Plata in the Island of Hispaniola in the year 1660, after having been forced to show the road from the town of St. Iago in the said island, was accused of having massacred the illustrious Prince Maurice. He denied it, but said that in 1652 a great nobleman, having lost his vessel near Porta Rica, came on to the island with his crew, who were all massacred, with the exception of the Lord, who was put in the prison of the Inquisition by order of the Governor, he forbidding his being called Prince, and not wishing him to be known.

2. La Brose, a filibuster, being prisoner on the island of Porta Rica in the years 1656 and 1657, said that the common

report was that there was a great Lord in prison, who had lost his ship, and that it was Prince Maurice.

3. A French sailor, whose barque traded to Porta Rica, pointing out a woman, whose husband was in the Inquisition at Porta Rica, said that there was a much greater Lord than he in that same prison." *French.* 1¼ *pp.*

SIR RICHARD FANSHAW to ARCHBISHOP BOYLE OF DUBLIN.

[1663 ?]—" Your Lordship's 15th of the last I received, in which I read your Lordship's affection to me so very great as that must needs be which blinds so clear a judgment as yours in the choice of an office for me, not that I think it incongruous or disproportionable either to step from the present employment I have the honour to hold of Master of Requests to Lord Chancellor of Ireland, or to hold them both together, since as to the first, in a time of so great regularity as that of Queen Elizabeth, Sir Christopher Hatton was removed from Captain of the Guard to Lord Chancellor of England, and as to the second [*left blank*] Lord Chancellor of Ireland, by her Majesty's special favour and dispensation made Master of Requests here, which, together with the warrant for it, appears upon regard [*sic*]. Neither do I find in myself any doubt at all of my integrity, in which opinion, without vanity, I can fully concur both with [your] Lordship and the many in that kingdom, for whom your Lordship does me the honour to undertake that they conceive it of me. So that, if I had science equal to conscience, and then eloquence proportionable to both, I should get the victory so much over my natural and customary backwardness, as, upon this hint from your Lordship, to stand candidate for the place. But really, my Lord, I find the former and the [*torn*] of those necessary requisites so very defective in me that, not to lose wholly the benefit of this intimation, I must beg of your Lordship to cast timely about how upon the vacancy some fitter person may be removed [to] that office, who quitting a lesser, yet of good importance too, and which may admit of more non-residence, especially when his Majesty's service even in reference to the advantages of Ireland may require it, I, by the favour of his Majesty and of my Lord Lieutenant, may be accommodated and richly satisfied with his leaving.

In order hereunto I remit unto your Lordship herewith a letter or warrant, which I had from his Majesty upon my departure for Portugal, to be sworn a councillor in Ireland, and at the same time my Lord Lieutenant will remember how graciously and seriously, in the Privy Garden at Hampton Court, his Majesty did recommend me to his Grace, to build upon that foundation such a structure as I am now speaking of, whether in lands or office within the gift of the crown there." *Draft.* 1¾ *pp.*

THOMAS MARSDEN * to SIR RICHARD FANSHAW.

1664, January [4-]14. Lisbon—It has been no small ingredi-

---

* *See* Alumni Oxonienses, Early Series, p. 972.

ent in the comfort of my life that heaven gave me the opportunity of being employed as one of your servants, for nowhere could I have met with " so fair a complication of wisdom and candour as is eminently conspicuous in your Lordship, which perfections do not stand in need of my trumpet when both our King and Court proclaim them so loudly. . . . I know likewise that your readiness to do good is far greater than your desire to hear yourself called a benefactor. I shall therefore be silent both as to the one and the other, not doubting but your Lordship will remember that the seat of gratitude is the heart, not the tongue, and that the most genuine characters it can be writ in are mutes, not vowels." In pursuance of your instructions I have given what time I could spare from other studies to the Spanish tongue, and if I fail in what you wish, "it is for want of parts, not industry, and to prove such errors venial, I need but to quote that worn maxim *ultra posse non est esse.* . . . Mr. Fanshaw's society is sweet to me. I could wish my sullen temper was capable of requiting him. The frequent remembrance of your Lordship, my honourable lady, with my hopeful young ladies, cheers us up exceedingly." This is a copy of one which I sent to London, but which I believe never came to your hands. 1 *p.*

CHARLES II. to PHILIP IV., King of Spain.

1663-4, January 13—Letter of credence for Sir Richard Fanshaw. *Draft.* 1 *p.*

SIR HENRY BENNETT to DON JUAN OF AUSTRIA.

[1664], January 19th—Expressing the esteem which he himself and the King, his master, have for his Highness, and recommending Sir Richard Fanshaw, now sent as Ambassador to Madrid. *French. Copy.* 1 *p.*

SIR HENRY BENNETT to the DUKE D'AVEIRO.

[1664], January 19th—Announcing that Sir Richard Fanshaw is sent by the King, his master, to arrange terms of peace between Spain and Portugal, and hoping that he may be well received and assisted in his endeavours. *French. Copy.* 1 *p.*

SISTER MARIA DE LA CRUZ to SIR RICHARD FANSHAW.

1664, February [2-]12—As your Excellency's secretary has received orders to set out for Castile, I profit by the opportunity to send the enclosed (*missing*), knowing that it will run none of the perils which have, for long, compelled me to silence, and also to offer the assurance of my affection to yourself and to the Ambassadress, whom I love with all my heart, not forgetting my precious Margaret—to whom I send this little carriage—and your other daughters. I hope that when convenient I may have a reply to this paper, sent with all necessary caution. I greatly long to see your Excellency here once again, and pray God so to dispose affairs, as to give us all the happiness

which we desire. *Spanish.* ¾ *p.* *Endorsed by L. Fanshaw:*—
"From the Lady Abbess at Alcantra, near Lisbon, Donna Maria
de Guzman, dated 12 February, 1664, s.n."

CONDE DE CASTELMELHOR to SIR RICHARD FANSHAW.

1664, February [3-]13. Salvaterra de Magos—I have now received, all at the same time, five letters from your Excellency
written last year, for which I offer you my hearty thanks. The
news of the improvement in your Queen's health has given as
much pleasure in this Court as in England. You do me a favour
by touching on the business of the Marques de Liche and Dom
Annello de Gusman, as having spoken to the King, my master,
I can tell you what you may say to your King. Time will not
permit me to go fully into the matter, but I can assure you of
the pleasure it will give my master to accede to his brother's
wishes if he can. Taking this for granted, and believing that
my master will arrange the business if possible, your Excellency
will realize and represent to your King that this is the fruit
which Portugal derives from the battle in which she risked so
much, hoping to gain from it a space of breathing-time. It is
the holding of these gentlemen which encourages the people of
these kingdoms in carrying on the war, and in their hopes of
making peace. *Portuguese. Signed.* 2 *pp. Endorsed by Fanshaw :*—"Rec. March 13, stylo novo, by J. Price."

The SAME to the SAME.

1664 [February 23-]March 4. Lisbon—I thank you for your
letter written in London, with a postscript from Portsmouth,
and for the information concerning your instructions. I hope
you will meet with all success. As regards the liberation of
the Marques de Liche and Dom Annello de Gusman and the
mediation which his Britannic Majesty wishes to make on their
behalf, if it be not against the interests of the King, my master,
I have to say that the matter is already under consideration,
and I assure your Excellency that, if I succeed in it, the chief
cause will be my desire to please the King of Great Britain,
but I beg to repeat what I said in my letter of February 13th,
written in Salvaterra, that upon the fact of keeping these gentlemen here the Portuguese found their great hopes for the success
of the war, thus holding such pledges as may, lead to peace, from
the desire which the Spaniards must feel for their liberation.
I again pray your Excellency to be good enough to tell me
how we can communicate with safety, as I desire to tell you
the court news with all the sincerity which I can, and must
hope for from yourself. *Portuguese. Signed.* 1¾ *pp.*

DON ANTONIO DE SOUSA DE MACEDO to SIR RICHARD FANSHAW.

1664 [February 24-]March 5. Lisbon—I have received your
letter, written in London on November 28, and another from
Portsmouth of the 31st of January, and was much pleased to
hear good news of you and yours.

The announcement that you are going as ambassador to Castile consoles us a little for your loss here, as we believe that you will be of great service to the common welfare, undeceiving his Catholic Majesty by giving good testimony of our union, strength and constancy. The successes of our arms have, thanks be to God, been happily continued since you left us. In the business of the gentlemen concerning whose liberty you wrote, we would do much to give pleasure to his Britannic Majesty and to be serviceable to yourself, but you will understand that many things have to be taken into consideration in the matter. It will give me great pleasure if I can be the means of arranging it to your satisfaction. *Portuguese.* 1¼ *pp.*

Consul Thomas Maynard to Sir Richard Fanshaw.

1664 [February 24-]March 5. Lisbon—It was very welcome news to our ministers that your Excellency had passed by for Spain, and the hopes of the whole nation are that you will bring about a treaty with that Crown, "which hath been more wished than hoped for, for many years together. All endeavours are tried here to have a considerable army in the province of Alentejo next campaign, and . . . the Conde de Castelmelhor hopes to have two thousand English and French well mounted, which they now begin to be sensible that they will do them as much service as twice that number of their own nation." Our English have grown extremely thin through sickness but are in good heart, having been lately indifferently well paid. "Monsieur Schomberg was lately disgusted because his articles were not kept, and had some thoughts of quitting the service, or at least he made show of his going away, but now things are accommodated." Our Brazil fleet has sailed, and two ships will shortly be ready to depart for Goa. "The Conde Duque and Don Anello de Guzman have entreated me to beseech your Excellency to intercede for them that they may have their liberty, but I seemed strange in the business," and will go no further until I have your commands. My wife sends her humble duty to your Excellency, your lady and the young ladies. 1½ *pp.*

M. de Fremont to Sir Richard Fanshaw.

1664 [February 24-]March 5. Lisbon—If your Excellency had remembered that I understand a little Castilian, you might easily have let me hear from you, but I thank you much for honouring me with a word from your hand. I have already congratulated you upon your embassy to Spain, and I pray God that we may have cause to meet upon the frontiers and help to bring about a good agreement. I know that it is vanity on my part to imagine that I may be employed in so important a matter, but your Excellency's glory will be so great that I may well appropriate a little of it without robbing you. *French. Signed.*

COMTE DE SCHONBERG to SIR RICHARD FANSHAW.

1664 [February 24-]March 5.   Lisbon—I thank you for letting me hear from you, and wish you a happy arrival and all prosperity in your negotiations, knowing well that you will do all in your power to give to this kingdom the peace which I desire, although I am a soldier.   I wish we could have met, that I might have heard your news of the King and given you mine concerning those in this country.   I pray you to command me in all things, and to believe that I have no greater desire than to continue in your good graces.   *French.*   1 *p.*   *This and the five preceding letters all received together, by J. Price.*

LIONEL FANSHAW to SIR RICHARD FANSHAW.

1664 [February 26-]March 7.   Seville—On Sunday, February 10th, *stilo novo*, there arrived at Lisbon the frigate *Advice*, commanded by Captain William Poole, who told me he believed you were then at sea.   The next day I received your letter, commanding me to attend you in Spain, and so thought it best to go in Captain Poole's frigate.   I went two or three times to the Secretary, Antonio de Sousa de Macedo, hoping to get a letter from him to you, but could obtain nothing but empty compliments.   The King and the Conde de Castelmelhor were both at Almeyrin, and I had not time to go to them.   I also wrote to the chaplain of the Lady Abbess at Alcantra, asking him to tell her that I should wait on her the next afternoon, which I did, and received letters from her for you and for her father.   On Thursday, the 4th-14th, we set sail, I having then received by Consul Maynard a letter from the Marques de Liche to the Duke de Medina Celi, and from Don Anello Gusman to his father, the Duke of Medina de las Torres.   On the Saturday following we met the *Antelope* and the *Hector*, who by Lord Teviot's orders were seeking some Algiers men-of-war. Next morning I landed at Cadiz, and went to Consul Westcombe's house.   In the afternoon the Governor honoured me "with a visit, and many courteous expressions therein, which I repaid the next day save one."   On the 1st inst., this style, I began my journey for Seville, and in my way delivered the Marques de Liche's letter to the Duke de Medina Celi, who took it very kindly, and offered me letters to the chief persons in Seville, or any other assistance he could do me.   I thanked him, and told him I should not need to give him that trouble, having your Lordship's pass, but that should I meet with any molestation I would presume to beg his assistance. At St. Lucar the Governor sent word that "he intended me a visit, which I endeavoured to prevent by waiting on him; but meeting him in the way he caused his coach to stop while he came out to salute me." On the 4th inst., this style, I came to Mr. Andrew Duncan's in this city, where I have offers of the greatest kindness imaginable from all the chief merchants.   I have sent off the letter to the Duke of Medina de las Torres.   I am told of a set of good mules to be sold here, but have not yet seen them. March 8, *stilo novo*. This morning we have news of your Lordship's arrival, for which God be praised. 4½ *pp.*

NEWS LETTER.

[1664], February 1 to March 16—Sent [by Williamson] to Sir Richard Fanshaw.

"Monday, February 1st, the Earl of Bristol put his plea into his Majesty's Court of Exchequer, grounded upon a certificate under the hand of the minister and some persons of credit in Wimbleton, certifying that on Sunday fortnight he attended the whole divine service at his parish church, and demeaned himself in all things conformable to the Church of England.

January 31st his Majesty was at the Lord Chancellor's, holding conference about the disposing the estates of the late traitors in Yorkshire, and ordered that they should be distributed amongst such persons as had been most instrumental in the discovery, and, that this should be a lasting precedent for the better discovering of all treasons, for the future the discoverer should have a recompense out of the estate of the convicted traitor.

Edinburgh, January 26th.—An order is sent down for an High Commission Court in Scotland, wherein either of the Archbishops is president. His Majesty's letter to the Council, concerning the Archbishop's primacy and having the place in Scotland, was read and approved, so that now he hath the precedence of the Chancellor in all places and entries.

There have lately been orders given out concerning some prisoners in the Tower. Major Salway is discharged his imprisonment, Mr. [Col. Henry] Nevill hath obtained liberty to go beyond sea, giving security not to return into England nor to remove to any part besides what first he goes to without leave from his Majesty. [Edward] Bagshaw, having some seditious papers found about him, was put in the dungeon February 4th.

Monday, February 8th, in the evening the Duchess of York gave a great entertainment with comedy and ball at St. James's to their Majesties and all the ladies about town, as a respect to Mrs. Blagge, one of her maids of honour, married last week to Sir Thomas Yerbury, a person of very good quality and fortune.

Bantam, September 18th.—The Dutch have sent twenty sail of ships, pretending for Twyann,* though their design is upon an island 'twixt Twyann and China. The Dutch have had twenty-five sail arrived from Holland this year, have as many on the coast of India and Zeilam [Ceylon], at least forty sail more to the eastward, and thirty-two riding in Batavia Road. They declare they will never deliver Poleron to the English, call themselves masters of the South Sea coast from Malabar to Cape Commaroon [Comorin], upon pain of loss of ships and lives of all such as shall trade thither.

---

* Formosa—called Toyan or Taiouan in old maps.

Mr. Bagshaw, Saturday, February 6th, was removed out of the dungeon, but is still kept close prisoner in the Tower.

Friday, February 12.—A motion was made on the behalf of the Earl of Bristol at the Exchequer bar. His plea was only upon a bare averment—for it was not thought safe since his Majesty's proclamation to appear [by] certificate—and the Court ordered that he should give security for payment of 220*l*.—at the rate of 20*l*. per month—and so proceedings to be stopped, unless the Attorney General should show cause.

[Capt. Robert] Atkinson—the great engineer in the late troubles in Yorkshire—was brought up by two justices of Westmoreland, and by insinuation of further discovery prevailed to so much liberty as to make an escape.

At the Common Pleas an action was brought by the Marquess of Dorchester against —— Probe, Esquire, upon a *Scandalum Magnatum*, for saying my Lord is no more to be regarded than that dog that lay by him, for which the jury gave his Lordship 1,000 marks.

Monday, February 15.—The Earl of Elgin's child was christened, the Archbishop of Canterbury godfather; the Duchesses of York and Somerset godmothers.

The same day Major Miller, sometimes deputy to [John] Baxter in the Tower, was sent prisoner to Windsor Castle.

The Council, Wednesday, 17th, sent the minister of Wimbleton [Thos. Luckin] and three of the Earl of Bristol's servants prisoners to the Gatehouse, for not obeying his Majesty's proclamation in discovering him, and have given orders to send for the churchwardens and constable of the parish to appear before them.

A Frenchman, having been observed several times to have returned this last summer to Hull and to have viewed too nearly the works of the place, was by Colonel Gilby, the Deputy-Governor, last week secured till he produce a good account of his business. He is said to be the person that fortified the French fortifications in Dunkirk, 1658.

Saturday, February 20th.—Twynne, the printer, had his trial at the Old Bailey for printing a treasonable pamphlet, and received his sentence to be drawn, hanged and quartered.

Sir Richard Everard was before the Council for seizing several Popish books and trinkets, but dismissed with thanks.

Monday, February 22nd.—[Simon] Dover, [Thos.] Brewster and [Nathan] Brooks were arraigned for publishing seditious libels. They were ordered to the pillory, and one fined 100, the others 40 marks apiece, and then not to be set at liberty till his Majesty's further pleasure be known concerning them.

The *Greyhound* and *Concord*, two very rich ships, which were much feared, are both escaped the hands of the pirates, and come up the river in safety, the former valued at the Custom House at 150,000*l*.

Edinburgh, February 17th.—This day his Majesty's letter was read concerning the fines, and proclamation is to be made on Thursday next, ordering the first moiety of the fines to be paid in at Martinmas next.

The Earl of Bristol's plea was accepted in the Exchequer, it being found by several precedents in that Court that hand and seal were sufficient evidence for conformity, though the Bishop had not declared it, which as to that was the only point then depending.

Wednesday, February 24th.—The Earl of Bristol's servants were upon their petition discharged by the Council from their imprisonment. The constable and churchwardens, giving notice of their attendance, were ordered to be released from the messenger's custody without payment of fees, but the minister of Wimbleton remains still prisoner in the Gatehouse.

Saturday, February 27th.—Twynne, the printer's head, was set upon Ludgate. He said upon the ladder that he forgave all men, that his judgment was just, and had he had such an example he should never have been betrayed into that treason.

At the assizes at Southwark three were pressed to death for refusing to plead, of the others only·six condemned, and not above two to suffer.

Monday, February 29th.—The Lord Chancellor went to take the air, being the first day he had gone out for fourteen weeks. On Tuesday, March 1st, he found himself in some distemper, which yet is not such—since the taking away of some blood— as is thought will confine him any long time to his chamber.

By letters November 20th from the Earl of Carlisle, his Majesty's Ambassador Extraordinary to the Emperor of Russia, dated at Vologda, we find his Excellency received with very extraordinary honour, and such as the Emperor is not used to give to any Prince's minister. The winter was so backward that his Excellency was forced to expect at Vologda till the frosts were harder ere he could reach Moscow, whence it is supposed he returns this March.

Hull, March 5th.—On Sunday last a party of horse of Doncaster troop went to secure a runegado—son of a sequestrator from York—upon the late plot. They found him at his brother's house, four miles beyond Doncaster, who submitted himself prisoner, but his brother, who—'tis like—by this means feared a further discovery, ran out with a fork, thrust the horse into the breast, and had made further mischief if the commander of the party had not given him a shot, of which he is since dead.

By a vessel arrived from Guinea the Royal Company find a very good account of the improvement of their trade; that in one very [sic] place, Cormantine, there will be a ready debit of 100,000l. for ready gold, but they evidently discover that the Dutch will leave no stone unturned to discourage and ruin that trade. The company had, when this vessel came off, three ships of force to secure their trade there, and by this time five or six more are there.

Edinburgh, 4th.—The High Commission Court is set in Scotland; have appointed several sub-committees, in each of which a Bishop is to be of the quorum, and to give an account to the High Court the 14th of next month at Glasgow. The Lord Lauderdale is Governor of Edinburgh Castle, in place of the Earl of Middleton, hath possession delivered to one deputed for him, and appointed a new Deputy-Governor.

The Lord Hollis had his audience Thursday 10th at St. Germains, with very great honour, being brought from Paris by the Mareschal de Clerembault, and after usual compliments passed to him that night, which was Wednesday, by persons of honour, in the name of the King, the two Queens, Monsieur and Madame, the next day he was conducted to audience by Comte d'Armagnac, a Prince of the house of Lorraine, the Prince d'Harcour, his father, being absent from Court. The King received his compliment with particular kindness, it being made in English by his master's order, as the ambassador expressly owned to the King, and interpreted by a gentleman of the Ambassador's.

Wednesday, 16th.—The Parliament met according to the prorogation, where Mr. Secretary Morrice delivered a message from his Majesty to this effect, viz.:—That his Majesty did passionately desire to see his House of Parliament, and thought the time long till he did meet them, but he did hear that there were several members upon the road who would be here in a few days, and that his Majesty had occasions which did at present somewhat impede his coming to meet his Houses of Parliament, upon which the House adjourned till Monday morning eight o'clock.

The same day search was made by Serjeants-at-Arms, assisted with some of the guards, at the several houses of the Earl of Bristol, but they could not find him." 6¼ *pp.*

Lord Holles to Sir Richard Fanshaw.

1664, March 26-April 5—Describing his reception at the French Court. *Extract.* [*Printed in Original letters of Sir Richard Fanshaw, p.* 51, *ed.* 1702.]

Lord Chancellor Clarendon to the Duke of Medina de las Torres.

1664, March 27. London—Assuring him of the earnest desire of the King, his master, for the alliance and friendship of Spain, and recommending Sir Richard Fanshaw, now sent as ambassador to his Catholic Majesty, a man of the greatest fidelity and singular prudence, experienced in affairs, well acquainted with the Spanish Court, and a particular friend of his own. *Latin. Copy.* 1¾ *pp.*

LORD CHANCELLOR CLARENDON to the DUKE OF MEDINA DE LAS TORRES.

1664, March 27. London—Recommending Sir Benjamin Wright, who hopes by assistance of his Excellency to despatch his important financial business at the Court of Madrid, and stating that if he obtains the justice which he desires, it will be very pleasing to the King of Great Britain, who has often earnestly recommended the matter to his Catholic Majesty. *Latin. Copy.* 1¼ *pp.*

SIR JOHN LAWSON to SIR RICHARD FANSHAW.

1664, March 28. On board H.M.S. *Resolution* in Algiers Bay—We have a war with Algiers. They are more perfidious every day, and the most treacherous people in this part of the world. We have got eighteen English ships from them, "but till it please God they feel some smart, no peace can be made with them but what is worse than war." My humble service to your lady and the young ladies and gentlemen. 1 *p.*

EARL OF TEVIOT to CONSUL WESTCOMBE, at Cadiz.

1664, April 15-25. Tangier—Thanking him for sending letters and news books, which is a charity to those who see nothing but Moors and the four elements ; describing a repulse of the Moors ; stating that, although they are short of lime, they will either get it from Portugal or make it themselves, as "a gallant man never wanted arms," and expressing his conviction that in two years, Tangier, unless given away or sold, will be a very comfortable place and pleasant too. *Copy in Westcombe's writing.* 1 *p.* [*Another copy, by Lionel Fanshaw, is amongst the Tangiers Correspondence, and is quoted by Colonel Davis in his History of the 2nd, Queen's Royal Regiment, Vol. 1, p.* 60.]

NEWS LETTER.

1664, April 21—Sent [by Williamson] to Sir Richard Fanshaw.

The Bishop of Carlisle being removed to the Archbishopric of York, Dr. Rainbow is appointed to succeed in Carlisle.

Monday, April 18—The House of Commons gave leave for a Bill to be brought in for appointing a register for sale of lands in every county,. read a Bill for the better making of brick and tile and a Bill for preventing merchants cheating their creditors, and committed the Bills for regulating the law for settling lands gained from the sea, and for preventing fraudulent conveyances.

The same morning the Jews at the Exchange offered four for an hundred to insure no war to be with the Dutch in three months,* and order is given at the office to that purpose.

* *See* Pepys' Diary, under date,

In the afternoon her Majesty went to take a divertisement on horseback, her habit thus, a scarlet coat, richly laced and trimmed with sky-coloured ribbon, a falling band, and on that a carnet [carcanet?], with an hat heaped [*sic*] with sky-coloured ribbon, which I tell not so much to discover the novelty of the fashion as to assure you that all were generally taken with it, who, though they ever admire her Majesty, yet did commend this dress as that which did more particularly with better grace present her perfections.

Tuesday, 19.—The House of Commons read a Bill for physicians, a Bill for making the river navigable from Bristol to London, and a third for regulating elections of members to serve in Parliament, and then adjourned into a grand committee for hearth money.

The same day at the Committee appointed to consider of the trade of the nations, it was resolved *nemine contradicente* that several and respective wrongs, dishonours and indignities done to his Majesty by the subjects of the United Provinces by invading of his rights in India, Africa and elsewhere, and the damages, affronts and injuries done by them to our merchants be reported to the House as the greatest obstructions of our foreign trade, and that it is the opinion of this Committee that the said respective dishonours, indignities and grievances be humbly and speedily presented to his Majesty, and that he be most humbly moved to take some speedy and effectual course for the redress thereof and all other of the like nature, &c., for prevention of the like in the future.

Hague, April 15.—Since the news of his Majesty's order concerning Zealand they have resolved to send a civil letter to his Majesty, and the East India Company have sent in their list of damages. A ship from the New Netherland says that the English have taken possession by the South river and forced out the Hollanders.

Complaints are made at Ratisbon that the King of France infringes upon the liberty and jurisdiction of Alsace, there being ten towns that pretend to be free. However, upon their refusal to take the oath of fidelity to him, it is discoursed the forces designed for Germany will be ordered in their way under Duke Mazarin to besiege Colmaer.

Several reports run of an engagement betwixt the English and Dutch upon the coasts of Guinea, some to our advantage but the most to the Dutch, as if they had beaten our ships, and by false insinuations to the inhabitants gained them on their side, and took our fort. The truth of it is so [*sic*] much feared by such as have had experience of their former treachery, and know them still of that principle to use all base means whatsoever to hinder us of a trade that is so eminently profitable to the kingdom.

Wednesday, 20th.—The House of Commons read a Bill for the physicians, ordered the Bill for hearth money to be engrossed, and agreed to the amendments made by the Lords in the Bill tor preventing the disturbance of seamen and preserving his Majesty's stores.

Upon Mr. Clifford's report from the Committee of Trade, and reading their order, the House agreed *nemine contradicente* to the whole words in the order, *mutatis mutandis*, with this addition, that in prosecution thereof they will with their lives and fortunes assist his Majesty against all impositions whatsoever. They further resolved to desire the concurrence of the Lords, and a conference to be held with them concerning it.

Paris, 15th.—The French King hath given order for demolishing the churches belonging to the Protestants in Languedoc, built—as is pretended—contrary to the Edict of Nantes; and that Mr. de Lionne's clerk, who gave copies to [*sic*] the papers of State to foreign ministers, was hanged. 4 *pp.*

JOSEPH WILLIAMSON to SIR RICHARD FANSHAW.

1664, April 28—"Though I am conscious how little worth the postage this sheet is, yet at the distance, and in the agitation of so weighty a matter—of a war with Holland—I hope it may quit costs to inform your Excellency a little. In fine. the Dutch really apprehend it, and I know not how far that may bring them to do what will prevent it. In the meantime we expect to hear what is done between us in Guinea, something material no question, and we hope the best. This day a smart Bill passed the Commons against Sectaries."

Postscript.—"Comte de Konigsberg is here yet, well feasted, but what answer he will have I know not. Others are concerned to put to their hands first." ½ *p.*

On the same sheet,

NEWS LETTER.

[1664], Friday, April 22—The Bill for confirming his Majesty's Charter to the Physicians was committed with provisoes on the behalf of the surgeons and apothecaries, as also the Bill against unlawful meetings. The same day the report was made to the House of Lords, concerning the damages by the Dutch, viz. :—Upon ships and goods belonging to the East India Company, 148,000*l.*; for burning and spoiling their factories, 87,000*l.*; to the particular traders to the coasts of Africa, 330,000*l.*; to the Turkey Company, 110,500*l.*; to the Portugal merchants, 160,000*l.*; and besides, four millions for Poleron. The Lords, after some debate, agreed fully to the Commons, and sent two judges on the message, desiring them that a message might be sent to his Majesty to know what time he would be pleased to appoint that both Houses might wait upon him to acquaint him with their humble resolution in that case, but just as the judges came to the stairs of the House, the Commons were adjourned till Tuesday, 26th, which when the Lords heard they also adjourned till the same day.

At the High Commission Court in Scotland, April 14th, one Hamilton, near Glasgow, and Francis Galway, two great remonstrators, for non-conforming and not attending the Church, both denying to take the oath of supremacy, were adjudged to lose the fourth of their estates, each of them being 100*l.* per annum, and the collector appointed to levy it. Tallidafe, a minister, and Semple, a scrivener, committed to tue Tolbooth; the cause this: Mr. James Wood, a minister of St. Andrew's, being then upon his death bed the Archbishop visited him, and having received good satisfaction from him as to the episcopal government gave an account of it to others. Tallidafe and Carstairs, hearing of it, never left the dying man till they forced from him a contrary declaration, writ by Semple, and witnessed by them two, giving out withal the Archbishop's relation as a forgery. Carstairs, late minister at Glasgow, not appearing, is to be criminally prosecuted.

The House of Commons, April 26th, ordered the Bill for securing English ships against pirates to be engrossed, passed the Bill for better collecting of hearth money, and agreed to the vote of the Lords in attending his Majesty in a full body concerning the Dutch, &c., when he shall please to appoint.

Edinburgh, April 18th.—The High Commission Court sat again, and after admonition took bail of the scrivener and witness to the forced declaration of Mr. Wood to appear upon summons, and ordered the declaration to be burnt by the hand of the common hangman of St. Andrew's. Upon complaints of several ministers that they, notwithstanding they were lately turned out, did still baptize, preach, &c., it was ordered that any who should presume so for the future should be immediately sent to the Tolbooth at Edinburgh or Glasgow. Several others were ordered to appear before them the first Tuesday of June next, till which time they adjourned.

That likewise those of Argier have by message assured the Earl of Teviot that although many seizures have been made of English ships, yet the ships and goods are all preserved by the Government, and shall be all restored and the men all set at liberty, and what shall be found wanting shall be satisfied for by those that made the seizure.

From Tangier by a fresh packet we have news that besides the late advantages in repulsing Gaylan, those of Tituan have sent to offer to enter into a free trade, &c., with the town of Tangier, and in case Gaylan shall oppose it, then to shake off his obedience and give themselves into the protection of Tangier.

Hague, April 22nd.—Vangoch, having received his commission, is preparing for his embassy to England. Spain doth not yet give leave to Holland to unload any goods there. Trump is come home, but de Ruyter not yet gone, by reason of the alarms from England. The States of Zealand have ordered the libels against the Duke of York to be publicly disowned by proclamation, and affixing them in all their towns, and the authors of the libels and those which posted them up to be tried at Middleburgh.

Wednesday, April 27th.—The House of Commons read an Act concerning the Customs, and referred it to a committee to regulate the fees that the merchants may receive no injury. A petition was read of Colonel Man and officers on behalf of themselves and soldiers in Scotland under the command of Major-General Morgan, which was referred to a committee. In the afternoon both Houses, in a full body, attended his Majesty in the banqueting-house with their vote concerning the Dutch, to which his Majesty promised he would send answer in writing.

Thursday, April 28th.—The Commons read a Bill for making navigable some rivers in Cornwall, an additional Bill concerning Corporations, and passed the Bill against conventicles, entitled, "An Act to prevent and suppress seditious conventicles." In this Act five above the family make a conventicle. 3 *pp.*

VISCOUNT DONGAN to SIR RICHARD FANSHAW.

1664, May [1-]11. Xeres de la Frontera—Welcoming him to the Court of Spain, sending greetings to himself, his wife and daughters, in which he is joined by his wife, Donna Maria, and begging to be of any possible service to him during his stay in the country. *Spanish.* 2 *pp.*

DONNA MARIA EUFEMIA DONGAN to ISABEL [*sic*] LADY FANSHAW.

1664, May [1-]11. Xeres—To the same effect as the preceding. *Spanish.* 1½ *pp.*

COLONEL SIR TOBIAS BRIDGE to SIR RICHARD FANSHAW.

1664, May 8. Tangier *—Announcing the calamity that has befallen the garrison in the loss of the Earl of Teviot, with other officers and soldiers. *Endorsed by Fanshaw as* "enclosed in one from Mr. Wilson, dated at Malaga 19th of the same. Both to me. Received at Ballecas on the 15-25th May." [*Printed in Original letters of Sir Richard Fanshaw, p.* 99, *ed.* 1702.]

ENGLISH PRISONERS in Seville to SIR RICHARD FANSHAW.

1664, May [14-?]24. Prison in Seville—"The joyful news of your Honour's safe arrival at Madrid [*sic*] doth very much revive our drooping spirits, hoping the time will not be long before we enjoy our long expected freedom from miserable captivity." The Council here have taken our examinations and sent them to Madrid. They threaten us very hard, especially our commander, who was pressed into the service by Captain Minnes, and has never acted beyond his commission. ¾ *p.*

---

* The officers at Tangier date old style. Lord Teviot was killed 3-13 May.

SIR RICHARD FANSHAW to the DUKE OF MEDINA DE LAS TORRES.

1664, May [14-]24. Ballecas—Hearing that your Highness had cause for anxiety the other night, I send the bearer of this— Mr. Lionel Fanshaw, my secretary,—to enquire after your health, and also to place in your hands—more quickly than I could do myself—a letter which I have received for your Highness from the Lord Chancellor of England. *Spanish. Draft.* ½ *p.* [*The answer to this is amongst the published letters, p.* 86.]

VISCOUNT DONGAN to SIR RICHARD FANSHAW.

1664, May [18-]28. Xeres—Recommending the bearer, Don Juan Lopes de Espinola. *Signed.* 1 *p.* [*Referred to in the published letter of June 1st, p.* 102.]

COLONEL TOBIAS BRIDGE to SIR RICHARD FANSHAW.

1664, May 20. Tangier—Mine of the 8th acquainted your Excellency with the sad disaster which had befallen this garrison, but understanding from Cadiz that the report of our loss makes it much greater than it is, I send you a true account of it. Besides our noble Governor and nineteen commission officers we lost sixteen gentlemen and reformadoes and three hundred and ninety-six private soldiers; but the garrison being still pretty considerable I do not doubt but that we shall be able to give his Majesty a good account of its safety. Our lines and fortifications are so far from being rased—as the report goes in Spain—that we are still in possession of all we ever had and are actively proceeding with them. 1 *p.*

CONSUL MAYNARD to SIR RICHARD FANSHAW.

1664 [May 23-]June 2. Lisbon—The King of Portugal's ministers are still averse to compliance with the articles of peace, and I am remitting the particulars to my Lord Chancellor, hoping that the King will constrain them to a more punctual observance of the treaty. As regards the islands of the Azores and Madeira, the Condé de Castelmelhor and the Secretary of State tell me that you have promised to say no more about them until our King replies to their request to have that article mitigated. Meanwhile the merchants there "continue under an intolerable burden, and are like to continue so without your Excellency's favour to mind my Lord Chancellor to signify the King's pleasure touching that article to this Court." Our armies have been ready to meet the Spaniard at least twenty days, but now we hear that the enemy will not invade us this year, so this campaign is likely to be only offensive. The King of Portugal has twenty thousand foot and six thousand horse in Alenteixo, which cost a vast sum to bring together, and they certainly will not disperse without some action against the enemy's garrisons.

Three hundred and thirty English soldiers have arrived here, and four hundred more are expected, the King of Portugal's minister in London and Lieut.-Colonel Belasyse having promised that they shall be better paid than formerly. But I see no improvement in this respect, they being already six months in arrears " and like to be more, insomuch I have some apprehensions there will be a great disorder amongst them." About a thousand French have arrived, conducted by the Count de Marea, and with them came Mons. Carleton, *alias* Colbert, but he is to return to France immediately. Our trade is extremely obstructed by the piracies of the Galicia men-of-war, and we much hope that your Excellency will do all in your power to put a stop to their proceedings. I desire my duty to my lady and the young ladies. Sir Thomas da Crux left the world about three months since. 2 *pp.*

Viscount Dongan to Sir Richard Fanshaw.

1664 [May 26-]June 5. Xeres—Recommending the bearer, Captain John Frederisco Velosques, a German, who is anxious to obtain a licence from the Spanish Court to go to his own country. 2 *pp.*

T. Goddard to Sir Andrew [King].

1664 [May 31-]June 10th—The Duke asked me whether his Excellency was come to town and whether he was contented with the house, as also when he had resolved to have audience of the King, to which I answered that I knew nothing of his intentions. I next went to Don Domingo, who will come to see his Excellency to-morrow evening.

"This afternoon I did particularly note the manner of the curtains that I might the better answer my lady another time, and also informed myself of Don Domingo. The curtains for the doors must be either of taffeta or damask; those for the windows must be of an indifferent good linen, and in this manner is the palace fitted, having linen curtains within and without for the windows and silk for the doors. If it be not too much trouble, you may please to acquaint my lady with this." [*Margin, in Fanshaw's hand*:—"Manner of summer furnishing in the palace, &c., of Madrid."]

Endorsed by Fanshaw:—"The Duque de Medina de las Torres having upon the 10th of June, 1664, sent for Mr. Goddard to come and speak with him, this letter of the same contains his Excellency's queries to the said Mr. Goddard, so far as they related to me.—Ric. F. My coming into Madrid was the 8th of the same."

Sir John Lawson to Sir Richard Fanshaw.

1664, June 1st. H.M.S. *Resolution,* Alicante Road—Having heard the sad news from Tangier, by a letter from Sir Tobias Bridge, I am going thither at once with the whole squadron. There is a rumour of a war with the Dutch, but Mr. Coventry writes me " all is fair yet, but doubtful. . . . Those of Algiers are yet stubborn, but if we be not otherwise diverted I hope ere six months goes about they will seek peace." My humble service to your right honourable lady and the young ladies. *Signed.* 1 *p.*

Ceremonies of the SPANISH COURT.

1664, June [5-]15—Memorandum by Sir Richard Fanshaw that on this day Don Pedro de Roco, Master of the Ceremonies, was with him, the substance of whose discourse was as follows, viz.:—That the ambassadors of the first class nowhere treat the public ministers *de señoria illustrissima.*

That the upper hand or chair they will not give them in their own houses, but would unto such as have the character of ambassador for their own masters, though not reputing them ambassadors so called.

"That my audience being on Wednesday, and Thursday a day of some other solemnity in the palace, likewise their Majesties on Friday to remove to the *Buen Retiro,* those three days once past he conceived my wife might obtain leave to kiss her Majesty's hand upon short notice whensoever she requested it."

In passing towards the door he asked me whether I had notified the day of my audience to the ambassadors here, "in order to their sending their families to make part of my *accompaña-mente.*" I answered that if I had fully expected this function from them—as for anything yet passed I do if it has been the custom, the supposition to the contrary being only this Master of the Ceremonies' advice—I yet should not have advertised them my exact day, for I did "hold it not decent to ask in direct terms a customary courtesy as a positive due." *Copy.* 1½ *pp.*

[*This interview is alluded to by Sir Richard in his account of his reception. See Spanish Correspondence, June 8-18, 1664.*]

WILLIAM BLUNDEN to SIR RICHARD FANSHAW.

1664, June 6-16. Alicante—Stating that Sir John Lawson left that road on the 12th instant with his fleet, and the next day met Admiral de Ruyter, "who struck his flag and saluted Sir John with all demonstrations of friendship, and was answered with the like in point of salute, but not in the flag." 1½ *pp.*

CONSUL SAMUEL TRAVERS to SIR RICHARD FANSHAW.

1664, June [10-?]20. Pontevedra—Complaining of the depredations of rovers and pirates of Spain upon English ships bound or pretended to be bound for Portugal, and also of the unjust proceedings of the judges and *cursitos* with regard to the same. 5 *pp.*

SIR HENRY BENNETT to SIR RICHARD FANSHAW.

1664, June 13—Six pages of cipher, undeciphered, headed: "This is a duplicate of that part of Mr. Secretary's letters in cipher to your Excellency of April 8th, May 12th and June 2nd, now put into Mr. Coventry's cipher, and in case your Excellency finds your last cipher erroneous or too difficult and that the old one you had in Portugal will decipher the enclosed note, your Excellency may be pleased to make use of the said cipher until an occasion offers of sending you a better."

[The cipher does not agree with the only key to W. Coventry's ciphers in the collection at the Public Record Office, although it is constructed something on the same plan. When worked out, the extracts here proved to be all contained in the letters of the above three dates in the printed collection.]

COLONEL ROGER ALSOPP to SIR RICHARD FANSHAW.

1664, June 13. Tanger—I should have sent you an account of the occurrences here had there not been a kind of prohibition, "lest, by scribbling, things might be falsely represented." I understand that you wish to know what officers of fidelity yet remain here. "To that I have only this to say, that the officers now remaining are very obedient to command and observant to their duty. Of old officers there is Col. Sir Tobias Bridge, Major Fairborne, Captain Mordent, Lieut.-Colonel Molloy, Captain Danell, Captain Carr, and about twelve lieutenants and ensigns. The officers slain in the conflict was his Excellency the Earl of Teviot, Major Knightley, Major Fitzgerald, Captain Langton, Captain Rudyard, Captain Brookes, Captain Boulger, with five lieutenants, seven ensigns, and sixteen gentlemen and reformadoes, yet notwithstanding our great loss, through the incomparable prudence and conduct of his Excellency, as the Moors themselves confess since, we lost our lives at a very dear rate to Guyland's army, for we killed above two for one, which I believe hath caused the enemy ever since to be very cautious of his attempts. Upon the occasion of our going thither I do not so well understand as to give your Excellency a particular account of it, but my Lord of Teviot, being a person of so active a spirit and having nothing to do in the fortifications for want of lime, he had, as I understand, long before designed to cut down or burn the brushwood on the other side of the Jues [Jew's] river, that he thereby might the more clearly see the parties coming down from the hill to the ambuscades. But I am afraid the business was not well timed, for on that day two years before Guyland obtained so great a victory over this garrison by cutting off near four hundred men of the best soldiers and officers that was then in the place, and it is said that Guyland observes the day wherein he doth anything remarkable. My Lord of Teviot also observed the day of month wherein Guyland obtained that victory, and to that end drew out a party of near five hundred soldiers, with the best officers in the two regiments. I should myself have added my poor life, that signifies little, but that I was then sick in my bed, and had been so for above three weeks before, yet notwithstanding, when the alarum bell rang, I made a shift to get out, and crept up to the Fort Royal, which I found exceedingly badly manned, but some soldiers upon the alarum being got together, and there not being anyone to command them, I took upon me to command that place, not knowing how the business might go with my Lord and the party abroad. Things, as you may believe, were then very much distracted, but I made it my business with all expedition to settle and compose all things, so that in a trice we began to think of the worst, and consider of the best way how we might defend our spacious lines and rugged fortifications, which were then very far from being defensive, and to that end, I being myself altogether unable by reason of sickness to take upon me the government of this place, Sir Tobias Bridge, Sir Bernard de Gunne [Gomme], the King's engineer general, who was then here, and myself considered of a way how this place might be absolved and kept for his Majesty's interest and service, and immediately convened the commissioned officers then remaining to make choice of one to command us in chief. My own ability caused me to decline the command of the place, though of due it fell to me. Colonel Bridge being well and an active man I made it my desire to him before the whole council of war that he would for the preservation of this place accept of the government until his Majesty's pleasure should be further known, to which the officers then assembled gave their consent by reason of my sickness, and truly we have no reason to repent our election, for Sir Tobias hath been ever since exceedingly active and stirring, and leaves no stone unturned whereby he may advance or preserve his Majesty's interest." We have raised a fort with lime and stone, which Lord Teviot before his death had named Fort Ann, and have also made a very pretty earth fort. Another small stone redoubt will be finished to-morrow, and Fort Royal has been put into such a condition that I believe we may defy Guyland and all his Moors. "In truth we are as poor as may be, for excepting the provisions in the King's stores we have scarce an officer in the garrison that is able to buy himself a good dinner, but courage and fidelity is ever most known and set forth in the greatest want." All hands are at work, and the horse of the garrison, contrary to anything I have seen elsewhere, "after they have made their discoveries," willingly bring us lime for our work. "Notwithstanding our great watching, working and poverty we are knit together, so as I may be bold to say it must be a more knowing enemy than Guyland, through the providence of God, can break us." I am glad that war with Holland has not yet broken out, and hope it may be delayed until we are more prepared for it, although "those peoples are so insolent if they have the least power that I could heartily wish that his Majesty of England might be the rod to humble them." *Copy.* 4 *pp.*

Endorsed :—" Copy of a letter from Col. Roger Allsopp . . sent to Mr. Sec. Bennett 9 July." *The letter is not now in either the Tangiers or the Spanish Correspondence, although in his despatch of that date Fanshaw writes to Bennett :* " *The enclosed from Tangier I take to be both a very true and a very judicious relation of the state of that place." See Foreign Correspondence, Spain, July 9, 1664.*

ENGLISH PRISONERS in Seville to LORD AMBASSADOR RICHARD
FANSHAW, Madrid.

1664, June [13-]23—Stating that they had hoped long ago to
hear the joyful news of their enlargement from the miserable
captivity which has now lasted twelve months, and praying his
Excellency to pardon their importunity, they fearing that the
weightiness of his affairs may cause him to be oblivious of them,
although they have little reason to suspect it, having so lately
received a signal token of his tender affection and care towards
his countrymen in distress. ½ p.

COLONEL TOBIAS BRIDGE to RICHARD LORD FANSHAW.

1664, June 14. Tanger—Notwithstanding our great loss
we still daily face the Moors, and have not lost an inch of
ground nor a single man since the Earl's death. I am every
day expecting Sir John Lawson and his fleet. "If God in his
providence have designed honour and advantage to our King
and nation by this place, it is now left to his care to maintain
it by very weak instruments indeed" until his Majesty shall
provide better ones. "The Countess of Teviot arrived here the
3rd instant full of hopes and joy, but now most disconsolate."
Colonel Alsoppe is in good health, and will write to you himself.
Postscript.—June 20. For want of conveyance this letter
has not been sent. Sir John Lawson and his fleet came into
the road last night, and has honoured us with his company a
great part of this day, whose counsel we readily hearken to and
comply with. I have secured Mr. James Wilson, a merchant
in this place, he being charged by Captain Poole, commander
of one of his Majesty's ships, with reviling the late Earl of
Teviot, and being "otherwise very factious and seditious." 1½
pp. Seal with crest.
Endorsed :—"Received at Madrid 8-18 July." [*Compare
Bridge's letter to Col. Fitzgerald, in Foreign Correspondence,
Spain, July 21-31.*]

SIR JOHN LAWSON to SIR RICHARD FANSHAW.

1664, June 14. H.M.S. *Resolution* in Malaga Road—Requesting him to obtain the King of Spain's orders that the ships
of his Britannic Majesty may have the freedom of the ports
for careening, and especially desiring an order to the Governor
of Gibraltar, that being a more convenient place than Cadiz.
1 p.
Endorsed :—"Received at Madrid 3-13 July."

ENGLISH PRISONERS in Seville to LADY FANSHAW.

1664 [June 28-]July 8. Prison in Seville—Her favour to
them being fresh in their memory, they beg her to remember
her promise and use her influence for their release. ¾ p.
Endorsed as received in Madrid July 8-18.

LIONEL FANSHAW to [the SECRETARY OF STATE?].

1664, July [5-]15—My master the Ambassador, having seen this memorial [*see below*], said it was a great distress to him that any servant should be dissatisfied in his house, and that he should be much annoyed if, on the one hand, his major domo did not punctually pay the petitioners what was agreed upon, but that, on the other hand, he considered four reales a day, besides two suits of livery a year, sufficient remuneration for them. He therefore ordered his major domo—on completing the payments for the current week—to dismiss the petitioners, and begs that your Excellency's chamberlain will procure him others in their place not exceeding the same number. *Spanish. Draft by Fanshaw.* 1 *p.*

Overleaf,

Petition of the FOUR SPANISH PAGES to SIR RICHARD FANSHAW.

[No date]—Stating that the four reales a day allowed them merely cover their daily board, and that they are not able to provide themselves with other things—such as white stuffs, gloves, ruffles, stockings, &c.—which they need to appear with the splendour and neatness requisite in the servants of so great a Prince, and praying for an increase of wages. *Spanish. Copy.* ½ *p.*

SIR TOBIAS BRIDGE to SIR RICHARD FANSHAW.

1664, July 9. Tanger—Stating that he has received a letter pretending to come from the Saint Abdala of Sally, and that as it came unsealed and seemed to have been broken open, he has detained the Moor who brought it; also that there are skirmishes with the Moors almost every morning, but that only one man of the garrison has been wounded. 1 *p.*

With note on the cover by Consul Westcombe that this letter came to his hands at Cadiz on Wednesday [13-]23 July.

SIR RICHARD FANSHAW to SIR JOHN LAWSON.

1664, July 12-22. Madrid—"Ever since I parted from you I have had my eye, and at this time have—more or less—my hand upon every particular you hinted to me" concerning our fleet, the garrison of Tangier and the West Indies, "of all and every of which, if you expect a speedy account, you know not Spain, and if you suspect I will give you none at all—because hitherto I have not—you know not me." As to the accommodation of the fleet, I hope despatches, if not sent already, will go by this post, and that "the good disposition which the Duke of Medina Celi hath ever exprest in words will render further orders—otherwise than from himself—in those points unnecessary. By the last from England his Majesty and all the Royal Family—God be praised—were in perfect health. Whether war or peace with Holland, for aught appears to me, as then uncertain, so as no reason for any abroad to build upon either." Young Sir Edward Turner has had a dangerous fever, but is now perfectly recovered. He and I and all mine send our service to you. *Copy.* 1½ *pp.*

SIR JOHN LAWSON to SIR RICHARD FANSHAW.

1664, July 24. H.M.S. *Resolution,* in the Bay of Cadiz—I have received a letter of yours from the Consul at Cadiz, by which I rejoice to understand that your Excellency and your noble family are in good health, and that Sir Edward Turner is so well recovered from his fever. I hear only dubious reports of the rumoured war with the Dutch. Tanger is now in a good condition, Colonel Fitzjerrald, Deputy-Governor, having arrived, and most of the recruits. Common bruit gives me to understand that the Spaniards are not the quickest people in the world, but methinks that the Council might by this time have sent orders to two or three of the ports to allow the King of Great Britain's ships to have the free use of them. "I have only desired liberty for Port Mayon and Gibralter's new Mole. For the former, though we had fair promises, yet we were little better used than on the Barbarian coast, for we could obtain no pratique at Mayorke, Alicant, nor none of those ports," although the Dutch fleet was allowed it. "The Duke of Medina Celi hath given many fair words, but few good deeds," and I believe he was never a greater enemy to Tanger than now. 1¾ *pp.*
Endorsed :—"Received at Madrid 5-15 August."

CONSUL THOMAS MAYNARD to SIR RICHARD FANSHAW.

1664 [July 29-]August 8. Lisboa—"I have, in obedience to your Excellency's command, advertised you of all passages in this place. This year hath been hugely propitious to this Crown, which I wish may not make our ministers forget that the fortune of war is changeable. Our countrymen have added to the reputation they got last year in the field, which cost them dear at Valensa, where they had foul play, for the two English regiments of foot had order to storm at a breach which was made in the wall, and the *terzo* [regiment] *da Armada* were to fall on upon the right hand of the English and a French regiment, and a regiment of Portuguese upon the left hand, and in another part of the town the regiment of Casquais was to storm. So about nine o'clock at night, the 9-19 June, the sign was given, and the English, according to their orders, ran directly to the breach, but not a man besides them stirred out of their quarters but one Portuguese captain, who was so gallant to say, it is a shame to see the English fight and we to stand looking on, but before he could get to the breach he was slain with a musket shot. The English fought it out above half an hour, to the admiration of all those that stood and looked on, in which short time were slain Lieutenant-Colonel Hunt, Major Wetmore, Captain Travers, Captain William More, Captain Noland, Captain Fitzpatrick, two lieutenants, three ensigns, nine serjeants, and one hundred and fifty-eight common soldiers; and wounded Captain Stansby, Captain Hill, Captain Turner, Captain Roch, Captain Landy, Captain Baxter, Captain Maynard, my brother, and many others; very few came off without wounds, besides two hundred common soldiers. Colonel Person, who got abundance of honour by his gallantry that day, received two shots in his body, but having good arms they did him little harm, and notwithstanding all this good service and expense of their blood the Court endeavour to bring them to new conditions; first, by delaying to pay their arrears according to promise, being indebted to the soldiers almost eight months' pay; secondly, to abate above a fifth part of their pay for the time to come; thirdly, that henceforward they shall not receive their commissions from my Lord Schonberg—which doth a little entrench upon his authority and gives him no small disgust— but from the King of Portugal; and fourthly, that they shall at all times receive orders from the General of the horse, Campmaster General, General of the Artillery, &c., which doth hugely disgust the whole party, who have by their commissioners,— Colonel Person and Major Romsey for Colonel Person's regiment, Major Trelawny and Captain Russell for the regiment of horse, Captain Hill and Captain Maynard for the General's regiment of foot,—given the King their answer that rather than they will abate anything of their pay or alter the conditions made with the Condé de Castelmelhor the 10th of January last, they will all lay down their commissions, except our Sovereign Lord the King order them the contrary. So they have given my Lord Chancellor and Sir Henry Bennet a full account of all, desiring they may receive what is their due from this Crown, and then they will serve them to the last drop of their blood; if not, that his Majesty will be pleased to order them to be transported from this place to any part of the world, where they will do all the service that can be expected from soldiers; however, submitting to the King's gracious pleasure, that if his Majesty sees it needful to continue them here, though under never so hard conditions, they have unanimously resolved to undergo all the hardships in the world rather than to disobey so gracious a master, and serve this Crown with the last drop of their blood." 1¾ pp.

Sir Richard Fanshaw to Sir John Lawson.

1664, August 6-16. Madrid—I received yours of the 24th July from Cadiz on the 5-15 instant, and answer it by way of Alicante, as you advise. "You do with much reason wonder it should be so tedious a task to obtain from the Spanish Council order to two or three of their ports, the King our master's ships may have the free use of them; and the rather since the

Hollands fleet, with less reason in respect of fear of infection, had from the same Governors who refused pratique to you, not only pratique, but the highest and most joyful entertainment almost that you have heard of, De Ruyter with a score of Dutch grandees being admited on shore, and feasted with a collation and comedy in the King's Palace at Valencia by the Viceroy, who the next day, in person, with a number of the principal of that kingdom, were highly feasted on board De Ruyter, receiving upon [arrival] three hundred guns, with as many protestations as [sic] true love and friendship to Spain. You must now have a very great deal of charity for me if you can persuade yourself that I have used those which I ought to this Court in behalf of his Majesty's ships, seeing no effect thereof in all this time, and yet much more charitable to the Spanish Court and nation, if, being of that persuasion, you can induce yourself further to believe that they are not very partial to the Dutch." I am sure I thought so until two or three days ago, when "letters from Malaga advertised us that De Ruyter coming thither, where they have lodged a magazine and therefore one would think should look upon themselves as at home, was flatly denied pratique." I believe you were better used there, and think "chance and variety of humour in variety of Governors, and fits sometimes in one and the same Governors, sway these things in these parts of the world." Mr. Blunden believes that the Holland resident at this Court procured De Ruyter's admission to Valencia, but I read the very letter of the Viceroy, the Marques de St. Roman, in which he gives particulars of the entertainment on both sides, " and adds—without mentioning any command for it from Madrid—that he admitted De Ruyter, though he came from the Barbary coast, because he, the said Vice-king, was satisfied he had no communication with Algiere." In conclusion I assure you I have done my utmost in urging your wishes, and have sent copies of your letters to Secretary Bennet, by which both the King and the Duke of York will understand your condition. *Copy.* 2½ *pp.*

COLONEL JOHN FITZGERALD to SIR RICHARD FANSHAW.

1664, August 9. Tanger—Reporting the good condition of the garrison, but complaining that the Duke of Medina [Celi] has revived an old proclamation to forbid all commerce with the ports of Africa. 1 *p.*

With note on the cover by Consul Westcombe that it was received at Cadiz on the [12-]22 August. [*A translation of the Duke's proclamation, in Westcombe's writing, is in the Tangiers Correspondence, dated July* 16.]

The SAME to the SAME.

1664, August 16. Tanger—I thank you for your good advice and beg you to continue it to me in the future. Col. Reymes left yesterday, and will write to you from Cadiz concerning the condition of this place. I do not think the new town now a building will do us any harm in time of war, and the markets there will be an advantage in time of peace. "As for the Spaniards, although I have several intelligences come to my hand, I cannot believe they would show any ways [?] to these people, lest by the same means they might lose all their interest in Africa, yet I trust neither Moor nor Spaniard, their interest being so much concerned in this place, and being at this distance from England." I rejoice much at the news you send me that the Duchess of Orleans has a son. If you will send your letters to me to our Consul at Cadiz he will forward them by a barque which I have established as a packet-boat to go once a week between this place and Cadiz. 1 *p.*

Sir Richard Fanshaw to Sir John Lawson.

1664, August 20-30. Madrid—Last Tuesday night an express passed through this town from Holland, who was heard to say that the English had taken six Holland ships in the Channel, that war was declared, and that he was posting to the Spanish ports to give notice thereof to the Dutch consuls. "This, whether true or false—I mean the matter of fact, for that he said it is true enough," I conceive you ought to know, and thought of sending an express myself to Alicante, but as my last was robbed and wounded at his first setting out "I look upon this of the ordinary as a safer way, and not much a slower." If there be any truth in the report "I apprehend it must look forward; that is to say that the Hollanders, having by fair promises of satisfaction gained time for their preparations, and gotten home their adventures from the Indies and elsewhere, intend to surprize us with a breach on their part, rather than to expect till we break with them. This I hold improbable enough, too, yet howsoever that it is not amiss upon whatsoever alarum to be awake to all things but absolute impossibilities." I am sending this same advertisement to Tanger and to our countrymen in the ports.

Postscript.—"The last letters from England spake not a word of the Hollanders," but said that the King had perfectly recovered "from a sickness which gave some fear to those who were nearest about his sacred person. God be blessed for it." *Copy.* 2 *pp.*

Philip Strange to Sir Richard Fanshaw.

1664, August [21-]31. Cadiz prison—Petitioning that he and other English taken at sea have now been in prison fourteen months without one word of comfort, although they have written three letters before, and that if they had been "rovers" they could not have been worse dealt with, having no provision allowed them, and being only kept by the charity of their countrymen from absolute starvation, from which one man has already died, and two more are like to follow him. 1 *p.*

Endorsed as received [*at Madrid*] *August* 31-*September* 10.

COLONEL FITZGERALD to SIR RICHARD FANSHAW, at Madrid.

1664, August 29. Tanger—Stating that De Ruyter with his fleet is now at Malaga, and that the *Mathias* sailed on the 27th to go to Sir John [Lawson], who is said to be at Alicante. ½ *p.*
Endorsed :—" Received 13-23 September." [*Compare letter of same date to Bennet, Tangiers Correspondence.*]

COL. ROGER ALSOPP to SIR RICHARD FANSHAW.

1664, August 29. Tanger—I thank your honour for yours of the 2nd, wherein you "confer more honours and favours upon me than I am afraid you will find me deserving of, but however your Lordship shall find that I have solely devoted myself to do his Majesty the best service that lieth in the power of my declining age. I do duly consider that all I can do will be too little to redeem the time I have lost, when I was more able to serve his Majesty. Believe this, my Lord, not to be a compliment, but as real as may be spoken from a faithful soldier and loyal subject. Since the arrival of Col. John Fitzgarald, our present Governor, Col. Reames, and Col. Henry Norwood, unto whom I am now Lieutenant-Colonel, all things here are very well settled. . . . After the building of one redoubt more we shall fall upon the repairing of the houses in the town, which are ragged and torn, and when that is finished, to our solid fortifications against a Christian enemy." The garrison is paid off for the Earl of Teviot's time, and we shall spur on the Mole with all vigour when Esquire Cholmely arrives with materials. It is to be wished that his Majesty would make this place a corporation, "for the better encouragement of merchants and other inhabitants to settle themselves here, for in my opinion, though the military power may be never so honest, it is not so well understood as that of magistracy." Our Governor sent Col. Norwood, Lieut.-Col. Fitzgarald and Mr. William Staines, merchant, as commissioners with proposals of peace to Guyland. They stayed at Arzilla three or four days, but little was done. Guyland said he could do nothing of himself, but would assemble his great ones, and send an answer in four days. This was a month since, and the answer is not yet come, and I believe "that the next time we shall see Guyland will be with his army in hostility, and truly my opinion is, if we stand to our business bravely, his flag of truce will be sent in the very same day, and I do assure your Lordship he is like to get little but knocks." My Colonel, being indisposed with the flux, begs you to excuse his not writing this time. 1 *p.*
Seal of arms.
Note by Westcombe :—" Received at Cadiz 10 September."

GASPAR DE HARO, Marques de Liche, to SIR RICHARD FANSHAW.

1664 [August 31-]September 10.   Castle of St. George, Lisbon—Consul Thomas Maynard tells me of the favour which your Excellency is pleased to show me by remembering me in your letter, and manifesting your kind desire to procure my liberation, for which I offer you my grateful thanks, not doubting the power of his Majesty of Great Britain and the honour which he does me. I hope that I may have an opportunity at some time of proving my gratitude and good will. *Spanish.* 1¼ *pp.*

CHARLES II. to SIR RICHARD FANSHAW.

1664, Sptember 7. Whitehall—Recommending to him the case of John Wilmot, merchant, now a prisoner in Porta Santa Maria in Spain, at the suit of one Humphrey Holcombe, his creditor. *Sign Manual. Countersigned by Sir Henry Bennet.* 2½ *pp.*

ADMIRAL THOMAS ALLIN to SIR RICHARD FANSHAW.

1664, September 9. H.M.S. *Plymouth*—I tender my humble service " to your Excellency and consort, with the virtuous young ladies. I am to intimate unto you that his Royal Highness hath sent me into the Straits to take the command of that squadron in place of Sir John Lawson, who is sent for home for some greater employment, and with him goeth home Captain Berckly. I am to receive from Sir John the cipher by Mr. Coventry's order to correspond with you, and shall be glad to hear from you, and who are your correspondents at Cales [Cadiz], Malaga, and Alicante, that letters may not fail of quick passages. I shall upon all occasions and accidents give your honour account of what passes, either on this coast or Argiers. News out of England little, we see the Hollanders get before us in making provisions for war, having my Herr Updam riding before the Maze [Maas] and Goree with twenty-two sails of good men-of-war, but the plague is amongst them. Trump hath eighteen sail coming in with eleven East India men, and these for ought we know may join together; they have eight or ten with their fleet of busses, and all our fleet as yet when together with the Earl of Sandwich about sixteen, now I and the *Crown* are come away; and Sir John and the *Bristol* going to them will make eighteen. It is certain we have thirty great ships that have all their standing rigging and graved, which will be soon ready. I left my Lord Sandwich lying off Beachy and the coast of France to see who passes. I have in my convoy for Cales Captain Coale, from thence to Legorne and the Morea one Stafforfe, those two with piece goods, and one Yarmouth ship laden with lead, Captain Hudson, Smyrna factor, Captain Hill, London merchant, bound both to Scanderoone. My respects to Sir Andrew King and the rest of your noble company." *Signed.* 1 *p. Seal of arms.*

SIR JOHN LAWSON to SIR RICHARD FANSHAW.

1664, September 27. Bay of Bulls, H.M.S. *Resolution*—We were denied pratique both at Alicante and Malaga, and at Gibraltar " they were so uncivil as not to let us have the least

refreshment for our moneys, but coming hither the Governor
hath been very civil in giving pratique, that we might have all
things we stood in need of, and had prepared guns to have
answered my salute, but that I went in no further than this
place." I sail for England to-day, leaving Captain Allin in
command of the fleet. Captain Berkeley only goes with me.
1 *p.*

Sir John Lawson to Sir Richard Fanshaw.

1664, September 27, twelve o'clock at night. H.M.S. *Resolution* off Cadiz—Stating that De Ruyter has taken in great stores
of wine, oil, bread and flesh, and is believed to have sailed for
the coast of Guinny; and requesting that this information may
be at once forwarded to his Majesty. 1 *p.*

George Bromydge to Sir Richard Fanshaw.

1664 [September 27-]October 7. Seville prison—Six weeks
ago we received the joyful news that the King had ordered our
release, yet we are still in durance. We beseech your Excellency
to find out why our order is stopped, and to have it sent down
here, as the winter is drawing on, "and if it should be our
unhappy fortune to stay here another winter I am confident
the major part of us must of necessity perish, we having neither
hose, shoes nor clothes to defend us from the cold." ¾ *p.*

Sir Henry Bennet to Sir Richard Fanshaw.

1664, October 6—Eight pages of cipher, not deciphered,
but the key for which is amongst the papers. They prove to be
the cipher part of the letter dated August 25th in the printed
letters (p. 283), and thus give the true date of the letter, that
printed being manifestly incorrect.

Sir George Downing to Sir Richard Fanshaw.

1664, October 6. Hague—"My Lord Carlisle hath had his
audience at Stockholm, and both thereat and at his entering
more honour done him than hath been known done to any,
all the burgesses being in arms, &c." I send you a paper in
relation to the ships *Bona Esperanza* and *Henry Bonaventure*,
from which you will see they take the usual way with men who
have other people's money in their hands, wishing to draw the
matter from one court to another, and so keep up the dispute.
The Guiny fleet has not gone yet, nor have Obdam's ships—
which are to convoy them through the Channel—got in their
provisions. There has been much ado in the Estates of Holland
about levying the two hundredth penny on every man's estate,
which still finds opposition, and also "which way to find moneys
to carry on their occasions, for though the country is full of
money yet the Estates have none; on the contrary they are
infinitely in debt," and only pay at the rate of four per cent.
interest. 1½ *pp.*

Colonel Fitzgerald to Sir Richard Fanshaw.

1664, October 8-18. Tanger—Stating that he has finished the line and all the out works, so that he now cares little whether the Moors choose peace or war, though, for the honour of the place and better encouragement to trade, he will endeavour to bring them to a good correspondency; to which end he has entertained about twenty of them, who have brought him in three or four hundred head of cattle. This has enabled him to give fresh meat instead of salt to his men, " to the preserving many from falling sick at this time of the year." 1 *p.*
Endorsed :—" Received 1-11 November."

Sir George Downing to Sir Richard Fanshaw.

1664, October 13. Hague—The Estates of Holland are still trying to find money to carry on their design against the English, but several towns still oppose the tax of the two hundredth penny " so that as yet I see no way before them but borrowing, and that way they can have enough as long as their credit lasts, but if they come to get a blow at sea, it was found by experience in Cromwell's time that their credit did shrink, and it would so again." Obdam's fleet is now victualled, and as soon as the wind serves for the Guiny ships to get out of the Texel and come before Goree, it is said he will take them down the Channel. Holland has proposed the building of twenty-four great ships, but Zealand and some other provinces have given their consent to eighteen only. " All their confidence and talk is in France, yet on the other hand they see plainly that as in relation to their trade, France doth them all the hurt they can possible. The peace or truce between the Emperor and the Turk doth very much startle them here, fearing that if they should come to odds with his Majesty that the Princes of the Empire, their neighbours, and particularly the Bishop of Munster, should give them trouble by land." I enclose a copy of my memorial to the Estates, which will show you what cause his Majesty has " not to be very well pleased with these people, especially upon the coast of Guiny."

Sir Edward Turnor, sen., to Sir Richard Fanshaw.

1664, October 13—I received your very kind letter of the 9th of July, and returned an answer, which however I find by my son's letters has miscarried, and so must now thank you for your extraordinary care of him, both in sickness and in health. In the letters which immediately followed his illness he seemed to have no affection for Spain, but now I find him somewhat reconciled to the country and not very desirous to return till next spring, and I have commanded him not to come back unless by your advice. I told you in my former letter that Sir Thomas Ingram is in possession of his desires, and that I will do my best in the business which you have intrusted to me. I suppose you hear " that the Dutch and we are likely to fall out. As yet we ride upon the fore-horse, but we hear De Ruyter is stolen to Guynney with a design to do us some mischief. . . . Prince Rupert is gone out with a strong party to see what they do there; Sir John Lawson is returned, and the Earl of Sandwich is abroad with a good strength to watch their motions nearer home; and the Duke of York is now preparing . . . to go himself and see the issue of the business. God bless you all. Our Parliament meets again the 24th of November." 1 *p.*

VISCOUNT DONGAN to SIR RICHARD FANSHAW.

1664, October [15-]25. Xeres—"I had the honour of your Excellency's of the 14th current with the greatest regret imaginable; your enclosed paper has eased our minds a little, whereby we may guess which way to govern our small affairs for home. I cannot requite your Excellency with much news from hence, only some reports which your Excellency will be a better judge of. It is confidently reported here, and not undesired, that there is a treaty with Portugal and that it passes by your Excellency's way; here they would seem to particularise the conditions too. Here the justices are so insufferable in their thieving and extortion that they are daily knocked in the head and abused by both gentry and commonalty, that it presages some great change. In one from the Duke of Ormond to me by this post he says that a license will be sent to me to transport some horses for him. It is not come, neither do I know where to apply myself for it, in the meantime I will provide the horses. I suppose it must be from thence. The fall of the money has done no small mischief in these parts, and does not little discontent the people. My wife and family kisses your Excellency's, your lady and young ladies' hands." *Holograph.* 2½ *pp.*

COLONEL JOHN FITZGERALD to SIR RICHARD FANSHAW.

1664, November 6-16. Tangier—Since Saly came into Guylan's hands his boats have done much injury to our merchants, and will be more prejudicial to the Newfoundland men than Argier has been. If his Royal Highness would send three or four of his sixth-rate frigates " to ply before that place and Tetuan, it would not be difficult in a short time to ruin them both." The free commerce which you have procured from the Spanish Court between this place and the coasts of Spain is of great concernment to this city, and in the name of the whole garrison I thank you, for the countenancing of us is a slight to Guylan. He has detained two of my men, whom I sent with an answer to his last letter.

Postscript.—November 12-22. I have received your Excellency's letter with the welcome proclamations of the King of Spain, and congratulate you particularly upon your success. I have received the enclosed from Guylan or he that there commands in chief. He has kept my two men nearly six weeks. "The reason thereof I do not so well understand, but be it either war or peace I am prepared for both." 2½ *pp.*

Endorsed :—"Received and answered 29 November-9 December."

WILLIAM BLUNDEN to SIR RICHARD FANSHAW.

1664, November [13-]23. Alicant—This Sunday morning I have received your Excellency's of the 9-19 current. We hear that peace has been re-established with Argeir upon the same articles formerly concluded by Sir John Lawson, and the fleets going to Tunis and Tripoley to effect the same with them, Capt. Chicherly immediately set sail in search of the Admiral. I have acquainted all our nation here to be wary. The Dutch have many gallant rich merchant ships in these Mediterranean seas, but not any men-of-war that I know, more than two which are convoys for Turkey." The peace with Argier will I conceive prevent our having pratique in any port of Spain, but the orders should be continued for relieving the frigates with necessaries. Those to come hither must be issued to the Marques de St. Roman, Vice-rey of Valencia. "It is likely Admiral Allin may mistake in his advice of the loss of Gigiarie, for by a Spanish captive who came out of Argier the next day after him, we understand that the French, having undermined some out-works, voluntarily retired from them, suffered the Moors to enter, and afterwards sprung their mines; which although proved to the loss—of no moment— of some number of Moors, is esteemed a disrepute to the French and a weakening of their main fortification." *Signed.* 1 *p.*

ADMIRAL THOMAS ALLIN to SIR RICHARD FANSHAW.

1664, November 16. H.M.S. *Plymouth*, Bay of Fuorsy— Stating that he has left the *Phœnix* at Alicante and is about to sail for Tangier; that they of Alicante are very ill-satisfied at the peace with Argier; and that the news concerning the French at Gigirie is certainly true if the Turks are to be believed, who would have given any satisfaction if they might have borrowed three of the English ships to fetch thence the guns and ammunition. ½ *p.*

SIR RICHARD FANSHAW to COLONEL FITZGERALD, Deputy-Governor of Tangier.

1664, November 22-December 2. Madrid—Draft of letter printed in the published letters, p. 347.

COLONEL FITZGERALD to SIR RICHARD FANSHAW.

1664, November 28-December 7 [*sic*]. Tanger—If the Spaniards be sincere in the declaration which your Excellency has procured from them of correspondency with this town, I cannot see but that Guylan must make peace. However, I shall always be prepared for either peace or war, " and the probability of the one shall not make me neglect the possibility of the other. . . . . There are two forts built at the two coves where the mole men work, so that now, in their own opinion, they work very secure." I am going to begin the fortifications of the upper castle, according to the figure sent me from England for completing the citadel begun by Don Sebastian. 2 *pp*.

[*Compare letter* [*to Sec. Bennet?*], *same date. Tangiers Correspondence.*]

SIR RICHARD FANSHAW to SIR GEORGE DOWNING.

1664, November 30-December 10. Madrid—You appear not to have received mine of August 24th, old style, telling you that a Dutch express had passed through this town, who said that war was declared between Holland and England. I hinted to you that I thought it possible he might be sent to De Ruyter, with orders to begin hostilities on a certain day, and I have since found that he carried orders to be dispatched to Guinea.

The Dutch Ambassador has arrived at Madrid, and sent to ask that my coach and family might attend him at his first public audience. I went to visit him, and after wishing him joy told him that I desired to explain why I could not send my coach and family to accompany him and " to stop the mouths of those who might therefore be likely otherwise to say that war is already declared between England and Holland," but that the King my master had forbidden this ceremony, both as to foreign ambassadors in his own Court and to his own in foreign Courts, desiring us "to seek out other ways to express our respects to the ambassadors of his Majesty's allies." He had his first audience on November 16-26, going in good style, accompanied by fifty or sixty gentlemen on horseback, and the coaches of the ambassadors of Germany, France, Venice, Lucca and Parma. In the afternoon "he came in all his trim to pay me my visit," but found me not at home. *Copy.* 1¾ *pp*.

[*Compare letter to Bennet, November* 16-26. *Spanish Correspondence.*]

NEWS LETTER.

[1664], November—The *Dunkirk, Assistance* and *Henry* are now in the Downs with others, but the *Royal James,* Sir William Penn Commander, has not yet arrived. A fleet of twelve or fourteen Hollanders are off the Isle of Wight, standing all hazard rather than put into port. One Yarmouth man with wines was cast away in a storm near Brixton.

"Dublin, Nov. 9, upon a difference between Col. Demsey and Mr. Lutterell, they went into the field, the former having for his second one MacAvering, the other Ensign Buckley. The principals, after some passes, parted without harm, but the seconds engaging were both wounded, but Buckley more dangerously, though 'tis hoped not mortally."

Mr. Nicholas Bacon, a barrister of Grey's Inn, being found guilty of endeavouring the death of Sir Harbottle Grimston, Master of the Rolls, has been sentenced to 1,000 marks fine, three months' imprisonment, and to make public acknowledgment of his offence at the King's Bench bar and Chancery. Major Holmes has reached Lisbon on his way to England. Captain Tiddiman, Rear-Admiral to the Earl of Sandwich, is sent into the Channel to stop the Dutch men-of-war, and the Customs House has received orders to seize all Dutch vessels and take from them their sails and rudders, no satisfaction having been given for the outrages upon his Majesty's subjects.

"The Lord Fitzharding returned to Court the 20th, having given his Majesty ample satisfaction of his message and a fair account of the high respects that Court [of France] gave him and his company, which speaks a good correspondency betwixt the two Crowns. The Lord Fitzharding was presented with a ring to the value of 2,000l." The *Colchester* frigate has brought in the *King Solomon* of Amsterdam, and twenty-two Dutch ships have been seized in Torbay.

"Edinburgh, November 15, Sunday last in all churches they prayed for the good success of his Royal Highness and the navies under his conduct." His Majesty has granted letters of reprisal against the Dutch. 3¼ *pp.*

CONSUL MAYNARD to SIR RICHARD FANSHAW.

1664, December [12-]22. Lisboa—"My late afflictions have made me incapable of all business, but I do not know that the neglect of any troubles me so much as my breach of promise in the sending those things you desired for your lady, for which I beg both her and your pardon. I have lost a good wife. God of his mercy sanctify all his dispensations." If you will send me two lines of intelligence from your parts I shall esteem it a great favour. "At this time here appears a prodigious comet, which hath been seen these twelve nights in the constellation of Hydra, betwixt Corno and the Pot, in twenty-four degrees south latitude, and comes upon the meridian about half an hour past five o'clock in the morning, the influence of which is extremely feared in this country. You will do me a favour to let me know how it appears with you." My humble service to your lady. ¾ *p.*

COLONEL HENRY NORWOOD to SIR RICHARD FANSHAW.

1664, December 15. Tangier—"If I thought your Excellency had as much time to read my impertinences as I have to write them," no occasion should pass without your hearing from me. I gave you in August a flying relation of my embassy to Gayland, and since then have heard from our Governor of the good effects of your negotiation for us. "The sad news of the King's fleet under Admiral Allin will accost you with noise enough. On Sunday morning last it came here by a *barca luenga*, and made a great allay to the several sorts of happy tidings that we had lately received from England and elsewhere, as the return of poor—nay rich—Robin Holmes from his conquest of the river Gambo with Dutch prizes, the equipage and forwardness of his Majesty's fleet in great advance to the Dutch, his Royal High-

ness there in person, and the excellent peace with Algier. . .
I wish the Admiral may be able to satisfy the King that nothing
can be imputed to ill-conduct. I am persuaded it was his forward zeal to examine the Dutch fleet that made him thus
unhappy." Gayland still keeps our messengers at Arsila, and I
believe means to attempt something against us. "If scaling
suddenly be his design, I am well assured he must be deceived,
because our redoubts are palisadoed and much higher than to
him they seem to be. In fine, when he shall perceive himself
neglected in Spain, he will seek our friendship, not till then.
. . . I hope the malevolent portent of the blazing star,
which for fourteen days past hath appeared in this horizon,
south east, hath already wrought its effects upon the King's
interest in these parts by endamaging his fleet. The King of
France at Jugerer hath felt its influence more sharply. If it
be true, as is reported, that your Excellency is summoned to
return, _re infecta_, it will concern us to prosecute the Mole at
another kind of vigour than at present. 'Tis pity so public
a good for our nation should stand still for the private business
of Mr. Cholmley. What friendship can we expect in the Spanish
ports when your Excellency is gone?" $2\frac{1}{4}$ _pp._
Endorsed:—"Received 30 December-9 January."

ADMIRAL THOMAS ALLIN to SIR RICHARD FANSHAW.

1664, December 17. H.M.S. _Plymouth_, in the Bay of Bulls—
Describing the disaster which has befallen his fleet—his own
and four other ships having got ashore in a night of dismal
rain and darkness, and the _Phœnix_ and _Nonsuch_ being lost,
which has half broken his heart. 1 _p._ _Seal of arms and crest._
[_Calendared S.P. Dom., Chas. II._, 1664-1665, _from a copy,
under this date._]

VISCOUNT DONGAN to SIR RICHARD FANSHAW.

1664, December [18-]28. Xeres—I and my wife thank you
and my lady heartily for your kind words, and wish you both
all imaginable happiness. "I have the same your Excellency
sends me of his Royal Highness embarking, as also the Duke
of Monmouth, Duke of Buckingham, Duke of Richmond and
Mr. Harry Ford of Norfolk, as also all the young nobility and
gallantry of the Court. I am also advertized that my Lord Fitzharding is married to Mrs. Bagot, one of the Duchess's maids
of honour, the night before he went for France, being employed
by his Majesty thither, as also of Mr. Onel's [Daniel O'Neill]
death." No doubt you have heard of the loss of two of our
frigates near Gibraltar by foul weather. "You will not doubt
how little troubled these people are at it, as I saw in a letter from
one of their prime men here. God reward their good wills, and
send us never any need of their kindness. I am sorry to hear of
your Excellency's preparations for home. I wish it may be this
way, that I may go under your shelter. If not, God send us a
happy meeting in England." _Holograph._ 3 _pp._

ADMIRAL THOMAS ALLIN to SIR RICHARD FANSHAW.

1664, December 25. H.M.S. *Plymouth*, in the Bay of Cadiz—Describing an encounter with the Dutch upon the 19th, when he took two ships and sunk two more. *Signed.* [*Calendared S.P. Dom., Chas. II.*, 1664-1665, *from a copy, under this date.*]

SIR RICHARD FANSHAW to ADMIRAL ALLIN.

1664-5, December 27-January 6. Madrid—The sad news of your disaster came to me but a few days before the good news of your victory against the Dutch, which I received from the Duke of Medina de las Torres. I hope that our shipwrecked men—for to my great joy I hear both they and the guns were saved—will be recruited with Dutch ships, and our Mold at Tangere supplied with Dutch workmen upon liberal and Christian terms. *Copy.* 1 *p.*

COLONEL L[UCAS] TAAFE to LORD [AMBASSADOR FANSHAW].

[1665, January?]—I would have esteemed my long service to this Crown well repaid had I been allowed to go to Madrid to kiss your hands, " but as strangers must endure mortifications, which in time of peace are more ordinarily offered than in war, merely to weary them of their employments, I have fixed my resolution of retiring homewards and resigning my command to my nephew Nick," who served for seven years in my regiment, and has lately arrived here from London. I hear from my brother that the King has been pleased to recommend this suit to your care. I have sent a memorial to the Duke of Medina de las Torres, which, seconded by you, will I doubt not be easily granted. 1¼ *pp.*

VISCOUNT DONGAN to SIR RICHARD FANSHAW.

1665, January [1-]11. Xeres—"Your Excellency is resolved before this of the doubt of the war with Holland." I hear that you are thinking of returning home, and wish I knew when and if by land, that I might arrange my affairs so as to wait for you, "for Donna Mary has no inclinations to go by sea, and the rather for the Holland wars." Our General has gone out from this port, we believe towards the Straits. He tells me he will be going for England at the beginning of next month. *Holograph.* 2 *pp.*

CONSUL WESTCOMBE to SIR RICHARD FANSHAW.

1665, January [8-]18. Cadiz—Informing him of the movements of the English fleet and mentioning a report that De Ruyter has retaken all the English forts in Guinea and ten or twelve of their ships on that coast. 2 *pp.*
Endorsed as received on January 19-29.

Sir Thomas Allin to Sir Richard Fanshaw.

1664-5, January 15. H.M.S. *Plymouth*, Gibraltar Bay—
Stating that he is now bound for home, with twelve men-of-
war and twelve merchant ships, and means to touch at Tangier
and Cadiz on his way. *Signed.* ½ *p.* *Seal of arms.*

Sir Thomas Allin to William Coventry.

1664[-5], January 15. H.M.S. *Plymouth* in Gibraltar Bay—
I have, thank God, got off the *Bonadventure* in spite of the
weather, which is so foul that when we tried to go for Cadiz we
were obliged to stand in for Tanger, and there were kept five
days by the storm. Our prize lost three anchors and nearly
fell foul of the *Antelope.* I have sent Capt. Mauhun [Mohun?]
to bring him to Gibraltar, whither I have come myself, having
heard from my brother that Capt. Parker and about a dozen
English ships were riding here, with cargoes to the value of
300,000*l.* "We are intending homeward, according to instructions, with this fleet; Capts. Jo. Born [Brown?], Haddock,
Hasellgrove, Hosier, Fenny, Talbot, Crane and Mathews; these
rich ships, besides some small Marcellis [Marseilles] and Mallaga
men. . . . [The Dutch] talk of fitting some merchant men
to join with the three men-of-war which are making clean at
Cadiz, who will be out so soon as they understand of our going
home, and then their trade will on again, which now have order
to stay in all ports wheresoever their intelligence meet them,
laden or light. This puts a great stop to the King of Spain's
proceeding against Portugal," as the ships laden with provisions
for his army dare not stir. I have just received a request from
the Governor here to give a *segoura* to a Dutch ship laden
with corn to pass to Cadiz. After consultation in a council of
war I have done so. *Copy.* 2 *pp.*

Joseph Williamson to Sir Andrew King.

1664-5, January 16. Whitehall—"I am much obliged to you
for your punctuality. This hour comes to us your happy news
of what hath been begun by Captain Allen, and we hope will
be carried on to a perfect issue. Certainly if he finds himself
in a condition, he will not want even the law of nations and
nature to pursue his enemy fighting into any Prince's port
whatsoever, though some question might be made whether he
could begin to fight him there. God give good success, and
there will not want right to justify it.

We long to hear this news from Gibraltar of the loss of our
two frigates strongly contradicted.

Van Beuninghen cannot yet obtain a peremptory declaration
from the French Court, though he makes his masters hope,
and they the poor people believe, it will at last follow. In the
meantime France takes time to examine:—

1. Whether this quarrel, being for pretensions and rights

out of Europe, be within their treaty with Holland, which expressly limits it to Europe.

2. And more particularly whether we or they are the first aggressors in the quarrel, for that is expressly a condition in their warrants.

Now it is without all doubt most notorious that they are so, since the evidence of what De Ruitter hath done on the coast of Guiney, and that by their instructions, and now owned to be so, since they can no longer hide it, for till now it is to be observed that all along to the French King, to Sir George Downing, to the King and all the world they denied any such thing or that he was gone that way, which the French King takes himself much affronted in and justly.

And the plain truth is, Holmes, upon his examination, as he was examined at the Tower on Saturday by the two Secretaries,* gives so good account of whatever he hath done in his late expedition to Guiney that it will appear plainly he hath done no hostility or damage to them there, for which—besides all their former injuries and oppressions to our trade there, which it might have been otherwise not unjust to have resented— he did not first receive the just provocations from the Dutch at each particular place. And so the world will see in time, when a narrative is made out of his papers, which are most in the Dutch and Portuguese tongues. A copy of one I send you for a pattern of their perfidy, having as you will see now very lately attempted to engage the King of Barca to join with them in a war against us.

Great vigour is used in our naval preparations, whatever false rumours are thrown about by the Dutch and their partisans the fanatics amongst us that a peace is intended, whereof there is no ground at all.

The Prize Office is settled, and all the sub-commissioners, being thirty-nine or forty in number, are House of Commons men except three or four, so perfect a harmony of duty and kindness is there between the subject and his Prince respectively.

The passage about Scotland doth not proceed so well to our neighbours as they hoped, for two of three East India ships are returned back to Amsterdam, their men having by extremity of weather lost fingers, teeth and noses in the service; the third they give for lost. And yet they must try that or none, for they dare not attempt the Channel.

I pray you procure me the present names, qualities, marriages and children of the grandees, chief officers and ministers of state of that [Spanish] Court."

Postscript.—"Our own Straits fleet of between twenty and thirty are well arrived at Plimouth, blessed be God." 3 *pp.*

SIR RICHARD FANSHAW to VISCOUNT DONGAN.

1664-5, January 24-February 3. Madrid—Thanking him for his letter of January 11th, and stating that some of his company

---

* *See* Cal. S.P. Dom., 1664-5, p. 170.

have already gone, and others will start on their journey home by land in a few days, but which way he himself will go or when he will set out he cannot say until he hears from England. *Copy.* ½ *p.*

COLONEL LUCAS TAAFE.

1665 [January 28-]February 7. Madrid—Pass from Sir Richard Fanshaw for "Don Lucas Taafe," who has honourably served his Catholic Majesty as *Mestre de Campo* in his armies, and now holds his license to depart, to go to England with three servants and their arms. *Spanish.* ½ *p.*

DON FRANCISCO DE AYALA.

1665, January—Papers concerning the imprisonment of Don Francisco de Ayala. *Spanish.* 12 *pp.*

SIR GEORGE DOWNING to SIR RICHARD FANSHAW.

1664[-5], February 2. The Hague—Many capers are putting to sea with letters of marque, and Banckert has sailed from Zealand with twelve or thirteen, "to try what exploits he can do again, and they doubt not but they shall ruin the English plantations in the Caribes and those parts, and many letters of marque are also sent to Italy and Cadiz. . . . They begin to talk that notwithstanding the greatness of their preparations, yet that if in the upshot they should find much hazard in the adventuring a battle in these parts, that possibly they may keep their fleet within doors, at least for a time . . . and so wear away the English fleet, while in the meantime they do their business in the East and West Indies, Straits and those parts." The States General of Holland have made known their resolutions for the raising of money, viz.: The two hundredth penny to be levied twice; the addition of a fifth more upon all that pass by boat or waggon, a chimney or fire-hearth tax, and a moiety more upon the land tax.

Postscript.—"Much alarm upon the account of the Bishop of Munster and other neighbouring Princes of Germany, whose deputies are now together, about adjusting matters among themselves." *Signed.* 1 *p.*

THOMAS MARSDEN to SIR RICHARD FANSHAW.

1665, February [3-]13. Lisbone—I thank your Excellency for honouring me with a letter, and hold myself bound to give you an account of my affairs here. "Immediately upon my being deprived of the protection of your presence, I thought it needful to put some more sweat into my sermons than formerly I did, lest any might watch for an occasion to say that my pains were not answerable to my pay; the which I have done from that time to this, and that not without the success wished for. But

I thank God, not being carped at is the least part of the success I have had in my ministry, if I may believe my auditors, some· of whom—upon occasion of my preaching my farewell sermon last Lord's Day upon Gal. IV., 11, "I am afraid of you, lest I have bestowed upon you labour in vain"—have told me not without tears that I have not laboured in vain, that they have looked deeper into eternity, and do value a Saviour far more than they did when first I came amongst them. The whole body of them are so passionately covetous of my stay that they have offered to augment my salary to obtain it, or to dispense with my absence for ten or twelve months for settling my affairs in England in case of return." But as I do not see any possibility of this I have begged them to transfer their respect to my successor, whereon they have cheerfully renewed their subscriptions for whatever minister my Lord of London shall send them, which subscriptions I shall deliver to him, together with the testimonials given me by the merchants here, one of which I enclose to your Lordship. Since you left this Court I have only omitted preaching on two Lord's Days, once for indisposition, and the second time because the merchants desired me to forbear "by reason the *Auto da fee* [*sic*] fell upon a Sunday."

I count myself happy in my acquaintance with your house, where "I was no less a learner than a teacher." I have rubbed off much ignorance since I came to Lisbon, and have also "gotten a competent treasure into my purse," my moneys—amounting to 344*l*. 3*s*. 4*d*.—being put into two bills of exchange, payable by Mr. Wm. Bird and Mr. Edward Norwood, merchants of London. I hope by long and hard study in England to fit myself for your Lordship's countenance, and entreat your "concealing my infirmities and imperfections, a greater number whereof your Lordship and my lady have seen both in my person and my pen than any, I think, in the world besides." I shall try always by God's help to carry myself as becomes a Gospel minister, and hope that this promise to you "may contribute something to my establishment in good and manly resolutions." Mr. Price will explain to you the reasons which require my return to England. 1 *p*.

Enclosing,

> *Certificate, signed by M. Frogiert, "French minister, hearer of the same Mr. Marsden," Thos. Maynard, English Consul, Chris. Maynard, Vice-Consul, and twenty-four English merchants, that Thomas Marsden has been "assiduous and laborious in his studies, constant and orthodox in his preachings, pious and exemplary in his life," and has discharged himself in all things as well befits a Gospel minister. Lisbon [January 31-]February 10, 1665. 1 p.*

CONSUL WESTCOMBE to SIR RICHARD FANSHAW.

1665, February [5-]15. Cadiz—Admiral Allin and his fleet are detained at Gibraltar by contrary winds. The *Essex*, Capt.

Utbert, is waiting for him at Cadiz, that they may all go together for England.

De Reyter is hourly expected from Guinea, and is said to have reduced all that coast. The French King has offered 600,000 pieces-of-eight for the garrison of Tangier.

A ship arrived this week from Dublin (in twelve days) reports "that the Scots Irish are up in arms about a place there called Belturbet, near Black Bog, several thousands of them, and headed by one Sir Fylum O'Neel [Phelim O'Neill], who newly came thither out of France."

The States of Holland are said to have demanded from the French King the men whom, as their protector, he promised to send them when required.

All is well at Tangier.

It is to be feared that the Dutch will domineer much when the English frigates have left, as besides De Ruyter's fleet of fourteen or sixteen sail, Van Tromp is expected with ten or twelve more from Holland, convoying the Smyrna ships. 3 *pp.*

SIR RICHARD FANSHAW to SECRETARY MORICE.

1664-5, February 8-18. Madrid—The bearer, Sir Andrew King, goes express to England at my request, on business which I pray you to favour so far as you can.

"He carries likewise incidentally the success of my negociation in this Court, the sum whereof is, I am no forwarder therein to this day than I was when I left London, so that if this shall be thought sufficient ground for my return, your honour may be attended shortly in person" by your humble servant. *Copy.* ¾ *p.*

[*Compare letters to the King, Clarendon and Duke of York, in the published letters, same date.*]

MONS. DE FREMONT to SIR RICHARD FANSHAW.

1665, February [10-]20. Bellem—I am kept here by storm and tempest, waiting a favourable wind to carry me to England. I wished to return by way of Spain, not so much to satisfy my curiosity, as in order to pay my respects to your Excellency and your family; but the Comte de Schomberg and my other friends think it better for me to go by sea. I do this very reluctantly, especially since your letter has redoubled my desire to see Madrid, and I venture to hope that you, too, will be a little sorry, as I might have diverted you for a day or two by a relation of what has passed here since you left. But wherever I am I shall always be your very humble servant. *French.* 1 *p.*

WILLIAM SCOWEN to SIR RICHARD FANSHAW.

1664[-5], February 13. Molinnick in Cornwall—"In the

midst of many unhappinesses of the late wars here—which the
Lord hath blessed us to overlive—it was my good fortune to be
a little known to your Lordship, and somewhat more to my
lord, your honourable brother and my singular good friend,"
on which account I venture to speak to your Lordship on behalf
of Don Juan Scone, a kinsman of mine, born in Spain, but son
to one of my name. His father left England "very young,
when he was not well able to write his own name, nor was he
curious—it seems—to reform it afterwards, and so perhaps there
may have been some scruple thereupon of his descent; but I do
hereby certify your Lordship that it was right and without any
blemish at all." Having attained an estate fit to support it, the
son desires to receive the habit of knighthood, and if you could
say a few words in his favour to his Catholic Majesty in this
behalf, both he and I should be very grateful to you. 1 *p.*
Seal of arms.

Consul Westcombe to Sir Richard Fanshaw.

1665, February [18-]28—Sends certificate concerning the
goods taken out of the *Good Hope*, Ellyas Hyne, commander,—
bound from Newfoundland to Cadiz,—by an Ostend man-of-war,
and also his correspondence with Admiral Allin and the
Governor of Gibraltar in relation to saving certain things from
the two English frigates stranded near the Rock.

Admiral Allin is still detained there. Three Dutch men-of-
war are at Cadiz with the Smyrna ships, who seem to have
had orders not to stir for some time, as they have discharged
a thousand mariners.

The only news is in the enclosed paper received from Rouen.
2½ *pp.*

Enclosing,

> 1665, *January* [10-]20. *Rouen—English letters state that
> orders are given for raising five thousand land soldiers. His
> Majesty, with consent of Parliament, has given full power
> over the fleet to the Duke of York. The States of Holland
> have imprisoned the Princess Dowager and Admiral Opdam,
> "pretending they have conspired with many others to betray
> them to the English for the Prince of Orange." A rich
> West India Hollander has been taken, and it is proposed
> in Parliament to block up the ports of Holland. Some ships
> have been already taken out of the Texel.* ½ *p.*

Comte de Schonberg to Sir Richard Fanshaw.

1665 [February 25-]March 7. Lisbon—After having been so
long without hearing from you, I rejoice to receive your letter
and to know that you and your family are well. We are hoping
for a happy issue to your negociations for a peace between Spain
and Portugal, and for myself I desire it ardently that I may

withdraw from here and find some opportunity of serving his
Majesty of Great Britain with his troops more usefully and more
to my own satisfaction than I have done this last year. M. de
Fremont has left this kingdom. I hope that I shall soon follow
him, and that I may have the honour of seeing your Excellency
in England. *French. Holograph. 2 pp.*

GASPAR DE HARO, MARQUES DE LICHE, to SIR RICHARD FANSHAW.

1665 [February 25-]March 7. Castle of St. George, Lisbon—
Your letter of January 13th was delivered me by the bearer
of this, and the news that you and the Consul are well has
comforted me in my close imprisonment, as also the information
that his Majesty of Britain has taken it upon him to try to
procure my release, a work fitting for the piety and greatness
of his royal person, and of which I doubt not that I shall see
the result, especially as your Excellency is the principal instrument in it. Knowing your kind favour to me I do not need to
remind you of my great necessity, but the twenty-one months
which I have spent in a prison, destitute of all the conveniences of life, oblige me to pray you to continue your good offices
that my liberation may be speedy, and so the more valued. I
have seen the heads of a letter from Sir Henry Bennet, and perceive that the favours which his Britannic Majesty is pleased
to show me now equal those bestowed on me by his royal
generosity at other times, and also the confidence with which I
avail myself of his mediation, in which alone I have always
placed all my hopes. And I beg your Excellency to be not so
much an intercessor in this matter as a godfather, placing me at
his Majesty's feet to beg that he will be pleased to act in it. I
rejoice at the friendly zeal of Baron de Bativila, of which
you assure me by his request for the continuance of my
friendship, as I am very sure of his, and I thank your Excellency
most gratefully for your kindness, hoping that I may some day
have the chance of employing myself in your service. *Spanish.
3 pp.*

SECRETARY ANTONIO DE SOUSA DE MACEDO to SIR RICHARD
FANSHAW.

1665 [February 27-]March 9. Lisbon—I received with much
pleasure your letter of the 13th of January. The bearer of this,
John Price, carries my master's reply to the papers sent to
this Court. His Majesty and his ministers are well assured
of your Excellency's goodwill, and although we know that the
ministers of Castile are not disposed to be reasonable as regards
Portugal, yet we believe that if it were possible to effect anything it would be entirely by means of your zeal, prudence
and industry. The truth is that the Castilian ministers are
trying to deceive England, wishing to delay matters until they
see how affairs go between that country and Holland, but they
have to do with your Excellency, who knows well how to

circumvent them. My wife sends her greetings to your lady and to your daughters. I asked this bearer on her behalf whether there was nothing which she could send which might be agreeable to Madame, but I could not draw any declaration from him, and as he travels à la legère, it is impossible to send sweetmeats or anything heavy, which would be a burden to him. But we beg you to tell us if we can do anything for you here. *French.* 1½ *pp.*

ANTONIO DE SOUSA DE MACEDO to SIR RICHARD FANSHAW.

1665 [February 27-]March 9—Stating that he encloses a cipher, whereby his Excellency may more conveniently communicate with him. *Portuguese.* ½ *p.* [*Cipher enclosed.*]

SIR HENRY BENNET to CONSUL WESTCOMBE.

1664-5, March 1st. Whitehall—I send this by Lord Belasyse, going as Governor to Tangier, "a very gallant man, and particularly my friend, so I have made it much my care to recommend you very kindly to him." You must punctually correspond with him, and have a care of his correspondence with our Ambassador at Madrid, for which and other services you shall find your account and have your expenses paid, besides a salary from the King, which I have delayed asking for, expecting that the merchants would answer me better than they have done concerning your allowances. "Your friend, Sir Thomas Clifford, hath been charged with negotiating this on your behalf, but yet he hath concluded nothing, not for want of goodwill in him to oblige you," but because of the difficulty with the merchants. With this there also goes a packet of commissions from his Royal Highness for you to distribute to Englishmen or strangers who are willing to take them and serve his Majesty against the Dutch. You will receive instructions from Mr. Coventry upon what conditions you are to dispose of them. You will remember we depend principally upon your care to send us constant accounts of what happens on your coasts, in relation either to Tangier, his Majesty's fleets or our merchants. Pray fail not herein. *Copy by Westcombe.* 2 *pp.*

MARTIN WESTCOMBE to SIR RICHARD FANSHAW.

1665, March [5-]15. Cadiz—On Tuesday last, the 18th inst., Admiral Allin, all his frigates and about twenty merchantmen left Gibraltar "with a brave Levant" for England. On the 12th news came from Madrid that the King was very sick, whereupon *rogativos* were made in all the churches in this city for his recovery.

A soldier from Tanger reports that two Moors of importance, well clad in outward vests of scarlet and attended by several servants, have been at Tanger with letters from Gueland to Col. Fitzgerrald, stating that the two Englishmen detained at Arzeela are well, and shall one day be at liberty, and that the

Moors will not hearken to a peace with Tanger until they have a brush first against it. Gueland has had above twenty thousand Moors above Tanger all this cold and wet weather, which must have killed many of them. They still remain about the garrison, dispersed and hid in the bushes, according to their custom, but, thank God, Tanger is in a good condition and quite ready for them. My belief is that they will make no attempt until the 3rd of May, a day "which these barbarous people build upon for success to their enterprises, which indeed by sad remembrance those villains have had twice, in my Lord of Peterborough's time, and the most noble Lord of Teviot then lost his life." 2 *pp.*

CONSUL MARTIN WESTCOMBE to SIR RICHARD FANSHAW.

1665, March [12-]22. Cadiz—Letters from St. Malo's state "that Ludlow, the grand traitor, is in Holland, and assures that nation that his interest in England is so great that he can raise a new distraction in the kingdom again. [Complaints about his own ill-treatment by the merchants.] 2½ *pp.*

SIR RICHARD FANSHAW to MR. CROONE.

1664-5, March 21-31. Madrid—I have received yours of the [7-]17th, and have acquainted these ministers with the suspected design upon Oran by the Turks of Algier. I shall be glad to hear the sequel from time to time. Concerning the rumour of the Duke of Beaufort having gone towards Tanger my letters received to-day from that place and from Cadiz say nothing of it, and therefore I do not credit it. I hear no complaints from this Court of the Knight of Malta whom you mention as spoiling the subjects of his Catholic Majesty in a Portugal ship with English colours, "which methinks should be, were it but to stop my mouth, that is not at all mealy in reference to those many occasions of complaints the Spaniards give to us," especially their imposition of new duties and reviving of the *reprisalia* of Oliver's time. I thank you for your enquiries after the miserable English captives in Tetuan, and pray you to continue to do all you can to obtain their liberty, a pious and charitable office, in which I will willingly join both in word and deed as occasion may offer. Secretary Bennet writes that he has sent orders to all the Consuls to warn English ships not to stir out of any ports without convoys. *Copy.* 1¾ *pp.* [*The letter of March 17, to which this is an answer, is in the Spanish Correspondence.*]

SIR RICHARD FANSHAW to LORD HOLLES.

1665, March 29-April 8. Madrid—The party of horse and foot whom I mentioned in my last as marching against the Portuguese, aimed at Valencia de Alcantra, but finding their design discovered retired without doing anything. Count Marchin, who commanded them, has arrived here, and tells me that he only left the army because "he could not in point of military honour serve under any general but a Prince, having so often commanded armies in chief." When he served under this very Marquis of Caracena in Flanders the Marquis stood *loco principis*, as now does the Marquis of Castel-Rodrigo,* under whom he would not scruple to execute his old command, and to whom I believe he is going again. Sir George Downing sends me Holland's answer to his memorial. "If they prove as good at downright blows as they are at downright railing we shall have the worst end of the staff, but because those two go seldom together I trust in God it will fall out quite otherwise. My Lord Bellasis' arrival at Tanger will now doubtless cure the world of a general error, which without any shadow at all of truth hath constantly prevailed for many months, that his Majesty hath sold the place." I hope his Lordship will have ships enough with him "to make our stake good in the Mediterranean against an upstart fleet which the Dutch are there scrambling together." The King has resolved to go to Aranjuez the middle of this month. *Copy.* 2¼ *pp.*

J[OHN] LORD BELASYSE to CONSUL WESTCOMBE.

[1665], April 6-16. H.M.S. *Foresight*—Announces his arrival in those parts, and desires that Messrs. Andrew and John Duncan, Mr. John Frederick and Messieurs Lasnier and Gentill may be informed that he has letters of credit upon them from their correspondents in London for considerable sums, for the payment of the garrison of Tangier, and that he desires them to have at least the moiety of the moneys in readiness, as he will require supplies shortly. Hopes to arrange that Westcombe,—who has been recommended to him by Secretary Bennett,—shall be better recompensed for his services than formerly.

Postscript.—Prays him to forward a letter to his wife in England. *Copy by Westcombe.* 1 *p.*

WILLIAM BLUNDEN to SIR RICHARD FANSHAW.

1665, April [10-]20. Alicante—Secretary Morice sends me "two blank commissions for private men-of-war against the Dutch, with freedom to carry and sell the prizes in Tanger, which is much more at hand than England." I will endeavour to bestow them upon some active persons of our nation, but this port is not much frequented by strangers, and at present I do not know certainly of any who could undertake the employment. I see he is sending the same to several other ports, and Sir Henry Bennett writes to me to the same purpose.

Don Sevastian del Hoyo will speedily wait upon you. The Dutch *barco longo* still keeps about Cartagena. Ten days since,

---

* Don Luis de Benavides, Carrillo y Toledo, Marques de Fromista et de Caracena, Spanish governor of the Low Countries, 1661-1664, recalled to take the command against Portugal. Don Francisco de Moura Cortereal, 3rd Marques de Castel Rodrigo, governor of the Low Countries, 1664-1668.

they set upon an English vessel, but she killed and hurt some of their men and forced them to leave her.

"We frequently receive letters from Oran, and I have not seen nor heard any mention of attempts to be feared from Argier. The Marques de Leganes hath that garrison in a good condition, and hath intelligence by land from Argier and other in parts of Barbary, the town is well peopled and stored with provision . . . and the place is so strong and well fortified that they fear not all Barbary," so I conceive there is no ground for that report, as I am very glad that of the sale of Tanger is the same. I now understand it had its first rise in France, from the money which the *Ann,* one of his Majesty's third-rate frigates, carried to Lisboa for the dowry of one of the Mademoiselles d'Orleans, to be married with the King of Portugal, which not being known or remembered, the fame ran that money was the price of Tanger. I conceive it is the most important place in Christendom for his Majesty and good of our nation, and when the Mold is built and magazines it may maintain itself with little or no charge to the Crown. It was an obscure place and not known till delivered to his Majesty, and now the whole world sees how much the case is altered by the change of possessor. Yesterday one of the State of Genoa's galleys arrived, come for their ambassador. She touched at Mallorca, where Don Francisco Cottoner, brother to the great Master of Malta, embarked on her. He is going to Madrid. 3 *pp. Endorsed as received* 18-28 *ditto."*

SIR RICHARD FANSHAW to CONSUL WESTCOMBE.

1665, April 11-21. Madrid—The King and Queen of Spain have gone to Aranjuez for a month. The Marques de Caracena has taken his leave and will speedily repair to the army. The Bishop of Metz, uncle to the French King, left Paris on the 30th past with his assistant in the embassy and a very splendid train of three hundred persons. "I am very heartily sorry for the persecution of Don Antonio Pimentell, whom I always took for an exceeding honest gentleman and most accomplished minister, both in martial and civil affairs, of whose person also I have a particular affectionate esteem, wishing I knew how to serve him . . . and wondering as much as you upon what account the *oydor* [of Granada], his judge, should proceed to the rigour of imprisonment of any of our nation." Have not our nation a judge conservador of their own in those parts? I wish likewise further certainty of the Saint's diversion of Guylan, and what progress his supposed army is making. *Copy.* 1½ *pp.*

J[OHN] LORD BELASYSE to SIR RICHARD FANSHAW.

1665, April 15. Tangier—His Majesty having honoured me with the command of this place and enjoined my correspondence with you I send this to inform you of my safe arrival, after a prosperous passage, and that I find all here in a good condition.

"Our neighbours in Africa we may perhaps expect upon that superstitious our unfortunate day, May the 3rd, but that which threatens a greater danger is the strength of the Hollanders at Cales, in case de Rutter return thither and should block us up by sea." If this should happen, pray advise his Majesty of it at once that he may send ships to our relief. I have brought letters from the King to the Duke of Medina Celi, Governor of Andalusia, which I shall send next week, your Excellency's solicitation having much improved our correspondence with Spain. *Holograph.* 2¼ *pp.*

WILLIAM BLUNDEN to SIR RICHARD FANSHAW.

1665, April [17-]27. Alicante—Thanks him for agreeing to represent to the English Court their request that Don Sevastian del Hoyo may be Consul in Cartagena. Hears that four Smyrna ships are passed, convoyed as far as Tanger by three men-of-war, of which the *Foresight*, bringing over Lord Bellasis, is one, and will remain there. The other two, with the *Crown*, return homeward with all speed. Last week the Duke of Beaufort with three men-of-war and a fireship came into port, but has left again to lie by Cape Martin. "They say they have burnt the Admiral of Argeir and another great ship of theirs near Tunis. All the country about Oran is in peace with that garrison. It is probable the Turks of Argeir, when they go to recover their tribute at Tremesen, as they yearly do, may molest the *Advares* [*i.e.*, nomadic villages] of the Moors for having peace with Oran, as their custom is continually, but now somewhat more than ordinary, in regard no Governor hath had peace so far within the country as this Marques de Leganes now hath, but they cannot attempt anything against the place." *Signed.* ¾ *p.*
Endorsed :—"Received 25 April-5 May."

SIR RICHARD FANSHAW to LORD BELLASIS.

1665, April 18-28. Madrid—Congratulating him on his assuming the government of Tangier and begging to be honoured with his commands both in public and private affairs. *Copy.* 1 *p.*

SIR RICHARD FANSHAW to CONSUL WESTCOMBE.

1665, April 18-28. Madrid—This King, with the Queen and Empress, have been almost a fortnight at Aranjuez, and his Majesty is so vigorous as "to have sat on horseback a matter of three hours, and in that posture to have killed a wolf from his own hand," whereas before his going there it was doubted whether he had strength to perform the seven leagues journey in a coach or litter, and that in two days. "The Marques de Caracena is gone to the army against Portugal, and people are big with expectation of what will be done this *campaña.*" The Duke of Avero will speedily depart for Cadiz to take command of the Spanish navy royal. *Copy.* 1 *p.*

Sir Richard Fanshaw to Lord Holles.

1665, April 19-29. Madrid—"I have not lately received any from your Excellency. All people grow big now with expectation of what will be the success of this Spanish campaign against Portugal, of the great French embassy into England, and above all of the Duke of York's personal expedition against the Hollanders, whose princely person and undertaking God Almighty preserve and prosper. [*This letter is almost identical with one to Bennet in the Harley MSS., and the middle part is printed in Lady Fanshaw's memoirs, p.* 300.]

We have good news from Tangier, and hear "that the Saint is upon the back of Guylan with a considerable army. If this prove true I should think a very good game—as the state of things may be at home—might suddenly be played there, nipping and crushing the Hollanders in those seas into the bargain." *Copy.* 1¾ *pp.*

Lord Belasyse to Consul Westcombe.

1665, April 22. Tanger—Thanking him for his warning concerning a design of the Hollanders and saying that if Captain Wagger can engage their privateers he dare contribute to the wager that he will come off victorious. *Copy by Westcombe.* 1¼ *pp.* [*Two other copies in the Tangiers Correspondence.*]

Martin Westcombe to Sir Richard Fanshaw.

1665 [April 23-]May 3. Cadiz—I have received your Lordship's of the 11-21, and humbly thank you for it. Last Friday, the 1st inst., twelve Dutch men-of-war left this place, avowedly to accompany their Smyrna ships, but I have sent notice thereof to Lord Belasyse, in case they should attempt anything against that garrison or the ships in its port. Here we have only the *Crown* frigate and a few merchantmen.

"As to the Granada *oyidor* and judge against Don Antonio Pimentell, our late Governor, his proceeding against my Vice-Consul and one Mr. Richards, merchant, even to imprisoning them, I am informed it was because they did not upon their oath declare the truth of what they knew and acted with their own hands." A day or two after, they and the judge became very good friends, so all is well. This city never had a judge Conservador. They are only in Seville and Malaga. "This judge is generally reported to be as upright a judge as the world affords; prosecutes the whole truth against the late Governor, and 'tis said will not admit an untruth against him nor any other if he knows it, not for the world's treasure."

"The Saint Banbuquer and his son are fallen out, as I hear, which now puts a stop to the intended expedition against Gueland. All well at Tanger two days since, praised be God.·

This is the sad day, my Lord, on which the Earl of Teviot
and five hundred men with him perished, and the like number
on said day in the Lord of Peterborough's time."

The Dutch men-of-war are still riding before Rotta. Yesterday they chased in here an English ship, the *John*, Capt. James
Bonnel, from Bilboa, laden with iron. It would be much for
our honour and the safety of the English merchant men if
we had six or eight frigates on this coast. As it is " the Dutch
crow very much over us."

I assure you there is not a word of truth in what Mr. Cuningam
and his consorts lay to my charge. Mr. Southerland and Mr.
Courtney are ashamed of it, and say they were drawn into it
by others. Mr. Cuningam, whom one may term a Spaniard,
thinks of nothing but of engratiating himself with this nation,
and cares not what prejudice he may do to ours. 4 *pp.*

Endorsed :—" Received 1-11 ditto."

Alexander Southerland to Lionel Fanshaw.

1665 [April 23?-]May 3. Cadiz—I have received your
courteous lines of the 21st ultimo, and shall be glad to serve
you. "As to the bad understanding the nation and Consul
[Westcombe] have together, I consider it very obnoxious to
all in these times especially, but in reality the Consul is totally
the occasion of it, pretending a power and jurisdiction over all
beyond that of any of his predecessors." He seems now to
be sensible of his errors. "He is a criminal person, and his
place not able to maintain him and his family, except he can
oblige the nation to assist him."

Sir Richard Fanshaw to Lord Belasyse, at Tangier.

1665 [April 25-]May 5. Madrid—"Having received your
Excellency's, dated at Tanger 15th of the last, I do now upon
more absolute certainty, with the same cordialness as in mine
by the last post, give your Excellency a joyful welcome into
that Government and my neighbourhood, beginning my correspondence with public news that will not displease you.

From Mr. Secretary Benet—now Lord Arlington—as followeth
of the 6th of the last.* Our news from Guiney is infinitely
much better than we could have expected. Most of our ships
are safely come off the coast, and places in a resolution and
condition of holding out, but what is become of De Ruyter
we do not yet know.

This same news is a little more explained to me by my brother
Warwick, viz.:—We have a good return from Guiney this day,
Cormention [Cormantin] and all safe 18th of December, and
40,000*l.* in gold and good cargoes.

The Spanish Ambassador, likewise the two from France,
arrived that day.

---

* This letter of Lord Arlington's is among the Fanshaw letters at the
British Museum. Harley MSS. 7010, f. 231.

A good peace and league concluded between his Majesty and Sweden.

A very ill understanding at that time between the French and the Hollanders upon the account of two great frigates built in Holland for the French King and detained by the States for their own service; how far this will be resented by France more than already it is and what further influence it may have as to our affairs a little time will show.

The Duke of York at sea with more than eighty great ships already: difference of opinion, whether the Hollanders will venture out or no; if they do a most bloody battle cannot be avoided. God protect the person of his royal Highness and prosper his Majesty's cause.

Another clause in my Lord Arlington's letter is as followeth:—The rumours you hear of rising and troubles in Scotland or Ireland have not the least foundation for them. The King since he came home was never so obeyed everywhere as he is now, neither was there ever so little discontent appeared. The whole people of what opinion or interest soever are generally fond of this war and the vigorous prosecution of it is the most popular thing the King can pursue. The particulars of this I leave to your other correspondents.

Thus far my Lord Arlington, and indeed many particular friends of mine—who have no relation to Court—write largely to the same effect.

Your Excellency's two packets enclosed with your letter to me, I shall send forward for England by to-morrow's post, and advance your wishes of a squadron in those parts as much as lies in me and may stand with his Majesty's service elsewhere for several reasons, especially in case De Ruyter should come up that way, who I think is dived into the sea."

Postscript.—" My private news is very unsuitable to that of the public, and will be some grief to your Excellency for the honour you did the deceased to love him. Upon Easter Day last in England, God took to himself my most dear and loving brother, my Lord Fanshaw. To qualify this great loss in some measure his son—now Lord Fanshaw—about the same time was married to a fair and very exceedingly rich young lady." *Copy.* 2 *pp.*

F[ILIBERT] VERNATTI to SIR RICHARD FANSHAW.

1665, May 2-12. Port St. Mary—Lord Belasyse sent me here with letters from his Majesty and himself to the Duke of Medina Celi, and whilst I was here he sent the *Crown* frigate to this port, which at the mouth of the bay fought with two Holland's men-of-war—who went out on purpose to meet him—forced them both on shore, and killed the Captain and other officers of one of them. For this the Dutch have much abused the Captain, and when he put off to sea he was followed by two Hollanders, who fired after him. They returned next day with other Dutch men-of-war and gave out that the frigate had run away to Tanger, " and since have posted more libels, and sufficiently scandalous, but the Duke of Medina caused them to pull [them] down, with great threats against the person that put them up, if he could but find him. . . . I yesterday desired the Consul to go with me to kiss the Duke's hands, who, after he had passed his compliments to my Lord Belasyse, asked the Consul why the frigate went away without his license. The Consul answered he had given the Captain notice of the orders he had received, but he was the Commander of a man-of-war, and received no instructions but what came from England. The Duke turned to me and commanded me to tell the General of Tanger that the Consul proceeded very ill, and that he must proceed against the Consul, and that if there had been no King in Spain it was sufficient he was upon this place; then commanded his adjutant to put the Consul in the prison, which was done. And a while after a letter wrote from the Duke to the Governor of Cadiz, and the Consul sent over, and order given the said Governor to proceed against the Consul as he should find cause, so the Governor sent him to the gaol of Cadiz, and immediately after the Dutch Consul was also brought in to keep him company, where at present both are. What will be the end I know not, but it is apparently evident that the Hollanders are more favoured than the English, and the affections of the Spaniards in these places are totally for the Dutch." Having been an eye-witness of all this I thought it my duty to give you an account thereof. 2¼ *pp.* [*There is a copy of this letter in the Spanish Correspondence, but it is calendared here at some length as explaining Westcombe's letters of this time.*]

MARTIN WESTCOMBE to SIR RICHARD FANSHAW.

1665, May [2-]12. Cadiz—Giving the circumstances of his own and the Dutch Consul's imprisonment, by order of the Duke of Medina Celi, stating that his only crime was having permitted Captain Wager to depart from the bay without the Duke's license—as if his Majesty's frigates were at his disposal—and praying his Excellency to acquaint Lord Arlington with what has happened. 3 *pp.* [*There is a copy of this in the Spanish Correspondence.*]

The SAME to the SAME.

1665, May [3-]13. Cadiz—Stating that he is informed by his fellow-prisoner, the Dutch Consul, that in answer to the Dutch Admiral the Duke of Medina Celi had declared that he put the Consuls in prison because the English and Dutch frigates had gone out, as it was reported to fight; and marvelling, if this were a crime, that the Duke himself, with the young Duke of Alcalla, went out in the expectation of seeing them fight, as did the Governor of Cadiz, and thousands of people there and at St. Mary port. 3 *pp.* [*Copy in the Spanish Correspondence. These two letters are endorsed as received on the 9-19 May.*]

Lord Belasyse to Sir Richard Fanshaw.

1665, May 4. Tanger—We are in a more secure and prosperous condition than ever, I having already succeeded "in rectifying several disorders, dissipating of factions, putting the civil government into a way of settlement and the martial into better discipline. . . . We did yesterday—being the Moors' superstitious and our formerly unfortunate day—draw our garrison into arms," but Guyland did not appear. I hear that Benbuker is advancing towards him with considerable strength. Sir Bernard de Gomme will tell you more of our affairs. His merit and prudence in settling our fortifications has contributed much to his Majesty's service and our security. *Autograph.*

Postscript.—If you have not yet received an account of Captain Wager's success against two Holland men-of-war, Sir Bernard will give it you. 2½ *pp.* [*Compare his letter to the King of the same date, in the Tangiers Correspondence.*]

John Bland to Sir Richard Fanshaw.

1665, May 7-17. Port St. Mary—Has been to Sevilla and other parts on business for Tanger, but is now returning thither. The Consul of Cadiz is in prison " by the Duke of Medina Celi, to serve his humour," and the people are much against the English and in favour of the Dutch, whose part they take on all occasions. Hearing that Mr. John Vassall, Consul at Malaga, is dead, he prays for the place, which would be a good second to his business at Tanger. 2 *pp.*

Madrid.

1665, May [8-]18—Paper concerning the arrangements made by the town of Madrid for fitting up a platform or balcony from which the English ambassador may see the " *Fiesta de los Toros.*" *Copy. Spanish.* 1½ *pp.*

Sir Richard Fanshaw to Lord Belasyse.

1665, May 9-19. Madrid—Giving an account of the taking of three Dutch ships by Captain [John] King of the *Diamond* between Yarmouth and Holland. *Copy.* 1 *p.*

Sir Richard Fanshaw to Consul Westcombe.

1665, May 9-19. Madrid—Yours of the 10th came yesterday to my hands, confirmed by one from Mr. Vernatty. "I do not see what reason the Dutch or anybody else have to scoff at us for what you write was lately done by the *Crown* frigate or the Commander thereof, Captain Wagger, but if they think they have it is to be wished they may have such occasion every day." I am very sorry for what has befallen you, and shall do my utmost for you. I have drawn up a memorial for his Majesty, who has to-day returned from Aranjuez, and sent it to the Council of State, and when I have an answer will acquaint you speedily therewith. It is reported from Brittany that the English and Holland's fleet have been seen fighting. "For the present I give little credit to this, appealing, as my author doth, to the next." I hope you and your good wife will be of good heart. *Copy.* 1¾ *pp.*

JOSEPH WILLIAMSON to SIR RICHARD FANSHAW.

1665, May 11. Whitehall—My Lord Arlington commands me to excuse his not writing, "his Lordship, it seems, finding nothing of business to be worth it. Tuesday last you will see the French Ambassadors had their public audience in much ceremony, being led to it by the Earl of Oxford." We are expecting our fleet on our own coasts, "so as our neighbours will then have one excuse less for not coming out, which it seems they begin now to be ashamed of, and have much ado to answer to their people." 1 *p.*

INTELLIGENCE FROM ENGLAND.

1665, May 11. London—Mrs. Steele has been committed to the King's Bench for complicity in the murder of one Perkins, a bailiff. It appears that Mr. Francis Fortescue, Mr. — Fortescue, Mr. Sheldon and Mr. Dudley—all of the King's Guards—were the men concerned in it, and that one of the Fortescues and Mr. Dudley killed him, the other two assisting.

The Bill against the coal merchants and woodmongers is found, and three of them are to come to their trial next term. On May 3rd the Grand Jury found the Bill for the murder of Mr. Hastings against my Lord Morley and Capt. Bremengham, an *ignoramus* as to Mr. Mark Trevor.

Hull, May 2nd.—The coasts are full of capers, who cause much loss. Sixty sail going north were forced into Scarborough and "some about Whitby, where the Dutch fired several guns into the town."

Edinburgh, April 29.—The suspected persons in the west of Scotland are all disarmed and about twenty seamen seized, two of which are said to have kept correspondence with the Dutch.

From Ireland we have advice of one Dutch caper taken and another that escaped by night, but so maimed that it is judged she could not make a port.

May 5th.—"The Duke of Newcastle came to town, and the next day waited on his Majesty to render his humble thanks for the addition of honour lately conferred on him, which his Majesty was pleased to accept with such favour as showed not only a regard to his merit, but an affection for his person."

The King has made Sir John Finch—brother to the Solicitor General—Resident at Leghorn, "a gentleman, whose parts and travel have rendered him eminently fit for public employment."

Yarmouth, May 5th.—There are many ships in our Roads, and on May 4th several guns were heard at sea.

"The Queen Mother is upon her return into France, being, upon advice of her physicians, to take of the waters of Bourbon for her health."

Mr. Barker has got 1,000*l.* damages upon an action of battery against Mr. Percival, Mr. Godfrey and Mr. Wilford, all three of whom are imprisoned for a month without bail or mainprize, and to give security for their good behaviour for seven years. News of the 5th tells us that our fleet, lying northwest of the Texel, surprized a fleet of Dutch coming from Scotland. . . . The two men-of-war that were their convoy ran first. Eight were taken, seven Bordeaux men and a West India man of good value. The rest, about twenty, are pursued by Capt. [Sir Jeremy] Smith in the *Mary*, formerly called the *Speaker*, with other ships, who we hope will give a good account. Here died by the account of the weekly bills nine this last week: One at Woolchurch, one at St. Andrew's, Holborn, three St. Giles in the Fields and four in St. Clement's Danes, besides spotted fever six, and yet in the general bill it is decreased forty-one, for prevention of which the King's Bench Court made an order requiring and empowering all constables in and about the city to shut up any house suspected to have the sickness, and to prohibit persons from conversing with them. The King's Bench Court gave Mrs. Steele her liberty upon bail till the next term. The Countess of Falmouth is lately delivered of a daughter.

There is no further account given of the German forces intended for the Netherlands, and it is judged they will not proceed in their march till the Infanta begins her journey. That Holland is in great disorder may be easily guessed by the cause [*sic*] our fleet still continues to block them up, but give they out what they will the true reason [is] that they want yet two thousand men to supply even those ships at the Texel.

"The most of the counties in England have made very considerable progress in raising money for a present supply to his Majesty upon the security of the royal aid at six per cent., to which his Majesty adds three per cent. gratuity."

There is no further news from the fleet. 2¼ *pp.*

Endorsed as "received in a letter from Mr. Williamson of the same date."

J. Lord Belasyse, to Consul Westcombe.

1665, May 12-22. Tanger—Assuring him of the resentment with which he has heard of his imprisonment, and desiring to know whether "in relation to the Hollanders and the Duke of Medina's unkindness" to the English, it would be safe to send a frigate to Cadiz for the moneys which he urgently needs for the great arrears of his garrison. Twelve Hollands men-of-war have sailed before the bay, but durst not come within reach of the cannon, and now an easterly Levant wind has forced them back towards Cadiz. *Signed.* ½ *p.*

Endorsed:—"Received in Cadiz Sunday morning, the 24th May, 1665."

SIR RICHARD FANSHAW to CONSUL WESTCOMBE.

1665, May 16-26. Madrid—Enclosed you will find a copy of my memorial to his Catholic Majesty for your liberty, and also of his answer, ordering your speedy release without security. I hope to prevent such disturbances for the future. Sir George Downing writes that a part of the English fleet was supposed to be before the Texel, and that on the 27th ult. there was a great alarum at the Hague and all the beacons at Sckeev-ling and along the coast were fired, so I presume we shall soon hear of some action. *Copy. 1 p.*

Enclosing,

1. *The above-mentioned memorial, dated May* [9-]19. *Spanish. 1 p.*

2. *Secretary Blasco de Loyola to Sir Richard Fanshaw.*

1665, *May* [15-]25—*The King, my master, having seen the representation made by your Excellency concerning the Consul, Mr. Martin Westcombe, now held prisoner in Cadiz, has been pleased to determine that he shall be immediately released, without giving any security. And he has ordered me to take this opportunity of requesting your Excellency in his name to give notice to the Captains of his Britannic Majesty's ships to observe punctually and carefully the conditions of the peace, as regards entrance into, stay in and departure from our ports; that they may not fail in the respect which they owe to those of his Majesty, nor embarrass and obstruct the intercourse and free commerce between friendly nations and this Crown. Spanish. Copy.* ½ *p.*

MARTIN WESTCOMBE to SIR RICHARD FANSHAW.

1665, May [21-]31. Cadiz—I have already thanked you for your care towards my releasement from the Duke's action. I hope you will "procure a *cedulla* that Consuls shall not be subject to imprisonment for his mere fancy or the pleasure of Governors, nor for anything but grave matters alleged, and then not in a common gaol but in places decent to what Consuls represent." Mr. Nathaniel Marston of Seville died, as it were suddenly, last week of a dead palsy, "and the Consul of Malaga, Mr. John Vassall, died in England very lately of a fistula. My disease, my Lord, I fear me will be only starving, which, well considered, is a disease bad enough." I made little enough in time of peace, when ships came to the port, but now "that no ships have come of a great while and God knows when they will" I am at my wits' end. I have written to Lord Arlington "to be pleased to purchase a handsome subsistence for me by one means or other, as all other Consuls have for the honour of their countries," and I beg your Lordship to send him a

24. M

certificate of what you know of me in reference to his Majesty's service.

There are now sixteen or seventeen Dutch ships before Tangier, which, if ten or twelve English frigates were sent, might be beaten all to pieces. We do not know what mischief they will do, nor how long they will block up the place. They have taken several *barcos longos* from hence and from Malaga, going with wine, sheep and other provisions to Tangier.

I am told that the garrison there and the Dutch ships have exchanged above five hundred pieces, and the Dutch ship *St. Lewis* received four great shot in his hull; also that the Dutch are resolved " to remain before Tangier until they starve it, that the Moors may take it from us if they cannot. Praised be God, Tanger hath above fifteen months' provision." Your Lordship will see by the letters I send that Lord Belasyse acknowledges the seasonable advice I gave him of the intentions of the Dutch, which enabled him to get the great guns down to the water side and to bring the ships close to the shore, to the chain, when otherwise they would all have been surprized and taken. 4 *pp.*

Sir Richard Fanshaw to Lord Bellasyse.

1665, June [6-]16. Madrid—Yours to Lord Arlington and my brother Warwick shall be forwarded to England to-morrow. I shall always concur with you " so far as may stand with his Majesty's main design near home, which only himself can positively judge of, having all before him." I doubt not but the best will be done for the important place under your command. " For a whole week at least, till within these two days, Hollanders' intelligence had sunk fifty of our men-of-war in one—by them reported—battle. That invention failing they have now shipwrecked of ours perhaps more. For this latter they have more colour, but—I trust in God—no more truth." The enclosed will lay the facts impartially before you. *Copy.* 1 *p.*

Joseph Williamson to Sir Richard Fanshaw.

1665, June 8. Whitehall—My lord wishes me to say " that he hopes the enclosed will content you in point of news for one week. God grant us much more such, though I hope we shall not have occasion for the wish, so great is the victory God hath given his Majesty at this blow. The enclosed is a copy of the letter written on this argument to my Lord Mayor this night,* and will satisfy your Excellency of the most material circumstances of this glorious action. Never was people so transported with joy as is this city and country universally. His royal

---

* This fixes the date of the letter to the Lord Mayor, put to June [5?] in the Cal. S.P. Dom. for 1664-1665.

Highness is yet on the coast of Holland, and picking up the stragglers, if any be left. Banker [Vice-Admiral Bancquaert] of Zealand had his leg shot off, which was omitted in the relation."

Postscript.—" The fight began off Sole Bay, on our own coast, with several signal circumstances of God's favour to us, as the arrival of a hundred and fifty collier ships that very morning from Newcastle, which filled up our numbers of men; the safe arrival of four frigates of ours and a rich merchant fleet from the Baltic; the advantage of the wind, which turned for us the very hour we engaged, and stood right all day." 1¼ *pp.*

VISCOUNT DONGAN to SIR RICHARD FANSHAW.

1665, June [9-]19. Bayonne—We have been alarmed by letters sent from Madrid to Victoria to the secretary of the Franciscan order with news of a great victory got by the Hollanders, who also reported for certain that Prince Rupert's squadron were all cut off, but both news have proved false. The Dutch fleet has gone to the North Sea to meet De Ruder, and I believe ours is not far from them. " I advertise your Excellency lest you should be *asustared* [*i.e.*, frightened] as I was by the Hollanders' well-framed stories and the Spaniards' credulity of the blind man's dreams." *Holograph.* 2½ *pp.*

MARTIN WESTCOMBE to SIR RICHARD FANSHAW.

1665, June [11-]21. Cadiz—I thank your Lordship for yours of the 9th and the certificate, which I shall keep as an honour to me and my children after me.

All is well at Tanger. " The Dutch men-of-war are hovering about the Straits' mouth, sometimes in and so out, to wait for our merchants ships and for the *Crown* frigate, Capt. Wagger, which they heartily endeavour to snap if they can. By the Lord Belasyse's order, I have settled a post twixt this place and Tanger for letters to go and come every week." The boat comes to Tarrifa, which confronts Tanger, and from thence the letters reach me on Saturday or Monday and go on by this day's post to Madrid and England.

The *propio* I keep till our post comes on Tuesday and then despatch him back to Tarrifa, and there our *barco longo* waits to carry him over the six leagues to Tanger.

Sir Benj. Wright arrived from Madrid three days since. It is said the Duke of Avero will go to sea in eight or ten days. The *Admirante* General Don Paublos de Contrera was buried last Thursday. It is believed our present Governor, Don Diego de Zbarro, will succeed him, " although the Principe Montesarcho be in a fair way for it, but his art at sea is short of Don Diego's.

" I pray your honour to notice the third article of what the Dutch Consul wishes to have put in his *cedulla*, for it is very important. I have sometimes been sent for by the Duke to St.

M 2

Mary Port, kept two or three days, and then merely told by his secretary that the Duke esteemed my care in coming but had nothing to say to me, while, all the time, ships and matters of commerce were urgently needing my assistance, and the Dutch Consul has been served in the same way.

"A Consul cannot duly execute his charge if he be liable to any Duke or Governor that may either disturb him upon design or mere fancy, for I humbly conceive, my Lord, that Consuls ought to be free and absolute in their ways that are just and warrantable.

"The Spaniards in these parts promise themselves great success against the Portugals this summer. *El tiempo lo dira.*"

Three days since about twenty Dutch merchant men set sail for the north. It is believed they will not venture into the Channel but will go for Norway. They are mostly laden with salt. The rich Smyrna men are still here and dare not stir. $3\frac{1}{2}$ *pp.*

Endorsed :—"Rec. 19-29 ditto."

SIR RICHARD FANSHAW to CONSUL WESTCOMBE.

1665, June 13-23. Madrid—Our last news from England makes us question whether the Dutch fleet will put to sea at all at present. "The English navy royal, that the Hollanders might have the less excuse for their not coming out, were all well upon our own coast on the 4th instant, new style, notwithstanding those several Dutch reports . . . of most of our fleet being destroyed, sometimes by storm and sometimes by fight; but we are now so well accustomed to hear such flams that they find no credit with us." No doubt you know more about the late Portuguese victory than I do. *Draft.* 1 *p.*

JOHN BLAND to SIR RICHARD FANSHAW.

1665, June 15. Tanger—I thank you for your kind information to Lord Bellasis concerning me. I have always found him very kind since I got to Tanger, "yet I find my being in Spain at his arrival, which I thought might have been the better, proved somewhat to my disadvantage." If the Consulship of Malaga be confirmed to me it will not only help my own affairs here in Tanger but likewise enable me "to assist forwards the public." I can be all the vintage time in Malaga and the rest of the year in Tanger. "I supposed these things had been absolutely in your Excellency's disposal, the merchants there consenting therein. If it must come by my Lord Benitt's hands I doubt much, because I fear he hath no kindness for me, because I appeared so much for Sir Francis Bedingfield, whom it seems, contrary to my knowledge, he had a pique [against], although what I did therein was merely out of a respect I bore to my Lord Benitt, but it was not then so taken." I have written to Mr. Povey to bespeak him the right way and "if it take, well, if not I shall not be much troubled," but go on with what presents itself here. If the soldiery of the Irish party here bore less sway and would not meddle in other than military affairs this place would soon render the King profit and commerce would quickly settle, but so long as "none must live here but subject to their ways and power, your Excellency may judge what encouragement men of business can find amongst armed men." For want of some good frigates the Hollanders much disturb this port, as do also the Moors of Guylan's party. "In England they are not so sensible as they should of the advantages of this place, and of what consequence it is to our King's glory and honour to have a small navy here." We are in daily expectation of Guylan and his army towards the settling of a peace one way or another. *2 pp.*

Endorsed as received at Madrid July 6, new style.

Martin Westcombe to Sir Richard Fanshaw.

1665, June [18-]28. Cadiz—The enclosed came for you yesterday from Tangier. [*Probably Bland's letter, above.*] We hear that all is well there, and that the *Crown* frigate has arrived safely in spite of the endeavours of the Dutch vessels to entrap her on the way. We are hourly hoping for news of the success of our encounter with the Dutch in the Channel. "The Portugal army about Villa Viciossa, where our Queen of England was born, fought a pitched battle with the Spaniards the 17th current, and after six hours' dispute, from one of the clock at noon, the Spaniards were totally routed of their whole army with bag and baggage and guns by the Portugals, which makes this nation in these parts look very blue upon it."

It is thought that the Duke of Avero, having now little to do, will take his fleet out of danger of the Turks and wait about the Southward Cape for the coming of the galleons, which are expected in August.

It is remarkable "that Don Paublos de Contrera, *Admirante* General, that was to go and fight against the Portugals, died the 17th of this, which was the very day the Spaniards were routed by the Portugals, and we have it here how that very day the King of Spain was in great danger in his coach, which was crushed to pieces by some building that fell upon it as his Majesty was going to some convent to his devotions." It is said that Guyland means to conclude a peace with Lord Belasyse. I doubt not his Lordship will observe the Spanish maxim, *en paez o en guerra, guarda bien tu tierra*. I wish some salary could be procured for me from his Majesty for my better subsistence and discharge of the duties of my office. I hope also that you will procure the general *cedulla* in favour of Consuls, such as the Dutch ambassador is about to get. It will be of high concern to his Majesty's affairs, and a means to unite to me all the affections of his subjects here, if they know that my house is a sanctuary for protection of their goods and persons in case of need. 3¼ *pp.*

Endorsed:—"Received 6 July, 65, n.s."

SIR RICHARD FANSHAW to CONSUL MARTIN WESTCOMBE.

1665, July 4-14. Madrid—In answer to yours "I formerly prepared you to expect nothing but dismal alarms of the Dutch beating us before our own doors; we had them here in plenty and for no less than a whole month together, one upon the neck of another, hardly delivered from them yet, though the contrary have come so fully confirmed from all parts, not excepting Holland itself, and that from hands that wished it enough otherwise. . . . For my own part, I do not wonder to find that nation spread these inventions far from home, having a letter by me from the Hague * which assures me that when the certain news of all came thither, in an open note of five or six lines to one of the States, in the midst of a great crowd of people, he read it to himself, had a guard kept upon the fellow that brought it," and sent the pink in which he came from the fleet out to sea again immediately, whereon "a report ran presently as if they had got the victory, and a note was put up to one of the ministers there, after the seven o'clock sermon, to thank God for the same, as he accordingly did and there was a strange echoing for joy among the people present; but for all that, within an hour or two after, the truth began to get out by little and little, turning their joy into mourning; this was short and sweet."

A great man of this Court asked me why they spread such false news. I answered that whatever moved them to it, "it was a content I did not grudge to an enemy, hurting nobody but themselves."

You have done very well to warn Lord Bellasyse of the suspected underhand dealing against Tangier. We must all be awake to the possibility of surprize or combination and be able to distinguish our friends from our foes.

I am sorry that your bodily indisposition continues. "If it were a sickness of the mind, the contents of the enclosed for my Lord Bellasyse—which therefore I leave unclosed for your perusal—would cure you." Pray show them to Sir Benjamin Wright, if he is still in Cadiz. *Copy.* 3½ *pp.*

JOHN WESTCOMBE to SIR RICHARD FANSHAW.

1665, July [10-]20. Bayonne—I suppose we shall soon hear of another fight with the Dutch. Their last beating "hath, it seems, given great jealousy to this kingdom," and we hear constant talk of a war with England.

M. Colbert has written to the first president and jurats of Bordeaux to stay all vessels in the river. "The English frigates take all the French vessels they meet, pretending them to be bound for Holland or Zealand." The Dutch report that De Ruyter has taken seventeen English ships near Barbadoes, which is as true as many other things they have proclaimed. "Sir John Lawson much regretted in London, where the sick-

---

* *See* Downing's letter of June 8. Harley MSS., 7,010.

ness increaseth much. There died the last week two hundred and sixty-seven. God withdraw his heavy hand from them. It is most about St. Giles' and the Long Acre. The Court was about to remove to Hampton Court." 1 *p.*
Endorsed :—" Received 18-28 ditto."

Sir Richard Fanshaw to Don Antonio de Sousa de Macedo.

1665, July [12-]22. Madrid—Stating that the chief reason for his despatch to Lisbon is in regard of the affairs of Don Francisco de Alarçon [Conde de Torres Vedras], now a prisoner in the Tower of Belem, but that he does not intercede with his Excellency in that behalf, believing that his wife's application to Donna Mariana—to which she is urged by the unhappy mother of the Count—will be still more effectual. *Draft. Spanish.* 1 *p.*

Sir Richard Fanshaw to Don Anelo de Gusman.

1665, July [12-]22. Madrid—Expressing pleasure at hearing that he is well, and assuring him of the continuance of his efforts to procure his release. *Spanish. Draft.* ½ *p.*

Consul Martin Westcombe to Sir Richard Fanshaw.

1665, July [16-]26. Cadiz—Three or four Dutch ships of war of the old squadron are careening at Puntall. The rest are about the Straits' mouth and Malaga, watching for Captain Wager in the *Crown*, and some Smyrna ships. "God send us a dozen English frigates upon this coast and then all these Dutch men-of-war, which are poorly manned and victualled, will vanish away and leave us masters of these seas also, and we shall be free of a most lying nation." Letters from London tell us that the sickness increases and that a hundred odd had died that week of the plague. The report has come to the Spaniards, who have sat in *Cabildo* about it. "This nation needs but a feather for a subject to debar us from any commerce with Tangier, to gratify Guiland's desires," and it would be well for that garrison not to depend upon us here for provisions. 2½ *pp.*

Sir Richard Fanshaw to Consul Westcombe.

1665, July 18-28. Madrid—The contents of your last are so material that I shall send a copy to England. We have heard nothing certain thence since I wrote to you, save that a squadron of Dutch men-of-war " was gone to the north for securing their adventures that way, and Prince Rupert, not ill attended, in the rear of them. . . . The Hollanders give out they will come suddenly forth with a fleet more numerous than their last, to expect which—according to computation—his Royal Highness with another more numerous and strong than his last is before the date hereof before their ports the third time, and consequently, if they sallied, the second blow struck. God preserve his princely person" and send us success.

Postscript.—"We hear to our great grief that Sir John Lawson is dead of his hurt received in the battle." *Copy.* 1½ *pp.*

Sir Thomas Ingram to Sir Richard Fanshaw.

[16]65, July 28. Hampton Court—Praying him to forward a packet to Lord Bellasyse containing orders of importance, and wishing him all happiness and a safe return. *Seal, with device.* ½ *p. Endorsed as received 2 November, s.n.*

Sir Richard Fanshaw to Lord Belasyse.

1665, August 1-11. Madrid—I have received yours,* telling me of the King of Portugal's most generous present, sent upon the report that you were besieged both by sea and land. Letters from the Hague † tell me that the Hollanders brag much that they have blocked you up; and also "that they have endeavoured all they can to make the world believe their loss by our late victory upon them to be very inconsiderable, yet now at last they universally acknowledge that they were beaten, and that most shamefully." The officers at the Texel have declared that John Everson—who was so much abused at his coming ashore—" behaved himself in the fight, no man better, yet as to satisfaction for throwing him into the water and the like, he is like to get none. Both he and Trump, especially the latter, are discontented with De Witt and the rest of the Estates' deputies at the Texell," and the Admiralty of Amsterdam has complained to the Estates General that they take too much upon them. There have been mutinies on several of the ships and in various parts of the country "when the drums beat for men in the name of the Estates, without mentioning the Prince of Orange." They are trying to get their fleet together again, but men come in slowly and there is great animosity between the marine soldiers and the seamen " touching their behaviour in the fight, the first being now observed to have but little courage to the business, more than what they have from brandy-wine." They had not yet pitched upon their Commander-in-Chief, having lost their best men in this fight. John Bancker of Zeeland has died of his wounds. Their loss of officers and men is thought to be more irreparable than that of their ships.

Adrian Bancker went out with twenty ships, but has returned without doing anything. De Ruyter's wife had received a letter from him from Martinique, telling her that he had nine men killed and twenty-two wounded on his own ship at the Barbadoes. It is acknowledged that he has not taken Cape Coreo [Corço], nor is anything said of his having taken Cormantine. Three Captains have been condemned to be shot at the Texel,

---

* Lord Belasyse's letter is in Harley MSS., 7,010 (f. 325).   †*See* Downing's letters. *Ibid.*

and three or four others to be punished, "such as had but few friends."

My last letters from England said that the fleet was putting to sea, the *Royal Sovereign* carrying a hundred and six brass guns and being commanded by Sir Jeremy Smith. His Majesty has "with much ado prevailed with his Royal Highness to stay at home this time, as Prince Rupert doth also."* The three squadrons are commanded by Lord Sandwich, Sir William Penn and Sir Thos. Allin. *Copy.* 4½ *pp.*

Sir Richard Fanshaw to Consul Westcombe.

1665, August 8-18. Madrid—Thanking him for his news and stating that it will be of little purpose to prohibit the merchants in London from writing to their factors in Spain concerning the sickness unless the bills of mortality are suppressed, and the Spanish ambassador and resident in England and their followers persuaded not to write thereof. *Copy.* 1 *p.*

Sir Richard Fanshaw to Sir George Downing.

1665, August 9-19. Madrid—We here have had as many reports of victories by the Dutch as you have had of the blocking up of Tangier, the truth of all which "will give them as little cause to brag as to rejoice, unless . . . to come alive off, though lame, [is] a matter of jubilee." The last news from Tangier was good. Guyland was said to have drawn near the garrison, sending a present to Lord Belasyse "with other shows of desiring peace." I hear that the Duke of Beaufort is or soon will be upon the coast of Andalusia, bringing French mariners to supply the Dutch ships about Cadiz, but of this last "I do make a very great question." The galleons arrived at St. Lucar have brought about eighteen millions of plate. The patache *Margarita* from the pearl coast was carried off by the Argereens after small dispute. "What was become of the Spaniards' twenty sail of men-of-war under the command of the Duke of Avero no man there then knew." The French fleet was then said to be about the Straits' mouth. "The Palace here talks aloud of the Empress beginning her journey by all means the next month, but the Court looks upon the variableness that is in the circumstances of her conveyance as no sign at all of any such haste, and upon this occasion a hundred political surmises are whispered abroad."† *Draft.* 2 *pp.*

Lord Belasyse to Sir Richard Fanshaw.

1665, August 10-20. Tanger—I enclose a relation of what has passed between us, the Hollanders, and those of Algeres, who brought in the Spanish prize. I have defended and secured what remained of her cargo, "yet I confess 'tis a little against my conscience to contribute to serve Turks against Christians," although I am obliged to do it to preserve peace with those

* *See* Arlington's letter of July 6th. Harley MSS., 7,010. † Compare letter to Arlington. *Ibid.*

people. Guyland has sent me a present of fresh provisions and overtures tending to a peace. He is so "hard put to his defence against the armies of Ben Bowcar and the King of Taffaletta, an African prince beyond Morocco, his neighbour and ally . . . as he may soon lose all his holds, for Alcassar and Arsilli cannot defend themselves if he quit the field, and Sally and Tituan will revolt from him most certainly when Benbowcar is master of the campania." We are in a very good condition here. I pray you to send the enclosed to Lord Arlington safely, as it is of importance. *Holograph.* 2½ *pp.* [*The enclosure to Lord Arlington is in the Tangiers Correspondence, and also an extract from the above.*]
Endorsed :—" Received 21-31 ditto."

WILLIAM SCOWEN to SIR RICHARD FANSHAW.

1665, August 15. Molynick—Renewing his request that "the habit of knighthood in Spain" may be procured for his kinsman, and referring to a letter written by the late Lord Fanshaw to Sir Richard in this behalf, sent by a vessel which was blown up at sea. 1 *p. Seal of arms.*
Endorsed :—" Received 14-24 November, 65."

SIR RICHARD FANSHAW to LORD HOLLES.

1665, August 16-26. Madrid—Lord Dongan left this Court on the 6th of June for England, by way of France, with Sir Bernard de Gomme and Captain Carr, but I have heard nothing of them since they passed Bordeaux. Sir Hugh Cholmely reports that Tanger is in an excellent condition. Guylan is said to be busy attending the saint, Cidi Abdaly, who has reduced Fesse [Fez] and has joined the King of Tafeletts, as report goes, against Guylan. A letter from Alicante tells us that the Duke of Beaufort lies hovering about the islands of Majorca and is thought to have some design against them. "The same letter adviseth that the said Duke met with the three Sardenia galleys that carried the Marques de Camarassa (*Viceroy of Sardenia and grandee of Spain*), from whom he demanded a salute, as conceived, to the flag, but the Prince Lodovicio, General of the Sardenia galleys, answered that he also bore his flag and expected the same ceremony; but it was replied that it was for the Duke's royal person and not the flag, so the Prince saluted him and the other answered, and both passed without other dispute. *This a gloss, which, it seems, some in those parts put upon that action,* but the truth is the Duke forced the Spanish Viceroy and General to give the first salute to the standard *of France,* the which is very much—inwardly at least—resented by this Court, the articles between the two Crowns providing that meeting in French seas the Spaniards shall salute first and in Spanish seas the French." [*The words in italics are added in Fanshaw's own hand.*] 2 *pp. Draft.*

LAURENCE BRADY.

1665 [August 22-]September 1. Madrid—Pass from Sir Richard Fanshaw for Laurence Brady, Irishman, to return to Ireland. *Two copies, in English and in Spanish.* ½ *p. each.*

TORLAGH MORPHY.

1665 [August 22-]September 1. Madrid—A like pass for Torlagh Morphy. *Draft.* ½ *p.*
Annexed,
    Petition of Torlagh Morphy to be allowed to pass to Ireland, he having served his Majesty in his frigates at Brest and St. Sebastian the space of five years, in which service he has lost his right hand. 1 *p.*

CONDE DE CASTELMELHOR to SIR RICHARD FANSHAW.

1665 [August 26-]September 5—Joined to my rejoicings over the glorious victory which God has been pleased to give to the arms of the King my master and to my pleasure at receiving good tidings from your Excellency, there is the pain of not being able to execute your commands, but the matter in question having been referred to the *Ministros de letras,* no others are free to meddle therein. Your intercession however has such power with his Majesty that he has given Don Francisco d'Alarçon permission to write the note enclosed. The Secretary of State tells me that he is writing to you with full details, from a repetition of which I hold myself excused. I enclose a narrative of the late victory. It is a great satisfaction to me that our army has been so powerful during the two years in which I have had the management of affairs, and I trust that it may be the same in the future. All is being done for the Marques de Liche and Don Anello de Guzman which the good of the state permits.
Postscript.—Don Francisco must send his letter to the Marques de Caraçena. *Portuguese.* 1¾ *pp.*

ANTONIO DE SOUSA DE MACEDO to SIR RICHARD FANSHAW.

1665 [August 26-]September 5. Lisbon—Your letter of July 22 [*see p.* 199, *above*] gratifies me with the news of your health and your kind remembrance of me. The business of Don Francisco d'Alarçon, as soon as it came to this Court, was referred to the *Ministros de letras,* to whom it belongs. They must proceed conformably to the laws, and in matters which may be said to belong to the public his Majesty is accustomed to leave things to run their ordinary course, without using his royal power. But to show what weight is attached to your intercession, he has given orders that Don Francisco may send home tidings of his health and may use any clothes or money conveyed to him from thence. I may add as a friend that he would probably be allowed to receive letters also, under proper restrictions. *Portuguese.* 1¾ *pp.*

DONNA MARIANA LEMERCIER to LADY FANSHAW.

1665 [August 28-]September 7. Lisbon—I cannot express the pleasure which it has given me to receive tidings of you and your daughters, and to know that I still have a place in your remembrance. By this kindness you put me under fresh obligation, although it may seem impossible to add to the many favours which I have received from you. As regards the business of Don Francisco de Alarçon, I have used all my influence with Antonio de Sousa according to your desire, considering the cause which his country and his wife have to be overcome with grief. We women are apt to give more weight to feelings of pity than to reasons of state, but I have found Antonio de Sousa very wishful to do anything which his service to the King permits, and he will not fail to act if opportunity offers. *Portuguese.* 1 *p.*

Endorsed in Spanish by Fanshaw;—"From the wife of the Secretary of State, Antonio de Sousa de Macedo, to my wife."

DON JUAN XIMENO DE BOHORQUES.

1665 [August 28-]September 7. Madrid—Pass from Sir Richard Fanshaw for Captain Don Juan Ximeno de Bohorques, Knight of the Order of Calatrava, with his servants, to go to England. *Draft.* 1 *p.*

Annexed,

> A long undated paper by Don Juan Ximeno about his affairs. 4 *pp. Spanish.*

SIR RICHARD FANSHAW to CONSUL WESTCOMBE.

1665 [August 29-]September 8. Madrid—I thank you for your letter and the enclosed papers and am particularly glad to have the note concerning the privileges of consuls.

"Our last letters from the north assure us that De Ruyter hath gone home, creeping safe through all our watches, and was immediately chosen to command the Holland fleet, the which, by all probable computation and some confident letters of advice likewise, hath been now a matter of nine weeks at sea to the number of between ninety and a hundred ships, so that by the next we may in likelihood have the success of a second battle, suitable, if God pleases, to the former, and till then I forbear writing to my Lord Belasyse.

"For news here, Don Luis de Oyanguren is dead, regretted as may seem by many, and [by] all accounted a very able minister." *Draft.* 1½ *pp.*

---

* *See* Downing's letter of August 3rd. Harley MSS., 7,010.   † *See* Fanshaw's letter to Arlington of Sept. 7th, N.S. *Ibid.*

Sir Richard Fanshaw to Lord Arlington.

1665, September 7-17. Madrid—Announcing the death, between four and five in the morning, of his Catholic Majesty Philip IV., with the steps taken immediately afterwards, and the contents of his will. 2¼ pp. Copy. [*The original of this letter is in the Spanish Correspondence, under date.*]

King of Spain.

1665, September [7-]17. Madrid—"Papers of relation of the King of Spain's death," being a repetition in Spanish of the above, with the addition of a clause that his Majesty is said to have declared that he had a natural son by a young lady of noble birth and high degree—whom he did not name—when he was a widower, and that this son was about eighteen years of age. *Spanish.* 1¾ pp.

Lord Arlington to Consul Westcombe.

1665, September 11. Sarum—I have commanded Robin Lye from time to time to answer your letters. I have not yet been able to do what I desire as to "establishing you a convenient subsistence, in recompense of the many good services you have always rendered his Majesty," but I hope to content you with all speed, and shall likewise take care that the merchants both pay you what consulage they ought and carry themselves towards you as becomes your character. I have written to my Lord Ambassador at Madrid, telling him to receive your complaints and see you righted, "and that not being effectual to your satisfaction, then to send hither the names of those which have slighted and abused you, upon which they shall see that his Majesty's arm is long enough to reach them wherever they are." Robert Lye is going to Ireland on my own business and is like to stay there some time, so in future direct your letters to me and I will take care that they are duly answered. *Copy.* 1 p.

Earl of Bath to Sir Richard Fanshaw.

1665, September 18. Fort of Plymouth—I take this occasion of presenting an earnest request on behalf of Don Juan Scawen of Cadiz, who was born of an English father, of the family of Mr. William Scawen of Molinnick, co. Cornwall, well known to me "to be of an ancient descent of gentry and allied to most of the gentlemen and worthy families of the county. The father of this Don Juan was a long time Consul for the English at Cadiz and well reported of by our nation," and his son desires so far to ingratiate himself with the King of Spain as to receive the honour of knighthood from him, in which matter I beg your favourable assistance. I have been commanded by his Majesty into Cornwall, in order to the securing of the peace of the county and am now at my government here. I shall return to Court in about a fortnight. *Signed. Seal of arms, with coronet.* 1 *p.*

LORD BELASYSE to SIR RICHARD FANSHAW.

1665, September 26. Tanger—As to the prize ship defended here from the Hollanders, those of Algeires have sent demanding an account of the cargo, and charging me with double what was preserved, "rather as a factor of theirs than as a person of condition who hath obliged them in the securing the goods from many difficulties; first, from the enemy and after from the fury of a Levant wind which ran that ship upon the rocks . . . and then from the Turks themselves and from my own people, who endeavoured to plunder what they could get, besides great quantities of goods stolen and conveyed into Spain by the merchants here, notwithstanding my strict proclamation to the contrary, so as in truth, without my authority and personal toil, very little had been saved." Yet they refuse to gratify my officers and are unwilling to pay the charges, which—together with your advice—has made me suspend permission to them to sell the goods here. They have returned to Tituan for further orders, and meanwhile I should be glad to have such orders from England as might justify my allowing the Spaniards, rather than these enemies to Christians, to have the advantages of what remains. But if no orders come and the Turks return with reasonable satisfaction, I fear it would be unsafe to refuse them the goods.

The Spanish Governors are very severe to us, and at Malaga and Tariffe have shot at the *Crown* and our *barco longo*, refusing all pratique and not even allowing us to receive our letters. I pray you if possible to procure orders to the Governor of Tariffe to allow this last, "we being, I thank God, not only free from all pestilential diseases, but so careful to preserve ourselves as I have made commissioners for health, and appointed a Lazaretta, and no ships from England shall have pratique with us but in landing provisions for the garrison."

We hope soon to hear of a second victory in the north, of the diminution of the sickness and the arrival of supplies. The *Crown* frigate has sailed for England with Sir H. Cholmley and about fifty disabled soldiers. She has by this I hope safely passed the Hollands fleet, which is watching for her outside our bay. *Holograph.* 4 *pp.*
Endorsed:—"Received 16-26 October."

SIR RICHARD FANSHAW to CONSUL WESTCOMBE.

1665 [September 26-]October 6. Madrid—I thank you for your letter, and especially for the good news of Col. Bellasyse being free. I should like to know upon what terms, whether by exchange or otherwise, and also to hear how they proceed against the Dutch Consul.

"That news you had from Dunkerque could not at that time be true, but presuming the two fleets have long before this time met and fought, I hope it will not be long before we have the certainty of as good news as that would have been if true.

"What we have here at present is only that preparation is making for the proclamation of the young King upon Thursday next." 1 *p.*

CONSUL M. WESTCOMBE to SIR RICHARD FANSHAW.

1665, October [1-]11. Cadiz—The English ketch laden with French wines, which was robbed and seized in the bay by a Dutch man-of-war, has been offered back to me by the Dutch Commandant of the squadron, but she is in such a sad condition (much of the wine having been taken away and most of the casks broken or vented) that I have refused to take her without further compensation.

I send you a letter received from Mr. Robert Downe, a captive at Tetuan, whose account is confirmed by other trustworthy evidence. The Duke of Medina Celi is doing his utmost to destroy Tangier, and it is certain that the Spaniards have an absolute peace with Gueland. Although the Moors sometimes take Spanish boats and keep the men as slaves, yet this is done with the connivance of the Duke in order to delude the world, and also to punish boatmen who have carried provisions to Tangier. It is in order to prevent provisions being thus taken that the prohibition of intercourse with Tangier has been issued, though done under pretence of the plague.

I also send copies of the letters exchanged between the Governor of the city and the Dutch Commandant about the ketch, but his saying that he offered her to me as she was taken is against all truth.

Enclosing,

1. *Robert Downe to Consul Westcombe.*

1665, September 22. *Tituan—The Turks, who have been to Tanger about selling the goods of the galleon, report that there is great want of provisions there, and three English soldiers who have run away from thence say the same thing, but neither Mr. Wilson nor Mr. Jones mention it in their letters.*

There arrived here yesterday from Arzeela (where Gueland makes his abode), a Spaniard, whom the Duke of Medina of Port sent to the said Gueland with eight thousand pieces of eight and a letter from the King of Spain, promising him munitions of war against the English. I send the enclosed to advise my Lord at Tanger of this and also of what passes here about my liberty, "which

*some time I have and some time I have not." I hope to
hear from you by the Armenian, David Jacob. 1 p.*
    2. *The above-mentioned letters from the Commander of
the Dutch fleet, Don Juan Gidienson Vurburch (September
8, n.s.), and the Governor of Cadiz, Don Martin de Sayas
Vazan (September 18 and October 6, n.s.), concerning the
English ship taken by the Dutch. Spanish. Copies.
4½ pp.*

MONSIEUR DE FREMONT to SIR RICHARD FANSHAW.

1665, October [7-]17. Paris—I would gladly have written
to you at once on my arrival in France, but your Excellency
knows by experience that one cannot do just what one likes in
this world. I have now to acquaint you that a vessel named
the *Fortune,* bound from Rochelle for Cadiz, has been taken
and carried in to Galicia by a Biscay ship. In her there was
a certain Changuion, now kept prisoner at Pontevedra, who
was going as valet to the Lord of Tanger,. who introduced
us to each other, and I know is well loved by you. I beg you
to get the man set at liberty and that he may have his goods
restored to him, especially a case of guns, pistols and books
which he was taking from me to his master, that the latter
might enjoy the diversions of the chase and of reading. If
you can bring them together, you will oblige both the master
and the man. "Songez y Monseigneur, je vous en conjure,
pour l'amour de ce Milord et de cet autre Anglois qui devint
un jour amoureux a la priere de Madame l'Ambassadrice de la
Signora Silva da Gloria. Pour moy, je me contenteray de
l'honneur d'estre dans vostre souvenir et dans la memoire de
Madame vostre femme et de Mesdemoiselles vos filles, et surtout
de celle a qui l'on avoit donné pour gouverneur cet Anglois
amoureux dont je viens de parler. Je m'imagine, Monseigneur,
qu 'il n'i a rien de si obscur pour vous dans Luis de la Camoens
que cette lettre, aussi me flatai je de l'esperence que lors que
vostre Excellence en aurra trouvé le sens, qu'elle y prendra
quelque plaisir par celuy qu 'elle prendra a obliger un aussi
gallant homme qu'est le Milord dont il s'agit." *French.*
1¼ *pp.*

CONSUL WESTCOMBE to SIR RICHARD FANSHAW.

1665, October [8-]18. Cadiz—I have this morning written
to you in Spanish concerning the ketch of wines taken from
us by the Dutch. If no pressing order comes from Madrid, I
fear those here will delay to do justice to us.
    The Duke of Avero, with his squadron and four prizes, Dutch,
Hamburger, Italian and Portuguese, arrived yesterday, "and
the Duke permits no man to *saltar en tierra* until he hears
from Madrid whether he is to stay here or proceed."
    A French ship has arrived in the bay "from the city where
Consul Maynard lives" [Lisbon], and brings letters from the

English merchants there, stating that a merchant ship, called the *Royal Catherine*, Captain John Shaw, arrived there at the end of September from Plymouth, having made the voyage in twelve days, and brought news that our fleet had totally routed the Dutch. " God send it true."

Here is another French ship arrived from Rochelle in twelve days, and she reports that there was no news there of any fight.

" Col. John Belasyse made his escape, but it was by private consent of his Captain, who had two or three pieces of eight for his connivance. He is now at Tanger. . . . That garrison much wants an open commerce with Spain, who do us much injury, who without any reason deny it us merely upon a report of pest, which, God be thanked, is no more than what their own tongues have raised, the better to achieve with Gueland their designs against Tanger."

The Dutch men-of-war continue to sell all their English prizes, and the Spaniards use no diligence to execute his Catholic Majesty's *cedullas*, prohibiting such sales. 3 *pp.*

Enclosing,

1. *Consul Westcombe to Sir Richard Fanshaw.*
1665 [8-]18—*Concerning the English ketch or ballandra of French wines taken by the Dutch. Spanish.* 2 *pp.*

2. *Protest of the Dutch Consul against Westcombe and his reply thereto. Spanish.* 4 *pp.*

LORD BELASYSE to SIR RICHARD FANSHAW.

1665, October 10-20. Tanger—I last night received yours of the 17th and 22nd September, new style, and thank you for your relation concerning the change of Government occasioned by the death of his Catholic Majesty in Spain. I have told you what has passed concerning the patache *Margarita*, wherein I am delaying as much as possible in hopes of direction from England. " I confess it is a very uneasy thing to find the employment of this place encumbered with the protection I am forced to give the Turks' ships, and prizes taken from the Christians here, having lately another accident happened, wherein I am forced to employ my utmost skill how to behave myself on the one side lest any succeeding breach of peace should be imputed to me by the Algerines, if I deny what their articles allow—in the interpretation whereof they are over partial to themselves—and on the other side lest our Christian neighbours, and even his Majesty's own subjects who are concerned, should have just cause of complaint against us."

Four days ago, some Algerines brought in a supposed French prize, but from the oath of the captain, an Irishman, who died of his wounds within twelve hours, I have reason to suppose she was Irish, and only shewed the French flag to defend herself from the Hollanders. I have therefore ordered the Turks to take her on to Algeire, where the English Consul will lay claim on behalf of the owners, I having sent to him the attestation of the deceased captain.

Your Excellency's intelligence of Guylan's defeat and being slain is not true. The last we had reports him to be at Salley, and no way inclined to a peace with us, being courted by the Duke de Medina Celi and the Hollanders to the contrary, who, though managed very secretly, do I am confident lay many designs to engage him to attack or distress us, which, were it not for Benbucar's diversion, we should hear more of; though no ways apprehended by me as of dangerous consequence to this place by any open acts of hostility either by land or sea, we being, I thank God, in a condition resolved and powerful to oppose any such attempts. And if our friends in England be so just and kind to us as to send by strong convoys our long expected supplies of provisions, with recruits of men and money, I shall not doubt but to give his Majesty a good account of his service here, and that the place will every day grow more important by the vigorous prosecution we make in the Mould, fortifications, civil justice and government, as well as regulation of the military, and notwithstanding the severe proclamations from Spain against pratique with us, their boats do daily steal refreshments to us, however, I desire your Excellency to continue your complaints against the severity which is exercised by the several Governors of Malaga, Tarifa and Cadiz, &c., whereby when it pleases God the sickness in England abates, orders may be procured from the Court of Madrid to open a correspondency with us again, though I assure you those very ports are not more strict than myself in denying access to English vessels, of which there are some now on quarantine in the bay. There is a report here that our fleet has gained a second victory over the Dutch, greater than the former. 3 *pp.* [*Last sentence only in Lord Belasyse's own hand.*]

Endorsed :—" Received with one from Consul Westcombe 2 November, s.n. Answered 3 ditto."

LORD BELASYSE to SIR RICHARD FANSHAW.

1665, October 12-22. Tanger—I beg you to forward the enclosed as safely and speedily as you can. It is of great importance, advising the arrival of a fleet from Plymouth, consisting only of sixteen merchantmen, one of the two frigates which convoyed them being gone to Salee, and the other, as we believe, taken by the Hollanders, together with two of the provision ships and one bound for Smyrna, richly laden. A more acceptable piece of news is that a squadron of our ships met with the Holland fleet going home from Bergen, and took ten men-of-war, two large and rich East Indiamen, and twenty other merchant ships. *Signed.* 1½ *pp.* [*The enclosed letter (to Arlington) is in the Tangiers Correspondence.*] *Received at the same time as the preceding.*

CONSUL WESTCOMBE to WILLIAM COVENTRY.

1665, October [13-]23. Cadiz—An English ship's boat has just brought in eighteen mariners belonging to the victuallers bound for Tanger, who were all taken yesterday, to the number of about twenty, by nine Hollands men-of-war within three leagues of Tanger. His Majesty's frigate, the *Merlin*, is also taken. The want of these ships will be a sad loss to Tanger, and unless provisions are sent to it under safe convoy with all imaginable haste, the garrison will be exposed as a prey to the enemy. For God's sake let these things be taken into serious consideration, in order to the preserving "that incomparable jewel of Tanger." 1 *p. Copy by Westcombe.*

CONSUL WESTCOMBE to LORD AMBASSADOR FANSHAW.

1665, October [15-]25. Cadiz—States that the Dutch Consul is still in prison in the common gaol, and that the commissary Gilberto Melce, a Dutchman, who fits out the Dutch men-of-war and disposes of the prizes taken from the English, is also clapt up at St. Mary Port. Has presented a petition to the General about the *Fidelity*, John Stafford, commander, "as being unjustly taken as [*sic*] by a *barco lungo*, which by a *cedulla* of his Catholic Majesty neither English nor Dutch cannot build, buy nor set out as men-of-war, nor any other embarcation of this kingdom." The rumour of the taking of twenty English ships by the Dutch near Tangier proves false, as they have taken only four or five, amongst which is the *Merlin*, whose commander, Captain Charles Howard, "behaved himself bravely with his twelve guns." 2½ *pp.*
Enclosing,
        Captain Charles Howard to Consul Westcombe.
        1665, October 14. Aboard the St. Charles—Announcing the capture of himself and his ship, the Merlin, by the Dutch after five or six hours' dispute, whilst he was defending the victualling ships going for Tangier. Copy. 1 p.

GILES WOODWARD to SIR RICHARD FANSHAW.

1665, October [18-]27. Malaga—Acknowledging his Excellency's letter of 20th current, and stating that the news of the English victory has so cast down the Holland merchants that they are ashamed to walk the streets. Hopes it may work some alteration in the cross-grained disposition of their crabbed Governor, who refuses to admit English ships, notwithstanding the orders sent to him. 1 *p.*

CAPTAIN EDMOND FARRELL.

1665 [October 30-]November 9. Madrid—Pass from Sir Richard Fanshaw for Captain Edmond Farrell, Irishman, aged about thirty-four years, to return to his own country, either directly or by way of England. 1 *p. Copy.*

ROBERT DOWNE to his cousin, CONSUL WESTCOMBE.

1665, November 4. Tituan—I embrace this opportunity of writing to you by a gentleman, taken in coming from your port to Tanger about fourteen months past, who has now ransomed himself for eleven hundred pieces of eight.

"Gilan hath been out of Alcazer above this month to wait on the King of Tafalett, who is come down the second time upon him, and hath fired and destroyed all the stately gardens and vineyards about Fez," taking divers castles and killing about fifty of the chiefest horsemen and many ordinary soldiers. It is said that the saint Benbucker is newly come against the said King, and has put his son Abdalle into Fez while he goes to look after him. $\frac{3}{4}$ *p.*

SIR RICHARD FANSHAW to CONSUL WESTCOMBE.

1665, November 7-17. Madrid—Informing him that the sickness in England is so much decreased that he hopes it will soon be extinguished; and that the Bishop of Munster goes on prosperously against the Hollanders. *Copy.* $\frac{3}{4}$ *p.*

The CANARY COMPANY to SIR RICHARD FANSHAW.

1665, November 13. Putney—Having been told by Mr. Thomas Goddard of your Excellency's readiness to own our concerns in the Court of Spain, we are emboldened to trouble you again, being assured that we need not prescribe to you "the most proper way to chastise the ringleaders of the Islanders that oppose us, whereby the whole rabble of them may be reduced to consider their own interest and incline to an amicable conformity with us in the commerce." His Majesty has sent for two of our nation from Tenerife, "who have with open face encouraged the said islanders in their mutinous proceedings, to answer the same at the Council Board," and we doubt not that they will be reduced to obedience. Signed by Sir Arthur Ingram, governor, John Turner, deputy, Nicholas Warren, John Paige, Robert Belin, Will. Maskelyne. $1\frac{1}{2}$ *pp.*

LORD BELASYSE to SIR RICHARD FANSHAW.

1665, November 13-23. Tanger—I have received yours with the enclosed from Lord Arlington, and shall observe his Majesty's commands about the patache *Santa Margarita.* The King of Portugal has agreed that all vessels going hence shall have free admittance to his ports, upon my certificate that this place is in good health, and has likewise given order to the Governor of Algarvie to furnish us with what that kingdom affords. "It seems strange that our neighbours of Spain should be so rigorous as not only to deny pratique and correspondency with this place, which is in as good health as any part of that kingdom, but also refuse to admit those ships which have not been at London these six months, and have already performed one quarantine in this port, upon a second quarantine to be kept in Spain; a thing that Italy itself, which is the strictest place in the world, in the case of health, does not deny."

Our enemies show themselves much in the fields, "being about to till their grounds, as we imagine. What their number or design is, or whether Guylan be there in person, we cannot certainly say, but, however, we are in a readiness for all occasions, wanting for nothing, thanks be to God." I have just received your welcome news of the abatement of the sickness, which God grant may utterly vanish by the cold season. 2 *pp.* [*Last sentence only in Lord Belasyse's own handwriting.*]

Giles Woodward to Sir Richard Fanshaw.

1665, November [14-]24. Malaga—Complaining of his imprisonment by the Governor, in consequence of the presence of a certain "fish ship," which "doth so exasperate this little man" that he will probably proceed to further extremities unless prevented. 1½ *pp.*

Sir Richard Fanshaw to Consul Westcombe.

1665 [November 28-]December 8. Madrid—I cannot tell what more to say as to your differences with our merchants until I have your answer to my last; but if they continue, you might do well to petition the King, our master, "by some clear act of state to settle certain points that are too often controverted between consuls and merchants in all places where I have been; and certain I am that if I were in England present at such a debate, I would take more than a little pains it might receive a final determination. . . . As to the matter of those ministers' partiality to the Hollanders, with other hard measure to our nation, my complaints to this Court continue almost as constant as the occasions they give for them, of which also I believe they hear some measure from their superiors, so as to make them, if not more conscientious of his Catholic Majesty's *scedulas*, yet more cautious in what manner they break them. A thorough cure I hope will follow in a short time.

Fresh news here is none from England worth your knowledge or our friends in Tanger, but the continued abatement (God Almighty be blessed for it) of the infection; bad news, none at all but what is coined, and of such black money I need send you none, your mints (according to what I hear) going faster than ours, or even in Holland itself." 1¼ *pp.*

P[HILIBERT] VERNATTY to SIR RICHARD FANSHAW.

1665, [November 28-December 8? Malaga]—I find nothing
here but complaints of the unheard of usage which the merchants receive from the Governor of this place. "It appears
to all men of all nations that inhabit here that there is nothing
but passion that bears sway with him. He is so severe against
poor Tanger that did he know of anyone that either goes or
comes from thence, no punishment would satisfy his anger but
fire and sword. It is true money will not tempt him, but his
great zeal will utterly destroy this place, for scarce anybody
of the citizens can procure money to cultivate their vineyards,
only for his not giving pratique to ships that come bound hither
and not from England." I beg to recommend to you the condition of Donna Teresa Colin, to whom and to her friends "all
the nation acknowledges themselves obliged.' 1 *p.*

Endorsed :—"From Mr. Vernatty, supposed to be written
at Malaga about the 8 December, 1665. Received 5-15 ditto.

CONSUL NICH. PARKER to LORD BELASYSE.

1665, December 2. Algeire—I send your Excellency the
Duana's letter and a translation thereof, with the Pashaw's
seal upon it. Concerning the goods in the prize ship, I humbly
suggest that by what you have written and I (by your order)
have said, we are so much bound to these people that we cannot draw back without prejudice to the peace. I do not say
this for fear of any ill conveniency to myself, for I would
willingly bear all and more than was inflicted on my predecessor, but anything to disturb the peace would much trouble
me, and your Lordship well knows " how ticklish these people
are." I am glad that in future the pirates are not to make
Tanger their mart, "for these people are so ignorantly covetous
that although they have all the right imaginable, yet they will
return with complaints and upon the first occasion they can
find of advantage, all frivolous pretences shall be reckoned for."
Copy. 1½ *pp.*

CONSUL WESTCOMBE to SIR RICHARD FANSHAW.

1665, December [3-]13. Cadiz—Complaining that in the two
years and a half of his consulship he has spent, with all
good husbandry, above three thousand pieces of eight more than
his office has produced, and that he is now upon his last legs,
and knows not what in the world he shall do unless Lord
Arlington can be persuaded to succour him. 1¾ *pp.*
Endorsed :—"Received 12-22, late at night."

SIR FRANCIS BEDINGFIELD to SIR RICHARD FANSHAW.

1665, December [3-]13. Porta Santa Maria—Prays forgiveness, "in this benign time of *Pasquas*," for some offence

which he fears that he has given, and solicits his Excellency's help in behalf of one of the poor Englishmen that were condemned for four years to the galleys, and who has ended his time, but whom the General of the galleys, the Marquis of Bayona, refuses to release without a letter from Fanshaw himself. *2 pp.*

Endorsed :—" Received 12-22 ditto, at night. Answered 19-29 ditto, with a letter for the Marques de Bayona in behalf of the English galley-slaves."

CONSUL WESTCOMBE to SIR RICHARD FANSHAW.

1665, December [3-]13. Cadiz—The Dutch are still on the coast and part of them in the bay. A *propio* has arrived from Holland to say that eight or ten more men-of-war will be here directly, and another has gone from Paris with a packet for the Duke of Beaufort, ordering him to repair to the bay with his fifteen men-of-war and join with the Dutch against the English. It may be they have a design against Tangier. 1¼ *pp.*

LORD DONGAN to SIR RICHARD FANSHAW.

1665, December 6. [Dublin]—I delivered all your commands in England, but " your letter to my Lord Lieutenant and Council here I could not find at Salisbury, Secretary Morice being with his Royal Highness at York." When it is sent hither, my Lord Lieutenant will see it complied with. Lord Chief Justice Smith sends you a great bottle of Irish aqua vitæ. My Lord Chancellor, my Lord Primate and Sir Paul Davis say they will write to you. 1½ *pp.*

CONDE DE MARCHIN to SIR RICHARD FANSHAW.

1665, December [10-]20. Madrid—Recommending to his protection Don Diego Pacheco and Don Carlos del Castillo. *Spanish.* ¾ *p.*

RICHARD CHAMBRES to SIR RICHARD FANSHAW.

1665, December [10-]20. Xeres—Apologises for not having written earlier. Now that Lord Dongan has gone, makes bold to offer his respects and to wish his Excellency and his lady " a most contented Christmas." Hears that the Portuguese have besieged Ayamonte in the Condado and two other small villages, and are doing great harm in parts of Gallicia. Preparations are being made in Xeres for sending some troops thither. Encloses a letter from his daughter, Lady Dongan. 1 *p.*

GILES WOODWARD to LIONEL FANSHAW.

1665, December [12-]22. Malaga—I have made bold to relate to his Excellency what has passed here with our Governor, "as peevish a piece of ill-favouredness that ever a people were troubled with." Unless his Catholic Majesty stops the unjust proceedings of this man he will drive the English from the town, for he is our declared enemy. Indeed he has no respect for anybody. Mr. Vernatty is still here. 1 *p.*

DR. BRUNE RYVES, Dean of Arches, to SIR RICHARD FANSHAW.

1665, December 14. Haseley—"The miserable distractions of these times, by reason of that dreadful contagion which hath raged amongst us this whole summer and is not yet ceased, but scattered not only in London but in many places of the country, must plead my apology that it is so late that I return my humble thanks unto your Lordship for those many favours showed to my son, and that in the midst of your many and weighty affairs you can remember that you have such a poor servant as myself and vouchsafe to honour me with your letters. Truly, my Lord, we have been afraid one of another, as if the curse of Cain had been upon us, to fear that every man that met us would slay us. The highways have been unoccupied, all intercourse of letters obstructed, and no man thought himself secure in his closest retirements. Now God be praised, as the sun begins to draw nearer unto us, so we hope the sun of righteousness will arise upon us with healing on his wings, which God grant.

"For the affairs of this kingdom, I presume you have an account of them from many better hands. I shall only condole unto you the declining of that honourable order which might have had the happiness to receive an addition of honour and preservation of its lustre by your Lordship's relation to it, but since your Lordship was taken up from that employment that dignity doth decline. Since your Lordship's departure the doors of St. George's Hall have been shut; we have not seen a knight of the order in Windsor. The truth is, the honour of that order and the dignity and profit of the Masters of Request both do want your presence and support. Though your Lordship laid the foundation of a register, yet Sir Harry De Vic, having gotten the papers into his hands under a pretence to perfect the remainders, I could never get any papers, either your Lordship's or his own, out of his hands, but I hope to live to see your Lordship one of the order, that so you may restore that, and it honour you.

"My son presents his most humble duty, service and thanks to your honour, and desires me to acquaint your Lordship that he is very mindful of your Lordship's commands in relation to Sir Andrew King, but by reason of the contagion he hath not had the opportunity to speak with him. My son, ever since his arrival in England, hath been retired to my house at Haseley in Oxfordshire, and as yet hath not done anything in order to that concern which drew him over hither. Good my Lord, present my most humble service to your most noble and virtuous lady. That God would bless you and her and all your children, and return you all into your own country full of honour and wealth and favour with God and the King, whom you serve, is the daily prayer" of your devoted servant. 1 *p.*

Wm. Blunden to Sir Richard Fanshaw.

1665, December [18-]28. Alicant—A small vessel from Tunis brings word that about a month since the Duke of Beaufort made peace with the King of that country, and that they are to redeem all their captives at a hundred and seventy-five pieces of eight per head; also that in going thither the Duke unfortunately met with and captured the *Advice*, Capt. George Deacon, and the *Bilboa Merchant*, both laden with currants, and another small vessel with Gallipoly oil, as well as several ships of other nations, all which they released, but the English ones they have carried into Thollon [Toulon]. ½ *p.*

John Bulteel [Secretary to Lord Chancellor Clarendon] to Sir Richard Fanshaw.

1665, December 22. Oxon—Can it be possible that you will pardon me for not having answered your letter, received three months ago? "I will plead no excuse, though really I could allege many . . . as my Lord's not often writing to you, and sometimes, when he did, I not being with him, and in the hurry this late contagion put all men in, my not knowing how to convey my letters to you, for in this progress I have not always been where the Court was, and now, last of all, when Sir Patrick Hamoleda [*sic*] went hence, my being accidentally drawn from that design by an employment would not give me leisure to perform it, nor indeed take my leave from him, for which omission, with my most humble service to him, I beg your Lordship would be pleased to make my excuse." I hope to be able to find you such a seat as you desire, and a little cottage for myself near to it, "and then I shall be content from my hermitage daily to walk to your palace," and to plant trees—which I think should be lime, for their quick growth, unless the Hollanders, who are masters of the best and cheapest, prohibit their importation. "And though my Lord Cornbury—who, by the way, commands me to salute you in his name and is very much your Excellency's servant—should not be seated just by you, yet I hope it will not be at so great a distance but your coach may carry us thither to dinner and return us back at night." I pray you to make up your mind, "for otherwise that noble Lord, with a melancholy lodge that lies in Whichwood Forest, will tempt me from you, and haply if that should fall before your Lordship could extricate yourself out of the great affairs of the world it would not be improvidently done of me to accept it, that so with Philemon—and you do not know but with Baucis too, bating her age—I may treat you both, as he did the Thunderer and his nimble company, only I will take care the wine shall be better—for if I remember, the poet says it was not of the oldest—and to it, instead of some of those rustical dainties which our clime affords not, make it up with a haunch of venison.'' I refer you to the bearer of this, Sir Robert Southwell, for news, and will write again when my Lord Sandwich goes for Madrid.

I pray you '' present my humble service to your most excellent lady and your fair daughters, especially she that, when I had the honour to dine with her at your Lordship's in Lincoln's Inn Fields, defied all mankind and thought of nothing but a nunnery, from which resolution, if her years and value of the world hath not by this time redeemed her, yours and my lady's authority must, or you will have a sin to answer for the brave youth of England will never pardon you."

Postscript.—" My Lord Cornbury, Sir Richard Beling—now secretary to the Queen—Mr. Wren and Mr. Clutterbooke present their most humble service to your Lordship." 3 *pp.*

Sir Thomas Beverley to Sir Richard Fanshaw.

1665, December 23.   Magdalen College, Oxford—Yours of the 5th of June only reached me in the middle of October, " in a corner of my native country, the place of my retreat from the common calamity, and far distant from the post roads; no carriers being permitted to have recourse to London."

The same thing prevented my meeting Lord Dongan, but from your friends here I have heard news of you, and rejoice with them over the birth of your little son.

"Though we are all Athenians in this place, yet I can meet with no news your Lordship will not have by better hands, unless it be some that in this great sweep of mortality I find none of your Lordship's and my acquaintance missing." The Exchequer Barons, Mr. Moore and my brother Berkenhead are here and send their service, as does also Mr. Attorney. "We dined together at the President's of this College about two or three days since, where we had the happiness of Sir Philip Warwick and your sister's company, and to drink your good health in as generous wine as any Spain affords. . . . I hope, though there be cause enough to fear the contrary—the sickness increasing these two last weeks—to be at London about the beginning of February." Mr. Williamson—Lord Arlington's secretary—tells me [the] post goes early to-morrow. I hope you will make a shift to read these rude lines. *Seal of arms.* 1 *p.*

Sir Andrew King to Sir Richard Fanshaw.

1665, December 24.   Cowper's Hill—What I hinted at in my last is confirmed. "The good Duke of Albemarle commands the fleet.   Prince Rupert hath been dangerously sick, but recovers and takes the command under the Duke. Several of the last summer's commanders are put off and more will follow. We may expect by God's blessing a good issue, for we are for fitting men and such as value the King's honour. The Tangier fleet left Portsmouth on the 18th. "The Earl of Sandwich went out of Oxford about that time to settle his domestics, and said [he] should return and be ready to depart on his extraordinary embassy for Madrid by the beginning of January. His preparations are chiefly mourning, and that's not long in hand. Lord Arlington's secretary, Mr. Godolphin, goes secretary to the Embassy, and Mr. Fras. Godolphin accompanies my Lord of Sandwich." Mr. [torn]thell has returned from the Bishop of Munster, who, with his army, is in the States' country, and is going to-day express to the Emperor and the said Bishop again. He says the Bishop has twenty-two thousand men, and that they value not the French assistance. "We have had hard frosts with pleasant serene weather, the sun shining all day. Notwithstanding, the sickness hath these two last weeks increased from 428 to 525, which gives us both sorrow and fear. It's said the great concourse of people thither is the cause, but we hope an abatement this week." God bless you and your family and send us a happy meeting. 2 *pp.* *Seal of arms.*

CONSUL WESTCOMBE to SIR RICHARD FANSHAW.

[1665, December 24-]1666, January 3· Cadiz—The report that a cessation of arms for thirty years has been agreed upon between Spain and Portugal "has ravished for joy" both Spanish and Portuguese in those parts; and the settling of the *treguas* is entirely attributed to his Excellency's good management. It is said that English ships are now admitted into the Flemish ports without any scruple. 2 *pp.*

JUAN SCOWEN to SIR RICHARD FANSHAW.

[1665, December 24-]1666, January 3. Cadiz—Transmitting a letter sent for his Excellency from William Scowen. *Spanish.* ½ *p.*
Enclosing,
    1. *Duplicate of the letter of William Scowen, dated August 15. See above, p. 202.*
    2. *Certificate by the kindred of Juan Scowen, that William Scowen, Esq., Judge of the Admiralty, has appeared before them and declared that Don Juan Scowen is lawfully and righteously descended out of his family, and is a member thereof ; the said Wm. Scowen's family being of "long continuance of gentry here, having loyally, eminently, and faithfully served his Majesty and his father of blessed memory during the late times of rebellion, together with all those of his name and kindred." Signed by Richard Arundel, Baron of Trerise; Sir John Trelawny and Sir John Corydon, Barts.; Sir Richard Edgcombe, Knight of the*

Bath; Sir Peter Courteney, Sir John Arundel, Sir Sam. Coseworth and Sir William Godolphin, Knights; and seven others. Dated, August 10, 1665, Cornwall. 1 p.

Sir Richard Fanshaw to Consul Westcombe.

[1665, December 26-]1666, January 5. Madrid—I am sorry to hear how insolent the Dutch are, and how partial the Spaniards are to them. I hope to get these things remedied in time, and intend, God willing, ere long to prefer another memorial to this Queen. "I am still thinking how I may best serve you in your own private concerns, being sorry you have not as yet a comfortable subsistence settled to you. I do remember that in a copy you sent me of a letter you received from my Lord Arlington, he was pleased in a very friendly manner to promise you his assistance, whereof I shall, before it be long, put his Lordship in mind. The last we heard of the sickness in London was six hundred that week. I hope by this time it is not six." *Copy.* 1 p.

Consul Westcombe to Sir Richard Fanshaw.

[1665, December 31-]1666, January 10. Cadiz—Both Spanish and Portuguese are beyond expression joyful at the *Treguas*, and invoke a thousand benedictions upon your Excellency for so great a work. The Dutch men-of-war are still in the bay or about the Strait's mouth. I have been so curious as to trace the actions of these eighteen Dutch men-of-war, from the beginning of December, 1664, till the end of December, 1665, and to see "what purchase they have taken." I enclose an account of their captures, with my calculations of their value, which I make to be 332,500 pieces of eight, and the charges of the Dutch men-of-war in taking these ships at least 540,000 pieces of eight, "and therefore they need not brag much of the profit made upon the English nation on this coast."

I pray your Lordship to think of me, for I get nothing but put offs from Mr. James Cuningam and others here, who, "with their lawyers' tricks and quillets," try to entrap me and have even bribed my own lawyer to persuade me to sign papers in their favour. I send you the copy of a letter received from Amsterdam. 2 pp.

Enclosing,

1. *A list of the ships taken by the Dutch squadron from the English, beginning of January,* 1664, *to end of January,* 1665, *most of them being sold in the Bay of Cadiz:—*

Pieces of eight.

Puny, *Capt. Mathews, taken in Alicante Road* .... *Value* 10,000

Adventure *of Plymouth, John Cole, taken in Malaga Road* .... „ 3,500

Pieces of eight.

William, *Capt. Wm. Snowden, taken under the fort of Rhotta*	*Value*	2,500
Speedwell, *Stephen Williamson, with lime*	„	1,200
Loyal Merchant, *William White, with New England fish*	„	8,800
Dove, *John Fasset, with ditto*	„	5,400
Tiger *ketch, William Eadrum, with provisions for Tanger*	„	5,200
Angel Gabriel, *Edmond Ravens, from Ireland*	„	8,200
Pearl, *of Bristol, Thomas Dyer*	„	5,000
Salamander *frigate, Capt. John Belasyse, provisions for Tanger*	„	18,000
Fidelity, *of Apsum, Captain Stafford, with Sherry wines, redeemed.*		
——, *a new Pink of Yarmouth, with herrings*	„	5,300
Endeavour, *of North Yarmouth, Capt. Hugh Crafford, with salt*	„	3,000
Royal Catherine *ketch, Walter Webber, with French wines*	„	5,600
Marling [Merlin] *gally, Capt. Chas. Howard, a man-of-war*	„	9,500
William and Mary, *of London, Francis Allin, with pack goods*	„	156,000
William and John, *Capt. Sheppard, a victualler for Tanger*	„	12,500
Thomas, *of Plymouth, John Barkley, with hoops and iron*	„	8,500
——, *of Plymouth, with pilchards* ...	„	4,000
Rose, *Capt. Crow, with dry fish*	„	5,800
John, *a pink, another victualler for Tanger*	„	8,400
Lily, *of Bastable [Barnstaple], with bacallao [i.e., cod-fish]*	„	6,200
Benjamin *pink, George Lewis, with dry fish*	„	8,500
Deliverance, *Capt. John Summers, with wax and almonds*	„	18,800
Elizabeth, *with bacallao*	„	12,600

Pieces of eight   332,500

Charges of the Dutch men-of-war.

Three States ships ten [sic] *months, and* 15 *hired merchant ships, one with the other at* 3,000 *pieces of eight per month amounts to* 540,000 *pieces of eight.*

2. *A letter from Amsterdam, signed "A constant friend," stating the Coorgas, the Munster General, is reported to be taken, and that the French forces "are very unruly, the*

inhabitants standing in as much fear of them as of the Munsters, these ravishing the women and borrowing of the Dutchmen . . . but now to prevent further clamour it is said they are ordered to go into Munsterland to repay the Bishop in his own coin of burning and plundering the country." By reason of a spring tide and high wind the water has broken down the dykes and done much damage, both at Amsterdam and Rotterdam. Dated December 7, 1665. Copy. ¾ p.

Robert De Lander.

[1665]—Statement by Sir Richard Fanshaw, that in August of the previous year 1664, Robert Lander, bound from Jamaica to New England, being distressed by tempest, desired leave of the Governor of Havana in the West Indies to take his ship in there for repairs, to which he agreed. But when the ship and crew were in his power he sold the vessel, and sent the men as prisoners in the orange ships for Spain. His Catholic Majesty is therefore prayed to order liberty for the men and restitution of their ship. *Spanish.* 3 *pp.*
Enclosing,
 Depositions signed by Robert De Lander and others. [Comp. De Lander's letter to Consul Westcombe in the Spanish Correspondence.]

Sir Richard Fanshaw to the Queen of Spain.

1666, January [3-]13—Interceding on behalf of Thomas Couling, Consul at Teneriffe, in the Canary Islands, and the merchants trading and residing there. *Spanish. Draft.* 1½ *pp. Endorsed as presented on this date.*

Duke and Count of Oñate to Sir Richard Fanshaw.

1666, January [4-]14. Madrid—The Queen my mistress, in consideration of the particular zeal and diligence with which you have acted in the arrangement of the articles of the peace concluded by your Excellency and myself between the two crowns of Spain and England, by virtue of the powers given us by our sovereigns—from which it is hoped so much good will result to all Christendom, and especially to the subjects of the two kingdoms—has been pleased to grant a hundred thousand pieces-of-eight to yourself and fifty thousand to your wife. *Spanish. Copy.* 1 *p.*

Consul Maynard to Sir Richard Fanshaw.

1666, January [7-]17. Lisbon—I cannot express how much cast down I was to receive no line from you by Mr. Price. I made bold to tell you "of our last campaign and the gallant behaviour of this small party of English, who are now so few that no considerable service can be expected from them, although they should all lay down their lives for the honour of their King and country. At the late siege of La Guarda were slain Capt. Charles Langley, Lieutenant Sinous, Ensign Perry and about forty private sentinels. There is now a good understanding betwixt the Court and them, they having but four months' pay due to them." You will have all news of this Court better from the ministers by Mr. Price. 1 *p.*

RICHARD FANSHAW to his WIFE.

[1666] [8-]18 January, Monday. Toledo—" My dearest life, hitherto—God be thanked—all well, the air and motion agreeing exceedingly well with me, as I believe it will with thee and the children as often as the weather shall prove favourable. God bless us all, and send us soon and happily to meet, whereof I have already met with something of good omen, as lodged in the house now belonging to a rich Portuguese and in a city most interested of any in Spain in, and most greedy of a peace with Portugal in respect of their trade, for which reason they express among themselves great joy at my passing through in order to that end, for sufficiently public it is everywhere. Once more and ever, God bless us all. Dearest only love, thine own ever.

I do not know that I left anything forgot there. Services to all friends.

CATHERINE FANSHAW to her father, SIR RICHARD FANSHAW.

1666 [January 8-]18. Madrid—I hope your Excellency will not think that I have not wished to write and beg for your blessing, and that you will grant my desire to hear that you are well. I pray you to be assured of the goodwill of my heart, although my hand does not know how to explain it as it ought. May God preserve you to us, who are much saddened by your absence, but my consolation is that God will restore you happily to us, in which hope I remain your very obedient daughter. *Spanish.* ½ *p.*

MARGARET FANSHAW to her father, SIR RICHARD FANSHAW.

1666, January [10-]20—The greatest pleasure that I can have is your Excellency's company, for lack of which I am very unhappy, but not without hope that God will grant you a safe journey here, and a long life with my mother and my brother and sisters and myself, who, begging for your blessing, am always your obedient daughter. *Spanish.* ½ *p.*

ANNA FANSHAW to her father, SIR RICHARD FANSHAW.

[1666, January 10?]—I am very sorry that I do not know enough to write to your Excellency as I should like to do, but I hope that in God's good time you will return safely to us, until when I pray for your blessing. My sisters and my brother Richard kiss your hands and entreat your blessing. *Spanish.* ½ *p.*

Lord Belasyse to Lord Holles, Ambassador in Paris.

1665-6, January 10-20. Tanger—A French ship laden with tobacco and sugars has been chased into the bay by the Turk's Admiral, but was secured and protected by some shots from the guns on the Mole. The Turks sent to demand their prize, but I refused to give her up, whereupon they have departed in a fury and will no doubt complain to the Duana at their return to Algiere, as they have done before, when "both my reason and inclination have induced me to favour Christians against infidels."

I am staying the ship here until his Majesty's pleasure be known, because the French have been so discourteous in seizing our merchant ships, but "I hope the good intelligence betwixt the two Crowns will procure me speedy orders from his Majesty to discharge her, together with his commands how to deport myself in the like accidents for the future." *Copy.* 1½ *pp* [*There is another copy of this letter in the Tangiers Correspondence.*]

Consul Valentine Morgan to Sir Richard Fanshaw.

1666, January [10-]20. St. Sebastian—Regrets that he cannot show his loyalty and zeal by employing his life and fortune in his native sovereign's service. He is " enclosed in this nook " as his King's minister, though without the least stipend to defray his charges or the help which he must of mere compassion give to his countrymen, both seamen and soldiers, but is well content if his endeavours be well construed. Sends relation of what has passed touching the *Charles* of Boston and her cargo, which has been discharged against the orders of the King of Spain, under pretence of repairing and graving the ship.

Postscript.—Did not send off the above, in hopes to have had it put in better form, but "could not since compass the notary," who was doubtless bribed by his adversaries. February 2 [stilo novo], 1666. 1 *p.*

Ann, Lady Fanshaw, to her husband, Sir Richard Fanshaw.

1666, January ⌊18-]28. Madrid—"My dear soul, thine from Tolethey [Toledo] I have received, but much long to hear from thee since how thou goest on thy journey. God of his mercy bless thee and prosper thee and send us a happy meeting here again suddenly, for I believe when thou hast examined well all thy letters thou wilt find cause as well in thy reason as

affection to hasten hither. Thou wilt find by Lord Ar[lington]
that in his canting language he would fain have his cast general
reap the fruit that thou hast sown, but he will be much mistaken, and I find here would have been so if his design had
been promoted sooner, for yesterday the Du[ke] de Me[dina]
las To[rres] was to visit me with his Duchess, and told me that
he had newly received a letter, but said not from whence, but
by circumstances I believe from his brother-in-law from Flanders,
in which, says he, I find that foul [? fool] Molinay hath advised
their sending of Ea[rl] San[dwich] to this Court without ever
having advertised either the Queen of his design or me, but, says
he, I have communicated this to the Queen, and yesterday her
Majesty called a council thereupon, and upon their advice
this was resolved, that a letter of grace and encouragement should
be sent post after thee, and a post sent immediately into England
to command the Conde de Moliney to depart that Court in twenty-
four hours, and to come hither here to give an account of this
presumptuous action. Likewise the Duke added that the King
his master said to him upon occasions that if this ambassador
of England, who is so discreet and careful both to follow his
master's instructions and to assist me, should either be called
home before he hath finished his business here or any other
sent to treat over him, I will never give him more than the
accustomed ceremonies of my Court, but to treat if this fail
none will do. Said the Duke, the like say I; first, I hope
our post will stop him that is coming, but if not I will assure
your Excellency he shall have from this Court a very quick
despatch, speaking much more of resentment of this than I
can here say, not forgetting to tell me that he was never a man
that cared to deal with two persons about one business, nor
knew what he should say when he was assured that thou hadst
gained those conditions for England that never any had before,
nor the best statesman of England could expect from this
Court, remembering a little those that did precede thine. To
all this and much more I replied that I was very sorry that I
was not capacitated to understand the things of state that I
might reply to them to his Excellency's content, but that which
I knew of these things were all general, and more at this time
than ever by his Excellency's favour; that for the Conde
Moliney, he was altogether unknown to thee, but well known
to our King, who had a great esteem for him; that it was
possible his letters of information of the Earl coming might
miscarry or come hereafter; that for the Earl he was a great
person and that I supposed he might be sent upon some extraordinary occasion, and that I did not doubt but that he would
fully satisfy him so much at his coming if so, for I had
no particular news thereof, but that I saw it in the news books
from London; that I had letters for thee from the Secretary,
which had lain some time by the way, and I did not doubt, God
willing, thou would quickly give his Excellency an account of
what thou foundest therein of concern to this Court. Then his

Excellency offered me his service with much compliment, and so did the Duchess too, and so we parted.

Now my sense upon this whole business is this, which indeed the Du[ke] and the father Pa[trick] told me almost at large; that the Count Moliney and the Se[cretary] with Lord Chan[cellor], finding that the Duke had quite turned the stream from their mill, began to be concerned, and thought by this means to bring it to them again, but lord what a loud laugh it will make when their pitiful designs are known and the rage this Court is in thereat, for first, why did not he, if this was disliked, not presently signify the King's pleasure thereupon, having the papers in their hands five months; secondly, why did not he send a post with such as was agreeable to their designs; *thirdly, why any and at their own time in the name of God; fourthly, it infinitely concerns us to make an end for many reasons, says another*, and now after this and more thou should stop thy hand. Truly, my dear, God hath both in his justice and mercy dealt with thee and them, for them, to do the King and kingdom good notwithstanding these little and weak men to turn their own private designs, and in his favour to thee in not suffering them to hurt thee, and in spite of them this negotiation of thine will prove wise and honest and honourable to the end of the world, for thou hast made this business of England better than any can suppose, nay, better than they themselves knew till they had received thy agreement, and therein thou followed thy instructions to the full, as it is well thou didst. As we have often talked and withal as I suppose thou meanest to answer his letter, *thou hast left room in the league to add what his Majesty shall be pleased to think fit, concerning anything at home or abroad*, which must always be allowed to be so discreet a reservation and copious that their ambassador may have an ample employment thereupon, and we to satisfy ourselves in that part thou hast acted, for which to God be the glory, and be cheerful, my soul, and as thou hast always had God and honour before thy eyes, so thou wilt never want his blessing thereupon, for as for our back friends, if we were to live upon their approbation, we should be as poor as if we lived upon their purse. I have had very many visits since thou went thy journey, amongst whom a very great man said, well, madam, my Lord Ambassador hath made the greatest and happiest negotiation that hath been this many hundred years, and is at this time the most envied man, both at home and abroad, by all foreign ministers in the world, and this peace that he is now gone about, whether it succeed or no, is the greatest trust that ever any one man had. My dear, probably Sir Robert Southwell will be at Lisbon before thou canst meet the Con[de] de Cas[tel]me[lhor], because he is supposed to come in these ships of Sir Jeremy Smith's; if not he is to come with Sir Christopher Mins, who sets sail, as is supposed, about this time.

Dear lamb, it is much to be wished thy sudden return, for what they do not do there quickly they will never do, and these express a great longing to have thee suddenly bring them a peace back, though I confess I am heartily glad that all this dispute hath fallen out in thy absence, so that it will appear that thou hadst no hand in it. I want that cipher very much, for what may come then, and I may have need to say. There is no post come yet back from England; so soon as any doth or any other imminent thing happen I will not fail to send to thee an express. I have sent thee all thy letters of these ten days last past from all parts as they came to my hands, there is a packet gone to Tanger from Lord Arl[ington] and another from Tanger to Lord Arl[ington]. My dear soul, this is what of news at present is here known. Now as to our particular, God's name be praised, we are all in health, and I earnestly desire thee to have a care of thy health and safety, and then to remember our discourse of the park. Prithé if I do not do well in anything, correct me and I will mend, for I am very diffident of my carriage in this place, as I have great reason to be, as thou well knowest. I long to hear what hopes there is in thy business, my dear. If it will not do, either public or private, be not troubled, but leave it to God; it is much what hitherto thou hast done relating thereto, and likewise prithé send me word when thou thinkest thou shall be back again in grace of God, thus with my perpetual prayers to God for thee and thy prosperity," I remain thine ever.

Postscript.—"The prayers and good wishes that thou hast from this whole Court are very great. I never have seen such expressions of joy as all here show upon this occasion, nor so general an anger from great and small of anything to be said from England but by thee, and though I shut my mouth I cannot but open my ears with wonder to hear what is said of this Earl, for all his old sins are here with a prospective seeing, the Duke telling me he knew him by hearsay to be a Cromwellist, which will not down [*sic*] here; in fine great heat is expressed hereupon, as thou wilt find by the Du[ke]'s letter and Father Pa[trick's] to thee, which is enclosed. This must not be forgot, that amongst the many visits I have had the Marques[a] de Liche's was one, nor must I likewise forget that your friend, Mr. La Strange,* hath amongst his news put in a letter from Madrid, highly in thy commendations, and his own sense thereupon higher, for which I do not doubt but he will have a good reprimand. Lord Holles is detained fifteen days longer in Paris and the Government of Jersey is taken out of Lord St. Alban's hands and given to one Lieutenant-General or Sir Thomas Morgan; who that is I know not. It is supposed there will be a war with England, but not of the French seeking, but yet I think it is uncertain. The plague is not gone, rather increased a little in London the beginning of January. I have had no letters from private hands this week. Again and again God bless thee, my soul." 5¾ *pp.*

Endorsed :—"Received at Benavente 7th February, at noon, *per propio.*"

[The words in italics are underlined in the letter.]

---

* Roger L'Estrange, Surveyor of the Press.

LYONELL FANSHAW to LADY FANSHAW.

1666, January [19-]29. Frexinall—Explaining a cipher, and reporting that his Lord has had his health well all the journey hither. 1 *p*.

ANN, LADY FANSHAW, to her husband, SIR RICHARD FANSHAW.

1666 [January 24-]February 3. Madrid—My dearest life, thine of the 19th of the last from Frexinall I did receive by the hands of Don Nicholas, whom the Duke sent with it to me the same hour that he received it. I am sorry to see so little hopes of the fruit of thy long labours, but we must submit ourselves to God's will and remember that if he takes care for the birds of the air he doth not slightly decree his will in the fortunes of kingdoms, and as for thee those principles with which thou didst both begin and persevere in this peace are so religiously wise that I do not doubt but God will give thee and thine a blessing for the good intent of thy heart, and the honour of going thus far will appear in all ages a great and honourable work when it shall be laid open to the world, and therefore, my love, be cheerful and animate thyself therein, by putting a confidence and value of thy own understanding, which to have done, being a young man, doubtless had been a fault—though now the English fashion—but besides thy natural parts that great experiences, especially in these Courts, thou hast, as likewise been longer experienced in State matters, both by practice and books, than our directors, in the consideration of which it would now in thy years be as great a fault not to reflect on these points and therein to be positive, as it was a virtue in thee in thy youth to submit thy judgment to riper years, and thou art now on that vantage ground of truth, as my Lord Bac[on] saith, from which to behold one's enemies or no friends in the vale beneath with their many shufflings and arts, great and small, is a pleasant sight, so it be, as the same author says, with pity, which truly they deserve, for whenever day shall appear all their mummeries will prove trash. To conclude this discourse, my soul, be cheerful, make much of thyself, be not surprised either with their want of their former kindness, which is always a loose garment put on over statesmen's clothes, nor be not too thoughtful, but do the best that in thee lies for God's glory, for thy country's good and thy own honour and profit, and then submit cheerfully to God's decrees, who, with glory to him be it ever by us spoken, hath brought us to this, hath delivered us out of many dangers and chooses for us such good things as we neither had foresight nor power to choose.

The packets that I sent to thee on the 28th of the last not being yet gone, by reason, says the Du[ke], that a despatch which the Queen sends therewith was not ready till this day, I have put these up with them. This day no letters are come for thee from Andalusia, but Mr. Godart's letters say that Sir

Jeremy Smith is arrived at Calles, and with him Don Patricio
Mulede, and that there are four frigates and seventeen ships
that carry victuals for Tanger, and that Sir Robert Southwell
is at Lisbon, who put in with six ships, which after his landing is to come hither for Calls [*sic*]. This day Don Alonso,
the Du[ke's] Secretary, came hither from the Du[ke] and
Duch[ess], and in much discourse told me that the Condé de
Sandwich would not come, with more than ordinary heat, saying that Condé Moliney would be here in few days to answer
this insolent action, which the Queen, says he, is most highly
displeased with, as she hath great cause, for his complaining
of that ambassador that both her Majesty and all this Court
hath such kindness for, to which I replied that for the first,
there was nothing more ordinary, as he well knew, than for
Princes to send their extraordinary ambassadors when they
pleased, and many times occasions required them, and that
I was fully satisfied that his Majesty did it upon good reasons
though I knew them not, and so I knew would thou be, as
both of us to see in this Court an honourable person of our
own country. For the latter, I hoped the Condé would clear
himself of all things that might disgust this Queen and Court,
being a person for whom I have heard our King had a great
kindness; for my husband, though he hath not the honour to
be known to the Condé, yet his actions were and would be
I suppose, from which I [*torn*] that he is his friend. But
in fine they are all here raging mad at the Condé, time will
tell why. It is said that there is a great number of soldiers
going from Ireland to the Bish[op] of Mun[ster], likewise
it is said that one Lord Rotorford [Rutherford] comes to
Tanger in the next fleet in the room of Lord Bell[asyse],
but I have neither of these from a sure hand. My dear love,
I have no more to say by this post, but to tell thee that if any
letters come for thee from Lord Ar[lington] or any other of
concern, be sure I will send a post, as likewise if any extraordinary accident happens in this Court. God in heaven bless
thy business and send it a prosperous end if it be his will,
and keep thee in health and send thee well back to me."

Postscript.—" The enclosed that my cousin Fan[shaw] wrote I
thank thee for, and shall make use of it upon any occasion that
requires it. I have sent thee in this packet a ring for a token,
of those that Fa[ther] Pa[trick] gave me. Dick, God be praised,
is both a very fine boy and very well, as is all thine and myself, and present their duty to thee." 3 *pp.*

Addressed by Lady Fanshaw :—" For my dear life."

Endorsed :—" Received at Benavente 7 die, at noon, *per
propio.*"

The SAME to the SAME.

1666, [January 31-]February 10. Madrid—Dearest life, I
send this post to bring thee the news of England and our good
healths, which God be praised we all perfectly enjoy notwith-

standing we have had all very great colds by reason of the change of the weather, which hath been very rigorous here, though now most sweet. *From England I have been shown several letters that upon the receipt of thine of the 20th of the last, new style, the King did express openly a very great joy of the work of thy hands and particularly spoke much in thy praise with great esteem, and so did the Duke of York, with the Secretary, Lord Ar[lington], and all the whole Court—* one thing observe by the way that we have here all letters four days date later than the Secretaries—but our dear friend, the Lord Ch[ancellor], said truly he did not expect this work to be so finished, and showed himself very melancholy, at which the King laughed and so doth many a one, and write that now he will be much troubled how to provide for his cast Condé, but I hear that he will now make him Governor of Tanger— and that from a good hand—in fine, to God be the glory, thou art very successful in all thy undertakings and so understood. No post returned from England nor any letters yet sent me for thee from Don Patr[icio] Mol[edi]. This place is very disconsolate in fear thou wilt not make a peace, and some, and not the simplest, think they may send a white paper to sign and it will be granted, indeed their case is sad. The Queen Mother of France is dead, and departed this life with these blessed words in her mouth to the King, her son: Love peace and make peace with all the world that you may have eternal peace. The French would, now declared, have peace with England on any conditions and are for certain providing against Spain with much eagerness. The Hollander is in a very ill condition, and every day worse and worse. The Prince of Munster—for that is the title our King is pleased we should call him—is in a very good condition, and it is said that he is to come in person to a place in Flanders, there to meet the Du[ke] of Yor[k] and the Mar[quis] of Bran-[denburg] and Lu[xembourg] and Mar[quis] de Cas[tel] Ro-[drigo], with many other Princes of Germany, some time this next month. Great preparations are making in England for this summer, the last news of the plague from England was seventy in all thereof, and but fourteen in the city. Lord Bell[asyse] going home.

Now, my dear, to return to thy present business. I hope it will have a good end notwithstanding all their tricks that have employed themselves to make this void, and the airy part gives way to the more solid body, and necessity will speak plainer than the most eloquent, and better is half a loaf than no bread, and I hope by this time thou art near returning, though I could wish that this letter might find thee there, being a clear light to thee in three points. First, that thou art well received with honour by our master; the next, that England is very prosperous; and thirdly, that I find a peace here is desired upon any terms. I forgot to tell thee that we have taken upon the coast of England two Holland ships, besides three others that are worth three or four and twenty thousand pounds sterling, and some French ships, which our King says he only deposits till his Majesty is satisfied for the losses he hath received by the French King at sea.

My love, prithé make much of thyself and have a care of cold, and send me by this bearer what thou hast to say, and likewise the day's journeys thou art to make at thy return to me, that so, God willing, I may know how thou makest thy way, to send to thee if need be, that I should receive any extraordinary news. This being all that I have at present to say, with my perpetual prayers to Almighty God for thy health and prosperity and safe return to all thine."

Postscripts.—Prithé let Mr. Cooper and the Arguisil [*Alguacil*, *i.e.*, steward] draw me a note of the way of thy return.

"Just as I am making up this letter I am showed one from London that says that Lord San[dwich] hath sent to Bristol for many young merchant men to come with him to be put into Tanger, and likewise that Dunkirk is now more than ever spoke of, upon which, with many other things, I have much to tell thee to make thee merry, but they are not fit to be written, but shall not be forgot, God willing, at our meeting.

"As thou will see by Father Pa[trick]'s letter, I have nothing but good words for my money as yet, but they often repeated, and he himself came just as I was naming him in this to me, and was very full of discourse of many things, amongst which he told me that the Du[ke] would very suddenly be the favourite, likewise of the high expression that our King made of joy at thy concluding the peace here, and of many other things that rejoiced him that he had heard out of England by this day's post. Amongst which one thing is said not unpleasant, which is that the King had a play acted, in which many nations met, and the Frenchman made them all afraid, but the Englishman coming by him as he was vapouring, he gave over and said nothing, but the Englishman, not contented, then withdrew his sword and told him he would make him take notice of him, with which the Frenchman replied that he desired friendship with him and therefore desired him to accept of a present and gave him a purse of gold. This makes much talk and laughter, and is writ also from Bayonne. The friar told me that thou wast jealous that there was some underhand dealing in this treating with Portugal by a friar employed by Caracena, but swears that there is none, and that this Crown by the Duke doth wholly put their confidence in thee, and to that purpose either with these or within two days after the Queen and Duke will not fail to write by an express to thee to that purpose. I told him I knew nothing at all of this business, as in truth I did not, nor well know whether I did well understand him now, but this I plainly perceive, that either they are innocent or ashamed they are not. I had like to forgot to tell thee the last week four Turks men.

of-war fought two French men-of-war off Cadiz and took them."
3½ pp.
Addressed by Lady Fanshaw :—" For thyself, my dear love."

NEWS LETTER.

1666, January—Cadiz [December 31-]January 10. Many
ships have brought corn from the Levant, or this country would
be starved. The Duchess of Aveiro departs for Seville in the
galleys within two days, and Sir Benjamin [Wright] means
to go also.

Seville, January [2-]12. All here are in fear of a mutiny.
There are so many robberies every night that the *Assistente*
has ordered that no man stir out of his house after six o'clock.
Three coaches of cavaliers were robbed at eight o'clock the
other night, and the rogues were so impudent as to go into
a shop hard by to divide the money.

Malaga, January [2-]12. Several Argier frigates are at
Tanger. That Divan has agreed with Lord Bellasis for the
cargo of the *Margarita*. The Marquis shot yesterday at two
small English vessels bound home from the Levant. He has no
mercy on us, though he admits the Hamburghers.

Granada, January [1-]11. The Venetians and the Pope are
said to be in league with France, and to have procured the
admission of Florence and Genoa. All Italy is disturbed since
in Germany the princes of the house of Saxony and many others
have joined with the title of *defenders against their enemies.*
The Bishop of Munster draws very near the Hollanders, and
the States have asked for a contribution of twelve millions to
prosecute the war.

Madrid, January [10-]20. Seven new Counsellors of State
have been sworn, viz., the Duke of Alburquerque, the Cardinal
Colona, the Duke of Montalto, the Count of Ayala, Don Luis
Ponce de Leon, the Confessor of the Queen* and the Marques
de Fuente, ambassador in France. They are called in a
pasquinade the seven deadly sins. It is said on good authority
that the Duke of Medina Celi is coming to Madrid voluntarily,
by persuasion of his daughter, the Marquesa de Liche.
Partly in Spanish. 1¾ pp.

Enclosing,
A note of the Counsellors of State that are now chosen :—
*Montalto, Pride; Ayala, Avarice; Fuente, Lewdness;
Ponze, Anger; Colona, Gluttony; the Confessor, Envy;
Alburquerque, Sloth. Spanish.*

CONSUL VALENTIN MORGAN TO SIR RICHARD FANSHAW.

1666 [February, early in. San Sebastian]—The war between
England and France was published in France on the 27th ultimo,
and no doubt "the wars with Spain and France will soon
follow." In such case it will be dangerous to send any packet

---

* Eberhard von Neidhart, called in Spain *el padre Nithard or Everardo.*

of importance by way of France, and the best way will be with packet-boats. Sir Andrew King asked me on your behalf how I could procure two frigates to go constantly between Spain and England, and I sent him "an ample form" how it might be done, and with such secrecy that no man living would know the design save the master that carried the packets, as the frigates would carry some small matter of goods and be known only for merchant men. He was well pleased with the sugges-. tion, but " the matter was notwithstanding ordered to the King's minister's management, by which it came, the same day he received the orders, to be public over all the city." For better secrecy, if needful, I will, as owner, keep three frigates, which shall go and come constantly for an annual payment of 18,000 pieces of eight, which, to colour the design, may bring English goods, not drapery, lest there be scruple of the sickness, but lead, shot, beeswax, tanned leather or wheat. If there be any difficulty about these goods, the ships shall come only in ballast, and they shall not stay an hour longer either in England or here than to take in their packets, wind and weather permitting. I shall gladly receive your Excellency's resolutions, but cannot abate a real of my proposition and must be paid beforehand every three months, otherwise I will not hazard it. 1 *p.*

Endorsed :—" Received at Estremos 24 February, 1666, s.n."

PRINCE DE CHALAIS TALLERAND DE PERIGORD to SIR RICHARD
FANSHAW.

1666, February [1-]11. Lisbon—Your kind promise of friendship when we met at Madrid with the Comte de Marchin emboldens me to hope that you will not refuse your help in obtaining permission for me to go on parole to the frontiers of Navarre. The Council of Portugal granted permission to my brother, the Marquis de Noirmoustier, for me to do so, but since the King of England asked the same thing for the Marques de Liche and Don Annielo de Gusman without their obtaining it, I am not allowed to go for fear of vexing his Majesty. I have sent to London about it, but as it is very important for me to go at once, I beg your assistance. If the treaty breaks off—which is not likely since it is in your hands— I will return, and if needful the Comte de Chomberg and my brother will be securities for me. *French.* 1¼ *pp.*

COMTE DE SCHONBERG to SIR RICHARD FANSHAW.

1666, February [1-11?]. Salvaterra—The bearer of this is a servant of Mons. de Challay [Chalais], who wishes to obtain permission from the Comte de Castelmelhor to visit his wife on the frontiers of Navarre for two or three months. If the King returns to-morrow evening, I shall come to see you, not wishing

to let you go without assuring you of my respect. *French.*
Holograph. 1¼ *pp.*

LADY FANSHAW to her husband, SIR RICHARD FANSHAW.

1666 [February 2-]12. Madrid—My dear life, the Duke did
promise me that I should have a post to send to thee yesterday,
but yet he is not gone, therefore I write this to add to the latter.
This day the Duke de Avero was to visit me. I can find nothing
to say to thee new but only this, that whatever thy business
proves, send as little of it by writing as thou canst possible
to this Court till thou comest to declare it at large, and I
believe for many reasons thou wilt be of my opinion. I believe
this will find thee on the way hither; prithé dispatch him back
with what brevity thou canst after thou hast answered the letters
sent thee by the Du[ke] with this, the writing whereof I suppose hath been the reason that this post hath been detained
till this time. *Just as I am writing this the Duke sent Father*
P[atrick] to tell me that he had received news from England
that the King had sent to the Emperor, and that from thence
the Queen received letters this day from her brother in which
he did much rejoice at the peace concluded and league too,
as he hoped, for that he and other Princes should immediately
declare the league they had and were a finishing with the King
of England, wishing heartily a match with the fair lady of
his house and the King of Portugal. Likewise the Du[ke]
sent me word that he was now ready to assign the payment of
a hundred and fifty pieces of eight, which Mr. Godart should
suddenly pay me. In fine, thus stands matters, that now the
Confessor is not only a councillor but very near a declared
favourite, and the Du[ke] his Governor. The Marques[a?] de
Liche this day sent me a little greyhound puppy, so fine a
creature I never saw in my life, which I take care of much for
thee, but Dick lugs her by the ears and is very fond of her.
God's name be praised, he grows a lovely fine boy and all the
girls are very well, and so am I, but wish thee with me a
thousand times, and if thou mayst be so happy to conclude
this business now, or to lay there a foundation so as to do it
hereafter in this place, it will be most happy, if not, God's will
be done, to whom I perpetually pray that he will bless, preserve
and keep thee, and send us a happy meeting."

Postscript.—" Never was any people so thirsty as these are
for good news from thee, which God of his mercy send." 1¾ *pp.*
Addressed by Lady Fanshaw :—" For thyself, my life."
Endorsed :—" Received at Benavente 9-19 February, 1666,
per propio."

GASPAR DE HARO, MARQUES DE LICHE, to SIR RICHARD FANSHAW.

1666, February [6-]16. Castle of St. George, Lisbon—
Thanking him for past kindnesses, and praying him to continue his efforts to procure his liberation. *Spanish.* 1½ *pp.*

CONSUL THOMAS MAYNARD to SIR RICHARD FANSHAW.

1666, February [7-]17. Lisboa—Stating that Sir Jeremy
Smith passed by Cadiz, but only looked into the bay without
making any stay. He took a Hollander laden with figs upon
the coast of the Algarves and a French ship laden with sherry
sacks near the bar of St. Lucar, and it is reported that he took
another French ship near the Straits' mouth. 1 *p.*

LADY FANSHAW to her husband, SIR RICHARD FANSHAW.

1666, February [9-]19. Madrid—My dearest life, I am
infinitely troubled that I have not yet heard from thee, we
here guessing that that post first sent might have been here
long since. This is the third post that hath been sent to thee
since thy going from hence; what the other two carried I
knew, because I was told, but this errand is kept so secret that
yet I cannot find it out; flying reports there are, first, that
a post came from England, then that the Duke's son came
home privately from Lisbon, and that, say others, the Duke
hath received private packets from Lisbon; but this is sure,
that on the 27th of the last the King of France declared publicly
a war against England, and as sure that on Tuesday last here
in the morning the Queen called a full council, both of state
and war, and I do conjecture from thence is this post sent, but
as I am at this point in comes Fa[ther] Pa[trick] from the
Du[ke] to me and unriddles the riddle, which, says he, is this:
that this post is sent to inform thee that there is a declared
war from France to England; and for the Duke's son, it was
Don Domingo that unhappily killed the Marquis the year we
came into Spain. So that is all the news of this Court, but it
is talked that the Condé de Pen[aranda] shall be president of
Castile and the Condé de Vilinbrose [Villa Umbrosa] president
de la Assienda. I have here enclosed sent thee all the news that is
stirring in thy letters from England, I having this week received
no more. The last news of the plague of the 20th of last
month, this style, died eighty-nine of the plague. The Du[ke]
continues very civil to me, and now begins to think it long
till he hears how the business of Portugal goes, for it concerns
them much here, their punctilios falling and their desires
increasing daily with violence for a peace on any terms. My
dear life, I need not to tell thee how many fears and hopes
I have daily and what disorder of mind I am often in, and
the more because I must not in point of honour show it but
to God that sees my heart, and I hope hears my perpetual
prayers for thy health and prosperity. I desire [him] to send
thee to me safe back, if he please, with an olive branch in thy
mouth to these distressed people, and to my everlasting joy
to return into our own country, there to praise God for all his
infinite mercies to us. God be praised, Dick and all thine

are very well and beg thy blessing. Dear love, have a care of thyself and be cheerful, and so God preserve thee." 1¾ *pp.*
Addressed by Lady Fanshaw :—" For thyself, my life."

SIR RICHARD FANSHAW to [the DUKE OF MEDINA DE LAS TORRES].

1666, February [11-]21. Benavente—With regard to the coming of the Earl of Sandwich to this Court as ambassador extraordinary, I cannot count it bad news, both for the reasons which I have already mentioned and because he is my very good friend, although this does not prevent my acknowledging my infinite indebtedness to the kindness of the Queen and yourself in vouching for my innocence on being informed that complaints have been made to our English Court of my ill-carriage in Spain by a minister who has neither seen nor treated with me in his life. If this were so, I am very sure that upon the King, my master—by whom I have been proved so many years—no hearsay testimony would make the least impression to my prejudice. I hold it for certain that his Majesty has taken this resolution in order, by the talents and rank of the new ambassador, to bring quickly to an end some fresh negotiations of importance, and also to show how greatly he esteems the persons and desires the friendship of the Catholic Sovereigns. One thing I confess will grieve me, and that is if there is any omission in giving the Count as hearty a reception at Madrid as I had upon coming into Spain—and more, if more is possible—since, on the one hand, I have certain information that it will be noticed in England, and, on the other, any failure herein might, by malevolent or mistaken persons, be imputed to me. *Spanish. Copy.* 1 *p.*

SIR RICHARD FANSHAW to his wife, LADY FANSHAW.

1666, February [12-]22. Cruche in Portugal—" My dear life, this I write to thee, being four leagues from Benevente, where my station was, on my way back to Madrid, and it is by the first express of two that have come to me from thence, reserving the second to follow after I shall be out of this kingdom.

The packet herewith enclosed for the Duke, bearing date yesterday, could not say so much, therefore, together with it, send advice to his Excellency I have been in my journey and am from this day forward.

Thine by the latter reached me at Benevente, very opportunely for me to make use—as I did—of the three notes therein specified.

A list of my gists [*sic*] from Badajos goes herewith enclosed, reckoning I may arrive there four days hence, so to one day more or less my arrival with thee may be estimated.

With me comes Sir Robert Southwell, in manner as thou

wilt see by my enclosed for Mr. Hodser. His stay being so short, I wish my girls will give us their *Querer* over again, and that Dick also lug his new puppy by the ears very unconcerned.

Much I have to talk, and much I have to hear then, opening my mouth and not shutting my ear, between thee and me. Services to all friends, and blessings God shower upon us and all ours." 1 *p. Seal of arms.*

Addressed by Sir Richard:—" For thyself, my soul."

Sir Jeremy Smith to the Duke of Medina Celi.

1665-6, February 13-23. On board the *Mary*, Cadiz Bay—Has come hither with the King of Great Britain's fleet, intending to water and take in provisions, but has been denied pratique by the Governor. Is sorry that his master's interests "should be so little where his deserts and confidence have been so great, and his devotion so clear to befriend this Crown," as their coming hither will shortly manifest, and prays his Excellency to afford them suitable entertainment. ½ *p. Copy.*

Duque de Medina Celi to Don Geronimo Smith.

1666, February [13-]23. Port St. Mary—Acknowledges Sir Jeremy's letter and congratulates him on his safe arrival. As regards the refusal of the Governor of Cadiz to allow pratique to the fleet, orders have come from his Majesty (in respect of the plague in England) not to admit any vessels from that kingdom into the ports, in order not to risk the health of the people; but if Sir Jeremy finds it necessary to careen and take in water, arrangements shall be made to enable him to do so. *Spanish. Copy.* 1 *p.*

Sir Richard Fanshaw to Lady Fanshaw.

1666, February [18-]28. Merida—My dearest dear, by the date of this informing thyself, thou wilt find I draw near thee as fast as I can, having never in my whole life more longed to be with thee, and that is a proud one. Till then I am silent, but very well and comfortable as to our particular, however the public shall determine of their own concerns, whereunto no endeavours of mine have or ever shall be wanting neither.

Thine of the 3rd post I received in my way at Estremos, and was very welcome.

Sir Robert Southwell comes with me. I wish D. Patricio Hodser would meet [me] at Casa Rubias to tell what is provided as to him. I reckon I shall be there—at Casa Rubias—on Saturday or Sunday next at night. God bless us all. The Duke bestows to me high commendations on Dick. This night I lodge at Medellin." 1 *p.*

SAMUEL SMALL to SIR RICHARD FANSHAW.

1666 [February 21-]March 3. Oporto—Has heard nothing
of his business since he left Madrid, and should be in despair
if he were not confident of his Excellency's *amparo* [support].
His kinsman, Edward Mellish, as chiefly interested in the
matter, is writing more at large concerning it, and also touching
some grievances of his own. 1 *p.*
Endorsed:—"Received 10 April, s.n., *per* Mr. Crisp."

EDWARD MELLISH to SIR RICHARD FANSHAW.

1666 [February 22-]March 4. Oporto—The renown of your
Excellency's virtues emboldens me to beg your interposition at
this [Portuguese] Court, for the redress of the unheard of wrongs
and oppressions under which I have suffered, owing to the malice
of two wicked villains who, because I would not let them rob
me of my goods, have exhibited false articles against me to the
officers of the Custom House at Figueira, how that I have
imported there in several barrels 700,000 pieces-of-eight, stamped
in England with this King's mark, and have bribed some of
the officers to connive at my landing them. The barrels were
proved to contain only shot and butter, and I made only culpable
of defrauding the King of his customs, of which also I was
innocent, for the barrels did not at all belong to me but to the
mariners of the ships, as I have demonstrated in a remonstrance
sent to Sir Robert Southwell and the Consul. But being supposed culpable, I am obliged to run a suit of law against these
villains, which has already cost me three times more than the
penalty would have done, and my enemies are so powerful at this
Court that they persist in the impeachment concerning the
moneys and a fresh examination has been ordered, although
I was pronounced guiltless by the other.

I have always paid duty for my goods, but the truth is that
the officers in the Custom House have been guilty of many
misdemeanours, and the *Dezembargador* says the King must not
be a loser, and therefore, right or wrong, he has extorted the
money from us. English. Hitherto, God be praised, my innocency has borne me out, but fearing to be engulfed at last,
I pray your Excellency to pity me so far as to demand my
redress of his Majesty at Salvaterra. I the rather venture
to ask this as knowing the protection you gave to my kinsman,
Sam. Small, at Madrid, concerning the ship *William and
Elizabeth*, unjustly taken and carried into Vigo, for though he
could not then effect his business, he acknowledged himself
infinitely bound to your Excellency, and brought me great hopes
of accomplishing it, especially as the matter has been particularly recommended to your Excellency by his Majesty in
letters granted to my brother-in-law, Mr. William Sherrington
of London. 2¾ *pp.*
Endorsed:—"Received 10 April, s.n., *per* Mr. Crisp."

Sir Richard Fanshaw to Lady Fanshaw.

1666 [February 23-]March 5. Oropesa—"My dearest life, this is only to tell thee what is already above said, and that myself—I thank God—and all my company are and have continued hitherto in perfect health, hoping to find thee and all at home with the like, so remain my only dear love, thine ever."

Prewritten:—"Oropesa, Friday morning, 5th March, 1666. At night at Talavera de la Reyna, six leagues. Saturday night, St. Olalla, six leagues. Sunday night, at Casa Rubias, six leagues. Monday night, at Madrid, seven leagues. ½ p. *Seal of arms.*

Addressed by Sir Richard:—"Para mi muger Doña Ana Fanshaw, que Dios guarde muchos años."

Lady Fanshaw to Sir Richard Fanshaw.

1666 [February 25-]March 7. Madrid—My dearest life, a thousand times I praise God for his mercy to me in bring[ing] thee so well near me. I hope on Monday, God willing, I shall see thee about two leagues off, but not to go into any house, because it is needful to make haste hither, especially if thou wilt do as the Duke advises by Father Patr[ick]. For Sir Rob[ert] Sou[thwell], the master of the ceremonies says that the style of this Court hath always been to have the envoyé to come secretly to the ambassador's house of his King, and then upon the ambassador's advertising the Queen thereof he shall be after three or four days put into a house of the Queen's providing, with all necessaries and ceremonies belonging to his quality, to which end I have provided the lower quarter well dressed up for him and his man that waits on him; for his other servants they must lodge abroad. If thou likest it I think it were well that he with his people might pass over the river as we use to do by the Castle Decampaye, and so come to our house by Santa Barberica in thy litter, if he have no conveyance of his own, when thou comest into my coach, at which time I do wish he may not use the northern custom to salute me and mine—a thing never to be forgiven or forgotten in this Court—therefore I do earnestly desire that my cousin Fanshaw or some other way may be found to advertise him that here that is not to be done. So much for that.

Now, my love, take great care what thou sayest to F[ather] P[atrick], who is to play a double game. Much he will tell thee, and it is requisite thou should discover to him for the Duk[e's] satisfaction so much of thy business as will stay his stomach, but no more. For the pulse of this Court is this, that they have been very high with the Duke, not because a peace is not concluded with Portugal, but that the Duke did rest assured, and so persuaded them, it should be so without fail, upon which confidence there is neither money, commanders, nor men provided for a war either offensive or defensive against that country, the fault of which is laid at his door. If thunder from heaven had struck them they could not remain more stunned than they have been, and since distracted with calling daily Councils of State and War, and all without resolution and to no purpose, but in fine they suspend the resolution till they have heard thee, hoping, as some of them have told me, that there is some door open for a treaty, which is more longed for than ever fruit was by a woman with child, notwithstanding all their punctilios. And all their hopes is in thy hands, what ill words ever they may vent according to their customs, either to make them a peace with Portugal or to help them to make a war, in case the Portuguese be unreasonable, by the assistance of England. Therefore it is requisite that thou should be at once kind to F[ather] P[atrick], respective to the Duke, but withal to keep thy dignity, as having spent thy time, thy money, and endured a hard perilous journey for their sakes, all which, in case it should have no effect as to their redress, deserves both a reward and much thanks, which thou wilt do well to let them see thou expects.

The President and Penneirandy [Peñaranda] at war with the Duke, the Baron de Lesley suspected very false to the Duke, the Confessor the same.

The Condé de Villin Brossey [Villa Umbrosa], now President of the *Assienda*, much the Duke's, by love as well as by blood. Caracena very ill relished, and not known how he will come off.

My love, I had not writ thus largely to thee, being so near me, but that I judged it necessary to give thee these few hints, upon which, God willing, we shall discourse more at large. In the meantime thou mayst make use of this according to thy discretion and the condition of thy business, in which God Almighty ever with his mercy direct thee to his glory, the honour of thy master and our good." 2½ *pp.*

Sir Richard Fanshaw to Sir Jeremy Smith.

1666 [February 27-]March 9. Madrid—I arrived here from Portugal yesterday evening, and at the same time came your letter, informing me of his Majesty's frigates being denied pratique in the Spanish ports. I have not yet had time to wait upon the Queen or her ministers, but will do so before the next post. "I question not but you have heard before this time of the French King's having declared war against England." I hope the ships which set Sir Robert Southwell ashore at Cascayes have got safely to you. As yet we have no certain news of my Lord Sandwich's arrival in Spain. All the news from England is good. When we last heard the King was at Whitehall. *Copy.* 1 *p.*

Sir Richard Fanshaw to Consul Morgan.

1666, March 3-13. Madrid—Received at Estremos his letter suggesting a way for the safe conveyance of letters, and thanks him for his care, but being only newly arrived at the Court, has not yet had time to consider the proposition. ¼ *p. Copy.*

CONSUL MARTIN WESTCOMBE to SIR RICHARD FANSHAW.

1666, March [4-]14. Cadiz—We have notice of your Lordship's return to Spain. It will be joyful news to the Spaniards to hear that you have ended the differences with Portugal, but the report here is that the treaty is broken off.

"All well at Tanger, praised be God. The 8th of last month, Gueland with his fifteen thousand Moors of foot and two thousand horse, attacked the Spanish garrison of Alarache, scaling it with thirty ladders early in the morning, but was repulsed and lost fourteen hundred men and many of the best of Barbary, and so Gueland departed. I hope now he hath lost the favour of this nation by being unfaithful to his great promises of friendship to this Crown, which persuades me to believe that he will soon apply himself to a peace with Tanger.

"The Duque de Beaufort with his thirty men-of-war, with the seven of the Dutch, are still in Thollon."

The frigate *Antelope*, Captain Hollis, arrived here a week ago, and went to join Sir Jeremy Smith's squadron, which is cruising off the Straits' mouth.

The Spanish armada ships here are fitting with all possible haste. It is believed the Spaniards are afraid of the French and Dutch design against their Nova Espana fleet, which is expected about next August.

No English ships may have pratique here as yet, "though, God be praised, now in perfect health in England; London the place objected." 2 pp. [*Compare letter to Lord Arlington of this date. Spanish Correspondence.*]

CONSUL SAMUEL TRAVERS to SIR RICHARD FANSHAW.

1666, March [13-]23. Pontevedra—Master Thomas Goddard and company have informed me of your Excellency's safe return to Madrid, upon which I heartily congratulate you.

An hour ago I received a letter from Philip Stafford, my substitute at the Groyne, dated yesterday, and informing me that the Earl of Sandwich had entered the port accompanied by two frigates. The Governor would not permit any to go aboard, "but went himself in a shallop and showed the King's order for not admitting English vessels by reason of the contagion, to whom was delivered the testimony of health from Portsmouth, which he sent hither, *per coreo* to the Condestable, and being in Latin he caused it to be translated into Spanish and perused it." He has promised to let the Earl land, not in the city of the Groyne but at some *quinta* near, and that those on board the ship may have any supplies they need. I have told Stafford to attend diligently on his Excellency. 1¼ pp.

SIR RICHARD FANSHAW and SIR ROBERT SOUTHWELL to the CONDE DE CASTELMELHOR.

1666, March [14-]24. Madrid—We arrived here on the 8th inst., "and delivered the project brought with us to the Duke
24.   P

of Medina de las Torres, desiring him to present it to the Queen and that we might have speedy audience, that so I, the envoy, might be back in Portugal by the latter end of the month. . . . This Court was now already full of the report that the treaty carried by me, the ambassador, into Portugal was refused and larger conditions insisted upon, whereupon they spread abroad that I had bound up the King of England, my master, by the said treaty to oblige Portugal to accept it," or else that he must turn his arms against the said kingdom. According to this groundless report, the Duke returned us answer "that we were both highly blamed here for setting to that project in Portugal," and that they would do nothing until they heard the King of England's opinion by an envoy who would presently be sent, expecting the treaty to be ratified and Portugal forced to accept it. To this we returned that it was impossible for our King to ratify the treaty relating to Portugal without Portugal's consent and that I, the envoy, had brought instructions to meet all cases, and so there was no need to send an envoy to England. The Secretary of State next sent me, the ambassador, a letter returning the project and forbidding us to talk to the Queen of it, whereupon I, the envoy, desired my passport to be gone; but yesterday Don Blasco de Loyala gave me some expectation of audience from the Queen, and said I might send a servant into Portugal to comply with my promise. And I, the ambassador, finding how much this Court continued to reflect on my reputation, wrote again to the Duke, who sends me word by my secretary that what I say is true, so all this time has been spent in groundless contentions and not about the great affair which we have not been permitted to approach. I, the envoy, now have promise of audience for to-morrow, and will then in all haste return to Portugal, where we beg you will keep yourselves free to accept what terms may be obtained.

We have news from England, to our sorrow and our joy that her Majesty, our mistress, "has miscarried at Oxford out of apprehensions of danger the King was in, who was gone to London, and where she herself now is in safety with him. This is an earnest from heaven of the blessing we may expect in a Prince of Wales," which will confirm the amity between England and Portugal.

We see little reason for his most Christian Majesty having declared war against England, mentioning no provocation but his inclination to support the Dutch, "who have affronted and invaded the rights of all the Princes in Europe but himself." The said King has drawn thirty thousand men to the waterside, it may be in order to invade England, where, "between soldiers in pay and the militia of the provinces well armed and equally valuable to the others in our account, near eighty thousand men are ready to watch his landing." His ambassador here wishes Spain to trust him with the mediation of the peace and engages to oblige Portugal to accept less than was offered by the King of England's mediation, and that if Spain will join against England, he will assist her to regain Tanger and Jamaica.

Your Excellency will beware of suffering Portugal to enter into any league with this Prince, whereby your design of joining with England, your inseparable ally against the common enemy in the Indies, would be disappointed. *Copy.* 3½ *pp.*

Don Martin de Cayas Vasan, Governor of Cadiz, to "Don Geronimo Esmite."

1666, March [19-]29. Cadiz—Explaining the reasons why he cannot insist on the Dutch making satisfaction for their taking of an English *balandra* in the bay. *Spanish.* 2 *pp.*

Sir Jeremy Smith to the Governor of Cadiz.

1665-6, March 19-29. Cadiz Bay—Stating that he has received his letter of this date (as to the small vessel of wines taken by the Dutch), but does not find therein the satisfaction which the King, his master, commands him to receive for wrongs done to the English nation. If the applications for redress of what they have suffered from the Dutch be not at once attended to, a course will be taken to seek it another way. ½ *p.*

William Blunden to [Lionel Fanshaw?].

1666, March [19-]29. Alicante—Cannot tell how the report of Sir Jeremy Smith having met and worsted the Duke of Beaufort got about, as news from Marseilles states that the French fleet will not be ready to sail for a month, the delay being caused by their extreme want of men. It is said they are fitting up five more ships, and that they will have twelve fire-ships, "which more signifies their fear than discretion, for such an extravagant number are unusual in fleets far superior to theirs." The Governor [of Alicante] promises to protect all merchant ships in the port. ½ *p.*

Sir Richard Fanshaw to Consul Westcombe.

1666, March [20-]30. Madrid—Hears that Lord Sandwich has arrived at Corunna, and presumes that some ships have come with him to join Sir Jeremy Smith's squadron. Sends a list [wanting] of the French men-of-war at Toulon, which is to be communicated to Sir Jeremy. All well in England. ¾ *p. Copy.*

Henry Croone to Lionel Fanshaw, at Madrid.

1666, March [20-]30. Malaga—Regrets to hear that the treaty with Portugal has not yet been effected, but is confident that it will be concluded ere long, and trusts that it will be before the Earl of Sandwich's arrival, as it would be a great pity that another should have the glory when Sir Richard has had all the trouble. The *Lion* and the *Swallow* have arrived at Tanger and Sir Jeremy Smith is in Cadiz Bay. 1 *p.* *Seal of arms.*

Consul Martin Westcombe to Sir Jeremy Smith.

1666, March [21-]31. Cadiz—Stating that orders have come from the King of Spain to the Duke of Medina Celi to admit the Earl of Sandwich and his retinue to land where they please, and to treat them with all possible courtesy, and complaining that he is in danger of being clapped into the common gaol in consequence of the Dutch vessel from the East country having been taken by the boats of the English frigates within the limits of the port. Does not wish to question his honour's proceedings, but must pray to be indemnified by him in this matter. 1½ *pp.* *Copy.*

Antonio de Sousa de Macedo to Sir Richard Fanshaw.

1666 [March 24-]April 3. Lisbon—I thank your Excellency for your much valued letter of March 25. We rejoice to hear that you are all well, and my wife, Donna Marianna, sends especial greetings to my lady, the ambassadress.

As regards business, the ministers of that [the Spanish] Court are deceived by the delay of the King of France in proceeding to war against Castile, not understanding that the hesitation of Portugal is the cause, and that it will break out when Portugal desires. No one can hope that Castile will have aid from his Britannic Majesty, because he must give this either of his generosity or in the interests of his State. If the former, it is clear that his help must go to his brother-in-law and friend, who fights in a just cause; if the latter, it is also clear that he cannot join Castile if this power carries on war with Portugal, since in this case Castile would not be important, and the alliance would be only a burden and no profit. And if Castile thinks that England will help her in order that France may not advance further, she is mistaken, for if France allows England to dominate Holland, France will also wish her to advance against Spain. Finally, in the way in which this people become agitated and down-hearted on the slightest occasion, your Excellency will recognize their natural condition, and still more in the equivocation—to give it no other name—with which they desire to persuade people that your Excellency will promise them things which they cannot imagine. May God dispose all things better than men know how to desire, so that means fail not for the good of both Portugal and England.

I send you the papers concerning what passed on the frontiers with the Jesuit fathers. It is no new thing that they deny everything there. In what they say of your Excellency's promises we may see their sincerity in the affair. The Comte de Castelmelhor will tell you the intentions of the King of Great Britain, by our master's orders. *Signed. Spanish.* 2½ *pp.*

Endorsed:—"Received at Madrid 10 ditto, s.n., per Mr. Edward Crispe."

CONSUL WESTCOMBE to SIR RICHARD FANSHAW.

1666 [March 25-]April 4. Cadiz—The Earl of Sandwich is daily expected here from England, and it is said that a house is to be provided for him in Seville. It is generally reported that the hoped-for adjustment with Portugal is quite broken off, and the bruit runs that the Portuguese are in arms again and doing daily mischief on the frontiers. "All well in Tangier, praised be God, and believed that Gueland will suddenly court a peace with that garrison, now that he hath totally lost his credit with the grandees of this nation. We hear nothing of the Duque de Beaufort, which makes us believe he is still in Thollon." Sir Jeremy Smith, with his squadron of fifteen or sixteen frigates, is supposed to be about the Straits mouth. I pray you write to him to keep me indemnified from suffering by any of his actions—as I am like to do about the Dutch vessel taken by his boats—for "our King's affairs will in these parts go at six and seven if I am clapped up in prison." 2 *pp.*

Enclosing,
> An *invoice of the cargo of the Dutch vessel taken by Sir Jeremy Smith, consisting of yellow beeswax, pigs of lead, "tripitrapes," pipe staves, cases of bottles and fifty boxes of amber to make beads.*

LORD BELASYSE to CONSUL WESTCOMBE.

1666, March 26, April 5. Tanger—On receipt of your last I went aboard the Admiral and urged Sir Jeremy to make restitution of the ship taken from the Dutch, "which he no way inclined to do, alleging her lawful prize and out of the power of the Spanish guns or protection, but in truth the ship is delivered up here to the Commissioners (after condemnation), so plundered by the boats that took her as she is not fit or worth the re-delivery." However, as she is, anyone may have either ship, goods or both at the rates expressed in your letter. All the prizes brought in by Sir Jeremy are of small value, "and I assure you I gratify none of my friends in good bargains, being rather obliged in my honour and trust to hold them up to good values, lest his Majesty should be abused. · · · I hope there will be no cause from the Spaniards to be severe upon you about a business you are no way concerned in, and most undoubtedly my Lord Sandwich at his arrival will protect you from any trouble, when so many great occasions for union betwixt the two crowns interpose."

I have written to Lieut.-Col. Fitzgerald, now at Cadiz, about the purchase of the barco longo. Sir Jeremy Smith set sail this morning for England. 1 *p.* *Copy by Westcombe.*

SIR RICHARD FANSHAW to SIR JEREMY SMITH.

1666 [March 27-]April 6. Madrid—I have received yours from Cadiz, and with it a list of the ships which are to come out with the Duke of Beaufort, and a letter to Sir Robert Southwell, which is already delivered, as he is at this Court. You speak of touching at Lisbon on your way back to England, in which case I beg you to advertise me thereof, as some of my family may be awaiting such an opportunity to return home. "Here are at present several news by way of Flanders very exceeding good for England, whereof you will hear from other hands. I dare not be the author of any of them further than through an implicit faith that God Almighty will ever bless us, as he ever hath done in all ages whenever we were ourselves, that is to say England, united; and as to yourself in particular, I do hope and expect from your tried valour and vigilance—although I confess you have a tough task in hand, and therefore worthy of you—you will make as good news in performance as can be sent you in rumour or reality either from the north, whereof I despair not in the least to make a double echo. This, above all, take as a high instance of blessings from above, that the first week of March there died in London but twenty-eight of the plague." *Draft.* 2¼ *pp.*

TANGIER.

1666, April 2. Tangier—Manuscript copy in Spanish of the Articles of Peace between Lord Belasyse and *Cedi Hamet el Hader Ben Ali Gaylàn*, of which there is a printed copy in English in the Tangiers Correspondence. 2¾ *pp.*

[*Printed in Davis's* "History of the Second, Queen's Royal Regiment," *Appendix D.*]

CONSUL WESTCOMBE to SIR RICHARD FANSHAW.

1666, April [8-]18. Cadiz—The prison keeper has this morning given me leave (for my money) to come home and write my letters. Being a prisoner, I could not myself deliver what you enclosed for the Duke of Medina Celys, but have sent it by a person of quality.

Lord Belasyse is now at Sevilla, and intends to go for England on the *Hampshire* frigate, Captain Pratt, which is now in the port. He has made a firm peace with Gueland. Col. Norwood has arrived at Tanger, where he is now Lieutenant-Governor.

I pray your Lordship to give his Majesty of England an account of the abuses to his subjects here "by the Governor

protecting the Dutch in all their villanies and imprisoning of me and slighting the character of being his servant and consul in this factory as in other occasions. If your Lordship stand not by me in this time of need, farewell all consuls." *2 pp.*
Endorsed:—" Received 16-26 ditto. Ans. 17-27 ditto."
And by Lady Fanshaw:—" Marchands afares and sey afares."
Enclosing,
Another letter from himself to Sir Richard, in Spanish, complaining of his wrongs, and praying Sir Richard to represent them to his Catholic Majesty. 2¼ pp.
[*Sir Richard's answer to these letters, dated April* 17-27, *is in the Spanish Correspondence.*]

CONSUL WESTCOMBE to SIR RICHARD FANSHAW.

1666, April [15-]25. Cadiz—Stating that the *Hampshire* frigate is still waiting Lord Belasyse's return from Sevilla, and that advices from Alicante say that Mons. de Beaufort and his fleet will not come out of Toulon before the end of May. *1 p.*
Endorsed:—" Rec. May the 3rd, 1666. Ans. 4th ditto."

CONSUL WESTCOMBE to SIR RICHARD FANSHAW.

1666, April [15-]25. Cadiz—Complaining of his imprisonment by the malice of the Dutch, aided by the Governor of the city, and of the confiscation of all his goods, even to the very bed on which he sleeps, and begging his Excellency to move the King of Spain to order his release and the restoration of his goods and also to reprehend the officers, that such violent proceedings may not take place in future without express orders from his Majesty and notice given to the representative of the King of England. *Spanish.* 1½ *pp.*

SIR RICHARD FANSHAW to LORD BELLASYSE.

1666, April [17-]27. Madrid—Acknowledging the receipt of a copy of the articles of peace with Guyland, congratulating his Lordship on having arranged them, and stating that there is no news in the country save the one important but long looked-for event, " namely, the marriage of the Empress on Sunday last—Duke of Medina de las Torres proxy—and her imperial Majesty's journey to begin to-morrow, Wednesday, towards Vienna." *Copy.* ½ *p.*

CONSUL GILES WOODWARD to SIR RICHARD FANSHAW.

1666, April [17-]27. Malaga—I have nothing to offer you but complaints of our sub-governor or *Alcalde mayor,* the Marques de Aquila Fuente being gone to Granada about a fortnight since, whom we thought too harsh and rigid, but this man is abundantly worse. Some ten days since three English ships came here, but the Alcalde drove them out into the bay by firing seven or eight guns at them, which must have done them no small mischief. "The fear they had of some ships off at sea made them creep in a little nearer" again, and the Alcalde using this against me last Wednesday seized me and hath kept me in the common prison ever since. The whole place crys shame on him, and most of the gentlemen of the town have spoken with him about it and demanded his reason for it, but he is resolved to keep me prisoner until the ships are gone. I beg your Excellency to procure me redress from the tyranny of this madman, and that "for the future their hands may be bound up . . . or else a consul here will signify very little." I made my address to Don Christoval Munez de Escovan, our Judge-Conservador at Granada, who sent me the enclosed despatch, but this Alcalde refused observance thereof. 2 *pp.*

Enclosing,
  The above-mentioned despatch. Spanish. 5½ *pp.*

CONSUL WESTCOMBE to SIR JEREMY SMITH.

1666, April [18-]28. Cadiz—The storm which I feared about the taking of the Dutch vessel is now come upon me, and I have been a close prisoner in the common gaol since the 8th inst., everything in my house, even to my very bed, being sequestered. "All this had been excused had your honour been pleased to let the Dutch merchants redeem or buy their ship and goods again, according to my earnest request." I believe you were persuaded against it by Mr. James Coningan, "that false Scot and embroiler of the whole world." If you had known him as well as I do, you would have made no account of his advice. He is no ways concerned with our nation, being here married and naturalized as a subject to this Crown. I have given my Lord Ambassador Fanshaw an account how I am used, and am now writing to Lord Arlington. *Copy.* 1½ *pp.*

[*The letter to Lord Arlington is in the Spanish Correspondence under date, and also another copy (sent to him) of this letter.*]

CONSUL WESTCOMBE to SIR RICHARD FANSHAW.

1666 [April 22-]May 2. Cadiz—I am much engaged to your Lordship for your care in procuring my release. If you could obtain a *cedulla* that the Consul in future shall not be imprisoned nor his house visited (which hitherto any Governor or inferior minister have done at their will and pleasure) it would be a great piece of service to his Majesty, as then his servants would always be free to do him service, and all their letters and papers secure in their houses. Also it will unite the factories to the Consul (if only for their own interest), as his house would be a sanctuary for both their persons and estates. The privilege can hardly be denied, as the only reason the Spaniards allege for searching is the fear that his Majesty's customs may be defrauded, whereas the consuls " do not traffic or commerce." This would be much better than if the factors should obtain it for their own houses, as it said they mean to solicit to my Lord of Sandwich, for then we shall never have but confusion and disorder amongst us, and then they will slight and scorn the Consul, as they have been so apt to do.

The *Hampshire* left last Tuesday for England, with Lord Belasyse on board.

The Duke of Beaufort is ransoming the French captives at Argier for 100 pieces-of-eight apiece, and will use them to furnish his fleet. I send you a letter received from Sir Henry Cholmley.

The Spanish squadron of eleven sail are making ready to depart. Some say they go for the Straits with the galleys to convoy the Emperatrice, others that they are going to the coast of Portugal to hinder the entry of provisions into that country, " but the most certain account is, they go to surprize the French ladies that are to come with six ships to Lishboa to match with the King of Portugal and his brother."

Postscript.—I hear that the Governor is sending up all the *autos* about the ballandra of French wines taken from us by the Dutch, the Queen having commanded him to do so. 3 *pp.*

Enclosing,

Sir Henry Cholmley to Consul Martin Westcombe.

1666, *April* 16-26. *Tangier—Requesting him to forward a package to England, and stating that on the following Wednesday they proclaim the peace with Gayland.* ⅓ *p.*

WILLIAM BLUNDEN to SIR RICHARD FANSHAW.

1666 [April 29-]May 9. Alicante—The French fleet has been eleven days out of Toulon, and yesterday appeared before this port with thirty-two men-of-war, the eight Hollanders, ten fireships and eighteen sail of merchantmen under their convoy; the Duke of Beaufort Admiral. Twelve galleys are to follow them. " They make great enquiry after our fleet, and it is generally believed they will make a bravado before Tanger." They report themselves that they are bound for Rochelle, where they are to join with a hundred and four sail of Dutch men-of-war, who are to come about by the north of Scotland. None of their fleet have been to Argier, but the Consul is treating for the redemption of the French mariners there. The *Reyna,* one of their new and best ships, proves so leaky that she will have to put into Cartagena for repairs. ¾ *p.*

Consul Westcombe to Sir Richard Fanshaw.

1666 [April 29-]May 9. Cadiz—Complaining that he is still a prisoner, and has to pay exorbitant sums to the gaoler and *escrivano* for permission to go occasionally to his house, besides all other charges, whereby he is almost ruined and made weary of his life. *3 pp.*

William Blunden to Lyonel Fanshaw.

1666 [April 30-]May 10. Alicante—Wrote to Sir Richard by the Valencia post, of the passing of the French armada. The twelve galleys have now passed, and it seems they intend to visit Tanger, but they carry no land soldiers, more than the number customary to man their fleet. They are commanded by the Marquis of Biuon. ¼ *p.*

Consul Westcombe to Sir Richard Fanshaw.

1666, May [6-]16. Cadiz—I expected by yours of the 4th to receive tidings of my releasement, and an order "for my howsel stuff and one slave to be disembargued . . . pray, my Lord, get me out of this unreasonable confinement" and procure a remedy for the future.

The bruit here is general that the French and Dutch fleets intend to attack Tanger. I have given notice of it to Col. Norwood, and hear from him that they are "in a posture to entertain their enemies better than they think." *2 pp.*

Colonel H. Norwood to Sir Richard Fanshaw.

1666, May 9-19. Tangier—It is reported here "that my lady was already gone for England, and that your Excellency was upon the point of going. If the premises be true, I dare pronounce the conclusion so. . . . We are looking out sharply for Mons. Beaufort with the French armada to attack us, as is given out from all parts. I am so charitable for that nation as to think their affairs are not managed by such weak counsels, for if they force us to set our wit to theirs, we shall—to human understanding—use them no better than they were treated at Gigery." ¾ *p.*

Endorsed :—"Rec. 21-31 ditto."

Consul Westcombe to Sir Richard Fanshaw.

1666, May [13-]23. Cadiz—I am still waiting for the good hour when your Lordship shall have procured my liberty, and "have me excluded from the persecution I receive here for the actions of our English Admirals, as that of Admiral Allin. I am sued for one million of pieces-of-eight, the impost of the Smyrna ships taken from the Dutch, and now 13,000 pieces-of-eight for the ship and cargo of the ship Sir Jeremy took in sight of this bay the 30th of March last."

The Duke of Medina's Auditor General, Ferdinand Ximines, a man ripe for any mischief, has put it into the head of the Dutch Commissary, Gilberto Melce, at St. Mary Port, to bring a process against me concerning the Smyrna ships taken and sunk by Admiral Allin, and by order of the *Consejo de guerra*, the *autos* or *pleito* goes up to Madrid this very day. It imports much that a defence should be made on our side to the said *Consejo*, who, it is reported, will give any sentence for money.

The *pleito* of the balandra of French wines taken from us by the Dutch goes up also to-day. " If the Spaniards have any shame in them or Christianity " they cannot but order us satisfaction.

Last Wednesday the Duke of Beaufort's fleet came to an anchor in sight of this bay, near Rotta. [*List of ships, as on p.* 249.] " Ships that came in their convoy from Malaga, Genoveses, were ashamed to see how they handled their sails. Twenty English frigates would rout them all to pieces." Their design is variously reported, some saying they are to lie off this coast this summer, others that they sail to-morrow for Lishboa to land the corn and soldiers they have for them. The most probable is that they are going for the north and will touch at Lishboa on the way, for the French living ashore here have sent aboard above two millions of pieces-of-eight as returns for linens the French merchants have sold here. A French ship of St. Malo's, the *St. Joseph*, goes hence with them very richly laden. I heartily wish a competent number of our frigates may meet them. 4 *pp.*

The French Fleet.

1666 [May 13-23]—' Separation des escadres de l'armee de Roy en Levant, l'anée 1666."

Escadre de l'Amiral.

		Brusleaux [fireships].
L'Amiral.	Matelote de	Le *St. Cyprien* brus-
La Thérese.	*l'Amiral.*	leau de *l'Amiral.*
Le St. Joseph.		
Le St. Louis.	Malelote de *St.*	Le *Bilbeaud* [brus-
	Louis.	leau] du *St. Louis.*
La Ville de Rouen.		
L'Escureuil.		
L'Infante.		
Le Cesar.		Les *Trois Roy* brus-
		leau du *Cesar.*
La Vierge.		
L'Hercule.		Le *St. Augustin* brus-
		leau pour *l' Hercule.*
Le Croissant.		

Escadre du Vis-Amiral.

La *Royalle,* Vis-Amiral.		Le *Guillaume,* brusleau du Vis-Amiral.
Le *Jullue* [sic].		
L'*Estoille de Dianne.*		
La *Reyne.*	Matelote de *la Reyne.*	Le *Roy David* brusleau de *la Reyne.*
Le *Sauveur.*		
La *Ste. Anne.*		
La *Palme.*		
La *Françoise.*	Matelote de *la Françoise.*	La *Concorde* brusleau de *la Françoise.*
Le *Ligournois.*		
Le *Soleil d'Affrique.*		

Escadre du Contre Amiral.

Le *Dauphin,* Contre Amiral.	Matelote du *Dauphin,* Contre Amiral.	Le *Flambeau,* brusleau du *Dauphin,* Contre Amiral.
Le *Soleil.*		
Le *Lion d'Or.*		
L'*Anna.*		Le *St. Anthoine,* brusleau de *l'Anna.*
Le *Dragon.*		
L'*Elbeuf.*		
Le *Lion Rouge.*		
Le *Palmier.*		
La *Perle.*		
La *Nostre Dame.*		

Ordres pour la Route.

"Pendant la route, la vice-amiral et son escadre seront tousjours a tribord de l'Amiral, et Contre-amiral et son escadre a besbord, assez esloignez pour laisser les baisseaux de son escadre avec lui, et chaque vaisseau de son escadre sy bien dans son poste qu'il ny ayt pont d'ambras [embarras] sy on rencontroit le ennemy. Le Contre-amiral avec son escadre serrera la fille quand il en sera besoin et ne caissera [laissera?] aucune navire merchand de l'arriere et pandant une chasse ne les abandonnera point, a moinge que l'amiral par son signal particulier ne les faict chasser l'escadre des Messieurs les Estates Genereaux d'Holande, sera tousjours soubs le vent de l'armée du roy, sy Monsieur le Commandant n'ayme mieux estre de l'arriere de Monsieur l'amiral." 1½ *pp.*

Underwritten,

Consul M. Westcombe to Sir Richard Fanshaw.

1666, *May* [13-]23. *Cadiz—Stating that this paper of orders of the Duke of Beaufort and the arrangement of his ships has been given to him this morning by one that*

" privately procured the same out of the secretaria of the Duke," and suggesting that it would not be amiss to send it to the King. $\frac{1}{2}$ p.

[SIR RICHARD FANSHAW] to the [DUKE OF MEDINA DE LAS TORRES].

1666 [May 22-]June 1—The Earl of Sandwich, ambassador extraordinary from the King, my master, brings two commissions for her Majesty the Queen, one of condolence, the other concerning business of much importance to both Crowns; and as his Excellency feels that he ought to lose no time in beginning the latter, while he prepares for his public audience—for which he reserves the former—he has requested me to ascertain in what way he may obtain a private audience of her Majesty. Trusting to the kindness which I have so often experienced from your Excellency, I beg you to arrange this private audience, at whatever time is least inconvenient to her Majesty, and that I may accompany the Earl to introduce him, such being his desire. *Spanish. Draft.* $\frac{1}{2}$ p.

[*In a letter to Arlington (June 2nd, Spanish Correspondence), Fanshaw says that he has applied to the Duke for this private audience.*]

CONSUL WESTCOMBE to SIR RICHARD FANSHAW.

1666, June [3-]13. Cadiz—"I cannot without much regret hear of your Lordship's leaving this Court. Seeing it must be so I have nothing to say but to wish your Lordship and all your concerns all happiness and prosperity." I beg you to recommend me to my lord of Sandwich and to do what you can for me when you arrive in England. I cannot but tell you afresh how much I suffer by my continual imprisonment, and "no longer than yesterday, being in the street by connivance of the gaoler, I met with the *Auditor de lo maritimo* and [he] asked me how I dared to appear in the streets, and in a very scornful manner bid me to prison presently, as if I had committed some great crime," when I am only suffering for what was done by Sir Jeremy Smith. The Duke of Beaufort is said to be on the Portuguese coast, "and will there tarry until the two ladies expected at Lishboa, his nieces, arrive there safe from the interception of the seventeen Spanish men-of-war which are before the mouth of Lishboa. 3 pp.

CONSUL WESTCOMBE to SIR RICHARD FANSHAW.

1666, June [17-]27. Cadiz—Thanks his Excellency for promising to represent his condition *viva voce* in England. Reiterates his complaints against the Spanish authorities and the English merchants, and also against the Dutch Commissary in relation to the ships taken by Sir Thomas Allin, and prays that Lord Sandwich may be fully acquainted with the matter.

In evidence of his attention to his Excellency's commands,
sends the enclosed paper of April 1st, 1664, concerning which
he went over to St. Mary Port, but could not by any means
prevail for the thing desired. Also encloses a relation of the
taking of another English ship, the *Waterhouse*, by the Spanish
armada. They mean to condemn all, right or wrong, nor can
he find any lawyer who will draw him up a petition in this
case. They are a strange people, and no justice can be expected
of them, by reason of which and other things he is quite
weary of his office. 3 *pp.*
Endorsed :—" Rec. 6th July, s.n."
Enclosing,
    1. 1664 [*March* 22-]*April* 1. *Sevilla—Memorandum
that the Lord Ambassador Fanshaw wishes copies to be
procured, if possible, of the letters interchanged by the
Condé de Peñaranda and the Duque de Medina Celi "concerning Blake's hovering on the coast of Andalusia and
Cromwell's fleet at the same time in the West Indies."* ¼ *p.*
    2. 1666, *June* [9-]19. *Cadiz Bay—Declaration of Chris-
topher Tronco, gunner's mate, and seven others of the ship*
Waterhouse *of London that on May 18th last, being then
about the rock of Lisboa, they were chased and boarded by
a Spanish vessel, when they made no resistance, but cried
for quarter, notwithstanding which the Spaniards, entering
the great cabin and gun room, killed the Captain, mortally
wounded several others, and brought the ship and goods into
the bay of Cadiz, where deponents are kept close prisoners.*
1 *p.*

CAPT. ROBERT FERRERS to LIONEL FANSHAW.

1666 [June 23-]July 3—My Lord Sandwich bids me tell you
that he has this afternoon to make visits to several of the
Council, and at six o'clock to meet the Duke of Medina at
the *Buen Retiro*, but about eight o'clock he will not fail either
to wait upon my lady himself or send Mr. Godolphin, in order
to give her satisfaction for all such things as are agreed upon
according to Sir Benjamin Wright's and Mr. Goddard's arbitra-
ment. 1 *p.*

SIR ROBERT SOUTHWELL to LADY FANSHAW.

1666 [September 23-]October 3. Madrid—The sight of this
place " does very sensibly renew the grief I sustained for the
loss of my dear Lord Fanshaw, so eminent a subject of his
Majesty's and so worthy a friend to myself. It is true I had
eased somewhat my mind in contemplation of his happiness,
and that the virtues he died withal had conveyed him to that
rest which God Almighty provides for those who give so happy
an account of their lives, but I am sufficiently amazed to hear
that soon after my departure for Portugal and his Excellency's

death some of his domestic servants should confidently affirm that I used an insupportable insolence to his Excellency, and that the same was a chief part of his disease and a great occasion of his death." I am confident that I need not assure you how clear my conscience is herein, and all my letters will show the veneration with which I spoke of him. Also he himself frequently assured me that it was a happiness to him to have employed with him "one who was his friend and the son of his friend, and he did hope that it should therefore not be unhappy to me neither." I beg your ladyship "to conjure those persons who so easily cast on me this black aspersion to be friends to truth if not to me, for I do protest unto your ladyship that my zeal is so great to pay by all the good offices of my life in whatever I am able to the memory of my dear Lord Fanshaw, now in heaven, and to all the shares and portions of him that are left, that none shall quietly disturb my intentions or blast the friendship that was between us." I wish your ladyship, with your daughters and son, a happy end to your travels." $2\frac{1}{4}$ *pp.*

SIR RICHARD FANSHAW.

[1666?]—Certificate written and signed by Lionel Fanshaw, stating that Sir Richard despatched Major Fairborne to England on November 1, 1665, n.s., with a rough draft of the articles which he signed with the Duke of Medina de las Torres on the 7-17 December, and that Major Fairborne delivered the said despatches to Lord Arlington on November 13-23, as appears by his Lordship's letter of November 14. So that twenty-four days elapsed between the time of the receipt of the letters in England and the signing of the articles. $\frac{1}{2}$ *p.* [*Apparently written in England, as the water mark is not like any of those in the paper used in Spain, but is the same as that of the order of the Queen Mother's Council, below.*]

HUMPHREY, BISHOP OF LONDON, to [LADY FANSHAW].

1667[-8], January 7—"I first render my thanks to your ladyship for the great favour for twice coming to visit me, and I should most gladly [have] attended your ladyship if my condition would have given me leave, but my physicians have strictly enjoined me to reserve myself from company, so that I have not seen any lady these four months, though many have come and desired to see me, and I must use the same privacy until the spring. Your ladyship I know will favourably interpret this my defence.

As to the lease of Frunton [Frinton] I know your ladyship hath had possession thereof but since Michaelmas, 1667 [*sic*], and these two sad years I believe might render no other profit than what your ladyship mentions in your letter, for a worthy person that holds a manor in Essex worth 300*l.* by the year made this year last past but 100*l.* It was a bad year all over England but specially in that county, as the oldest man living did never know the like, and I hope no future age will feel such a misery. The preceding year, by the misery of war at sea, interruption of trade and cheapness of all native commodities, reduced the land to very low revenue, but these two years must not be the measure of future valuations, peace and God's blessing upon the kingdom will in human judgment advance the value of land to ancient rents and rates. And particularly Frunton was in the year 1647, when the Parliament invaded church land, surveyed and returned to be worth two hundred and fourteen pounds, six shillings, eight pence. It was bought then by Mr. Wakering, that was very serviceable to that generation of men, and the surveyors did not use to prepare hard bargains for their good friends. Add that above forty years since the Bishop's accounts and memorials mention near about that value, and these are competent rules for me to proceed by, so that your ladyship will have just cause to judge that I have great respect unto you when I demand one hundred and thirty pounds and no more to change your present estate into twenty-one years. I have set your ladyship the price and hope your ladyship will not dislike it. I pray for your ladyship." *Holograph.* 1¼ *pp.*

Lady Fanshaw.

1668[-9]February 25. Queen [Mother's] Council Chamber in Denmark House—Order by her Majesty's Council that Lady Fanshaw, tenant of the Queen [Mother's] manors of Hitchin and Tring, co. Hertford, having prayed that she might be admitted to account for the rents, &c., of the said manors as bailiff and not as lessee, and then to surrender the leases, the said lady Fanshaw is to pay the sum of 105*l.* 17*s.* 3¼*d.*, due to her Majesty, and is then to be discharged of all debts and accounts concerning the manors and to render up her leases. Signed by Sir John Wintour, Sir Robert Long, Sir Peter Balle and Edward Walpoole. 1 *p.*

Annexed,
> Receipt by *John Watts, receiver for co. Hertford, for the above sum. March 4th,* 1668-9. ¼ *p.*

Lady Fanshaw and Thomas Hawes.

1672, June 28—Articles of agreement whereby, in consideration of the payment of 50*l.*, Dame Anne Fanshaw of Lincoln's Inn Fields assigns to Thomas Hawes of Poplar the residue of

her lease of a messuage in the parish of Hertingfordbury, co. Hertford. *Signed and sealed by Thomas Hawes.* 1 *sheet.*
Annexed,
> Bond of Thomas Hawes to Lady Fanshaw in 100l., con- ditioned for the due performance of the covenants of the above agreement. Same date. Signed and sealed. ½ p.

DUKE OF SOMERSET to the DOWAGER LADY FANSHAW, Lincoln's Inn Fields.

1672, November 4th—I have received your letter proposing to purchase Hewish Farme, allowing its value—1,000l.—out of the moneys I owe you. Concerning the planting of young trees, I shall readily comply with your ladyship's proposal, "I being never scrupulous in trifles. Ryder has promised me to pay in the remainder of your moneys betwixt this and Christmas, which will afford me that satisfaction that I am so much nearer being out of debt." If you will send your servant to Mr. Thomas in Gray's Inn he will draw up your lease, and I will seal it without delay. *Signed.* 1 *p.*

FANSHAW FAMILY.

Undated draft by Lady Fanshaw of an inscription "for a plain stone to be set up over the vault of the family of the Fan- shawes in Ware Church in the county of Hertford."
"Here lies buried Thomas Fanshaw of Inkens [Jenkins] in Essex, son of John Fanshawe of Fanshaw-gate in Derbyshire, bought Ware Park. He was Remembrancer of the Exchequer in the beginning of Queen Elizabeth's time; he inherited it from his uncle. He married first the daughter of Anthony Bourchier, Esq., by whom he had only one son, Sir Henry Fan- shaw of Ware Park, Remembrancer of the Exchequer, and after her decease he married the daughter of Customer Smith, by whom he had Sir Thomas Fanshaw, Clerk of the Council, and William Fanshaw, auditor of the Duchy, and three daughters. The eldest married Sir Christopher Hatton of Cerbey [Kirby] in Northamptonshire; the second married Sir Benjamin Ayloffe of Braxted in Essex; the third married Thomas Bullock, Esq., of Norton in Derbyshire. Sir Henry Fanshaw left Sir Thomas Fanshaw, after Lord Visc. Fanshaw, Remembrancer of the Exchequer; Henry Fanshaw, Esq., soldier, died in Holland; John Fanshaw, Esq., Sir Simon Fanshaw and Sir Richard Fanshaw, who was Remembrancer of the Exchequer to Charles I. and Secretary of the Council of War to Charles II., and Secretary of the Latin and Master of Requests, and his Majesty's ambassador to Portugal and Spain. He likewise left four daughters, the eldest married Sir Capell Bedells of Homerton in Huntingdonshire, and the second to Thomas * Nues [Newse]

---

* Lady Fanshaw calls him William in her "*Memoirs.*"

of Hadham, Esq., in Hertfordshire, and the third died unmarried, the fourth married Sir William Butler of [Teston]
in Kent.

The Lord Viscount Fanshaw left four sons, Thomas, Lord
Viscount Fanshaw, and Henry, Charles and Simon, and four
daughters, Ann, Mary, Katherine and Elizabeth. This Lord
Viscount Fanshaw sold Ware Park to Sir Thomas Bidd [Byde]
in the year of our Lord 1668, having been three generations
complete in the family of the Fanshaws." 1 *p.*

INDEX.

A.

Abdala or Abdalla, the saint, son of Ben ·Bowcar, 159, 186, 212.
Abrahamson, Abraham, 137.
Acuna, Juan Nuñez de. *See* Nuñez.
Admiralty, judge of, in Cornwall, 219.
Africa, 59, 125, 149, 150, 163.
—— commerce with the ports of, forbidden by Spain, 162.
African prince, 202.
Africans, the, 121.
Alarache, Spanish garrison of, 241.
Alarçon, Don Francisco de, Conde de Torres Vedras, 199, 203 (2), 204.
—— wife of, 204.
—— mother of, 199.
Albemarle, Duke of. *See* Monck.
Alburquerque, Duke of, 39, 232 (2).
Alcacer. *See* Alcasser.
Alcacevas, 102, 107.
Alcalla, Duke of, son of the Duke of Medina Celi, 189.
Alcantra, abbess of. *See* Cruz, sister Maria de la.
Alcassar or Alcazer, Afriea, 202, 212.
Alcasser or Alcacer da Sal, 100, 102, 107.
Alentejo, province or frontiers of, 50, 85 (2), 92.
—— generalissimo in. *See* Marialvá, Marques de.
—— English troops in, 29.
—— Portuguese army in, 55, 142, 153.
—— Don Juan marches into, 101.
Algarve or Algarves, province of, 119, 121, 212, 235.
—— governor of, 121 (2), 212.
Algarves honey, 71.
Algibarrota, battle of, 85.
Algiers, Algiere, Argiers or Argiere, 30, 151, 165, 168, 184.
—— bay, letter dated from, 148.
—— captives or slaves at, 88, 249 (2).
—— Divan of, 232.
—— Duana at, 214, 224.
—— English consul at, 209, 249.

Algiers—*cont.*
—— fear of infection from, 162.
—— letter dated at, 214.
—— Pashaw at, 214.
—— peace concluded with, 51, 169 (2), 172, 209.
—— people or Turks of, Algerines or Argereens, 88, 182, 185, 224.
—— character of, 148, 154, 214.
—— preservation of peace with, 201, 209, 214.
—— ships taken by, 151, 201 (2), 202, 206, 207, 209, 214.
—— the plague at, 110.
—— ships of, 143, 232.
—— burnt by the French, 185.
—— war with, 148.
Alicante, 160, 161, 163, 164, 165, 169, 183, 202, 247, 249.
—— English Consul at. *See* Blunden, William.
—— Governor of, 243.
—— letters dated at, 155, 169, 183, 185, 217, 243, 249, 253.
—— Road, English fleet in, 154, 155.
—— ship taken in, 220.
Allestree, Dr., 130.
Allin or Allen:
—— Francis, 221.
—— Admiral or Captain Sir Thomas, 45 (2), 51, 169, 174, 177, 179, 201, 250, 251, 253.
—— fleet under command of, 35, 165, 166, 177, 181.
—— letters from, 165, 169, 172-174.
—— letters to, 40, 173.
—— ships of, lost, 171, 172.
—— victory of, over the Dutch, 173 (2).
—— is going for England, 173, 174, 178, 181.
—— brother of, 174.
Almeyrin, the King of Portugal at, 143.
Alonso, Don, secretary to the Duke of Medina de las Torres, 229.
Alsace, free towns of, 149.
Alsopp, Col. Roger, 158.
—— letters from, 156, 164.
Alva, Duke of, 39.

Ambassadors. *See the several countries, Ambassadors to and from.*
precedency of, 45.
Amboyna, the business of, 4, 5.
Ameixial or El Canal, battle of, 104, 106 (2), 110 (2), 112 (2), 113 (2), 121, 122, 124, 125, 141.
—— descriptions of, 103-105, 107-109.
—— English share in, 115, 121, 122 (2).
—— list of Spanish killed or taken prisoners at, 108.
(Masiel) letter dated at, 106.
America, 125.
Amsterdam, 171, 175, 220.
Admiralty of, 200.
breaking of the dykes at, 222.
letter dated at, 221.
Anabaptists, plot of the, 46, 48.
Andalusia, 36, 132, 201, 228, 254.
Governor of. *See* Medina Celi, Duke of.
Anglesey, Earl of (Arthur Annesley), 127.
Angoren. *See* Oyanguren.
Angulo or Aquella, Estevan or Stephen de, Mestre de Campo, taken prisoner, 105, 108.
Apsley :
Sir Allan, 116.
—— letter from, 124.
—— brother of. *See* Apsley, Col. James.
or Appesley, Col. James, 49, 101, 124.
—— letter of, 115.
—— relation by, of the proceedings of the armies, 101-105.
—— has redeemed his reputation, 112, 124.
—— regiment of, 105.
Apsum [Topsham, co. Devon], ship of, 221.
Aquila Fuento, Marques de, 247.
Aranjuez, visits of the Spanish royal family to, 183-185, 190.
Arches, Dean of. *See* Ryves, Dr. Brune.
Arlington, Lord. *See* Bennet, Sir Henry.
Armagnac, Comte de, 147.
—— father of. *See* Harcourt, Prince de.
Armenian, an, 208.
Aronches or Aruntias, 102, 107, 125, castle of, 125.
Arsila. *See* Arzilla.
Arson, Monsieur, 33.
Arthur, King, time of, 95.
Arundel :
Sir John, signature of, 220.
Richard, Baron of Trerise, signature of, 219.
Aruntias. *See* Aronches.
Arzilla or Arsila, in Morocco, 32, 202.
Commissioners sent to, 164.
Gayland at, 207
messengers detained at, 172, 181.

Ashburnham (Aspernam), John, 54.
Ashley-Cooper, Anthony, Baron Ashley, 30, 46, 65, 80.
—— letter from, 35.
" Athenians," 218.
Atkinson, Captain, killed, 105.
Capt. Robert, 145.
Atougia, Conde de, formerly vice-roy in the Indies, 96.
Attorney-general (Sir Geoffrey Palmer), 145, 218.
Austria, Don Juan of. *See* Juan, Don.
House of, 125, 127, 234.
Auyz, Governor of, 56.
Avero or Aveiro :
Duke of, 185, 195, 197, 208, 234.
—— fleet of, 197, 201, 208.
—— letter to, 140.
Duchess of, 232.
Avignon, kept by the King of France, 55.
Ayala :
Count of, 232 (2).
Don Francisco de, papers relating to, 176.
Ayamonte, siege of, 215.
Ayloffe, Sir Benj., wife of, 257.
Azores, islands of, 153.
merchants in, 153.

B.

Babel, builders of, 60.
Baçaim. *See* Bazaim.
Backwell, Alderman, 30.
Bacon :
Francis, Lord, quotations from, 116, 228.
—— essay of, *De Vana Gloria*, 116.
Nicholas, 170.
Badajos, 256.
bridge of, 101.
Bagot, Mrs., maid of honour to the Duchess of York, 172.
Bagshaw, Edward, 144, 145.
Balle, Sir Peter, order signed by, 256.
Ballecas, letter dated at, 153.
letter received at, 152.
Baltic, the, ships from, 195.
Banckert, Bancker or Banker, Adrian, 200.
Admiral John, 176, 195, 200.
Bantam, intelligence from, 144.
Barbadoes, 67, 138, 198.
De Ruyter at, 200.
Barbary, 58, 59, 184, 241.
or Barbarian Coast, 160, 162.
Barca, King of, 175.
Barcelona, 63, 64.
Barker, Mr., 192.
Barkley, John, 221.
Barnstaple or Bastable, ship of, 221.

Bassine, island of, East Indies, demanded by England, 18.
Batavia Road, ships in, 144.
Bataville or Bativila, Baron de, 39, 180.
Bath, Earl of [John Grenville] letter of, 205.
Bath, knight of, 220.
Bath (the Bath), 80, 130.
Bativila, Baron de. *See* Bataville, Baron de.
Baubigny, Mons. de, 109.
Bavaria, Duke of, Prince Rupert addressed as, 117.
Baxter :
  Captain, 161.
  John, 145.
Bayona, Marques de, General of the galleys, 215.
Bayonne, 231.
  letters dated at, 195, 198.
Bazaim or Baçaim, demanded by England, 116, 121, 122.
Beachy Head, fleet off, 165.
Beaucham, William, deposition of, 117.
Beaufort, Duke of (French Admiral), and his fleet, 182, 185, 201, 202, 215, 217, 241, 243, 245-247, 249-253.
  —— list of his ships, 251, 252.
  —— orders for his fleet, 252.
  —— secretaria of, 253.
  —— nieces of. *See* Orleans, Princesses of.
Bechtman, Martin, engineer, 130.
Bedells, Sir Capell, and his wife, 257.
Bedingfield, Sir Francis, 196.
  —— letter of, 214.
Beia or Beja (Beze), 55, 56, 98, 99, 109.
  —— Chamber of, 56.
Beira (Bera), province of, 84.
Belasyse, Bellasyse, Bellasis :
  John Lord, 186, 188, 189, 194-198, 200, 204, 207, 208, 232.
  —— letters from, 183, 184, 186, 190, 192, 201, 206, 209, 210, 212, 224, 245.
  —— letters to, 185, 187, 190, 194, 200, 214, 247.
  —— appointment of, as Governor of Tangier, 181, 184.
  —— congratulations to, 185, 187.
  —— arrival of, at Tangier, 183, 185.
  —— presents sent to, 200, 201 (2), 208.
  —— dislikes to serve Turks against Christians, 201, 206, 209, 224.
  —— peace with Gayland concluded by, 246.
  —— is returning to England, 229, 230, 246, 247, 249.
  —— wife of, 183.
  —— officers of, 206.
  —— valet of, 208.
  Major or Lieut.-Colonel, brother of Lord Fauconberg, 114, 116, 118, 153.
  Col. John, 206, 209, 221.
Belem, Belin or Bellyn [Bethlehem] Tower of, Governor of. *See* Bravo, **Miguel.**

Belem, Belin, or Bellyn—*cont.*
  letter dated from, 178.
  prisoners in, 25, 68, 72, 199.
Belin, Robert, 212.
Beling :
  Mr., 83.
  Sir Richard, secretary to the Queen, 218.
Bellasis or Bellasyse. *See* Belasyse.
Belturbet, Ireland, Irish rising at, 178.
Benavente, 236.
  letter dated at, 236.
  letters received at, 227, 229, 234.
Ben Bowcar, Ben Buker, or the "Saint" (Cidi Mahomet Ben el Hadge Ben Bowcar), a Moorish chief, 32, 184, 186, 202 (2), 210, 212.
  —— army of, 184, 186, 190, 202.
  —— expedition of against Gayland, 184, 186 (2), 190.
  —— son of. *See* Abdalla, Cidi.
Benisfield [? Bedingfield], Mr., Governor of St. Christophers, 135.
Bennet, Sir Henry, and (in 1665), Lord Arlington, Secretary of State, 5, 37, 72, 73 (2), 75, 76, 99, 161, 162, 189, 191, 193, 214, 220, 230.
  —— letters from, 33, 65, 80, 83, 86, 87, 132, 140 (2), 155, 166, 181, 205.
  —— —— alluded to, 70, 87-91, 98, 111, 112, 180, 182, 183, 187, 188, 205, 212, 220, 225, 227, 229, 255.
  —— letters to, 50, 56, 73, 75, 86, 92, 110 (2), 123, 130, 132 (2), 133, 205.
  —— —— alluded to, 121, 194, 202, 210, 227, 248.
  —— letter countersigned by, 165.
  —— notes or papers for, 36, 43, 157.
  —— made Secretary of State, 48, 50, 73.
  —— is like to be very powerful, 55
  —— has charge of the affairs of Portugal, 74 (2), 75.
  —— recommendations by, 111, 183.
  —— created Lord Arlington, 187.
  —— message from, 194.
  —— pique of, against Sir Fras. Bedingfield, 196.
  —— his "cast general" (*i.e.* Sandwich), 225.
  —— rough draft of Fanshaw's treaty sent to, 255.
  —— and Lord Sandwich's embassy, 225, 226.
  —— secretaries of. *See* Williamson, Joseph, and Godolphin, William.
Bentivoglio, Cardinal, 42.
Bera. *See* Beira.
Bera, the river. *See* Tera.
Bere, Mr., merchant, 56.
Bergen, ships from, 210.
Berkeley or Berckly, Captain, 165, 166.
  Sir William, Governor of Virginia, letter to, from the King, 6.

Berkenhead, [Sir John], 218.
Beverley, Sir Thomas, letter of, 218.
Beverley, co. York, 5.
Beze. *See* Beia.
Bible, the, 133.
Bieque, Birque or Crab Island, West Indies, 135.
Bilbao (Bilboa), English merchant at, 1.
    ship from, 187.
Bird:
    Mr., 25.
    William, 177.
Biscay, an old soldier of, 111.
    ships, or Biscayers, 61, 70, 208.
Bishops, 146.
Bishops' accounts, alluded to, 256.
Biuon, Marquis of, 250.
Black Bog, Ireland, 178.
Blagge, Mrs., maid of honour to the Duchess of York, 144.
Blake, Admiral Robert, 254.
Bland, John, letters of, 190, 196.
Blunden, William, English Consul at Alicante, 162.
    —— letters from, 155, 169, 183, 185, 217, 243, 249, 250.
Bohorgues, Don Juan Ximeno de, memorial by, 204.
    —— pass for, 204.
    —— servants of, 204.
Boito or de But, Conde de, Mestre de Campo, 105, 108.
Bombay or Bombaim, island of, 88.
    cession of to England, 18.
    English fleet to go to, 18.
    refusal of the Portuguese to deliver up, 87 (2), 89, 111, 113, 116, 121, 122.
    Sir Abraham Shipman to have the command of, 89, 90.
    vice-roy at. *See* Goa, vice-roy of.
Bonnel, Captain Jas., 187.
Books or pamphlets, popish or seditious, 144, 145.
Boothhouse, Samuel, 72.
    —— letter of, 78.
Bordeaux, 192, 198, 202.
    —— president and jurats of, 198.
Boston, co. Lincoln, ship of, 224.
Boswell:
    Humfrey, 5.
    Sir William, 4.
    —— death of, 4.
Boulger, Captain, 156.
Boulion, house of, 117.
Bourbon, waters of, 192.
Bourchier, Sir Anthony, daughter of, 257.
Boyle, Dr. Michael, Archbishop of Dublin, letter to, 139.
Bradall, Roger, 67.
Brady, Laurence, pass for, 203.
Brandenburg (Frederick William), Marquis of, 230.
Bravo, Miguel, Governor of the Tower of Belem, 72, 73 (2).
    —— letter to, 73.

Braxted, co. Essex, 257.
Brazil, 82.
    affairs of, Council for managing, 51.
    —— —— president of, 51.
    Company in Portugal, dissolution of, 51.
    English trade with, 18, 23.
    fleet (Portuguese), 39, 51, 66, 71, 94.
    —— arrives at Lisbon, 118.
    King of (the King of Portugal), 38.
    ships to be sent to, by the Duke of York, 82, 87 (2), 123 (3).
    ships trading to, 30, 34 (2), 47.
    —— dues owing by, 46, 47, 49, 56, 80.
    trade of Portugal with, 18.
Breda, 10, 12.
    letter dated at, 5.
Bremengham, Captain, 191.
Brest, 203.
Brett, Sir Edward, 7.
    —— officer of, 7.
Brewster, Thomas, 145.
Brick and tiles, Bill for the better making of, 148.
Bridge, Col. Sir Tobias, 154, 156.
    —— letters of, 152, 153, 158, 159.
    —— appointed *ad interim* Governor of Tangier, 157.
Bridgewood, Edward, 67, 79.
    letter of, 32.
Bristol, Earl of (George Digby), 71.
    —— charge brought by, against Clarendon, 127.
    —— animosity of the King and Duke of York towards, 127.
    —— conformity of, 144-146.
    —— plea of, in the Exchequer, 144-146.
    —— cannot be found, 147.
    —— houses of, 147.
    —— servants of, 145, 146.
    —— his wife, Countess of Bristol, 71.
Bristol, 149, 221, 231.
British Pale (in Africa), 99.
Brittany, 136, 191.
Brixton, Isle of Wight, ship lost near, 170.
Bromydge, George, letter from, 166.
Brookes, Captain, 156.
Brooks, Nathan, 145.
Broughton, ——, 6.
Brown or Born, Captain Jo, 174.
Brussels, 8, 10, 15.
    —— letters dated at, 7-15.
Bryn, Captain, 112.
Buccleuch, Duchess of [Lady Anne Scott], marriage of, 80.
Buckingham, Duke of (George Villiers), 172.
Buckley, Ensign, 170.
Buen Retiro, palace of the Spanish King near Madrid, 155.
Bullock, Thos., Esq., and his wife, 257.
Bulls, Bay of, Cadiz, 165, 172.

Bulteel, John, secretary to the Earl of Clarendon, letter of, 217.
Burborough, Queen Elizabeth's commissioners at, 43.
Bushell, Richard, and his wife, 134.
Butler, Sir William and his wife, 258.
Byde (Bidd), Sir Thomas, 258.

C

Cadaval (Carevall), Duque de, Nuño Alvares Pereira, Marques de Fereira, Ambassador from Portugal to France, 25.
Cadiz (Cales, Calles, Calls), 153, 158, 161, 163, 165, 174, 181, 198, 232, 235, 246 (2).
  Auditor de lo Maritimo at, 253.
  bay, 160, 173, 220, 254.
  —— English fleet in, 160, 244.
  —— letters dated from, 237, 243.
  Cabildo of, 199.
  capture of, by the Earl of Essex, 38.
  churches of, 181.
  Dutch at, 185, 247, 248, 253.
  —— Commissary at, 211, 253.
  —— Consul at, 189, 195, 196, 207, 209, 211.
  English Consul at. *See* Rumbold Henry *and* Westcombe, Martin.
  —— ——, a former, 205.
  —— factory at, 247.
  —— merchants at, 187, 205, 213, 249.
  Escrivano at, 250.
  French at, 251.
  gaol of, 244.
  —— keeper of, 246, 250, 253.
  —— letter dated from, 163.
  —— prisoners in, 163, 189 (3), 193, 211, 246-248, 253, 254.
  General at, 211.
  Governor of, 143, 166, 189 (2), 207, 210, 237, *and see* Zbarro, Don Diego de, *and* Cayas Vasan, Don Martin de.
  late Governor of. *See* Pimentel, Antonio.
  intelligence from, 88, 232.
  letters dated at, 71, 173, 177, 181, 182, 186, 187, 189 (2), 193, 195, 197, 199, 207, 208, 211 (2), 214, 215, 219 (2), 220, 241, 243-248, 250 (2), 252-254.
  letters received at, 159, 162, 164, 192.
  officials at, 247, 253.
  ships to or at, 37, 39, 165, 174, (2), 178, 179, 186, 187, 192, 193, 208, 229, 244, 250.

Cadiz—*cont.*
  slaves to be sold at, 132.
  travellers to or from, 25, 143, 185, 229.
  Vice Consul of, 186.
Cagaway, Point, Jamaica, 35.
Cain, the curse of, 216.
Calatrava, Knight of the Order of, 204.
Calderon, Maria, Spanish actress, mother of Don Juan, 37.
Cales or Calles. *See* Cadiz.
Camarassa, Marques de, Viceroy of Sardinia, 202.
Cambridge:
  Vice Chancellor of, 72.
  Jesus College, Master and Fellows of, letter of, 133.
  —— injuries to their chapel by the Puritans, 133.
Camoens, Luis de la, translation of, by Fanshaw, alluded to, 208.
Canal, el, battle of. *See* Ameixial.
Canary Islands and islanders, 71, 212, 222.
Canary Company, letter from, 212.
  —— Governor and Deputy governor of, 212.
Canterbury, Archbishop of [Dr. Juxon], 72, 145.
Capuchin's robe, 118.
Caraccas, the, 134.
Caracena, Marques de (Don Luis de Bonavides), Spanish Governor of Flanders, 183, 184, 185, 203, 240.
  —— a friar employed by, 231.
Carcamo, Diego de, 39.
Cardinal, the. *See* Mazarin.
Cardinals, the, letter to, from the King of France, 63.
Caribees, English plantations in, 176.
Carleton. *See* Colbert.
Carlisle, Bishops of. *See* Sterne, Richard, and Rainbow, Edward.
Carlisle, Earl of (Charles Howard), Ambassador to Russia, 146.
  —— audience of, at Stockholm, 166.
Carmes, Convent de, near Evora, 84.
Carneton. *See* Colbert.
Carr, Captain, 156, 202.
Carstairs [John], minister at Glasgow, 151.
Cartagena, 183, 249.
  Consul for, 185.
Carteret, Sir George, letter of, 33.
Casa Rubias, near Madrid, 237, 239.
Cascaes (Cascales, Cascayes, Cascays), 55, 59, 90, 91, 95, 240.
  Lord Peterborough at, 120.
Casquais, regiment of, 160.
Castañeda, Conde de. *See* Marialva.
Casteladavida, troops at, 56.
Castelmelhor, Conde de, Don Luis de Sousa Vasconcellas, secretario de la puridad, favourite of the King of Portugal, 36, 83, 84, 108, 109, 115, 120, 121, 123, 128, 130 (2), 142, 143, 153, 161, 226, 233, 245.

Castelmelhor, Conde de—*cont.*
—— letters from, 85, 113, 121, 141 (2), 203.
—— —— extract from, 122.
—— letters to, 74, 85, 91, 111, 116, 122 (2), 126, 241.
—— complaints by and against, 48.
—— information from or interviews with, 36, 38, 41, 49, 52, 58, 63.
—— popularity of, 96.
—— must send pay for the troops, 98, 99, 106, 109, 113.
—— his desire for a battle, 109.
—— success of the army under his management of affairs, 203.
—— servant of, 96.
Castel-Rodrigo, Marques de [Don Francisco de Moura], Spanish Governor of the Low Countries, 183, 230.
Castile. *See* Spain.
—— crown of, 89, *and see* Spain, crown of.
Castilians. *See* Spaniards.
Castillo, Don Carlos del, 215.
Castrillo, Conde de, 36, 43.
Catalan, a, 71.
Catherine, Infanta of Portugal and Queen of England, 17, 20, 23-26, 29, 32, 62, 69-71, 128.
—— letters to, 16, 17, 27 (2), 129, 132.
—— letters from, 22, 23, 24, 26.
—— her dowry or portion, 21, 40, 43, 44, 47, 50, 55, 56, 59, 66, 69, 76, 129.
—— —— delay in the payment of, 46, 49, 52, 53, 56, 131.
—— —— statements concerning, 30, 34, 46.
—— —— English troops paid out of, 54, 57, 74, 81, 111.
—— —— last part of, not expected to be paid, 69.
—— preparations for her journey to England, 16, 17, 21.
—— her husband's affection to, 20, 21, 28, 30, 46.
—— assures King Charles of her affection for him, 22, 24.
—— asks that Sir Richard and Lady Fanshaw may be of her household, 23.
—— has sailed for England, 26.
—— landing of, in England, 27 (3), 76.
—— goes to Hampton Court, 27, 101.
—— has assured her mother of her happiness, 28.
—— her possible claim to the Crown of Portugal, 38.
—— health of, 66, 141, 242.
—— hopes of her having a child, 80, 242.
—— goes to Tunbridge, 80, 127.
—— the Pope does not answer her letter, 83.
—— entertainment given to, 144.

Catherine, Queen—*cont.*
—— costume of, described, 149.
—— birthplace of, 197.
—— her household, 26, 76.
—— keeper of the jewels to, 23.
—— woman of the bedchamber, to, 23.
—— master of the horse to, 24.
—— page of the back stairs to, 26.
—— priests in attendance on, 74.
—— secretary to. *See* Beling, Sir Richard.
Catholic King. *See* Spain, King of.
Catholic Sovereigns. *See* Spain, King and Queen of.
Cayas Vasan, Don Martin de, Governor of Cadiz, 246, 247, 249.
—— letters from, 208, 243.
—— letter to, 243.
Ceylon (Zeilam), 144.
Chalais Tallerand de Perigord, Prince de, 233.
—— letter from, 233.
—— wife of, 233.
—— brother of. *See* Nourmoustier, Marquis de.
—— servant of, 233.
Chambres, Richard, letter of, 215.
—— daughter of. *See* Dongan, Lady.
Chancery, Court of, 171.
Changuion, a valet, 208.
Channel, the English, 163, 166, 167, 171, 175, 197.
Charles I., agent of, 67.
—— esteem of, for the King of Spain, 1.
—— credentials from, alluded to, 1-3.
—— instructions of, 1.
—— portion assigned to his daughter by, 4.
—— Remembrance of Exchequer to. *See* Fanshaw, Sir Richard.
—— service or loyalty to, 67, 219.
—— sign manual of, 3.
Charles II., 8, 10, 26, 27, 175, *and passim.*
—— letters from, 6, 16, 17 (2), 22 (2), 28-31, 81, 165.
—— —— alluded to, 24, 28, 43, 55, 88, 144, 145, 184, 188.
—— letters to, 4-6, 16, 22-24, 26, 28, 29, 56, 57.
—— advowson in the hands of, 82.
—— allies of, 170.
—— Ambassadors extraordinary of, to Spain, 3.
—— birthday of, 100 (2), 101 (2).
—— Commissioner for, 52.
—— Court of. *See* Court, the.
—— —— at Brussels, 7.
—— debts due to, 78.
—— document signed by, 29.
—— Engineer General of. *See* Gomme, Sir Bernard de.
—— favour of, 191, 217.
—— friends of, in exile, 33.

Charles II.—*cont.*

—— gentlemen of the bedchamber of, 30.

—— guards of, 191.

—— health of, 66, 159, 163.

—— household of, 17.

—— instructions from, to Fanshaw, 3, 18, 20.

—— —— asked for, 60, 64, 119, 122.

—— loyalty, zeal or affection for, 16, 67, 79, 164, 205, 219, 223, 224.

—— marriage of, 17 (2), 21, 64.

—— matters to be laid before, 128, 149, 162, 166, 213, 246, 253.

—— as mediator between Spain and Portugal, 36, 37, 47, 58, 63, 65, 88-90, 131 (2).

—— memorial to, 80.

—— message from, 253.

—— ministers of, 53.

—— moneys assigned by, 5.

—— moneys for, 30, *and see* Catherine, dowry of.

—— moneys paid on behalf of, 30.

—— money from, needed for the troops in Portugal, 37, 48.

—— orders, intentions, or wishes of, 5, 33, 34, 148, 205, 212, 224.

—— portraits of, 62, 90.

—— proclamations of, alluded to, 145.

—— promises of, 7-9.

—— recommendation by, 31, 32, 139, 140, 173.

—— revenue of, debates concerning, 83.

—— —— management of, 83.

—— Secretary of the Council of War to. *See* Fanshaw, Richard.

—— servants of, miserable condition of, 14.

—— —— arrears due to, 14.

—— sign manual of, 3, 6, 20, 165.

—— support or succour of Portugal by, 52, 58, 59, 63, 65, 74, 81, 99, 131, 244, *and see* Portugal.

—— tutor of, 62.

—— father of. *See* Charles I.

—— mother of. *See* Henrietta Maria, Queen.

—— wife of. *See* Catherine, Queen.

—— brother of. *See* York, James, Duke of.

—— sisters of. *See* Mary, Princess of Orange, and Henrietta Anne, Duchess of Orleans.

—— Aunt of. *See* Elizabeth, Queen of Bohemia.

—— his journey to Scotland, 4.

—— coronation of (in Scotland), 6.

—— his return to England, anticipated, 11, 15.

—— difficult to persuade of Willis's treachery, 13.

Charles II.—*cont.*

—— his journey to the frontiers, 13, 15 (2).

—— —— hopes of his speedy return from, 15.

—— poverty of, 14.

—— places bestowed by, 16, 67 (2).

—— progress of, 17.

—— and the Queen, 16, 17 (2), 20, 21, 27, 28, 30, 46, 129.

—— delight of his subjects at his return, 17.

—— and the affairs of Portugal, 18, 20, 49, 53, 153, 242, 243.

—— forbids Clarendon to go to receive the Queen, 27.

—— his knowledge of Spanish, 36, 50.

—— his interest in the succession to the crown of Portugal, 38, 52.

—— memorial sent to, by the Portuguese Ambassador, 46.

—— plot against, 48.

—— debate before, in Council, 48.

—— sends congratulations to the King of Portugal, 49.

—— Lord Inchiquin's discourse with, 54, 57.

—— dismisses Secretary Nicholas, 54.

—— proposed co-operation of France with, 58, 64.

—— dispositions or appointments of, for Tangier, 58.

—— gifts from, 62.

—— his anxiety about his troops, 66.

—— and the House of Commons, 74, 77.

—— his attempts to procure toleration in religion, 74, 77.

—— grants the army in Portugal payment from the Queen's dowry, 74, 76, 86, 112, *and see* Catherine, dowry of.

—— sends a letter to the troops in Portugal, 76.

—— granting of supplies for 77, 192.

—— celebration of St. George's day by, 79, 80.

—— good affection of the Parliament towards, 84.

—— refers the petition of the English officers to Fanshaw, 86.

—— anger of, at the refusal to deliver up Bombay, 87, 89, 90, 116.

—— his return to London, anniversary of, 100.

—— is expected by Portugal to remount his troops, 122.

—— lends ships to his brother, 123 (2).

—— movements of, 127.

—— proclamation of, against dissenters, asked for, 127.

—— animosity of, against the Earl of Bristol, 127.

Charles II.—*cont.*
—— esteem of, for Don Juan, 140.
—— his mediation on behalf of the Spanish prisoners in Portugal, 141 (2), 142, 165, 180, 233.
—— entertainment given to, 144.
—— holds conference at the Lord Chancellor's, 144.
—— friendship of, to Spain, 147, 237.
—— message of, to Parliament, 147.
—— the States of Zealand are sending a letter to, 149.
—— the two Houses to attend on, 150, 151.
—— has forbidden the ceremony of attendance upon Ambassadors, 170.
—— letters of reprisal granted by, 171.
—— messenger sent by, to France, 171, 173.
—— harmony of, with his subjects, 175.
—— gives the Duke of York full power over the fleet, 179.
—— peace concluded with Sweden by, 188.
—— gratuity given by, 192.
—— persuades the Duke of York to stay at home, 201.
—— and Fanshaw's treaty with Spain, 226.
—— "kindness" of, for Molina, 229.
—— holds French ships as pledges, 231.
—— amused by Clarendon's vexation, 230.
—— play acted before, 231.
—— has expressed his satisfaction with Fanshaw, 230, 231.
—— league of, with the Emperor, 234.
—— supposed reasons of, for sending Sandwich to Spain, 236.
—— letters granted by, 238.
—— his return to London, 240, 242.
Cherny, regiment of, 109.
Cheshire, royalist rising in, 13.
Chesterfield, Earl of (Philip Stanhope), 55.
Chicherly, Captain, 169.
Chiffinch, Tom, 62, 90.
—— letter to, 62.
China, island near, 144.
Cholmeley, Mr. or Sir Hugh, 24, 25, 164, 172, 202, 206, 249.
—— letter from, 249.
Chouet, Monsieur, 97.
Christopher, Don, the old Governor of Jamaica, 35.
Church:
    non-attendance at, 151.
    of England, conformity to, 144.
    lands, invaded by the Parliament, 256.
Church, Percy, 7, 8, 10, 13-16, 23.

Cimbre, Bishop-elect of. *See* Rosario, Frey Domingo del.
Cipher, letters written in, 3, 9, 16, 155, 166.
    sent to Fanshaw, 181.
    explanation of, 228.
Cirencester, 130.
Claran. *See* Cleran.
Clarke, Joshua, 134.
Cleran or Claran, Mons. de, 109, 115.
Clerembault, Mareschal de, 147.
Cleves, Elector of, 6,
Clifford, Mr., 150.
    Sir Thomas, 181.
Clutterbooke, Mr., 218.
Coal merchants and woodmongers, bill found against, 191.
Coale, Captain, 165.
Coavans, Captain, 136.
Cocke, Robert, 33, 67, 70, 79 (2).
—— letter of, 66.
Colbert :
    Jean Baptiste de, French minister, 41, 43, 198.
    du Terron, Mons. Charles, *alias* Carleton or Carneton, Marquis de Bourbonne, intendant of Marine and Counsellor of State in France, agent to Portugal, 41, 43, 44, 63, 109 (2), 111, 154.
Cole, Captain John, 220.
Colin, Donna Teresa, 214.
Colmaer in Alsace, intended siege of, 149.
Cologne (Collein), Elector of, 6.
Colona, Cardinal, 232 (2).
Colonel, Sir Augustine, agent of the King of Portugal in London, 34, 46, 47.
Comet, appearance of, 171, 172.
Cominges-Guitant, Gaston Jean Baptiste de, Lieut.-General and Captain of the Guard to the Queen Mother of France, Ambassador to Portugal in 1657, and to England in 1663, 58, 63, 64.
—— his opinion of Portugal, 64.
—— challenge sent to, 64.
—— his public entry, 83.
—— Commissioners to treat with, 83.
Common Prayer, Book of, 133.
Commons, House of :
    adjournment of, 150.
    behaviour of, 77.
    bills in, 148-152.
    conference of with the Lords. *See* Lords.
    debates in, 83.
    members of, 175.
    proceedings of, 74, 148-152.
    goes into Committee for the hearth money, 149.
    reports to be made to, 149.
    Speaker of. *See* Turner, Sir Edward.
Common Pleas, Court of, action in, 145.
Commonwealth, the, "the rebels," or the Parliament party, 14.

Commonwealth, the—*cont.*
—— Ambassadors of, to the Hague, 5, 6.
—— army of, 14.
—— ——, has not dissolved the Parliament, 12.
Comorin or Commaroon, Cape, 144.
Conge, Frenchman, 137.
Consuls, 193, 195-197, 247-249, *and see under the several Spanish and Portuguese ports.*
Contrera, Don Paublos de, *Admirante* General of Spain, 195, 197.
Conventicle Bill, 127, 150, 152.
Conventicles, laws against, to be put in force, 127.
Cooper, Mr., 231.
Coorgas, General, 221.
Corço (Corco), Cape, 200.
Cormantin (Cormantine, Cormention), in Guinea, 146, 187, 200.
Cornbury, Lord (Henry Hyde), son of the Earl of Clarendon, 72, 113, 217, 218.
—— is his father's amanuensis, 10.
—— letter to, 70.
Cornbury, co. Oxon., 130.
Cornwall, 178, 205, 220.
rivers in, bill for making navigable, 152.
Corporation bill, 152.
Corpus Christi, celebration of the feast of, 92.
Corunna or the Groyne:
Earl of Sandwich arrives at, 241, 243.
English Vice-Consul at, 241.
Governor of, 241.
Coryton, Sir John, Bart., signature of, 219.
Coseworth, Sir Sam, signature of, 220.
Cottington, Sir Fras. or Lord, embassies of to Spain, 31, 130.
—— letter from, to the King, 4.
Cottoner, Don Francisco, 184.
—— brother of, 184.
Council of State, 29.
—— report to, 34.
Council Chamber, 132.
Couper, John, narrative of, 135.
Court, the English, 54, 56, 60, 148, 206.
Lord Inchiquin át, 48.
entertainments at, 78.
persons returning to, 171.
removes from London on account of the plague, 199.
the young nobility of, 172.
Molina recalled from, 225.
complaints made to, concerning Fanshaw, 236.
Courtenay, Sir Peter, signature of, 220.
Courtney, Mr., 187.
Coventry:
Harry, 7.
William, secretary to the Duke of York, 41, 79, 134, 154, 165, 181.

Coventry, William—*cont.*
—— letters of, 82, 87.
—— letters to, 61, 123, 174.
—— cipher of, 155, 156.
Cowkillers in the West Indies, 138.
Cowling, Thomas, Consul at Teneriffe, 222.
Cowper's Hill, co. Middlesex, letter dated at, 218.
Crab Island. *See* Bieque.
Crafford, Captain Hugh, 221.
Crane, Captain, 174.
Crato, Commissary General Juan de, 56.
Craven, Lord, talked of as Governor of Jamaica, 88.
Crawford, William, 132.
Creed John, secretary to the Earl of Sandwich, 32.
Creighton, Dr. [Robert], Dean of Wells, 72.
Créqui, Duc de, Ambassador extraordinary from France to the Pope, 71.
—— attack upon, in Rome, 62.
—— his wife, 62.
Crispe, Edward, 238 (2), 245.
Cromwell, Oliver, "the great traitor and usurper," 66.
—— appointment by, 66.
—— fleet of, 254.
—— rebels in service of, 67.
—— "tampering" of, with Spain, 39.
—— death of, alluded to, 128.
—— government or time of, 24, 166, 182.
Cromwellist, a, 227.
Crook or Cruck, Lieutenant, 84, 98.
—— valet of, 84.
Croone, Henry, letter of, 243.
—— letter to, 182.
Crow, Captain, 221.
Crowder, Hans, 34.
Cruce, Thomas de, 25.
Cruche, in Portugal, letter dated at, 236.
Cruck, Lieutenant. *See* Crook.
Crux, Sir Thomas da, death of, 154.
Cruz, Señora, sister Maria de la [Donna Maria Guzman], Abbess of Alcantra, 79, 141, 143.
—— letter of, 140.
—— chaplain of, 56.
—— father of. *See* Medina Sidonia, Duke of.
Cuba, city of, 56.
troops at, 56.
Cuba, Island of, Havanna in. *See* Havanna.
Lord Windsor's action in, 71.
prisoners in, 136.
St. Iago in. *See* St. Iago.
Culpeper or Culpepper, John, Lord, 5.
Cumberland, Duke of (Prince Rupert), 117.
Cuningham (Cuningam), Mr., 187, 220.
Cunha, Juan Nuñez da. *See* Nuñez.
Curtius [William, agent in Germany], 6.

Custom House :
  farmers of, letters to, 134.
  orders sent to, 171.
  valuation of ships at, 145.
Customs, Act concerning, 152.
  Commissioners of, 34.

D

D'Ablancourt, Sieur. *See* Fremont, Nicholas de.
Daniel or Danell, Captain, 156.
Davis, Sir Paul, 215.
Deacon, Captain George, 217.
De But, Conde de. *See* Boito.
Dee Pee, Captain Anthony, narrative of, 136.
Degebi (Eudigbe, Eugebe, Zigebe), the river, 100, 102, 103, 107.
Dempsey, Dempsy or Demsy, Major Laurence, 106.
—— as Lieut.-Colonel, 112, 114, 122, 170.
—— letters from, 55, 122.
—— troop of, killed and wounded in, 122.
Derby, co., 257.
De Ruyter. *See* Ruyter, Michael de.
Detangres, engineer, 84.
—— valet of, 84.
Dickenson, Mr., 133.
Digby :
  Sir John (afterwards Earl of Bristol), embassy of, to Spain, 132.
  Sir Kenelm, 72.
  —— letter to, 71.
Discoverers, payment of, 144.
Dissenters, 77.
Domanico [Dominica ?] island of, 136.
Domingo, Don, son of the Duke of Medina de las Torres, 154, 235.
Doncaster, 146.
—— troop of horse at, 146.
Dongan :
  Viscount, 132, 202, 215, 218.
  —— letters from, 152-154, 168, 172, 173, 195, 215.
  —— letter to, 175.
  —— family of, 168.
  Maria Eufemia, Lady, 152, 168, 172, 173, 215.
  —— letter of, 152.
  —— father of. *See* Chambres, Robert.
  or Dongham, Lieut.-Colonel Michael, 86, 101.
  —— his death, 104-106, 111, 122.
  —— his troop, killed and wounded in, 122.
Dongham. *See* Dongan.

Dorchester, Marquess of [Henry Pierrepoint], 145.
Dover, Simon, 145.
Downe, Robert, 207.
—— letters of, 207, 212.
—— cousin of. *See* Westcombe, Martin.
Downing, Sir George, Ambassador to the Hague, 83, 183, 186, 193.
—— letters from, 166, 167, 176.
—— letters to, 170, 201.
Downs, the, 41, 55, 57, 170.
Dublin :
  Archbishop of. *See* Boyle, Dr.
  letter dated at, 215.
  news from, 170.
  ship from, 178.
Dudley, Mr., 191.
Duncan :
  Andrew (Consul at Seville), 143, 183.
  John, 183.
Duncum, Mr., 90.
Dunkirk or Dunkerque :
  the Earl of Teviot at, 130.
  fortifications at, 145.
  news from, 207.
  sale of, 44, 48 (2), 58, 61, 231.
Duras, house of, 117.
Dutch or the Dutch, *passim.*
  Admirals, 189, *and see* Tromp, De Ruyter, Evertsen *and* Banckert.
  affection of, to Spain, 162.
  Ambassador at Madrid, 197.
  —— audience of, 170.
  ' a most lying nation," 199.
  at Tangier, 201.
  Bishop of Munster's campaign against, 212.
  Consuls, 163.
  —— at Cadiz. *See* Cadiz.
  damage done by, to English trade, 149-152.
  dealings of, with Gayland, 210.
  designs of, 144, 176, 186, 194, 241.
  dissatisfaction of the people of Algiers with, 88.
  express, 163, 170.
  false reports spread by, 175, 194-196, 198 (2), 213.
  fleet, 249, 250, 252. *See* Ruyter, De, fleet of. *See* Dutch ships.
  —— captains in, condemned to be shot, 200.
  —— command of, given to De Ruyter, 204.
  —— commander of, at Cadiz. *See* Vurburch, Juan Gidienson.
  —— defeat of, in Cromwell's time, 166.
  —— reported engagement with, 149.
  —— and pratique in Spain, 160, 162.
  —— disposition of, 165, 170, 182, 195, 204, 206.
  —— the plague in, 165.
  —— defeat of, 173 (2), 194, 195, 198, 200 (2), 211.
  —— strength of, at Cadiz, 184.

Dutch fleet—*cont.*
—— delay of, in leaving their ports, 188, 191, 196.
—— another fight with, expected, 198, 200, 204, 206, 207.
—— reinforcement of, 199.
—— difficulty in manning, 200.
—— mutiny in, 200.
—— a second defeat of, reported, 209, 210.
French forces borrow from, 222.
French support to, 242.
Goa besieged by, 19.
grandees, 162.
ill-understanding of, with the French, 188.
in Spain, 211.
in Guinea, 146.
in the East Indies, 90.
in the West Indies, 137.
in the New Netherlands, 149.
insolence or boas..ul words of, 157, 178, 183, 187, 188, 190, 199-201, 220, 242.
letters of reprisal against, 171.
mariners, 200.
—— hardships endured by, 176.
—— killed or wounded, 184, 200.
officers, killed, 188.
partiality to, in Spain. *See* Spain.
preparations of, for war, 165.
prisoners in the West Indies, 135.
privateers to be set out against, 183.
prospect of war with. *See* Holland.
provocation given by, 175.
service against, 181.
ships, 71, 138, 144, 169, 173-175. 186, 187, 191, 192, 194-197, 199, 201, *and see* Dutch fleet.
—— engagement of, with English vessels, 183, 188-191.
—— poorly manned and victualled, 199.
—— off Spain, &c., 215, 220.
—— (prize), 82, 171, 208.
—— seizure of, 171.
—— taken by the English, 163, 179, 190-192, 210, 230, 235, 244, 245 (3), 248, 250.
—— with letters of marque, 176.
—— with the Duke of Beaufort, 241.
—— East Indiamen, 165, 175.
—— West Indiamen, 179.
ship claimed by the, 206.
ships taken by the, 173, 207-211, 220, 221, 243 (2), 249, 251.
—— list of, 220, 221.
treachery of, 149, 175.
workmen, 173.
war with England apprehended by, 150.
the Duke of York to take command against, 185.
have lost their best officers, 200.
are in an ill condition, 230.
Dyer, Thomas, 221.

E.

Eadrum, William, 221.
Earle, Dr. John, Dean of Westminster, 72.
East country, the, vessel from, 244.
Eastern seas, Dutch and English claims in, 144.
East India Company :
  claim of, for damages, 149, 150.
  factories of, 150.
East Indiamen, 210.
—— Dutch, 165, 175.
East Indies, the, 18, 24, 90.
  Dutch designs in, 176.
  English factories in, 19.
—— fleet going for, 23.
  Portuguese in, 18.
Edgecombe, Sir Richard, K.B., signature of, 219.
Edinburgh :
  castle of, governors of. *See* Middleton and Lauderdale, Earls of.
—— deputy governor of, 147.
  churches of, prayers in, 171.
  intelligence from, 144-146, 151, 191.
Edward, Prince [Palatine], son of the Queen of Bohemia, 6.
Elizabeth, Queen :
—— Captain of the Guard to, 139.
—— Commissioners of, 43.
—— help given to Holland by, 37, 39.
—— help given to Portugal by, 39.
—— Remembrancer of Exchequer to. *See* Fanshaw, Thomas.
—— Walsingham's queries to, 45.
Elizabeth, Queen of Bohemia, sister of Charles I, 5.
—— letter from, 6.
—— her godson, 6.
Elgin, Earl of [Robert Bruce], child of, christened, 145.
Ellvas. *See* Elvas.
Elvas, Luis Mendez de, 94.
Elvas or Ellvas, battle of, 93.
  letter dated at, 74.
Embrun, Archbishop of (Georges d'Aubusson de la Feuillade), French Ambassador at Madrid, 43.
Emperor [Ferdinand II.], Sir H. Wotton's embassy to, 132.
  [Leopold], agent sent to, 219.
—— league of with England, 234.
—— truce of, with the Turks, 167.
—— sister of. *See* Spain, Queen of, 234.
Empire, Princes of the, 167.
England, *casual notices, passim.*
  alliance of with Portugal. *See* Portugal.
  Ambassadors from and to, 132, 170.
  Ambassadors from :
  to France. *See* Holles, Lord.

England, Ambassadors from—*cont.*
  to the Hague. *See* Downing, Sir George.
  to Spain and Portugal. *See* Fanshaw, Sir Richard, and Sandwich, Earl of.
  Ambassadors to:
  from France. *See* Cominges, Mons. de.
  from Holland. *See* Vangoch.
  trom Portugal. *See* Sande, Marques de.
  from Spain. *See* Molina, Conde de.
  from Sweden. *See* Friesendorff.
  Ambassadors to, priests in attendance upon, 74.
  bad years in, 256.
  banishment from, 144.
  capture of Cadiz by. *See* Cadiz.
  certificate of titles and laws of precedence in, 75.
  civil war, or "the troubles" in, alluded to, 2, 3, 6, 81.
  counties of, are raising supplies for the King, 192.
  Court of. *See* Court, the.
  Crown of, 35, 75.
  Great Seal of, 21.
  intelligence from, 163, 179, 196, 230, 231, 234, 235, 240, 242, *and see* News letters.
  laws of, 82.
  mediation of, 42, *and see* Charles II., as mediator between Spain and Portugal.
  messenger sent to, 110.
  militia of, 242.
  Parliament party in, 12-15. *And see* Commonwealth.
  passes for, 176, 204.
  power of, by sea, 38.
  preparations in, to resist invasion, 242.
  prosperous or contented state of, 188, 230.
  quarrel of with Holland. *See* Holland.
  Royalist party in, 12-15.
  —— rising in [under Sir George Booth], 12, 13.
  ships to and from, *passim.*
  ships from, suspected, on account of the plague, 206.
  Spanish agents in, 47, *and see* Moledi.
  territories of, enlargement of, 18.
  trade of, advancement of, 18.
  —— with Brazil. *See* Brazil.
  —— with Portugal. *See* Portugal.
  treaty of, with Portugal. *See* Portugal.
  travellers to, 178 (2), 202.
  troops in, 242.
  —— raising of, 179.
  anticipated return of the King to, 11.
  joy in, at the King's return, 17.
  Portuguese agent sent to, 30.
  plot discovered in, 46, 48.

England—*cont.*
  evil or restless spirits in, 54, 77.
  want of money in, 75.
  hostility of, towards Spain, 88.
  has now a King, 128.
  stake of, in the Mediterranean, 182.
  French embassy to, 185.
  arrival of Ambassadors in, 187.
  popularity of the war with Holland in, 188.
  is not sensible of the importance of Tangier, 197.
  war with, talked of, in France, 198.
  the youth of, 218.
English, or the English:
  animosity to, in Spain, 189, 190.
  army in Portugal. *See* Portugal.
  —— a former, 31.
  captives in Spain, 152, 158, 215, 254.
  —— in the West Indies, 134-138.
  —— with the Moors, 182.
  fleet. *See* Fleet, the.
  goods, fear of infection from, 233.
  the Governor of Tituan makes overtures to, 25.
  language, translations into, 11.
  mariners, prisoners in Spain, 254.
  merchants, 46, 47.
  —— in Portugal. *See* Portugal.
  —— in Spain. *See* Spain.
  piracies committed upon, 51.
  ships. *See* Ships.
  surgeon, in the West Indies, 134.
Englishman, in a play, 231.
Escalante, Conde de, Mestre de Campo, 105, 106, 108.
Escovan, Don Christoval Munez de, judge-conservador at Granada, 248.
Espinola, Juan Lopes de, 153.
Espinosa, General, 71.
Essex, late Earl of [Robert Devereux]:
  —— expedition of, to Cadiz, 38.
  —— said to have stuck his dagger into Lisbon gates, 39.
Essex, co., 257.
  manor in, 256.
Estramadura, commander in, 37.
Estremos, 85, 103, 107, 237, 240.
  letters dated at, 82, 84, 106, 109.
  letter received at, 233.
  Portuguese army at, 101, 116, 121.
Everard, Sir Richard, 145.
Evertsen or Everson, John, Dutch Admiral, 200.
Evora:
  camp before, letters dated from, 113, 115.
  convent near, 116.
  country near, letter dated from, 99.
  Dean of, 96, 97.
  Fort St. Antonio (St. Anthoene) at, 84, 98, 114-116, 118.
  Portuguese Governor of. *See* Miranda, Manuel de.
  Spanish commander in, 111, 114.
  approach to and siege of, by the Spaniards, 83-86, 101, 102.

Evora—*cont.*
surrender of, to the Spaniards, 92, 94, 96, 97, (2), 102, 103, 107, 119.
—— riot at Lisbon in consequence of, 92, 125.
garrison of, temporary prisoners of war, 97.
held by the Spaniards, 98, 101, 103, 107, 109.
march of the Portuguese army towards, 97, 98, 100, 122.
Schonberg wishes to attack, 106.
engagement near, 107, 110, *and see* Ameixial, battle of.
" re-siege of," 111, 114, 116, 118.
capitulation of, 114-116, 118, 119, 125.
Evora-Monte, 103, 107.
castle of, 83.
Exchange, the, transactions at, 148.
Exchequer, the, 53, 69, 120.
Bar, motion made at, 145.
Barons of, 218.
Chancellor of, 68.
—— (in 1647). *See* Hyde, Sir Edward.
Court of, order made by, 145.
—— plea entered in, 144, 145.
—— precedents in, 146.
moneys due from, 21, 68.
Remembrancers of. *See* Fanshaw, Sir Richard, *and* Thomas.
Under Treasurer of, 1.

F.

Fairborne, Major, 156, 255.
Falmouth, Countess of, 192.
—— daughter of, 192.
Fanshaw :
Ann or Anna, Lady, 25, 27, 49, 177, 218, 223, 254.
—— letters from, to her husband, 224-239.
—— letters to, 152, 158, 204, 223, 228, 236, 237, 239, 254, 255, 257.
—— articles of agreement by, 256.
—— bond given to, 257.
—— endorsements by, 116, 247.
—— father of. *See* Harrison, Sir John.
—— illnesses of, 61, 120.
—— information sent to, 154.
—— inscription written by, 257.
—— intercession of, 199, 204.
—— —— asked for, 158.
—— messages from, 54, 71.
—— presents to, 222, 229, 234.
—— remembrances sent to, 13, 46 (2), 48, 55, 78, 91, 124, 140 (2), 142, 148, 152, 154 (2), 165, 168, 171, 172, 181, 208, 217, 218, 244.
—— rents and leases of, 255-257.

Fanshaw Ann, Lady—*cont.*
—— Queen Catherine prays that she may be woman of her bedchamber and lady of the jewels, 23.
—— her audience of the Spanish Queen, 155.
—— her return to England, 250, 255.
Ann (daughter of first viscount), 258.
Anna (daughter of Sir Richard), letter from, 223.
Catherine (daughter of first viscount), 258.
Catherine (daughter of Sir Richard), letter from, 223.
Charles (son of first viscount), 258.
Elizabeth (daughter of first viscount), 258.
Sir Henry (son of Thomas), of Ware Park, Remembrancer of the Exchequer, 257.
—— son of, 257.
—— daughters of, 257, 258.
Henry, soldier (second son of Sir Henry), 257.
Henry (son of first viscount), 258.
John, of Fanshaw-gate, co. Derby, 257.
—— son of, 257.
John, Esq. (third son of Sir Henry), 257.
Lionel, cousin and secretary to Sir Richard, 35, 120, 133, 140 (2), 153, 229, 239.
—— letters of, 25, 130 (2), 143, 159, 228.
—— letters to, 187, 215, 243 (2), 250, 254.
—— certificate by, 255.
Margaret (daughter of Sir Richard), 140.
—— letter from, 223.
Mary (daughter of first viscount), 258.
Sir Richard, Bart. (youngest son of Sir Henry), Remembrancer of Exchequer to Charles I., Secretary of the Council of War to Charles II., Latin Secretary, Master of Requests, and Ambassador to Portugal and Spain, 257, *and passim.*
letters from, to :
the King, 56, 57, 131.
Allin, Admiral, 40, 173.
Belasyse, Lord, 185, 187, 190, 194, 200, 247.
Bennet, Sir Henry, 50, 56, 73, 75, 86, 92, 110 (2), 118, 123, 130, 132 (2), 133, 205.
Bravo, Señor, 73.
Castelmelhor, Conde de, 74, 85, 91, 111, 116, 122 (2), 126, 241.
Chiffinch, Tom, 62.
Clarendon, Earl of, 36, 37, 39, 40, 49-51, 60, 63, 91, 112.
Commanders of ships, 100.

Fanshaw, Sir Richard, letters from, to :
Cornbury, Lord, 70.
Coventry, William, 61, 123.
Croone, Mr., 182.
Digby, Sir Kenelm, 71.
Dongan, Lord, 175.
Downing, Sir George, 170, 201.
Dublin, Archbishop of, 139.
Fanshaw, Lady, 223, 236, 237, 239.
Fitzgerald, Colonel, 169.
Guzman, Don Anelo de, 199.
Harrison, Sir John, 71.
Holles, Lord, 182, 186, 202.
Holmes, Major Robert, 61, 126.
Inchiquin, Earl of, 59.
Lawson, Sir John, 159, 161, 163.
London, Bishop of, 81, 113.
Macedo, Don Antonio de Sousa de, 73, 74, 85, 100, 101, 199.
Maynard, Consul, 33, 128.
Medina de las Torres, Duke of, 153, 236, 253.
Mennes, Sir John, 70.
Molesworth, Colonel, 66.
Morgan, Consul, 240.
Morice, Secretary, 45, 51, 60, 69, 178.
Norwood, "Squire," 126.
O'Brien, Major General, 68, 72.
Peterborough, Earl of, 120.
Russell, Bishop, 60.
Sande, Marques de, 27, 56, 62.
Schonberg, Comte de, 99, 105, 111, 126.
Smith, Sir Jeremy, 240, 246.
Spain, Queen of, 222.
Teviot, Earl of, 99, 121.
Warwick, Sir Philip, 53, 68.
Westcombe, Consul, 184, 185, 190, 193, 196, 198, 199, 201, 204, 206, 212, 213, 220.
Winchester, Bishop of, 113.
York, Duke of, 45.
letters to, from :
his wife, 224-239.
his daughter Catherine, 223.
—— Margaret, 223.
—— Anna, 223.
the King, 3, 22, 165.
Allin, Admiral, 165, 169, 172-174.
Alsopp, Col. 156, 164.
Apsley, Sir Allan, 124.
Apsley, Colonel, 115.
Bath, Earl of, 205.
Bedingfield, Sir Francis, 214.
Belasyse, Lord, 184, 190, 201, 206, 209, 210, 212.
Bennet, Sir Henry, 33, 65, 80, 83, 86, 8/, 132, 155, 166.
Beverley, Sir Thomas, 218.
Bland, John, 190, 196.
Blunden, William, 155, 169, 183, 185, 217, 249.
Boothhouse, Samuel, 78.
Bridge, Colonel, 152, 153, 158, 159.
Bromydge, George, 166.
Bulteel, John, 217.
Canary Company, the, 212.

Fanshaw, Sir Richard, letters to, from :
Carteret, Sir George, 33.
Castelmelhor, Conde de, 85, 113, 121, 141 (2), 203.
Chambers, Richard, 215.
Cocke, Robert, 66.
Coventry, William, 82, 87.
Dempsy, Major, 55, 122.
Dongan, Lord, 152, 154, 168, 172, 173, 195, 215.
Downing, Sir George, 166, 167, 176.
English officers, 74.
English prisoners in Seville, 152, 158.
Fanshaw, Lionel, 25, 130 (2), 143.
Fitzgerald, Colonel, 32, 162 (2), 164, 167-169.
Fremont, Mons. de, 120, 142, 178, 208.
Gilpin, Captain B., 111.
Hodges, Captain, 74.
Holles, Lord, 147.
Holmes, Major Robert, 90.
Hyde, Sir Edward, or Clarendon, Earl of, 7-16, 23, 75, 89.
Inchiquin, Earl of, 35, 46, 54, 127.
Ingram, Sir Thomas, 200.
Jesus College, Cambridge, 133.
King, Sir Andrew, 218.
Lawson, Sir John, 148, 154, 158, 160, 165, 166.
Liche, Marques de, 164, 180, 234.
Loyala, Blasco de, 193.
Macedo, Ant. de Sousa de, 34, 68 (3), 72, 85, 86, 100 (2), 101, 106, 110, 115 (2), 129, 141, 180, 203, 244.
Marchin, Count, 215.
Maria de la Cruz, 140.
Marsden, Thomas, 139, 176.
Maynard, Consul, 128, 142, 153, 160, 171, 222, 235.
Mennes, Sir John, 79.
Montague, Edward, 79.
Morgan, Consul, 224, 232.
Morice, Secretary, 48, 73, 79.
Norwood, Col. Henry, 171, 250.
Oñate, Duke of, 222.
Rumbold, Henry, 71.
Russell, Bishop, 47.
Ryves, Dr. Brune, 216.
Sande, Marques de, 49.
Sandwich, Lord, 22 (2).
Schonberg, Comte de, 82, 84, 97, 99, 106, 113, 143, 179.
Scowen, Juan, 219.
Scowen, William, 178, 202, 219.
Strange, Philip, 163.
Taafe, Colonel Lucas, 173.
Tallerand, Prince, 233.
Teviot, Earl of, 90.
Travers, Consul, 155, 241.
Turner, Sir Edward, 167.
Vernatti, Philibert, 188, 214.
Warwick, Sir Philip, 46, 77.
Westcombe, John, 198.

Fanshaw, Sir Richard, letters to, from :
  Westcombe, Martin, 173, 177, 179,
    181, 186, 189 (2), 193, 195, 197,
    199, 207-209, 211 (2), 214, 215,
    219, 220, 241, 245-248, 250-253.
  Williamson, Joseph, 88, 150, 191,
    194.
  Woodward, Giles, 211, 213, 247.
  York, Duke of, 78, 79, 87.
Fanshaw, Sir Richard, drafts or copies
  by, *passim.*
  —— apology to, 214.
  —— chaplain of. *See* Marsden,
    Thomas.
  —— cipher sent to, 181.
  —— coach of, 170.
  —— commendation or praise of,
    17 (2), 27, 31 (2), 48, 78, 79,
    129, 131, 132, 139, 140 (2), 147.
  —— entertainments or arrears of,
    21, 53, 54, 69, 129, 131, 132,
    134.
  —— grant to, by the Queen of
    Spain, 222.
  —— his house or *Quinta,* near
    Lisbon, 25.
  —— —— in Lisbon, 41, 62.
  —— —— —— French services held
    at, 130.
  —— —— in Madrid, 154.
  —— —— in Lincoln's Inn Fields,
    218.
  —— household of, 159, 176.
  —— —— major domo or Alguacil
    of, 159, 231.
  —— —— pages in, petition of,
    159.
  —— —— servants of, 25, 133, 255.
  —— instructions to, from Charles
    I., 1.
  —— —— from Charles II., 3, 18,
    20, 131.
  —— memoranda by, 22, 155, 202,
    204.
  —— "Original letters of," papers
    printed in, 147, 152, 153, 170.
  —— passes given by, 176, 203 (2),
    204, 211.
  —— petition to, 159.
  —— recommendations to, 205, 215,
    238.
  —— secretary of, 242, *and see*
    Fanshaw, Lionel.
  —— statement by, 222.
  —— his studies and writings, 10,
    11.
  —— goes to France, 1.
  —— is to go to Hyde and Cotting-
    ton in Spain, 3.
  —— is still at Madrid, 4.
  —— the Duke of York asks for, 6.
  —— in Paris, 7, 8 (2).
  —— young Lord Herbert under the
    care of, 8, 14.
  —— sent as Ambassador extra-
    ordinary to Portugal, 17-20.

Fanshaw, Sir Richard—*cont.*
  —— his appointment as ordinary
    Ambassador to Portugal, 22.
  —— his return to England, 22-24
  —— Queen Catherine asks that ne
    may be of her household, 23.
  —— is returning to Portugal, 27,
    28, 31.
  —— letter of credence for, to the
    King of Spain, 29.
  —— audience of, at the Court of
    Lisbon, 33, 36.
  —— visits paid to and by, 41.
  —— arrival of, at Lisbon, 49.
  —— congratulates Sir Henry Ben-
    net, 50.
  —— complains of not hearing from
    the English ministers, 51 (2), 56,
    57, 60, 70.
  —— anxiety of, concerning the
    intentions of France, 63, 64.
  —— his love for his King and
    country, 64.
  —— certificate by, concerning
    titles and laws of precedence, 75.
  —— wishes to go with the King
    to the army, 85 (2).
  —— is to be present at the treaty
    between Spain and Portugal, 89,
    90.
  —— invited to a conference of the
    ministers, 110, 111.
  —— loss of his infant daughter,
    alluded to, 120 (2).
  —— thanked for his kindness to
    Colonel Apsley, 124.
  —— inquiries after the health of,
    by the King of Portugal, 126.
  —— high tone of, towards the
    Portuguese Court, 129.
  —— the King of Portugal sends
    for, 129.
  —— his return to England, 119,
    122 (2), 123, 126, 129 (2), 131.
  —— writes to the King concerning
    his mission to Spain, 131.
  —— intended return of, to Lisbon,
    131.
  —— plate, Bibles and Prayer
    Books, and Communion linen for,
    133.
  —— appealed to for help by Jesus
    College, Cambridge, 134.
  —— is a Councillor for Ireland,
    139.
  —— suggested as Lord Chancellor
    of Ireland, 139.
  —— his mission to Spain, 131,
    132 (2), 140 (2), 142 (2).
  —— goes to Spain, 142-144.
  —— arrival of, at Madrid, 152,
    154, 236.
  —— his audience of the Spanish
    King, 154, 155.
  —— reported to have arranged a
    treaty between Spain and Por-
    tugal, 168, 219, 220.

Fanshaw, Sir Richard—*cont.*
—— mediation, &c., of, at the Spanish Court, 162, 168, 182, 212, 213, 220, 222, 247 (2).
—— —— asked for, 152, 158, 163, 166, 215, 233, 238 (2).
—— cannot send his coach and family to attend the Dutch Ambassador, 170.
—— his intended return to England, 172, 173, 176, 250, 253.
—— arrangements for the witnessing a bull fight by, 190.
—— birth of a son [Richard], 218.
—— treaty of, with Spain, 222, 225, 226, 230, 231, 255.
—— —— defence of his conduct in signing, 255.
—— his journey to Portugal, and negotiations there, 223-231, 234, 244.
—— proceedings of, approved by the Spanish Court, 225-227, 229, 231.
—— good health of, 228, 237, 239.
—— the Queen of Spain's "kindness" for, 229.
—— the King has expressed approval of, 230.
—— his return to Madrid, 236, 237, 239, 240, 241.
—— prays that Lord Sandwich may be well received, 236.
—— his friendship for Sir Robert Southwell, 255.
—— death of, 254.
—— his family, 34, 78, 127, 132, 160, 170, 178, 219, 246.
—— his wife. *See* Fanshaw, Ann, Lady.
—— his son. *See* Fanshaw, Richard.
—— his daughters, 25, 46, 48, 91, 204, 217, 223, 234, 237, *and see* Fanshaw, Anna, Catherine, and Margaret.
—— —— messages to, 140 (2), 142, 148, 152, 154 (2), 165, 168, 181, 208, 218, 255.
—— his brother. *See* Fanshaw, Thomas, Lord.
—— his cousin, Lionel. *See* Fanshaw, Lionel.
Richard or Dick (son of Sir Richard), 218, 223, 224, 229, 234, 235, 237, 255.
Sir Simon (fourth son of Sir Henry), 257.
Simon (son of first viscount), 258.
Thomas, of Jenkins (son of John), Remembrancer of Exchequer to Queen Elizabeth, 257.
—— wives and children of, 257.
Sir Thomas, first Viscount Fanshaw, Remembrancer of Exchequer (eldest son of Sir Henry), 179, 202, 257.
—— death of, 188.

Fanshaw, Sir Thomas—*cont.*
—— son of. *See* Fanshaw, Thos , second Viscount.
—— children of, 258.
Sir Thomas (son of Thomas), Clerk of the Council, 257.
Thomas, second Viscount Fanshaw (eldest son of first Viscount), 188, 258.
William (son of Thomas), auditor of the Duchy of Lancaster, 257.
Fanshaws, inscription for the family vault of, 257.
Fanshaw-gate, co. Derby, 257.
Faro (Faeror), 38, 111, 120.
Farrell, Captain Edmond, pass for, 211.
Fasset, John, 221.
Fauconberg or Faulconbridge, Lord (Thomas Belasyse), 118.
—— brother of. *See* Belasyse, Major.
Fell, Dr. John, Dean of Christchurch, 130.
Fenny, Captain, 174.
Fereira, Francisco, 110.
Ferns, Fernes or Fearns, Captain Henry, 117, 135-138.
—— extract from the journal of, 136.
Ferrers, Captain Robert, letter of, 254.
Fez (Fesse), in Morocco, 32, 202, 212.
—— gardens and vineyards round, 212.
Fiesco, Faisco, or de Fiesque, Marques or Conde Luis de, taken prisoner, 105, 108.
Figueira, Custom House and officers at, 238.
Finch :
Sir Heneage, Solicitor General, 191.
—— brother of. *See* Finch, Sir John.
Sir John, made resident at Leghorn, 191.
Fish, ships laden with, 1, 221.
Fitzgerald :
Lieut.-Colonel or Colonel John, deputy governor of Tangier, 160, 164, 172, 181, 246.
—— letters from, 32, 162 (2), 164, 167-169.
—— letter to, 169.
Lieut.-Colonel [Edward], 164.
Major, killed, 156.
Mrs., 25.
Fitzharding, Viscount (Charles Berkeley), 171, 172.
—— wife of. *See* Falmouth, Countess of.
Fitzpatrick, Captain, killed, 161.
Flanders or the Low Countries, 52, 88, 225, 230, 246.
—— Spanish Governors of, 183.
Fleet, the English, *casual notices, passim. And see* Allin, Admiral ; Lawson, Sir John ; *and* Smith, Sir Jeremy, fleets of.
commanded by the Duke of York, 172, 179, 188.

Fleet, the English—*cont.*
   commanded by the Duke of Albe-
     marle, 218.
   commanders of the three squadrons
     of, 201.
   commanders of, cashiered, 219.
   —— fitting men appointed as, 219.
   disaster to, 171-173.
   Dutch ships taken by. *See* Dutch
   ships.
   engagement of, with Dutch fleet,
     192.
   for Bombay, 18.
   for the East Indies, 23.
   for Portugal, 29 (2), 65, 76, 81, 87,
     91.
   for Tangier. *See* Tangier.
   liberty of the Spanish ports desired
     by or refused to, 158-162, 166,
     169.
   movements of, 18, 22, 40, 168, 169,
     173, 191, 196.
   on the coast of Holland, 192, 193.
   on the coast of Spain, 181, *and see
     under names of the several
     Admirals.*
   salutations of or to, 155.
   strength of, 165.
   victory of, 173 (2), 194, 195.
   victualling of, 33.
Flemish boors, 44.
   ports, English ships admitted to,
     219.
   ship, 117.
Florence, State of, 232.
Fontaines, Mons. des, 109.
Ford, Harry, of Norfolk, 172.
Formosa. *See* Twyann.
Fortescue:
   Francis, 191.
   Mr., 191.
France, King of [Louis XIV.], 43, 44,
   58, 127, 149, 150, 175, 178, 231, 242,
   244.
   —— letter of, to the Pope, 62.
   —— —— to the Cardinals, 63.
   —— order by, 63.
   —— printed letters to, 38.
   —— Ambassador extraordinary of,
     to Rome. *See* Crequi.
   —— Commissioners of, 71.
   —— frigates built for, 188.
   —— ministers of, 41.
   —— pretensions of, in Spain, 37,
     41.
   —— and Portugal, 52, 63, 64, 81,
     99, 125.
   —— and the Pope, 55, 62, 71.
   —— has offered to buy Tangier,
     178.
   —— his mother's dying words to,
     230.
   —— has declared war against Eng-
     land, 235, 240, 242.
   —— uncle of. *See* Metz, bishop
     of.

France, King of—*cont.*
   —— brother of. *See* Orleans,
     Duke of.
   Queen of (Maria Theresa), 147.
   Queen Regent or Mother of (Anne
     of Austria), 147.
   —— illness of, 78.
   —— death and dying words of,
     230.
   —— brother of. *See* Spain, Philip
     IV, King of.
   —— jeweller of, 63.
France, 1, 50, 109, 110.
   agents of, in Portugal, 83, *and see*
     Colbert, Mons.
   allies of, 42, 125.
   Ambassadors from, 45.
   —— to England, 187, 191, *and see*
     Cominges, Mons. de.
   —— to Madrid, 45, 170, 242, *and
     see* Embrun, Archbishop of.
   Ambassadors to :
   —— from England. *See* Holles,
     Lord.
   —— from Portugal. *See* Soure,
     Conde de, and Sande, Conde de.
   —— from Spain. *See* Fuente,
     Marquez de.
   coast of, English fleet off, 165.
   Court of, 171.
   —— at St. Germains, reception of
     Lord Holles at, 147 (2).
   —— examines into the quarrel
     between Holland and England,
     174.
   Crown, influence of, in Portugal,
     64.
   —— negotiations with, 26, 75.
   Intendant de Finances in, 41.
   messenger sent to, 83, 110.
   news from, 58, 183.
   Princess of, King of Portugal's
     proposed marriage with, 71.
   Princesses of, go to Portugal, 249,
     253.
   sale of Dunkirk to. *See* Dunkirk.
   salute to the flag of, 202.
   State papers of, betrayed to foreign
     ministers, 150.
   travellers to and from, 63, 64, 111,
     132, 154, 178, 192, 202, 208.
   treaties with, 83, 174, *and see* Spain.
   disorders in, 5.
   tries to prevent the English and
     Portuguese marriage, 39.
   intrigues of, in Spain and Portugal,
     40-43, 44, 49, 63, 64, 88, 89, 241,
     242.
   Walsingham's embassy to, 45.
   help from, for Portugal, 54, 57,
     64, 110, 125, 131.
   money given by, to Holland and
     Sweden, 125.
   expected renewal of the war with,
     127.
   reliance of Holland upon, 167.
   friendship of England with, 171,
     224.

R 2

France—*cont.*
  Lord Fitzharding sent to, 171, 172.
  embassy from, to England, 186.
  prospect of war with, 198, 227.
  Venice and the Pope said to be
    in league with, 232.
  war with England, proclaimed,
    232, 235.
  war with Spain, expected, 232.
  danger of sending letters through,
    233.
Francis, Richard. *See* Fanshaw, Sir
  Richard.
Franciscan order, the, 195.
Frankfort [on Main], assembly of
  deputies at, 6.
Fraudulent conveyances, bill for preventing, 148.
Frederick, John, 183.
Freeman, Sir Ralph, 78.
—— his daughter, 78.
Fremont [Nicholas de] Sieur D'Ablancourt, 99, 106, 130, 180.
—— letters from, 120, 124, 126,
  142, 178.
—— letter to, 108.
French, the, *casual notices*, *passim*.
  captives in Tunis or Algiers, 217,
    249 (2).
  flag, the, 209.
  fleet, 201, 243, 249-251, *and see*
    Beaufort, Duke of, fleet of.
—— list of ships in, 251, 252.
—— orders for, 252.
  incognito, 110.
  language, letters, &c., written in,
    63, 83, 85, 99, 100, 107-109, 115,
    117, 118, 121, 126 (3), 139, 140
    (2), 142, 143, 178, 180, 181,
    208, 233, 234.
  mariners, 139, 201, 249.
  merchants, 251.
  minister at Lisbon, 130, 177.
  prisoners in the West Indies, 134-
    138.
  prizes, 209.
  sea captain, 41.
  ships, 137, 202, 209, 251.
—— English ships taken by, 217.
  224.
—— taken by the English, 198,
  231, 235.
—— taken by the Turks, 232.
  troops, 127, 149.
—— in Holland, 221, 222.
—— for or in Portugal, 40-42, 44,
  63, 80, 91, 97, 100 (2), 109, 111,
  118, *and see* Schonberg, regiments of.
—— —— officers of, 91.
  wines, ships laden with, 207,
    209, 221, 249, 251.
  reported loss of Gigerie by. *See*
    Gigirie.
  attack upon, in Rome, 62.
  accounts of the battle of Ameixial,
    by, 107, 109.
  ill-understanding of, with the
    Dutch, 188.

French, the—*cont.*
  desire peace with England, 230.
Frenchman, seized for viewing the
  works at Hull, 145.
  in a play, 231.
Frenchmen, depositions of, 117, 136.
Fresqui [Ferexqui, Fiasetri], Conde de,
  Mestre de Campo, 105, 108.
Frexinall, letter dated at, 228.
Friesendorff, Lord John Frederick Van,
  plenipotentiary from Sweden to Eng-
  land, 22.
Frinton or Frunton, co. Essex, estate
  of, 255, 256.
Frogiert, Mons., French minister at
  Lisbon, certificate signed by, 177.
Frunton. *See* Frinton.
Fuensaldaña or Fuensaldague, Conde
  de, Ambassador from Spain to France,
  63.
Fuente, Marques de, Spanish Ambassa-
  dor in France, 232 (2).
Fuorsy, Bay of. 169.

G.

Galizia or Galicia, province or frontiers
  of, 29, 50, 52, 96, 154, 208, 215.
  army of, 47.
  General of horse in, 36.
Gallipoly oil, ship laden with, 217.
Galway, Francis, 151.
Gambia (Gambo), river, 171.
Garner, Nicholas, signature of, 136.
Garter, Order and Knights of the, 216.
  prelate of the, 62.
Gaylan [Gayland, Guiland, Guyland,
  Guylan], Cidi Hamet el Hader Ben
  Ali, a Moorish chief, 32, 151, 157,
  164, 168, 169, 172, 181, 182, 190, 210,
  213, 241.
  abode of. *See* Arzilla.
  army of, 156, 157, 164.
  Benbucar's expedition against.
    See Benbucar.
  boats of, 168.
  chief men or party of, 164, 197.
  Commissioners sent to, 164, 172.
  and Spain, 37, 130, 172, 199,
    207-210, 241, 245.
  defeat or repulse of, 151, 241.
  victory of. *See* Tangier, defeat
    of the garrison of.
  former victory of, 156.
  prospect of peace with, 197 (2),
    201, 202.
  sends a present to Lord Belasyse,
    201, 202.
  expedition of other chiefs against,
    202, 212.
  peace with, 241, 246, 247.

Geneiro, Sir Manuel de, 56.
Genoa, State of, 232.
   Ambassador from to Spain, 184.
Gentill, Mons., 183.
German Colonel, 114.
   forces, 192.
   (i.e., Prince Maurice), in the West
   Indies, 137.
Germans, 154.
Germany, 149, 154.
   Ambassador of, to Spain, 170.
   Princes of, 230, 232, 234.
   —— friendly towards Charles II.,
   6.
   —— deputies of, 6, 177.
   Sir Thos. Roe's embassy to, 132.
Gibraltar, 158, 165, 172, 174 (2), 177,
   181.
   Governor of, 158, 174, 179.
   new Mole at, 160.
   Rock of, English frigates stranded
   near, 179.
Gigirie (Gigarie, Gigery, Jugerer), loss
   of, by the French, 169 (2), 172, 250.
Gilby, Colonel Anthony, deputy Gover-
   nor of Hull, 145.
Gilderslewe, Robert, 135.
   —— information by, 134.
Gilpin, Captain B., 119, 120.
   letter from, 111.
Glasgow, 151.
   High Commission Court at, 147.
   minister at, 151.
   Tolbooth in, prisoners committed
   to, 151.
Gloria, Signora Silva da, 208.
Goa, East Indies, 18, 19, 24, 142.
   —— besieged by the Dutch, 19.
   —— island near, 89.
   —— vice King of, 89.
Goddard, Thomas, 154, 212, 228, 234,
   254.
   —— letter from, 154.
Godfrey, Mr., 192.
Godolphin:
   Francis, 219.
   William, secretary of Lord Arling-
   ton, is to be secretary to the
   Spanish embassy, 219, 254.
   Sir William, signature of, 220.
Godshill, Isle of Wight, 134.
Golden Fleece, order of, 97.
Gomme, Sir Bernard de, Engineer
   General, 157, 190, 202.
Goodward, Giles, Consul at Malaga,
   letters from, 211, 213, 215, 243, 247.
Goree, Dutch fleet at, 165, 167.
Gorer, Frederick, 138.
Gosport, near Portsmouth, 134.
Goudinge, Captain, 105.
Granada, 247.
   judge-conservador of, 248.
   oyidor of, 184, 186.
Great Seal, the, 4, 87, 89.
Grimston, Sir Harbottle, Master of the
   Rolls, attempt against, 170.
Groyne, the. See Corunna.
Grun, John, 80.

Guadiana, the river, the Spanish army
   crosses, 101.
Guinea (Guinny, Guiny), 146, 149, 150,
   166, 167, 170, 187.
   De Ruyter's fleet off, 166-168, 175,
   178.
   Holmes' expedition to, 175.
   reported capture of the English
   forts, in, 173.
Guinea or Royal Company, 146.
   —— ships of, 146.
Gusman. See Guzman.
Guylan or Gayland. See Gaylan.
Guzman or Gusman, Don Añelo or
   Daniel de, son of the Duke of Medina
   de las Torres, 105, 108, 141-143, 199,
   203, 233.
   —— letter to, 199.
   Donna Maria. See Cruz, sister
   Maria de la.

H.

Haddock:
   Captain, 174.
   Mr., 131.
   Richard, signatures of, 136 (2).
Hadham, co. Hertford, 258.
Hague, the, 7.
   alarm at, 193.
   Ambassadors from the Common-
   wealth to, 5, 6.
   intelligence from, 149, 151, 200.
   false report of victory at, 198.
   letters dated at, 4, 6, 166, 167, 176.
   minister at, 198, and see Downing,
   Sir George.
Halbord, Captain, 120.
   Mr., 25.
Hall, Captain, of the Princess, 20.
Hamburg, ships of or Hamburgers, 88,
   208, 232.
Hamilton:
   Monsieur, 78.
   remonstrator, 151.
Hampton Court, 28, 33, 69, 199.
   letters dated at, 1, 22, 29-31, 200.
   prepared for the Queen, 27.
   privy garden at, 139.
Harcourt or Harcour, Prince de, 147.
   —— son of. See Armagnac, Comte
   de.
Haro, Don Luis Mendez de, Marques
   del Carpo y de Liche, Conde Duque
   de Olivares, chief minister of the King
   of Spain, 13, 15.
   —— son of. See Liche, Marques
   de.
Harrison, Sir John, father of Lady
   Fanshaw, 53, 62 (2), 72.
   —— letter to, 71.

Haseley, co. Oxford, 216.
   letter dated at, 216.
Hasellgrove, Captain, 174.
Hasset, Mons., letter to, 126.
Hastings, Mr., murdered, 191.
Hatton, Sir Christopher, Captain of the Guard to Queen Elizabeth, made Lord Chancellor, 139.
   Sir Christopher of Kirby, wife of, 257.
Havanna in Cuba, city of, 136, 222.
   Governor of, 222.
   prisoners at, 134, 135.
Havre de Grace, 110.
Hawes, Thomas, articles of agreement by, 256.
   —— bond of, 257.
Hazard:
   Margaret, information by, 134.
   Robert, 134.
Hearth money, bill for, 149, 151.
   Committee for, 149.
Heath, Mr., 8, 10, 11.
Heavers, Dr., prebendary of Windsor, 72.
Heenvliet, Monsieur, 4, 5.
Henchman, Humphrey, Bishop of London, 177.
   —— letter from, 255.
Henrietta Maria, Queen Dowager of England, or the Queen Mother, 5, 192.
   Council of, order by, 256.
   Council Chamber of, in Denmark House, 256.
   manors of, 256.
   moneys due to, 256.
   physicians of, 192.
   portion of, 53.
   priests in attendance on, 74.
Henriques, Don Juan, Mestre de Campo, 105.
Herbert, William, Lord, son of the Earl of Pembroke, 8, 14, 15.
Herrings, ships laden with, 221.
Hertford, co., 256-258.
   receiver for, 256.
Hertingforaoury, co. Hertford, messuage in, 257.
Hewish farm, 257.
Hich [Hicks ?], Dr. 72.
Hill, Captain, 161, 165.
Hispaniola, St. Dominique or San Domingo, island of, 117, 137, 138.
   —— president of, 137.
Hitchin, co. Hertford, manor of, 256.
Hodges, Captain Richard, of the Westergate, 72, 73.
   —— acknowledgment by, of papers entrusted to him, 72.
   —— letter of, 74.
Hodser, Don Patricio, 237 (2).
Holcombe, Humphrey, 165.
Holland, 110, 190, 198, 244.
   Ambassador to, from England. See Downing, Sir George.
   —— from Portugal, 19.
   discontent or disorder in, 192, 200.
   English fleet on the coast of, 195.

Holland—cont.
   English officer in, 257.
   Estates General of. See States General, below.
   express from, 163, 215.
   fleet of. See Dutch fleet.
   frigates built in, 188.
   messenger sent to, 110.
   money given to by France, 125.
   peace of, with Portugal. See Portugal.
   peace or treaty of, with Spain. See Spain.
   ports of, proposal to blockade, 179.
   provinces of, 167.
   reported conspiracy for betrayal of, to the English, 179.
   ships from, 178, and see Dutch ships.
   ships to be built in, 167.
   States or Estates General of, 167, 178, 179, 188, 198, 200, 252
   —— deputies of, 178.
   —— have no money and are in debt, 166.
   —— taxes imposed by, 166, 167, 177.
   —— war contribution demanded by, 232.
   trade of, 19, 167.
   treaty of, with France, 175.
   war with, prospect of, 148, 150, 151, 154, 157, 160 (2), 163, 165, 167, 168, 170.
   war with, 173, 175.
   —— popular in England, 188.
   help given to, by Queen Elizabeth, 37, 39.
   Sir George Downing to go as Ambassador to, 83.
   rumour of intended peace with, 176.
   Col. Ludlow in, 182.
   false reports in, 198.
   difficulty of, in finding a commander for the fleet, 200.
   war of, with the Bishop of Munster, 219, 232.
   province of, proposals of, 167.
Holles, Denzil, Lord, 227.
   —— letter from, 147.
   —— letters to, 182, 186, 202, 224.
   —— embassy of, to Paris, 83, 132.
   —— reception of, at the French Court, 147 (2).
   —— gentleman in the suite of, 147.
Hollis, Captain, 241.
Holmes, Major or Captain Robert or Robin, 61, 62, 77, 79, 82, 87, 91, 95, 110, 124, 171 (2).
   —— letter of, 90.
   —— letter to, 61.
   —— affront offered to, 127-129.
   —— examination of, 175.
Homerton, co. Huntington, 257.

Hopton, Sir Arthur, 132.
Hosier, Captain, 174.
Howard, Captain Charles, of the
  Merlin, 211.
—— letter of, 211.
Hoyo, Don Sevastian del, 183, 185.
Hudson, Captain, 165.
Hull, Dutch capers near, 191.
  fortifications of, 145.
  deputy governor of, 145.
  intelligence from, 146.
Hunt, Lieut.-Colonel, killed, 161.
Huntingdon, co., 257.
Hyde, Sir Edward, Earl of Clarendon
  and Lord Chancellor, 65, 72, 88, 91,
  113, 130, 153, 161, 217.
—— letters from, 4, 7-16, 23, 27
  (2), 31 (2), 75, 89, 147, 148.
—— letters to, 26 (2), 36, 37, 39,
  40, 49-51, 60, 63, 91, 112, 129.
—— endorsements by, 29 (2).
—— illness of, 12, 23, 54, 57, 60,
  75, 91, 146.
—— secretary of. *See* Bulteel,
  John.
—— as Chancellor of the Exchequer, 1.
—— as Ambassador extraordinary
  to Spain, 3.
—— anxiety of, concerning Portugal, 31.
—— recommends Sir Richard Fanshaw, 31 (2).
—— information given to, 54, 57.
—— cannot interfere in favour of
  Nicholas, 54, 55.
—— meddles only with matters
  relating to his office and affairs
  of state, 55.
—— is not apprehensive concerning France, 89.
—— indignation of, at the refusal
  to deliver up Bombay, 89.
—— charge brought against, by
  the Earl of Bristol, 127.
—— the King holds conference
  at his house, 144.
—— and Lord Sandwich's embassy,
  226.
—— annoyance of, at Fanshaw's
  action in Spain, 230.
—— sons of, 9.
—— eldest son of. *See* Cornbury,
  Lord.
—— sister of, 14 (2).
—— —— her son, 14 (2).
Hyne, Captain Ellyas, 179.

Inchiquin, Earl of—*cont.*
—— letter to, 59.
—— as commander of the English
  troops in Portugal, 29 (2), 32,
  55, 64, 86.
—— in England, 48, 51, 55, 57,
  95, 128.
—— accused of a design to pass
  the English soldiers over to
  Spain, 67, 68, 127.
—— son of, cashiered in France,
  127.
—— brother of. *See* O'Brien,
  Christopher.
India, Dutch ships on the coast of, 144.
  English rights in, 149.
Indies, the, 125, 243, *and see* East
  Indies.
  former Viceroy in. *See* Atougia,
  Conde de.
Ingram :
  Sir Arthur, Governor of the Canary
  Company, signature of, 212.
  Sir Thomas (Chancellor of the
  Duchy of Lancaster), 167.
—— letter from, 200.
Ipswich, 134.
Ireland, 76, 139, 188, 205, 212.
  bill for the settlement of, 127.
  Commissioners for, 30.
  Council of, 215.
  Councillors of, 139.
  intelligence from, 191.
  leave of absence from, 3.
  license to return to, 203 (2).
  Lord Chancellor of, 139.
  Lord Chief Justice of. *See* Smith.
  Lord Primate of [Dr. Margetson],
  215.
  Lord Lieutenant of. *See* Ormond,
  Duke of.
  Lord Ormond in, 127.
  Scots in, rising of, 178.
  soldiers going from, to Munster,
  (Germany), 229.
  Strafford's government of, 1.
Irish aqua vitæ, 215.
  fish, sent to Spain, 1.
Irishmen, 209.
—— abroad, 26, 88, 137, 197, 203,
  211.
  ships, 209, 221.
Iron, ships laden with, 187, 221.
Italian ship, prize, 208.
Italy, disturbed state of, 232.
  letters of marque sent to, 176.
  soldiers from, 71.
  strict measures taken in, against
  infection, 213.

I.

Immaculate Conception of our Lady,
  festival of, 49.
Inchiquin, Earl of (Murrough O'Brien),
  40, 41, 43, 49, 57, 60, 61, 66, 72 (2),
  127, 128.
—— letters from, 35, 46, 127.

J.

Jackson, Philip, merchant, 1, 2.
Jacob :
  Abraham, 63.
  David, an Armenian, 208.
  Mr., 46, 123.

Jacous, Matte, 138.
Jamaica, 35, 89, 222, 243.
    Governor of. *See* Windsor, Lord.
    Governor and Lieut.-Governor for,
      88, 89.
    the old Governor of (Don Christo-
      pher), 35.
Japan, 70.
Jardin, Joseph, secretary of the French
    embassy at Madrid, 63.
    —— his father and brothers, 63.
Jenkins (Inkens), co. Essex, 257.
Jersey, Governors of. *See* St. Albans,
    Earl of, and Morgan, Sir Thomas.
Jeruminhe (Jerumena, Jerumania), 97,
    102, 10*l*.
Jesuit fathers, 244.
Jesuits. *See* Priests and Jesuits.
Jewel house, master of. *See* Talbot,
    Sir Gilbert.
Jew, person "miscalled" a, 94.
Jews, 148.
Jews or Jues river, near Tangier, 156.
Job's messengers, 45.
Jocquet, 84.
Johnson, Mr., 120, 121.
Jones, Mr., at Tangier, 207.
Juan, Don, of Austria, natural son of
    Philip IV. of Spain, General of the
    Spanish army invading Portugal, 37,
    52, 125, 186.
    —— campaign of, in Portugal, 84,
      85, 92, 96-109, 114, 115, 125.
    —— siege and taking of Evora by.
      See Evora.
    —— defeat of. *See* Ameixial,
      battle of.
    —— carriage, standard and plate
      of, captured, 109.
    —— letter to, 140.
Judges, sent to the King, 150.
Jugerer. *See* Gigirie.
Jury, a grand, bills found by, 191.

K.

Keiserstein, regiment of, 109.
Kent, co., 258.
King :
    Sir Andrew, 165, 178, 216, 233.
    —— letter from, 218.
    —— letters to, 154, 174.
    Captain John, 190.
King's Bench :
    Bar of, 171.
    Court of, 192.
    prison, committal to, 191.
Kirby (Cerbey), co. Northampton, 257.
Kirkhouse, letter dated at, 132.
Knightley, Major, killed, 156.
"Knot," the, 13.
Konigsberg, Comte de, 150.

L.

La Brose, a filibuster, 138.
Lagos, 38.
La Guarda, siege of, 223.
Lancashire, royalist rising in, 13.
Lancaster, Duchy of, auditor of, 25*l*.
Lander, Robert de, 222.
    —— depositions signed by, 222.
Landroal, 121.
    army or camp at, 100, 102, 107.
    letter dated at, 97.
Lands gained from the sea, bill relating
    to, 148.
Landy, Captain, 161.
Langdon, Captain, killed, 156.
Langley, Captain Charles, slain, 223.
Languedoc, Protestant churches in, to
    be demolished, 150.
Lasnier, Mons., 182.
La Strange. *See* L'Estrange.
Latin, letters written in, 129 (2), 134,
    147, 148.
Latin secretary, 9, 11, *and see* Wecker-
    lin, *and* Fanshaw, Sir Richard.
    salary of, 9.
Lauderdale, Earl of [John Maitland].
    —— made Governor of Edinburgh
      Castle, 147.
    —— called as a witness by Bristol,
      127.
Lawson, Admiral Sir John, and his
    fleet, 25, 32, 37, 82, 87 (2), 91 (2),
    123, 124, 155, 158, 164, 165 (2), 169.
    —— letters from, 148, 154, 158,
      160, 165, 166.
    —— letters to, 159, 161, 163.
    —— statement by, 123.
    —— concludes a peace with Tripoli,
      51.
    —— returns to England, 168.
    —— death of, 198, 200.
Lead, ship laden with, 165.
Leech, Sir Robert, 35.
Leganes, Marques de, Governor of
    Oran, 184, 185.
Leghorn or Legorne, 88, 165.
    English Resident at, 191.
Leifrid, Dr., Professor at Tubingen,
    book written by, 6.
    —— is imprisoned, and his book
      burnt, 6.
Lemercier, Donna Mariana, wife of
    Antonio de Sousa, 181, 199, 244.
    —— letter from, 204.
Lesley, Baron de, 240.
L'Estrange or La Strange, Roger,
    surveyor of the press, 227.
Letters of marque, or reprisal, alluded
    to, 170.
Levant, corn from, 232.
    ships from, 232.
Lewis, George, 221.

Liche or Lixe, Gasper de Haro, Marques de (son of Don Luis de Haro), prisoner in Portugal, 105, 106, 108, 141 (2), 143, 165, 203, 233.
—— letters from, 164, 180, 234.
—— attempt at escape by, 131.
Marquesa de, daughter of the Duke of Medina Celi, 227, 232, 234.
Lincoln, Bishop of [Dr. Sanderson], 72.
Lincoln, Earl of [Theophilus Clinton], 78.
Lionne, Mons. de, clerk of, 150.
Lisbon, Lisboa, or Lishboa, 22, 33, 34, 47, 49, 52, 61, 76, 79, 98, 132, 141, 184, 199, 253.
Archbishop of, 41, 42.
—— palace of, plundered by the mob, 93.
arrival of the Brazil fleet at, 118.
Auto da fé at, 177.
castle of St. George at, letters dated at, 164, 180, 234.
convents of, procession of the friars of, 94.
English chaplain at, 67, 81, 177, and see Marsden, Thomas.
—— church at, 81.
—— College at, President of, 48, 60.
—— Consul at, 66, 67, and see Maynard, Thomas, and Robinson, Mr.
—— embassy at, secretary of, 133.
—— merchants at, 81, 177, 209.
—— certificate signed by, 178.
—— fleet going to, 80, 91, 246.
Exchequer of, 123.
Fanshaw's house in, 41.
French agent at, 49.
—— minister at, 130, 177.
—— Princesses expected at, 249, 253.
gates, the Earl of Essex sticks his dagger into, 39.
houses of the nobility in, plundered, 93, 94.
letters dated at, 16, 22, 24-26, 28, 29 (3), 32, 35-37, 39, 40 (2), 45 (2), 49-51, 53, 55-57, 59-63, 66 (2), 68-73, 75, 81, 86 (2), 91, 92, 100 (2), 105, 110-113, 118, 120, 121, 123 (2), 124, 126, 128-132, 140-143, 153, 160, 171, 176, 179, 180, 203, 204, 222, 233, 235, 244.
letters received at, 48, 49, 55.
map or "draught" of, alluded to, 62.
merchants of, 123.
nunnery in, 93.
palace of, 34, 49 (2), 68, 92, 93, 120, 126, 128, 130.
—— the Broad Place or Terrero, and yard of, 92, 93.
—— Secretaria in, 92.
—— letters dated at, 68 (2), 72, 85 (2), 100 (2), 101, 113, 115 (2), 121.
port or road of, 41, 90.

Lisbon, Lisboa, or Lishboa, port of—cont.
—— ship wrecked in, 51.
Quinta de Alleyro, near, 25, 34.
Prince Rupert at, 79.
riot in, 92-94, 125.
—— quenched "with buckets from the church," 94.
river of. See Tagus.
rock of, 254.
ships to and from, 82, 89, 100, 123, 126, 143, 183, 208, 209, 251.
Sir Robert Southwell at, 226, 229.
Spanish prisoners in, 114, and see Guzman, Don Anello de; Liche, Marques de, and Alarçon, Francisco de.
"the town of Ulysses," 120.
travellers to or from, 16, 19, 91, 171, 235.
troops to be sent from, 84, 98.
Littleton, Sir Christopher, 89.
Liturgy, banishment of, 133.
restoration of, 134.
Lodestein, Conde de, 108.
Lodovicio, Prince, 202.
London, Bishops of. See Sheldon, Gilbert, and Henchman, Humphrey.
Aldermen of, 30.
bankers in, 34.
carriers forbidden to go to, 218.
constables of, order to, 192.
correspondents in, 183.
intelligence from, 199, 231.
letters dated at, 16, 17 (2), 27 (2), 33 (2), 47, 49, 54, 79, 127, 130, 141 (2), 147, 148.
Lord Mayor of, 194.
merchants of, 81, 82, 201, 238.
plague in, 192, 198, 199, 216, 220, 227, 230, 241, 246.
prisoner in, 53.
rejoicings in, 194.
ships of, 165, 221, 254.
Streets, buildings, &c., in:—
Bristol House, 71.
Denmark House, Queen Mother's Council Chamber in, 256.
Gray's Inn, 170, 257.
Lincolns Inn Fields, 218, 256, 257.
Long Acre, 199.
Ludgate, head set upon, 146.
Old Bailey, trial at, 145.
Palace in, letter dated at, 16.
Poplar, 256.
St. Andrew's, Holborn, parish of, 192.
St. Clement Danes, parish of, 192.
St. Giles, 199.
St. Giles in the Fields, parish of, 192.
St. James' [Palace], comedy and ball at, 144.
—— letters dated at, 87 (2), 124.
Woolchurch, 192.
Worcester House, letters dated at, 23, 75, 89.

London—*cont.*
    suspected houses in, to be shut up, 192.
    travellers to and from, 1ɔʋ (2), 131, 178, 218.
    troops to be shipped from, 91.
Long, Mr., 4, 5.
    Sir Robert, order signed by, 256.
Lord Chamberlain. *See* Manchester, Earl of.
Lord Chancellor. *See* Hyde, Earl of Clarendon.
    —— *temp.* Elizabeth, 139.
Lord Treasurer. *See* Southampton, Earl of.
Lords, House of, adjournment of, 150.
    amendments made in, 149.
    charge brought in against Clarendon, 127.
    conference of, with the Commons, 150.
    vote of, alluded to, 151.
Lord's Supper, or Holy Communion, the, administered in French, 130.
Lord's Table, furniture and napery for, 133.
Lorraine, Duke of, 127.
    Prince of the House of, 147.
    French army goes into, 127.
Low Countries, late Governor of. *See* Juan, Don.
Loyola, Blasco de, Spanish Secretary of State, 242.
    —— letter of, 193.
Lucca, resident from in Spain, 170.
Luckin, Thomas, minister of Wimbledon, 144.
    —— imprisoned in the Gatehouse, 145, 146.
Ludlow, Colonel Edmund, boasts of his interest in England, 182.
Lutcerell, Mr., 170.
Luxemburg, Marquis of, 230.
Lye, Robin, 205.

M.

Maas or Maze, the, 165.
McAvering, —, 170.
Macedo, Antonio de Sousa de, Secretary of State in Portugal, formerly Resident in England, 25, 33 (2), 41, 45, 46, 49, 71, 73, 89, 97, 108, 111, 128, 130, 143, 153, 203, 204.
    —— letters from, 34, 68 (3), 72, 85, 86, 100 (2), 101, 106, 110, 115 (2), 129, 141, 180, 181, 203, 244.
    —— letters to, 74, 85, 100, 101, 199.
    —— certificate by, 129.
    —— complaints by and against, 48.

    —— marriage of his son, 25.
    —— wife of. *See* Lemercier, Donna Marianna.
Madeira, island of, 153.
Madrid, 51, 88, 152, 162, 173, 178, 181, 195, 208, 233, 238 (2), 251.
    Ambassadors at. *See* Spain, Ambassadors to.
    —— quarrels of, 43.
    Buen Retiro, palace of, near, 254.
    bull fight at, 190.
    Castle De Campo (Decampaye), near, 239.
    celebration of festival in, 92.
    French embassy at, secretary of, 63.
    informations or intelligence from, 68, 195, 232.
    letters dated at, 4, 130, 132, 159, 161, 163, 169, 170, 173, 175, 176 (2), 178, 182 (2), 184-187, 190 (2), 193, 194, 196, 198-206, 211-213, 215, 222-224, 228, 229, 234, 235, 239-241, 243, 246, 247, 254.
    —— printed, 227.
    letters received at, 158 (4), 160, 163, 164, 197, 243.
    palace of, 201.
    —— solemnities at, 155.
    —— summer furnishing of, 154.
    river at, 239.
    Santa Barberica in, 239.
    Sir Richard Fanshaw at. *See* Fanshaw.
    travellers to, 15, 64, 170, 195, 218, 219, 232.
Majorca or Mayorke, 160, 202.
Malabar, 144.
Malacre, West Indies, 117.
Malaga, 152, 162, 164, 165, 196, 232.
    English Consul at. *See* Woodward, Giles.
    English merchants at, 214, 216.
    gentlemen or citizens of, 214, 248.
    governor of, 206, 210, 211, 213-215, 247.
    judge-conservador in, 186.
    letters dated at, 211, 213-215, 243, 247.
    prison in, 248.
    road, ship taken in, 220.
    ships of, to or from, 51, 158, 174, 194, 199, 251.
    sub-governor or *Alcalde Major* of, 247, 248.
Mallorca (? Majorca), 184.
Malta, knight of, 182.
    Master of, 184.
    —— brother of, 183.
Man, Colonel, 152.
Manchester, Earl of (Edward Montague), Lord Chamberlain, 65.
    —— warrants of, 132 (2), 133 (3).
Marcyn or Marchin, Count, Commander in the Spanish army, 97, 182, 233.
    —— letter from, 215.

Marea, Comte de, 154.
Marialva, Marques de, Dom Antonio Luis de Ménésés, Conde de Cantanhede, generalissimo in Alentejo, 25, 93, 94, 114, 116.
—— house of, plundered by the mob, 93.
—— Quinta of, 94. ·.
—— brother of, the Regidor, 93.
Marlborough, Earl of (James Ley), at Bombay, 87 (2), 89.
Marsall, in Lorraine, garrison at, 127.
Marsden, Thomas, chaplain to Fanshaw and to the English at Lisbon, letters from, 139, 176.
—— certificate in favour of, 177.
Marseilles or Marcellis, intelligence from, 243.
—— ships of, 174.
Marsham, Ferdinando, 72.
Marston, Nathaniel, Consul at Seville, death of, 193.
Martin, Cape, 185.
Martinique, De Ruyter at, 200.
Masiel. See Ameixial.
Maskelyne, Will, signature of, 212.
Masters, Thos., 134.
Mathews, Archbishop [of York], 78.
—— Captain, 174, 220.
Maurice, Prince, depositions concerning, 117, 134-139.
—— his shipwreck, 117, 134, 135, 137, 138.
—— his imprisonment, 118, 134-139.
—— his death, 117 (2).
Maynard :
Captain, 161.
Anthony, 34.
Chris., Vice-Consul at Lisbon, certificate signed by, 177.
Thomas, English Consul at Lisbon, 16, 24, 25, 43, 52, 58, 66, 81, 82, 115, 131, 164, 180, 208, 238.
—— letters from, 128, 142, 153, 160, 171, 222, 235.
—— letters to, 33, 128.
—— certificate signed by, 177.
—— his wife, 55, 59, 142.
—— —— death of, 171.
—— brother of. See Maynard, Captain.
Mazarin, Cardinal, 10.
—— confidant of, 41.
—— secretaries of, 40, 41.
Duke of, forces under, 149.
Meakinge, Cornet, 105.
Medellin, 237.
Medina Celi, Duque de, Governor of Andalusia, 71, 143, 159, 160, 162, 185, 188-190, 192, 193, 195, 196, 232, 244, 246, 254.
—— letter from, 237.
—— letters to, 130, 237.
—— dealings of, with Gayland, 207, 210.
—— adjutant of, 189.
—— Auditor-General of, 251.

Medina Celi, Duque de, Governor of Andalusia—cont.
—— daughter of, See Liche, Marquesa de.
of Port, Duke. See Medina Celi.
Medina de las Torres, Duque de (Don Ramero Nuñez Felipez de Gusman, Marques de Toral), chief minister of Spain, 36, 88, 130, 143, 154, 173 (2), 228, 229, 231, 234-236, 239, 240, 254.
—— letters to, 147, 148, 153, 236, 253.
—— visits Lady Fanshaw, 225.
—— views and policy of, 225-227, · 242.
—— is proxy at the Infanta's marriage, 247.
—— treaty signed with, by Fanshaw, 255.
—— secretary of, 229.
—— sons of. See Guzman, Don Añelo, and Domingo, Don.
—— brother-in-law of, 225.
Duchess of, 225, 226, 229.
Medina Sidonia, Duke of, father of the Abbess of Alcantra, 143.
Mediterranean sea, 169, 183.
Melce, Gilberto, Dutch Commissary at Cadiz, 211, 251.
Mellish, Edward, 238.
—— letter of, 238.
—— kinsmen of, 238.
Melo :
Sieur Denys de, General of Artillery and Commander in Alentejo, 55.
Don Francisco de. See Sande, Marquis of.
Don Francisco de (junior), 64.
Meneses, Don Luys de, Marques de Panalva, General of horse in Galicia, 36, 47, 49.
Mennes, Sir John, 51, 72.
—— letter from, 79.
—— letter to, 70.
—— wife of, 70.
Merchants, cheating of their creditors by, bin tor prevention of, 148.
Mercurio Portuguez, copy of, 75.
Merida, letter dated at, 237.
Metz, Bishop of, uncle to the French King, 184.
Meynell, Alderman, 30.
Middleburgh, libellers to be tried at, 152.
Middleton, Earl of, government of Edinburgh Castle taken from, 147.
Militia, debates concerning, 83.
Miller, Major [John], 145.
Mines, Mins or Myngs, Captain, or Sir Christopher, 226.
—— letter of, 34.
—— capture of St. Iago upon Cuba by, 34.
Minho or Minio, province of, frontiers of, 49, 52, 84, 98.
Minnes, Captain (Sir John Mennes?), 152.
Mins. See Mines.

Miranda:
Conde de, Ambassador from Portugal to Holland, 19, 20.
Henri Henriques de, gentleman of the bedchamber, 97.
Manual de, his brother, Governor of Evora, 97.
Mohun (Mauhun), Captain, 174.
Moledi (Muledi, Mollery, O'Moledi, Hamoleda), Don Patricio or Sir Patrick, Spanish agent in England, 68, 128, 217, 229, 230.
Molesworth, Colonel Guy, Lieut.-Colonel of the English troops in Portugal, 46, 66, 86.
—— condemned to be shot, 74.
—— letter to, 66.
Molina (Moliney, Molinay), Conde de, Spanish Ambassador in England, 187, 201, 225, 226, 229, 236.
Molinnick or Molynick, in Cornwall, 205.
letters dated at, 178, 202.
Molloy, Lieut.-Colonel, 156.
Monck, George, General, 12.
—— his army, 12.
—— as Duke of Albemarle and Lord General, 65, 84, 86.
—— is to command the fleet, 218, 219.
Monmouth, Duke of [James Scott], 172.
—— marriage of, 80.
Montague:
Edward, Master of the horse to Queen Catherine, 24, 26, 27.
—— letter of, 79.
Admiral Edward, 12, and see Sandwich, Earl of.
Montalto, Duke of, 232 (2).
Monte Mor, troops sent to, 98.
Montenegro, Don Antonio de, Commissary General, 108.
Montesarcho, Principe, 195.
Moore or More:
Captain William, 116, 161.
(brother-in-law of Sir Thos. Beverley), 218.
Moors, 148, 163, 169 (2), 181, 182, 186, 190, 194, 213, and see Turks.
advares or nomadic villages of, 185.
boats captured by, 207.
losses of, 156.
prisoners of, kept as slaves, 207.
repulse of, 148.
skirmishes with, 159.
Moralis, Don Pedro de, Governor of St. Iago upon Cuba, 35.
Mordaunt or Mordent, Captain, 156.
More. See Moore.
Morea, the, ships to, 165.
Morfoue, Don Whan [Colonel Murphy?], 137.
Morgan:
Major-General or Lieut.-General Sir Thomas, 59.
—— forces under, 152.
—— made Governor of Jersey, 227.

Morgan—cont.
Valentine, English Consul at San Sebastian, 224.
—— letter from, 232.
—— letter to, 240.
Morice or Morris, Sir William, Secretary of State, 45, 49, 72, 91, 147, 215.
—— letters from, 48, 73, 79.
—— letters to, 45, 60, 178.
—— blank commissions sent by, 183.
—— documents countersigned by, 20, 29.
Morley, Lord, 191.
Morley, Dr. George, 11.
—— as Bishop of Winchester, 72.
—— letter to, 113.
Morocco, 202.
Morphy, Torlagh, pass for, 203.
—— petition of, 203.
Mortality, bills of, alluded to, 192, 201.
Moscow, 146.
Mostyn, Colonel, 89.
Munster:
Bishop or Prince of, 167, 177, 212, 222, 229.
—— agent sent to, 219.
—— movements of, 230, 232
—— troops of, 219, 222.
General of, 221
Munsterland, 222.
Murray, Charles, 6.

N.

Nantes, 136.
Edict of, 150.
Naval preparations in England, 175.
Navarre, frontier of, 233 (2).
Navy, Commissioners of, 70, 78.
Negro slaves, sale of, 132.
Netherlands, forces for, 192.
Nevill, Colonel Henry, 144.
Newcastle, Duke of (William Cavendish), 191.
Newcastle, ships from, 195.
New England, fish from, 221 (2).
traveller to, 222.
Newfoundland ships, 168, 179.
New Netherland, ship from, 149.
Newse (Nues), Thomas or William, 257.
News letters, 144, 148, 150, 170.
—— Spanish, 232.
Nice, Marques de. See Niza.
Nicholas, Don, 228.
Sir Edward, Secretary of State, 6, 11, 37 (2), 50.
—— dismissal of, 48, 54, 73.
—— money and title offered to, 54.
—— title refused by, 55.
Niza or Nice, Marques de (Don Luis Vasco de Gama, Conde de Vidiguera), 25, 94.
Nobales [Novalia ?] Don Juan, 108.

Noirmoustier, Marquis de, 233.
Noland, Captain, killed, 161.
Norfolk, 172.
Norris, Sir John, 39.
Northampton, co., 257.
North Sea, Dutch fleet gone to, 195.
Norton, co. Derby, 257.
Norwood :
    Edward, 177.
    Colonel Henry, or "Squire," 164.
    —— letters from, 171, 250.
    —— letter to, 126.
    —— affront offered to, 127-129.
    —— made Lieut.-Governor of
    Tangier, 246.
Nova Espana fleet, 241.
Nuñez da Cunha or d'Acuna, Juan,
    Portuguese officer, 36, 45, 49 (2).
    —— letter of, 47.

O.

Obdam. See Opdam.
O'Brien, Major General Christopher,
    brother of the Earl of Inchiquin, 52,
    60, 66, 68, 72, 73 (2), 112, 128.
    —— letters to, 68, 72, 73.
    —— accused of a design to take
    the English troops over to Spain,
    67, 68, 84, 127.
    —— imprisonment of, 68.
    —— Albemarle and Bennet report
    upon, 86.
    —— servants of, 68.
Oieras (Oyers, Wyers), Bay of, 74.
    letter dated from, 46.
O'Moledi. See Moledi.
Oñate, Duke and Count of, letter of,
    222.
O'Neill :
    (O'Nell), Daniel, death of, 172.
    (O'Neel), Sir Phelim, 178.
Opdam, Obdam or Updam, Admiral,
    165, 179.
    —— fleet of, 165, 166, 167.
Oporto, 38.
    letters dated at, 238 (2).
Oran, Governor and garrison of, 182,
    184, 185.
    country round, 185.
Orange, William, Prince of, 4, 179,
    200.
    Mary, Princess of, daughter of
    Charles I., 5.
    —— letter of, 4.
    —— her portion and jointure, 4, 5.
    [Amelia], Princess Dowager of,
    imprisonment of, 179.
Orleans, Duke of, or Monsieur, brother
    of the French King, 147, 168.
    —— daughters of, 44.
    —— Mademoiselle, his eldest
    daughter, 44, 63.

Orleans, Duke of, eldest daughter of
—cont.
    —— —— to marry the King of
    Portugal, 184.
    Duchess of or Madame, his wife
    (Princess Henrietta Anne of Eng-
    land), 147.
    —— birth of her son, 163.
    Princesses of. See Orleans, Duke
    of, daughters of.
Ormond, James Butler, Marquis, and
    (in 1660), Duke of, 3, (2), 8, 9, 16,
    139.
    —— letter to, 24.
    —— as Lord Lieutenant of Ireland,
    215.
    —— called as a witness by Bristol,
    127.
    —— his wife, the Duchess of
    Ormond, 24.
Oropesa, letter dated at, 239.
Ossati, Cardinal de, 37.
Ostend, Commissioners of Queen Eliza-
    beth at, 43.
    ships of, or Ostenders, 51, 61, 70,
    179.
Otoguia or Outoguia, Conde de, 51.
Oxford, Earl of (Aubrey de Vere), 191.
Oxford, 219, 242.
    "Athenians" at, 218.
    Charles I. at, 67.
    letter dated at, 217.
    Magdalen College, letter dated at,
    218.
    —— President of, 218.
Oxfordshire, 216.
Oyanguren or Angoren, Don Luis de,
    Spanish Secretary of State, 36.
    —— letter to (?), 159.
    —— death of, 204.
    —— chamberlain of, 159.
Oyers, Bay of. See Oieras.

P.

Pacheco, Don Diego, 215.
Paige, John, of the Canary Company,
    signature of, 212.
Palatine, Princes. See Rupert, Maurice
    and Edward.
Palme, Val de, 100.
Palmer, Sir Geoffry, Attorney General,
    145, 218.
Panalva, Marques de. See Meneses,
    Don Luys de.
Pantoja, Don Balthazar de Roixas,
    Governor of the army of Galizia, 47.
Papists, bill against, not passed, 127.
    laws against, to be put in force,
    127.
Paris, 43, 147, 215, 227.
    Bastile at, prisoner in, 33.
    letter dated at, 208.
    travellers to and from, 5, 7, 8, 184.

Parker :
Captain, 174
John, 80.
Nicholas, Consul, at Algiers, letter of, 214.
Parliament (of the Commonwealth), 12, 15.
—— the Rump, "sits and governs three kingdoms," 16.
—— invasion of church land by, 256.
Parliament of Charles II., 77, 79, 127, 179.
adjournment or prorogation of, 79, 127, 147.
and supplies or revenue, 77, 80, 87.
and the Act of Uniformity, 80.
attends the King, 152.
bills in, 127.
consents to the Duke of York having full power over the fleet, 179.
dissolution of, 27.
meeting or session of, 48, 66, 147, 168.
members of, 147.
—— Bill for regulating the election of, 149.
message to, from the King, 147.
proscription of priests and Jesuits demanded by, 74.
refuses the King's wish for toleration, 77, 80.
temper of, 80, 84, 87.
Parliamentary affairs, 79
Parma, resident from, in Spain, 170.
Pasquas, the benign time of, 214.
Patrick, Father, 226, 227, 229, 231, 234, 235, 239, 240.
Paulinge, Captain, killed, 104, 105
Peach, William, 67.
Pearson or Person, Colonel, 161.
—— regiment of, 161.
Pembroke, Earl of (Philip Herbert), 10, 14.
—— his wife, 14.
—— his son. See Herbert, William, Lord.
Penn, Sir William, 170, 201.
Pennaranda (Penneirandy), Conde de, 235, 240, 254.
Percival, Mr., 192.
Perkins, a bailiff, murdered, 191.
Perry, Ensign, 223.
Person. See Pearson.
Peterborough, Earl of (Henry Mordaunt), Governor of Tangier, 37 (2), 80, 119, 121, 182, 187.
—— his return to England, 91, 110, 111, 120.
Physicians, Bill for granting a charter to, 149 (2), 150.
Pillory, persons set in the, 145.
Pimentell, Don Antonio, 184, 186.
Pinheros, convent dos, 100.
Pirates, 70.
Plague, the, 192, 206, 210, 235, and see London, the plague in.
increase of, 218, 219.

Plague, the—cont.
decrease of, 212, 213 (2), 230.
disappearance of, 241.
distraction caused by, 216-218.
news of, cannot be suppressed, 201.
precautions against in Spain, 199, 207, 209, 210, 237.
Play, acted in England, 231.
Plesse, or Plece, Mons. de la, 109 (2), 114.
Plymouth (Plimouth), 41, 175, 209, 210.
fort of, letter dated at, 205.
French troops embarking from, 91, 118.
ships of, 220, 221 (2).
Poleron, island of, 144, 150.
Pollen, Lieutenant, killed, 122.
Ponce or Ponze de Leon, Don Luis, 232 (2).
Ponte, Conde de. See Sande, Marques de.
Ponteval, Conde de, 41.
Pontevedra, Condestable at, 241.
letters dated at, 155, 241.
prisoner at, 208.
Poole, Captain William, 143, 158.
Pope, the (Alexander VII.), 36, 55, 71, 83, 232.
—— letter to, 62.
—— Commissioners of, 71.
—— Corsican Guard of, attack upon the French Ambassador by, 62.
Popish books and trinkets, 145.
Port Alegre, Bishop of. See Russell.
troops at, 56.
Porta Santa Maria. See Port St. Mary.
Port au Prince (Porto Prince), Cuba, 136.
Port de la Plata, Hispaniola, 138.
Portland, Earl of, 72.
Port Mahon or Mayon, Minorca, 160.
Porto del Rey, 102, 107.
Porto Rico. See Puerto Rico.
Port St. Mary or Porta Santa Maria, 130, 189, 196, 254.
Dutch Commissary at, 251.
letters dated at, 188, 190, 214, 237.
prisoner at, 165, 211.
Portsmouth, 134, 141, 219.
bill of health from, 241.
Queen Catherine lands at, 27.
letter dated at, 28.
Portugal
Don Antonio of, 39.
Don Sebastian of, 36, 170.
King John I. of, victory of, 85.
John IV., late King of, 36, 49, 67.
—— anniversary of the proclaiming of, 49.
—— Councillors of, 97.
—— persons "marked with a black coal by," 96.
Alfonso VI., King of, 17, 19-21, 24, 26, 36, 40, 51, 55, 57, 64, 66, 69, 73 (2), 78, 81, 82, 89, 92, 96, 123 (3), 128, 180, 203, 204, 212, 238, 244, 245.

Portugal, Alfonso VI., King of—*cont.*
—— as Señor or Conde of Portugal, 40.
—— as King of Brazil, 38.
—— letters from, 16, 26, 29 (2), 129 (3), 131, 132.
—— letters to, 22, 28, 30, 31, 47, 75.
—— agent of, in London. *See* Colonel Sir Augustine.
—— audiences of, 33, 50, 52.
—— Commissioners of, 52.
—— Commissioners to, 161.
—— dues owing to. *See* Brazil ships.
—— favourite of. *See* Castelmelhor, Conde de.
—— gentleman of the bedchamber to, 97.
—— message from, 53, 121.
—— his payment of his sister's dowry. *See* Catherine, Queen, dowry of.
—— brother of. *See* Infante Pedro, *below.*
—— takes the government, 29-32.
—— and Sir Richard Fanshaw, 33, 49, 56, 85, 121, 126, 129, 131, 132.
—— demands to sign as King, 36, 38, 39.
—— and the English troops, 37, 45, 55, 91, 161.
—— danger of his yielding to Spain, 38.
—— proposed marriage of, with a Princess of Orleans, 44, 63, 71, 184, 234, 249.
—— raises the price of gold, 51, 69.
—— movements or plans of, 61, 85 (2), 92, 94, 143, 233.
—— a yacht suggested as a present for, 62.
—— sends Major-General O'Brien to England, 68.
—— and the delivery of Bombay to England, 89, 90.
—— keeping of the feast of Corpus Christi by, 92.
—— tries to pacify the people, 93.
—— report that he is killed, 93.
—— orders the army to give battle, 98.
—— information of the battle of Ameixial sent to, 106.
—— Don Juan's standard sent to, 109 (2).
—— invitation from, to the English commanders, 126.
—— Lord Teviot visits, 130.
—— renewed negotiations of, with Spain, 131, 132, 140.
—— and his Spanish prisoners, 141.
—— present sent by, to Tangier, 200.

Portugal—*cont.*
Queen regent of, Luisa [de Guzman], widow of King John IV., 19-21, 23-25, 28, 61, 62, 70, 80, 128.
—— documents signed by, 16, 26.
—— letters from, 26 (2), 28, 29.
—— letters to, 16, 17, 28, 31 (2).
—— chaplains of, 56.
—— character of, 16, 17, 21, 30.
—— Confessor of. *See* Rosario, Frey Domingo del.
—— Counsellors of, 97.
—— ministers of, 69.
—— physician of, 51.
—— regency of, 36, 57.
—— resigns the government, 29-31, 53, 57, 69, 70, 94.
—— accused of exhausting Portugal for the sake of her daughter, 69.
—— sends her people to help against the mob, 94.
Infante Pedro of, the King's brother, 38, 93, 130.
—— marriage of, 249.
Portugal, *casual notices, passim.*
affairs of, 22, 56, 70, 83, 123, 124, 129, 131, 244.
agent sent to England by, 30.
alliance of, with England, 16, 18-21, 23, 38, 42, 89, 90, 244.
Ambassadors of, 45, 64.
—— to England. *See* Sande, Marques de.
—— to France. *See* Soure, Conde de.
—— to Holland. *See* Miranda, Conde de.
Ambassadors to, 45.
—— from England. *See* Fanshaw, Sir Richard, and Sandw'ch, Ea.l of.
—— —— (*temp.* John I.), 85.
—— from France (late), 64.
and Spain, relations of, *passim.*
army of, 18, 50, 85, 92, 97, 153, 203.
—— character of, 84, 95, 106, 114, 160.
—— commanders of, incapacity or indolence of, 84, 97, 106, 107, 114, 116.
—— desertions from, 98.
—— Generals of, 101, 104, *and see* Marialva *and* Villa Flor, Marques de.
—— —— lodgings of, 116.
—— Lieut.-General of, 116.
—— movements of, 98-105, 107, 215, 222.
—— officers of, 36.
—— —— Camp-Master General, 161.
—— —— General of the Artillery, 161.
—— —— General of the Horse, 161.
—— prisoners taken by, 115 (2).
—— Viador of, 109.

Portugal, army of—*cont.*
—— march of, to relieve Evora, 92, 102, 107.
—— skirmishes of, with the rebels, 100, 101.
—— victory of. *See* Ameixial, battle of.
—— campaign of, will be stopped by the heat, 114, 119.
aversion of, to the admittance of strangers, 65.
Bishops in, 72.
Brazil fleet of, 142.
bull-fights in, 22, 127, 129.
business of, delayed by the Lord Chancellor's illness, 54, 57, 60.
cautionary towns in, 59, 65.
cipher used in, 156.
coast of, piracies upon, 51.
—— Spanish fleet going to, 249.
coinage of, raising of the value of, 51, 69, 94.
Condado in, 215.
condition of, 37, 52, 57, 58, 60, 61, 91, 142.
correspondence with, falls to Bennet, 74 (3), 75.
Council of, 40, 84, 86, 91, 92, 98, 111, 123, 233.
Court of, or Court of Lisbon, 40, 41, 49, 56 (2), 61, 64, 84, 98, 105, 141, 153, 161, 180, 203, 223, 238.
—— bribery at, 33.
—— ceremonies or festivities of, 33, 34, 49, 92, 118.
—— factions in, 18.
—— French agents at, 83.
—— the Governor of Evora afraid to appear at, 97.
—— negligence or affront shown by, 127-129.
Crown or Kingdom of, 18, 34, 37, 45, 53, 56, 71, 160.
—— affection for, or desire to help, 16, 28 (2), 31 (2), 32.
—— devolution of, 38, 52.
—— has been on the verge of ruin, 124.
—— help for, from England, 18, 31, 52, 53, 58-63, 74, 75, 99, 244.
English army or troops, for or in. 29 (3), 37, 38, 43, 44, 55, 59, 60, 66, 76, 80, 98, 111, 114, 118, 121, 122, 153, 161.
—— at Ameixial and Evora, 101-109, 114-116, 118.
——"comical passages" told of, 118.
—— commissioners from, to the King, 161.
—— discontent or desertion of, 32, 42, 44, 51, 71, 84.
—— endeavours of the Spaniards to entice over, 52.
—— good conduct and valour of, 56, 84, 101-106, 109, 110, 115, 116, 118, 119, 121, 122, 142, 160, 223.
—— late Lieut.-Colonel of. *See* Molesworth, Guy.

Portugal, English army or troops, for or in—*cont.*
—— losses of, 105, 122, 223.
—— necessities of, or money needed for, 32, 37, 40, 43, 44, 46, 48, 51, 52, 54, 57, 60, 66, 76, 83, 84, 86, 98, 106, 110, 114, 117, 122, 125, 126, 142, 153, 161.
—— officers of, 32, 45, 83, 111.
—— —— letter and petition of, 74, 86.
—— —— letter to, 86.
—— —— killed and wounded, 161.
—— to be paid from the Queen's portion, 54, 57, 66, 74, 76, 81, 86, 91, 111.
—— paymaster general to, 61.
—— Count Schonberg appointed to the command of, 64, 74, 76, 86.
—— proposed removal of, 76, 81, 119, 122, 126.
—— reduced numbers of, 119, 142, 223.
English army in (former), 29, 31.
English envoy to. *See* Southwell, Sir Robert.
—— merchants in, 18, 52, 56.
—— minister for, 23.
fleet of, 18.
French agent in. *See* Colbert.
—— troops for or in, 40-42, 44, 63, 91, 98, 105, 111, 124, 142, 153, 160, *and see* Schonberg, regiment of.
garrisons of, 92, 101.
lack of shipping in, 44.
ministers or government of, 18, 43, 53-55, 57 (2), 60, 61, 63, 65, 68, 69, 73, 86, 92, 93, 110, 112, 125, 129, 142, 153, 160, 180, 203, 204, 223.
Ministros de letras, 203 (2).
nobility of, 32, 93, 94.
patron saints of, 50.
payments by, to the English troops, 43, 44.
—— for the Infanta's dowry. *See* Catherine, Queen.
Regidor of, 93, 96.
royal family of, restoration of, 49.
Secretary of State. *See* Macedo, Antonio de Sousa.
—— *de la puridad*. *See* Castelmelhor, Conde de.
Spanish prisoners in, 105, *and see* Liche, Marques de ; Guzman, Don Añello : *and* Alarçon, Don Francisco de.
succour given to, by Queen Elizabeth, 39.
title of Señor or Conde de, 40.
towns of, in correspondence with Don Juan, 125.
—— governors of, 56.
trade of, 18, 19, 89.
treaty of, with England, *passim.*
—— with Holland, 19, 20.
—— with Spain, proposed, *passim.*

Portugal, treaty of, with Spain—cont.
—— —— preliminary articles of,
36.
—— —— Commissioners for, 49,
51, 64.
victory or successes of, 142, 203,
and see Ameixial, and Villa
Viciosa, battles of.
—— the fruit gained by, 141 (2).
want of horses in, 119.
war with Spain, passim.
and France, 131, 243.
and Holland or the Low Countries,
19, 20, 52, 125.
Sir Richard Fanshaw sent to. See
Fanshaw.
Portuguese or the Portuguese, casual
allusions, passim.
cáptain, gallantry of, 160.
character of, 18, 39, 40, 61, 64, 83,
95, 114, 124.
crown or crusado, value of, 30, 34,
46, 53.
in Brazil. See Brazil.
in the West Indies. See West
Indies.
in the East Indies. See East
Indies.
language, letters, &c., written in,
16, 25-27, 29 (2), 34, 47 (2), 49,
63 (2), 68 (3), 72, 75, 85 (2), 86,
100 (2), 101, 106, 110, 113, 115
(2), 121, 129 (2), 141 (2), 181,
203, 204 (2).
sent away from England, 33.
ships, 182, 208.
Povey [Thomas], 196.
Powell, a prisoner at Havanna, 135.
Pratt, Captain, 246.
Price, John, 26, 141, 143, 178, 180, 222,
223.
Pride, Captain William, declaration by,
136.
Priests and Jesuits, proscription of, demanded by Parliament, 74.
Privy Council, 46, 48, 54, 57, 73, 83,
145, 212.
—— clerk of (Thomas Fanshaw),
257.
Privy Seals, alluded to, 1, 2, 21, 53,
132.
Prize office and commissioners, 175.
Probe, ——, Esq., 145.
Proverb quoted, 112.
Puerto Rico, Porto Rico, or Porta Rica,
island of, West Indies, 117 (2), 134-
139.
castle, governor, inquisition, &c., in,
135-139.
Prince Maurice at. See Maurice.
St. Joan de, town of, 135.
Puntall (near Cadiz), ships at, 199.
Putney, letter dated at, 212.
Pyrenees, treaty of, 10.

Q

Quama, village of, island of St Germans, 138.
Querer pro solo querer, Spanish play
translated by Fanshaw, 11, 237.

R

Rainbow, Dr. Edward, made Bishop of
Carlisle, 148.
Rand:
Andrew, 34.
John, 34.
Ratisbon, 149.
Ravens, Edmond, 221.
Rawdon:
Sir Marmaduke, 67.
Col. Thomas, his son, 67.
Rear Admiral, 171.
Rebellion, the late, 219.
Requests, Master of, 9, 10, 78, 139,
216, and see Fanshaw, Sir Richard.
Reymes or Reames, Col. [Buller], 162,
164.
Rhotta or Rotta, fort of, 187, 221, 251.
Richards, Mr., 186.
Richmond, Duke of (Charles Stuart),
172.
Rioles, the Spaniards march towards,
83.
Roach. See Roch.
Robinson:
Captain, 51.
Consul (at Lisbon), 66.
Roch or Roach, Captain, 116, 161.
Roche, John, an Irish gentleman, 26.
Rochelle, ships to or from, 208, 209,
249.
Roco, Don Pedro de, Master of the
Ceremonies at the Spanish Court,
155.
Rodonde, near Evora, 98.
Rolls, Master of. See Grimston, Sir
Harbottle.
Roman Catholics, 78.
Rome, 37.
agent to, 83.
attack upon the French Ambassa-
dor in, 62.
Romsey, Major, 161.
Rosario, Frey Domingo del (O'Daly),
Confessor of the Queen Regent of Por-
tugal, and Bishop elect of Cimbra,
26, 33.
—— —— letter from, 24.
Roscarrock, Col., 36, 51 (2).
Rotta. See Rhotta.

Rotterdam, breaking of the dykes at, 222.
Roubinet, Martin, 118.
Rouen, 179.
 letter dated at, 179.
Row, Thomas, declaration by, 136.
Rowe, Sir Thos., embassy of, to Germany, 132.
Royal aid, money raised on the security of, 192.
Royal Company. *See* Guinea Company.
Royal Family, the, good health of, 160.
Rudyard, Captain, 156.
Rumbold, Henry, 32.
 —— letter of, 71.
Rupert (Robert), Prince Palatine of the Rhine, 79, 136, 168, 199, 201, 218, 219.
 letter to, 117.
 fleet or squadron of, 135, 137, 138, 168, 195, 199.
 brother of. *See* Maurice, Prince.
Russell, R., Bishop of Port Alegre, 20, 23, 47, 58, 69, 77.
 —— letter of, 47.
 —— letter to, 60.
Russia, Emperor of, 146.
 —— ambassador to, 146.
Rutherford:
 Andrew, Lord, and (in 1663), Earl of Teviot, 130.
 —— letters from, 90, 148.
 —— letters to, 99, 121.
 —— his wife, the Countess of Teviot, 158.
 —— his chaplain, at Dunkirk, 130.
 —— kinsman of, 90, 95.
 —— goes as governor to Tangier, 58, 59, 65, 80, 90, 95, 99.
 —— at Tangier, 110, 111, 119, 120, 143, 151, 164.
 —— death of, 152, 153, 156-158, 182, 187.
 (Roterford) Sir Thomas, Lord, 229.
Ruyter (Rutter, Ruder), Adrian Michael de, Dutch Admiral, and his fleet, 151, 155, 162, 164, 166, 168, 170, 173, 175, 178, 185, 187, 188, 193, 200, 204.
 wife of, 200.
Ryder, ——, 257.
Ryves, Dr. Brune, Dean of Arches, letter of, 216.
 son of, 216.

S

St. Ageo, West Indies, 137.
St. Albans, Earl of (Henry Jermyn), Governor of Jersey, 227.
St. Andrews, hangman of, 151.
St. Antonio, fort of. *See* Evora.
St. Christophers, island of, 137, 138.
 —— governor of, 135, 137.

St. George, the patron saint of Portugal, 50.
St. George's Day, keeping of, 79, 80.
St. Germains:
 the French Court at, 147.
 letters dated at, 3, 62.
St. Germans, island of, West Indies, 137, 138.
St. Iago upon Cuba, capture of, by the English, 34, 35.
 castle, governor, &c., of, 35.
St. Iago, Hispaniola, 138.
St. Julian, castle and governor of, 74.
St. Lucar, 143, 201, 235.
 —— governor of, 143.
St. Malo's, 182, 251.
St. Mary Port. *See* Port St. Mary.
St. Olalla, 239.
St. Peter's Island, West Indies, 136.
St. Roman, Marques de, viceroy of Valencia, 162, 169, 232.
St. Sebastian. *See* San Sebastian.
St. Uvall, 38.
Sale of lands, bill appointing registrars for, 148.
Salee, Sallee, or Sally, 32, 168, 202, 210.
 the Saint Abdala of. *See* Abdala.
Salisbury, Bishop of [Dr. Henchman], 72.
Salisbury or Sarum, 215.
 —— letter dated at, 205.
Salmon, Francisco, accountant of the Spanish navy, 132.
Salt, ship laden with, 221.
Salvaterra de Magos, 141, 238.
 —— letters dated at, 141, 233.
Salway, Major, 144.
Samana, West Indies, 118.
Sande, Marques de (Francisco de Melo, Conde de Ponte), Portuguese Ambassador in England, 16-18, 20, 21, 26, 34, 45, 46, 48, 53, 55-57, 60, 64, 69, 72, 76, 77, 80, 86-88, 91, 95, 98.
 letters, &c., to, 27 (?), 34, 56, 62, 81.
 memorial by, 80.
 brother of, 34.
 servants of, 25.
San Domingo or St. Dominique, island of. *See* Hispaniola.
San or St. Domingo, town of, 117 (2), 137.
 —— fort of St. Jeronymo at, 137.
Sandwich, Earl of (Edward Montague), ambassador extraordinary to Portugal, 17, 21, 23, 25.
 letters of, 22 (2).
 as Master of the Wardrobe, warrants to, 133.
 fleet of, 17, 165, 166.
 rear-admiral of, 171.
 retinue of, 244.
 secretary of. *See* Creed, John.
 father of, 255.
 to command one squadron of the fleet, 201.

Sandwich, Earl of—*cont.*
- embassy of, to Madrid, 218, 219, 225, 227, 229-231, 236, 240-245, 249, 253, 254.
San Sebastian, 3, 203, 233.
letters dated at, 224, 232.
English Consul at. *See* Morgan, Valentine.
Santirena or Satirani, Conde de, 114.
Sardinia (Sardenia) galleys, 202.
viceroy of, 202.
Sarmento, Don Garcia, 108.
Saussay, Mons. de, 109.
Saxony, house of, 232.
Scanderoone, ships to, 165.
Scarborough, ships to, 191.
Schamps, Fedric de, letter from, 117.
Scheveningen (Sckeevling), 193.
Schonberg (Schomberg, Chomberg), Frederic Armand, Comte de, 26, 41, 52, 58, 115, 116, 120, 122, 124, 142, 161, 178, 180, 233.
letters from, 82, 84, 97, 99, 106, 108, 113, 143, 179, 233.
letters to, 99, 105, 111, 126.
chaplain of, 130.
house of, at Lisbon, 40.
lieutenant of. *See* Plesse, Sieur de la.
praise of, 64, 105, 106, 109, 110.
regiment of, 109 (2), 113.
— horse, 122.
— foot, 161.
trumpeter of, 109.
[Mainhardt], eldest son of, 114.
"winding discourses," of, 64.
appointed commander of the English troops, 64, 74, 76, 86, 97.
is a Protestant and speaks English, 76, 86.
is dissatisfied with the conduct of the war, 97, 98, 106.
proceedings of, in the campaign, 101, 105-110, 119, 120.
Scotland, 127, 152, 175, 188, 192, 249.
Archbishop or Primate of. *See* Sharp, James.
Archbishops of [St. Andrew's and Glasgow], 144.
Charles II.'s expedition to, 4.
Chancellor of, 144.
Council of, 144.
fines to be paid in, 145, 146.
High Commission Court established in, 144, 146, 147, 151 (2).
ministers in, turned out for nonconformity, 151.
west of, suspected persons in, 191.
Scots, Irish, rising of, 178.
in Spain, 248.
Scowen or Scawen, William, Judge of the Admiralty in Cornwall, 205, 219.
— letters from, 178, 202, 219.
— family of, 205, 219.
— kinsman of. *See* Scowen, Juan.
or Scone, Don Juan, 179, 202, 205.
— letter of, 219.
— father of, 205.
— kindred of, certificate by, 219.

Secretaries of State, 9, 48, 78, 89, *and see* Nicholas, Sir Edward, Morice, Sir William and Bennet, Henry, Lord Arlington.
examination by, 175.
partition of provinces between the two, 74.
Semple, a scrivener, 151.
Sentences or punishments, 145, 146, 171.
Serjeants-at-arms, 53, 147.
Serpa, near Evora, 109.
Setuval, intended march of Don Juan to, 52.
Seven deadly sins, the, Spanish Counsellors of State called, 232.
Sevila, Don Gasper de, 33.
Seville, 143, 190, 232, 245-247.
Assistente of, 232.
Consul of, 193.
Council at, 152.
gaol, English prisoners in, 152, 158 (2), 166.
judge conservador in, 186.
letters dated at, 143, 152, 158 (2), 166, 254.
Seymour (Seamor), Harry, 5 (2).
— servant of, 5.
Sharp, James, Archbishop of St. Andrew's, Primate of Scotland, 144, 151.
Sharpe, Captain, troop of, 122.
Shaw, Captain John, 209.
Sheldon :
Dr. Gilbert, Bishop of London, 72, 82.
— letters to, 81, 113.
— intended promotion of, 113.
Mr., 191.
Sheppard, Captain, 221.
Sherrington, William, 238.
Shipman, Sir Abraham, 89, 90.
Ships, English, *casual notices, passim, and see* Fleet, the
admitted to Flemish ports, 219.
at Tangier. *See* Tangier.
bill for securing of, against pirates, 151.
captain of a, killed by the Spaniards, 254.
captains of, to observe the conditions of the peace with Spain, 193.
commanders of, letter to, 100.
engagement of, with Dutch vessels, 183, 188, 191.
French ships taken by, 198.
lent to the Duke of York, 123 (2).
lost, 171, 172, 179.
— in the West Indies. *See* Maurice, Prince, shipwreck of.
pratique demanded by and refused to, in the Spanish ports, 158-161, 166, 169, 206, 209-211, 213, 214, 240, 241 (2), 248.
precautions to be taken by, regarding the plague, 110.
"private men-of-war," to be set out against the Dutch, 183.
prize, 148, 151, 172, 174.

Ships, English—*cont.*
taken by the Dutch. *See* Dutch.
——, list of, 220, 221.
taken by the French, 217.
value of, 145.
victuallers, taken, 2.0, 211, 221.
named ;—
Adventure, 220.
Advice, 143, 217.
Amiral (French), 251.
Angel Gabriel (French), 221.
Ann, 183.
Anna, 252.
Antelope, 143, 174, 241.
Assistance, 170.
Augustine, 123.
Benjamin, 221.
Bilbao Merchant, 217.
Bilbeaud (French), 251.
Bonadventure, 174.
Bona Esperanza, 166.
Briar, 136.
Bristol, 165.
Bristol Merchant, 97.
Centurion, letter dated aboard, 34.
Cesar (French), 251.
Charles, 132, 224.
Colchester, 171.
Concord, 34, 145.
Concorde (French), 252.
Croissant (French), 251.
Crown, 165, 185, 186, 188, 190,
195, 197, 199, 206.
—— captain of. *See* Wager, Captain.
Dauphin (French), 252.
Deliverance, 221.
Diamond, 190.
Dove, 221.
Dragon (French), 252.
Dunkirk, 170.
Elbeuf (French), 252.
Elizabeth, 221.
Endeavour, 221.
Escureuil (French), 251.
Essex, 177.
Estoille de Dianne (French), 252.
Fidelity, 210, 221.
Flambeau (French), 252.
Foresight, 185.
—— letter dated aboard, 183.
Fortune, 208.
Françoise (French), 252.
Good Hope, 179.
Great Charity, 123.
Greyhound, 32, 145.
Guillaume (French), 252.
Hampshire, 246, 247, 249.
Hector, 34, 143.
—— letter dated aboard, 111.
Henry, 170.
Henry Bonaventure, 166.
Hercule (French), 251.
Honest Seaman, 136.
Infante (French), 251.
John, 187, 221.
Jullue (French), 252.
King Solomon, 171.
Ligournois (French), 252.

Ships, named—*cont.*
Lily, 221.
Lion, 244.
Lion d'Or (French), 252.
Lion Rouge (French), 252.
Little Lewis, 34.
Loyal Merchant, 221.
Margarita. See Santa Margarita.
Mary, formerly the *Speaker*, 192.
—— letter dated aboard, 237.
Mathias, 123, 164.
Merlin (Marling), 211 (3), 221.
Mermaid, 32.
Nonsuch, loss of, 172.
Norwich, 32.
Nostre Dame (French), 252.
Palme (French), 252.
Palmier (French), 252.
Pearl, 221.
Perle (French), 252.
Phœnix, 110, 169.
—— loss of, 172.
Plymouth, letters dated aboard,
165, 169, 172-174.
Portland, 40.
Princess, 20.
Puny, 220.
Reserve, 95, 99, 126.
—— letters dated aboard, 90 (2).
Resolution, letters dated aboard,
148, 154, 158, 160, 165, 166.
Reyne or *Reyna* (French), 249, 252.
Roi David (French), 252.
Rose, 221.
Royal Catherine [merchant], 63,
64, 209.
Royal Catherine (ketch), 221.
Royal James, Earl of Sandwich's
admiral ship, 21, 170.
—— letters dated aboard, 22, 26.
Royal Sovereign, 201.
Royalle (French), 252.
Ruby, 55.
Ste. Anne (French), 252.
St. Anthoine (French), 252.
St. Augustin (French), 251.
St. Charles (Spanish), letter dated
aboard, 211.
St. Cyprien (French), 251.
St. Joseph (French), 251 (2).
St. Lewis (Dutch), 194.
St. Louis (French), 251.
Salamander, 221.
Sampson, 34.
Santa Margarita (Spanish), 201,
209, 212, 252.
Sauveur (French), 252.
Soleil (French), 252.
Soleil d'Afrique (French), 252.
Speaker. See Mary.
Speedwell, 221.
Swallow, 244.
Thérese (French), 251.
Thomas, 221.
Tiger, 221.
Trois Roy (French), 251.
Turtugo, 136.
Unicorn, 55.
Vierge (French), 251.

Ships, named—*cont.*
　Ville de Rouen (French), 251.
　Waterhouse, 254.
　—— declaration by the crew of, 254.
　Westergate, 72, 73 (2).
　—— letter dated aboard, 74.
　William, 221.
　—— *and John*, 221.
　—— *and Mary*, 221, 238.
Signet book extracts, 133
Signet Office, 132.
Silva, Duerte [Edward] da, 46, 47, 53, 69, 77, 80.
　statement by, 30.
Sinous, Lieutenant, 223.
Small, Samuel, 238.
　letter of, 238.
　kinsman of, 238.
Smith :
　Lord Chief Justice of Ireland, 215.
　"Customer," daughter of, 257.
　Admiral (Captain) Sir Jeremy, 110, 111, 192, 201, 243-246, 250, 253.
　—— letters from, 237, 243.
　—— letters to, 237, 240, 243, 244, 246, 248.
　—— fleet of, 226, 229, 235, 237, 241, 243 (2), 245.
Smyrna factor, 165.
　ships or fleet, 178, 179, 185, 186, 199, 210, 250, 251.
　mariners of, 179.
Snowden, Captain William, 221.
Soldiers, disabled, 206.
Sole Bay, 195.
Solicitor-General. *See* Finch, Sir Heneage.
Somerset :
　Duke of (John Seymour), letter from, 257.
　Duchess of, 145.
Sound, the, 12.
Sousa, Antonio de. *See* Macedo.
Southampton, Earl of (Thomas Wriothesley), Lord High Treasurer of England, 34, 46, 53, 65, 68, 77, 80, 132, 133.
　—— letter from, 134.
　—— report by, 34.
Southerland, Alexander, 187.
　—— letter of, 187.
Southn river (North America), 149.
South Sea coast, claimed by the Dutch, 144.
Southward Cape, 197.
Southwark, assizes at, 146.
Southwell, Sir Robert, envoy to Portugal, 218, 226, 229, 236-240, 246, 255.
　—— letters of, 241, 254.
　—— servants of, 239.
Souvre or Soure, Juan da Costa, Conde de, ambassador from Portugal to France, 64.
Spain, King of :
　John I., defeat of, 85.
　Philip II., 38.
　Philip IV., 1, 2, 36, 38-40, 43, 47,

Spain, Philip IV., King of—*cont.*
　49, 52, 81, 88, 89, 138, 142, 148, 158, 166, 168, 174, 176, 183, 195, 207, 209, 211, 213, 233.
　letters of, 130, 132.
　letters of credence to, 29, 140.
　chief minister of. *See* Haro, Don Luis Mendez de.
　commanders of, 97, *and see* Juan, Don.
　knighthood desired from, 179, 202, 205.
　memorial to, 193.
　infirmity or illness of, 36, 78, 181, 185.
　has written concerning Lord Windsor's action in Cuba, 71.
　movements of, 155, 182, 185, 190, 197.
　death of, 205 (2), 209.
　—— (false) report of, 129.
　second wife of. *See* Spain, Queen of.
　son of. *See* Charles II., *below*.
　illegitimate sons of, 205, *and see* Juan, Don.
　daughter of. *See* Infanta, the. *below.*
　sister of. *See* France, Queen dowager of.
　Queen of [Marie Anne of Austria, second wife of Philip IV.], 36-38, 155, 185 (2), 186, 220, 222, 229, 231, 234, 236, 239, 240, 242, 249, 253.
　gives birth to a son, 22.
　and Lord Sandwich's embassy, 225, 228, 229, 235.
　confessor of [Eberhard von Neidhart], 232 (2), 234, 240.
　brother of. *See* Emperor [Leopold].
　Infante or Prince of, death of, 22.
　Infante Charles of, 36, 37, 185.
　birth of, 22.
　as King Charles II., 207, 216, 222, 224, 237, 241, 247 (2).
　Infanta of, 37, 192.
　as "the Empress," 185 (2), 186, 201, 247, 249.
　marriage of, to the Emperor, 247.
Spain, *passim.*
　Admirante General of, 195.
　agent of, in England, 47, *and see* Moledi, Don Patricio.
　ambassadors of, 45, *also ;*—
　　to England. *See* Molina, Count.
　　to France. *See* Fuente, Marques de.
　ambassadors or ministers to, 155, 170, 239, *also ;*—
　　from England. *See* Fanshaw, Sir Richard.
　　from France, 43, 242, *and see* Embrun, Archbishop of.
　　from Holland, 170.
　ambassadors extraordinary to. *See* Cottington, Lord ; Hyde, Sir Edward.

Spain—*cont.*
Sir John Digby's and Sir Francis Cottington's embassy to, 132.
animosity to the English in, 173, 192, 232.
and England, 13, 38, 47, 74, 81, 88, 182, 240.
and Gayland. *See* Gayland.
and Holland, 99, 151, 241.
and Portugal, *passim.*
and Tangier. *See* Tangier.
army, of, campaigns of, against Portugal, 25, 50, 82-84, 98-107, 174, 182, 185, 186, 196.
—— capture and loss of Evora by. *See* Evora.
—— defeat of. *See* Ameixial and Villa Viciosa, battles of.
—— commanders of, 36, 202, *and see* Juan, Don ; Caracena, Marquis of ; Castel-Rodrigo, Marquis of ; Marcyn, Count.
—— losses of, 85, 100, 101, 104, 105, 108, 116.
—— nobles in, lose their baggage and coaches, 104.
——, officers in :—
—— —— Mestres de Campo, 105, 108, 176.
—— —— Lieut.-Colonel, 108.
—— —— Commissaries General, 108.
—— —— other officers, 108.
Assienda of, President of, 235, 240.
bad faith of, 37, 119.
change of government in, 125, 209.
Commissioners from, 45.
Council or Council of State of, 160, 161, 191, 225, 235, 240, 254.
—— of war in, 235, 240.
Counsellors of State called the seven deadly sins, 232.
or Madrid, Court of, 1-4, 17, 147, 148, 152, 154, 162, 168, 175, 182, 185, 198, 202, 210, 229, 234-236, 246.
—— ceremonies of, 155, 225, 239.
—— dilatoriness of, 159-161, 178.
—— master of the ceremonies at, 155, 239.
—— temper or views of, 50, 201, 202, 225-227, 229, 231, 239, 242.
Crown or kingdom of, 173, 176.
—— friendship of England to, 1, 147, 237.
—— title of the French King to, 41.
Dutch admiral entertained in, 162.
—— resident in, 162.
English Consuls in, 182, 204, *and see under the various ports.*
—— deserters to, 42, 98.
—— factors or merchants in, 1, 181, 182, 201.
—— prisoners in, 163, 164, 166, 254, *and see* Seville.
—— subjects in, 181, 196, 248.
—— naturalized in, 187, *and see* Scowan, Juan.

Spain—*cont.*
fall of money in, 168.
former rule of, over Portugal, 124, 125.
galleons of, 197.
garrison of, 153, 241.
general of the galleys in, 215.
grandees of, 175, 202, 235.
horses from, 168.
inclinations of the people of Portugal towards, 18, 94, 124, 125.
judge conservadors for the English in, 184, 186.
ministers of, views of, 180, 213, 244.
Navy of, accountant of, 132.
—— Duke of Aveiro is to command, 185.
negotiations with, by Cromwell, 39.
orange ships to, 222.
overtures from, 96, 128.
partiality to the Dutch in, 162, 189, 190, 213, 220, 247.
pirates and rovers of, 155.
precautions against the plague in, 199, 210, 213, 237.
recovery of Jamaica and Tangier desired by, 243.
Secretaries of State in. *See* Oyanguren, Don Luis, *and* Loyala, Don Blasco de.
—— chamberlain of, 159.
secretary of war, 56.
stolen goods conveyed into, 206.
travellers to or from, 1, 3, 130, 132, 140, 176, 178, 235.
treaty of peace made by, with England, 66, *and see* Fanshaw, treaty concluded by.
—— with Queen Elizabeth, 43.
—— with France, 63, 202.
—— with Holland, 39.
—— (proposed) with Portugal, *passim.*
unpreparedness of, for war, 239.
a viceroy of, 202.
war of, 4.
—— with France, expected, 232.
—— with Portugal, *passim.*
Spaniards or Castilians, 39, 97, 98, 170, 206, 209, 234, 235, 240, 241.
captured by the Moors, 169, 207.
character or conduct of, 71, 130, 163, 195, 244, 254.
in the West Indies, 89, 117, 134-139.
Spanish Armada or fleet, 39, 110, 241, 249, 250, 254.
—— the great, alluded to, 43.
clime, business does not ripen as fast as fruit in, 119.
ensign, 118.
language, letters, &c., written in, 16, 17 (3), 25-29, 31 (3), 32, 47, 56, 57, 62, 68, 73-75, 85 (2), 91, 101 (2), 111, 117, 122 (2), 126, 129, 130-132, 141, 142, 152 (2),

Spanish language, letters, &c., written in—*cont.*
153, 159 (2), 165, 176 (2), 180, 190, 193 (2), 199, 203-205, 208, 209 (2), 215, 219, 222-224, 232 (2), 234, 236, 237, 243, 246-248, 253.
—— study or knowledge of, 140, 142.
letters, collection of, suggested, 11.
officials, unjust proceedings of, 155.
prisoners in Portugal, 114, *and see* Liche, Marques de ; Guzman, Don Añello de, *and* Alarçon, Francisco de.
—— —— list of, 123.
proverb, 197.
resident in England, 201.
ships, 135, 138.
—— rules for saluting, 202.
—— taken, 201, 207.
wine, 218.
Spragg, Captain, of the *Portland*, 40.
Stafford :
Captain John, 211, 221.
Philip, 241.
Stafforfe, Captain, 165.
Stainer or Stayner, Sir Richard, 25, 32.
Staines, William. 164.
Stansby, Captain, 101.
Stashous, Hollanders at, 137.
Steelé, Mrs., 191, 192.
Stephens, Major, 25.
Sterne, Dr. Richard, Bishop of Carlisle, translated to York, 148.
Stirling, camp at, 6.
Stockholm, burgesses of, 166.
Lord Carlisle's audience at, 166.
Stone, Mr., portra.t of the King by, 62.
Strafford, Earl of [Thomas Wentworth], as governor of Ireland, 1.
Straits, the, 176, 235.
ships in or near, 165, 173, 195, 201, 241, 245, *and see* Cadiz, ships at.
fleet from, has arrived at Plymouth, 175.
Strange, Philip, letter from, 163.
Subsidy Bill, passed, 127.
Sugar, trade in, 19, 23.
Summers, Captain John, 221.
Surgeons and apothecaries, 150.
Sutton, Captain, 114.
—— troop of, 122.
Suzel, 107.
Sweden, King of, 22.
plenipotentiary from, to England, *See* Friesendorff.
Sweden, money given to, by France, 125.
peace concluded with, 188.

T.

Taafe :
Col. Lucas, letter from, 173.

Taafe, Col. Lucas—*cont.*
—— pass for, 176.
—— regiment of, 173.
—— brother of, 173.
Nicholas, his nephew, 173.
Tafilet or Taffaletta, King of, 202 (2), 212.
Tagus, or river of Lisbon, 45, 62, 65, 74, 94.
Talavera de la Reyna, 239.
Talbot :
Captain, 174.
Sir Gilbert, master of the jewel-house, warrant to, 133.
Tallerand de Perigord, Prince de. *See* Chalais.
Tallidafe, Mr., a minister, 151.
Tangiér (Tanger), 25, 38, 59, 65, 122. 151, 160, 163, 181 (2), 182 (2), 187. 190, 194-197. 200, 201, 210, 211, 213, 215, 227, 231, 249, 250.
bay, 206.
—— letter dated from, 22.
commerce of, with Spain, 168, 169, 172, 185, 199, 207, 210.
Commissioners at, 206, 245.
committee for (in England), 58.
—— president of. *See* York, Duke of.
a corporation desired for, 164.
difficulties between the soldiers and merchants at, 197.
English fleet going to, or at, 22, 154, 158, 169, 174 (2), 219.
engineer at, 130.
fortifications at, 111, 119, 153, 156, 157, 164, 167, 169, 172, 190, 210.
Fort Ann at, 157.
Fort Royal at, 156, 157.
the French King has offered to buy, 173.
garrison of, 119, 124, 159, 186, 190, 194, 199.
—— defeat of, 152-154, 156, 186.
—— in Lord Peterborough's time, 186
—— good condition of, 32, 37, 121, 153, 157, 158, 160, 162-164, 167, 178, 182, 184, 186, 190, 194, 195, 201, 202 (2), 210, 212, 213, 241, 245, 250.
—— money, provisions, &c., for, 111, 119-121, 164, 167, 183, 194, 206, 207.
—— —— needed, 192, 207, 210. 211.
—— officers of, 156.
—— —— slain, 106.
—— poverty of, 157.
—— soldiers from, detained by Gayland, 169, 172, 181.
—— skirmishes of, with the Moors, 159.
governors of. *See* Peterborough, Earl of ; Rutherford, Lord (after Earl of Teviot), Belasyse, Lord.
—— *pro tem*. *See* Bridge, Sir Tobias.

Tangier, governor of—*cont.*
—— report that Lord Sandwich is to be, 230.
houses at, 25, 50, 80, 90, 99, 164.
importance of, to England, 184, 197, 210.
Irish party at, 197.
King's stores at, 157.
lazaretta at, 206.
letters dated at, 32, 148, 153, 156, 158, 159, 162 (2), 164 (2), 167, 168, 169, 171, 184, 186, 190, 192, 196, 201, 206, 209, 210, 212, 224, 245, 249, 250.
Lieutenant-governors of. *See* Fitzgerald *and* Norwood, Colonels.
merchants of, 99, 158, 164, 168, 206.
mole or mould at, 58, 87, 119, 164, 172, 173, 184, 210, 224.
Moors near, 197, 213, *and see* Gayland.
new town building near, 163.
precautions against the plague at, 206, 210, 213.
reported sale of, 183, 184.
runaway soldiers from, 207.
ships to or from, 51, 59, 11°, 124, 185, 186, 194, 232, 244, 250.
—— —— prize, 183, 214, 245.
—— —— victuallers, 210, 211 (2), 221, 229.
Spanish designs against, 37, 39, 130, 198, 207, 209, 214, 243.
—— governor of, 36.
state-house needed at, 99.
unlucky day for, 156, 184, 186, 190.
Upper Castle at, 170.
Tarifa or Tariffe, governor of, 206, 210.
packet-boat to and from, 195.
Tarroro, Conde de, 36.
—— son of. *See* Meneses, Don Luys de.
—— family of, 36.
Tenerife, 212.
consul and merchants at, 222.
Tera (Terra, Bera), the river, 83, 103, 107.
Terena, near Evora, 98, 121.
Teston, co. Kent, 258.
Tetuan or Tituan, in Morocco, 32, 151, 168, 202, 206, 207.
English captives in, 182, 207.
governor of, 25.
letter dated at, 207.
Teviot, Earl of. *See* Rutherford, Lord.
Texell, the river, 167, 179, 192, 193.
deputies sent to, 200.
Thames, the river, 145.
Bill for navigation of, 149.
Thomas, Mr., of Gray's Inn, 257.
Thore, Conde de, 25.
Thurlow, John, 13.
Tiddiman, Captain and Rear-Admiral, 171.
Tituan. *See* Tetuan.
Toledo (Tolethy), 223, 224.
letter dated at, 223.

Torbay, Dutch ships seized in, 171.
Torres Vedras, Conde de. *See* Alarçon, Francisco de.
Tortola (Tortolea), island of, 136.
deputy governor of, 137.
Tortuga, Turtugeo, or La Tortue, island and governor of, 117, 136-138.
—— letter, &c., dated at, 117, 136.
Toulon (Thollon), 32, 136, 217, 249.
Beaufort's fleet at, 241, 243, 245, 247.
Tower, the, officers of, 145.
plot to seize, 48.
prisoners in, 144, 145.
Trade, Committee for, 149, 150.
Tras los Montes, province of, 98.
Travers:
Captain, 126.
—— death of, 161.
—— wife of, 126.
Samuel, consul at Pontevedra, letters of, 155, 241.
Trelawny:
Captain or Major, 55, 86, 90, 111, 112, 114, 161.
—— company or troop of, 98, 122.
—— brothers of, 90.
Sir John, Bart., signature of, 219.
Tremesen, Turkish tribute at, 185.
Trerise, Baron of. *See* Arundel, Richard.
Trevor, Mark, 191.
Tring, co. Hertford, manor of, 256.
Tripoli, 169.
peace concluded with, 51.
Tromp, Trump or Van Tromp, Martin Haspertzoon, Dutch Admiral, 151, 200.
—— fleet of, 165, 178.
Tronco, Christopher, declaration by, 254.
Trump. *See* Tromp.
Tubingen, professor at, 6.
Tunbridge, the King and Queen at, 80, 127.
Tunis, 169, 185.
captives in, 217.
King of, 217.
peace concluded with, 51.
Turenne, Marshal or Prince de, 41, 91, 109, 127.
—— letter to, 124.
Turkey Company, 150.
Turkey, convoys for, 169.
Turks, 197, 209, *and see* Moors.
ot Algiers. *See* Algiers.
of Barbary, 206, 207.
Admiral's ship, 224.
[Christian] prisoners taken by, 63.
prizes taken by, 224, 231.
truce of, with the Emperor, 167.
Lord Belasyse dislikes to serve, against Christians, 201, 206.
Turner:
Captain, 161.
Sir Edward, sen., Speaker of the House of Commons, 127.
—— letter from, 167.

Turner—*cont.*
 Sir Edward, junior, his son, 160 (2), 168.
 John, deputy governor of the Canary Company, signature of, 212.
Twyann, Toyan, or Taiouan [Formosa], island of, 144.
Twynne, ——— (printer), execution of, 145, 146.

U.

Ulysses, the town of [Lisbon], 120.
Uniformity, Act of, 74, 80.
Utbert, Captain [Richard], 110, 178.

V.

Valador, Don Francisco, commissary General, 108.
Valença (Valensa), storm of, by the English troops, 160.
Valencia, 250.
 King's palace at, 162.
 viceroy of. *See* St. Roman, Marques de.
Valencia de Alcantra, Spanish forces at, 182.
Van Beuninghen, 174.
Vangoch, Dutch ambassador to England, 151.
Van Tromp. *See* Tromp.
Vassall, John, Consul at Malaga, death of, 190, 193.
Velosques, Captain John Frederisco, 154.
Venetians, the, 232.
Venice, ambassador from, to Spain, 170.
Venta del Duque or Vinda de Duque, 103.
Vernatti, Filibert or Philibert, 190, 216.
 ——— letters from, 188, 214.
Vic, Sir Harry de, 216.
Victoria or Vittoria, 195.
 secretary of the Franciscan Order at, 195.
Vienna, the Empress's journey to, 247.
Vigo, prize taken into, 238.
Villa Flor, Conde de (Don Sancho Manoel), commander in chief of the Portuguese army, 84, 98, 122.
 ——— accused of inactivity and incapacity, 98, 107, 109, 114.
Villa Umbrosa (Vilinbrose, Villin Brossey), Conde de, President of the *Assienda*, 235, 240.
Villa Viciosa, birthplace of Queen Catherine, 83, 197.
 ——— ——— Portuguese victory at, 197.
Vincennes, letter dated at, 63.
Vinda de Duque. *See* Venta del Duque.
Virginia, governor of. *See* Berkeley, Sir William.
 ——— plantation of, 6.

Virgin Islands, West Indies, 134, 137.
Vologda, in Russia, 146.
Vurburch, Juan Gidienson, commander of the Dutch fleet at Cadiz, 207 (2).
 ——— letters from and to, 208.
Vyner, Sir Thomas, 30.

W.

Wager or Wagger, Captain [Charles], commander of the *Crown* frigate, 186, 188-190, 195, 199.
Wakering, Mr., 256.
Walpoole, Edward, order signed by, 256.
Walsingham [Sir Francis], embassy of to France, 45.
War, Council of, 74.
 ——— on shipboard, 174.
Wardrobe, master of. *See* Sandwich, Earl of.
Ware Church, co. Hertford, vault of the Fanshaw family in, 257.
 Park, co. Hertford, 257, 258.
Wares, bay of. *See* Oieras, bay of.
Warren, Nicholas, signature of, 212.
Warwick, Sir Philip, 72, 187, 194, 218.
 letters of, 46, 77.
 letters to, 53, 68.
 wife of, 46, 54, 218.
 brother-in-law of. *See* Fanshaw, Sir Richard.
Watts, John, receiver for co. Hertford, receipt by, 256.
Webber, Walter, 221.
Webster, Mr., 5.
Weckerlin (Wakerly), Latin secretary, 9.
Westcombe :
 John, letter from, 198.
 Martin, consul at Cadiz, 160, 163, 187, 209, 210, 220.
 ——— letters from, 173, 177, 179, 181, 182, 186, 189 (2), 193, 195, 197, 199, 207-209, 211 (2), 214, 215, 219, 220, 241, 244-248, 250-253.
 ——— letters to, 148, 181, 183-186, 190, 192, 193, 196, 198, 199, 201, 204, 205, 206, 207, 211, 212 (2), 213, 220, 243, 245, 249.
 ——— house of, 143, 197, 248, 250.
 ——— imprisonment of, 189 (3), 190, 192, 193 (2), 244, 245, 247, 248 (2), 250 (3), 253.
 ——— notes or endorsements by, 159, 162, 164.
 ——— slave of, 250.
 ——— wife of, 291.
 ——— family of, 187.
West India Company, 82.
 ships, 192.
West Indies, the, 19, 39, 134-139, 177, 222.
 Cromwell's fleet in, 254.
 depositions taken in, 117, 134-136.

West Indies, the—*cont.*
priests in, 118.
trade with, 19, 23, 24, 88.
Westminster, 78.
Dean of. *See* Earle, Dr.
Gatehouse at, prisoners in, 145, 146.
Westmoreland, justices of, 145.
Wetmore, Major, killed, 161.
Wharton, Cornet, 105.
Whichwood Forest, lodge in, 217.
Whitby, fired on by the Dutch, 191.
White, William, 221.
Whitehall, 41, 49, 78, 131, 240.
banqueting hall at, 152.
letters dated at, 18, 48, 65, 78-80, 83, 86, 87, 165, 175, 181, 191, 194.
plot to attack, 48.
Whitehead, Thomas, signatures of, 136 (3).
Whitney, Edward, 6.
Wight, Isle of, 134, 170.
Wilford, Mr., 192.
Williamson :
Joseph, secretary to Nicholas and to Arlington, 66, 132, 192, 218.
—— letters from, 88, 150, 174, 191, 194.
—— news letters sent by. *See* News letters.
—— house of, 130.
Stephen, 221.
Willis, Sir Richard, treachery of, 13 (3).
Wilmot, John, 165.
Wilson, James, merchant at Tangiers, 152, 158, 207.
Wimbledon Church, constable and churchwardens of, 144-146.
—— minister of. *See* Luckin, Thos.
Winchester, Bishop of. *See* Morley, George.
Windsor, Thomas Hickman, Lord, 71.
—— letter to, 34.
Windsor, 80, 216.
Castle, 48, 145.
St. George's Hall at, 216.
prebendary of, 72.
Wines, French, 221.
sherry, 221.
ships laden with, 171, 207, 208, 221, 249, 251.
Wintour, Sir John, order signed by, 256.
Wirtemberg, Duke of, 6.
his country, 6.
Witt, John de, Grand Pensionary of Holland, 19, 200.
Wood, James, a minister of St. Andrew's, 151.
Woodward, Giles, English consul at Malaga, 190, 193, 196, 213, 248.
—— letters of, 211, 213, 215.
Wotton, Sir Henry, 132.
Wren, Mr., 218.
Wright, Sir Benjamin, 145, 195, 198, 232, 254.
Wyche or Weich, Sir Peter, 51, 67.

X.

Xeres de la Frontera, 98, 168, 215.
letters dated at, 152 (2), 154, 168, 172, 173, 215.
Ximenes, Ferdinand, auditor-general of the Duke of Medina Celi, 251.

Y.

Yarmouth, 190, 191.
roads, ships in, 191.
ships of, 165, 170, 221.
North, ship of, 221.
Yerbury, Sir Thomas, marriage of, 144.
York, Archbishop of. *See* Sterne, Dr. Richard.
York, James, Duke of, Lord Admiral, 20, 30, 61, 65, 87, 123, 151, 162, 165, 168, 181, 215, 230.
letters from, 5, 78, 79, 87.
letters to, 45, 129.
as president of the committee for Tangiers, 58.
the Earl of Chesterfield's jealousy of, 55.
proposed trading venture by, 79, 82, 87 (2), 123 (3).
has " no superfluity," 87.
animosity of, against the Earl of Bristol, 127.
as commander of the fleet, 168, 171, 172, 179, 186, 188, 195, 199.
is to stay at home, 201.
godmother of. *See* Elizabeth, Queen of Bohemia.
secretary of. *See* Coventry, William.
York, Duchess of, entertainment given by, 144.
is godmother to Lord Elgin's child, 145.
maids of honour to, 144, 172.
York, city of, sequestrator of, 146.
Yorkshire, 72.
conspiracy in, 144-146.

Z.

Zbarro, Don Diego de, governor of Cadiz, 195.
Zealand, province of, 149, 151, 167, 176, 195, 198, 200.
—— states of, 151.
Zeilam. *See* Ceylon.

HISTORICAL MANUSCRIPTS COMMISSION.

REPORTS OF THE ROYAL COMMISSIONERS APPOINTED TO INQUIRE WHAT PAPERS
AND MANUSCRIPTS BELONGING TO PRIVATE FAMILIES AND INSTITUTIONS ARE
EXTANT WHICH WOULD BE OF UTILITY IN THE ILLUSTRATION OF HISTORY,
CONSTITUTIONAL LAW, SCIENCE AND GENERAL LITERATURE.

Date.	— —	Size.	Sessional Paper.	Price.
				s. d.
1870 (Reprinted 1874.)	FIRST REPORT, WITH APPENDIX - - Contents : — ENGLAND. House of Lords ; Cambridge Colleges ; Abin·don and other Corporations, &c. SCOTLAND. Advocates' Library, Glasgow Corporation, &c. IRELAND. Dublin, Cork, and other Corporations, &c.	f'cap	[C. 55]	1 6
1871	SECOND REPORT, WITH APPENDIX AND INDEX TO THE FIRST AND SECOND REPORTS - - - - - Contents : — ENGLAND. House of Lords; Cambridge Colleges ; Oxford Colleges ; Monastery of Dominican Friars at Woodchester, Duke of Bedford, Earl Spencer, &c. SCOTLAND. Aberdeen and St. Andrew's Universities, &c. IRELAND. Marquis of Ormonde, Dr. Lyons, &c.	,,	[C. 441]	3 10
1872 (Reprinted 1895.)	THIRD REPORT, WITH APPENDIX AND INDEX - - - - - Contents :— ENGLAND. House of Lords; Cambridge Colleges ; Stonyhurst College ; Bridgewater and other Corporations; Duke of Northumberland, Marquis of Lansdowne, Marquis of Bath, &c. SCOTLAND. University of Glasgow ; Duke of Montrose, &c. IRELAND. Marquis of Ormonde ; Black Book of Limerick, &c.	,,	[C. 673]	6 0
1873	FOURTH REPORT, WITH APPENDIX. PART I. - - - - - Contents : — ENGLAND. House of Lords; Westminster Abbey ; Cambridge and Oxford Colleges ; Cinque Ports, · Hythe, and other Corporations, Marquis of Bath, Earl of Denbigh, &c. SCOTLAND. Duke of Argyll, &c. IRELAND. Trinity College, Dublin ; Marquis of Ormonde.	,,	[C. 857]	6 8

T 2

Date.		Size.	Sessional Paper.	Price.
				s. *d.*
1873	FOURTH REPORT. PART II. INDEX - -	f'cap	[C. 857 i.]	2 6
1876	FIFTH REPORT, WITH APPENDIX. PART I. Contents:— ENGLAND. House of Lords; Oxford and Cambridge Colleges; Dean and Chapter of Canterbury; Rye, Lydd, and other Corporations, Duke of Sutherland, Marquis of Lansdowne, Reginald Cholmondeley, Esq., &c. SCOTLAND. Earl of Aberdeen, &c.	,,	[C.1432]	7 0
,,	DITTO. PART II. INDEX - - -	,,	[C. 1432 i.]	3 6
1877	SIXTH REPORT, WITH APPENDIX. PART I. Contents:— ENGLAND. House of Lords; Oxford and Cambridge Colleges; Lambeth Palace; Black Book of the Archdeacon of Canterbury; Bridport, Wallingford, and other Corporations; Lord Leconfield, Sir Reginald Graham, Sir Henry Ingilby, &c. SCOTLAND. Duke of Argyll, Earl of Moray, &c. IRELAND. Marquis of Ormonde.	,,	[C.1745]	8 6
(Reprinted 1893.)	DITTO. PART II. INDEX - - -	,,	[C 2102]	1 10
1879 (Reprinted 1895.)	SEVENTH REPORT, WITH APPENDIX. PART I. Contents:— House of Lords; County of Somerset; Earl of Egmont, Sir Frederick Graham, Sir Harry Verney, &c.	,,	[C 2340]	7 6
(Reprinted 1895.)	DITTO. PART II. APPENDIX AND INDEX Contents:— Duke of Atholl, Marquis of Ormonde, S. F. Livingstone, Esq., &c.	,,	[C. 2340 i.]	3 6
1881	EIGHTH REPORT, WITH APPENDIX AND INDEX. PART I. - - - - - Contents:— List of collections examined, 1869-1880. ENGLAND. House of Lords; Duke of Marlborough; Magdalen College, Oxford; Royal College of Physicians; Queen Anne's Bounty Office; Corporations of Chester, Leicester, &c. IRELAND. Marquis of Ormonde, Lord Emly, The O'Conor Don, Trinity College, Dublin, &c.	,,	[C.3040]	[*Out of print.*]
1881	DITTO. PART II. APPENDIX AND INDEX - Contents:— Duke of Manchester.	,,	[C. 3040 i.]	[*Out of print.*]
1881	DITTO. PART III. APPENDIX AND INDEX - Contents:— Earl of Ashburnham.	,,	[C. 3040 ii.]	[*Out of print.*]

Date.	—	Size.	Sessional Paper.	Price.
				s. d.
1883 (Reprinted 1895.)	NINTH REPORT. WITH APPENDIX AND INDEX. PART I. - - - - Contents :— St. Paul's and Canterbury Cathedrals ; Eton College ; Carlisle. Yarmouth, Canterbury, and Barnstaple Corporations, &c.	f'cap	[C 3773]	5 2
1884 (Reprinted 1895.)	DITTO. PART II APPENDIX AND INDEX Contents : — ENGLAND. House of Lords. Earl of Leicester ; C. Pole Gell, Alfred Morrison, Esqs , &c. SCOTLAND. Lord Elphinstone, H. C. Maxwell Stuart, Esq., &c. IRELAND. Duke of Leinster, Marquis of Drogheda, &c.	,,	[C.3773 i.]	6 3
1884	DITTO. PART III. APPENDIX AND INDEX - - - - - Contents :— Mrs. Stopford Sackville.	,,	[C.3773 ii.]	[Out of print.]
1883 (Reprinted 1895.)	CALENDAR OF THE MANUSCRIPTS OF THE MARQUIS OF SALISBURY, K.G. (or CECIL MSS.). PART I. - - -	8vo.	[C.3777]	3 5
1888	DITTO. PART II. - - - -	,,	[C.5463]	3 5
1889	DITTO. PART III. - - -	,,	[C 5889 v.]	2 1
1892	DITTO. PART IV. - - -	,,	[C.6823]	2 11
1894	DITTO. PART V. - - -	,.	[C.7574]	2 6
1896	DITTO. PART VI. - - -	.,	[C.7884]	2 8
1899	DITTO. PART VII. - - -	,,	[C.9246]	2 8
1885	TENTH REPORT - - - - This is introductory to the following :—	,,	[C.4548]	[Out of print.]
1885 (Reprinted 1895.)	(1.) APPENDIX AND INDEX - - - Earl of Eglinton, Sir J. S. Maxwell, Bart., and C. S. H. D. Moray, C. F. Weston Underwood, G. W. Digby, Esqs.	,,	[C.4575]	3 7
1885	(2.) APPENDIX AND INDEX - - - The Family of Gawdy.	,,	[C.4576 iii.]	1 4
1885	(3.) APPENDIX AND INDEX - - - Wells Cathedral.	,,	[C 4576 ii.]	[Out of print.]
1885	(4.) APPENDIX AND INDEX - - - Earl of Westmorland ; Capt. Stewart ; Lord Stafford ; Sir N. W. Throckmorton ; Sir P. T. Mainwaring, Lord Muncaster, M.P., Capt. J. F. Bagot, Earl of Kilmorey, Earl of Powis, and others, the Corporations of Kendal, Wenlock, Bridgnorth, Eye, Plymouth, and the County of Essex ; and Stonyhurst College.	.,	[C 4576]	Ditto.
1885 (Reprinted 1895.)	(5.) APPENDIX AND INDEX - - - The Marquis of Ormonde, Earl of Fingall, Corporations of Galway, Waterford, the Sees of Dublin and Ossory, the Jesuits in Ireland.	,,	[4576 i.]	2 10

Date		Size.	Sessional Paper.	Price.
				s. d.
1887	(6.) APPENDIX AND INDEX - - - Marquis of Abergavenny, Lord Braye, G. F. Luttrell, P. P. Bouverie. W. Bromley Davenport, R. T. Balfour, Esquires.	8vo.	[C.5242]	1 7
1887	ELEVENTH REPORT - - - This is introductory to the following:—	,.	[C.5060 vi.]	0 3
1887	(1.) APPENDIX AND INDEX - - - H. D. Skrine, Esq., Salvetti Correspondence.	.,	[C 5060]	1 1
1887	(2) APPENDIX AND INDEX - - - House of Lords. 1678-1688.	,,	[C.5060 i.]	2 0
1887	(3.) APPENDIX AND INDEX - - - Corporations of Southampton and Lynn.	,.	[C.5060 ii]	1 8
1887	(4.) APPENDIX AND INDEX - - - Marquess Townshend.	,,	[C.5060 iii.]	2 0
1887	(5.) APPENDIX AND INDEX - - - Earl of Dartmouth.	,,	[C.5060 iv]	2 8
1887	(6.) APPENDIX AND INDEX - - - Duke of Hamilton.	,,	[C.5060 v.]	1 6
1888	(7.) APPENDIX AND INDEX - - - Duke of Leeds, Marchioness of Waterford, Lord Hothfield, &c.; Bridgewater Trust Office, Reading Corporation, Inner Temple Library.	,.	[C 5612]	2 0
1890	TWELFTH REPORT - - - - This is introductory to the following:—	,,	[C.5889]	0 3
1888	(1.) APPENDIX - - - - Earl Cowper, K.G. (Coke MSS., at Melbourne Hall, Derby). Vol I.	,,	[C.5472]	2 7
1888	(2.) APPENDIX - - - - Ditto. Vol. II.	,,	[C.5613]	2 5
1889	(3.) APPENDIX AND INDEX - - - Ditto. Vol. III.	,,	[C.5889 i]	1 4
1888	(4.) APPENDIX - - - - The Duke of Rutland, G.C.B. Vol. I.	,,	[C 5614]	3 2
1891	(5.) APPENDIX AND INDEX - - - Ditto. Vol. II.	,,	[C.5889 ii.]	2 0
1889	(6.) APPENDIX AND INDEX - - - House of Lords, 1689-1690.	,.	[C.5889 iii.]	2 1
1890	(7.) APPENDIX AND INDEX - - - S. H. le Fleming, Esq., of Rydal.	,,	[C.5889 iv.]	1 11
1891	(8.) APPENDIX AND INDEX - - - The Duke of Atholl, K.T., and the Earl of Home.	,,	[C.6338]	1 0
1891	(9.) APPENDIX AND INDEX - - - The Duke of Beaufort. K.G , the Earl of Donoughmore, J. H. Gurney, W. W. B. Hulton, R. W. Ketton, G. A. Aitken, P. V. Smith, Esqs.; Bishop of Ely; Cathedrals of Ely, Gloucester, Lincoln, and Peterborough; Corporations of Gloucester, Higham Ferrers, and Newark; Southwell Minster; Lincoln District Registry.	,,	[C.6338 i.] .	2 6

Date.	---	Size.	Sessional Paper.	Price.
				s. d.
1891	(10.) APPENDIX - - - - The First Earl of Charlemont. Vol. I. 1745–1783.	8vo.	[C. 6338 ii.]	1 11
1892	THIRTEENTH REPORT - - - This is introductory to the following :—	,,	[C.6827]	0 3
1891	(1.) APPENDIX - - - - The Duke of Portland. Vol. I.	,,	[C.6474]	3 0
	(2.) APPENDIX AND INDEX. Ditto. Vol. II. - - -	,,	[C 6827 i.]	2 0
1892	(3.) APPENDIX. J. B. Fortescue, Esq., of Dropmore. Vol. I. - - - -	,,	[C.6660]	2 7
1892	(4.) APPENDIX AND INDEX. - - - Corporations of Rye, Hastings, and Hereford. Capt. F. C. Loder-Symonds, E. R. Wodehouse, M.P., J. Dovaston, Esqs., Sir T. B. Lennard, Bart., Rev. W. D. Macray, and Earl of Dartmouth (Supplementary Report).	,,	[C.6810]	2 4
1892	(5.) APPENDIX AND INDEX. House of Lords, 1690–1691. -	,,	[C.6822]	2 4
1893	(6.) APPENDIX AND INDEX. Sir W. Fitzherbert, Bart. The Delaval Family, of Seaton Delaval ; The Earl of Ancaster ; and General Lyttelton-Annesley.	,,	[C.7166]	1 4
1893	(7.) APPENDIX AND INDEX. The Earl of Lonsdale - - -	,,	[C.7241]	1 3
1893	(8.) APPENDIX AND INDEX. The First Earl of Charlemont. Vol. II. 1784–1799.	,,	[C.7424]	1 11
1896	FOURTEENTH REPORT - - - This is introductory to the following :—	,,	[C.7983]	0 3
1894	(1.) APPENDIX AND INDEX. The Duke of Rutland, G.C.B. Vol. III.	,,	[C.7476]	1 11
1894	(2.) APPENDIX. The Duke of Portland. Vol. III. -	,,	[C.7569]	2 8
1894	(3.) APPENDIX AND INDEX. The Duke of Roxburghe ; Sir H. H. Campbell, Bart. ; The Earl of Strathmore ; and the Countess Dowager of Seafield.	,,	[C.7570]	1 2
1894	(4.) APPENDIX AND INDEX. Lord Kenyon - - -	,,	[C.7571]	2 10
1896	(5.) APPENDIX. J. B. Fortescue, Esq., of Dropmore. Vol. II.	,,	[C.7572]	2 8
1896	(6.) APPENDIX AND INDEX. House of Lords, 1692–1693 - -	,	[C.7573]	1 11
1895	(7.) APPENDIX. The Marquis of Ormonde, K.P. -	,,	[C.7678]	1 10

Date.		Size.	Sessional Paper.	Price.
				s. d.
1895	(8.) APPENDIX AND INDEX. Lincoln, Bury St. Edmunds, Hertford, and Great Grimsby Corporations; The Dean and Chapter of Worcester, and of Lichfield; The Bishop's Registry of Worcester.	8vo.	[C.7881]	1 5
1896	(9.) APPENDIX AND INDEX. Earl of Buckinghamshire; Earl of Lindsey; Earl of Onslow; Lord Emly; T. J. Hare, Esq.; and J. Round, Esq., M.P.	,,	[C.7882]	2 6
1895	(10.) APPENDIX AND INDEX. The Earl of Dartmouth. Vol. II. American Papers.	,,	[C.7883]	2 9
	FIFTEENTH REPORT. This is introductory to the following:—	,,	[C.9295]	0 4
1896	(1.) APPENDIX AND INDEX. The Earl of Dartmouth. Vol. III.	,,	[C.8156]	1 5
1897	(2.) APPENDIX. J. Eliot Hodgkin, Esq., of Richmond, Surrey.	,,	[C.8327]	1 8
1897	(3.) APPENDIX AND INDEX. Charles Haliday, Esq., of Dublin; Acts of the Privy Council in Ireland, 1556–1571; Sir William Ussher's Table to the Council Book; Table to the Red Council Book.	,,	[C.8364]	1 4
1897	(4.) APPENDIX. The Duke of Portland. Vol. IV.	,,	[C.8497]	2 11
1897	(5.) APPENDIX AND INDEX. The Right Hon. F. J. Savile Foljambe.	,,	[C.8550]	0 10
1897	(6.) APPENDIX AND INDEX. The Earl of Carlisle, Castle Howard.	,,	[C.8551]	3 6
1897	(7.) APPENDIX AND INDEX. The Duke of Somerset; The Marquis of Ailesbury; and Sir F. G. Puleston, Bart.	[In the Press.]		
1897	(8) APPENDIX AND INDEX. The Duke of Buccleuch and Queensberry, at Drumlanrig.	8vo.	[C.8553]	1 4
1897	(9.) APPENDIX AND INDEX. J. J. Hope Johnstone, Esq., of Annandale.	,,	[C.8554]	1 0
1899	(10.) APPENDIX AND INDEX. Shrewsbury and Coventry Corporation; Sir Walter Corbet, Bart., &c.	..	[In the Press.]	

Date.		Size.	Sessional Paper.	Price.
				s. d.
1898	MANUSCRIPTS IN THE WELSH LANGUAGE. Vol. I. Lord Mostyn, at Mostyn Hall, co. Flint.	8vo.	[C.8829]	1 4
	Vol. 2. Mr. Wynne at Peniarth	,,	[*In the Press.*]	
1899	REPORT ON THE MANUSCRIPTS OF THE DUKE OF BUCCLEUCH, K.G., K.T., AT MONTAGU HOUSE, WHITEHALL. VOL. I.	,,	[C.9244]	2 7
1899	DITTO DITTO OF THE MARQUIS OF ORMONDE, K.P., AT THE CASTLE, KILKENNY. VOL. II.	,,	[C.9245]	2 0
1899	DITTO DITTO OF THE DUKE OF PORTLAND. VOL. V.	,,	[*In the Press.*]	
	DITTO DITTO OF J. B. FORTESCUE, ESQ., OF DROPMORE. Vol. III.	,,	[*In the Press.*]	

Lightning Source UK Ltd.
Milton Keynes UK
UKHW050843241218
334233UK00008BA/743/P